PARSONS

Gary L. Parsons

THE INSECTS
STRUCTURE AND FUNCTION

BIOLOGICAL SCIENCE TEXTS

General Editor

PROFESSOR W. S. BULLOUGH, Ph.D., D.Sc.,
Professor of Zoology
Birkbeck College, University of London

THE INSECTS
Structure and Function

R. F. CHAPMAN

Visiting Professor,
Birkbeck College, University of London

ELSEVIER New York

American edition published by
AMERICAN ELSEVIER PUBLISHING COMPANY, INC.
52 Vanderbilt Avenue, New York, NY 10017

Second Edition © 1971 by R.F. Chapman
First Edition published in 1969

Library of Congress Cataloging in Publication Data

Chapman, Reginald Frederick.
The insects: structure and function.

(Biological science texts)
Bibliography: p.
Includes indexes.
1. Insects. I. Title.
QL463.C48 1976   595.7   76-28262
ISBN 0-444-19456-8

Printed in the United States of America

PREFACE

My own interest in insects started from a behavioural–cum–ecological approach, but the need to try to understand what the insects were doing and how they were doing it extended my interests to morphology and physiology. This brought with it the realisation that in order fully to appreciate any problem, be it basically morphological, physiological or ecological, a broad understanding of the insect is essential. I have adopted this point of view in teaching entomology to first degree and postgraduate students.

Although there are a number of admirable textbooks dealing with the morphology, physiology and natural history of insects, none of these, perhaps advisedly, makes any real attempt to bring the different approaches together. In this book I have tried to fill the gap, bringing morphology and physiology together and relating these studies to the behaviour of the insect under natural conditions. It is not intended that the book should be comprehensive, but it is hoped that it gives a general picture of what makes an insect tick, at least as far as present-day knowledge allows.

The arrangement of the chapters and sections reflects my own line of thinking. One could justify almost any arrangement, and I hope that the brief introductions to each chapter will serve to link sections whose relationships may not otherwise be apparent. At the end of each introductory section I have included a list of some of the more important reviews on each topic. In addition to these, other references are included in the text only where a point is not fully dealt with in the reviews or if it is subject to controversy. In most chapters some more recent references are included not only for the value of the work which they contain, but also because they give the most up-to-date entry to the literature. The sources of the illustrations are given since the inability to trace the origin of an illustration is a common cause of annoyance.

I am indebted to many people for help and advice given in the course of preparing the manuscript, but the chief sufferers have undoubtedly been my family. Their forbearance and understanding have been quite overwhelming; without them the book would certainly not have been completed. In addition my wife has made the very real contribution of checking and criticising the whole manuscript.

My friend Dr. Lena Ward has offered the most valuable criticisms which have added materially to the book, and this is also true of Mr. T. E. Hughes who has read many chapters and contributed in many other ways from his wealth of zoological knowledge. Others who have offered valuable advice are Dr. J. W. L. Beament, Mr. J. W. Charter and Dr. L. Rathbone. Not least in this category are my students who all too frequently have picked up a glib statement or an inconsistency when I thought they were dozing. Despite these combined efforts and my own, I am afraid that errors will remain. These, of course, are my own responsibility.

I am indebted in many ways to Professor W. S. Bullough, the editor of this series. Throughout he has encouraged and proffered advice on many aspects of the production and presentation of the book. Among other things he introduced me to scraper board as a means of illustration. I hope my efforts do him justice. The English Universities Press have been most helpful throughout.

Finally, I am indebted to the ladies who typed the manuscript and especially to Miss M. D. Pickard who did by far the greater part. Her retirement was admirably timed! Mrs. H. Llewellyn and Miss D. Speller also helped with some parts.

CONTENTS

SECTION F   THE BLOOD, HORMONES AND PHEROMONES

SECTION A

The Head, Ingestion and Utilisation of the Food

CHAPTER I
THE HEAD AND ITS APPENDAGES

The characteristic feature of arthropods, including the insects, is a hard, jointed exo-skeleton or cuticle. This consists of a series of hard plates, the sclerites, which may simply be joined to each other by membranes giving flexibility, or may be closely articulated together so as to give a more precise movement of one sclerite on the next.

Insects and other arthropods are built up on a segmental plan. Each segment basically has a dorsal sclerite, the tergum, joined to a ventral sclerite, the sternum, by lateral membranous areas, the pleura. Arising from the sterno-pleural region on each side is a jointed appendage. In the insects such segments are grouped into three units, the head, thorax and abdomen, in which the various basic parts of the segments may be lost or greatly modified. Typical walking legs are only retained on the three thoracic segments. In the head the appendages are modified for feeding purposes and in the abdomen they are lost, except that some may be modified as the genitalia and in Apterygota some pregenital appendages are retained.

The insect head is a strongly sclerotised capsule joined to the thorax by a flexible membranous neck. It bears the mouthparts, comprising the labrum, mandibles, maxillae and labium, and also important sense organs. On the outside it is marked by grooves most of which indicate ridges on the inside, and some of these inflexions extend deep into the head, fusing with each other to form an internal skeleton. These structures serve to strengthen the head and provide attachments for muscles as well as supporting and protecting the brain and foregut.

The head is derived from the primitive pre-oral archecerebrum and a number of post-oral segments. Embryological evidence shows that the mandibles, maxillae and labium are derived from typical appendages so that the head includes at least three post-oral segments and it is generally believed that there is also a premandibular segment, although there are no corresponding appendages in the adult. Apart from this there is much controversy concerning the inclusion of other segments in the head and the extent of the archecerebrum (see Snodgrass, 1960).

The main sense organs on the head are a pair of compound eyes, typically three ocelli and a pair of antennae. The latter are very variable in form and functions, but are usually concerned with mechanoreception and chemoreception.

The mouthparts consist of upper and lower lips and two pairs of jaw-like structures, the mandibles and maxillae. In many insects which feed by biting off fragments of food and chewing them up these structures retain their jaw-like form, but in many which are fluid feeders various elements of the mouthparts become tubular for sucking up the food, while others may be stylet-like, serving to pierce the tissues of the host plant or animal.

3

Important works dealing generally with the insect head are DuPorte (1957), Matsuda (1965) and Snodgrass (1960). The form and functioning of the antennae is reviewed by Schneider (1964), while mouthparts are most fully dealt with in various specialist books and papers on specific insects (see p. 19).

1.1 Head

1.11 Orientation

The orientation of the head with respect to the rest of the body varies. The hypognathous condition with the mouthparts in a continuous series with the legs is probably primitive (Fig. 1). This orientation occurs mostly in vegetarian species living in open habitats. In the prognathous condition the mouthparts point forwards and this is found in

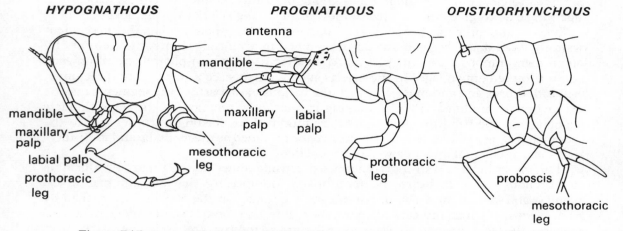

Fig. 1. Different positions of the head and mouthparts relative to the rest of the body. Hypognathous—grasshopper; prognathous—beetle larva; opisthorhynchous—aphid.

carnivorous species which actively pursue their prey, and in larvae, particularly of Coleoptera, which use their mandibles for burrowing. Finally, in Heteroptera and Homoptera there is the opisthorhynchous condition in which the elongate proboscis slopes backwards between the front legs.

1.12 Grooves of the head

The head is a continuously sclerotised capsule with no outward appearance of segmentation, but it is marked by a number of grooves. Commonly all these grooves are called sutures, but Snodgrass (1960) recommends that the term suture should be retained for grooves marking the line of fusion of two formerly distinct plates. Grooves with a purely functional origin are called sulci. The groove which ends between the points of attachment of maxillae and labium at the back of the head is generally believed to represent the line of fusion of the maxillary and labial segments and it is therefore known as the postoccipital suture. The remaining grooves on the head indicate only the presence of strengthening ridges on the inside and hence should be called sulci.

Since these are functional mechanical developments to resist the various strains imposed on the head capsule the sulci are variable in position in different species and any one of them may be completely absent. However, the needs for strengthening the head wall will be similar in the majority of insects so that some of the sulci are fairly constant in their occurrence and position.

The most constant is the epistomal (frontoclypeal) sulcus which acts as a brace between the anterior mandibular articulations (Fig. 2). At each end of this sulcus is a pit, the anterior tentorial pit, which marks the position of a deep invagination to form the anterior arm of the tentorium (p. 7). The lateral margins of the head above the mandibular articulations are strengthened by a submarginal inflexion, the subgenal sulcus, which is generally a continuation of the epistomal sulcus to the postoccipital suture. The part of the subgenal sulcus above the mandible is called the pleurostomal sulcus, the part behind the mandible is the hypostomal sulcus. Another commonly occurring groove is the circumocular sulcus which strengthens the rim of the eye and may develop into a deep flange protecting the inner side of the eye. Sometimes this sulcus is connected to the subgenal sulcus by a vertical subocular sulcus which, with the circumocular sulcus, acts as a brace against the pull of the mandibular muscles which arise on the top of the head. The circumantennal sulcus strengthens the head at the point of insertion of the antenna, while running across the back of the head, behind the compound eyes, is the occipital sulcus.

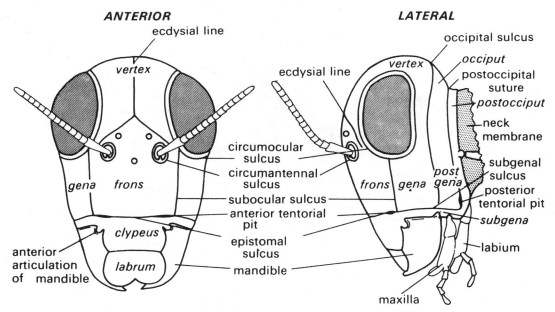

Fig. 2. The common lines or grooves on the insect head and the areas which they define. Names of areas are italicised (modified after Snodgrass, 1960).

Immature insects nearly always have a line along the dorsal midline of the head dividing into two lines on the face so as to form an inverted Y (Fig. 2). There is no groove or ridge associated with this line which is simply a line of weakness, continuous with that on the thorax, along which the cuticle splits when the insect moults. It is therefore called the ecdysial cleavage line, but has commonly been termed the epicranial suture. The anterior arms of this line are very variable in their development and position (Snodgrass, 1947) and in Apterygota they are reduced or absent. The ecdysial cleavage line may persist in the adult insect and sometimes the cranium is inflected along this line to form a true sulcus.

Other ecdysial lines may be present on the ventral surface of the head of larval insects (see Hinton, 1963a).

1.13 Areas of the head

The different areas of the head defined by the sulci are given names for descriptive purposes, but they do not represent primitive sclerites. Since the sulci are variable in position so, too, are the areas which they delimit. The front of the head, the fronto-clypeal area, is divided by the epistomal sulcus into the frons above and the clypeus below (Fig. 2). It is common to regard the arms of the ecdysial cleavage line as delimiting the frons dorsally, but this is not necessarily so (Snodgrass, 1960). From the frons muscles run to the pharynx, the labrum and the hypopharynx; from the clypeus arise the dilators of the cibarium (see below). The two groups of muscles are always separated

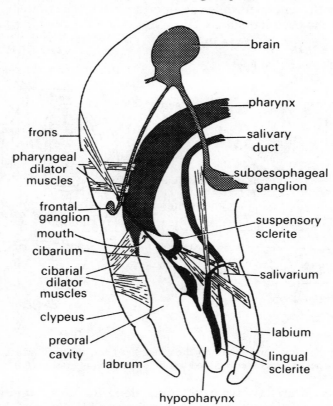

Fig. 3. Diagrammatic vertical longitudinal section through the head of a biting insect showing the preoral cavity and the musculature of the hypopharynx (after Snodgrass, 1947).

by the frontal ganglion and its connectives to the brain (Fig. 3) and Snodgrass (1947) believes that on the basis of the muscles frons and clypeus can be distinguished even in the absence of the epistomal sulcus. DuPorte (1946) does not believe that the muscles are necessarily so constant in their origins.

Dorsally the frons continues into the vertex and posteriorly this is separated from the occiput by the occipital sulcus. The occiput is divided from the postocciput behind it by the postoccipital suture, while at the back of the head, where it joins the neck, is an opening, the occipital foramen, through which the alimentary canal, nerve cord and some muscles pass into the thorax.

The lateral area of the head beneath the eyes is called the gena from which the subgena is cut off below by the subgenal sulcus, and the postgena behind by the occipital sulcus. The region of the subgena above the mandible is called the pleurostoma and that part behind the mandible is the hypostoma.

1.14 Ventral region of the head

Ventrally, in a hypognathous insect, the head is extended by the mouthparts with the labrum forming the upper lip anteriorly, the mandibles and maxillae laterally and the labium, the lower lip, posteriorly. These appendages enclose a cavity, the preoral cavity, with the mouth at its base (Fig. 3). Behind the mouth is the hypopharynx, the proximal membranous part of which is continuous with the pharynx. The part of the preoral cavity enclosed by the proximal part of the hypopharynx and the clypeus is known as the cibarium. Behind the hypopharynx and between it and the labium is a smaller cavity known as the salivarium, into which the salivary duct opens.

1.15 Modifications of the head

The most marked differences in the structure of the head capsule occur at the back of the head. Typically the hypostomal sulci bend upwards posteriorly and are continuous with the postoccipital suture (Fig. 4A). The posterior ventral part of the head capsule is membranous and is completed by the labium. In some insects, however, the hypostomata of the two sides meet in the midline below the occipital foramen to form a hypostomal bridge which is continuous with the postocciput. This is particularly well-developed in Diptera (Fig. 4B). In other cases, Hymenoptera and the water bugs *Notonecta* and *Naucoris*, a similar bridge is formed by the postgenae, but the bridge is separated from the postocciput by the postoccipital suture (Fig. 4C).

Where the head is held in the prognathous position the lower ends of the postocciput fuse and extend forwards to form a median ventral plate, the gula (Fig. 4D), which may be a continuous sclerotisation with the labium. Often the gula is reduced to a narrow strip by enlargement of the postgenae and sometimes the postgenae meet in the midline so that the gula is obliterated. The median ventral suture which is thus formed at the point of contact of the postgenae is called the gular suture (but see Hinton, 1963a).

1.16 Tentorium

The tentorium consists of two anterior and two posterior apodemes which form the internal skeleton of the head serving as a brace for the head and for the attachment of muscles. The anterior arms arise from the anterior tentorial pits which in Apterygota and Ephemeroptera are ventral and medial to the mandibles. In Odonata, Plecoptera and Dermaptera the pits are lateral to the mandibles while in most higher insects they are facial at either end of the epistomal sulcus (Snodgrass, 1960). DuPorte (1946), however, believes the anterior tentorial pits to lie on the sulcus between the frons and the gena.

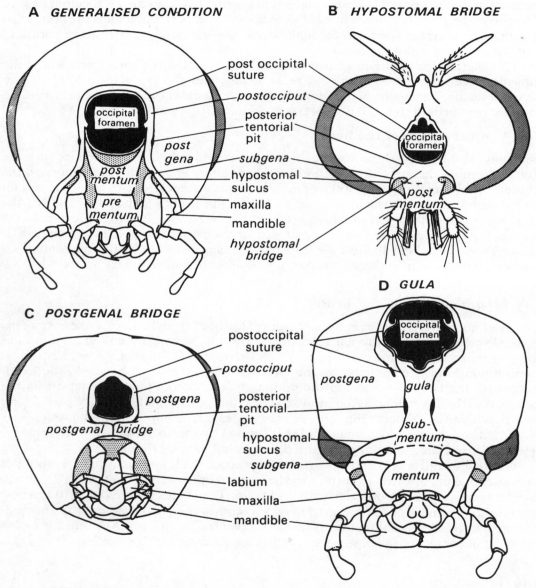

Fig. 4. Modifications occurring at the back of the head. A. Generalised condition; B. *Deromyia* (Diptera) with a hypostomal bridge; C. *Vespula* (Hymenoptera) with a postgenal bridge; D. *Epicauta* (Coleoptera) with a gula. Membranous areas stippled, compound eyes cross-hatched (after Snodgrass, 1960).

The posterior arms arise from pits at the ventral ends of the postoccipital suture and they unite to form a bridge running across the head from one side to the other. In Pterygota the anterior arms also join up with the bridge (Fig. 5), but the development of the tentorium as a whole is very variable (see Snodgrass, 1935). Sometimes a pair of dorsal arms arise from the anterior arms and they may be attached to the dorsal wall of the head by short muscles.

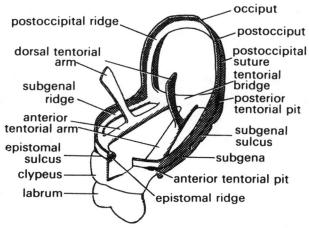

Fig. 5. Diagram of the tentorium and its relationship with the grooves and ridges of the head. Greater part of head capsule cut away (after Snodgrass, 1935).

In Machilidae (Thysanura) the posterior bridge is present, but the anterior arms do not reach it, while in Lepismatidae the anterior arms unite to form a central plate near the bridge and joined to it by very short muscles. In *Tomocerus* (Collembola) two branching anterior tentorial arms are present, while the posterior arms are long and unite above the hypopharynx. In addition, the tendons joining the transverse mandibular and maxillary muscles (see Fig. 12A) form square plates which are linked together and with the posterior tentorial arms by fibrous connectives. These structures, together with extensions from the mandibular tendon, form a complex endoskeleton in the head. *Campodea* (Diplura) has no anterior tentorial arms, but the posterior arms are long and again unite over the hypopharynx. Transverse tendons are also present, but they are simpler than in *Tomocerus*. The association of the tentorium with the hypopharynx in these entognathous insects (p. 14) is probably connected with the feeding movements and protrusibility of the hypopharynx.

Manton (1964) indicates that the basic elements occurring in the head endophragmal skeleton are homologous throughout the insects; other authors have believed the structure in entognathous insects to be mesodermal in origin.

1.2 Neck

The neck or cervix is a membranous region which gives freedom of movement to the head. It extends from the occipital foramen at the back of the head to the prothorax, and possibly represents the posterior part of the labial segment together with the anterior part of the prothoracic segment. Laterally in the neck membrane are the cervical sclerites, typically two on each side. The first articulates anteriorly with the occipital condyle at the back of the head and posteriorly with the second cervical sclerite which in turn articulates with the prothoracic episternum. Muscles arising from the postocciput and the pronotum are inserted on these sclerites (Fig. 6A) and their contraction increases the angle between the sclerites so that the head is pushed forwards (Fig. 6B). A muscle arising ventrally and inserted on to the first cervical sclerite may aid in retraction or lateral movements of the head.

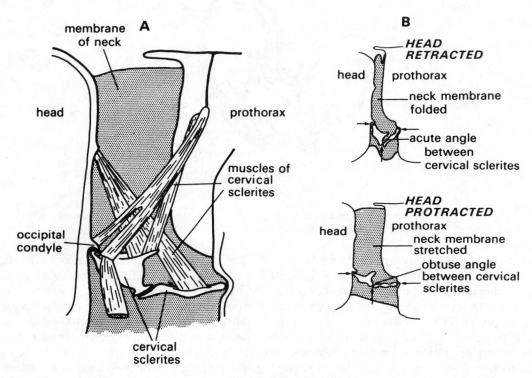

Fig. 6. A. The neck and cervical sclerites of a grasshopper seen from the inside (from Imms, 1957). B. Diagrams showing how a change in the angle between the cervical sclerites retracts or protracts the head. Arrows indicate points of articulation.

Running through the neck are longitudinal muscles, dorsal muscles from the ante-costal ridge (p. 128) of the mesothorax to the postoccipital ridge, and ventral muscles from the sternal apophyses of the prothorax to the postoccipital ridge or the tentorium. These muscles serve to retract the head on to the prothorax while their differential con-traction will cause lateral movements of the head.

1.3 Antennae

All insects except Protura possess a pair of antennae, but they may be greatly reduced, especially in larval forms.

1.31 Antennal structure

The antenna consists of a basal scape, a pedicel and a flagellum. The scape is inserted into a membranous region of the head wall and pivoted on a single marginal point, the antennifer (Fig. 8A), so that it is free to move in all directions. Frequently the flagellum is divided into a number of similar annuli joined to each other by membranes so that the flagellum as a whole is flexible. The term segmented should be avoided with reference to the flagellum of Pterygota since the annuli are not regarded as equivalent to leg segments (Schneider, 1964).

In Pterygota and Thysanura the antennae are moved by levator and depressor muscles arising on the anterior tentorial arms and inserted into the scape, and by flexor and extensor muscles arising in the scape and inserted into the pedicel (Fig. 7A) (Imms, 1940). There are no muscles in the flagellum and the nerve which traverses the flagellum is purely sensory. This is the annulated type of antenna.

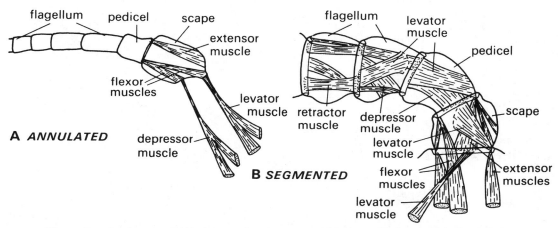

Fig. 7. Proximal parts of (A) the annulated antenna of *Locusta* (Orthoptera) in lateral view, and (B) the segmented antenna of *Japyx* (Diplura) in dorsal view (after Imms, 1940).

In Collembola and Diplura the musculature at the base of the antenna is similar to that in Pterygota, but, in addition, there is an intrinsic musculature in each unit of the flagellum (Fig. 7B), and, consequently, these units are regarded as true segments. Five muscles run from the base of each segment to the base of the next and produce various movements, but in the more distal segments the muscles are reduced and all but one of them may be absent. This type of antenna is called segmented.

1.32 Growth of the antenna

In hemimetabolous and amelabolous insects (p. 396) the number of annuli in the antennal flagellum increases during postembryonic life (see Fig. 258). Thus, the first instar larva of *Dociostaurus* (Orthoptera) has antennae with 13 annuli, while in the adult there are 25. The manner in which new annuli are added varies. In annulated antennae division of the proximal annulus, termed the meriston, results in the production of new elements between it and the second annulus, but in segmented antennae the growth zone is apical, new segments arising from the most distal segment.

1.33 Variation in form of antennae

The form of the antenna varies considerably depending on its precise function (Fig. 8). Sometimes the modification produces an increase in surface area; for instance, the surface area of the pectinate antenna of a male *Bombyx* (comparable with Fig. 8C) is 29·0 sq.mm.; without the branches it would only be 4·8 sq.mm. (Schneider, 1964). The partial significance of this is probably to permit the presence of more sensilla. Elongation, such as occurs in the cockroach, is possibly associated with the use of the antennae as feelers.

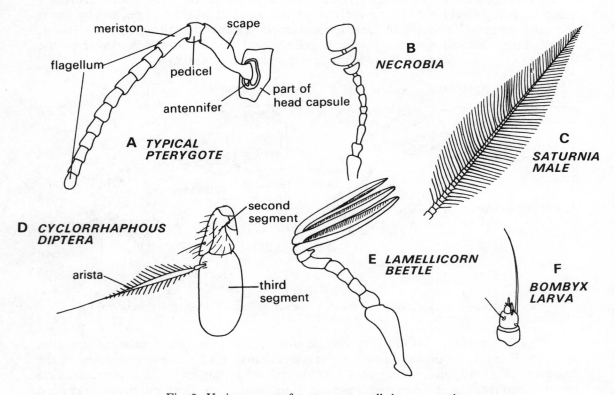

Fig. 8. Various types of antennae, not all the same scale.

Sexual dimorphism in the antennae is common, the antennae of the male often being more complex than those of the female. This often occurs where the male is attracted to or recognises the female by her scent (p.737). Conversely, in chalcids scent plays an important part in host-finding by the female and in this case the female's antennae are more specialised than the male's (Richards, 1956).

The antennae of larval holometabolous insects are usually considerably reduced. The larval antennae of Neuroptera and Megaloptera contain a number of annuli, but in larval Coleoptera and Lepidoptera (Fig. 8F) the antennae are reduced to three simple segments. In some larval Diptera and Hymenoptera the antennae are very small and may be no more than swellings of the head wall.

1.34 Functions of antennae

The antennae function primarily as sense organs. In forms with annulated antennae a major sense organ, Johnston's organ (p. 605), occurs in the pedicel. This is a chordotonal organ which perceives movements of the flagellum. Smaller sensilla occur on various parts of the antennae and the most important are sensory hairs, basiconic and coeloconic pegs, plate organs and campaniform sensilla (Chapter XXIX and XXX). Schneider (1964) gives a full list. The sensilla are often concentrated in particular regions and in *Melanoplus* (Orthoptera), for instance, there are no basiconic or coeloconic pegs on the proximal annuli, while most of these sensilla are found on the annuli in the middle of the flagellum (Fig. 9). The various types of sensilla function as tactile and smell receptors, contact chemoreceptors, hygroreceptors and temperature receptors.

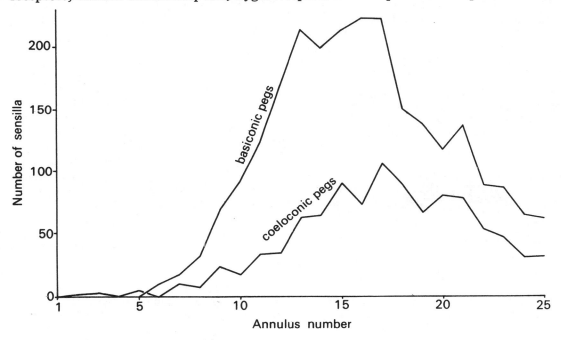

Fig. 9. Distribution of some sensilla on the flagellum of a male *Melanoplus*. 1 = most proximal annulus, 25 = most distal annulus (from data in Slifer *et al.*, 1959).

Sometimes the antennae have other functions. The adult water beetle *Hydrophilus* submerges with a film of air over its ventral surface which it renews at intervals when it comes to the surface. At the surface the body is inclined to one side and a funnel of air, connecting the ventral air bubble to the outside air, appears between the head, the prothorax and the distal annuli of the antenna which is held along the side of the head. The four terminal annuli of the antenna are enlarged and are clothed with hydrofuge hairs to facilitate the formation of the air funnel (Miall, 1922).

In the newly hatched larva of *Hydrophilus* the antennae assist the mandibles in masticating the prey. This is facilitated by a number of sharp spines on the inside of the antennae.

Finally, in fleas and Collembola the antennae are used in mating. Male fleas use the antennae to clasp the female from below. In many Collembola the males have prehensile antennae with which they hold on to the antennae of the female and in *Sminthurides aquaticus* the male may be carried about by the female, holding on to her antennae, for several days.

1.4 Mouthparts

The mouthparts are the organs concerned with feeding, comprising the unpaired labrum in front, a median hypopharynx behind the mouth, a pair of mandibles and maxillae laterally, and a labium forming the lower lip. In Collembola, Diplura and Protura the mouthparts lie in a cavity of the head produced by the genae which extend ventrally as oral folds and meet in the ventral midline below the mouthparts (Fig. 10).

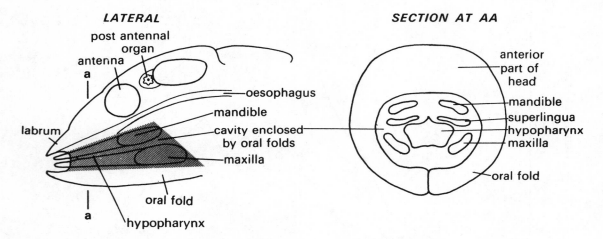

Fig. 10. Diagram to illustrate the entognathous condition of the mouthparts. In the lateral view the hatched area represents the cavity enclosed by the oral folds (modified after Denis, 1949).

This is the entognathous condition (see Manton, 1964). In the rest of the insects the mouthparts are not enclosed in this way, but are external to the head, the ectognathous condition (*e.g.* Fig. 1).

The form of the mouthparts is related to diet, but two basic types can be recognised: mouthparts adapted for biting and chewing solid food, and mouthparts adapted for sucking up fluids. The biting and chewing form is considered to be primitive.

1.41 Biting mouthparts

Labrum

The labrum is a broad lobe suspended from the clypeus in front of the mouth and forming the upper lip. On its inner side it is membranous and may be produced into a median lobe, the epipharynx, bearing some sensilla. The labrum is raised away from the mandibles by two muscles arising in the head and inserted medially into the anterior margin of the labrum. It is closed against the mandibles by two more muscles arising in the head and inserted on the posterior lateral margins on two small sclerites, the tormae (Fig. 11). Differential use of these muscles can produce a lateral rocking movement of the labrum.

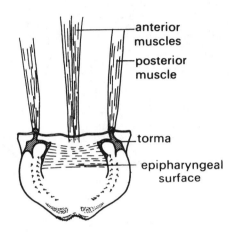

Fig. 11. The labrum from the posterior, epipharyngeal, surface (after Snodgrass, 1944).

Mandibles

In the Apterygota, other than Lepismatidae, the mandibles are relatively long and slender and they have only a single point of articulation with the head capsule. The mandible is rotated about its articulation by anterior and posterior muscles arising on the head capsule and on the anterior tentorial arms. The principal adductor muscles are transverse and ventral, those of the two sides uniting in a median tendon (Fig. 12A) (see Manton, 1964).

In Lepismatidae and the Pterygota the mandibles are articulated with the cranium at two points, having a second more anterior articulation with the subgena in addition to the original posterior one (Fig. 12B). These mandibles are usually short and strongly sclerotised and often the biting surface is differentiated into a more distal incisor region and a proximal molar region, the mandibles of the two sides being asymmetrical so as to oppose each other in the midline. The development of incisor and molar areas varies with the diet. The mandibles of carnivorous insects are armed with strong shearing cusps; in grasshoppers feeding on vegetation other than grasses there is a series of sharp pointed cusps, while in grass-feeding species the incisor cusps are chisel-edged and the molar area has flattened ridges for grinding. These cusps may become worn down during feeding (Chapman, 1964).

The original anterior and posterior rotator muscles of Apterygota have become abductors and adductors in the Pterygota, the adductor becoming very powerful. The apterygote ventral adductor is retained in most orthopteroids and arises from the hypopharyngeal apophysis, but in Acrididae and the higher insects this muscle is absent (Fig. 12B), or, in insects with sucking mouthparts, may be modified as a protractor muscle of the mandible.

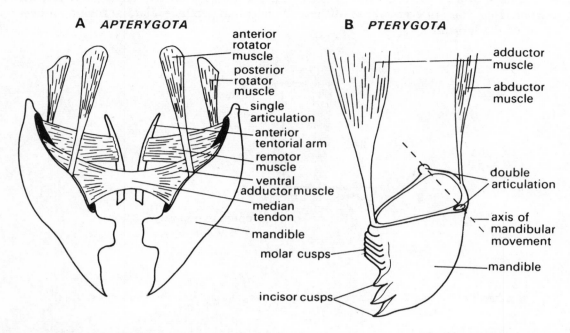

Fig. 12. Diagrams of the mandibles of (A) an apterygote, in which only some of the muscles are shown, and (B) a pterygote insect (after Snodgrass, 1935, 1944).

Maxillae

The maxillae occupy a lateral position on the head behind the mandibles. The proximal part of the maxilla consists of a basal cardo, which has a single articulation with the head, and a flat plate, the stipes, hinged to the cardo. Both cardo and stipes are loosely joined to the head by membrane so that they are capable of movement. Distally on the stipes are two lobes, an inner lacinea and an outer galea, one or both of which may be absent. More laterally on the stipes is a jointed, leg-like palp made up of a number of segments; in Orthoptera there are five (Fig. 13A).

The muscles of the maxilla are comparable with those of the mandible. Anterior and posterior rotator muscles are inserted on the cardo and a ventral adductor muscle arising on the tentorium is inserted on both cardo and stipes. Arising in the stipes are flexor muscles of lacinea and galea and a lacineal flexor also arises in the cranium, but neither lobe has an extensor muscle. The palp has levator and depressor muscles arising in the stipes and each segment of the palp has a single muscle causing flexing of the next segment (Fig. 13B).

The palps are sensory organs used to test the quality of the food. During feeding in the cockroach the whole maxilla makes rapid backwards and forwards movements at the side of the hypopharynx and at the same time the terminal lobes are moved. By this action particles of food are scraped back into the preoral cavity. The maxillary lobes are also used for cleaning antennae, palps and front legs, the appendage being drawn through the galeal pads which work rapidly over its surface.

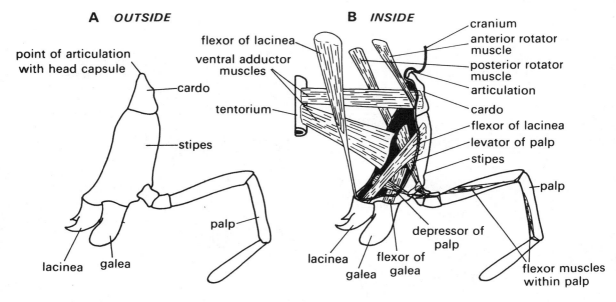

Fig. 13. Diagrams of the maxilla from the outside (A) and the inside (B) to show the musculature (after Snodgrass, 1935).

Labium

The labium is similar in structure to the maxillae, but with the appendages of the two sides fused in the midline so that they form a median plate. The basal part of the labium, equivalent to the maxillary cardines and possibly including a part of the sternum of the labial segment, is called the postmentum. This may be subdivided into a proximal submentum and a distal mentum. Distal to the postmentum, and equivalent to the fused maxillary stipites, is the prementum. Terminally this bears four lobes, two inner glossae and two outer paraglossae, which are collectively known as the ligula. One or both pairs of lobes may be absent or they may be fused to form a single median process. A pair of palps arise laterally from the prementum, often being three segmented (Fig. 14A).

The musculature corresponds with that of the maxillae, but there are no muscles to the postmentum. Muscles corresponding with the ventral adductors run from the tentorium to the front and back of the prementum; glossae and paraglossae have flexor muscles, but no extensors, and the palp has levator and depressor muscles arising in the prementum. The segments of the palp each have flexor and extensor muscles. In addition there are other muscles with no equivalent in the maxillae. Two pairs arising in the prementum converge on to the wall of the salivarium at the junction of labium with hypopharynx. A pair of muscles opposing these arises in the hypopharynx and the combined effect of them all may be to regulate the flow of saliva or to move the prementum (see Fig. 3). Finally a pair of muscles arising in the postmentum and inserted into the prementum serves to retract or flex the prementum (Fig. 14B).

The prementum closes the preoral cavity from behind and the palpi, like the maxillary palpi, are mainly sensory in function.

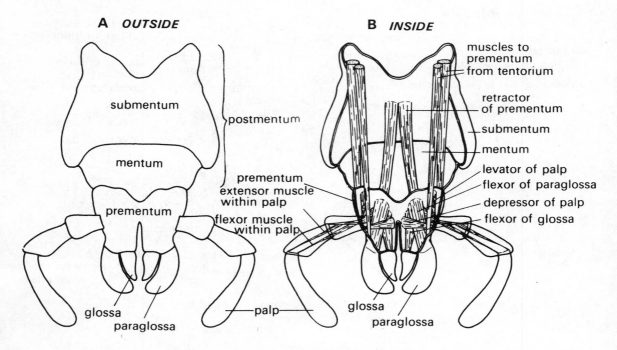

Fig. 14. Diagrams of the labium from the outside (A) and the inside (B) to show the musculature (after Snodgrass, 1944).

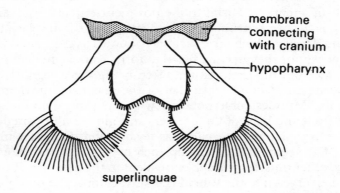

Fig. 15. The hypopharynx of a larval ephemeropteran showing the large superlinguae (after Snodgrass, 1935).

Hypopharynx

The hypopharynx is a median lobe immediately behind the mouth. The salivary duct usually opens behind it, between it and the labium. Most of the hypopharynx is membranous, but the adoral face is sclerotised distally, and proximally contains a pair of suspensory sclerites which extend upwards to end in the lateral wall of the stomodaeum. Muscles arising on the frons are inserted into these sclerites which distally are hinged to a pair of lateral lingual sclerites. These in turn have inserted into them antagonistic pairs of muscles arising on the tentorium and the labium. The various muscles serve to swing the hypopharynx forwards and back and in cockroach there are two more muscles running across the hypopharynx which dilate the salivary orifice and expand the salivarium (Fig. 3).

In Apterygota, larval Ephemeroptera and Dermaptera there are two lateral lobes of the hypopharynx called the superlinguae (Fig. 15).

1.42 Sucking mouthparts

The mouthparts of insects which feed on fluids are modified in various ways to form a tube through which liquid can be drawn and the saliva injected. This results in elongation of some parts and often some of the typical structures are lost. In *Apis* (Hymenoptera) the galeae and labial palps form a tube round the elongate fused glossal tongue (Snodgrass, 1956). The proboscis of Lepidoptera is formed from the galeae, the

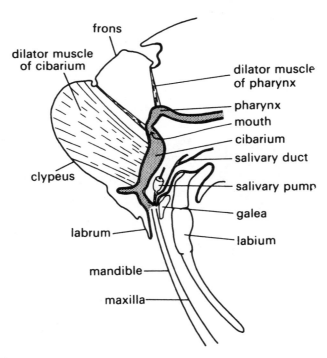

Fig. 16. Median vertical section of the head of a cicada showing the enlargement of the cibarial dilator muscles in the formation of a sucking pump (after Snodgrass, 1944).

rest of the mouthparts, apart from the labial palps, being reduced or absent (Eastham and Eassa, 1955). The Homoptera and Heteroptera have separate food and salivary canals between the opposed maxillae which are styliform (Snodgrass, 1944), while in Diptera the food canal is formed between the labrum and labium and the salivary canal runs through the hypopharynx (Snodgrass, 1944). In addition the higher Diptera have specialised pseudotracheae in the labium. These are small channels which open to the exterior and pass liquid food to the food canal.

Associated with the production of a tube for feeding is the development of a pump for drawing up the fluids and a salivary pump for injecting saliva. Often the feeding pump is developed from the cibarium which, by extension of the lateral lips of the mouth, becomes a closed chamber connecting with the food canal. The cibarial muscles from the clypeus enlarge so that a powerful pump is produced (Fig. 16). In Lepidoptera and Hymenoptera the cibarial pump is combined with a pharyngeal pump which has dilators arising on the frons.

CHAPTER II
FEEDING

Insects feed on a very wide variety of animal, vegetable and dead organic materials. Some are virtually omnivorous, but the majority are more specific, being restricted to a particular category of food or even to a particular plant or animal. Food preference may be based on nutritional or non-nutritional factors and appears to be of significance in that survival is better or fecundity greater with the preferred food. The finding and recognition of such food involves various mechanisms depending on the insect and its particular mode of life, but vision and olfaction are of widespread importance.

Feeding and ingestion involve modifications of the mouthparts and physiological adaptations. Fluid feeders often inject enzymes into the food and in blood-sucking insects an anticoagulant may be injected. Predaceous insects restrain their prey by force or by means of a venom injected with the saliva or, in Hymenoptera, via the sting.

A few insects grow fungi as food and social insects store food. Amongst the social insects feeding of one insect by another commonly occurs and this behaviour may provide a basis for the whole social system.

A general account of feeding in insects is given by Brues (1946). Other more specialised reviews are as follows:— food preference: Dethier (1947b), Lipke and Fraenkel (1956), Thorsteinson (1960); feeding behaviour: Dadd (1963), Dethier (1966), Kennedy and Stroyan (1959), Mittelstaedt (1962); venoms: Beard (1963), Edwards (1963); fungus feeding: Grassé (1949), Baker (1963); social insects: Richards (1953), Wheeler (1922).

2.1 Feeding habits

Any classification of feeding habits is arbitrary, but Brues (1946) recognises four fairly comprehensive categories:— plant feeders, predators, scavengers and parasites.

Nearly half of the species of insects feed on plants and these may be further subdivided into those feeding on green plants (phytophagous) and those feeding on fungi (mycetophagous). Predominantly phytophagous groups of insects are:— Orthoptera, Lepidoptera, Homoptera, Thysanoptera, Phasmida, Isoptera, Coleoptera (families Cerambycidae, Chrysomelidae and Curculionidae), Hymenoptera (Symphyta) and some Diptera. Most of these feed on higher plants, but, for instance, the aquatic larvae of Ephemeroptera and some Plecoptera and Trichoptera feed on algae. Fungus-feeding larvae are frequent amongst Diptera (particularly Mycetophilidae) and the habit also occurs in various Coleoptera. In many other insects fungi form at least a part of the diet. This is true in many dung-feeding insects and others, such as some termites, which cultivate their own fungi.

Some predators occur in most of the insect orders, some groups being entirely predaceous. Predominantly predaceous groups are:— Odonata, Dictyoptera (Mantodea), Heteroptera (Reduviidae and others), larval Neuroptera, Mecoptera, Diptera (Asilidae and Empididae), Coleoptera (Adephaga, larval Lampyridae and Coccinellidae) and Hymenoptera (Sphecidae and Pompilidae). These feed mainly on other insects, but larval Lampyridae, for instance, prey on snails.

Saprophagous insects occur mainly in the higher insects with larvae differing from the adults. Decaying organic matter is a common source of food for many larval Diptera and Coleoptera. In this habitat fungi may also form an important part of the diet.

Parasites may live on the outside or inside their hosts. Amongst ectoparasites are all Siphonaptera, Anoplura and Mallophaga and some Dermaptera, Heteroptera, such as *Cimex* and some Reduviidae, and various Diptera—mosquitoes, Simuliidae, Ceratopogonidae, Tabanidae and the Pupipara for example. Many of these are bloodsucking, in many cases on vertebrates. Sometimes both sexes suck blood, as in Siphonaptera and tsetse flies, or only the females do so, as in Nematocera and Brachycera. In the latter instance the females also regularly feed on nectar, which is the only food of the males (Downes, 1958).

Internal parasites, most of which are parasitic only as larvae, include all the Strepsiptera, the Ichneumonoidea, Chalcidoidea and Proctotrupoidea amongst Hymenoptera and Bombyliidae, Cyrtidae, Tachinidae and Sarcophagidae amongst Diptera.

In holometabolous insects (p. 398) larval food is often different from that of the adult; compare the caterpillar and the butterfly.

2.2 Finding and recognising the food

For some insects the problem of finding food does not arise since they are surrounded by an abundance of food from the time of hatching. This usually results from the oviposition habits of the parent as in many phytophagous forms in which the female oviposits on the plant which forms the larval food. Similarly amongst saprophagous and endoparasitic insects the female lays her eggs in suitable detritus or in the appropriate host (see p. 331). The larvae of social insects are presented with food by the workers (p. 36) and are incapable of searching for it, but, with these exceptions, food-finding must play an important part in the lives of many insects.

The initial attraction of insects to their food from a distance is often not very specific. Final recognition of the food usually occurs at closer quarters and involves different stimuli from those involved in attraction from a distance.

2.21 Food-finding and recognition in phytophagous insects

Attraction to a food plant from a distance can occur visually or by olfaction, probably varying very much with the species and the situation. *Schistocerca* (Orthoptera), for instance, is attracted by the sight of any solid object of an appropriate size and especially by a pattern of vertical stripes (Wallace, 1958), but such attraction can usually only be very general because of the variability in form of most plants (Thorsteinson, 1960).

Colour may also play a part in recognition. Under experimental conditions aphids are attracted by yellow and this may be related to the fact that they prefer young or senescent leaves, which are often yellowish, to mature, green ones. Form and colour are important to bees in finding flowers and colour is probably important in many species feeding on the flowers themselves.

Because of the general lack of specificity of visual factors, olfaction must usually play an important part in arriving at and recognising the food. Thorsteinson (1960) suggests that the initial effect of odours is to inhibit locomotion so that once a plant is found, presumably largely as a result of random searching, there is little tendency for the insect to move away again. Such odours he calls 'aggregants' and they are only effective over short distances. There are, however, instances of attraction to a more distant source of smell. Larval *Schistocerca*, for instance, respond to the smell of food over a metre away by moving upwind towards it (Haskell, *et al.*, 1962), but only if they are starved beforehand.

At close quarters chemoreception—olfaction, contact chemoreception and gustation—are important in food plant recognition. Bees, having made a visually directed approach to a flower, are guided by the flower smells and by their own colony smells previously left on the flower (p.745). Contact chemoreceptors commonly occur on the tarsi, and stimulation of the tarsi of blowflies and butterflies with sugar leads to extension of the proboscis. Similar receptors on the proboscis promote feeding and others within the mouthparts lead to continued feeding provided the food is suitable. In nectar-sucking insects such as the bee, the strength of these responses increases with the concentration of sugars so that the insect always takes the most concentrated food available.

Host plant selection in aphids occurs mainly after alighting (Kennedy and Stroyan, 1959) when the insect probes the plant with its proboscis, testing the physical and chemical properties of the sap. Kennedy and Booth (1951) suggest that selection is based on two sets of stimuli. Some stimulating factors are non-nutritious, but are specific chemicals relating to the taxonomic position of the plant as a result of which the aphid tends to prefer particular plant species. Other factors are nutritional and indicative of the physiological condition of the plant. These act via the plant sap or physiologically related factors. The two sets of factors may oppose each other since often a taxonomically suitable host is not in a suitable physiological condition, and *vice versa*. The choice made by the aphid is a balance between the two.

In biting and chewing insects like the locust, once contact is made with potential food the insect rapidly vibrates its palps so that these touch the surface of the food and are stimulated chemotactically. Biting, which follows, is a non-specific response and if the insect is sufficiently hungry it will bite substances which are normally rejected although these may subsequently be rejected as a result of gustatory stimuli. Continued feeding results from the presence of attractive substances, including nutritive ones, in the food (Dadd, 1963) and in *Camnula* (Orthoptera) feeding is induced by the sugars and amino acids normally present in wheat leaves on which the insect feeds (Thorsteinson, 1960). In the larva of *Bombyx*, Hamamura *et al.* (1962) have analysed the factors promoting feeding and have isolated separate factors which lead to attraction, biting and continued swallowing. The chemicals β-sitosterol and morin have been isolated as biting factors, and cellulose is a swallowing factor whose effect is enhanced by a number of co-factors such as sucrose, inositol, inorganic phosphate and silica. In general it appears that suitable gustatory stimuli are important for continued feeding.

2.22 Food-finding and recognition by predators

Predators catch their prey either by sitting and waiting for it to come their way or by actively pursuing it. *Mantis*, for example, sits and waits for its prey and, as it has a very mobile head, the movements of the prey can be followed without the whole mantis moving. The eyes are large and wide apart enabling the mantis to judge its distance from the prey accurately (p. 567). When striking at the prey, *Mantis* can compensate for the position of the head relative to the thorax, which is indicated by proprioceptive hairs at the front of the prothorax, and for deviation of the prey from the optical axis between the two eyes (Mittelstaedt, 1962). The front legs of the mantis are raptorial and armed with spines (Fig. 17) so that when the prey is within range it is caught and held by a rapid movement of the forelegs (extension only takes 30–60 msec.) and then brought back to the mouth. In a comparable way some dragonfly larvae wait for their prey, lying concealed in the mud at the bottom of a pool and seizing the prey with the labial mask. This is a modification of the labium in which pre- and post-mentum are elongated and the palps are modified to form grasping organs (Fig. 18). The mask can be extended in front of the head by an increase in blood pressure and the palps are used to catch the prey. By withdrawal of the mask the prey is carried back to the mandibles.

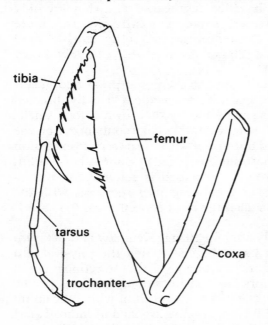

tibia

femur

tarsus

coxa

trochanter

Fig. 17. Raptorial foreleg of a mantis (from Imms, 1957).

A few insects make traps in which they catch their prey. Ant lions (larval Myrmeleontidae, Neuroptera), for instance, dig pits one to two inches in diameter with sloping sides in dry sand and then bury themselves at the bottom with only the head exposed (Fig. 19). If an ant walks over the edge of such a pit it has difficulty in regaining the top because of the instability of the sides. In addition, the larva, by sharp movements of the head, flicks sand at the ant so that it falls to the bottom of the pit and is captured by the ant lion.

Adult Odonata are active hunters, pursuing other insects in flight, and, in order to facilitate catching, the thoracic segments are rotated forwards so as to bring the legs into an anterior position (Fig. 20). Tiger beetles hunt on the ground and have long legs, which increase their speed, and prognathous mouthparts with large mandibles.

The majority of hunters have well-developed eyes since only vision can give a sufficiently rapid directed response to moving prey. This reaction is usually not specific and the predator will pursue any moving object of suitable size. Thus dragonflies turn towards small stones thrown into the air and the wasp *Philanthus* orientates to a variety of moving insects of appropriate size, although it only catches bees. This subsequent recognition involves other senses and only if the insect has the smell of a bee does *Philanthus* attempt to capture it. Provided it has the appropriate smell the wasp will attack any insect of the right size, but, having caught it, stinging does not follow unless the insect really is a bee, other insects experimentally given the smell of a bee are released. This final recognition is presumably tactile. Comparable behaviour is probably common amongst other parasites and predators.

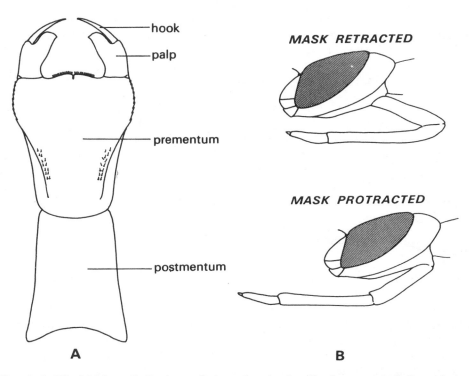

Fig. 18. A. The labial mask of a dragonfly larva (partly after Gardner, 1960). B. Lateral view of the head of a dragonfly larva showing the labial mask retracted and protracted (diagrammatic).

Fig. 19. Section through the pit made by an ant lion showing the larva lying in wait for its prey at the bottom of the pit (from Berland and Grassé, 1951).

In predaceous larval forms with poorly developed eyes and often with subterranean habits, such as tabanid larvae, the finding of prey must be largely olfactory. *Dytiscus* (Coleoptera) also responds to chemical stimuli in the water, rather than the sight of prey.

Mechanical stimulation is sometimes important in finding prey and some dragonfly larvae depend on mechanoreceptors on the antennae or tarsi for this. *Notonecta* is able to locate prey trapped in the air–water interface as a result of the ripples which radiate from it, perceiving the vibrations with sensory hairs on the swimming legs. Amongst terrestrial insects the response of ant lions to their prey depends on mechanical stimulation from the falling sand as well as on vision.

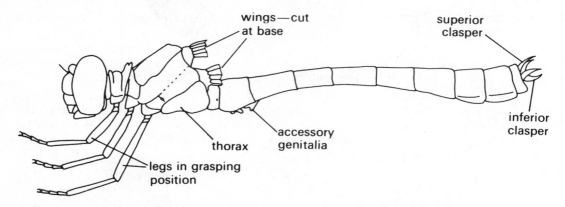

Fig. 20. Diagram of a male dragonfly to show the oblique development of the thorax bringing the legs into an anterior position which facilitates grasping the prey.

Coccinellid (Coleoptera) larvae preying on aphids only respond to the prey on contact. They move across a leaf, searching to either side as they go, but after finding and eating an aphid they tend to remain in the same area by making numerous small turning movements. Since aphids usually occur in large numbers this is clearly an advantage and this type of behaviour is only suited to prey which is more or less sedentary and locally abundant.

2.23 Host-finding by blood-sucking insects

Perception of a host at a distance may arise from visual, olfactory or mechanical stimulation, depending on the species and the situation. *Glossina swynnertoni*, a tsetse fly inhabiting relatively open savannah, can see cattle moving 450 ft. away, but *G. medicorum*, from dense forest and thicket, only reacts to a moving screen at distances under 25 ft. Movement of a potential host increases the likelihood of the insect reacting to it. The smell of the host is also important and where vision is limited, as in *G. medicorum*, may be particularly important. If an insect responds to the smell of a host by taking off and then orientates upwind it will fly into the vicinity of the source of smell. At closer quarters vision may become more important again (Buxton, 1955; Chapman, 1961). Mosquitoes react to hosts at a distance in similar ways (Kalmus and Hocking, 1960).

At closer quarters other factors also play a part in attraction. In addition to smell, moisture and warmth are important to mosquitoes (Brown, 1958) and settling depends on the nature of the surface. Mosquitoes settle more rapidly on rough than on smooth surfaces and often on dark rather than light ones. After settling, probing the host tissues with the proboscis is induced by olfactory stimuli and also by the warmth of the host.

2.24 Host-finding by internal parasites

In the majority of internal parasites the parent insect oviposits in a suitable host. Smell, and possibly also contact chemoreception, are involved in this (see p. 331). In some cases, however, the parent does not seek out the larval host, but oviposits or larviposits in places frequented by the host so that the larvae make their own way on to the host when the occasion presents itself. For instance, the human warble fly, *Cordylobia anthropophaga,* oviposits in sand fouled with urine. The larvae hatch in a day or two and then remain inactive until the area is visited by a potential host, man or some other mammal. They are activated by the vibrations and warmth of the host and bore in through the skin.

In a very few insects the larvae act as the dispersive phase and reinfect new hosts. This is the case in Strepsiptera and the meloid beetles, both of which produce vast numbers of larvae known as triungulins (see Fig. 264A). Strepsipteran triungulins escape from the female, which is an internal parasite, when the host is visiting a flower. They remain in the flower until another insect arrives and then jump on to it. If this is the correct host they remain clinging to it and, depending on the species, parasitise it or its offspring; if it is not the appropriate host they jump off again (Clausen, 1940). Some meloids find their hosts in essentially similar ways, while in others, parasitic in grasshoppers' eggs, the triungulins actively seek out the eggs.

2.3 Food preferences

2.31 Food preferences of phytophagous insects

The degree of specificity of insects to particular plants varies considerably. Some species, particularly amongst Homoptera and sawflies, are restricted to one particular plant species and are regarded as monophagous. *Coccus fagi*, for instance, only feeds on beech, and the larvae of the sawfly, *Xyela julii,* only on *Pinus sylvestris.* Some such species may feed on other plants if they are forced to do so, but others will die in the absence of the correct plant. Other insects are less restricted, but nevertheless feed on only a limited range of plants. They are called oligophagous. *Pieris rapae* (Lepidoptera), for instance, feeds only on Cruciferae and other plants which contain mustard oils. Finally there are polyphagous insects which feed on a very wide range of plants, but even these show preferences for particular foods. *Schistocerca* is polyphagous.

There are two points of view with regard to the basis of food preference. One suggests that choice is governed by non-nutritional factors (Dethier, 1947b; Lipke and Fraenkel, 1956). It is argued that the leaves of most plants are adequate for insects from the nutritional standpoint so that nutritive factors cannot be the basis of selection. Rather, selection is based on physical factors and secondary chemical substances such as glycosides, alkaloids and essential oils. For instance, *Nomadacris* (Orthoptera) selects the softest and moistest grass irrespective of species (Chapman, 1957) and *Plutella* (Lepidoptera) can be induced to feed on normally unacceptable plants by coating them with mustard oil. Mustard oil is an essential constituent of the normal food plant with no known metabolic significance to the plant.

The alternative point of view is that preferences are related to nutritive substances in the plant (Kennedy and Booth, 1951; Thorsteinson, 1960). Thorsteinson has shown, for instance, that the·sugars and amino acids of the normal food plant stimulate feeding in *Camnula* and, whereas Dethier (1947b) believes selection to be based on the variation in attraction by different chemicals, Thorsteinson considers that the inhibition of feeding is often more important. He divides phytophagous insects into two major .groups. In one, including the grasshoppers, feeding is induced by chemical stimulants present in all plants, but tends to be limited by the presence of inhibitors in some. These inhibitors, which will be different for different insects, may be scattered at random throughout the plant kingdom or may be present in all except certain taxonomic groups. By this balance between attraction and inhibition oligophagous feeding habits result. In the second group of insects, such as *Pieris,* feeding is induced by some extraordinary chemical stimulant only present in some particular taxonomic group of plants. Oligophagy may also arise in this way (and see Fraenkel, 1969, *Entomologia exp. appl.* **12**).

2.32 Prey specificity in predators

Some predaceous insects, particularly amongst Hymenoptera, are relatively specific in their choice of prey. *Philanthus* only catches bees, pompilid wasps only take certain spiders, and *Eumenes* only collects caterpillars, although of different species, for its nest. Other predators, such as asilids (Diptera), appear to take anything of a suitable size and exhibiting suitable behaviour, including even members of their own species.

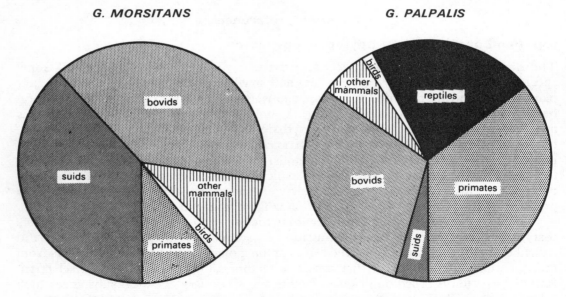

Fig. 21. The hosts of *Glossina morsitans* and *G. palpalis.* The angle subtended by each sector of the centre of the circle represents the proportion of flies feeding on each particular host (after Weitz, 1964).

2.33 Host preferences of blood-sucking insects

In general the free-living blood-sucking insects, such as mosquitoes and tsetse flies, bite a wide range of hosts, although most are restricted to mammals and birds. Within this range tsetse flies, at least, show distinct preferences. *Glossina morsitans* feeds primarily on ungulates, which are essential for its continued existence, while man and reptiles are particularly important to *G. palpalis* (Fig. 21).

The less mobile blood-suckers are more specific. This is true to some extent of fleas, although here the specificity is largely ecological. Development of fleas usually occurs in the nest of the host and particular species tend to be restricted to a particular type of nest with a characteristic micro-environment. Nests may, for instance, be subterranean, on the surface of the ground or in trees. This clearly limits the type of host which a particular species of flea is likely to encounter, but, given the opportunity, most fleas will bite unusual hosts. Lice, on the other hand, which spend the whole of their life history on the host, are extremely host specific (Hopkins, 1950).

2.34 Significance of food preferences

Although many insects can be reared on abnormal food substances, food preferences are often of considerable significance. *Melanoplus,* for instance, fails to survive on some food plants, but on its preferred food, hedge mustard, development and survival are good. Even so development takes longer and fewer eggs are laid than with a diet containing a variety of plants (Barnes, 1955). Similarly, mosquitoes can survive solely on nectar, but many species require a blood meal if they are to produce eggs. Such species are called anautogenous; others, which can produce eggs on a diet of nectar alone, are called autogenous.

2.4 Conditioning to food

There is some evidence that insects can become conditioned to particular foods. *Carausius* (Phasmida) normally feeds on privet and will reject ivy, but if it is forced to feed on ivy it ultimately tends to prefer this to privet and, comparably, locust larvae reared on an artificial diet can only be induced to eat grass, the normal food, with difficulty (Haskell, *et al.,* 1962). In the case of *Carausius* the altered preference is passed on to the next generation. There is some suggestion that the food first eaten by a phytophagous insect conditions its subsequent behaviour so that it shows a preference for this food (Haskell, *et al.,* 1962).

2.5 Feeding and ingestion

Once the insect has recognised its food as suitable it starts to feed. The processes by which food is ingested vary considerably.

2.51 Feeding in phytophagous insects

Typical plant-feeding insects with biting mouthparts bite off fragments of food and pass them back to the mouth with the aid of the maxillae while grasshoppers also help to guide the food into the mouth by holding it between their forelegs. Often such insects feed at the edge of a leaf, moving on towards the centre, and usually the more woody parts are avoided.

Fluid feeders may obtain their food from the cell sap or directly from distributive vessels. Aphids, for instance, usually tap the phloem. When an aphid lands it inserts its mouthparts into the plant tissue using the protractor and retractor muscles of the stylets in the head, probably aided by a clasping action of the labium. In the course of penetration through the leaf epidermis and parenchyma it encounters mechanical resistance and this to some extent affects selection of the feeding site, but it is probable that this resistance is partially overcome by the saliva dissolving the middle lamellae between the plant cells. As the stylets penetrate the tissues saliva flows from the tip and gels so that a sheath is formed round them (p. 54). In some species, at least, no feeding takes place until the stylets reach the phloem and in *Aphis* penetrating to this tissue takes about an hour. The subsequent intake of sap is largely passive due to the pressure within the plant forcing sap into the stylets, but the rate of flow is controlled by the aphid since if it is starved or is attended by ants the rate of feeding is increased (Kennedy and Stroyan, 1959; Auclair, 1963).

2.52 Feeding in predaceous insects

Having captured their prey some predaceous insects, such as the mantis, restrain the victim by sheer mechanical strength and then tear it to pieces with powerful mandibles, ingesting the whole insect. Many other forms, including Heteroptera and some Diptera (Asilidae), inject salivary secretions which kill the prey and then, following extra-intestinal digestion of the contents, ingest the digested remains and discard the cuticular shell. Finally, in a different category, are the predaceous Hymenoptera which capture other animals and store them alive for use as food by the larvae. The prey in this case is paralysed by a venom injected via the sting of the predator.

2.53 Venoms of predaceous insects

The venoms injected by Heteroptera, such as *Platymeris,* are produced in the salivary glands which are enlarged and have a muscular coat. Following penetration of the stylets into the prey the venom is forcibly injected by a powerful salivary pump and is then transported round the body of the victim in the haemolymph. Injection is followed by convulsive struggling, rapidly leading to tremors and then to death. These venoms are non-specific, being toxic to a wide range of insects and their action is to cause a general lysis of the tissues so that nervous activity rapidly stops. Similar venoms are probably used by larval Neuroptera and by Asilidae and Empididae (Diptera) and Odonata (Beard, 1963; Edwards, 1963).

Hymenoptera which paralyse their prey inject the venom via the sting, which is a modified ovipositor (see p. 326). There is no real evidence that the wasp attempts to inject its venom into a nerve ganglion of the victim as is suggested in the literature, but localised stinging in particular regions of the prey probably indicates the presence of relatively weak spots in the integument at these points. These venoms also circulate in the haemolymph, but they do not kill the prey, only paralysing the musculature of the body wall, possibly by a neuromuscular block. The heart and alimentary canal continue rhythmic activity and the nervous system remains active, but, although such a state of paralysis may last for several months, degenerative changes set in and the insect eventually dies. The injected venom does not help to keep the prey 'fresh' for the larvae to feed on subsequently, but rather the prey is in the position of an insect deprived of food which can survive as long as its food reserves allow. These paralysing venoms may be very specific, affecting only one or a small number of species so that injection into an inappropriate species has no effect. This indicates very specialised and specific chemical configurations for the venoms.

2.54 Feeding in blood-sucking insects

After a tsetse fly lands on its host it spreads its legs apart, grips the skin with its claws and braces itself so as to be able to exert a downward pressure. Then it lowers the haustellum and pierces the skin by the rasping action of the labella (see Buxton, 1955). Feeding never follows the initial probe and the haustellum is partly withdrawn, the head moved and a new thrust made in a different direction. In this way the fly causes a local haemorrhage in the tissues and it drinks from the pool of blood which is produced. The whole process of feeding to repletion takes about two minutes in *G. morsitans*. In mosquitoes the stylets bend inside the host tissues and often penetrate a blood capillary from which blood is then drawn directly. This also occurs in *Rhodnius* where, as in mosquitoes, the stylets penetrate the tissues as a result of the action of their protractor and retractor muscles following an initial thrust from the leg musculature.

Blood-sucking insects inject saliva into the wound and often this saliva contains an anticoagulant. This prevents the blood from clotting in the wound and in the proboscis of the insect, but the saliva of some such insects, notably *Aedes aegypti,* contains no anticoagulant and the blood clots in the stomach within 15 minutes of feeding. The absence of the anticoagulant, however, does not impair feeding.

Blood is sucked up by the action of the cibarial pump and feeding continues until the insect is enormously distended; *Rhodnius* may increase its weight by more than six times in a 15-minute feed. The size of the meal in *Rhodnius* is limited by the extent to which the abdomen will enlarge, which is determined by the epicuticle. The abdominal cuticle consists only of undifferentiated endocuticle and strongly folded epicuticle and expansion can continue only until the epicuticle is smooth. Expansion is facilitated by plasticisation of the endocuticle so that it becomes less rigid at an early stage during the meal. This plasticisation is probably brought about by a neurosecretion which reaches the body wall through the abdominal nerves. It is only a temporary effect and decreases after feeding (Maddrell, 1966a).

2.6 Fungus-growing insects

Some termites and ants grow fungi on specially prepared substrates. All the Macrotermitinae are fungus growers and they produce a 'comb' of chewed wood on which the fungal hyphae grow and produce conidia. Some of the fungi, such as *Xylaria,* an Ascomycete, are not confined to termite nests, but the Termitomyces, which are Basidiomycetes, occur only in termitaria. *Xylaria* only produces fruiting bodies when the nest is deserted by the termites. The fungus is eaten in small amounts by the workers and is fed to some of the larvae (Grassé, 1949).

Other insects, especially some of those boring in wood, also have constant associations with particular fungi although they do not prepare specific substrates. Amongst these are the ambrosia beetles, various species of Scolytidae and Platypodidae and all Lymexilidae. These beetles make their tunnels in and under the bark of trees, but the bulk of their food is derived from fungi growing in the tunnels. The fungi are mostly rather specialised ones some of which may be connected with a variety of different beetles while others are constantly associated with one or a few species. They are transmitted by the female beetle in depressions of the body surface in which secretions of oil from associated glands accumulate. When the beetle starts actively boring the output of oil is increased and the oidial cells of the fungus are washed out. These then germinate on the tunnel walls to produce a new growth of ambrosia (Baker, 1963).

2.7 The timing of feeding activity

Feeding behaviour results from the summation of a series of internal and external stimuli. Pupae do not feed at all and in Ephemeroptera, Lepidoptera and Oestridae (Diptera) there are some species which do not feed as adults, often having reduced mouthparts. Feeding does not occur in newly emerged insects and is reduced or non-existent during diapause (Fig. 22) and at the time of moulting (Fig. 23). Female mosquitoes do not feed while they are producing eggs. The state of feeding is also important and the tendency to feed is greatly reduced after a meal and may even be physically impossible as in *Rhodnius* (see above), which only takes a single large meal in each larval instar. Tsetse flies are not attracted to their hosts for two or three days after feeding and phytophagous insects have a period of postprandial quiescence during which feeding activity, as well as other activities, is reduced.

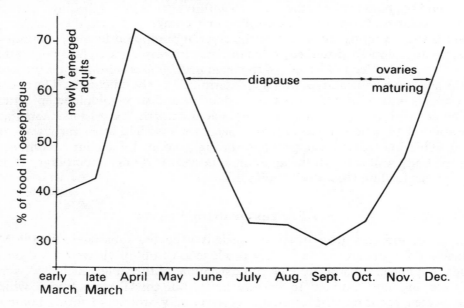

Fig. 22. Seasonal variation in the amount of feeding by adult female red locusts (after Chapman, 1957).

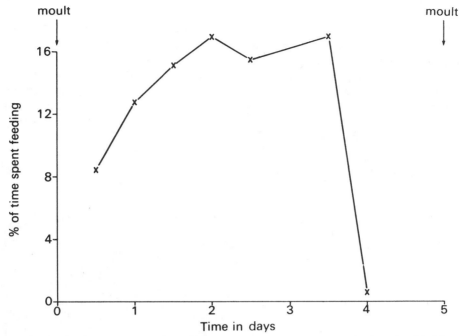

Fig. 23. Variations in the amount of time spent feeding by *Locusta* during the third larval instar (after Ellis, 1951).

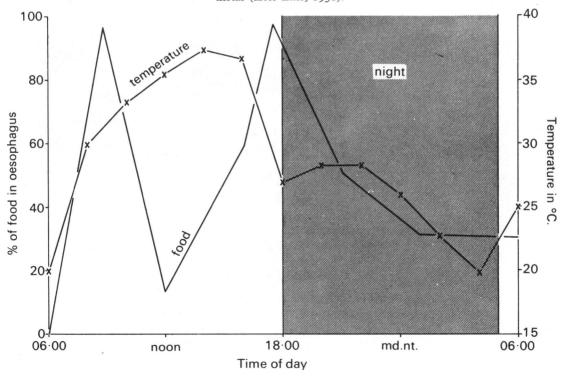

Fig. 24. Daily variation in the amount of feeding by adult male red locusts (after Chapman, 1957).

Apart from these factors there is often also some diurnal variation in feeding. This is, in part, directly related to the existing environmental conditions, such as light and temperature, which may be limiting, but, as with other activities, changes in these conditions may be important in stimulating feeding. *Nomadacris,* for instance, feeds mainly in the morning and evening (Fig. 24) when conditions are changing rapidly. Many mosquitoes are crepuscular in their biting habits and, although biting is influenced by climatic factors, the timing appears to result partly from an endogenous rhythm of activity, changes of light intensity merely acting as time cues (Clements, 1963). Biting activity also varies with the habitat. In forest regions *Aedes africanus* bites by day at ground level, but is crepuscular in the canopy, and *Mansonia fuscopennata* also bites at different times in different situations (Fig. 25).

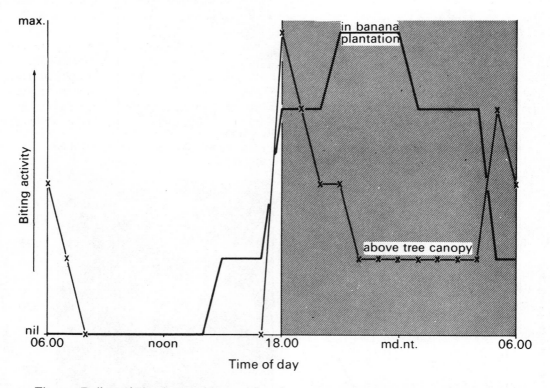

Fig. 25. Daily variation in the biting activity of *Mansonia fuscopennata* in the forest canopy and in a banana plantation (adapted from Haddow, 1961).

2.8 Food storage

Many insects build up temporary internal stores of food in the fat body or, in fluid feeders, in the crop, but external storage is a characteristic of the social and subsocial insects. Many solitary Hymenoptera (Sphecoidea and Pompiloidea) build cells and provision them for the use of their larvae. Some, such as *Ammophila,* exhibit progressive provisioning of the nest. *Ammophila* excavates a hole in the ground, provisions it with a caterpillar and then lays an egg and closes the cell. The wasp then starts a new nest.

Each morning on her first flight the female visits each nest, of which there may be three at any one time, and examines its state of provisions. If there is an ample supply she closes the nest and leaves it until the following day, but if there is not much food she brings a fresh supply. The female continues to bring food to the nest whenever it is required until the larva is well grown when she puts in a final store and seals the nest for the last time. Other solitary wasps, like *Eumenes,* and solitary bees put a large stock of provisions into the nest at the time the egg is laid and this suffices for the whole of larval development, for the cell is never visited again. This type of provisioning is known as mass provisioning.

Honey ants, such as *Myrmecocystus,* store nectar and other sweet substances in the crops of certain workers known as repletes. These are fed sugars until their gasters become enormously distended so that their movement is greatly restricted and they remain hanging from the roof in special chambers in the nest. The sugar is regurgitated to other workers as it is required (Wheeler, 1926).

There are many other examples of food storage, but this becomes most significant in *Apis* with perennial colonies in temperate regions where there is a long period during which fresh food is unobtainable. *Apis* feeds on honey and pollen. Honey is derived from nectar, which has a variable composition, but may consist of some 60% water and a very high proportion of sugars of which 40–50% is sucrose. Only traces of protein are present. When nectar is collected the enzyme invertase is secreted on to it so that sucrose is broken

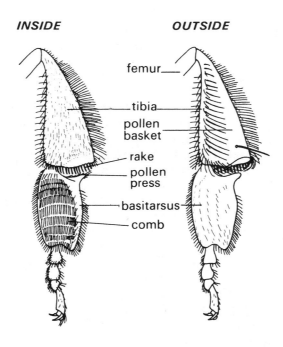

INSIDE   **OUTSIDE**

femur

tibia

pollen basket

rake

pollen press

basitarsus

comb

Fig. 26. The hind tibia and tarsus of the honey bee, from inside and outside, showing the pollen collecting apparatus (partly after Snodgrass, 1956).

down to glucose and fructose. On reaching the nest the forager gives its nectar to a house bee who has the task of reducing its water content to about 20%. To achieve this the worker regurgitates a small drop of nectar from the honey stomach, manipulates it with the mandibles and then swallows it again, repeating this process some 80 or 90 times in 20 minutes. By this process water is evaporated and the nectar concentrated. When it has reached a suitable concentration the honey is put into a cell and used for food or is sealed up for use later.

Honey provides the carbohydrates and water for adults and larvae; protein is derived from pollen. Pollen collecting is facilitated by the pectinate hairs characteristic of Apoidea since the pollen grains tend to become caught up in these hairs. The bee may actively collect pollen, biting anthers so as to increase the amount released, or it may simply become dusted with pollen while in search of nectar. Pollen collected on the head region is brushed off with the forelegs and moistened with a little regurgitated nectar or honey before being passed back to the hind legs which also collect pollen from the abdomen using the combs on the inside of the legs (Fig. 26). The pollen on the combs of one side is then removed by the rake of the opposite hind leg and collects in the pollen press between the tibia and metatarsus. By closure of the press pollen is forced outwards and upwards on to the outside of the tibia and is then held in place by the hairs and spines of the pollen basket. On returning to the nest the pollen is kicked off by the middle legs into an empty cell, house bees break up the masses of pollen and pack it down and the cell is then capped or left open for current use (Butler, 1962).

2.9 Social feeding

Feeding of one insect by another sometimes occurs in non-social insects during courtship as in the presentation of food to the female empid (Diptera) by the male (see p. 304), but in general such behaviour occurs only in the social insects. Here there are often stages—larvae, soldiers or reproductive forms—which are incapable of feeding themselves and must be fed by the workers.

In wasps the larvae are fed on the masticated remains of other insects. Bees use honey and pollen, but also brood food, a secretion of the hypopharyngeal and mandibular glands of the workers containing protein derived from pollen. Brood food is fed to all larvae for the first three days after hatching and subsequently probably forms an important part of the diet of larvae destined to become queens. The quantity of food eaten also plays some part in queen determination (see Butler, 1962). In a similar way queen determination in the ant Myrmica is related to feeding, larvae destined to become queens apparently having more protein in their diet. This varies with the physiological condition of the workers tending the larvae and possibly again involves glandular secretions by the workers (Weir, 1959).

Termites practise social feeding and in Kalotermitidae proctodaeal feeding occurs. These insects produce two types of excrement, solid faeces and a liquid containing fragments of wood and intestinal flagellates (see p. 61). Production of this second type of excrement is stimulated by other individuals placing their antennae on the dorsal or perianal region of the worker. Apart from any direct nutritive value this behaviour is important in renewing the intestinal fauna of newly moulted individuals because this fauna is lost each time a termite moults. This behaviour does not occur in Termitidae with no comparable intestinal fauna, although faeces may be eaten.

2.91 Trophallaxis

Often in the social insects a mutual exchange of food occurs, such behaviour being known as trophallaxis. When, for instance, an ant feeds a larva it receives from the larva a drop of salivary fluid, which may be so attractive to the worker that it solicits saliva from the larva without giving anything in return. This mutual exchange of food has been regarded as the basis of social systems in insects (see Wheeler, 1922; Richards, 1953), but in the wasp *Vespula sylvestris* it has been shown that the larval saliva, although taken by the workers, is not especially attractive to them. It is probable that the secretion of saliva is a means whereby the larvae eliminate excess water, and its removal by the workers prevents the nest from becoming fouled. Thus in this insect, at least, typical trophallaxis does not occur, and if such a relationship ever existed it has become modified in the course of evolution (Brian and Brian, 1952).

CHAPTER III

THE ALIMENTARY CANAL

The alimentary canal comprises three regions, foregut, midgut and hindgut, various parts of which may become modified anatomically or physiologically to perform various functions. The foregut is commonly concerned with the storage of food and sometimes helps to fragment the food before it passes to the midgut. The latter, which in most insects is lined by a delicate membrane, is primarily concerned with the production of enzymes and the absorption of the products of digestion. In some fluid-feeding insects it is specialised, together with other parts of the gut, to facilitate the rapid elimination of water from the body. The hindgut conducts undigested food to the exterior via the anus, but also has other functions. In particular the rectum is concerned in salt and water regulation.

The gut is innervated by motor nerves from the stomatogastric and central nervous systems which control the movements of the gut and the passage of food along it.

Various glands, associated with the mouthparts, function mainly in the production of saliva, but have other important roles as in the production of pheromones in social insects and silk in Lepidoptera.

A general account of the structure of the alimentary canal is given by Snodgrass (1935). Goodchild (1966) reviews the evolution of the alimentary canal in the bugs.

3.1 General structure

The alimentary canal in insects is divided into three main regions; the foregut or stomodaeum which is ectodermal in origin, the midgut or mesenteron which is endodermal, and the hindgut or proctodaeum which is again ectodermal. In many insects these regions are subdivided into various functional parts of which the most usual are the pharynx, oesophagus, crop and proventriculus in the foregut, the caeca and ventriculus in the midgut, and the pylorus, ileum and rectum in the hindgut (Fig. 27). The gut is supported in the body by muscles anteriorly and posteriorly, but elsewhere only by connective tissue and especially by tracheae which, in insects, form an important element of the connective tissue.

Usually the gut is a continuous tube running from the mouth to the anus, but in some insects feeding on a fluid diet containing little or no solid waste material the connection between the midgut and the hindgut is occluded. This is the case in some plant-sucking Heteroptera (Goodchild, 1963b) and in larval Neuroptera which digest their prey extra-orally. A similar modification occurs in the larvae of social Hymenoptera with the result that the larvae never foul the nest; in this case a pellet of faecal matter is deposited at the larva-pupa moult.

The length of the gut is roughly correlated with diet, insects feeding on a largely protein diet tend to have a shorter gut than those feeding largely on carbohydrates, but this is not always true.

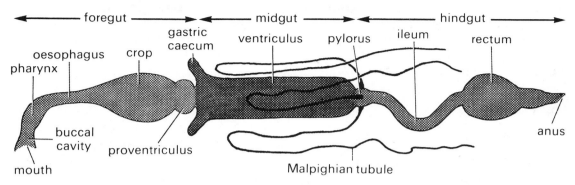

Fig. 27. Diagram showing the usual subdivisions and appendages of the alimentary canal (after Snodgrass, 1935).

3.2 Foregut

Since the foregut is ectodermal in origin it is lined with a layer of cuticle, known as the intima, which is shed at each moult in the same way as the rest of the cuticle. The foregut epithelium consists of flattened cells with indistinct boundaries. Outside the epithelium

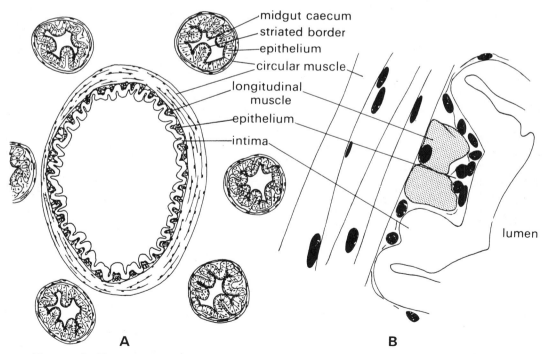

Fig. 28. A. Transverse section of foregut and midgut caeca of *Chorthippus*. B. Section of the foregut more highly magnified.

is a layer of longitudinal muscle and a layer of circular muscle, the latter often being relatively well developed (Fig. 28). The circular muscles are not inserted into the epithelium, but are continuous all round the gut so that their contraction leads to the development of even longitudinal folding (Fig. 28A). When the gut is distended with food these folds are flattened out. In addition, especially in the proventriculus, there may be six or eight permanent infoldings of the wall. The longitudinal muscles may be inserted into the circular muscles or into the epithelium. Outside the muscle layers is a delicate connective tissue sheath.

3.21 Pharynx

The pharynx is the first part of the foregut following on from the buccal cavity. Apart from the typical foregut musculature the pharynx has a series of dilator muscles inserted into it. These arise ventrally on the tentorium and dorsally on the frons and are best developed in sucking insects, especially Lepidoptera and Hymenoptera where the pharyngeal pump is used to draw up fluids. They are also present in biting and chewing insects and play a part in passing food back from the mouth to the oesophagus.

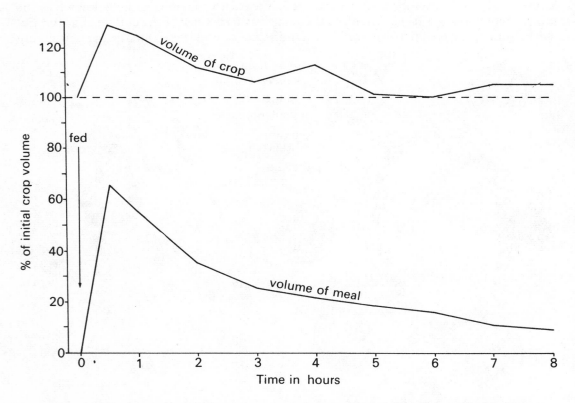

Fig. 29. The change in volume of the crop and the meal after ingestion by *Periplaneta*, showing the relative constancy of crop volume (after Davey and Treherne, 1963a).

3.22 Oesophagus

The oesophagus is an undifferentiated part of the foregut serving to pass food back from the pharynx to the crop.

3.23 Crop

The crop is an enlargement of the foregut in which food is stored. Usually it represents the posterior part of the oesophagus, but in some fluid feeders it is a lateral diverticulum (Fig. 45). Frequently when empty the crop is folded longitudinally and transversely, but in *Periplaneta* (Dictyoptera), at least, it undergoes very little change in volume since when it does not contain food it is filled with air (Fig. 29) (Davey and Treherne, 1963a).

In general, secretion and absorption do not occur in the crop, being limited by the impermeable intima. Digestion can occur, however, as a result of salivary enzymes passing back to the crop with the food and midgut enzymes being regurgitated from the midgut. Although the proventriculus acts as a valve limiting the backward movement of food, it does not prevent the regurgitation of fluids.

3.24 Proventriculus

The proventriculus is variously modified in different insects. In fluid feeders it is absent except for a simple valve at the origin of the midgut. A valve is also present in many other insects (Figs. 30, 31) and often the circular muscles form a sphincter at the entrance to the midgut.

In the cockroach and cricket the intima in the proventriculus is developed into six strong plates or teeth, which serve to break up the food (Fig. 30). The proventriculus as a whole controls the passage of food from the crop to the midgut (p. 61). In Acridoidea there are six longitudinal folds with small cuticular teeth, and here the proventriculus serves simply as a valve, retaining food in the crop while permitting the forward passage of enzymes.

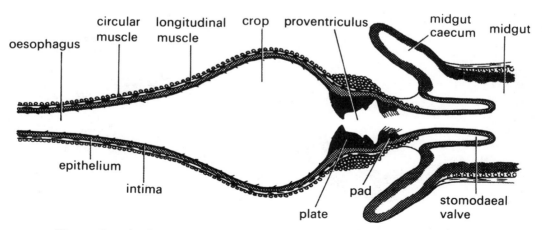

Fig. 30. Longitudinal section of the foregut of *Periplaneta* (after Snodgrass, 1935).

The proventriculus of the bee is very specialised (Fig. 31). An anterior invagination into the crop ends in four mobile lips each armed with a number of spines. Again the proventriculus controls the movement of food from the crop to the midgut, but it is also able to remove pollen from a suspension in nectar in the crop while the nectar is retained. Writhing movements of the crop keep the pollen dispersed while the lips of the proventriculus make snapping movements in such a way that the spines strain off the grains of pollen and retain them. In this way a bolus of pollen is formed and is then passed back through the proventriculus to the midgut. Nectar is retained in the crop for regurgitation and processing to form honey (p. 36).

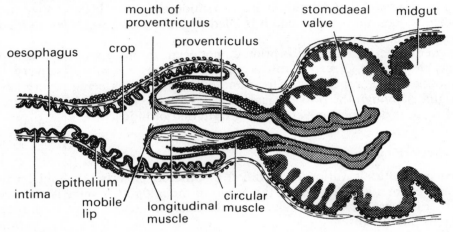

Fig. 31. Longitudinal section of the proventriculus of *Apis* (after Snodgrass, 1956).

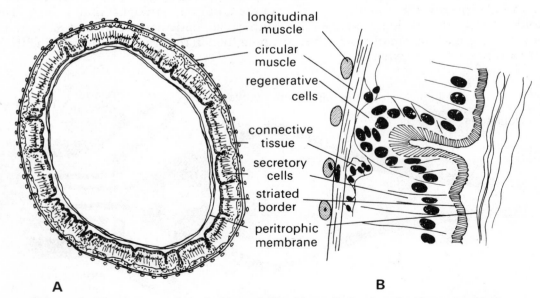

Fig. 32. A. Transverse section of midgut of *Chorthippus*. B. Section of midgut more highly magnified.

3.3 Midgut

The midgut does not have a cuticular lining but, in the majority of insects, it is lined by a delicate peritrophic membrane (see p. 46). The most characteristic cells of the midgut epithelium are tall and columnar with microvilli forming a striated border bounding the lumen (Fig. 32). Typically, the basal membrane is very deeply infolded and large numbers of mitochondria are associated with the folds (Fig. 33, cuprophilic cell). Rough endoplasmic reticulum is also often extensive and it is probable that this is concerned with enzyme production. A variety of cell types may be present. In larval *Lucilia*, for instance, there are lipophilic and cuprophilic cells. The former are packed with lipoid spheres and glycogen, and the striated border is unusual in consisting of parallel lamellae rather than microvilli. Mitochondria are evenly distributed through-out the cell (Fig. 33). Cuprophilic cells contain esterases and cytochrome oxidase and the microvilli are sparse and squat. Mitochondria are associated with the infoldings of the basal membrane (Waterhouse and Wright, 1960).

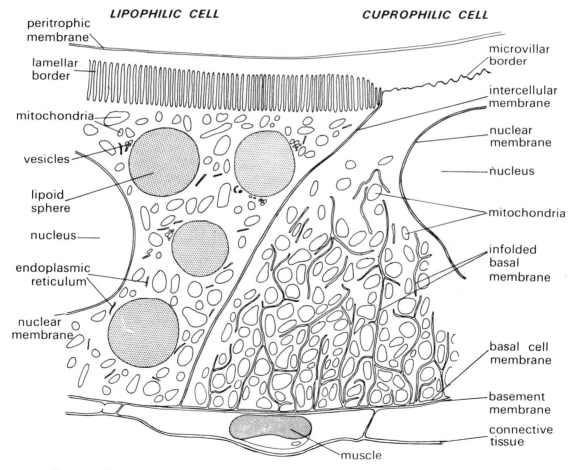

Fig. 33. Diagram of adjacent lipophilic and cuprophilic cells from the midgut of *Lucilia* larva (modified after Waterhouse and Wright, 1960).

The columnar cells are concerned with enzyme secretion and with absorption. Histological changes are visible during a secretory cycle; at first granules appear in the cytoplasm and these give rise to vacuoles which may be liberated separately into the gut lumen through the striated border or they may first coalesce into a single large

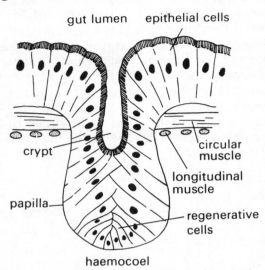

vacuole. Secretion may involve the complete breakdown of the cell which is then replaced by the regenerative cells. Such breakdown may occur randomly throughout the gut or it may pass in waves along the length of the epithelium. Secretion which involves the complete breakdown of a cell is called holocrine secretion; where the cell does not break down completely, but recovers and functions again, the process is known as merocrine secretion.

In caterpillars, and in Ephemeroptera and Plecoptera (Wigglesworth, 1965) there are goblet cells in addition to the columnar cells. These cells have an internal cavity the lining of which is faintly striated, but which, according to Waterhouse (1957), does not open into the midgut lumen. Goblet cells probably play a part in secretion, but, in addition, they appear to be concerned with storage excretion (p. 498). In *Tineola* (Lepidoptera) they accumulate metals and dyes in the goblet cavity or in the cytoplasm of the cell. These substances are discharged at the following moult when the whole of the epithelium is renewed.

Fig. 34. Diagram of a midgut crypt extending through the muscle layer to form a papilla (after Snodgrass, 1935).

Midgut cells also play some part in excretion in *Rhodnius*. Here haemoglobin is broken down in the cells to haematin, a verdohaem pigment and biliverdin. The latter is accumulated and then discharged into the lumen of the gut for disposal.

When cells of the midgut break down during secretion new ones are formed by the division and differentiation of regenerative cells (Fig. 32). These are small cells lying at the base of the epithelium either scattered or in groups (nidi) as in Orthoptera. Sometimes they occur at the bottom of folds or crypts in the epithelium and in many Coleoptera these crypts are visible as small papillae on the outside of the midgut (Fig. 34).

The muscle layers outside the epithelium are usually poorly developed, but the circular muscles lie adjacent to the epithelium, the reverse of the position in the foregut. The muscle layers are bounded by a delicate connective tissue sheath.

3.31 Anatomical differentiation

Anatomically the midgut is usually a simple tube, undifferentiated except for the presence of four, six or eight caeca at the anterior end. In some Diptera, however, the midgut is differentiated into an anterior cardiac chamber (Snodgrass, 1935; but called the proventriculus by other authors) and a long ventriculus, and in Heteroptera there are four regions, the last giving rise to numerous caeca which house bacteria.

The Homoptera and some Heteroptera feed on plant fluids. In order to obtain adequate nourishment large quantities of fluid must be ingested and modifications of the gut occur which provide for the rapid elimination of the excess of water taken in. This is necessary to avoid excessive dilution of the haemolymph and to concentrate the food to facilitate enzyme activity. This problem is less acute in other fluid feeders because their needs are smaller. Those Lepidoptera, Hymenoptera and Diptera which feed on nectar as adults only need this for maintenance; growth is complete and the

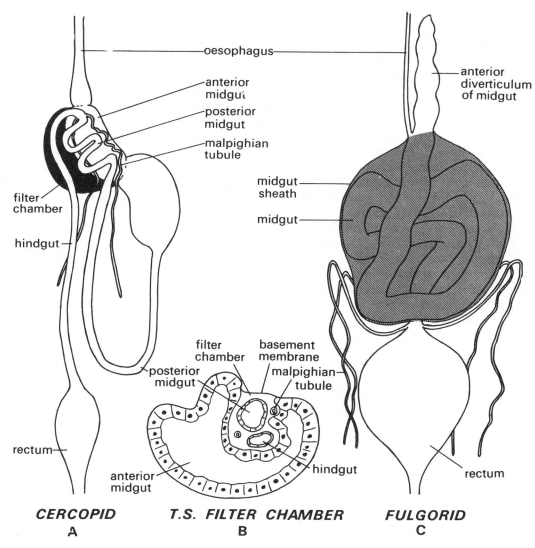

Fig. 35. A. Diagram of the alimentary canal of a cercopid showing the filter chamber (after Snodgrass, 1935). B. Transverse section of filter chamber (from Imms, 1957). C. Alimentary canal of a fulgorid (after Goodchild, 1963a).

larval reserves often suffice for egg development so that only small amounts of fluid are taken in. This fluid is stored in the crop which is lined by an impermeable cuticle and from which small quantities are passed back to the midgut as they are required. In this way over-dilution of the haemolymph resulting from the absorption of too much fluid is avoided. The volumes ingested by bugs are too large for this and the insects have no crop, but they do have a large rectum to which water is passed as quickly as possible.

In Cicadoidea the rapid removal of water to the rectum is achieved by the anterior midgut forming a large thin-walled bladder which is closely bound to the anterior hindgut and Malpighian tubules by its own basement membrane. The chamber formed within the folds of the anterior midgut is called the filter chamber (Fig. 35A). Water passes directly from the midgut to the hindgut along an osmotic gradient and there may be no significant flow of fluid through the lumen of the gut; in some species the lumen is occluded so that no flow is possible. Fulgoroidea have the midgut enclosed in a sheath with oenocytes (p. 426) inside it (Fig. 35C) and it is suggested that the sheath cells play an active role in limiting dilution of the haemolymph. An anterior, air-filled diverticulum of the midgut is not enclosed by the sheath and this may allow for the swallowing of air for expansion at each moult without damaging the sheath.

In plant-sucking Pentatomomorpha the midgut is divided into four regions, as in other Heteroptera. It is believed that the caeca of the fourth region actively remove water from the haemolymph so that excessive dilution does not occur, and between the third and fourth regions there is a constriction or a complete discontinuity which ensures the backward flow of this water to the rectum (Goodchild, 1963b). Finally, in some bryocorine Miridae the anterior midgut makes contact with a large accessory salivary gland. After feeding a clear fluid is exuded from the mouthparts suggesting that water is withdrawn from the midgut to the salivary glands and then eliminated via the mouth.

The problem in blood-sucking insects is different. It is common for a large amount of blood to be ingested at one meal, but, since feeding is discontinuous and the bulk of the nutriment is in the blood corpuscles rather than in solution in the serum, the fluid contents can be eliminated with little loss of nutriment. In *Glossina*, for instance, water is removed from the blood in the anterior half of the midgut and very quickly eliminated via the Malpighian tubules so that a very clear urine may be passed while the insect is still feeding (and see p. 712).

3.32 Functional differentiation

Even if there is no anatomical differentiation of the midgut there may be functional differentiation. For instance, in nematoceran larvae absorption of different substances apparently occurs in different parts (Wigglesworth, 1942) (see p. 68) and this is also the case in the blowfly larva where on histochemical grounds the midgut is divided into three regions and the middle part is further differentiated into five zones (Fig. 45) (Waterhouse, 1957). Similar differentiation occurs in larval Lepidoptera.

3.33 Peritrophic membrane

The peritrophic membrane forms a delicate lining layer to the midgut, although it is absent in many fluid-feeding insects, in *Anthrenus* (Coleoptera) larvae and in carabid beetles. It contains chitin and sometimes also some protein.

Two types of peritrophic membrane are recognised according to their modes of formation. In Diptera the membrane is usually a single layer made up, in *Glossina* at least, of disorientated fibres in an amorphous matrix. It is secreted as a viscous fluid at the anterior end of the midgut. This fluid is forced through a mould or press formed by the stomodaeal invagination and the wall of the midgut so that it forms a tube which becomes the membrane. To form a satisfactory mould the cells of the invagination are large and turgid so that they press against the midgut wall (Fig. 36). They can be pulled away by longitudinal muscles, and spines at the tip of the invagination help to draw out the membrane during this movement. This type of membrane is formed continuously at a rate, in *Eristalis* (Diptera) larvae, of about 6 mm./hr.

The second type of membrane is formed by delamination from the whole surface of the midgut. This type occurs in Orthoptera, Odonata, Coleoptera and Hymenoptera and because of the mode of formation there are often several membranes lying one inside the other. In *Periplaneta* the membrane consists of a regular fibrillar network, usually with three systems of fibrils at 60° or 90° to each other, overlaid by, and sometimes continuous with, a less regular network. The pores in the network are up to 0·2 μ across and a thin, structureless film is stretched across them (Fig. 37A) (Mercer and Day, 1952). The fibrils forming the network are approximately 100 Å in diameter and each strand of the net is made up of about four such fibrils.

It is possible that the microvilli of the midgut cells form a template on which the fibrils are laid down (Fig. 37B) so that a network is formed (Mercer and Day, 1952). The less regular networks could arise from fibrils laid down more distally on the microvilli and the amorphous matrix from the secretion of a second substance alternating with the secretion of fibrillar material. A period of secretion might be followed by a period in which material was elaborated, but not secreted, and in this way separate mem-

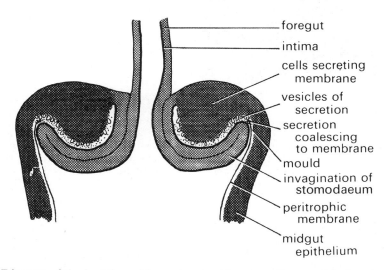

Fig. 36. Diagram of the junction of foregut and midgut in a dipteran showing the origin of the peritrophic membrane and the mould formed by the stomodaeal invagination and the midgut wall (modified from Wigglesworth, 1965).

branes would be formed. Wasp larvae form six such membranes in a day and starved *Aeschna* (Odonata) larvae two. In Dermaptera and Lepidoptera this mode of formation seems to occur together with that observed in Diptera so that the membranes have a dual origin.

The function of the peritrophic membrane is to protect the cells from damage by the gut contents and this is consistent with its absence or delicate nature in many blood-sucking insects.

In general the membrane acts as a barrier to microflora so that infection is prevented, while it may also facilitate absorption in fluid feeders. In the blowfly larva food passes through the gut, within the membrane, at the rate of about 50 mm./hr., but the peritrophic membrane is only produced at about 5 mm./hr. Consequently, the fluid between the membrane and the epithelium is relatively still and substances will be absorbed from it more readily.

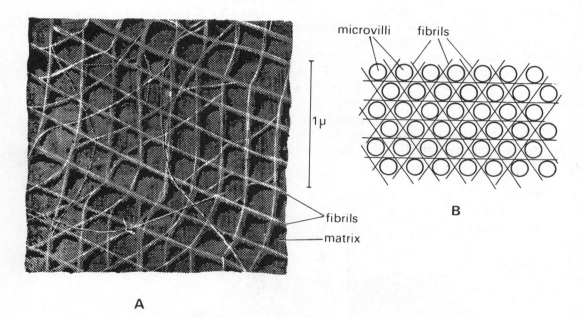

Fig. 37. A. Part of a fibrillar membrane from the peritrophic membrane of *Periplaneta*. B. Diagram of a surface section of a midgut epithelial cell showing the microvilli (in section) forming a template for the fibrils of the peritrophic membrane (after Mercer and Day, 1952).

If digestion is to occur the membrane must be permeable to enzymes and the products of digestion. In *Calliphora* (Diptera) it is freely permeable to water, salts, glucose and amino acids, but, although it allows enzymes to pass in from the outside, it does not permit the outward movement of polysaccharides or proteins from the gut lumen. It is thus polarised to some extent as a result of its structure and it is not a simple ultra-filter (Zhuzhikov, 1964).

3.4 Hindgut

The hindgut is lined by a layer of cuticle which is thinner and more permeable than that of the foregut. The epithelium generally is thin, but the cells are more cuboid than in the foregut (Fig. 38) while those of the rectal pads are tall with a clear cytoplasm

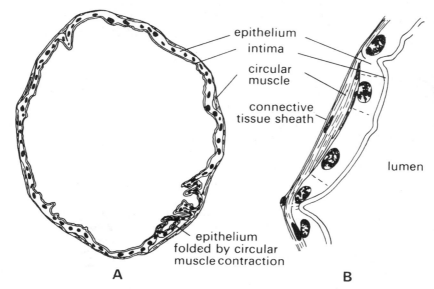

Fig. 38. A. Transverse section of the ileum of *Chorthippus*. B. Section of ileum more highly magnified.

(Fig. 39). Except round the rectum the musculature is poorly developed, but where it is present the longitudinal muscles are usually external to the circular. Along the rectum the longitudinal muscles are often collected into strands opposite the gaps between adjacent rectal pads (Fig. 39).

3.41 Pylorus

The pylorus is the first part of the hindgut and from it the Malpighian tubules often arise. In some insects it forms a valve between the midgut and hindgut.

3.42 Ileum

In most insects the ileum is an undifferentiated tube running back to the rectum, but in some termites it forms a pouch in which the flagellates concerned with cellulose digestion live, and in larval Scarabaeoidea there is a comparable fermentation chamber in which the intima is produced into spines (see p. 61). In Heteroptera it is suggested that the ileum is concerned with the removal of water from the haemolymph (Goodchild, 1963b) and in blowfly larvae certain cells are concerned in the excretion of ammonia (Waterhouse, 1957).

3.43 Rectum

The rectum is often an enlarged sac and is thin walled except for certain regions, the rectal pads, which have a columnar epithelium. There are usually six rectal pads and they may extend longitudinally along the rectum or they may be papilliform as in Diptera. In Odonata and Orthoptera each pad consists of a single layer of cells (Fig. 39B), but in Neuroptera, Lepidoptera and Hymenoptera there are two layers. The pads have a good tracheal supply indicating a high level of metabolism.

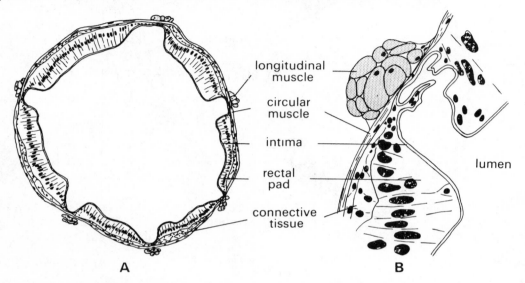

Fig. 39. A. Transverse section of the rectum of *Chorthippus*. B. Section of rectum more highly magnified.

The rectum, and in particular the rectal pads, are important in the reabsorption of water, salts and amino acids from the urine (Ramsay, 1958) (see p. 507). In addition in some aquatic insects, such as larval Anisoptera and Helodidae, there are tracheal gills in the rectum. In larval Anisoptera water is pumped in and out of the rectum so that the water round the gills is constantly renewed (p. 479) and by the forcible ejection of water the insect is able to propel itself forwards rapidly.

3.5 Innervation of the gut

The foregut is innervated from the frontal and ingluvial ganglia, from the intervening recurrent and oesophageal nerves and from the ingluvial nerve (p. 524). These nerves may also extend to the midgut. In *Schistocerca* the ingluvial ganglion is autonomous and exerts a major influence on movements of the proventriculus. The hindgut receives nerves from the last abdominal ganglion and in *Apis* the nerves extend to the midgut.

The nerve endings do not usually penetrate the basement membrane of the gut epithelium so that they are not in general sensory, but rather motor nerves concerned with the control of the muscles of the gut. There are sense organs in the pharynx of *Periplaneta*.

3.6 Passage of food through the gut

Food is pushed back from the pharynx by the pharyngeal pump, aided by the cibarial pump when this is present, and subsequently passed along the gut by peristaltic movements. The movement of food from the crop to the midgut is controlled by the proventriculus and its associated sphincter. In *Periplaneta* the rate of emptying of the crop is inversely proportional to the concentration of food in it so that food in high concentration is passed back to the midgut very slowly. With dilute solutions the proventriculus opens more frequently and probably also wider and for a longer time than with concentrated solutions. It is suggested that the ingested fluid stimulates a sense organ in the pharynx which is innervated from the frontal ganglion. From the latter a nerve passes to the ingluvial ganglion and so to the proventriculus, and it is probable that stimulation of the sense organ determines the rate of opening of the proventriculus (Davey and Treherne, 1963a, b).

In the midgut the passage of food is aided by the peritrophic membrane which, as it moves down the gut, will carry the enclosed food with it. In some Diptera a rectal valve possesses spines which help to draw the peritrophic membrane backwards.

Food may or may not enter the midgut caeca; in *Locusta* both anterior and posterior arms of the caeca are lined with peritrophic membrane and the food can pass into them, but in *Schistocerca* the anterior arms are closed off by the membrane so that no food can get into them (Goodhue, 1963).

The movements of the hindgut are primarily concerned with the elimination of undigested material. In *Schistocerca* the ileum is usually thrown into an S-bend and at the point of inflexion the muscles constrict the gut contents so that the peritrophic membrane bends and is broken. The separated posterior part of the membrane encloses a pellet of faecal material. When the insect is about to defaecate it elongates its abdomen, thereby straightening out the S-bend, and at the same time contractions of the posterior part of the ileum and the rectum force the pellet out of the anus (Goodhue, 1963). The faeces are thus enclosed in old peritrophic membrane, but this is not the case in all insects as in some the membrane is broken up in the hindgut.

The time taken by food in its passage through the gut is very variable. In *Periplaneta* food is retained longer in the gut if the insect is active or if it is starved—in a starved insect some food can still be found in the crop after two months. On the other hand a large meal or high temperature result in food passing through more rapidly. With food readily available the midgut can be filled in an hour and food reaches the rectum in six hours. The relative times vary very much from one insect to another.

3.7 Head glands

Associated with the mouthparts are the mandibular, maxillary, pharyngeal and labial glands although they are not usually all present together.

3.71 Mandibular glands

These are found in Apterygota, Isoptera, Coleoptera and Hymenoptera and are usually sac-like structures in the head opening near the bases of the mandibles. In *Apis* (Fig. 501) the glands are larger in the queen than in the worker and are very small in the drone.

In the queen they produce the pheromones concerned with colony control (p. 747), while in workers they probably produce some saliva and serve to soften the cocoon at the time of emergence.

The mandibular glands are particularly large in larval Lepidoptera where they are the functional salivary glands, but they are absent from adult Lepidoptera.

3.72 Maxillary glands

Maxillary glands are found in Protura, Collembola, Heteroptera and some larval Neuroptera and Hymenoptera. They are usually small, opening near the bases of the maxillae, and may be concerned with the lubrication of the mouthparts. In carnivorous Heteroptera they may play a part in producing the toxin which kills the prey (p. 30) (Edwards, 1963).

3.73 Pharyngeal glands

Pharyngeal glands (hypopharyngeal glands of Snodgrass, 1956) occur in Hymenoptera and are particularly well developed in worker honeybees. They are vestigial in the queen bee and absent from the male. There is one gland on each side of the head, each consisting of a long coiled tube to which large numbers of solid lobules are attached. The glands open at the base of the hypopharynx by separate ducts (Snodgrass, 1956). They produce brood food with which young larvae are fed and which probably plays some part in caste determination (p. 36) It also provides a major part of the diet of laying queens and possibly also of drones (Ribbands, 1953). In addition the glands produce an invertase.

The pharyngeal glands of worker honeybees undergo changes in development which are associated with changes in the bees' behaviour. The newly emerged worker has poorly developed pharyngeal glands, but after feeding on pollen the glands become bigger and by the fifth day of adult life they start to produce brood food. At this time the worker acts as a nurse bee, feeding the young larvae. Subsequently, corresponding with the tendencies of older bees to leave the hive and forage for nectar and pollen, the pharyngeal glands retrogress. The secretion of intervase at first increases and then decreases in a way comparable with the secretion of brood food.

3.74 Labial glands

These glands are found in the majority of insects, although they are absent from some Coleoptera. They are large and extend back into the thorax. In most insects the labial glands are acinous glands (Fig. 40), the acini containing two cell types, but in the larvae of Diptera, Lepidoptera and fleas they are tubular and contain a single cell type (Fig. 333). In larval Diptera the cells are enormous and contain polytene chromosomes as in *Drosophila*. Part of the gland may be differentiated to form a salivary reservoir, while in Heteroptera the gland consists of a number of separate lobes (Fig. 42).

Anteriorly the glands open into a narrow duct on each side and these join to a single median duct opening into the salivarium (Fig. 3). In fluid-feeding insects the salivarium is modified to form a pump. This has a rigid lower wall and a flexible upper one which can be drawn upwards by dilator muscles so that fluid is sucked into the lumen and then, when the muscles relax, the upper wall springs down by virtue of its elasticity and forces saliva out (Fig. 41). In some insects, at least, there are valves which ensure the forward flow of saliva. For fine structure see Kendall (1969, *Z. Zellforsch.* **98**) and Kloetzel and Laufer (1969, *J. Ultrastruct. Res.* **29**).

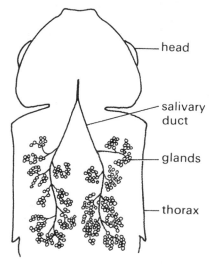

Fig. 40. Salivary glands of a locust (modified after Albrecht, 1956).

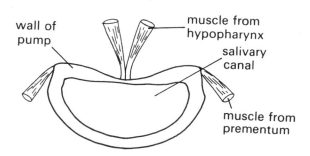

Fig. 41. Diagrammatic transverse section of a salivary pump (after Snodgrass, 1935).

3.75 Functions of the labial glands

In most insects the labial glands are the functional salivary glands. The saliva serves to lubricate the mouthparts, more is produced if the food is dry, and it also contains enzymes which start digestion of the food. The presence of particular enzymes is related to diet, but an amylase, converting starch to sugar, and an invertase, converting sucrose to glucose and fructose, are commonly present. Sometimes proteases and lipases are also present and in insects which digest their prey extra-intestinally these may be particularly important (p. 56). The saliva of some blood-sucking insects also contains an anticoagulant and if the salivary glands of *Glossina* are removed the blood eventually clots in the mouthparts. Not all blood-sucking insects have an anticoagulant (p. 31).

In larval Lepidoptera and Trichoptera the labial glands produce silk which is used in the construction of larval shelters and the cocoon. The silk glands are cylindrical and the cells are characterised by the possession of large, branched nuclei. Silk consists of an inner tough protein, fibroin, enclosed by a water-soluble gelatinous protein, sericin. In *Bombyx* the fibrinogen, which on extrusion is denatured to fibroin, is secreted in the posterior part of the gland, while sericin is secreted in the middle regions. The ducts from these glands in Lepidoptera are joined by the duct from another small gland, Lyonnet's gland, which possibly lubricates the tube through which the silk passes. Finally, the silk is moulded to a thread as it passes through the silk press which resembles a typical salivary pump.

Male scorpion flies, *Panorpa* (Mecoptera), have enlarged salivary glands and produce large quantities of saliva which are eaten by the female during copulation.

Plant-sucking Heteroptera and Homoptera produce two types of saliva, a viscous substance which hardens to form the sheath and a more fluid substance. In *Oncopeltus* (Heteroptera) the sheath material is produced in response to resistance encountered by the stylets during penetration of the leaf. If the leaf is tough the sheath is short and thick, but if the leaf is more easily penetrated the sheath is longer and thinner. It is secreted by the anterior and lateral lobes of the salivary glands (Fig. 42) and an oxidising substance comes from the accessory gland (Miles, 1960). The lipoprotein forming the sheath is exuded as the stylets are temporarily withdrawn during penetration and it

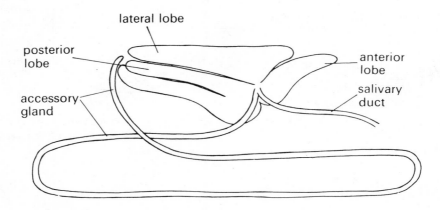

Fig. 42. Salivary gland of *Oncopeltus* (after Miles, 1960).

gels in contact with air due to the formation of hydrogen bonds and disulphide bonds. Bonding does not occur within the salivary gland because of the reducing conditions and dielectric effects produced by companion materials. At the same time as these bonds are formed it is possible that a phenolase oxidises some substance such as DOPA (p. 443), which is known to be present, to quinones and further bonding between the quinones produces the compact gelling of the sheath (Miles, 1964). As the stylets are pushed down again they punch a hole in the lump of sheath material, moulding it to their form, and by a repetition of this process as the stylets penetrate the leaf an elongate sheath is produced.

The function of the sheath is not clear, but the fact that it is open at the inner end suggests that it is not acting as a filter. It may serve to prevent loss of plant sap and loss of the more fluid saliva through the wound in the epidermis (Miles, 1959).

The more fluid saliva is produced in the posterior lobe of the glands and some of the mucoids it contains come from the accessory gland. In *Oncopeltus* it is secreted on to the surface of a leaf before penetration starts and is then sucked back in by the bug. This presumably stimulates gustatory sense organs and is concerned with the selection of a feeding site. More saliva is secreted during feeding, but only if the food is not fluid since the passage of fluid up the stylets inhibits the production of saliva. In more solid food the saliva digests starch and leaches the medium in which the bug is feeding.

In the aphid *Myzus*, which feeds from phloem, saliva is secreted during penetration of the stylets, but not while it is feeding, whereas in *Adelys*, feeding in parenchyma, salivary production is continuous. The saliva contains a pectinase which aids penetration by breaking down the middle lamellae of the plant cells, and in addition there are a number of amino acids and amides. *Aphis pomae* secretes relatively large amounts of alanine and glutamic acid, some aspartic acid, valine and serine and traces of leucine and histidine. It is suggested that these substances are unutilised dietary products from the haemolymph which are excreted in this way and which might be the cause of the injuries which aphid saliva causes to the plant (Auclair, 1963).

No sheath is produced by aquatic Heteroptera or Cimicomorpha in which the salivary glands produce a toxin killing and partially digesting the prey (p. 30).

In social insects the larval saliva is of great importance in trophallaxis (p. 37).

The labial glands of Collembola may have an excretory function (p. 496).

CHAPTER IV

DIGESTION AND ABSORPTION

The alimentary canal is concerned primarily with the digestion and absorption of foodstuffs, and different parts of the gut are concerned with different aspects of these functions. In some insects, especially fluid feeders, digestion may begin before the food is ingested through the injection or regurgitation of enzymes on to the food, but in general digestion occurs largely in the midgut where most of the enzymes are produced. These enzymes break down the complex substances in the food into more simple substances which can be absorbed and later assimilated. Most carbohydrates are degraded to monosaccharides, but in the majority of insects there is no enzyme which breaks down cellulose although this is commonly present in the diet. Some insects, notably the termites and wood-eating cockroaches, harbour micro-organisms which facilitate cellulose digestion. Proteins are broken down to polypeptides which are then absorbed before being further digested. Fats may be absorbed unchanged, but often are broken down to fatty acids and glycerol.

The enzymes carrying out these activities only function optimally within a limited range of pH and temperature.

Absorption in some cases is a passive process, but in other instances active transport occurs. Passive movement is only possible as long as the concentration in the gut exceeds that in the haemolymph, and in some cases there are special mechanisms which ensure that this is so. The absorption of water is particularly important in terrestrial insects, and the rectum plays an important part in removing water from the faeces.

The efficiency with which insects utilise their food is very variable, but most phytophagous insects digest and absorb only a relatively small proportion of the food they eat and the bulk is passed out unchanged as the faeces.

Digestion in insects is reviewed by Day and Waterhouse (1953), Gilmour (1961), House (1965a), Waterhouse (1957) and Wigglesworth (1965), and absorption by Treherne (1962) and Waterhouse and Day (1953). See also Treherne (1965c, 1967).

4.1 Digestion

Enzymes concerned with digestion are present in the saliva and in the secretions of the midgut. In addition, digestion may be facilitated by micro-organisms in the gut.

4.11 Extra-intestinal digestion

Since saliva contains enzymes, digestion often starts before the food is ingested. This is particularly true of fluid-feeding insects where enzymes are injected into the host, and in carnivorous Heteroptera and Asilidae the contents of the prey are completely histolysed before ingestion. It is not clear whether salivary enzymes or regurgitated midgut enzymes are responsible for this.

Extra-intestinal digestion also occurs in *Dytiscus* (Coleoptera) larvae which have no salivary glands so that the midgut enzymes must be involved. These are injected into the prey through the mandibles which are perforated by a narrow tube and when, in a short time, the contents of the prey have been digested the resulting fluid is withdrawn via the same route. A similar mode of feeding is employed by larval Neuroptera and Lampyridae.

Proteolytic enzymes persist in the excreta of larval blowflies so that the meat in which they live is partially liquified before it is ingested. Another instance of extra-intestinal digestion occurs in *Bombyx* where the moth on emergence secretes a protease attacking the sericin of silk so that its escape from the cocoon is facilitated.

4.12 Internal digestion

Most digestion occurs in the midgut in which the enzymes are secreted, but, because of the regurgitation of midgut juices, some also takes place in the crop. In Orthoptera the bulk of digestion occurs in the crop and this is reflected in the distribution of enzymes; in *Schistocerca* the greatest α-glucosidase activity occurs in the lumen of the foregut (Fig. 43), although in the tissues most activity is found in the midgut and caecal epithelia (Evans and Payne, 1964). Some α-glucosidase activity does occur in the foregut epithelium, but this is intracellular and is probably not secreted into the lumen. Little digestion occurs in the hindgut apart from cellulose digestion in a few insects and in these, micro-organisms, rather than the insects' own enzymes, are responsible (p. 61).

The enzymes present in the midgut are adapted to the diet (Table 1); if an insect, like a larval blowfly, feeds on a primarily protein diet proteases are important, whereas in an adult, nectar-feeding lepidopteran they are absent. In aphids feeding on phloem containing no polysaccharides or proteins the presence of amylase and proteinase has not been confirmed, but invertases do occur (Auclair, 1963).

Micro-organisms may produce enzymes which are utilised, directly or indirectly, by the insect. This is the case in cellulose and wax digestion (p. 63) and even in *Apis* the only enzymes produced by bacteriologically sterile bees are invertase, protease and lipase; the other carbohydrases normally present are produced by bacteria.

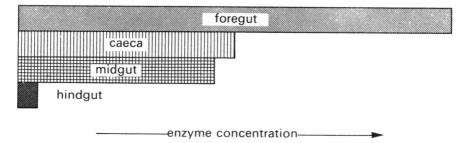

Fig. 43. Relative concentrations of α-glucosidase in different parts of the lumen of the alimentary canal of *Schistocerca* (modified after Evans and Payne, 1964).

TABLE I

THE MIDGUT ENZYMES SECRETED BY INSECTS WITH DIFFERENT DIETS

(* indicates presence of enzyme) (Data from Wigglesworth, 1965)

Insect	diet	protease	lipase	amylase	invertase	maltase
Cockroach	omnivorous	*	*	*	*	*
Carausius	phytophagous	*	*	*	*	*
Lepidoptera						
larvae	phytophagous	*	*	*	*	*
adults	nectar	—	—	—	*	—
adults	non-feeding	—	—	—	—	—
Lucilia						
larvae	meat	*	*	—	—	—
Calliphora						
adults	sugars	weak	—	*	*	*
Glossina	blood	*	?	weak	—	—

Carbohydrates

Carbohydrates are generally absorbed as monosaccharides so that, before they are absorbed, disaccharides and polysaccharides must be broken down to their component monosaccharides. This may be a complex reaction taking place partly in the gut wall and a variety of enzymes is involved. Different enzymes are usually necessary to hydrolyse different series of sugars, for instance those built up from glucose or from galactose, and different linkages, α or β, between the sugar residues also require different enzymes.

Disaccharides. The common disaccharides maltose, trehalose and sucrose all contain a glucose residue which is linked to a second sugar residue by an α-linkage.

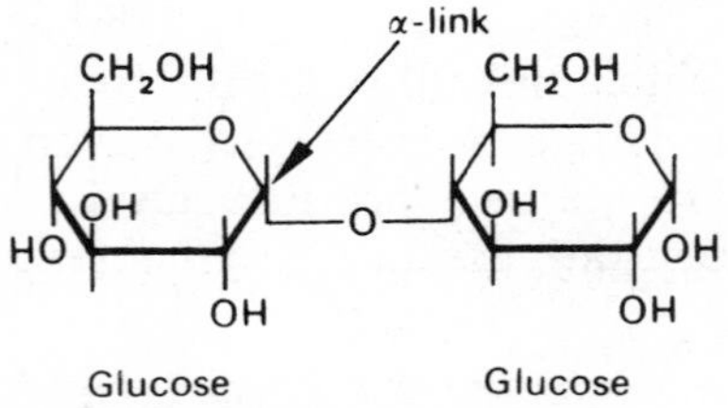

MALTOSE

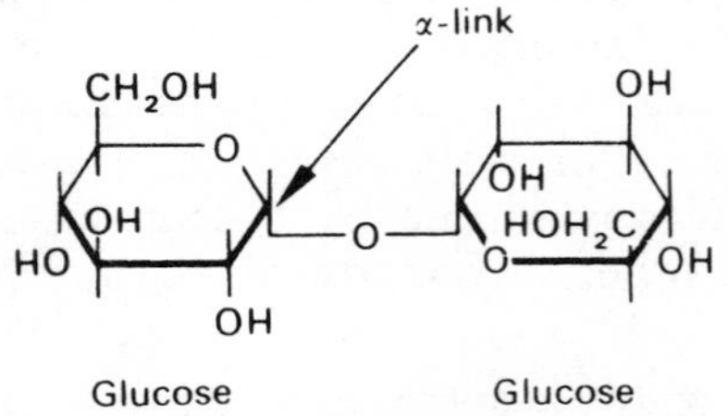

TREHALOSE

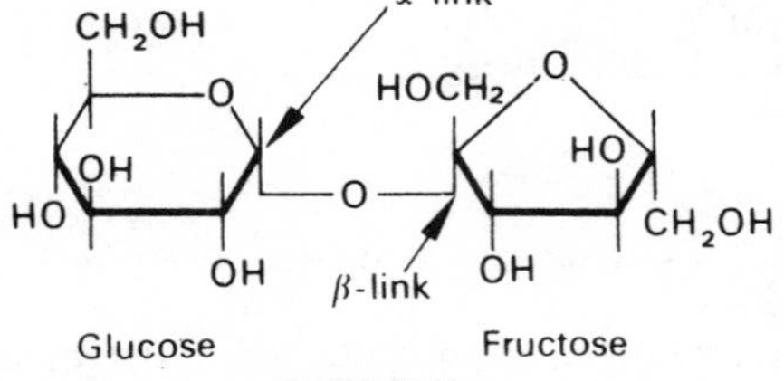

SUCROSE

All these are hydrolysed by an α-glucosidase (*i.e.* an enzyme attacking the α-link of a glucose residue) and this is the usual invertase found in insects although in *Calliphora* a β-fructosidase also occurs.

The naturally occurring β-glucosides (salicin, arbutin and cellobiose) are usually of plant origin and the highest β-glucosidase activity is found in phytophagous insects.

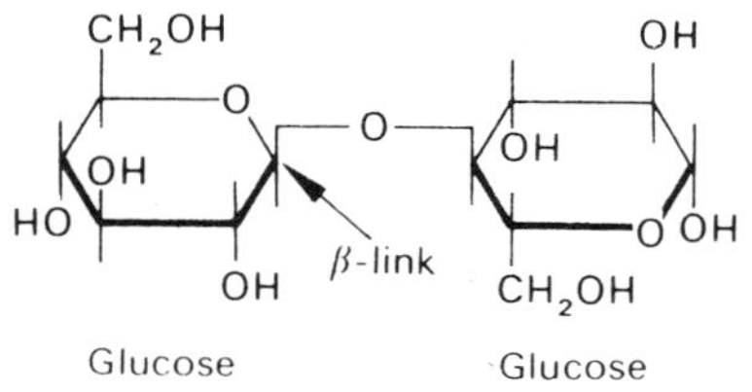

CH₂OH OH
O O
OH OH
HO O OH
OH β-link CH₂OH
Glucose Glucose
CELLOBIOSE

The glucosidases are the commonest glycosidases, but α-galactosidase, hydrolysing substances such as melibiose, is recorded from Diptera and *Schistocerca*, and β-galactosidase, hydrolysing lactose, is also present in *Schistocerca*.

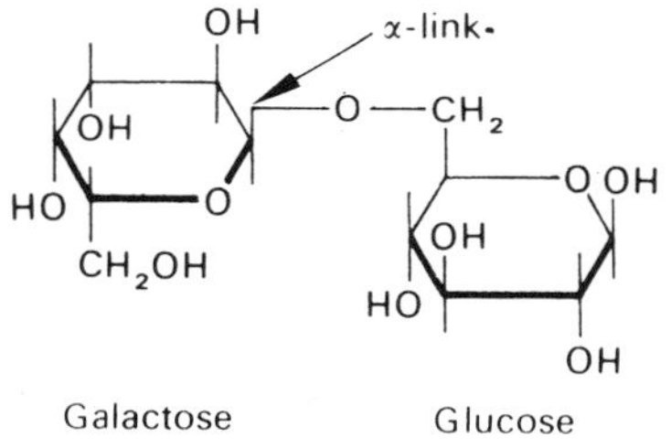

OH α-link·
O—CH₂
OH O OH
HO O OH
CH₂OH
HO
OH
Galactose Glucose
MELIBIOSE

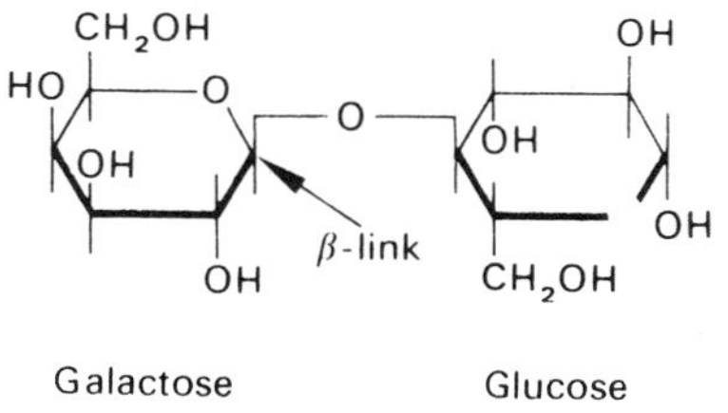

CH₂OH OH
HO O O
OH OH
β-link CH₂OH OH
OH OH
Galactose Glucose
LACTOSE

Apart from the group/bond specificity shown by these enzymes there are others which are much more specific, only hydrolysing a single substrate. Thus in *Schistocerca*, in addition to the general α-glucosidase, which hydrolyses trehalose among other α-glucosides, there is probably a specific α-glucosidase which only hydrolyses trehalose (Evans and Payne, 1964).

In the hydrolysis of carbohydrates water is the typical acceptor for the sugar residues:—

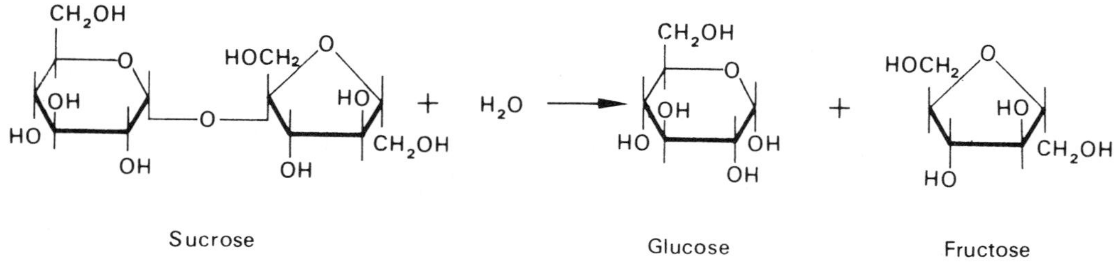

CH₂OH
O HOCH₂ O
OH HO
HO O CH₂OH + H₂O ⟶
OH OH
Sucrose

CH₂OH
O
OH HOCH₂ O
HO OH + HO
OH HO CH₂OH
Glucose Fructose

but other sugars may equally well act as acceptors with the formation of oligosaccharides. Thus in the hydrolysis of sucrose other sucrose molecules may act as acceptors to form the trisaccharides glucosucrose and melezitose.

Glucose   Sucrose   Glucosucrose

Melezitose

These in turn may accept further glucose to form tetrasaccharides. This process is known as transglucosylation and a similar process occurs in the hydrolysis of maltose where, in addition, maltose is reformed by the glucose produced in hydrolysis acting as an acceptor in its turn (Payne and Evans, 1964).

With trehalose no transglucosylation occurs, perhaps because the relevant enzyme has a high degree of specificity for water as an acceptor as well as a high specificity to the substrate. In some aphids there appear to be two α-glucosidases with different acceptor specificities to different ends of the sucrose molecule. The effect of one is to add glucose to the C-4 of the glucose in sucrose to form glucosucrose, while the effect of the other is to add glucose to the C-3 of the fructose in sucrose to form melezitose which is common in honeydew, the watery fluid continually excreted by feeding aphids (Auclair, 1963).

Polysaccharides. Starch is broken down to maltose, and glycogen to glucose by the action of amylase, which specifically catalyses the hydrolysis of $1:4$-α-glucosidic linkages in polysaccharides, but there are two types of amylase working in different ways. An exoamylase splits off maltose residues from the ends of the starch molecule leading to a rapid increase in the concentration of maltose, while an endoamylase attacks bonds well within the starch molecule so that there is only a slow build-up of maltose to start with. The products are then further digested in the normal way by α-glucosidases.

Although many insects feed on plants and wood, only a minority of them have an enzyme, cellulase, capable of hydrolysing cellulose. Where there is no cellulase the insects must either feed on the cell contents without digesting the cell walls or they must rely on micro-organisms to digest the cellulose for them.

Amongst the larvae of wood-boring beetles various methods are adopted. Lyctids have no cellulase and feed only on the cell contents; Scolytidae have no cellulase, but do have a hemicellulase so that hemicelluloses, mixtures of pentosans, hexosans and polysaccharides, are attacked; finally, Anobiidae and Cerambycidae do possess a cellulase and can utilise the cell walls as well as the contents.

A cellulase has also been identified in *Ctenolepisma* (Thysanura) and in *Schistocerca* (Evans and Payne, 1964). The activity of the cellulase in *Schistocerca* is so slight that it can normally be of little value because the food passes through the alimentary canal too quickly, but if the insect is starved food already in the gut may be retained for several days so that the cellulase might then have some effect. Cellulase acts by breaking cellulose down into cellobiose units which are then further hydrolysed by a β-glucosidase.

Larval Scarabaeoidea have no cellulase although they feed on rotten wood, but the wood is retained in a pouch in the hindgut by branched spines arising from the intima. In the pouch the bacteria ingested with the wood continue to ferment it and as they die they in turn are digested by the insect's enzymes passing back from the midgut. The digested remains are absorbed through the wall of the pouch where, between the spines, the intima is very thin.

In some other wood-eating insects there is a permanent gut flora or fauna concerned with cellulose digestion. Thus, in the larvae of the beetle *Rhagium* there are cellulose fermenting bacteria, while in the cockroach, *Cryptocercus*, various flagellates are responsible for cellulose digestion. This is also true of the larvae, soldiers and workers of most wood-eating termites, but it is not true of Termitidae. The flagellates occur in vast numbers in an expansion of the hindgut and in workers of *Zootermopsis* (Isoptera) constitute about a third of the wet weight of the insect. They phagocytose fragments of wood which they hydrolyse to glucose, and in *Cryptocercus* the glucose is passed out into the gut of the insect and then, by contraction of the hindgut, it is forced forwards to the midgut for absorption. In *Zootermopsis*, however, the glucose is retained by the flagellates and the process of anaerobic fermentation continued with the ultimate release of carbon dioxide, hydrogen and organic acids, especially acetic. These acids are then used as a source of carbon by the insect (Grassé, 1949) and as a result of the activity of the flagellates some two-thirds of the food ingested is rendered assimilable.

Since the flagellates live in the hindgut they are lost at each moult when the intima is shed. In termites, however, the habit of proctodaeal feeding soon results in recolonisation of the intestine (p. 82). Many flagellates are damaged in the passage through the mandibles and proventriculus and are digested in the midgut, but the remainder pass on undamaged to the hindgut where they stay. The passage through the gut takes about two hours. *Cryptocercus* is not a social insect so that recolonisation of the gut cannot occur by social feeding and here a proportion of the flagellates move into the space which forms between the hindgut epithelium and the intima before the latter is shed. At the moult these flagellates, which may remain active or may encyst, are not lost, but form the nucleus of the population in the next instar.

The flagellates occurring in the insects are specific, and six orders of flagellates as well as certain families of the order Trichomonadina are composed entirely of gut-dwelling forms. The fauna is presumed to have originated in the cockroaches since they are the older group. In *Cryptocercus* there are 13 genera and 25 species of flagellate.

Two genera have free-living representatives, but the remainder are only found in the alimentary canals of insects. The genera *Oxymonas* and *Trichonympha* occur in termites as well as in the cockroach. Amongst the termites there is some specificity, some flagellate genera only occurring in certain genera of termites, but Grassé (1952a) suggests that this is largely fortuitous and depends on the ethological isolation of the hosts. It is known that flagellates can be experimentally exchanged between termite species.

Proteins

Insects possess a series of proteases. A trypsin-like proteinase is produced in the midgut which breaks protein down to peptones and polypeptides. These, in turn, are acted on by peptidases, some of which occur in the gut lumen, but most of which are found in the epithelial cells indicating that most of the polypeptides are absorbed before being further digested. There are different types of peptidase: carboxypolypeptidase attacks the peptide chain from the —COOH end, provided tyrosine or other specific amino acids are present in the chain; aminopolypeptidase attacks the chain from the —NH₂ end; and dipeptidase hydrolyses all dipeptides.

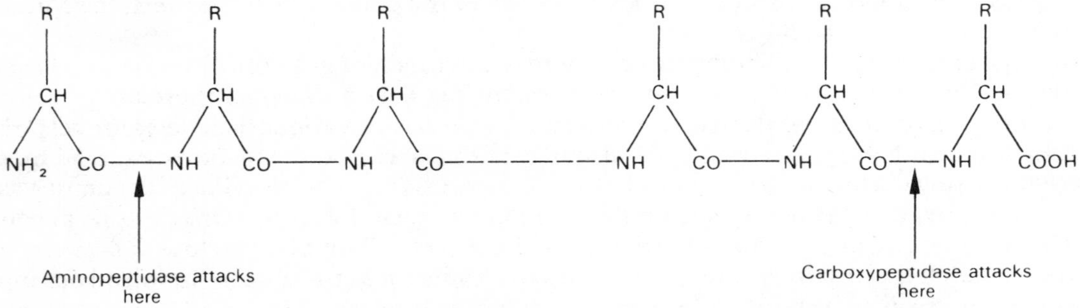

Aminopeptidase attacks here

Carboxypeptidase attacks here

Some insects are able to digest the inert animal proteins keratin and collagen. Keratin is the protein found in wool, hair and feathers. It consists of polypeptide chains, including sulphur-containing amino acids, which are linked together by disulphide bonds rendering the whole protein stable. Only the Mallophaga of birds, some dermestid larvae and some tineid larvae are able to digest it. *Tinea* (Lepidoptera) larvae utilise some 47% of the wool ingested.

Tineola, at least, has a keratinase capable of digesting keratin under anerobic conditions. This releases cystine which is probably reduced to cysteine by cystine reductase:—

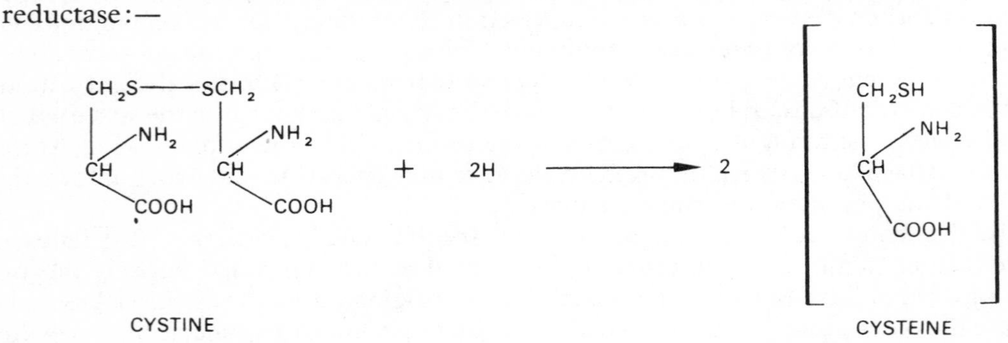

CYSTINE   CYSTEINE

and cysteine is further broken down by cysteine desulphydrase to form hydrogen sulphide. Both cysteine and hydrogen sulphide are reducing agents and will promote the breaking of the disulphide bonds in the keratin, so facilitating enzyme activity.

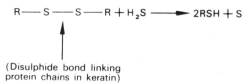

$$R—S—S—R + H_2S \longrightarrow 2RSH + S$$

(Disulphide bond linking
protein chains in keratin)

They will also lower the redox potential (see p. 65) so that the very low potential (−200 mv. compared with up to +200 mv. in other insects) characteristic of insects which digest keratin is probably largely a consequence of, rather than an essential condition for, keratin digestion (Gilmour, 1965).

The larvae of *Hypoderma* (Diptera) and of some blowflies are known to produce a collagenase acting on the collagen of animal tissues. *Hypoderma* lays its eggs on hairs of the host and its larvae bore through the skin and into the host tissues. Blowfly larvae may be the cause of strike in sheep where, again, they live in live animal tissues, or they may live in carrion.

Lipids

Many insects produce lipases which hydrolyse fats to fatty acids and glycerol. This hydrolysis apparently does not proceed to completion because the fatty acids become enclosed within an accumulation of partly hydrolysed fat which displaces the enzyme from the oil-water interface on which the lipase acts so that further hydrolysis is prevented.

A specialised case of lipid digestion is the digestion of beeswax by larvae of the wax moth, *Galleria*. Honeycomb normally forms a large part of the diet of these larvae although they can survive without it. Beeswax, from which honeycomb is made, is a mixture of esters, fatty acids and hydrocarbons (see p. 100), and the larva of *Galleria* is able to utilise some 50% of the wax, mainly the fatty acids and some of the unsaponifiable material, but also some hydrocarbons. It is not known to what extent bacteria are important in digestion of the wax. Bacteriologically sterile larvae can digest stearic acid, hexadecyl alcohol and octadecyl stearate, but not the esters of myricyl alcohol which form a large part of the wax. The insect is known to produce a lipase and possibly also lecithinase and cholinesterase, but it seems likely that most digestion of the esters and fatty acids results from the activities of the bacteria (Gilmour, 1961).

4.13 Enzyme activity

Enzymes only exhibit maximal activity under certain conditions in which pH, redox potential and temperature play a large part.

pH

The pH of the foregut is greatly influenced by food and varies with the diet since there is no appreciable buffering of the foregut contents. Thus with a cockroach fed on a protein diet the foregut pH is 6·3, fed with maltose it is 5·8 and with glucose 4·5–4·8. The more acid pH with the sugars results from micro-organisms producing organic acids.

The midgut is usually buffered so that pH is maintained relatively constant. In *Apis* there are two buffering systems, one is a complex of organic acids and their salts having its maximum effect at pH 4·2, the other a series of mono- and di-hydrogen phosphates with a maximum effect at pH 6·8 (Fig. 44). These two systems tend to maintain the pH

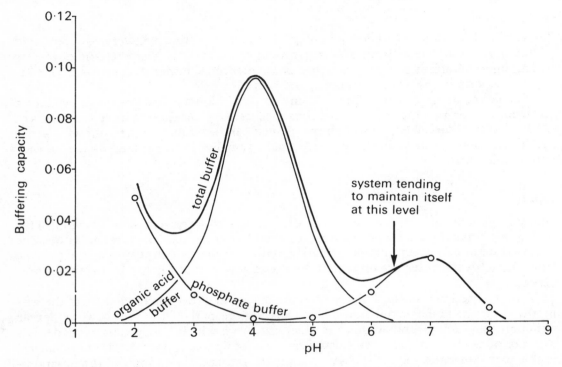

Fig. 44. The buffering capacity of the midgut contents of *Apis*. The measured pH of the midgut would be expected to bear some simple relationship to the buffering capacity (from Day and Waterhouse, 1953).

at about 6·3. In the cricket, grasshoppers and Lepidoptera larvae, however, phosphate has little buffering effect and here the main buffers are probably weak acids, including amino acids and their salts, and proteins. Mosquitoes have little buffering facility and after a blood meal the midgut pH rises to 7·3, the normal value for blood.

In the midgut the pH is usually in the range 6·0–8·0 (see Day and Waterhouse, 1953; House, 1965a), but in larval Lepidoptera and Trichoptera pH 8·0–10·0 is usual. An alkaline pH is more usual in phytophagous insects than in carnivorous ones, but there are many exceptions. In *Periplaneta* and *Cydia* (Lepidoptera) pH is uniform throughout the midgut, but there may be localised differences in pH indicating differences in the activities of the different parts of the midgut. In *Lucilia* larva, for instance, the anterior and posterior ends of the midgut are weakly alkaline while the middle is strongly acid (Fig. 45).

The hindgut is usually slightly more acid than the midgut, partly due to the secretions of the Malpighian tubules.

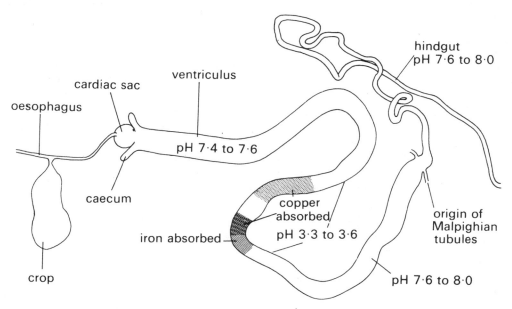

Fig. 45. Diagram of the gut of *Lucilia* larva showing pH of gut contents and regions of iron and copper absorption (from Waterhouse and Day, 1953).

Redox potential

The redox potential is an important factor in digestion and absorption. It is a measure of the oxidising or reducing power of a substance expressed in terms of its tendency to lose or gain electrons. A negative potential characterises a reducing substance, a positive potential an oxidising substance, while the greater the potential, positive or negative, the stronger the oxidising or reducing powers of the substance. Thus in *Tineola* a redox potential of -200 mv. in the midgut indicates very powerful reducing conditions. Usually the potential in the midgut is positive and it may reach as much as $+200$ mv. In *Lucilia* larva the redox potential is positive throughout the gut whereas in *Blattella* (Dictyoptera) the hindgut contents have a negative potential.

Temperature

Enzyme activity increases with temperature and in *Schistocerca* the rate of increase in activity of α-glucosidase for a 10°C. rise in temperature (Q10) is 2·25. The greatest activity occurs at 45–50°C., but only for short periods because enzymes are denatured at high temperatures, and long periods over 40°C. result in inactivation of this enzyme. The optimum for long-term activity must be a balance between higher activity and more rapid denaturing at higher temperatures.

In *Tenebrio* (Coleoptera) larva changes of protease activity occur to compensate for changes in temperature. If the larva is transferred from 23°C. to 13°C. protease activity first falls and then increases so that after ten days protease activity is twice as high as it was initially. On returning to 23°C., protease activity returns to its original level. Amylase activity shows no comparable compensating changes (Applebaum *et al.*, 1964).

4.14 Control of enzyme secretion

In insects living in a constant supply of food, enzyme production is continuous whereas in others it is probably intermittent. Enzyme activity is diminished by starvation, but in *Blattella* some activity still persists after several days of starvation. When food is taken again there is a temporary fall in activity followed by a gradual increase lasting several hours, all the enzymes being stimulated irrespective of the nature of the food. Enzyme activity also changes with development and season; in *Bombyx* larva amylase activity doubles in the first six days of the fourth instar and *Apis* workers exhibit relatively little invertase activity in early spring and in autumn.

The innervation of the gut appears to be largely motor, controlling the muscles, so that there is no anatomical basis for the nervous control of enzyme secretion. Secretion may be the result of direct stimulation of the secreting cells by food or it may be under endocrine control. In *Calliphora* the ingestion of protein stimulates the median neurosecretory cells to produce a hormone which, in turn, acts on cells in the midgut epithelium and results in the release of protease (Thomsen and Møller, 1963).

The fate of enzymes in the alimentary canal is not known, but they are only rarely found in the hindgut.

4.2 Absorption

The products of digestion are absorbed in the midgut and to some extent also in the hindgut, where some reabsorption from the urine also occurs (p. 507), but there is no evidence of any absorption in the foregut. The cells concerned with absorption are, at least in some cases, the same as those producing enzymes in a different phase of their cycle of activity. Phagocytosis of food particles does not occur, all the substances are absorbed in solution.

Absorption may be a passive or an active process. Passive absorption depends primarily on the relative concentrations of a substance inside and outside the gut, diffusion taking place from the higher to the lower concentration. In addition, in the case of electrolytes, the tendency to maintain electrical equilibrium inside and outside the gut will interact with the tendency to diffuse down the concentration gradient. Passive movement of water involves movement from a solution of lower osmotic pressure to one of higher osmotic pressure. Active absorption depends on some metabolic process for movement of a substance against a concentration or electrical potential gradient.

4.21 Carbohydrates

Carbohydrates are mainly absorbed as monosaccharides and in *Periplaneta* and *Schistocerca* their absorption takes place in the midgut and especially in the midgut caeca. The process of absorption of the sugars resulting from the hydrolysis of more complex carbohydrates depends on diffusion from a high concentration in the gut to a low one in the haemolymph. This is facilitated by the immediate conversion of glucose to trehalose in the fat body which surrounds the gut so that the concentration of glucose in the blood never builds up. If, however, the concentration of glucose in the gut is very high it diffuses very rapidly at first so that the mechanism converting it to trehalose is unable to keep pace and glucose accumulates in the haemolymph. As a result the diffusion gradient across the wall of the gut is reduced and the rate of absorption falls off. Normally a very high concentration in the midgut is avoided by the rate of crop emptying which is low when the concentration of sugar is high (p. 51).

The conversion of glucose to trehalose, a disaccharide, increases the molecular weight so that the possibility of diffusion back into the gut is reduced. Another factor favouring inward diffusion is the absorption of water which results in an increased concentration of sugars in the gut so that the diffusion gradient becomes greater.

Mannose and fructose are absorbed in a similar manner to glucose, but rather more slowly because their conversion to trehalose is less rapid so that their concentration gradients across the gut wall are less marked.

In *Aedes* (Diptera) larva glycogen appears in the posterior midgut cells soon after glucose is ingested. It is possible that rapid conversion to glycogen might maintain a concentration gradient of glucose inwards from the gut lumen so that glucose diffuses in, but in *Phormia* (Diptera) and other dipterous larvae the concentration of glucose in the haemolymph is normally high so that glucose absorption must entail another, possibly active, process.

4.22 Proteins

It is presumed that, in general, proteins are absorbed after degradation to amino acids. Absorption takes place primarily from the midgut, and the caeca are especially important in the absorption of glycine and serine by *Schistocerca,* but amino acids passed out in the urine from the Malpighian tubules are also reabsorbed in the rectum (p.507). Sometimes proteins are absorbed unchanged and then digested within the cells, and the midgut cells of *Rhodnius* and *Pediculus* (Siphunculata), for instance, are known to absorb haemoglobin unchanged.

The mode of absorption of amino acids depends to some extent on their relative concentrations in the food and the haemolymph. Some are present in higher concentrations in the food than in the haemolymph and these may be absorbed by passive diffusion. Others, such as glycine and serine in *Schistocerca,* are in higher concentration in the blood, but the absorption of water from the gut reverses the relative concentrations so that again diffusion can account for their absorption. There is also evidence that a diffusion gradient may be maintained by the rapid metabolism of the absorbed amino acids. This is suggested by the accumulation of glycogen in the caecal cells of *Aedes* larva after it has been fed on casein, alanine or glutamic acid. It is, however, probable that the absorption of other amino acids depends on a specific, active mechanism rather than on diffusion alone. This probably varies from one insect to another, depending on the composition of the diet and the haemolymph.

4.23 Lipids

Very little is known about the absorption of fats, but it is possible that they are sometimes absorbed unchanged. The products of wax hydrolysis are absorbed in a phosphorylated form and dephosphorylation follows in the epithelium. It is suggested (Gilmour, 1961) that cholesterol is esterised as a preliminary to absorption.

Fat absorption takes place mainly in the midgut, for instance in the caeca in *Periplaneta*, the anterior midgut in *Aedes* larva, the anterior and posterior midgut in blowfly larva, and there is some evidence for the absorption of fats from the hindgut of adult Hymenoptera.

4.24 Water

Water is absorbed in various parts of the midgut: in *Schistocerca* and *Aedes* larva, for example, water is absorbed in the caeca, in *Glossina* in the anterior midgut, and in *Lucilia* larva in the middle zone of the midgut. In addition, many insects reabsorb water from the urine via the rectal pads (p. 507), but where there is little need for water conservation, as in freshwater insects, Homoptera, Heteroptera and holometabolous larvae living on a fluid diet, reabsorption does not occur and the rectal pads may be absent (Waterhouse and Day, 1953). In *Carausius* some water from the urine is reabsorbed in the ileum.

Water absorption involves active and passive movements of the water. Passive absorption depends on the osmotic pressure of the blood exceeding that of the gut contents and if the converse is true water may be withdrawn from the haemolymph. In *Lucilia* larva the acidity of the midgut coagulates the protein in the food. This reduces the osmotic pressure of the gut contents and so facilitates absorption. Active transport takes place against an osmotic gradient, the steepness of which is increased by absorption. In *Sialis* (Megaloptera) larva this active transport appears to be linked with sodium uptake.

The insect can regulate the amount of water absorbed from the rectum according to its needs. In *Schistocerca* this regulation is probably brought about by changes in the passive permeability of the rectal wall (Phillips, 1964b).

4.25 Inorganic ions

Inorganic ions are absorbed in the midgut and reabsorbed from the fluids in the rectum (see p. 507). There may be specific zones for the absorption of different ions in the midgut and in *Lucilia* larva there is a small zone in the centre of the midgut where iron is absorbed, while copper is absorbed in two small zones characterised by a mosaic of cuprophilic and lipophilic cells (Fig. 45). Adult *Lucilia* absorb copper in the anterior and posterior parts of the midgut.

The potential of the rectal contents of *Schistocerca* is positive with respect to the haemolymph ($+15$ to $+30$ mv.) so that anions (Cl^-) must undergo active absorption. Cations (Na^+, K^+) may be absorbed passively, but not in sufficient quantities to account for their concentrations in the haemolymph, suggesting that they too are absorbed actively. Potassium is absorbed about ten times more rapidly than sodium at the same rectal concentration, indicating selective permeability of the rectal wall (Phillips, 1964b). All three ions (K^+, Na^+, Cl^-) may be taken up against very steep concentration gradients and this is not related to water uptake since the flux of water may be in the opposite direction. This may not always be true and in *Sialis* larva the active uptake of sodium ions appears to be linked to water uptake, while the potential difference between rectum and haemolymph is sufficient to account for the uptake of potassium. Similarly in *Aedes aegypti* larva sodium uptake from the rectum is active while potassium uptake is passive

No storage of ions takes place in the rectal epithelium, at least in *Schistocerca*, and extrusion from the epithelium to the haemolymph must be active because sodium, for instance, is present in higher concentration in the haemolymph than in the epithelium (120 m.equiv. compared with 57 m.equiv.) and the epithelium is negatively charged with respect to the haemolymph (Phillips, 1964b).

4.3 Efficiency of food utilisation

The efficiency with which food is utilised varies from insect to insect. In many fluid feeders there is little or no solid waste and the gut may be occluded as in larval Neuroptera. Utilisation in these insects must be very high. In aphids, on the other hand, utilisation is generally poor. A continuous flow of sap is taken from the plant and most of this is passed out at the anus as honeydew. Some 50–60% of the ingested nitrogen is removed from the sap and although utilisation of sugars is usually low some hydrolysis does occur leading to the production of hexoses and oligosaccharides which are also found in the honeydew (Auclair, 1963).

In phytophagous insects generally utilisation is poor. Fifth instar larvae of *Schistocerca* utilise only 35% of the dry weight of their food, but first instar larvae use 78% (Davey, 1954). This is true with an abundance of food. If the insect is starved, food is retained in the gut for long periods and utilisation is probably more efficient. Lepidopterous larvae utilise 25–40% dry weight of their food and the utilisation of different materials may vary from one species to another. Thus *Pieries brassicae* (Lepidoptera) larvae utilise more fat than *Aglais urticae* (Lepidoptera) larvae (Evans, 1939).

More recent work has tended to consider energy utilisation as being a more accurate measure of selective absorption than gross food utilisation. Thus the caterpillar of *Hyphantria* (Lepidoptera) utilises some 23% of the food it ingests, but assimilates 29% of the calorific value of the ingested food (Gere, 1956) and the grasshopper, *Orchelimum*, assimilates 27% of the calorific value of the food (Smalley, 1960).

Although high levels of utilisation will be efficient from the nutritional standpoint this may be partly offset by other considerations. Thus Dadd (1960a) obtained faster growth rates and better survival of *Schistocerca* and *Locusta* when large amounts of cellulose were added to an artificial diet and utilisation fell to 45–50% as compared with 70–80%. This suggests that mechanical factors, as well as the nutritional value of the food, are important.

CHAPTER V
NUTRITION

The food ingested and digested by the insect must fulfill its nutritional requirements for normal growth and development to occur. These requirements are complex and although most nutrients must be present in the diet, some may be obtained from other sources. Some nutrients may be accumulated and carried over from earlier stages of development, others may·be synthesised by the insect from different dietary constituents, while others may be supplied by micro-organisms. A number of substances, particularly amino acids and vitamins, are essential for any development to occur; others, while not essential, are necessary for optimal development. The balance between different constituents is also important.

Carbohydrates are a common source of energy and, although not always essential, they are usually necessary for normal growth. Some ten amino acids are essential for tissue and enzyme production, but fats are usually essential only in very small quantities. A dietary source of sterols is necessary for all insects since they are unable to synthesise these compounds. Various vitamins are essential in the diet and a source of inorganic salts is also necessary.

In the absence or imbalance of certain requirements growth may not occur or may be impaired, or moulting may not occur. Colouration is also affected by some elements of the diet and in social Hymenoptera dietary differences are involved in caste determination. An adequate source of protein is essential for egg production.

All insects in the course of feeding and other activities become infested with micro-organisms, but in some species the micro-organisms are always present and may be essential for normal development. Sometimes they are housed in special cells and the biology of the insect is such that they are transferred from one generation to the next. Micro-organisms are usually present in insects with a restricted diet which is deficient in some essential nutrients and these are probably provided by the micro-organisms.

Insect nutrition is reviewed by Dadd (1963), Friend (1958), Gilmour (1961), House (1961, 1963, 1965b, 1969, *Entomologia exp. appl.* **12**), Johansson (1964), Lipke and Fraenkel (1956) and Trager (1953). Micro-organisms in insects are discussed by Brooks (1963a, 1963b), Musgrave (1964), Tóth (1952), Richards and Brooks (1958) and Wigglesworth (1952).

5.1 Nutritional requirements

It is to be expected that the basic nutritional requirements of all insects will be the same since their basic metabolic processes must be similar, but there are, nevertheless, differences in the dietary requirements of different species. These differences may arise as a result of real differences in metabolism, or as a result of sufficient nutrient reserves being accumulated at a previous stage of development, or as a result of the ability of the insect or associated micro-organisms to synthesise certain nutrients (see p. 81).

5.11 Storage

Sometimes an essential nutrient is not required in the diet because sufficient reserves have been accumulated during an earlier feeding period. There are two important reserves of nutrients:— the yolk in the egg and the fat body of the larva and adult.

Because of their relatively small size insect eggs cannot store major nutrients, such as glucose, in excess of the needs of the embryo, but minor nutrients, such as vitamins, may be present in sufficient quantity to accommodate the needs of the developing larva as well (Gordon, 1959). Not all the minor nutrients are stored to the same extent and while, for instance, there is a good deal of linoleic acid in the egg of *Blattella,* there is no thiamine.

Once these stores have been used up the insect needs a supply of the appropriate nutrients in the diet. Thus the egg of *Blattella* contains sufficient inositol for development as far as the third larval instar, while in the egg of *Schistocerca* there is enough β-carotene for normal growth throughout the whole of larval life, but if eggs are obtained from adults with a deficiency of carotene, no carotene is stored and it becomes an essential item in the larval diet (Dadd, 1961c).

Larger amounts of nutrients, including the major types, may be stored in larval and adult fat bodies. This is the case, for instance, in those Lepidoptera which do not feed as adults. Sufficient reserves are accumulated by the larva to supply the adult metabolic processes. Similarly, if locusts are fed on grass during the first two larval instars they can continue development up to the last larval instar without carbohydrate in the diet because they have accumulated a sufficient quantity in the fat body (Dadd, 1963). Minor nutrients may also be stored and larval *Anthonomus* (Coleoptera) store sufficient choline and inositol to permit egg development even if these substances are absent from the adult diet.

In some cases nutrients are obtained from the degradation of tissues. Thus the nutrients required for egg development in autogenous mosquitoes (p. 295) and for the development of young in *Aphis* may be derived from the autolysis of flight muscles.

5.12 Synthesis by the insect

The ability of insects to synthesise essential nutrients varies. Some substances, such as nucleic acids, are synthesised by all insects. Such synthesis may be adequate for growth, but in *Drosophila* growth is improved by the presence of RNA in the diet. Vitamins are also sometimes synthesised. Choline and ascorbic acid are synthesised by the majority of insects and a smaller number, *Tenebrio* amongst them, are able to synthesise linoleic acid, but many require it in the diet. Insects may also have some ability to synthesise pyridoxine. *Chilo* (Lepidoptera) is able to synthesise many of the non-essential amino acids.

5.13 Dietary requirements

Carbohydrates

Carbohydrates serve as a source of energy and may be converted to fats for storage and to amino acids. Although they often form a major part of the diet, carbohydrates are not always essential. They can be replaced by protein or fats, but this depends on the ability to convert the proteins and fats to intermediate products suitable for use in the cycles of energy transformation (p. 92) and the speeds with which these conversions take place. Some such conversion probably occurs in most insects and may serve for the whole of energy production. Thus in *Musca* (Diptera) development can proceed in the complete absence of carbohydrate and in the diet of *Galleria* carbohydrate can be entirely replaced by wax (Dadd, 1964). On the other hand carbohydrate cannot be replaced by lipids or proteins in *Schistocerca*, *Locusta* or *Pseudosarcophaga* (Diptera) (House, 1959) and some insects need very large amounts. *Tenebrio*, for instance, fails to develop unless carbohydrate constitutes at least 40% of the diet and growth is optimal with 70% carbohydrate.

The utilisation of different carbohydrates depends on the ability to hydrolyse polysaccharides, the readiness with which different substances are absorbed and the possession of enzyme systems capable of introducing these substances into the metabolic processes. Some insects can use a very wide range of carbohydrates. *Tribolium* (Coleoptera), for instance, uses starch, the alcohol mannitol, the trisaccharide raffinose, the disaccharides sucrose, maltose and cellobiose and the monosaccharides mannose and glucose among others. Other insects living in stored products, and *Schistocerca* and *Locusta* are also able to utilise a wide range (Dadd, 1960c), but many phytophagous insects, such as *Melanoplus*, are unable to utilise polysaccharides and some insects are only able to use a very restricted range of sugars. *Chilo*, for instance, only uses sucrose, maltose, fructose and glucose. The pentose sugars do not generally support growth and may be actively toxic, perhaps because they interfere with the absorption or oxidation of other sugars which are normally utilised (Lipke and Fraenkel, 1956).

There may be differences in the ability of larvae and adults to utilise carbohydrates. For instance, the larva of *Aedes* can use starch and glycogen, while the adult cannot.

Amino Acids

Amino acids are required for the production of tissues and enzymes. Usually present as protein, they form a major part of the diet, 30–40% in most synthetic diets, and growth is poor with too little (p. 76). There are ten essential amino acids, the absence of any one of which usually prevents growth. These are arginine, lysine, leucine, isoleucine, tryptophan, histidine, phenylalanine, methionine, valine and threonine, but there is some variation in the requirements of different insects. For instance, glycine is essential for several dipterous species, alanine for *Blattella* and proline for *Phormia*, but in this case methionine is not essential and can be replaced. Other amino acids, although they are not essential, are necessary for optimal growth because their synthesis from the essential acids is difficult. In this category in *Pseudosarcophaga* are alanine, glycine, serine and tyrosine.

It is probable that the balance between different amino acids is particularly important.

Lipids

Fats are the chief form in which energy is stored and the ability to synthesise fats for storage is widespread, but, except for specific items in small amounts, they are not usually essential constituents of the diet. Only small quantities of fat are present in leaves so that it would not normally form an important source of energy in phytophagous insects and even in the wax moth, *Galleria,* beeswax is not an essential part of the diet although growth is improved when it is present (Dadd, 1964). The reserves of fat in the body are affected qualitatively and quantitatively by the fat in the diet (Friend, 1958), but this does not imply simple storage of the ingested fats, these are extensively changed before they are stored.

All insects need a dietary source of sterol for normal growth and reproduction, but the range of sterols used is limited to those essentially similar to cholesterol, with a hydroxyl group at position 3.

Cholesterol

Plant feeders amongst Orthoptera, Lepidoptera, Coleoptera, Diptera and Hymenoptera can use plant sterols, converting them to cholesterol or 7-dehydrocholesterol, whereas *Dermestes* (Coleoptera), feeding exclusively on animal material, can only use cholesterol and 7-dehydrocholesterol (Levinson, 1962).

The amount of cholesterol required can be reduced by the inclusion of 22-dehydro-cholesterol or Δ^7-ergosterol in the diet, but these substances cannot entirely replace cholesterol. Such substances are called 'sparing' agents and it is probable that they can replace cholesterol where this only plays a structural role in other compounds, but that cholesterol itself is required for some specific metabolic role. This role is unknown. Cholesterol may be stored and this accounts for the reduced dietary requirements of older *Tenebrio* and *Calliphora* larvae.

Linoleic acid is an essential requirement of some insects, such as *Ephestia* (Lepidoptera) and *Schistocerca*. It is concerned in the formation of lipid phosphatides and in its absence moulting is abnormal suggesting that it plays a part in the production or functioning of moulting fluid. *Tenebrio* is able to synthesise linoleic acid and this may be true of other insects.

β-carotene (provitamin A) is not usually regarded as an essential dietary requirement, but it is important in *Schistocerca*. Normally in this insect there is a sufficient reserve of β-carotene in the egg to permit growth, but in insects reared on a carotene-free diet from eggs already deficient in carotene growth is retarded and the moult delayed. In addition, the insects are smaller, lighter and less active than usual. The normal yellow or orange colour of locust larvae, due to a carotenoid, does not develop in the absence of carotene and melanisation is also reduced (Dadd, 1961c).

Carotenoids may be necessary in small amounts in the diets of all insects since the visual pigment retinene is derived from them (p. 553).

B vitamins

Vitamins are organic substances, not necessarily related to each other, which are required in small amounts in the diet since they cannot be synthesised. They mostly provide structural components of coenzymes. It is generally considered that the only vitamins needed by insects are the water-soluble B vitamins.

The B vitamins thiamine, riboflavin, nicotinic acid, pyridoxine and pantothenic acid are essential to most insects (Table 2), while biotin, folic acid and choline are also required by many (see *e.g.* Gilmour, 1961). Other vitamins may be specific requirements of particular insects. For instance, *Tenebrio* needs a source of carnitine, but this can be synthesised by *Dermestes* and *Phormia*. Other vitamins, although not essential, may promote growth; this is true of inositol in *Ephestia* and lipoic acid in *Hylemya* (Diptera).

TABLE 2

MINIMAL VITAMIN REQUIREMENTS FOR NORMAL GROWTH OF *SCHISTOCERCA*
(from Dadd, 1961)

Vitamin	Minimal requirement between these values (μg/g diet)
Thiamine	2·5–5·0
Riboflavin	2·5–50·0
Nicotinic acid	0·0–10·0
Pyridoxine	12·5–50·0
Folic acid	0·0–2·5
Pantothenate	5·0–25·0
Inositol	125·0–500·0
Choline chloride	500·0–1250·0

There is some interchange between the B vitamins, and in *Phormia* carnitine can replace choline suggesting either that the substances are interconvertible or that they are interchangeable in phospholipids.

Choline is required in relatively large amounts by *Blattella, Schistocerca, Locusta* and *Acheta* (Orthoptera) suggesting that it forms a structural unit in a complex lipid rather than a coenzyme. Other substances may have a sparing action (p. 73) on choline; dimethylaminoethanol, for instance, accelerates growth on a diet containing suboptimal amounts of choline. Inositol is also required by locusts in relatively large amounts (Table 2).

In some insects some B vitamins are provided by associated micro-organisms (see p. 81). Thus *Stegobium* (Coleoptera) only needs thiamine and pyridoxine in its diet because riboflavin, nicotinic acid, pantothenic acid, folic acid, biotin and choline are supplied by intracellular symbionts.

Ascorbic acid (vitamin C)

Ascorbic acid is not usually an essential dietary constituent, but it is widely distributed in insect tissues indicating that it is synthesised. *Schistocerca, Bombyx* and *Anthonomus*, however, have a dietary requirement for ascorbic acid and it may be that this is true for most, but not all, phytophagous insects (Dadd, 1963). In the absence of ascorbic acid *Schistocerca* undergoes abortive moults and dies. The level of ascorbic acid in the blood fluctuates and is minimal just after the moult in *Schistocerca* and has a similar fluctuation in *Bombyx*.

Nucleic acids

No insect is known with an absolute requirement for nucleic acid which is normally synthesised, but a dietary supply improves growth in *Drosophila* and other dipterous larvae. The requirement in this instance is primarily for adenylic acid perhaps because this is synthesised less readily or is required in greater quantities, as in ADP and ATP, than the other constituents of nucleic acid.

Inorganic salts

A dietary source of inorganic salts is essential, but relatively little work on salt requirements has been carried out because traces of salts are often present as impurities in other dietary factors. Their importance lies in the maintenance of an ionic balance suitable to the activity of living cells, as co-factors of some enzyme systems and as integral parts of others. *Schistocerca* develops on a diet containing only sodium, calcium, potassium, magnesium, chloride and phosphorus with other elements present only as impurities (Dadd, 1961b). Known essential trace elements are iron, copper, iodine, manganese, cobalt, zinc and nickel (Trager, 1953).

Most insects appear to be relatively insensitive to wide variations in levels and proportions of the different elements in the diet.

5.2 The effects of dietary deficiencies

Dietary deficiencies, resulting from inadequate amounts of nutrients in the food, may manifest themselves in various ways (see House, 1963). They may impair growth or moulting, or they may affect body form, or they may have detrimental effects on reproduction.

5.21 Nutrition and growth

Some nutrients are essential for growth to occur at all. For instance, all insects require a sterol in the diet and in the absence of a suitable one soon die (*e.g.* Dadd, 1960b). This is also true of certain amino acids and vitamins. The absence of other substances may lead to impaired growth, although growth will occur in their absence. *Drosophila* larvae, for instance, can survive without RNA in the diet, but growth is more rapid if RNA is available (Sang, 1959). Similarly in *Schistocerca* the vitamins carnitine, lipoic acid, glutathione and B_{12} result in faster growth, although they are not essential (Dadd, 1963).

The amounts in which the essential nutrients are present are important and they must exceed certain minimal values if development is to proceed normally. *Schistocerca,* for instance, needs at least 20% sugar in the diet for good growth (Fig. 46) (Dadd, 1960c), while the minimal requirement for cholesterol is about 1·0 mg./g. of diet (Dadd, 1960b) and for the various B vitamins ranges from about 2·5 to 1000 μg./g. of diet (Table 2; Dadd, 1961). In *Schistocerca* the tolerance to excess nutrients, such as vitamins and inorganic salts is wide and growth is not inhibited by concentrations ten times as high as the minimum (Dadd, 1961a, 1961b), but this is not always true. There is an optimal

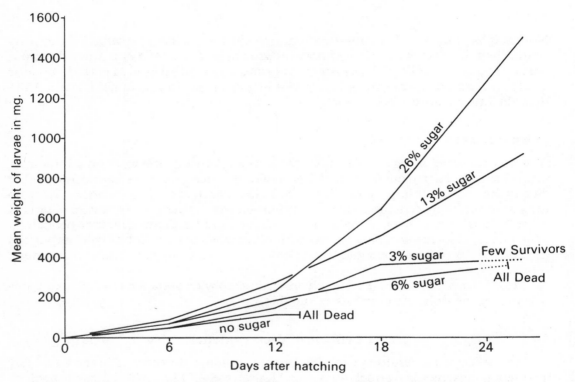

Fig. 46. The effect of various concentrations of sucrose on the growth of *Schistocerca* (after Dadd, 1960b).

level of casein and other substances in the diet of larval *Drosophila* above and below which the rate of development is reduced (Fig. 47; Sang, 1959), and the growth of *Tribolium* is slowed by too high a concentration of biotin.

The relative proportions of nutrients may also be important. Thus the concentration of RNA needed for optimal development of *Drosophila* is doubled if folic acid is not also present and an increase in the dietary concentration of casein from 4% to 7% necessitates a doubling of the concentrations of nicotinic acid, pantothenic acid, biotin and folic acid for optimal growth. This doubling of the vitamins reflects the greater activity of the enzyme system in dealing with the higher concentration of protein.

Nutritional requirements may alter at different stages of development. *Schisto-cerca* needs more carbohydrate in the later larval instars than in earlier ones and *Pyrausta* (Lepidoptera) larvae can develop without any for the first three instars. In this case the increased requirements in the later instars are associated with the accumulation of food reserves in the fat body. *Blattella* is able to develop as far as the third larval instar without inositol and young *Schistocerca* can survive without ascorbic acid, but these substances are required by the later instars. In these instances sufficient nutrients for the early instars are stored in the egg, but once these reserves have been used up a dietary supply is essential.

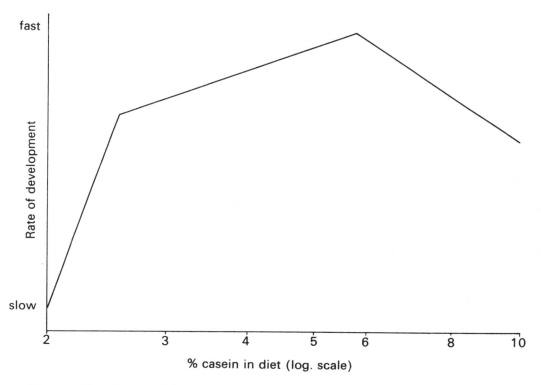

Fig. 47. The effect of different concentrations of casein on the rate of development of *Drosophila* larvae (modified after Sang, 1959).

5.22 Nutrition and moulting

Nutritional deficiencies may affect moulting. Thus in the absence of linoleic acid or ascorbic acid *Schistocerca* fails to moult properly. *Ephestia* also requires an adequate supply of linoleic acid for the final moult to be successful; with a suboptimal dose the wings are devoid of scales because these do not separate from the pupal cuticle, and with no linoleic acid the insect fails to emerge.

5.23 Nutrition and body form

Colouration may be affected by nutrition either through the absence of some constituent of a pigment or through interference with pigment metabolism. The absence of
β-carotene has both effects in *Schistocerca*. The carotene is an essential constituent of
the yellow carotenoid giving the background colour, but in the absence of carotene
melanisation is also reduced (Dadd, 1961c). *Aedes* larvae also lack pigmentation if there
is no tyrosine and only a little phenylalanine in the diet.

If the diet is adequate qualitatively, but only available in limited amounts the
resulting adults will be reduced in size. *Ephestia kühniella*, for instance, needs about
0·13 g. of wholemeal flour for normal development. On smaller amounts, even as little as
0·04 g., the moths emerging are normal, but smaller (Norris, 1933). The proportions of
the wings relative to the body may also be altered by the diet.

Differences in diet may lead to polymorphism. The chalcïd *Melittobia* is parasitic
on the wasp *Trypoxylon* and the first 12 to 20 larvae to develop within a host do so rapidly.
The resultant adults emerge with short crumpled wings and proceed to mate and
oviposit in the same host. Later larvae develop more slowly and give rise to fully-winged
adults which leave the host. These differences are due to changes in the food supply
from the host.

Dietary differences are often involved in polymorphism in the social Hymenoptera
(Michener, 1961). Some larvae of the honeybee, *Apis*, for instance, are fed by the workers
in a qualitatively and quantitatively different way from the rest of the larvae and as a
result they develop into queen bees (see p. 36). In the ant, *Myrmica rubra*, whether or
not a larva becomes a queen depends on the treatment it receives early in the third
instar. Of particular importance is the condition of the workers feeding the larvae.
Workers in the spring (vernal) condition promote rapid growth of the larvae and these
become workers, but if the larvae are fed by workers in the autumn (serotinal) condition
their development is slow, they overwinter as larvae, and the larger ones amongst them
develop into queens in the following spring (Weir, 1959). These differences result from
differences in the food in which the glandular secretions of the workers in various physiological conditions may be particularly important.

5.24 Nutrition and reproduction

The diet plays an important part in egg production by female insects (Johansson, 1964).
For instance, *Leptinotarsa* (Coleoptera) females feeding on young potato plants with a
high lecithin content produce 30 to 50 eggs in each batch; on older plants with a lower
lecithin content only 8–20 eggs are laid, while feeding on *Solanum commersonii* instead
of *S. edinense* prevents any egg production at all. In insects, such as some Lepidoptera,
which do not feed as adults nutrients are stored by the larva and the larval diet is important in egg production. In the majority of insects, however, fecundity is largely
related to adult nutrition, although food reserves derived from the larva may have some
importance.

Protein is important for yolk production and the diet of the female insect may be
modified to provide this protein. In virgin *Musca* females the ratio of sucrose to protein
in the diet is 16:1, while in egg-laying females it is 7:1. In *Calliphora*, food selection
changes cyclically during yolk formation. During the early stages of egg development

much protein is ingested and the intake of protein stimulates the corpora allata which secrete a factor leading to increased carbohydrate intake during the period of yolk deposition in the egg. The removal of protein metabolites from the blood at this time leads to a reduction in corpus allatum activity and so to less carbohydrate intake (Strangways-Dixon, 1959) (and see p. 710).

The need for protein for egg production is reflected in the sexual difference in feeding behaviour in many biting flies, such as mosquitoes and tabanids, where the female is blood-sucking and the male feeds exclusively on nectar. Some female mosquitoes lay no eggs until they have had a blood meal, these are known as anautogenous; others are autogenous and can lay their first batch of eggs without a blood meal. The protein for yolk production comes from the reserves in the fat body in autogenous *Culex pipiens* or from the flight muscles, which are degraded at this time, in autogenous *Aedes communis*. In some mosquitoes, however, the differences between autogenous and anautogenous forms result from differences in hormonal control rather than differences in food reserves (Clements, 1963).

Nutritional factors other than protein influence egg production. For instance, the fecundity of the flea *Xenopsylla* is reduced by feeding on rats deficient in thiamine. *Culex* lays twice as many eggs per mgm. of blood after feeding on canary blood as compared with human blood and comparable results in *Aedes* are correlated with the level of isoleucine in the blood. These requirements may be such that a diet suitable for larval development is not optimal for reproduction. Thus in *Drosophila* fructose is important for egg production, but is of little importance to the larva.

The quantity of food is again important. In *Ephestia* the number of eggs laid is related to the amount of flour ingested as a larva and in *Cimex* the number of eggs laid increases with the size of the blood meal.

Dietary deficiencies may result in a disturbance of yolk synthesis (House, 1963). In *Rhodnius* no yolk is deposited in the absence of a blood meal because there is no protein to form yolk, but the effect may not always be a direct one. Protein synthesis is under endocrine control (p. 710) and failure to stimulate the corpora allata may result in a failure of protein synthesis despite adequate reserves. In *Calliphora* the corpora allata are stimulated by the ingestion of protein.

Even if eggs are produced their viability depends in part on the adult diet. The eggs of *Anthonomus* fail to hatch if there is no cholesterol in the adult diet and in *Musca* the number of eggs hatching is proportional to the amount of cholesterol in the diet.

5.3 Micro-organisms

Many insects take in micro-organisms casually with their food while others have a constant association with micro-organisms living either in the gut or intracellularly in various tissues.

5.31 Casual associations

Micro-organisms are almost inevitably ingested during feeding so that an intestinal flora is present in most insects. The alimentary canal of grasshoppers, for instance, is sterile when the insects hatch from the egg, but soon acquires a bacterial flora which increases in numbers and species throughout life. In general, insects with straight alimentary canals contain fewer micro-organisms than those with complicated guts with a range of pH, providing a number of different niches. The micro-organisms occurring in the gut in these cases of casual infection largely reflect what is present in the environment (Brooks, 1963a).

These casual associations with micro-organisms are important in the nutrition of some insects. Scarabaeoid larvae have a fermentation chamber in the hindgut in which decaying wood with its content of micro-organisms is retained. The micro-organisms continue to ferment the wood and without them the larvae would be unable to utilise the cellulose of the wood (p. 61). In other cases, although they are not essential, contamination of a diet with micro-organisms accelerates the rate of development. Thus larval *Hylemya* living on a sterile diet take 27 days to reach the pupal stage compared with 10 days on the same diet containing bacteria (Friend, *et al.*, 1959). Such micro-organisms may make an otherwise unsuitable diet adequate by supplying essential vitamins or other substances. Friend *et al.* (1959) suggest that the onion bulb may only provide an inadequate diet for *Hylemya*, but the bacteria living in the tunnels made by the larva supply some essential substances which would otherwise be lacking and so enable the larva to survive.

Micro-organisms also assist with wax digestion in *Galleria* although the insect can survive without them.

5.32 Constant associations

In general constant associations with micro-organisms occur in insects with a restricted diet deficient in certain essential nutrients, suggesting that the micro-organisms make good these deficiencies. Thus micro-organisms are found in insects feeding on wood, dry cereal, feather, hair and wool, in sap-feeding Heteroptera and Homoptera and in those blood-sucking insects which never feed on anything except blood. Those blood-sucking insects which at some stage partake of other food do not house micro-organisms. Thus symbionts are found in blood-sucking bugs and lice, and *Glossina* and Nycteribiidae, which are viviparous, amongst Diptera, but not in fleas, blood-sucking Nematocera or Tabanidae since these have free-living larvae (Wigglesworth, 1952).

Micro-organisms are also found in cockroaches and some ants. These are omnivorous insects and hence in this instance the presence of micro-organisms is not correlated with a restricted diet. In the case of the cockroach, *Blattella*, however, it is suggested that in the normally rather poor diet the balance of amino acids is not optimal and a good deal of degradation and reformation takes place. For this considerable amounts of riboflavin and pyridoxine are needed, often in excess of the amounts in the diet, and the micro-organisms supplement the dietary supply of these and other substances (Gordon, 1959).

Types of micro-organism

The most commonly occurring micro-organisms in insects are bacteria or bacterium-like forms which are found in Blattaria, Isoptera, Homoptera, Heteroptera, Anoplura, Mallophaga, Coleoptera, Hymenoptera and Diptera. In addition flagellates are found in wood-eating cockroaches and termites, yeasts in Homoptera and Coleoptera and an actinomycete in *Rhodnius*. In many cases the precise nature of the micro-organisms is not known.

Location in the insect body

In some insects the symbionts are free in the gut lumen. This is the case with the flagellates which live in the hindguts of wood-eating cockroaches and termites and with the bacteria living in the caeca of the last segment of the midgut in plant-sucking Heteroptera. In *Rhodnius*, *Actinomyces* lives in crypts between the cells of the anterior midgut.

Most micro-organisms are intracellular in various parts of the body. The cells housing the symbionts are known as mycetocytes and these may be aggregated together to form organs known as mycetomes.

Mycetocytes are large, polyploid cells occurring in many different tissues. Normally the micro-organisms are incorporated into them when the cells are first differentiated in the embryo, but sometimes the cells develop some time before they are invaded. Most commonly the mycetocytes are scattered through the fat body, as they are in cockroaches and coccids, but in *Haematopinus* (Siphunculata) they are scattered cells in the midgut epithelium and in other insects they may be in the ovarioles or free in the haemolymph.

Mycetomes may originate in the gut wall, as in Anoplura and *Glossina,* where the mycetome is a ring of enlarged midgut cells, or in modified Malpighian tubules, as in some Coleoptera, but frequently they are independent of the gut. In *Calandra* (Coleoptera) larva the mycetome is a U-shaped structure well supplied with tracheae lying below the foregut, but not connected to it (Musgrave, 1964). Nycteribiidae have mycetomes in the abdomen and *Cimex* has a small mycetome near the gonads. In holometabolous insects the mycetomes are often only found in immature stages. At metamorphosis they fragment into mycetocytes which become lodged in adult organs, in the case of *Calandra* in the anterior midgut caeca.

The wood-eating cockroaches have two sets of symbionts, intestinal flagellates and intracellular bacteroids in the fat body. This situation also occurs in the termite *Mastotermes darwiniensis,* but the remainder of the wood-eating termites only retain the intestinal fauna.

The roles of micro-organisms in the insect

It is known that the intestinal flagellates of cockroaches and termites are concerned with the digestion of wood and that they release products which can be utilised by the insect (p. 61). In other cases it is presumed that the organisms provide essential nutrients, but this has only been shown conclusively in a few cases. The yeasts of *Stegobium* provide B vitamins and sterols which may be secreted into the gut or released by the digestion of the micro-organisms. The symbionts of *Blattella* provide certain amino acids and possibly a tripeptide as well as B vitamins (see above). Blood is normally sterile and contains some of the B vitamins in smaller amounts than are required by insects. This deficiency is made good, at least in *Rhodnius* and *Triatoma* (Heteroptera), by the symbionts.

There is some evidence that the micro-organisms, particularly those in Homoptera and Heteroptera, are concerned with nitrogen metabolism (Tóth, 1952). This may result from the fixation of free nitrogen or by the breakdown of the insect's metabolic waste products, urea and uric acid, into nitrogenous compounds that can be used. Although it seems certain that the organisms can perform these functions *in vitro,* there is no proof that they do so when inside the host insect.

In the coccid *Stictococcus sjoestedti* the bacterium-like micro-organisms may be concerned with sex determination. In the mature insect mycetocytes invade the ovary, but only infect those oocytes to which they are adjacent. Consequently two types of eggs are produced: those with and those without micro-organisms. The eggs develop parthenogenetically and the uninfected eggs develop into males, while the infected ones give rise to females (Richards and Brooks, 1958).

The effect of loss of micro-organisms varies with the insect and will also depend on the diet available to the insect. *Rhizopertha* (Coleoptera) apparently suffers no loss from the absence of symbionts, *Calandra* is smaller and lighter in their absence, while *Rhodnius* deprived of its intestinal flora rarely reaches the adult stage. It appears that many insects can live equally well with or without their micro-organisms provided the diet is adequate. If, however, the diet is not adequate, as must often be the case, the micro-organisms become vital.

Transmission

Since these organisms are constantly associated with insects there must be some provision for their transfer from parent to offspring. There are essentially four different methods by which this is brought about (Brooks, 1963b).

In the cockroaches, and in *Mastotermes, Camponotus* (Hymenoptera) and some beetles, mycetocytes migrate to the ovary and the bacteria are surrounded and drawn into the oocyte by microvilli of the vitelline membrane. The oocytes of Homoptera are infected in a similar way, but the bacteria only enter the oocytes through the follicle cells at one end (see Fig. 245). Alternatively, micro-organisms from the female accessory glands may be smeared on to the outside of the egg as it is laid. The chorion and the micro-organisms are then eaten by the insect when it hatches. This occurs, for instance, in a number of Chrysomelidae and in this case the symbionts are able to survive on the outside of the chorion for longish periods. Some male bostrychid beetles transfer symbionts in the seminal fluid, but, with this exception, micro-organisms are always transmitted by the female.

Where the symbionts live in the gut other methods of infection are employed. Termites and some bugs exhibit behavioural adaptations facilitating transfer; in termites, for instance, proctodaeal feeding ensures that newly moulted individuals receive a fresh infection of flagellates (p. 61). Finally, reinfection may simply be a chance process as in the wood-eating cockroaches and *Rhodnius*. These insects live in restricted habitats already fouled and contaminated by their own excreta so that they readily pick up a fresh infection.

Symbionts may exhibit polymorphism with special transmission forms, perhaps stimulated to develop by the hormones of the insect (Richards and Brooks, 1958). The flagellates of termites and *Cryptocercus* have sexual stages which are related to the moulting cycles of the insect and transmission forms, concerned with the infection of oocytes, are described for several intracellular symbionts.

CHAPTER VI

THE FAT BODY AND GENERAL METABOLISM

The fat body of insects is made up of cells resembling blood cells aggregated to form a rather irregular and diffuse tissue. It serves as a store for food reserves and, in some insects, for the storage of excretory materials. In a few it becomes modified as a light-producing organ. The fat body is of major importance as a centre in which many metabolic processes occur.

Metabolism involves, among other things, the utilisation of substances absorbed from the gut, their assimilation into the substance of the body or their oxidation to provide energy. Carbohydrates are the usual source of energy in insects, but in some species fats are utilised during flight. The carbohydrate is oxidised in a series of small steps so that the energy which is released can be conserved in high energy phosphate bonds. In this form the energy is made available to the insect for driving other metabolic and particularly synthetic processes, and as a source of muscular energy

Food reserves are stored in insects as particular forms of fats and carbohydrates. These substances are synthesised from the food taken in and mechanisms are also available for their subsequent utilisation in energy or tissue production. Proteins, too, must be synthesised in the forms characteristic of the insect from the amino acids derived from the food.

Much fuller accounts of various aspects of insect biochemistry and metabolism are to be found in Chefurka (1965a, b and c), Chen (1966), Edwards (1953), Gilby (1965), Gilmour (1961 and 1965), Harvey and Haskell (1966), Kilby (1963) and Sacktor (1961, 1965). See also Gilbert (1967, *Adv. Insect Physiol.* **4**) and Wyatt (1967, *Adv. Insect Physiol.* **4**). Detoxication mechanisms by which insects counter the effects of toxic substances, and in particular of insecticides, are reviewed by Smith (1955). The anatomy and functioning of light organs are considered by Buck (1948), Gilmour (1961), McElroy (1965) and Smith (1963).

6.1 Fat body

The insect fat body consists of loosely aggregated or compact masses of cells enclosed in a membranous sheath and freely suspended in the haemocoel so that they are intimately bathed by the blood. The cells are arranged in irregular strands or sheets, but the arrangement is relatively constant within a species. Often there is a parietal layer of fat just beneath the body wall; less frequently a visceral layer ensheathes the gut (Fig. 48).

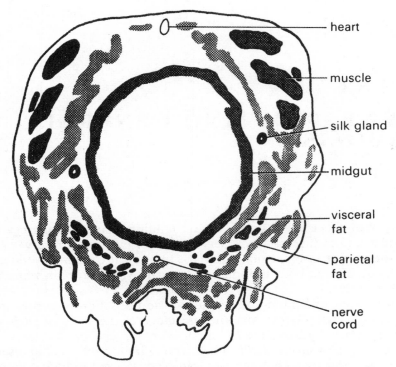

Fig. 48. Transverse section of *Pieris* larva to show the distribution of fat.

6.11 Trophocytes

The greater part of the fat body is made up of cells called trophocytes. In the young larva these cells contain few inclusions and have rounded nuclei, but subsequently they become vacuolated and distended by stores of glycogen, fat or protein. The nuclei are compressed and become elongate or stellate and the cell boundaries may no longer be apparent, although they become visible again if the cell contents are depleted. At the time of metamorphosis in holometabolous insects, albuminoid granules appear in the trophocytes. They are usually regarded as the products of protein or lipoprotein synthesis, but Nair and George (1964) regard them as definite organelles concerned with fat synthesis.

The trophocytes are very like some blood cells and there may be a close relationship between the two. There is a good deal of evidence suggesting that blood cells enter and add to the substance of the fat body, and in the aquatic Heteroptera, for instance, the fat body increases in size throughout life by the inclusion of free adipohaemocytes (p. 677). In *Aleyrodes* the cells of the fat body float freely in the haemolymph and there is no sharp distinction between them and the haemocytes.

The trophocytes accumulate reserves of food of which fat is the most usual, being stored in variable forms which depend, among other things, on the diet and the temperature of synthesis (p. 99). Carbohydrate in the fat body is usually in the form of glycogen and protein may also be present. Protein is not usually stored in quantity in adult insects, but it does occur in the trophocytes of overwintering worker bees where it is used in the production of the salivary secretions with which larvae are fed in the following spring.

Food reserves usually increase throughout the larval period, especially in holometabolous insects, so that in the mature larva of *Apis*, for instance, the fat body comprises 33% of the dry weight.

These food reserves are of particular importance to the insect during non-feeding periods, whether these are of short or long duration and whatever their cause. During long flights, for instance, the stores in the fat body provide a major source of energy and it is generally true that insects can go on flying until their reserves in the fat body are consumed (p. 233). They also enable the insect to survive periods of quiescence or diapause' and usually, as a preliminary to diapause, extensive reserves are accumulated (see p. 719). For instance, the female *Culex* builds up her reserves in the autumn so that at the beginning of the winter they constitute about 30% of the wet weight. By the end of the winter, however, they are severely depleted and only amount to about 6% of the wet weight.

The reserves of larval holometabolous insects are largely used at metamorphosis when the adult tissues are built up. The fate of the fat body at this time is very variable. The cells generally survive, but in Hymenoptera and some higher Diptera their breakdown is almost complete (p. 416). The adult fat body is then rebuilt from the few remaining larval cells or from embryonic tissue. Egg production may also depend on reserves in the fat body, especially in insects which do not feed as adults, and it is often the case that the fat body is more prominent in female than in male insects.

6.12 Urate cells

Scattered amongst the trophocytes in the fat body of Collembola, *Blatta* and larval Apocrita are the urate cells in which uric acid accumulates. In these insects the Malpighian tubules are absent or do not excrete uric acid and the accumulation in the urate cells may be regarded as a form of storage excretion. In some other insects, such as larval Lepidoptera, with fully functional Malpighian tubules, uric acid accumulates in some of the trophocytes during the larval instars and then is passed to the Malpighian tubules at pupation. It is probable that these accumulations are the end products of metabolic processes within the individual cells and there is no evidence that the cells are depots in which products from other parts of the body are accumulated.

It is possible that the uric acid in the urate cells provides a store of nitrogen for use in the production of new tissues or that after reduction to hypoxanthine it is available to supply purines, such as adenine, for nucleoprotein synthesis, but the enzymes appropriate to these reactions are not known in insects (Kilby, 1963).

Uric acid   Hypoxanthine   Adenine

6.13 Mycetocytes

Mycetocytes are cells containing micro-organisms. In many insects, such as cockroaches, they are scattered through the fat body and the organisms they contain are responsible for the synthesis of nutritional elements (p. 81). In *Blaberus*, at least, the mycetocytes do not differ in structure from ordinary trophocytes and each bacterium is enclosed by a membrane (Walker, 1965).

6.14 Tracheal cells

Tracheal cells, which are characterised by having numbers of intracellular tracheoles, occur in the larva of the bot fly, *Gasterophilus*. They are very large cells, 350–400 μ in diameter, and almost completely fill the posterior third of the body (see Fig. 328). The larva of *Gasterophilus* spends part of its life attached to the wall of the stomach of a horse and during this period it contains haemoglobin. At first the haemoglobin is dispersed throughout the fat body, but later it becomes concentrated in the tracheal cells which differentiate from typical trophocytes. These cells, with the haemoglobin, appear to enable the larva to make better use of the intermittent supply of air brought to it as gas bubbles in the food of the horse (Keilin and Wang, 1946).

6.15 Other cells

In queen termites the fat body differs structurally and chemically from the fat body of other castes, including the larvae. The change from the larval structure occurs in *Kalotermes* when the queen is first fed entirely by other members of the colony, and at this time specialised cells develop (Grassé and Gharagozlou, 1963, 1964). The fat body of the queen contains little glycogen or fat, but is probably specialised for protein synthesis. This is in keeping with the high level of nitrogen in the secretions fed to it by other members of the colony and with the large amounts of protein required to produce the enormous numbers of eggs.

The larvae of phytophagous Diptera accumulate calcium in the fat body in the form of calcospherites.

6.2 Luminescence

A number of insects appear to luminesce, but in many cases this luminescence is due to bacteria. Self-luminescence, not involving bacteria, is only known to occur in a few Collembola, such as *Onychiurus armatus*, in the homopteran *Fulgora lanternaria*, in a few larval Diptera belonging to the families Platyuridae and Bolitophilidae, and in a relatively large number of Coleoptera, primarily in the families Lampyridae, Elateridae and Phengodidae. In these families luminescence may occur in both sexes or be restricted to the female; it also occurs in some larval forms.

The light-producing organs occur in various parts of the body. *Onychiurus* emits a general glow from the whole body, but in most beetles the light organs are relatively compact. They are often on the ventral surface of the abdomen. In male *Photuris* (Coleoptera) there is a pair of light organs in the ventral region of each of the sixth and seventh abdominal segments. In the female the organs are smaller and often only occur in one segment. The larvae have a pair of small light organs in segment eight, but these disappear at metamorphosis when the adult structures form. A review of the positions and anatomy of light organs in fireflies is given by Buck (1948). In *Fulgora* the light organ is in the head.

The light organs are generally derived from the fat body, but in *Bolitophila* (Diptera) they are formed from the enlarged distal ends of the Malpighian tubules.

6.21 Structure of a light-producing organ

The structure of the light organ of *Photuris* has been studied in detail by Smith (1963) and the following description is based on his account.

Each light organ consists of a number of large cells, the photocytes, lying just beneath the epidermis and backed by several layers of cells called the dorsal layer cells (Fig. 49). The cuticle overlying the light organ is transparent. The photocytes are so arranged that they form cylinders running at right angles to the cuticle, and within each cylinder are tracheae and nerves. Each trachea gives off branches at right angles and as these branches enter the region of the photocytes they break up into a number of tracheoles which run between the photocytes parallel with the cuticle. The tracheoles are spaced 10 to 15 μ apart and since the photocytes are only about 10 μ thick the diffusion path for oxygen is short. The origin of the tracheoles is enclosed within a large tracheal end cell,

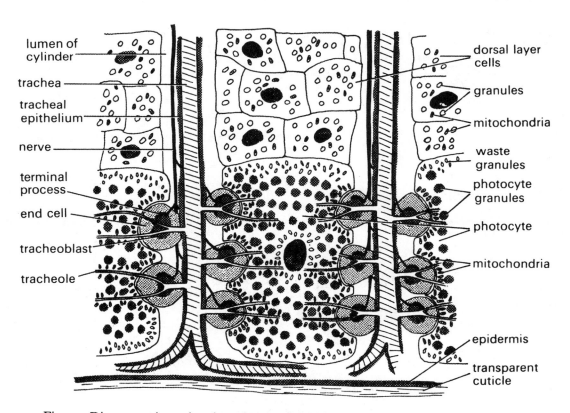

Fig. 49. Diagrammatic section through part of the light organ of *Photuris*. The tracheoles pass between the photocytes, but do not penetrate into the cells (based on Smith, 1963).

the inner membrane of which, where it bounds the tracheoblast (p. 450), is complexly folded. In some species the end cells are only poorly developed.

The nerves entering the photocyte cylinder end as spatulate terminal processes between the plasma membranes of the end cell and the tracheoblast within which the tracheoles arise. There are two types of vesicles within the terminal process; large vesicles, about 1000 Å across, resembling neurosecretory droplets, and smaller ones, 200–400 Å across, which are typical of the vesicles found in presynaptic positions and containing acetylcholine (p. 534).

The photocytes are packed with photocyte granules, each of which contains a cavity connecting with the outside cytoplasm via a neck. It is presumed that the reactants involved in light production are housed in these granules. Smaller granules also occur dorsally and ventrally. Mitochondria are sparsely distributed except where the cell adjoins the end cells and tracheoles. The dorsal layer cells also contain granules, generally regarded as urate granules, and it has been supposed that the cells form a reflecting layer. There is, however, no evidence for this and it has also been suggested that the oxyluciferin irreversibly produced in light production (section 6.22) is stored in them.

In *Photinus* (Coleoptera) it is estimated that the two lanterns together contain about 15,000 photocytes forming some 6,000 cylinders, each with 80–100 end cells.

6.22 Mechanism of light production

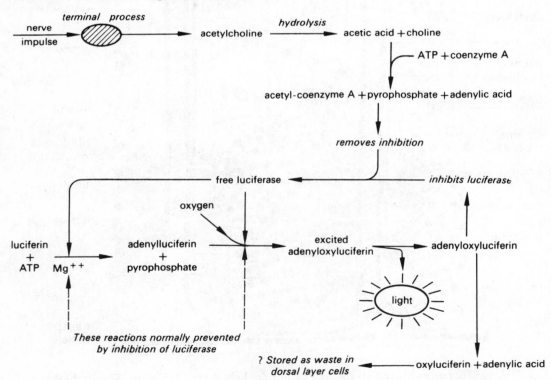

Scheme of the reactions involved in light production.

Basically, light is produced by the oxidation of luciferin, in the presence of the enzyme, luciferase. Luciferin is first activated by ATP in the presence of magnesium and luciferase to produce adenylluciferin. This is oxidised by an organic peroxide, again in the presence of luciferase, to form so-called excited adenyloxyluciferin which decays spontaneously to low energy adenyloxyluciferin with the production of light. The energy for this reaction is obtained directly from the oxidation process, not from the ATP, and it is released in one large step. The reaction is very efficient, some 98% of the energy involved being released as light.

The low energy adenyloxyluciferin produced inhibits further reaction, perhaps by becoming bound to the luciferase; pyrophosphate, however, removes the inhibition. It is suggested that when the light organ is stimulated by a nerve the acetylcholine released at the nerve ending (section 6.24) reacts with ATP and coenzyme A to yield pyrophosphate. This diffuses to the photocyte granules and stimulates the production of light by removing the inhibition of luciferase. During the reaction in the photocyte more pyrophosphate is released and this may spread through the cell, extending the reaction (Gilmour, 1961; McElroy, 1965).

6.23 Colour of light produced

In many insects the light produced by the light organs is yellow-green in colour, extending over a relatively narrow band of wavelengths, 520–650 mμ in *Photinus* and *Lampyris* (Coleoptera). The light is blue-green in *Bolitophila*, white in *Fulgora*. *Phrixothrix* (Coleoptera) larvae and adult females have 11 pairs of green light organs on the thorax and abdomen, and a pair of red ones on the head.

6.24 Control of light production

The light organs of *Photuris* are innervated from the last two abdominal ganglia. The axons, acting via the end cells, supply small parts of each organ and these units can be stimulated to produce light independently of the rest of the organ. There is a long delay between the time of stimulation of the nerve and the production of light, suggesting that a chemical diffuses a certain distance before light is produced. Possibly the arrival of the nerve impulse at the nerve ending leads to the release of acetylcholine which then diffuses out, initiating the reaction in the photocytes (section 6.22). The flash produced by each unit is very short, but different units are usually out of phase so that the organ as a whole produces a relatively long flash. See also Carlson (1969, *Adv. Insect Physiol.* **6**).

In *Photinus* each flash from the whole organ lasts a few hundred milliseconds, flashes following each other at regular time intervals, but in some larval insects and in *Lampyris* and *Platyura* (Diptera) the light is emitted as a sustained glow. In these insects the end cells are less well-developed than they are in *Photinus* and the mechanism by which light production is controlled may be rather different.

6.25 Light production in the field

In most insects light production appears to have sexual significance. The male *Photinus* produces a flash at intervals of about 5.8 sec. while flying about 50 cm. above the ground. Females perch on suitable eminences and if a flashing male comes within about two metres the female flashes in response. There is a delay of about two seconds between male and female flashes, the length of the delay being characteristic of the species. The male turns towards the female flash and as a result of further flashing is ultimately led right up to her. The continuous glow of female *Lampyris* also serves to attract the male.

Certain species of fireflies in Burma and Siam form groups which flash synchronously, but the control of this flashing is not understood.

The luminescence of *Bolitophila* larvae possibly serves as a lure, attracting insects on which they feed into networks of glutinous silk threads which they spin.

6.3 Respiratory metabolism

Energy is usually obtained from the oxidation of carbohydrate:

$$C_6H_{12}O_6 + 6O_2 \rightarrow 6CO_2 + 6H_2O + ENERGY$$

but this reaction does not occur in one step at normal body temperatures. Instead, it occurs as a series of small steps each facilitated by the action of a specific catalyst or enzyme. By this means much of the free energy of the reaction can be conserved, whereas if the breakdown was direct most of this energy would be dissipated as heat. The first part of this breakdown is an anaerobic process known as glycolysis which occurs in the extra-mitochondrial cytoplasm. Glycolysis commonly leads to the formation of pyruvate which is then oxidised within the mitochondria by the enzymes of the citric acid cycle (also known as the tricarboxylic acid or Krebs cycle) (see diagram, p. 92). The energy released in these reactions is finally conserved in a terminal oxidase system involving the cytochromes (see below).

In insect flight muscle, however, there is a suggestion that the normal pathway is short-circuited so that energy is released more rapidly to meet the demands of the muscle. The enzyme system in this muscle is such that glycolysis produces α-glycerophosphate rather than pyruvate and this is then oxidised with a direct transfer of energy to the cytochrome system. In this way the whole of the citric acid cycle is by-passed (see p. 95).

Other work, however, suggests that α-glycerophosphate may not be any more important than pyruvate in supplying energy to the flight muscles. The production of pyruvate depends on a supply of a suitable hydrogen acceptor (see below) of which nicotinamide-adenine dinucleotide (NAD; also known as diphosphopyridine nucleotide, DPN) is most important. The availability of NAD depends on its regeneration from the reduced form (NADH$_2$) and this occurs in the course of the formation of α-glycerophosphate from dihydroxyacetone phosphate (see diagram, p. 95). The importance of α-glycerophosphate may be in this rather than in the direct transfer of energy to the cytochrome system (see Chefurka, 1965c).

6.31 Sources of energy

In general it is probable that carbohydrates such as glucose and glycogen form the initial substrates for oxidation, but the pentose cycle provides a path for the interconversion of sugars containing different numbers of carbon atoms, making the oxidative metabolism of most carbohydrates possible (see Gilmour, 1961; Chefurka, 1965a).

The citric acid cycle also serves as a pathway for the final oxidation of fats which are used as fuel in the flight of some insects (p. 223). The end product of degradation of fatty acids is acetyl-coenzyme A which can enter the citric acid cycle (see diagram).

Deamination of some amino acids also yields intermediates in the citric acid cycle so that these too can provide a source of energy. Thus in the fat body of *Schistocerca* glutamate is converted to α-ketoglutarate, one of the intermediates in the citric acid cycle:

$$\text{GLUTAMATE} + H_2O + \text{NAD} \rightarrow \alpha\text{-KETOGLUTARATE} + NH_3 + NADH_2$$

6.32 Release and conservation of energy

Before sugars enter into metabolic reactions they are phosphorylated by the addition of a phosphate group. Their subsequent oxidation usually involves the removal of hydrogen, a process known as dehydrogenation. This results in structural changes in the molecule which are accompanied by a redistribution of the intrinsic energy in the system so that most of it is concentrated in a bond linking a phosphate radical to the rest of the system. In this way an energy-rich bond is created. By the process of dephosphorylation this bond energy is transferred to a molecule of adenosine diphosphate (ADP) converting it to adenosine triphosphate (ATP) (see *e.g.* Baldwin, 1949).

The hydrogen which is removed in dehydrogenation is not transferred directly to oxygen, but passes to some other hydrogen acceptor which is usually NAD or nicotinamide-adenine dinucleotide phosphate (NADP or TPN). In accepting hydrogen these are converted to the reduced forms $NADH_2$ and $NADPH_2$. These in turn pass the hydrogen to flavoproteins (FP) which then become reduced (FPH_2), but α-glycerophosphate, formed in glycolysis, and succinate, formed in the citric acid cycle, transfer hydrogen directly to the flavoprotein:

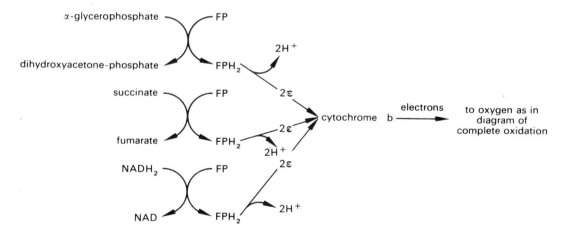

From the flavoproteins electrons (ε) are passed to the cytochrome system and H^+ ions are released into solution.

Cytochromes have a central iron atom which is capable of reversible oxidation and reduction by the removal or addition of electrons:

$$Fe^{+++} + \varepsilon \quad Fe^{++}$$

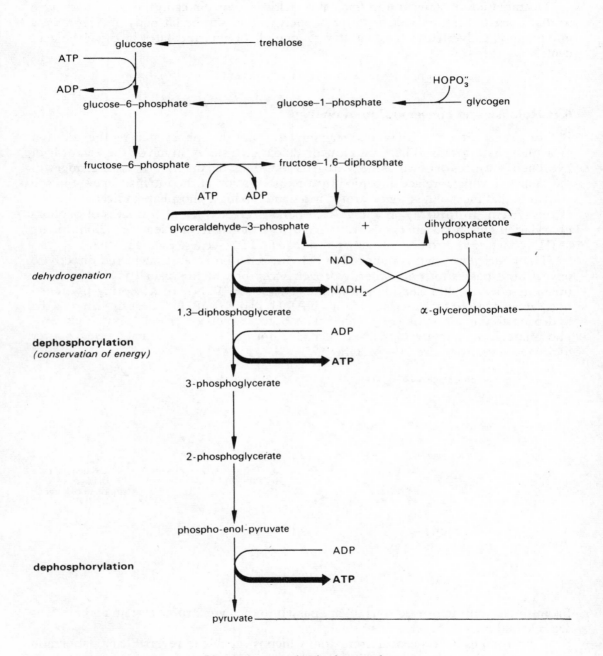

Glycolysis, occurring in the cytoplasm

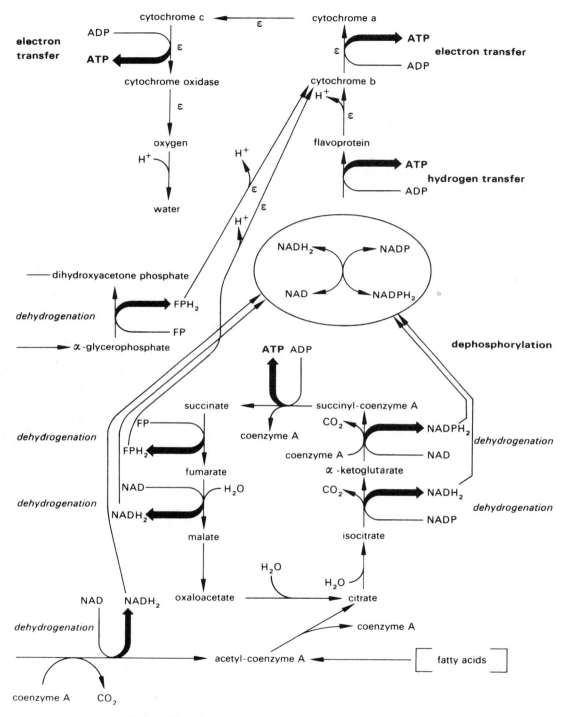

Citric acid cycle and terminal oxidation in the mitochondria

Thus in the transfer of electrons from flavoprotein to cytochrome b, the first in the series, the reaction can be summarised:

$$FPH_2 + 2Fe^{+++} \rightarrow FP + 2Fe^{++} + 2H^+$$

The various cytochromes are arranged in a series of ascending redox potential (p. 65) from $-0 \cdot 1$ volt at the flavoprotein to $+0 \cdot 8$ volt at the oxygen. That is to say each stage is a successively stronger oxidising agent than the previous one. This means, for instance, that cytochrome a will accept electrons more readily than cytochrome c, while the latter, being the stronger reducing agent, will give up its electrons more readily. Hence there is a smooth flow of electrons from the flavoprotein to oxygen, the final transfer from cytochrome a to oxygen being catalysed by cytochrome oxidase.

In some insect tissues there is a cytochrome, b_5, which, unlike all the other cytochromes, occurs outside the mitochondria and it is probable that the first step in electron transfer is from flavoprotein to cytochrome b_5. The subsequent path of the electrons is unknown, but there is no evidence that cytochrome b_5 is a terminal oxidase comparable with cytochrome oxidase (Gilmour, 1961). It is present in developing muscles, although it is absent from the mature muscles, and it has been suggested that it might be concerned in protein synthesis (see Chefurka, 1965c).

With the rise in the state of oxidation, free energy is liberated which serves to produce a high energy bond linking phosphate to ADP with the production of ATP. The greater part of the energy of the reaction is conserved at this stage, but some ATP is also formed in the course of glycolysis and the citric acid cycle. In all, the oxidation of one molecule of glucose yields a net gain of 38 high energy bonds combined in ATP. ATP is the only known source of energy which can be directly utilised in animal processes, but other nucleotide phosphates are concerned in energy conservation. These are inosine, guanosine, uridine and cytidine triphosphates.

In general, energy is produced as it is required and very little is stored in an immediately available form. Some energy can be stored in ATP, but the supply of the latter is limited because ADP, from which it is derived, is essential for the transfer of energy so that ADP and ATP must be continually recirculated. The store of energy can be increased by the transfer of the high energy bonds to phosphagens, of which arginine is known to occur in insects, although only in low concentrations. It is most abundant in muscle where the most urgent needs for large amounts of energy are to be expected. The energy stored in arginine phosphate is not immediately available, but can rapidly be transferred to ADP:

$$\text{ARGININE PHOSPHATE} + \text{ADP} \rightleftharpoons \text{ATP} + \text{ARGININE}$$

6.33 Utilisation of energy

The energy conserved during the respiratory processes is utilised in muscular activity (see p. 214), in biosynthesis and in other active mechanisms of the cell. It is probable that all the cells of the body possess an ATPase, an enzyme hydrolysing ATP, and it is presumed that this splits off a phosphate group and its high energy bond from ATP. The phosphate group may be transferred to various acceptor molecules which are thus phosphorylated. The effect of phosphorylation is to activate the acceptor molecules so that they readily take part in reactions. For instance, glucose is activated by conversion to glucose-6-phosphate:

$$\text{GLUCOSE} + \text{ATP} \rightarrow \text{GLUCOSE-6-PHOSPHATE} + \text{ADP}$$

The energy thus provided also enables the glucose to be actively absorbed by a cell against a concentration gradient.

In Odonata and Orthoptera two phosphate groups, each with an associated high energy bond, may be split from ATP and the enzymes responsible for this are known as apyrases. These are extremely dependent on temperature for their activity and this is reflected in the restriction of insect activity, and flight in particular, to relatively high temperatures. The fibrillar flight muscles of Diptera and Hymenoptera (see p. 212) are more specialised with an ATPase capable of splitting off only one phosphate group from ATP.

6.34 Anaerobic respiration

The supply of oxygen to the tissues via the tracheae is very efficient and even in flight, when oxidative processes are extremely active, the supply normally keeps pace with the rate at which the substrate is dehydrogenated and electrons transferred to the cyto-chromes. Thus it is unusual for oxidation to be incomplete, but anaerobic respiration may sometimes occur during flight (see p. 225) and insects can survive under anaerobic conditions for quite long periods.

In anaerobic respiration the breakdown of the substrate does not proceed beyond glycolysis and in vertebrates pyruvate, the end product of glycolysis, is reduced to lactate. In insect flight muscle, however, very little lactate is produced because lactic dehydro-genase, the enzyme which catalyses its production from pyruvate, is only present in low concentration. Consequently the main end products of glycolysis are pyruvate and α-glycerophosphate in roughly equi-molar amounts:

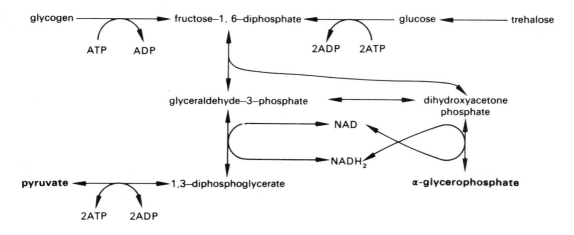

With glycogen as the initial substrate glycolysis yields two molecules of ATP for each glucose residue utilised, but with trehalose or glucose, themselves requiring energy from ATP for their initial phosphorylation, there is no net gain in ATP (see diagram).

Thus glycolysis in insect flight muscle is very inefficient compared with the process in vertebrates, this inefficiency presumably being outweighed by the importance of the α-glycerophosphate pathway in aerobic respiration in flight muscle (see p. 223).

Tissues other than flight muscle do have a lactic dehydrogenase leading to the formation of two molecules of lactic acid for every molecule of glucose used, with a consequent net gain in energy. This system is known to occur in insects or tissues where oxygen is likely to be in short supply. Thus it is found in the leg muscle of *Belostoma,* an aquatic bug, and in the aquatic larva of *Chironomus.* It also occurs in the femoral muscles of grasshoppers where there is, during jumping, a momentary very high demand for energy in a tissue far removed from the spiracles and with a relatively poor oxygen supply (Zebe and McShan, 1957).

When anaerobiosis does occur the end products are oxidised as soon as sufficient oxygen becomes available again. The oxygen requirement for this oxidation is called an oxygen debt and such a debt is indicated by a rate of respiration higher than normal when the insect returns to aerobic respiration. Thus, during sustained flight, *Schisto-cerca* builds up a small oxygen debt. When flight stops the rate of oxygen consumption exceeds the normal resting rate for a short time while the products of glycolysis are oxidised (the oxygen debt is paid off) (Fig. 50).

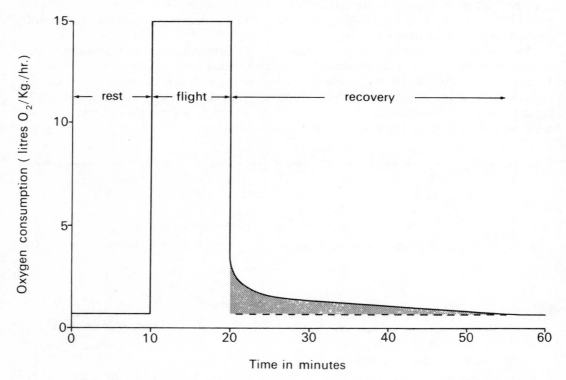

Fig. 50. Oxygen consumption of *Schistocerca* at rest and during flight showing the elevated consumption during flight and afterwards during the recovery from an oxygen debt (hatched area) (after Krogh and Weis-Fogh, 1951).

6.4 Intermediate metabolism

Intermediate metabolism includes all the cellular reactions which are not immediately concerned with the release of energy. These reactions are concerned with the formation of special secretions and the synthesis and breakdown of cellular constituents. Only the better known processes and substances will be considered.

6.41 Carbohydrate metabolism

Trehalose

Trehalose is a disaccharide widely distributed amongst insects and usually occurring in appreciable amounts in the blood, representing a store of carbohydrate in readily mobilisable form. It is utilised as a source of energy in flight, during metamorphosis and during periods of starvation. In *Schistocerca* it is synthesised in the fat body from glucose and more slowly from other sugars. The probable path of synthesis involves uridine diphosphate glucose (UDPG):

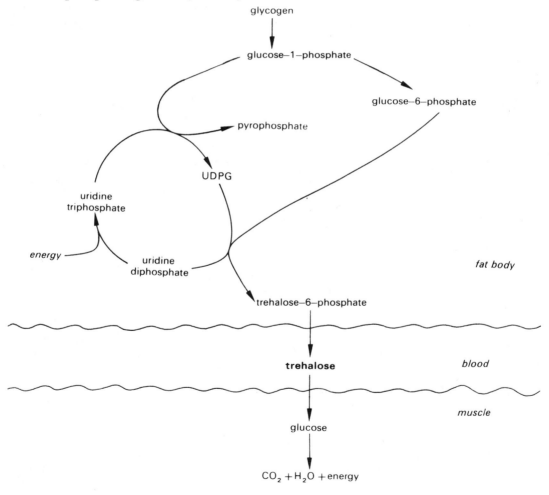

This process is expensive for the insect because it involves the utilisation of energy in the synthesis of UDPG so that trehalose must have considerable selective advantages from other points of view to have developed as the main carbohydrate transport substance of insects. One possible advantage is that it is a relatively unreactive substance and can therefore be stored in high concentrations in the haemolymph. Synthesis takes place very rapidly and in *Phormia* 50% of the radioactive glucose injected in an experiment was converted to trehalose within two minutes.

Trehalose does not readily penetrate into muscle, but is hydrolysed by trehalase to give glucose which is then utilised. A trehalase is present in the fat, in the wall of the gut, in muscle and in the blood (Chefurka, 1965c; Kilby, 1963).

Chitin

Chitin, a constituent of insect cuticle, is a polymer of acetyl glucosamine units (p. 432). In *Schistocerca* it is formed during and just after a moult from carbohydrate reserves, of which trehalose is probably the most important. The synthesis of chitin possibly involves uridine triphosphate leading to the formation of uridine diphosphate acetylglucosamine (UDPAG) followed by condensation to form chitin (Candy and Kilby, 1962).

Much of the cuticular material is digested by the moulting fluid and reabsorbed by the insect when it moults. The carbohydrate present in the old cuticle may thus be resynthesised and re-used in the new one.

Glycogen

The polysaccharide glycogen is an important reserve in some insects such as *Drosophila* where accumulations occur in the fat body, the halteres, the flight muscle and the midgut cells. It is formed from glucose, probably by two methods: by phosphorylation followed by condensation of glucose molecules, or by a method involving UDPG comparable with trehalose formation. Glycogen can also be derived from amino acids and when, for instance, *Aedes* larva is fed on glycine and alanine, glycogen is rapidly deposited in the midgut cells. There is no evidence for the production of glycogen from fats.

6.42 Lipids

Lipids are not precisely defined substances, but they are organic compounds related to fatty acid esters (fatty acids form an homologous series with the general formula $C_nH_{2n+1}COOH$), insoluble in water, but soluble in organic solvents.

Triglycerides and fatty acids

Lipids are the major food reserves of insects, probably usually occurring in the form of triglycerides in which the fatty acids are combined with glycerol:

$$\begin{array}{l} CH_2O.CO.R \\ CHO.CO.R' \\ CH_2O.CO.R'' \end{array}$$

Reports of high proportions of free fatty acids may be artefacts (Gilby, 1965). The fatty acids combined in the triglycerides are usually long chain acids, both saturated and unsaturated, the proportions of which vary considerably, depending, among other things, on the fats in the food and the temperature at which synthesis occurs. The most abundant saturated fatty acids are palmitic and stearic; the common unsaturated ones are oleic, with a double bond at position 9, and the polyunsaturated linolenic acid with double bonds at positions 9, 12 and 15.

$$\overset{9}{C}H(CH_2)_7.COOH \\ \parallel \\ CH(CH_2)_7.CH_3$$

$$CH_3CH_2CH = \overset{15}{C}HCH_2CH = \overset{12}{C}HCH_2CH = \overset{9}{C}H(CH_2)_7.COOH$$

OLEIC ACID   LINOLENIC ACID

Fatty acid synthesis takes place in the fat body and elsewhere from amino acids, sugars and simpler fatty acids. Synthesis from acetate involves ATP, coenzyme A, CO_2, NAD and possibly a member of the citric acid cycle such as α-ketoglutaric acid. By repeated condensations long chain acids are built up (see Kilby, 1963). In *Eurycotis* (Bade, 1964) synthesis first involves the production of even-numbered saturated fatty acids by the condensation of 2-carbon units. The saturated acids are then desaturated to give the unsaturated acids; thus, stearic is converted to oleic.

The fatty acids provide an energy reserve which can be used during periods of starvation or, in some insects such as *Schistocerca*, during sustained flight activity (p. 224).

Following degradation to acetyl-coenzyme A fatty acids can enter the citric acid cycle. It is probable that the whole process of mobilisation does not occur in the fat body. Lipase activity is high in the fat body and it is suggested that the fatty acids are first hydrolysed to glycerol and then phosphorylated to glycerophosphate. In this form they are transported to the flight muscle where the conversion to acetyl-coenzyme A is completed.

Waxes

Small amounts of wax are found in the cuticle of most insects where it forms the water-proofing layer (p. 500). Much larger amounts are produced by coccids and related insects, which cover themselves and their eggs with strands or plates of wax, and by bees which construct their cells of wax.

Natural waxes are mixtures, often of large numbers of compounds, and differ widely in their composition. The major components are even-numbered, long-chain alcohols and acids or their esters and odd-numbered, long-chain paraffins. Beeswax, for instance, contains 12% paraffins, 72% esters and 13% free long-chain acids.

The fat cells and oenocytes play a major part in the synthesis of beeswax and in the process material passes from the fat cells to the oenocytes and from both fat cells and oenocytes to the wax glands in the abdomen. Piek (1964) suggests the following scheme of synthesis with esters being produced by the fat cells and wax acids and paraffins by the oenocytes:

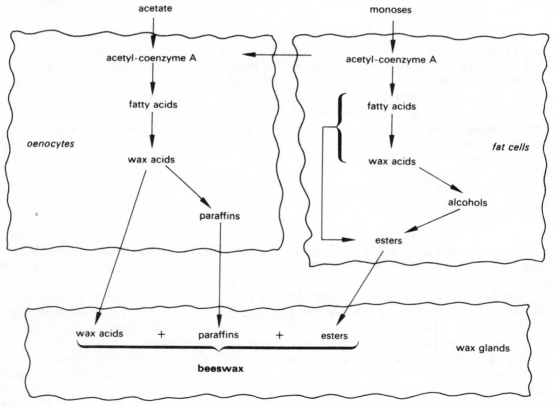

The oenocytes are also concerned with the metabolism of lipoprotein which is used in cuticle formation (p. 437).

Other lipids

Other lipids occurring in insects are phospholipids, which are lipids containing phosphorus, and steroids, complex ring compounds, occurring as free sterols or sterol esters (see *e.g.* Walsh, 1961). Sterols are essential dietary constituents (p. 73) and it is possible that some insect hormones are steroids (p. 701.).

6.43 Amino acid and protein metabolism

Amino acids

A good deal of amino acid synthesis occurs in the fat body. In *Schistocerca*, for instance, carbon from acetate is incorporated into glutamate, proline, aspartate and alanine in the fat body (Clements, 1959). Since these amino acids correspond with keto acids occurring in the citric acid cycle (*e.g.* glutamic with α-ketoglutaric, aspartic with oxaloacetic) and can be derived from the keto acids by transamination mechanisms, it is suggested that the intermediates of the citric acid cycle provide the carbon skeletons of these amino acids.

Transamination, the transfer of amino groups from an amino acid to a keto acid without the intermediate formation of ammonia and resulting in the formation of a second amino acid, occurs in a variety of tissues.

AMINO ACID	KETO ACID	KETO ACID	AMINO ACID
$CH(NH_2).COOH$	$CO\ COOH^-$	$CO.COOH$	$CH(NH_2).COOH$
$CH_2.COOH$	CH_2	$CH_2.COOH$	CH_2
	$CH_2.COOH$		$CH_2\ COOH$
ASPARTIC	α-KETOGLUTARIC	OXALOACETIC	GLUTAMIC

$$\text{ASPARTIC} + \alpha\text{-KETOGLUTARIC} \rightleftharpoons \text{OXALOACETIC} + \text{GLUTAMIC}$$

Insect tissues contain many transaminases and in *Bombyx,* for instance, 19 amino acids are known to act as donors in transamination reactions. The glutamate-aspartate conversion is the most widespread and the most active, being recorded from the nerve cord, the muscles, the gut wall and the Malpighian tubules as well as from the fat body. Activity is highest in the Malpighian tubules, while little or no transaminase activity occurs in the blood.

Keto acids (R.CO.COOH) such as pyruvic and oxaloacetic may be produced in transamination reactions and also by the oxidative deamination of amino acids, involving amino acid oxidases and glutamic dehydrogenase. These acids may be used in fat synthesis or as substrates in the citric acid cycle. In *Schistocerca* the fat body uses glycine and leucine as respiratory substrates and it is suggested that the fat body is important in transdeaminating amino acids and making them available for further metabolism by other tissues (Clements, 1959).

Glutamate plays a central role in the transfer of nitrogen from one compound to another. Ammonia is more actively incorporated into it and aspartate than into other amino acids and glutamate is also involved in the most active transamination reactions. Thus it serves to incorporate nitrogen into the system and then to distribute it. The general reactions of amino acids in insects can be summarised:

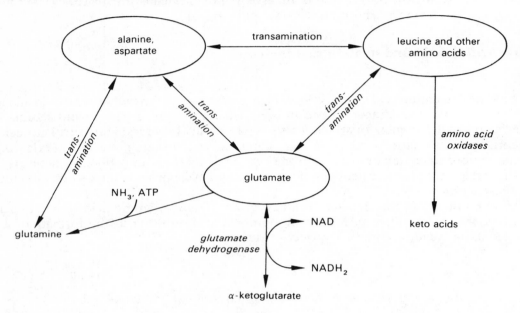

Protein synthesis

Amino acids are the units from which body proteins are synthesised. They are joined by peptide bonds to form peptides and further bonding of polypeptide chains produces proteins. By analogy with other organisms it is presumed that RNA acts as a template for protein synthesis, determining the order in which amino acids are linked.

Increased protein synthesis is often related to an increase in RNA. In *Tenebrio* the ratio RNA:DNA is high at the beginning of the pupal period when the adult tissues are forming. Subsequently the ratio falls, but then it rises again just before adult emergence when the adult cuticle is being produced.

Protein is an essential component of all cells and many special secretions, so that its synthesis must occur in many cells. The midgut epithelium, for instance, produces the digestive enzymes and the silk glands of lepidopterous larvae elaborate the proteins of silk. Blood protein is produced in the cells of the fat body.

6.5 End products of catabolism

The breakdown of carbohydrates and fats ultimately results in the production of water and carbon dioxide. The water may be eliminated via the Malpighian tubules (p. 490) and the carbon dioxide via the tracheal system (p. 463). Protein catabolism leads to the production of ammonia in addition to water and carbon dioxide and since ammonia is toxic to cells it must be eliminated from the body. In insects ammonia is not commonly excreted as such, but is usually converted into the less toxic uric acid which requires less water for its safe elimination. There are also other possible end products of nitrogen metabolism which may, or may not, be derived from uric acid.

Uric acid

The synthesis of uric acid probably utilises glycine, glutamine and aspartate as substrates and involves formate, ribose-5-phosphate and ATP. The fat body is probably important in this synthesis but whether or not it is the only or even the most important tissue involved in the synthesis is not known.

Uric acid is also derived from the metabolism of purines such as adenine and guanine which may be released during the breakdown of nucleic acid.

Other end products

Allantoin is excreted by aquatic insects, and uricase, producing allantoin from uric acid, is present in Orthoptera, Coleoptera, Lepidoptera and Diptera. The larva of *Lucilia* accumulates uric acid in the tissues, but excretes allantoin and ammonia.

Allantoic acid occurs in the excreta of larval and adult Lepidoptera and larval Hymenoptera, constituting 0·2–0·4% of the wet weight of the excreta compared with 1–40% of uric acid. It also comprises up to 25% of the meconium, the waste products of pupal metabolism discharged when the adult emerges. Allantoic acid is produced from allantoin by the action of allantoinase.

Urea is commonly present in small amounts in the excreta of insects. Sometimes, as in *Rhodnius*, it may be derived directly from the diet, but in most cases it is synthesised by the insect. It is not certain if an allantoicase occurs by which urea might be derived from allantoic acid. In *Schistocerca* and some other insects there is some evidence for an ornithine cycle (see *e.g.* Gilmour, 1961) as in vertebrates, but in Diptera it is concluded that no ornithine cycle is present.

Ammonia is excreted in large amounts by the larvae of aquatic insects and blowflies. It is not derived from the breakdown of urea, but may be carried in a bound form to the excretory organs and there released by deamination. *Lucilia* larva has an adenosine deaminase with high activity in the gut and Malpighian tubules.

6.6 Metabolic rate

The rates at which metabolic processes proceed vary considerably (Edwards, 1953), but for resting insects oxygen consumption, used as a measure of metabolism, is greater in the adult than in the larva, while the pupal consumption is lower than either (Fig. 51). Even within these stages the rate is variable and in the pupa oxygen consumption is at first high, then falls off, but rises again before adult emergence (Fig. 52). The oxygen consumption of diapausing insects follows a similar pattern, being high during phases of morphogenesis, but low during the period of diapause development (see Fig. 495).

Activity results in sharp increases in metabolism. Thus in resting *Apis* energy is consumed at the rate of 9 cal./kg./hr; during flight the figure may be up to 48 times as high and in *Schistocerca* oxygen consumption increases by a factor of 25 or more during flight (Fig. 50). Usually larger insects have slightly lower metabolic rates than small ones.

Extrinsic factors also influence metabolism, and temperature is particularly important. Metabolism increases with temperature up to a maximum and then sharply declines at the upper lethal temperature (Fig. 51).

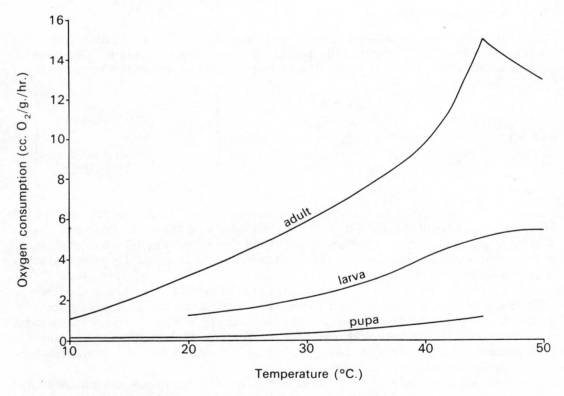

Fig. 51. Oxygen consumption of larval, pupal and adult *Calliphora vomitoria* showing the increase in consumption with temperature and, in adults, the sharp fall at the upper lethal temperature (data from Battelli and Stern, 1913).

The respiratory quotient, $\dfrac{CO_2 \text{ output}}{O_2 \text{ input}}$, varies with the substrate which is being oxidised. If the substrate is completely oxidised, carbohydrate metabolism is associated with an R.Q. of 1·0 and fat metabolism with an R.Q. of 0·7. Thus a cockroach has an R.Q. of 1·0, but after several days' starvation, when it is using fat reserves, the R.Q. falls to 0·7. The respiratory quotient of *Drosophila* in sustained flight is 1·0, that of *Schistocerca* 0·7, indicating the utilisation of carbohydrates and fats respectively.

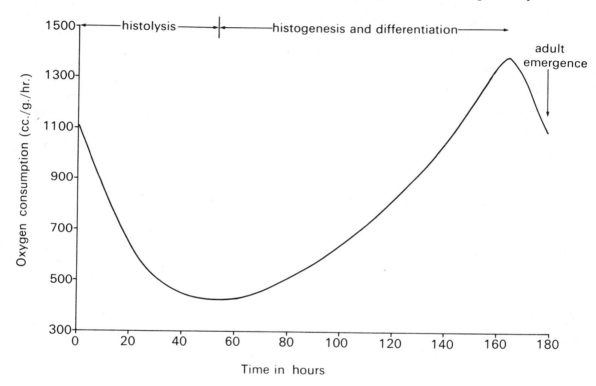

Fig. 52. Oxygen consumption of the pupa of *Galleria*. Not all insects show the fall in consumption just before adult emergence (from Wigglesworth, 1965).

6.7 Control of metabolism

Cell metabolism in many instances is controlled by hormones. Thus, hormones are known to be concerned in the control of growth and differentiation, cuticular tanning, development of the gonads, rate of heartbeat, diuresis, the mobilisation of energy reserves and the activity of the central nervous system. The mode of action of the hormones is not understood, but it is possible that they act directly on the cell nucleus so activating or depressing the activity of certain genes (see Chapter XXXIV).

Within the cell some regulation results from the structural organisation of the cell, some components being spatially isolated from others. Thus, part of the respiratory cycle occurs in the cytoplasm, part in the mitochondria and the enzymes and substrates involved are effectively isolated from each other. The rates of enzyme reaction are regulated by the availability of substrate or coenzymes and by the accumulation of the products of enzyme activity. For instance, the oxidation of α-glycerophosphate in the mitochondria is inhibited by the accumulation of the oxidation product, dihydroxyacetone phosphate, and only becomes appreciable when the ratio concentration of substrate/concentration of product exceeds 3·0 (Gilmour, 1965). This reaction may also be limited by the activity of the α-glycerophosphate dehydrogenase. It is suggested that in the resting flight muscle this enzyme is inhibited so that oxidation takes place via the citric acid cycle. During flight the inhibition is removed by divalent cations released during nervous stimulation of the muscle so that the α-glycerophosphate is rapidly oxidised to dihydroxyacetone phosphate and the citric acid cycle is by-passed (see p. 92).

The availability of ADP as a phosphate acceptor also limits, and may completely inhibit, oxidative metabolism in other animals, but it is not certain that this is so in insects since, in experimental work, the addition of ADP does not always increase the rate of oxidation (see Sacktor, 1965).

CHAPTER VII

COLOUR

Some pigments play a vital role in metabolic processes and their production is often linked with other processes in the body. Several different classes of pigment exist and they are responsible for many of the colours of insects. Most whites, blues and metallic colours, on the other hand, result from the physical structure of the surface of the cuticle and not from pigments.

Short-term, reversible colour change resulting from the movement of pigments only occurs in a few insects, but long-term changes in the deposition of pigment commonly occur. These often result in the insect matching its background, and if the background undergoes a permanent alteration the colour of the insect may undergo a parallel evolutionary change.

The colour of many insects tends to conceal them from potential predators. Other insects have markings which help to frighten off predators, or they may have a conspicuous colouration associated with distastefulness so that predators soon learn to avoid them. Different species, which may or may not themselves be distasteful, may have a similar colouration to a distasteful species so that they benefit from the learned avoidance by predators of this particular colour pattern.

Colours are also important in intraspecific recognition, and sometimes excretory products are stored in a coloured form.

Animal colours are reviewed by Broughton (1965), Cromartie (1959), Fox (1953) and Fox and Vevers (1960). The significance of colour is considered extensively by Cott (1957).

7.1 The nature of colour

Colour is produced from white light when some of the wavelengths are eliminated, usually by absorption, and the remainder are reflected or transmitted. The wavelengths of the reflected or transmitted component determine the colour which is seen (Fig. 53). If all wavelengths are reflected equally the reflecting surface appears white; if all are absorbed the colour is black.

Differential reflection of light to produce colours occurs in one of two ways: the physical nature of the surface may be such that only certain wavelengths are reflected, or pigments may be present which, as a result of their molecular structure, absorb certain wavelengths and reflect the remainder. Colours produced by these methods are known, respectively, as physical (or structural) and pigmentary colours.

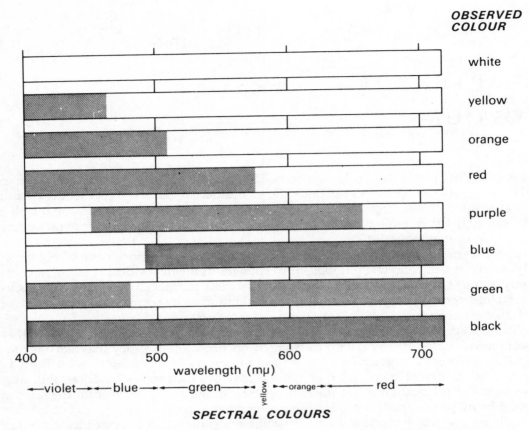

Fig. 53. Colour production by the elimination (*e.g.* absorption) of certain wavelengths from white light. Eliminated wavelengths are hatched, reflected wavelengths clear (from Fox, 1953).

7.2 Physical colours

Surface structures are mainly responsible for the production of whites, blues and iridescent colours. Such colours may be produced by scattering, interference or diffraction.

7.21 Scattering

Light may be scattered, that is, reflected in all directions, by irregularities of a surface or by granules just beneath it. If the irregularities or granules are large relative to the wavelength of light all the light is reflected and the surface appears white. Most whites in insects are produced in this way, although some white pigments also occur. Matt whites are produced by an even scattering of the light in all directions and in Lepidoptera, such as Pieridae, this results from deep longitudinal corrugations and fine, unordered striations on the surface of the scales (but see also p. 114). Pearly whites, such as occur in *Argynnis* (Lepidoptera), are produced by scattering from a number of thin, overlapping lamellae separated by airspaces. In butterflies the lamellae are the upper and lower laminae of overlapping scales (Mason, 1926).

If the granules near the surface are very small, with dimensions similar to the wavelengths of blue light (o·6 μ or less), the short, blue waves are reflected while the longer wavelengths are not. This type of scattering is called Tyndall scattering and produces blue or green. It depends for its effect on an absorbing layer of dark pigment beneath the fine granules. In the absence of this layer the blue is masked by light reflected from the background.

Tyndall blues are rare in insects, but the blue of dragonflies is produced in this way, the dark background being provided by a brown–violet ommatin.

7.22 Interference

Interference colours result from the reflection of light from a series of superimposed surfaces separated by distances comparable with the wavelengths of light. As a result of this spacing some of the wavelengths reflected from successive surfaces will be in phase and so are reinforced, others are out of phase and are cancelled out. The net result is that only certain wavelengths are reflected and the surface appears coloured (Fig. 54). The wavelength of the reflected colour depends on the refractive index of the material and the distance between the reflecting surfaces. Viewing the surface from an oblique angle is

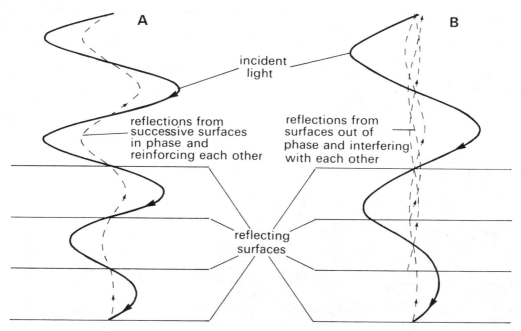

Fig. 54. Diagrammatic representation of colour production by interference. At each of the reflecting surfaces some light is reflected while the remainder is transmitted at a lower intensity (as indicated by the reduced amplitude). The diagram shows two components of incident white light, the wavelength of one of which (A) bears a simple relationship to the distance between the reflecting surfaces so that its reflections from these surfaces reinforce each other. The other component (B) has a wavelength unrelated to the distance between the surfaces so that its reflections interfere with each other (after Richards, 1951).

equivalent to reducing the distance between successive surfaces so that the colour changes in a definite sequence as the angle of viewing becomes more oblique (Newton's series). This change in colour with the angle of viewing is called iridescence and is a characteristic of interference colours (Mason, 1923, 1927a, 1927b). The brightness of the reflected colour increases with the number of reflecting surfaces.

Interference colours are common in Lepidoptera, being produced by the scales. In *Uranio* the iridescent scales are hollow with an upper lamina composed of five to ten lamellae which produce colour by interference (Fig. 55). Viewed from immediately

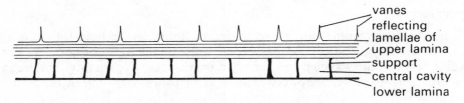

Fig. 55. Diagrammatic transverse section of a scale of *Uranio* (modified after Mason, 1927).

above, different scales appear green, blue or reddish-purple, depending on the spacing of the lamellae, changing to purple, orange and yellow-green when viewed obliquely. In *Lycaena* the iridescence is produced by the lower lamina of the scale seen through the grid-like upper surface (Mason, 1927a).

The blue of *Morpho* (Lepidoptera) is produced by a different type of scale which consists of a flat basal plate carrying a large number of vertical vanes running parallel to the length of the scale on Y-shaped supports (Fig. 56). Each vane is made up of a

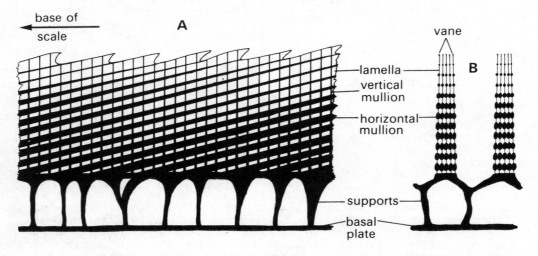

Fig. 56. A. Diagrammatic representation of a lateral view of part of an iridiscent scale of *Morpho*. B. Transverse section of part of the scale (after Anderson and Richards, 1942).

number of delicate vertical lamellae supported by a series of vertical and obliquely horizontal mullions (thickenings). There are twelve horizontal mullions spaced about 0.19μ apart and becoming thicker towards the base of the vane. Collectively the mullions of adjacent lamellae form a series of reflecting surfaces so spaced that a blue colour is produced by interference effects (Anderson and Richards, 1942).

The metallic colours of many beetles are produced by layers in the cuticle of the elytra, the predominant colour depending on the spacing of the layers. A metallic effect is produced by an underlying layer of pigment. In the tortoise beetles, Cassidinae, the lamellae in the cuticle are separated by a fluid or a substance with a high moisture content. Normally the beetles are brassy-yellow or green, but the colours change on dehydration due to changes in the spacing of the lamellae. This occurs in life if the insect is disturbed and the colours change from gold to green to violet and finally to brown-orange, as the background pigment shows through, in less than one minute. After a short time the original colour is restored.

The iridescence of membranous insect wings is due to reflection from the surfaces of a series of cuticular layers, 0.2μ apart.

7.23 Diffraction

A series of fine grooves or ridges separated by spaces corresponding with the wavelength of light will split white light into its component spectral colours. This is known as diffraction. Diffraction colours are rare in insects, but the beetle *Serica* has transverse striations on the elytra at 0.8μ intervals so that they form a diffraction grating. In diffuse light the beetle looks brown, but when viewed along its axis in a narrow beam of light the grating produces an iridescence.

7.3 Pigmentary colours

Pigmentary colours result from the molecular structure of certain compounds. Particularly important in the production of colour are double bonds, $C = C, C = O, C = N$, and $N = N$, the number and arrangement of these being important. Particular groupings are also important. The $-NH_2$ and $-Cl$ radicals, for instance, shift the absorptive region of a particular compound so that it tends to absorb longer wavelengths. The colour-producing molecule, known as the chromophore, is often conjugated with a protein molecule, forming a chromoprotein.

7.31 Brown and black of cuticle

The black or brown colour of much insect cuticle is attributed to the pigment melanin, but, if the definition of melanin is restricted to compounds composed of polymerised indole rings, this is not entirely true. Hardening of the cuticle involves cross-linkages between the protein molecules, quinones providing the links (p. 443), and some darkening does result from this tanning process. However, hardening and darkening may be independent of each other. Thus, albino *Schistocerca* have a hard, but colourless cuticle and when a normal locust moults it exhibits some dark markings before it hardens. This suggests that darkening may involve some deposition of melanin as well as the production of sclerotin.

Melanin synthesis involves tyrosine and DOPA-quinone:

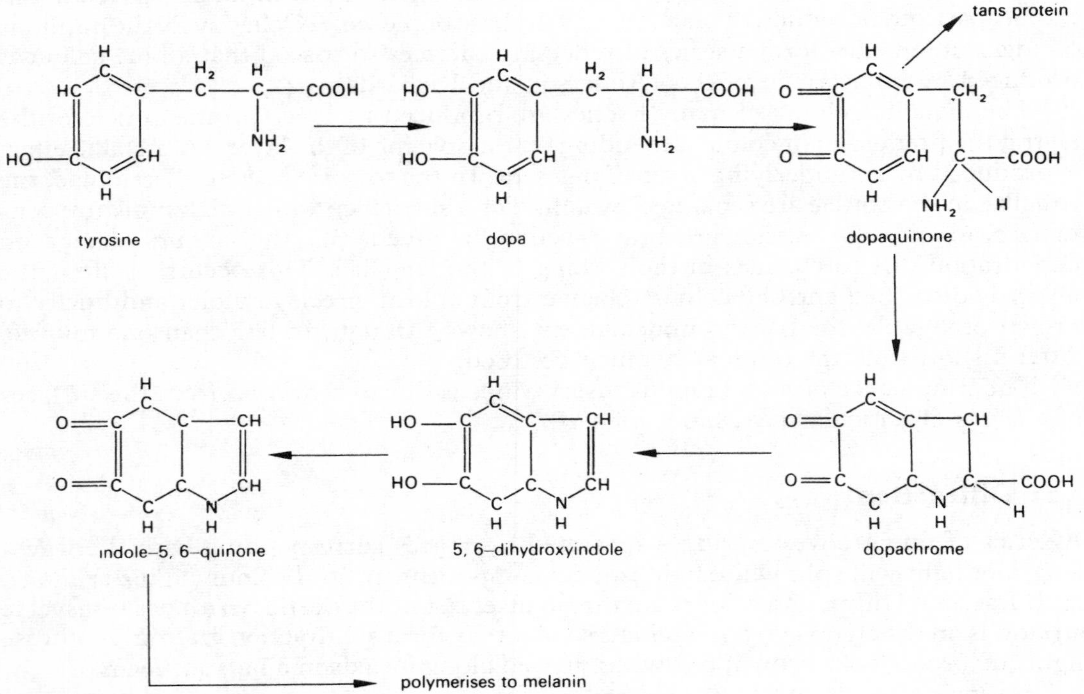

tyrosine

dopa

tans protein

dopaquinone

indole-5, 6-quinone

5, 6-dihydroxyindole

dopachrome

polymerises to melanin

It is possible that quinones are produced in excess of those needed in sclerotisation and the excess polymerise to melanin. Such polymerisation could take place round the quinones linking the proteins provided that these still have substitutable positions (Cottrell, 1964).

The dark colouring of cuticle is diffuse, but typically melanin occurs in a granular form. Dark granules, which may be melanin, do exist in the epidermis of *Carausius*.

7.32 Carotenoids

Carotenoids are a major group of pigments, soluble in fats and containing no nitrogen. They are built up from isoprene residues:

$$CH_2 = C(CH_3) \quad\text{---}\quad CH = CH_2$$

isoprene

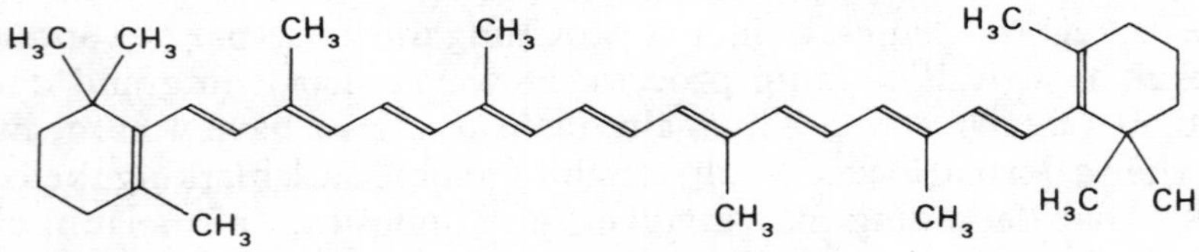

β-carotene

Carotenoids are of plant origin and are not synthesised by insects. There are two groups: the carotenes, and their oxidised derivatives, the xanthophylls. The latter may be obtained in the diet, but can also be produced by insects by the oxidation of carotene.

Yellow, orange and red are commonly produced by carotenoids, the colour depending largely on the form of the terminal isoprene residues—whether or not they form a closed ring and the degree of unsaturation.

The yellow of larval and mature adult *Schistocerca* is produced by β-carotene which also occurs in internal organs, and in various insect secretions, such as the silk of *Bombyx* (Lepidoptera) and beeswax.

The red colour of *Coccinella* (Coleoptera) is due to α- and β-carotenes together with lycopene, and the latter also produces the red of *Pyrrhocoris* (Heteroptera). Astaxanthin, a xanthophyll, is produced from carotene in the cuticle of *Schistocerca* and contributes to the pink colour of the immature adult, although this is mainly due to insectorubin (p. 115).

In grasshoppers of the genus *Oedipoda* carotenoid proteins produce the blue, red and yellow of the hind wings of different species.

In combination with a blue pigment, usually mesobiliverdin, carotenoids produce greens (green produced in this way is sometimes known as insectoverdin). The yellow component is β-carotene in *Carausius* (Phasmida) and *Schistocerca* blood, β-carotene and astaxanthin in the integument of solitary *Schistocerca* larvae, and lutein, a xanthophyll, in the larva of *Sphinx* (Lepidoptera).

The functions of carotenoids in cell metabolism are not known, but small quantities are probably concerned in the production of the visual pigment retinene (p. 553).

7.33 Pterines (pteridines)

The pterines are nitrogen-containing compounds, all having the same basic structure, but differing in the radicals attached to this nucleus (Ziegler-Gunder, 1956; Ziegler-Gunder and Harmsen, 1969, *Adv. Insect Physiol.* **6**).

Xanthopterin   Erythropterin

Pterines may be synthesised from purines and the fall in the concentration of uric acid in the pupa of *Drosophila* when the eye pigments are synthesised supports this (see Chefurka, 1965b). Possibly flavins, also closely related compounds, are involved in pterine synthesis.

White (leucopterin), yellow (xanthopterin) and red (erythropterin) are commonly produced by pterines, xanthopterin being the most widely distributed. Other pterines, such as biopterin, fluoresce in ultraviolet light, although they do not appear coloured in daylight.

Pterines are important pigments in Lepidoptera. Leucopterin and xanthopterin are common in the wings of Pieridae where they supplement the structural white. The yellow of the brimstone butterfly is due to chrysopterin, the brighter colour of the male resulting from its higher concentration, while the red of the orange-tip butterfly is due to erythropterin. The yellows of Hymenoptera are produced by crystalline granules of pterine in the epidermis overlying areas of metabolically inactive tissue (Fig. 60).

The pterines are also important eye pigments, occurring with ommochromes in the accessory pigment cells separating the ommatidia. In *Drosophila* five pterines have been isolated from the eye: two yellow compounds, another (isoxanthopterin) with a purple fluorescence, and two (including biopterin) with a blue fluorescence.

Pterines are important metabolically as cofactors of enzymes concerned in growth and differentiation and they may act as controlling agents in these processes. Their association with ommochromes arises because they are cofactors of the enzymes involved in ommochrome synthesis. The vitamin folic acid is possibly derived from pterines.

7.34 Ommochromes

The ommochromes are a group of pigments derived from the amino acid tryptophan via kynurenine and 3-hydroxykynurenine. Oxidative condensation of the 3-hydroxy-kynurenine gives rise to the ommochromes.

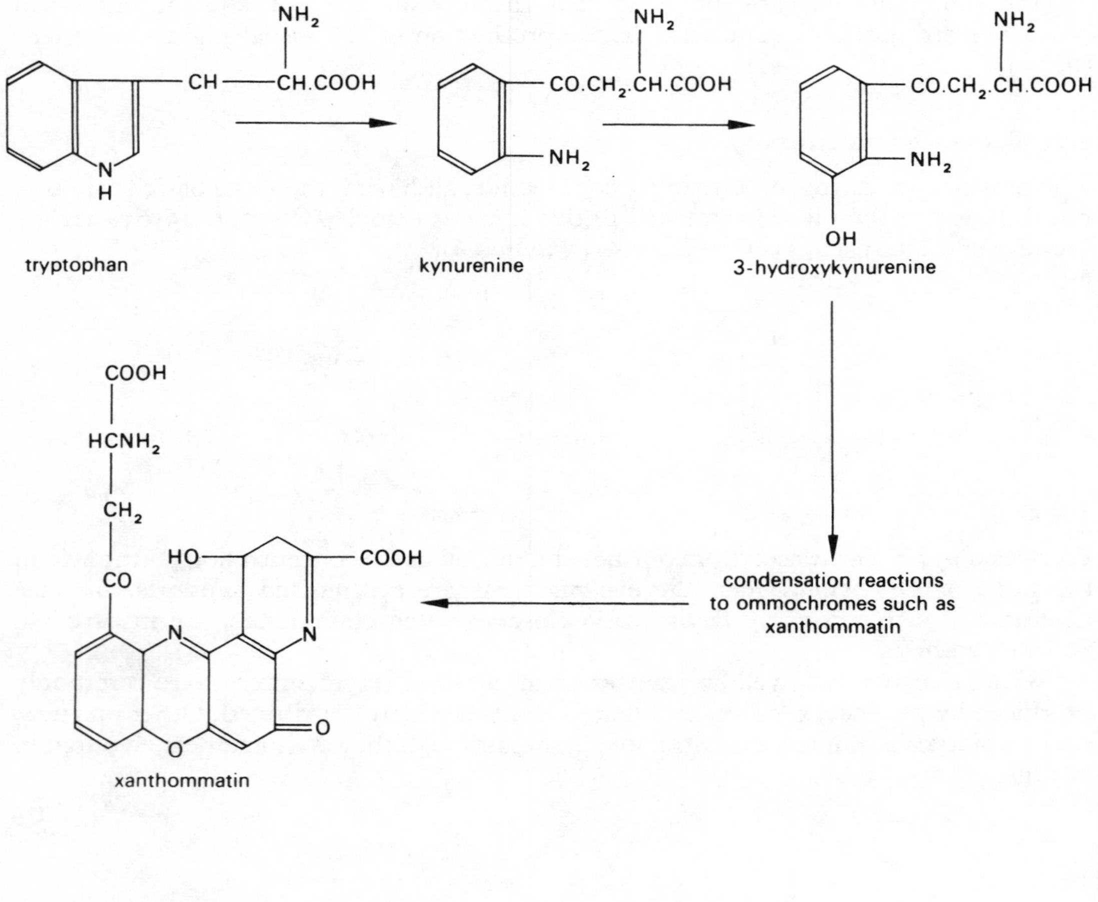

tryptophan

kynurenine

3-hydroxykynurenine

condensation reactions
to ommochromes such as
xanthommatin

xanthommatin

This condensation is coupled with the production of DOPAquinone from DOPA (p. 112), involving the same enzyme as in melanin formation. DOPAquinone acts as an electron acceptor, inducing the condensation (Gilmour, 1965).

Ommochromes are widely distributed as masking pigments in the accessory cells of the eyes, serving to isolate the ommatidia.

Yellow, red and brown body colours are produced by ommochromes. The pink of immature adult *Schistocerca* is due to an ommochrome, insectorubin, which is synthesised in the integument and then slowly decreases in amount as the insect gets older. Red Odonata and probably also the reds and browns of nymphalid butterflies are due to ommochromes, while in blue Odonata a dark brown ommochrome provides the background for the production of Tyndall blue.

Ommochromes may be produced during the breakdown of proteins since they are found in the faeces of starved locusts, in the meconium of butterflies and also in the eyes of the vermilion mutant of *Drosophila* (Diptera) after starvation. Ommochromes are normally lacking from this mutant.

7.35 Tetrapyrroles

There are two major classes of tetrapyrroles, the porphyrins in which the pyrroles form a ring:

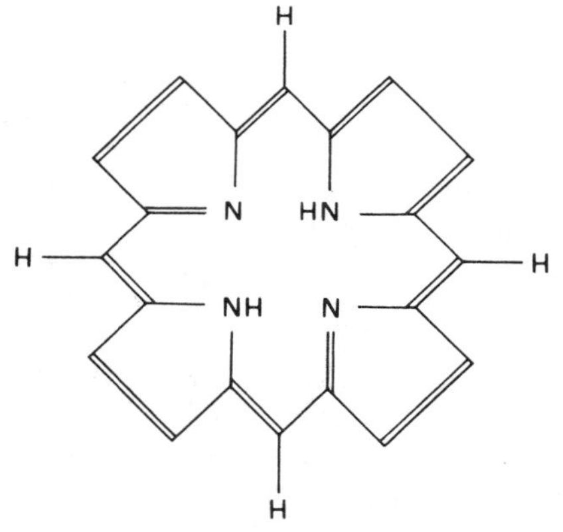

and the bilins with a linear arrangement of the pyrroles:

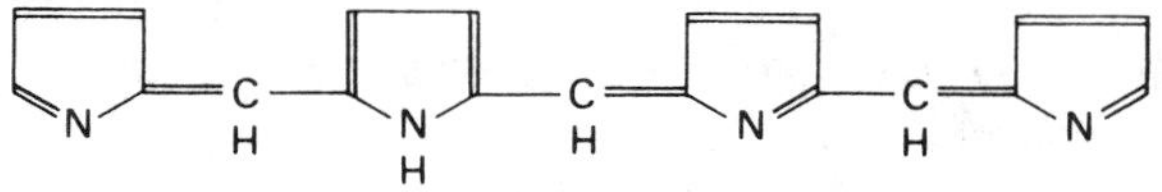

A porphyrin with an atom of iron in the centre is called a haem molecule and this forms the basis of two important classes of compounds, the cytochromes and the haemoglobins. In each case the haem molecule is linked to a protein.

All insects are able to synthesise cytochromes, which are essential in respiration (p. 91), the different cytochromes differing in the forms of their haem groupings. Normally they are only present in small amounts so that they produce no colour, but where, as in flight muscle, they are present in high concentrations, they produce a reddish-brown colour.

Only a few insects, living in conditions subject to low oxygen tensions, contain haemoglobin and these are coloured red by the pigment showing through the integument. In *Chironomus* (Diptera) larva the haemoglobin is in solution in the blood, while in the larva of *Gasterophilus* it is in the fat body. Haemoglobin serves a respiratory function (p. 487).

Bilins, bilirubin and biliverdin, may arise from the opening out of porphyrins as a result of oxidation. Typically they are blue or green. In *Chironomus* bilins from the haemoglobin of the larva accumulate in the fat of the adult and impart a green colour to the newly emerged fly. Similarly in *Rhodnius* the pericardial cells become green due to the accumulation of bilins derived from ingested haemoglobin.

Mesobiliverdin is commonly present combined with protein and in association with a yellow carotenoid produces the green colour of many insects.

7.36 Quinone pigments

The quinone pigments of insects fall into two categories: anthraquinones and aphins.

Anthraquinones are formed from the condensation of three benzene rings and three of these pigments, each produced by a different coccid, used to be important as commercial dyes. The best known is cochineal from *Dactylopius cacti*. The purified pigment is called carminic acid:

Carminic acid

The pigment, which is derived from the food-plant *Opuntia coccinellifera*, is present in globules in the eggs and fat body of the female, constituting up to 50% of the body weight. The male contains relatively little pigment.

Aphins are quinone pigments with a nucleus of seven condensed benzene rings. They are found in the blood of aphids, sometimes in high concentration, and impart a purple or black colour to the whole insect. Two series are known, one characteristic of *Aphis*, the other of *Tuberolachnus*.

7.37 Flavones (anthoxanthins)

These are plant pigments found in a few insects. They are responsible for the red colour of the bugs *Leptocoris* and *Lygaeus* and also occur in Lepidoptera. The yellow colour of the marbled white butterfly is due to a flavone obtained unaltered from the grass, *Dactylis glomerata*, on which it feeds.

The related anthocyanins, responsible for the colours of many plants, have not certainly been identified in insects.

7.4 The colours of insects

The colours of insects may result from a variety of structures and pigments which it may be useful to summarise.

Black and browns result from sclerotin and melanin. Aphins produce a black or very dark purple colour in aphids, while iridescent purples, as in the purple emperor butterfly, result from interference effects.

Red is commonly produced by carotenoids (Coccinellidae, *Pyrrhocoris*), but may be due to pterines (orange-tip butterfly) or ommochromes (Odonata, probably the reds and browns of Nymphalidae, pink of immature *Schistocerca*). Pterines and ommochromes are also responsible for eye colours. Chironomid larvae may be red due to the presence of haemoglobin and some coccids have red quinone pigments. Orange-reds and coppery colours of many beetles are interference colours.

Yellow is produced by pterines (brimstone butterfly, Hymenoptera) and carotenoids (locusts). Carotenoids also colour some secretions (silk, beeswax). Flavones may contribute to yellow, usually with other pigments. Brassy yellows are interference colours.

Green frequently results from a mixture of a blue bile pigment and a yellow carotenoid (*Carausius*, Lepidoptera larvae), but in Pieridae is produced by the juxtaposition of yellow and black scales. Bile pigments alone may produce green (adult Chironomidae) and in others (emerald moths) the pigments have not yet been isolated. Interference effects produce the metallic greens of beetles and Zygaenidae.

Blues are usually produced by interference phenomena (Lycaenidae) and rarely by Tyndall scattering (Odonata). Blue pigments are uncommon, but *Oedipoda caerulescens* (Orthoptera) has a blue carotenoid in the wings.

White primarily results from scattering, sometimes associated with a white pigment, such as leucopterin in Lepidoptera.

7.5 Colour change

Colour change may occur in two ways: by the physical movement of pigment or by the production or destruction of pigment. A change in colour produced by the movement of pigment is called a physiological change and differences in colour may be produced quickly. Colour changes involving the metabolism of pigments are called morphological changes and they take place more slowly.

7.51 Physiological colour change

Physiological colour changes are unusual in insects. In *Carausius* (Phasmida) individuals which are brown in the daytime become black at night due to the movement of pigment in the epidermal cells (Fig. 485). Similar changes due to the movement of pigment occur in the Australian grasshopper *Kosciuscola*, but in response to temperature rather than light (Key and Day, 1954a). Above 25°C. the males are blue, below 15°C. they are a dull black. Females show similar, but less marked changes. Under natural conditions the grasshoppers are black at night when the temperature is low and on a clear day they become pale two or three hours after sunrise as the temperature rises. They darken again in the late afternoon as it becomes cooler. In these changes the epidermal cells are independent effectors, responding directly to stimulation; nerves and hormones are not involved (Key and Day, 1954b). The changes may have a thermoregulatory function since dark insects absorb more radiation than paler ones (p. 640) and *Kosciuscola* is a montane species with only a limited range of movement.

Changes in the physical colours of Cassidinae as a result of disturbance (p. 111) and of Chrysididae with humidity are also known to occur.

7.52 Morphological colour change

Changes in the amount of pigment may be produced in many different ways in response to external or internal factors. The colours of grasshoppers and related insects tend to have a general resemblance to the prevailing colour of the environment, a phenomenon known as homochromy, and a change in the environment leads to a change in the colour of the insect. Thus *Acrida* (Orthoptera) changes from straw-yellow to green if put on to the appropriate background, some specimens changing in three days, but most taking rather longer. Such changes in the colour of the integument only occur at a moult, but this is not true of darkening which can occur in the absence of moulting. Black grasshoppers are commonly found in Africa after bush fires and some individuals of *Phorenula werneriana* change from grey to coal black in two days. This change occurs in recently emerged and old adults, but only in bright sunlight. In diffuse light the change is much less marked and in general the contrast between incident and reflected light is an important factor in this type of colour change (Uvarov, 1966). In *Mantis* (Dictyoptera) the green biliverdin breaks down in high light intensities forming products which are initially brown and subsequently become almost colourless (Passama-Vuillaume, 1965). Differences due to background colour also occur in other groups. Pierid pupae, for instance, may be dark or pale according to their surroundings.

Temperature is important in pigment development. Locusts bred at 40°C. have very little pigmentation and are pale yellow with a few dark markings. At lower rearing temperatures the darkening becomes progressively greater and at 26°C. the larvae are largely black with some yellow pattern (Goodwin, 1952). Similar changes occur in Lepidoptera and probably also in other insects.

Crowding influences colour in some insects. Locust larvae reared in isolation are green or fawn, while rearing in crowds produces yellow and black individuals. The colours and patterns change as the degree of crowding alters (Stower, 1959). The larvae of some Lepidoptera, such as *Plusia*, undergo comparable changes, some of them occurring in the course of an instar, but the most marked alterations only at moulting (Long, 1953).

Many changes occur in the course of development, the reasons for which are unknown. Thus the early larva of *Papilio demodocus* (Lepidoptera) is brown with a white band at the centre; the late larva is green with purple markings and a white lateral stripe. Some, at least, of these changes are under hormonal control and just before pupation the larva of *Cerura* (Lepidoptera) turns from green to red, the change being controlled by the moulting hormone.

Colour change is often associated with ageing and maturation. Male *Schistocerca* change from pink to yellow as they mature and *Mesopsis* (Orthoptera) slowly develops a black patch on the hind wings over a period of about six months, again possibly associated with maturation (Burtt and Uvarov, 1944). The male of the dragonfly *Brachythemis leucosticta* develops dark patches on the wings as it matures.

7.53 Seasonal colour change

In some insects marked differences in colour occur between successive generations correlated with seasonal changes in the environment. This is particularly well shown in some African butterflies such as *Precis octavia* which is rusty red in the wet season and violet-blue in the dry. In butterflies from temperate regions the spring and summer generations often look different and in *Arachnia levana* they are quite distinct. The form which develops depends on the length of day to which the larvae are subjected. Larvae experiencing short days give rise to diapause pupae and adults of the spring form, larvae experiencing long days have no diapause in the pupa and the adults are of the summer form (Müller, 1955).

7.54 Long-term evolutionary changes

The best known evolutionary colour changes are those associated with industrial melanism (Kettlewell, 1961). During the last 120 years there has been a marked increase in the incidence of melanism amongst moths which is well shown by *Biston betularia*. The typical form is peppered black and white, while the melanic form *carbonaria* is almost entirely black. In 1848 form *carbonaria* was a rarity in the Manchester area, but by 1895 it constituted 95% of the *B. betularia* population of this region. At the same time and subsequently it has spread through Britain so that in 1958 the black form was known from all parts of Britain except the extreme west of England and the north of Scotland, often being the dominant form.

Biston betularia is a night-flying moth spending the day at rest on tree trunks. Originally the typical form blended well with its background of bark and lichens, but industrial pollution has blackened the bark and killed the lichens so that over the past 150 years the background against which these moths rest has been completely altered and form *carbonaria* is now much better concealed than the typical form. Field experiments show that in a polluted wood birds take more typical forms than black forms. The effects of pollution are not restricted to industrial areas because the prevailing south-westerly winds drift dust over the greater part of the country so that even in the less industrialised east of England form *carbonaria* now comprises at least 80% of the population.

As well as increasing protection from predators, the form *carbonaria* is also more viable than the typical form under prevailing conditions and the rate of spread of this form indicates a 30% advantage over the paler variety.

Some 70 to 100 of the 780 macrolepidoptera found in Britain are undergoing similar changes, but only those species which spend the day on backgrounds affected by pollution and which depend on concealment are involved. Similar changes are occurring elsewhere in Europe and North America, but they are not known from the tropics.

7.6 Significance of colour

The pigments of insects probably have some metabolic significance, but, in addition, the colours which they produce are of significance in the relations of the insect with other animals. Colour is frequently used as a defence against vertebrate predators and it may also be important in intraspecific recognition.

Colours are interpreted in terms of human vision, but their appearance, and hence significance, may be different for other animal groups. For instance, the male brimstone butterfly, which to us appears uniform yellow, has markings on the forewing which become visible in a photograph taken on film which is sensitive to ultraviolet (Nekrutenko, 1965). At least some insects are sensitive to ultraviolet so that the appearance of this butterfly to them might be quite different from its appearance to humans. Of the potential predators of insects, birds and probably also lizards, are relatively less sensitive to light of short wavelength, but more sensitive to long wavelengths, while insectivorous mammals are believed to be colour blind (Walls, 1942). This, however, only means that they may be unable to discriminate between light of different wavelengths, it tells us nothing of the range of wavelengths to which they are sensitive.

7.61 Concealment from predators

Colour often helps to conceal insects from predators (Cott, 1957). This may result simply from a general similarity of colour between the insect and its background (homochromy), as in grasshoppers which become black on burnt ground or green in fresh grass. Given the choice these insects are able to select a background of the appropriate colour and experiments on *Biston betularia* show that this resemblance and behaviour do afford the insects some protection from predators. Often homochromy is associated with some appropriate body form and behaviour as in Phasmida and many mantids and grasshoppers.

Protection may also be afforded by obliterative shading. Objects are made conspicuous by the different light intensities which they reflect as a result of their form. Usually a solid object looks lighter on the upper side and darker beneath because of the effect of shadows (Fig. 57A), but by appropriate colouring this effect can be eliminated.

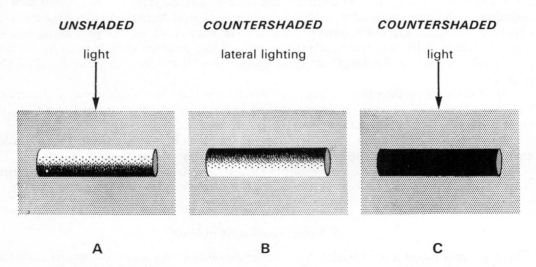

Fig. 57. Diagrams to illustrate the appearance of (A) an unshaded object in overhead light, (B) a countershaded object in lateral light and (C) a countershaded object in overhead light (after Cott, 1957).

The object is shaded in such a way (Fig. 57B) that when viewed in normal lighting conditions all parts of the body reflect the same amount of light so that it loses its solid appearance (Fig. 57C). Such countershading is well-known in caterpillars where the side towards the light is most heavily pigmented and the side normally in shadow has least pigment. To be successful this type of pigmentation must be combined with appropriate behaviour patterns since if the larva were to sit with the heavily pigmented side away from the light it would become more, not less, conspicuous. Countershading with the appropriate behaviour does afford some protection from visual predators (de Ruiter, 1955).

Colour may also afford protection if the arrangement of colours is such as to break up the body form. This is disruptive colouration and is most efficient when some of the colour components match the background and others contrast strongly with it (Fig. 58). Disruptive colouration occurs, for instance, in moths such as *Xanthorhoë fluctuata,* which rests on tree trunks.

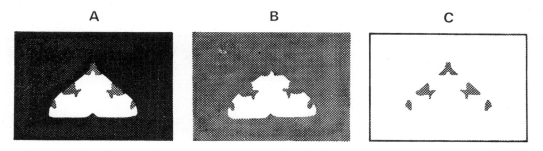

Fig. 58. Diagram of a moth with disruptive pattern on (A) an unsuitable background, (B) and (C) backgrounds blending with one of the insect colours and contrasting with the other (after Cott, 1957).

7.62 Advertisement

The colour patterns of some insects are used to attempt to intimidate predators or to deflect their attention to parts of the body which are least vulnerable. Eyespots play an important part in this behaviour and they are found in various positions on the wings of Lepidoptera and some other insects.

The peacock butterfly has one eyespot on the upper surface of each wing. These eyespots are primarily black, yellow and blue, surrounded by dark red. At rest the butterfly sits with its wings held up over its back, the upper surfaces of the forewings being juxtaposed so that the eyespots are concealed. If the insect is disturbed by visual or tactile stimuli it lowers the wings so that the eyespots on the forewings are displayed and then protracts the forewings so as to expose the hindwing eyespots. At the same time the insect makes a hissing sound by rubbing the anal veins of the forewings against the costal veins of the hindwings. The forewings are then retracted and partly raised and the sequence of movements repeated, sometimes for several minutes. While displaying, the body is tilted so that the wings are fully exposed to the source of stimulation and at the same time the insect turns so as to put the stimulus behind it (Blest, 1957). This display does release an innate escape response in birds and some birds learn to avoid peacock butterflies altogether, but in others the effectiveness of the display wanes.

Other experiments show that the attacks of birds are usually directed at eyespots so that these do serve, temporarily, to deflect attacks away from vulnerable parts. There is no sharp distinction between eyespots used for intimidation and those concerned with deflection. In general it may be that deflecting spots are smaller than those used in intimidation, but it is possible that some may serve either function depending on the nature and experience of the predator.

Other types of colour advertisement by insects are associated with distastefulness so that predators learn to associate a particular colour pattern with distastefulness and so, subsequently, avoid taking insects displaying this pattern. Such patterns must be bold and readily recognisable and frequently involve red or yellow with black. Thus the black and yellow of the bee and wasp is associated with a sting and the red and dark green of the burnet moth with extreme distastefulness.

In experiments, toads learned to avoid bees, some after eating only one bee, others only after repeated trials, but after a week all of 33 toads had stopped eating bees. The distasteful association was remembered by the toads so that when they were offered bees again two weeks after the original experiment very few of them would accept the food. Complete avoidance was soon re-established in spite of the fact that, apart from the bees, each toad had eaten only one mealworm during the whole experiment (Fig. 59) (Cott, 1957).

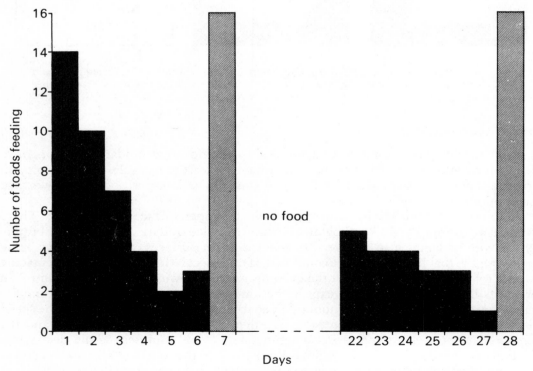

Fig. 59. The number of toads out of 18 which accepted bees (black) on successive days and the number which accepted mealworms (hatched) when they would no longer take bees (after Cott, 1957).

7.63 Mimicry

Predators learn to avoid distasteful insects with distinctive colours, but theoretically a predator must learn to avoid each individual species separately. If, however, the colour patterns of some species are similar to each other, learning to avoid one also produces an avoidance of the other so that it is an advantage for distasteful insects to look similar because in this way wastage is reduced. Thus various wasp species have the same basic black and yellow pattern, and burnet and cinnabar moths have comparable red markings on a dark green or black ground.

Resemblance of one species by another is called mimicry and the principle on which it is based may be extended to include species which are not distasteful or are only mildly so. If a predator learns to avoid a particular pattern because the insect having it is distasteful it will subsequently avoid other species with the same pattern, even though they may not be distasteful. As a result of this, palatable species gain some advantage from a resemblance to distasteful ones. The distasteful species is called the model, those that resemble it in appearance are mimics.

In this type of mimicry it is important that the mimic is uncommon relative to the model. If this was not the case a predator might learn to associate a particular pattern with palatability rather than distastefulness. This limits the numbers or distribution of a mimetic form, but such a limit may be circumvented by the mimic becoming polymorphic with each of the morphs resembling a different distasteful species. The best known example of genetic polymorphism is that of the female *Papilio dardanus* (Lepidoptera) which has a large number of mimetic forms mimicking a series of quite different butterflies (Carpenter and Ford, 1933). See Rettenmeyer (1970, *A. Rev. Ent.* **15**).

7.64 Intraspecific recognition

In some insects colour is important in the recognition of one sex by the other. Thus the male of *Hypolimnas misippus* (Lepidoptera) responds to the brown of the female wings by pursuing her, but his response is inhibited by the presence of white in the wings (Stride, 1957). Similar use of colour is known in other insects.

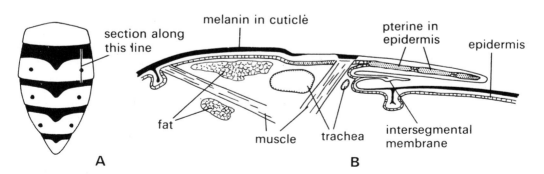

Fig. 60. A. The pigment pattern on the abdomen of *Vespa*. B. Longitudinal section through a tergite and associated tissues showing the distribution of pigments (from Wigglesworth, 1965).

Some dragonflies exhibit territorial behaviour, a male in his home territory chasing off other males of the same species (p. 302). Threatening sign stimuli are employed in this behaviour and, for instance, the male of *Plathemis lydia* raises its abdomen so that its blue upper surface is displayed to other males. In the presence of the female the abdomen is depressed (Corbet, Longfield and Moore, 1960).

7.65 Storage excretion

Some pigments may be regarded as metabolic waste products so that their accumulation may be regarded as a form of storage excretion (see also p. 498). Pterines, for instance, may be derived from purines, such as uric acid. Similarly melanin production might be a method of disposing of toxic phenols arising from metabolism and it may be significant that melanin is often produced over metabolically active tissue such as muscle (Fig. 60).

SECTION B

The Thorax and Movement

CHAPTER VIII

THE THORAX AND LEGS

The six-legged condition of insects is probably derived from some myriapod condition. The development of longer legs to facilitate fast running necessitates a reduction in the number of legs for functional efficiency and six is the smallest number which gives continuous stability during movement at a variety of speeds (see Chapter IX). Mechanical efficiency also requires the placing of these legs close together behind the head and it is believed that as a result of these mechanical and functional requirements the insect thorax was evolved (see Manton, 1953).

Independently of this, wings also developed on the thorax so that it became the locomotor centre of the insect. Hence the skeleton of the thoracic segments is modified to give efficient support for the legs and wings and the musculature is adapted to produce the movements of the appendages. The legs themselves, starting from a typical walking leg, are also adapted to various functions with appropriate modifications in their form.

For a general review of the morphology of the insect thorax and legs see Snodgrass (1935). Matsuda (1963) considers certain specialised aspects.

8.1 Segmentation

In larval holometabolous insects the cuticle is soft and flexible, or only partially sclerotised, and the longitudinal muscles are attached to the intersegmental folds (Fig. 61A). This represents a primitive condition comparable with that occurring in the annelids, and the segments delimited by the intersegmental folds are regarded as the primary segments. Insects with this arrangement move as a result of successive changes in the shapes of the thoracic and abdominal segments (p. 154), these changes of shape being permitted by the flexible cuticle.

When the cuticle is sclerotised the basic arrangement is believed to comprise dorsal and ventral plates associated with narrow intersegmental sclerites which develop in the intersegmental folds and have the longitudinal muscles attached to them (Fig. 61B). Clearly, such an arrangement permits very little movement and the intersegmental sclerites usually become fused with the segmental sclerites behind. The large sclerite on the dorsal surface of a segment is called the tergum, or, in the thorax, the notum, the groove of the intersegmental sclerite is the antecostal sulcus, and the narrow rim in front of the sulcus is called the acrotergite (Fig. 61C). An acrotergite never occurs at the front of the prothorax because the anterior part of this segment is involved in the neck (p. 9) and the muscles from the head pass directly to the acrotergite of the mesothorax.

An area at the back of each segment remains membranous, forming a new intersegmental membrane. This does not correspond with the original intersegmental groove

127

so that a secondary segmentation is superimposed on the first. Thus the visible segmentation of adult insects is, in fact, this secondary segmentation and may not correspond precisely with the larval segmentation (Snodgrass, 1935).

This basic condition occurs in the abdomen where this is sclerotised, in the meso- and meta-thoracic segments of larval insects with a sclerotised thorax, in the Apterygota and in adult Dictyoptera and Isoptera where the wings are not moved by indirect muscles (see p. 185). With this arrangement contraction of the longitudinal muscles produces telescoping of the segments.

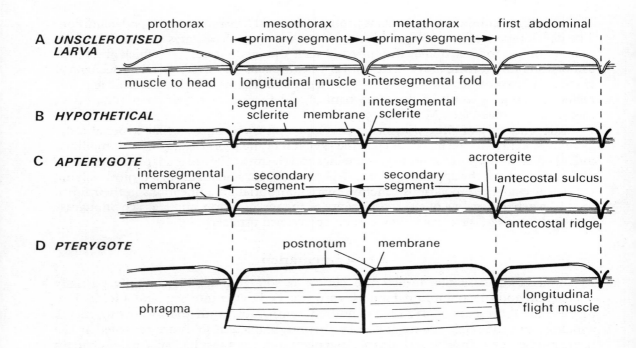

Fig. 61. Schematised diagrams showing changes in segmentation and the derivation of the postnotum and phragmata in pterygote insects. Sclerotised areas are indicated by a solid line, membranous areas by a double line.

8.2 Thorax

The thorax consists of three segments known, respectively, as the pro-, meso- and meta-thorax. In most insects all three segments bear a pair of legs, but this is not the case in larval Diptera, larval Hymenoptera Apocrita, some larval Coleoptera and a small number of adult insects which are apodous. In addition, winged insects have a pair of wings on the meso- and meta-thoracic segments and these two segments are then collectively known as the pterothorax.

8.21 Tergum

The tergum of the prothoracic segment is known as the pronotum. It is often small as it serves only for the attachment of the leg muscles, but in Orthoptera, Dictyoptera and Coleoptera it forms a large plate affording some protection to the pterothoracic segments. The meso- and meta-nota are relatively small in wingless insects and larvae, but in winged insects they become modified for the attachment of the wings. In the majority of winged insects the downward movement of the wings depends on an upward distortion of the thorax (p. 185). This is made possible by a modification of the basic segmental arrangement. The acrotergites of the metathorax and the first abdominal segment extend forwards to join the tergum of the segment in front and in many cases become secondarily separated from their original segment by a narrow membranous region. Each acrotergite and antecostal sulcus is now known as a postnotum (Fig. 61D). There may thus be a mesopostnotum and a metapostnotum if the wings are more or less equally important in flight, but if only the hind wings are important, as in Orthoptera and Coleoptera, only the metapostnotum is developed. The Diptera on the other hand, using only the forewings for flight, have a well developed mesopostnotum, but no metapostnotum. To provide attachment for the large longitudinal muscles moving the wings the antecostal ridges at the front and back of the mesothorax and the back of the metathorax usually develop into extensive internal plates, the phragmata (Figs. 61D and 66). Which of the phragmata are developed again depends on which wings are most important in flight.

Various strengthening ridges develop on the tergum of a wing-bearing segment which are local adaptations to the mechanical stresses imposed by the wings and their

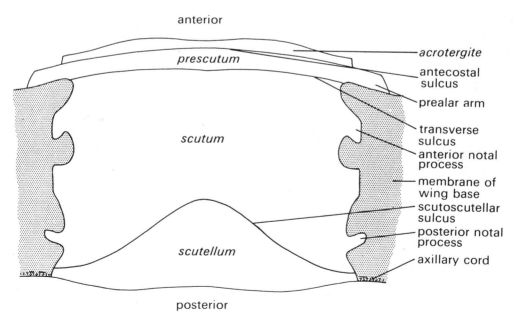

Fig. 62. Diagram showing the main features of the notum of a wing-bearing segment (from Snodgrass, 1935).

muscles. The ridges appear externally as sulci (see p. 4) which divide the notum into areas. Often a transverse sulcus divides the notum into an anterior prescutum and a scutum, while a V-shaped sulcus posteriorly separates the scutellum (Fig. 62). These areas are commonly demarcated, but, because of their origins as functional units, plates of the same name in different insects are not necessarily homologous. In addition the lateral regions of the scutum may be cut off or there may be a median longitudinal sulcus. Commonly the prescutum connects with the pleuron by an extension, the prealar arm, in front of the wing, while behind the wing a postalar arm connects the postnotum to the epimeron. Laterally the scutum is produced into two processes, the anterior and posterior notal processes which articulate with the axillary sclerites in the wing base (p. 177). The posterior fold of the scutellum continues as the axillary cord along the trailing edge of the wing.

8.22 Sternum

As on the dorsal surface, the primary sclerotisations are separate segmental and intersegmental plates and commonly in the thorax these remain separate. The intersegmental sclerite is produced internally into a spine and is called the spinasternum, while the

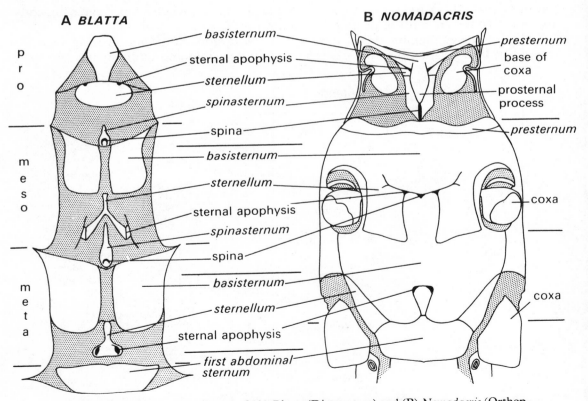

Fig. 63. Ventral view of the thorax of (A) *Blatta* (Dictyoptera) and (B) *Nomadacris* (Orthoptera) (after Snodgrass, 1935; Albrecht, 1956).

segmental sclerite is called the eusternum (Fig. 66). Various degrees of fusion occur so that four basic arrangements may be found:

a) all elements separate—eusternum of prothorax; first spina; eusternum of mesothorax; second spina; eusternum of metathorax (see Fig. 63A. Notice that in the diagram eusternum is divided into basisternum and sternellum)

b) eusternum of mesothorax and second spina fuse, the rest remaining separate

c) eusternum of prothorax and first spina also fuse so that there are now three main elements—compound prosternum; compound mesosternum; eusternum of metathorax

d) complete fusion of meso- and meta-thoracic elements to form a pterothoracic plate (Fig. 63B).

Arising from the eusternum are a pair of apophyses (p. 431), the so-called sternal apophyses (Fig. 66). The origins of these on the sternum are marked by pits joined by a sulcus (Fig. 63B) so that the eusternum is divided into a basisternum and sternellum, while in higher insects the two apophyses arise together in the midline and only separate internally, forming a Y-shaped furca (Fig. 64). Distally the sternal apophyses are associated with the inner ends of the pleural ridges, usually being connected to them by short muscles. This adds rigidity to the thorax, while variation in the degree of contraction of the muscles makes this rigidity variable and controllable. The sternal apophyses also serve for the attachment of the bulk of the ventral longitudinal muscles, although a few fibres retain their primitive intersegmental connections with the spinasterna (Fig. 66).

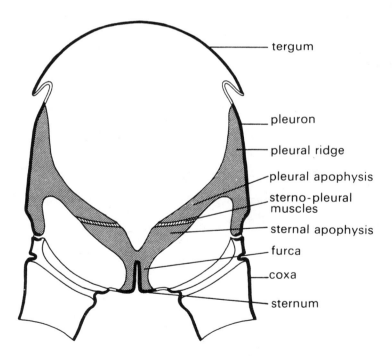

Fig. 64. Diagrammatic cross-section of a thoracic segment showing the pleural ridges and sternal apophyses (from Snodgrass, 1935).

Some insects have a longitudinal sulcus with an internal ridge running along the middle of the sternum. This is regarded by some authorities as indicating that the whole of the primitive sternum has become invaginated and that the apparent sternum in these insects is really derived from subcoxal elements (see Matsuda, 1963). The median longitudinal sulcus is known as the discrimen.

The sternum is attached to the pleuron by pre- and post-coxal bridges. The sternum of the pterothoracic segments does not differ markedly from that of the prothorax, but usually the basisternum is bigger, providing for the attachment of the large dorsoventral flight muscles.

8.23 Pleuron

The pleural regions are membranous in many larval insects, but typically become sclerotised in the adult. Basically there are probably three pleural sclerites, one ventral and two dorsal, which may originally have been derived from the coxa (Snodgrass, 1958). The ventral sclerite, or sternopleurite, articulates with the coxa and becomes fused with the sternum so as to become an integral part of it. The dorsal sclerites, anapleurite and coxopleurite, are present as separate sclerites in Apterygota and in the

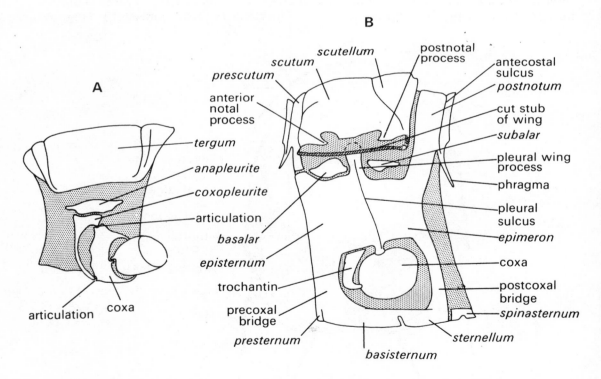

Fig. 65. A. Lateral view of the prothorax of *Perla* (Plecoptera). B. Diagrammatic lateral view of a typical wing-bearing segment. Anterior to left, membranous regions stippled (from Snodgrass, 1935).

prothorax of larval Plecoptera (Fig. 65A). In other insects they are fused to form the pleuron, but the coxopleurite, which articulates with the coxa, remains partially separate in the lower pterygote orders forming the trochantin and making a second, more ventral articulation with the coxa (Fig. 65B).

Above the coxa the pleuron develops a nearly vertical strengthening ridge, the pleural ridge, marked by the pleural sulcus externally. This divides the pleuron into an anterior episternum and a posterior epimeron. The pleural ridge is particularly well developed in the wing bearing segments where it continues dorsally into the pleural wing process which articulates with the second axillary sclerite in the wing base (Fig. 65B).

In front of the pleural process in the membrane at the base of the wing and only indistinctly separated from the episternum are one or two basalar sclerites, while in a comparable position behind the pleural process is a well-defined subalar sclerite. Muscles concerned with the movement of the wings are inserted into these sclerites.

Typically there are two pairs of spiracles on the thorax. These are in the pleural regions and are associated with the mesothoracic and metathoracic segments. The

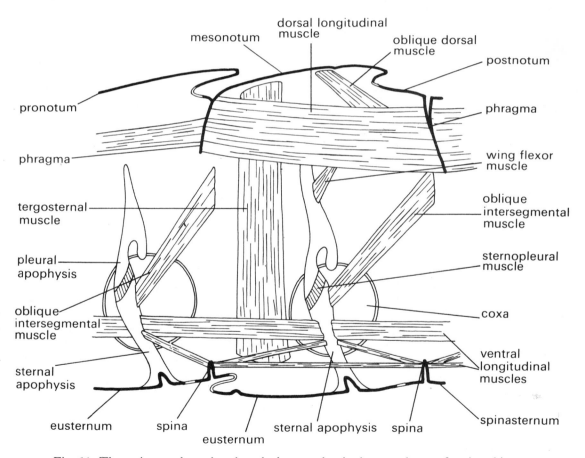

Fig. 66. The main muscles, other than the leg muscles, in the mesothorax of a winged insect (from Snodgrass, 1935).

mesothoracic spiracle often occupies a position on the posterior edge of the propleuron, while the smaller metathoracic spiracle may similarly move on to the mesothorax. The Diplura are exceptional in having three or four pairs of thoracic spiracles. *Heterojapyx*, for instance, has two pairs of mesothoracic and two pairs of metathoracic spiracles.

8.24 Muscles of the thorax

The longitudinal muscles of the thorax, as in the abdomen, run from one antecostal ridge to the next. They are relatively poorly developed in sclerotised larvae, in adult Odonata, Dictyoptera and Isoptera which have direct wing depressor muscles (p. 185), and also in secondarily wingless groups such as Siphonaptera. In these cases they tend to telescope one segment into the next while the more lateral muscles rotate the segments relative to each other. In unsclerotised insects contraction of the longitudinal muscles shortens the segment.

In most winged insects, however, the dorsal longitudinal muscles are the main wing depressors and they are strongly developed (see p. 185, Fig. 66), running from phragma to phragma so that their contraction distorts the segments. The ventral longitudinal muscles run mainly from one sternal apophysis to the next in adult insects, producing some ventral telescoping of the thoracic segments.

Dorso-ventral muscles run from the tergum to the pleuron or sternum. They are primitively concerned with rotation or compression of the segment, but in winged insects they are important flight muscles (p. 185). In larval insects an oblique intersegmental muscle runs from the sternal apophysis to the anterior edge of the following tergum or pleuron, but in adults it is usually only present between prothorax and mesothorax.

The other important muscles of the thorax are concerned with movement of the legs and are dealt with separately (p. 143).

8.3 Legs

8.31 Basic structure

With the exception of apodous larval forms and a few specialised adults, all insects have three pairs of legs, one pair on each of the thoracic segments. Each leg consists typically of six segments, articulating with each other by mono- or di-condylic articulations set in a membrane, the corium. The six basic segments are coxa, trochanter, femur, tibia, tarsus and pretarsus (Fig. 67A).

The coxa is often in the form of a truncated cone and articulates basally with the wall of the thorax. There may be only a single articulation with the pleuron (Fig. 68A), in which case movement of the coxa is very free, but frequently there is a second articulation with the trochantin (Fig. 68B). This restricts movement to some extent, but because the trochantin is flexibly joined to the episternum the coxa is still relatively mobile. In some higher forms there are rigid pleural and sternal articulations limiting movement of the coxa to swinging about these two points (Fig. 68C). In the Lepidoptera the coxae of the middle and hind legs are fused with the thorax and this is also true of the hind coxae in Adephaga.

The part of the coxa bearing the articulations is often strengthened by a ridge indicated externally by the basicostal sulcus which marks off the basal part of the coxa as the basicoxite (Fig. 69A). The basicoxite is divided into anterior and posterior parts by a ridge strengthening the articulation, the posterior part being called the meron. This is very large in Neuroptera, Mecoptera, Trichoptera and Lepidoptera (Fig. 69B), while in the higher Diptera it becomes separated from the coxa altogether and forms a part of the wall of the thorax.

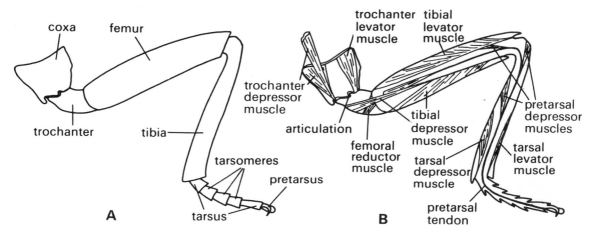

Fig. 67. Typical insect leg. A. External view. B. Internal arrangement showing the intrinsic muscles (after Snodgrass, 1927).

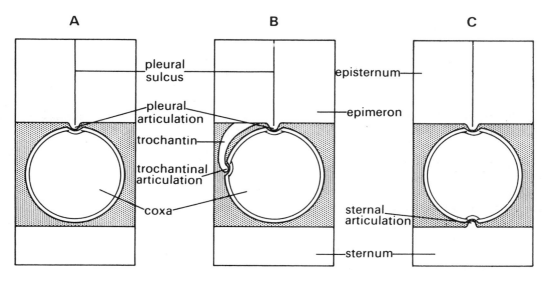

Fig. 68. Diagrammatic representations of different types of coxal articulation with the thorax. Membranous regions stippled (from Snodgrass, 1935).

The trochanter is a small segment with a dicondylic articulation with the coxa such that it can only move vertically (Fig. 70A). In Odonata there are two trochanters and this also appears to be the case in Hymenoptera, but here the apparent second trochanter is, in fact, a part of the femur.

The femur is often small in larval insects, but in most adults it is the largest and stoutest part of the leg. Often the femur is more or less fixed to the trochanter and in this case there are no muscles to move it, but sometimes a single muscle arising in the trochanter is able to produce a slight backward movement, or reduction, of the femur.

The tibia is the long shank of the leg articulating with the femur by a dicondylic joint so that it moves in a vertical plane (Fig. 70B and C). In most insects the head of the tibia is bent so that the shank can flex right back against the femur (Fig. 67).

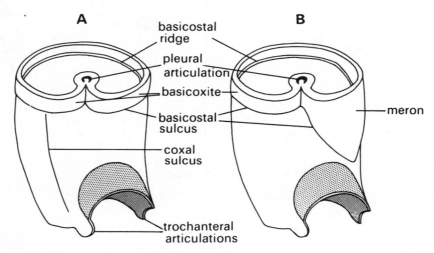

Fig. 69. Outer view of (A) typical insect coxa, and (B) coxa with a large meron (from Snodgrass, 1935).

In Protura, some Collembola and the larvae of holometabolous insects the tarsus is simple (Fig. 71A) or, in the latter, may be fused with the tibia. In most insects, however, it becomes subdivided into from two to five tarsomeres. These are differentiated from true segments by the absence of muscles (see Fig. 67). The basal tarsomere, or metatarsus, articulates with the distal end of the tibia by a single condyle (Fig. 70D), but between the tarsomeres there is no articulation; they are connected by flexible membrane so that they are freely movable. Levator and depressor muscles of the tarsus arise in the tibia and are inserted into the proximal end of the metatarsus.

The pretarsus consists of a single claw-like segment in Protura, some Collembola and many holometabolous larvae (Fig. 71A), but in the majority of insects its consists of a membranous base supporting a median lobe, the arolium, which may be membranous or partly sclerotised, and a pair of claws which articulate with a median process of the last tarsomere known as the unguifer. Ventrally there is a basal sclerotised plate, the unguitractor, and between this and the claws are small plates called auxiliae (Fig. 71B).

In Diptera a membranous pulvillus arises from the base of each auxilia while a median empodium, which may be spine- or lobe-like, arises from the unguitractor (Fig. 71C). There is no arolium in Diptera other than Tipulidae. The development of the claws is variable. Commonly they are more or less equally well-developed, but in Thysanoptera they are minute and the pretarsus consists largely of the bladder-like arolium. In other groups the claws develop unequally and one may fail to develop altogether so that in Mallophaga, for instance, there is only a single claw.

The muscles of the leg are described in Chapter IX.

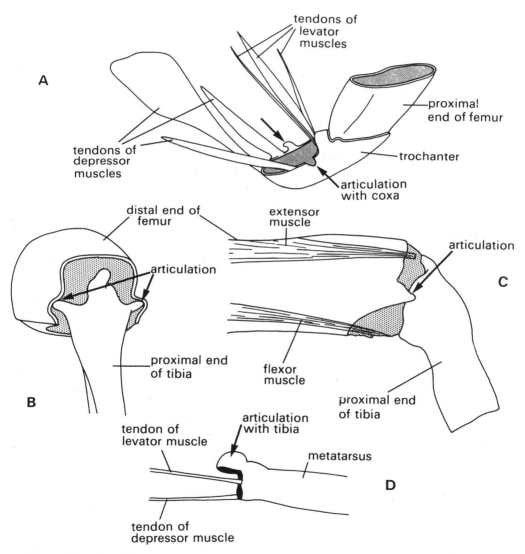

Fig. 70. Details of articulations of the leg joints. A. Articulation of trochanter with coxa and the muscles moving the trochanter. B and C. Articulation of tibia and femur, (B) end view, (C) side view. D. Articulation of tarsus with tibia (after Snodgrass 1935, 1952).

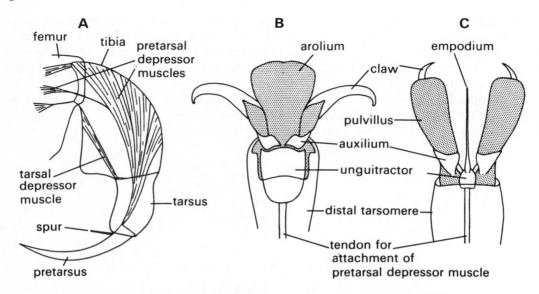

Fig. 71. A. Distal part of prothoracic leg of *Triaenodes* (Trichoptera) larva showing a primitive pretarsal segment. B. Pretarsus of *Periplaneta,* ventral view. C. Pretarsus of a dipteran, ventral view (after Tindall, 1964; Snodgrass, 1935).

8.32 Modifications of the basic pattern

The basic insect walking leg may be modified in various ways to serve a number of functions. Amongst these are jumping, swimming, digging, grasping, grooming and stridulation. Modifications associated with jumping and swimming are considered in Chapter IX.

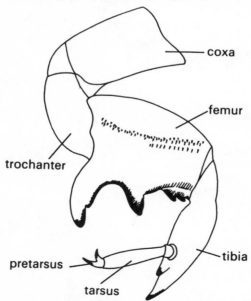

Fig. 72. Foreleg of a larval cicada (from Pesson, 1951a).

Digging

Legs modified for digging are best known in the Scarabaeoidea and the mole cricket, *Gryllotalpa*. In *Gryllotalpa* the forelimb is very short and broad, the tibia and tarsomeres bearing stout lobes which are used in excavation. In the scarab beetles the femora are short, the tibiae are again strong and toothed, but the tarsi are often weakly developed. Larval cicadas are also burrowing insects. They have large, toothed fore femora, the principal digging organs, and the strong tibiae may serve to loosen the soil (Fig. 72). The tarsus is inserted dorsally on the tibia and can fold back. In the first instar larva it is three-segmented, but it becomes reduced in later instars and may disappear completely.

Grasping

Modifications of the legs for grasping are frequent in predatory insects. Often pincers are formed by the apposition of the tibia on the femur and this occurs in the forelegs of mantids (Fig. 17), in some bugs such as Phymatidae and Nepidae, and in some Empididae and Ephydridae among the Diptera. In some Empididae the middle legs are modified in this way, while in *Bittacus* (Mecoptera) the fifth tarsomere folds back on the fourth.

The legs may be adapted for grasping in other ways and for other purposes. In the male *Dytiscus*, for instance, the first three tarsomeres of the foreleg are enlarged to form a circular disc. On the inside this disc is set with stalked cuticular cups, most of which are very small, but two of which, on the metatarsus, are very much larger than the rest (Fig. 73A). A viscous secretion from a gland in the tarsus is discharged from these suckers so that they adhere to surfaces to which they are applied (Miall, 1922). The suckers are chiefly employed in holding the female during mating, but may also be used occasionally to grasp prey. Suckers are also possessed by the males of some other beetles belonging to the families Hydrophilidae, Carabidae, Cicindelidae, Meloidae and Silphidae.

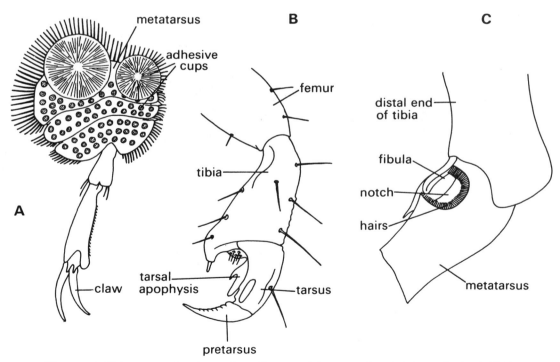

Fig. 73. A. Foretarsus of male *Dytiscus*. B. Leg of *Haematopinus* (Siphunculata). C. Toilet organ on the foreleg of *Apis* (after Miall, 1922; Séguy, 1951a; Snodgrass, 1956).

The ability to hold on is also important in ectoparasitic insects. These usually have well developed claws and frequently the legs are stout and short as in Hippoboscidae, Mallophaga and Siphunculata. In the latter two groups the tarsi are only one or two segmented and often there is only a single claw which folds back against a projection of the tibia (Fig. 73B).

In free-living insects the claws are used to grip on to normally rough surfaces, while if the surface is very smooth a purchase can be obtained by the adhesion of the hairs on the arolia or pulvilli. In Orthoptera there are adhesive pads on the undersides of the tarsomeres, and in *Rhodnius* (Heteroptera) and some other Reduviidae there are specialised adhesive pads on the distal ends of the tibiae of the front and middle legs. These pads are closely set with about 5000 adhesive spines, which do not arise from sockets in the usual manner. Glandular cells in the epidermis open into the spines and presumably discharge at the tips which are somewhat dilated and cut back (Fig. 74). The glands produce an oily secretion which forms a film on the surface and it is believed that the breakdown of this oil film causes the tips of the spines to adhere to the surface on which the insect is walking. The pads are used by the insect when it is walking up smooth surfaces on which the claws cannot obtain a grip (Gillett and Wigglesworth, 1932).

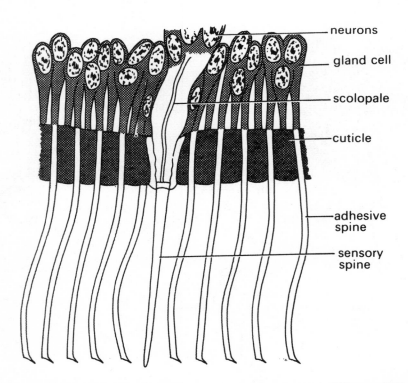

Fig. 74. Section through part of the adhesive organ of *Rhodnius* (after Gillett and Wigglesworth, 1932).

Grooming

In a number of insects the forelegs are modified as toilet organs. In *Apis* there is a basal notch in the metatarsus lined with spinelike hairs. A flattened spur called the fibula extends down from the tip of the tibia in such a way that when the metatarsus is flexed against the tibia the fibula closes off the notch so as to form a complete ring (Fig. 73C). This ring is used to clean the antenna. First it is closed round the base of the flagellum and then the antenna is drawn through it so that the hairs clean the outer surface and the fibula scrapes the inner surface (Snodgrass, 1956).

A similar, though less well developed organ, occurs in other Hymenoptera and some Coleoptera of the families Staphylinidae and Carabidae.

Lepidoptera have a mobile lobe called the strigil on the ventral surface of the fore tibia. It is often armed with a brush of hairs and is believed to be used to clean the antenna and possibly the proboscis.

The hind legs of Apoidea are modified to collect pollen from the hairs of the body and accumulate it in the pollen basket (see p. 35).

Reduction of legs

Some reduction of the legs occurs in various groups of insects. Many Papilionoidea, for instance, have the anterior tarsi reduced, and the Nymphalidae are functionally four-legged, the front legs being held permanently withdrawn against the thorax. In the male nymphalid the tarsus and pretarsus of the foreleg are completely lacking, while in the female the tarsus consists only of very short segments. In the male of *Hepialus*, on the other hand, the hind leg lacks a tarsus.

More usually reduction of the legs is associated with a sedentary or some other specialised habit, such as burrowing, in which legs would be an encumbrance. Thus female coccids are sedentary and are held in position by the stylets of the proboscis. The legs are reduced, sometimes to simple spines, and in some species are absent altogether. Similarly female Psychidae which never leave the bags constructed by their larvae show varying degrees of reduction of the legs, some species being completely apodous. Legs are also completely absent from female Strepsiptera which are parasitic in other insects.

Apart from the Diptera, all the larvae of which are apodous, legless larvae are usually associated with particular modes of life. There is a tendency for the larvae of leaf-mining Lepidoptera, Coleoptera and Tenthredinoidea to be apodous (see Hering, 1951). Parasitic larvae of Hymenoptera and Strepsiptera are apodous and in Meloidae the legs are greatly reduced. Finally in the social and semisocial Hymenoptera in which the larvae are provided with food by the parent apodous forms are also the rule.

CHAPTER IX

LOCOMOTION

Mobility at some stage of the life history is a characteristic of all animals. They must move in order to find a mate, for dispersal and, in many cases, in order to find food. The success of insects as terrestrial animals is in part due to their high degree of mobility arising from the power of flight (see Chapter XI), but more local movements by walking or swimming are also important. Most insects move over the surface of the ground by running or hopping, the power for these movements coming from the legs. The legs move in sequences which are varied at different speeds in such a way that stability is always maintained. Co-ordination of these movements involves central mechanisms, but segmental reflexes are also important.

The legs can only function in this way when the skeleton is rigid. In soft-bodied larval forms the muscles work against a hydrostatic skeleton maintained by the turgor pressure of the haemolymph. These forms crawl by extending the body anteriorly, obtaining a fresh purchase on the substratum and then drawing up the rest of the body. Some forms have abdominal appendages which assist in crawling.

Aquatic insects also use the legs in movement, the swimming legs being modified to expose a maximum area on the power stroke and a minimum on the return stroke. With other adaptations this ensures a maximal thrust on the backstroke so that the insect swims forwards. Larvae of aquatic Diptera which are legless move by lateral flexure of the whole body and larval Anisoptera use a method of jet propulsion.

Insect locomotion on land is reviewed by Hughes (1965a) and aquatic locomotion by Nachtigall (1964). Wilson (1966a) considers the patterns of insect walking and their possible control. See also Wendler (1966).

9.1 Walking

9.11 Movements of the leg

In describing the movements of the legs the following terms are used (Hughes, 1952).

Protraction—the complete movement forwards of the whole limb relative to its articulation with the body

Promotion—the movement of the coxa resulting in protraction

Retraction—the backward movement of the leg between the time it is placed on the ground and the time it is raised

Remotion—the corresponding movement of the coxa

Adduction—the movement of the coxa towards the body

Abduction—the movement of the coxa away from the body

Levation—the raising of the leg or a part of the leg, part of protraction

Depression—lowering the leg, or a part of the leg. The terms levation and depression are to some extent interchangeable with:

Extension—an increase in the angle between two segments of the leg

Flexion—a decrease in the angle between two segments of the leg

The muscles which produce these movements fall into two categories, extrinsic, arising outside the leg, and intrinsic, wholly within the leg and running from one segment to the next. The coxa is moved by extrinsic muscles arising in the thorax and a fairly typical arrangement is shown in Fig. 75 with promotor and remotor muscles arising on

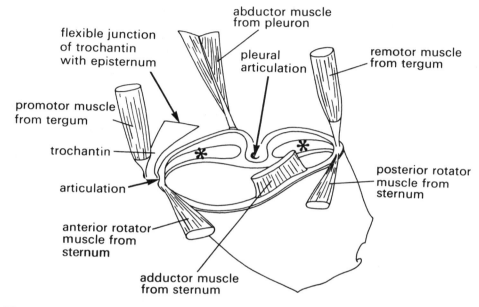

Fig. 75. Inner view of coxa showing the extrinsic leg muscles which move it. Muscles arising from the points marked with asterisks and inserted at the wing base are omitted (from Snodgrass, 1935).

the tergum, abductor and adductor muscles from the pleuron and sternum and rotator muscles also from the sternum. The functions of the muscles may vary, depending on the activities of other muscles and also on the type of articulation. In *Apis* (Hymenoptera), which has rigid pleural and sternal articulations, promotor and remotor muscles from the tergum are absent.

In the pterothoracic segments, muscles (marked with an asterisk in Fig. 75) run from the coxae to the basalar and subalar sclerites. They are concerned with wing movements.

The intrinsic musculature of the leg is much simpler than the coxal musculature, typically consisting only of pairs of antagonistic muscles in each segment (Fig. 67B). In *Periplaneta* (Dictyoptera) there are three levator muscles of the trochanter arising in the coxa and three depressor muscles, two again with origins in the coxa and a third arising on the pleural ridge and the tergum.

The femur is usually immovably attached to the trochanter, but the tibia is moved by extensor and flexor muscles arising in the femur and inserted into tendons from the membrane at the base of the tibia. Levator and depressor muscles of the tarsus arise in the tibia and are inserted into the top of the metatarsus, but there are no muscles within the tarsus moving the tarsomeres.

It is characteristic of the insects that the pretarsus has a depressor muscle, but no levator muscle. The fibres of the depressor occur in small groups in the femur and tibia, being inserted into a long tendon which arises on the unguitractor (Figs. 67B, 71B and C). Levation of the pretarsus results from the elasticity of its basal parts.

9.12 Mechanism of walking

The forces which act on the body to produce locomotion arise in various ways from the activities of the legs.

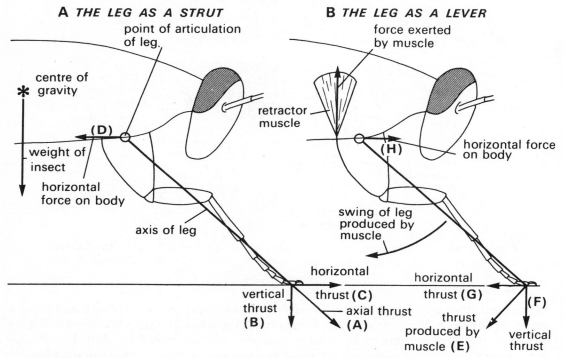

Fig. 76. A. Diagrammatic representation of a leg acting as a strut. The axial thrust (A) is exerted down the length of the leg by virtue of the weight of the insect. The size of the axial thrust depends, among other things, on how much of the weight is borne by the other legs. It can be resolved into vertical and horizontal components (B and C), but because the foot is held by friction with the substratum it does not move. Instead, an equal and opposite horizontal force (D) acts on the body and, in this case, tends to push it back unless balanced by other forces. B. Diagrammatic representation of a leg acting as a lever. Contraction of the retractor muscle tends to swing the leg back so that the foot exerts a thrust (E) on the ground. This can be resolved into vertical and horizontal components (F and G), but since the foot is held still by friction an equal and opposite horizontal force (H) acts on the body pushing it forwards. For a fuller consideration of the mechanics involved see Gray (1944).

A leg may act simply as a strut with the forces acting down it depending on its angle of inclination to the body and the weight of the insect (Fig. 76A). Equal and opposite forces will be exerted by the leg on the body. The force acting down the leg can be resolved into two components, horizontal and vertical, and because the leg is splayed out lateral to the body the horizontal force can be resolved into longitudinal and transverse components (Fig. 77). The relative sizes of the longitudinal and transverse components will vary according to the position of the leg (Fig. 77). In this diagram it is assumed that

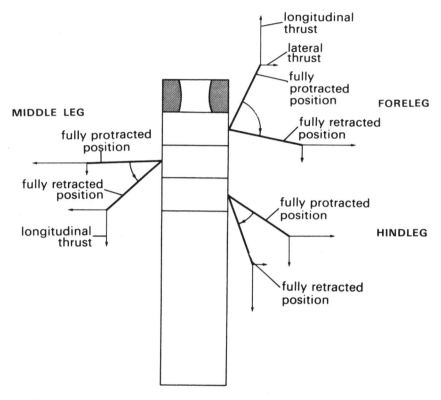

Fig. 77. Diagram to show the positions of the legs forming a typical triangle of support when fully protracted and fully retracted, together with the longitudinal and lateral components of the horizontal strut effect which the legs exert on the ground at these times. The forces acting on the body will be in the opposite directions (after Hughes, 1952).

only three legs are on the ground (see p. 148) and it is clear that for most of its movement the strut effect of the foreleg tends to retard forward movement, while that of the middle and hind legs promotes forward movement. So long as all the longitudinal and lateral forces balance each other there will be no movement, but if the forces are not balanced the body will be displaced due to a fall in the centre of gravity.

A leg can also act as a lever, that is a bar on which external work is done so that it rotates about a fulcrum. This effect is produced by the extrinsic muscles which move the leg relative to the body and so lever the insect along (Fig. 76B).

The leg, however, is not a simple, rigid strut or bar. It also has intrinsic muscles which can exert forces on the body by flexing or extending the leg. If a leg is extended anteriorly flexion of the joints will pull the body forwards (Fig. 78B), while in a leg directed backwards straightening the joints will push the body forwards (Fig. 78A).

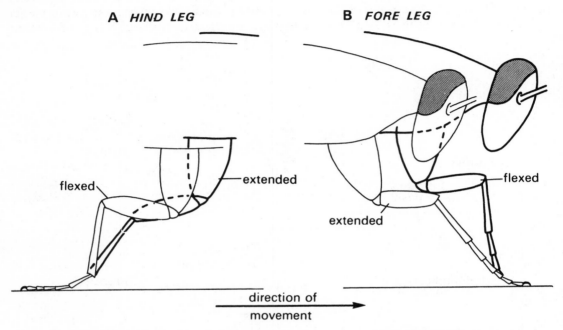

Fig. 78. Diagrams to show the effects of extension and flexion of the coxo-trochanteral and femoro-tibial joints on the movement of the body, while the feet remain still. A. Extension of the hind leg pushes the body forwards. B. Flexion of the foreleg pulls the body forwards.

When *Periplaneta* starts to move the foreleg is fully protracted due to maximum promotion of the coxa and extension of all the leg segments. At this stage it exerts a strut action retarding forward movement. Retraction begins by remotion of the coxa which produces a lever effect drawing the animal forwards, an effect which is added to by flexion of the trochanter on the coxa and the tibia on the femur. This phase continues until the leg is at right angles to the long axis of the insect. When it has passed this position it exerts a strut effect which, aided by extension of the leg, tends to push the insect forwards.

During protraction the leg is lifted and flexed so that it exerts no forces on the body. The promotor muscle of the coxa probably starts to contract before retraction is complete so that the change over from retraction to protraction is smooth. As the leg swings forwards it extends again so that in each cycle of movement the intrinsic muscles undergo two phases of contraction and relaxation, while the extrinsic muscles only contract and relax once.

The tarsi of the middle and hind legs are always placed on the ground behind their coxae so that their longitudinal strut effect always assists forward movement (Fig. 77).

The main propulsive forces of both pairs of legs are derived from extension of the trochanter on the coxa and of the tibia on the femur pushing the insect forwards.

The longitudinal forces produced by these movements are mostly such that the insect moves forwards. At the same time lateral forces are produced and when, for instance, the right foreleg is on the ground it tends to push the head to the left. This is partly balanced by the other legs, but there is some tendency for the head to swing from side to side during movement (see Hughes, 1952).

Only *Periplaneta* has been fully studied in this way, but it is probable that the leg movements and forces involved in walking are broadly similar in other insects.

9.13 Patterns of leg movement

When an insect is walking its legs move in a definite sequence following two general principles. First, no leg is raised until the leg behind it is in a supporting position and, second, the movements of the two legs of a segment alternate.

The pattern of leg movements and the number of legs on the ground at any one time depend on the relative times of protraction, when they are in the air, and retraction, when they are on the ground. Changes in the pattern occur automatically following changes in the relative periods of protraction and retraction (but see Wilson (1966a) for a slightly different interpretation of the manner in which these changes may be brought about). At low speeds the retraction time is long relative to protraction so that $\frac{\text{protraction}}{\text{retraction}}$ is low. Thus $\frac{\text{protraction}}{\text{retraction}} = 0.31$ for *Blatta* (Dictyoptera) moving at 3.2 cm./sec. and at lower speeds the value is still lower. Under these circumstances most of the legs are on the ground for most of the time and the legs are protracted singly in the sequence R3 R2 R1 L3 L2 L1 R3 etc. (where R and L indicate right and left, and 1, 2 and 3 the fore, middle and hind legs) (Figs. 79A, 80A). As the speed increases retraction

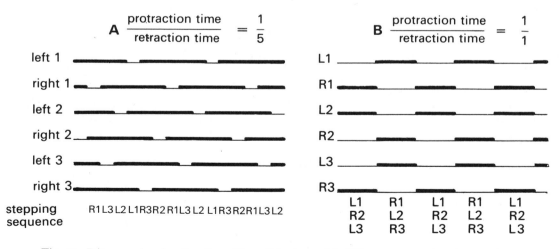

Fig. 79. Diagram showing the disposition of the legs with different protraction time: retraction time ratios. Thick lines indicate retraction with the foot on the ground, thin lines protraction with the foot in the air (modified after Hughes, 1952).

time becomes relatively shorter and $\dfrac{\text{protraction}}{\text{retraction}}$ approaches unity. With $\dfrac{\text{protraction}}{\text{retraction}}$

1.0 only three legs remain on the ground at any one time. The three are the fore and hind legs of one side and the middle leg of the opposite side. Between them they form a triangle of support. As they are protracted the other three are retracted and *vice versa* in

the sequence $\begin{matrix} \text{R1} & \text{L1} & \text{R1} \\ \text{L2} & \text{R2} & \text{L2} \\ \text{R3} & \text{L3} & \text{R3} \end{matrix}$ etc. (Fig. 79B), the insect thus being supported on alternate

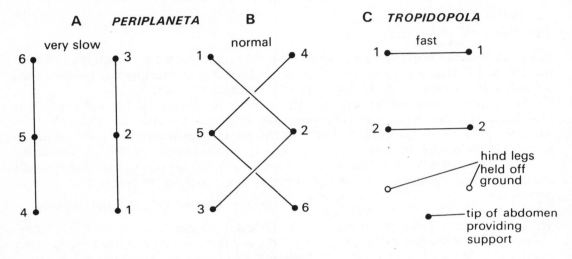

Fig. 80. Diagrams showing the order in which the feet are lifted (A) in *Periplaneta* at very low speeds, (B) in *Periplaneta* and most other insects at normal speeds, and (C) in *Tropidopola* at high speeds. Numbers indicate the sequence of stepping; points joined by straight lines indicate legs stepping together or in rapid succession (from Hughes, 1965a).

triangles of legs. This occurs in *Carausius*, but in *Periplaneta* the legs of one triangle are not all protracted simultaneously, but follow each other in rapid succession (Fig. 80B). This pattern of movement based on alternating triangles of support is commonly observed. The insect never has less than three legs on the ground and can stop at any point without losing its stability since the three legs enclose the vertical axis through the centre of gravity. Stability is enhanced by the fact that the body is slung between the legs so that the centre of gravity is low (Fig. 81).

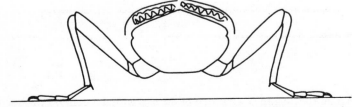

Fig. 81. Transverse section through the mesothorax of *Forficula* (Dermaptera) to show the body suspended between the legs (after Manton, 1953).

Other patterns of movement also occur. Thus *Petrobius* (Thysanura) moves the two legs of a segment together and this is also true of the climbing grasshopper *Tropidopola*. This insect is effectively quadrupedal, using only the anterior two pairs of legs, while the tip of the abdomen provides an additional point of support (Fig. 80C). At fast speeds the legs are moved in the sequences $\frac{L_1 \; L_2 \; L_1}{R_1 \; R_2 \; R_1}$ etc. At slow speeds mantids are also functionally quadrupedal using only the posterior two pairs of legs, but the sequence of stepping is L3 L2 R3 R2 L3 etc., or $\frac{L_3 \; L_2 \; L_3}{R_2 \; R_3 \; R_2}$ etc.

The speed of movement varies very greatly from one insect to another, but in general is higher at higher temperatures. At 25°C. *Periplaneta* moves at about 70 cm./sec. with top speeds up to 130 cm./sec. (see Hughes, 1965a). Speed also depends to some extent on size because insects with longer legs can take longer paces so that for the same frequency of pacing they will move further than smaller insects. Thus first instar larvae of *Blattella* (Dictyoptera) can move at about 3 cm./sec., while adults are capable of speeds up to 20 cm./sec.

9.14 Co-ordination of leg movements

The movements of the legs are controlled by the central nervous system and by feedback from the proprioceptors in the legs. The ganglia of the head, influenced by the

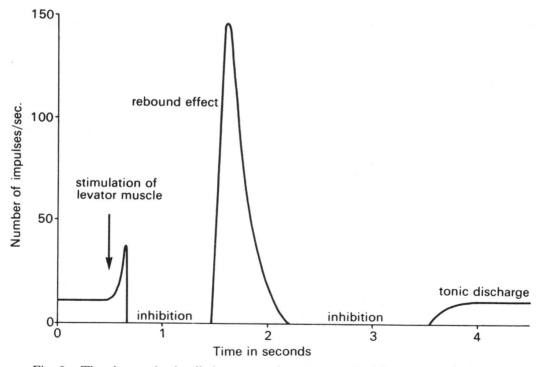

Fig. 82. The changes in the discharge to a depressor muscle following stimulation of a levator muscle. After an initial rise the discharge is briefly inhibited and then rebounds at a high frequency which might cause contraction of the muscle (after Pringle, 1940).

peripheral sense organs, exert an overall control, both inhibitory and stimulatory (see p. 536), but movements of an individual leg may depend largely on a system of reflexes. Stimulation of the campaniform sensilla of the legs causes a reflex contraction of the depressor muscles; touch on the upper side of the leg produces reflex levation. The excitation of one set of muscles inhibits the nervous discharge to the antagonistic muscles (see p. 218), but, if the excitation is strong, its removal is followed up by a sharp peak, known as a rebound effect, in the discharge to the antagonistic muscles which may lead to their contraction (Fig. 82). Thus the stimulation of one muscle could lead to the contraction of its antagonistic muscles and if the input is sufficiently strong the alternation could be maintained (Pringle, 1940). It has been shown that the rate of reaction of the sensilla and the speed of conduction through the reflex is adequate to account for the fastest movements of the legs seen in running. Thus the reflexes almost certainly do have a role in the control of leg movements, although they may be overridden by stronger nervous outputs from other sources (Wilson, 1965a).

Some reflex inhibition in the muscles in the contralateral leg also occurs so that, for instance, stimulation of the depressor muscles of one side inhibits the discharge to the depressor muscles on the other side of the segment. As a result of this the two legs of a segment are out of phase.

Clearly there must also be co-ordination between the segments to maintain stepping and control timing. This might involve intersegmental reflexes, but there is little evidence for their existence. Some measure of intersegmental co-ordination could arise from the perception by the sensilla of each leg of changing drag and gravitational effects resulting from the activities of the other legs, but there are good arguments suggesting that such explanations are not adequate and it seems certain that autonomous central nervous processes are involved (see Wendler, 1966; Wilson, 1966a).

9.2 Jumping

Jumping normally involves some modification of the hind legs as in Orthoptera, Siphonaptera and Homoptera (see p. 153), but other mechanisms occur in Collembola, Elateridae and *Piophila* (Diptera). In most cases jumping is a form of escape reaction, but Orthoptera, in addition to this, may also use short hops as a normal means of progression.

9.21 Jumping with legs

Orthoptera and jumping beetles

In Orthoptera, the flea beetles, Halticinae, and *Orchestes,* a weevil, the hind femora are greatly enlarged, housing the powerful extensor (levator) tibiae muscles, which in Orthoptera consist of two large masses of muscle fibres arising obliquely from the wall of the femur and inserted into a long, flat apodeme (Fig. 83). The jump in this case results from the sudden straightening of the femoro-tibial joint, extending the tibia which is also elongate.

Fifth instar larvae of *Locusta* (Orthoptera) can make long jumps of up to 70 cm., reaching a height of 30 cm. The power for the jump is provided by the sudden extension of the hind tibiae which at rest are folded under the femora. Before a jump a locust raises the front part of the body and flexes the femoro-tibial joint. The hind femora are moved forwards and the tibiae of both sides suddenly extended, pushing against the ground and projecting the insect into the air (Fig. 84).

The power for this movement comes from the extensor tibiae muscles which occupy the femur. Since they consist of a series of short fibres inserted obliquely into the apodeme (Fig. 83) they have a large cross-sectional area and hence are very powerful. They can exert a peak tension of over 800 g. on the apodeme. The latter is inserted into the tibia above the articulation with the femur (Fig. 83A) so that, in imparting movement to the foot, there is a marked lever effect (Fig. 85). Because of the nature of the joint the

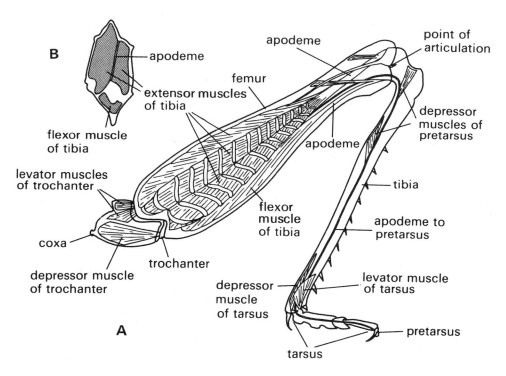

Fig. 83. Hind leg of a grasshopper showing (A) the musculature and (B) a transverse section of the femur (from Snodgrass, 1935).

lever ratio is 1:60 in the fully flexed or fully extended positions, falling to 1:35 with the tibia half extended. Thus each foot exerts a thrust of approximately 20 g. against the ground, ample to lift the insect, weighing about 1·5 g., into the air.

The measured take-off velocity in an adult locust weighing 3 g. is 340 cm./sec. This can be resolved into horizontal and vertical components which will determine the length and height of the jump (Fig. 84). The height increases with the angle of take-off, which is usually about 60°, and also with the distance through which the legs move. The heavier the insect, however, the less high will it jump (Hoyle, 1955).

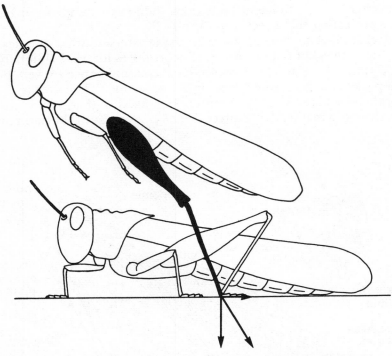

Fig. 84. Diagram of a locust jumping, showing the thrust exerted by the hind leg and its vertical and horizontal components.

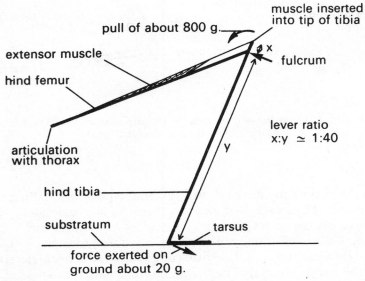

Fig. 85. Diagram to show the lever effect of the hind tibia of a locust with the tip of the femur acting as a fulcrum.

Homoptera

In the jumping Homoptera of the families Cercopidae, Jassidae, Membracidae and Psyllidae the jump is produced by a rotation of the leg on the coxo-trochanteral joint. Powerful muscles from the furca, pleuron and notum are inserted into a tendon from the edge of the trochanter and the coxa opens very widely to the thorax to permit the entry of these muscles. In psyllids the coxa is fused with the thorax and the position of the trochanteral articulations is altered so as to bring the femora parallel with the trunk.

Siphonaptera

The muscles producing the jumps of the flea are those of the femur which arise in the thorax. These muscles are so inserted relative to the point of articulation of the leg with the thorax that they draw it up against a pad of resilin (p. 434) without rotating it. The system is thus in unstable equilibrium and a slight sideways movement of the muscle, produced by a laterally inserted muscle, causes the femur to swing suddenly downwards as the tension in the system is released. This has the effect of throwing the insect into the air (Bennet-Clark and Lucey, 1967).

9.22 Mechanisms of jumping not involving legs

Collembola

Collembola jump using modified abdominal appendages. Arising from the posterior end of the fourth abdominal segment is a structure called the furca which consists of a

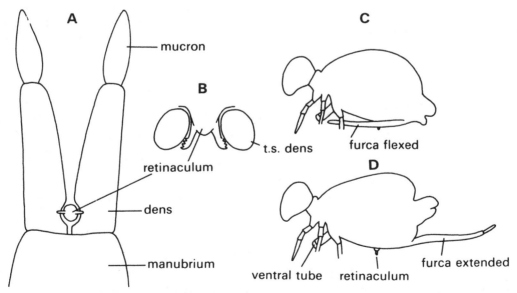

Fig. 86. Jumping in Collembola. A. Furca and retinaculum seen from below. B. Diagram showing the retinaculum holding the dentes. C and D. Diagrams of a collembolan with the furca in the flexed and extended positions. Jumping is produced by the swing from the flexed to the extended position (partly after Denis, 1949).

basal manubrium bearing a pair of rami, each divided into a proximal dens and a distal mucron (Fig. 86). The furca can be turned forwards and held flexed beneath the abdomen by a retinaculum on the posterior border of segment three (Fig. 86C). The jump is produced by the sudden release of the furca following the development of tension at its base so that it swings backwards very quickly and throws the insect into the air.

It is probable that the mechanism of furcal extension is not the same in all Collembola. Entomobryidae have powerful extensor muscles arising on the fourth abdominal tergite and it is probable that these muscles develop the tension extending the furca. In Tomoceridae and Isotomidae on the other hand these muscles are not well developed and the tension is produced by the elasticity of the cuticle following its distortion by the flexion of the furca. In *Allacma,* for instance, the furca is pulled round by flexor muscles distorting the cuticle at the base of the manubrium so that it is under tension. Once the furca is held by the retinaculum all the muscles relax so that when the furca is released it springs back as the distorted cuticle assumes its normal shape again (Denis, 1949).

Other insects

Jumping as a result of the sudden release of tension previously developed also occurs in Elateridae and the larvae of various Diptera. Elaterids jump if they are turned on their backs and the jump serves as a means by which they can right themselves. The insect first arches its back between the prothorax and the mesothorax so that it is supported anteriorly by the prothorax and posteriorly by the elytra with the middle of the body off the ground. Then it contracts the ventral muscles which would tend to straighten the body, but a stout process on the prosternum catches on the edge of a cavity in the mesosternum so that the muscle contraction is isometric. The muscles consequently develop a considerable tension until suddenly the prosternal process slips into the cavity. As a result the prothorax straightens with respect to the mesothorax and the insect is jerked into the air. It has no control over its orientation in the air, but sometimes lands on its feet.

The larva of *Piophila* (Diptera) lives in cheese and in the last instar it is able to jump. It does this by bending the head back beneath its abdomen so that the mandibles engage in a transverse fold near the posterior spiracles. The longitudinal muscles on the outside of the loop so formed contract and build up a tension until suddenly the mandibles are released and the larva jerks straight and strikes the ground so that it is thrown into the air, sometimes as high as 20 cm. A similar phenomenon occurs in the larvae of some Clusiidae and Trypetidae, while in cecidomyid larvae anal hooks catch in a forked prosternal projection producing a leap in the same way as *Piophila* by building up muscular tension and then suddenly releasing it.

9.3 Crawling

The larvae of many holometabolous insects move by changes in the shape of the body rather than by movements of the legs as in walking or running by adult insects. This type of locomotion can be differentiated as crawling. In the majority of crawling forms the cuticle is soft and flexible and does not, by itself, provide a suitable skeleton on which the muscles can act. Instead, the pressure of the haemolymph within the body provides a hydrostatic skeleton. Special muscles lining the body wall of caterpillars keep the body turgid and, because of the incompressibility of the body fluids, a change in the shape of one part of the body due to muscular contraction must be compensated by an opposite change in some other part. The place and form of these compensating changes will be controlled by the degree of tension of the muscles throughout the body.

Caterpillars typically have, in addition to the thoracic legs, a pair of prolegs on each of abdominal segments three to six and another pair on segment ten (Fig. 262). The prolegs are hollow cylindrical outgrowths of the body wall, their lumen being continuous with the haemocoel (Fig. 87). An apical area, less rigid than the sides, is known as the planta and it bears a row or circle of outwardly curved hooks, or crochets, with which the leg obtains a grip. Retractor muscles from the body wall are inserted into the centre of the planta so that when they contract it is drawn inwards and the crochets are disengaged. The leg is evaginated by turgor pressure when the muscles relax. On a smooth surface the prolegs can function as suckers. The crochets are turned up and the planta surface is first pressed down on to the substratum and then the centre is slightly drawn up so as to create a vacuum (Hinton, 1955).

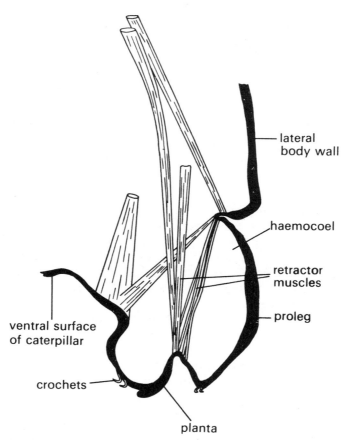

Fig. 87. Transverse section through part of an abdominal segment of a caterpillar showing the proleg (after Hinton, 1955).

Caterpillars move by serial contractions of the longitudinal muscles coupled with leg movements. The contractions start posteriorly and the anal claspers are lifted and moved forwards, followed by similar movements of the more anterior legs, the two legs of a segment moving together. Each segment is lifted by contraction of the dorsal longitudinal muscles of the segment in front, while at the same time the prolegs are retracted (Fig. 88). Subsequently contraction of the ventral longitudinal muscles brings the

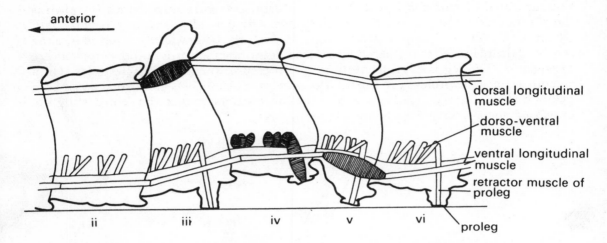

Fig. 88. Diagrammatic section through a caterpillar showing a wave of contraction which passes along the body from behind forwards and produces forward movement. Contracted muscles are shown hatched (modified from Hughes, 1965a).

segment down again and completes the forward movement as the legs are extended and obtain a fresh grip. As the wave of contraction passes forwards along the body at least three segments are in different stages of contraction at any one time. This calls for a high degree of co-ordination and it appears that control is largely a central nervous process, the muscles being stimulated by impulses passing down the nerve cord. It is probable, however, that this central control is modified by local reflexes involving the stretch receptors (see p. 617) (Weevers, 1965).

Many geometrid larvae have prolegs only on abdominal segments six and ten. These insects loop along, drawing the hind end of the body up to the thorax and then extending the head and thorax to obtain a fresh grip.

In the apodous larvae of Diptera a different method is used, although movement again depends on changes in the shape of the body as a result of muscles acting against the body fluids. The posterior segments of the body are often provided with prolegs (see Fig. 175) or with creeping welts (Fig. 263F). These are raised pads usually running right across the ventral surface of a segment and armed with stiff, curved setae which may be distributed evenly or in rows or patches. Each welt is provided with retractor muscles (Hinton, 1955). In the larva of *Musca* there are locomotory welts on the anterior edges of segments six to twelve and also on the posterior edge of segment twelve and behind the anus.

In movement the anterior part of the body is lengthened and narrowed by the contraction of oblique muscles, while the posterior part maintains a grip with the prolegs or welts. Hence the front of the body is pushed forwards over, or through, the substratum. It is then anchored and the posterior part drawn forwards by a wave of longitudinal shortening which passes down the body from front to back. The anterior region is anchored in the soil-dwelling larvae of Tipulidae, Bibionidae and Hepialidae (Lepidoptera), and probably in other burrowing forms, by the broadening of the body which accompanies shortening (Fig. 89), while in the larva of *Musca* crawling on a plane surface, anchorage is provided by the mandibles which are thrust against the substratum until they are held by an irregularity of the surface (Hewitt, 1914).

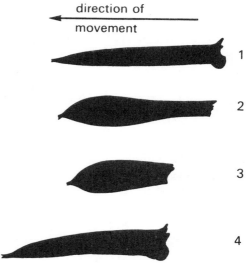

Fig. 89. Diagram of the movement of *Tipula* (Diptera) larva during locomotion through the soil (after Ghilarov, 1949).

9.4 Movements on the surface of water

Some insects are able to move on or in the film at the surface of water. Collembola, such as *Podura aquatica,* sometimes occur on the surface film in large numbers. These insects have hydrofuge cuticles which prevent them from getting wet, but the ventral tube on the first abdominal segment is wettable and anchors the insect to the surface, while the claws, which are also wettable, enable it to obtain a purchase on the water. These insects can spring from the water surface using the caudal furca in the same way as terrestrial Collembola (p. 153).

Gerris (Heteroptera) stands on the surface film and rows over the water surface with its middle and hind legs which have powerful retractor muscles inserted into the trochanters. The muscles of the middle legs are the most powerful and these legs supply most of the thrust. It is presumed that the backward movement of the legs causes the surface film to become packed up behind them, building up a pressure which imparts a forward thrust to the insect. During protraction the tibiae and tarsi are trailed backwards so that they offer a minimum of resistance to forward movement and then the middle legs are lifted off the surface and swing forwards, while the insect is supported by the fore and hind legs. Steering may be achieved by the unequal contractions of the retractor muscles of the two sides and fast turning is produced by movement of the legs of one side while the legs on the other side, towards which the insect is turning, remain still (Brinkhurst, 1959b).

Stenus (Coleoptera) species live on grass stems bordering mountain streams in situations such that they fall into the water quite frequently. The beetle can walk on the surface of the water, but only slowly. More rapid locomotion is produced by the secretion of a substance from the pygidial glands opening beneath the last abdominal tergite. This substance lowers the surface tension of the water behind the insect so that it is drawn forwards by the higher surface tension in front, and by moving its abdomen from side to side the insect can direct its movements (Billard and Bruyant, 1905).

9.5 Movement under water

The activity of aquatic insects is affected by their respiratory habits (see Chapter XXIV). Permanently submerged forms which respire by gills or a plastron have a density greater than that of the water and can move freely over the bottom of their habitat. In swimming these must produce a lift force to take them off the bottom. Many other insects come to the surface to renew their air supply and submerge with a store of air which tends to give them buoyancy. In swimming the buoyancy must be balanced or overcome by the forces of propulsion. A few insects, such as larval *Chaoborus* (Diptera) and *Anisops* (Heteroptera), can control their buoyancy so that they can remain suspended in mid water (p. 488).

9.51 Bottom dwellers

Bottom-dwelling aquatic insects, such as *Aphelocheirus* (Heteroptera) and larval Odonata and Trichoptera, can walk over the substratum in the same way as terrestrial insects. The larva of *Limnephilus* (Trichoptera) basically uses an alternation of triangles of support (see p. 148), but because of the irregularity of the surface the stepping pattern tends to become irregular. The forelegs may step together instead of alternating and the hind legs may follow the same pattern. Normally the power for walking comes primarily from traction by the fore and middle legs and pushing by the hind legs, but under difficult conditions the hind legs may be extended far forwards outside the middle legs so that they help the other legs to pull the larva along (Tindall, 1963).

In the bottom-dwelling *Triaenodes* (Trichoptera) the larval case is built of plant material arranged in a spiral, the last whorl of which extends dorsally beyond the rest of the case (Fig. 90). The dorsal position is essential since otherwise the movements of the hind swimming legs are hindered, and in this position it also provides a certain amount of lift, carrying the case off the bottom. This lift is controlled by the movements of the legs which tend to produce a downward thrust (Tindall, 1964).

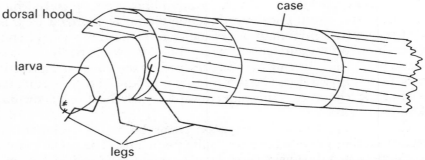

Fig. 90. Diagram of *Triaenodes* larva in its case (after Tindall, 1964).

Larval Anisoptera can walk across the substratum using their legs, but they are also able to make sudden escape movements by forcing water rapidly out of the branchial basket (p. 479) so that the body is driven forwards. The branchial basket is compressed by longitudinal and dorso-ventral contractions of the abdomen, the contractions being strongest in segments six to eight in which the branchial basket lies. Before this contraction the anal valves close and then open slightly leaving an aperture about 0·01 sq. mm. in area. The contractile movement lasts about 0·1 sec. and water is forced through the anus at a velocity of about 250 cm./sec. propelling the larva forwards at 30–50 cm./ sec. As the abdomen contracts the legs are retracted so as to lie along the sides of the body, offering a minimum of resistance to the forward movements (Hughes, 1958). Co-ordination involves giant fibres running in the ventral nerve cord (p. 523).

9.52 Free-swimming insects

Larval and pupal Diptera, larval and adult Heteroptera and adult Coleoptera form the bulk of free-swimming insects and, apart from the Diptera, most of these use the hind legs, sometimes together with the middle legs, in swimming. The hind tibiae and tarsi, and sometimes also those of the middle legs, are flattened antero-posteriorly to form a paddle which is often increased in area by inflexible hairs or, as in *Gyrinus* (Coleoptera), by cuticular blades 1 μ thick and 30–40 μ wide (Fig. 91). In *Acilius* (Coleoptera) the hairs constitute 69% of the total area of the hind tibiae and 83% of the tarsi. The hind legs of these insects are relatively shorter than the hind legs of related terrestrial insects, but the tarsi are relatively longer.

The point of attachment of the hind legs is displaced posteriorly compared with terrestrial insects and in dytiscids and gyrinids the coxae are immovably fused to the thorax. This limits the amount of movement at the base of the leg and the basal muscles are concentrated into two functional groups, a powerful retractor group and a weaker protractor group. Intrinsic muscles of the legs tend to be reduced and the movements of the distal parts of the legs during swimming are largely passive.

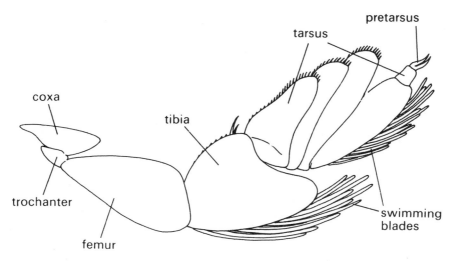

Fig. 91. Hind leg of *Gyrinus* (after Miall, 1922).

The two legs of a segment move together, contrasting with the alternating movement of the legs in terrestrial insects (p. 147), but *Hydrophilus* (Coleoptera) is an exception. This beetle uses the middle and hind legs in swimming, the middle leg of one side being retracted simultaneously with the hind leg of the opposite side, but out of phase with the contralateral middle leg.

Buoyancy

Many free-swimming insects are buoyant and when they stop swimming come to rest at the surface of the water in a characteristic position which results from the distribution of air stores on and in the body. Most forms float head down and *Notonecta* (Heteroptera), for instance, rests at an angle of 30° to the surface. As it kicks with its swimming legs this angle is increased to 55° so that the insect is driven down, but as it loses momentum during the recovery stroke of the legs it will tend to rise again (Fig. 92A). If the driving movements of the legs are repeated rapidly, before the insect rises very much, the path

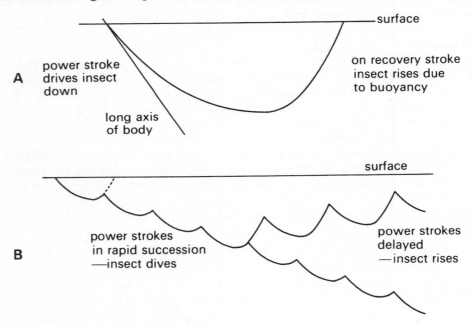

Fig. 92. Diagram of the path through water of an insect such as *Notonecta*. A. The path due to a single swimming stroke by the legs. B. Different paths produced by differences in the timing of successive strokes (after Popham, 1952).

may be straightened out and by controlling the rate of leg movement the insect can dive, move at a constant level or rise to the surface (Fig. 92B). The beat tends to be faster at higher temperatures so that movement becomes more uniform as the temperature rises (Popham, 1952). In *Dytiscus* the buoyancy effect is offset at faster speeds by using the middle and hind legs alternately, while *Hydrophilus* achieves the same effect by using the legs of the two sides out of phase. Hence these insects produce a continuous driving force which offsets their buoyancy.

Thrust

The thrust which pushes the insect down through the water is developed during retraction of the legs, but, because the insect is surrounded by the medium, protraction of the legs also produces forces. These tend to drive the insect backwards and if it is to move forwards the forward thrust produced on the backstroke must exceed the backward thrust produced on the forward, recovery stroke of the legs.

The thrust which a leg exerts in water is proportional to its area and the square of the velocity with which it moves. Hence to produce the most efficient forward movement a leg should present a large surface area and move rapidly on the backstroke, while presenting only a small surface and moving relatively slowly on the recovery stroke.

To achieve a large surface area during the backstroke the swimming legs of *Dytiscus* are straight with the fringing hairs, which are articulated at the base, spread to expose a maximum area (Fig. 93A and B). On the forward stroke, however, the femorotibial joint flexes so that the tibia and tarsus trail out behind (Fig. 93D–F). At the same

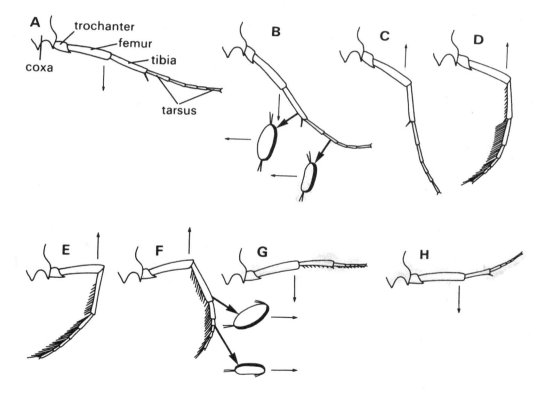

Fig. 93. Diagram showing successive positions of the right hind leg of *Dytiscus* during swimming. G, H, A and B show stages of retraction, C–F stages of protraction. Insets are cross-sections of the tibia and tarsus showing their orientation during retraction (B) and protraction (F). Small arrows indicate the direction of movement of the femur relative to the body of the insect (after Hughes, 1958).

time the tibia rotates through 45° so that the previously dorsal surface becomes anterior and the fringing hairs fold back. The tarsus, which articulates with the tibia by a ball and socket joint, rotates through 100° in the opposite direction. These movements are passive, resulting from the form of the legs and the forces exerted by the water, and they ensure that the tibia and tarsus are presented edge on to the movement, producing a minimum of thrust. Subsequently, at the beginning of the backstroke the leg and hairs extend passively to expose a maximum surface area again. There is no extensor tarsi muscle and the extensor tibiae is weak. The power for the stroke comes from the muscles moving the trochanter on the fixed coxa (Hughes, 1958).

Similar devices are employed by other insects for exposing a maximum leg area during the power stroke and a minimum during the recovery stroke. The swimming blades fringing the leg of *Gyrinus* (see Fig. 91) are placed asymmetrically so that they open like a venetian blind, turning to overlap and produce a solid surface during the power stroke. In the recovery stroke the tarsomeres collapse like a fan and are concealed in a hollow of the tibia which in turn is partly concealed in a hollow of the femur. These changes decrease the area of the middle leg by 35% and of the hind leg by 28%.

The relative power developed on the forward and backward strokes also depends on the relative speeds of the strokes. In *Acilius* (Coleoptera) the backstroke is faster than the forward stroke so that for a given leg area the forward thrust on the body exceeds the backward thrust. In *Gyrinus*, on the other hand, the backstroke is slower than the forward

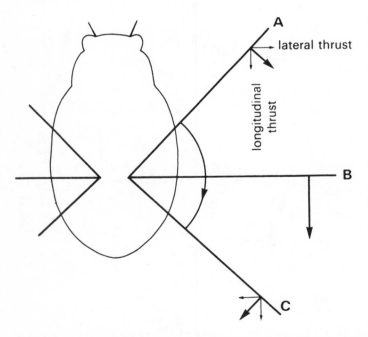

Fig. 94. Diagram of a water beetle showing the thrust exerted by the hind leg at different points of the power stroke. It is assumed that the velocity of the leg at A and C is only half its velocity at B, where, since the leg is at right angles to the body, only longitudinal thrust is produced. Equal and opposite forces act on the body (modified after Nachtigall, 1965).

stroke so that for a given area the backward thrust is greater than the forward thrust. Hence if the area of the legs of *Gyrinus* remained constant the insect would tend to move backwards and it is only because the reduction in area of the leg on the forward stroke reduces the backward thrust on the body that the net effect is to push the insect forwards.

The legs move in an arc so that lateral thrust is produced in addition to the longitudinal thrust (Fig. 94). In most insects, where the legs of the two sides move in phase, the lateral forces developed on the two sides balance each other out, but in *Hydrophilus*, where the legs are used alternately, there is some deviation to either side, although the lateral thrust of the hind leg on one side is largely balanced by the opposite lateral thrust of the contralateral middle leg.

Forward thrust is minimal at the beginning and end of each stroke (Fig. 94, leg at A and C), but when the legs are at right angles to the body the whole of the thrust developed is longitudinal (Fig. 94, leg at B). It is advantageous if the velocity of the leg is greatest at this point and is low at the beginning and end of the stroke so that the lateral forces, which are produced mainly during these phases, are kept to a minimum. This is the case, at least in *Acilius* and *Gyrinus*. In the latter the leg is moving most rapidly when it is at an angle of 90–135° to the body. After this the velocity rapidly falls to zero.

Streamlining

Most aquatic insects are streamlined and dorso-ventrally flattened so that they offer a minimum of resistance as they pass forwards through the water. *Acilius*, for instance, only creates about three times the resistance of an ideal streamlined body and deviations of up to 10° on either side do not markedly increase the resistance. There is, however, a marked increase in resistance if the insect turns broadside or ventral side to the direction of movement and this facilitates turning and braking. Turns are made by producing strokes of unequal amplitude on the two sides or, in making a sharp turn, the leg on the inside may be extended and kept still while the contralateral leg paddles.

Stability

The dorso-ventral flattening of many aquatic insects provides stability in the rolling and pitching planes (see p. 200). The control of yawing involves the eyes, antennae and possibly also receptors on the legs, these receptors acting so that any unequal stimulation as a result of deviation from a straight course is corrected for. The head ganglia are involved in these responses. In *Triaenodes* the long case (Fig. 90) acts as a rudder giving some stability in the pitching and yawing planes. Rolling may be controlled by the long, outstretched hind legs.

Speed

The speed of movement depends on the frequency with which strokes are made and the lengths and velocities of the strokes. *Gyrinus* can swim on the surface at up to 100 cm./sec. in short bursts, the hind leg making 50–60 strokes/sec. Beneath the surface its speed rarely exceeds 10 cm./sec. *Acilius*, making 3–10 strokes/sec., can reach 35 cm./sec., while *Triaenodes*, with hind legs making 13 strokes/sec., only moves at about 1·7 cm./sec. because of the high drag effect of the larval case.

Other forms of swimming

Appendages other than the legs are sometimes used in swimming. Mosquito larvae when suspended from the surface film or browsing on the bottom can glide slowly along as a result of the rapid vibrations of the mouth brushes in feeding. In *Aedes communis* this is the normal method of progression. *Caraphractus cinctus* (Hymenoptera) parasitises the eggs of dytiscids which are laid under water. The parasite swims jerkily through the water by rowing with its wings, making about two strokes per second. Larval Ephemeroptera and Zygoptera move by vertical undulations of the caudal filaments (see Fig. 261) and the abdomen, while in the larva of *Ceratopogon* (Diptera) lateral undulations pass down the body from head to tail driving the insect through the water (Fig. 95A). Many other dipterous larvae flex and straighten the body alternately to either side, often increasing the thrust by a fin-like extension of the hind end. Mosquito larvae, for instance, have a fan of dense hairs on the last abdominal segment and as a result of the lateral flexing of the body move along tail first (Fig. 95B). The density of mosquito larvae is very close to that of water and affects their locomotion. Early instar larvae are usually less dense than the medium so they rise to the surface when they stop swimming. This is also true of the pupae, but last instar larvae may be slightly denser so that they sink when they stop moving actively. The larvae of *Chaoborus* and other Diptera make similar movements to those of mosquito larvae. The mechanics of undulating propulsion are considered by Gray (1953).

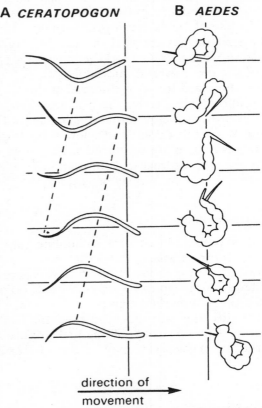

A CERATOPOGON   **B AEDES**

direction of movement

Fig. 95. Diagrams showing successive positions in swimming of the larvae of (A) *Ceratopogon* and (B) *Aedes*. Dashed lines indicate the movement of a lateral undulation along the body from front to back (from Nachtigall, 1965).

CHAPTER X
THE WINGS

The success of insects as terrestrial animals is at least partly due to their ability to fly. Typically, adult insects have two pairs of wings articulating with the thorax and consisting of flattened lobes of the integument supported by hollow veins. The wings are modified in various ways and often the fore wings are hardened and serve to protect the hind wings. In some insects the two pairs of wings are to some extent independent of each other in flight, but this appears to be relatively inefficient and most insects tend to become functionally two-winged either by the loss of one pair of wings or by coupling the wings on each side so that they function as one. At the bases of the wings small sclerites articulate with the thorax, permitting not only the movements of the wings in flight, but also enabling them to be folded back over the body when at rest. At the base of the wings are sense organs concerned with the control of wing movements and in the Diptera the hind wing has become wholly modified as a sense organ. The muscles moving the wing fall into two classes; those directly inserted into the base of the wing and others which move the wings indirectly by distorting the thorax.

The structure of the wings is considered by Comstock (1918) and Snodgrass (1935), wing coupling in Panorpoidea by Tillyard (1918), and various aspects, including the articulation of wings, by Pringle (1957).

10.1 Occurrence and structure of wings

Fully developed and functional wings occur only in adult insects, although the developing wings may be present in the larvae. In hemimetabolous larvae they are visible as external pads (p. 407), but they develop internally, and so invisibly, in holometabolous forms (p. 412).

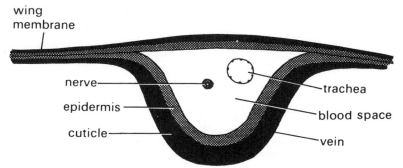

Fig. 96. Diagrammatic section through part of a wing including a transverse section of a vein.

The Ephemeroptera are exceptional in having two fully winged stages. The final larval instar moults to a subimago which resembles the adult except for having fringed and slightly translucent wings and rather shorter legs. It is able to make a short flight after which it moults and the adult stage emerges. In the course of this moult the cuticle of the wings is shed with the rest of the cuticle.

The fully developed wings of all insects appear as thin, rigid flaps arising dorso-laterally from between the pleura and nota of the meso- and meta-thoracic segments. Each wing consists of a thin membrane supported by a system of tubular veins. The membrane is formed by two layers of integument closely apposed, while the veins are formed where the two layers remain separate and the cuticle is more heavily sclerotised (Fig. 96). Within each of the major veins is a nerve and a trachea, and since the cavities of the veins are connected with the haemocoel blood can circulate round the wing (see Fig. 462).

On the anterior margin of the wing in some groups is a pigmented spot, the pterostigma (Fig. 101). This is present on both pairs of wings of Odonata and on the forewings of many Hymenoptera, Psocoptera, Megaloptera and Mecoptera. Along the posterior margin of the wing near its base is a hollow tube, the axillary cord, which arises from the posterior lateral angle of the notum (Fig. 101). This serves to strengthen the edge of the membrane and, in some insects at least, as a channel for the return of blood from the wings to the thorax.

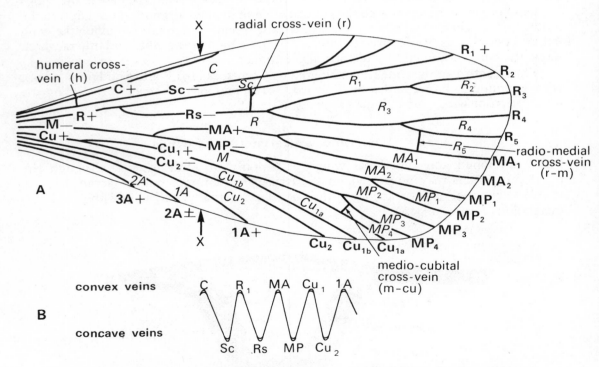

Fig. 97. A. Diagram of the hypothetical basic wing venation showing also the main cross-veins and the names of the cells (italicized). B. Section at X–X in (A) showing the concave and convex veins with the depth of pleating greatly exaggerated.

10.11 Venation

In many fossil insects the venation consists of an irregular network known as the arche-
dictyon. This may persist in present-day insects in the reticulum of veins occurring in
the wings of Odonata and at the base of the fore wings of Tettigonioidea and Acridoidea
(Fig. 100), but in most living insects the venation consists of a number of well-marked
longitudinal veins running along the length of the wing connected by a variable number
of cross-veins. It is possible to a large extent to homologise the longitudinal veins
occurring in different orders of insects and these can be derived from a basic hypothetical
arrangement (Fig. 97A). Homologies are based on studies of fossil forms, the presence
and arrangement of tracheae in the veins, the form and position of the veins and their
association with particular axillary sclerites (see p. 177). In addition, there is a tendency
for the wings of the lower orders of insects to fold in a fanlike manner (Fig. 97B). A vein
on the crest of a fold is called convex (indicated by + in fig. 97A), while a vein in a trough
is called concave (— in fig. 97A). Further, a row of trichoid sensilla (p. 597) may be
associated with each vein and they may persist in the absence of the vein. Hence whether
the vein is concave or convex and the presence of rows of trichoid sensilla may give further
assistance in homologising the veins of different insects (see Comstock, 1918 and e.g.
Ragge, 1955).

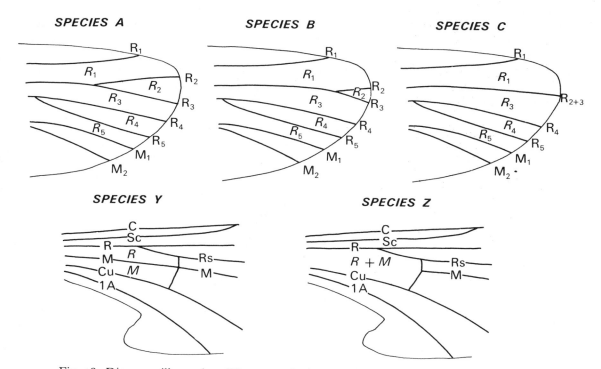

Fig. 98. Diagrams illustrating different methods by which veins are lost. In species A, B
and C the veins R_2 and R_3 show progressive degrees of coalescence so that ultimately, in C,
cell R_2 is lost. In species Y the base of vein M is present and cells R and M (italicized) are
separate, but in Z the stem of M has atrophied so that cells R and M combine to form one
large cell R+M.

The basic longitudinal veins from the leading edge of the wing backwards are:—

Costa (abbreviated to C) on or just behind the leading edge.

Subcosta (Sc), may be two-branched.

Radius (R), divides into two main branches R_1 and the radial sector (R's) which further divides into four branches, R_2, R_3, R_4, R_5.

Media (M) dividing into anterior media (MA) with two branches, MA_1, MA_2, and the posterior media (MP) with four branches, MP_1, MP_2, MP_3, MP_4.

Cubitus (Cu), dividing into two branches Cu_1 and Cu_2, and Cu_1 may further divide into Cu_{1a} and Cu_{1b}.

Anal veins (A), three separate veins labelled 1A, 2A and 3A.

Connecting the longitudinal veins across the wing are the cross-veins. These are variable in number and position, but the more usual cross-veins are indicated in fig. 97. It is not certain that these can be homologised in the different orders of insects.

Modifications occur in the basic venation. For instance, both major branches of the medial vein are present in many fossil insects and in present-day Ephemeroptera and Orthoptera (Ragge, 1955), but in the majority of living insects the anterior media is lost. Odonata are exceptional in having lost the posterior media. Reduction in venation may occur by the complete atrophy of a vein or by its coalescence with another vein; which of the two processes accounts for the loss of a vein in a particular insect can only be determined from the study of a series of related forms (Fig. 98). In some very small insects the venation may be very greatly reduced and in the Chalcidoidea, for instance, only the subcosta and part of the radius are present (Fig. 99). Conversely an increase in the venation may occur by the branching of existing veins to produce accessory veins or by the development of additional, intercalary veins between the existing ones as in the hind wing of Orthoptera (Fig. 100). Large numbers of cross-veins are also present in some forms as in the Neuroptera.

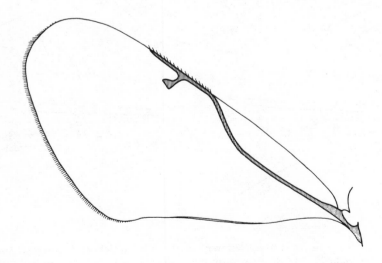

Fig. 99. Forewing of *Perilampus* (Hymenoptera) showing extreme reduction of venation (after Clausen, 1940).

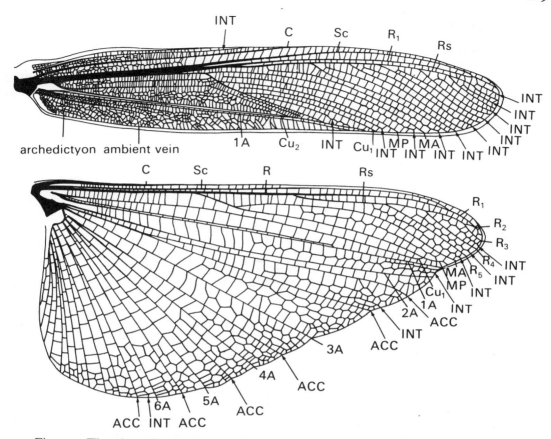

Fig. 100. The wings of *Locusta* showing the venation. Some of the secondary veins are indicated by arrows. INT = intercalary vein, ACC = accessory vein (after Ragge, 1955).

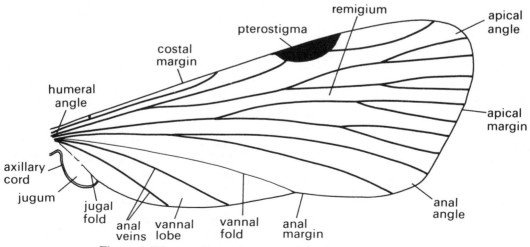

Fig. 101. Diagram illustrating some of the features of the wing.

10.12 Areas of the wing

In order to give maximum efficiency and support to the wing during flight the longitudinal veins tend to be concentrated towards the anterior margin of the wing. The
region containing the bulk of the veins is called the remigium (Fig. 101) and behind it
the area supported only by the anal veins is called the vannal or anal region. The remigium and the vannal region are separated by the vannal fold which may lie before or
behind the vein 1A.

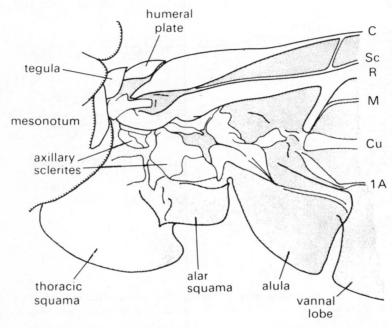

Fig. 102. Base of the right wing of a tabanid showing the arrangement of the various structures
(after Oldroyd, 1949).

Proximal to the vannus in some insects is another membranous lobe called the
jugum. In some Diptera there are three separate lobes in this region of the wing base
(Fig. 102) known from proximally outwards as the thoracic squama, alar squama and
alula. There is some confusion in the terminology and homologies of these lobes, but it
appears that the thoracic squama is derived from the posterior margin of the scutellum,
the alar squama represents the jugum and the alula is a part of the vannal region which
has become separated off from the rest. Some Coleoptera have a lobe called an alula
folded beneath the elytron. It appears to be equivalent to the jugum.

The wing margins and angles are also named (Fig. 101). The leading edge of the wing
is called the costal margin, the trailing edge is the anal margin and the outer edge is the
apical margin. The angle between the costal and apical margins is the apical angle, that
between the outer and anal margins is the anal angle, while the angle at the base of the
wing is called the humeral angle.

10.13 Cells of the wing

The veins divide the area of the wing into a series of cells which are most satisfactorily named after the vein forming the anterior boundary of the cell (Fig. 97A). If a vein atrophies the cell which remains includes two previous cells (*e.g.* R + M in fig. 98Z), but coalescence of veins results in the disappearance of the cell between them (Fig. 98C). A cell entirely surrounded by veins is said to be closed, while one which extends to the wing margins is open.

10.2 Modifications of the wings

10.21 The wing membrane

Typically the wing membrane is semitransparent as it is in Odonata and Hymenoptera. Such wings often exhibit iridescence as a result of their structure (see p. 111), but sometimes, in addition, the wings are patterned by pigments contained in the epidermal cells. This is true in some Mecoptera and Trypetidae, while in many insects which have the fore wing hardened, such as Orthoptera and Coleoptera, the fore wing is wholly pigmented.

10.22 Hairs and scales on the membrane

The surface of the wing membrane is often set with small non-innervated spines called microtrichia. Typically trichoid sensilla (p. 597) are confined to the veins, but in Trich-optera comparable hairs, known as macro-trichia clothe the whole of the wing membrane.

In Lepidoptera the wings are clothed in scales. These vary in form from typical hair-like structures to flat plates (Fig. 103A) and they usually cover the body as well as the wings. A flattened scale consists of two lamellae with an airspace between, the inferior lamella, that is the lamella facing the wing membrane, being smooth, the superior lamella usually with longitudinal and transverse ridges. The two lamellae are supported by internal struts called trabeculae (Fig. 103B). The scales are set in sockets of the wing membrane so that they are inclined to the surface and overlap each other to form a complete covering. In primitive Lepidoptera their arrangement on the wings is random, but in Papilionoidea, for instance, they are arranged in rows.

Pigments in the scales are responsible for the colours of many Lepidoptera, the pigment being in the wall or the cavity of the scale. In other instances physical colours

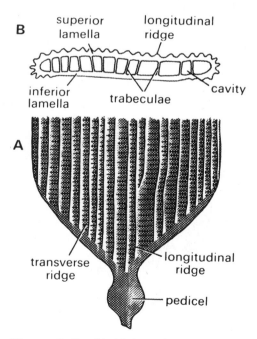

Fig. 103. A. Basal half of a typical lepidopteran scale. B. Transverse section of a scale (after Bourgogne, 1951).

result from the structure of the scale (see Figs. 55, 56). Some specialised scales are asso-ciated with glands (p. 733), while the scales may also be important in smoothing the air-flow over the wings and body. On the body they are important as an insulating layer helping to maintain the high temperature of the thorax (p. 641).

Scales also occur on the wing veins and body of Culicidae and on the wings of some Psocoptera and a few Trichoptera and Coleoptera.

10.23 Wing form

In Odonata, Isoptera, Mecoptera and male Embioptera the two pairs of wings are similar in form, roughly shaped like elongate triangles, but in most other groups of insects one or other of the wings becomes modified from this basic form. Thus the hind wings of Plecoptera, Dictyoptera and Orthoptera have large vannal lobes so that they are generally much more extensive than the fore wings (Fig. 100). Sometimes the hind wings have a projection from the hind margin as in swallow-tailed butterflies and some Lycaenidae, while in the Nemopteridae the hind wings are slender ribbons trailing out behind the insect (Fig. 104A). The hind wings are similarly modified in some Zygaenidae.

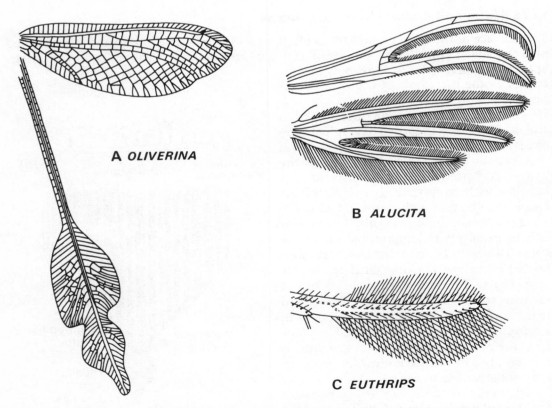

A OLIVERINA

B ALUCITA

C EUTHRIPS

Fig. 104. A. Wings of *Oliverina* (Neuroptera) (after Comstock, 1918). B. Wings of *Alucita* (Lepidoptera) (from Bourgogne, 1951). C. Forewing of *Euthrips* (Thysanoptera) (from Pesson, 1951b).

Sometimes the hind wings are very small, as in Ephemeroptera, Hymenoptera and male coccids, while in some Ephemeroptera, such as *Cloëon*, and some male coccids they are absent altogether. In Diptera the hind wings are modified to form the halteres (p. 181), while in male Strepsiptera the fore wings form similar dumb-bell-shaped structures.

Sometimes the outline of the wings is irregular, as in *Polygonia c-album* (Lepidoptera) where it serves to break up the outline of the resting insect. In the plume moths, Pterophoridae and Orneodidae, the wings are very deeply cleft and divided into a number of lobes fringed with scales (Fig. 104B). Wing fringes are common in Lepidoptera and Culicidae and in some Tinaeoidea they are so extensive as to greatly increase the effective area of the wing. The wings of very small insects are often reduced to straps with one or two supporting veins and long fringes of hairs (Fig. 104C). This occurs in Thysanoptera, in Trichogrammatidae and Mymaridae amongst the Hymenoptera and in some of the small Staphylinoidea amongst the Coleoptera.

Some insects have both pairs of wings reduced and they are said to be brachypterous or micropterous. This occurs, for instance, in some Orthoptera and Heteroptera. The completely wingless, or apterous, condition is also widespread. Winglessness occurs as a primitive condition in the Apterygota, while the ectoparasitic orders Mallophaga, Anoplura and Siphonaptera are secondarily wingless. Wingless species are also widespread in most other orders, but apparently do not occur in Odonata or Ephemeroptera. Sometimes both sexes are wingless, but frequently the male is winged and only the female is apterous. This is the case in coccids, Embioptera, Strepsiptera, Mutilidae and some Chalcididae. In the ants and termites only the reproductive caste is winged and here the wings are shed after the nuptial flight, breaking off by a basal suture so that only a wing scale remains (Fig. 105). The break is achieved in different ways, but termites frequently rest the wing on the ground and then break it off by twisting the wing base. After loss of the wings the flight muscles degenerate.

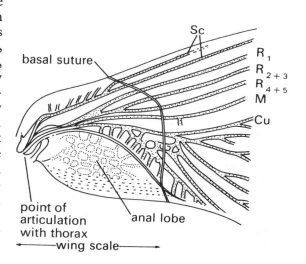

Fig. 105. Wing base of a termite showing the basal suture at which the distal part of the wing breaks off (from Grassé, 1949).

Quite commonly the development of the wings varies within a species either geographically or seasonally. Such wing polymorphism occurs in various groups, but is particularly well known in Heteroptera. For instance, *Gerris lacustris* is bivoltine in Britain and the overwintering generation is largely macropterous, that is fully winged, while the summer generation contains a relatively high proportion of micropterous individuals. In this case the wing length is determined largely by the environment and to a lesser extent by genetic segregation (see *e.g.* Brinkhurst, 1959a, 1963; Lees, 1961; Young, 1965a).

10.24 The protective function of the fore wings

The fore wings of many insects become more fully sclerotised than the hind wings and serve to protect the latter when they are folded up at rest (Fig. 106). Fore wings modified in this way are known as elytra or tegmina. Leathery elytra occur in Orthoptera, Dictyoptera and Dermaptera, while in Heteroptera only the basal part of the wing is hardened, such wings being known as hemelytra (Fig. 107). The basal part of the hemelytron may be subdivided into regions by well-marked veins and in capsids, where the development is most complete, the costal margin of the wing is cut off as a proximal embolium and distal cuneus, the centre of the wing is the corium, and the anal region is cut off as the clavus. In lygaeids only the corium and the clavus are differentiated.

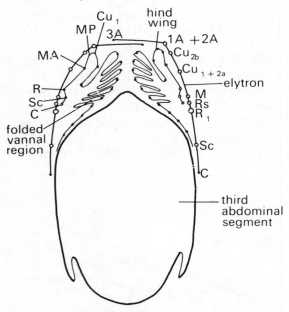

Fig. 106. Transverse section through the abdomen of *Dociostaurus* (Orthoptera) showing the hindwings folded beneath the elytra (from Uvarov, 1966).

The elytra of Coleoptera are very heavily sclerotised and the basic wing venation is lost, although it may be indicated internally by the arrangement of tracheae. The two surfaces of the elytron are separated by a blood space (Fig. 108) running across which are cuticular columns, the trabeculae, arranged in longitudinal rows and marked externally by rows of striations. Primitively there are eight such striae, although the number may be increased in some Adephaga. The elytra of beetles do not overlap in the midline, but meet and are held together by a tongued and grooved joint while in some Carabidae, Curculionidae and Ptinidae they are fused together so that they cannot open and in these species the hind wings are also atrophied. At the sides the elytra are often reflexed downwards, the vertical part being called the epipleuron and the horizontal part the disc.

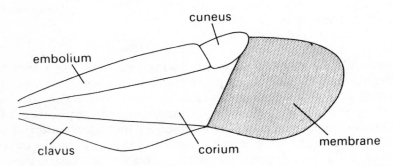

Fig. 107. Forewing of an anthocorid (Heteroptera) (after Comstock, 1918).

10.25 Sound production

In various groups of insects the wings are modified for sound production and they may be retained for this function when they are no longer used in flight (see Chapter XXVIII).

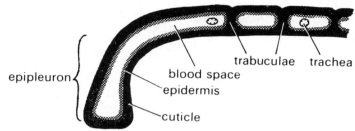

epipleuron

blood space

trabuculae   trachea

epidermis

cuticle

Fig. 108. Diagrammatic transverse section through part of an elytron of a beetle.

10.3 Wing coupling

The wings of most insects are moved by distortions of the thorax (see p. 185) and, because they are so closely associated, the movements of each of the thoracic segments must influence the other. Hence it is impossible for the fore and hind wings to beat completely independently of each other and in Orthoptera and Odonata, where the wings are not otherwise linked, both pairs of wings vibrate with the same frequency and with the hindwing beat consistently more advanced than the forewing beat (see Fig. 127). Such mechanical linking of the wings also involves the timing of the nerve impulses to the flight muscles.

The two-winged condition is apparently more efficient than the four-winged and in the majority of insects the mechanical coupling of the wings is supplemented, and possibly made more precise, by an anatomical coupling of the fore and hind wings so that they move together as a single unit.

This wing coupling may take various forms, but in many species involves lobes or spines at the wing base. A primitive arrangement is found in some Mecoptera of the family Choristidae in which there is a jugal lobe at the base of the fore wing and a humeral lobe at the base of the costal margin of the hind wing. Both lobes are set with setae, those on the humeral lobe beging termed frenular bristles (Fig. 109A), and, although they do not firmly link the wings, they overlap sufficiently to prevent the wings moving out of phase. From this the types of coupling occurring in other Mecoptera, Neuroptera, Trichoptera and Lepidoptera can be derived (see Tillyard, 1918).

In some of the older forms of Trichoptera only the jugum is present on the fore wing. It lies on top of the hind wing so that it is not a very efficient coupling mechanism, but the Hepialidae have a strong jugal lobe which lies beneath the costal margin of the hind wing so that this is held between the jugum and the rest of the fore wing (Fig. 109B). This is called jugate wing coupling. In Micropterygidae the jugum is folded under the fore wings and holds the frenular bristles. This is jugo-frenate coupling.

Many other Lepidoptera have the frenulum well developed and engaging with a catch or retinaculum on the underside of the fore wing so that the wings are firmly coupled. This is frenate coupling. Female noctuids, for instance, have from two to 20 frenular bristles and a retinaculum of forwardly directed hairs on the underside of the cubital vein (Fig. 109C); in the male the frenular bristles are fused together to form a single stout spine and the retinaculum is a cuticular clasp projecting down from the radial (Tillyard, 1918) or subcostal (Bourgonge, 1951) vein (Fig. 109D). Thysanoptera have the wings coupled in a comparable way by hooked spines at the base of the hind wing catching a membranous fold of the fore wing.

The wings of the Papilionoidea and some Bombycoidea are coupled by virtue of an extensive area of overlap between the two. This is known as amplexiform wing coupling. A similar arrangement occurs in some Trichoptera, often together with some other method of coupling.

Other insects have the wings coupled by more distal modifications which hold the costal margin of the hind wing to the anal margin of the fore wing. Thus Hymenoptera have a row of hooks, the hamuli, along the costal margin of the hind wing which catch

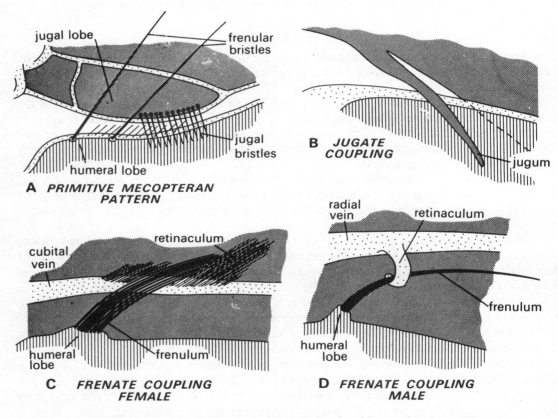

Fig. 109. Wing coupling mechanisms involving the jugal and humeral regions of the wings. A. Primitive mecopteran pattern in *Taeniochorista* (Mecoptera). B. Jugate coupling in *Charagia* (Lepidoptera). C. Frenate coupling in female *Hippotion* (Lepidoptera). D. Frenate coupling in male *Hippotion* (Lepidoptera). All diagrams represent the mechanisms as seen from below with the attachment to the thorax immediately to the left. Membrane of the forewing shown diagonally hatched, that of the hindwing with vertical hatching (after Tillyard, 1918).

into a fold of the fore wing; Psocoptera have a hook at the end of Cu_2 of the fore wing which hooks on to the hind costa; and Heteroptera have a short gutter edged with a brush of hairs on the underside of the clavus which holds the costal margin of the hind wing. Homoptera exhibit a variety of modifications linking the anal margin of the fore wing to the costal margin of the hind wing (see Pesson, 1951a).

Other insects have become functionally two-winged by the reduction or complete loss of one pair of wings. In Diptera and some Ephemeroptera the fore wings alone function as propulsive organs, while in the Coleoptera the hind wings provide the power for flight. The elytra are not vibrated, but are extended at 30–45° above the horizontal by tonic contractions of the flight muscles aided by self-locking apodemes at the base. In Cetoniinae the elytra are raised only sufficiently to allow the wings to unfold and the wings then vibrate through lateral emarginations of the elytra.

10.4 Articulation of the wings with the thorax

The basal region of the wing, where it joins the thorax, is membranous and in this membrane are the axillary sclerites which permit the wing to move freely on the thorax. Typically there are three axillary sclerites (Fig. 110). The first is in the dorsal membrane and articulates proximally with the anterior notal process and distally with the

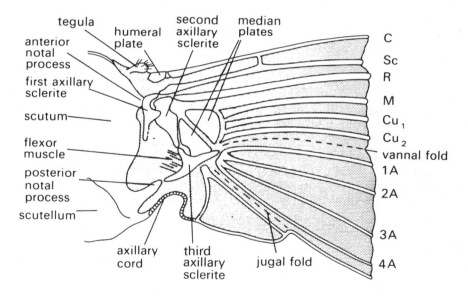

Fig. 110. Diagram of the articulation of a wing with the thorax (modified after Snodgrass, 1935).

subcostal vein and the second axillary sclerite. The second extends to both membranes and articulates ventrally with the pleural wing process (see Fig. 114) and distally with the base of the radius. It is also connected with the third axillary sclerite which articulates proximally with the posterior notal process and distally with the anal veins. The third axillary sclerite is Y-shaped with a wing flexor muscle inserted into the crutch of the Y. In Hymenoptera and Orthoptera there is a fourth axillary sclerite between the posterior notal process and the third axillary sclerite.

In addition to the axillary sclerites there are other plates in the wing base. Connected with the third axillary, and perhaps representing a part of it, may be one or two median plates from which the media and the cubitus arise. At the base of the costa is a humeral plate and often, proximal to it, is another plate derived from the edge of the articular membrane and called the tegula. In Lepidoptera the tegula is very large and overlaps the wing base, while it is also well-developed in Hymenoptera and Diptera (Fig. 102). The tegula only rarely occurs in association with the hind wing.

All present-day insects other than Ephemeroptera and Odonata are able to fold their wings back over the body when at rest. It might be expected that this folding would be associated with greater complexity of the sclerites at the wing base and that in Ephemeroptera and Odonata the arrangement would be simpler. The wing base of Ephemeroptera is very similar to that in other insects (see Snodgrass, 1935), but Odonata have only two large plates hinged to the tergum and supported by two arms from the pleural wing process. The plates are called the humeral and axillary plates.

Although the movement of the wings on the thorax involves some condylic movement at the pleural process, a great deal of movement is permitted by the presence of resilin ligaments, such as the wing hinge ligament of Orthoptera (see p. 434). In this way the problems of friction and lubrication which would occur at a normal articulation moving at the high frequency of the wings are avoided. The wings of Hymenoptera and Diptera are suspended by two opposing ligaments (Neville, 1965c).

10.5 Wing folding

Homoptera, Psocoptera and Neuroptera hold their wings in a roof-like manner over the back when at rest, while most of the other groups of insects hold their wings flat over the back. In addition to being folded backwards the hind wings of Orthoptera and the fore wings of Vespoidea are longitudinally pleated.

Folding is produced by a muscle arising on the pleuron and inserted into the third axillary sclerite in such a way that when it contracts the sclerite pivots about its points of articulation with the posterior notal process and the second axillary sclerite. As a result, the distal arm of the third axillary sclerite rotates upwards and inwards so that finally its position is completely reversed. The anal veins are articulated with the sclerite so that when it moves they are carried with it and become flexed over the back of the insect. The rest of the wing is pulled back by the vannal region. Extension of the wings probably results from the contraction of muscles attached to the basalar sclerite or, in some insects, to the subalar sclerite.

The wings of Coleoptera and Dermaptera fold transversely as well as longitudinally so that they can be accommodated beneath the elytra. This transverse fold necessitates a modification of the venation and in Coleoptera there is a discontinuity between the proximal and distal parts of the veins (Fig. 111). The folding results automatically from the structure and flexibility of the veins.

Sometimes the wings are held in the folded position by being coupled together or fastened to the body. For instance, in Psocoptera the costal margin of the hind wing is held by a fold on the pterostigma of the fore wing. The elytra of Coleoptera are held together by their tonguing and grooving, but are also held to the body by a median longitudinal groove in the metathorax which holds the reflexed inner edges of the elytra. Dermaptera have rows of spines on the inside edge of the elytron which catch into combs on the metathorax, while many aquatic Heteroptera have a peg on the mesothorax which fits into a pit in the margin of the hemelytron. Symphyta have specialised lobes, the cenchri, on the metanotum which engage with rough areas on the undersides of the fore wings to hold them in place.

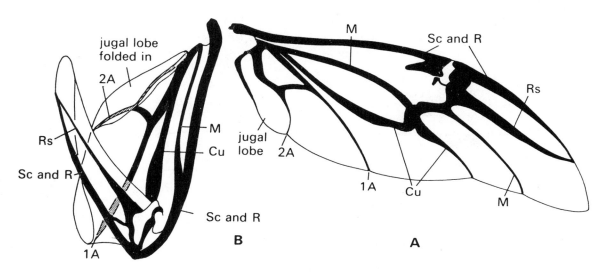

Fig. 111. Wing folding in *Melolontha* (Coleoptera). A. Wing extended. B. Wing folded (from Jeannel, 1949).

10.6 Sense organs and the haltere

The macrotrichia along the veins are probably mechanoreceptors responding to touch and possibly to the flow of air over the wings in flight. At the base of the wing are several groups of campaniform sensilla (p. 615), generally three groups on the underside of the subcosta and three on the dorsal side of the radius (Fig. 112 and see Pringle, 1957). These groups are not always well defined and in Acrididae, Blattaria and Plecoptera the radial groups are absent altogether. More distally on the veins are other scattered campaniform sensilla, but these are large and circular, so that, unlike those in the basal groups, they can have no directional sensitivity. The sensilla in the groups are oval, all those in a group being similarly orientated, so that they are sensitive to distortions of the wing base in particular planes. The number of sensilla in each group varies, there being more in more highly manoueverable species. Thus *Apis* has about 700 campaniform sensilla at the base of each fore wing, while *Panorpa* (Mecoptera) has only about 60. Some of these sensilla, at least, are concerned in the control of stability in flight (see p. 203).

In addition to the campaniform sensilla there are up to four chordotonal organs at the base of each wing. One of these is inserted into the costa, arising proximally at the wing base, while the others run obliquely across the radial, medial and sometimes also the cubital veins.

Most insects do not have internal proprioceptors connected with the wings or their muscles, but in Orthoptera each wing has a stretch receptor and a chordotonal organ in the thorax associated with the wing base. The two organs of a mesothoracic wing of *Schistocerca*, for example, arise together on the mesophragma. The stretch receptor extends to just behind the subalar, while the chordotonal organ is attached a little more ventrally (Gettrup, 1962). The stretch receptor is already present in the third instar and appears to be homologous with the abdominal stretch receptors. These organs have been identified in acridids, gryllids and tettigoniids, but not in a gryllotalpid or a blattid. They are concerned with the control of wing movement (see p. 197).

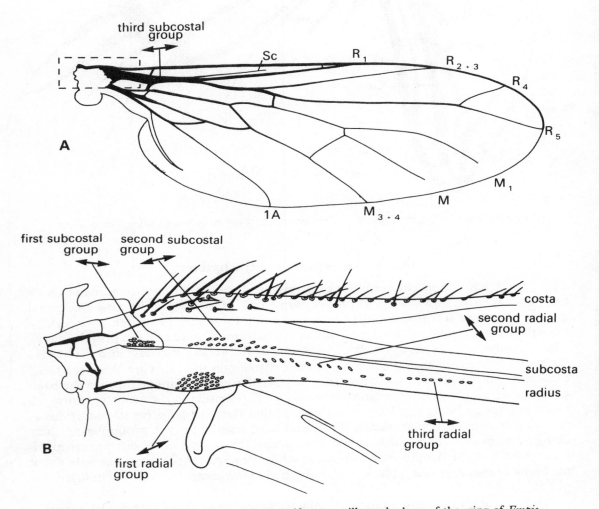

Fig. 112. Distribution of groups of campaniform sensilla at the base of the wing of *Empis* (Diptera). A. Whole wing showing, enclosed within the broken line, the position of the area enlarged in B. Arrows indicate the orientation of the long axes of the sensilla (after Pringle, 1957).

Halteres

The hind wings of the Diptera are modified to form the halteres which are sense organs concerned with the maintenance of stability in flight (see p. 203). Each haltere consists of a basal lobe, a stalk and an end knob which projects backwards from the end of the stalk so that its centre of gravity is also behind the stalk. The whole structure is rigid except for some flexibility of the ventral surface near the base which allows some freedom of movement, while the cuticle of the end knob is thin, but is kept distended by the turgidity of large vacuolated cells inside it. The haltere is larger in less specialised forms such as *Tipula*; in *Calliphora* it is only 0·7 mm. long.

On the basal lobe of the haltere are groups of campaniform sensilla which can be homologised with the groups at the base of a normal wing (see Pringle, 1948, 1957). Dorsally there are two large groups of sensilla each containing, in *Calliphora*, about 100 campaniform sensilla (Fig. 113). One group, forming the basal plate, has the sensilla orientated with their long axes at about 30° to the axes of the longitudinal rows in which they are arranged; the second group, forming the dorsal scapal plate, has the sensilla parallel with the axis which passes through the main point of articulation and the centre

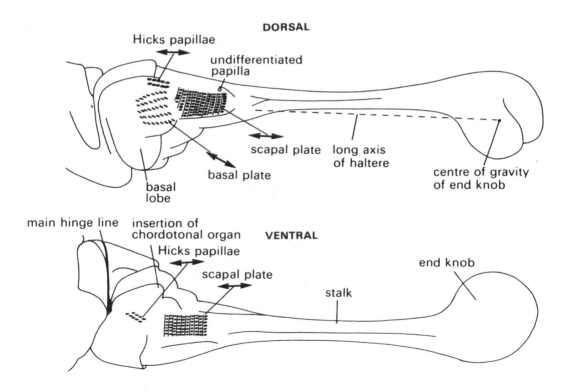

Fig. 113. Dorsal and ventral views of the halteres of *Lucilia* showing the basal groups of sensilla. The orientation of the campaniform sensilla is indicated by the arrows (after Pringle, 1948).

of gravity of the haltere (indicated as the long axis of the haltere in Fig. 113). Near the basal plate is a further small group of campaniform sensilla known as Hicks papillae. These are set below the surface of the haltere and are orientated parallel with its long axis. There is also a single round, so-called undifferentiated papilla near the scapal plate. On the ventral surface there is another scapal plate with about 100 sensilla and a group of ten Hicks papillae. These are orientated parallel with the long axis of the haltere.

Also attached to the ventral surface is a large chordotonal organ orientated at about 45° to the long axis of the haltere. A smaller chordotonal organ runs vertically across the base.

These sensilla react to the forces acting at the base of the haltere during flight. They perceive the vertical movements of the haltere and also the torque produced by lateral turning movements of the fly (p. 203).

10.7 Muscles associated with the wings

A number of muscles are inserted directly into the sclerites of the wing base; they are called the direct wing muscles (Fig. 114). One of these, arising on the pleuron and inserted into the third axillary sclerite, flexes the wing backwards and in Diptera this muscle may be assisted by another inserted into the first axillary sclerite. Extension of the wing from the flexed position is produced by one or more muscles inserted into the basalar. These muscles arise on the episternum, the sternum and the coxa. Another muscle, arising on the meron, is inserted into the subalar, accompanied in gryllids,

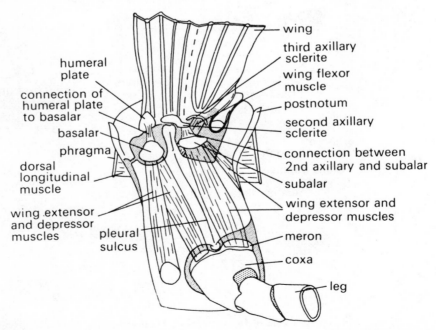

Fig. 114. Lateral view of the thorax showing the direct wing muscles. The pleural region is assumed to be transparent (after Snodgrass, 1935).

Trichoptera and Lepidoptera by a second muscle from the epimeron. The basalar and subalar muscles extend and depress the wing. Odonata have two muscles arising from the episternum inserted into the humeral plate and two from the edge of the epimeron inserted into the axillary plate.

In addition to the direct muscles there are other muscles which, although not directly associated with the wings, move the wings as a result of the distortions which they produce in the shape of the thorax (see p.185). These are the indirect flight muscles. The most important indirect flight muscles are the dorsal longitudinal muscles and the tergosternal muscles (see Fig. 116) of which there may be two or more pairs. These muscles are usually well developed, while the oblique dorsal muscles, which run from the postphragma to the scutum are often small or absent altogether. In Diptera and Cicadidae, however, the oblique dorsal muscle becomes almost vertical by extension of the postphragma and in these groups it is well developed.

CHAPTER XI

MOVEMENT AND CONTROL OF THE WINGS

Insects fly by beating their wings up and down and only a few large species are known to glide for any distance between wing strokes. Little is known about the flight of very small insects, but a completely different set of principles may be involved (see Horridge, 1956; Pringle, 1957). They are not considered here.

Some of the movements of the wing are produced by muscles directly inserted into the wing base, but others result from distortions of the thorax produced by muscles not directly associated with the wings. In some insects, such as the Diptera, all the wing movements are produced by such indirect muscles. The movement is aided by the elasticity of the wing hinge, the flight muscles and the thorax itself and this elasticity may result in the wings clicking automatically into the up or down positions after the muscles have pulled them into a position which is unstable.

The frequency with which the wings vibrate varies considerably. In some insects with a low wingbeat frequency each cycle is produced by a nervous impulse and the oscillating rhythm of the flight muscles results from an inherent oscillation in the motor neurons driving the muscles. The basic oscillation is modified by the input from peripheral sensilla. In Hymenoptera and Diptera, in which the wings commonly vibrate at over 100 cycles per second, there is no direct relationship between nervous stimuli and muscle contraction. A steady flow of nerve impulses keeps the muscles activated, but the frequency of muscle contraction is a function of the muscles and the resonant frequency of the thorax.

The movements of the wing during the stroke are complex and the twisting of the wings is particularly important because this controls the aerodynamic forces which are produced and which propel the insect through the air.

Normally when the insect is in contact with the ground, the activity of the nerve cells controlling flight is inhibited, but once the tarsi lose touch with the substratum the inhibition is removed. During flight the insect tends to deviate from a steady path, but peripheral sensory mechanisms enable it to correct for such deviations.

Flight in general is reviewed by Chadwick (1953a and b) and Pringle (1957, 1965, 1968, *Adv. Insect Physiol.* 5) and the papers of Jensen (1956), Jensen and Weis-Fogh (1962), Weis-Fogh (1956a, b, 1964b) and Weis-Fogh and Jensen (1956) should also be consulted. The control of flight is reviewed by Gettrup (1965), Weis-Fogh (1964c) and Wilson (1965b, 1966b, 1968, *Adv. Insect Physiol.* 5).

11.1 Movements of the wings

The up and down movements of the wings are produced by direct and indirect wing muscles, but they also involve the elasticity of the thorax, the wing base and the muscles themselves.

11.11 Movements produced by the muscles

In all insects the upward movement of the wings is produced by indirect dorso-ventral muscles inserted into the tergum of the segment bearing the wing. By contracting they pull the tergum down and hence also move down the point of articulation of the wing with the tergum. The effect of this is to move the wing membrane up with the pleural process acting as a fulcrum (Fig. 115A, 116A). The muscles producing this movement are not always homologous. In many insects they arise on the sternum or the coxae, but in Auchenorrhyncha and Psyllidae the tergosternal muscles are small and are functionally replaced as wing elevators by the oblique dorsal muscles. These arise on

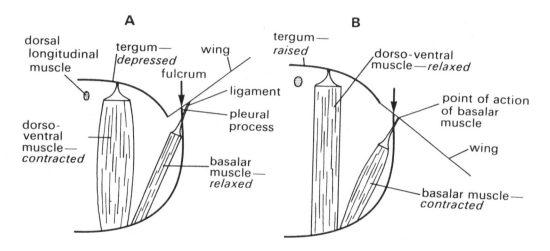

Fig. 115. Diagrammatic cross-section of the thorax illustrating the wing movements in an insect, such as a dragonfly, in which the direct wing muscles cause depression of the wings.

the postphragma and so are normally obliquely longitudinal (Fig. 66), but in the groups mentioned the phragma extends ventrally carrying the origins of the muscles with it so that they come to exert their pull vertically instead of horizontally (see Pringle, 1957).

The downward movement of the wings in Odonata and Blattaria is produced by direct muscles inserted into the basalar and subalar sclerites which are connected to the axillary sclerites by ligaments (see Fig. 114). Hence contraction of these muscles exerts a pull on the wings outside the fulcrum of the pleural process and so pulls the wings down (Fig. 115B).

In Diptera and Hymenoptera the downward movement is produced by the dorsal longitudinal indirect muscles. Because the dorsum of the pterothorax is an uninterrupted plate, without membranous junctions (see Fig. 61D), contraction of the dorsal longitudinal muscles cannot produce a telescoping of the segments as in the abdomen. Instead, the centre of the tergum becomes bowed upwards (Fig. 116D) so that the tergal articulation of the wing is also moved up and the wing membrane flaps down (Fig.

116C). At the same time the anterior and posterior notal processes become approximated because of the hinging of the scutellum to the scutum (see Fig. 119), and this also assists in the movement of the wing (Pringle, 1957).

In Coleoptera and Orthoptera the downward movement is produced by the direct and indirect muscles acting together. The direct muscles are then dual purpose since they are also concerned in twisting the wing during the course of the stroke (see p. 192).

A number of the muscles moving the wings arise in the coxa which is itself moveable. Whether these muscles move the legs or the wings appears to be determined by the position of the appendages; if the wings are closed the muscles move the legs, but in flight with the legs in the flight position (p. 197) the wings are moved.

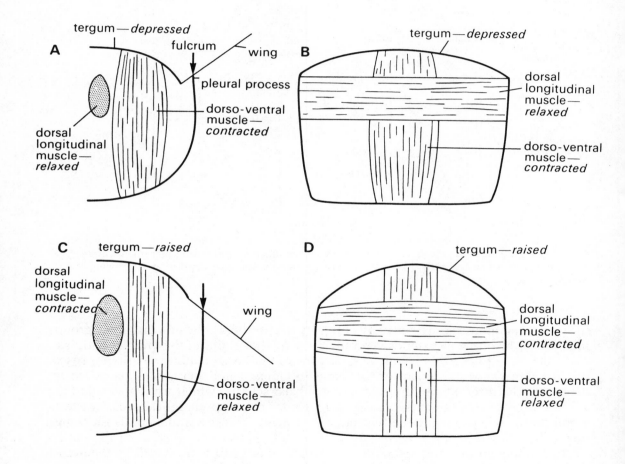

Fig. 116. Diagrams illustrating the movements of the wings in an insect, such as a fly, in which both up and down movements of the wing are produced by indirect muscles. A and C. Cross-sections of the thorax. B and D. Views of the wing-bearing segment from the inside showing, in D, the shortening and bowing of the tergum produced by contraction of the dorsal longitudinal muscles.

11.12 Movement due to elasticity

In *Schistocerca* (Orthoptera), and probably in other insects, much of the energy involved in the upstroke is stored as elastic forces for use in the downstroke. This is possible because the aerodynamic forces produced at this time act in the same direction as the wing movement so assisting its movement. Thus the muscles have only to overcome the forces of inertia of the wing and elasticity of the wing base, and as a result some 86% of the energy they produce is stored for use in the downstroke.

The elasticity of the system results partly from the pad of resilin which forms the main wing hinge (see Fig. 286). The elastic properties of this pad are almost perfect so

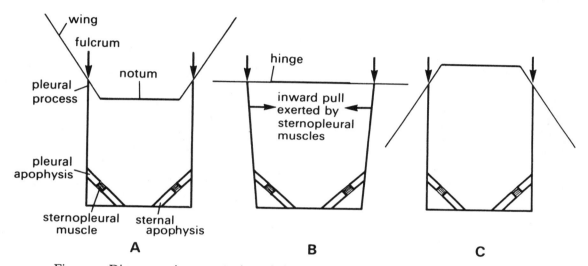

Fig. 117. Diagrammatic cross-section of the insect thorax illustrating the distortion of the thorax produced by wing movement. A. Wings stable in the up position. B. Unstable position due to the inward pull of the sternopleural muscles. C. Wings stable in the down position.

that it absorbs less than 3% of the energy imparted to it when it is stretched in the upward movement of the wings. The remaining energy is available for pulling the wing down.

The elasticity of the flight muscles is also important. These muscles are characterised by a greater resistance to stretch compared with other muscles due to the elastic properties of the contractile system. The sarcolemma seems to add little to the elasticity of the muscle (Buchthal *et al.*, 1957).

Contraction of the indirect flight muscles distorts the thorax so that the elastic properties of the thorax as a whole are also significant factors in wing movement. Figure 117 shows diagrammatically the manner in which the movement of the wings involves a lateral movement of the wall of the thorax. This movement is resisted by the elasticity of the thorax which is largely due to the sternopleural articulation and, to a lesser extent, the tergopleural articulation. In the mesothorax of Coleoptera and the metathorax of Hymenoptera the pleural and sternal apophyses are fused so that lateral stiffness of the thorax is considerable and constant, but in other insects the apophyses are joined by a muscle, alterations in the tension of which can regulate the lateral stiffness.

As a result of this lateral stiffness the position of the wings is unstable for much of the stroke and they will tend to return automatically either to the fully up or fully down positions (Fig. 117), these being the only stable positions. Thus in flight the wings are moved by the muscles to the position of maximum instability (Fig. 117B) and then they will swing into the up or down position as a result of the thoracic elasticity. This arrangement is called a 'click' mechanism.

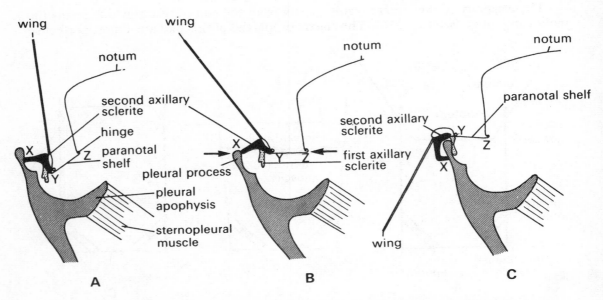

Fig. 118. Diagrammatic section through the wing base of a fly illustrating the click mechanism in the wing movement. A. Wing stable in the up position. B. Unstable position with the system XYZ in a straight line and under pressure between the arrows. C. Wing stable in the down position (partly from Pringle, 1957).

In an insect the wing articulation is more complex than in the diagrams, but the method of working is basically the same. Thus in *Sarcophaga* (Diptera) both dorsoventral and dorsal longitudinal indirect flight muscles produce a lateral extension of the notum, exerting forces outwards, while the pleural process is pulled inwards by the sterno-pleural muscle. Hence the system XYZ in Figure 118 is only stable at the extreme ends of the stroke (Fig. 118A and C).

Contraction of the dorsal longitudinal muscles of *Sarcophaga* lowers the scutellum which is hinged to the scutum. This raises the anterior end of the scutellar lever, which arises from the side of the scutellum (Fig. 119), and this pushes the first axillary sclerite up until it reaches the unstable position (Fig. 118B) when the forces exerted at X and Z cause the wing to click into the stable down position (Fig. 118C). In raising the wings the scutellar lever pulls the first axillary sclerite down to the position of maximum instability and then the wing automatically clicks up. Click mechanisms have been demonstrated in Orthoptera, Diptera, Coleoptera and possibly Odonata.

At the end of each wing-stroke the movement produced by the click is limited by a stop. This gives greater efficiency in flight since it eliminates the necessity of doing work in stopping the movement. Thus in *Sarcophaga* the upstroke is limited by the scutellar lever hitting against the pleural sclerites, but the lower limit is more variable. It is determined by the nature of the articulation between the first and second axillary sclerites which can be varied to some extent by the direct muscles altering the lateral tension.

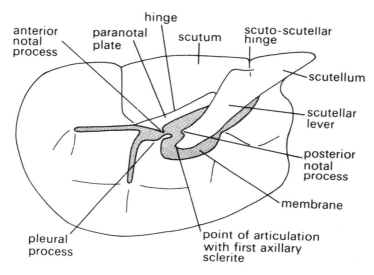

Fig. 119. Lateral view of the thorax of *Sarcophaga* (from Pringle, 1957).

In *Schistocerca* the movement of the wings may be stopped by the contraction of antagonistic muscles before the wingstroke is complete. Thus the dorsal longitudinal muscles may start to contract before the end of the upstroke. This requires a greater muscular output than is necessary in *Sarcophaga,* but in this way the amplitude of the wing beat is reduced, enabling the wings to be driven at a higher frequency.

11.13 Frequency of wingbeat

The frequency with which the wings vibrate varies considerably in different insects. Thus in butterflies the wingbeat frequency is 4–20/second, in *Schistocerca* it is 15–20/second, while in *Apis* and *Musca* the frequency is about 190/second. *Forcipomyia* (Diptera), a very small insect, has a wingbeat frequency of about 1000/second.

The lower wingbeat frequencies of 30/second and less are associated with tubular or close packed flight muscles (see Chapter XII) which show a normal 1 : 1 relationship with the nervous input. That is, each nerve impulse produces a single muscle contraction. At the higher wingbeat frequencies, however, this is not the case. These frequencies are associated with fibrillar flight muscles in which each nerve impulse leads to a succession of muscular contractions. These contractions are said to be myogenic and the frequency with which the wings vibrate in this case depends on the natural frequency of the thorax and its muscles.

Even within a species the frequency of wingbeat may vary, being generally higher in smaller individuals. The frequency is greater in males than in females, although this may only reflect the generally smaller size of male insects. Frequency also varies with age, being higher in older insects (Fig. 120), while it tends to decrease as the insect fatigues. In *Drosophila* (Diptera) the wingbeat frequency increases with temperature (Fig. 120), but in Hymenoptera temperature has no effect. The wingbeat frequency of *Schistocerca* is constant within the normal flight range of 25–35°C., but alters at lower and higher temperatures.

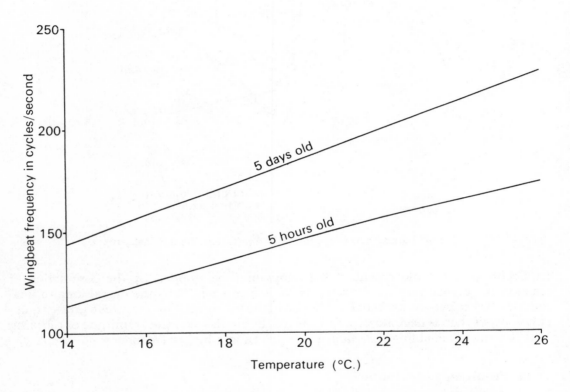

Fig. 120. Variation with age and temperature of the wingbeat frequency of *Drosophila* (from Chadwick, 1953a).

Frequency can be controlled to some extent and in *Schistocerca* a higher frequency is used to increase lift. This involves an increased rate of firing of the motor nerves to the muscles moving the wings, but in Diptera frequency can be modified by alterations in the tension of certain muscles, such as the sternopleural muscles, which alter the natural frequency of the thorax.

The wings do not move at a constant speed throughout the stroke, the downward movement of the wings being rather slower than the upward movement (see Fig. 121).

11.14 Stroke plane

The wings do not make simple up and down movements, but in the course of each cycle of vibration they also move backwards and forwards to some extent. As a result, the tip of the fore wing of *Schistocerca* moves in an ellipse relative to the body (Fig. 121), moving forward and down on the downstroke, up and back on the upstroke. In some other insects, such as bees and flies, the wing tip traces a figure-of-eight relative to the body. When the insect is moving the path of the wing tip through the air follows a rather irregular path (Fig. 121).

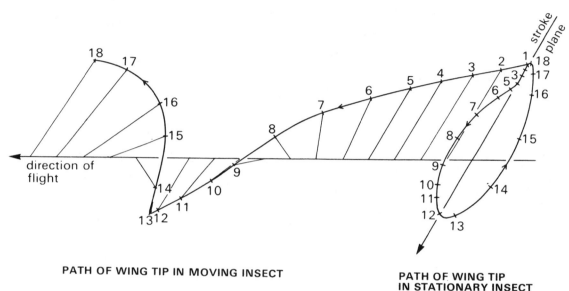

PATH OF WING TIP IN MOVING INSECT

PATH OF WING TIP
IN STATIONARY INSECT

Fig. 121. Movement of the tip of the forewing of *Schistocerca*. The ellipse on the right shows the movement relative to the body of the insect, while the irregular curve shows the path of the wing-tip as the insect moves through the air. The numbers indicate the positions of the wing at regular time intervals throughout the stroke and the lines joining the wing-tip path to the flight axis show the angle which the long axis of the wing makes with the body at different stages of the stroke (after Jensen, 1956).

The plane in which the wings vibrate relative to the body is called the stroke plane and in *Schistocerca* this is at a more or less constant angle of 30° to the long axis of the body. In *Apis* the plane is variable and when a bee hovers the stroke plane almost coincides with the horizontal plane through the long axis of the body. Differences in the plane of movement of the two sides produce turning movements.

11.15 Amplitude of wingbeat

The amplitude of the wing stroke, measured in the stroke plane, varies from one species to another. Thus in *Aeschna* (Odonata) the amplitude is about 70°, while in *Lucanus* (Coleoptera) it is 160°. In *Schistocerca* where the wings are not linked anatomically the forewing amplitude is 60–70°, while that of the hind wing is 110°. Variation of the amplitude of wingbeat on the two sides of the body may be used in steering, the insect turning away from the side of greatest amplitude. A reduction in amplitude may be associated with a higher wingbeat frequency.

11.16 Wing twisting

In addition to variations in the form of the wingbeat the wing may twist in different ways in different phases of the stroke thereby altering the forces which it exerts. In many insects the twisting is produced by two direct flight muscles, the basalar muscle which pronates the wing, that is it causes the ventral surface to face downwards by pulling down the leading edge, and the subalar muscle which supinates the wing, causing the ventral surface to face obliquely forwards by pulling down the trailing edge. Since these muscles also act as direct wing depressors they are active only during the down-stroke when the balance between them determines the degree of pronation of the wing. In addition there is some passive bending of the wing as a result of its flexibility and this is evident in the hind wing of the locust which always assumes a smooth camber. During the upstroke, when the direct muscles are inactive, the twisting of the wing is entirely passive. In *Sarcophaga* wing twisting results automatically from the relative movements of the first and second axillary sclerites (see Pringle, 1957).

The wings undergo a regular sequence of changes in twisting, being fully pronated during most of the downstroke with, in *Schistocerca*, a posterior flap coming forwards towards the end of the movement (Fig. 122). In the upstroke the wing is supinated and Z-shaped in cross-section.

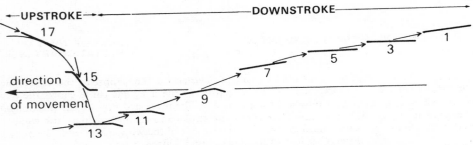

Fig. 122. Changes in the twisting of the mid-section of the forewing of *Schistocerca* in the course of a single stroke. The relative size of the wing is greatly exaggerated for clarity. Short arrows indicate the direction of the relative wind and the numbers correspond with those showing the wing-tip positions in figure 121 (after Jensen, 1956).

11.2 Aerodynamics

11.21 Flapping flight

The forces which keep an insect airborne and propel it along are produced by the move-ments of the wings. They vary throughout the wingbeat due to changes in the twisting of the wings and changes in the velocity of the relative wind. The relative wind is the movement of the air relative to the wing and it has two major components; one due to the airspeed of the insect and a second due to the velocity of the wing in the stroke plane. The relative wind may be regarded as the resultant of these two forces (Fig. 123).

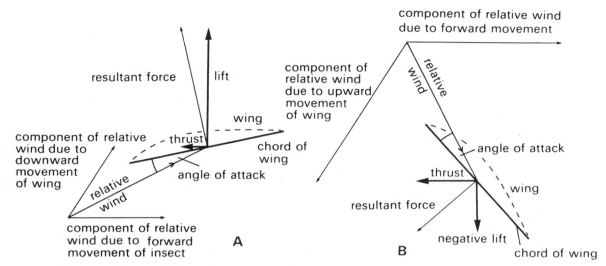

Fig. 123. Diagrams illustrating the forces acting at the mid-point of the wing at different phases of the wingbeat corresponding roughly with positions 7 and 15 in figure 122. A. Downstroke of wing with positive angle of attack. B. Upstroke of wing with negative angle of attack. The lengths and thicknesses of the arrows have no significance in indicating the strengths of the forces.

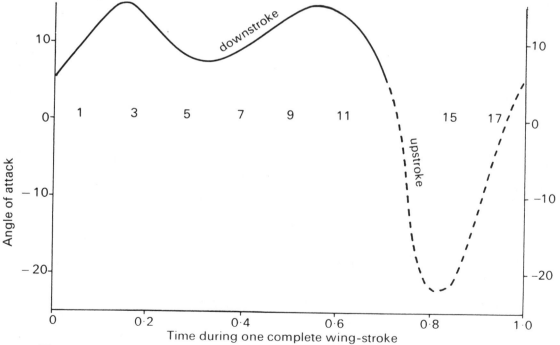

Fig. 124. Changes in the angle of attack at the mid-point of the forewings of *Schistocerca* during a single cycle of movement of the wings. Since the angle of attack varies along the length of the wing, no negative lift is produced by the wing as a whole (see Fig. 125). Numbers along the zero axis indicate intervals corresponding with those in Fig. 122 (after Jensen, 1956).

The forces which the relative wind exerts on the wing depend on the angle at which it strikes the chord of the wing. This angle is known as the angle of attack and it may be either positive or negative (Fig. 123A, B). Because of the twisting of the wing the angle of attack varies along its length, while the twisting also modifies the angle of attack at any one point in the course of the wingbeat (Figs. 122 and 124). Thus in *Schistocerca* the angle of attack at the mid-point of the wing is positive and fairly constant throughout the downstroke, but becomes negative during the upstroke.

Lift

The force which the relative wind exerts on the wing can be resolved into two components, the lift and the thrust. The lift is the vertical force produced and to keep the insect steady in the air the lift force must roughly equal the weight of the insect. Lift becomes minimal during the upstroke of the wings, but, in *Schistocerca*, because of the adjustment of the angle of attack, it never becomes negative, that is the wings as a whole never produce a force pushing the insect down (Fig. 125). Because of their bigger area and greater amplitude of movement the hindwings produce more lift than the forewings, about 71% of the total, and because of the adjustment of the angle of attack 20% of the total lift is produced during the upstroke of the wings. The resulting variation in lift

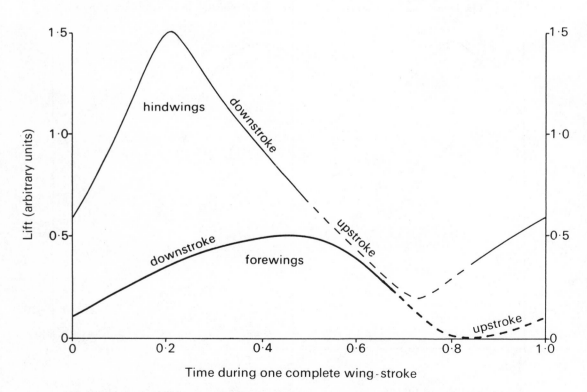

Fig. 125. Changes in the lift produced by the wings of *Schistocerca* during a wing-stroke (after Jensen, 1956).

in the course of a wingbeat leads to a cycle of vertical displacements of the insect as it flies along so that instead of following a horizontal path it loops up and down (Fig. 126).

Lift is also produced by the action of the relative wind on the body as distinct from the wings, but the force is insignificant compared with that produced by the wings, amounting to less than 1/20th of the total lift in *Schistocerca* (Jensen, 1956). In *Drosophila* lift is proportional to the body angle (p. 202) (Vogel, 1966).

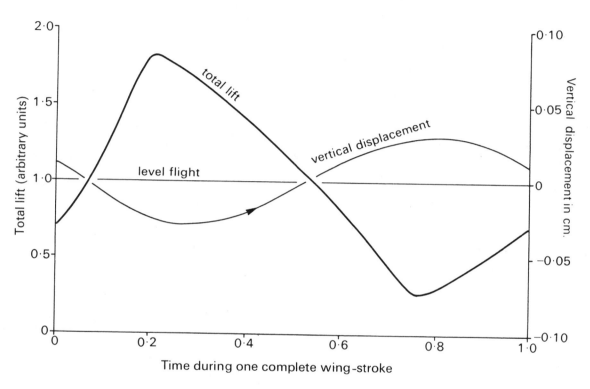

Fig. 126. Changes in the total lift and associated vertical displacements of *Schistocerca* during a wing-stroke. There is a time lag between the period of maximum lift and the corresponding rise of the insect (after Jensen, 1956).

Thrust

In order to move forwards the insect must also produce a horizontal force known as the thrust. This must be sufficiently great to overcome the drag forces which resist the motion of the insect through the air. Drag results partly from the profile of the insect, that is the area which it presents to the air, but largely from an induced drag due to the development of vortices at the wing tips which dissipate much of the kinetic energy of the wings as heat. These vortices result from the mixing of air at different pressures from the two sides of the wing.

The thrust, like lift, varies in the course of a wingbeat and the hind wing of *Schisto-cerca* produces thrust maximally in the middle of the downstroke and again in the up-stroke (Fig. 127). This variation results in slight changes in the forward speed of the insect in the course of a wingbeat.

Propelling the insect forwards requires relatively little energy compared with that needed to keep it in the air and in *Schistocerca* the average thrust is only 7% of the average lift.

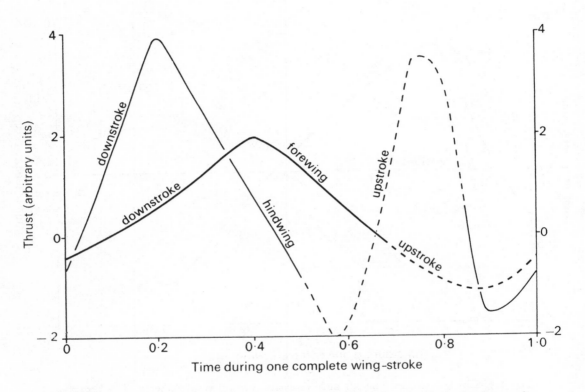

Fig. 127. Changes in the thrust produced by the wings of *Schistocerca* during a wing-stroke (after Jensen, 1956).

11.22 Gliding

Occasionally insects are seen to glide with the wings outstretched, the lift forces produced by rising air being sufficient to keep them airborne without any wing movements (and see p. 242). Thus during a glide an insect expends very little energy. Various Lepidoptera, locusts and Odonata have been seen to glide and it is suggested that the inability of dragonflies to fold their wings is a secondary adaptation to this, since wings locked in a stretched position are an asset in gliding. Locusts are also able to lock their fore wings in the outstretched position (Neville, 1965c).

11.3 Control of wingbeat

11.31 The initiation of wing movements

In most insects the wings start to beat as a result of loss of tarsal contact with the substratum and in the locust this occurs when the insect jumps into the air. When the legs are touching the ground movement of the wings is inhibited, the contact probably being perceived through the proprioceptors of the legs. The wings may also be induced to beat by various shock stimuli.

11.32 Maintenance of wing movements

The loss of tarsal contact with the substratum is sufficient to maintain the movement of the wings of *Drosophila* as well as initiating it, but in most other insects flight soon stops unless the insect receives further stimulation. This is provided by the movement of wind against the head. A wind speed of only 2 m./sec. is sufficient to maintain the wing movements of *Schistocerca* and since this is less than the flight speed of the insect the relative wind produced in flight will provide sufficient stimulus. The air movement is perceived in locusts by hair beds on the face (see Fig. 407). In Diptera the wind is perceived by movements of the third antennal segment relative to the second, probably involving Johnston's organ (see p. 605) (Hollick, 1941).

These stimuli also result in the legs being drawn up close to the body in a characteristic manner. Thus in locusts stimulation of the hair beds causes the fore legs to assume the flight position, but the hind legs only do so when the sensilla at the base of the wing are stimulated by the wing movement. Diptera hold their legs in the flight position when their antennae are stimulated in flight.

11.33 Nervous control of wing movements

The basic rhythm of the muscular contractions involved in the flight of the locust is inherent and continues in the complete absence of nervous input from peripheral sensilla. There is no centre in the nervous system concerned with flight control and it is probable that the basic oscillation results from inherent properties of the motor neurons supplying the muscles. Basically it may be supposed that the neurons of two antagonistic muscles inhibit each other (Fig. 128). One neuron is at first dominant, but it fatigues and is suppressed by its antagonist, which in its turn fatigues so that the first neuron becomes dominant again (Fig. 128B). Experimental work indicates that such simple reciprocal inhibition cannot account for the observed flight pattern in which each muscle unit receives only one or two impulses in each cycle with a relatively long time interval between successive firings. Hence it is suggested that the oscillatory cells have follower cells which fatigue rapidly and so produce only one or two impulses. In this way the oscillation of nerve impulses and hence of muscle contractions might be maintained.

This central oscillation is modified by the input from peripheral sensilla amongst which the stretch receptors at the base of the wing of the locust (see p. 180) are particularly important. Each stretch receptor fires one, two or three times towards the top of the upstroke, the first impulse always being produced when the wing is in a particular position. The number of spikes produced is a measure of the velocity and amplitude of the wing movement (Gettrup, 1963). Hence the stretch receptors transmit some precise information on the wingbeat, but it appears that this information is lost in the central nervous system and is not made use of by the insect. Instead the impulses from the receptors appear to summate over several cycles of wing movement.

A major effect of the input from the stretch receptors is to double the basic rate of oscillation of the wings, but apart from this they may tend to keep the frequency more or less constant by means of a negative feedback mechanism. As wingbeat frequency increases the amplitude of the wingbeat is reduced due to muscular braking. This possibly results in less input from the stretch receptors so that stimulation of the central oscillators is reduced and the wingbeat frequency declines (Wilson and Gettrup, 1963).

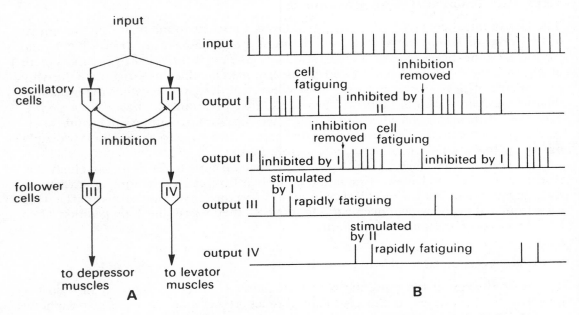

Fig. 128. A. Hypothetical arrangement of motor neurons which could account for the observed activity in locust flight motor neurons. B. The supposed activity of the cells in A. Each vertical line represents a nerve impulse. The input may be regular (as shown) or irregular, but the output of cells I and II is not altered. For explanation see text (after Wilson, 1964).

Despite the complexity of the flight movements of the locust each of the muscles involved comprises only a small number of units and, for instance, the first basalar muscle consists of only a single unit, while the subalar muscle consists of two muscle units. Each unit has its own motor fibre and so can act independently.

The force exerted by a muscle can be increased either by increasing the number of units which are active or by increasing the strength of the pull exerted by each unit. Although the units of the flight muscles are only innervated by fast axons (p.216) they are caused to contract more strongly if, instead of being stimulated by a single nerve impulse, they are stimulated by two impulses following close together, the time between the impulses probably being determined by the relative refractory period of the nerve and the muscle membrane (Wilson, 1964). This provides a means by which graded information can be transmitted to muscles despite the all-or-nothing code of the nervous system (see p. 529). Thus when the insect is producing only low lift forces the second basalar muscle and some units of the dorsal longitudinal muscle of the hind wing may be inactive, whereas in producing high lift forces all the units come into action and the forces exerted by the individual units are increased by double firing of the motor neurons (Fig. 129).

The twisting of the wings by the controller muscles is precisely timed by the pattern of motor impulses to the muscles (Fig. 129). Only in the case of one muscle, the meso-thoracic subalar muscle, is the firing of the motor nerve very variable in its timing and this is the muscle which varies the twisting of the fore wing to control lift (Wilson and Weis-Fogh, 1962). The precise co-ordination of the other neurons does not arise from a fixed pattern of connections between them since they can function in other sequences than that involved in flight (D. Wilson, 1962).

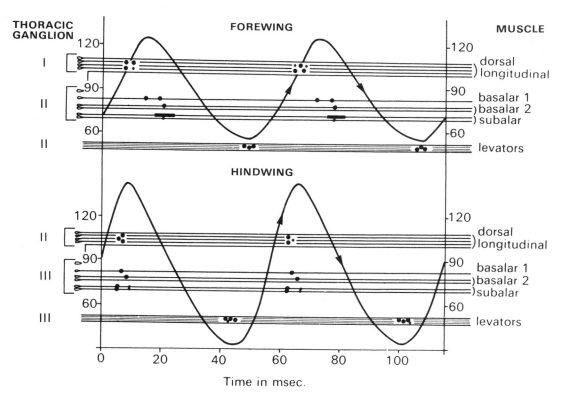

Fig. 129. Diagram illustrating the timing of firing of motor neurons to the flight muscles of fore and hind wings in relation to the wingbeat cycle. Each neuron is shown by a horizontal line with its origin in the appropriate ganglion on the left-hand side. Each dot on a line represents a nerve impulse occurring at that time; a small dot indicates that an impulse may or may not occur, a large dot that it always occurs. The heavy bar on the motor neuron to the forewing subalar muscle indicates that firing occurs within this period, but not at a precisely fixed time as with the other units. The heavy curve and the numbers along the ordinate indicate the angular displacement of the wings in degrees; 90° indicates wing horizontal, above 90° wings up, below 90° wings down (after Wilson and Weis-Fogh, 1962).

The problem of control of the wingbeat is different in insects in which the wingbeat is myogenic. Here also the muscles must act in a precise sequence, but this sequence is not directly related to nervous input and the timing of firing of the motor neurons does not coincide with a particular phase of the wingbeat cycle. The nervous input to the flight muscles serves only as a general stimulator maintaining the muscle contractions. Control of the movements is exerted by the muscles which control the mechanical properties of the thorax; an increase in the lateral stiffness of the thorax produces an increased wingbeat frequency, while a decrease in stiffness leads to a reduced frequency. These changes only take effect over a number of cycles of wing movement; there is no stroke by stroke control and such precise control is unnecessary because the insect only travels a very short distance in the course of a single wingbeat (Wilson and Wyman, 1963).

11.4 Stability in flight

Because of the variations in the forces acting on an insect during flight it has a tendency to deviate from a steady path. This instability may involve rotation about any of the three major axes passing through the centre of gravity of the body (Fig. 130). Rotation

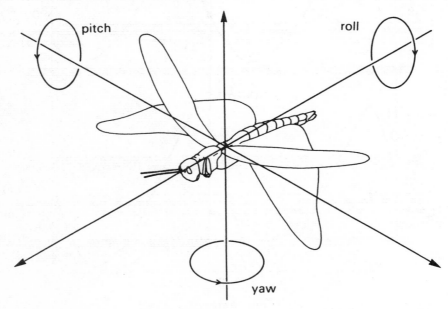

Fig. 130. Diagram showing the main axes about which an insect may rotate due to its instability in flight (after Weis-Fogh, 1956).

about the long axis of the body is called rolling, rotation about the horizontal, transverse axis is pitching, and rotation about the vertical axis is yawing. Deviations from a steady path are perceived by various sensilla and the nervous input from these exerts a controlling influence on the wingbeat cycle so that the deviation is corrected and the steady path maintained. The sensilla at the base of the wings and in the halteres of Diptera are of particular importance in this control and they are considered separately.

Rolling

Vision plays an important part in the control of rolling. Odonata and Orthoptera, and probably also other insects, have a dorsal light reaction by which they align the head so that the dorsal ommatidia receive maximal illumination. To produce a dorsal light reaction a number of ommatidia must be illuminated, but the response does not depend on stimulation of a particular part of the eye since it is still apparent if the most dorsal ommatidia, which are normally concerned in the response, are covered. The response is improved by stimulation of the ocelli, although they do not play a direct role in orientation (see p. 570) (Goodman, 1965).

Since normally most light comes from the sun or the sky overhead the dorsal light reaction ensures that the head is usually held in a vertical position. In Odonata, where the head is loosely articulated to the thorax, it also tends to keep in a vertical plane due to its own inertia, but this is not the case in the locust where the head and thorax are broadly attached so that rolling by the thorax is immediately transmitted to the head. As a result, a locust flying in complete darkness is unable to orientate in this plane and will fly upside down or at any other angle (Fig. 131).

The dorsal light reaction gives stability to the head, and the rest of the body is aligned with the head. Any deviation from this alignment is signalled by proprioceptors between

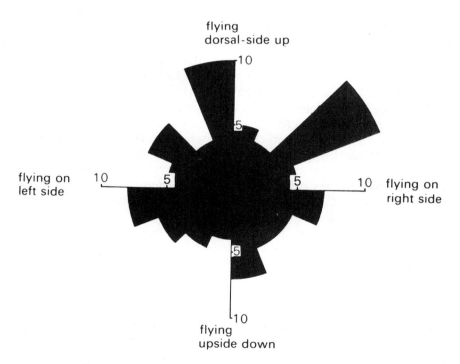

Fig. 131. Diagram showing the orientation of a locust in a series of observations made when it was flying in complete darkness. The figures indicate the percentage frequency with which orientation occurred in each sector (based on Goodman, 1965).

the head and the thorax. In *Schistocerca* there are hair beds on the cervical sclerite and hairs along the anterior border of the pronotum which are involved in this orientation (see p. 600). Unequal stimulation of the sensilla on the two sides due to a turning of the thorax relative to the head leads to differential twisting of the wings so that the thorax is brought back into alignment again.

If insects controlled rolling exclusively by a dorsal light reaction they would sometimes have a tendency to fly at unusual angles. This might occur, for instance, with the sun low in the sky just before sunset. That this does not occur indicates that other stimuli are also important. *Schistocerca* also orientates to the horizon, keeping this transversely across the eyes with the upper ommatidia more brightly illuminated than the lower ones. The orientation is accurate and the insect can follow a slow change of 5° so that it is able to perceive any tendency to roll. This and the dorsal light reaction give *Schistocerca* good control of rolling (Goodman, 1965).

Pitching and lift control

When flying steadily insects tend to keep the body at a more or less constant angle with the horizontal. In locusts this body angle is usually 6–7°. Any tendency to pitch is counteracted by changes in the twisting of the fore wing so that the forces which it exerts are modified, but even if locusts are subjected experimentally to changes of up to 15° in body angle they are able to keep the lift force more or less constant. This constancy is achieved by regulating the twist of the fore wing during the downstroke so that the amount of lift which it produces is altered. There is no regulation of the upstroke or of the hind wing in any phase. Thus an increase in body angle will increase the angle of attack of the hind wings on the downstroke so that they produce more lift, but this is compensated for by a reduction in the lift produced by the fore wings so that the total lift force remains constant. In addition the balance between the fore and hind wings is disturbed so that there is a tendency for the insect to pitch forwards and so to counteract the imposed change in body angle.

The twisting of the fore wing in this compensating reaction and in the control of pitch is regulated by the campaniform sensilla at the bases of the wings. To produce the reaction in the fore wings the sensilla of both pairs of wings are necessary and the change in twisting which they produce is not instantaneous, but occurs in the course of 100 to 150 wing strokes (Gettrup, 1966). There is no evidence for a comparable lift-control reaction in *Drosophila* (Vogel, 1966).

In Diptera the halteres are important in controlling pitching, but it is also probable that Johnston's organ in the antenna exerts some controlling influence over the wing movements.

Yawing

In the control of yaw vision probably plays a part together with the sensilla at the base of the wings or halteres. In addition, in *Schistocerca* the sensilla in the facial hair beds have some degree of directional sensitivity and there is some evidence that oblique stimulation of the hair beds, such as would occur in an insect tending to yaw, produces a modification of the wingstroke to correct for the deviation (see Fig. 405) (Haskell, 1960b).

Sensilla at the wing base

In the normal vibration of a wing a twisting-force, or torque, is produced in the cuticle at the wing base. If the wing was to move up and down in a vertical plane only vertical torque would be produced. Thus with the wing in the up position the cuticle at the base on the upper side would be compressed, while that on the ventral side is stretched, and *vice versa* with the wing in the down position; all the forces would be acting parallel with the long axis of the wing. But because of the complexity of the wing movement this torque will differ in strength and direction in different parts of the wing stroke (Fig. 132). The torque is perceived by the sensilla, and particularly the campaniform sensilla, of the wing base. These sensilla are arranged in groups, all those within a group having a similar orientation (see Figs. 112 and 113), so that each group will respond maximally to torque in a particular direction and, if the sensitivity of the sensilla is appropriately adjusted, they may respond only once during a wing cycle. It is possible that any tendency for the insect to deviate from a stable orientation would result in differential changes in the stimulation of these sensilla which could thus exert a controlling influence on the wingbeat to correct for the deviation. This is certainly the case in the control of lift and pitching in *Schistocerca*, but the situation is best understood in the halteres of Diptera which are specialised organs of stability.

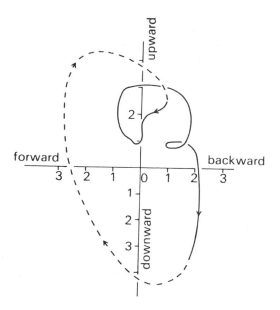

Fig. 132. Graph of the magnitude, in g.cm., and the direction of the torque in the basal veins of the forewing of *Schistocerca* during one stroke. Solid line indicates downstroke, broken line upstroke (based on Jensen, 1956).

Halteres

The halteres vibrate with the same frequency as the fore wings, but in antiphase. Their movement is less complex than that of the wings because of their structure and the nature of their articulation with the thorax. The centre of gravity of the haltere lies in the end knob (see Fig. 113) so that when the haltere vibrates it swings forwards until the long axis passing through the hinge and the centre of gravity is at right angles to the long axis of the body. As a result, the haltere vibrates in a vertical or near vertical plane without making the complex fore and aft movements of the wing. Hence the forces acting at the base of the haltere and stimulating the campaniform sensilla are limited to a vertical plane when the haltere is oscillating with the insect in steady flight, and dorsal and ventral torques oscillate with the same frequency as the vibration of the halteres (Fig. 133B). These torques are perceived by the dorsal and ventral scapal plates which are believed to maintain a constant amplitude of oscillation of the haltere.

The path of the end knob during vibration represents an arc of a circle about the long axis of the insect and the haltere may thus be regarded as a gyroscope whose axis of rotation corresponds with the long axis of the insect. As in a gyroscope the halteres possess inertia, tending to maintain a fixed orientation in space so that if the insect rotates about any of its axes torques will be produced at right angles to the stroke plane. In yawing the haltere on the outer side of the rotation will tend to swing back relative to the insect, while that on the inside will swing forwards (Fig. 134). The campaniform sensilla respond to compression forces along their long axes and bending the haltere forwards will compress the campaniform sensilla of the basal plate, while bending backwards will extend and stimulate the chordotonal organ. A single haltere can distinguish the direction and rate of yawing by the relative timing of the impulses from these two sets of sensilla, while there may, in addition, be central summation of the input from the halteres of the two sides. Stimulation of the halteres by yawing leads to a reflex modification of the twisting of the fore wings on the downstroke so that the deviation is corrected and the insect maintains a steady path.

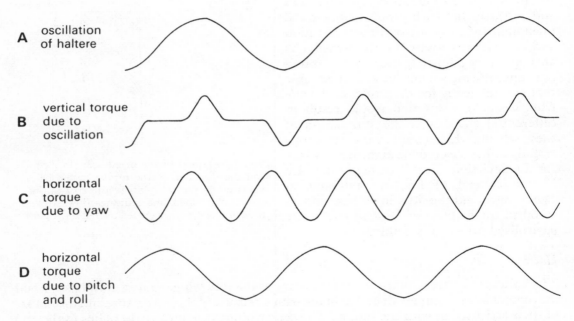

Fig. 133. Diagrams showing oscillation of the torques occurring at the base of a haltere as a result of vibration of the haltere and turning movements of the insect (after Pringle, 1948).

Rolling and pitching also produce torque at the bases of the halteres at right angles to the stroke plane, but the torques are differentiated from yaw by the timing and frequency of their oscillation. Yawing produces a torque which oscillates at twice the frequency of vibration of the halteres (Fig. 133C), pitching and rolling produce torques which oscillate with the same frequency as the halteres (Fig. 133D). Although the torques generated by pitching and rolling are identical the two movements are differentiated by the fact that in pitching the torques produced by the two halteres are in phase, while in rolling they are in antiphase. Summation in the thoracic ganglion would enable the insect to distinguish instability in these two planes and to adjust the wing twisting to correct for the instability. This adjustment of the wings does occur and the halteres are important in controlling stability in all planes (Pringle, 1948, 1957).

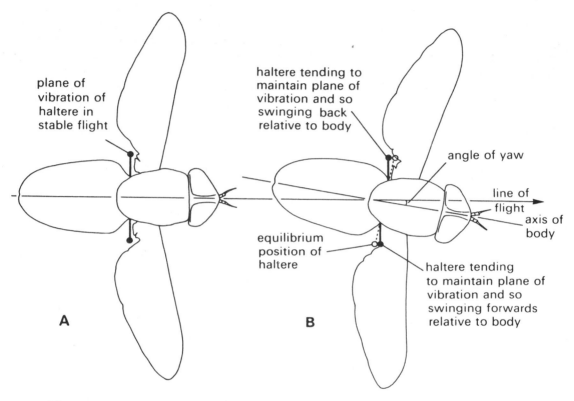

plane of vibration of haltere in stable flight

haltere tending to maintain plane of vibration and so swinging back relative to body

angle of yaw

line of flight

axis of body

equilibrium position of haltere

haltere tending to maintain plane of vibration and so swinging forwards relative to body

A

B

Fig. 134. Diagrams to illustrate the action of the halteres. A. In stable flight the halteres swing outwards and vibrate in a plane with their long axes at right angles to the long axis of the body. B. If the insect makes a yawing movement the halteres have a tendency to continue vibrating in their original plane and a horizontal torque is created at the base of the haltere. If the yaw is not corrected the halteres rapidly assume the equilibrium position.

Control of flight speed

Flight speed relative to the ground may be controlled by an optomotor reaction with a tendency to keep images moving over the eye from front to back at a certain speed (see p. 565), while in *Apis* and *Calliphora*, at least, airspeed is also controlled by the antennae. The antennae are held forwards against the airflow, their static position probably being perceived by sensory hairs at the base of the flagellum. Oscillations of the flagellum due to the wing movements are perceived by Johnston's organ (p. 605). The position of the antennae and the oscillations of the flagellum control the amplitude of wingbeat and in this way influence thrust and flight speed (see Schwartzkopff, 1964).

11.5 Landing

During flight the legs of an insect are held close to the body (p. 197), but before it lands it is obvious that the legs must be extended so that the insect lands on its feet. In *Lucilia* extension of the legs results from visual stimuli mediated via the compound eyes. Particularly important in producing leg extension is a marked contrast in the stimulation of adjacent ommatidia and a rapid change in the illumination of successive ommatidia. Such changes might occur as the insect approaches a surface since the angular movement will increase as it gets closer and details with contrasting shadows will become more apparent. In addition, to produce the leg movements a relatively large number of ommatidia must be stimulated and hence the insect will not continually respond to small features of the environment which are visible in normal flight (Goodman, 1960).

CHAPTER XII

THE MUSCLES

Since much of the work on insect muscles has been concerned with flight muscles it is convenient to consider muscles in general in this section. All the muscles of insects are built on a similar plan with elongate cells housing the contractile elements and, in many cases, inserted into the integument at either end. The internal arrangement of the muscle cells, however, varies in different muscles and is particularly characteristic in muscles moving the wings. Shortening of the muscles involves the filaments of which they are composed sliding between each other, but there may also be some shortening of the individual filaments. The muscles are stimulated to contract by the arrival of nerve impulses which cause local changes in the electrical properties of the muscle membrane and induce chemical changes within the cell. Usually one nerve impulse causes one contraction, but in specialised muscles which can oscillate at high frequency the muscles may contract several times as a result of a single nervous stimulus. The speed with which they oscillate in these cases depends on the mechanical properties of the muscles and the structures to which they are attached. The output of power by flight muscles may be very high and the associated metabolic rate higher than in any other tissue. To maintain such a high level of metabolism the supply of oxygen and of fuel must be adequate and insects are adapted anatomically, physiologically and biochemically to ensure that this is the case.

The fine structure of insect muscles has been studied in particular by Smith (see Smith, 1966, for references). Structure and functioning of flight muscles is reviewed by Pringle (1957, 1965) and Boettiger (1960), and biochemical aspects are covered by Maruyama (1965) and Sacktor (1961, 1965). Hoyle (1965a) considers the neural mechanisms concerned in the control of insect muscles and see also Aidley (1967, *Adv. Insect Physiol.* **4**) and Usherwood (1969, *Adv. Insect Physiol.* **6**). For a discussion of the physical and chemical bases of muscular contraction see Huxley *et. al.* (1964).

12.1 Structure

12.11 Basic muscle structure

Each muscle is made up of a number of fibres which are long, usually multinucleate, cells running the whole length of the muscle. Each fibre is bounded by the sarcolemma which comprises the plasma membrane of the cell plus the basement membrane (Smith, 1961). The cytoplasm of the fibre is called sarcoplasm and the endoplasmic reticulum, which is not connected to the plasma membrane, is known as the sarcoplasmic reticulum. The plasma membrane is deeply invaginated into the fibre, often as regular radial canals between the Z and the H bands (see below), and this sytem of invaginations is called the transverse tubular, or T, system. It is associated with vesicles of the sarcoplasmic reticulum (Fig. 135). The nuclei may occupy various positions in the cell.

The characteristic feature of muscle cells is the presence of myofibrils (fibrils) embedded in the sarcoplasm and extending continuously from one end of the fibre to the other. The arrangement of the fibrils varies, but they are always in close contact with the mitochondria, which are sometimes known as sarcosomes.

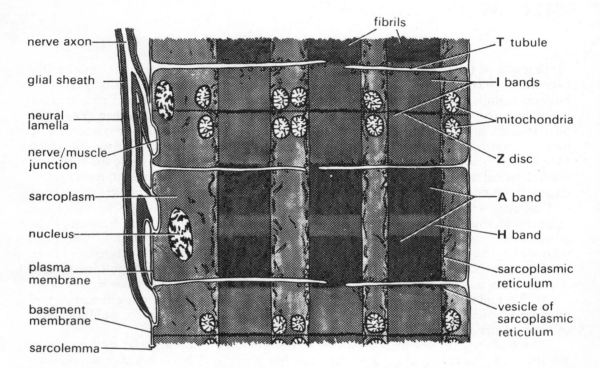

Fig. 135. Diagram of a lateral view of part of a muscle fibre showing the arrangement of the major constituents.

The fibrils in their turn are composed of molecular filaments consisting mainly of two proteins: myosin and actin (see Fig. 140). The myosin filaments are stouter and are made up of numerous myosin molecules. These are elongate structures with a globular 'head' at one end, and in each sarcomere (see below and Fig. 140) all the molecules in one half are aligned in one direction, while all those in the opposite half are aligned in the opposite direction (Fig. 136). Myosin by itself has never been extracted from the thick filaments of insect muscles, but is always accompanied by some actomyosin, suggesting that this protein is also normally present. The thick filaments are each surrounded by six thin, actin filaments (Fig. 137A) which consist of two chains of actin molecules twisted round each other. The actin filaments are orientated in opposite directions on the two sides of a Z disc (Fig. 136) where they are cemented together by an amorphous material (Ashhurst, 1967, *J. Mol. Biol.* **27**).

The actin and myosin filaments are linked at intervals by cross-bridges formed from the 'head' ends of the myosin molecules. These cross-bridges are responsible for structural and mechanical continuity along the whole length of the muscle fibre (Huxley, 1965). A further protein, tropomyosin, is also present in the contractile elements in small quantities.

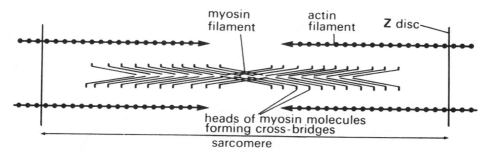

Fig. 136. Diagrammatic representation of the orientations of the actin and myosin molecules and filaments in a muscle (after Huxley, 1965).

All the filaments in a fibre tend to be aligned so that the whole fibre appears to be transversely striated. Essential features of these striations are the Z discs which run across the fibre at regular intervals cutting off a series of units called sarcomeres. On either side of the Z discs actin filaments extend towards, but do not reach the centre of the sarcomere, while the myosin filaments do not reach the Z discs. Hence each sarcomere has a lightly staining band at each end and a darkly staining band in the middle, known respectively as the isotropic, I, and anisotropic, A bands. In the centre of the A band, where actin filaments are absent, is the rather paler H zone. Other bands may also be present and changes occur when the muscle contracts (see Figs. 135, 140).

The muscle fibres are collected into units of 10–20 fibres separated from neighbouring units by a tracheolated membrane. Each muscle consists of one or a few such units and, for instance, there are five in the dorsal longitudinal flight muscles of *Schistocerca*. Each muscle unit may have its own nerve supply, independent of all the others, and in this case it is the basic contracting unit of the muscle, but in other cases several muscle units may have a common innervation so that they function together as the motor unit.

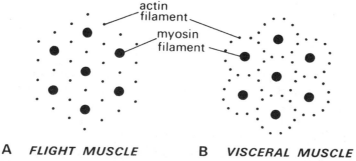

A   *FLIGHT MUSCLE*   B   *VISCERAL MUSCLE*

Fig. 137. Diagrams showing the arrangement of the muscle filaments in (A) flight mucle and (B) visceral muscle (after Smith *et al.*, 1966).

Innervation

The nervous supply to a muscle consists of a small number of large axons. Basically each unit is innervated by a fast axon and a slow axon (see p. 216) and sometimes also by an inhibitory axon (p. 539). Such multiple innervation is called polyneuronal. Within the unit each muscle fibre receives endings from the fast axon, and some may also be innervated by the slow axon (Fig. 138). In the jumping muscle of the locust about 40% of the fibres receive branches from both axons, but in the flight muscles of Odonata, Orthoptera, Diptera and Hymenoptera only fast axons are present. Sometimes different

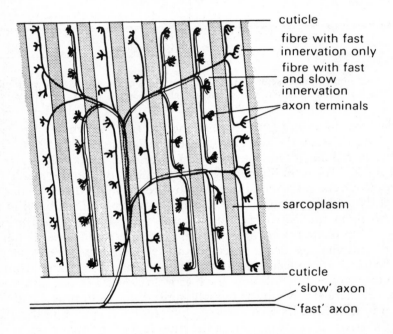

cuticle

fibre with fast innervation only

fibre with fast and slow innervation

axon terminals

sarcoplasm

cuticle

'slow' axon

'fast' axon

Fig. 138. Diagram illustrating the innervation of a typical muscle unit. All the fibres receive branches of the fast axon, while some also have endings from the slow axon (from Hoyle, 1965a).

parts of a muscle serve different functions and in this case the two parts have separate nerve supplies. Thus the posterior part of the basalar muscle of *Oryctes* is concerned only with wing depression and has only a fast innervation, but the anterior part also controls wing twisting and its innervation is complex, consisting of up to four axons, one of which is inhibiting (Ikeda and Boettiger, 1965).

Characteristically in insects there are many nerve endings spaced at intervals of 30–80 μ along each fibre (Fig. 138). Where a fibre has a double innervation it is probable that both axons have endings in the same terminals (see Fig. 351).

Oxygen supply

Since muscular contraction requires metabolic energy the muscles have a good tracheal supply and this is particularly true of the flight muscles where often the respiratory system is specialised to maintain the supply of oxygen to the muscles during flight (see p. 454). In most muscles the tracheoles are in close contact with the outside of the muscle fibre, but in the flight muscles of many insects they indent the muscle membrane so that they become functionally, but not anatomically, intracellular within the muscle fibre.

Muscle insertion

Skeletal muscles are fixed at either end to the integument, spanning a joint in the skeleton so that contraction of the muscle moves one part of the skeleton relative to the other. Typically such muscles are said to have an origin in a fixed or more proximal part of the skeleton, and an insertion into a distal, movable part, but these terms become purely relative in the case of muscles with a dual function (see p. 186) (D. Wilson, 1962).

At the point of attachment of the muscle fibre to the epidermis, the plasma membranes interdigitate and are held together by desmosomes. Within the epidermal cell, microtubules run from the desmosomes to hemidesmosomes on the outer plasma membrane, and from each hemidesmosome a dense attachment fibre passes to the epicuticle through a pore canal. In earlier studies the microtubules and attachment fibres were not separated and were called tonofibrillae. Only actin filaments reach the terminal plasma membrane of the muscle fibre, inserting into the dense material of desmosomes or hemidesmosomes (Caveney, 1969, *J. Cell Sci.* **4**).

The muscle attachment fibres are not digested by moulting fluid so that during moulting they retain their attachment to the old cuticle across the exuvial space between the new and old cuticles. As a result, the insect is able to continue its activities after apolysis during the development of the new cuticle. Finally, at about the time of ecdysis, the connections to the old cuticle are broken (see also Lai-Fook, 1967).

Muscle attachment fibres which extend to the epicuticle can only be produced at a moult and most muscles appear to form their attachments at this time. Muscle attachment can occur later on, however, if cuticle production continues in the post-ecdysial period, but in this case the attachment fibres are only connected to the newly formed procuticle and do not reach the epicuticle (see Hinton, 1963b).

12.12 Variations in structure

The structure of muscles varies in different part of the body and in different insects. Some of the more significant of these variations will now be described.

Tubular muscles

The leg and trunk muscles of many insects have a tubular appearance due to the myofibrils being arranged radially round a central core of sarcoplasm containing the nuclei. The mitochondria, which are adjacent to the fibrils, may be on either side of the Z discs or irregularly scattered. Each fibre is 10–30 μ in diameter with extensive I bands constituting up to 50% of the sarcomere length.

The flight muscles of Odonata and Dictyoptera are also of this type (Fig. 139A), but between the fibrils are large, slab-like mitochondria which occupy some 40% of the volume of the fibres. Very large mitochondria are a feature of all insect flight muscles, their size being correlated with the very high metabolic rate of the muscles (p. 223). T-tubules run in regular pairs along the sides of the fibrils between the Z discs and the H band, while the sarcoplasmic reticulum forms a perforated sheet covering the fibrils (Smith, 1966). The I bands constitute about 30% of the sarcomere length.

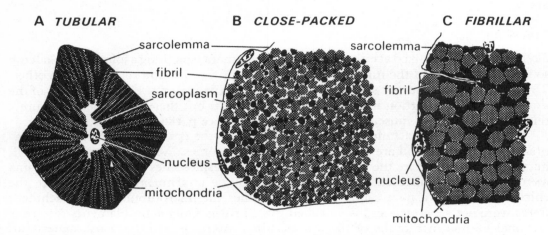

Fig. 139. Transverse sections of flight muscle fibres, all to approximately the same scale. A. Tubular muscle of *Enallagma* (Odonata) (after Smith, 1965). B. Part of a close-packed fibre of *Locusta* (based on Bücher, 1965). C. Part of a fibrillar fibre of *Tenebrio* (based on Smith, 1961).

Close-packed muscles

In the muscles of some larval insects, in Apterygota, and in the legs of some adult winged insects the myofibrils form a mass occupying the centre of the fibre with the nuclei in the peripheral cytoplasm. A similar arrangement, but with the peripheral cytoplasm greatly reduced, occurs in the flight muscles of Lepidoptera and Orthoptera and is described as close-packed. The fibres in these muscles are larger than those in tubular muscles, reaching 100 μ in diameter, but the fibrils are still only one micron or less in diameter. Mitochondria are large, occupying much of the space between the fibrils (Fig. 139B). Unlike the flight muscles of Odonata, in which the tracheoles are restricted to the periphery of the fibres, in close-packed muscles tracheoles push into the fibre, indenting the muscle plasma membrane.

Fibrillar muscles

The flight muscles of Hymenoptera, Coleoptera, Diptera, Homoptera and Heteroptera are characterised by the large size of the fibrils, up to 5 μ in diameter, with a corresponding increase in the diameters of the fibres which range from 30 μ in carabid beetles to 1·8 mm. in *Rutilia* (Diptera). The fibrils, with nuclei scattered between them, are distributed through the entire cross-section of the fibre (Fig. 139C).

The sarcolemma is weakly developed. It is invaginated in a T-system as in other muscles and in *Polistes* (Hymenoptera) the T-tubules are aligned with the H band, but in the fibrillar muscles of *Tenebrio* (Coleoptera) and *Megoura* (Homoptera) the system is more complex and less regular. In these insects invaginations of the plasma membrane are produced by indenting tracheoles and from these invaginations fine tubules of plasma membrane extend in to entwine each fibril. Associated with the T-system are vesicles of the sarcoplasmic reticulum, but this differs markedly in its development from the sarcoplasmic reticulum of other muscles, since it consists only of a number of unconnected vesicles scattered without reference to the sarcomere pattern.

Mitochondria are large, as in all flight muscles, and almost the whole surface of each myofibril may be in direct contact with mitochondria. These may be regularly arranged, as between the Z and H bands in *Polistes,* or without any regular arrangement, as in *Calliphora.* The mitochondria increase in size and number over the first few days of adult life and in *Drosophila*, at least, this is paralleled by an increase in wingbeat frequency (see Figs. 120, 152). Subsequently as flight activity declines so does the size of the mitochondria (Rockstein and Bhatnagar, 1965). The high concentrations of cytochromes found in these large mitochondria give these muscles a pink or yellow colour which contrasts with the white of other muscles.

Fibrillar muscles may contain only a few fibres because these are so big. Thus the dorsal longitudinal flight muscles of Muscidae consist of only six fibres. Further, sarcomere length is short, only one or two microns in *Tenebrio,* and the I band makes up less than 10% of this. In some cases the myosin filaments taper towards the Z disc so that there is no distinct I band.

Visceral muscles

Apart from the large number of skeletal muscles attached to the cuticle at either end, the body also contains numerous visceral muscles which produce movements of internal organs such as the heart, the alimentary canal and the reproductive ducts. Often their activity is irregular or slow and rhythmic, contrasting with the more rapid, precise movements of skeletal muscle.

Visceral muscles differ in structure from skeletal muscles in several respects. Adjacent fibres are held together by desmosomes, which are absent from skeletal muscle, and in some cases the fibres may branch and anastomose. Further, each fibre is uninucleate and the contractile material is not grouped into fibrils, but packs the whole of the fibre. As in other muscles it consists of thick and thin filaments, presumably representing myosin and actin, but the filament array is different in having a ring of twelve actin filaments round each myosin filament (Fig. 137B). A T-system is present with a regular arrangement in *Periplaneta,* but it is irregularly disposed in *Carausius* and *Ephestia* (Lepidoptera).

The muscles appear striated due to the alignment of the filaments and thus they resemble skeletal muscle, but contrast with the visceral muscle of vertebrates which is not striated. The Z and H bands are irregular, and sarcomere length is about seven or eight microns, some two or three times the length of flight muscle sarcomeres (Smith *et al.,* 1966).

Visceral muscles may be innervated from the autonomic nervous system or from the ganglia of the ventral nerve cord, but sometimes are without any innervation. This is the case, for instance, in the heart of *Anopheles* (Diptera) larvae.

12.2 Physiology

12.21 Excitation of the muscle

With the exception of some visceral muscles, muscles are stimulated to contract by the arrival of a nerve impulse at the nerve/muscle junctions. Transmission across the synaptic gap between the nerve and muscle membranes involves a chemical, but probably not acetylcholine which is concerned in typical synaptic transmission (see p. 534).

As with the nerve, there is a difference in potential across the muscle membrane so that it has a resting potential of about 60 mV., the inside being negative with respect to the outside. The arrival of a nerve impulse causes a change in the permeability of the muscle membrane so that there is an influx of sodium ions and a rise in potential. Subsequently an increase in the permeability to potassium ions leads to their movement out from the muscle so that the potential falls to its original level (see p. 530). The short-lived increase in potential produced by these changes is called the post-synaptic potential and it is suggested that changes in the relative permeability to sodium and potassium determine its size (see Hoyle, 1965a). The post-synaptic potential spreads from the synapse, but decreases rapidly so that its effect is localised and in order to stimulate the whole fibre a large number of nerve endings are necessary.

It is probable that the invaginations of the T-system are important in conveying the changes in potential deep into the muscle and close to the fibrils. This is important since it is believed that activation of the fibrils involves chemical transmission within the fibres and the diffusion of a chemical from the surface membrane to the central fibrils would involve a considerable delay in contraction. The T-system greatly reduces this delay by bringing the plasma membrane to within a few microns of each fibril.

12.22 Activation of the muscle fibre

The mechanism by which the myofibrils are activated so that they contract is not understood, but it involves the release of calcium ions within the muscle fibre. Smith (1965a) suggests that the calcium is released from the vesicles of the sarcoplasmic reticulum associated with the T-system and that it stimulates the activity of an ATPase. Alternatively, the calcium may act more indirectly on a relaxing factor which in turn affects the ATPase (Gilmour, 1965). In *Calliphora* ATPase activity is localised in the myosin filaments, probably in the cross-bridges, and it is also sometimes found in the mitochondria, but not if calcium ions are present (Tice and Smith, 1965; and see also Huxley, 1965). The effect of the ATPase is to break down ATP to ADP with the release of energy which is used in muscle contraction. It is believed that the actin and myosin filaments first become linked together by the cross-bridges and that movement of these links with subsequent breaking and recombination causes the actin filaments to slide further between the myosin filaments so that the sarcomere, and hence the muscle, shortens (see Huxley and Hanson, 1960, and Huxley *et al.*, 1964, for discussion of the possible mechanisms of movement). As a result of the sliding of the filaments the I bands shorten and may disappear as the myosin filaments approach the Z discs (Fig. 140). Extreme contractions may cause crumpling of the myosin filaments at the Z disc so that a dark band, C_z, is formed. Thus the length of the I band in relaxed muscle is roughly proportional to the degree of shortening which the sarcomere can undergo and body muscles may shorten by as much as 50% of their length, while flight muscles may shorten by as little as 1%.

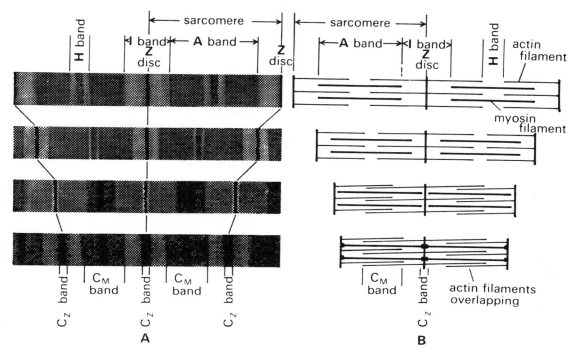

Fig. 140. A. The appearance of a muscle fibre in various states of contraction. B. Diagrams showing the presumed arrangement of the muscle filaments in positions corresponding to (A). This diagram does not take into account the possibility that shortening of the filaments may also occur (see text) (after Smith, 1965).

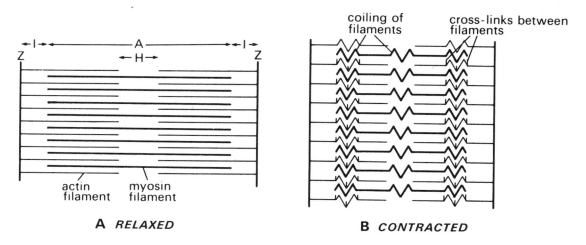

Fig. 141. Diagrams illustrating the manner in which muscle shortening could arise by the coiling of the myosin filaments. A. One sarcomere relaxed. B. Sarcomere contracted (after Gilmour and Robinson, 1964).

At the same time as the I band is obliterated by the myosin filaments the H band disappears as the ends of the actin filaments approach each other (Fig. 140). Ultimately the actin filaments from the two ends of a sarcomere may come to overlap each other so that another dark band, C_m, forms.

Muscle shortening in insects may also involve other mechanisms than the sliding of filaments since some shortening of the A band is also observed. This suggests that the thicker, myosin, filaments themselves shorten, perhaps by coiling, and this is in keeping with the presence of actomyosin in these filaments. Actomyosin is known to shorten in the presence of ATP *in vitro*. Gilmour and Robinson (1964) suggest that in relaxed muscle the filaments are free to slide between each other (Fig. 141A), but when the muscle is activated they become linked together by the cross-bridges. Thus as the thick filaments shorten they also shorten the actin filaments and hence the sarcomere and the muscle (Fig. 141B). Coiling of the thick filaments may occur preferentially at the ends and possibly also in the middle and in this way the characteristic banding of contracted muscle may arise.

Relaxation of the muscle possibly involves the sequestration of calcium ions so that ATPase activity is suppressed.

12.23 Fast and slow axons

The size of the twitch produced by the arrival of a nerve impulse varies, depending on whether stimulation occurs via the fast or slow axons. It must be understood that the terms 'fast' and 'slow' do not refer to the speed of conduction of the impulse, but to the type of post-synaptic potential, and hence muscle twitch, which is produced. Stimulation via the fast axon produces a post-synaptic potential of constant size and a brief, powerful contraction of the muscle (Fig. 142A). Contractions tend to fuse if the rate of stimulation exceeds 10/second and with 20–25 stimuli/second the muscle undergoes a smooth, maintained contraction; it is in a state of tetanus.

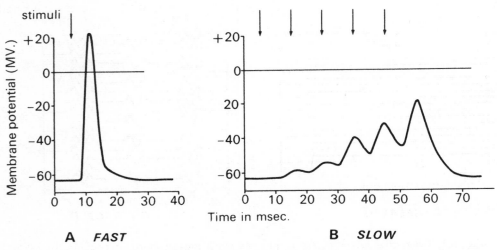

Fig. 142. Electrical changes at the muscle membrane following stimulation by (A) fast and (B) slow axons (after Hoyle, 1965).

A single impulse from the slow axon, on the other hand, produces only a small post-synaptic potential and a very small twitch, but with successive stimuli the potential and the strength of the contraction increase due to summation or facilitation (Fig. 142B). The response is thus said to be graded and this is important in the production of slow and precise movements. In vertebrates such movements are brought about by using different numbers of muscle units, but in insects, where the number of units per muscle is small, the variation in response is very limited and the gradation of response by individual units becomes significant. The velocity and force with which a muscle contracts increases with the frequency of stimulation and in the extensor tibiae muscles of the locust stimulation below five per second produces no response in the muscle, 15–20 stimuli per second produce muscle tonus, and stimulation by over 70 stimuli/second produces rapid extension of the tibia. The speed of response increases up to a stimulus frequency of 150/second.

In many cases the fast axon reinforces the slow axon when this is firing at high frequency, but in some cases the two axons function quite independently of each other. Thus stimulation of the extensor tibiae muscle of the hind leg of a locust via the fast axon produces a jump or a kick; all other movements are controlled via the slow axon alone. When only a fast axon is present some grading of the strength of contractions is produced by impulses following each other in rapid succession. This occurs, for instance,

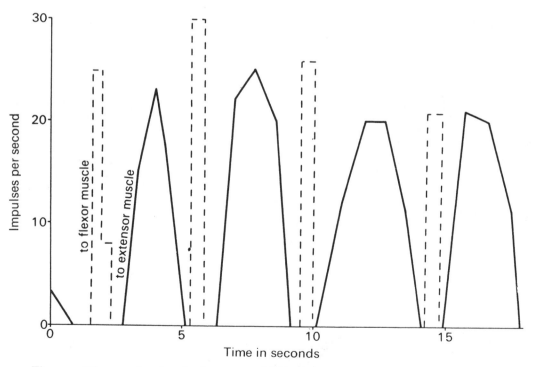

Fig. 143. Diagram showing the frequency of firing from the slow axons to the extensor and flexor tibiae muscles of the hind leg of *Schistocerca* during slow walking. There is complete reciprocal inhibition of the two muscles (after Hoyle, 1964).

in the double firing of the axon to the second basalar muscle of *Schistocerca* (p. 198)
which may result in the muscle more than doubling the amount of work which it does.
The extra force exerted varies with the timing of the second impulse relative to the
first and in the basalar muscle at 40°C. is maximal when the second stimulus follows
about 8 msec. after the first (Neville and Weis-Fogh, 1963).

12.24 Oscillation of antagonistic pairs of muscles

Skeletal muscles usually occur in antagonistic pairs, as, for instance, the extensor and
flexor muscles of the tibia. In slow movements these muscles are mutually inhibited by a
central control so that as one contracts the other relaxes and *vice versa* (Fig. 143), but in
faster movements one muscle is maintained in a continual state of mild contraction,
while the other alternately contracts and relaxes so that the appendage is moved (Fig.
144). In this case either the flexor or the extensor may act as the driver (Hoyle, 1964).

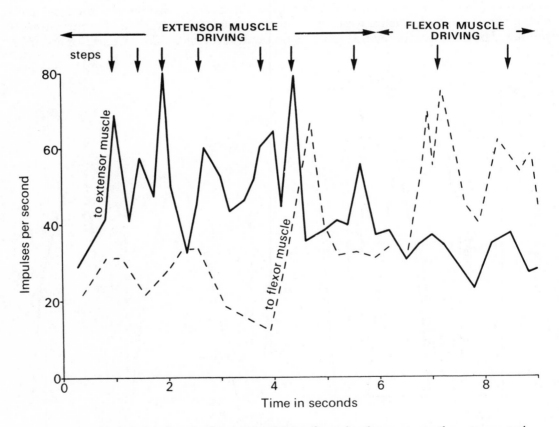

Fig. 144. Graph showing the frequency of firing from the slow axons to the extensor and
flexor tibiae muscles of the hind leg of *Schistocerca* during fairly rapid walking. There is a
continuous discharge to both muscles with first the extensor and then the flexor acting as
the driver (after Hoyle, 1964).

This mechanism increases the speed at which repeated movements can occur since the continually contracting antagonist helps to restore the position of the limb rapidly on relaxation of the driver. Further, the driver itself does not relax fully in these circumstances so that a shorter time is needed for it to develop the necessary force on contraction than would be the case if it was fully relaxed (Hoyle, 1965a).

Sometimes a muscle is opposed only by the elasticity of the cuticle. Thus depression of the pretarsus is produced by a muscle, but extension results entirely from the elasticity of the cuticle at the base of the segment.

12.25 Oscillation of flight muscles

The high wingbeat frequencies necessary for flight are produced by the rapid oscillation of pairs of antagonistic muscles (see Fig. 116) and this is achieved despite the relatively low rate of shortening of about 40 mm./sec. in *Schistocerca* and only 11 mm./sec. in *Sarcophaga*. Three factors combine to reduce the duration of the muscle twitch and so to make flight possible; these are the loading of the muscle, the temperature of the muscle and the very slight contraction necessary to move the wing.

A maximum rate of shortening is achieved if the tension and loading of the muscle are maximal at the beginning of its stroke. Loading of the flight muscles involves the inertia of the wings, elastic loading due to the straining of the thorax (p. 187), the mechanical leverage of the wings which changes in the course of a stroke, damping of the movement

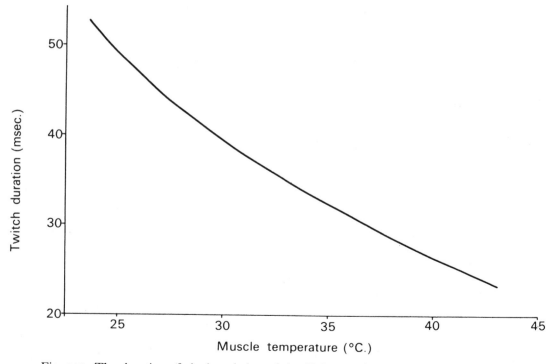

Fig. 145. The duration of single twitches of the flight muscle of *Schistocerca* at different temperatures (after Neville and Weis-Fogh, 1963).

of the wings by the air, and elastic loading due to the stretching of the antagonistic muscle. The first three of these factors are high during the first part of the stroke so that conditions favour a high rate of muscle contraction.

The duration of each muscle twitch is also influenced by temperature (Fig. 145). In *Schistocerca* contraction and relaxation of the metathoracic dorsal longitudinal muscle takes 59 msec. at 22°C. A cycle of movement of the wings takes about the same time so that in flying at this temperature about 50% of the work done by this muscle would be wasted due to interaction with the antagonistic muscle. It is therefore not surprising that sustained flight does not occur at such a temperature. Sustained flight is only observed above 24°C., at which temperature the duration of the muscle twitch is about 49 msec. and still some 25% of the output of work is wasted. Double firing, which increases the force exerted by the muscle, lengthens the duration of the twitch and, outside the range 30–35°C., much of the force is wasted in opposing the antagonist. It follows from these considerations that twitch duration is only short enough for efficient flight to occur within a limited range of temperature (Neville and Weis-Fogh, 1963) (and see p. 229).

Finally, the flight muscles are inserted in such a way (see Figs. 115, 116) that only a very small contraction is necessary to produce a large movement of the wing, and the flight muscles of *Sarcophaga*, for instance, only shorten by 1 or 2% in the course of a wingstroke. Because of this the muscle twitch is brief despite the low rate of shortening.

Synchronous muscles

Each contraction of the flight muscles of Odonata, Orthoptera and Lepidoptera is produced by the arrival of a nerve impulse (Fig. 146A) and the muscles are described as synchronous. Most insect skeletal muscles are of this type. Usually the wingbeat frequency of insects with synchronous flight muscles is low, not more than about 25 beats/second, but in some instances it is much higher, reaching 100 cycles/sec. in *Hemaris*, the bee hawk moth.

Asynchronous muscles

In insects which possess fibrillar muscles the wingbeat frequency is often in excess of 100 cycles/sec. and it is a characteristic of these muscles that several contractions follow the arrival of each nerve impulse. The tymbal muscle of *Platypleura* (Homoptera) is also a fibrillar muscle and in this case four contractions follow one nerve impulse (Fig. 146B), while the frequency of contraction of the flight muscle of *Oryctes* is independent of the frequency of stimulation, which only affects the amplitude of the contraction. These muscles in which the ratio of contractions to stimuli differs from the normal 1 : 1 ratio are said to be asynchronous.

Asynchronous muscles can contract and relax at very high frequencies, but high frequency stimulation causes them to contract tetanically. A nerve impulse is necessary to initiate contractions, but subsequent contractions are products of the muscles themselves and are said to be myogenic. Further nervous stimulation is necessary only to maintain the level of activity of the muscles, perhaps through the release of calcium from the vesicles of the reduced sarcoplasmic reticulum (Smith, 1965b; and see p. 214).

Myogenic contractions only occur in an oscillating system such as the thorax. Here the contraction of a flight muscle moves the wings and at the same time lengthens the antagonistic muscles. This lengthening will at first take place slowly, but will occur much more rapidly towards the end of the stroke if the wing movement involves a click mechanism (p. 188). At the same time the active muscle at first shortens slowly and then, following the click, very rapidly. These sudden changes in length will produce corresponding changes in tension in the muscle, a sudden increase in length produces a sudden increase in tension and *vice versa,* and it is an intrinsic property of the contractile proteins of fibrillar muscle that a sudden change in tension is followed, after a delay, by a further change (Fig. 147) (Jewell and Ruegg, 1966). Thus a sudden increase in tension due to stretching is followed by a further rise in tension, and a delayed fall follows a sudden drop in tension. Since the flight muscles are antagonists a decrease in tension in one corresponds to an increase in tension in the other. The increased tension acting on a pliant system will produce movement and as a result of this the muscles alternately contract and relax, the rate of oscillation being determined by the mechanical and elastic properties of the thorax and the muscles.

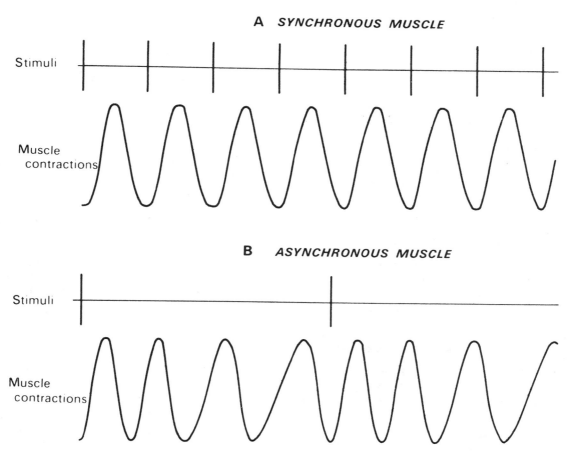

Fig. 146. Relationship between nervous stimulation and muscle contraction in (A) synchronous muscle and (B) asynchronous muscle, such as the tymbal muscle of *Platypleura*.

The precise relationship between muscle length and tension varies with the temperature, and the muscles of *Oryctes,* for instance, only produce maximum work at the resonant frequency of the system when they are at 40°C. Thus the thoracic temperature is of considerable importance in insects with asynchronous flight muscles and this accounts for the period of warming up by wing vibration, or fanning (p. 230), which commonly precedes flight.

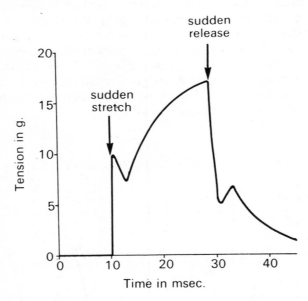

Fig. 147. The effect of sudden small changes of length on the tension developed by fibrillar muscle. Initial tension=0 (from Pringle, 1965).

12.26 Visceral muscles

The control of visceral muscles probably differs from that of normal skeletal muscles since their response to drugs is often rather different. In those cases, such as the heart of *Anopheles* larva, which have no innervation the rhythmic contractions are probably under neurosecretory control (see discussion in Davey, 1964 and p. 672).

12.3 Energetics of muscle contraction

The tension exerted by insect muscles is not exceptional. For instance, the mandibular muscles of various insects exert tensions of 3·6–6·9 Kg./sq.cm., and the extensor tibiae muscle of *Decticus* (Orthoptera) 5·9 Kg./sq.cm. compared with values of 6–10 Kg./sq.cm. in man. The power exerted by a muscle is proportional to its cross-sectional area and, in general, this is not very great in insects, but in some muscles, such as the extensor tibiae of a locust, a considerable cross-sectional area is achieved by an oblique insertion of the muscle fibres into an apodeme (see Fig. 83A). As a result, this muscle can exert a pull of some 800 g.

The forces exerted by flight muscles are in no way unusual, but the muscles are exceptional in their frequencies of contraction in flight and hence in their total power output which varies from 35 to 175 watts/Kg. compared with 15–17 watts/Kg. in man (Weis-Fogh, 1961). Such a power output requires an enormous expenditure of energy and the metabolic rates of active insect flight muscles are the highest of any tissue known. In the locust flight muscle the metabolic rate during flight ranges from 400 to 800 Kcal./Kg./hr. and in *Apis* from 1300 to 2200 Kcal./Kg/hr. These figures represent increases of up to 100-fold over the resting level.

12.31 Conversion of energy

The very rapid conversion of chemical energy to mechanical work in insect flight muscle appears to demand some special mechanism facilitating the rapid oxidation of substrate, and controversy centres round the role of α-glycerophosphate (see Chefurka, 1965b; Sacktor, 1965). Glycolysis (p. 95) occurs in the extra-mitochondrial cytoplasm and the first oxidation reaction to occur is the removal of hydrogen from glyceraldehyde phosphate and its transfer to nicotinamide adenine dinucleotide (NAD). The supply of NAD is limited so that the reduced form ($NADH_2$) must be reoxidised as quickly as possible, but in the process the hydrogen must be transferred to the mitochondria in which the cytochrome system is housed. A cytoplasmic α-glycerophosphate dehydrogenase appears to be particularly important in this reaction, catalysing the oxidation of $NADH_2$ by dihydroxyacetone phosphate to produce NAD and α-glycerophosphate, which now contains the hydrogen. The α-glycerophosphate passes into the mitochondria and is then oxidised giving up the hydrogen to the cytochrome system and reforming dihydroxyacetone phosphate which is thus made available for further oxidation of the extra-mitochondrial $NADH_2$ (see diagram, p. 92). The oxidation of α-glycerophosphate proceeds at a very high rate, more than ten times as fast as with most other substrates, and there is a correspondingly high rate of transfer of hydrogen to the cytochrome system. This mechanism is believed to account for the greater part of the oxygen uptake during the first part of flight, but subsequently the importance of α-glycerophosphate may be reduced, perhaps because the availability of phosphate is limited since it is employed in the phosphorylation of ADP. In this case $NADH_2$ is oxidised by a malic dehydrogenase and oxidation in the citric acid cycle becomes more important.

Other authorities believe that the citric acid cycle is important at all times, although α-glycerophosphate may be important in maintaining the supply of NAD (see p. 91). Certainly where fat is used as a major substrate, as in the locust, α-glycerophosphate is not particularly important. Fats enter the citric acid cycle as acetyl coenzyme A, condensing with oxaloacetate to form citrate. In locust muscle the condensing enzyme catalysing this reaction is 130 times more active than the same enzyme in frog gastrocnemius muscle and so a ready supply of substrate for oxidation is maintained (see Neville, 1965c).

12.32 Fuels

The fuels from which energy is derived vary in different insects. Hymenoptera and Diptera use carbohydrates and so does *Periplaneta*, although in this case the oxidation is not complete. Locusts and aphids use carbohydrate at the beginning of flight, but subsequently burn fat, which also provides the substrate in Lepidoptera. The locust first uses the glycogen stored in the wing muscles since this is readily available and quickly mobilised. The use of this fuel is associated with a flying speed of 4 m./sec. or more (Fig. 148), but local supplies of glycogen are soon exhausted and the flying speed falls. The mobilisation of fat takes some time, but once achieved the flying speed rises to 3 m./sec. and more and remains steady for several hours (Weis-Fogh, 1952).

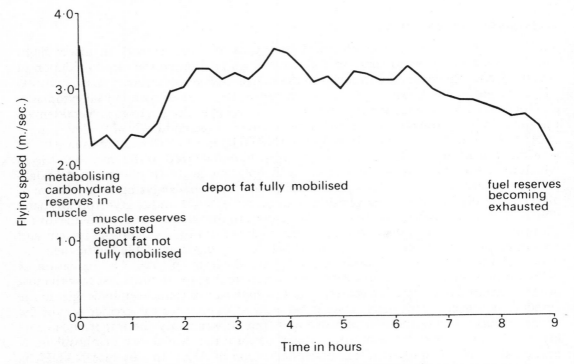

Fig. 148. The flying speed of male *Schistocerca* on a flight mill showing changes in speed with changes in the fuel supply (after Weis-Fogh, 1952).

In any insect the reserves in the flight muscles are limited and further supplies of fuel must be drawn from elsewhere. Trehalose in the blood forms an important carbohydrate reserve in many insects, although in *Apis* glucose is more important. Glycogen present in the muscle and fat body is withdrawn during flight by *Drosophila* and *Culex* (Diptera), while sugars in the crop of *Tabanus* (Diptera) and the honey stomach of *Apis* provide fuels for these insects. In general the carbohydrates are transported in the blood as trehalose (see p. 97). The main fat reserves used by *Schistocerca* in flight are in the fat body and their transport to the muscles involves esterification (Beenakkers, 1965; and see p. 100).

Fat is more suitable than carbohydrate as a reserve for insects which make long flights because it produces twice as much energy per unit weight. Thus a gram of fat yields 9·3 kcal., a gram of carbohydrate only 4·1 kcal., while glycogen, which is a common carbohydrate reserve, is strongly hydrated so that it is eight times heavier than isocaloric amounts of fat. Thus an insect can store large amounts of energy more readily as fat and 85% of the energy stored by the locust is in this form (Weis-Fogh, 1952). Fat has the further possible advantage over carbohydrate that it produces approximately twice as much water on combustion so that the effects of water loss during prolonged flight may be offset.

12.33 Supply of fuels

The transport of fuels in the blood to the flight muscles is facilitated by the movement of blood into and out from the spaces between the fibres of the muscles. In *Aeschna*, for example, blood constitutes 15–20% of the muscle volume so that considerable movement occurs as the muscle contracts and expands (Weis-Fogh, 1964b). The T-system, with narrow canals connecting with the extracellular spaces and extending deep into the fibres, may also play an important part in maintaining the fuel supply by reducing the length of the diffusion path through the tissue.

Diffusion through the tissues is very slow so that to maintain an adequate supply of fuel within the muscles very high concentrations may be necessary in the blood. Weis-Fogh (1964a) does not consider the possible relevance of the T-system, but calculates that in the dragonfly a carbohydrate concentration of 100 mg./100 g. of haemolymph is necessary and in the Diptera and Hymenoptera, with bigger fibres even higher concentrations are required. These figures can be correlated with the high levels of carbohydrate found in the blood. At the end of the fifth larval instar the concentration of carbohydrate in the blood of *Schistocerca* exceeds 2000 mg./100 g. haemolymph and at most times the concentration is greater than 500 mg./100 g. (Howden and Kilby, 1960). Assuming comparable figures in other adult insects the fuel supply is clearly adequate to meet the demands.

Fats are less soluble than carbohydrates and, having larger molecules, diffuse more slowly through the tissues. Weis-Fogh (1964b) calculates a concentration of 20 mg./ 100 g. haemolymph as necessary for diffusion at a rate sufficient to maintain the known rate of metabolism. The blood of *Locusta* contains about 800 mg. of esterified fatty acids per 100 g. haemolymph so that again the supply is ample for the needs of the insect.

12.34 Oxygen supply

During flight insects incur little or no oxygen debt (p. 95) and, in keeping with the high metabolic rates, rates of oxygen consumption are very high. The locust flight muscles, for instance, use some 80 litres O_2/Kg./hr. and for other insects consumption may exceed 400 l.O_2/Kg./hr., but the special adaptations of the thoracic tracheal system enable these demands to be met. In the locust pterothoracic ventilation produces a supply well in excess of the needs, and the specialised system of tracheae and tracheoles in the muscle (p. 455) ensures that the oxygen reaches the site of consumption. Other than in Odonata and blattids tracheoles indent the flight muscle fibres and approach very close to the mitochondria so that tissue diffusion is reduced to a minimum. It is calculated that the muscles have a safety factor of two or three with respect to their oxygen supply.

In Odonata and blattids, on the other hand, tracheoles remain superficial to the muscle fibres and these fibres, with a radius of about 10 μ, are believed to be approaching the limiting size for the efficient diffusion of oxygen in sufficient quantities (Weis-Fogh, 1964b).

12.35 Control of metabolism

It is not clear how the metabolism of flight muscles is controlled. Possibly α-glycero-phosphate dehydrogenase is important. It is suggested that when the insect is at rest this enzyme is inhibited or inactivated and respiration is maintained at a low level via the citric acid cycle. In flight the inhibition is removed, possibly by calcium ions released by the arrival of nerve impulses, so that the enzyme becomes active and respiration proceeds at a much higher rate. Alternatively control could be exerted through the availability of ADP since only if adequate amounts of ADP are present can energy be transferred through the synthesis of ATP (but see p. 106).

12.36 Elasticity of muscle

Not all the energy used during muscle contraction need be derived directly from the combustion of fuels; in flight muscles energy may be stored in elastic elements of the muscle. Flight muscles, and especially fibrillar muscles, have a much higher elasticity than other muscles. Some of this elasticity is attributed to the sarcolemma, but the greater part is due to elastic elements in parallel with the contractile system, or perhaps to the contractile system itself. Energy is stored in this elastic system when the muscle is stretched by the antagonistic muscle and, in the locust depressor muscles at least, when work is done on the wing by aerodynamic forces during the upstroke (see p. 187). This energy is then used when the muscle shortens and as a result much energy is used which would otherwise be wasted.

CHAPTER XIII

FLIGHT ACTIVITY

The mechanisms by which insects fly have been discussed in the previous chapters (Chapters X, XI and XII); in this chapter the functions of flight and the factors limiting and stimulating flight activity are considered. For physiological reasons flight only occurs under particular conditions, being limited by factors of the external and internal environment. The functioning of the flight muscles is particularly important in this respect and for these to work properly body temperature must be sufficiently high. Often the flight muscles are not fully developed until some time after emergence and during this period of development flight activity is restricted. Even when conditions are favourable for flight insects do not necessarily fly unless they are stimulated to take off. Many external factors may promote take-off and it is probable that sometimes internal factors are responsible. Once in flight various stimuli will induce an insect to land, the precise stimuli depending on the habits and behaviour of the insect.

Flight activity may be concerned with routine behaviour such as feeding and reproduction or it may take the form of a dispersal flight or migration from the habitat in which these other activities are suppressed. In some insects the direction of migration is controlled by the insect, but in many cases, where the insects fly in winds whose speed exceeds their own speed through the air, direction is determined mainly by the wind. Return migrations sometimes occur, the return movement occasionally being made by the original migrants, but in other cases by members of a later generation. The distances flown vary from a few metres to thousands of kilometres, but in general the function of migratory flights is the same, the invasion of new habitats.

Haskell (1966) gives a general review of flight activity, but other reviews are concerned mainly with migration and dispersal. This aspect of flight is dealt with by C. Johnson (1954, 1965, 1966, 1969, *Migration and dispersal of insects by flight*), Rainey (1963), Schneider (1962), Southwood (1962) and Williams (1930, 1958).

13.1 Factors limiting flight activity

Flight only occurs within a limited range of conditions, being inhibited by various external and internal factors, the external factors presumably acting through the peripheral sensilla. Although the factors are separated below it must be remembered that the insect responds to the whole complex of its environment, external and internal, although at various times different factors may become dominant.

13.11 External limiting factors

Light

The flight activity of many insects is limited by light intensity and Lewis and Taylor (1965) conclude that this is the major factor controlling times of flight. For instance, many day-flying insects, such as butterflies and Hymenoptera, are not active in the dark and aphids will not take off when the intensity falls below 20 ft.-candles. On the other hand, many Orthoptera, moths, Neuroptera, Trichoptera and Nematocera are essentially nocturnal and do not fly when it is light. In some instances these differences in behaviour are known to be coupled with morphological and physiological adaptations, as in the eyes of Lepidoptera (p. 548), and probably can be correlated with the development of different senses. Thus day-flying predators and flower- and leaf-eating insects rely to a large extent on sight, while crepuscular and nocturnal forms depend largely on scent to find their food or a mate (p. 24).

Wind-speed

Most insects tend to fly only when the wind-speed is relatively low and if the wind-speed is high over long periods flight occurs mainly during lulls (Fig. 149). It appears in part that take-off is inhibited by high winds, although after a time aphids will take off in spite of the wind (see p. 235). In addition, insects in flight tend to land when the

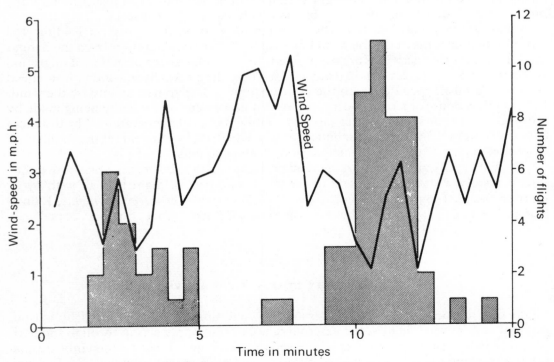

Fig. 149. The number of *Nomadacris* seen flying in successive half-minutes in relation to wind-speed (after Chapman, 1959a).

wind-speed increases and this behaviour probably involves an optomotor reaction (p. 565). If the insect is flying high above the ground, however, it may be unable to distinguish the pattern of features on the ground or their images may move so slowly over the eye that they do not evoke a response from the insect. In these circumstances wind-speed is unlikely to be limiting and the insects will remain airborne in the highest winds (see Kennedy, 1951).

Humidity

It is doubtful if flight is ever completely inhibited, in the sense that it is physically impossible, by the humidity of the environment, but in some cases there is a correlation between humidity and the continuity of flight. In laboratory experiments the longest flights made by *Schistocerca* occur at high humidities (Weis-Fogh, 1952) and field observations on both *Schistocerca* and *Nomadacris* also suggest that the most continuous flight is observed at high humidities (Chapman, 1959a; Waloff, 1953). The flight of *Aphis*, however, is not shortened at low humidities.

Temperature

Environmental temperature is of the greatest importance as a factor limiting flight, but since it exerts its effect largely through the body temperature of the insect it is considered with other internal limiting factors.

13.12 Internal limiting factors

Temperature

The body temperature of an insect is of overriding importance in limiting flight and all insects have a minimum body temperature below which flight is quite impossible. Figure 150 shows the percentage of field observations at various air temperatures during which *Nomadacris* is observed in flight. Very occasional short spontaneous flights are also observed at 19°C. so that the limiting air temperatures for flight are about 19° and 38°C. with peak flight activity between 29° and 35°C. Comparable ranges are known for other insects and in the laboratory the lowest air temperature at which *Schistocerca* flies for any length of time is 22°C., and no sustained flight occurs above 38°C. (Weis-Fogh, 1956a). In *Culex* the minimum air temperature for flight is 15°C., but the Arctic *Aedes punctor* can fly at 2·5°C.

It is probable that at the lower temperatures given above body temperature is much the same as air temperature, but at higher temperatures the insects are probably several degrees hotter than the figures given because their temperature is raised by radiation from the sun and by muscular activity (see p. 639).

The lower temperature limits for flight activity are related to the physiology of the flight muscles. Thus the length of time taken for the completion of a flight muscle twitch is so long at temperatures below 24°C. that flight of *Schistocerca* is extremely inefficient and the twitch is only sufficiently short above 30°C. for really sustained flight to occur (p. 220). Also the apyrases, enzymes concerned in the utilisation of energy, are only efficient at high temperatures (p. 95), while in insects with asynchronous flight muscles the power output is maximal only within a limited range of temperatures, with an optimum at about 40°C. in *Oryctes* (p. 222). Thus the lower limit for flight is set by the inefficiency of the muscles at these temperatures.

If a locust is disturbed at a temperature which is too low for flight it can raise its body temperature by vibrating its wings, fanning, so that flight becomes possible (p. 644). Some moths and dragonflies also exhibit this behaviour. Many insects, including locusts and some Hymenoptera, raise their body temperature in the morning or at other times when the temperature is low by basking in the sun and in this way body temperature may be raised to a level at which flight is possible.

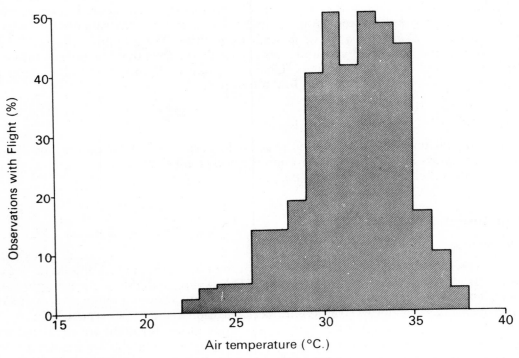

Fig. 150. Flight activity of *Nomadacris* in relation to air temperature (after Chapman, 1959a).

The upper limit may be set by the upper lethal temperature. For instance, sustained flight of *Schistocerca* in the laboratory is not observed at air temperatures above 38°C. Because of the heat output by the flight muscles body temperature in these experiments is probably close to 45°C. and clearly any further increase in temperature would approach dangerously close to the lethal limit (p. 650). Hence sustained flights at high temperatures are not to be expected, although short flights are possible.

A flying locust has no special mechanism to prevent it from overheating (Church, 1960a), but in experiments with the moth *Celerio* the thoracic temperature while in flight only increased from 32°C. to 40°C. as the air temperature was raised from 10°C. to 35°C. This suggests that at the higher air temperatures heat production is regulated so that the possibility of overheating is reduced (Heath and Adams, 1965).

Muscle development

For a time after emergence the flight pattern of adult insects is not fully developed
and this period is known as the teneral period. Thus adult locusts usually remain with
the larvae for a week to ten days after becoming adult. At first they are unable to fly,
then they begin to make short flights which get progressively longer until the full
flight pattern is developed. In other insects the teneral period may be much shorter, a
matter of hours in aphids, and its length is proportional to temperature (Fig. 151).

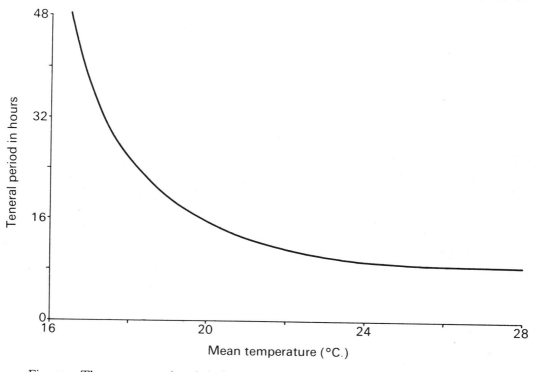

Fig. 151. The mean teneral periods from emergence to uninhibited take-off of *Aphis fabae*
in relation to air temperature (from Johnson, C., 1965).

The initial inability to fly may be partly related to the softness and incompleteness
of the cuticle. In most insects a period of an hour or two is required after emergence for
the hardening of the cuticle to occur (p. 443) and during this period no flight is possible.
Complete development of the cuticle may take some time after this (p. 446), but probably
much more important in limiting flight is the degree of development of the flight muscles
which in many insects are known to undergo extensive changes during the first few days
of adult life. Thus in *Locusta* the flight muscle mitochondria increase in size over the
first eight days of adult life (Fig. 152) and there are corresponding changes in the enzyme
systems with increases of glycerol-1-phosphate oxidase and α-glycerophosphate dehydrogenase, both essential enzymes in the flight mechanism (see p. 223). During the
same period the number of myofibrils increases from about 30 to approximately 1000
in each muscle and the number of filaments in each fibril is doubled (Bücher, 1965).

Similar changes occur in other insects. In *Apis* the muscles are fully developed after about 20 days and only after this are the bees able to make long flights (Herold and Borei, 1963). Similarly in *Glossina* (Diptera) the changes extend over several days and it is possible that in holometabolous insects the delay in development of the muscles reflects a limitation of the reserves available during the pupal period (Bursell, 1961).

Other fully winged insects may be unable to fly at any stage because the wing muscles never develop fully and some corixids are polymorphic with regard to the development of flight muscles. In the flightless forms the full number of muscle fibrils is present, but they are thin and white compared with the large, yellowish muscles of flying forms. The differences in colour probably reflect differences in mitochondrial development and hence in the concentrations of cytochrome present (Young, 1965b).

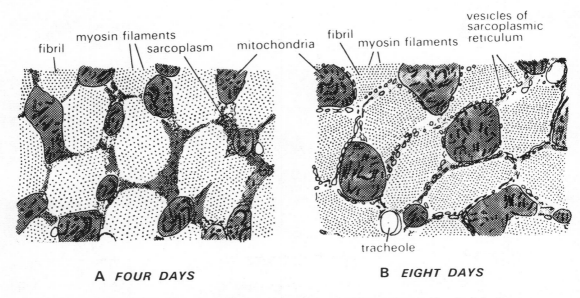

Fig. 152. Cross-sections of parts of the dorsal longitudinal flight muscle of adult *Locusta* (A) four days and (B) eight days after emergence. Notice the larger mitochondria and increased number of filaments in B (after Bücher, 1965).

In many insects after the teneral development there is a period of extensive flight activity, followed by a further period of reduced activity which may be associated with the breakdown, or autolysis, of the flight muscles. This usually occurs in aphids within two or three days of emergence, depending on when the insects settle down on a host plant. If they do not settle down the muscles, and the capacity to fly, are retained. The breakdown involves the dissolution of the fibrils of all the large direct and indirect wing muscles. The sarcolemma remains, but the nuclei become pycnotic and scattered through the cytoplasm. This breakdown, which is probably controlled by a hormone, is accompanied by an increase in the size of the fat body and embryos in the reproductive ducts resume their development which is inhibited during the flight period (B. Johnson, 1957, 1959).

A similar process is known to occur in some mosquitoes, such as some races of *Aedes communis*, in *Musca*, in some Scolytidae and *Leptinotarsa* (Coleoptera) and in the queens of ants and termites which shed their wings after a short nuptial flight. In general it is believed that the degenerating muscles provide essential reserves for egg development, but this may not be so in aphids which have access to ample nitrogenous nutrients, nor in some beetles such as *Sitona* and *Hydroporus* where the reduction occurs in generally unfavourable circumstances (Jackson, 1952; B. Johnson, 1957).

Availability of fuel

Flight can only occur as long as there is fuel to drive the muscles and experiments on *Schistocerca* suggest that, on the average, fuel in this insect is sufficient for about ten hours of uninterrupted flight, although this period could be greatly prolonged if flight was intermittent with periods of feeding in between. Flight might also be prolonged if periods of active flight were interspersed with glides on rising air currents and certainly some flights are much longer than the experimental figures suggest is possible. For instance, it is estimated that a swarm of locusts which moved from the Canary Isles to Southern Britain must have been in the air for some 60 hours.

Various estimates are given for the flight range of other insects based on their performance on flight mills in still air (see Hocking, 1953). For instance, the range of *Aedes* species is estimated at roughly 20–50 km., and for various *Simulium* (Diptera) species at over 100 km., but it is doubtful if these figures bear very much relationship to performances in the field.

Apart from its effect in some migrations it is doubtful if the availability of fuel ever limits flight. Migrants often use fat as a fuel because it provides more energy per unit weight (p. 224).

State of feeding

Feeding often reduces activity and there is some evidence that this applies to the flight activity of *Nomadacris* in the field (Chapman, 1959a). *Glossina* tends to remain inactive after a blood meal, only becoming active again when the meal is well digested, but conversely migrating locusts often feed as they progress and in *Ascia* (Lepidoptera) a series of short feeding flights leads into migration (p. 241).

State of maturity

The state of maturity may not, in general, limit flight, but there is some evidence that gravid females of *Nomadacris* do not fly readily and tend to drop down into the vegetation when disturbed. On the other hand migration by swarms of mature locusts does occur. In many insects, such as aphids, locusts and *Ascia,* the long-range migratory flights occur mainly in the immediate post-teneral period before the insect becomes mature.

13.2 Factors promoting take-off

It does not follow that, if conditions are suitable for flight, flight necessarily occurs. Some stimulus is necessary to cause the insects to take off and then, provided conditions are suitable, they will continue flying. Take-off may sometimes occur when conditions are unsuitable for sustained flight and in this case the insect lands almost immediately.

Many different stimuli may cause an insect to start flying and in many cases it appears that a change in stimulation rather than the absolute level of stimulation is important in this respect.

Light and visual stimulation

There is some evidence that flight may be initiated in some insects by light of a particular intensity. Thus *Anax* (Odonata) is probably stimulated to take off by a certain low light intensity (Corbet, Longfield and Moore, 1960) and in *Calliphora* the frequency of take-off increases with the light intensity above a low level (Digby, 1958a). On the other hand in some insects a change in light intensity appears to provide an important stimulus. Thus in locusts bursts of flying are often seen following changes in light intensity on an intermittently cloudy day, either an increase or a decrease in intensity apparently being effective, although it is impossible to separate the effects of light and temperature in these cases (Chapman, 1959a; Waloff and Rainey, 1951). Night flight in *Schisto-cerca* starts at about half-an-hour after sunset irrespective of other conditions and it is probable that in this instance the rapid decrease in light intensity promotes take-off (Roffey, 1963; Waloff, 1963).

Visual stimuli other than changes in intensity may promote take-off in some predatory and parasitic insects. Experiments indicate that movement of an object in

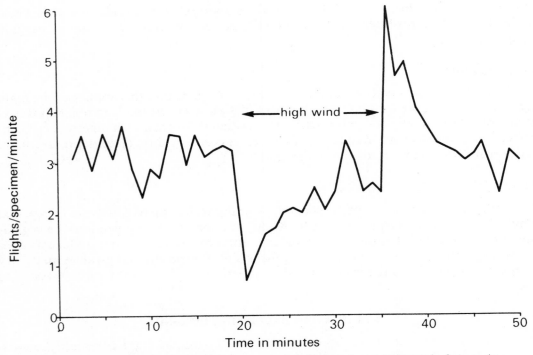

Fig. 153. The mean flight activity in a group of *Calliphora* in a wind-speed of 0·5 m./sec. with a short period of 3·0 m./sec. (after Digby, 1958b).

the visual field of *Glossina* causes the fly to take off and approach the host (see p. 26). Similarly the parasitic fly *Pachyophthalmus,* which detects the nest of its host *Eumenes* (Hymenoptera) by pursuing the wasp, normally sits on some vantage point and is stimulated to fly by any insect flying within about two feet. Pursuit only ensues if the passing insect is *Eumenes,* otherwise the fly lands again (Chapman, 1959c). Many Asilidae and dragonflies catch their prey by darting out from a vantage point on which they sit until the insect comes sufficiently close (Corbet, Longfield and Moore, 1960; Oldroyd, 1964).

Wind-speed

It is believed that high winds inhibit take-off, causing the insect to cling more strongly to its perch. This is true in aphids, but only over short periods; if the high wind persists the aphids take off regardless of its speed. This suggests some degree of adaptation to the high winds, and experimental work on *Calliphora* shows that this does occur in this insect. After a sudden increase in wind-speed the flies take off less frequently, but gradually the number taking off increases in spite of the high wind (Fig. 153). In *Calliphora* it has been suggested that wind-speeds below 0·7 m./sec. have a stimulating effect and increase the numbers of flies taking off, but at higher speeds the numbers taking off decrease (Fig. 154) (Digby, 1958b).

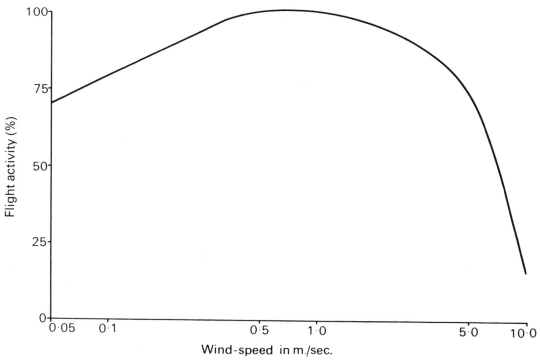

Fig. 154. Flight activity of *Calliphora* in relation to wind-speed. The figures are expressed as a percentage of the activity at 0·5 m./sec. and show the activity 30 minutes after a change from this level (after Digby, 1958b).

A sudden fall in wind-speed leads to a sharp increase in the numbers of insects taking off and in *Calliphora* the number taking off is greater than would be expected from the simple relationship between wind-speed and flight activity indicated above (Fig. 153). This suggests that the fall in wind-speed is itself important, irrespective of the speed of the wind and Kennedy (1951) concludes that this is also true in *Schistocerca*. Conversely, in locusts there is an occasional suggestion that sudden strong gusts of wind stimulate take-off, but this could arise from the sudden cooling effects produced by the wind rather than being a direct effect of the wind. Temperature changes may also follow more normal changes in wind-speed and it is possibly these, rather than the wind itself, which promote take-off (see Chapman, 1959a).

Humidity

There are some suggestions from field work that the flight of locusts may be initiated by an increase in humidity, such as might be caused by a moist wind blowing from a wet to a dry area, but there is no general agreement on this point (see *e.g.* Davey, 1959).

Smell

Some insects are stimulated to take off when they perceive particular smells, take-off being followed by an upwind orientation which takes the insect to the source of the smell. Field and laboratory experiments indicate that the smell of the host stimulates take-off by *Glossina medicorum* (Chapman, 1961), and this may also be true in some other blood-sucking insects. In a similar way some male moths are stimulated to take off by a pheromone produced by the female (p.737).

Temperature

Activity is promoted by sharp changes in temperature (p. 649) and there is good evidence that this applies also to flight activity in the field. Often under these circumstances temperature changes are accompanied by changes in wind-speed or light intensity and it is impossible to separate the effects of the different stimuli with certainty (Chapman, 1959a). In *Calliphora*, an increase in temperature at the rate of 5°C./minute at first reduces take-off, but subsequently more flights occur at the higher temperature (Digby, 1958a).

Other stimuli

Many different stimuli may promote take-off in various insects. Disturbance by other animals, for instance, may sometimes be important and the flight responses of locusts to each other may simply be a special case of this. Thus an individual locust may be stimulated to take off by the mechanical agitation of its fellows or visually or aurally by the passage of other locusts overhead.

Under some circumstances it is possible that insects take off in the complete absence of external stimuli, and in this case intrinsic stimuli must be involved. Behaviour which probably falls in this category is sometimes observed in predaceous insects such as Asilidae which move their perch from time to time if no potential prey appears. This can be interpreted in terms of the build-up of an internal drive, but it is impossible to be certain that external stimuli play no part in these movements.

13.3 Stimuli leading to landing

Very little is known of the factors which cause an airborne insect to land, but landing at any time must depend on whether or not the insect has the opportunity to do so, and can only occur if the insect is close to the ground and can control its own movements.

Since sustained flight only occurs under certain conditions a change resulting in adverse conditions will lead to landing by the insect. This will occur, for instance, if the temperature falls below the minimum for flight and similarly landing will follow quickly if take-off occurs in suboptimal conditions.

On the other hand, insects often land although the environmental conditions remain suitable for flight, and landing may be promoted by special stimuli appropriate to the particular insect. For instance, a food-collecting bee is stimulated to approach and land on a flower with the appropriate smell and colour. However, since it may only just have taken off from a similar flower the landing clearly results from a change in the responses of the insect itself. This is seen in aphids and some other insects where the positive photo-tactic reactions which are important at take-off become weaker or even reversed so that the insect moves towards the vegetation. The change in behaviour is regarded as arising through a change in a central nervous balance mechanism which is modified by different inputs (Kennedy and Booth, 1963a). Flight itself influences this balance so that after a period of flight an aphid is more ready to settle down on a leaf and the longer the period of flight the more readily will it settle. Settling is said to be induced by flying (Kennedy and Booth, 1963b).

13.4 Speed of flight

The speed of an insect in flight can be measured in terms of its movement relative to the ground, its ground-speed, or its movement relative to the air, its air-speed. Ground-speed depends on the air-speed of the insect, the speed of the wind and the orientation of the insect relative to the wind. If air-speed is greater than wind-speed the insect can orientate at any angle to the wind and make headway (Fig. 155A), although its path relative to the ground, known as its track, will not generally coincide with the direction in which it is heading, its course. If the air-speed is less than wind-speed the insect will move downwind irrespective of its course (Fig. 155B).

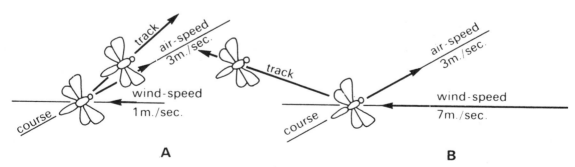

Fig. 155. Diagrams showing the interrelationships between course, track and wind direction (A) where the air-speed of the insect exceeds wind-speed and (B) where the air-speed is less than the wind-speed.

Laboratory and field observations on *Schistocerca* indicate that it has an air-speed of 15–20 km./hour, the speed being greatest soon after take-off and subsequently falling to a steady level (see Fig. 148). Experiments on a flight mill indicate air-speeds of about 9 km./hr. for *Apis* and various Tabanidae and speeds of 3–4 km./hr. for *Aedes*. Field observations suggest air-speeds of the same order with maximum speeds over short distances of approximately double these figures (Hocking, 1953).

If the insect is moving downwind its ground-speed may exceed its air-speed, but in upwind orientation the converse must be true. There is evidence that insects can regulate their ground-speed by adjusting the air-speed to some extent and this is most obvious in some hovering insects such as syrphids, *Apis* and *Macroglossa* (Lepidoptera) and in others, such as some Diptera and Ephemeroptera, which form swarms (p. 299). These insects are able to remain stationary over one spot despite changes in wind-speed and this involves balancing the air-speed against the wind-speed. The insect maintains its station by means of a visual fix on some feature of the environment.

Adjustment of air-speed also occurs in forward progression into the wind. For instance, in still air *Aedes* has an air-speed of 17 cm./sec.; in a wind of 33 cm./sec. the air-speed is increased to 49 cm./sec. so that the ground-speed is only slightly less than in still air, falling to about 16 cm./sec. Further increase in wind-speed is compensated by an increased air-speed so that the insect is able to maintain its forward movement against

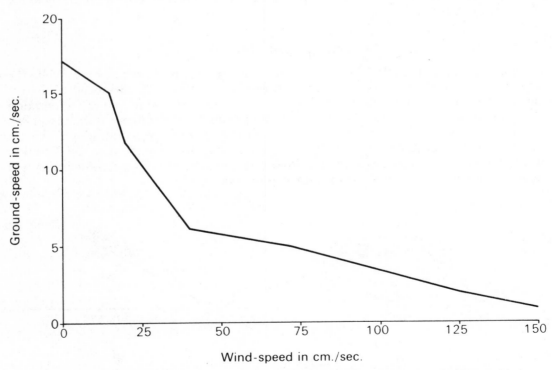

Fig. 156. The ground-speed of *Aedes aegypti* when flying into winds of varying force. Air-speed is adjusted so that ground-speed does not fall as quickly as would otherwise be expected (from Clements, 1963).

the wind, although with a gradually decreasing ground-speed (Fig. 156). Observations on *Ascia* and locusts also suggest that air-speed is regulated to maintain a fairly constant ground-speed despite changes in the velocity of the wind (Kennedy, 1951; Nielsen, 1961).

This regulation is believed to involve an optomotor reaction, the insect preferring to perceive the movement of images of the background across the eye from front to back at a certain moderate rate (see p. 565). There is also evidence that air-speed may be perceived through the stimulation of Johnston's organ in the antennae and that changes in stimulation lead to modifications in the amplitude of wingbeat (p. 197).

13.5 Types of flight

Flight activity is broadly divided into two categories, trivial flight which is concerned with feeding and mating, and migration in which these vegetative activities are suppressed so that flight behaviour dominates. There is no clear separation between the two types of flight and one may grade into the other. For instance, in termites the migration of winged reproductives away from the nest leads to the finding of a mate. Conversely, the trivial feeding flights of *Ascia* gradually become longer until the insect is migrating. Either type of flight may lead to dispersal, but migration, which frequently carries the insect beyond the confines of its habitat is probably more important in this respect.

13.51 Trivial flights

Trivial flights are local movements concerned with the finding of food, a mate or a suitable oviposition site, or with escaping from a potential enemy. Thus they show great diversity in their length and orientation. They may involve no more than the flitting from flower to flower of some insects within a limited habitat, or they may involve movements over some kilometres as in the attraction of some male moths to the scent of females (see p. 737). In other cases the trivial flight may lead to no displacement at all, as in the mating swarms of male mosquitoes and Ephemeroptera (p. 299) and the territorial behaviour of some male dragonflies. For instance, the males of *Tholymis tillarga* (Odonata) fly up and down a narrow stretch of water driving off other males, and despite a good deal of flight activity there is no effective displacement of the individual, although his behaviour does lead to some dispersion of the species by driving others away from his stretch of water (Corbet, Longfield and Moore, 1960).

Vision is important in many cases of trivial flight. For instance, bees and butterflies orientate to flowers, the colour and size of the flowers being important. Similarly, predatory insects, such as Odonata, and blood-sucking insects may orientate visually to their food (p. 26). Visual means may also be employed in finding a mate, as in *Hypolimnas* (Lepidoptera) (p. 123).

Smell also plays a part in flight orientation, the insect orientating to a wind carrying some specific smell as in the mating behaviour of some moths and host-finding by some species of *Glossina* (pp. 737, 26). Water vapour may act in a similar way and it has been suggested that locusts move upwind into a moist wind. The orientation to wind in these cases probably involves vision and possibly also stimulation of the antenna, or, in locusts, the facial hair beds (p. 600).

Most insects fly when disturbed and in some insects special types of flight are associated with this escape reaction. Solitary *Schistocerca*, for instance, 'rocket' into the air and then crash down again very quickly. Often an escaping insect flies on an erratic course with frequent sharp turns or high-speed climbs (Callahan, 1965), or, as in the case of some moths pursued by bats, high-speed power dives to the ground. The stimuli evoking these responses are probably normally visual or mechanical, and some night-flying moths are able to perceive and react to the sounds emitted by bats (p.614).

13.6 Migration

In the course of the adult life of many, perhaps most, insects there is a phase during which flight activity dominates over all other forms of behaviour. The flight occurring during this period is called migration. Often it is the immediate post-teneral flight and in many insects migration is restricted to a short period, only a few days at most in aphids and 15–30 hours in *Ascia*. Following this the insect matures and only trivial flights occur, or the flight muscles may break down so that no further flight is possible (p. 232). Sometimes, however, migration follows a prolonged period of diapause and usually in such cases the movement is additional to an immediate post-teneral migration. *Eurygaster* (Heteroptera), for instance, migrates to and from its place of aestivation, only maturing when it finally settles in its breeding grounds. Finally, a number of insects also migrate when they are mature. This is true, for instance, of some locust movements, some instances of migration by *Catopsilia* (Lepidoptera) (see Williams, 1958) and some migrations of dragonflies (Corbet, Longfield and Moore, 1960), but again in these species migration is more commonly an immediate post-teneral flight.

Migration is regarded as a dispersal mechanism and it always includes females, but not necessarily males, this depending on the mating behaviour of the species. Thus the migration of *Schistocerca* involves both sexes, and in *Eurygaster* the outward flight to the aestivation quarters includes both sexes, but only the females return to the breeding grounds. In *Rhyacionia* (Lepidoptera) only the females migrate, having been fertilised before they start, while the migrations of aphids involve parthenogenetic females.

13.61 Direction of migration

The direction of migration is strongly influenced by wind-speed and direction (Fig. 155). Wind-speed increases with the height above the ground so that, for all insects, there is a layer of air close to the ground in which their air-speed exceeds the wind-speed, while at higher levels the converse is true. The layer of relatively low wind-speeds is called the boundary layer and its thickness varies with different insects having different air-speeds, with the presence and form of vegetation, and with the wind-speed. Within the boundary layer an insect can orientate and make progress in any direction, but at higher levels the wind-speed exceeds the air-speed and displacement will be predominantly downwind irrespective of the orientation of the insect.

Migration within the boundary layer

The migrations of some insects are made largely or entirely within the boundary layer and hence their direction is controlled by the insect. Thus *Ascia monuste* in Florida flies low, only 1–4 m. above the ground, and it tends to fly in situations sheltered from the wind. Moreover, it is a strong flier and can make headway against a wind of 10 km./hr. so that its movement is not much affected by wind direction. Flights from the coastal colonies are directed to the north and to the south at the same time and it is suggested that in this case the direction of migration is determined by the behaviour immediately before the migration. At this time the insect feeds at flowers and the colonies of flowers extend in a north–south direction along the coast. Hence there is some tendency for feeding flights to be similarly orientated and as intervals between feeding become longer and the insects start to migrate they continue the tendency to fly in a northerly or southerly direction. Subsequently the direction may become fixed by a sun compass reaction or by orientation to polarised light (p. 563). In this way the main trend of the migration is fixed, but the insects follow landmarks, such as roads and the coastline, when these head in the right general direction (Nielsen, 1961).

The migrations of *Melolontha* also occur within the boundary layer. In this case the beetles fly from their site of emergence to woodland up to two miles distant. The initial orientation is visual, involving fixation on the highest visible point in the woodland, but again this appears to be supplemented by orientation to the sun or the pattern of polarised light from the sky. This orientation is remembered by the insect and serves to direct it on the return course to the breeding grounds (Schneider, 1962). Thus in species migrating within the boundary layer it appears that a variety of factors may be involved in the initial orientation, but this subsequently becomes fixed with reference to the sun or the pattern of polarised light.

Migration outside the boundary layer

Even species which normally migrate within the boundary layer are sometimes seen flying outside it. For instance, *Ascia monuste* in Argentina has been observed migrating at all levels up to 5000 ft. At the lower levels the insects were variously orientated to the wind, but the higher flights were all downwind (see Haywood, 1953).

This applies also to locusts. For instance, *Nomadacris*, after fledging, flies in relatively low density and within about 20 ft. of the ground. Such flight is only observed in low wind-speeds and often involves flying into, and making headway against, the wind. This movement leads to concentration of the locusts, and the denser swarms which result fly at higher levels and in higher wind-speeds so that they tend to drift downwind (see p. 246).

In the flight of solitary *Schistocerca* at night the insects do not have any particular orientation to the wind if the wind-speed is below 2·5 m./sec., but at higher wind-speeds movement is downwind. The air-speed of locusts is about 3 m./sec. and these observations indicate that within the boundary layer, with air-speed exceeding wind-speed, the insect can control its progress, but outside the boundary layer, with winds in excess of the air-speed, it is largely at the mercy of the wind. In the daytime insects flying outside the boundary layer probably turn and fly with the wind as a reaction against the tendency for images to pass forwards over the eye if the insect is blown backwards, but at night no optomotor reaction is possible and some insects are carried backwards by the wind (Roffey, 1963; Waloff, 1963). The behaviour of locust swarms is rather a special case because of the gregariousness of the locusts and they are considered separately (section 13.63).

Aphids have an air-speed of about 0·6 m./sec. so that with them flight within the boundary layer is relatively unusual. Further at the start of flight they climb steeply due to a positive phototactic reaction to the shorter wavelengths of light. Hence they are quickly carried beyond the boundary layer and are transported by the winds. Many other insects amongst the Odonata, Coleoptera, Lepidoptera and Diptera launch themselves upwards beyond the boundary layer in a similar manner and as methods of observation improve and become more critical it is found in an increasing number of insects that the direction of migration is determined largely by the movements of the mass of air in which the insects find themselves (see *e.g.* Johnson, 1966; French, 1965).

This is not to say that the insect plays a purely passive role. Its original launching into the air is an active movement different from that seen in trivial flights. Further, the insect is heavier than air and so, in general, will remain airborne only so long as it is actively flying. If it stops flying the insect descends to the ground unless it is held up by rising air currents.

In order to support an insect the velocity of a convection current must exceed the sinking speed of the insect and such velocities do commonly occur at certain times. Rainey (1958) estimated a sinking speed for locusts with the wings outstretched at about 1 m./sec. and in one observation obtained evidence for some 50 up-gusts per square kilometre with a velocity equivalent to or greater than this. In Canada vertical velocities of up to 8 m./sec. are recorded (Wellington, 1945) and these currents would be capable of supporting many insects. Convection due to the heating of the ground by the sun will be of great importance in carrying insects high into the air and this is primarily a diurnal phenomenon, dying down in the evening as the ground cools. Hence many insects will be carried upwards into the air and occasional records are obtained of insects at 10,000 ft.; at midday, with convection approaching its maximum, half the population of *Oscinella* (Diptera) in Britain is normally above 1300 ft.

These up-currents are not continuous, but have down-draught zones between them. Hence insects may not, in general, remain airborne due to convection for very long periods and convection will not necessarily result in the insects being transported over long distances. It will, however, distribute them over a considerable area because of the turbulent movement of the air in the up-currents.

If, having been carried upwards by convection currents, the insects keep flying they may be transported by high winds over considerable distances. Rapid long-range movements of locust swarms may be accounted for in this way as, for instance, the movement of swarms of *Schistocerca* from southern Morocco to Portugal, a distance of some 1200 km., in about 24 hours. It is thought that these insects were carried up by strong convection currents to a height of about 2000 ft. where they encountered winds from the south approaching 45 km./hr. Carriage on the wind would account for the observed displacement of the locusts (Waloff, 1946).

13.62 Return movements

Few insects are known to make return migrations comparable with those made by birds, but evidence is accumulating which indicates that such movements are not uncommon. In many instances the return flight is not made by the initial migrants, but by members of a subsequent generation, this reflecting the general brevity of the life of adult insects.

The best documented example of a return migration is that of *Danaus plexippus*, the American monarch butterfly. In the summer months this insect is found right across the United States and extending into southern Canada (Fig. 157A). The adult insect, however, can survive only for short periods at low temperatures and requires constant access to nectar which is not available in the northern winter. Hence it is unable to over-winter in the more northern parts of its range. In the autumn it moves south into areas beyond the range of the cold air masses or into areas in which, as in the Gulf of Mexico, the cold air is moderated by warm-water currents (Fig. 157B).

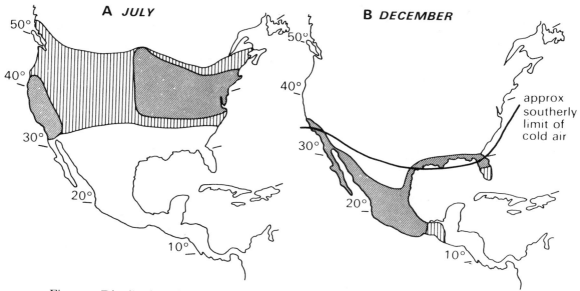

Fig. 157. Distribution of *Danaus plexippus* in North America in (A) July and (B) December. Vertical hatching indicates low densities, diagonal hatching high densities (after Urquhart, 1960).

The southward movement begins in July in the northern parts of the range, reaching its climax in September and finally fading out in October. Flight is usually within 15 ft. of the ground, within the boundary layer, although higher flights are made to avoid obstacles. On the way south the butterflies roost in trees, clustering together on cold nights and remaining in the roosts until the temperature rises above about 13°C.

In the warmer parts of the overwintering range (Fig. 157B) the insects remain free-flying and breeding occurs, but in some localities in Florida and California which are within the range of the cold northern air masses the butterflies roost in dense colonies in the trees, flitting out on warm days to feed on nectar.

In February and March as the temperature rises the colonies start to break up and a return movement to the north begins. The individuals leaving the Californian colonies are the same as those which flew south in the autumn and this may also be true of some individuals from Florida, but here some winter breeding is known to occur so that at least some of the individuals flying north are the offspring of those that originally came south. The return to the extreme north of the range takes about two months (Urquhart, 1960).

Outward and return movements by the same individual are also known in a few other insects. For instance, *Agrotis infusa* (Lepidoptera) in Australia moves to the mountains in the summer, so avoiding the excessive aridity of the plains, and returns to the plains to breed in the autumn. The pentatomids *Eurygaster integriceps* and *Aelia rostrata* make similar movements in middle eastern countries, but here it is believed that the movements are purely fortuitous, depending on the prevailing winds at the time of migration so that many insects are lost and never return to their breeding grounds (E. S. Brown, 1965). The two-way movement of *Hippodamia convergens* (Coleoptera) is believed to occur in a similar way (Hagen, 1962).

In many other instances the return movement is made by members of a subsequent generation and not by the original insects. For instance, *Vanessa atalanta* (Lepidoptera) in Britain is generally observed moving in a northerly direction in spring and, after breeding, in a southerly direction in the autumn (Fig. 158), and evidence is accumulating for comparable movements in other Lepidoptera in Europe and elsewhere (see Williams, 1958).

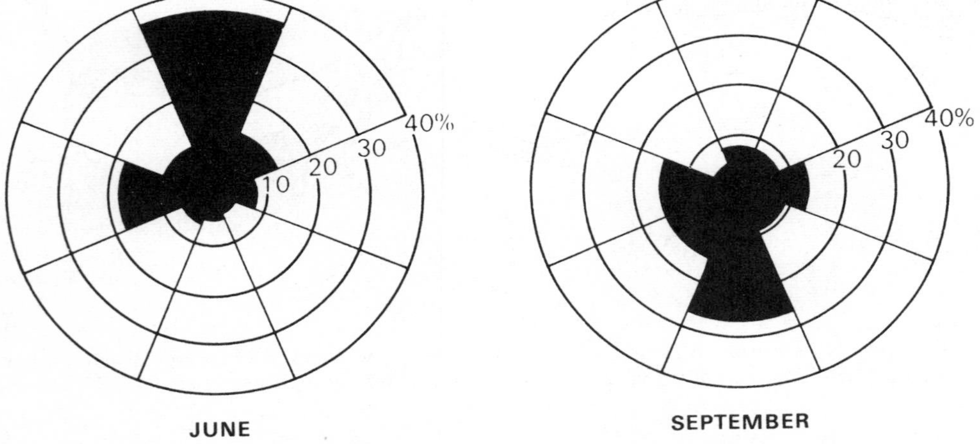

JUNE   SEPTEMBER

Fig. 158. The direction of flight of *Vanessa atalanta* in Britain in June and September. Expressed as a percentage of the total numbers of observations (based on Williams, 1951).

13.63 Locust migration

Locust migrations are conspicuous because they involve swarms consisting of enormous numbers of individuals which move over hundreds of kilometres. There are many locust species, but the best known is *Schistocerca gregaria* which extends across north and central Africa to the Middle East, Arabia and India. Swarms of *Schistocerca* commonly have an area of over 10 sq. km. and big swarms may extend over 250 sq. km. This involves vast numbers of insects and a swarm with an area of 20 sq. km. was estimated to contain 1,000,000,000 locusts. The distance moved by such swarms is very variable, but is often 30–40 km./day and not infrequently 100 km./day.

Swarms in flight may be roughly classified into two types depending on their form. They may be flat with all the locusts flying within a few metres of the ground or they may extend upwards in a towering form to over 1000 m. above the ground. These types are called stratiform and cumuliform swarms respectively. In the first the locusts are highly concentrated with densities usually between one and ten locusts per cubic metre, but in cumuliform swarms the insects are much more widely dispersed and density ranges from 0·001–0·1 locusts/cu. m.

A single swarm may occur in either of these forms at different times since the differences arise from differences in the air currents in the swarm. Stratiform swarms are formed when there is no marked temperature gradient above the ground, indicating the absence of convective up-currents, but cumuliform swarms occur where there is a marked temperature gradient and associated convection. The convection currents in this case carry the locusts upwards, but they will only do so provided they exceed the sinking speed of the locusts. Up-gusts of sufficient velocity to do this may occur with a frequency of 50/sq. km. and they are probably responsible for the towering pillars of locusts often seen in cumuliform swarms. The top of such a swarm is close to the limit of the temperature gradient in the air, this being associated with the limit of convective air movements (Fig. 159).

Small swarms, with an area of less than one square kilometre, are often stratiform even in turbulent conditions and this probably reflects some difference in the behaviour of the locusts in the smaller group.

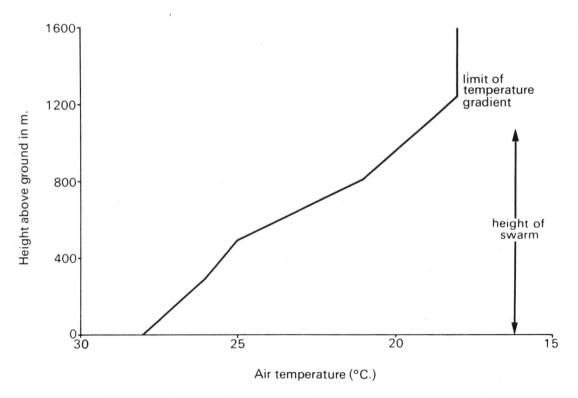

Fig. 159. The height of a cumuliform swarm of *Schistocerca* in relation to the temperature gradient above the ground (based on Rainey, 1958).

Photographic analysis shows that, although in any one part of the swarm all the locusts tend to be similarly orientated, in the swarm as a whole the locusts are randomly orientated with respect to each other. It might be expected that this randomness, together with the disruptive effects of air turbulence would lead to the dispersal of the swarm, but it is found that at the edge of the swarm all the locusts are heading towards the body of insects (Fig. 160) so that the cohesion of the swarm is maintained. It is believed that whenever a locust heads out of the swarm it turns and flies back again into the rest of the locusts, possibly reacting to visual and auditory stimuli provided by the swarm (Haskell, 1960b).

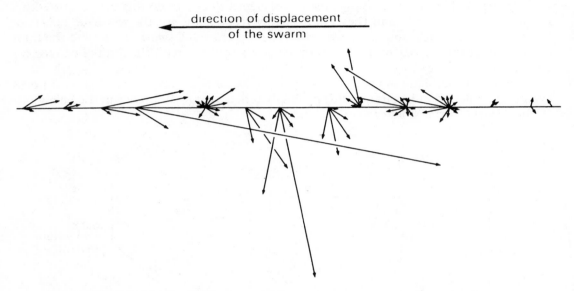

Fig. 160. Diagram illustrating the orientations of individual locusts in a swarm, based on a series of photographs taken at intervals as the swarm passed overhead. The length of each arrow is proportional to the number of locusts orientated in the direction shown (from Haskell, 1960b).

Since the locusts in a swarm are randomly orientated the swarm will inevitably tend to be displaced downwind. Other directions are possible if orientation is co-ordinated instead of random and there are many reports in the literature of swarms flying into the wind, but these reports have yet to be substantiated by critical analysis. Where critical methods have been employed it is found that swarm displacement is downwind (Fig. 161) (Rainey, 1963). The speed with which the locusts move downwind is very variable and is usually less than half the wind-speed. This is due in part to the fact that flight is intermittent, with locusts continually landing and taking off, so that although the swarm as a whole is continually airborne the individual locusts are only in the air for a part of the time. It is rare for the whole of a swarm to be airborne for any length of time. The slow downwind progress of swarms could also result from a preponderance of upwind orientation by the locusts.

The effect of downwind displacement is to bring the locusts into convergence areas, that is areas in which there is a net excess of inflowing air over outflowing air across the boundaries (Fig. 162). Often these areas are somewhat ephemeral, but some are more permanent and one of these, the Inter-Tropical Convergence Zone between winds originating on either side of the Equator, is of particular importance in the biology of *Schistocerca*. The convergent winds tend to carry locust swarms into the convergence zones and once there they tend to remain so that swarms accumulate and this is especially true in the Inter-Tropical Convergence Zone (Fig. 163). Swarms may continue to fly when in these zones, but the irregularity of the winds tends to limit displacement. For instance, there is a record of a swarm in the Sudan in June, 1955 which flew 150 km. in two days, but at the end of this time it had undergone no net displacement because of the irregularity of its movements.

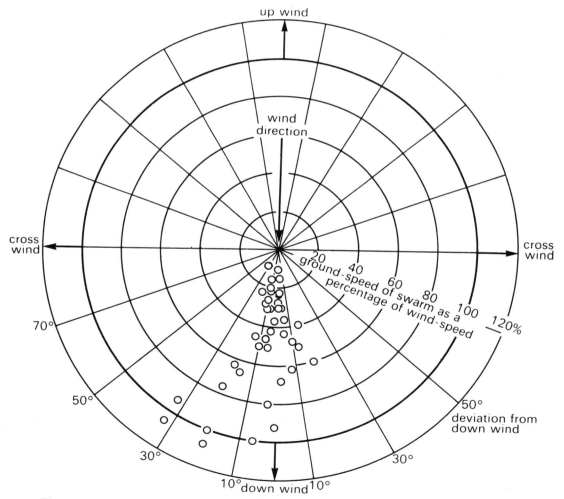

Fig. 161. Direction and speed of displacement of 49 desert locust swarms in relation to wind (after Rainey, 1963).

The association of the locusts with convergence areas is important because convergence results in rising air and this leads to precipitation. Hence their behaviour pattern brings the locusts into areas in which rain is almost assured, providing suitable conditions for oviposition and fresh food for the larvae. It also has important practical applications since the Inter-Tropical Convergence Zone moves regularly over the seasons so that it is possible to predict the seasonal movements of the locusts to some extent (see Rainey, 1963).

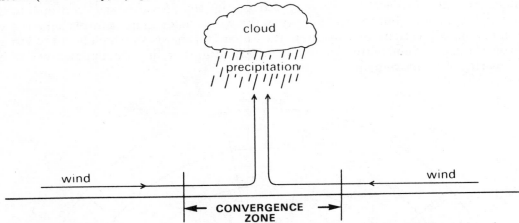

Fig. 162. Diagram of a convergence zone showing convergent winds producing rising air currents and hence leading to precipitation.

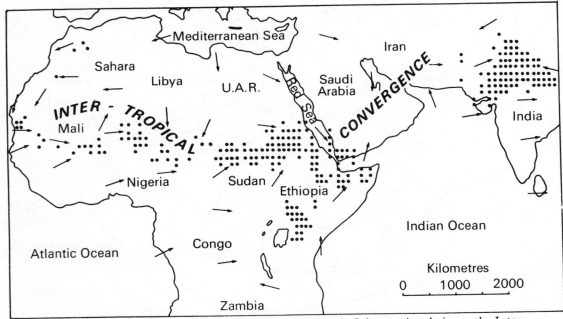

Fig. 163. The distribution of swarms of *Schistocerca* (•) in July 1954 in relation to the Inter-Tropical Convergence Zone. Arrows indicate the general wind direction at mid-day 900 m. above the ground (after Rainey, 1963).

Swarms of locusts usually migrate in the daytime although their flight sometimes continues into the night, but solitary locusts also migrate extensively and apparently mainly at night. Solitary migratory locusts, *Locusta*, for instance, make seasonal movements from the semi-desert areas surrounding the Niger flood plain into the plain, recolonising the semi-desert areas again in a later generation following the onset of the rainy season. The movement to the plain appears to be a downwind movement into a moister, more clement region.

13.64 Mass flights

Although migration of small numbers of insects occurs and is probably more common than it appears to be, migration frequently involves mass flights. Aphid migration, for instance, commonly involves very large numbers often reaching two daily peaks, one in the morning and a second in the afternoon (Fig. 164). The numbers of aphids in the air at any one time depend primarily on the numbers of insects becoming adult, the length of the teneral period and the presence or absence of limiting weather conditions. Aphids emerging in the morning with the temperature rising have a short teneral period and fly in the afternoon, but those emerging in the afternoon are inhibited from taking off

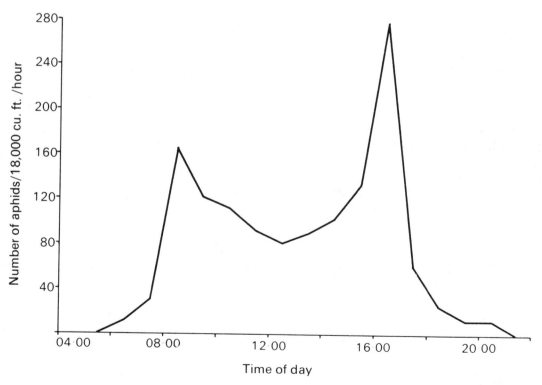

Fig. 164. Daily changes in the density of *Aphis fabae* in the air above a bean crop (after Johnson and Taylor, 1957).

by the low light intensity and temperature of the evening. These all leave together the following morning when light and temperature become suitable and, together with others emerging and completing the teneral period overnight, they provide the morning peak of numbers. It is important to notice here that the two peaks arise from the activity of different individuals and not from changes in the activity of the same aphids (see Johnson and Taylor, 1957).

Similarly in *Aedes taeniorrhynchus* adult emergence reaches a peak between 09.00 and 12.00 hours, but flight is inhibited by the light intensity until 18.00 hours when it is getting dark so that all the insects take off together in a mass flight (Nielsen, 1958). Probably in many insects with a short teneral period mass exodus on migration follows mass adult emergence and limiting flight conditions as in these examples. In some cases emergence is synchronised by a diapause (p. 717). The mass flights of some other insects appear to result largely from some common reaction to the environment since emergence may take place over a relatively long period. For instance, winged termites and ants accumulate in the nest, only flying when particular weather conditions prevail. Possibly some social factor is also relevant in these insects.

In locusts the synchronising of take-off arises from the gregarious behaviour of the insects which at some earlier period have aggregated as a response to environmental conditions.

13.65 Beginning of migration

Migration is to be regarded as an evolved adaptation and not a reaction to current adversity. This is suggested by the fact that migration in many cases is not immediately referable to prevailing adverse conditions, but commonly begins before these conditions are met. *Danaus*, for instance, begins to move south before the onset of cold weather (p. 243), and locust swarms leave their habitats while food supplies are still abundant. Sometimes the movements may involve all the individuals of every generation as in *Danaus* or a population may show genetically determined polymorphism with some individuals in every generation migrating as in *Dysdercus* (Heteroptera) (Fig. 165). In these cases the onset of migration may be spontaneous, not involving environmental signals. In other cases, however, migration is facultative and only occurs in certain generations, sometimes again involving polymorphism which in this case is controlled by the environment.

In the case of facultative migration the insect must be put into a state of readiness to migrate by environmental factors. This state of readiness may be simply a physiological and behavioural phenomenon, but it may also involve the production of fully winged forms in an otherwise flightless population. Possibly in some cases photoperiod provides the stimulus for such development and photoperiod is known to affect wing polymorphism in aphids. In corixids, temperature and the availability of food may be important in controlling the development of flying forms (Young, 1965b). Crowding also appears to be of some importance, possibly because over a long term it tends to be correlated with food shortage. Thus crowding stimulates the production of winged forms in aphid populations and the mass migrations of locusts are associated with crowding.

The stimuli which initiate take-off when the insects are in a state of readiness to migrate are considered above (section 13.2).

13.66 Displacement as a result of migration

The displacements resulting from migration are extremely variable from species to species and even within a species, the distance moved depending on the speed of flight, the duration and frequency of single flights and the duration of the migratory period. The southerly movement of *Danaus plexippus* in the autumn involves a migration of over 1600 km. for the individuals in the north of the range and one marked individual was recovered in Mexico 2800 km. from its origin in Ontario four months previously. The rate of movement was probably faster than this would suggest since another recovery had travelled 1700 km. in 18 days, an average speed of almost 100 km. per day (Urquhart, 1960).

These movements are made largely within the boundary layer as are those of *Ascia* which, in Florida, migrates from 16 to 150 km., the longer distances occurring where more insects are involved in the migration.

With insects moving outside the boundary layer displacements are equally variable. Many insects may not be displaced particularly far because of the pattern of convection currents, but some may be carried on the wind for considerable distances and Gressitt *et al.* (1962) collected a number of terrestrial insects in mid-Pacific, a pyralid and a pentatomid being 500 km. or more from the nearest land. It is not certain that these insects were airborne for the whole of this distance, but it is quite probable since it is known that Lepidoptera may be carried as much as 3000 km. on the wind (French, 1965). On the other hand the wind-borne movements of *Eurygaster* only extend over 20–30 km. (E. S. Brown, 1965).

Locust swarms may remain in one place without effective displacement (see above), but conversely there are records of swarms moving from northern Arabia to the Niger Republic, some 3500 km., in a month (Rainey, 1963). Solitary *Locusta* fly for distances of up to 300 km. in and around the Niger flood plain (Davey, 1959).

Many migratory movements are on a much smaller scale than these figures would suggest and for instance the dispersal flights of termites and ants may extend over distances of 100 m. or less.

13.67 End of migration

Although migration many occasionally come to an end because the insects are exhausted such evidence as is available suggests that this is usually not the case. Various environmental factors may ultimately be responsible, but the readiness to react to these factors probably depends on some physiological changes within the insect so that signals which evoked no response during migration now produce a reaction. Thus in aphids there is some neuro-physiological relationship between flight and settling with settling becoming more prolonged and stable after longer flights (see p. 237).

The stimuli promoting landing behaviour in an insect ready to respond are variable and appropriate to the particular insect. Thus aphids respond to leaves reflecting relatively long light wavelengths, *Ascia* to the smell of salt marshes in which it breeds (Nielsen, 1961), and *Melolontha* to the trees to which its flight is directed.

When the migration is an immediate post-teneral flight it is often followed by maturation. It is unlikely that maturation is the immediate cause of the end of migration, but the two phenomena are clearly related, perhaps hormonally, since maturation is known to be under hormonal control (p.708).

13.68 Significance of migration

The probable long-term advantage of migration is that it enables a species to keep pace with changes in the location of its habitats (Southwood, 1962). This is suggested by the fact that migration is most fully developed in insects living in temporary habitats; those living in stable habitats have much less tendency to migrate. This can be illustrated by reference to the British Anisoptera. Six species live in streams which are regarded as permanent habitats and none of these migrates, 14 species occupy only slightly less permanent lakes and canals and six of them (43%) migrate, while of 19 species living in relatively temporary pools ten (53%) migrate.

The impermanence of a habitat may result from a number of causes. Often seasonal climatic changes make a habitat untenable for part of a year. In north temperate regions the winter is the unfavourable period while in the tropics many insects are unable to survive the dry season in an active form. In these cases suitable and unsuitable conditions alternate in a regular sequence, but in other cases climatic changes may occur in an irregular manner. A habitat may also become untenable because of ecological changes, as in the progress of an ecological succession where, for instance, open grassland may be replaced by scrub. Or the habitat itself may be ephemeral in the case of species breeding in flowers or fungi or carrion. Finally in some cases the impermanence of the habitat may arise through alterations in the requirements of the insect at different stages in the life cycle; Acrididae, for instance, have different requirements for feeding and for oviposition.

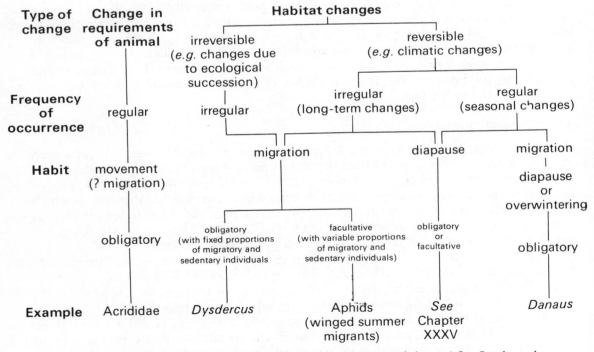

Fig. 165. The relation of movement and diapause to environmental change (after Southwood, 1962).

An unfavourable period arising through the impermanence of the habitat may be survived either by migration to some other more suitable habitat or by diapause. If the change in habitat is reversible, as with seasonal changes, diapause may be an advantage since it does not subject the insect to the possibility of completely failing to find a suitable habitat as may occur with migration (see Chapter XXXV). Sometimes a migration precedes diapause, carrying the insect to a suitable site in which to survive. This occurs, for instance, in *Eurygaster*, in thrips which leave the vegetation to overwinter under the bark of adjacent trees, and in *Danaus*. Where changes in the habitat are irregular migration has a clear advantage over diapause. The interrelationships of the various types of migration, diapause and environmental change are summarised in figure 165.

SECTION C

The Abdomen, Reproduction and Development

CHAPTER XIV
THE ABDOMEN

The insect abdomen is more obviously segmental in origin than either the head or the thorax, consisting of a series of similar segments, but with the posterior segments modified for mating and oviposition. The musculature of the anterior segments is fairly uniform and it is concerned primarily with compressing and distending the abdomen in ventilatory movements. In general the abdominal segments are without appendages except for those concerned with reproduction and a pair of terminal, usually sensory, cerci. Pregenital appendages are, however, present in Apterygota and in many larval insects. Aquatic larvae often have segmental gills, while many holometabolous larvae, especially amongst the Diptera and Lepidoptera, have lobe-like abdominal legs called prolegs. It is not clear whether or not these are serially homologous with the thoracic legs.

The general structure of the insect abdomen is considered by Snodgrass (1935), and for a discussion on the origins of abdominal appendages see Hinton (1955).

14.1 Segmentation of the abdomen

14.11 Number of segments

The basic number of segments in the abdomen is eleven plus the post-segmental telson which bears the anus. Only in adult Protura and the embryos of some hemimetabolous insects is the full complement visible. In all other instances some degree of reduction has taken place. The telson, if it is present at all, is generally represented only by the circumanal membrane, but larval Odonata are exceptional in that three small sclerites surrounding the anus may represent the telson.

In general, more segments are visible in the more generalised hemimetabolous orders than in the more specialised holometabolous insects. Thus in Acrididae all eleven segments are visible (Fig. 166A) whereas in Muscidae only segments 2–5 are visible and segments 6–9 are telescoped within the others (Fig. 166B). Collembola are exceptional in having only six abdominal segments, even in the embryo.

The definitive number of segments is present at hatching in all insects except Protura. All the segments differentiate in the embryo and this type of development is called epimorphic. In Protura, on the other hand, the first instar larva hatches with only eight abdominal segments plus the telson; the remaining three segments are added at subsequent moults, arising behind the last abdominal segment, but in front of the telson (Fig. 167). This type of development is called anamorphic.

In general, the abdomen is clearly marked off from the thorax, but this is not the

257

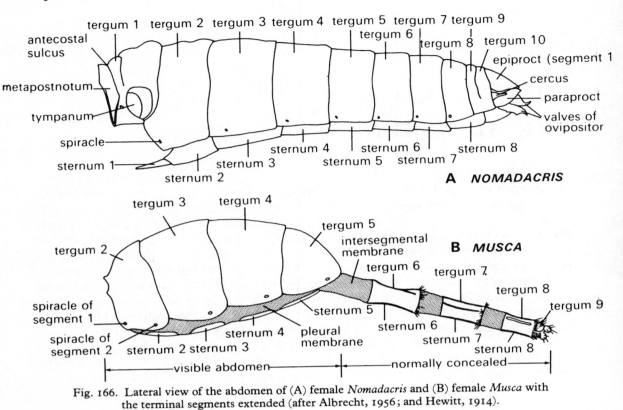

Fig. 166. Lateral view of the abdomen of (A) female *Nomadacris* and (B) female *Musca* with the terminal segments extended (after Albrecht, 1956; and Hewitt, 1914).

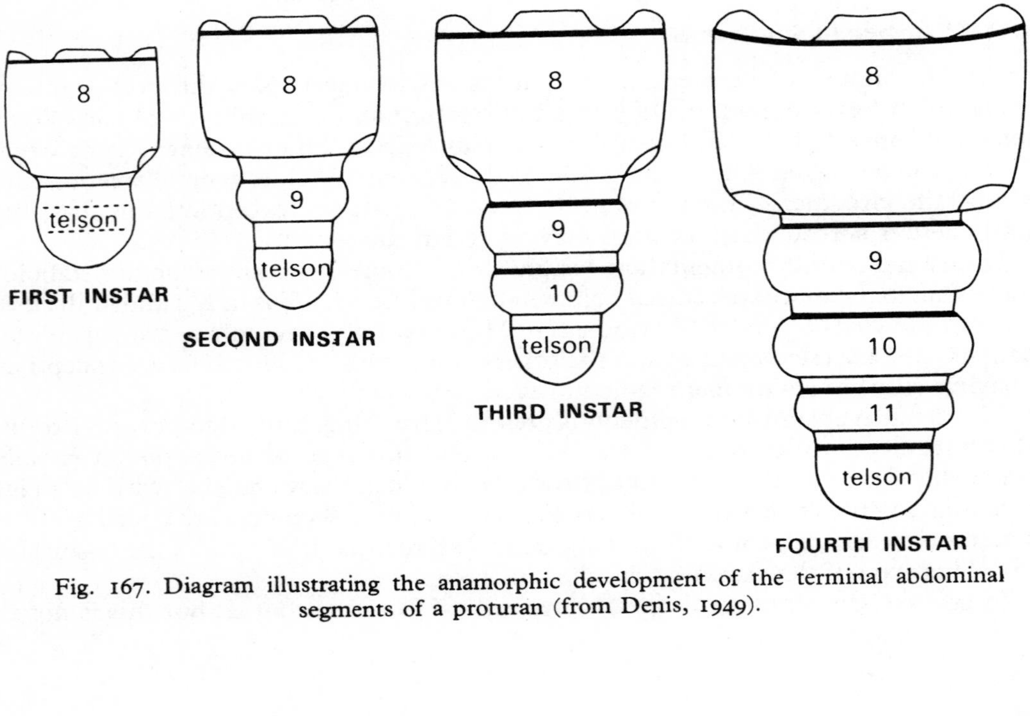

Fig. 167. Diagram illustrating the anamorphic development of the terminal abdominal segments of a proturan (from Denis, 1949).

case in the Hymenoptera where the first abdominal segment is intimately fused with
the thoracic segments and is known as the propodeum. The waist of Hymenoptera
Apocrita is thus not between the thorax and abdomen, but between the first abdominal
segment and the rest of the abdomen. Often segment 2 forms a narrow petiole connecting the two parts. The swollen part of the abdomen behind the waist is called the gaster
(Fig. 168).

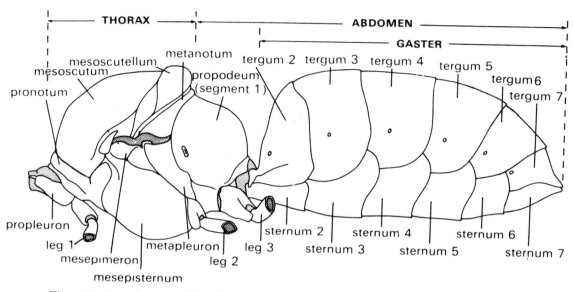

Fig. 168. Lateral view of the thorax and abdomen of *Apis* (after Snodgrass, 1956)

14.12 Structure of abdominal segments

A typical abdominal segment, such as the third, consists of a sclerotised tergum and
sternum joined by membranous pleural regions (Fig. 171). In many holometabolous
larvae, however, there is virtually no sclero-
tisation and the abdomen consists of a series
of membranous segments. This is true in
many Diptera and Hymenoptera, some
Coleoptera and most lepidopterous larvae.
In these the only sclerotised areas are small
plates bearing trichoid sensilla, while in
others, such as larval Thysanoptera, the
membrane is studded with small sclerotised
plaques. Even where well-developed terga
and sterna are present these may be divided
into a number of small sclerites as in the
larva of *Calosoma* (Coleoptera) (Fig. 169).

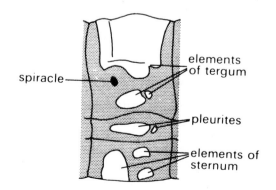

Fig. 169. Lateral view of an abdominal segment
of a larva of *Calosoma* (after Snodgrass, 1935).

In other insects, however, the extent of
sclerotisation may be increased by sclerites

in the pleural regions (Fig. 169), and these pleural sclerites sometimes bear appendages. The styli of Thysanura (p. 265) and the gills of Ephemeroptera arise from such plates. Sometimes the tergum, sternum and pleural elements fuse to form a complete ring and this is true in the genital segments of many male insects, in segment 10 of Odonata, Ephemeroptera and Dermaptera and segment 11 of Machilidae.

Typically the posterior part of each segment overlaps the anterior part of the segment behind (Fig. 170), the two being joined by a membrane, but segments may fuse together, wholly or in part. For instance, in Acrididae the terga of segments 9 and 10 fuse together (Fig. 166), while in some Coleoptera the second sternum fuses with the next two so that the sutures between them are largely obliterated.

The more anterior segments have a spiracle on either side. This may be set in the pleural membrane (Fig. 169), or in a small sclerite within the membrane, or on the side of the tergum (Fig. 166) or sternum.

The reproductive opening in male insects is usually on segment 9, while in the majority of female insects the opening of the oviduct is on or behind segment 8 or 9. The Ephemeroptera and Dermaptera are unusual in having the opening behind segment 7. These genital segments may be highly modified, in the male to produce copulatory apparatus (see p. 309), and in the females of some orders to form an ovipositor. This may be formed by the sclerotisation and telescoping of the posterior abdominal segments, or it may involve modified abdominal appendages (p. 323).

In front of these genital segments the abdominal segments are usually unmodified, although segment 1 is frequently reduced or absent. Behind them segment 10 is usually developed, but segment 11 is often represented only by a dorsal lobe, the epiproct, and two lateroventral lobes, the paraprocts. In Plecoptera, Blattidae and Isoptera the epiproct is reduced and fused with the tergum of segment 10, while in most holometabolous insects segment 11 is lacking altogether and segment 10 is terminal.

Modifications of the terminal abdominal segments often occur in aquatic insects and are concerned with respiration (see Chapter XXIV). In some larval Diptera segment 8 may become long and thin, forming a respiratory siphon, and this development is most marked in *Eristalis* where segment 8 forms a telescopic tube. In mosquito larvae the siphon is a dorsal projection from segment 8 and in *Mansonia* this siphon is modified for piercing plant tissues. A similar modification of the terminal abdominal segment occurs in the larva of the syrphid *Chrysogaster*.

In *Nepa* and *Ranatra* (Heteroptera) the spiracles are not on a siphon, but air is conveyed to the terminal abdominal spiracles while the insect is under water by a tube formed from two processes held together by fine hooks.

14.13 Musculature

Where the cuticle of the abdomen is largely membranous, as in many holometabolous larvae, most longitudinal muscles run from one primitive intersegmental fold to the next (see Fig. 61), but in well-sclerotised insects a secondary segmentation becomes superimposed on this primary pattern with the intersegmental sclerites fusing with the anterior ends of the following terga and sterna (see p. 127) to produce antecostal ridges. In most insects the dorsal and ventral longitudinal muscles are in two series, external and internal (Fig. 170). The internal muscles run from one antecostal ridge to the next and so retract the segments within each other. The external muscles are much shorter and only extend from the posterior end of one segment to the anterior end of the next and, because of the degree of overlap between the segments, the origins may be posterior to the insertions (Fig. 170B). Hence they may act as protractor muscles, extending the abdomen, and their efficiency is sometimes improved by the development of apodemes so that their pull is exerted longitudinally instead of obliquely. If such a protractor mechanism is absent extension of the abdomen results from the elasticity of the cuticle and the pressure of blood in the abdomen. In the grasshopper the external dorsal muscles are so placed that they produce some lateral twisting of the abdomen.

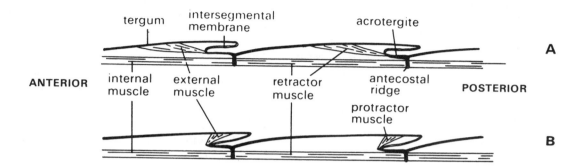

Fig. 170. Diagram of the dorsal longitudinal musculature in an abdominal segment. A. Typical arrangement of external and internal muscles, both acting as retractors. B. Origin of external muscle shifted posteriorly so that it acts as a protractor (from Snodgrass, 1935).

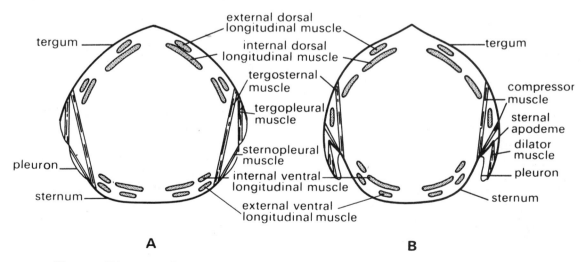

Fig. 171. Diagrammatic transverse sections of an abdominal segment. A. Typical arrangement of the muscles. B. Lateral muscles differentiated into compressor and dilator muscles (from Snodgrass, 1935).

There are also lateral muscles which usually extend from the tergum to the sternum, but sometimes arise or are inserted into the pleuron. They are usually intrasegmental, but sometimes cross from one segment to the next. Their effect is to compress the abdomen dorso-ventrally. Dilation of the abdomen often results from its elasticity and from blood pressure, but in some insects some of the lateral muscles function as dilators. This occurs when the tergal origins of the muscles are carried ventrally by extension of the terga, while the sternal insertions may also be carried dorsally on apodemes (Fig. 171B).

In addition to the longitudinal and lateral muscles others are present in connection with abdominal appendages, especially the genitalia, and the spiracles (p.458), while transverse bands of muscle form the dorsal and ventral diaphragms (p.665).

14.2 Abdominal appendages

Insects are generally believed to have been derived from some myriapod-like ancestor with a pair of typical walking legs on each segment. Typical legs, such as are found on the thorax, never occur on the abdomen of insects, but various appendages do occur and some of these are probably derived from typical appendages. Others are probably secondary structures which have developed quite independently of the primitive appendages.

14.21 Primitive appendages

The appendages of segment 11 form a pair of structures called cerci which arise from the membranes between the epiproct and the paraprocts, and even where segment 11 is absent the cerci may be present, appearing to arise from segment 10.

Cerci are present in the Apterygota and the hemimetabolous orders other than the hemipteroids. Only Mecoptera, and possibly the Symphyta, amongst the holometabolous insects have cerci. They may be simple, unsegmented structures as in Orthoptera (Fig. 172A), or annulated as in Dictyoptera (Fig. 172B). They may be very short and barely visible or form long filaments as long or longer than the body as in Thysanura, Ephemeroptera and Plecoptera. Even within a group, such as the Acridoidea, the range of form of the cerci is considerable (see Uvarov, 1966).

The cerci usually function as sense organs, being set with large numbers of trichoid sensilla with a complex articulation at the base. Thus they are sensitive to tactile stimuli and to air movement and sometimes may act as sound receivers (p. 599).

Sometimes the cerci are different in the two sexes of a species, suggesting that they play a role in copulation. Thus the cerci of female *Calliptamus* (Orthoptera) are simple cones, but in the male they are elongate, flattened structures with two or three lobes at the apex armed with strong inwardly directed points. There is similar dimorphism in Embioptera where the male cerci are asymmetrical with the basal segment of the left cercus forming a clasping organ (Fig. 172C) and amongst the earwigs the cerci form powerful forceps which are usually straight and unarmed in the female, but incurved and toothed in the male (Fig. 172D). Similar forceps-like cerci in the Japygidae are used in catching prey.

In larval Zygoptera the cerci are modified to form the two lateral gills (see Fig. 319), while in the ephemeropteran *Prosopistoma* the long, feather-like cerci, together with the median caudal filament, can be used to drive the insect forwards by beating against the water.

The primitive segmental appendages are not known to persist on segment 10, but those of segments 8 and 9 may be modified as the external genitalia (p. 323). In the more anterior segments many insects have appendages, but it is generally agreed that they are derived from segmental appendages only in the Apterygota.

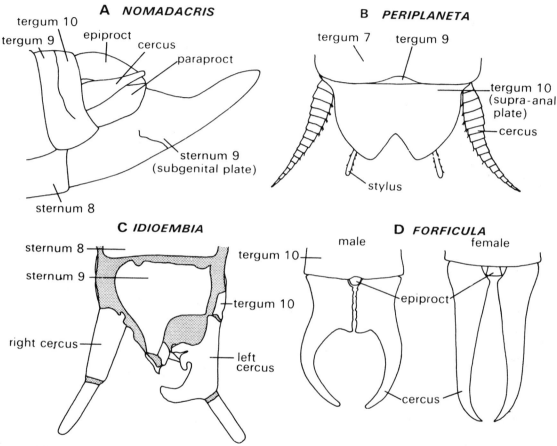

Fig. 172. Different types of cerci. A. *Nomadacris* (Orthoptera)—lateral view of tip of abdomen of male. B. *Periplaneta* (Dictyoptera)—dorsal view of the tip of the abdomen of male. C. *Idioembia* (Embioptera)—ventral view of tip of abdomen of male. D. *Forficula* (Dermaptera) —male and female forceps (cerci) (after various authors).

Collembola

The Collembola have pregenital appendages on three abdominal segments. From the first segment a median lobe projects forwards and down between the last pair of legs (see Fig. 86C, D). This is known as the ventral tube and at its tip are a pair of eversible vesicles which in many Symphypleona are long and tubular. The unpaired basal part of the ventral tube is believed to represent the fused coxae of the segmental appendages and the vesicles are thus coxal vesicles. The vesicles are everted by blood pressure from within the body and are withdrawn by retractor muscles.

The ventral tube appears to have two functions. In some circumstances it functions as an adhesive organ enabling the insect to walk over smooth or steep surfaces. To facilitate this on a dry surface the vesicles are moistened by a secretion from cephalic glands opening on to the labium and connecting with the ventral tube by a groove in the cuticle in the ventral midline of the thorax. The ventral tube also enables Collembola to adhere to the surface film on water since it is the only part of the cuticle which is wettable, all the rest is strongly hydrofuge.

The second function of the vesicles of the ventral tube is the absorption of water from the substratum (p. 505).

The appendages of the third and fourth segments of the abdomen of many Collembola form the retinaculum and the furca which are used in locomotion (see p. 153).

Protura

There are pairs of appendages on each of the first three segments of the abdomen of Protura. At their most fully developed they are two segmented with an eversible vesicle at the tip (Fig. 173A). The appendages are moved by extrinsic and intrinsic muscles which include a retractor muscle of the vesicle.

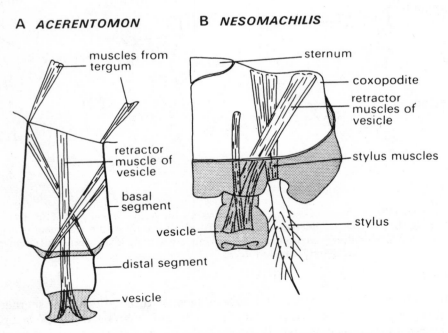

Fig. 173. A. Abdominal appendage of *Acerentomon* (Protura). B. Abdominal appendage of *Nesomachilis* (Thysanura). The sternum and coxopodite are seen from the inside (from Snodgrass, 1935).

Thysanura and Diplura

On abdominal segments 2–9 of Machilidae, 7–9 or 8–9 of Lepismatidae, 1–7 of Japygidae and 2–7 of Campodeidae there are pairs of small, unjointed styli, each inserted on a basal sclerite which is believed to represent the coxa (Fig. 173B). Since similar styli are present on the coxae of the thoracic legs of *Machilis* (Thysanura) these styli are regarded as coxal epipodites.

Associated with the styli, but occupying a more median position, are eversible vesicles. These are present on segments 1–7 of Machilidae and 2–7 of *Campodea* (Diplura), but in Lepismatidae and Japygidae there are generally fewer or none. The vesicles evert through a cleft at the posterior margin of the segment, being forced out by' blood pressure. At the tip there are large nuclei, but cell boundaries are not visible and the epithelium here may be syncytial (Fig. 174). The retractor muscles of the vesicles arise close together on the anterior margin of the sternum. As in the Collembola, these vesicles can absorb water from the substratum (Drummond, 1953).

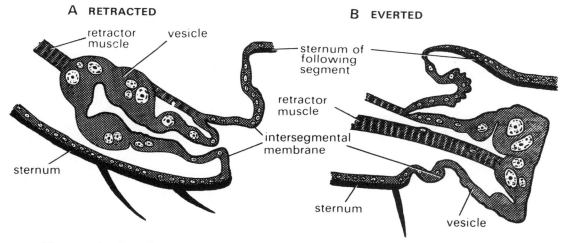

Fig. 174. Sections through an eversible vesicle of *Campodea* (A) retracted and B everted (after Drummond, 1953).

14.22 Secondary appendages

Appendages are absent from the pregenital segments of adult insects other than Apterygota, but are widely present in the larvae of holometabolous insects and, as gills, in diverse aquatic larval forms. Some authorities regard these appendages as being derived from primitive segmental appendages (see *e.g.* Snodgrass, 1935), but it is probably more reasonable to regard most of them as secondary developments (Hinton, 1955) and this point of view is taken here.

Gills are present on the abdominal segments of the larvae of many aquatic insects. Ephemeroptera usually have six or seven pairs of plate-like or filamentous gills (Fig. 261) which are moved by muscles and may play a direct role in gaseous exchange, but perhaps are more important in maintaining a flow of water over the body (p. 480). Gill tufts may also be present on the first two or three abdominal segments, or in the anal region of larval Plecoptera. The larva of *Sialis* (Megaloptera) has seven pairs of five-segmented gills, each arising from a basal sclerite on the side of the abdomen (Fig. 177A), and a similar terminal filament arises from segment 9. Similar, but unsegmented gills are present in other larval Megaloptera and in some larval Coleoptera. Larval Trichoptera have filamentous gills in dorsal, lateral and ventral series.

Leg-like outgrowths of the body wall, known as prolegs, are common features of the abdomen of holometabolous larvae. These appendages are expanded by blood pressure and moved mainly by the normal muscles of the adjacent body wall together with others inserted at the base of the proleg and a retractor muscle extending to the sole or planta surface (see Fig. 87). Frequently the prolegs are armed distally with spines or crochets which grip the substratum and sometimes, when prolegs are not developed, their position is occupied by a raised pad armed with spines. Such a pad is called a creeping welt and is clearly comparable with a proleg (Fig. 263).

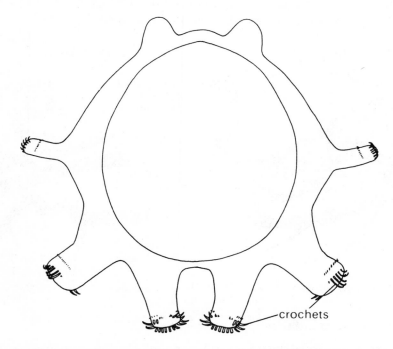

Fig. 175. Cross-section of an abdominal segment of a tabanid larva showing numerous prolegs, including dorsal and lateral pairs (after Hinton, 1955).

Creeping welts and prolegs are present in many dipterous larvae some of which have several prolegs on each segment (Fig. 175) while others have creeping welts which extend all round the segment. The larvae of a number of families of Diptera have abdominal suckers which may be derived from prolegs. Thus the larva of the psychodid *Maruina* has a sucker on each of abdominal segments 1–8 and these enable the larva to maintain its position along the sides of waterfalls, and in another larva, of *Horaiella,* a single large sucker, bounded by a fringe of hairs, extends over the ventral surface of several segments.

Larval Blepharoceridae, which live in fast-flowing streams and waterfalls, have a sucker on each of abdominal segments 2–7. Each sucker has an outer flaccid rim with an incomplete anterior margin. The central disc of the sucker is supported by close-packed sclerotised rods and in the middle a hole leads into an inner chamber with strongly sclerotised walls and an extensive folded roof (Fig. 176). Muscles inserted into the roof and the rim of the sclerotised walls of the inner chamber increase the volume of the chamber when they contract and if at the same time the rim of the sucker is pressed down on to the substratum a partial vacuum is created so that the sucker adheres to the surface.

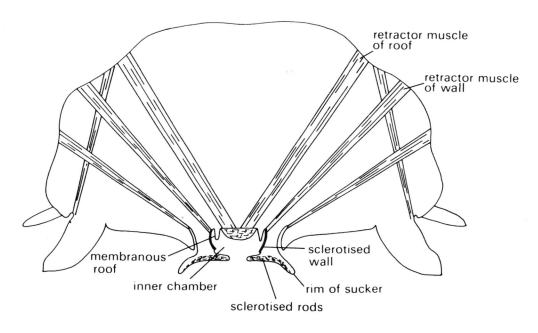

Fig. 176. Transverse section through the sixth abdominal segment of a blepharocerid larva showing the ventral sucker (after Hinton, 1955).

Even if a well-formed sucker is not present many dipterous larvae can produce a sucker-like effect by raising the central part of the ventral surface while keeping the periphery in contact with the substratum, the sucker being sealed and made effective by a film of moisture.

Finally, in a few larval Diptera prolegs may be used for holding prey. The larva of *Vermileo* lives in a pit in dry soil and feeds in the same way as an ant lion (p. 24). It lies ventral side up and prey which fall into the pit are grasped against the thorax by a median proleg on the ventral surface of the first abdominal segment.

Thus prolegs are present in many different families of Diptera and have a variety of functions. Hinton (1955) suggests that prolegs have evolved separately in at least twenty-seven different groups within the order.

Well-developed prolegs are also a feature of lepidopterous larvae which usually have a pair on each of abdominal segments 3–6 and 10 (Fig. 262). Embryological evidence suggests that these prolegs may be serially homologous with the thoracic legs, but the bulk of other evidence is opposed to this suggestion (Hinton, 1955). The prolegs are armed distally with crochets (see Fig. 87) which may form a complete ring, but climbing forms have the prolegs pointed mesally with a median row of crochets so that they are suited for grasping twigs. Climbing caterpillars occur in several families including the Geometridae and Sphingidae.

Variations occur in the numbers of prolegs in lepidopterous larvae. Megalopygidae have prolegs on segments 2–7 and 10, but those on segments 2 and 7 have no crochets. More frequently the number of prolegs is reduced and in Geometridae there are usually only two pairs, on segments 6 and 10. Prolegs are completely absent from some leaf-mining larvae and from the free-living Eucleidae, some of which, however, have weak ventral suckers on segments 1–7.

In some Notodontidae the anal prolegs are modified for defensive purposes. Thus in *Cerura* they are slender projections which normally point posteriorly, but if the larva is touched the tip of the abdomen is flexed forwards and a slender pink process is everted from the end of each projection. At the same time the larva raises its head and thorax from the ground and emits formic acid from a ventral gland in the prothorax. This reaction is presumed to be a defensive display.

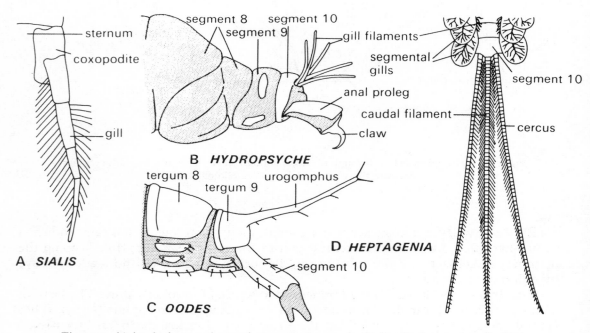

Fig. 177. Abdominal appendages of pterygote larvae. A. *Sialis* gill, dorsal view. B. *Hydropsyche* (Trichoptera) lateral view of terminal abdominal segments showing gills and anal proleg. C. *Oodes* (Coleoptera) lateral view of terminal abdominal segments showing urogomphus. D. *Heptagenia* (Ephemeroptera) dorsal view of terminal abdominal segments showing gills, cerci and median caudal filament (mainly from Snodgrass, 1935).

Digitiform prolegs without crochets occur on the first eight abdominal segments of larval Mecoptera. They have no intrinsic musculature, but are moved by differences in blood pressure and by the action of muscles on adjacent parts of the ventral body wall. Prolegs without crochets also occur on the abdomen of larval Symphyta and particularly in the Tenthredinoidea. The number varies from six to nine pairs.

Finally, larval Trichoptera have anal prolegs on segment 10 (Fig. 177B). Their development varies, but in the Limnephilidae, where they are most fully developed, there are two basal segments with a terminal claw, having both levator and depressor muscles. These appendages, together with a dorsal and two lateral retractile papillae on the first abdominal segment, enable the larva to hold on to its case.

14.23 Other appendages

Apart from the segmentally arranged prolegs and gills some insects have other abdominal appendages, commonly in the form of a median process from the last segment. Thysanura and Ephemeroptera have a median caudal filament which resembles the two cerci (Fig. 177D). Larval Zygoptera have a median terminal gill on the epiproct, while in larval Sphingidae a terminal spine arises from the dorsum of segment 10. In larval mosquitoes and chironomids a group of four papillae surrounds the anus (see Fig. 341). These papillae are concerned with salt regulation (p. 509).

Some larval Coleoptera have a pair of processes called urogomphi which are outgrowths of the tergum of segment 9 (Fig. 177C). They may be short spines or multiarticulate filaments and they may be rigid with the tergum or arising from the membrane behind it so that they are mobile. Jeannel (1949) regards them as homologous with cerci, but see Crowson (1960). Aphids have a pair of tubes, known as cornicles, projecting from the dorsum of segment 6. They permit the escape of a waxy fluid which perhaps serves as a protection against predators, but see Lindsay (1969, *Ann. ent. Soc. Am.* **62**).

CHAPTER XV

THE REPRODUCTIVE SYSTEM

The male and female reproductive systems generally consist of paired gonads connected to a median duct leading to the gonopore. Accessory glands are often present which, in the male are usually concerned with spermatophore formation and sperm maintenance, and in the female provide a glue for sticking the eggs to the substratum or provide the substance for a complex egg-case. The female has, in addition, a spermatheca for storing sperm after copulation.

Each gonad typically consists of a series of tubes each with a germinal area at the tip which contains the primordial sex cells. From these spermatogonia or oogonia are produced which, as they pass down the tube, are to be seen in successive stages of development. Each secondary spermatogonium gives rise to four spermatozoa, but only a single oocyte is formed from each secondary oogonium. In some cases nutriment is provided for the oocytes by special nurse cells, but yolk is laid down largely by the incorporation of protein from the blood. The production of yolk is under hormonal control and its deposition results in the formation of an extremely large egg cell which is enclosed in a shell and then passed into the oviduct. Sometimes, if conditions are adverse, oocytes are resorbed.

Insects are not always sexually mature when they have completed the final moult to adult and in species with an adult diapause there may be a considerable delay before mature sex cells are produced. Hence it is necessary to distinguish between becoming adult and becoming sexually mature.

A general review of insect reproduction is given by Davey (1965a), while the structure of reproductive organs is considered by Snodgrass (1935). For a general review of oogenesis see Raven (1961) and for aspects of oogenesis in insects see Bonhag (1958), King (1964) and Telfer (1965). Control of reproduction is reviewed by Highnam (1964) and de Wilde (1964a, b), while nutritional aspects are considered by Johansson (1964).

MALE

15.1 Anatomy of male internal reproductive organs

The male reproductive organs typically consist of a pair of testes which connect with paired seminal vesicles and a median ejaculatory duct (Fig. 178). In most insects there are also a number of accessory glands which open into the vasa deferentia or the ejaculatory duct.

Testis

The testes may lie above or below the gut in the abdomen and are often close to the mid-line. Usually each testis consists of a number of testis tubes or follicles. Sometimes, as in Coleoptera Adephaga, there is only a single follicle, in lice there are two, while in Acrididae there may be over 100. In other cases, as in Lepidoptera, the follicles are incompletely separated from each other (Fig. 179B), and the testes of Diptera consist of simple, undivided sacs, although these may be regarded as single follicles. Sometimes the testis consists of a series of lobes each of which consists of a number of follicles. Thus in the cerambycid *Prionoplus* each testis comprises 12 to 15 lobes each with 15 follicles (and see Fig. 178B). The testes of Apterygota are often undivided sacs, but it is not certain in this case that they are strictly comparable with the gonads of other insects since the germarium occupies a lateral position in the testis instead of being terminal.

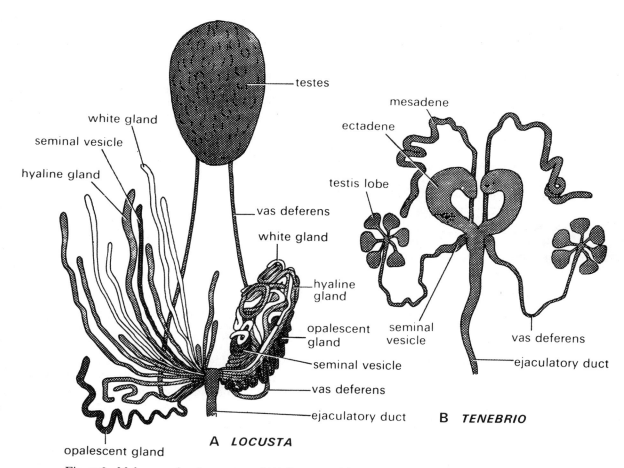

Fig. 178. Male reproductive system of (A) *Locusta,* with the accessory glands in their normal position on the right and separated on the left, and (B) *Tenebrio* (from Uvarov, 1966; Imms, 1957).

The walls of the follicles consist of a thin epithelium standing on a basement membrane and in some cases the epithelium consists of two layers of cells (Snodgrass, 1935). The follicles are bound together by a peritoneal sheath and if the two testes are close to each other they may be bound together. This occurs in some Hymenoptera and Lepidoptera, and in some of the latter the testes may fuse completely to form a single median structure.

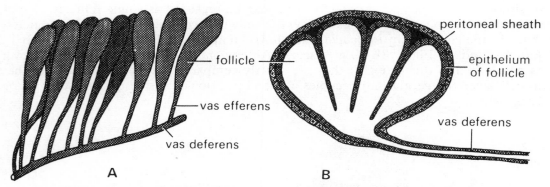

Fig. 179. A. A series of testis follicles opening independently into the vas deferens as in Orthoptera. B. Section through a testis in which the follicles are incompletely separated from each other and have a common opening to the vas deferens, as in Lepidoptera (from Snodgrass, 1935).

Vas deferens

From each testis follicle a fine, and usually short, vas efferens connects with the vas deferens (Fig. 179A) which is a tube with a fairly thick bounding epithelium, a basement membrane and a layer of circular muscle outside it. The vasa deferentia run backwards to lead into the distal end of the ejaculatory duct and often they are dilated to form the seminal vesicles (Fig. 178B). In other cases, as in Acrididae, the seminal vesicles are separate diverticula arising from the ejaculatory duct (Fig. 178A), while in some Diptera there is a common median seminal vesicle.

Ejaculatory duct

The ejaculatory duct, which leads to the aedeagus (p. 309), is ectodermal in origin and is lined with cuticle. Often at least a part of the wall is muscular, but the ejaculatory duct in *Apis* is entirely without muscles (Snodgrass, 1956).

Where a complex spermatophore is produced the ejaculatory duct is also complex. Thus in *Locusta* (Orthoptera) the ejaculatory duct consists of upper and lower ducts connected via a funnel-like constriction (Fig. 180A). The lumen of the upper part of the duct is a vertical slit bounded laterally by columnar epithelium (Fig. 180D). In the funnel the cuticle forms a series of, usually nine, ridges on either side. These curve upwards posteriorly as they run back to meet in the dorsal midline and they project so that they almost completely divide the lumen (Fig. 180C). The lumen of the lower duct is circular and leads to the ejaculatory sac and spermatophore sac (Fig. 180A, B). Scattered muscle fibres are present in the wall of the upper duct, but are absent elsewhere (Gregory, 1965).

The ejaculatory duct of *Oncopeltus* (Heteroptera) is also extremely complex, being specialised for the erection of the penis (Bonhag and Wick, 1953).

Ephemeroptera have no ejaculatory duct and the vasa deferentia lead directly to the paired genital openings. Dermaptera, on the other hand, have paired ejaculatory ducts, although in some species one of the ducts remains vestigial. Thus in *Forficula* the right-hand ejaculatory duct is fully functional, while the left-hand duct is vestigial (Popham, 1965).

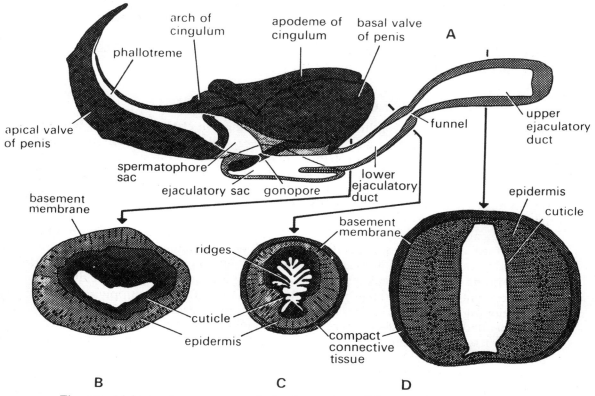

Fig. 180. Male copulatory organ and ejaculatory duct of *Locusta*. A. Lateral view with musculature removed. B. Transverse section of lower ejaculatory duct. C. Transverse section of funnel. D. Transverse section of upper ejaculatory duct (after Gregory, 1965).

Accessory glands

The male accessory glands open into the vasa deferentia or the distal end of the ejaculatory duct. They may be ectodermal in origin, when they are known as ectadenia, and in this case they open into the ejaculatory duct. Ectadenia occur in Coleoptera and possibly other groups, but lack of embryological information makes this uncertain. Glands of mesodermal origin, mesadenia, are found in Orthoptera (see D. S. Anderson, 1966) and in some cases, *Tenebrio* (Coleoptera) for instance, both ectadenia and mesadenia are present (Fig. 178B).

The number of accessory glands varies considerably. Apterygota and some Diptera have none at all, but others have several pairs. Thus in *Locusta* there are 15 pairs of accessory glands, not counting the seminal vesicles with which they are closely associated (Fig. 178A), and *Periplaneta* has a very large number of glands. Where large numbers of glands occur it is probable that they produce various secretions and this is certainly the case in Acrididae where white, opalescent and hyaline glands are recognisably different and it is quite probable that there is functional variation even within one of these categories. Each gland in *Locusta* is differentiated into a thin-walled distal part, sometimes with a visible brush border and probably secretory in nature, and a proximal thick-walled part which is presumed to conduct the secretions down to the ejaculatory duct (Gregory, 1965).

The secretions of the accessory glands mix with the sperm in the seminal fluid and produce spermatophores in some insects (p. 313).

15.2 Spermatogenesis

At the distal end of each testis follicle is the germarium in which the germ cells divide to produce spermatogonia (Fig. 181). In Orthoptera, Dictyoptera, Homoptera and Lepidoptera, the spermatogonia probably obtain nutriment from a large apical cell with which they have cytoplasmic connections, while in Diptera and Heteroptera (Bonhag and Wick, 1953) there is a comparable apical complex consisting of a syncytium with numerous nuclei. In Diptera the transfer of mitochondria from this complex to the spermatogonia has been observed (Carson, 1945).

These apical connections are soon lost and the spermatogonia associate with other cells which form a cyst around them (Fig. 181). One, or sometimes more, spermatogonia are enclosed in each cyst and, in *Prionoplus,* there are initially two cyst-cells round each spermatogonium. The cyst-cells may be spermatogonia which lack adequate nutrition and therefore fail to continue their normal development. They may supply nutriment to the developing sperm and, in *Popillia* (Coleoptera), the sperm at one stage have their heads embedded in the cyst-cells, this perhaps facilitating the transfer of nutrients (J. Anderson, 1950). In Heteroptera, trophocytes, large cells with irregular nuclei, are scattered amongst the cysts.

As more spermatogonia are produced they push those which have developed earlier down the follicle so that a range of development is present in each follicle with the earliest stages distally in the germarium and the oldest in the proximal part of the follicle adjacent to the vas deferens. Three zones of development are commonly recognised below the germarium (Fig. 181). These are:—

I   a zone of growth in which the primary spermatogonia, enclosed in cysts, divide and increase in size to form spermatocytes

II   a zone of maturation and reduction in which each spermatocyte undergoes the two meiotic divisions to produce spermatids

III   a zone of transformation in which the spermatids develop into spermatozoa, a process known as spermiogenesis.

Since, in general, all the cells in a cyst are derived from a single primary spermatogonium they remain synchronised in their subsequent development. The number of sperm which a cyst ultimately produces depends on the number of spermatogonial divisions which occur and this is fairly constant for a species. In Acrididae there are between five and eight spermatogonial divisions and *Melanoplus,* which typically has seven divisions before meiosis, usually has 512 sperm per cyst. Normally four spermatozoa are produced from each spermatocyte, but in many coccids the spermatids which possess heterochromatic chromosomes degenerate so that only two sperm are formed from each spermatocyte and 32 are present in each cyst (Nur, 1962). In *Sciara* (Diptera) only one spermatid is formed from each spermatocyte because of the unequal distribution of chromosomes and cytoplasm which occurs at the meiotic divisions (Phillips, 1966).

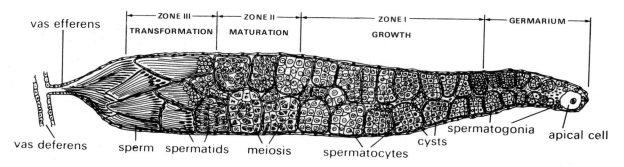

Fig. 181. Diagram of a testis follicle showing the stages of development of the sperm (from Wigglesworth, 1965).

Biochemical changes occur in the course of spermatogenesis. The repeated cell divisions entail the synthesis of large amounts of DNA and RNA, but the synthesis of DNA stops before meiosis occurs, while RNA synthesis continues into the early spermatid. Subsequently no further synthesis occurs and the RNA is eliminated first from the nucleus and then from the cell as the nucleus elongates. The reduction in RNA synthesis is associated with a rise in the production of an arginine-rich histone which forms a complex with DNA stopping it from acting as a primer for RNA synthesis. It is suggested that this mechanism insulates the genetic material during transit from one generation to the next (Bloch and Brach, 1964; Das, *et al.*, 1964; Muckenthaler, 1964).

The time taken for the completion of spermatogenesis varies, but in *Melanoplus* the period is about 28 days, the spermatogonial divisions occupying eight or nine days and spermiogenesis ten (Muckenthaler, 1964). In most insects meiosis is complete before the final moult and in insects which do not feed as adults spermatogenesis may be complete before the adult emerges.

15.21 Structure of mature spermatozoa

The mature sperms of *Parlatoria* (Homoptera), *Rhodnius* (Heteroptera) and *Orgyia* (Lepidoptera) are filamentous in form, about 300 μ long and less than a micron in diameter, while the sperm of *Drosophila* (Diptera) may be as much as 1·7 mm. long. The head and tail of the sperm are of approximately the same diameter (Fig. 182). The greater part of the head region is occupied by the nucleus with only a thin coating of cytoplasm, and in front of the nucleus is the acrosome which in *Acheta* (Orthoptera) has a double conical structure (Fig. 184D). The acrosome is probably concerned with attachment of the sperm to the egg and possibly also with the lysis of the egg membrane, thus permitting sperm entry.

A centriole is usually present immediately behind the nucleus and from it arises the axial filament, which runs the length of the tail of the sperm. The axial filament is formed of a number of very fine microtubules which in the sperm of *Drosophila*, grasshoppers and various other insects are arranged in a ring of nine doublets, with arms on one of the subfibres, surrounding two central tubules. Outside the ring of doublets is a further ring of nine accessory tubules (Fig. 183). It is presumed that the action of

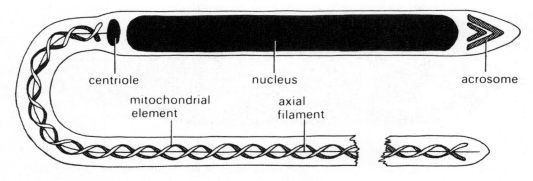

Fig. 182. Diagram showing the possible structure of an insect spermatozoon (after Davey, 1965a).

these rings of microtubules produces the lashing of sperm tails in the same way that the tubules in a flagellum are believed to produce movement (Bishop, 1962). On either side of the axial filament, or spiralling round it, are the long mitochondrial derivatives (see below) which, it is presumed, provide the power for movement by the sperm.

The sperm of coccids, which occur in sperm bundles, are lacking in all the typical organelles. In *Parlatoria* the nucleus is apparently represented by an electron opaque core which has no limiting membrane. Mitochondrial derivatives are absent, but Robison (1966) suggests that the homogeneous cytoplasm of the sperm is a mitochondrial product and serves as a store of energy so that mitochondria themselves are not necessary. There is no plasma membrane, but the outer wall of each sperm is formed by a ring of 45–50 microtubules about 200 Å in diameter. These run the whole length of the sperm and may be concerned with its mobility, replacing the typical axial filament.

The typical 9 + 2 arrangement of tubules in the axial filament is also lacking in the sperm of *Sciara*. In this species there are 72–76 pairs of tubules arranged in a curved row or a spiral which posteriorly encloses the mitochondrial derivative. The latter is single, not paired, and extends for almost the whole length of the sperm. It comprises two regions: an amorphous mitochondrial body with a paracrystalline rod running along one side. Comparable paracrystalline regions of the mitochondrial derivative are known in *Thermobia* (Thysanura), *Macroglossa* and *Pieris* (Lepidoptera), while in *Drosophila* this is the only mitochondrial component present. It is suggested that this region represents a maximal concentration of mitochondrial cristae with a corresponding concentration of respiratory enzymes (Makielski, 1966).

In *Sciara* the amorphous part of the mitochondrial derivative is sloughed off a few hours after the sperm reach the female spermatheca and at this time the sperm become motile. Makielski (1966) suggests that only after this are the sperm capable of fertilising the eggs. Sperm of some other animal groups are known to require a period of development in the female before they are capable of fertilising eggs and this phenomenon is known as capacitance.

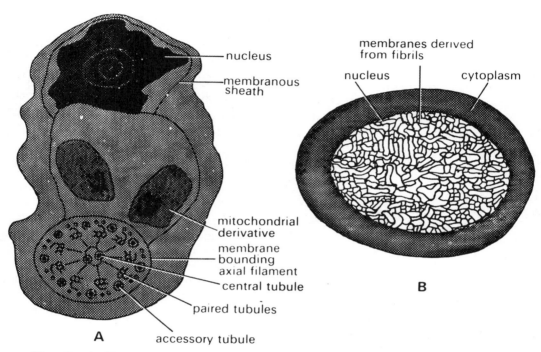

Fig. 183. A. Transverse section through a sperm of *Thermobia* (after Bawa, 1964). B. Transverse section through a differentiating spermatid of *Chortophaga* showing the reticulate appearance of the nucleus (after Dass and Ris, 1958).

Sperm bundles

In a number of insects sperm are grouped together in bundles for at least some of their existence and sometimes the bundles persist even after transference of the sperm to the female. The sperm of *Thermobia* normally occur in pairs, the two individuals being twisted round each other, and although their plasma membranes remain distinct an electron opaque substance is visible between them where they are close together. In addition, a continuous membrane appears to be present round both spermatozoa in some places (Bawa, 1964). Pairs of sperm also occur in Coleoptera.

Coccids have much more specialised sperm bundles. In these insects each cyst commonly produces 32 sperm and these become separated into two bundles of about 16 sperms. Each bundle becomes enclosed in a membranous sheath and the cyst wall degenerates. The bundles of *Pseudococcus* are much longer than the sperm which occupy only the middle region and the head-end of the bundle has a corkscrew-like form which may be concerned in locomotion (Nur, 1962). The sperm bundles of *Parlatoria*, on the other hand, are only the same length as the sperm which are all orientated in the same direction within the bundle. Movement of the bundle results from the combined activity of the sperm within (Robison, 1966).

In Orthoptera and Odonata different types of sperm bundle are formed. These are known as spermatodesms and consist of all the sperm from one cyst held together by a hyaline cap in which their heads are embedded. Usually the sperm separate when the spermatodesm enters the vas deferens, but in the Acrididae, the spermatodesms persist until they are transferred to the female.

15.22 Spermiogenesis

The spermatid which is formed after meiosis is typically a rounded cell containing the normal cell organelles. Subsequently it becomes modified to form the sperm and this process of spermiogenesis entails a complete reorganisation of the cell. It is convenient to consider separately each organelle of the mature sperm.

Acrosome

The acrosome is derived, at least in part, from Golgi material which in spermatocytes is scattered through the cytoplasm in the form of dictyosomes. There may be 30 or 40 of these in the cell and they consist of several pairs of parallel membranes with characteristic vacuoles and vesicles (Fig. 184A). After the second meiotic division the dictyosomes in *Acheta* fuse to a single body called the acroblast which consists of 6–10 membranes forming a cup with vacuoles and vesicles both inside and out (Fig. 184B).

In the later spermatid a granule, called the proacrosomal granule, appears in the cup of the acroblast and increases in size. The acroblast migrates so that the open side faces the nucleus and then the granule, associated with a newly developed membrane, the interstitial membrane, moves towards the nucleus and becomes attached to it (Fig. 184C). As the cell elongates the acroblast membranes migrate to the posterior end of the spermatid and are sloughed off together with much of the cytoplasm and various other cell inclusions. The proacrosomal granule then forms the acrosome, becoming cone-shaped and developing a cavity in which an inner cone is formed (Fig. 184D) (Kaye, 1962).

In *Gelastocoris* (Heteroptera) the proacrosome is formed from the fusion of granules in the scattered Golgi apparatus and no acroblast is formed. This may also be the case in Acrididae (Payne, 1966).

Nucleus

In the early spermatid of grasshoppers the nucleus appears to have a typical interphase structure with the chromosome fibrils unorientated. Each of the fibrils, which constitute the basic morphological units of the chromosomes, is about 200 Å in diameter and is made up of two subunits about 100 Å in diameter. The nucleus becomes very long and narrow and as it does so the chromosome fibrils become aligned more or less parallel with its long axis. The 100 Å microfibrils appear to separate into 40 Å fibrils and at the same time the non-histone protein, which in *Acheta* is largely in granules in the nucleoplasm, disappears from the nucleus (see above). The 40 Å fibrils are arranged so that they appear to form an anastomosing network when the nucleus is seen in cross-section (Fig. 183B) and as the nucleus elongates and narrows the nucleoplasm between them is progressively reduced until finally the whole of the nucleus appears to consist of a uniformly dense material (Dass and Ris, 1958). A similar linear arrangement of the chromosomes occurs in other groups, but in *Periplaneta* the chromosome fibrils become aggregated into granules. In *Acheta* Kaye and McMaster-Kaye (1966) suggest that the nucleus at this time does not consist wholly of chromatin, but also contains thin fibres containing non-histone protein.

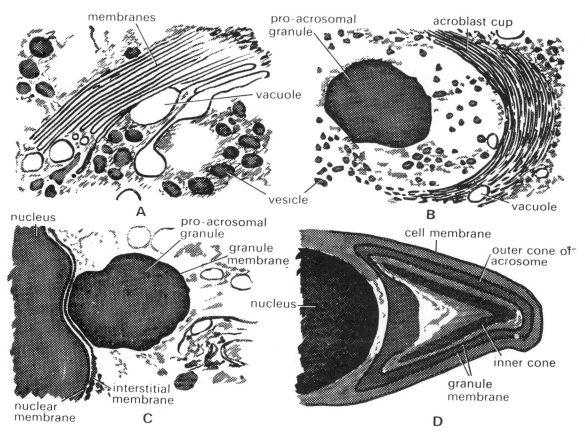

Fig. 184. Development of the acrosome of *Acheta*. A. A dictyosome. B. Acroblast with pro-acrosomal granule. C. Pro-acrosomal granule attached to the nucleus. D. Acrosome of a mature spermatozoon. Not all to same scale (after Kaye, 1962).

Mitochondria

In the spermatid the mitochondria fuse to form a single large body, the nebenkern, which consists of an outer limiting membrane and a central pool of mitochondrial components. The nebenkern divides into two parts which are associated with the developing axial filament. These parts elongate to form a pair of ribbon-like structures which, in *Buenea* (Heteroptera), have the limiting membrane replaced by a lamellated crystalline-like lattice (Collins and Richter, 1961).

Centriole and axial filament

The axial filament complex arises in the spermatid from the centriole. This process has been studied in *Sciara* (Phillips, 1966) and, although in the sperm of this insect the number of tubules in the centriole and axial filament is very high, it probably does not differ in its essentials in other insects. The centrioles of spermatogonia of *Sciara* are composed of 50–90 short, singlet tubules arranged in an oval with fibrous material on either side and a dense band on the inside. After the second meiotic division a single truncated cone-shaped centriole is present at the future head-end of the spermatid and at this stage the tubules are probably in doublets. Soon afterwards microtubules are observed extending out from the centriole, possibly having 'grown' out from it.

As the spermatid elongates the centriole migrates towards the tail, finally assuming a position adjacent to the posterior end of the nucleus. The microtubules continue to elongate and become orientated parallel with the long axis of the spermatid, extending into the tail. They thus now form the beginnings of the axial filament complex the pattern of which, as a result of its mode of formation, reflects the pattern of tubules in the centriole. The whole complex becomes surrounded by a smooth double membrane and the definitive condition arises from the addition of side arms to the tubules and the formation of more tubules peripherally.

15.3 Transfer of sperm to the seminal vesicle

In some Heteroptera and *Chortophaga* (Orthoptera), and possibly in other insects, the sperm make a complex circuit of the testis follicle before they leave the testis, migrating in a spiral path to the region of the secondary spermatocytes and then turning back and passing into the vas deferens. In *Chortophaga* the movement occurs after the spermatodesm is released from the cyst, but in the heteropteran *Leptocoris* the sperm are still enclosed in the cyst. In this case the movement starts while the spermatids are still differentiating and is at least partly due to the elongation of the cyst which occurs in the development of the sperm (Payne, 1934).

The fate of the cyst-cells is variable. In *Prionoplus* the cyst-cells break down in the testis (Edwards, 1961), but in *Popillia*, although the sperm escape from the cysts as they leave the testis, the cyst-cells accompany the sperm in the seminal fluid into the bursa of the female. Here they finally break down and it is suggested that they release glycogen which is used in the maintenance of the sperm (J. Anderson, 1950).

The sperm are inactive in the vas deferens and are carried along by peristaltic movements of the wall of the tube (Payne, 1933, 1934). They remain immobile in the seminal vesicle where they are often very tightly packed and in some cases, as in *Apis*, the heads of the sperm are embedded in the glandular wall of the vesicle.

FEMALE

15.4 Anatomy of female internal reproductive organs

The female reproductive system consists of a pair of ovaries which connect with a pair of lateral oviducts. These join to form a median oviduct opening posteriorly into a genital chamber. Sometimes the genital chamber is closed to form a tube, the vagina, and this is often developed to form a bursa copulatrix for reception of the penis. Opening from the genital chamber or the vagina is a spermatheca for the storage of sperm and frequently a pair of accessory glands is present (Fig. 185).

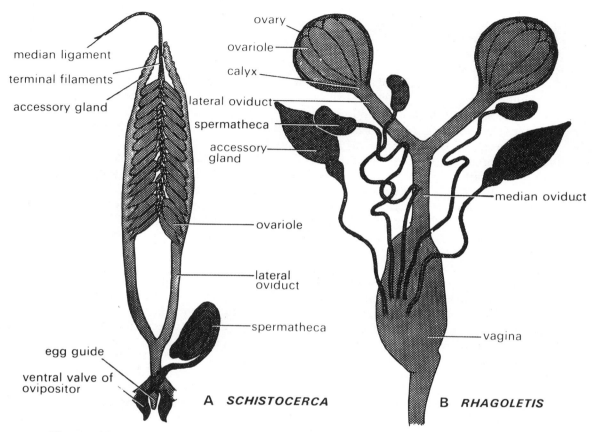

Fig. 185. Female reproductive systems of (A) *Schistocerca* and (B) *Rhagoletis* (Diptera) (after D. S. Anderson, 1966; Snodgrass, 1935).

Ovary

The ovaries lie in the abdomen above or lateral to the gut. Each consists of a number of egg-tubes, or ovarioles, comparable with the testis follicles in the male. Development of the oocytes takes place in the ovarioles.

The number of ovarioles is roughly constant within a species, although in locusts it is affected by the treatment of the parental population. Thus *Schistocerca* reared from parents bred in a crowd have an average of 96 ovarioles in the two ovaries, while others after three generations of breeding in isolation have about 116 (D. S. Anderson, 1966, and see Uvarov, 1966). There is also evidence of geographical variation in the numbers of ovarioles in African grasshoppers (Phipps, 1962) and within the Acridoidea some families tend to have more than others. Pyrgomorphidae, for instance, tend to have more ovarioles than Gomphocerinae of the same size. In general larger species have more ovarioles than small ones; thus the small British grasshoppers commonly have a total of eight ovarioles, the larger locusts about 100.

Similar variation occurs in other orders. *Calliphora* (Diptera) has about 100 ovarioles in each ovary, *Drosophila* 10–30, while the viviparous Diptera, *Melophagus* and *Hippobosca*, have only two, and *Glossina* only one in each ovary. Some viviparous aphids exhibit extreme reduction in the number of ovarioles, having only one functional ovary with a single ovariole. At the other extreme are queen termites which have large numbers of ovarioles, over 2000 in each ovary of *Eutermes*. Most Lepidoptera have only four ovarioles on each side.

The ovaries of Collembola are not composed of ovarioles, but are sac-like with a lateral germarium from which files of oocytes are produced. The ovaries are probably not homologous with those of other insects.

Other than in the Diptera there is no sheath enclosing the ovary as a whole, but each ovariole has a wall which, frequently at least, is made up of two layers; an outer ovariole sheath and an inner tunica propria (Fig. 188A). The external sheath is a cellular network of modified fatty tissue. The cells of this net are rich in lipids and glycogen and are metabolically active, but there is no evidence that they are directly concerned with oocyte development. Tracheoles also form part of the external sheath, but they do not penetrate it and all the oxygen utilised by the ovariole diffuses in from these elements. In *Periplaneta* mycetocytes (p. 81) are present in the sheath, but there are no muscle fibres such as are present in the sheaths of *Bombyx* (Lepidoptera) and *Drosophila* (see King and Aggarwal, 1965).

The tunica propria is an elastic membrane containing fine fibrils. It surrounds the whole of the ovariole and the terminal filament. During the early stages of development it increases in thickness, but subsequently, when the oocytes enlarge rapidly during vitellogensis, it becomes stretched and very thin. It is possibly a secretion of the terminal filament and follicle cells. The tunica propria has a supporting function, and in addition, because of its elasticity, it plays a part in ovulation (section 15.7) (Bonhag and Arnold, 1961). Amoeboid cells in the space between the ovariole sheath and the tunica propria may be concerned with repairing the latter if it is damaged (Koch and King, 1966).

Distally each ovariole is produced into a long terminal filament consisting of a syncytial core bounded by the tunica propria. Usually the individual filaments from each ovary combine to form a suspensory ligament and sometimes the ligaments of the two sides merge into a median ligament (Fig. 185A). The ligaments are inserted into the body wall or the dorsal diaphragm and so suspend the developing ovaries in the haemocoel.

Proximally the ovariole narrows to a fine duct, the pedicel, which connects with the oviduct. In the immature insect the lumen of the ovariole is cut off from the pedicel by an epithelial plug (Fig. 188B), but this is destroyed at the time of the first ovulation and subsequently is replaced by a plug of follicular tissue (p. 296).

The ovarioles may enter the oviduct in a linear sequence so that if there are only a few, as in some Apterygota and Ephemeroptera, they may appear to be segmental. This arrangement is probably of no particular significance and is not apparent in insects with a larger number of ovarioles (Fig. 185A). In other groups, such as the Lepidoptera and Diptera, the ovarioles open together into an expansion of the oviduct known as the calyx (Fig. 185B).

Oviducts

The oviducts are tubes with walls of a single layer of cuboid or columnar cells standing on a basement membrane and with a muscle layer outside. In Acridoidea a part of the wall is glandular. Usually the two lateral oviducts join a median oviduct which is ecto-dermal in origin and hence is lined with cuticle, but the Ephemeroptera are exceptional in having the lateral oviducts opening separately by two gonopores. The median ovi-duct is usually more muscular than the lateral ducts, with circular and longitudinal muscles. It opens at the gonopore which, in Dermaptera, is ventral on the posterior end of segment 7, but in most other groups opens into a genital chamber invaginated above the sternum of segment 8 (Fig. 186A). Sometimes the genital chamber becomes tubular

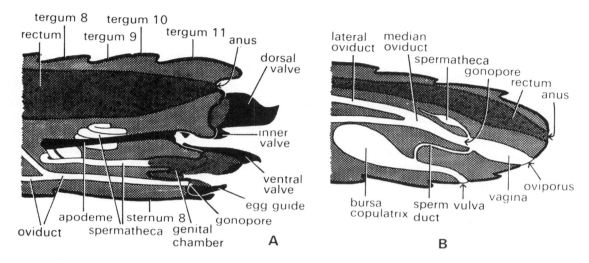

Fig. 186. Diagrammatic sagittal sections of the end of the abdomen of (A) *Locusta* and (B) a ditrysian lepidopteran (from Uvarov, 1966; Imms, 1957).

and is then effectively a continuation of the oviduct through segment 9. This continua-tion is called the vagina and its opening the vulva. It is often not distinguishable in struc-ture from the oviduct, but its anterior end, and the position of the true gonopore, is marked by the insertion of the spermatheca (see Snodgrass, 1935). Frequently the vagina is developed to form a pouch, the bursa copulatrix, which receives the penis, while in viviparous Diptera the anterior part of the chamber is enlarged to form the uterus in which larval development occurs (p. 371).

Most female Lepidoptera are unusual in having two reproductive openings. One on segment 9 serves for the discharge of eggs and is known as the oviporus, while the other on segment 8 is the copulatory opening, the vulva. The latter leads to the bursa copulatrix which is connected with the oviduct by a sperm duct (Fig. 186B).

Two openings also occur in the water beetles *Agabus*, *Ilybius* and *Hydroporus*, but here both openings are terminal with the opening of the bursa copulatrix immediately above the vaginal opening (Jackson, 1960).

Spermatheca

A spermatheca, which serves for the storage of sperm from the time the female is impregnated until the eggs are fertilised, is present in most female insects. Sometimes

two are present, as in *Blaps* (Coleoptera) and *Phlebotomus* (Diptera), and most of the
higher flies have three (Fig. 185B). In the lower orders of insects, as in Orthoptera, the
spermatheca opens into the genital chamber independently of the oviduct (Fig. 186A),
but where the genital chamber forms a vagina the spermathecal opening becomes
internal and is effectively within the oviduct (Fig. 186B).

The spermatheca is ectodermal in origin and is lined with cuticle. Typically it consists of a storage pouch with a muscular duct leading to it, and often there is an
associated gland, or the spermathecal epithelium may itself be glandular, producing
secretions which probably provide nutrients for the sperm.

Accessory glands

Female accessory glands often arise from the genital chamber or the vagina, but in
Acrididae they are simply anterior extensions of the lateral oviducts (Fig. 185A). Where
such glands are apparently absent the walls of the oviducts may be glandular, and this is
the case in Pyrgomorphidae (D. S. Anderson, 1965). Often the glands produce a substance for attaching the eggs to the substratum during oviposition and hence they are
often called colleterial glands, but there are frequent instances of specialised functions
which have been most fully investigated in *Periplaneta*. In this insect the eggs are laid in
an ootheca consisting of a tanned, cuticle-like substance which is produced by the
accessory glands. The two glands open into the genital chamber and each consists of a
mass of branched tubules lined with cuticle. The cuticle is secreted by epidermal cells,
but opening between these are the gland cells. These differ in different parts of the
glands and in the left gland, which is larger than the right, three types are recognisable,
but all of them possess a structure called the end-apparatus which forms the secreting
surface of the cell. It consists of an invagination of the free margin lined with radially
directed microvilli projecting into it (Fig. 187). In the most distal cells (Type 4 of
Brunet, 1952) the ends of the microvilli are free, but in the more proximal types 2 and
3 they end in a dense feltwork. The type 4 cells occupy the bulk of the gland and they,
perhaps together with the type 2 cells, produce the protein from which the ootheca is
formed. In addition this gland produces a β-glucoside of protocatechuic acid and an
oxidase, the latter possibly from the type 2 cells. The type 4 cells may become inactive
after a time and they may be replaced by the type 3 cells. The right-hand gland has
two types of secretory cell both of which are columnar with a tubular end-apparatus.
It secretes a β-glucosidase which liberates protocatechuic acid from its β-glucoside
when the secretions of the two glands mix in the genital chamber. The protocatechuic
acid is oxidised to a quinone by the oxidative enzymes and this tans the protein to
produce a cuticle-like structure (see p. 443) (Brunet, 1952; Mercer and Brunet, 1959).

The frothy secretions which form the eggpods of grasshoppers and the gelatinous
sheath of *Chironomus* (Diptera) eggs are also produced by the accessory glands. In
Hydrophilus (Coleoptera) the accessory glands produce silk which forms the cocoon
in which the eggs are laid. The cocoon is moulded to the shape of the abdomen with the
aid of the forelegs, then the abdomen is withdrawn and the eggs are laid. Finally the
cocoon is sealed off and remains floating on the surface of the water. It is equipped with
a silken 'mast' about an inch high which serves a respiratory function (Fig. 211A).

Glands associated with the genitalia perform a variety of functions in female Hymenoptera. The poison used by Pompilidae and others to paralyse their prey, and that used

in a defensive manner by *Apis* and various ants, is derived from such glands. Another gland may serve to lubricate the ovipositor, while in many ants pheromones used in marking trails are produced by glands discharging via the sting (p. 743).

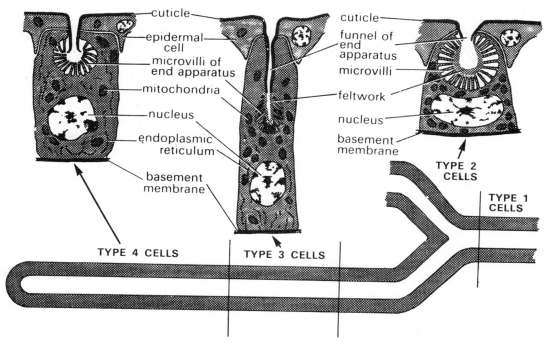

Fig. 187. Diagram of the left colleterial gland of *Periplaneta* showing the different types of secretory cells and their positions in the gland (based on Brunet, 1952; and Mercer and Brunet, 1959).

15.5 Oogenesis

Each ovariole consists of a distal germarium in which oocytes are produced from oogonia, and a more proximal vitellarium in which the oocytes grow as yolk is deposited in them. The vitellarium in a mature insect forms by far the greater part of the ovariole.

The germarium contains prefollicular tissue (see below) and the stem line oogonia and their derivatives. The stem line oogonia are derived directly from the original germ cells (p. 364), and in *Drosophila* there are only one or two of these in each ovariole (Chandley, 1966; Koch and King, 1966). When they divide, one of the daughter cells retains the function of the stem line cell, while the other becomes a definitive oogonium and develops into an oocyte. Oocytes pass back down the ovariole, enlarging as they do so, and as each oocyte leaves the germarium it is clothed by the prefollicular tissue which forms the follicular epithelium. At first this may be two- or three-layered, but ultimately it comes to consist of a single layer of cells. Oocyte growth continues and the follicular epithelium keeps pace by cell division so that its cells become cuboid or columnar. In *Drosophila* the number of follicle cells round each oocyte increases from an initial figure of about 80 to about 1200. Subsequently, during yolk deposition, growth of the oocyte is very rapid, but at this time the follicle cells do not divide and they become stretched over the oocyte as a flattened, squamous epithelium. Nuclear division may continue without cell division so that the cells become binucleate or endopolyploid and this may have the effect of maintaining a suitable ratio of genetic material to actively synthesising cytoplasm in these relatively large cells.

As the oocyte grows the nucleus also increases in size, due largely to the production of more karyolymph, while the strands forming the chromosomes are dispersed and lose their basophilic staining properties. The nucleus is now known as the germinal vesicle and at first it increases in size as rapidly as the oocyte, but during yolk deposition the oocyte grows much more rapidly and the germinal vesicle becomes relatively smaller (Seshacher and Bagga, 1963).

Typically each ovariole contains a linear series of oocytes in successive stages of development with the most advanced in the most proximal position at the greatest distance from the germarium (Fig. 188). An oocyte with its surrounding follicular epithelium is termed a follicle and successive follicles are separated by interfollicular tissue derived from the prefollicular tissue. The number of follicles in a mature ovariole is variable between species, but roughly constant for a species. Thus *Schistocerca* commonly has about 20 follicles in each ovariole and this number is present even in senile females which have oviposited several times, suggesting that more oocytes are produced as the older ones are ovulated (D. S. Anderson, 1966). In *Oncopeltus* there are often eight follicles per ovariole and in *Drosophila* six, while *Melophagus* has only one follicle in each ovariole at any one time.

In most insects the meiotic divisions are not completed in the ovary and oocytes usually leave the ovarioles in the metaphase of the first maturation division. This, however, is not true of viviparous species such as *Hemimerus* (Dermaptera) or in *Cimex* (Heteroptera) and related species in which fertilisation takes place in the ovary; in these, maturation of the oocytes is completed in the ovary.

15.51 Types of ovariole

There are two broad categories of ovarioles, panoistic in which there are no special nurse cells, and meroistic in which nurse cells, or trophocytes, are present. Further, there are two types of meroistic ovariole: telotrophic, in which all the trophocytes are terminal in the germarium, and polytrophic, in which trophocytes accompany each oocyte and are enclosed within the follicle.

Panoistic

Panoistic ovarioles, which have no specialised nurse cells, are found in the more primitive orders of insects, the Thysanura, Odonata, Plecoptera, Orthoptera and Isoptera. Amongst the holometabolous insects only Siphonaptera have ovarioles of this type. The prefollicular tissue may be cellular, but sometimes, as in *Thermobia* (Thysanura) (Fig. 188A) it consists of small scattered nuclei in a common cytoplasm.

Telotrophic

Telotrophic ovarioles are characterised by the presence of trophic tissue as well as oogonia and oocytes in the germarium. This arrangement is found in Heteroptera and many Coleoptera Polyphaga. The trophocytes are derived, with the oocytes, from the oogonia and in some species the production of oocytes and trophocytes continues in the

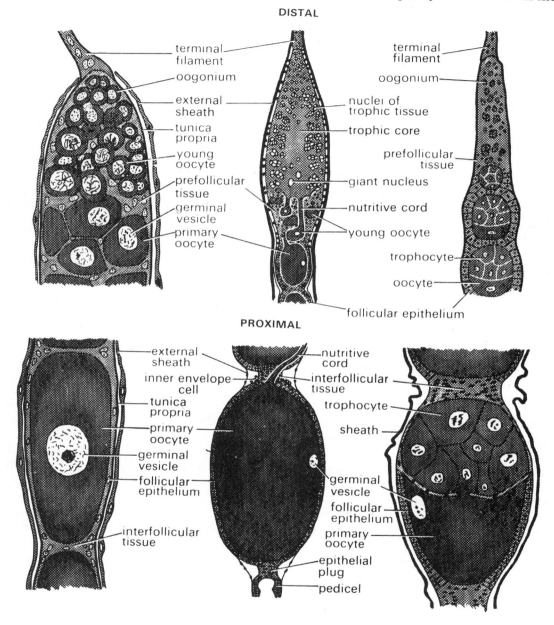

DISTAL

PROXIMAL

A   *PANOISTIC*   B   *TELOTROPHIC*   C   *POLYTROPHIC*

Fig. 188. Diagrams illustrating the structure of the distal region of the ovariole, including the germarium (above) and a proximal part with well-developed oocyte (below) in (A) panoistic, (B) telotrophic and (C) polytrophic ovarioles (from Bonhag, 1958; Davey, 1965a).

adult, but in *Oncopeltus* oogonial division is completed in the larva so that the adult germarium contains only oocytes and trophic tissue (Fig. 188B). In this species the trophic tissue can be divided into three zones:—

1. in which the cells are distinct and undergo mitosis before passing down to the next zone,

2. in which the cell boundaries are lost and the nuclei, often bigger than in zone 1, aggregate in clusters,

3. in which the nuclei are bigger still, apparently as a result of fusion, and occupy the periphery so that a mass of cytoplasm, forming the trophic core, is present in the centre of the ovariole. Nuclei migrate from the periphery into the core and some of them fuse to form giant nuclei, but ultimately they all break down, releasing their contents into the cytoplasm.

In *Gerris* (Heteroptera) some of the trophic cells break down to form a trophic core, but others retain their identity. These cells contribute material which is extruded from the nuclei to the core along cytoplasmic strands (Eschenburg and Dunlap, 1966). The trophic tissue also remains cellular in *Tenebrio* and in this species no trophic core is formed.

Behind the trophic tissue are the oocytes and prefollicular tissue and, as in other types of ovariole, oocytes become clothed by follicle cells as they leave the germarium. Each oocyte remains connected to the germarium by a cytoplasmic nutritive cord which extends to the trophic core, elongating as the oocyte passes down the ovariole. Finally, at the time of vitellogenesis, the nutritive cord breaks and the follicle cells form a complete layer round the oocyte. In Coleoptera the nutritive cords, which develop from the individual trophocytes, are much finer than in Heteroptera and they may disappear as the follicles are completed. In other cases nutritive cords may be absent altogether.

Polytrophic

Polytrophic ovarioles have trophocytes enclosed in the follicles with each oocyte (Fig. 188C, 190). They occur in Dermaptera and the lice and throughout the holometabolous orders, except for the Siphonaptera. The distal end of the germarium is occupied by the oogonia, of which there are about 50 in *Drosophila*. An oogonium divides to produce an oocyte and a trophocyte, but the division is incomplete so that the two cells remain attached by a narrow cytoplasmic bridge. Further divisions usually occur and these too are incomplete so that a complex of interconnecting cells is produced (Fig. 189). Cytoplasmic bridges do not occur in *Aedes* (Diptera), however, and presumably in this case cell division is complete (Roth and Porter, 1964). The number of trophocytes associated with each oocyte is characteristic for each species, although in those species with larger numbers of trophocytes some variation may occur. Dermaptera have only one trophocyte with each oocyte, *Aedes* and *Melophagus* (Diptera) seven, *Drosophila* and *Dytiscus* (Coleoptera) 15, *Apis* and *Bombus* (Hymenoptera) 48 and *Carabus* (Coleoptera) 127. In addition to oocytes and trophocytes, prefollicular tissue is present in the germarium and in *Anisolabis* (Dermaptera) the prefollicular nuclei are scattered in a common cytoplasm.

As each oocyte with its trophocytes leaves the germarium the oocyte always occupies a posterior position. All the cells become enclosed within a common epithelial layer which soon becomes flattened over the trophocytes, but is thicker, with cuboid cells, round the oocyte. A fold of follicular epithelium pushes inwards separating oocyte from trophocytes except for a median pore (Fig. 188C). In Neuroptera, Coleoptera and Hymenoptera the trophocytes are pinched off in a separate follicle from the beginning (Fig. 190).

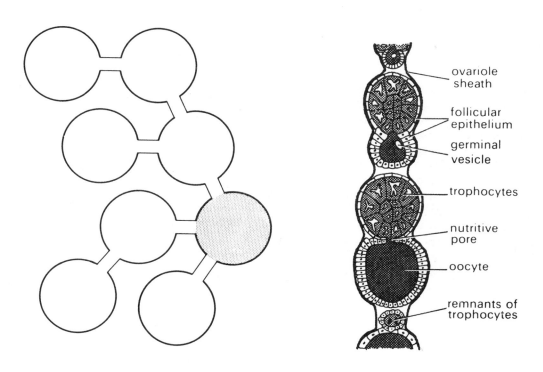

ovariole
sheath

follicular
epithelium

germinal
vesicle

trophocytes

nutritive
pore

oocyte

remnants of
trophocytes

Fig. 189. (*left*) Diagram showing the interconnections of the oocyte (stippled) and the trophocytes at the 8-cell stage in *Drosophila*. Each cell will divide again to produce the final, 16-cell, stage. The oocyte always occupies the most posterior position, to the right in the diagram (after King, 1964).

Fig. 190. (*right*) Diagram of part of an ovariole of *Bombus*, a polytrophic ovariole in which the trophocytes are in a separate follicle from the oocyte (after Hopkins and King, 1966).

At first the trophocytes are bigger than the oocyte and the trophocyte nuclei enlarge considerably. In *Drosophila* the trophocyte nuclei increase in volume about 2000-fold and the chromosomes undergo eight or nine doublings so that polytene chromosomes are produced. The chromosomal strands do not adhere together, but form a tangled mass in the nucleus. In *Drosophila* the trophocytes adjacent to the oocyte have larger nuclei, and their chromosomes undergo one more replication, than the anterior trophocytes. Subsequently they lose their DNA, but the anterior cells do not. Later in development the trophocytes become smaller and finally degenerate and are cut off from the oocyte by the follicle cells. The stages of oogenesis in *Drosophila* are summarised by Cummings and King (1969, *J. Morph.* **128**).

15.52 Oocyte growth

Oocyte growth occurs in two stages. First there is a period of relatively slow growth during which oocyte and trophocytes, if they are present, grow at approximately the same rate. During this period various essential substances are passed to the oocyte. It is followed by a period of rapid growth of the oocyte due to the laying down of yolk, but it does not follow that all the other processes come to an end at this time. Yolk deposition is known as vitellogenesis.

During the period of growth before vitellogenesis, RNA, DNA, protein, lipids and sometimes carbohydrates are passed into the oocyte by the trophocytes in meroistic ovarioles. In some cases a transfer of mitochondria and ribosomes has been observed. The follicle cells are also active at this time and the microvilli on their inner faces interdigitate with those on the surface of the oocyte. Pinocytosis is observed to occur at the oocyte membrane suggesting that substances, presumably from the follicle cells, are being transferred to the oocyte (E. Anderson, 1964). Synthetic activity may also occur within the oocyte itself and extrusion of nuclear material from the germinal vesicle has been observed in many insects.

In telotrophic ovarioles DNA from the nuclei of the trophic cells is present in the trophic core, but cannot be traced in the nutritive cords. Nevertheless, it is assumed that it is transferred to the oocyte. Transfer of DNA from trophocytes also occurs in polytrophic ovarioles and there is also the possibility that it is contributed by the follicle cells.

RNA plays an essential role in controlling protein metabolism in the oocyte. In meroistic ovarioles it is derived from the trophocytes and it may be that a prime function of the trophocytes is the production of reserve ribosomes for protein synthesis in the oocyte during early embryonic development. In most cells ribosomes are probably produced in the nucleus, but in the oocyte at this time there is no evidence of RNA synthesis in the nucleus, the chromosomal DNA being in a dispersed condition or forming an amorphous body, the karyosome. In panoistic ovarioles, however, the chromosomes of the oocyte have a lampbrush configuration suggesting RNA formation, and nucleolar budding and the transfer of nucleolar material to the cytoplasm is also observed, indicating that in this instance RNA is produced in the germinal vesicle (Telfer, 1965).

15.53 Vitellogenesis

Vitellogenesis, the deposition of yolk in the oocyte, occurs in the lower parts of the ovariole and it results in a very rapid increase in size. In *Drosophila* the oocyte volume increases about 100,000 times during the course of its development, which takes about three days after leaving the germarium, and in *Nomadacris* (Orthoptera) the oocytes grow from less than two millimetres to over six millimetres long in about a week. Normally vitellogenesis is largely restricted to the terminal oocyte, the following oocyte remaining relatively small until the first is discharged from the ovariole. Hence there is an interval between successive ovulations (p. 296) which is determined by the rate of vitellogenesis.

In some insects, such as those Lepidoptera which do not feed as adults, Ephemeroptera and Plecoptera, vitellogenesis is completed in the late larva or pupa. In most cases, however, a period of maturation is required in the adult before the eggs are ready to ovulate. Commonly this period is only a matter of days, but in cases of adult diapause it may be very prolonged (see p. 717). Hence it is necessary in insects to differentiate between becoming adult and becoming mature. Having matured, successive ovulations occur at regular intervals.

The yolk may be broadly categorised as protein yolk, which is a protein–carbohydrate complex, and lipid yolk, while in some insects glycogen is also present in granules between the other yolk bodies. The protein yolk is most abundant and forms the richest deposit of protein in the oocyte. The different types of yolk have different origins and will be dealt with separately.

Protein yolk

The protein which forms the protein yolk is derived from proteins in the blood. In *Hyalophora* (Lepidoptera) the haemolymph of the female contains a protein which is not present in the male and this is absorbed preferentially by the oocyte. The other blood proteins are also absorbed, but to a much smaller extent and it may be that there is selective absorption of the proteins on some component of the uptake system, such as the oocyte membrane. Sexual differences in the blood proteins are known to occur in Orthoptera and other Lepidoptera and such differences may reflect the development of special proteins in the females for yolk synthesis. The origin of these proteins is unknown, but probably the fat body is involved.

At the time of vitellogenesis in *Hyalophora*, *Panorpa* (Mecoptera), *Aedes* and *Calliphora* the follicle epithelium retracts from the surface of the oocyte and gaps appear between the follicle cells. Thus there is a free access of haemolymph to the surface of the oocyte since the only potential barrier, the tunica propria, is permeable to large molecules. A substance, presumably protein, in the space round the oocyte becomes concentrated at the surface of the oolemma, the membrane bounding the oocyte (Fig. 191), and is then taken up by pinocytosis, pinosomes appearing in the cell membrane at points indicated by a series of bristle-like striations on the inside. In *Aedes* the number of pinosomes present during vitellogenesis is 15 times as high as during the preceding period with an estimated 300,000 on the surface of the oocyte facing the follicle cells (Roth and Porter, 1964). The pinosomes become cut off as vesicles which fuse together, ultimately becoming crystalline and forming the yolk spheres. In *Hyalophora* it is estimated that about 1,000,000 vesicles are required for the formation of each yolk sphere. Since each vesicle is bounded by an element of the cell membrane there must be a rapid turnover in this membrane with rapid production to make good the loss.

The role of the follicle cells in yolk deposition is not clear and it may be purely permissive, their separation simply permitting access to the oocyte. Nevertheless active synthesis is occurring in the follicle cells at this time and in a number of insects some of the cells break down after a period of secretion during vitellogenesis. It is possible that they are contributing some element which is then passed into the intercellular spaces and taken up with the blood protein. That they have some such role is suggested by the presence of long microvilli and most active pinocytosis opposite the follicle cells in *Bombus* (Hopkins and King, 1966).

The oocyte itself may also synthesise protein at this time since the cytoplasm is rich in RNA, but it is suggested that, at least in *Periplaneta*, this synthesis is concerned with maintenance rather than yolk production (E. Anderson, 1964).

In *Anisolabis* a polysaccharide which may contribute to the protein–carbohydrate complex is derived from the trophocytes (Bonhag, 1956).

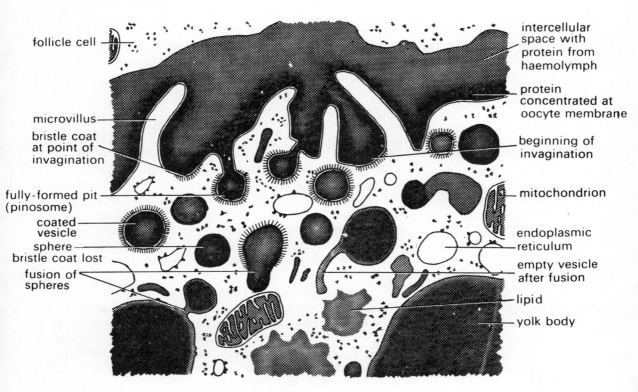

Fig. 191. Diagram illustrating the uptake of protein by micropinocytosis and its subsequent incorporation into yolk bodies in the oocyte of *Aedes* (after Roth and Porter, 1964).

During vitellogenesis in Hymenoptera, Lepidoptera and some other insects, vesicles, known as secondary yolk nuclei because of their superficial resemblance to nuclei, are present in the peripheral cytoplasm. These vesicles arise as emission bodies from the nucleus during the germarial phase of development and subsequently increase in number by division. They have a double membrane and, in *Bombus,* contain two inclusions one of which increases in size during vitellogenesis. They also contain RNA and it is suggested that they are concerned in the control of protein uptake by pinocytosis and possibly also control vitelline membrane production since they disappear shortly after it is formed (Hopkins, 1964).

Lipid yolk

Lipid yolk probably arises in the oocyte in the Golgi apparatus, the vesicles of which become filled with lipid, grow and ultimately develop into the lipid yolk bodies. The nature of the lipid may vary in the course of development and often at first only phospholipid droplets are present. Subsequently droplets having a triglyceride core and phospholipid sheath are found and finally only homogeneous triglyceride bodies remain. It is suggested that these represent successive stages in the development of the lipid yolk and that the phospholipid is utilised in the synthesis of the yolk platelets (Seshacher and Bagga, 1963).

The follicle cells probably play an important part in the transfer of lipids to the oocyte, but in meroistic ovarioles, although not in *Culex* (Diptera), lipid is obtained early in development from the trophocytes.

Glycogen

Glycogen is not present in all insect oocytes, but when it is present it is derived from the trophocytes or the follicle cells. In *Anisolabis* and *Bombus,* sugars from the blood are metabolised to form glycogen in the trophocytes and the glycogen is then transferred to the oocyte (Bonhag, 1956; Hopkins and King, 1966). In other insects the glycogen only appears in the oocyte after the trophocytes have degenerated and it is believed that it may be contributed by the follicle cells. It is also possible that, in *Apis,* it is synthesised from glucose in the oocyte itself.

15.54 Vitelline membrane formation

The vitelline membrane, which forms the outer layer of the oocyte, is laid down at the end of vitellogenesis. In some cases it may be a modification of the existing plasma membrane, but in others it forms in the intercellular space between the oocyte and the follicle cells. Droplets of material are contributed largely by the follicle cells, but also by the oocyte, and these condense to form the membrane.

15.55 Formation of the egg-shell

The shell of the egg is formed largely, and in many cases wholly, by the follicle cells, but in Acrididae a secretion of the common oviduct is added to that of the follicle cells.

The part of the shell secreted by the follicle cells is known as the chorion and this typically consists of two layers, an inner endochorion and an outer exochorion. In *Rhodnius,* at least, the endo- and exo-chorion are not chemically homogeneous and their development entails the production of a series of secretions. First, in the production of the endochorion, a polyphenol is secreted in droplets over the vitelline membrane and this is followed by a protein which subsequently becomes tanned and resistant due to the addition of more polyphenol, which also forms another layer of droplets outside the protein. Then follows an amber-coloured layer, produced by the addition of oil to tanned protein, which cements a second layer of protein to the rest. This layer is not produced uniformly, but is deposited more rapidly at the edges of the follicle cells than at their centres so that pits appear in the chorion opposite each cell. This protein also becomes tanned, but less strongly than the inner layer.

The exochorion of *Rhodnius* is added during a second phase of secretion by the follicle cells and, unlike the endochorion, it is not modified after its production. First a layer of soft lipoprotein is added to the outside of the endochorion and again more is added round the edges of the follicle cells so that the pits are accentuated. Subsequently a uniformly thin layer of resistant lipoprotein is added to complete the chorion. As in many eggs the outside of the chorion is marked with a series of hexagons which are the imprints of the follicle cells which produce it (Beament, 1946a).

Specialised parts of the chorion in *Rhodnius* involve the same secretions as produce the more generalised regions, but the secretions are produced in different amounts and some may be omitted altogether. Thus there are rings of cells in the follicular epithelium which by differential secretion produce the cap, the junction of the cap with the rest of the chorion, and the micropyles and aeropyles (Fig. 192, and see Beament, 1947). The cells forming the junction, for instance, produce no exochorion, while the aeropyles

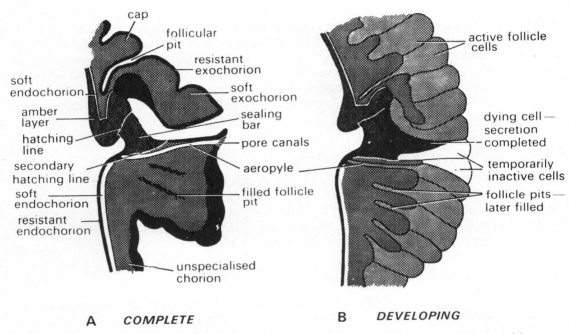

A COMPLETE   B DEVELOPING

Fig. 192. Section through the chorion of the egg of *Rhodnius* at the junction of the cap with the main shell. A. Completed chorion. B. Chorion in process of secretion by the follicle cells (after Beament, 1946b).

are deep follicular pits comparable with the shallower pits produced by all the other follicle cells.

In Acrididae the common oviduct secretes an extrachorion over the outside of the exochorion. It is produced as a layer of uniform thickness, but starts to shrink while the eggs are still in the oviduct and continues to do so after they are laid. It does not shrink evenly so that islands of extrachorion remain which contribute to the typical pattern of sculpturing on the outside of the egg (Hartley, 1961).

15.56 Control of oogenesis

The development of mature oocytes is dependent on suitable environmental conditions and various factors may be important for different species (see Johansson,

1964; Norris, 1964). For instance, in many insects with an adult diapause maturation only occurs when the daylength is long and the temperature is high (see p. 720). Adequate nutrition is probably of general importance and in the absence of sufficient food or a lack of protein many insects fail to produce mature oocytes. Many mosquito species and *Cimex*, for instance, require a blood meal before they produce eggs, although mosquitoes will live for long periods on a diet of sugars. In *Schistocerca* the presence of mature males accelerates oogenesis.

Although for oogenesis to occur an adequate supply of protein in the diet is essential, the environmental phenomena generally exert their influence via the neurosecretory system. The median neurosecretory cells of the brain have two possible effects: a direct effect on protein synthesis, including the synthesis of yolk protein, and an indirect effect via the corpora allata. The hormone produced by the corpora allata may have a direct effect on metabolism, but in *Schistocerca* its effect is to control the uptake of protein by the oocyte (see p. 708, and Highnam, 1964; Telfer, 1965; Wigglesworth, 1964; de Wilde, 1964b).

15.6 Resorption of oocytes

In a number of insects, Orthoptera, Heteroptera, Diptera, Hymenoptera and Coleoptera, oocytes in the ovarioles may be destroyed and their contents resorbed by the insect. This process is usually associated with starvation or other adverse conditions (see *e.g.* Hopkins and King, 1964). In *Cimex* the absence of fertilisation results in resorption, while in *Schistocerca* less resorption occurs if the females are in the presence of mature males. In this insect the availability of protein in the blood and a hormone which facilitates the entry of protein into the oocytes are known to be factors which influence resorption (Highnam, Lusis and Hill, 1963). Similarly in *Culicoides barbosai* (Diptera) the number of oocytes which develop for a second oviposition is proportional to the size of the blood meal which the insect takes and commonly about 75% of the oocytes degenerate after starting to develop (Linley, 1966). In parasitic Hymenoptera resorption may occur if the insect fails to find a suitable host, but it goes on synchronously with oogenesis so that the parasite is always able to lay some eggs if it encounters an appropriate host (Flanders, 1942).

Resorption may occur when an oocyte is in any stage of development, but it is most commonly observed in terminal oocytes containing yolk. It is an orderly process in which the follicle cells act as vitellophages. They increase in size and project in folds into the oocyte. Then the epithelium breaks down and the cells phagocytose and digest the yolk before they also break down. The remains of the follicle cells form a resorption body which resembles a corpus luteum. In locusts it is frequently coloured yellow due to the accumulation of lipids (Lusis, 1963).

15.7 Ovulation

The passage of the oocyte into the oviduct, a process known as ovulation, involves escaping from the follicular epithelium and the breakdown of the epithelial plug at the entrance to the pedicel. In *Periplaneta* the elasticity of the tunica propria helps to force the oocyte into the oviduct where it may be stored temporarily before oviposition. In species where the external ovariole sheath contains muscle fibres these probably assist the movements of the oocyte. Sometimes, as in Orthoptera, all the ovarioles ovulate simultaneously, but in other cases, as in viviparous Diptera, they function alternately or in sequence. In Lepidoptera, which commonly lay large batches of eggs although possessing a total of only eight ovarioles, the oocytes may accumulate in the very long pedicels until a large number is present. Similarly in some parasitic Hymenoptera, such as *Apanteles,* large numbers of eggs may be stored, in this case in the lateral oviducts, thus enabling the insect to lay a large number of eggs quickly when it finds a suitable host (Flanders, 1942).

The elasticity of the tunica propria causes it to fold up after the oocyte is shed and this pulls the next oocyte down into the terminal position. The empty follicle epithelium of the first oocyte usually persists, but it becomes greatly folded and compressed and comes to form a new plug at the entrance to the pedicel (Fig. 193). The compressed follicle epithelium is known as a corpus luteum and sometimes the corpora lutea of two

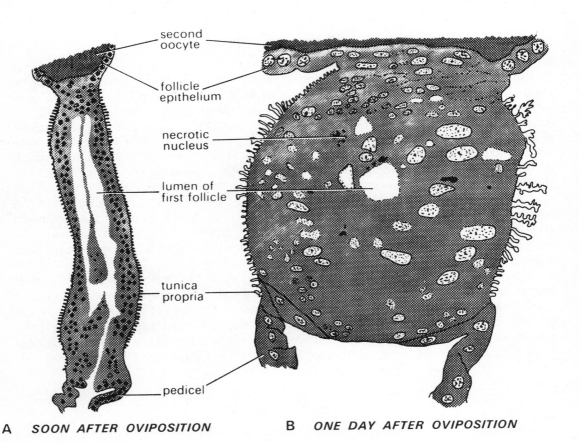

A   SOON AFTER OVIPOSITION   B   ONE DAY AFTER OVIPOSITION

Fig. 193. The corpus luteum formed by the empty follicle cells of *Locusta*. A. Soon after oviposition. B. 24 hours later. Not to same scale (after Singh, 1958).

or three successive ovulations may be present together despite the fact that they break down progressively (Singh, 1958). In *Melophagus* much of the debris from the follicle cells and trophocytes is passed out of the ovariole when this contracts after ovulation so that only a small relic of the follicle epithelium persists. In this case the ovariole contraction is slow and is not completed until the next oocyte is well developed (Saunders, 1964).

CHAPTER XVI

MATING BEHAVIOUR AND THE TRANSFER OF SPERM TO THE FEMALE

Mating behaviour may be defined broadly as the events surrounding the insemination of the female by the male. Typically this involves a whole sequence of events which are not always clearly separable from each other, but which it is convenient to treat separately. Before mating can occur the sexes must come together, or aggregate, and in this scent and sound, both of which can be specific and carry over considerable distances, are important. Vision is important in some day-flying insects and the swarming behaviour which occurs in some species may also be concerned in aggregation for mating. The attractants leading to aggregation may be specific, but sometimes, particularly with visual attraction, this is not so and further recognition is required. In this specific recognition a variety of signals are used including visual and chemical stimuli. Commonly aggregation results in a number of males courting a single female and this may lead to aggression between the males, but in some insects male aggression results in the setting up of territories which facilitate undisturbed mating.

In some species the female accepts the male immediately they meet, but often she requires some further stimulation before she will allow him to copulate. This may involve elaborate courtship behaviour by the male using a variety of stimuli and including, in some instances, the presenting of food or a token to the female. Following this the pair come together in a characteristic position, in which one sex usually sits on the back of the other, and then copulation occurs with the coupling of the external genitalia which, in the male, are specialised to grasp the female.

In more primitive insects sperm are transferred to the female in a structure known as the spermatophore produced by the male, but in many groups sperm are transferred directly via a long penis. The spermatophore is usually placed or formed in the copulatory pouch of the female and from here the sperm pass to the spermatheca where they are stored until the eggs are fertilised. In direct insemination the sperm may be deposited directly in the spermatheca. Some insects have a characteristic post-copulatory behaviour.

Various aspects of reproductive behaviour are reviewed by Alexander (1964), Davey (1960, 1965a), Hinton (1964a), Jacobson (1965), Manning (1966) and Richards (1927). Interpretation of the male genitalia is discussed by Snodgrass (1957).

MATING

16.1 Aggregation

For mating to occur it is obvious that the male and female must be in the same place and various devices are employed by one or other sex for attracting the other. Scent is commonly emitted by female insects to attract males, and since these scents, or pheromones, are carried by air currents and are effective in very low concentrations they are effective over long distances so that, at least in Lepidoptera, large numbers of males may be attracted to a single female. Female scents are also known in some cockroaches, Coleoptera, Hymenoptera and Isoptera. Less commonly attractant scents are emitted by male insects. These scents are usually highly specific (see Chapter XXXVI, and Jacobson, 1965).

Sound also carries for long distances and is equally effective during the day or at night and it is used by various insects to attract other members of the species. Sound production is particularly important in cicadas and Orthoptera (see Chapter XXVIII) where, except in a few geographically separated species, different species have characteristic songs. These may be attractive to both sexes, and acridids of either sex tend to move into a stridulating group of the same species. This is also true of cicadas, and in North America, where three species of *Magicicada* may occur in a single locality, the species are aggregated and sexually isolated from each other by their specific songs. Amongst most Orthoptera only males stridulate, but in some Acrididae both sexes do so, male and female responding to each other as they approach.

Vision is often employed by day-flying insects when searching for a mate, but, unlike scents and sounds, distance perception is usually not specific. The males of the butterfly *Hypolimnas*, for example, fly up towards anything moving which is of a size appropriate to the female, and *Eumenis* (Lepidoptera) is attracted by any dark object with a fluttering flight. A non-specific response also occurs in many Diptera and probably in other insects. Vision is occasionally employed in mating at night by insects, mainly beetles of the families Lampyridae and Elateridae, which exhibit luminescence. Both sexes or the female only may be luminous and the characteristics of the light, such as wave-length and frequency of flashing, are specific (see p. 89).

Sometimes a particular reaction to the environment tends to bring about aggregation and in some species this behaviour plays an important part in mating. Males of *Andrena flavipes* (Hymenoptera) are attracted by the scent of the area in which the females nest and outside these areas, even quite close to them, the males fail to recognise the females (Butler, 1965). Comparably the male of *Culicoides nubeculosus* (Diptera), although it does not feed on blood, is attracted to the same host as the female, and mating may follow.

16.11 Swarming

Swarming behaviour, in which a group of insects remains more or less stationary, flying over one spot, may be regarded as a special instance of insects showing a common reaction to a feature of the environment. This behaviour is not always known to be concerned with mating, but in some cases, at least, mating occurs within the swarms. Swarming is best known in the Diptera where it occurs in many Nematocera, in some species of Tabanidae and Stratiomyidae and occasionally in members of other families.

Swarming does not involve any gregarious reaction on the part of the insects, but results from a common response to some visual marker by a number of individual insects. Hence a swarm may contain from one to several hundred insects. Usually the marker is some feature which contrasts with its background; in *Culicoides nubeculosus* it may be a dark patch of damp sand or a cow pat, or in *C. riethi* a light patch (Downes, 1955).

Often swarms form over tall objects and in forest swarms may occur over the tops of tall trees. The marker need not always be below the insect since *Serromyia* forms swarms beneath the tips of branches silhouetted against the sky.

The insects maintain their positions relative to the marker visually, flying into the wind and adjusting their air-speed so as to remain in one place, or allowing themselves to drift back slightly and then flying forwards again. Their ability to hold station in the wind depends on their flying strength and *Tabanus thoracinus* can maintain its position against a 5 km./hr. wind without difficulty, while a 3 km./hr. wind disperses a swarm of *Culicoides*. The insects do not normally hover in a stationary position even under ideal conditions, but perform a 'dance', making up and down or side to side movements within the swarm. The height at which swarms develop varies, but frequently they are between two and ten feet above the marker. In high winds the swarms may be nearer the ground and if the marker is a solid object they may develop on its lee side.

In the tropics swarms commonly occur in the twilight after sunset or before sunrise, but in temperate regions swarming may be conspicuous at other times of day, twilight swarming perhaps being limited by low temperatures. Various species form swarms at particular times. Thus over high forest in Uganda mosquitoes swarm at dusk rather than dawn, being most abundant about half-an-hour after sunset (Haddow and Corbet, 1961). The common *Mansonia fuscopennata* first appears in numbers about 15 minutes after sunset and *M. aurita* about five minutes later, but despite these characteristic differences in arrival time all the mosquito species stop swarming about 40 minutes after sunset. Tabanids on the other hand swarm mainly in the morning. *Tabanus thoracinus* appears within a few minutes of Nautical twilight, when the sun is 12° below the horizon and only the general outlines of objects are visible, and disappears after 25 minutes when *T. insignis* is just arriving (Corbet and Haddow, 1962). Tabanids in temperate regions may, however, swarm late in the morning after sunrise, while *Culicoides* often swarms in the afternoon. Swarms at this time of day may persist for an hour or more, but crepuscular swarms are, of necessity, much shorter-lived and often persist for 15 minutes or less.

The timing of crepuscular swarms is related to light intensity, but the times of appearance of mosquito swarms are very precise and do not always occur at particular intensities. Possibly in the evening the sharp fall in intensity acts as a stimulus, provided the level is below a threshold intensity which may differ for different species, but it is not certain that all species react in a similar way (see *e.g.* Nielsen and Nielsen, 1958). Swarming activity stops when the light intensity falls below a certain very low level. In morning swarms the converse may be true, swarms forming when light intensity rises above a threshold, but at this time low temperature may also be a limiting factor.

Because of their mode of formation swarms of Diptera are not always monospecific, although they often are so, and the swarms observed by Haddow and Corbet (1961) always contained several species of mosquitoes and sometimes small tipulids and other insects. The majority of dipteran swarms consist only of males, but mixed swarms are recorded in some species of *Mansonia*, *Ceratopogon* and *Bezzia*, while in *Serromyia* and a few mosquito and empid species wholly female, as well as male, swarms occur.

In some species females are known to fly into the male swarms and mate. This occurs, for instance, in *Culicoides nubeculosus*, *C. riethi* and *Mansonia fuscopennata*. These same species are also known to mate outside swarms so that swarming is not essential for mating and in many other instances mating has not been observed at all in swarms. Thus it may be that swarming is not concerned primarily with mating, but in *Tabanus thoracinus*, although mating does not occur in the male swarms, females do congregate at the same site so that the species becomes aggregated (Corbet and Haddow, 1962). It is also suggested that swarming increases the sexual excitement of the participants even though it may not lead directly to mating.

Swarming, usually by males over water, also occurs in some Ephemeroptera, Trichoptera and Plecoptera. Females are often seen to fly into these swarms and mate.

16.2 Recognition

It is necessary that an insect should recognise another member of its own species so that, following aggregation, it does not waste time and energy in trying to mate with a member of another species. Sometimes the initial attractants are quite specific and this is true of many female pheromones. Male *Saturnia* (Lepidoptera), for instance, will attempt to mate with any object which emits a high concentration of the female attractant without any further stimulus, but, since the factors leading to aggregation are not always specific, some further means of recognition is often necessary. Often vision is involved. Thus the male *Hypolimnas*, having been attracted non-specifically, recognises the female by virtue of her brown colour, the effect of which is enhanced by the contrasting margin of black. White inhibits pursuit by the male (see Stride, 1957). In *Drosophila* the initial approach of the male to the female is also visual, but specific recognition involves tapping with the fore legs. If the stimulus, presumably a chemical one, is not appropriate courtship is broken off at this point. In newly emerged *D. melanogaster* and *D. similis*, two sibling species, the females are mainly responsible for specific recognition, but within a few days the males are also capable of picking a female of the right species (Manning, 1959). The male of *Andrena* is attracted to the nest area by smell, but the orange legs of the female are important in his final recognition of her. Sound is also involved in species recognition. Thus female mosquitoes flying into male swarms are recognised by their wingbeat frequencies (see p. 605).

Even though an insect may recognise another member of its species, sexual recognition is often poor and many males court and attempt to copulate with other males. Such behaviour is particularly common when females are scarce. Sometimes the assaulting male is simply kicked off by the other as in locusts, but sometimes more specific stimuli inhibit the activity of the aggressor. Thus *Drosophila* males when assaulted flick their wings in the same way as unreceptive females; this behaviour inhibiting the advances of other males.

16.3 Male aggression

If females are scarce the competition between males may lead to aggression. This is not always clearly separated from attempts to mate with other males, but certainly occurs in some Hymenoptera and in grasshoppers which have a specific song which is sung if a male intrudes during courtship (p.576). The males sing against each other in the rivals duet until the intruder retires. In crickets actual fighting occurs whenever they meet and not only in the presence of a female. The contestants rear up, lash each other with their antennae or kick with their hind legs. The longer the fight goes on the fiercer it gets, the insects stridulating and grappling with each other and one may be thrown on to its back, but mutilation is rare. If a group of male crickets is together in a restricted area they rapidly establish a hierarchy which is stable over short periods. The position of an individual in the hierarchy depends on his age, how recently he has copulated, or been in isolation, whether or not he occupies a crevice, and on his dominance in recent bouts of fighting (Alexander, 1961).

Territory

If male crickets are not confined to a small space in which fighting is frequent each insect tends to remain in a particular burrow or crevice on many successive nights. In and around this burrow he becomes dominant and so a small territory is established. This has the effect of reducing the numbers of encounters between males so that they sing the normal mating song more frequently at times appropriate to attract the females. Further, the territorial habit disperses the males over a bigger area and this makes for maximum size and continuity of the acoustic field to which the female is attracted. Finally, once the female is within the territories she is able to localise the position of a calling male more easily than if the males are all together in a confined space (Alexander, 1961).

   Territorial behaviour with similar functions is exhibited by the sphecid *Sphecius*. Most males of this species emerge before the females and each male establishes a territory, usually at a site where emergence holes are already numerous, driving off intruders of other species and sometimes grappling with males of its own species. There is some tendency for the boundaries between adjacent territories to become learned so that the amount of grappling is reduced and a single male occupies the same territory for a week or more. If a receptive, unfertilised female enters the territory the male follows her and mates with her. As a result of this behaviour males are spread over a maximum area, increasing the chances of a female finding a mate, while at the same time interference by other males during mating is reduced (Lin, 1963).

   Territorial behaviour also occurs in some dragonflies. Males fly over particular stretches of water, clashing with intruders so that individual territories are established. These may be very temporary, different territories being occupied on successive days, but often the boundaries are learned by the insects so that there is a tendency for clashes to be avoided. In some cases fighting has been replaced by ritualised behaviour involving sign stimuli. For instance, *Plathemis* displays the bluish-white upper surface of its abdomen to other males which fly off with the abdomen depressed, and in *Perithemis* the amber-coloured wings provide the stimulus. The effect of this behaviour may be to reduce disturbance by other insects during mating and subsequent oviposition, while it also leads to dispersal of the species within and away from the habitat (see Corbet, 1962; Corbet, Longfield and Moore, 1960).

16.4 Stimulation of the female

Once a male has recognised a female he may mount her and attempt to copulate immediately. This occurs, for instance, in *Ammophila* (Hymenoptera), *Musca* (Diptera) and some Odonata. In other cases, however, the female is not immediately receptive of the male, she is said to be coy, and needs to be stimulated by the male before she will permit him to mount. Females are often completely non-receptive for a time after the final moult and again after copulation.

Non-receptive females repulse males either by simply kicking them away or by specific inhibiting stimuli. For instance, a male *Drosophila* can only mount and copulate with a female if she spreads her wings and genitalia. To avoid copulation a virgin female flicks her wings and twists the abdomen sideways, while a female which has already copulated extrudes the terminal abdominal segments. These activities not only prevent the male from copulating, but also inhibit his courtship to some extent.

It is not clear what controls responsiveness, but it is not necessarily related to maturation of the oocytes since female locusts will copulate before yolk is laid down in the oocytes. Roth and Barth (1964) have shown that in *Byrsotria* (Dictyoptera) a small meal increases receptiveness, even though it may be quite inadequate for vitellogenesis, and they have suggested that the meal triggers some element of the neurosecretory system which controls receptiveness. In grasshoppers there is some evidence that a blood-borne factor, perhaps from the gonads, is responsible (p. 715).

16.41 Functions of courtship

The biological significance of coyness and the male courtship which it entails is not clear although various possibilities may be suggested. In species in which the female is aggressive courtship may represent some form of appeasement by the male so that he is not attacked. The courtship feeding of the female empid by the male could be interpreted in this way. Some male empids present food to the female and she feeds while he copulates with her. In other species this behaviour is ritualised and the male presents the female with an inanimate object, such as a petal, wrapped in a silken cocoon, or even with an empty cocoon. Similarly the male *Panorpa* secretes drops of saliva on to the surface of a leaf. These harden and are eaten by the female while the male copulates with her.

In other cases female coyness cannot be interpreted in this way, but may be regarded as a way in which disturbance of the female by the male is reduced to a minimum, and perhaps as a means by which more time is given for correct identification of the mate so that fewer mistakes are made (Bastock and Manning, 1955; Richards, 1927). It is suggested that a specific and elaborate courtship helps to isolate closely related species which might otherwise interbreed, although Manning (1966) considers that there are no clear-cut examples of discrimination based on close courtship.

Sexual isolation does result from some mating behaviour as in the auditory attraction of cicadas (see p. 592), but cases of isolation resulting from close range courtship behaviour are less clear. In the case of *Chorthippus brunneus* and *C. biguttulus* (Orthoptera), however, courtship is certainly involved in sexual isolation. In these very similar species males attempt to copulate more frequently and females are more receptive if stimulated by the song of their own species. Amongst sibling species pairs of *Drosophila* slight differences in courtship behaviour occur, the differences residing mainly in the frequency with which various elements in the behaviour pattern are used, rather than in qualitatively different behaviour patterns. Thus *D. simulans* males fan far less than *D. melanogaster* males, and *simulans* tends to use visual stimuli in species recognition to a greater extent than *melanogaster*.

In some cases courtship behaviour has an obvious functional significance. For instance, when the male of *Byrsotria* is stimulated by the female pheromone he starts to court by turning away from the female and opening his wings. This exposes a gland on

the metanotum and incites the female to climb on his back and feed on the secretion of
this gland. When she is in this position the male is able to copulate with her.

It is possible that courtship is not simply a measure of female coyness, but that it
also serves to bring the male himself into a state of readiness to copulate. This is suggested
by the behaviour of the male of *Gomphocerus* (Orthoptera) which may fail to copulate
successfully with a singing and receptive female, but after courting her is able to mate
immediately with a second female without or with only a brief courtship (Loher and
Huber, 1966).

16.42 Mechanisms of courtship

Courtship involves a variety of different mechanisms and senses in different insects.
Chemoreception may be involved, as in *Eumenis* in which the male bows towards the
female so that her antennae are brought into contact with his alary scent glands (p.
740). Hearing may be important, as in grasshoppers in which the male hops excitedly
round the female singing his courtship song at the end of which he leaps on to her back
(p. 592). In *Drosophila melanogaster* mechanoreception is important in stimulating the
female. A courting male extends the wing nearest to the female and vibrates it in a vertical
plane so that a current of air impinges on her antennae. Individuals with small wings are
less successful in their courtship and take longer to rouse the females (Ewing, 1964).
Visual displays are used by many insects to stimulate females and often the markings of
these insects serve to emphasise their movements. For instance, the movements of the
wings which male sepsids perform in front of the females are made more conspicuous
by the black wing tips.

Courtship feeding

In some insects feeding may have a special role in inducing receptiveness in the female
(Richards, 1927) and this has been shown to be true in *Byrsotria* (see above). Courtship
feeding occurs in many insects in addition to the predaceous species mentioned above.
In the cockroaches feeding on a secretion produced by the male induces the female to
mount on his back so that copulation can ensue. Various Diptera, such as *Rivellia* and
some Sepsidae, are known to regurgitate a drop of fluid and pass this to a female before
mating.

The bug *Stilbcoris* feeds on fig seeds and an adult male usually carries a seed impaled
on his proboscis. He approaches a female from behind and presents the seed to her so
that she can see it and so that it comes into contact with her antennae. By flexing his legs
the male vibrates the seed, alternating periods of stillness with periods of vibration,
and at the same time he injects saliva into the seed. This makes the seed more acceptable
to the female who now investigates it and may insert her proboscis into it. If she does
the male slowly approaches her until he is able to grasp her and copulate. The female
continues to feed on the seed. Males which do not have a seed do not normally attempt
to court (Carayon, 1964).

Courtship feeding also occurs amongst the wasps of the subfamily Thynninae. In
some genera the females feed themselves while they are copulating, but in others the
male carries the wingless female to a feeding site where he feeds her either directly from
his mouth or by first regurgitating food on to his abdomen or a leaf. The female feeds

from the regurgitated drops with her reduced mouthparts. In yet other species the male collects nectar and honeydew into a cavity beneath his head where the food is held by hairs. The food bolus may be larger than the head of the insect and the female is fed from it without being transported to the feeding ground (Given, 1954).

Sequences in courtship behaviour

In many instances courtship does not involve a single stimulus from the male, but entails a whole sequence of activities. These may be controlled endogenously within the male once he has been stimulated to perform them, or they may require further stimulation from the female who responds to the signals of the male.

The courtship of *Drosophila melanogaster* is controlled entirely endogenously and a male will readily court an etherised female. In this species the male approaches the female, taps her once with his fore legs and then opens and vibrates the wing nearest to the female. He then circles the female, facing her all the time, and may repeat the wing vibration several times until finally he licks the genitalia of the female, mounts her and attempts to copulate. The different activities are regarded as expressing successively higher levels of excitation, vibration expressing greater excitement than merely facing the female and licking representing a still higher level of excitation (Bastock and Manning, 1955).

In *Drosophila subobscura*, on the other hand, courtship consists of a series of responses by each sex, each successive response stimulating a further step in the behaviour sequence of the opposite sex (Fig. 194). Thus the male orientates towards the female and taps her with his fore legs, while the female stands still. The visual and tactile stimuli which she presents cause the male to extend his proboscis and move face to face with her. She continues to stand still and he taps her head, whereupon both begin to dance. The dance consists of a series of side to side steps in which the two insects remain facing each other. In the course of this the male gradually opens his wings and when the dance stops he spreads his wings in an attitude called wing posturing. In this the wings are raised at right angles to the body with the leading edge down and this posture prompts the female to stand still. Then the male circles her and finally jumps on her, attempting to copulate at the same time (R. G. B. Brown, 1965). Even in this case, however, the pattern of behaviour is not fixed and some elements may be omitted. Similar sequences of events are known to occur in other insects such as crickets (see *e.g.* Alexander, 1961) and *Mormoniella* (Hymenoptera) (Barrass, 1960).

16.5 Pairing

Courtship behaviour culminates in the male and female coming together, one sex commonly mounting on the back of the other. Copulation may occur immediately or the insects may remain paired for a time before copulating. Various positions are adopted which are characteristic of the species (Fig. 195). In cockroaches and some gryllids and tettigoniids the female climbs on to the back of the male (Fig. 195C), and Alexander (1964) considers this to be the primitive condition since it occurs in the lower orders of insects. Another common position is with the male on the female (Fig. 195A); this occurs, for instance, in Tabanidae and this is often regarded as the primitive position because the male is usually the active partner and the female needs coercion (Richards, 1927). Sometimes, as in Acrididae, although the male sits on top of the female his abdomen is twisted underneath her, the false male above position (Fig. 195B). The abdomen of the male is also twisted under the female in insects, such as *Panorpa*, which lie side by side at the start of copulation. Sometimes the insects pair end to end (Fig. 195E, F and G) and often in this case the terminal segments of the male are twisted through 180°. This occurs, for instance, in some Heteroptera (see Fig. 199B) and in Tipulidae. In some tettigoniids and a few Diptera the end to end position is achieved with the male on his back, while in Culicidae male and female lie with their ventral surfaces in contact (Fig. 195D).

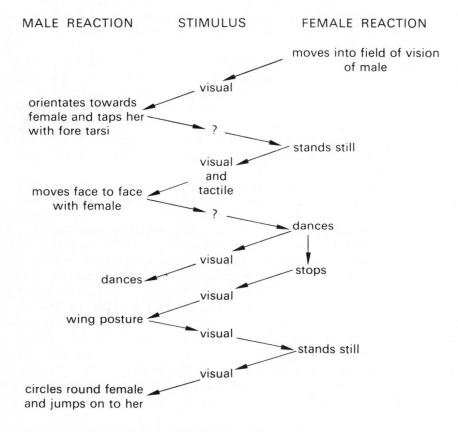

Fig. 194. Representation of the interactions between male and female *Drosophila subobscura* during courtship (after Brown, 1965).

There is considerable diversity in the positions assumed during copulation by insects within any one order. Thus all the above positions are to be seen in various families of Diptera. The same is true of Orthoptera except for the male above and venter to venter positions, while in Heteroptera only the female above and venter to venter positions do not occur. On the other hand Ephemeroptera always adopt the female above position and mantids the false male above. See also Alexander and Otte (1967, *Miscl. Publ. Mus. Zool., Univ. Mich.*, no. 133).

Once the genitalia of male and female are linked the insects may alter their positions and it is common among Orthoptera and Diptera for an end to end position to be adopted at this time.

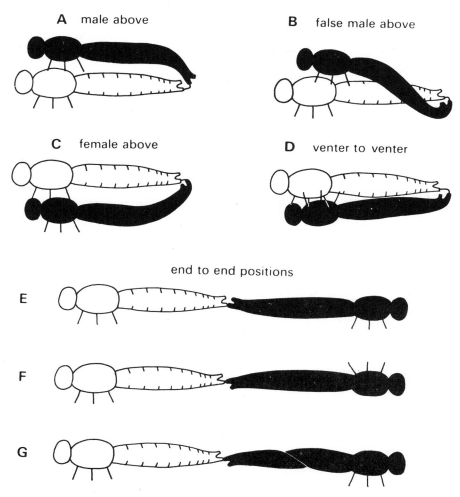

Fig. 195. Different positions assumed by the male and female during copulation, male black, female white. A. Male above (*e.g.* some Diptera). B. False male above (*e.g.* Acrididae). C. Female above (*e.g.* some Orthoptera). D. Venter to venter (*e.g.* Diptera, Culicidae—hypopygium inverted, cf. Fig. 198). E. End to end, male abdomen not twisted (*e.g.* some Hymenoptera). F. End to end, male inverted (*e.g.* some Tettigonioidea). G. End to end, male abdomen twisted (*e.g.* some Heteroptera, cf. Fig. 199) (based on Richards, 1927).

Usually in pairing the male grasps the female with his feet. In *Aedes aegypti*, for instance, the insects lie with their ventral surfaces adjacent and the male holds the hind legs of the female in a hollow of the distal tarsomere by flexing back the pretarsus. His middle and hind legs push up the female abdomen until genital contact is established and then his middle legs may hook on to the wings of the female, while his hind legs hang free.

Some male Hymenoptera, such as *Ammophila*, hold the female with the mandibles instead of, or, in some species, as well as, the legs.

In some insects the appendages are modified for grasping the female. Thus the fore legs of *Dytiscus* and some other beetles bear suckers (p. 139). *Hoplomerus* (Hymenoptera) has spines on the middle femora which fit between the veins on the wings of the female. In *Osphya* (Coleoptera) the male hind femora are modified to grip the abdomen and elytra of the female. A few insects have the antennae modified for holding the female as in Collembola.

The dragonflies are exceptional in their manner of holding the female. At first the male grasps the thorax of the female with his second and third pairs of legs, while the first pair touch the basal segments of her antennae. He then flexes his abdomen forwards and fits two pairs of claspers on abdominal segment 10 into position on the female. This completed he lets go with his legs and the two fly off 'in tandem'. The claspers consist of superior and inferior pairs and in Anisoptera the superior claspers fit round the neck of the female while the inferior claspers press down on top of her head (Fig. 196A). In most Zygoptera the claspers grip a dorsal lobe of the pronotum and in some Coenagriidae they appear to be cemented on by a sticky secretion, but this may be produced incidentally during sperm transfer (see Corbet, 1962).

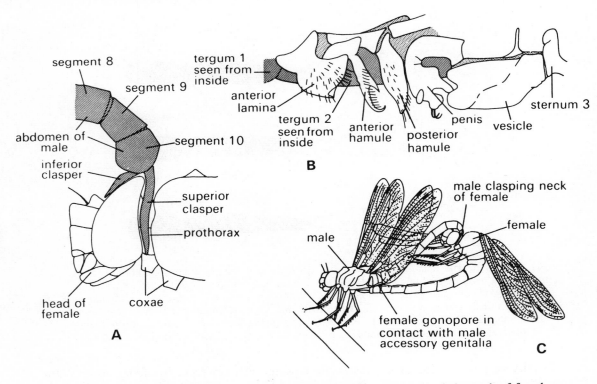

Fig. 196. Mating in Odonata. A. Position of the male claspers round the neck of female *Aeschna* during pairing (after Tillyard, 1917). B. Male accessory genitalia of *Onychogomphus*, terga of left side removed (based on Chao, 1953). C. Male and female *Aeschna in copula* (after Longfield, 1949).

SPERM TRANSFER

16.6 External reproductive organs of the male

The external reproductive organs of the male are concerned in coupling with the female genitalia and with the intromission of sperm. They are known collectively as the genitalia.

There is considerable variation in structure and terminology of the genitalia in different orders (see Tuxen, 1956, for terminology), but it is possible to homologise the basic elements (Snodgrass, 1957). These are derived from a pair of primary phallic lobes which are present in the posterior ventral surface of segment 9 (Fig. 197A). They are commonly regarded as representing limb buds and the structures arising from them as derived from typical appendages. Snodgrass (1957), however, believes that they may

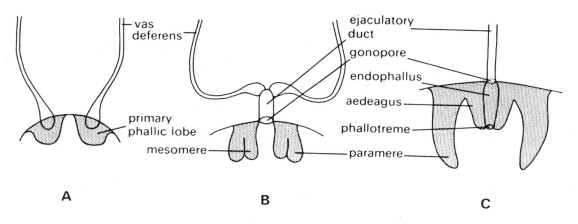

Fig. 197. Diagrams illustrating the origin and development of the phallic organ (after Snodgrass, 1957).

represent ancestral penes. These phallic lobes divide to form an inner pair of mesomeres and outer parameres, collectively known as the phallomeres (Fig. 197B). The mesomeres unite to form the aedeagus, the intromittent organ. The inner wall of the aedeagus, which is a continuation of the ejaculatory duct, is called the endophallus, and the opening of the duct at the tip of the aedeagus is the phallotreme (Fig. 197C). The true gonopore is at the junction of the ejaculatory duct and endophallus and hence is internal, but in many insects the endophallic duct is eversible so that the gonopore assumes a terminal position during copulation. The parameres develop into claspers which are very variable in form. They may be mounted with the aedeagus on a common base called the phallobase and in many insects these basic structures are accompanied by secondary structures which may develop on segments 8, 9 or 10. The term phallus is used by Snodgrass (1957) to mean the parameres together with the aedeagus, but is often used to mean the aedeagus alone; penis is sometimes used instead of phallus.

Some major variations in the development of the phallic lobes will be mentioned, but for a general account of the genitalia of insects see Snodgrass (1935, 1957). In Thysanura the phallic lobes unite without prior division to form the penis, while in

Ephemeroptera they remain separate and form paired penes. The Orthoptera and Dictyoptera also deviate from the basic pattern in that the phallomeres do not form a typical aedeagus and parameres.

Many male Diptera have the terminal abdominal segments rotated so that the relative positions of the genitalia are altered. In Culicidae, some Tipulidae, Psychodidae, Mycetophilidae and some Brachycera segment 8 and the segments behind it are rotated through 180° soon after adult emergence. Thus the aedeagus comes to lie above the anus instead of below it and the hindgut is twisted over the reproductive duct (Fig. 198A). The rotation may occur in either a clockwise or an anticlockwise direction. In *Calliphora*, and probably in all Schizophora, the terminal segments have rotated through 360° so that the genitalia are in their normal positions, but the movement is indicated

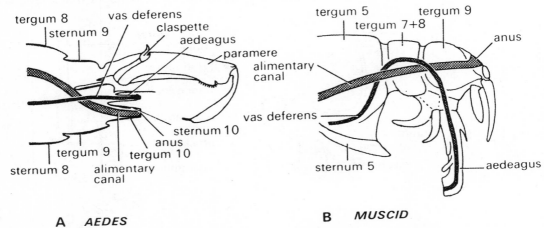

A   *AEDES*   B   *MUSCID*

Fig. 198. Diagrams illustrating torsion of the terminal segments of male Diptera. A. *Aedes* with the ninth and following segments rotated through 180°. B. A muscid with the terminal segments rotated through 360° as indicated by the twisting of the vas deferens over the alimentary canal (from Séguy, 1951b).

by some asymmetry of the preceding sclerites and by the ejaculatory duct looping right round the gut (Fig. 198B). This rotation occurs in the pupa and the degree of torsion between different segments varies in different groups. Amongst the Syrphidae a total twist of 360° is achieved by two segments rotating through 90° and one through 180° so that there is an obvious external asymmetry. Temporary rotation of the genital segments during copulation occurs in some other insects, such as Heteroptera (see Fig. 199).

Bilateral asymmetry of the genitalia occurs in Dictyoptera (Fig. 200), Embioptera (see Fig. 172C) and sometimes in other groups such as Lepidoptera and Heteroptera.

The Odonata differ from all other insects in having the intromittent organs on abdominal segments 2 and 3. Appendages are present on segment 10 which are used to clasp the female, but the genital apparatus on segment 9 is rudimentary. A depression on the ventral surface of segment 2 forms the genital fossa which opens posteriorly into a vesicle derived from the anterior end of segment 3. In Anisoptera the vesicle connects with a three-segmented penis and laterally various accessory lobes are present which guide and hold the tip of the female abdomen during intromission, the whole complex being termed the accessory genitalia (Figs. 20 and 196B). Sperm are transferred to the vesicle from the terminal gonoduct by bending the abdomen forwards. This may occur before the male grasps the female, as in *Libellula*, or after he has grasped her, but before copulation, as in *Aeschna*. The possible origins of the accessory genitalia are discussed by Corbet (1962).

16.7 Copulation

Copulation involves the linking of the male and female genitalia to form a firm connection between the two insects. While they are joined in this way the male transfers sperm to, or inseminates, the female, the sperm passing via the aedeagus. The details

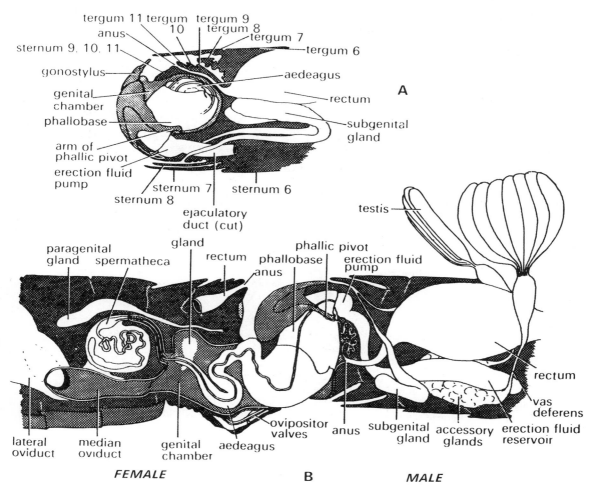

Fig. 199. A. Sagittal section of the genital capsule of a male *Oncopeltus* with the aedeagus retracted. B. Sagittal section of the posterior ends of copulating *Oncopeltus*. Notice the inversion of the male genital capsule and the insertion of the aedeagus into the spermatheca (after Bonhag and Wick, 1953).

of copulation vary from group to group depending on the structure of the genitalia, and only a few examples are given.

In Acrididae the tip of the abdomen of the male is twisted below the female and the edges of the epiphallus, a plate on top of the genital complex, grip the sides of the sub-genital plate of the female and draw it down into the anal depression of the male. The male uses his cerci to grip the female's abdomen and the aedeagus is inserted between the ventral valves of the ovipositor.

The male of *Oncopeltus* mounts the female, the genital capsule is rotated through 180°, mainly by muscular action, and the parameres grasp the ovipositor valves. Following insertion of the aedeagus the insects assume an end to end orientation in which they are held together mainly by the aedeagus (Fig. 199). An end to end position is also taken up by *Blattella* (Dictyoptera), but at first the female climbs on the back of the male who engages the hook on his left phallomere on a sclerite in front of the ovipositor. Then, in the end to end position, the lateral hooks on either side of the anus and a small crescentic sclerite take a firm grip on the ovipositor (Fig. 200).

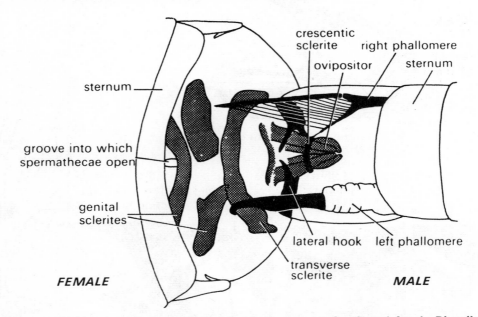

Fig. 200. Ventral view of the terminal abdominal segments of male and female *Blattella* showing the manner in which the male genitalia clasp the female. The insects are represented in the end-to-end position with the subgenital plates and endophallus of the male removed. Female sclerites shaded, male sclerites black (after Khalifa, 1950b).

Copulation in Odonata involves the male flexing his abdomen so that the head of the female touches his accessory genitalia and she then brings her abdomen forwards beneath her so as to make contact with the accessory genitalia (Fig. 196C). Some species, such as *Crocothemis*, copulate and complete sperm transfer in flight and in these copulation is brief, lasting less than 20 secs. Many species, however, settle before copulating and in these the process may last for a few minutes or an hour or more (see Corbett, 1962).

The duration of copulation in other insects is equally variable. In various mosquitoes the process is complete within a few seconds (see Clements, 1963), while in *Oncopeltus* the insects may remain coupled for five hours, in *Locusta* for eight to ten hours, and in *Anacridium* (Orthoptera) for up to 60 hours. Insemination is completed much more rapidly than this: in *Locusta* sperm reach the spermatheca within two hours of the start of copulation and in *Hetaerina* (Odonata) sperm transfer takes about 7·5 secs. in a copulation lasting some three minutes.

16.8 Insemination

In the insects the transfer of sperm to the female is a quite separate process from fertilisation of the eggs, which in some cases does not occur until some months after insemination. During this interval the sperm are stored in the spermatheca. Sperm may be transferred in a spermatophore produced by the male, or they may be passed directly into the spermatheca without a spermatophore being produced.

16.81 Spermatophore

The primitive method of insemination in insects involves the production by the male of a spermatophore, a capsule enclosing the sperm. Spermatophores are produced by the Apterygota, Orthoptera, Dictyoptera, some Heteroptera, all the Neuroptera except Coniopterygidae, some Trichoptera, Lepidoptera, some Hymenoptera and Coleoptera and a few Diptera Nematocera (Davey, 1965a; Davies, 1965; Nielsen, 1959).

Structure and transmission

In Collembola the male deposits spermatophores on the ground quite independently of the females. Sometimes spermatophores are produced in aggregations of Collembola so that there is a good chance of a female finding one and inserting it into her reproductive opening, but in other cases the male grasps the female by her antennae and leads her over the spermatophore. The spermatophores of *Campodea* are also produced in the absence of the female and, like those of Collembola, each one consists of a globule 50-70 μ in diameter mounted on a peduncle 50–100 μ high (Fig. 201A). The globule has a thin wall which encloses a granular fluid floating in which are from one to four bundles of sperm. The sperm can survive in a spermatophore for two days. A male may produce some 200 spermatophores in a week, but at least some of these will be eaten by himself and other insects (Bareth, 1964).

Lepisma (Thysanura) males also deposit spermatophores on the ground, but in this case in the presence of the females. By side to side movements of his abdomen a male spins silk threads over the female so that her movements are restricted and she is guided over the spermatophore which she inserts into her genital duct. In *Machilis* sperm droplets are deposited on a thread. Then the male twists his body round the female and with his antennae and cerci guides her genitalia into positions in which they can pick up the droplets.

In the Pterygota spermatophores are passed directly from the male to the female. Basically a spermatophore consists of a gelatinous protein capsule which is formed from the secretions of the male accessory glands. Two or more layers may be visible in the capsule and embedded in it are one or two sacs containing sperm. A single sperm sac is present in Grylloidea and Trichoptera, two are present in Tettigonioidea and *Sialis*. The outer gelatinous mass is prolonged into a neck and the sperm sacs may open on this (Fig. 201B) or they may be completely enclosed within the capsule. The whole structure is commonly of the order of two millimetres long.

In phasmids, gryllids and tettigoniids only the neck of the spermatophore penetrates the female ducts, the body of the structure remains outside and is liable to be eaten by the female or other insects. In Dictyoptera the body of the spermatophore, although still outside the female ducts, is protected by the enlarged subgenital plate of the female.

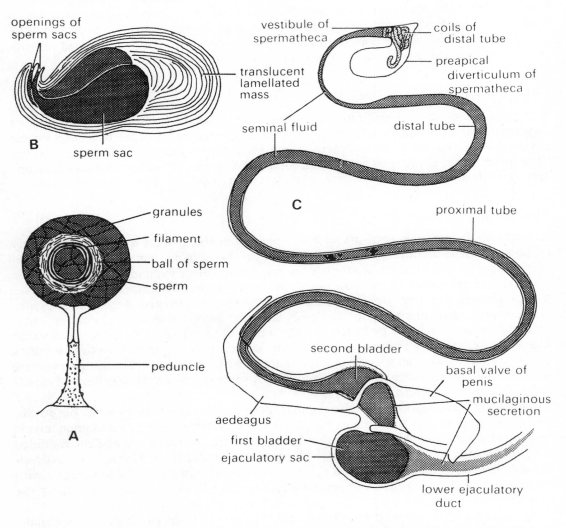

Fig. 201. Spermatophores. A. *Campodea* (after Bareth, 1964). B. *Blattella* (after Khalifa, 1950b). C. *Locusta* (after Gregory, 1965).

The spermatophore is specialised in the Acrididae to form a tube which is effectively a temporary elongation of the intromittent organ (Fig. 201C). It consists of two basal bladders in the ejaculatory and sperm sacs of the male (see Fig. 180) leading to a tube which is differentiated into proximal and distal parts and extends into the bulb of the spermatheca. In *Locusta* the whole structure is 35–45 mm. long, while the tube is only some 0·3 mm. in diameter.

Most other insects practise internal fertilisation and where a spermatophore is retained it is deposited directly into the bursa copulatrix of the female, and may be formed there as in Lepidoptera and Trichoptera. In these instances it is suggested that the spermatophore forms a plug which prevents loss of sperm from the female while they are in transit to the spermatheca (Davey, 1960). The structure of the spermatophore may be simplified in accordance with its altered function and in *Rhodnius* it consists only of a pear-shaped mass of transparent mucoprotein with an apical slit containing the sperm. There is no sperm sac.

Mating plugs, which are distinct from spermatophores (Hinton, 1964a), are produced in a number of insects. Thus in mosquitoes belonging to the genera *Anopheles*, *Aedes* and *Psorophora* a plug, formed from the accessory gland secretions of the male, is deposited in the genital chamber of the female. In *Psorophora* it is almost completely dissolved within 24 hours. A comparable structure present in some Lepidoptera, such as *Amauris* and *Acraea*, is called the spermatophragma or sphragis and it effectively prevents further mating by the female. Similarly, the bursa of *Apis* is occluded for some hours after the nuptial flight by a plug of mucus and often with parts of the male genitalia which become detached. See also Fuchs and Hiss (1970, *J. Insect Physiol.* **16**).

Spermatophore production

In gryllids and tettigoniids the spermatophore is produced before the male meets a female and these insects will only court when they carry a spermatophore. Other insects produce the spermatophore during copulation from secretions of the accessory glands. In *Rhodnius* the secretion becomes gelatinous as a result of a sharp change in pH from 7·0 in the transparent accessory gland to 5·5 in the spermatophore sac which moulds its form. The spermatophore sac is formed by the endophallus together with a part of the aedeagus which is inverted. The spermatophore of *Blattella* is formed in a pouch of the ejaculatory duct from three secretions produced in different glands. A milky secretion is surrounded by two others and sperm from the two seminal vesicles are injected into the middle layer to form two separate sperm sacs (Khalifa, 1950b).

The spermatophore is produced within the female in Lepidoptera and Trichoptera. Thus in *Galleria* (Lepidoptera) the aedeagus extends into the ductus bursae so that the male secretions are passed directly into the bursa copulatrix. First a yellow secretion is produced. This hardens and is followed by a white secretion which forms a mass in the bursa and the neck of the spermatheca, this part being moulded by the penis. Sperm are injected with other secretions into the vacuolated centre of the mass and the penis is withdrawn (Khalifa, 1950a).

In *Locusta* the spermatophore is produced largely in the male, although the ducts of the female serve to mould the tubular part. Its production begins within two minutes of copulation starting with the secretions of some of the accessory glands entering the ejaculatory duct. The secretions build up and so are forced down the ejaculatory duct and through the funnel (see Fig. 180), the shape of which produces a series of folds so that the secretions are moulded into a cylinder. A white semi-fluid secretion is then forced into the core of the cylinder so that it becomes a tube. This is enlarged in the ejaculatory sac to form the first bladder (Fig. 202A), while the part remaining in the ejaculatory duct, and known at this time as the reservoir tube, ultimately forms the second bladder in the sperm sac. At this stage seminal fluid is passed into the rudimentary spermatophore and then a separate cylinder of material is formed and pushed into the bladder where it becomes coiled up (Fig. 202B). This will form the distal tube and a further series of secretions forms the proximal tube (Fig. 202C). As the last part of the proximal tube enters the bladder it draws the wall of the reservoir tube with it so that this becomes invaginated, and finally the whole of the tube except for the tip is pushed inside the bladder by a mucilaginous secretion (Fig. 202D).

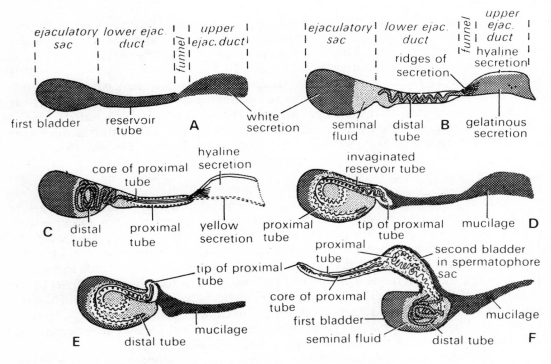

Fig. 202. Stages in spermatophore formation in *Locusta*. The parts of the male ducts in which the processes occur are indicated along the top (see Figs. 180, 201) (after Gregory, 1965).

At this time the ejaculatory sac starts to contract and so squeezes the tube of the spermatophore out of the bladder, while the pressure of mucilage in the ejaculatory duct forces the tip backwards through the gonopore, which is now open, and out through the aedeagus into the duct of the spermatheca (Fig. 202E, F). This process involves the tube being turned inside out and finally the second bladder is everted and moulded in the sperm sac (see Gregory, 1965, for a full account of this process).

Transfer of sperm to the spermatheca

Immediately following the transfer of the spermatophore the sperm migrate to the spermatheca where they are stored. Sometimes they are able to escape from the sperm sac through a pore, but in other cases, where the sperm sac is completely enclosed within the spermatophore, they escape as a result of the spermatophore rupturing. In Lepidoptera and *Sialis* the inside of the bursa copulatrix is lined with spines or bears a toothed plate, the signum dentatum, to which muscles are attached. The spermatophore is gradually abraded by movements of the spines until it is torn open. In *Rhodnius* the first sperm reach the spermatheca within about 10 minutes of the end of mating, while in *Acheta* transfer takes about an hour, and in *Zygaena* (Lepidoptera) 12–18 hours.

Although there is some evidence that the sperm move actively towards the spermatheca, guided by a chemical stimulus or a flow of fluid from the spermatheca, the bulk of evidence suggests that their movement is passive. In *Acheta* the sperm are held in the body of the spermatophore which remains external to the female, and the spermatophore is specialised to force the sperm out into the female ducts. An outer reservoir of fluid, the evacuating fluid, with a low osmotic pressure is separated by an inner layer with semipermeable properties from an inner proteinaceous mass called the pressure body which has a high osmotic pressure (Fig. 203A). When the spermatophore is deposited fluid passes from the evacuating fluid into the pressure body because of the

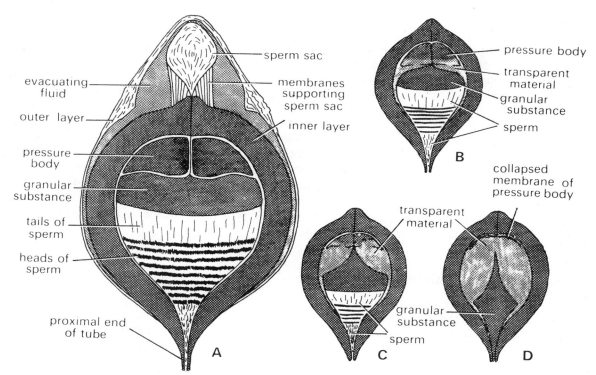

Fig. 203. A. Horizontal section through the ampulla of the spermatophore of *Acheta*. B, C, D. Stages in the evacuation of the spermatophore. The outer layer and evacuating fluid are not represented (after Khalifa, 1949).

difference in osmotic pressure. The pressure body swells producing a transparent material which forces the sperm out of the ampulla and down the tube of the spermatophore into the spermatheca (Fig. 203B–D). In *Locusta*, also, the sperm in the spermatophore are initially outside the female, in this case in the first bladder of the spermatophore. From here they are pumped along the spermatophore by contractions of the ejaculatory sac, first appearing in the spermatheca about 90 minutes after the start of copulation.

In many insects the spermatophore is placed in the bursa copulatrix of the female and the transfer of sperm to the spermatheca is probably brought about by the contractions of the female ducts. An opaque secretion from the male accessory glands of *Rhodnius* injected into the bursa with the spermatophore induces rhythmic contractions of the oviducts, probably by way of a direct nervous connection from the bursa to the oviducal muscles. The contractions cause shortening of the oviduct, and, it is suggested, cause the origin of the oviduct in the bursa to make bite-like movements in the mass of semen in the bursa so that sperm are taken into the oviduct. As this process continues the more anterior sperm are forced forwards along the oviduct and are passed into the spermathecae (see Davey, 1958).

Fate of the spermatophore

In some female insects the spermatophore is ejected some time after fertilisation. *Blattella* and *Rhodnius*, for instance, drop the old spermatophores some 12 and 18 hours respectively after copulation. The female *Sialis* pulls the spermatophore out and eats it and this commonly happens in Dictyoptera where the post-copulatory behaviour often has the effect of keeping the female occupied for a time to ensure that the sperm have left the spermatophore before she eats it.

The spermatophore is dissolved by proteolytic enzymes in other insects, such as Lepidoptera and Trichoptera, so that in many Trichoptera only the sperm sac remains one or two days after copulation. In *Galleria* digestion is complete in ten days, but the neck of the spermatophore persists. The spermatophore of *Locusta* breaks when the two sexes separate, either where the tube fits tightly in the spermathecal duct or at its origin with the bladders in the male. The part remaining in the male is ejected within about two hours by the contractions of the copulatory organ, while in the female the distal tube disappears, presumably being dissolved within a day, but the proximal tube, which dissolves much more slowly, persists for several days until it is ejected, probably by contractions of the spermathecal duct.

16.82 Direct insemination

Various groups of insects have dispensed with a spermatophore and sperm are transferred directly to the female ducts, and often into the spermatheca, by the penis which may be long and flagelliform to effect this transfer. Such direct insemination occurs, for instance, in some members of the orders Heteroptera, Mecoptera, Trichoptera, Hymenoptera, Coleoptera and Diptera.

Direct insemination occurs in *Aedes aegypti* and in this insect the paraprocts expand the genital orifice of the female while the aedeagus is erected by the action of muscles attached to associated apodemes. The aedeagus only penetrates just inside the female opening where it is held by spines which engage with a valve of the spermatheca. A stream of fluid from the accessory glands is driven along the ejaculatory duct and into the female by contractions of the glands and sperm are injected into the stream by the contractions of the seminal vesicles. Thus a mass of semen is deposited inside the atrium of the female and from here the sperm are transferred to the spermatheca (Spielman, 1964). The sperm of *Drosophila* are similarly deposited in the vagina and then pass to the spermatheca.

Oncopeltus has a long penis which reaches into the spermatheca into which sperm are deposited directly (see Fig. 199B). Erection of the phallus in this insect is a specialised mechanism involving the displacement of an erection fluid into the phallus from a reservoir in the ejaculatory duct. The fluid is forced back from the reservoir by pressure exerted by the body muscles, and this pressure is maintained throughout copulation. At the end of the ejaculatory duct the fluid is forced into a vesicle and then pumped into the phallus (see Bonhag and Wick, 1953). In those Coleoptera and Hymenoptera with a long penis erection is probably produced by an increase in blood pressure resulting from the sudden contraction of the abdominal walls.

16.83 Haemocoelic insemination

In some Cimicoidea the sperm, instead of being deposited in the female reproductive tract, are injected into the haemocoel. A good deal of variation occurs between the species practising this method and they can be arranged in a series showing progressive specialisation (Hinton, 1964a). In *Alloeorhynchus flavipes* the penis enters the vagina, but a spine at its tip perforates the wall of the vagina so that the sperm are injected into the haemocoel. They are not phagocytosed immediately, but disperse beneath the integument and later collect under the peritoneal membrane surrounding the ovarioles.

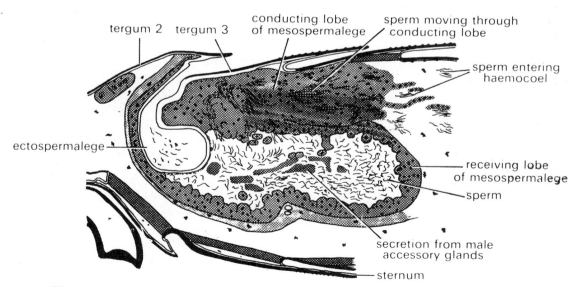

Fig. 204. Longitudinal section through the ectospermalege and mesospermalege of *Xylocoris galactinus* taken about an hour after copulation (after Carayon, 1953a).

These movements are possibly directed chemotactically. The sperm adjacent to the lowest follicle penetrate the follicular epithelium and fertilise the eggs via the micropyles.

Primicimex shows a further separation from the normal method of insemination. Here the left clasper of the male penetrates the dorsal surface of the abdomen of the female, usually between tergites 4 and 5 or 5 and 6. The clasper ensheathes the penis and sperm are injected into the haemocoel. They accumulate in the heart and are distributed round the body with the blood. Many are phagocytosed by the blood cells, but those that survive are stored in two large pouches at the base of the oviducts. The holes made in the integument by the claspers become plugged with tanned cuticle.

In other species the sperm are not injected directly into the haemocoel, but are received into a special pouch called the mesospermalege or organ of Ribaga or Berlese which is believed to be derived from blood cells. Other genera have a cuticular pouch, called the ectospermalege, for the reception of the clasper and the penis. There may be one or two ectospermalegia and their positions vary, but in *Afrocimex* they are situated in the membrane between segments 3 and 4 and segments 4 and 5 on the left-hand side. *Xylocoris galactinus* has a mesospermalege for the reception of sperm immediately beneath the ectospermalege (Fig. 204). It is formed from vacuolated cells surrounding a central lacuna into which the sperm are injected and from here they move down a solid

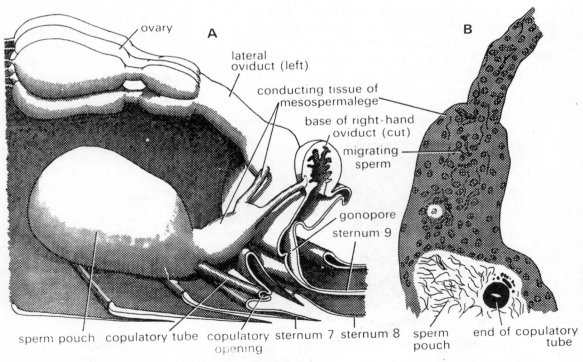

Fig. 205. A. Diagram of the internal reproductive organs of *Orius*. B. Longitudinal section of part of the mesospermalege showing the sperm pouch and conducting tissue (after Carayon, 1953b).

core of cells, forming the conducting lobe, into the haemocoel and finally arrive at the conceptacula seminis at the bases of the lateral oviducts where they accumulate. In *Cimex* this migration takes about 12 hours and after the female takes her next blood meal the sperm are carried intracellularly in packets to the ovaries through special conduit cells. At the base of each ovariole they accumulate in a corpus seminalis derived from the follicular cells (Davis, 1964).

Finally, in *Anthocoris* and *Orius* there is no temporary perforation of the integument because a copulatory tube opens on the left between the sternites of segments 7 and 8 and passes to a median sperm pouch where the sperm accumulate. From here the mesospermalege forms a column of conducting tissue along which the sperm pass to the oviducts so that they are never free in the haemocoel (Fig. 205).

In all these instances some sperm are digested by blood cells or by phagocytes in the mesospermalege. It is suggested that they are of nutritional value and perhaps haemocoelic insemination and its associated digestion of sperm facilitates more prolonged survival of the recipients in the absence of food (Hinton, 1964a).

In Strepsiptera sperm also pass into the haemocoel to fertilise the eggs, but they do so via the genital canals of the female (see Fig. 246).

16.9 Post-copulatory behaviour

The behaviour of insects immediately following copulation is as variable as that immediately preceding it. In *Oecanthus* (Orthoptera) and some blattids the female remains feeding on the metanotal gland of the male for some time. This behaviour prevents her from eating the spermatophore. The female mantid may eat the male and sometimes she starts feeding before copulation. The effect of eating the head of the male is to release copulatory behaviour by the removal of inhibitory centres (p. 538). The female is also known to eat the male in *Carabus auratus* and the ceratopogonid *Johannsenomyia*.

Odonata oviposit immediately after copulation and in Zygoptera and some Libellulidae the pair remain in tandem during this process. In other cases the male hovers over the female, driving off intruders. This is true in *Hetearina* in which the female submerges, the male remaining on guard for 30 minutes or more.

Male insects may copulate many times in rapid succession. Under experimental conditions a male *Mormoniella* has mated 154 times in four and a half hours, and a male of *Aedes aegypti* mated 30 times in 30 minutes. Although in the field such excessive copulation is unlikely to occur, multiple copulation by males must be common. When copulations follow each other in rapid succession only some of them result in successful insemination because the supply of sperm is limited. Thus of seven copulations performed by a male *Aedes* only four resulted in insemination of the female, but further insemination occurred on subsequent days as fresh sperm were produced (and see Jones and Wheeler, 1965). In species which produce a spermatophore the availability of material for the spermatophore may also be limiting. *Galleria* males which copulated within three hours of a previous copulation produced only small spermatophores, in some cases devoid of sperm. A normal spermatophore is produced after about 12 hours (Khalifa, 1950a).

The females of a few species, such as *Callitroga* (Diptera), are known to mate only once. Others commonly mate repeatedly, but the female is non-receptive for a time after copulating. The female of *Gomphocerus*, for instance, kicks away approaching males during this period. This inhibition of normal sexual behaviour results from nervous stimuli received from the spermatheca containing the spermatophore (Loher and Huber, 1966). After a few hours the female of *Locusta* will copulate again, but for the first three days these copulations do not lead to successful insemination because the spermathecal duct is blocked by the proximal tube of the original spermatophore. Later, however, when this is softer and can be flattened a successful second insemination may occur. All the spermatophores are ejected some 12–24 hours before oviposition and in the interval between ejection and oviposition the females are non-receptive (Gregory, 1965). In other insects the presence of a spermatophore in the female ducts may similarly prevent insemination for some time and the sphragis in Lepidoptera has a similar effect.

The relevance of multiple copulation is not clear. In mosquitoes it is probable that a single mating provides sufficient sperm to fertilise all the eggs which a female produces (Clements, 1963), but this is not certain in *Drosophila*. In this insect a female receives about 4000 sperm at one insemination. She may lay some 3000 eggs, and since eggs may receive more than one sperm a single insemination will barely suffice to fertilise all the eggs.

It is known, however, that insemination influences the metabolism and behaviour of the female as well as leading to the fertilisation of her eggs. In a number of cases, as in *Cimex, Pycnoscelus* (Dictyoptera) and *Schistocerca*, oocyte development is initiated or accelerated. In addition, in cockroaches insemination increases the number of oocytes which mature and which are laid and results in the production of a complete ootheca which is retracted into the brood sac (see p. 373) (Stay and Gelperin, 1966). Insemination produces these effects via its stimulation of the neurosecretory cells of the brain and especially of the corpora allata and it is possible that the importance of multiple copulation lies in these secondary effects rather than in the primary effect of fertilisation.

CHAPTER XVII

OVIPOSITION AND THE EGG

In some insects the female has no special structures associated with egg-laying, but in others the posterior part of the abdomen or some posterior abdominal appendages are modified to form an ovipositor. This enables the female to insert her eggs into special situations, within plant or animal tissue, for instance, instead of simply depositing them on a surface. The eggs may be laid singly or in masses and in some species they are deposited in special protective structures called oothecae formed from secretions of the female accessory glands. The oviposition site selected by the female is usually characteristic for the species and is of some importance since the survival of the egg and the availability of food for the larva when it hatches depend on her choice. The selection of the site involves a general attraction to some particular area and then a specific reaction which determines the precise spot at which the egg is laid within this area.

Insect eggs are relatively large because they contain a great deal of yolk. The shell of the egg is often complex and contains cavities connecting with the outside air by a number of small holes or, in some cases, through an open network. This system facilitates gaseous exchange all round the surface of the egg and in some cases, where the eggs of terrestrial insects are liable to flooding, it may function as a plastron. Water loss from the egg is restricted by a layer of wax on the inside of the shell and sometimes a second wax layer is formed in an embryonic cuticle. Many insect eggs absorb water during development so that they may increase considerably in size. One or more small holes are present in the shell, passing right through it to permit the entry of sperm.

The structure of the female genitalia is reviewed by Scudder (1961) and Snodgrass (1935), and the egg shell has been studied in particular by Hinton (see Hinton and Cole, 1965, for references). Respiration in the egg is considered by Hinton (1962b) and Wigglesworth and Beament (1950), and waterproofing mechanisms by Beament (1946b), and see Slifer and Sekhon (1963).

17.1 Female genitalia

The gonopore of the female insect is usually situated on or behind the eighth or ninth abdominal segment, but the Ephemeroptera and Dermaptera are exceptional with the gonopore behind segment 7. In many orders there are no special structures associated with oviposition, although sometimes the terminal segments of the abdomen are long and telescopic so that they form a type of ovipositor (see Fig. 166B). Such a structure is found in some Lepidoptera, Coleoptera and Diptera. In *Musca* the telescopic section is formed from segments six to nine and normally, when not in use, it is telescoped within segment five. This species has the sclerites of the ovipositor reduced to rods. In other species, as in trypetids, the tip of the abdomen is hardened and forms a sharp point which enables the insect to place its eggs in small holes and crevices.

Other insects have an ovipositor of a quite different form derived from the appendages of abdominal segments eight and nine. Such a structure is present in Thysanura, some Odonata, Orthoptera, Homoptera, Heteroptera, Thysanoptera Terebrantia and Hymenoptera. Scudder (1961) has attempted to rationalise the terminology associated with the ovipositor and his terms will be used together with the more generally used terminology of Snodgrass (1935).

Scudder (1961) believes *Lepisma* to possess a basic form of the ovipositor from which the ovipositors of other insects can be derived. At the base of the ovipositor on each side are the coxae of segments 8 and 9. These are known as the first and second gonocoxae (first and second valvifers of Snodgrass, 1935) (Fig. 206). Articulating with each of

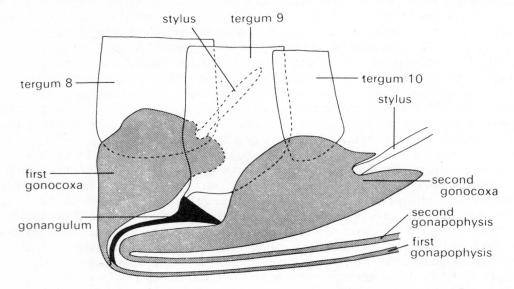

Fig. 206. Inner view of the genital segments of *Lepisma*. The forms and positions of some basal sclerites of the ovipositor have been slightly modified in order to show their interrelationships more clearly. Styli occur on other segments and are not an essential part of the ovipositor (after Scudder, 1961).

these plates is a slender process which curves posteriorly. These are the first and second gonapophyses (valvulae of Snodgrass, 1935) and they form the shaft of the ovipositor. In *Lepisma* the second gonapophyses of the two sides are united so that the shaft comprises three elements which fit together to form a tube down which the eggs pass. Finally, at the base of the ovipositor there is a small sclerite, the gonangulum, which is attached to the base of the first gonapophysis and articulates with the second gonocoxa and the tergum of segment 9. The gonangulum probably represents a part of the coxa of segment 9. It is not differentiated in *Petrobius* (Thysanura).

In some Thysanura and in the Pterygota an additional process is present on the second gonocoxa. This is the gonoplac (third valvula of Snodgrass, 1935). It may or may not be a separate sclerite and may form a sheath round the gonapophyses. The gonoplacs are well developed in the Orthoptera where they form the dorsal valves of the ovipositor with the second gonapophyses enclosed within the shaft as in tettigoniids (Fig. 207) or reduced as in the gryllids. Throughout the Orthoptera the gonangulum is fused with the first gonocoxa.

The Homoptera, Heteroptera and Thysanoptera have the gonangulum fused with tergum 9, while the gonoplac may be present or absent. In Pentatomomorpha and Cimicomorpha the development of the ovipositor is related to oviposition habit. If the insect oviposits in plant or animal tissue the valves are sclerotised and lanceolate and the

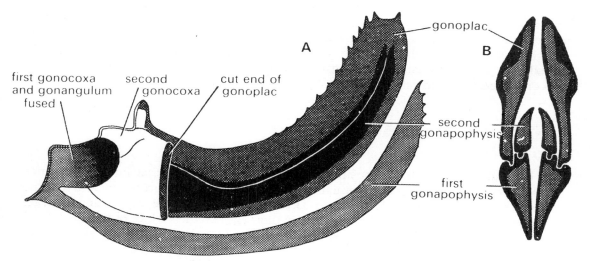

Fig. 207. The ovipositor of a tettigoniid. A. Lateral view with one gonoplac removed. B. Transverse section (from Snodgrass, 1935).

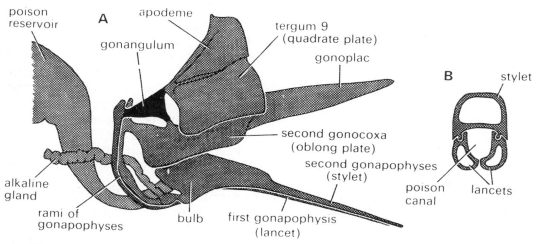

Fig. 208. Structure of the sting of a worker *Apis*. A. Lateral view. B. Transverse section through the shaft (after Snodgrass, 1956).

anterior strut of the gonangulum is heavily sclerotised. Species laying on leaf surfaces, however, have membranous and flap-like gonapophyses and the anterior strut of the gonangulum is membranous or absent (Scudder, 1959).

In the Hymenoptera the first gonocoxae are absent, although they may be present in Chalcidoidea, and the second gonapophyses are united. In the Symphyta and parasitic groups the ovipositor retains its original function, but in Aculeata it forms the sting. This does not involve any major modifications of the basic structure, but the eggs, instead of passing down the shaft of the ovipositor, are ejected from the opening of the genital chamber at its base. In *Apis* the first gonapophyses are known as the lancets and the fused second gonapophyses as the stylet. This forms an inverted trough which is enlarged into a basal bulb (Fig. 208) into which the reservoir of the poison gland discharges. The poison gland, sometimes known as the acid gland, consists of a pair of tubular glands which have a common duct leading to the poison reservoir. Another accessory gland, the alkaline gland, discharges at the base of the sting. Its function is unknown, but it may be concerned with lubrication of the sting.

17.2 Oviposition

17.21 Oviposition habits

The selection of a suitable oviposition site by the female is of great importance since it must ensure that the eggs are adequately protected from the environment and that the correct food will be available for the relatively immobile larvae when they emerge. Thus many Lepidoptera and Heteroptera lay their eggs on the surface of the larval food plant, often on the underside of a leaf so that the eggs are not exposed to extremes of heat and desiccation. The eggs are cemented to the surface by a secretion of the accessory glands and they may be laid singly, as in *Pieris rapae*, or in groups, as in *P. brassicae*.

The eggs of *Chrysopa* (Neuroptera) are laid on leaves, but raised on stalks which may be up to 15 mm. high. The stalk is produced as a viscous material which hardens in air as the insect draws it out. Some members of the genus lay their eggs in clusters so that the stalks become confluent.

Often eggs are laid in the soil as in some Asilidae and in *Tettigonia* (Orthoptera), and many Diptera oviposit on or in the surface of dung or carrion. *Orthellia*, for instance, makes a hole with its ovipositor in the surface of a freshly deposited cow pat. The hole is enlarged by pressing outwards with the ovipositor and a group of 25–35 eggs laid in the cavity so formed (Fig. 209A). Acrididae bore deep holes in the ground in which they lay groups of eggs.

Tettigoniids, Tenthredinidae and Thysanoptera often lay their eggs in plant tissues, using their ovipositor to do so. The oviposition site may be quite specific, as in thrips which differentiate between the petals and the bracts of a particular flower species, or unspecific, as in *Meconema* (Orthoptera) which inserts its eggs into crevices in bark or into fungi growing on bark.

Many parasitic Diptera lay their eggs on the appropriate host, while many parasitic Hymenoptera which have well-developed ovipositors lay their eggs in the host. In some instances, notably in *Rhyssa* which parasitises the larva of *Sirex* (Hymenoptera), the insect can locate and oviposit in its host by boring down with its ovipositor through the wood in which the host is burrowing.

In some parasitic species the female may oviposit in an area frequented by the host rather than on the host itself. The eggs of Trigonalidae are laid on leaves and must be eaten by a caterpillar or sawfly larva infected with an ichneumon or tachinid parasite in order for the larvae to reach their host. Because of the wastage which must occur these insects produce large numbers of eggs; several thousand in a few days are recorded (see Clausen, 1940). Meloid eggs are deposited near the host nesting or oviposition sites and the larvae search for the host. Meloids also produce large numbers of eggs.

Cordylobia (Diptera) also lays its eggs away from the host, while *Dermatobia*, the human warble fly, oviposits on other insects, especially mosquitoes, and ticks which then transport the eggs to the host. The female fly waits at a pool and as a mosquito emerges from the pupa she will capture it and lay a group of about 15 eggs on its abdomen. Such an association in which an animal of one species provides transport for another species is known as phoresy.

Other species have specialised oviposition habits. *Scarabaeus* (Coleoptera) constructs a subterranean chamber which is provisioned with one or more mounds of dung each containing an egg. The dung subsequently provides food for the larva. In *Copris* (Coleoptera) the chamber is constructed by the male and female working together. The social insects oviposit in specially constructed cells which they provision.

Insects with aquatic larvae show a similar range of variation in their oviposition behaviour. *Culex,* for instance, lands on the water and constructs a raft of 150–300 eggs between the hind tarsi which lie flat on the surface. The eggs float in an upright position because the micropyle cup at one end is hydrophile and the rest of the chorion is hydrofuge (Fig. 209B). Other mosquito species, such as *Anopheles*, lay their eggs singly on the surface and the position in which the eggs float, ventral surface uppermost, is determined by the presence of air-filled floats in the chorion (Fig. 209C). The eggs of dragonflies are also sometimes laid on the surface, either being dropped from above or washed off by the tip of the abdomen touching the water, but in this case the eggs slowly sink to the bottom. In other cases, as in *Chironomus*, the eggs are laid in a string which is anchored at the surface (Fig. 211).

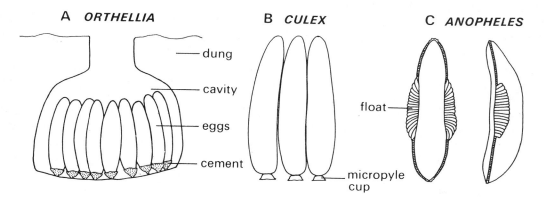

Fig. 209. A. Eggs of *Orthellia* in a cavity in cow-dung (after Hinton, 1960a). B. Eggs of *Culex* showing the hydrophile micropyle cup. C. Eggs of *Anopheles*, ventral and lateral views (after Marshall, 1938).

Other insects with aquatic larvae lay their eggs in floating vegetation. This is true of *Nepa* which lays its eggs so that their respiratory horns (see p. 339) remain above the water. Various species of Zygoptera also lay their eggs in surface vegetation such as *Potamogeton* and *Myriophyllum*.

Some species submerge to lay their eggs. This occurs in some Zygoptera which lay their eggs in the submerged parts of water plants. The female of *Hetaerina*, for instance, submerges to a depth of four or five inches and may remain submerged for nearly an hour while she lays her eggs in the roots of *Salix* (Bick and Salzback, 1966). Aquatic beetles also oviposit under water. Some, such as *Agabus*, lay their eggs on aquatic plants, the female in this species laying a row of eggs inside the leaf sheath (Jackson, 1958). *Ilybius* (Coleoptera) lays its eggs in the tissues of aquatic plants, making an incision so that the eggs are placed amongst the airspaces in the plant (Jackson, 1960). The mymarid *Caraphractus* swims under water in order to parasitise the eggs of these beetles (Jackson, 1966).

Finally, there are aquatic insects which oviposit in positions over or near water so that the larvae readily find their way to it. Some dragonflies and Trichoptera lay their eggs in or on emergent vegetation so that the larvae tend to drop into the water when they hatch. *Aedes*, on the other hand, lays its eggs on the ground near water in places liable to flooding and the eggs do not hatch until such flooding occurs.

17.22 Oothecae

Although in the majority of insects the eggs are simply glued on to, or inserted into, the substratum, a number of species lay their eggs in oothecae formed by secretions of the female accessory glands. Characteristic oothecae are produced by the Dictyoptera. *Blatta*, for instance, lays its eggs in two rows, each of eight eggs, inside a capsule which becomes tanned as it is formed (see p. 284) (Fig. 210A). Along the top of the capsule is a crest within which are cavities connecting, via small pores, with the outside and facilitating respiration by the eggs. Roth (1968) reviews the structure of oothecae in the Blattaria.

Acrididae lay their eggs in the ground in egg pods. A pod consists of a mass of eggs under the ground held together by a frothy secretion and sometimes also enclosed by a layer of the same substance. The hole above the egg-mass is plugged by more froth (Fig. 210B, C). The eggs within the mass are arranged irregularly in the Pyrgomorphidae and Cyrtacanthacridinae (Fig. 210B), but are in regular rows in the Acridinae and Truxalinae (Fig. 210C). Some species produce pods with only a few eggs; *Badistica*, for instance, lays between one and six, while at the other extreme *Phymateus* has been recorded to lay over 200 eggs in a pod.

The tortoise beetles also produce oothecae. The form and complexity of the ootheca varies from species to species, but *Basipta* attaches its ootheca to the stem of its food plant. The theca is formed of a large number of lamellae produced from an accessory gland secretion which is compressed into a plate-like form as it is extruded between the terminal sclerites of the abdomen. The lamellae are placed so as to form an open cup, the interior of which is occupied by about 30 cells also formed by the lamellae (Fig. 210D, E). An egg is placed in each of the cells as it is formed and round the outside of the cup the lamellae are plastered firmly together to form a hard 'shell' with looser lamellae outside it (see Muir and Sharp, 1904).

The heteropteran *Plataspis* forms a type of ootheca, laying its eggs in two rows and then covering them with hard elongage pellets of a secretion produced by specialised cells in the intestine. *Coptosoma* (Heteroptera) covers its eggs with an irregular layer of cement which traps pockets of air in deep follicular pits.

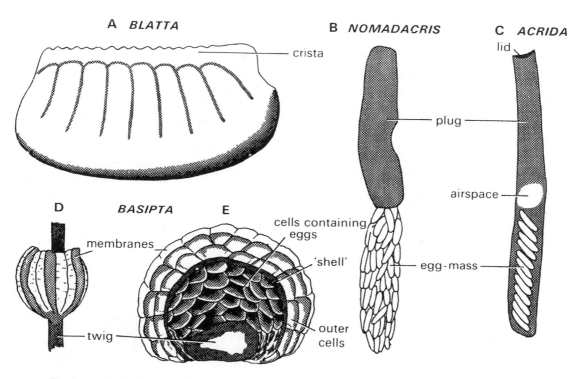

Fig. 210. A. Ootheca of *Blatta* (after Ragge, 1965). B and C. Egg pods of *Nomadacris* and *Acrida* (after Chapman and Robertson, 1958). D. Ootheca of *Basipta*. E. Transverse section of the ootheca of *Basipta* (after Muir and Sharp, 1904).

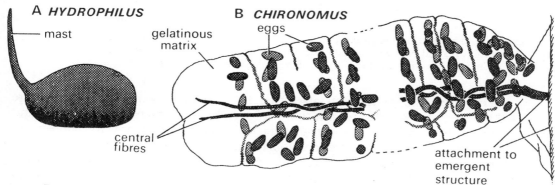

Fig. 211. A. Egg cocoon of *Hydrophilis* (after Miall, 1922). B. Egg-rope of *Chironomus*.

Amongst aquatic insects *Hydrophilus* constructs a silken cocoon with a mast (Fig. 211A, and see p. 284), while in many groups the eggs are enclosed in a gelatinous matrix. For instance, *Chironomus dorsalis* produces a structure in which the eggs loop backwards and forwards round the circumference of the matrix while a pair of fibres, which anchor the mass to the surface, run through the centre (Fig. 211B). Other species of chironomids and Trichoptera lay their eggs in masses or strands of gelatinous material.

17.23 Choice of oviposition site

Two phases can be recognised in the selection of an oviposition site. The first, or initial selection is based on a general reaction to the environment and this is followed by a final selection which depends on more specific responses.

Initial selection of a site involves various factors and pre-oviposition behaviour may be important as in locusts and grasshoppers. These insects tend to bask in warm spots on bare ground and often they oviposit at the basking site (Popov, 1958). Their choice is also influenced by the availability of suitable vegetation on which to feed and roost. Thus *Nomadacris* oviposits largely in areas where the vegetation has been burnt so that the ground is bare, but more eggs are laid, and later more larvae are present, adjacent to stands of unburnt grass than in extensive areas of bare ground (Fig. 212).

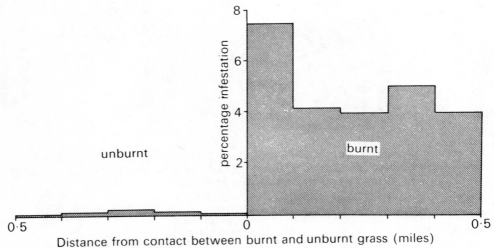

Fig. 212. The distribution of early instar larvae of *Nomadacris* in relation to a boundary between burnt and unburnt ground. The distribution of larvae at this stage can be taken as an indication of the distribution of the egg pods (after Symmons and Carnegie, 1959).

In other insects there is often attraction to a particular area. Mosquitoes are attracted to water, being influenced in this attraction by the presence of vegetation and the amount of light reflected from the surface. Female *Pieris* ready to oviposit are attracted to green surfaces whereas previously only blue or yellow are attractive. In other species olfactory, rather than visual, stimuli are important in determining the general area in which a species will oviposit. For instance, *Achroia*, a wax moth, is stimulated to probe with its ovipositor by the smell of beeswax (Makings, 1958) and *Mor-*

moniella keeps in an area contaminated by the smell of its host. Within this area it searches for the puparia of *Calliphora* which it parasitises (Edwards, 1955). *Nemeritis* (Hymenoptera) is similarly attracted by smell to the area occupied by its host, larval *Ephestia* (Lepidoptera) (J. R. Williams, 1951), and *Rhizopertha* (Coleoptera) is attracted to grain (Crombie, 1942).

These general stimuli, which result in the initial selection of the oviposition site, release behaviour patterns which lead to the final selection of the site. This often involves contact chemoreceptors on the antennae, tarsi and ovipositor (see Dethier, 1947a; Thomas, 1965). The female locust taps the surface of the soil with the tip of her abdomen and then probes with her ovipositor. Hard surfaces are rejected, but any soft sandy soil is accepted and she starts to dig (see p. 333). Oviposition only follows if the soil is moist, but saline soils are rejected. In *Schistocerca* the final choice of site is also influenced by the presence of other locusts, females exhibiting a preference for laying in groups rather than in isolation. Visual and olfactory stimuli are important in maintaining the groups (Norris, 1963).

Although mosquitoes are attracted to water they do not always oviposit once they have reached it. Oviposition depends, at least to a large extent, on the stimuli received by tarsal sensilla when the insect lands on the surface. *Aedes aegypti* and *Culex* reject water with a high salt content, the rejection possibly being based on the high osmotic pressure of saline solutions. In some species, although not these two, pH is also important (Hudson, 1956). *Pieris brassicae* also uses tarsal receptors, drumming on the surface of the plant with its fore legs. Normally this species only oviposits on plants which contain mustard oil and eggs are usually laid on the undersides of leaves partly because the female exhibits a preference for shade, but largely because she tends to hang down while ovipositing (David and Gardiner, 1962).

Nemeritis employs antennal sensilla, vibrating the antennae over the surface until it makes contact with its host. Having done so it stops and probes with its ovipositor. This makes the host recoil, exciting the parasite so that it thrusts more vigorously with its ovipositor and this increases its chances of penetrating the host cuticle. When the cuticle has been pierced *Nemeritis* can detect the presence of eggs laid by another parasite and may reject the host as unsuitable. This must involve sensilla on the ovipositor.

17.24 Mechanisms of oviposition

In the majority of species which lack an appendicular ovipositor, eggs are simply deposited on a surface or, if the terminal segments of the abdomen are elongated or telescopic, they may be inserted into crevices. In some cases, however, specialised structures are involved in the oviposition process. Many Asilidae, for instance, have spine bearing plates called acanthophorites at the tip of the abdomen. They push aside the soil as the insect oviposits so that the tip of the abdomen can be inserted and then, when the abdomen is withdrawn, the soil falls back and covers the eggs (Oldroyd, 1964). The beetle *Ilybius* has two finely toothed blades which form an ovipositor. The points of these blades are pushed into the surface of a suitable plant and then worked upwards by a rapid, rhythmic, saw-like action so that a tongue of plant tissue is cut away at the sides. An egg is laid in the hole beneath the blades and is covered by the tongue of plant tissue when the blades are withdrawn (Jackson, 1960).

Species which possess an ovipositor derived from the appendages of segments 8 and 9 penetrate tissues by a sliding movement of the valves relative to each other similar to that in the sting of *Apis* (see below). In an ichneumon the tip of the abdomen is turned down at the start of oviposition so that the valves point ventrally instead of posteriorly (Fig. 213). The gonapophyses then work their way into the host tissue, or through the wood in which the host is boring in the case of *Rhyssa*, by rapid to and fro movements. The gonoplacs do not enter the wound, but become deflected outside it. In this way *Rhyssa* can bore through 3 cm. of wood in 20 minutes.

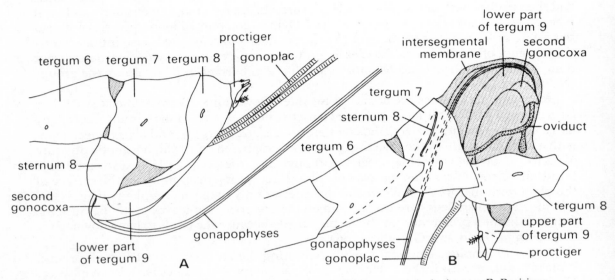

Fig. 213. Basal part of the ovipositor of *Megarhyssa* (Hymenoptera). A. At rest. B. Positions of abdominal sclerites and ovipositor during oviposition. Membranes stippled (after Snodgrass, 1935).

In *Apis*, although the ovipositor now forms a sting, the manner of functioning is essentially the same as in the ichneumon. When the insect is about to sting the basal parts of the apparatus swing up due to an upward movement of the anterior end of sternum 7, while the shaft of the sting is depressed by muscles (Fig. 214A, B). The initial thrust which pushes the tip of the valves into the host is produced by the downward deflection of the abdomen, but subsequently penetration results from the movements of the lancets on the stylet. These movements are produced by protractor and retractor muscles which run from either end of the second gonocoxa to the quadrate plate (see Fig. 208) which represents the lateral part of tergum 9. The quadrate plate is free to move because the central part of the tergum is membranous and the alternate contractions and relaxations of the muscles from the gonocoxa make it move backwards and forwards (Fig. 214C, D). This movement causes the gonangulum to rock on its articulation with the second gonocoxa (Fig. 214C, D, point X) and so moves the lancet relative to the stylet. The movements of the lancets of the two sides are out of phase and as they push into the wound they are held by their barbed tips. Hence the retractor muscles, instead of extracting the lancets from the wound, tend to depress the anterior ends of the second gonocoxae and so to restore the sclerites to their original positions, at the same time pushing the stylet into the wound. Successive thrusts carry the sting progressively deeper.

Poison is also injected by the action of the lancets since the poison reservoir itself has no muscles. Each lancet bears a concave valve which fits in the shaft of the sting (Fig. 214E). The movements of these valves as the lancets move in and out push poison along the shaft of the sting and out through a cleft near the tip of the lancets (Snodgrass, 1956).

In the Acrididae the action of the valves is quite different, involving an opening and closing movement of the dorsal and ventral valves rather than a sliding movement (Fig. 215). These movements are produced by muscles inserted on to an apodeme at the base of the valves, together with others inserted directly into the valves. The insect starts to dig a hole by raising the body on the first two pairs of legs and arching the tip of the abdomen downwards so that it presses more or less vertically on the ground. The opening movement of the valves scrapes particles of the substratum sideways and upwards and pressure is exerted down the abdomen so that the valves slowly dig a hole.

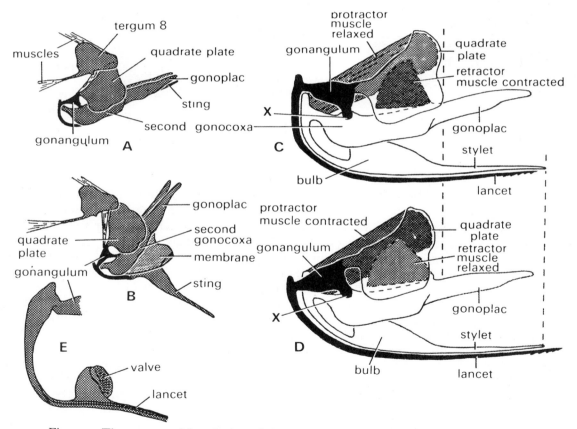

Fig. 214. The manner of functioning of the sting of *Apis*. A. Sting in retracted position. B. Sting protracted. C and D. Movements of lancet resulting from backwards and forwards movement of quadrate plate rocking the gonangulum on its articulation X. E. Basal part of lancet showing valve (after Snodgrass, 1956).

As the hole deepens the abdomen lengthens by the unfolding and stretching of the intersegmental membranes between segments 4 and 5, 5 and 6, and 6 and 7. The membranes are specialised to permit stretching, having a lamellated endocuticle under a thin epicuticle which is folded at right angles to the long axis of the body. As the abdomen lengthens these folds become smoothed out and the endocuticle stretches (Thomas, 1965). The intersegmental membranes of the male do not stretch to the same extent as in the mature female, nor do those of the immature female, indicating that some change occurs on maturation.

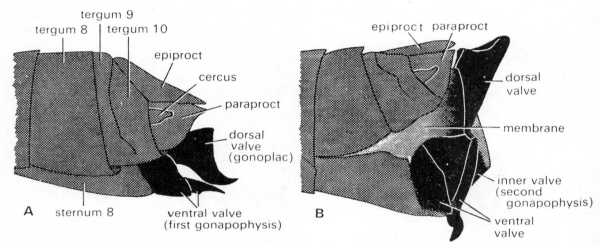

Fig. 215. Showing the manner in which the ovipositor valves of *Schistocerca* open. A. Valves closed. B. Valves open (after Thomas, 1965).

The extension of the abdomen which occurs may be very considerable. For instance, the abdomen of *Anacridium* stretches from 3·5 to 10·0 cm. in length and *Schistocerca* can dig to a depth of 14 cm. (Popov, 1958). The initial stretching of the membranes probably results largely from the pull of the ovipositor valves as they open during digging, but the extension is maintained by pressure from within the body. As the abdomen elongates there is some increase in the total body volume, but the pressure of haemolymph is maintained by the expansion of the airsacs and by swallowing air into the crop and midgut caecae. Air is pumped into the tracheal system by vigorous ventilatory movements of the head (see p. 466) synchronised with the opening and closing of the first thoracic spiracle, and as the eggs are laid more abdominal airsacs expand so that the haemolymph pressure is maintained. At the end of oviposition the airsacs fill the cavity of the first five abdominal segments and the volume of the tracheal system has increased by 117% above that at the start of oviposition (Woodrow, 1963).

At intervals during digging the female partly withdraws her abdomen and by small movements of the ovipositor valves together with twisting movements of the abdomen the walls of the hole are smoothed and compacted. Even in a suitable soil a female frequently abandons a hole and starts to dig again, but when a suitable hole has been constructed the process of oviposition proper begins. Just before an egg is laid the female pumps more air into her tracheal system by rapid movements of the head and then, with the thoracic spiracles closed, forces the air backwards so that the abdomen becomes turgid. It remains turgid until the egg is laid when the head moves forwards again and the pressure is released. Eggs are passed out micropylar end first and slowly the abdomen is withdrawn as more eggs are laid. When all the eggs have been laid the frothy plug is formed in the upper part of the hole and finally, having withdrawn her abdomen, the female scrapes soil over the top of the hole with her hind tibiae. The whole process may take about two hours of which egg-laying occupies some 20 minutes.

17.3 The egg

17.31 Structure

Typically insect eggs are very large since they contain a great deal of yolk. The eggs of Acrididae, for instance, may be 8 mm. long and 1 mm. in diameter and the eggs of smaller insects, such as *Musca,* are often a millimetre long. Some parasitic Hymenoptera, however, whose larvae develop internally in the fluids of other insects produce small eggs containing very little yolk. Thus the eggs of Platygasteridae, which parasitise cecidomyid larvae, are 0·02–0·10 mm. long and those of Mymaridae, which are laid in the eggs of other insects, 0·06–0·25 mm. long.

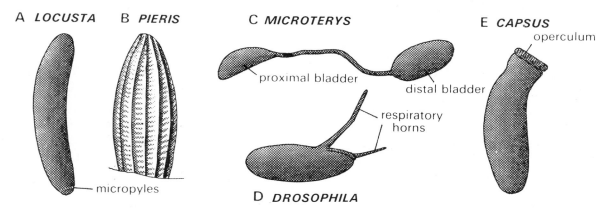

Fig. 216. Various forms of eggs. A. *Locusta.* B. *Pieris.* C. *Microterys* (Hymenoptera). D. *Drosophila.* E. *Capsus* (Heteroptera). Not all to same scale (after various authors).

Insect eggs occur in a variety of forms. Commonly, as in Orthoptera and many Hymenoptera, they are sausage shaped (Fig. 216A). Sometimes they are conical, as in *Pieris* (Fig. 216B), or rounded, as in many moths and Heteroptera. In the eggs of some Diptera and the Nepidae extensions of the chorion form one or more horns (Fig. 216D), while the eggs of many parasitic Hymenoptera have a projection called a pedicel at one end. The eggs of *Encyrtus* (Hymenoptera) are unusual in consisting of two bladders connected by a tube (Fig. 216C). During the process of oviposition the contents of the egg pass from the proximal to the distal bladder and the proximal bladder is lost. It is suggested that this may facilitate the entry of the egg into a host through a relatively small hole.

At the time of oviposition the cytoplasm of the egg forms a bounding layer, the periplasm, and an irregular reticulum within the yolk. The zygote nucleus usually occupies a posterior position. Round the outside of the ovum are the vitelline membrane and the chorion, or 'shell', with a layer of wax on the inside (Fig. 217). Later in the course of development the serosal cuticle is formed, consisting of a chitinous endocuticle, sometimes called the white cuticle, with an epicuticle having a second wax layer and incorporating the vitelline membrane on the outside. In the greater part of the epicuticle, which is sometimes known as the yellow cuticle, the wax layer is beneath a fibrous layer (Slifer and Sekhon, 1963).

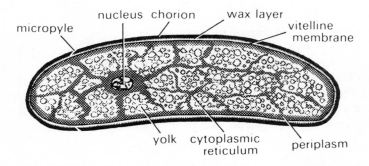

Fig. 217. Diagram of the structure of an egg at the time of oviposition.

Structure of the chorion

The chorion is a complex structure produced by the follicle cells while the egg is in the ovary (see p. 293). The outer surface is often sculptured, frequently with a pattern which is basically hexagonal, reflecting the form of the follicle cells. In other cases the surface may be ribbed or ridged and pitting also occurs, resulting from the uneven laying down of the chorion by the follicle cells (see Fig. 192B).

Sometimes two distinct regions of the chorion, the endochorion and exochorion, can be differentiated, the latter containing a tanned protein, chorionin, which resembles cuticulin in the insect epicuticle (see p. 435). In *Rhodnius* these two regions are formed from a number of chemically distinct layers (see Fig. 192) and this is also true in *Carausius* where the exochorion contains a tanned protein layer, a layer of fibrous protein impregnated with lime, and a layer of lipoprotein (Wigglesworth and Beament, 1950). In many accounts of the gross structure of the chorion, however, no clear distinction is made between these regions.

Usually some part of the chorion contains extensive airspaces. In *Tetrix* (Orthoptera), for instance, the basal layer of the chorion is a continuous sheet and arising from this are a number of struts with airspaces between them (Fig. 218A). The struts are buttressed at the base and branch laterally at their outer ends, the branches anastomosing and forming the outer layer of the chorion which is thus a perforated sheet (Fig. 218B).

Other insects have a more complex arrangement. In the egg of *Musca* there are extensive airspaces in the outer and inner meshworks of the chorion (Fig. 218C, D) and these are connected by fine tubes, the aeropyles, which run through the otherwise solid middle layer (Fig. 218C, E). The outer meshwork is absent over the greater part of the egg of *Calliphora*, but is present between the hatching lines (Fig. 219).

The outer surface of the chorion has strong hydrofuge properties in *Musca* and *Calliphora*, but in *Tetrix* and *Erioischia* (Diptera) the outer layers are readily wetted. A continuous basal layer is present adjacent to the oocyte in *Calliphora*, *Rhodnius* and *Nepa* as it is in *Tetrix*, but in the Muscinae this layer is perforated (see Hinton and Cole, 1965, and other papers by Hinton).

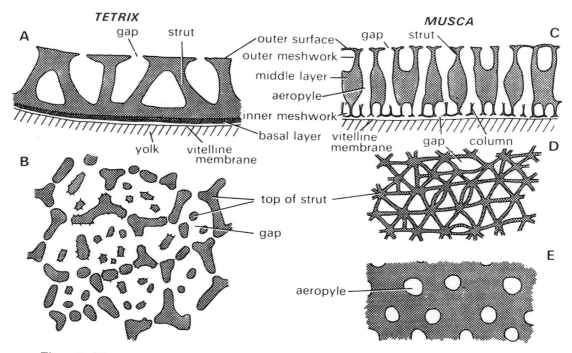

Fig. 218. The structure of the chorion of *Tetrix* and *Musca*. *Tetrix*: A. Transverse section. B. View of the surface. *Musca*: C. Transverse section. D. View of the surface. E. Horizontal section through the middle layer (after Hartley, 1962; Hinton, 1960a).

In *Apanteles* the eggs absorb nutriment from the host after oviposition and the chorion is very simple in structure (see King *et al.*, 1969, *Proc. R. ent. Soc. Lond.* A **44**).

The eggs of some species have a cap, or operculum, which is joined to the body of the egg along a line of weakness facilitating hatching (Fig. 216E). A cap is present in Cimicomorpha and, in *Rhodnius*, its structure differs from that of the rest of the chorion although the same elements are involved. The soft endochorion is much thinner than elsewhere on the egg, but the amber layer is much thicker and the follicular pits have slit-like openings and do not extend through the soft endochorion (see Fig. 192A). The cap is joined to the rest of the chorion by the sealing bar, which is formed from a very thin layer of resistant endochorion and a thick amber layer. There is a line of weakness where the sealing bar meets the cap (Beament, 1946a, 1947). Some pentatomids appear to have a cap, but this has the same structure as the rest of the chorion and is not joined to it by a sealing bar. A cap is present in the eggs of *Carausius*, Embioptera and the lice.

The eggs of some Diptera have hatching lines, which are lines of weakness along which the egg splits when the larva emerges. In *Musca* and *Calliphora* these take the form of two ridges which run longitudinally along the length of the egg (Fig. 219A). Along these lines the inner layer of the chorion extends outwards so that each ridge contains two inner layers which are back to back (Fig. 219C). In *Calliphora* the surface of the chorion between the hatching lines differs from that elsewhere (Hinton, 1960a).

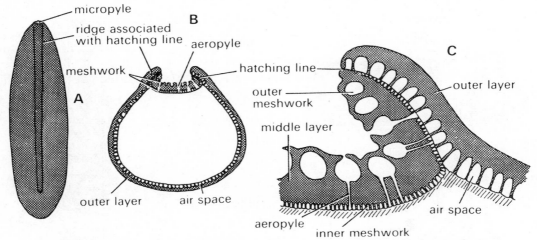

Fig. 219. Structure of the egg of *Calliphora*. A. Dorsal view showing hatching lines. B. Cross-section through the middle of the egg. C. Detail of section through one of the hatching lines (based on D. S. Anderson, 1960; Hinton, 1960a).

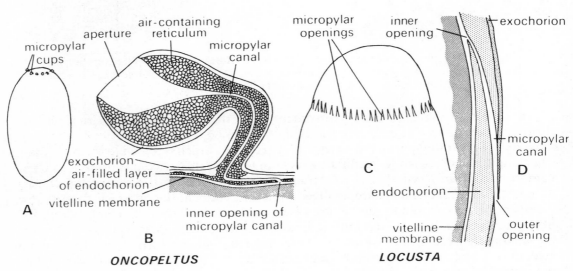

Fig. 220. A and B. *Oncopeltus:* whole egg and longitudinal section through a micropylar process (after Southwood, 1956). C and D. *Locusta:* posterior end of egg and longitudinal section through the chorion along the length of a micropylar canal (after Roonwal, 1954).

Micropyles

Since the chorion is laid down in the ovary some provision is necessary to allow the subsequent entry of the sperm. This takes the form of the micropyles which are funnel-shaped canals passing right through the chorion. Most dipterous eggs have only a single terminal micropyle, while Acrididae commonly have 30 or 40 arranged in a ring at the posterior end of the egg (Fig. 220C, D). In most Cimicomorpha the micropyles are present near the junction of the cap with the body of the egg, but there are no micropyles in the eggs of Cimicoidea which are fertilised in the ovary (see p. 319). The Pentatomomorpha have micropylar processes projecting from the chorion and in *Oncopeltus* each consists of a cup on a stem (Fig. 220A, B). The micropylar canal passes through the middle of the process and through the chorion and it is surrounded by an open reticulum of chorionin enclosing airspaces. There may be from two to several hundred such processes, depending on the species.

17.32 Respiration

Some gaseous exchange takes place through the solid chorion of most insect eggs, but the rate of diffusion of oxygen through this substance is not adequate to meet the demands of the developing embryo. Hence the majority of insect eggs have a series of air-filled cavities in the inner layers of the chorion which connect with the outside air through a

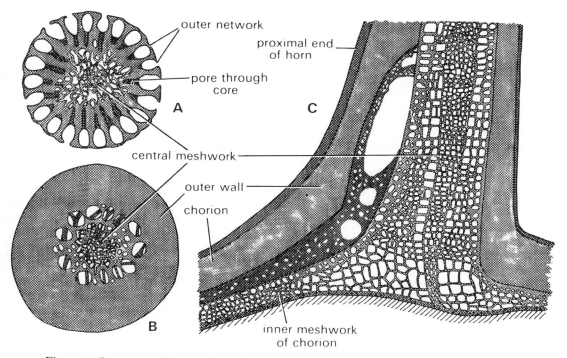

Fig. 221. Structure of the respiratory horn of *Nepa*. A. Cross-section of distal region. B. Cross-section of proximal region. C. Longitudinal section of the base of a horn showing its connection with the chorion (after Hinton, 1961b).

series of aeropyles. The aeropyles may be generally distributed as in *Musca* or restricted to a limited area, as in *Calliphora* where they occur only between the hatching lines and *Ocypus* (Coleoptera) which has an equatorial band of functional aeropyles. In *Rhodnius* they are restricted to a ring just below the cap (see Fig. 192). In other cases the cavities of the inner part of the chorion extend to the surface to facilitate gaseous exchange. Thus there is a small pore on the surface of the egg of *Carausius* at which the reticular endo-chorion is exposed, and the respiratory horns of some Diptera and the Nepidae serve the same function of connecting the inner layer of air with the atmosphere outside while at the same time restricting the area through which rapid loss of water can occur (Fig. 221). This is also true of the smaller respiratory horns of the Pentatomomorpha (Fig. 220B). In the egg of *Leptohylemyia* (Diptera) the middle layer of the chorion is a fine mesh-work which permits the access of air to the inner layers of the chorion all round the egg, but as a result of this the chorion provides virtually no resistance to the passage of water outwards from the egg (Hinton, 1962a).

Thus in all these cases there is a layer of air in the inner chorion which entirely or largely surrounds the ovum and which is connected to the outside air. This layer may have direct access to the ovum through pores in the innermost sheet of the chorion, but in some species, such as *Calliphora*, this sheet is imperforate. The chorion itself, however, is formed from a meshwork of fibrils with interstices of 20–50 Å so that oxygen can pass through this sheet although its movement will be impeded (Hinton, 1962b).

Wigglesworth and Beament (1950), studying respiration in the eggs of *Carausius*, *Rhodnius* and other species concluded that the cavities in the chorion were filled with some substance and did not contain air. The air was believed to reach the embryo through the porous protein of the chorion. However, the work of Hinton (1960a, 1961a, etc.) and of Wigglesworth and Salpeter (1962b) indicates that, at least in *Calliphora*, the cavities in the chorion are filled with air and it seems reasonable to suppose that this is true of the other species also.

Special provision for respiration by the eggs is made in the oothecae of cockroaches. In *Blattella* small cavities occur above each egg in the crest of the ootheca. These cavities connect with the outside air and a narrow duct leads down to a point above each egg at which the chorion is expanded to form an open meshwork. Each egg thus has a con-nection with the outside air (Wigglesworth and Beament, 1950).

The eggs of some terrestrial insects which are laid in the soil and other similar situations are subject to periodic flooding. Some eggs can survive this because the chorion, with its hydrofuge characteristics, maintains a layer of air round the egg into which gas from the surrounding water may diffuse. Thus the chorion acts as a plastron (see p. 481), but the effectiveness of a plastron depends on the area available for gaseous exchanges, that is on the extent of the air/water interface. In the eggs of Lepidoptera and most Heteroptera, *Rhodnius*, for example, the air/water interface is too small to be of significance, but the eggs may survive flooding by virtue of the fact that they can survive a great reduction in their metabolic rate. The plastron of *Ocypus* is more effective, but still not sufficiently large to permit continued development, but in *Calliphora*, where the plastron occurs between the hatching lines, and in *Musca*, where it covers the whole egg, normal development continues if the egg is immersed in well-aerated water. The respiratory horns of many dipteran eggs also form an efficient plastron if the eggs are flooded and this is true also in the eggs of Nepidae which are essentially terrestrial in their respiration since the horns normally project above the surface of the water.

The surface tension of water contaminated with organic acids and other surface active substances is lower than that of clean water, and the ease with which a plastron is wetted, and hence ceases to function, is inversely proportional to the surface tension. Thus the plastron of insect eggs which are laid in organic materials subject to flooding needs to have a high resistance to wetting if it is to continue functioning in spite of the low surface tension. It must also be able to withstand wetting by raindrops which, momentarily, may exert a pressure approaching half an atmosphere. Hence, although eggs in dung and similar situations can rarely be subject to flooding by more than a few centimetres of water, they possess a plastron capable of withstanding flooding by clean water to a much greater depth, and in some cases their resistance is greater than that exhibited by the plastron of some aquatic insects (see p. 482) (Hinton, 1960a, 1962b).

Eggs which are laid in water, such as those of dragonflies, obtain their oxygen from that dissolved in the water.

See Hinton (1969, *A. Rev. Ent.* **14**).

17.33 Water regulation

Water loss

In most eggs the chorion itself is not waterproof and at the time of oviposition water loss from the egg is limited by a layer of wax on the inside of the chorion. This is secreted by the oocyte at about the time it leaves the follicle and, in *Rhodnius*, it is complete over the micropyles where it is supported by the vitelline membrane. The wax has the characteristics of a monolayer (see p. 435) with a critical temperature above which the monolayer breaks down and water loss increases sharply (Fig. 222) (Beament, 1946b). The critical temperature for the eggs of *Rhodnius* is 42·5°C., and for the eggs of *Lucilia* (Diptera) and *Locustana* (Orthoptera) 38°C. and 55–58°C. respectively. Below this temperature water loss from the eggs of *Rhodnius* is negligible even in dry air, but not all insect eggs are as waterproof as this. The eggs of *Musca*, for instance, only develop at high humidities and even at 80% relative humidity only 15% of the eggs survive to hatching.

A second layer of wax is laid down, at least in *Rhodnius* and various Orthoptera, in the serosal cuticle. In *Melanoplus* and *Locustana* this layer is between the serosal endocuticle and an outer fibrous network. In the Orthoptera this secondary wax layer replaces the layer on the inside of the chorion since the latter probably becomes broken after a few days by the increase in size of the egg. The rate of evaporation from the egg of *Locustana* at 35°C. and 60% relative humidity drops from 0·35–0·54 mg./egg/24 hr. at oviposition, when only the primary wax layer is present, to 0 11–0·36 mg./egg/24 hr. five days later when the serosal cuticle and secondary wax layer are completed all over the egg except for the hydropylar area (see below). When this region is also sealed off the evaporation rate falls to 0·03–0·04 mg./egg/24 hr. (Matthée, 1951). The egg of *Aedes* is similarly not fully waterproofed until the serosal cuticle, presumably including the wax layer, is formed. McFarlane (1966) suggests that the serosal cuticle exhibits a polarised permeability, permitting the intake of water, but preventing its loss from the egg.

In some instances there is a suggestion that the chorion itself provides some resistance to desiccation. For instance, the endochorion of *Aedes*, which resists desiccation, is thicker and darker than that in the non-resistant eggs of *Culex*, and some tropical grasshoppers, such as *Tropidiopsis,* which survive the dry season in the egg stage have thick, tough chorions. A thick chorion and a reduction in the number of respiratory horns is also a characteristic of the eggs of heteropteran species which are laid in exposed situations subject to desiccation (Southwood, 1956).

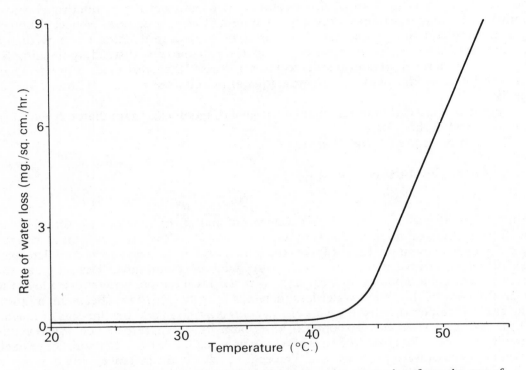

Fig. 222. Graph showing the relationship of temperature to water loss from the egg of *Rhodnius* in a dry atmosphere (after Beament, 1946b).

Under natural conditions water loss is normally restricted by the particular micro-environment of the oviposition site selected by the female. Thus many eggs are laid in crevices in bark or in the soil where transpiration will be restricted; or they may be in plant or animal tissues where, because of the moist environment, little or no water loss occurs. Sometimes the insect creates a micro-environment for its eggs by depositing them in an ootheca, such as that of the cockroaches and mantids, which, even if it does not possess a waterproofing wax layer, will limit transpiration by restricting air movement round the eggs. In the Acrididae the eggs are protected from desiccation to some extent by being some distance below the surface of the ground. In addition, in some tropical species which survive the dry season in the egg, the egg mass is enclosed in a layer of very hard, tough froth, as in *Cataloipus,* or has a conspicuous dark lid at the top of the plug, as in *Acrida* (Fig. 210C). These formations do not occur in species with different life cycles, suggesting that they have some role in the prevention of water loss from the egg.

Absorption of water

The eggs' of *Rhodnius*, and probably of many other Heteroptera and Lepidoptera which are laid in dry, exposed situations, develop without any uptake of water, but the eggs of many insect species absorb water from the environment in the course of development. This occurs in both terrestrial and aquatic insects and has been recorded, for example, in *Ocypus*, *Phyllopertha* and *Dytiscus* (Coleoptera), in *Notostira* and *Nepa* (Heteroptera), in *Culex* (Diptera) and in various Orthoptera. It results in a considerable increase in volume and weight (Fig. 223).

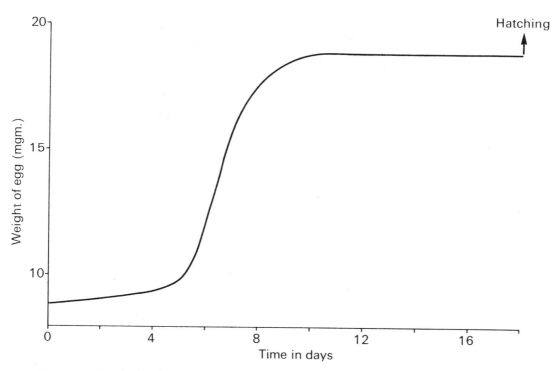

Fig. 223. Graph showing the change in weight of eggs of *Schistocerca* as they absorb water during development (after Hunter-Jones, 1964).

In some species, such as *Notostira* and *Gryllulus* (Orthoptera), water is absorbed over the whole of the egg, but at least in the Acrididae a specialised structure, the hydropyle, appears to be concerned in the uptake of water. It consists of a thickened region of the serosal epicuticle over a layer of endocuticle which is thinner than elsewhere (Fig. 224) and the area of contact between the two layers is greatly increased by interdigitation. There is no secondary wax layer over the hydropyle of eggs of *Locustana* and *Melanoplus*, but numerous wax-canal filaments (see p. 435), not found in other parts of the serosal cuticle, are present. It is presumed that water is taken up by the porous material on the outside of the hydropyle and held at the interface with the endocuticle which forms a semipermeable membrane. Slifer and Sekhon (1963) suggest that water is taken up osmotically and this is also probably the case in, for instance, *Notostira* and *Phyllopertha*. A type of hydropyle is also present in *Nepa,* but no such structure is present in the egg of *Deraeocoris* (Heteroptera). In the latter water may be taken up through the posterior end of the egg, which is embedded in plant tissue, or through the projecting anterior end (Hartley, 1965).

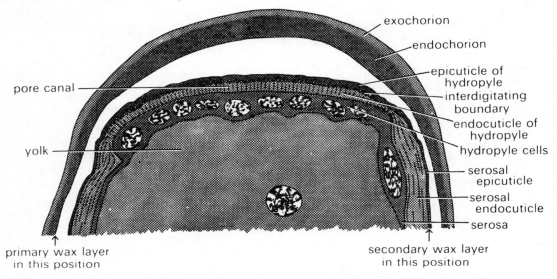

Fig. 224. Section through the posterior end of the egg of *Locusta* showing the hydropyle (based on Roonwal, 1954).

The uptake of water usually occurs during a limited period. Immediately after oviposition, no water is taken up. Then follows a period of rapid uptake, followed by a further period in which no increase in water content occurs (Fig. 223). At least in crickets, the chorion and serosa seem to be permeable at all times (Browning and Forrest, 1960) with constant interchange of water between the internal and external media. Limits are set on the amount of water taken up by the extent to which the chorion and serosa will stretch, and it is supposed that at the time of rapid increase in water content the chorion undergoes some change which makes it more extensible (Browning, 1967, in Beament and Treherne, *Insects and Physiology*). McFarlane (1966; and see Furneaux *et al.*, 1969, *J. Cell Sci.* 5) believes that the intake of water is prevented initially by the endochorion (his maternal epicuticle). Later this fragments and water enters the egg freely until further expansion is prevented by tanning of parts of the serosal epicuticle. In Heteroptera it is suggested that water uptake by the eggs of *Notostira* does not begin until osmotically active substances are produced within the egg, while water uptake by the eggs of *Phyllopertha* stops following a modification of the chorion which makes it waterproof.

The increase in volume of the egg which accompanies the uptake of water leads to the cracking of the chorion in Acrididae and *Dytiscus*, but in *Nepa* and *Ocypus* it stretches without breaking. In *Tetrix* the increase in size is partly taken up by expansion into an anterior horn of the chorion.

CHAPTER XVIII
EMBRYOLOGY

Development from egg to adult is a continuous process, but it is convenient to deal with development in the egg in this chapter and with postembryonic development in Chapters XX and XXI.

The insect egg is fertilised as it passes down the oviduct at the time of oviposition. Sperm entry initiates maturation of the oocyte and the subsequent development of the egg. The zygote nucleus divides and the daughter nuclei migrate to the periphery of the egg to form a layer of cells which surrounds the yolk. Part of this cell layer becomes thickened to form the band from which the embryo develops and then gastrulation occurs as a result of which an inner layer of cells is formed over the band. The details of gastrulation vary and the process is not immediately comparable with gastrulation in other animals. The embryo becomes cut off from the surface of the egg by extra-embryonic membranes which break and disappear when the embryo undergoes more or less extensive movements in the yolk. These movements bring the embryo to its final position with the·yolk now enclosed within the body wall.

The ectoderm forms the body wall, which invaginates to form the tracheal system, and the stomodaeum and proctodaeum, while the nervous system and sense organs are also ectodermal in origin. The mesoderm may at first form coelomic sacs, but these break down to form muscles and the circulatory and reproductive systems. The germ cells from which the sex cells are ultimately derived are differentiated early in development, sometimes after only a few nuclear divisions. The midgut is formed by the growth of two centres anteriorly and posteriorly. Physiological changes accompany the morphological developments.

These processes are controlled at first by various centres exerting their effects on the whole embryo. Later segmental centres appear and various structures have the effect of inducing the development of others. In the later stages there may be some overall hormonal control.

A general account of insect embryology is given in the textbook of Johannsen and Butt (1941), while Eastham (1930) reviews the development of the midgut and D. T. Anderson (1966) gives an account of the embryology of the Diptera. Agrell (1964), Counce (1961), Howe (1967) and Krause and Sander (1962) review the physiology of insect development.

18.1 Fertilisation

Within the spermatheca the sperm of most insects become active, the spermatodesms, in which up till now they have been aggregated, breaking down. They may remain alive

345

in the spermatheca for months or, in the case of *Apis* queens, years, and hence will require some nutriment. This may be provided initially in the seminal fluid from the male or from the degenerating cells of the testis cysts (see p. 280), but probably further nutriment is supplied in most cases from the spermathecal glands.

Fertilisation does not occur until the eggs are about to be laid and as each egg passes down the oviduct a few sperm are released from the spermatheca. It is not clear how this is brought about, although in some insects in which the spermatheca has compressor muscles it is likely that a few sperm are forced out each time these muscles contract. In other instances sudden pulses of haemolymph pressure due to contractions of the body musculature may be responsible, while in *Mormoniella* it is suggested that the sperm are activated in the spermatheca by a change of pH due to a secretion from the spermathecal gland and that they then actively swim from the spermatheca (King, 1962). The release of sperm from the spermathecae in Hymenoptera must be closely regulated since fertilised eggs give rise to females and unfertilised eggs to males.

The orientation of the egg in the oviduct often facilitates sperm entry. Thus in *Drosophila* the egg is orientated so that the single micropyle comes opposite the opening of the ventral receptacle of the oviduct which is filled with sperm. Comparable orientations occur in other insects.

Having reached the egg the sperm of *Periplaneta* swim in a curving path towards the surface and this tends to carry them into the funnel-shaped micropyles. The final entry into the egg probably involves a chemotactic response.

It is usually stated that several sperm penetrate each oocyte and where this happens fertilisation is effected by one of the sperms while the rest degenerate. The evidence, however, is conflicting and Hildreth and Luchesi (1963) conclude that in *Drosophila* it is usual for only one sperm to enter each egg.

In a few insects fertilisation occurs while the oocytes are still in the ovary. This is true of the Cimicoidea, which practise haemocoelic insemination (p. 319), and also of *Aspidiotus* in which the sperm become attached to large cells which proliferate in the common oviduct and then migrate to the pedicels.

18.2 Maturation of the oocytes

In most insects meiosis of the oocyte is initiated by sperm entry. In *Drosophila* the sperm head, after entering the oocyte, migrates towards the centre of the egg and resolves into a vesicular nucleus. During this period the oocyte undergoes its first meiotic division, while the second is not completed until some five minutes after the egg is laid. A few minutes later the mitotic spindles of the male and female pronuclei fuse together and the first mitotic division occurs. The polar nuclei resulting from the meiotic divisions of the oocyte fuse together and later degenerate (Fahmy, 1952).

18.3 Cleavage and formation of the blastoderm

18.31 Cleavage and the blastoderm

After oviposition the zygote nucleus of an insect egg starts to divide, the first division occurring within about 30 minutes of zygote formation in *Dacus* (Diptera). Nuclear division is not accompanied by cell division, but each daughter nucleus is accompanied by a halo of cytoplasm and each such unit of nucleus and cytoplasm may be called an energid. The first few, up to about eight, divisions of the daughter nuclei are synchronised, synchrony perhaps being facilitated by the fact that they are in cytoplasmic continuity. During interphase periods the cytoplasm of the energids increases at the expense of the cytoplasmic reticulum.

The energids move apart as they divide (Fig. 225A) and become arranged in a layer within the yolk, bounding a spherical or elongate mass of yolk which roughly corresponds with the form of the egg. In the eggs of hemimetabolous insects the nuclei at this time are more superficial than those of holometabolous insects and this may be connected with the amount of cytoplasm in the egg. The eggs of most hemimetabolous insects contain little cytoplasm and the periplasm is thin, while eggs of holometabolous insects have much more cytoplasm and a thick periplasm.

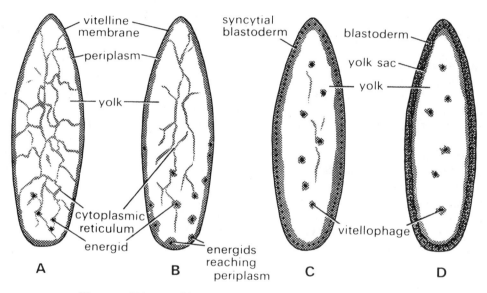

Fig. 225. Diagram illustrating the formation of the blastoderm.

Migration of the energids continues until they reach and enter the periplasm (Fig. 225B), but the point at which they do this varies, being at the posterior end of the egg in *Locusta*, for instance, but near the equator in *Panorpa*. In the higher Diptera their arrival at the periplasm appears to be synchronised, but in other cases this is not so.

The mechanism by which the energids move out to the periplasm is not understood. In *Calliphora* the centriole always leads during the movement and after division each nucleus rotates so that the centriole again assumes a leading position. This suggests that the nucleus itself is controlling the movement in some way, but in other species, *Pieris*, for example, cytoplasmic strands precede the energids to the periplasm.

Within the periplasm, which is commonly invaded after about the eighth cleavage, nuclear division continues, but is often no longer synchronised. Synchronous division does continue in *Dacus*, however, while in *Apis*, *Calandra* (Coleoptera) and *Calliphora* waves of mitoses pass along the egg from one end to the other. The nuclei spread all round the periphery of the egg (Fig. 225C) and at the same time, at least in Diptera, the periplasm thickens due to the addition of cytoplasm from the reticulum which becomes vacuolated.

In *Drosophila* folds of the plasma membrane develop between adjacent nuclei in the periplasm, retracting at each nuclear division. Finally, however, the folds extend beyond the nuclei and join together internally so that the undivided mass of yolk becomes surrounded by a layer of cells called the blastoderm (Fig. 225D) in which adjacent cells are held together by desmosomes (Mahowald, 1963b). As the cell walls form, the nuclei increase in size and a nucleolus becomes apparent for the first time. At first the nuclei are near the outer walls of the cells, but later they move inwards, their previous positions becoming occupied by complexes of granular and agranular membranes, ribosomes and mitochondria (Mahowald, 1963a). In *Dacus* and *Drosophila* the inner cell walls of the blastoderm cut off an inner undivided layer of cytoplasm. This anucleate layer is called the yolk sac (Fig. 225D). Subsequently it becomes nucleated due to the invasion of some of the vitellophages, but finally it is digested with the yolk in the midgut.

Cleavage of this type in which only the peripheral layer of cytoplasm divides is known as superficial cleavage.

Mitotic activity during this period of development is very high, but the time taken to complete a mitotic cycle is greater in the more primitive groups, such as Orthoptera, where it may take some hours, than in more advanced groups such as Lepidoptera and Diptera. Amongst the Lepidoptera a complete mitotic cycle normally takes less than an hour, while in *Drosophila* at 25°C. it takes only about ten minutes. This rapid division necessitates a rapid multiplication of the chromatin material and this is made possible by the large amount of DNA stored in the cytoplasm during oogenesis (see p. 290). Thus in *Drosophila* although nuclear multiplication in the first 13 hours of development exceeds 1000 with a corresponding increase in nuclear DNA, the total DNA content of the egg only increases five times. Presumably the cytoplasmic DNA is broken down to some extent before being incorporated in the nuclei.

18.32 Vitellophages

In many insects only some of the energids migrate to the surface to form the blastoderm, the rest remain behind in the yolk to form the yolk cells, or vitellophages. Thus in *Dacus* about 38 of 128 energids remain in the yolk to form the primary vitellophages and their subsequent division increases their number to about 300. Commonly the vitellophages begin to separate after the sixth or seventh divisions and become marked by the large size of the nucleus which increases through endomitotic division of the chromosomes. In some groups, including some Diptera, cells migrate back from the blastoderm to form secondary vitellophages. There is some evidence that vitellophages are derived from some of the pole cells (p. 365) and in *Dacus* some tertiary vitellophages are formed from the proliferating anterior midgut rudiment.

The vitellophages have a variety of functions. They are concerned with the breakdown of yolk at all stages of development and later, when the yolk is enclosed in the midgut, they may form part of the midgut epithelium. They are also involved in the formation of new cytoplasm and are responsible for the contractions of the yolk, producing the local liquefactions which are necessary for this.

In the eggs of Orthoptera, Lepidoptera and Coleoptera the yolk may become temporarily divided by membranes into large masses or spherules containing one or more
vitellophages. These yolk spherules are first formed close to the embryo and under the
serosa, but ultimately extend all through the yolk.

18.33 Other types of cleavage

Not all insects exhibit the superficial cleavage which is characteristic of the majority.
The superficial pattern is determined by the large amount of yolk present, but in species
with less yolk other forms of cleavage occur. The eggs of Collembola contain relatively
little yolk and early cleavage is complete. Each cell produced consists of a mass of yolk in
the centre of which is an island of cytoplasm containing the nucleus (Fig. 226A). In
Isotoma cleavage is equal so that cells of similar size result, but in *Hypogastrura* cleavage
is unequal with the formation of micro- and macro-meres. Total cleavage continues to

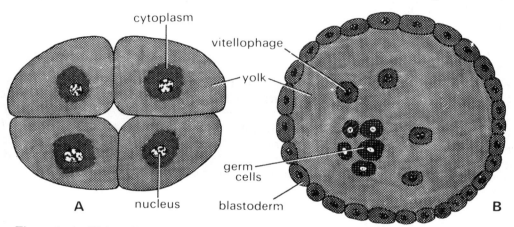

Fig. 226. A. Eight-cell stage in the development of *Isotoma* showing total cleavage. B.
Blastoderm stage of *Isotoma* (from Johannsen and Butt, 1941).

about the 64-cell stage at which the nuclei in their islands of cytoplasm migrate to the
surface and become cut off from the yolk by cell boundaries so that a blastoderm is formed
and subsequent cleavage becomes superficial (Fig. 226B). Some nuclei remain in the
yolk forming the vitellophages and the original boundaries within the yolk disappear
so that a single central mass remains.

An unusual form of cleavage also occurs in the small eggs of some parasitic Hymenoptera (see p. 376).

18.34 Control of cleavage and blastoderm formation

The initial stages of cleavage and migration are controlled by a cleavage centre situated
somewhere in the future head region. In general the cleavage centre is not recognisable
morphologically, but it is characterised as the region into which the zygote nucleus
moves before dividing and from which the energids subsequently move out. The
cleavage centre is probably activated by sperm entry.

In most insects the major axes of the embryo are determined before the egg is laid. Thus the end of the egg which is anterior while the egg is in the ovary becomes the head end of the embryo and the dorsal surfaces similarly correspond. This association presumably results from the position of some other orientating factor intimately associated with the oocyte. Thus in *Drosophila* the embryonic head always forms at the end of the egg which was adjacent to the nurse cells irrespective of this orientation with respect to the parent. The follicle cells are also variously differentiated (see *e.g.* p. 294) and these too may have a role in determining polarity. The dorso-ventral axis in *Drosophila* is probably determined by factors outside the follicle and, in most insects, the germinal vesicle is situated towards the dorsal side of the oocyte (Gill, 1964).

Changes probably occur in the cytoplasm between the time of maturation and blastoderm formation. At first the periplasm appears to inhibit further division of the polar bodies, but it does not have this inhibiting effect on the nuclei of the blastoderm later on. Despite these and other effects of the cytoplasm it is nevertheless true that the genes play an active role in controlling development from a very early stage (see Waddington, 1956).

18.35 Mosaic and regulation eggs

In the eggs of the higher Diptera and some Lepidoptera and Hymenoptera the fate of the different parts of the egg is already largely determined when the egg is laid and it is possible to map the presumptive areas at a very early stage (Fig. 227). This type of egg is called a mosaic egg. Preliminary studies do not indicate any marked differences in ultrastructure between the different areas, but in *Drosophila* there are differences in the degree of development of the membrane systems and the numbers of mitochondria in the cells of the dorsal and ventral surfaces of the blastoderm (Mahowald, 1963a).

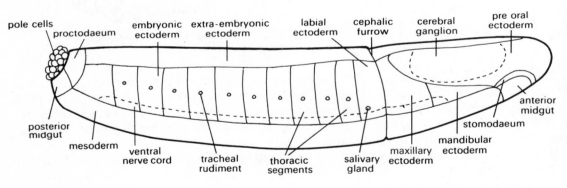

Fig. 227. The presumptive larval areas on the blastoderm of *Dacus* (after Anderson, 1966).

In other insects the fate of the various parts is not fixed for some time after laying; these are said to be regulation eggs. Thus a complete embryo may be formed even following injury, but the eggs usually become irrevocably determined soon after blastoderm formation, the major regions becoming fixed before minor features.

18.4 Early development of the embryo

18.41 Formation of the germ band

In most insect eggs the blastoderm forms a uniformly thin covering to the yolk and as a result of increased cell division it becomes thicker in the ventral region of the egg. This thickening is the germ band which develops into the future embryo, while the rest of the blastoderm remains extra-embryonic (Fig. 228). Sometimes, as in Mallophaga and *Apis*, the whole of the blastoderm is thick, but subsequently thins out except at the germ band, while in some Lepidoptera the blastoderm is differentiated into germ band and extra-embryonic tissue from the time of its first appearance.

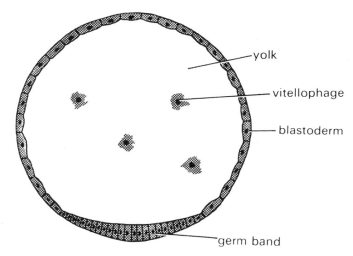

Fig. 228. Diagrammatic transverse section of a developing egg showing the ventral thickening which forms the germ band.

Initially, in eggs containing little cytoplasm, the germ band may be a small disc or streak of tissue, but it increases in size and becomes differentiated into a broad head region, the protocephalon, and a narrow 'tail', the protocorm (Fig. 229A). In Diptera, on the other hand, with ample cytoplasm, almost the whole of the blastoderm forms the germ band and there is very little extra-embryonic tissue (see Fig. 227).

The development of the germ band is regulated by two centres. In *Platycnemis* (Odonata) a posterior activating centre is present which is brought into action by the arrival of a cleavage nucleus. This stimulates the production of a substance which diffuses forwards through the egg and activates a differentiation centre in the prospective thoracic region. Activating centres probably occur in other insects, but these have not been fully investigated (see Counce, 1961).

The differentiation centre controls the development of the germ band by causing the yolk to make local contractions so that a space appears above the blastoderm. Within this space the thickened germ band is formed. Subsequently many processes such as mesoderm formation, segmentation and organogeny begin at the differentiation centre, extending forwards and backwards from it, and it continues to function until the embryo becomes segmented. At this time segmental centres assume the role of the differentiation centre which is thus the last centre to act while the embryo is still a single functional unit.

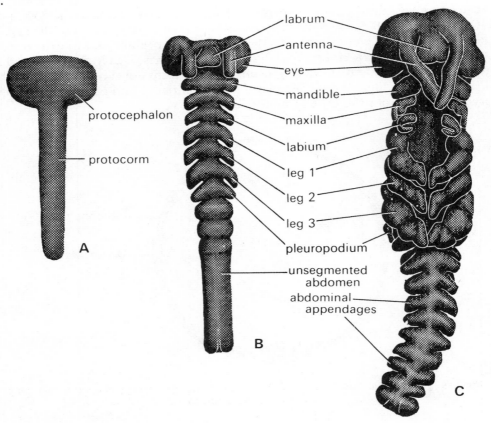

protocephalon

protocorm

A

labrum
antenna
eye
mandible
maxilla
labium
leg 1
leg 2
leg 3
pleuropodium
unsegmented abdomen
abdominal appendages

B

C

Fig. 229. Early stages in the development of *Ornithacris* showing the whole embryo with the embryonic membranes removed.

18.42 Gastrulation

Gastrulation is the process by which the mesoderm and endoderm are invaginated within the ectoderm, but as it occurs in insects it is not immediately comparable with the process in other animal groups (see Johannsen and Butt, 1941). No deep invagination occurs, but an inner layer of cells develops beneath the germ band.

The method by which the inner layer is formed varies in different groups and even at different stages in the same insect. In *Donacia* (Coleoptera), for example, an invagination develops along the midline of the embryo. It rolls up to form a tube, which later breaks down into an irregular inner layer of cells while the ectoderm closes beneath it (Fig. 230A). The middle plate also sinks in in *Apis*, but without rolling up, and the ectoderm extends inwards to cover it from its lateral edges (Fig. 230B). In Orthoptera cells proliferate from the upper surface of the germ band, either from the whole surface as in tettigoniids, or along the midline from which they spread out to form the inner layer as in Acrididae (Fig. 230C). In this case a temporary groove appears on the ventral surface which may be comparable with the blastopore in other animals. Finally, in *Isotoma* all the cells of the blastoderm divide tangentially to form an inner layer over the whole of the inside (see Fig. 237). Later the inner layer cells migrate to the region of the germ band so that the extra-embryonic region comes to consist of a single layer of cells (see Johannsen and Butt, 1941).

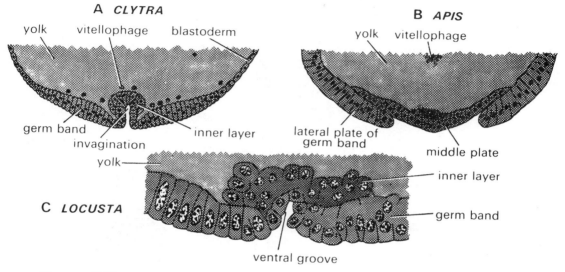

Fig. 230. Different types of gastrulation. A. Invagination in *Clytra* (Coleoptera). B. Overgrowth in *Apis*. C. Proliferation in *Locusta* (from various sources).

In the Diptera the latter part of gastrulation has a superficial resemblance to the process in other animals with the invagination of the posterior midgut rudiment deep into the yolk. Mesodermal invagination begins along the ventral surface, but extension of the mesoderm and the ectoderm which comes to cover it pushes the invagination of the posterior midgut rudiment and the proctodaeum anteriorly along the dorsal surface of the embryo (Fig. 231A, B). Invagination of the proctodaeum then carries the posterior midgut rudiment deep into the yolk (Fig. 231C).

Mesodermal and endodermal elements are commonly invaginated at the same time, the two ends of the inner layer then representing the endoderm and giving rise to the midgut. In other species, such as *Tenebrio,* however, the endoderm arises independently of the mesoderm by proliferation from the ends of the stomodaeum and proctodaeum. These differences probably result only from changes in the timing of development relative to the invagination of the stomodaeum and proctodaeum (Eastham, 1930).

18.43 Formation of embryonic membranes

The germ band usually does not remain exposed at the surface of the yolk, but becomes covered by one or more embryonic membranes. Soon after its formation folds appear at the periphery of the germ band (Fig. 232A) and these extend ventrally beneath the

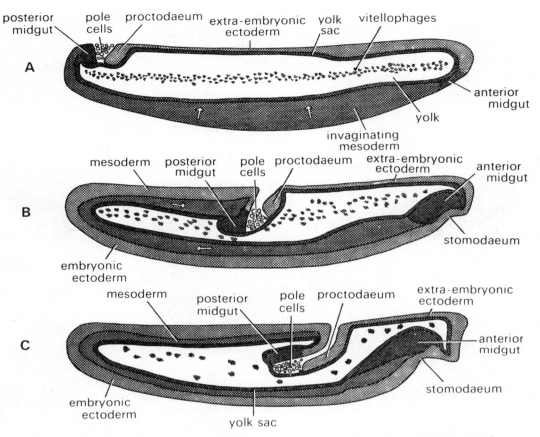

Fig. 231. Diagrammatic sagittal sections through the embryo of *Dacus*. A. Eight hours after laying. B. Nine hours after laying. C. Twelve hours after laying. Arrows indicate the movements of the mesoderm (after Anderson, 1962).

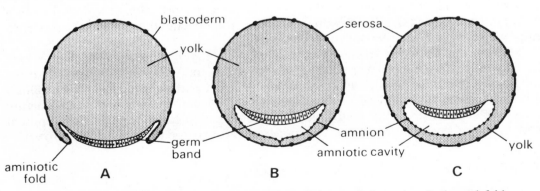

Fig. 232. Diagrams illustrating the development of the amniotic cavity. A. Lateral folds beginning to grow over germ band. B. Lateral folds meet beneath germ band. C. Amnion and serosa separated, embryo immersed in yolk.

embryo until they meet and fuse in the ventral midline (Fig. 232B). Thus the embryo lies on the dorsal surface of a small cavity, the amniotic cavity, bounded by a thin membrane, the amnion. The membrane round the outside of the yolk is now called the serosa, and amnion and serosa may remain connected where the embryonic folds fuse (Fig. 232B) or they may become completely separated, the embryo sinking into the yolk so that yolk penetrates between amnion and serosa (Fig. 232C). No further cell division occurs in the serosa, but endomitosis may occur so that the nuclei become very large and, in *Gryllus* (Orthoptera), they contain four times as much DNA as the nuclei in the germ band.

The embryo of Thysanura does not become cut off in an amniotic cavity, but it is invaginated within the yolk, while the extra-embryonic membranes are differentiated into a zone of cells with small nuclei adjacent to the embryo and a zone of cells with large nuclei over the rest of the egg (Fig. 233). From their superficial resemblance to amnion and serosa these zones are called proamnion and proserosa.

In the Cyclorrhapha the embryo occupies the whole egg from the beginning of development and in these insects the amnion is vestigial and the serosa absent.

After completion of the amnion and serosa further embryonic membranes are produced in tettigoniids from a thickening of the serosa in front of the head known as the indusium. This sinks in from the serosa and becomes separated into outer and inner layers which push between the serosa and the yolk, surrounding the egg except at the anterior pole. The outer layer of the indusium persists until the larva emerges, but the inner layer assumes the role of the serosa in other groups and, after fusing with the amnion, is broken during blastokinesis (see below). A similar structure is present in *Siphanta* (Homoptera) and, less well-developed, in a few other insects.

In Orthoptera the serosa secretes a cuticle to the outside and in tettigoniids this is supplemented by a second layer secreted by the inner indusial membrane. A subserosal layer is produced by Coleoptera while in *Isotoma* two successive cuticles are formed all round the outside of the egg (Fig. 237).

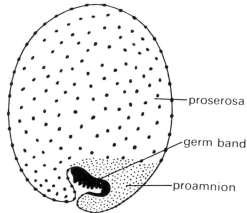

Fig. 233. Early stage of the invagination of the germ band in *Machilis* (from Johannsen and Butt, 1941).

18.5 Blastokinesis

18.51 Movements of the embryo

The early embryos of the lower orders of insects are relatively small compared with the size of the egg and in many of these groups the embryo makes extensive and regular movements within the yolk. All the displacements, rotations and revolutions of the embryo in the egg are collectively known as blastokinesis, although this term is also used in a more restricted sense (Johannsen and Butt, 1941). Often the movements can be differentiated into anatrepsis and katatrepsis, but these terms refer to different activities in different groups of insects. In Acrididae anatrepsis refers to the movement of the embryo away from the posterior pole of the egg, while katatrepsis refers to the movement which carries the embryo from the ventral to the dorsal surface of the egg (see *e.g.* Roonwal, 1937).

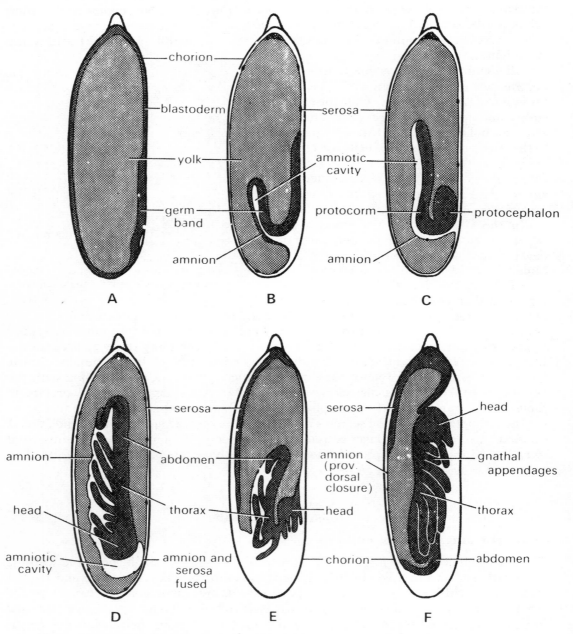

Fig. 234. Stages in the embryonic development of *Agrion* (from Johannsen and Butt, 1941).

The extent of the movements varies in different species. In Odonata and Tettigonioidea the movements are most extensive. In *Agrion* (Odonata), for instance, the germ
band is formed on the ventral surface of the egg (Fig. 234A). Its posterior end invaginates into the yolk, forming the amnion as it does so (Fig. 234B, C), and finally the embryo
becomes completely inverted in the yolk with its head towards the posterior pole of the
egg (Fig. 234D). The amnion and serosa remain fused at the head and ultimately rupture at this point. Then the embryo rotates back to its original position while the
extra-embryonic membranes shorten and thicken (Fig. 234E, F). Similar movements
occur in tettigoniids but the serosa is replaced by the inner layer of the indusium.

In Acrididae the movements are less marked. The embryo first moves down the
egg away from the posterior pole, but remains on the ventral surface. Then the amnion
and serosa join and rupture and the embryo passes through the yolk to the dorsal surface
of the egg. In some Coleoptera, such as *Chrysomela*, the movement is even less marked
with the tail of the embryo sinking temporarily into the yolk and then returning to the
surface again. Finally, in the Diptera no movements occur.

The mechanisms by which these movements are brought about are unknown, but it
appears that the driving force comes from within the germ band since extensive movements still occur when the extra-embryonic membranes are damaged experimentally.

18.52 Dorsal closure

One effect of blastokinesis in many insects is to reverse the relative positions of embryo
and yolk. At first the embryo lies on or in the yolk, but when the movements are completed the yolk is contained within the embryo. This results from the formation of the
dorsal wall of the embryo and in this process two phases can be recognised. The first,
or provisional, dorsal closure is formed by the extra-embryonic membranes as a result
of blastokinesis; later the provisional tissue is replaced by the embryonic ectoderm
which grows upwards to form the definitive dorsal closure.

Various methods are employed to achieve the dorsal closure. In Orthoptera blastokinesis results in the yolk becoming enclosed by the amnion and serosa (Fig. 235A).
As the ectoderm grows up to replace this provisional closure amnion and serosa shrink
and become confined to an antero-dorsal region where finally the serosa invaginates
into the yolk in the form of a tube (Fig. 236). This is the secondary dorsal organ and it is
ultimately digested in the midgut.

Where no marked blastokinesis occurs the dorsal closure is produced by rearrangement of the embryonic membranes even though the embryo itself remains relatively
static. In *Leptinotarsa* (Coleoptera) and other Chrysomelidae the amnion breaks and
grows up inside the serosa (Fig. 235B). Later it is replaced by the ectoderm while the
serosa remains intact round the outside. In *Chironomus* amnion and ectoderm grow
dorsally together so that the ectoderm forms the dorsal closure at an early stage while
the amnion forms a membrane all round the outside (Fig. 235C). The serosa is invaginated and destroyed. Similar growth of the membranes occurs in Lepidoptera and
Tenthredinidae, but the serosa also persists so that a layer of yolk is present all round
the embryo, held between the amnion and serosa (Fig. 235D). This provides the first
meal for larval Lepidoptera when they hatch.

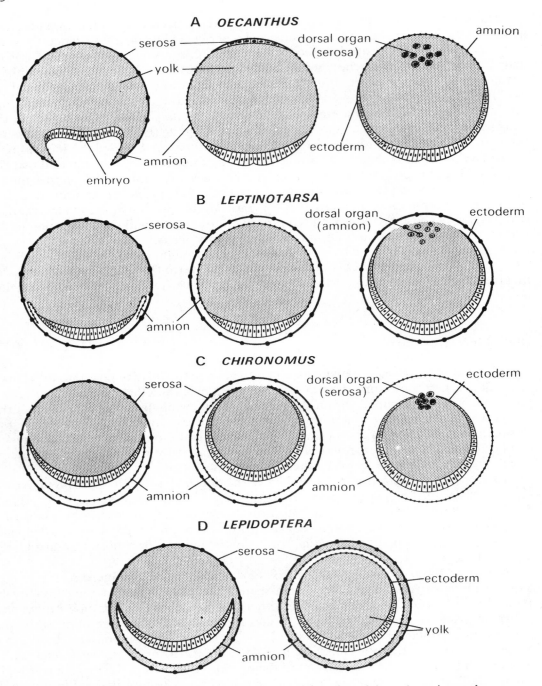

Fig. 235. Diagrams illustrating the dorsal closure and the fate of the embryonic membranes in (A) *Oecanthus* (Orthoptera), (B) *Leptinotarsa* (Coleoptera), (C) *Chironomus* (Diptera) and (D) a lepidopteran. The earliest stages figured on the left of the diagram can be derived from stage B or C in Fig. 232 (from Imms, 1957).

18.53 Dorsal organ

As the definitive dorsal closure develops the membranes forming the provisional closure are invaginated into the midgut and destroyed. The temporary structure which the membranes form during this process is known as the secondary dorsal organ (Fig. 236) and it is necessary to differentiate it from the primary dorsal organ which is most fully developed in the eggs of Apterygota. In *Isotoma* the primary dorsal organ first appears

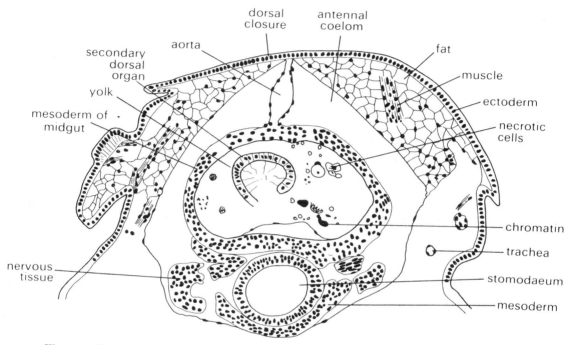

Fig. 236. Transverse section of the dorsal half of an embryo of *Ornithacris* after completion of the definitive dorsal closure.

at the anterior pole of the egg after the formation of the inner layer (Fig. 237). The ectodermal cells at this point are deep and become vacuolated, suggesting a glandular function. It is possible that the organ is concerned with moulting the cuticle which forms all round the egg at an early stage. At the time of the dorsal closure of the embryo the primary dorsal organ passes into the alimentary canal and is digested. Similar, but less well-developed structures, are formed in the early embryos of some beetles and *Apis*.

18.6 Development of organ systems

18.61 Appendages

The whole outer wall of the embryo represents the ectoderm and by outgrowths of the wall the appendages are formed. In front of the stomodaeum is the labrum and on either side on the protocephalon are the antennal rudiments (Fig. 229B). The protocorm becomes segmented and, in the lower orders, each segment extends laterally to form the rudiment of an appendage. Immediately behind the protocephalon are the rudiments of the mandibles, maxillae and labium. The latter arises in series with the rest as a pair of limbs which later fuse in the midline to form the definitive labium.

The appendages of the next three segments form the walking legs. These grow longer and become folded and grooved where later they will become segmented (Fig. 229C). By contrast the abdominal appendages disappear except that in some insects the appendages of segments 8 and 9 contribute to the ovipositor and those on segment 11 form the cerci. In Orthoptera and some other orders the appendages of the first abdominal segment also persist for a time (Fig. 239). They are known as the pleuropodia and in Orthoptera have a distal area in which the cells become very large and secrete an enzyme which digests the serosal endocuticle. They then degenerate, becoming torn off when the insect hatches. They probably serve the same purpose in *Belostoma* (Heteroptera) where they sink into the body so that only the tip of each cell projects from a bowl-shaped cavity. They reach their greatest development just before hatching.

In *Hesperoctenes* (Heteroptera) the egg has no yolk or chorion since it develops within the female parent, nutriment being obtained from the parent via a pseudo-placenta (see p. 370) formed from the pleuropodia. These grow and fuse together to form a membrane which completely covers the embryo and which makes contact with the wall of the oviduct.

The pleuropodia assume a variety of forms in Coleoptera, but in Dermaptera, Hymenoptera and Lepidoptera they are only ever present as small papillae which soon disappear (Hussey, 1927).

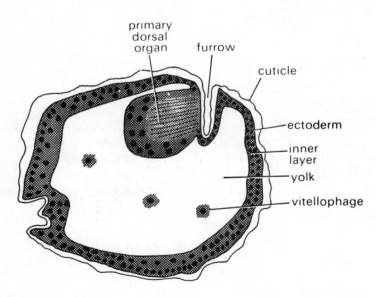

Fig. 237. Section through an early embryo of *Isotoma* showing the primary dorsal organ (from Johannsen and Butt, 1941).

18.62 Nervous system

The central nervous system arises as a thickening of the ectoderm on either side of the midline. The ectodermal cells divide tangentially cutting off large cells called neuroblasts which then divide several times in the same plane so as to form a column of nerve cells at right angles to the surface (Fig. 238). Usually there are four or five columns of cells on either side of the midline and a median row which forms the median neural strand. In *Pieris* and *Musca* the daughter cells of the neuroblasts do not divide again, but in *Apis* and *Calandra* they undergo lateral divisions.

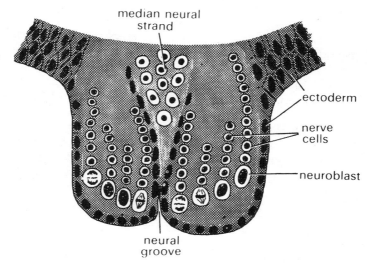

Fig. 238. Section through the developing ventral nerve cord showing the neuroblasts with their daughter cells (from Johannsen and Butt, 1941).

As the embryo segments the ganglia become differentiated. Three paired groups of neuroblasts corresponding with the protocerebrum, deutocerebrum and tritocerebrum (see p. 518) develop in the protocephalon and in addition, when the full complement of segments is present, 17 postoral ganglia may be recognisable: three in the gnathal segments, three in the thorax and eleven in the abdomen. The first three always fuse to form the suboesophageal ganglion and some fusion of abdominal ganglia always occurs, but the further extent of fusion varies, depending on the species (see p. 522).

The optic lobes which come to be associated with the protocerebrum arise separately from the nervous ganglia and contain no neuroblasts, although similar large cells are present. In Orthoptera they are formed by delamination from the ectodermal thickening which forms the eye, but in Hymenoptera and Coleoptera they develop from an ectodermal invagination arising outside the eye rudiment. Fibres grow out from the developing optic lobe to connect with the back of the eye.

The nervous system is enclosed within a sheath which secretes the neural lamella (p. 525). The sheath cells are probably ectodermal in origin, being derived from some of the outer ganglion cells (see Ashhurst, 1965, for references).

The ganglia of the stomatogastric system are formed from the ectoderm of the stomodaeum, and sensory structures arise from local modifications of the epidermis.

18.63 Other ectodermal structures

The tracheal system arises as paired segmental invaginations which become T-shaped. The arms of the T in adjacent segments fuse to form the longitudinal trunks and further invaginations from these develop into the finer branches of the system.

Oenocytes (see p. 426) are cut off from the epidermis of all the abdominal segments except possibly the last two.

18.64 Embryonic cuticle

Insects belonging to the hemimetabolous orders and at least some belonging to the Neuroptera, Trichoptera, Lepidoptera and Coleoptera, secrete a cuticle soon after blastokinesis. This embryonic cuticle soon separates from the epidermis and the first instar cuticle is laid down in its place, but the embryonic cuticle is not shed, remaining round the embryo until it hatches. The significance of the embryonic cuticle is unknown and the stage which possesses it is usually regarded as representing the true first larval instar, although it is not counted as such in the designation of the larval instars (see p. 387).

According to Mueller (1963) a very thin cuticle is formed in Acrididae and *Dysdercus* (Heteroptera) before the embryonic cuticle just described and a similar cuticle is present in *Hyalophora* (Lepidoptera). This thin cuticle is moulted when the embryonic cuticle proper is formed so that the latter is strictly the second embryonic cuticle.

18.65 Mesoderm and body cavities

The mesoderm is derived from the inner layer (see p. 352) forming two lateral strands which run the length of the body and are joined across the midline by a thin sheet of cells. In the lower orders the lateral strands become segmented and the somites separate off from each other, but in Lepidoptera and Hymenoptera the somites remain connected together. Amongst the Cyclorrhapha there is a tendency for the mesoderm to remain unsegmented as in *Dacus* in which the strands of mesoderm only become segmented as they differentiate into the definitive structures associated with the ectoderm. The mesoderm in the protocephalon arises *in situ* in the lower orders, but moves forwards from a post-oral position in the more advanced groups.

Cavities, which represent the coelom, appear in the blocks of mesoderm (Fig. 239). These cavities result from the development of clefts in the somites in *Carausius* and *Formica* (Hymenoptera), but by the block rolling up to enclose a cavity in *Locusta* and *Sialis*. In the Heteroptera the coelomic sacs remain open to the epineural sinus, while in Diptera the coelomic cavities are not formed.

Where they are most fully developed a pair of coelomic cavities is present in each segment of the protocorm, while in the protocephalon pairs of cavities develop in association with the premandibular and antennal segments. Sometimes one or two more pairs are present in front of the antennae. Subsequently in Orthoptera and Coleoptera the cavities of the thoracic and abdominal cavities become confluent forming a tube on either side.

At the same time as the coelom is forming, the primary body cavity develops as a space between the upper surface of the embryo and the yolk. This cavity is called the epineural sinus and in Orthoptera and *Pediculus* (Siphunculata) it is bounded dorsally by a special layer of cells forming the yolk cell membrane (Fig. 239).

Soon the walls of the coelomic sacs break down as the mesoderm which forms them differentiates to form muscles and other tissues. As a result the coelomic cavities and the epineural sinus become confluent so that the body cavities of those insects which develop coelomic cavities is a mixocoel, although it is usually called a haemocoel. Some of the coelomic sacs, particularly those associated with the antennae, may be quite large and make a significant contribution to the final cavity.

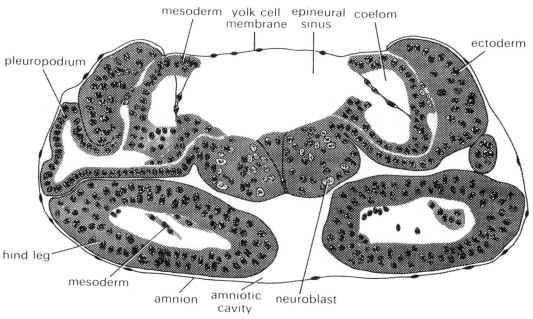

Fig. 239. Slightly oblique transverse section of an early embryo of *Ornithacris*. At this stage the embryo is completely immersed in the yolk.

After blastokinesis when the midgut is formed the mesoderm extends dorsally between the body wall and the gut so that the body cavity is also extended until finally it completely surrounds the gut.

The outer walls of the coelomic sacs form the somatic muscles, the dorsal diaphragm, the pericardial cells and the suboesophageal body. The latter is found in the Orthoptera, Plecoptera, Isoptera, Mallophaga, Coleoptera and Lepidoptera and consists of a number of large binucleate cells in the body cavity and closely associated with the inner end of the stomodaeum. The cells become vacuolated and usually disappear at about the time of hatching, but in Isoptera they persist until the adult stage is reached. It is usually assumed that these cells are concerned with nitrogenous excretion, but Kessel (1961) suggests that they are concerned with the breakdown of yolk.

The inner walls of the coelomic sacs form the visceral muscles, and the gonads; fat body and blood cells are also mesodermal in origin (see *e.g.* Ullmann, 1964). The heart is formed from special cells, the cardioblasts, originating from the upper angle of the coelomic sacs, while the aorta is produced by the approximation of the median walls of the two antennal coelomic sacs (Fig. 236).

18.66 Alimentary canal

The foregut and hindgut arise early in development as ectodermal invaginations, the stomodaeum and proctodaeum (Fig. 240), and it is now generally agreed that the midgut has a bipolar origin (see Johannsen and Butt, 1941). It is formed by bands of endoderm which grow out from rudiments at either end of the body and envelop the yolk (Fig. 240). At first the midgut is closed off anteriorly and posteriorly by the ends of the stomodaeum and proctodaeum, but these ends break down before the insect hatches.

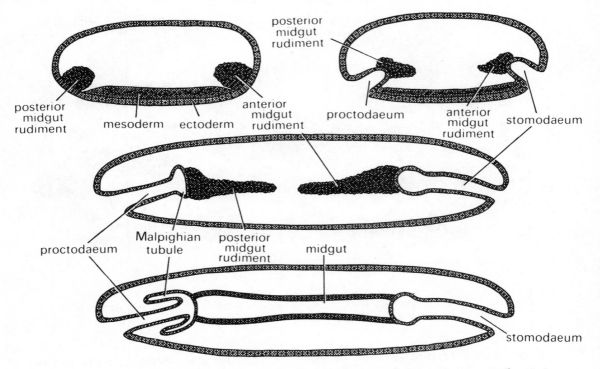

Fig. 240. Diagrams illustrating the development of the midgut (after Henson, 1946).

The Malpighian tubules arise from the tip of the proctodaeum. Usually only two or three pairs develop in the embryo, but others may be produced during larval development (see p. 394 , and Savage, 1956). Henson (1932) has argued that they are endodermal in origin, but the evidence for this is conflicting (Srivastava and Khare, 1966) and the argument is probably of little significance in the light of current views on the germ layer theory (see *e.g.* Waddington, 1956).

18.67 Reproductive system

In the Diptera, Coleoptera and Hymenoptera the cells destined to form the germ cells in the gonads are differentiated at the very start of embryonic development. At the posterior end of the egg is an area of cytoplasm, the pole plasm, which is differentiated from the rest and contains granules, called polar granules, rich in RNA. These granules differentiate during oogenesis. In *Drosophila* they first become apparent as small bodies which make contact with the mitochondria and increase in size. After fertilisation contact with the mitochondria is lost.

Cleavage nuclei move into the pole plasm and become surrounded by the polar granules which tend to coalesce. In Nematocera the numbers of energids which migrate into the pole plasm are constant for a species: one in *Miastor* and *Wachtliella*, two in *Sciara* and six in *Culex*. But in most of the Cyclorrhapha studied the number is variable, between three and eleven in *Drosophila*, for example. The invading nuclei divide so that in *Miastor* eight and in *Drosophila* about 40 pole cells are produced. These may be outside the blastoderm or, as in *Dacus*, in a circular polar opening of the blastoderm (Fig. 227).

The pole plasm appears to prevent the elimination of chromatin from the nucleus which occurs in other parts of the egg in these insects. In *Wachtliella* the cleavage nuclei contain some 40 chromosomes. After the third division one of the nuclei moves into the pole plasm, while the rest move towards the periphery elsewhere. At the next division the nucleus in the pole plasm divides normally, but in the others, although all the chromosomes start to move towards the poles of the mitotic spindle, only eight chromosomes in each half of the spindle complete the journey. The remainder return to the equator, agglomerate in large complexes and then degenerate (Geyer-Duszynska, 1959). This elimination probably arises as a result of some defect of the centromeres. Two more chromosomes are eliminated from the somatic cells of the male embryo at the seventh division.

The elimination of whole chromosomes from the somatic cells is known to occur in Cecidomyidae, Sciaridae and some Chironomidae, but even in *Drosophila* and *Calliphora* one of the chromosomes of the somatic nuclei loses a terminal segment (see Agrell, 1964). The chromosomes which are retained in the germ cells appear to be essential for oogenesis (Geyer-Duszynska, 1959), and Painter (1966) suggests that they serve to increase the ribosome forming capacity of the nurse cells. In some other insects, such as *Drosophila*, the same end is achieved by endomitosis in the nurse cells (see p.289).

In the Nematocera all the pole cells migrate in to form the germ cells in the gonads, but in Cyclorrhapha only a proportion of them do so, the rest becoming vitellophages or contributing to the midgut epithelium. Some of these cells migrate in through the blastoderm before gastrulation, but others only do so during or after gastrulation and during this process they are carried forwards and invaginated with the proctodaeum (Fig. 231). Controversy exists as to which of these cells form the germ cells, some authorities maintaining that the early migrating group is involved, others that the cells from the proctodaeum are responsible (see D. T. Anderson, 1962; Counce, 1963; Hathaway and Selman, 1961; Mahowald, 1962).

The early separation of the germ cells results in a very direct cell lineage from the gametes of one generation to the gametes of the next, in isolation from the structural cells of the body (Fig. 241). This presumably helps to ensure the integrity of the genetic system by reducing the possibility of abnormal divisions.

In other groups of insects the germ cells are not recognisable quite so early in development, but appear at about the time the mesoderm differentiates. In *Locusta* they first appear in the walls of the coelomic sacs in abdominal segments 2 and 5. Later they condense to a single group and become associated with ridges of mesoderm. There is some evidence that the development of these genital ridges is induced by the germ cells, but the bulk of existing work does not support this. The germ cells become enclosed by the mesoderm and increase in number before they become separated into columns by the ingrowth of the mesoderm. These columns form the germaria of the ovarioles or the testis follicles. The mesoderm thickens ventrally and gives rise to solid strands of cells in which cavities appear to form the lateral ducts. The median ducts arise from ectodermal invaginations.

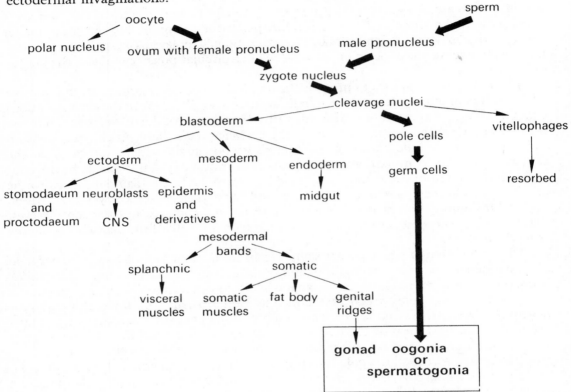

Fig. 241. Cell lineage during development, illustrating the early segregation and specialisation of the genital cells (based on Anderson, 1962).

In Orthoptera the mesodermal accessory glands of the male are formed from hollow ampullae which are remnants of the coelomic sacs of abdominal segment 10. The ampullae become divided into separate glands by the ingrowth of the walls.

18.7 Metabolic changes and control of organ development

Oxygen uptake by the egg increases throughout development as the embryo increases in size, while the respiratory quotient, which at first equals one, soon falls to a low level. This suggests that at first the small carbohydrate reserves of the egg are used and that subsequently fat is the main metabolic substrate. It has been calculated that in the egg of a grasshopper 75% of the oxygen uptake is concerned in the oxidation of fat.

The total nitrogen content of the egg remains constant throughout development, but its distribution varies, increasing in the embryo at the expense of the yolk. The amino acid pool in the developing egg is similar to that in the parent as is to be expected from the fact that amino acids can be taken up directly from the haemolymph. During embryogenesis the concentration of free amino acids at first increases due to the rapid breakdown of yolk reserves, probably by cathepsin-type enzymes which increase in activity to a maximum during this period (Kuk-Meiri, et al., 1966). These amino acids are used in the synthesis of proteins in the embryo and their concentration falls as the rate of protein synthesis increases (Chen, 1966). Changes in other substances during embryogenesis are reviewed by Agrell (1964).

The mechanisms which control later development, including organogeny are not clear. In general it is true that the ectoderm is self-differentiating, but that mesodermal development after the initial spreading out of the inner layer is induced by relatively undifferentiated ectoderm. There is also some evidence for the induction of some organs by others:—of the midgut by the splanchnic mesoderm, the anterior midgut by the stomodaeum, and ocelli by the wing buds. The eyes and optic lobes appear to have reciprocal inducing effects.

In *Locusta* and *Locustana* later developments are said to be under the general control of a hormone from the prothoracic gland, and in the absence of this the tissues fail to differentiate (B. M. Jones, 1956a), but Mueller (1963) found no evidence of this in *Melanoplus* nor is it true in Diptera (Anderson, 1966).

18.8 Duration of embryonic development

The times which insects take to complete their embryonic development vary considerably. Thus at 30°C. the complete development of *Culex* takes about 30 hours compared with 82 hours in *Ostrinia* (Lepidoptera), five days in *Oncopeltus*, 15 days in *Schistocerca* and 43 days in *Ornithacris* (Orthoptera).

The duration of development decreases as temperature increases and conversely the rate of development increases in a more or less linear manner with increasing temperature except at the extreme ends of the range for development (Fig. 242). Development is not completed if the temperature exceeds a certain level, often in the range 35–40°C., nor below a certain level, which in *Oncopeltus* is about 14°C. and in *Cimex* about 13°C. Some development does occur at lower temperatures, however, and in *Oncopeltus* some morphogenesis occurs even at 5°C. In addition to these developmental thresholds there is another temperature below which hatching of the fully developed embryo will not occur (see p. 384).

It is thus necessary to distinguish between the threshold temperature for some development, below which no differentiation occurs, the threshold for full development, and the hatching threshold. These distinctions are not always clear in the literature and in particular the thresholds for full development and hatching may be lumped as the developmental-hatching threshold or simply the hatching threshold (see Richards, 1957). This, however, can obscure the differences between different processes and the three thresholds are best considered separately.

Above the minimum temperature for full development the total heat input (temperature × time) necessary to produce full development and hatching is constant whatever the temperature. Thus in *Schistocerca* full development requires 224 degree days above a theoretical minimum for full development of 15°C. For instance, at 30°C. development takes about 15 days [(30–15°) × 15 days = 225 degree days] and at 20°C.

about 45 days [(20–15°) × 45 days = 225 degree days]. In *Schistocerca* this relationship also holds with fluctuating temperatures, including periods below the minimum for full development (Hunter-Jones, 1966), but in *Oncopeltus* and some other insects this is not entirely true because, although the development of *Oncopeltus* is not completed at temperatures below 14°C., some development does occur. Hence periods of low temperature do have an influence on the total number of degree days above 14°C. necessary for development (Richards, 1957, and see Howe, 1967).

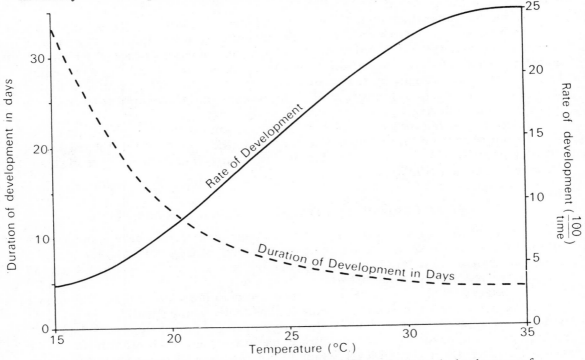

Fig. 242. The duration of the embryonic period and the rate of embryonic development of *Oncopeltus* in relation to temperature (from Richards, 1957).

Humidity also influences egg development in some species and in *Lucilia* there is a linear relationship between the time of development and saturation deficit. Many eggs must absorb water before they can complete their development (see p. 343), while if there is sufficient moisture in the environment to prevent death through desiccation, but not enough for development to continue, the eggs may remain quiescent for some time. Under such circumstances the eggs of *Schistocerca* develop to the beginning of blastokinesis and will then remain quiescent and viable for up to six weeks. At any time during this period development will proceed if more water becomes available. Locust eggs also fail to develop if they are in waterlogged soil (Hunter-Jones, 1966).

In some species the embryonic period is greatly prolonged by an egg diapause (p. 719) and as an extreme example the diapause eggs of *Locustana* may survive for over three years. Diapause occurs at different stages of development in different species: just after blastoderm formation in *Austroicetes* (Orthoptera), before blastokinesis in *Melanoplus*, or in the fully developed embryo in *Lymantria* (Lepidoptera).

CHAPTER XIX
UNUSUAL TYPES OF DEVELOPMENT

Sometimes eggs are retained by the female after they are fertilised so that they start to develop before they are laid. If this period of internal development is extended the larva may hatch within the parent and in a few species is nourished by her so that finally the female gives birth to a fully developed larva ready to pupate. In other instances eggs which are deficient in yolk are nourished via special placenta-like structures in the ducts of the female or in the haemocoel. Thus viviparity in insects takes various forms.

Amongst parasitic insects eggs sometimes give rise to a number of larvae instead of just one. This is known as polyembryony.

Eggs will develop without being fertilised, and sometimes this parthenogenesis is a normal occurrence. The sex of the offspring then depends on the behaviour of the chromosomes at meiosis and, in general, haploid eggs are male, diploid eggs female. A disadvantage of parthenogensis is that it reduces the adaptability of the insect, but in some cases this is overcome by an alternation of parthenogenetic and bisexual generations.

A few insects mature precociously and start to produce offspring while they are still larvae or pupae. This is known as paedogenesis.

Viviparity in insects is documented by Hagan (1951) and, in the Diptera, by Keilin (1916). Parthenogenesis is reviewed by Soumalainen (1962) and White (1954, 1964) and male haploidy by Whiting (1945). Kerr (1962) reviews sex determination.

19.1 Viviparity

The eggs of some insects are fertilised in the ovary or upper oviduct and in some of these species they are retained within the body of the female for some time before being laid. As a result the eggs start to develop while they are still within the parent and in *Cimex*, which practises haemocoelic insemination (p. 319), the embryo has almost reached the stage of blastokinesis by the time the egg is laid. In some other species internal development proceeds until the stage of hatching or even beyond, and such species are said to be viviparous.

19.11 Ovoviviparity

Many species retain the eggs in the genital tracts until the larvae are ready to hatch, hatching occurring just before or as the eggs are laid. All the nourishment for the embryo is present in the egg and no special nutritional structures are developed. Viviparity of this sort is called ovoviviparity and it differs from normal oviparity only in the retention of the eggs.

369

Ovoviviparity occurs spasmodically in various orders of insects: Ephemeroptera, Dictyoptera, Psocoptera, Homoptera, Thysanoptera, Lepidoptera, Coleoptera and Diptera, being particularly widespread in the last group from which the following examples are drawn. Sometimes species of *Musca* which are normally oviparous retain their eggs and deposit larvae, but numerous other Diptera, particularly the Tachinidae, are always ovoviviparous. In these the eggs are retained in the median oviduct which becomes enlarged as the uterus during gestation. Tachinids produce large numbers of eggs as do many oviparous Diptera, but in other ovoviviparous species, such as *Sarcophaga*, smaller numbers of bigger eggs are produced at each ovulation and in *Musca larvipara* only one large egg is produced at a time. This lower rate of egg production probably reflects the greater protection afforded to eggs carried by the female compared with eggs deposited in the environment.

The increased size of the eggs permits the accumulation of more nutriment so that the embryo may develop beyond the normal hatching stage and larvae are born in a late stage of development. In *Hylemya strigosa*, for instance, the larva passes through the first instar and moults to the second instar in the egg, casting the first instar cuticle immediately after hatching. In *Termitoxenia* development in the uterine egg goes even further. The egg hatches immediately it is laid, giving birth to a fully developed third instar larva which pupates a few minutes later, so that in this insect the larva never feeds as a free-living insect.

19.12 Viviparity

In some insects in which the eggs are retained after fertilisation the embryos receive nourishment directly from the parent in addition to or instead of that present in the yolk. Such insects are regarded as truly viviparous and some anatomical adaptations are present in the parent or egg which facilitate the exchange of nutriment. Viviparous species commonly produce fewer offspring than related oviparous species and this may be associated with a reduction in the number of ovarioles. Thus *Melophagus* (Diptera) has two ovarioles on each side, while *Glossina* (Diptera) has only one on each side (Fig. 243). In the related, oviparous, *Musca* there are about 70 ovarioles in each ovary. Similarly amongst the viviparous Dermaptera *Hemimerus* has 10–12 ovarioles on each side, but only about half these are functional. *Arixenia* (Dermaptera) has only three ovarioles on each side.

Sometimes the eggs are retained and development occurs in the ovariole, as in *Hemimerus*, the aphids and Chrysomedlidae. In other insects, such as the viviparous Diptera, the vagina is enlarged to form a uterus (Fig. 243). In Strepsiptera and a few parthenogenetic Cecidomyidae the eggs develop in the haemocoel of the parent.

Hagan (1951) recognises three main categories of viviparity and his scheme is followed.

Pseudoplacental viviparity

Insects exhibiting pseudoplacental viviparity produce eggs, containing little or no yolk, which are retained by the female and are presumed to receive nourishment via embryonic or maternal structures called pseudoplacentae. There is, however, no physiological evidence relating to the importance of these structures. Viviparous development continues up to the time of hatching, but the larvae are free-living.

In *Hemimerus* the fully developed oocyte has no chorion or yolk, but is retained in the ovariole during embryonic development. The oocyte is accompanied by a single nurse cell and enclosed by a follicular epithelium one cell thick. At the beginning of development the follicle epithelium becomes two or three cells thick and at the two ends

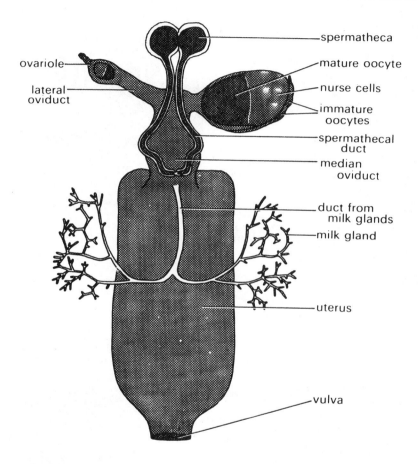

Fig. 243. Reproductive system of female *Glossina* (from Buxton, 1956).

thickens still more to form the anterior and posterior maternal pseudoplacentae (Fig. 244A). As the embryo develops it comes to lie in a cavity, the pseudoplacental cavity, produced by the enlargement of the follicle, but it becomes connected with the follicle by cytoplasmic processes extending out from the cells of the amnion and, later, of the serosa (Fig. 244B). Further, some of the embryonic cells form large trophocytes which come into contact with the anterior maternal pseudoplacenta. The follicle epithelium and pseudoplacentae show signs of breaking down and this is taken to indicate that nutriment is being drawn from them.

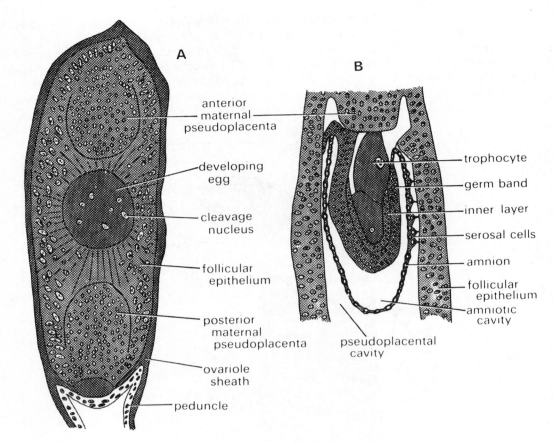

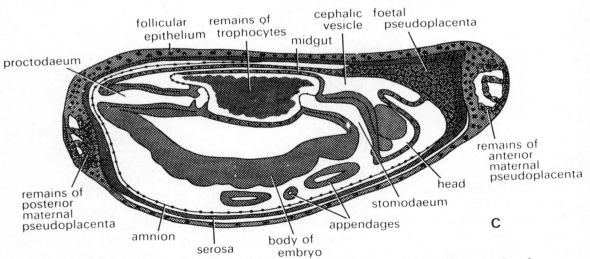

Fig. 244. Stages in the development of *Hemimerus*. A. Early cleavage. B. Fully developed germ band. C. End of blastokinesis (from Hagan, 1951).

Later in development the serosa spreads all round the embryo and, with the amnion, enlarges anteriorly to form the foetal pseudoplacenta (Fig. 244C). By this time the dorsal closure is complete except anteriorly where the body cavity is open to an extra-embryonic cavity, the cephalic vesicle. It is presumed that nutriment passes from the pseudoplacenta to the fluid in the cephalic vesicle and then is free to circulate into and round the embryo. The heart is probably functional at this time thus aiding the circulation.

The eggs of aphids also develop in the ovarioles and have no chorion. At first nutriment is received via the nutrient cords since aphids have telotrophic ovarioles (p. 286), but later a dominant role is played by the follicle cells. In *Macrosiphum* the follicle epithelium separates from the developing egg, but retains a connection posteriorly (Fig. 245). Through this connection reserve materials and symbionts are passed to the embryo, but the growth of the blastoderm restricts and finally severs the link. Possibly there is later some direct transfer of nutriment across the serosa from the follicle cells since the length of the egg increases by about 30 times in the course of development.

Pseudoplacental viviparity is also known to occur in a psocopteran, *Archipsocus*, in which the serosa is an important trophic organ, and in the Polyctenidae (Heteroptera) in which first the serosa and then the pleuropodia are important (see p. 360).

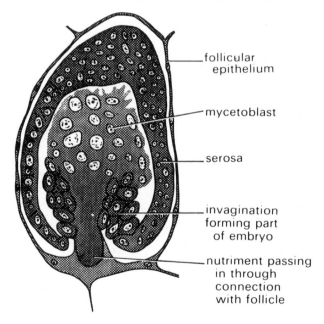

follicular epithelium

mycetoblast

serosa

invagination forming part of embryo

nutriment passing in through connection with follicle

Fig. 245. Section through an early embryo of *Macrosiphum* (from Hagan, 1951).

Viviparity in Dictyoptera

The position of the cockroaches with regard to viviparity is anomalous. Fundamentally all cockroaches are oviparous, laying their eggs in an ootheca (see Fig. 210A) which is extruded from the genital ducts. In some species the ootheca may be carried projecting from the genital opening, but in *Periplaneta* it is finally dropped some time before the eggs hatch. Other species such as *Blattella* continue to carry the ootheca externally until the time of hatching. Some others extrude the ootheca, but then withdraw it into the body again where it is held in a median brood sac which extends beneath the rest of the reproductive system. In this case the ootheca may be poorly developed and as the eggs increase in size they come to project beyond the ootheca. In most species the increase in size results only from the absorption of water, but in *Diploptera,* in which the eggs increase in length by five or six times during embryonic development, there is also an increase in dry weight indicating that some nutriment is obtained from the parent after ovulation.

It is not certain how *Diploptera* embryos obtain their nutriment, but it is possible that the pleuropodia function as pseudoplacentae. This is suggested by the fact that the pleuropodia are long hollow tubes which extend outside the serosal cuticle and lie beneath the chorion. Similar long pleuropodia occur in some other cockroaches such as *Leucophaea* which are not thought to obtain further nutriment from the parent after ovulation (Roth and Willis, 1958).

Adenotrophic viviparity

In adenotrophic viviparity fully developed eggs with chorions are produced and passed to the uterus where they are retained. Embryonic development follows as in ovoviviparity, but when the larva hatches it remains in the uterus and is nourished by special maternal glands. Parturition occurs when the larva is fully developed and pupation follows within a short time, there being no free-living feeding phase. This type of viviparity only occurs in *Glossina* and the Pupipara.

In *Glossina* the two ovarioles function alternately (Fig. 243) so that only one egg at a time passes to the uterus. Embryonic development is rapid, taking about three days at 24°C. in *G. palpalis,* and then the larva hatches. On the ventral wall of the uterus is a small pad of glandular cells with a cushion of muscle beneath and other muscles running to the ventral body wall. This structure is known as the choriothete and it is responsible for removing the chorion and the cuticle of the first instar larva. It undergoes cyclical development, degenerating during the later stages of larval development and starting to regenerate just before larviposition so that it is fully developed by the time the next larva is ready to hatch. The choriothete adheres to the chorion and when this is split longitudinally by an egg-burster (p. 386) it is pulled off by the action of the muscles of the choriothete, becoming folded up against the ventral wall of the uterus. The cuticle of the first instar larva is pulled off in the same way and its remains, together with those of the chorion, are expelled at parturition (Bursell and Jackson, 1957).

The first and second instar larvae feed on a secretion produced by 'milk' glands which open by a common duct into the uterus (Fig. 243). These glands undergo cyclical development, reaching a maximum during gestation. Their secretion accumulates in the uterus and is sucked up by the larva so that its midgut becomes distended, the contents being used during the latter part of the second instar and throughout the third when the larva grows considerably although it is not feeding. When the second instar moults, its cuticle is not immediately shed, but it is subsequently split by the growth of the pharate third instar and finally it is shed and voided shortly before parturition.

The larval respiratory system opens by a pair of posterior spiracles in the first two instars, but in the third instar larva the system is much more specialised. The terminal segment of the abdomen bears two heavily sclerotised lobes each of which is crossed by three longitudinal bands of perforations leading into the tracheal system. Each of these perforations is guarded by a valve which permits air to be drawn into the system, but not to be forced out. In addition to these openings in the polypneustic lobes the second instar spiracles on the insides of the lobes remain open because the second instar cuticle is not shed. Also as a result of this the tracheal system is lined by two layers of cuticle, the second instar cuticle being broken only at the inner ends of the system. Indirectly acting dorso-ventral muscles produce a piston-like movement in a specialised part of the tracheal system in the polypneustic lobes and it is suggested that this movement sucks air in through the valved perforations and forces it forwards between the two linings of the tracheae. An exhalent current flows through the loose second instar linings and out through the second instar spiracles. The respiratory muscles contract 15–25 times per minute (for details see Bursell, 1956).

By this means the larva is able to draw air in through the genital opening of the parent, but this mechanism can only function while the second instar cuticle persists, a period of four or five days at the beginning of the third larval instar. In the earlier instars oxygen may be obtained, at least partly, by diffusion from the female tracheal system which invests the uterus, while in the late third instar the valves in the polypneustic lobes disappear and a two-way airflow through the perforations is possible.

The hindgut of the larva is occluded at its connection with the midgut and again at the anus so that waste materials from the midgut are not voided and the hindgut forms a reservoir for nitrogenous waste. This arrangement prevents the larva from fouling the female ducts.

As far as is known the development of the Pupipara does not differ in essentials from that of *Glossina* outlined above, but there is no evidence for a complex air circulation similar to that which occurs in the larva of *Glossina*.

Haemocoelous viviparity

Haemocoelous viviparity differs from the other forms of viviparity in that development occurs in the haemocoel of the parent female. This type of development occurs throughout the Strepsiptera and in some larval Cecidomyidae which reproduce paedogenetically (p. 381).

Female Strepsiptera have two or three ovarial strands on either side of the midgut, but there are no oviducts and mature oocytes are released into the haemocoel by the rupture of the ovarian walls. In *Stylops* the eggs contain very little yolk, but some is present in other genera such as *Acroschismus*. Sperm enter through the genital canals which open in the ventral midline of the female (Fig. 246) and fertilisation and development continue in the haemocoel with a direct transfer of nutriment from the haemolymph to the embryo. The larvae hatch and find their way to the outside through the genital canals (see Hagan, 1951).

In *Miastor* (Diptera) the eggs are similarly liberated into the haemocoel from simple sacs. The developing egg is nourished via nurse cells, which arise independently of the oocyte (cf. p. 288), and later via the serosa which becomes thickened and vacuolated. When the larvae hatch they feed on the tissues of the female and any unhatched eggs, finally escaping through a rupture in the wall of the parent.

19.2 Polyembryony

Sometimes an egg instead of giving rise to a single larva may produce two or more, this process being called polyembryony. It occurs occasionally in Acridoidea and probably in other groups, but in some endoparasitic insects it is a regular phenomenon. This is true, for instance, in *Halictoxenos* (Strepsiptera) a parasite of *Halictus*; in *Aphelopus theliae* (Hymenoptera) a parasite of *Thelia* (Homoptera); in *Platygaster* (Hymenoptera) a parasite of Cecidomyidae; and in several genera of Encyrtidae and Ichneumonidae which parasitise the eggs and larvae of Lepidoptera. In all these cases the eggs of the parasite are small and relatively free from yolk, nutriment being derived from the host tissues in which they are situated.

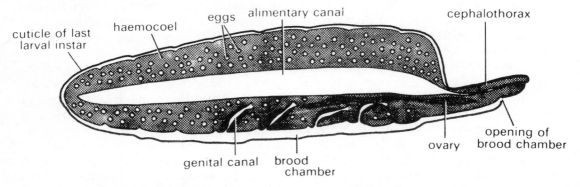

Fig. 246. Sagittal section through a female strepsipteran (from Clausen, 1940).

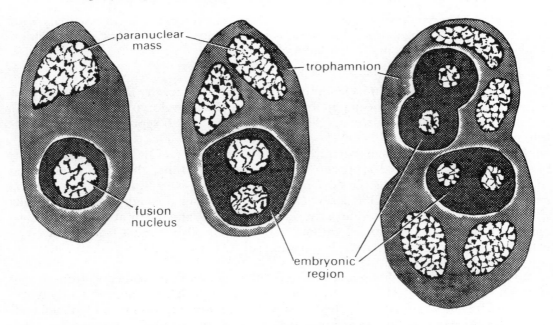

Fig. 247. Stages in the early development of *Platygaster hiemalis* showing the formation of two embryonic regions from a single egg (from Johannsen and Butt, 1941).

When the oocyte of *Platygaster hiemalis* matures two polar bodies are produced. They fuse together and the polar nucleus increases in size to form a paranuclear mass. Some of the cytoplasm in the egg is associated with the paranuclear mass and forms the trophamnion, the remainder is associated with the fusion nucleus and forms the embryonic region. The trophamnion surrounds the embryonic region and the paranuclear mass divides. At the same time cleavage occurs in the embryonic region, but after the second division the whole region divides into two so that two embryos are produced (Fig. 247). Nutriment is passed to the embryo from the host via the trophamnion, but later the paranuclear masses are absorbed and the trophamnion is represented by a very thin membrane. In *P. vernalis* several divisions of the embryonic region occur so that eight embryos are produced from each egg.

A somewhat similar, but more extensive, process occurs in *Litomastix* (Hymenoptera) a parasite of the moth *Plusia*. Three polar bodies are produced when the oocyte matures; two of these fuse to form the polar nucleus and the third degenerates (Fig. 248A). The zygote nucleus and its associated cytoplasm divides to form two blastomeres which become surrounded by the trophamnion. By further division (Fig. 248B) over 200 blastomeres are produced, some of them becoming spindle-shaped and

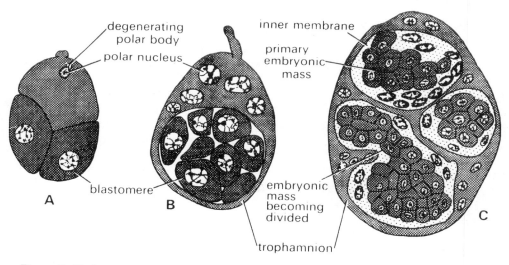

Fig. 248. Early stages in the development of the polygerm of *Litomastix* (from Johannsen and Butt, 1941).

pushing between the others to form nucleated inner membranes which divide the embryonic region into 15–20 primary embryonic masses each containing up to 50 blastomeres (Fig. 248C). These cells continue to divide and the embryonic masses are further divided into secondary and tertiary embryonic masses by ingrowths of the inner layer and the trophamnion. Finally the tertiary masses, which may become separated from each other, divide to form embryos of which 1000 or more may be derived from one egg.

The effect of polyembryony is to increase the reproductive potential of the insect, but the net effect is not always much greater than in related monembryonic species because polyembryonic forms tend to lay fewer eggs. Polyembryony may facilitate survival of the species through its relatively long life as a parasite during which time it is subjected to the reactions of the host (Clausen, 1940).

19.3 Parthenogenesis

Sometimes eggs develop without being fertilised and this phenomenon is known as parthenogenesis. Occasional parthenogenesis, resulting from the failure of a female to find a mate, is probably widespread, while in a number of insects parthenogenesis is a normal means of reproduction. It has been recorded from all the insect orders except Odonata, Dermaptera, Neuroptera and Siphonaptera.

The sex of the offspring developing from an unfertilised egg is dependent on the sex-determining mechanism of the insect and the behaviour of the chromosomes at the meiotic division of the oocyte nucleus. In the majority of insects the female is homogametic (XX) and the male heterogametic (XY or XO), but the Lepidoptera are exceptional with the females having the heterogametic constitution (see Kerr, 1962, for review of sex-determination). Hence the unfertilised eggs of most insects can contain only X-chromosomes since any Y-chromosome must come from the male. Whether the egg contains one or two X-chromosomes, that is, whether it is haploid or diploid, depends on the behaviour of the chromosomes at meiosis. Sometimes no reduction division occurs or reduction is followed by doubling of the chromosome number so that the diploid and XX composition of the egg is maintained. These eggs will give rise only to females. Eggs which undergo a normal reduction division and in which no chromosome doubling occurs remain haploid and, if they develop at all, become males. Such haploid males are characteristic of some insect groups.

Parthenogenesis may be classified according to the behaviour of the chromosomes at the maturation division of the oocyte:—

haplo-diploidy—A normal reduction division occurs in the oocyte, fertilised eggs developing into females, unfertilised eggs into males. This is characteristic of Hymenoptera and some smaller groups.

apomictic (ameiotic) parthenogenesis—No reduction division occurs so that the offspring have the same genetic constitution as the mother and all are female. This is of common occurrence in blattids, aphids, tenthredinids and curculionids.

automictic (meiotic) parthenogenesis—A normal reduction division occurs, but is followed by the fusion of two nuclei so that the diploid number of chromosomes is restored. Often the female pronucleus fuses with the second polar nucleus, or two cleavage nuclei may fuse. In *Solenobia* (Lepidoptera) two pairs of nuclei fuse after the second cleavage division. *Moraba* (Orthoptera) is exceptional in having a pre-meiotic doubling of the chromosomes followed by a normal division so that the diploid number is restored. This type of parthenogenesis, in which only females are produced, occurs in phasmids, coccids and psychids.

An alternative classification based on the sex of the offspring produced as a result of parthenogenesis is as follows:—

arrhenotoky—Only males are produced.

thelytoky—Only females are produced.

amphitoky—Individuals of either sex may be produced.

19.31 Arrhenotoky

Facultative arrhenotoky, in which the eggs may or may not be fertilised, is characteristic of a few groups of insects and has probably arisen only four or five times. It occurs throughout the Hymenoptera, in some Thysanoptera, the Coccidae Iceryini, some

Aleyrodidae and the beetle *Micromalthus*. In all of these the unfertilised, haploid eggs, produce males.

In the Hymenoptera the female determines whether or not an egg is fertilised by controlling the release of sperm from the spermatheca as the eggs pass down the oviduct. The stimuli prompting the female to withhold sperm are largely unknown, but in *Apis* the season and the size of the brood cell in which the female is ovipositing are relevant. In the parasitic Hymenoptera the size of the host is often important, relatively more unfertilised eggs being laid in small host (see *e.g.* Shaumar, 1966). For a discussion of male haploidy in Hymenoptera see Kerr (1962), White (1954) and Whiting (1945).

The coccid *Icerya purchasi* is of interest in that, apart from a few haploid males, the adult population consists entirely of hermaphrodites which are diploid with diploid ovaries, but which also have haploid testes. No true females occur. When the larva giving rise to an hermaphrodite hatches from the egg all the cells are diploid, but after a time haploid nuclei appear in the gonad. They form a core from which the testis develops surrounded by the ovary. Oocytes undergo a normal reduction division, but the spermatocytes, as in normal haploid males, do not. The hermaphrodites are normally self-fertilising, but they can be fertilised by the occasional males. Cross-fertilisation between the hermaphrodites does not occur. The few eggs which are not fertilised develop into males.

19.32 Thelytoky

Thelytokous parthenogenesis probably occurs occasionally in many species of insect and is known to occur in a number of species of Acrididae, for instance (see Hamilton, 1955). Unmated females of *Schistocerca* live for much longer than mated females, but lay about the same number of eggs. Nearly all of these start to develop, but only about 25% hatch and further heavy mortality occurs in the first larval instar. Thus the viability of unfertilised eggs is much less than that of fertilised eggs, but nevertheless *Schistocerca* has been reared parthenogenetically for six generations. It appears that the only eggs to survive are those in which the chromosomes double after meiosis. Unmated cockroaches also live longer than mated females, but they produce fewer eggs with poor viability (Roth and Willis, 1956). In *Bombyx* the tendency for sporadic parthenogenesis to occur varies in different strains.

In other insects thelytoky is a regular occurrence and, for instance, in *Carausius* and some Thysanoptera males are extremely rare, the whole population normally reproducing parthenogenetically. Sometimes, as in some Psychidae and Coccidae, a parthenogenetic race exists together with a normal bisexual race. Thus *Lecanium* (Homoptera) has one race consisting entirely of females which reproduce apomictically and another race which is bisexual and exhibits facultative thelytoky. In this case fertilised eggs may become males or females while unfertilised eggs develop automictically and so produce females. Commonly such races occur in different areas and in the weevil *Otiorrhynchus dubius*, for instance, a parthenogenetic race occurs in northern Europe and a bisexual race in central Europe. In general parthenogenesis occurs more commonly in the north than further south and in the genus *Otiorrhynchus* 78% of the species occurring in Scandinavia reproduce parthenogenetically, while only 28% of those occurring in the Austrian Alps do so.

Constant thelytoky occurs in a few Lepidoptera, such as the psychid *Solenobia*, and this raises the question of sex determination since the females of Lepidoptera are

heterogametic. Thelytoky in these insects may result from the passage of the
X-chromosome to the polar body at maturation so that only the Y-chromosome remains
in the egg; or two polar nuclei may fuse to give a female XO or XY constitution, while
the egg nucleus degenerates. A completely different explanation supposes that the
females are homozygous, YY, and so can give rise only to females (see Soumalainen,
1962; White, 1954).

An unusual type of thelytoky, known as gynogenesis, occurs in the form *mobilis*
of *Ptinus clavipes* (Coleoptera). The form *mobilis* exists only as triploid females which
reproduce parthenogenetically, but the development of eggs is triggered by healthy
sperm of *P. clavipes* or, less successfully, of *P. pusillus* (see Sanderson, 1961, for refs.).

Thelytoky occurs in many different and unrelated insects and is believed to have
arisen on a large number of occasions. It may result from apomixis or automixis and its
probable advantages over reproduction involving fertilisation are that the female spends
all her time in feeding and reproduction, no time is lost in finding a mate, and, since the
whole of the population is female, the reproductive potential is much greater than if
half the population are males. These advantages are, however, offset by the absence of
genetic recombination which normally occurs at mating. Thus the long-term effect of
thelytoky, in many cases at least, is to prevent a species from adapting to environmental
changes so that it is destined to die out or to return to bisexuality (see Soumalainen,
1962; White, 1954).

19.33 Alternation of generations

A number of insects combine the advantages of parthenogenesis with the advantages of
bisexual reproduction by an alternation of generations. This occurs, for instance, in the
Cynipidae which are commonly bivoltine, a generation of parthenogenetic females
alternating with a bisexual generation. *Neuroterus lenticularis* (Hymenoptera) forms
galls on the underside of oak leaves in which the species overwinters. Females emerge
in the spring and lay eggs. The eggs of some females undergo meiosis but, since, in the
absence of males, they cannot be fertilised, they remain haploid and so give rise to males;
other females produce eggs in which no reduction division occurs and which give rise
only to females. In this way the bisexual generation arises, the insects emerging from
catkin galls in early summer. After mating, the females of this generation lay eggs which
are fertilised and which produce the females of the following spring generation.

Aphids have a more complex alternation of generations with several parthenogenetic
generations occurring during the summer (Fig. 249). Sometimes, as in *Aphis fabae*,
an alternation of host plants also occurs. The first generation emerges on spindle in
spring from overwintering eggs. It consists entirely of females, the fundatrices, which
may or may not produce wingless generations of fundatrigeniae before a winged
generation, the migrantes, appears. These migrate to a bean plant and produce wingless
alienicolae of which there may be many successive generations, but ultimately these
produce the sexuparae some of which are winged and return to the spindle while others
are wingless. The former produce females, the latter winged males which then join the
females; they mate and winter eggs are produced. All these generations except for the
last reproduce parthenogenetically and consist entirely of females. In some species such
as *Tetraneura* only one class of sexuparae is produced and these individuals give birth
to both male and female sexual forms, an instance of amphitoky.

Female aphids are produced apomictically (but see Lees, 1966), while males result from the loss of an X-chromosome to a polar body at meiosis, although no reduction of the autosomes occurs. Thus an egg acquires the XO constitution of the male. The production of males is ultimately under environmental control, but how the environment controls chromosome behaviour is not known (Lees, 1966).

Spermatogenesis in male aphids is characteristic, ensuring that all the eggs produced are female. At the first meiotic division two kinds of spermatocytes are produced: some with an X-chromosome and some without. The latter degenerate so that only the

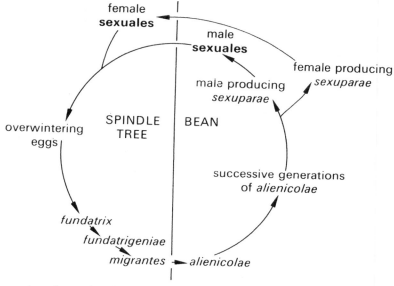

Fig. 249. Alternation of sexual and parthenogenetic generations in *Aphis*. Sexual generation in bold type; wholly female parthogenetic generations in italics (from Imms, 1957).

former undergo the second meiotic division and only one type of sperm, containing an X-chromosome, is produced. Hence the fertilised eggs can only be female.

The aphids reproduce very rapidly, combining the advantages of parthenogenesis with viviparity and paedogenesis so that successive generations are extensively telescoped. In the tropics, where conditions are continuously favourable, parthenogenesis may continue indefinitely without the intervention of a sexual generation.

An alternation of generations may also occur in Cecidomyidae (see below).

19.4 Paedogenesis

Sometimes immature insects mature precociously and are able to reproduce, this phenomenon being known as paedogenesis. It arises from a hormonal imbalance (p. 705) and most insects reproducing paedogenetically are also parthenogenetic and viviparous. Development of the offspring which are produced paedogenetically usually begins in the larval insect, but these insects may be grouped according to the stage which gives birth to the offspring.

In *Miastor* and *Micromalthus* the larvae give birth to other larvae or, occasionally, lay eggs. Paedogenesis occurs in *Miastor* only under very good or poor nutritional conditions. Young larvae are set free in the body cavity of the paedogenetic larva and they feed on the maternal tissues, eventually escaping through the body wall of the parent. Under average nutritional conditions normal adults are produced.

Micromalthus has five reproductive forms:— adult males, adult females, male-producing larvae, female-producing larvae, and larvae producing males and females. The species has a complex heteromorphosis (Fig. 250). The form emerging from the egg is a triungulin and this moults to an apodous larva which can develop in one of three ways. It can develop through a pupa to a normal adult female, or it can moult to a larval form which gives rise paedogenetically to a male, or to a paedogenetic larva which produces triungulins. Male-producing larvae lay a single egg containing a young embryo, but the egg adheres to the parent and when the larva hatches it eats the parent larva. If, for some reason the parent larva is not eaten, it subsequently produces a small brood of female larvae (J. A. Pringle, 1938; Scott, 1941).

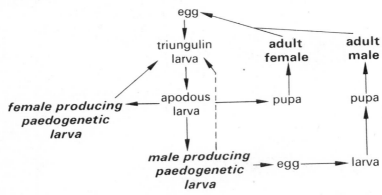

Fig. 250. Diagram of the life history of *Micromalthus*. Reproductive forms in bold type; paedogenetically reproducing larvae italicised (based on Pringle, 1938).

In the cecidomyids *Tekomyia* and *Henria* pupal forms give birth to larvae. The larvae of these insects are of two types; one type produces a pupa and, ultimately, a normal adult, but the other forms a hemipupa, a rounded structure with, in *Henria*, vestiges of wings and legs. A brood of larvae, commonly between 30 and 60 of them, escapes from the hemipupa by rupturing the cuticle (I. J. Wyatt, 1961). Wyatt (1963) also suggests that pupal paedogenesis occurs in *Heteropeza (Oligarces)*. Larvae are released into the haemocoel of the parent larva, but they escape from a form which he interprets as a hemipupa in which they can survive, if the conditions are moist, for up to 18 months. Paedogenesis is the normal method of reproduction in these insects and although normal adults may be produced it is not certain that they are capable of producing viable offspring.

Paedogenesis also occurs in aphids. Although the young are not born until the aphid has reached the adult stage, their development may begin before she is born while she is still in the ducts of the grandparental generation. Development of the offspring continues through the larval life of the parent.

The bug *Hesperoctenes* is an example of a paedogenetic form in which fertilisation occurs. Some last instar larvae are found with sperm in the haemocoel as a result of haemocoelic insemination (p. 319). These sperm fertilise the eggs which develop in the ovaries of the larva.

CHAPTER XX

HATCHING AND POSTEMBRYONIC DEVELOPMENT

When the larva is fully developed within the egg it escapes by rupturing the egg membranes and sometimes it has some special device which assists this process. In the course of hatching or immediately afterwards many insects shed an embryonic cuticle.

Once it has hatched the larva begins to feed and grow, but since the cuticle will only stretch to a limited extent growth is punctuated by a series of moults. The number of moults which occurs is variable, but is generally less in more advanced insects. In general, weight increases progressively, but linear measurements may increase in a series of steps corresponding with the moults, or more or less continuously if the cuticle is membranous as it is in many larvae. It is common for different parts of the body to grow at different rates so that simple mathematical relationships often do not hold. Growth of the epidermis and internal organs may entail an increase in cell size or an increase in cell number.

Growth from larva to adult usually involves some degree of metamorphosis. In many insects the larval form is tied to that of the adult by morphogenetic considerations, but in others a pupal instar interposed between the last larval instar and the adult has permitted a great divergence of form and habitat between larva and adult. In these a great variety of larval forms occurs. Sometimes the larva changes its habits during the life history and there is a corresponding change of form, a phenomenon known as heteromorphosis.

HATCHING

20.1 Escape from the egg

20.11 Hatching stimuli

The fully developed larva within the egg escapes by rupturing the vitelline membrane, the serosal cuticle when it is present (see p. 355), and the chorion. The stimuli which promote hatching are largely unknown and in many cases insects appear to hatch whenever they are ready to do so. Even in these instances, however, it is possible that some external stimulus influences hatching. There is a suggestion, for instance, that the larvae of *Schistocerca* hatch mainly at about dawn (see Hunter-Jones, 1966) and those of *Epitheca* (Odonata) at about sunset (Corbet, 1962).

In a few cases specific hatching stimuli are known. These vary, but are relevant to the insect concerned. The eggs of some *Lestes* (Odonata) species hatch when they are wetted provided the temperature is above a certain level. *Aedes* eggs hatch when immersed in deoxygenated water, the lower the oxygen tension the greater the percentage hatching (Fig. 251), but the responsiveness varies with age. The larvae are most sensitive soon after development is complete and will then hatch even in aerated water (Fig. 252), but if they are not wetted for some time they will only hatch at very low oxygen tensions. The low oxygen tension is perceived by a sensory centre in the head or thorax and maximum sensitivity coincides with a period of maximum activity of the central nervous system as indicated by the concentration of acetylcholine. Low oxygen tension has completely the opposite effect on the hatching of *Agabus* larvae which only occurs in oxygenated water (Jackson, 1958).

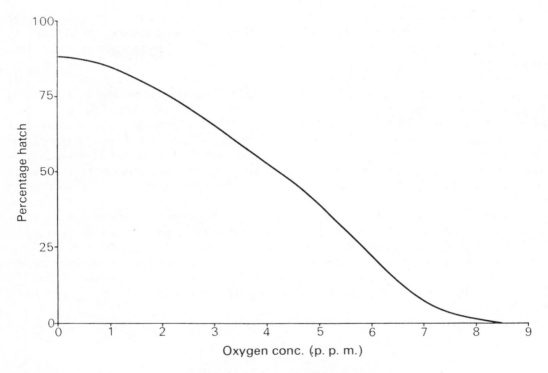

Fig. 251. The percentage of eggs of *Aedes* which hatch in water containing different concentrations of dissolved oxygen after incubation at 90–100% relative humidity (from Clements, 1963).

Amongst terrestrial insects the eggs of *Dermatobia* (Diptera) are stimulated to hatch by the warmth of the host (p. 327), while in grasshoppers the mechanical disturbance produced by one larva hatching activates other, unhatched larvae in the egg pod so that they all hatch within a short time (Uvarov, 1966).

Suitable temperatures are necessary for all insect eggs to hatch and there is a threshold temperature below which hatching does not occur. This temperature varies in different insects, but is about 8°C. for *Cimex*, 13°C. for *Oncopeltus* and 20°C. for *Schistocerca*. It is independent of the threshold temperature for full embryonic development which may be either higher, as in *Cimex* (13°C.), or lower, as in *Schistocerca* (about 15°C.). The failure to hatch at low temperatures may be related to the inactivity of the larva. Newly emerged *Schistocerca* larvae, for instance, are not normally active below about 17°C. and their activity remains sluggish below 24°C. (Hussein, 1937), and *Cimex* is not normally active below 11°C. Further, temperatures must be sufficiently high for the enzyme digesting the serosal cuticle to function efficiently (see below).

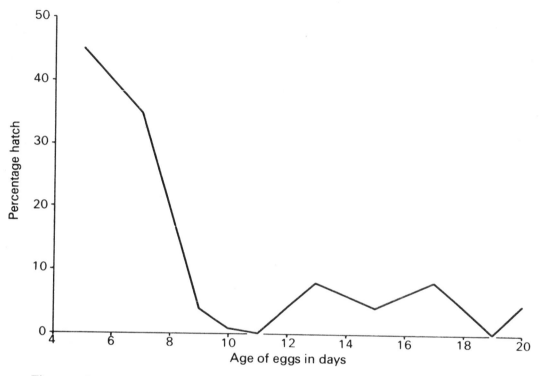

Fig. 252. The percentage of *Aedes* eggs of different ages which hatch under sub-optimal conditions, that is in aerated water. Only newly developed larvae hatch under these conditions, larvae which have remained some time in the egg require anaerobic conditions to induce them to hatch (after Judson *et al.*, 1965).

20.12 Mechanism of hatching

Most insects force their way out of the egg, first swallowing the amniotic fluid so as to increase their volume and then pumping blood forwards by contractions of the abdomen so that the head exerts pressure against the shell. In some cases the insects may increase their volume by swallowing air which diffuses through the shell or which enters following the initial rupture. In *Acheta* there are special muscles which assist the pumping movements and which degenerate after hatching. Similar muscles which are functional only at the time of a moult are known in other insects (p. 440).

The chorion may split in a more or less irregular manner depending on where the pressure is exerted; in *Agabus* a longitudinal slit develops. In other cases the chorion splits along a line of weakness such as those which occur at the longitudinal hatching lines of *Calliphora* (see Fig. 219) or at the junction of the body of the shell with the operculum in Heteroptera (see Fig. 192). *Aedes* has a line of weakness in the serosal cuticle and a split in the chorion follows this passively, perhaps because the serosa and chorion are closely bound (Judson and Hokama, 1965).

In a number of insects hatching is aided by cuticular structures, usually on the head, known as egg bursters. These are on the head of the embryonic cuticle of Odonata, Orthoptera, Heteroptera, Neuroptera and Trichoptera, but on the cuticle of the first instar larva in Nematocera, Carabidae and Siphonaptera. Their form varies, but in the pentatomids they are in the form of a T- or Y-shaped central tooth. Often, as in the fleas, mosquitoes and *Glossina,* the tooth is in a membranous depression which can be erected by blood pressure (Fig. 253A, B). In *Agabus* the egg burster is in the form of a spine on either side of the head, while in Cimicomorpha a row of spines runs along each side of the

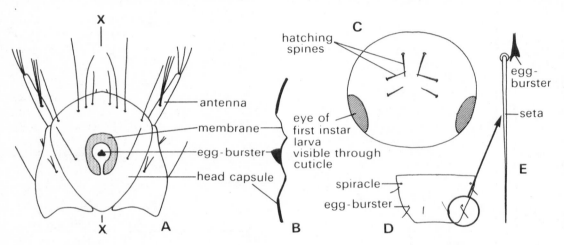

Fig. 253. Egg-bursters. A. The head of a first instar larva of *Aedes*. B. Diagrammatic vertical section through (A) along the line XX. C. Head of the embryonic cuticle of *Rhinocoris* (Heteroptera). D. Dorsal view of the eighth abdominal segment of the first instar larva of *Tenebrio*. E. Seta and egg-burster spine on (D) enlarged (after Marshall, 1938; Southwood, 1956; van Emden, 1946).

face from near the eye to the labrum (Fig. 253C). *Polyplax* (Siphunculata) has a pair of spines with lancet-shaped blades arising from depressions above them, while in *Pediculus* (Siphunculata) there are five pairs of these blades and in *Haematopinus* nine or ten pairs.

Many Polyphaga have egg bursters on the thoracic or abdominal segments of the first instar larva (van Emden, 1946). For instance, in *Meligethes* there is a tooth on each side of the mesonotum and metanotum, while larval tenebrionids have a small tooth on either side of the tergum of these and the first eight abdominal segments (Fig. 253D, E).

It is not clear how these various devices function and Jackson (1958) believes that in *Agabus*, the egg of which has a soft chorion, they are no longer functional. In other cases they appear to be pushed against the inside of the shell until finally they pierce it and then a slit is cut by appropriate movements of the head. The larva of *Dacus* (Diptera) uses its mouth hooks in a similar way, repeatedly protruding them until they tear the chorion (D. T. Anderson, 1962). The blades in *Polyplax* and the spines in *Cimex* are used to tear the vitelline membrane, the chorion then being broken by force (Sikes and Wigglesworth, 1931).

In Acrididae there is a thin membranous region of the neck which is expanded dorsally by blood pumped in from the abdomen. This cervical ampulla exerts pressure on the serosal cuticle which in these insects represents the main barrier to hatching since the chorion tends to crack away as the egg swells during development. In this group, and probably in the Heteroptera which also develop a thick serosal cuticle, hatching is aided by an enzyme, secreted by the pleuropodia, which digests the serosal endocuticle.

Larval Lepidoptera gnaw their way through the chorion and after hatching they continue to eat the shell until only the base is left. In *Pieris brassicae,* where the eggs are laid in a cluster, a newly hatched larva may also eat the tops off adjacent unhatched eggs (David and Gardiner, 1962).

When the egg is enclosed in an ootheca the larva escapes from this after leaving the egg. In the Blattaria the ootheca is split open before hatching by the swelling of the eggs as they absorb water. Acridids wriggle through the froth of the plug (see Fig. 210) enclosed in the embryonic cuticle and the thoracic dorsal longitudinal muscles may be specially developed to facilitate this since they become non-functional after hatching (Thomas, 1954). Movement is aided by the cervical ampulla which is collapsed as the head pushes into a narrow space and then expanded to give a purchase while the abdomen is drawn up. The larvae emerge from the eggs pointing upwards and then move up along the line of least resistance. Mantids probably make their way from the ootheca in a similar manner.

20.2 Intermediate moult

In those insects which possess an embryonic cuticle this separates from the underlying epidermis some time before hatching, but it is not shed so that when the larva hatches it is a pharate first instar (see p. 439). The embryonic cuticle is shed during or immediately after hatching and this process is commonly known as the intermediate moult. As the larva of *Cimex* or a louse emerges from the egg it swallows air and, by further pumping, splits the embryonic cuticle over the head. The cuticle is shed as the larva continues to hatch and finally it remains attached to the empty egg shell (Sikes and Wigglesworth, 1931). In Heteroptera the embryonic cuticle is attached inside the chorion at two or three places.

The intermediate moult in acridids begins as the larvae emerge on the surface of the soil, the cuticle being split by the action of the cervical ampulla so that the first instar larva can free itself.

POSTEMBRYONIC DEVELOPMENT

The life history of an insect is divided into a series of stages, each separated from the next by a moult. The form which the insect assumes between moults is known as an instar, that which follows the intermediate moult being the first instar which later moults to the second instar and so on until at a final moult the adult or imago emerges. No further moults occur except in the Apterygota (p. 703).

20.3 Numbers of instars

Primitive insects usually have more larval instars than advanced species. Thus *Ephemera* and *Stenonema* (Ephemeroptera) moult 30 and 40–45 times respectively, while Heteroptera commonly have five larval instars and Nematocera only four. Even within a group of related insects there is variation and amongst the Acridoidea the primitive Pyrgomorphidae have five or more larval instars while the advanced Gomphocerinae, which are also usually smaller, have four.

The number of larval instars through which a species passes is not absolutely constant. In the Orthoptera, in which the female is bigger than the male, she commonly has an extra larval instar, while larvae emerging from small eggs grow slowly and have an additional instar. *Nomadacris* may have six, seven, or occasionally eight larval instars depending on the treatment of the parents (see Albrecht, 1955). In *Plusia* and some other Lepidoptera, larvae reared in isolation may pass through five, six or seven instars, while nearly all of those reared in a crowd have only five (Long, 1953).

20.4 Growth

20.41 Weight

There is a progressive increase in weight throughout the larval instars and commonly the increase is faster during the early instars than in the later ones. For instance, during the first 14 days of the larval life of *Schistocerca* its weight increases 15 times, whereas

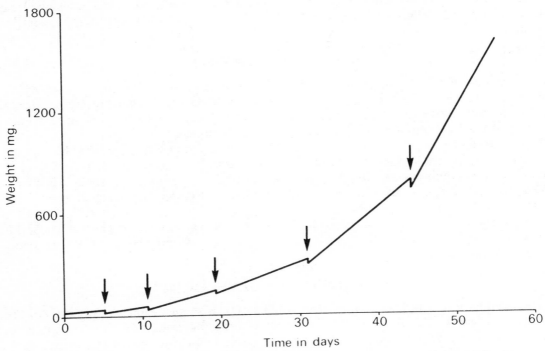

Fig. 254. The pattern of increase in weight of female *Locusta*. The times of the moults are indicated by arrows (after Clarke, 1957a).

during the following 14 days the increase is only about 4·5 times. The rate of increase in weight is greater in the female than in the male and her final weight is greater. From a hatching weight of about 18 mg. the male grows to a weight of about 1400 mg. on emergence and the female to about 1800 mg. (P. M. Davey, 1954).

Typically the weight increases steadily throughout a stage of development and then falls slightly at the time of moulting due to the loss of the cuticle and the loss of some water which is not replaced because the insect is not feeding. Following the moult the weight rapidly increases above its previous level (Fig. 254). In some aquatic insects the decrease in weight at the moult does not occur, but, conversely, there is a sharp increase due to the absorption of water, either through the cuticle or via the alimentary canal (Fig. 255).

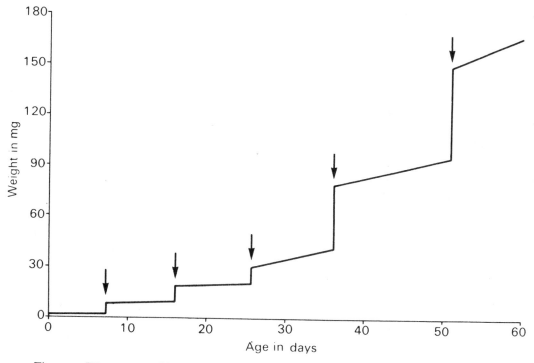

Fig. 255. The pattern of increase in weight of *Notonecta* (Heteroptera). Arrows indicate the times of the moults (from Wigglesworth, 1965).

In blood-sucking insects, such as *Rhodnius* which only feeds once during each instar, the pattern of growth is different. During the non-feeding period of each instar there will be a slow, steady loss in weight due to water loss, but feeding is accompanied by a sharp increase in weight followed by a fairly rapid fall as water is eliminated. There is, of course, a net increase in weight from one instar to the next.

The final weight of the adult insect varies according to the conditions under which the larva develops. Rapid development at high temperatures results in adults which are relatively light in weight. This occurs in *Dysdercus* (Heteroptera), for instance, but in this species an even greater reduction in weight is produced if the larvae do not have water for drinking. Crowding, possibly through its effect on the rate of development, also influences the adult size, insects from crowds being smaller than others bred in isolation. For instance, in one experiment on *Locusta,* Gunn and Hunter-Jones (1952) obtained adult females weighing 1·5 g. from larvae reared in isolation, while others from larvae reared in crowds weighed only 1·2 g. Where isolation is correlated with the production of an extra larval instar the difference in weight may be even more marked. Finally, adult weight may be influenced by the food on which the larva is nourished. This is particularly well illustrated in phytophagous insects such as *Melanoplus* in which the weight of females varies from 140 mg. to 320 mg. depending on the food available (Pfadt, 1949).

20.42 Growth of the cuticle

Fully sclerotised cuticle does not expand so that growth of sclerotised parts only occurs when an insect moults and a new, soft cuticle is produced and expanded. Consequently the growth of hard parts occurs in a series of steps (Fig. 256). Membranous regions can expand, however, both by the pulling out of folds and by stretching the cuticle itself. Thus a structure with a wholly membranous cuticle, or one, such as the abdomen of *Locusta,* in which the membranes are extensive, may grow continuously (Fig. 256). Other regions in which there is rather less membrane show an intermediate type of growth with some extension occurring in the course of each instar together with a marked increase at each moult.

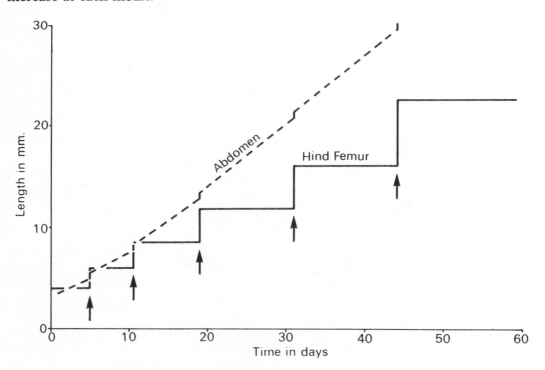

Fig. 256. The pattern of increase in length of the hind femur and abdomen of *Locusta.* Arrows indicate the times of the moults (after Clarke, 1957a).

Under the constant conditions of the laboratory and with an abundant supply of food the growth rate of sclerotised parts of the cuticle may be more or less constant so that it is possible to express the increase in size which occurs at each moult in simple mathematical terms. Dyar's law suggests that various parts of the body, such as head width, increase geometrically by a ratio which is constant for the species (often about 1·4). Richards (1949) showed that this relationship only holds if the duration of all the instars is the same, otherwise the change in size is proportional to the time for which an instar lasts and taking this into account an approximately straight line relationship may obtain between the size of an organ and the period of development which has elapsed (Fig. 257). Under natural conditions, however, with many variables growth rate is unlikely to be constant and there are many exceptions to these generalisations. They may, nevertheless, be used to give some check on the numbers of instars where this is not known.

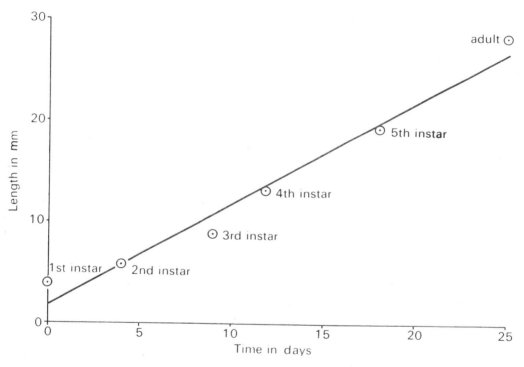

Fig. 257. The relationship between femur length and elapsed time in female *Locusta* (after Richards, 1949).

20.43 Allometric growth

The simple relationships suggested above apply to single, discrete structures. If different structures are compared it is commonly found that they are growing at different rates and this phenomenon is known as allometry or heterogonic growth. If the organ in question grows relatively faster than some other part taken as standard it is said to exhibit positive allometry, while slower growth is negative allometry. For instance, in *Hemi-*

merus the meriston grows faster than the antenna as a whole so that in the adult it contributes a greater proportion of the length than in the earlier instars (Fig. 258). Conversely the five apical annuli grow more slowly than the whole antenna so that their final contribution is proportionately less than their original one.

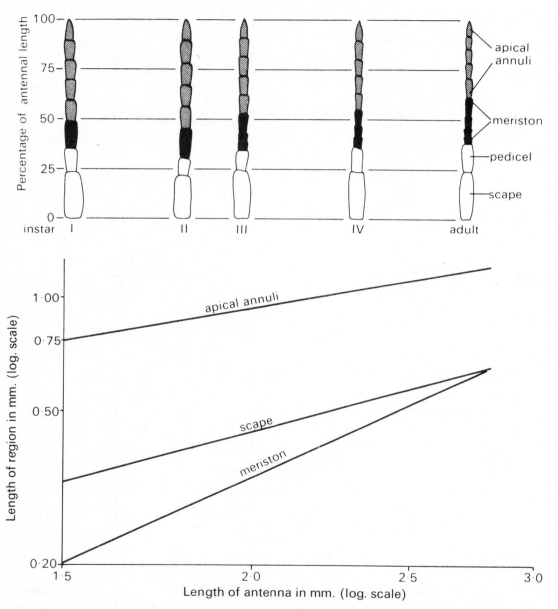

Fig. 258. Allometric growth in the antenna of *Hemimerus*. The diagram at the top illustrates the changes in the relative proportions of the different regions of the antenna in different instars. The graph shows these changes plotted against changes in the length of the antenna as a whole (after Davies, 1966).

The straight line relationship between two parts on a log./log. plot as illustrated in Figure 258 will only occur if the growth rates are consistent, but this is not always the case. In the first instar of *Dysdercus* the mesothorax grows at roughly the same rate as the body as a whole, but subsequently its growth is more rapid; the seventh abdominal segment grows slowly in the early instars, but very much faster in the final instar as the genitalia develop (Fig. 259). In none of the segments is growth relative to the body as a whole uniform throughout larval life (Blackith, *et. al.*, 1963).

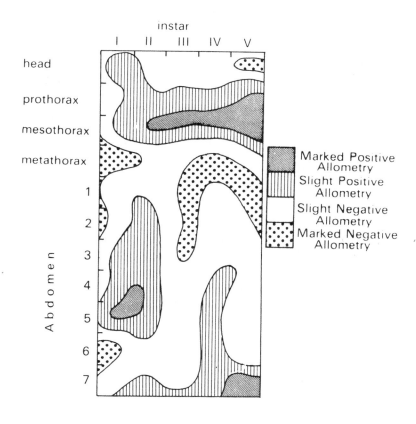

Fig. 259. Diagram showing the growth rates of different parts of the body of *Dysdercus* relative to the growth of the body as a whole in different larval instars (after Blackith *et al* 1963).

20.44 Growth of the tissues

The form of the cuticle depends on the epidermis, and growth of the epidermis may occur through an increase in cell number or an increase in cell size. Cell numbers increase just before moulting in many insects (p. 436), but in larval Cyclorrhapha the increase in size during larval life results entirely from an increase in the size of the epidermal cells. The number of cells influences the numbers of setae which may develop on the cuticle (see Lawrence, 1966a; Spickett, 1963; Wigglesworth, 1954b).

As with the epidermis, increase in the size of an internal organ may result from an increase in cell size or in cell number. The nervous system and fat body of *Aedes* grow through an increase in cell number, but most other tissues in this insect and in *Drosophila* have a constant number of cells and grow by cell enlargement. This enlargement is accompanied by endomitosis and occurs, for instance, in the salivary glands, abdominal muscles and Malpighian tubules. In the midgut both processes occur; the epithelial cells enlarge, but ultimately break down during secretion and each is replaced by two or more small cells derived from the regenerative cells. In some other insects the whole of the midgut epithelium is replaced at intervals by the regenerative cells (p. 44). Oenocytes may be produced progressively as in the water bugs or the same cells may persist throughout larval life, becoming progressively bigger so that in the last instar larva of *Drosophila* the oenocytes may be 80 μ in diameter. From this scant amount of data there is a general impression that tissues which are destroyed at metamorphosis grow by cell enlargement, while those that persist in the adult grow by cell multiplication. Cell enlargement is perhaps less wasteful of time and energy than cell division. For post-embryonic development of nervous system, see Edwards (1969, *Adv. Insect Physiol.* **6**).

The development of the Malpighian tubules varies. Henson (1944) differentiates between primary tubules, which arise as outpushings from the proctodaeum in the embryo, and secondary tubules which develop later and largely post-embryonically. There are four primary tubules in *Blatta,* while some other insects have six. *Schistocerca* has six primary tubules, but twelve more are added before the larva hatches and more develop in each instar up to the adult (see Fig. 331). Secondary tubules appear as buds at the beginning of each instar, but after their initial development they increase in length without further cell division as a result of an increase in cell size (Savage, 1956). The number of tubules similarly increases in each instar in *Carausius* and *Forficula,* and in the latter elongation of the existing tubules results partly from an increase in cell size, but also from rearrangement of the cells. At first each tubule consists of five rows of cells, but these later become rearranged to form two rows so that the tubule quickly trebles in length. In other insects, such as *Dysdercus* and *Pieris,* no increase in the number of Malpighian tubules occurs, but an increase in length again involves an increase in cell size and, particularly in *Pieris,* cell rearrangement.

20.45 Growth rate

The rate at which insects grow is influenced by the environment, and temperature is particularly important (see p. 646). Within the limits of temperature which permit growth, development generally proceeds more rapidly at higher temperatures. Thus in *Dysdercus* the time from hatching to adult emergence is 49 days at 20°C., 35 days at 25°C. and 25 days at 30°C. Humidity may also affect the rate of development. For instance, the larval development of *Locusta* occurs most rapidly between 60 and 70% relative humidity and mortality is also minimal within this range (Hamilton, 1950).

Availability of food is also important. If food is not available or is present in small quantities an insect may survive without growing for long periods. Thus a mosquito larva may survive for several months although normally its development is complete in a few days, and the larvae of many blood-sucking bugs can survive for months without a meal, growth being initiated only when they do feed (p.702). The rate of development may be influenced by the type of food and *Plusia* develops more rapidly on dandelion than on dock (Long, 1953). In the laboratory increased amounts of glucose or amino acid in the diet of *Pseudosarcophaga* (Diptera) reduce its rate of development (and see Fig. 47) and also alter the effect of temperature on growth. Thus with no glucose in the diet the larva grows faster at 30°C. than at 20°C., but with 2·25% glucose development is more rapid at 20°C. (House, 1966).

Crowding tends to increase the rate of development quite apart from changes which may be induced in the number of instars. Crowded larvae of *Plusia*, for instance, develop in 75–80% of the time taken by isolated larvae and this reflects the fact that the crowded insects spend 25% more time feeding.

20.46 Control of growth

Larval growth is characterised by periodic moults and to some extent internal changes are correlated with the moulting cycle. Moulting is initiated by the growth and moulting hormone and at larval moults the effect of this hormone is modulated by the juvenile hormone so that larval genes are stimulated and hence larval characters are produced (see p. 704).

While hormones exert an overall controlling influence, local factors, presumably chemical, control the form of particular areas. Thus the distribution of setae on the integument of *Rhodnius* is controlled by a determining substance which is absorbed by existing setae so that the development of new ones is inhibited. If, due to growth of the epidermis, the existing setae become widely spaced high concentrations of the determining substance may accumulate between them and so initiate the development of new setae. Where two or more integumental features are present in an integrated pattern they may be controlled by the same substance. In *Rhodnius,* for instance, it is suggested that a differentiating substance in high concentration produces the setae and that the same substance in low concentration initiates the development of dermal glands which are thus arranged round each seta. Where the integumental features are not arranged in an integrated manner, as with the hairs and scales on the abdomen of *Ephestia*, two determining substances might be involved. Further, in each abdominal segment of *Oncopeltus* and *Rhodnius* there appears to be a gradient of some factor which controls the orientation of integumental features such as the setae (see Lawrence, 1966a; Locke, 1959; Wigglesworth, 1959b).

There is relatively little information on the control of growth of internal organs, but some of these show cyclical activity which coincides with the moult. In the cells of the fat body of *Rhodnius,* for instance, there is a marked increase in the concentration of RNA and the number of mitochondria just before a moult and only at this time are the ventral abdominal intersegmental muscles fully developed (see p. 440). In insects in which the Malpighian tubules increase in number, mitosis and development of new tubules is phased with respect to the moult. On the other hand, in *Locusta* protein synthesis is continuous in various internal organs, being controlled by a hormone from the brain (see p. 703 ; and Clarke and Gillott, 1967a, b).

20.5 Types of development

During larval development there is usually no marked change in body form, each successive instar being essentially similar to the one preceding it, but the degree of change from last instar larva to adult varies considerably and may be very marked. This change is called metamorphosis (Snodgrass, 1954; Wigglesworth, 1965) and it is possible to define it in physiological terms as the change which accompanies a moult in the absence of the juvenile hormone (p. 704). In morphological terms Snodgrass (1954) relates metamorphosis to the loss of adaptive features peculiar to the larva and this is a reflection of the degree of ecological separation of the larva from the adult. The term metamorphosis is sometimes applied to all the changes occurring in the life history, from egg to adult (see *e.g.* Imms, 1957), but it is better not to use it in this wide sense.

The insects can be grouped in three categories, ametabolous, hemimetabolous or holometabolous, according to the extent of the change at metamorphosis. Ametabolous insects have no metamorphosis, the adult form resulting from a progressive develop-

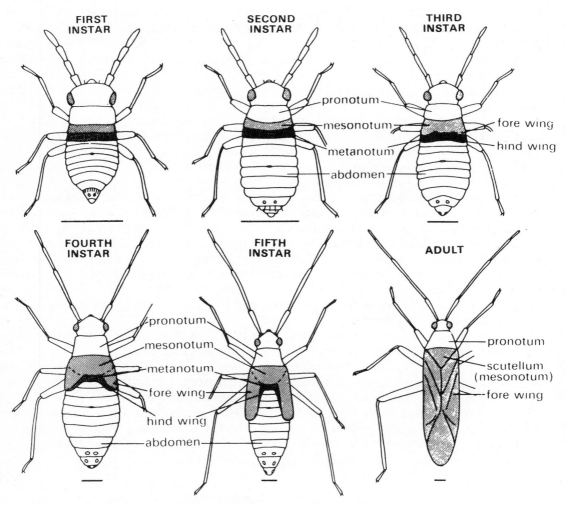

Fig. 260. Larval development of a hemimetabolous insect. The larval and adult stages of *Cyllecoris* (Heteroptera). The horizontal line under each **stage** represents 0·5 mm. (after Southwood and Leston, 1959).

ment of the larval form. This is characteristic of the Apterygota in which the larvae emerge from the egg in a form which essentially resembles the adult apart from its small size and lack of development of genitalia. At each moult the larva grows bigger and the genitalia develop. Adults and larvae live in the same habitat.

In hemimetabolous insects the larvae hatch in a form which generally resembles the adult except for their small size and lack of wings and genitalia (Fig. 260), but in addition they usually show some other features which are characteristic of the larva and which do not occur in the adult. At the final moult these features are lost. The Orthoptera, Isoptera, Heteroptera and Homoptera are commonly regarded as hemimetabolous. Snodgrass (1954) calls these groups ametabolous or paurometabolous, that is with a very slight metamorphosis, but a quantitative analysis of growth changes in *Dysdercus* shows a gradual transformation through the larval instars and a sharp discontinuity at the moult from larva to adult. This discontinuity applies not to typical adult features such as the wings and genitalia, but to other features which are not regarded as typically adult (Blackith, *et al.*, 1963). There is thus quantitative evidence of a metamorphosis and one of the changes which occurs at this time in *Rhodnius* is the loss of the larval cuticle with its stellate folds and abundant plaques bearing setae and its replacement by the adult cuticle which has transverse folds, a few setae and no plaques (see Lawrence, 1966b; Locke, 1959).

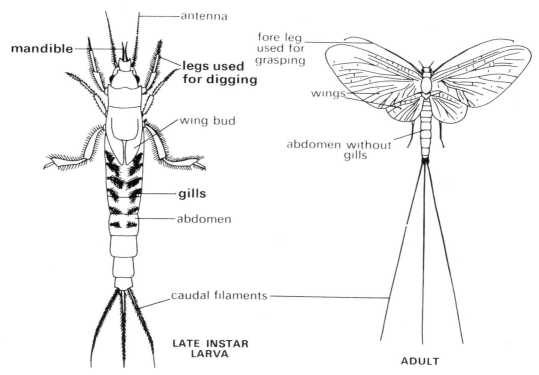

Fig. 261. Late larval instar and adult of *Ephemera*, a hemimetabolous insect showing conspicuous adaptive features in the larva. These features are indicated in heavy type (after Macan, 1961; Kimmins, 1950).

The Plecoptera, Ephemeroptera and Odonata have aquatic larvae and the typically larval adaptations are much more marked than in the previous groups. Hence these forms undergo a more conspicuous metamorphosis involving, among other things, the loss of the gills (Fig. 261). The general body form, nevertheless, resembles that of the adult and these insects are also regarded as hemimetabolous.

Finally, in holometabolous insects the larvae are quite unlike the adults and a pupal instar is present between the last larval instar and the adult (Fig. 262). The pupa is characteristic of holometabolous development which occurs in all the Neuroptera,

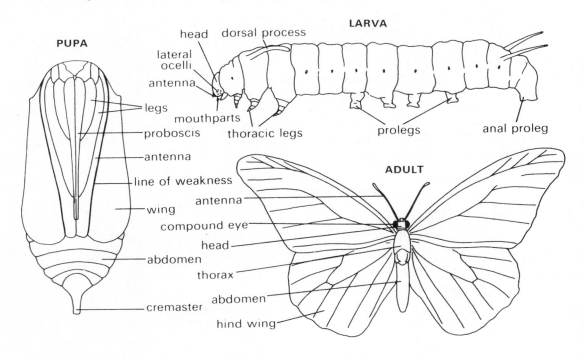

Fig. 262. Development of a holometabolous insect. Larva (lateral view), pupa (ventral view) and adult (dorsal view) of *Danaus* (Lepidoptera) (after Urquhart, 1960).

Trichoptera, Lepidoptera, Coleoptera, Hymenoptera, Diptera and Siphonaptera, in the Thysanoptera and Aleyrodidae, and in male Coccidae. The extensive differences between larval and adult structures are associated with the separation of larval and adult habitats. There is, however, no fundamental difference between the metamorphosis of hemimetabolous insects and that of holometabolous insects, both being associated with a moult in the absence of juvenile hormone (p. 704).

20.6 Types of larvae

It is convenient, for descriptive purposes, to group the insect larvae into broad categories based on their general appearance. Larvae of hemimetabolous insects essentially resemble the adults and they are sometimes called nymphs to distinguish them from the more radically different larvae of holometabolous insects. The most conspicuous difference between hemimetabolous and holometabolous larvae is in the development of the wings. In the former the wings develop as external buds which become larger at each moult, finally enlarging to form the adult wings (Fig. 260). In the latter, however, the wings develop in invaginations beneath the larval cuticle and so are not visible externally (see Fig. 274). The invaginations are finally everted so that the wings become visible externally when the larva moults to a pupa (Fig. 262). The separation of the forms exhibiting these types of development as nymphs and larvae respectively, however, suggests some basic difference between the two where none exists and the term nymph in this context is therefore better avoided.

There are many different larval forms amongst the holometabolous insects. The least modified with respect to the adult is the oligopod larva (but see also Chen, 1946). This is a hexapodous form with a well-developed head capsule and mouthparts similar to the adult, but no compound eyes. Two forms of oligopod larvae are commonly recognised: a campodeiform larva which is well sclerotised, dorso-ventrally flattened and is usually a long-legged predator with a prognathous head (Fig. 263A); and a scarabaeiform larva which is fat with a poorly sclerotised thorax and abdomen, and which is usually short-legged and inactive, burrowing in wood or soil (Fig. 263B). Campodeiform larvae occur in the Neuroptera, Trichoptera, Strepsiptera and some Coleoptera, while

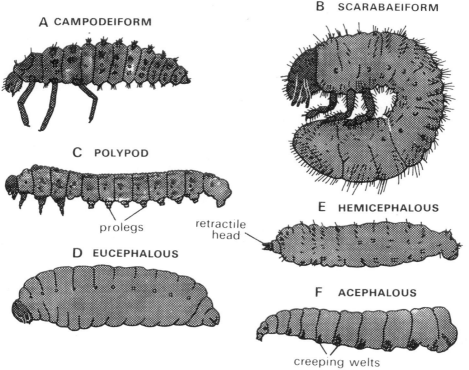

Fig. 263. Larval forms. A. Campodeiform—*Hippodamia* (Coleoptera). B. Scarabaeiform—*Popillia*. C. Polypod—*Neodiprion* (Hymenoptera). D. Eucephalous—*Vespula* (Hymenoptera). E. Hemicephalous—*Tanyptera* (Diptera). F. Acephalous—*Musca* (after Peterson, 1960, 1962; Hewitt, 1914).

scarabaeiform larvae are found in the Scarabaeoidea and some other Coleoptera.

A second basic form is the polypod larva. This, in addition to the thoracic legs, has abdominal prolegs. It is generally poorly sclerotised and is a relatively inactive form living in close contact with its food (Fig. 263C). The larvae of Lepidoptera, Mecoptera and Tenthredinidae are of the polypod type.

The third basic form is the apodous larva, which has no legs and is very poorly sclerotised. Several different forms can be recognised according to the degree of sclerotisation of the head capsule:

eucephalous—with a well-sclerotised head capsule (Fig. 263D). Found in Nematocera, Buprestidae, Cerambycidae and Aculeata.

hemicephalous—with a reduced head capsule which can be retracted within the thorax (Fig. 263E). Found in Tipulidae and Brachycera.

acephalous—without a head capsule (Fig. 263F). Characteristic of Cyclorrhapha.

Amongst the parasitic Hymenoptera the first instar larva hatches as a type known as a protopod larva. The protopod larva has many different forms and is often quite unlike a normal insect (see Fig. 265 and Clausen, 1940). These larvae hatch from eggs which contain very little yolk and some authorities regard them as embryos which hatch precociously (Chen, 1946), but others believe them to be specialised forms adapted to their peculiar environment (Snodgrass, 1954).

20.7 Heteromorphosis

In most insects development proceeds through a series of essentially similar larval forms leading up to metamorphosis, but sometimes successive instars have quite different forms, and development which includes such marked differences is termed heteromorphosis. (Hypermetamorphosis is commonly used for this type of development, but this implies the use of metamorphosis in the broad sense, referring to change of form throughout the life history.) Heteromorphosis is common in predaceous and parasitic insects in which a change in habit occurs during the course of larval development. Two types of heteromorphosis occur, one in which the eggs are laid in the open and the first instar larva searches for the host, and a second in which the eggs are laid in or on the host.

In the first type the first instar larva is an active form which, in Strepsiptera, for instance, is a campodeiform larva known as a triungulin (Fig. 264A). The triungulin attaches itself to a host when the latter visits a flower in which the larva is lurking. Subsequently it becomes an internal parasite and loses all trace of legs, while developing a series of dorsal projections which increase its absorptive area. Later, in the sixth and seventh instars it develops a cephalothorax (Fig. 264B, C).

A basically similar life history with an active first instar larva followed by inactive parasitic stages occurs in Mantispidae (Neuroptera), Meloidae and some Staphylinidae (Coleoptera), Acroceridae, Bombyliidae and Nemestrinidae (Diptera), Perilampidae and Eucharidae (Hymenoptera) and Epipyropidae (Lepidoptera) (see Clausen, 1940; Snodgrass, 1954).

The second type of heteromorphosis occurs in some endoparasitic Diptera and Hymenoptera. The first instar larva of *Cryptochaetum* (Diptera) has a pair of finger-like terminal processes which in the later instars develop into very long respiratory processes and greatly alter the appearance of the larva. A more marked heteromorphosis occurs in

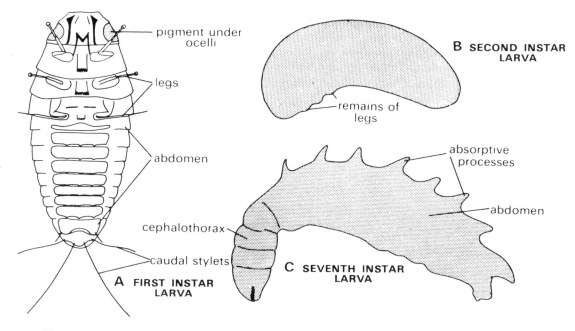

Fig. 264. Heteromorphosis. Larval stages of *Corioxenos* (Strepsiptera). A. Ventral view of the free-living first instar larva. B and C. Lateral views of older parasitic larvae (from Clausen, 1940).

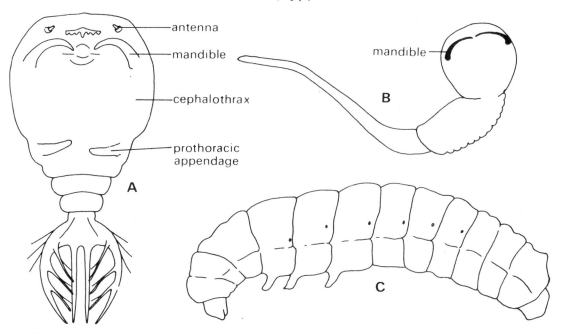

Fig. 265. Larvae of parasitic Hymenoptera. A. First instar larva of *Platygaster instricator* B. First instar larva of *Helorimorpha*. C. Mature larva of *Helorimorpha* (from Snodgrass, 1954).

those Hymenoptera which hatch as protopod larvae. The braconid *Helorimorpha*, for instance, has a big head, a small unsegmented body and a tapering tail in the first instar (Fig. 265B). The third instar larva, on the other hand, is a fairly typical hymenopterous larva (Fig. 265C). In the Platygasteridae the first instar larva is even more specialised with an anterior cephalothorax bearing rudimentary appendages, a segmented abdomen and various tail appendages (Fig. 265A).

CHAPTER XXI
METAMORPHOSIS

The changes which occur in the transformation of the larva to the adult may be more or less extensive depending on the degree of difference between the larva and the adult. Where the larva and adult are similar metamorphosis is relatively slight, but if the larva differs markedly from the adult a pupal instar may precede the adult. The pupa is probably to be regarded as the equivalent of the last larval instar of hemimetabolous insects and is a prerequisite for the greater divergence of larval and adult forms, permitting the larva to invade entirely new habitats. During the pupal period reconstruction of the tissues takes place involving particularly the eversion and growth of the wings and the development of the flight muscles.

Since the pupa is generally immobile and therefore vulnerable most insects pupate in a concealed cell or cocoon and they employ various means of escaping from this when they emerge as adults. Adult emergence is often synchronised, commonly occurring at night.

Insect pupae and their significance are considered by Hinton (1946, 1948b, 1963b), the morphological aspect of metamorphosis by Snodgrass (1954), and the physiological aspects by Agrell (1964) and Wigglesworth (1954b, 1959b, 1964).

21.1 The pupa

21.11 Form of the pupa

In the pupa of holometabolous insects all the features of the adult become recognisable so that the pupa has a greater resemblance to the adult than to the larva. At the larva/pupa moult the wings and other features which have been developing internally in the larva are everted and so become visible although they are not fully expanded to the adult form (see Fig. 262). In some pupae the appendages are free from the body and this condition is known as exarate, but in many others the appendages are glued down to the body by a secretion produced at the larva/pupa moult. This is the obtect condition and obtect pupae are usually more heavily sclerotised than are exarate pupae. A further differentiation can be made on the presence or absence of articulated mandibles in the pupa. When articulated mandibles are present, the decticous condition, they have apodemes which fit closely inside the mandibular apodemes of the adult (Fig. 266) and hence they can be moved by the mandibular muscles of the pharate adult. The alternative condition with immobile mandibles is known as adecticous.

Decticous pupae are always exarate. They occur in Megaloptera, Neuroptera, Trichoptera and some Lepidoptera. Some adecticous pupae are also exarate as in

Cyclorrhapha, Siphonaptera and most Coleoptera and Hymenoptera, but others are obtect. Most Lepidoptera, Neuroptera, Nematocera, Brachycera, Staphylinidae, some Chrysomelidae and many Chalcidoidea have obtect, adecticous pupae.

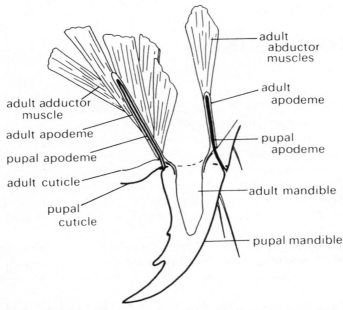

Fig. 266. Diagrammatic section through a mandible of a decticous pupa showing the pupal apodemes inside the adult apodemes (after Hinton, 1946).

Prepupa

The last instar larva is often quiescent for two or three days before the ecdysis to a pupa and in some cases the insect is a pharate pupa for a part of this time. This stage is sometimes known as a prepupa, but it does not usually represent a distinct morphological stage. A separate morphological stage known as the prepupa does exist in Thysanoptera and male Coccidae. In these insects the prepupa is a quiescent instar following the last larval instar and it is succeeded by a second, quiescent, pupal instar.

21.12 Protection of the pupa

The pupa of most insects is an immobile and hence vulnerable stage and a majority of insects pupate in a cell or cocoon which affords them some protection. Many larval Lepidoptera construct an underground cell in which to pupate, cementing particles of soil with a fluid secretion. *Cerura* (Lepidoptera) constructs a chamber of wood fragments glued together to form a hard enclosing layer and some coleopterous larvae pupate in cells in the wood in which they bore. Many larvae produce silk which may be used to hold other structures, such as leaves, together to form a chamber for the pupa, while in other species a cocoon is produced wholly from silk (Fig. 267B). Silken cocoons are produced by Bombycoidea amongst the Lepidoptera and by Siphonaptera, Trichoptera and Hymenoptera.

An exceptional protective structure is produced by the larvae of cyclorrhaphous Diptera from the cuticle of the last instar larva. Procuticle is laid down throughout the last larval instar and at the end of this stage the larva rounds off and the outer part of the

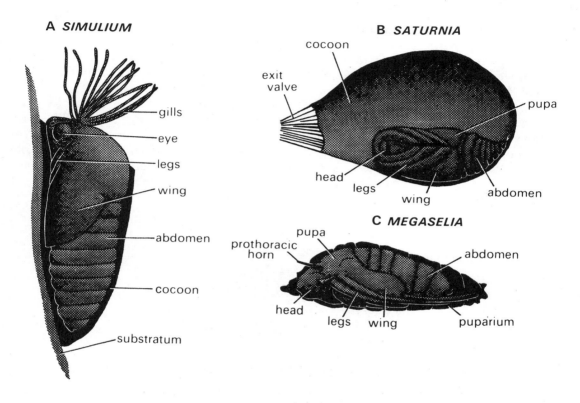

Fig. 267. Cocoons of various insects cut away to show the enclosed pupa. A. *Simulium*. B. *Saturnia*. C. Puparium of *Megaselia* (Diptera) (after various authors).

cuticle is tanned (p. 443) to form a rigid ovoid structure. The larva moults to the pupa, but its newly tanned and shaped cuticle remains unshed round the outside of the pupa, forming a protective structure known as the puparium (Fig. 267C). A thin membrane which adheres to the inside of the tanned cuticle probably represents the inner, untanned part of the larval cuticle, but alternatively, it is suggested that the larva undergoes an additional moult within the puparium to produce the pupa, and the thin membrane represents the cast cuticle from this moult (see Whitten, 1957).

A few insects form unprotected pupae. These are particularly well known in the Nymphalidae and Pieridae where the pupae are suspended from a silk pad. These exposed pupae exhibit homochromy (p. 118) whereas protected pupae are normally brown or very pale in colour.

21.13 Pupae of aquatic insects

The behaviour of aquatic insects on pupation varies considerably. Some larvae, such as the aquatic Arctiidae, Syrphidae and *Hydrophilus,* leave the water and pupate on land, but many others, particularly the aquatic Diptera, pupate in the water. Sometimes the pupae are fastened to the substratum. For instance, the pupae of Blepharoceridae have ventro-lateral pads on the abdomen with which they hold to stones, while Simuliidae construct open cocoons attached to stones and rocks (Fig. 267A). The pupa projects from the open end of the cocoon which is constructed more strongly in faster flowing water than it is in a weak current. Chironomidae pupate in the larval tubes or imbedded in the mud, while *Acentropus* (Lepidoptera) forms a silken cocoon with two chambers separated by a diaphragm. The pupa is in the lower chamber which is air-filled. In all these species oxygen is obtained from that dissolved in the water.

Other aquatic pupae obtain oxygen from the air, either directly or indirectly. The pupae of most Culicidae and Ceratopogonidae are free-living and active. They are buoyant so that, undisturbed, they rise to the surface and respire via prothoracic respiratory horns (Fig. 268). If disturbed their activity drives them downwards and the anal paddles assist in this movement. The pupae of some Culicidae and Ephydridae have their respiratory horns imbedded in the tissues of aquatic plants, obtaining their oxygen via the aerenchyma (p. 476).

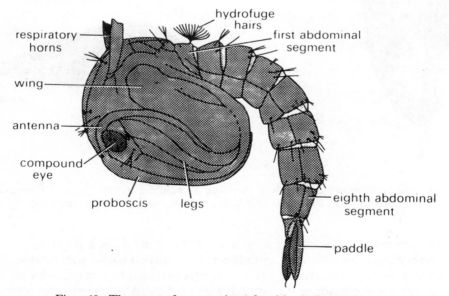

Fig. 268. The pupa of a mosquito (after Marshall, 1938).

21.14 Significance of the pupa

The pupa is indicative of the broad differences which occur between larval and adult forms of holometabolous insects. It is a stage during which major internal reconstruction may occur, but possibly its greatest importance is in permitting the full development of the wings. The internal development of the wings within the larva is restricted by lack of

space and this problem becomes more acute as the insect approaches the adult condition and the flight muscles also increase in size. Thus development can only be completed after the wings are everted and for this reason two moults are necessary in the
transformation from larva to adult. At the first, from larva to pupa, the wings are
everted and grow to some extent. Further growth occurs and the adult cuticle is laid
down at the pupa/adult moult (Hinton, 1963b).

Two moults may also be necessitated by extensive modifications to the muscular
system which occur at this time. Commonly all the muscles of the adult thorax are
different from those of the larva and they are not attached to the pupal cuticle. It has been
suggested that muscles will only develop in an appropriate form and length if they have
a mould in which to do so. The pupa provides a mould for the adult muscles. Hinton
(1948b) and Snodgrass (1954), among other authors, believed that the muscles could
only become attached to the cuticle when the epidermal cells were active and capable of
producing tonofibrillae, that is at a moult. Hence the second moult, from pupa to adult,
was necessary to provide this attachment. If the tonofibrillae are formed from epicuticle
(p. 211) which is only produced over a limited period this suggestion remains valid, but
in some insects, at least, tonofibrillae are formed long after the moult. These cannot be
epicuticular, but may be cuticular since the epidermal cells can go on producing
procuticle for some time. Thus it appears that muscle attachment may not be closely
dependent on moulting and hence that the pupa/adult moult is not primarily concerned with the attachment of the adult muscles (Hinton, 1963b).

The importance of the pupa in wing development and associated changes is empha-
sised by the absence of a pupal instar in the life histories of female Strepsiptera and
Coccidae which are wingless and larviform. The males in these groups are winged and
have a pupal instar.

The pupa is probably best regarded as equivalent to and derived from the last larval
instar of hemimetabolous insects, but for a summary of this and other points of view
see Hinton (1963b) and Novak (1966).

21.2 Development of adult features

Adult features may appear at the final moult, but commonly they undergo a progressive
development through the larval instars. This is most obvious in hemimetabolous insects,
but is equally true of many features of holometabolous insects.

21.21 Hemimetabolous insects

Epidermal mitosis and expansion only occurs at the time of a moult and in hemimetabolous insects a progressive development of the wing buds occurs at each moult. Apart
from their small size the wing buds differ from the adult wings in being continuous
sclerotisations with the terga and pleura; the basal region of the wing is not membranous
and no accessory sclerites are present. These appear at the final moult.

In general the wings arise in such a way that the lateral margins of the wing buds
become the costal margins of the adult wings (see Fig. 260), but in Odonata the buds
arise in an erect position, the margin nearer the midline ultimately becoming the costal
margin (Fig. 269). The wing buds of Acrididae originate as simple outgrowths of the
terga as in Heteroptera, but at the antepenultimate moult they become twisted into the

position found in the Odonata. This twisting results from the lower epidermis growing more rapidly than the upper. At the final moult the wings twist back so that the costal margin of the folded wings is ventral in position (Bland and Nutting, 1969, *Ann. ent. Soc. Am.* **62**).

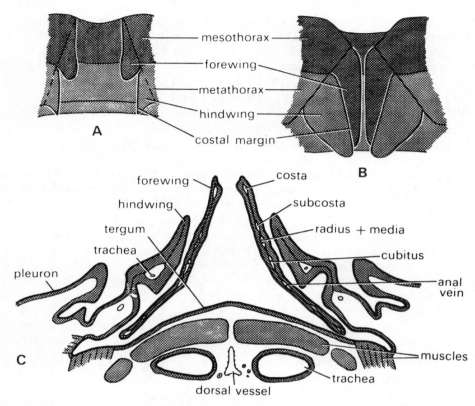

Fig. 269. A, B. Dorsal view of the pterothorax of (A) young and (B) older larvae of a dragonfly showing the wing buds. C. Transverse section through the dorsal part of the metathorax of a dragonfly larva (from Comstock, 1918).

In *Locusta* and dragonflies all the flight muscles are present in the larva although some are histologically distinct, lacking striations and presumably being non-functional. These muscles increase in size in various ways throughout the larval period. In Orthoptera they grow by the division of the existing elements; in Jassidae and some other Homoptera free myoblasts are incorporated into existing rudiments, while in *Bathylus* (Homoptera) both fibre division and myoblast incorporation occur. The incorporation of free myoblasts apparently takes place through a localised gap in the sarcolemma (Hinton, 1959; Tiegs, 1955). Further changes occur in the muscles in the young adult (p. 231). The phragmata to which the dorsal longitudinal flight muscles are attached become progressively bigger at each moult (Thomas, 1954).

Although accessory wing sclerites are not developed in the larva, the muscles which become attached to them in the adult are attached to appropriate positions on the larval cuticle. For instance, in *Locusta* the promotor-extensor muscle of the mesothoracic wing is inserted into the first basalar sclerite, but the equivalent muscle of the meta-thoracic wing is inserted into both basalar sclerites. In the larvae, although the sclerites are not developed, the muscle in the mesothorax has one point of attachment to the pleural cuticle, while that in the metathorax is attached at two points (Thomas, 1954).

The genitalia develop progressively by modification of the terminal abdominal segments (Fig. 270).

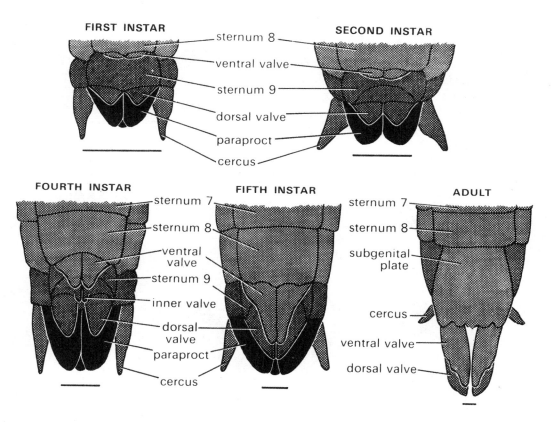

Fig. 270. Ventral view of the tip of the abdomen of various instars of the female *Eyprepocnemis* (Orthoptera) showing development of the genitalia. Horizontal bars under each figure represent 0·5 mm. (after Jago, 1963).

21.22 Holometabolous insects

The development of adult features in holometabolous insects varies in the degree of modification of larval features which is involved. In Neuroptera and Coleoptera, where the larvae have some resemblance to the adults, relatively little reconstruction occurs, but in Diptera the tissues are almost completely rebuilt following histolysis and phagocytosis of the larval tissues. It is generally agreed that phagocytes are not involved in the initial breakdown, but only attack tissue which is in the process of being histolysed.

Appendages

The development of adult appendages, including the mouthparts and antennae, may begin in the early larval instars and rudiments are commonly present in the embryo. If the adult appendage does not differ markedly from that of the larva it may be formed by a proliferation of the tissue within and at the base of the larval organ. This occurs in the legs of *Pieris*, for instance. Soon after the larva enters its final instar the epidermis becomes separated from the cuticle except at points of muscle attachment so that it is free to thicken and fold. The first thickening, well supplied with tracheae, develops at the junction of the second and third leg joints (Fig. 271A) and from this a wave of cell multiplication spreads out (Fig. 271B, C). As a result of the increase in area the epidermis becomes folded and a particularly large fold develops basally. Later, when the epidermis expands to form the pupal leg, this basal fold is divided by a longitudinal septum

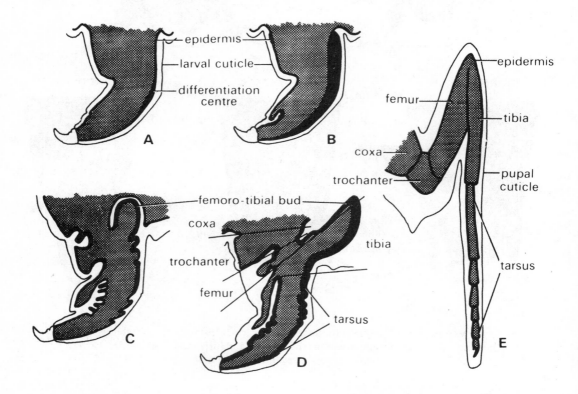

Fig. 271. Development of the adult leg in *Pieris*. A. Section through a leg of a last instar larva three hours after moulting. B. One day after moulting. C. Three days after moulting. D. Just before pupation. E. Section through a leg of a pupa. In (D) the presumptive areas of the adult leg are indicated (after Kim, 1959).

to form the femur and tibia. Epidermis from the more proximal parts of the larval leg forms the coxa and trochanter, and more distal tissue forms the tarsus. Further differentiation continues in the pupa to produce the adult leg (Fig. 271E) (Kim, 1959).

Where the difference between larval and adult organs is more marked the adult tissues develop from epidermal thickenings called imaginal buds or discs. In Diptera all the main adult features develop in this way (Fig. 272) and since the production of adult organs is thus restricted to small groups of cells the remainder of the epidermis

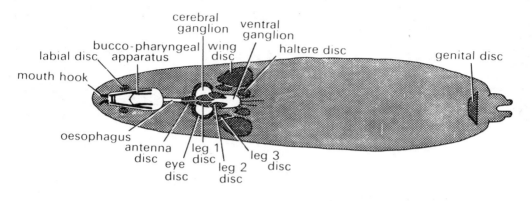

Fig. 272. Imaginal discs of a mature larva of *Drosophilia* seen from the ventral surface (after Bodenstein, 1950).

is free to undergo larval modifications (D. T. Anderson, 1964). The discs may be regarded as islands of embryonic tissue which remain undifferentiated until they give rise to the adult structures. They do not produce cuticle in the larva and the cells may continue to divide at all times, being independent of, or reacting in a different way to, the hormonal system which regulates growth in other parts of the epidermis (see Schneiderman and Gilbert, 1964).

The imaginal disc commonly becomes invaginated beneath the larval epidermis. In this way a cavity, the peripodial cavity is formed (Fig. 273A, B). It is lined with epidermis known as the peripodial membrane and as the imaginal disc enlarges the appendage forms and evaginates into the cavity (Fig. 273C). As the appendage grows it becomes folded inside the cavity until finally, at pupation, the rudiment is everted and the peripodial membrane comes to form part of the epidermis of the general body wall (Fig. 273D, E).

The details of development of the imaginal discs vary from one insect to another and from organ to organ. Where an appendage is present in the larva as well as the adult the imaginal disc is closely associated with the larval structure. Thus in *Pieris* the adult antenna is first apparent in the first larval instar as an epidermal thickening at the base of the larval antenna. The cells divide and in the succeeding instars an invagination is produced which pushes upwards deep into the larval head. In the fifth larval instar the adult antennal tissue grows more quickly than the peripodial membrane so that it is thrown into folds and towards the end of the instar the larval antenna starts to degenerate and is invaded by imaginal cells. When the peripodial cavity, which opens by a slit on the front of the epidermis of the head, evaginates, the antenna is carried to the outside and the peripodial membrane now forms a part of the wall of the head. The maxilla develops in an essentially similar way, but very little development of the labium takes place until the fifth instar (Eassa, 1953).

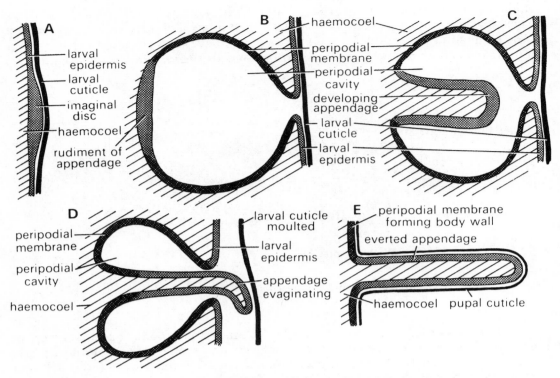

Fig. 273. Diagrams illustrating the manner in which an adult appendage of a holometabolous insect may develop in a cavity beneath the larval cuticle. A–C. In the developing larva. D. Larva in the process of moulting. E. Pupa with appendage everted.

The wings also develop from imaginal discs. In some Coleoptera they form as simple evaginations of the epidermis beneath the larval cuticle, but more usually they develop in peripodial cavities. In *Pieris* the imaginal disc is already apparent in the embryo and it invaginates in the second and third larval instars (Fig. 274). In the fourth instar the wing starts to develop as an evagination within the peripodial cavity, finally becoming everted at the larva/pupa moult. In *Drosophila*, on the other hand, invagination of the peripodial cavity is complete before the larva hatches, but the wing thickening does not develop until the second instar, growing more extensively in the third instar and becoming evaginated at the moult to the pupa.

The internal development of the wings is complex, involving great expansion and the formation of the veins. The development of a wing of *Drosophila* is used as an example. When the puparium is formed the wing projects backwards as a hollow cylinder of cells. The upper and lower surfaces come together except along certain lines which remain as lacunae (Fig. 275A, B) and where they meet their basement membranes may fuse to form a central membrane, but this soon disappears. There are four lacunae running along the length of the wing rudiment, the second dividing into two distally. A nerve and a trachea enter the second lacuna, and at about this stage, some six hours after the formation of the puparium, the pupal cuticle is laid down. After this the upper and lower surfaces of the wing are forced apart by an increase in blood pressure (Fig. 275C, D). The cells at first become stretched across the gap as narrow threads connecting the two surfaces, but finally these connections are broken except at the margins. A less extensive inflation occurs in *Tenebrio* and *Habrobracon* (Hymenoptera). Perhaps the inflation has the effect of expanding the newly formed pupal cuticle to the greatest possible extent so that the development of the adult wing can proceed.

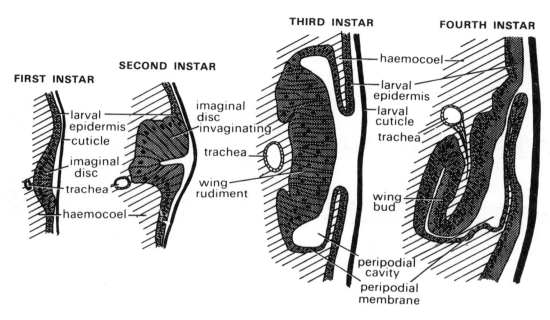

Fig. 274. Sections through the developing wing bud in the first four larval instars of *Pieris* (from Comstock, 1918).

Following the inflation, the wing contracts again. The epidermal layers on the two sides first become apposed round the edges (Fig. 275E) and then the contraction spreads inwards so that a flat double membrane is produced (Fig. 275F). During this process the definitive wing veins are formed along lines where the two epidermal layers remain separated (Fig. 275G). The veins are at first wide channels, but ultimately they become narrower as the membrane continues to expand. Cell division proceeds actively, especially above the veins so that here the cells become crowded and columnar, while elsewhere they are flattened. The fully developed wing finally secretes the adult cuticle (Fig. 275H) (Waddington, 1941).

Epidermis

When the imaginal appendages are everted from the peripodial cavities at the time of pupation the peripodial membrane contributes to the general epidermis of the adult body wall (Fig. 273). The extent to which the larval epidermis is replaced varies. In Coleoptera there is no extensive replacement, but in Hymenoptera and Diptera the epidermis is completely renewed from imaginal discs. The epidermis of the head and thorax are formed by growth from the imaginal appendage discs, while the abdominal epithelium is formed from special imaginal discs. In *Drosophila* most abdominal segments have pairs of dorsal, ventral and spiracular discs which expand to form the adult epidermis. As they do so the larval cells are sloughed off into the body cavity and are phagocytosed.

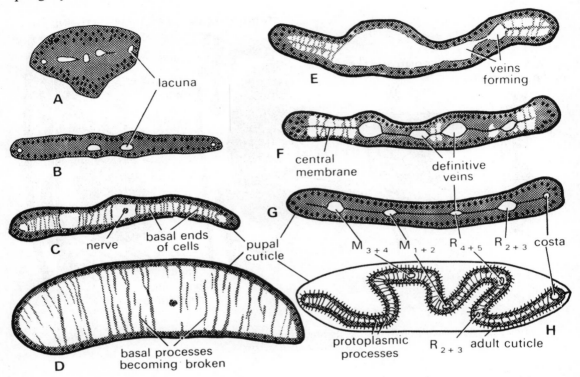

Fig. 275. Diagrammatic transverse sections of a developing wing of *Drosophila*. A, B. Successive stages in the resting larva before pupation. C–G. Further stages in the pupa. H. Pharate adult (after Waddington, 1941).

Muscles

The muscular system usually undergoes extensive modification at metamorphosis and the muscles fall into five categories according to their fate at this time:

1. Larval muscles may pass unchanged into the adult. This applies to some abdominal muscles.
2. Existing larval muscles are reconstructed.
3. Larval muscles may be destroyed and not replaced.
4. Larval muscles are destroyed, but are replaced in the adult by new muscles.
5. New muscles, not represented in the larva, may be formed.

In general larval muscles are histolysed and adult muscles rebuilt in the pupa, but the precise timing varies because some larval muscles have specific functions in pupal development and are destroyed much later than some other muscles. For instance, in *Drosophila* most muscles of the head and thorax start to break down before puparium formation and are fragmented before the larva pupates, but the dilator muscles of the pharynx remain unchanged until after pupation. They apparently are important in the evagination of the head region of the insect at pupation and after this they degenerate. In addition, one pair of muscles persists in each abdominal segment for about half the pupal period. It is suggested that they help to establish the segmentation of the pupal abdomen by telescoping each segment into the preceding one.

The first sign of muscle degeneration is liquefaction of the peripheral parts of the fibre. This is followed by a separation of the fibrils and in *Ephestia* phagocytes penetrate the sarcolemma and assist the destruction. The sarcolemma breaks down and the muscles separate from their attachments and fragment, the remains being consumed by phagocytes.

New muscles are always formed by free myoblasts, but muscles may be reconstructed in two ways. In the Neuroptera and Coleoptera the larval muscles contain two sets of nuclei, the functional larval nuclei and other small nuclei which are scattered through the cytoplasm. At metamorphosis the small nuclei multiply and, with associated cytoplasm, form myocytes. These migrate into the body of the muscle and associate in strands to form new fibres. In Diptera and some Hymenoptera, on the other hand, myoblasts which originate outside the larval muscle are concerned in the production of adult muscle, adhering to the outside or penetrating the sarcolemma in order to form new fibres.

Sometimes, as in *Simulium* and chironomids, the adult muscles are already present in the larva as rudimentary non-functional fibres. The dorsal longitudinal muscles in *Simulium*, for instance, are only about four microns in diameter in the first larval instar. They grow throughout the larval period and their nuclei increase in number. During the pharate pupal period they become divided up to produce the definitive number of fibres and at this time also myofibrils appear for the first time. They continue to grow until some time after the final moult (Hinton, 1959).

Alimentary canal

The alimentary canal is extensively remodelled at metamorphosis in species which have different larval and adult diets. In Coleoptera the reconstruction of the stomodaeum and proctodaeum is carried out by the renewed activity of the larval cells without any accompanying cell destruction, but in Lepidoptera and Diptera new structures develop from imaginal rings which are proliferating centres at the tips of the foregut and hindgut. The larval cells are sloughed into the body cavity.

The midgut is probably completely renewed in all holometabolous insects, usually being reformed from the regenerative cells at the base of the epithelium (p. 44). These cells proliferate and form a layer round the outside of the larval cells which thus come to lie in the lumen of the new alimentary canal. Sometimes this process occurs twice, once on the formation of the pupa and again when the adult tissues are forming and it is suggested that the special pupal midgut enables the insect to digest the sloughed remains of the larval midgut so that these can be assimilated and used in the reconstruction.

Malpighian tubules

Sometimes the larval Malpighian tubules pass unchanged to the adult or slight modifications may occur as in the Lepidoptera. Here the larval tubes have a cryptonephridial arrangement (p. 493), but at metamorphosis the parts associated with the rectum are histolysed while the more proximal parts form the adult tubules (Srivastava and Khare, 1966). In Coleoptera the tubules are rebuilt from special cells in the larval tubules, while in Hymenoptera the larval tubules break down completely and are replaced by new ones developing from the tip of the proctodaeum.

Fat body

The fate of the fat body at metamorphosis depends on the degree of reconstruction of the other tissues. Where, as in Coleoptera, many larval tissues remain unchanged the fat body shows little depletion, but where reconstruction is extensive the fat body may be almost or completely destroyed. It is then reformed in the adult from the few remaining larval fat cells or, as in *Musca*, from mesenchyme cells on the inside of the imaginal discs.

Other systems

In general the tracheal system shows little change other than the development of new branches to accommodate the particular needs of the adult, such as the supply to the flight muscles, and the elimination of some specifically larval elements. Sometimes, however, extensive renewal of the system occurs and in *Calliphora* this takes place from small groups of cells scattered through the walls of the larval tracheae.

The circulatory system undergoes little change from larva to adult.

In most holometabolous insects, particularly those that are more specialised, the central nervous system becomes more concentrated at metamorphosis. This concentration is accompanied by a forward movement of the more posterior ganglia resulting from the shortening of the interganglionic connectives. For instance, the larva of *Pieris* has, in addition to the head ganglia, three thoracic and eight separate abdominal ganglia. In the adult the meso- and meta-thoracic ganglia are fused with the first two abdominal ganglia to form a compound ganglion close behind the prothoracic ganglion. The next three abdominal ganglia remain separate, but the last three fuse together to form another compound ganglion. In the course of these changes the perineurium is histolysed and the neural lamella digested, the former being redeveloped from remaining glial cells. The nerve cells increase in number and this involves an accompanying increase in the numbers of glial cells (Heywood, 1965).

The higher Diptera are exceptional in having a more concentrated system in the larva than in the adult.

Biochemical changes

During the pupal period energy metabolism, as measured by the oxygen consumption, at first falls and then rises again, following a characteristic U-shaped curve (see Fig. 52). The fall in metabolic rate corresponds with the period of histolysis, while the subsequent rise occurs during the period of histogenesis and differentiation. These changes are produced by corresponding changes in the activity of the oxidative enzymes. The main substrates utilised during the pupal period are fats supplemented by small amounts of carbohydrate, but in *Apis* carbohydrate utilisation is high throughout.

There is relatively little information on nitrogen metabolism during metamorphosis despite its importance in histolysis and histogenesis. The total amount of nitrogen is constant throughout the pupal period and there are only relatively small changes in the ratio of protein nitrogen: nitrogen in compounds of low molecular weight such as peptides and amino acids. There is a small increase in the haemolymph concentration of some of the free amino acids during histolysis and a decrease during histogenesis, but these changes are smaller than would be expected considering the extent of tissue reconstruction. Other free amino acids in the haemolymph do not increase in concentration and it is possible that the larval proteins are only broken down to relatively complex peptides which are then rebuilt into the adult proteins (Chen and Levenbook, 1966). Ribosomal RNA, which is concerned in protein synthesis, increases during histogenesis (Fig. 276).

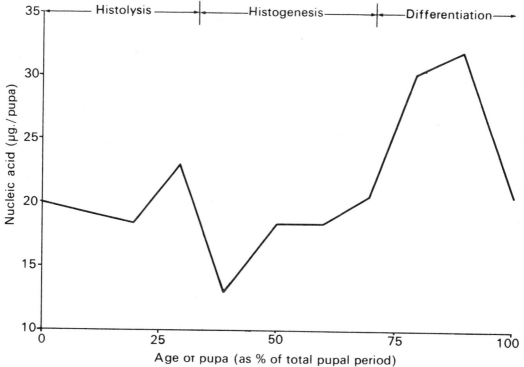

Fig. 276. Changes in the amount of ribosomal RNA present in different stages of the pupal instar of *Calliphora* (from Agrell, 1964).

There is a marked drop in the concentration of haemolymph protein at pupation due to the passage of the proteins into the tissues, some of which absorb particular proteins preferentially. It is suggested that these proteins may be involved in the transport of lipids and carbohydrates as conjugated groups (Loughton and West, 1965).

The waste products of pupal metabolism are discharged as the meconium when the adult emerges. Uric acid accumulates throughout the pupal period, but especially during histolysis, while in Lepidoptera and Hymenoptera allantoic acid comprises an appreciable part of the nitrogenous waste of the pupa. In *Phormia* (Diptera), urea accumulates during the development of the adult suggesting that it is the end product of nitrogen metabolism in this insect.

21.23 Control of metamorphosis

The development of adult characters is controlled by hormones (p. 704), but while the growth and moulting hormone causes the epidermis to adopt adult features it does not order the development of particular parts of the body. Some degree of determination of the adult tissues may be apparent in the embryo, the presumptive adult areas coinciding with the presumptive larval areas (see D. T. Anderson, 1966), but in *Drosophila* some lability of the adult tissues persists up to the time of pupation and even later (Waddington, 1956). More detailed features are not determined until after the more basic characters. For instance, the outline of the wing pattern of *Philosamia* (Lepidoptera) is determined before the details of the pattern.

There is some evidence that the various organs each have a differentiation centre which orders their development. For instance, in the leg of *Pieris* a basal thickening appears as an area of rapid cell division (Fig. 271) and mitosis spreads outwards from this point (Kim, 1959). Similarly the eye of *Aedes* begins as a thickening at the back of the future eye region from which a wave of mitosis passes forwards and a thickening, the optic placode, develops in an area which is already physiologically delimited. It is suggested that development of the optic placode is initiated by some factor which spreads forwards from the posterior region, while in the final larval instar a wave of ommatidial differentiation also starts at the back of the eye and spreads forwards (R. H. White, 1961). Finally, the pattern on the wings of *Ephestia* is determined in a regular sequence which again might be due to the spread of some factor from a differentiation centre in the middle of the wing (see Wigglesworth, 1965).

21.3 Adult emergence

The escape of the adult insect from the cuticle of the pupa or, in hemimetabolous insects, of the last larval instar is known as eclosion. The thorax of the enclosing cuticle splits along a line of weakness which in the pupa is T-shaped. To produce the split the adult swallows air to increase its volume and then further increases its thoracic volume by pumping blood forwards from the abdomen. In Lepidoptera and Diptera with an obtect pupa the mouth is sealed by a strongly sclerotised plate so that the adult insect cannot suck air directly into its gut. However, although some of the spiracles of the pharate adult connect with the pupal spiracles others do not, but open beneath the pupal cuticle. It is thus possible for the insect to pump air out of the tracheal system into the space between the adult and pupal cuticles and this air can be swallowed so as to increase the volume of the body (Hinton, 1946).

Having split the cuticle the adult pulls itself out, expanding the wings by pumping blood through them. In many insects the newly emerged adult hangs upside down so that the force of gravity assists the unfolding of the wings.

21.31 Escape from the cocoon

Where the pupa is enclosed in a cell or cocoon the adult also has to escape from this. Sometimes the pharate adult is sufficiently mobile to make its escape while still within the pupal cuticle. This is the case in species with decticous pupae which use the pupal mandibles, actuated by the adult muscles, to bite through the cocoon. Sometimes, as in Trichoptera, the adult mouthparts are non-functional and the sole function of the adult mandibular muscles is to work the pupal mandibles at emergence; subsequently they degenerate. The pupa moves away from the cocoon before the adult emerges and this is facilitated by the freedom of the appendages together with backwardly directed spines on the pupal cuticle which assist forward movement.

In species with adecticous pupae other methods are employed in escaping from the cocoon. In Monotrysia and primitive Ditrysia the pupa works its way forwards with the aid of backwardly directed spines on the abdomen, forcing its way through the wall of the cocoon with a ridge or tubercle known as a cocoon cutter on the head. The pupa does not escape completely from the cocoon, but is held with the anterior part sticking out by forwardly directed spines on the ninth and tenth abdominal segments. With the pupal cuticle fixed in this way the adult is able to pull against the substratum and so drag itself free of the pupal cuticle more readily. Cocoon cutters are also present in Nematocera although in this group they are usually multiple structures.

In many insects with adecticous pupae the adult emerges from the pupa while it is still in the cocoon, making its final escape later, often while its cuticle is still soft and unexpanded. This is true of the higher Ditrysia whose escape is facilitated by the flimsiness of the cocoon or the presence of a valve at one end of the cocoon through which the insect can force its way out, while the ingress of other insects is prevented. The cocoon of *Saturnia* is of this type (Fig. 267B), while in Megalopygidae a trap door is present at one end. Some Lepidoptera produce secretions which soften the material of the cocoon. *Cerura,* for instance, produces from its mouth a secretion containing potassium hydroxide which softens one end of its cell of agglutinated wood chips. This enables the insect to push its way out protected by the remnants of the pupal cuticle. The silk moth, *Bombyx,* produces a protease which attacks the sericin of silk and a few Noctuidae also produce softening secretions.

The Cyclorrhapha have a special structure, the ptilinum, which facilitates escape from the puparium and helps the insect to burrow to the surface of the debris in which the puparium is often buried. The ptilinum is a membranous sac which can be everted by blood pumped in by compression of the abdomen (see Fig. 291) so that it presses against the puparium and this splits along a line of weakness. The ptilinum is well developed in Schizophora, but is only rudimentary in Syrphidae.

The degree of hardening which these insects undergo before escaping from the cocoon varies. In some, most of the cuticle remains soft until after eclosion, but some parts, particularly those involved in locomotion, harden beforehand. Thus, in *Calliphora,* the legs and apodemes harden, so do the bristles which protect the soft cuticle, and such specialised parts as the halteres, antennae and genitalia. The remainder of the cuticle does not harden until after it is expanded when the insect is free (p.442, and see Cottrell, 1964). In Lepidoptera, however, the body does not expand greatly after emergence and here hardening of the cuticle is extensive before the insect emerges from the cocoon, although the wings remain limp.

Other insects emerge from the pupa and harden fully before making their escape from the cocoon and they may have specialised features to assist this. Coleoptera and Hymenoptera use their mandibles to bite their way out. Some weevils of the subfamily Otiorrhynchinae have on the outside of the mandible an appendage known as the false mandible (Fig. 277A) which is used in escaping from the cocoon and then, in most species, falls off. Amongst the Cynipidae which do not feed as adults, escape from the host in which the larva pupated is the sole function of the adult mandibles.

The cuticle of fleas also hardens before they escape from their cocoons and they may remain in the cocoon for some time after emergence. Their escape is stimulated by mechanical disturbances and in many species is facilitated by a cocoon cutter on the frons. In *Trichopsylla* the cocoon cutter is deciduous (Fig. 277B, C). Finally in the males of Strepsiptera the mandibles are used to cut through the cephalothorax of the last larval instar in which they pupate. The larval cephalothorax is earlier extruded through the cuticle of the host so that the adult insect can easily escape (Hinton, 1946).

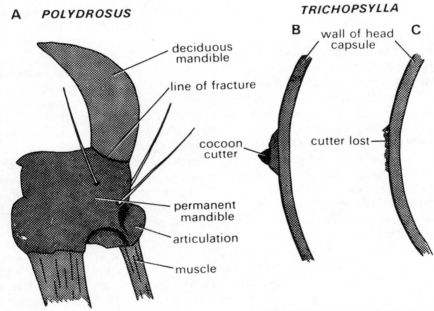

Fig. 277. A. The right mandible of *Polydrosus* (Coleoptera) at the time of emergence from the pupa. B. Front of the head of *Trichopsylla* showing the cocoon cutter. C. Front of the head of *Trichopsylla* after loss of the cocoon cutter (after Hinton, 1946).

21.32 Emergence of aquatic insects

Of the insects which pupate under water some emerge under water and swim to the surface, while in others the pupa rises to the surface before the adult emerges. In the Blepharoceridae the adult undergoes some degree of hardening within the pupal cuticle so that as soon as it emerges it rises to the surface and is able to fly. *Simulium* and *Acentropus* also emerge beneath the surface, but come up in a bubble of air. In *Acentropus* this is derived from the air in the cocoon, while *Simulium* pumps air out into the gap between the pupal and adult cuticles. Thus the adult emerges into a bubble of air and is able to expand its wings before rising to the surface.

The pupae of Culicidae are buoyant, while some other insects, such as *Chironomus*, whose pupae are normally submerged, increase their buoyancy just before emergence by forcing air out beneath the pupal cuticle or increasing the volume of the tracheal system. Aided by backwardly directed spines these pupae then escape from their cocoons or larval tubes and rise to the surface. Many Trichoptera swim to the surface as pharate adults, the middle legs of the pupae of these species being fringed to facilitate swimming and the insect may continue to swim at the surface until it finds a suitable object to crawl out on. In other Trichoptera the pharate adults crawl up to the surface, while the last instar larvae of Odonata and Plecoptera crawl out on to emergent vegetation so that the adult emerges above the water. Larval Ephemeroptera also come to the surface, but the form which emerges is a subimago, not the imago. The subimago resembles the imago, but its legs and caudal filaments are shorter and the wings are translucent instead of transparent and are fringed with hairs. The subimago flies off as soon as it emerges, but settles a short distance away and soon moults to the imago.

21.33 Timing of emergence

It is important that the emergence of species is timed so that the life history is synchronised with suitable environmental conditions and so that the meeting of the two sexes is facilitated. Synchrony with the environment results from the common reaction to the environment of the members of a species. Temperature is particularly important in this since to a large extent it governs the rate of development and the activity of the insect. Often a diapause is involved and in long-lived species a diapause may also be important in synchronising emergence so that the sexes meet (see Chapter XXXV).

It is common for male insects to emerge as adults a little before the females although the difference is not great. This is often the case with locusts (see Hamilton, 1936) and mosquitoes (Clements, 1963), for instance, and it probably reflects, in part, the smaller size of many male insects.

Apart from these general seasonal effects many insects emerge mainly at particular times of day, often at night or in the early morning. This may have some adaptive significance in giving the insect some degree of protection against predators while it is vulnerable in the period before it is able to fly. Thus in Britain, the last instar larvae of *Anax* (Odonata) which are ready to moult leave the water between 20.00 and 21.00 hours and by 23.00 hours most adults have emerged and are expanding their wings. The timing of emergence of *Sympetrum* (Odonata) and most tropical dragonflies is similar, although some temperate species emerge during the day, perhaps because activity is limited by low temperature at night.

Adult *Drosophila* emerge mainly in the first three or four hours of light in a 12 hours light: 12 hours dark regime and it has been suggested that this is due to a failure to emerge in the dark so that numbers of insects ready to emerge are inhibited from doing so until the light phase. However, Harker (1965), suggests that the lengths of various stages of development in the pupa are affected by the point in the light cycle at which they enter each stage and that a summation of these effects causes a mass emergence in the first few hours of light.

Aedes taeniorhynchus also emerges at particular times of day, but different broods emerge at different times depending on the temperature during the pupal period. The synchrony within a brood is brought about by a tendency of the larvae to pupate at about sunset.

SECTION D

The Cuticle, Respiration and Excretion

CHAPTER XXII

THE INTEGUMENT

The integument is the outer layer of the insect, comprising the epidermis (hypodermis) and the cuticle. It is a characteristic feature of arthropods and is, to a large extent, responsible for the success of insects as terrestrial animals. The cuticle affords support and protection through its rigidity and hardness and it is of primary importance in restricting water loss from the body surface. It is secreted by the epidermis and oenocytes and consists of a number of layers serving different functions.

As first secreted the cuticle is soft and flexible, but the outer part subsequently becomes hardened by a process known as tanning or sclerotisation, which involves the production of chemical bonds between the protein chains which make up the cuticle. Another important constituent of cuticle is chitin which acts as a packing, conserving the amount of protein used. The whole of the cuticle does not become hardened since flexible joints must occur between the hard plates for the insect to be able to move and in some joints a specialised rubber-like cuticle, resilin, develops.

The hardened cuticle by itself is not particularly waterproof. The waterproofing is provided by a thin, but complex epicuticle which is secreted to the outside.

Since hard cuticle will not expand it limits growth. Hence it is necessary for the insect to shed the existing cuticle from time to time and replace it with another which, before it hardens, is sufficiently flexible to permit some expansion. To conserve as much material as possible the untanned parts of the old cuticle are digested by moulting fluid and reabsorbed. The new cuticle is laid down, at least in part, before the old one is shed and the first layer to be produced is a layer of the epicuticle which protects the newly developing cuticle from digestion by the moulting fluid. Wax secretion is advanced by the time the old cuticle is shed so that water loss is restricted even at this time. The old cuticle is ruptured along lines of weakness by pressure exerted by the insect at various points. This and the subsequent expansion of the new cuticle may involve swallowing air or water and the presence of special muscles which degenerate soon after the moult.

The whole of the life history of the insect is geared to the moulting cycle and co-ordination of the various aspects of moulting involves a number of hormones.

Various aspects of the integument have been reviewed by Andersen and Weis-Fogh (1964), Cottrell (1964), Hackman (1964), Locke (1964), Richards (1951, 1958), Rudall (1963, 1965) and Wigglesworth (1957a). Neville (1967, *Adv. Insect Physiol.* **4**).

22.1 Epidermis and its derivatives

22.11 Epidermis

The epidermis is the outer cell layer of the insect. It is one cell thick and between moults the cells are flattened and their boundaries may be indistinct. They are bound together by septate desmosomes which are parallel lamellae bridging the intercellular spaces (Locke, 1961). During and just after a moult the cells may have long cytoplasmic processes on the outside extending into the pore canals of the cuticle (p. 428), but these processes may be withdrawn as the cuticle matures (Fig. 280).

22.12 Glands

Some of the epidermal cells may become specialised to form sense organs (see Chapters XXIX, XXX) or glands. The dermal glands commonly consist of three cells: a secretory cell, sometimes very large, and two other cells forming the duct from the secretory cell through the epidermis. The duct continues to the surface of the cuticle and its lining is probably continuous with the epicuticle. The products of the secretory cell accumulate in a vacuole and are discharged on to the surface during cuticle formation, forming the cement (p. 435). In *Rhodnius* (Heteroptera) there are two types of dermal glands secreting different components of the cement.

In all dipterous larvae there are glands, peristigmatic glands, surrounding the spiracles. They are usually single, large cells with intracellular ducts opening to the outside near the edges of the spiracles. Their secretion, which is produced continuously, is responsible for the hydrofuge properties of the cuticle surrounding the spiracles and prevents the entry of water into the tracheal system.

22.13 Basement membrane

The epidermal cells stand on a basement membrane which is an amorphous granular layer up to $0 \cdot 5 \ \mu$ thick (Locke, 1964). It forms a continuous sheet and at points where muscles are attached it is continuous with the sarcolemma (p. 207) (Fig. 284). In *Calliphora* (Diptera) larvae and some other insects stellate tracheal cells lie in the membrane (Wolfe, 1954a). Just before moulting in *Rhodnius* haemocytes thicken the membrane by the addition of a mucopolysaccharide (p. 679).

22.14 Oenocytes

The oenocytes are often large cells, more than 100 μ in diameter, in a group on either side of each abdominal segment. In Ephemeroptera, Odonata and Heteroptera, among others, the oenocytes remain close to their point of origin in the epidermis, lying between the bases of the epidermal cells and the basement membrane (Fig. 289); in Lepidoptera and Orthoptera they form clusters in the body cavity; while in Homoptera, Hymenoptera and some Diptera they are dispersed and embedded in the fat body. These cells may be formed continuously, or a new generation of cells may be produced at each moult, or, in holometabolous insects, there may be separate larval and adult generations. They show cycles of development which in immature insects are associated with the moulting cycle and they are probably concerned with the secretion of the lipoprotein of the epicuticle and perhaps with the synthesis of wax (see p. 437).

22.2 Cuticle

The cuticle is a secretion of the epidermis and covers the whole of the outside of the body as well as lining ectodermal invaginations such as the stomodaeum and proctodaeum and the tracheae. It is differentiated into two major regions: an inner region, up to 200 μ thick, which contains chitin and forms the bulk of the cuticle, and the thin outer epicuticle which contains no chitin and is only 1–4 μ thick.

The chitinous cuticle as it is first secreted is known as procuticle, but subsequently the outer part often becomes tanned or sclerotised to form exocuticle while the inner undifferentiated part is now called endocuticle (Fig. 278). Between the two there may be a region of hardened, but not fully darkened cuticle which is fuchsinophil (fully sclerotised cuticle does not stain readily) and such a layer is called mesocuticle.

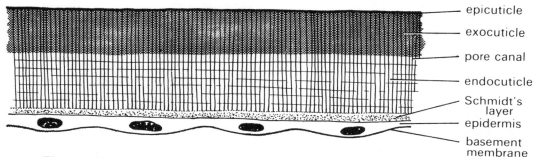

epicuticle
exocuticle
pore canal
endocuticle
Schmidt's layer
epidermis
basement membrane

Fig. 278. Diagrammatic representation of a section of mature cuticle and epidermis.

The cuticle has a lamellar structure resulting from the distribution of microfibres (see below) in the cuticle. These microfibres lie parallel to each other in the plane of the cuticle forming layers about 50 to 250 Å thick. The fibres in successive layers are at different angles, the direction of rotation being constant so that, in section, the cuticle appears to be made up of lamellae (Fig. 279). In the antennae of *Apis*, 15 to 20 such lamellae are laid down in one day, while in the fifth instar larvae of *Calpodes* kept in constant darkness, over 400 lamellae are produced in six days. As a result of this arrangement, oblique sections through the cuticle show a repeating parabolic pattern of the microfibres (Bouligand 1965, *C.r. hebd. Seanc. Acad. Sci. Paris* **261**).

In locust endocuticle, such lamellae are only produced during periods of darkness. In the light, all the microfibres assume a common preferred direction so that the cuticle is non-lamellate. Hence, in some insects such as Orthoptera and Dictyoptera, in which cuticle deposition extends over several days alternating layers of lamellate and non-lamellate cuticle occur, corresponding with cuticle laid down at night or during the day.

In other cases, notably the Heteroptera and Coleoptera, the chitin fibres are laid down with a constant orientation for 24 hours, but then are given a new orientation, varying from 30 to 90° from the original in different parts of the body. Thus in both these orders and in the Orthoptera and Dictyoptera, daily growth layers are formed which make it possible to estimate the age of insects from sections of the cuticle (Neville, 1967, *Adv. Insect Physiol.* **4**).

The rhythmic deposition of chitin with different orientations persists indefinitely in some insects, such as *Periplaneta* and belastomatid bugs, even under constant conditions. In *Schistocerca* the rhythm persists for some time if the insects are kept in the dark, but with constant light non-lamellate endocuticle is produced.

Between the endocuticle and the epidermis is an amorphous layer without any fibres, but which is granular near the epidermis (Fig. 278). This is the subcuticle or Schmidt's layer and probably represents endocuticle in the process of formation.

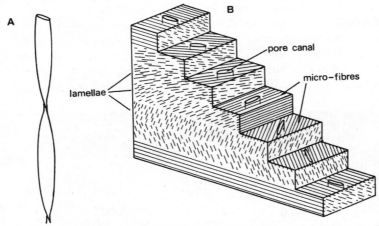

Fig. 279. A. Diagrammatic representation of a twisted ribbon pore canal. B. Diagrammatic section through a segment of cuticle showing microfibres of successive lamellae running in different directions and pore canals orientated parallel to the fibres (based on Neville *et al.*, 1969).

22.21 Pore canals

Running through the cuticle at right angles to the surface are very fine pore canals. They extend from the epidermis to the inner layers of the epicuticle and are usually stated to contain cytoplasmic extensions of the epidermal cells. Locke (1964), however, believes them to be extracellular, although containing filaments which arise from the cells and may extend to the peripheral ends of the canals. They have a flattened, ribbon-like form, the plane of flattening being parallel with the microfibres in each layer of the cuticle (Fig. 279). Thus, as the microfibres in successive layers change direction, the ribbon becomes twisted and the twisted-ribbon arrangement seems to be typical of lamellate cuticles (Neville *et al.*, 1969, *Tissue & Cell* 1). In non-lamellate cuticles the ribbon remains untwisted. In older larvae of *Sarcophaga* (Diptera) the cuticle thickens and the canals become straightened out by the intersusception of new cuticular material between the original layers (Fig. 280) (Dennell, 1946). Pore canals vary in diameter from about 1·0 μ in larval *Sarcophaga* to 0·15μ in the cockroach. Distally the pore canals contain filaments, probably of wax, and these continue into very fine wax canals which penetrate the cuticulin layers of the epicuticle (Fig. 287).

In mature cuticle pore canals may only occur in the outer parts, the inner parts being without them. This results from the laying down of endocuticle after the cytoplasmic processes have been withdrawn so that pore canals are no longer formed. After withdrawal of the cytoplasm the canals in the outer part become filled with cuticular material (Fig. 280B).

The pore canals are concerned with the transport of cuticular materials to the surface from the epidermal cells and to facilitate this they occur in large numbers. In larval *Sarcophaga* there are 50–70 canals associated with each epidermal cell giving a density of about 15,000 per sq. mm. In cockroach the density is about 1,200,000 per sq. mm. Locke (1964) suggests that the pore canal filaments may serve to anchor the cuticle to the epidermis.

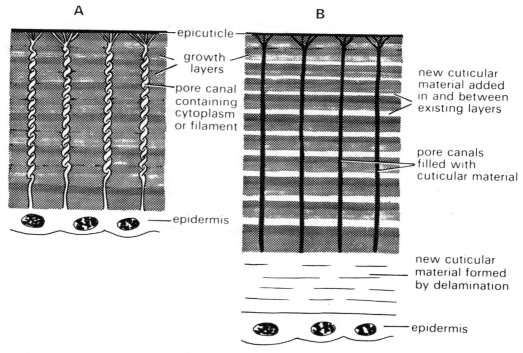

Fig. 280. A. Diagrammatic section through the integument of *Sarcophaga* larva soon after moulting. B. The integument of the mature larva.

22.22 Modifications of cuticle

In order to give flexibility to the cuticle only parts of it contain fully differentiated exocuticle. These parts are called sclerites and they are joined by regions in which the cuticle remains membranous (Fig. 281). The extent of the membrane and the method of articulation of the two adjacent sclerites determines the degree of movement which can

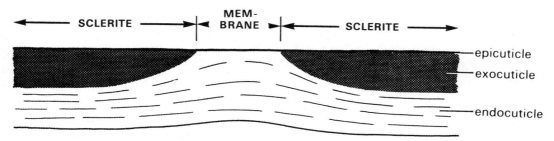

Fig. 281. Diagrammatic section through the cuticle showing a flexible membranous region between two rigid sclerites.

occur at the joint. Sometimes, as between abdominal segments, the membrane is extensive and there is no point of contact between adjacent sclerites so that movement is unrestricted (Fig. 282A). More usually the sclerites make contact with each other to form true articulations and the joints are called monocondylic or dicondylic depending on whether there are one or two points of articulation. Monocondylic articulations, such as that of the antenna with the head, permit considerable freedom of movement, whereas dicondylic articulations, which occur at many of the leg joints, give more limited, but much more precise movements. The articular surfaces may lie within the membrane,

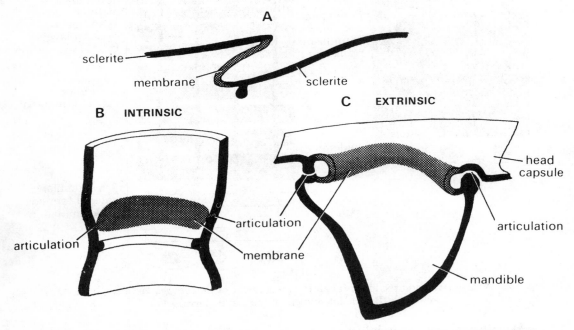

Fig. 282. Diagrams of different types of joints between sclerotised areas. A. Intersegmental. Extensive membrane with no articulation between sclerites. B. Dicondylic leg joint with intrinsic articulations. C. Dicondylic articulation of mandible with head capsule. Extrinsic articulations. Edges of sclerotised regions shown black, membrane hatched (from Snodgrass, 1935).

intrinsic, as in most leg joints (Fig. 282B), or they may lie outside it, extrinsic, as, for instance, in the mandibular articulations (Fig. 282C).

Apart from membranous areas, exocuticle is also absent along the ecdysial lines of larval hemimetabolous insects. The cuticle along these lines consists only of undifferentiated procuticle and, usually, epicuticle (Fig. 283) so that they constitute lines of weakness along which the cuticle splits at ecdysis (p. 440).

In many larval holometabolous insects the greater part of the cuticle remains undifferentiated (Dennell, 1946; Locke, 1960; Way, 1950). This facilitates growth, since undifferentiated cuticle is more extensible than sclerotised cuticle, it also enables some larvae to crawl in a manner quite unlike the adults, but well-suited to some environments (p. 154), and it is important for the conservation of materials. The bulk of the undifferentiated cuticle is digested and reabsorbed at moulting, while sclerotised parts are lost, hence an unsclerotised cuticle is more economic for a larval form which moults several times. Collembola moult continuously even when they are adult and, in keeping with this, their cuticle contains very little exocuticle. In addition, they eat their exuviae (p. 441) so that they conserve as much as possible from the cuticle.

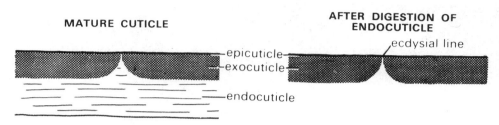

Fig. 283. Diagrammatic section of the cuticle transverse to an ecdysial line. Moulting fluid digests the endocuticle leaving the cuticle held together only by the epicuticle, producing a line of weakness.

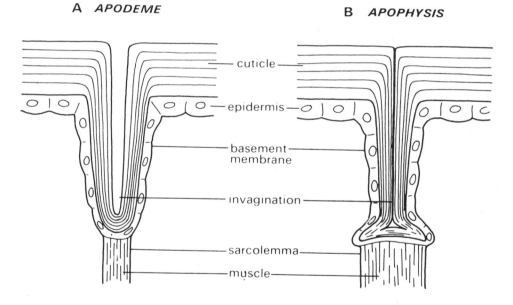

Fig. 284. Diagram of cuticular invaginations forming (A) an apodeme and (B) an apophysis (after Richards, 1951).

Invaginations and inflexions of the cuticle form the endophragmal skeleton. Hollow invaginations for muscle attachments are called apodemes, solid structures are apophyses (Fig. 284), but, in addition to muscle attachment, the endophragmal skeleton is also important in supporting and protecting various organs. In this category are the tentorium (Fig. 5) in the head and invaginations which are sometimes present covering the thoracic ganglia.

In the wing bases of Lepidoptera some apparently sclerotised parts are flexible. Here the exocuticle is more flexible than normal, but, in addition, the mesocuticle is not continuous but forms wedges which extend into the soft endocuticle so that bending is facilitated (Fig. 285) (Sharplin, 1963).

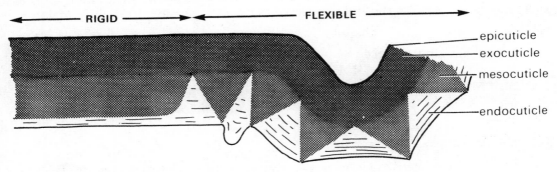

Fig. 285. Diagrammatic section of the flexible cuticle found in lepidopteran wing bases (after Sharplin, 1963).

22.23 Chemistry of chitinous cuticle

Chitin is an important constituent of arthropod cuticle, but it also commonly occurs in other animal groups. It is a polysaccharide made up largely of N-acetylglucosamine, but also probably containing some glucosamine (Rudall, 1963). The sugar residues are linked by 1–4 β linkages so that they form a chain in which all the residues are orientated in the same direction (*e.g.* in the following diagram C1 is always at the left-hand end of the sugar residue).

Acetylglucosamine   Acetylglucosamine   Glucosamine

Adjacent chitin chains are held together by hydrogen bonds to form micelles or micro-fibres, and hydrogen bonds probably also link the oxygen atoms of adjacent acetylglucosamine residues. Neighbouring chains run in opposite directions (*i.e.* with the C1 atoms at opposite ends of the molecules) and the suggested linkages are as follows:

Part of a chitin chain. It is suggested that every sixth or seventh residue is a glucosamine residue. Thick lines represent a chain of acetylglucosamine residues seen end on. Chains A, D and G run in one direction, chains B, C, E and F in the opposite direction.

Part of previous diagram seen in face view and with linkages distorted so that chains C and D are in the same plane.

Chitin constitutes 25–50% of the dry weight of the cuticle; the remainder is largely protein. Chitin is always associated with protein and in the cuticle the two are linked by covalent bonds to form a glycoprotein (Rudall, 1963).

The protein of undifferentiated cuticle is water-soluble and is called 'arthropodin', but it is not homogeneous, consisting of at least three major components with differing amino acid composition (Hackman, 1953). Sulphur-containing amino acids are absent. Part of the protein may later be tanned (p. 443), stabilised by cross-linkages between the molecules, to form a hard, inflexible and usually darkened structure. Such tanned arthropodin is called sclerotin, and this produces the hardness of the sclerites.

A cuticulin-like lipid is present throughout the refractile layers of the cuticle, in the pore canals and between the lamellae of the endocuticle (Wigglesworth, 1970, *Tissue & Cell* **2**).

22.24 Resilin

Some parts of the cuticle contain a colourless, rubber-like protein called resilin and such cuticle is called rubber-like cuticle (Andersen and Weis-Fogh, 1964). It is found in elastic hinges such as the wing-hinge ligament of *Schistocerca* (Orthoptera) which lies between the pleural process and the second axillary sclerite (Fig. 286A). The ligament is sharply differentiated from adjacent sclerotised cuticle and consists of a ventral region of tough, dense chitin and fibrous protein, and a dorsal region containing layers of resilin separated by chitinous lamellae, with a pad of pure resilin on the inside (Fig. 286B).

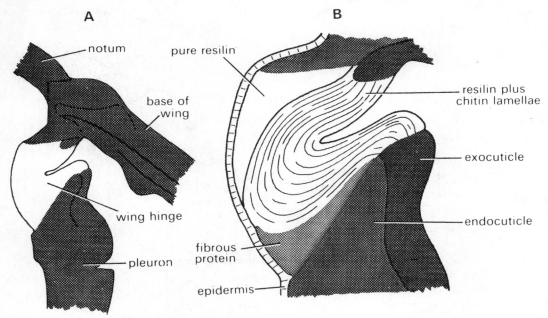

Fig. 286. A. Transverse section through the thoracic wall of *Schistocerca* showing the base of the wing and the wing hinge. B. Section through the wing hinge enlarged (modified after Anderson and Weis-Fogh, 1964).

Resilin contains various amino acids including two previously unknown ones which provide the links between the protein chains. These linkages are produced continuously as the resilin is laid down and so the process contrasts with the linking of protein in sclerotisation (p. 443) which is limited to a brief period and occurs some time after the protein is laid down (Neville, 1963). The amino acid sequence in the protein is such as to prevent other cross-links occurring, since these would impair the rubber-like properties.

Like rubber, resilin can be stretched under tension and stores the energy involved so that when the tension is released it returns immediately to its original length. In the locust between one quarter and one third of the recoil energy of the wing away from its equilibrium position is due to the elasticity of the wing-hinge ligament. Elsewhere resilin is found in the clypeo-labral spring which keeps the labrum pressed against the mandibles, while in beetles, where there are no inspiratory muscles, inspiration is produced by resilin ligaments between the terga and sterna.

22.25 Epicuticle

The detailed structure of the epicuticle varies from one insect to another. In general there is an inner cuticulin layer, then a layer of wax and frequently a layer of 'cement' over this (Fig. 287). This cuticulin layer has two components; an outer very thin, but very dense layer (called cuticulin *sensu strictu* by Locke, 1961, 1964) and a thicker dense, relatively homogeneous layer beneath.

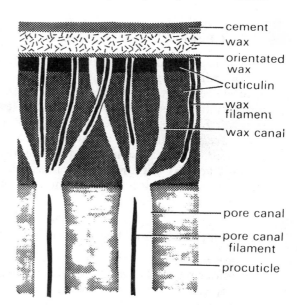

The wax of the epicuticle consists of long chain hydrocarbons and the esters of fatty acids and alcohols. It is probable that the molecules adjacent to the cuticulin are strongly orientated as a result of their polar, hydrophilic groups being adsorbed on to the surface of the cuticulin so that they form a layer only one molecule thick and hence called a monolayer. The monolayer may be in a liquid phase which is continually being moved and replaced and experiments on *Phormia* (Diptera) show that such movements can occur since an oil film can spread over the whole surface of an insect within 15 minutes. The molecules of the monolayer are very close together and inclined at an angle so that their packing is as close as possible (Fig. 336) and the spaces between

Fig. 287. Diagrammatic representation of a section through the epicuticle.

them are extremely small (Beament, 1964). This provides the waterproof layer of the cuticle since water molecules are unable to pass between the close-packed wax molecules. Due to their orientation the molecules also present a row of aliphatic groups to the outside and these are partly responsible for the hydrofuge properties of the insect cuticle.

Outside the monolayer the wax molecules are randomly orientated and may permeate the cement, while on the outside of the cement in many insects is a bloom in which the molecules are ordered and form thin plates. The pattern of blooming is characteristic, depending on the distribution of wax canals and the form of the cuticle beneath.

The cement is a very thin layer outside most of the wax, perhaps consisting of tanned protein with lipids or of a shellac-like substance. It may serve to protect the underlying wax, but where the cuticle expands, as it does in the larvae of holometabolous insects, it might be in the form of an open meshwork which provides a reservoir of lipids to replace lost surface lipids. It is absent from many adult insects which have scales.

22.3 Moulting and cuticle formation

Growth is limited by the cuticle which only undergoes a limited amount of stretching so that for any marked increase in size to occur the cuticle must be shed and replaced. Casting the cuticle is commonly known as moulting, but it involves two distinct processes which may be widely separated in time so that it is convenient to distinguish between them. The first process is the separation of the old cuticle from the underlying epidermal cells and this is called apolysis by Jenkin and Hinton (1966) although some authors use 'moulting' in a restricted sense to include only this process. The second process is the shedding of the remnants of the old cuticle, and this is known as ecdysis.

22.31 Changes in the epidermis

The onset of moulting is usually first indicated by changes in the epidermal cells which divide mitotically and so become close-packed and columnar in form. In *Rhodnius*, at least, cell destruction accompanies cell division and continues for a time after cell division stops, being dependent on the level of juvenile hormone in the blood. There is, nevertheless, a net increase in the number of cells per unit area (Fig. 288) so that when these are flattened the overall area of the epidermis, and hence of the cuticle, is increased. An increase in size does not always involve cell division and in the larvae of cyclorrhaphous Diptera growth takes place solely as a result of the cells increasing in size. In *Lucilia* (Diptera) larva the cells increase in area by a factor of 20 between the first and third instars.

22.32 Separation of the cuticle from the epidermis (Apolysis)

Perhaps as a result of the changes in cell shape, a tension is generated at the surface of the epidermal cells which results in their separating from the cuticle (Fig. 289B) (Passonneau and Williams, 1953). On the other hand in *Podura* (Collembola) the outer plasma membrane of the epidermal cells forms small out-pushings which separate off as vesicles and form a foam which lifts off the cuticle (Noble-Nesbitt, 1963c).

22.33 Digestion of the old endocuticle

As the cuticle separates from the epidermis moulting fluid is secreted into the space between the two. In *Podura* the fluid is elaborated as granules on the endoplasmic reticulum of the epidermal cells at points where this comes to penetrate the outer plasma membrane. The granules are formed in groups and these are released into the sub-cuticular space as granule bodies. Secretion continues until the cuticulin layer of the new cuticle is complete. In the pupa of *Hyalophora* (Lepidoptera) the moulting fluid at this time is in the form of a gel.

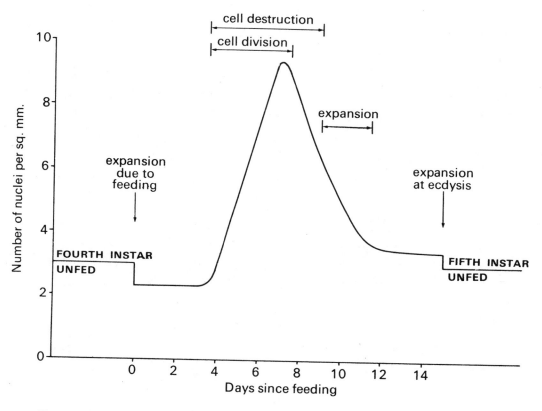

Fig. 288. The change in nuclear density (as an indication of cell density and size) in the tracheal epithelium of *Rhodnius*. Expansion and cell destruction decrease the density, cell division increases it. In this instance most expansion takes place before ecdysis (after Locke, 1964).

Moulting fluid contains enzymes, a proteinase and a chitinase, which will digest endocuticle, but when they are first secreted the enzymes are in an inactive state. The secretion of cuticulin follows the secretion of the moulting fluid, but precedes its activation (Fig. 289C). This is of great importance since otherwise the moulting fluid would digest the newly formed layers of the procuticle as well as the old endocuticle.

The substance of the cuticulin layer is probably produced in the oenocytes and then transferred to the epidermal cells which secrete it to the outside. In *Periplaneta* (Dictyoptera) a very resistant paraffin layer is secreted first (Dennell and Malek, 1955), while in *Rhodnius* polyphenols pass via the pore canals on to the outer surface of the cuticulin. These polyphenols do not form a discrete layer, but probably impregnate the cuticulin (Dennell and Malek, 1955).

At first the cuticulin layer is smooth, but then it increases in area and this produces complex surface patterns such as the taenidia in tracheae and the transverse ripples of adult *Rhodnius*. Once it is complete the epidermal cells begin to lay down the procuticle underneath it (Fig. 289D).

The mechanism by which the enzymes in the moulting fluid are activated is not known, but in *Hyalophora* it may be related to sclerotisation. They proceed to digest all the endocuticle of the old cuticle except for a thin layer which is modified in some way and

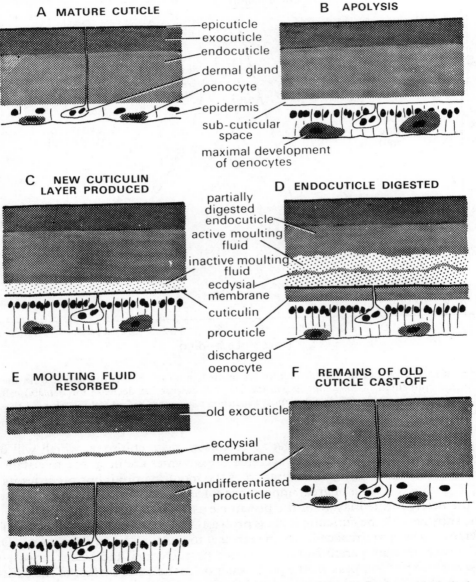

Fig. 289. Diagrammatic representation of the changes occurring in the integument during the moulting cycle.

persists as the ecdysial membrane (Fig. 289D; and see Locke, 1964), but they have no effect on the exocuticle or on the muscle and nerve connections to the old cuticle. These persist so that the insect is still able to move and receive stimuli from the environment, but these connections are finally broken at ecdysis by the muscular activity of the insect. The products of digestion of the cuticle are absorbed, it is said, through the integument, and up to 90% of the materials present in the cuticle may be conserved in this way.

As a result of the activity of the moulting fluid, lines of weakness appear in the cuticle along the ecdysial lines (Fig. 283). These vary in position, but in the locust there is a $\wedge$-shaped line on the head, the ecdysial cleavage line (p. 6), and a median dorsal line on the thorax.

22.34 Wax secretion

Shortly before ecdysis wax is secreted on to the surface of the new cuticle, and the layer adjacent to the cuticulin forms the orientated monolayer (Fig. 287). In the cockroach, at least, the orientation of the molecules in the monolayer is dependent on the water-saturated layer of cuticulin beneath. The cuticulin adsorbs the hydrophile polar groups so that the hydrofuge aliphatic groups are towards the outside. Tanned cuticulin has a very high affinity for the polar groups so that tanning is also important in the production and maintenance of the hydrofuge monolayer (Beament, 1960). Wax secretion is well advanced at ecdysis, but even so, in *Tenebrio*, the rate of water loss during the first 24 hours after ecdysis is four to six times as high as normal due to the incompleteness of wax production which continues to a greater or lesser extent through the intermoult period.

It is possible that the wax is transported to the surface as lipid-water liquid crystals. The polar groups of the wax molecules lie at the hydrocarbon/water interface and various arrangements are possible (see Locke, 1964). The wax filaments of the pore canals and wax canals may be liquid crystals and these would be pulled outwards as the surface wax, with which they are continuous, was absorbed in the meshwork of the cement or crystallised into the solid surface bloom. At the same time further molecules of polar lipids are added to the inner ends of the lipid crystals by the epidermal cells. Non-polar lipids, which form some of the surface bloom, could diffuse through the cylinders of polar lipids and even where, as in the larva of *Calpodes*, there are no pore canals the texture of the endocuticle is sufficiently coarse to allow lipids to pass from the epidermal cells to the surface (Locke, 1965a).

Soon after ecdysis a layer of cement produced by the dermal glands is formed over the surface of the wax.

22.35 Ecdysis

When the moulting fluid and the products of digestion of the moulting fluid are resorbed the old cuticle consists of little more than epicuticle and exocuticle and it is quite separate from the new cuticle (Fig. 289E). Usually ecdysis follows as soon as digestion is complete, but sometimes the old cuticle may be retained for some time and the insect enclosed in this way is referred to as a pharate instar (see Jenkin, 1966 for precise suggestions on terminology).

The old cuticle is split along the ecdysial lines as a result of the muscular activities of the insect inside. Usually the insect swallows air or water which swells the gut so that haemolymph pressure is increased. In *Schistocerca* the blood volume is highest just before ecdysis and the high blood volume also increases haemolymph pressure (Lee, 1961). Then by muscular action the blood is pumped into a particular part of the body, often the thorax, so that this expands and exerts pressure on the old cuticle causing it to split along its lines of weakness.

Special muscles may be concerned in these pumping movements. In *Rhodnius* the ventral intersegmental muscles of the abdomen develop just before a moult, are used during ecdysis to pump blood forwards by contracting the abdomen, and then degenerate, to re-develop again just before the next moult. Similarly in adult blowflies there are specialised muscles in the abdomen which persist during the period of escape from the puparium and expansion of the new cuticle and then break down (Fig. 290) (Cottrell, 1962a). The special abdominal muscles are internal to the definitive muscles and extend from the front edge of one presumptive sclerite to the front edge of the next so that, since they are not yet hardened, the sclerites are buckled when the muscles contract and the abdominal cavity is reduced in volume. Comparable muscles occur in Lepidoptera and probably in other groups.

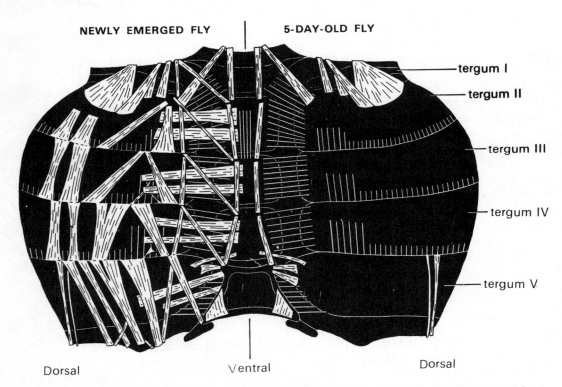

NEWLY EMERGED FLY | 5-DAY-OLD FLY

tergum I
tergum II
tergum III
tergum IV
tergum V

Dorsal   Ventral   Dorsal

Fig. 290. The abdominal musculature of a newly emerged *Sarcophaga* (left) and a 5-day-old fly (right). The abdomen has been split along the dorsal midline, laid out flat and viewed from the inside (after Cottrell, 1962a).

Cyclorrhaphous Diptera have a special structure called the ptilinum, an eversible sac at the front of the head which assists in their escape from the puparium (Fig. 291). It can be expanded in the newly emerged fly by blood forced into the head from the thorax and abdomen and then withdrawn again by muscles which force blood back to the thorax. The pressure of the ptilinum on the puparium splits off the cap of the latter and, if the puparium is buried in the soil, the ptilinum is also used by the fly to dig its way to the surface. Once the fly has hardened the ptilinum is no longer eversible and the muscles associated with it degenerate. Its position is indicated in the mature fly by the ptilinal suture.

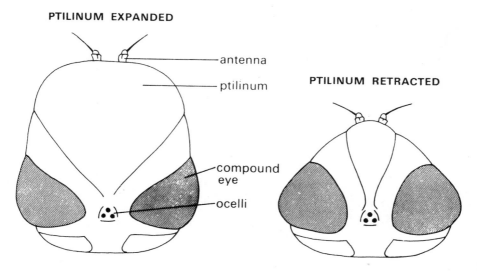

Fig. 291. Dorsal view of the head of a cyclorrhaphous fly showing the ptilinum expanded and retracted.

Having split the old cuticle the insect draws itself out, usually the head and thorax first, followed by the abdomen and appendages. Many insects suspend themselves freely from a support so that their emergence from the old cuticle is aided by the force of gravity. All the cuticular parts are shed, including the intima of fore- and hind-gut, the endophragmal skeleton and the linings of the tracheae except for some delicate parts which may break off. The old cuticle is referred to as the exuviae.

Immediately after emergence the new cuticle is still unexpanded and soft so that it provides the insect with little support. Probably the blood acts as a hydrostatic skeleton since its volume is still high and in *Calliphora* it constitutes 30% of the body weight at this time. After expansion is complete the blood volume is reduced so that it only constitutes about 10% of the body weight (see p. 683).

Some parts of the skeleton may be hard before ecdysis. Usually this pre-ecdysial hardening is restricted to the claws which are essential for the insect to hold on with, but it is more extensive in Cyclorrhapha and Ditrysia (Lepidoptera) which have to escape from a pupal cell or cocoon (see p. 419).

22.36 Expansion of the new cuticle

Having escaped from the old cuticle, the insect expands the new one before it hardens. This may again involve swallowing air or water. In the blowfly air is pumped into the gut by the pharyngeal muscles, producing a steady increase in blood pressure (Fig. 292), while at the same time simultaneous contractions of the abdominal and ptilinal muscles produce transient increases in pressure. In this way blood is forced into the wings so that they expand, but the high pressure does not expand the membranous regions between sclerites at this time because the presumptive sclerites are held tightly together by the

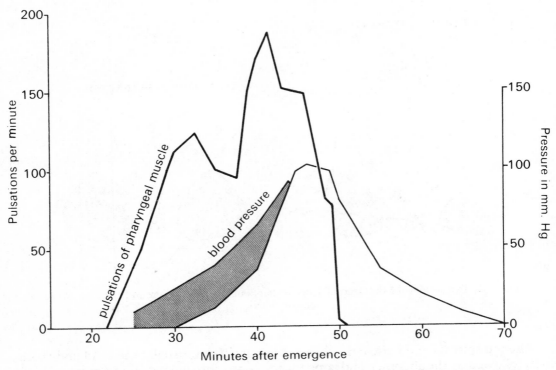

Fig. 292. The rate at which the pharyngeal muscle of an adult *Sarcophaga* pulsates while pumping air into the gut during the period of expansion after emergence. This produces an increase in blood pressure and further transient increases are produced by the simultaneous contraction of ptilinal and abdominal muscles. The hatched area indicates the range of fluctuation of blood pressure induced by these muscular efforts (after Cottrell, 1962a).

muscles. As a result the sclerites themselves are subjected to forces from inside the body and they expand by as much as 30%. This expansion is probably facilitated by a plasticization of the presumptive sclerites, perhaps due to a temporary reduction in the linking between the molecules of the cuticle before tanning begins (Cottrell, 1962b) (see also p. 31). Once tanning starts no further expansion is possible.

In Lepidoptera expansion occurs in a similar way, but the swallowing of air to increase haemolymph pressure is of less importance.

The extent of expansion after emergence depends partly on the temperature at the time. For instance, in *Aedes aegypti* (Diptera) wing length is slightly greater in insects emerging at low as compared with high temperatures after breeding under identical conditions up to the time of emergence. Possibly at low temperatures tanning takes place more slowly so that the wings have a longer period in which to expand (van den Heuvel, 1963).

22.37 Hardening the cuticle

Expansion of the new cuticle is brought to an end by the onset of tanning which involves the stabilisation of the protein in the cuticle by the formation of cross-links between the molecules. In insects these cross-links are provided by quinones:

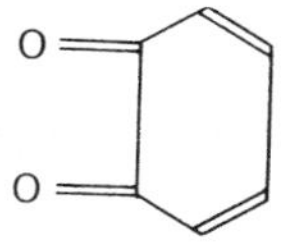

Ortho-quinone

Quinones are derived from tyrosine and just before ecdysis the concentration of tyrosine in the blood increases, falling off again when tanning occurs. The tyrosine is converted

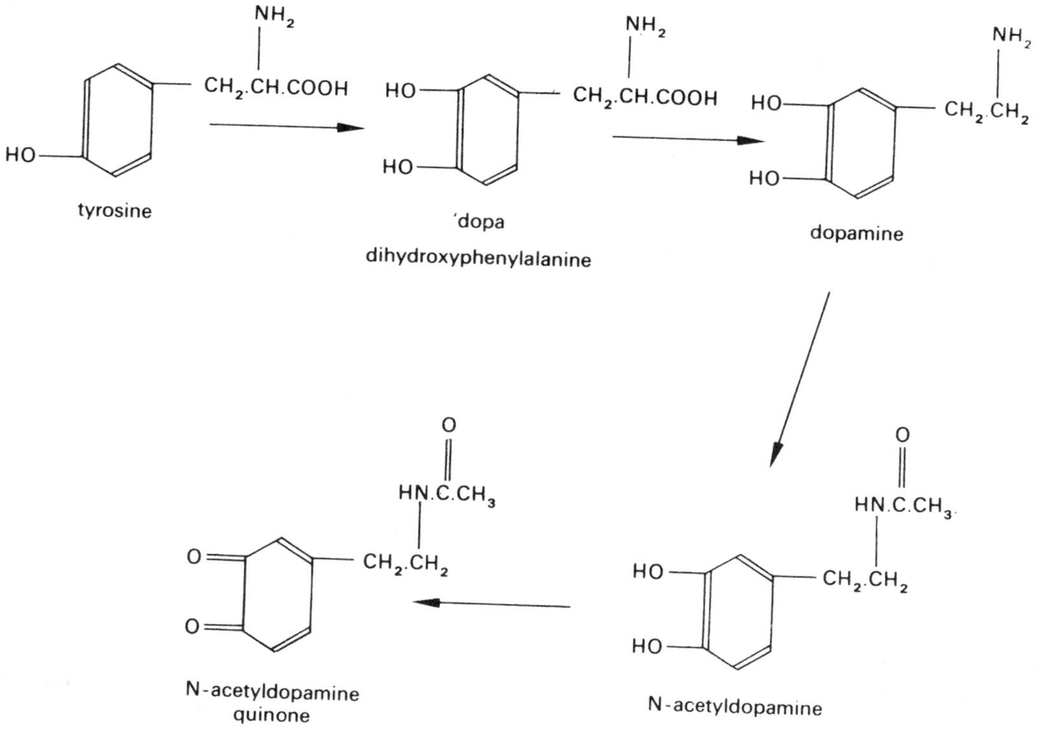
NH2
CH2.CH.COOH
HO
tyrosine
HO
NH2
CH2.CH.COOH
HO
'dopa
dihydroxyphenylalanine
HO
NH2
CH2.CH2
HO
dopamine
O
HN.C.CH3
CH2.CH2
O
O
N-acetyldopamine
quinone
O
HN.C.CH3
HO
CH2.CH2
HO
N-acetyldopamine

to DOPA (dihydroxyphenylalanine) and then to dopamine which in *Calliphora* larva is acetylated and oxidised to N-acetyldopamine quinone. This has also been detected in *Tenebrio* and *Schistocerca* (Cottrell, 1964). Earlier work on other insects suggests that deaminated derivatives of DOPA, such as protocatechuic acid, give rise to the quinones.

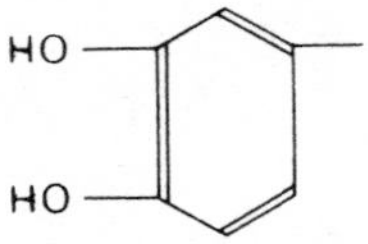

HO ——⬡—— COOH

Protocatechuic acid

HO ——⬡

It appears that a diphenol, N-acetyldopamine or perhaps protocatechuic acid, passes out through the pore canals of the newly formed cuticle and becomes concentrated in the outer parts. At the epicuticle the phenol is oxidised to a quinone by a phenol oxidase, which in *Calliphora* is specific to N-acetyldopamine. The quinone tans the protein of the cuticulin layer of the epicuticle and diffuses inwards tanning the proteins of the outer procuticle and so producing exocuticle.

In tanning, the quinone forms links with amino groups in the protein, but most of the amino groups are already involved in the peptide linkages, —CO.NH—, between adjacent amino acids forming the protein chain. Consequently, the only amino groups

Terminal amino group

NH$_2$

R

CO

NH

R'   Peptide links

Diagram of chain of 4 amino acids.
In the monobasic acids the amino
groups are involved in peptide linkages, but in lysine the ε-amino group
is not bound in this way.

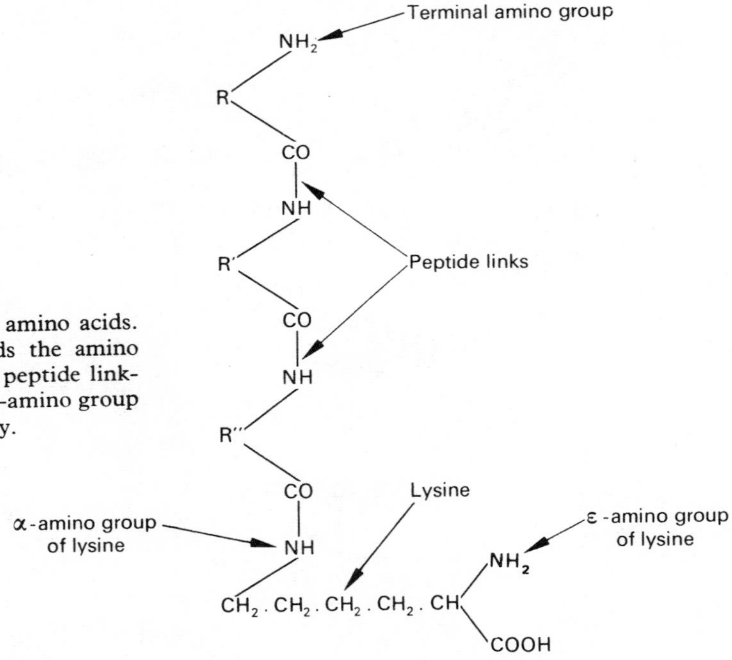

CO

NH

R''

CO   Lysine

α-amino group ——→ NH   ε-amino group
   of lysine   of lysine
                                    NH$_2$

CH$_2$. CH$_2$. CH$_2$. CH$_2$. CH

COOH

available for tanning are the terminal groups of the chains and those associated with dibasic amino acids, usually lysine. In the dibasic acid only one of the amino groups is involved in a peptide linkage, leaving the other available for tanning.

The quinone reacts first with the N-terminal amino groups of the protein to produce a catechol-type protein. In the presence of excess quinone this is oxidised to a quinonoid protein which then links on to another protein molecule.

In this way end-to-end linkages between protein molecules are produced. When all the N-terminal groups are occupied the quinones react with the ε-amino groups of lysine so that cross-linkages between the protein chains develop. In these reactions the nitrogen of the amino groups is linked directly to the quinone nucleus.

As a result of tanning the cuticle is made hard and brittle. Water-soluble arthropodin is converted to the insoluble protein sclerotin and there is also a considerable loss of water. This is associated with the alignment and closer packing of the chitin and protein micelles produced by the stretching of the new cuticle so that the cuticle as a whole becomes thinner. The close-packing of the micelles is also responsible for some of the hardening of the cuticle, quite independently of tanning (Wolfe, 1954b).

Some tanning may result from cross-linkages produced by quinones built into the proteins. These proteins contain tyrosine which might be oxidised *in situ* to form quinones and hence form direct links with adjacent protein molecules. This process is known as self-tanning, but there is as yet little evidence that it does occur.

In membranous regions and larval cuticle little or no hardening occurs so that the cuticle remains flexible.

As the cuticle hardens it usually also darkens. This darkening may simply result from sclerotin formation, probably depending on the type of bond between the protein chains, but it may also involve the polymerisation of excess quinones to form melanin (p. 112).

22.38 Post-ecdysial cuticle deposition

After moulting and tanning are complete the laying down of new endocuticle continues. This involves the production of new layers adjacent to the epidermis, but also, in *Sarcophaga* larva at least, the intersusception of material between the existing layers (Fig. 280) (Dennell, 1946). This process may continue for some time and in *Schistocerca* fresh cuticle is laid down continuously for the first three weeks of adult life. During this

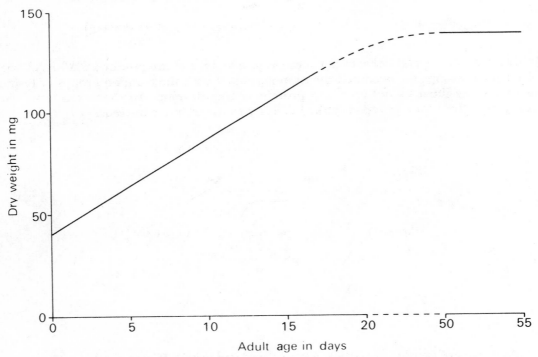

Fig. 293. Increase in the dry weight of the cuticle of adult *Schistocerca* after emergence (modified after Weis-Fogh, 1952).

time the dry weight of the cuticle more than doubles (Fig. 293), but after this the cuticle does not grow any more.

Wax secretion also continues in the intermoult period.

22.39 Control of moulting and associated processes

Moulting and cuticle formation are complex phenomena involving a number of discrete processes. Apart from wax formation and endocuticle production which may continue for some time there is a fairly distinct sequence of events:—

1. changes in the epidermal cells
2. secretion of the moulting fluid
3. secretion of the outer layer of cuticulin
4. secretion of the homogeneous layer of cuticulin
5. activation of the moulting fluid
6. absorption of digested remains of old cuticle
7. start of secretion of new procuticle
8. ecdysis and expansion of the new cuticle
9. sclerotisation
10. start of wax secretion

The hormone ecdyson plays a vital role in controlling these events (see p. 701), but evidence is accumulating which indicates that it does not simply trigger the epidermal cells so that the sequence follows automatically. Some of the processes are known to be controlled by other hormones or nervous stimuli, perhaps acting together with ecdyson, while the juvenile hormone exerts an overall modifying effect.

For instance, the period during which the cuticle of *Calliphora* is sufficiently plastic to be expanded is short and is restricted to the period during which the insect is swallowing air. This suggests that cuticular plasticity may be under nervous control. In *Rhodnius* the swelling of the abdomen at the time of feeding is controlled by neurosecretory axons to the abdominal wall (Maddrell, 1966a).

Sclerotisation is controlled by a hormone, called bursicon, which in *Sarcophaga* is released from the brain and the large compound thoracic ganglion, and it appears to be quite separate from other hormones produced in the brain. It is only produced at the time of moulting and its release is initiated by receptors in the cuticle operating when the fly is no longer confined to the medium in which it emerges. If the fly is forced to keep digging through soil after it has emerged from the puparium the release of this factor is delayed (Cottrell, 1964; Fraenkel and Hsiao, 1965). Bursicon is probably not involved in quinone formation, which may be controlled by ecdyson itself, but it may be concerned with some later step in tanning (Mills and Nielsen, 1967).

The secretion of wax by *Calpodes* larvae is controlled by a hormone released from the corpus allatum-corpus cardiacum complex, but produced elsewhere. This hormone, however, is only effective when together with ecdyson; endocuticle production is probably similarly controlled by ecdyson with another hormone (Locke, 1965b).

The factors which govern ecdyson secretion are considered in Chapter XXXIV.

22.4 Functions of the cuticle

The cuticle is one of the features of insects which is primarily responsible for their success. It plays an important part in supporting the insect, an essential requirement of terrestrial animals. Further, the presence of hard, jointed appendages makes accurate movements possible with a minimum of muscle, thus effecting an economy of muscle, and, by lifting the body off the ground, facilitates rapid movement. Flight depends on the possession of rigid wings and in insects the cuticle provides the rigidity. In the absence of the cuticle flight would not be possible.

Protection is also provided by the cuticle. Some insects, such as adult beetles, have hardened heavily sclerotised cuticles which make them difficult for predators to catch or parasites to parasitise. Protection from the physical environment is also afforded. Again in beetles, the upper cuticle of the abdomen, protected by the elytra, is very thin, but the cuticle of the ventral surface, exposed and subject to abrasion by the substratum, is very thick. The cuticular lining of the fore- and hind-guts also protects the epithelium from abrasion by the food while the wax layer is of great importance in the restriction of water loss (p. 500).

Finally, parts of the cuticle are modified to form sense organs (p.598) and its physical structure is also often important in the production of colour (p.110).

CHAPTER XXIII

THE TRACHEAL SYSTEM AND RESPIRATION IN TERRESTRIAL INSECTS

Gaseous exchange in insects is carried on through a system of internal tubes, the tracheae, the finer branches of which extend to all parts of the body and may become functionally intracellular in muscle fibres. Thus oxygen is carried directly to its sites of utilisation and the blood is not concerned with gas transport. The tracheae open to' the outside through segmental pores, the spiracles, which generally have some closing mechanism which permits water loss from the respiratory surfaces to be kept to a minimum. The spiracles open in response to a low concentration of oxygen or a high concentration of carbon dioxide in the tissues.

Diffusion alone can account for the gaseous requirements of the tissues of most insects at rest, but in larger insects or during activity demands on oxygen are greater. To meet these demands the insect pumps air in and out of the tracheal system by expanding and collapsing air-sacs which are enlarged parts of the tracheae whose volume can be changed by movements of the body. These movements are controlled by endogenous rhythms within the central nervous system.

In some insects which have low oxygen requirements the spiracles may open in such a way as to permit the entry of oxygen, but they prevent the exit of water and carbon dioxide except in occasional bursts. This is regarded as a water conserving mechanism. In some insects living in moist environments where water loss is not a problem gaseous exchange may take place through the permeable cuticle.

Insect respiration is reviewed by Buck (1962), Keister and Buck (1964) and Miller (1964, 1966a).

23.1 The tracheal system

23.11 Tracheae

The tracheae are the larger tubes of the tracheal system, running inwards from the spiracles and usually breaking up into finer branches the smallest of which are about 2 μ in diameter. Tracheae are formed by invaginations of the ectoderm and so are lined by a cuticular intima which is continuous with the rest of the cuticle (Fig. 294). A spiral thickening of the intima runs along each tube, each ring of the spiral being called a taenidium. The taenidia prevent the collapse of the trachea if the pressure within is reduced. The intima consists of a layer of cuticulin, probably with wax on the surface lining the lumen (Beament, 1964), and a protein/chitin layer on the outside. The micelles

449

in this layer are strongly orientated, those in the taenidia running round the trachea
and preventing its collapse, while between the taenidia they are parallel with the long
axis of the trachea and may serve to prevent over extension of the tube (Locke, 1964).

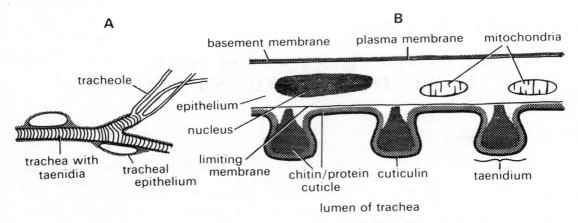

Fig. 294. A. Small part of the tracheal system showing tracheae, with taenidial thickenings,
and tracheoles (from Wigglesworth, 1954a). B. Longitudinal section of tracheal wall; body
cavity above, lumen of trachea below.

23.12 Air-sacs

In places the tracheae are expanded to form thin-walled air-sacs (Fig. 300) in which
the taenidia are absent or poorly developed and often irregularly arranged. Consequently, the air-sacs will collapse under pressure and they play a very important part
in ventilation of the tracheal system (p. 464) as well as having other functions (p. 470).
Air-sacs are widely distributed along the main tracheal trunks of many insects.

23.13 Tracheoles

At various points along their length, and especially distally, the tracheae give rise to
finer tubes, the tracheoles. There is no sharp distinction between tracheae and
tracheoles, but the latter are always intracellular and retain their cuticular lining at
moulting, which is not usually true of tracheae. Proximally the tracheoles are about $1\,\mu$
in diameter, tapering to about $0.1\,\mu$. They are formed in cells called tracheoblasts which
are derived from the epidermal cells lining the tracheae (Fig. 295). The intima of
tracheoles is some 16–20 mμ thick and is thrown into taenidial ridges, but, unlike the
taenidia of tracheae, these ridges are not filled with chitin/protein matrix (Edwards,
et al., 1958). The intima stands on a membrane, which may be a deep in-tucking of the
plasma membrane, and outside this are the cytoplasm and plasma membrane of the
tracheoblast.

The tracheoles are very intimately associated with the tissues and in fibrillar muscle,
for instance, they may indent the muscle plasma membrane and penetrate deep into the
fibre (Fig. 296), but it is probable that they never become truly intracellular. Distally
the tracheoles end blindly or they may anastomose.

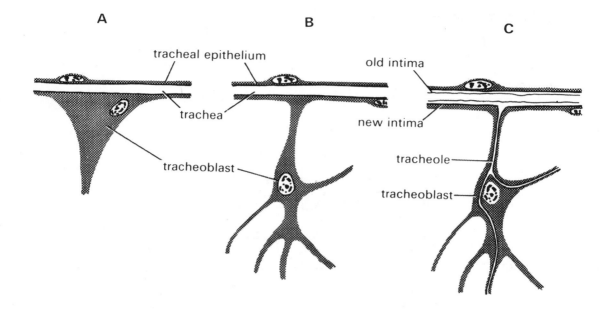

Fig. 295. The development of a tracheole. A. Tracheoblast developing from tracheal epithelial cell. B. Tracheoblast with extensive cytoplasmic processes. C. Tracheole develops within tracheoblast and connects with the trachea at the moult (after Keister, 1948).

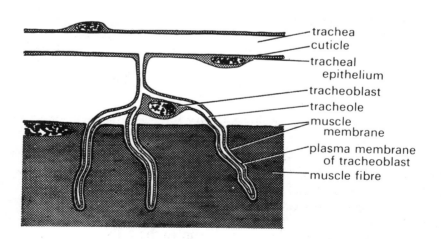

Fig. 296. Diagrammatic representation of tracheoles indenting the membrane of a muscle fibre to become functionally intracellular within the fibre.

23.14 Distribution of the tracheal system

The tracheal system arises externally at the spiracles and in many Apterygota, other than Lepismatidae, the tracheae from each spiracle form a series of unconnected tufts. In the majority of insects, however, the tracheae from neighbouring spiracles anastomose to form longitudinal trunks running the length of the body (Fig. 297). Usually

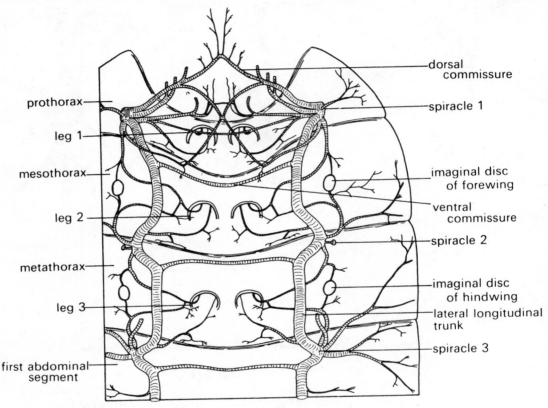

Fig. 297. Tracheation of the thorax and first abdominal segment of a caterpillar, dorsal view
(from Snodgrass, 1935).

there is a lateral trunk on either side of the body and these are often the largest tracheae, while, in addition, dorsal and ventral longitudinal trunks may also be present (Fig. 298). The longitudinal tracheae are connected to those of the other side of the body by transverse commissures, while smaller branches extend to the various tissues and in turn give rise to the tracheoles which run to the cells.

The arrangement of the tracheal system varies between different insects, but in general the heart and dorsal muscles are supplied by branches from the dorsal trunks, the alimentary canal, gonads, legs and wings from the lateral trunks and the central nervous system from the ventral trunks or transverse commissures. The head is supplied with air from spiracle 1 through two main tracheal branches on each side, a dorsal branch to the antennae, eyes and brain and a ventral branch to the mouthparts and their muscles. In *Schistocerca*, at least, the tracheal system of the head is largely isolated from that in the rest of the body by the small bore of some interconnecting tubes and the occlusion of

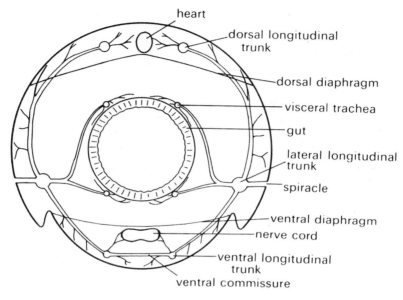

Fig. 298. Diagrammatic cross-section of the abdomen of an orthopteran showing the principal tracheae and tracheal trunks (from Snodgrass, 1935).

others (Fig. 299). This ensures a good and direct supply of air to the brain and major sense organs and since the exhalent trunk from the head supplies the thoracic ganglia these also have a good air supply (Miller, 1960c).

The tracheal system of the pterothorax (p. 128) in *Schistocerca* is similarly isolated (Fig. 300), while, in addition, the two sides are isolated from each other. This ensures a good supply of oxygen to the muscles during flight, but it also prevents the carbon dioxide produced by the muscular activity from being generally distributed throughout the body, and other tissues from being starved of oxygen by the excessive demands of the muscles.

The tracheal supply to the flight muscles follows a similar pattern in all larger insects. Each muscle has a primary supply consisting of a large tracheal trunk or air-sac running alongside or through the muscle. If a trachea forms the primary supply it widens to an air-sac beyond the muscle (Fig. 301). From the primary supply, small, regularly spaced tracheae arise at right angles, running into the muscle. These form the secondary supply and they are often oval proximally, permitting some degree of collapse, and taper regularly to the distal end. Finer branches pass in turn from these tracheae into the muscles (Weis-Fogh, 1964a). In Odonata the terminal tracheolar branches run alongside and between the muscle fibres, but in close-packed and fibrillar flight muscle they indent the fibre membrane and are functionally internal (Fig. 296).

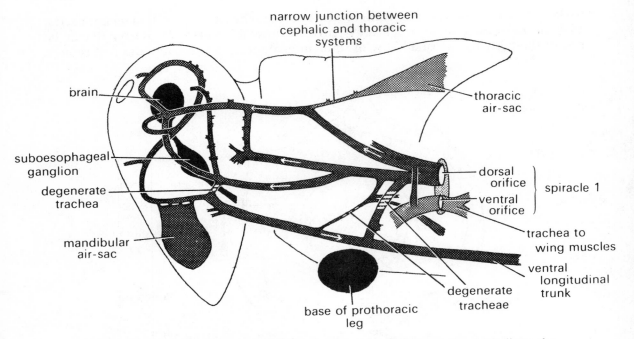

Fig. 299. Diagram of the main tracheae to the head of *Schistocerca*. Arrows indicate the probable direction of air-flow resulting from abdominal ventilation (after Miller, 1960c).

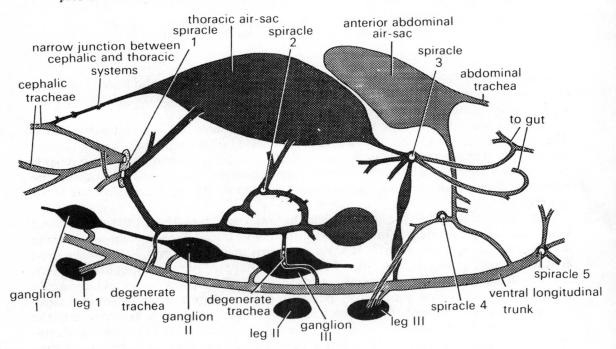

Fig. 300. Diagram of the pterothoracic tracheal system of *Schistocerca* (after Miller, 1960c).

To some extent the distribution and abundance of tracheae reflect the demands for oxygen by different tissues. Small changes may occur within an instar. For instance, in the event of damage to the epidermis the epidermal cells produce cytoplasmic threads

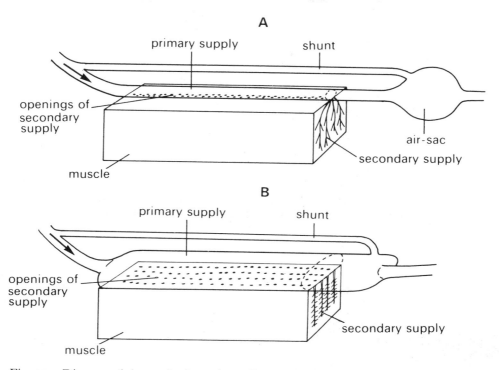

Fig. 301. Diagram of the tracheal supply to flight muscles in which the primary supply is (A) a trachea, or (B) an air-sac. Arrows indicate the inward flow of air (modified after Weis-Fogh, 1964).

which extend towards and ultimately attach themselves to the nearest tracheole. These cytoplasmic threads, which may be 150 μ long, are contractile and drag the tracheole to the region of the oxygen deficient tissue (Fig. 302). The normal distribution of tracheoles in the epidermis might arise in a similar way (Wigglesworth, 1959c).

Major changes in tracheation occur at the moult. For instance, the relative volume of tracheae in the ovaries of *Schistocerca* increases 18 times at the penultimate moult and a further 16 times at the final moult. Between moults the relative volume decreases because the ovary continues to grow, and similar changes occur in the testes and male accessory glands (D. S. Anderson, 1966). Thus as the tissue grows within an instar it becomes relatively less well supplied with oxygen and possibly shortage of oxygen stimulates mitosis in the tracheal cells so that at the moult new tracheae are formed. New tracheae arise as outgrowths, mainly terminal, of columns of cells from the existing tracheal epithelium (Fig. 303). They develop a lumen which subsequently becomes lined with cuticle and becomes connected to the existing system at the next moult (Wigglesworth, 1954a).

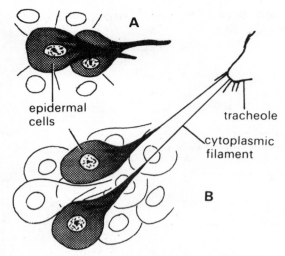

Fig. 302. A. Two epidermal cells sending out processes in the direction of a tracheole. B. Cytoplasmic filaments from epidermal cells attached to a tracheole and drawing it towards the cells (after Wigglesworth, 1959c).

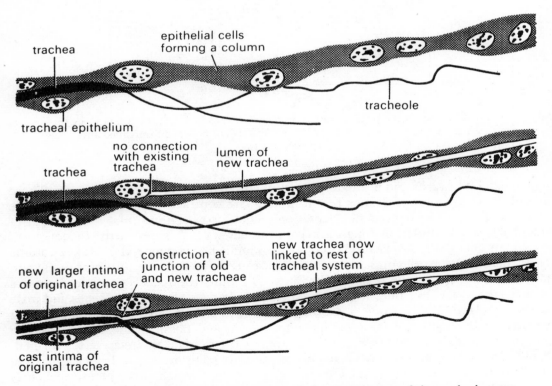

Fig. 303. Diagrams illustrating the development of a new element of the tracheal system (derived from Wigglesworth, 1954a).

At least partly related to altered oxygen demands, the tracheal system varies with the state of development and becomes more complex at each moult. This may involve changes in the functional spiracles as well as in tracheation. For instance, the first instar larva of *Sciara* (Diptera) is metapneustic, the second instar is propneustic and the fourth instar hemipneustic (see below). Each new system is built round that of the preceding instar, but on a larger scale and with new extensions (Fig. 303) (Keister, 1948).

23.2 Spiracles

The spiracles are the external openings of the tracheal system. They are lateral in position, usually on the pleura, and, except in *Japyx* (Diplura) with two pairs on the metathorax, there is never more than one pair of spiracles on a segment. Often each spiracle is contained in a small, distinct sclerite, the peritreme.

23.21 Number and distribution

With the exception of some Diplura, the largest number of spiracles found in insects is ten pairs, two thoracic and eight abdominal, and the respiratory system may be classified on the basis of the number and distribution of the functional spiracles (Keilin, 1944).

Polypneustic—at least 8 functional spiracles on each side
　　Holopneustic—10 spiracles; 1 mesothoracic, 1 metathoracic, 8 abdominal—as in bibionid larvae
　　Peripneustic—9 spiracles; 1 mesothoracic, 8 abdominal—as in cecidomyid larvae
　　Hemipneustic—8 spiracles; 1 mesothoracic, 7 abdominal—as in mycetophilid larvae
Oligopneustic—1 or 2 functional spiracles on each side
　　Amphipneustic—2 spiracles; 1 mesothoracic, 1 post-abdominal—as in psychodid larvae
　　Metapneustic—1 spiracle; 1 post-abdominal—as in culicid larvae
　　Propneustic—1 spiracle; 1 mesothoracic—as in dipterous pupae
Apneustic—no functional spiracles—as in chironomid larvae.
Apneustic does not imply that the insect has no tracheal system, but that the tracheae do not open to the outside. In numerous insects the first spiracle is on the prothorax, but is mesothoracic in origin (Hinton, 1966a). Where less than ten functional spiracles are present the others, nevertheless, persist. These 'non-functional' spiracles are open at the time of ecdysis and permit the cast intima to be shed (p. 461).

Some Diplura, such as *Japyx*, have 11 pairs of spiracles, including four pairs on the thorax, while the sminthurids (Collembola) have only a single pair of spiracles between the head and prothorax and from these tracheae extend, without anastomoses, to all parts of the body.

23.22 Structure

In its simplest form, found in some Apterygota, the spiracle is a direct opening from the outside into a trachea, but generally the visible opening leads into a cavity, the atrium, from which the tracheae arise. In this case the opening and the atrium are known collectively as the spiracle. Often the walls of the atrium are lined with hairs which filter out dust (Fig. 304). In some Diptera, Coleoptera and Lepidoptera the spiracle is covered by a sieve plate in which there are large numbers of small pores, which in the

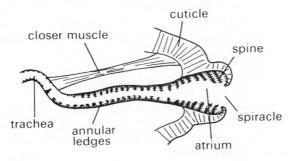

Fig. 304. Longitudinal section of the spiracle of a louse, *Haemotopinus,* showing the dust-catching spines and ledges (after Webb, 1948).

fifth instar larva of *Bombyx* (Lepidoptera) measure $6\,\mu \times 3\,\mu$. These sieve plates also serve to prevent the entry of dust or, especially in aquatic insects, water into the tracheal system.

The spiracles of most terrestrial insects have a closing mechanism which is important in the control of water loss (see Fig. 337). The closing mechanism may consist of one or two movable valves in the spiracular opening itself or it may be internal, closing off the atrium from the trachea by means of a constriction.

Spiracle 2 in grasshoppers is in the membrane between the meso- and meta-thorax. It is closed by two movable semi-circular valves which are unsclerotised except at the hinge and are thickened basally to form a pad into which a muscle is inserted (Fig. 305).

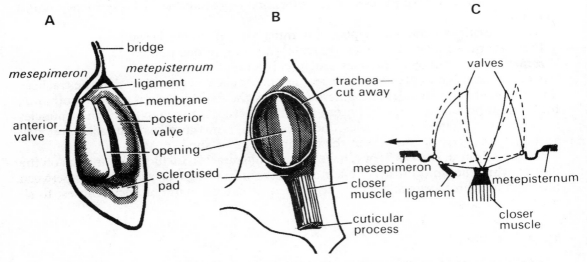

Fig. 305. The second thoracic spiracle of a locust. A. External view. B. Internal view. C. Diagrammatic transverse section showing how movement (indicated by arrow) of the mesepimeron causes the valves to open wide (after Miller, 1960b).

This muscle, by pulling down on the valves, causes them to rotate and so to close. The spiracle normally opens by virtue of the elasticity of the surrounding cuticle, but in flight it opens wider as a result of the slight separation of the mesepimeron and metepisternum. These two sclerites which surround the spiracle are normally held together by an elastic bridge, but when the basalar and subalar muscles contract the sclerites are pulled apart. This movement is transmitted to the spiracle largely through the ligament connecting the metepisternum to the anterior valve and the effect is to make the spiracle open wide (Fig. 305) (Miller, 1960b).

This 'one muscle' type of spiracle is usually present on the thorax, but in Orthoptera spiracle 1 has both opener and closer muscles. This spiracle is on the membrane between the pro- and meso-thorax, and consists of a fixed anterior valve and a movable posterior valve. It is unusual in having two orifices which lead directly from the external opening. A sclerotised rod runs along the free edge of the posterior valve, passing between the orifices and running round the ventral one (Fig. 306). The closer muscle arises on a

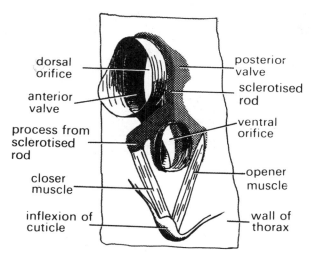

Fig. 306. The first thoracic spiracle of a locust, internal view (modified after Snodgrass, 1935; and Miller, 1960b).

cuticular inflexion beneath the spiracle and is inserted into a process of the sclerotised rod, while the opener muscle, also from the cuticular inflexion, is inserted on to the posterior margin of the posterior valve. When the insect is at rest and the closer muscle relaxes the spiracle opens some 20–30% of its maximum as a result of the elasticity of the cuticle; the opener muscle plays no part. Contraction of the opener muscle occurs with slow, deep ventilatory movements and this results in the spiracle opening fully (Miller, 1960b).

Closure of abdominal spiracles usually involves a constriction method. Commonly the atrium is pinched between two sclerotised rods, or in the bend of one rod, as the result of the contraction of a muscle. Opening may involve a muscle (Fig. 307A), an elastic ligament (Fig. 307B) or the elasticity of the cuticle (Fig. 307C). In other instances the atrium or trachea is bent so that the lumen is occluded.

23.23 Control of spiracle opening

The spiracles are normally open for the shortest time necessary for efficient respiration in order to keep water loss from the tracheal system to a minimum. Spiracle closure results from the sustained contraction of the closer muscle, while opening commonly results from the elasticity of the surrounding cuticle when the closer muscle is relaxed. The muscle is controlled by the central nervous system, but may also respond to local chemical stimuli which interact with the central control (Fig. 312).

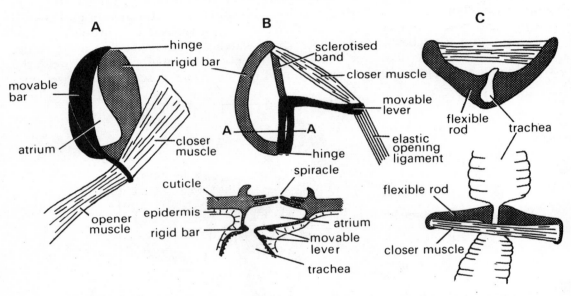

Fig. 307. Closing mechanisms internal to the spiracles. A. Abdominal spiracle of *Dissosteira* (Orthoptera) (from Snodgrass, 1935). B. Spiracle of lepidopterous larva; inner view above, horizontal section through AA below (from Imms, 1957). C. Constricting mechanism of trachea of flea; transverse section through the mechanism above, dorsal view below (after Wigglesworth, 1965).

The motor nerves to the spiracle muscles in each segment arise in the ganglion of the same segment or that immediately in front. The axons pass along the median nerve and then bifurcate, sending a branch to either side, so that the two spiracles receive the same pattern of motor impulses. In many insects a sensory nerve passes from each spiracle to the ganglion of the following segment.

The closer muscle is caused to contract by a stream of impulses from the central nervous system, but the frequency of the impulses, which determines the degree of contraction, may be altered by various factors acting on the central nervous system. Of particular importance are a high level of carbon dioxide and a low level of oxygen (hypoxia) in the tissues and both these conditions will arise while the spiracles are closed, due to the production of carbon dioxide and the utilisation of oxygen in respiration. Both conditions lead to a reduction in impulse frequency and so to spiracle opening, probably by stimulating an interneuron which inhibits the spiracle motor neuron. In 'two muscle' spiracles the impulse frequency to the opener muscle is increased by high carbon dioxide levels and hypoxia.

The frequency of motor impulses to the opener muscle is also affected by the water balance of the insect, possibly acting through the concentration of a particular ion. If the insect is desiccated the impulse frequency rises and the spiracles remain closed for longer; with excess hydration the converse is true so that the rate of water loss is increased.

Carbon dioxide also acts directly on the closer muscle of 'one muscle' spiracles, interfering with neuromuscular transmission so that the junction potential falls, muscle tension is reduced and the spiracle opens (Hoyle, 1960). The carbon dioxide has some other, internal, effect on the muscle, not concerned with neuromuscular transmission, and this also results in a reduction in tension.

The threshold of the peripheral response to carbon dioxide is set by the frequency of motor impulses from the central nervous system. The lower the impulse frequency, the lower is the threshold to carbon dioxide. In the adult dragonfly the impulse frequency is reduced by hypoxia and high carbon dioxide concentrations, and completely inhibited by flight so that under these conditions the spiracles tend to open more frequently. Desiccation and high temperature increase the impulse frequency, so that the peripheral threshold to carbon dioxide is raised and the spiracles open less frequently.

'Two muscle' spiracles do not respond to peripheral stimulation and are controlled entirely by the output from the central nervous system (Miller, 1960b).

Spiracle 2 of *Schistocerca* acts independently of the nervous system in its response to potassium. Concentrations of potassium above 30 mM/litre cause the closer muscle to contract even when it is isolated from the nervous system (Hoyle, 1961). Normally the concentration in the blood is not as high as this, but it may be exceeded as a result of desiccation and also at the moult. Consequently at these times the spiracles remain closed for most of the time, opening only when the concentration of carbon dioxide is high, and thus water loss is restricted. Such sustained muscular contraction due to high concentrations of potassium does not occur in other muscles.

23.3 Moulting the tracheal system

The cuticular lining of the tracheae is cast at each moult, and a new, larger intima is formed in its place. The longitudinal trunks break at predetermined points, the nodes, between adjacent spiracles and the old lining is drawn out through the spiracles and shed with the rest of the exuviae. In early *Sciara* larvae, with a relatively simple tracheal system, the whole of the cuticular lining is shed, but in older larvae with a more complex system the linings of the finest branches are persistent (Keister, 1948). In *Rhodnius* the linings of the tracheoles are never shed (Wigglesworth, 1954a). Instead, when a new tracheal lining is formed it pinches in on the old lining at the origin of the tracheoles. At the point of constriction the old cuticle breaks and the new tracheal intima becomes continuous with the original tracheole lining, but a marked discontinuity is apparent (Fig. 308).

Where the number of functional spiracles is reduced, the 'non-functional' spiracles persist and facilitate the shedding of the tracheal intima so that even in apneustic insects this can occur. The 'non-functional' spiracles may be visible as faint scars on the cuticle and from each scar a strand of cuticle connects with the longitudinal trachea. At each moult new cuticle is laid down round this thread in the form of a tube opening to the outside and through this the old intima is withdrawn. Subsequently the tube closes and forms the cuticular thread connecting the new intima with the outer cuticle. Similar ecdysial tubes are formed next to functional spiracles when the structure of the spiracles is so complex that it does not permit the old intima to be drawn through it. This occurs, for instance, in Elateridae, Scarabaeidae and some Diptera (Hinton, 1947).

The new cuticle lining the tracheae is smooth at first and only slightly larger than the layer which it is replacing. Subsequently it increases in diameter and becomes thrown into folds within which more cuticular material is deposited to form the taenidia.

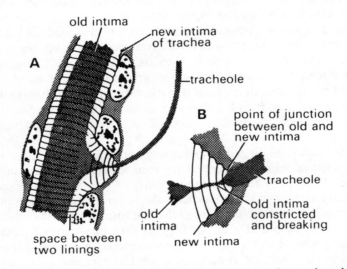

Fig. 308. A. Showing the development of a new tracheal intima at the moult and its junction with the original lining of a tracheole. B. The junction of trachea and tracheole enlarged (after Wigglesworth, 1954a).

23.31 Pneumatisation

Immediately following ecdysis, and in the embryonic insect, the tracheal system is liquid-filled. Subsequently the liquid is replaced by gas, a process known as pneumatisation, but this gas does not enter via the spiracles. It usually first appears in a main tracheal trunk and then spreads rapidly through the system so that this becomes completely gas-filled in 10–30 minutes. The gas is probably forced out of solution in the liquid by physical forces resulting from the active resorption of liquid from the trachea together with the change in the surface properties from hydrophile to hydrofuge which occurs when the cuticle is tanned (p. 439). These forces lead to the rupture of the liquid column and the appearance of gas in its place.

In most insects, but not in *Sciara*, some liquid normally remains in the endings of the tracheoles. During periods of high energy consumption the liquid is withdrawn from the system and air is drawn further into the tracheoles. At other times the liquid is secreted again and the air retreats. The level of liquid in the tracheoles represents the balance between the forces of capillarity and forces resulting mainly from imbibition by colloidal substances in the tracheoblast cytoplasm. These, in turn, are influenced by changes in the osmotic pressure of the tissues and so are related to metabolism. Similar forces may be responsible for the initial withdrawal of liquid from the tracheae after moulting (Buck and Keister, 1955).

23.4 Gaseous exchange

From the spiracles oxygen passes through the tracheal system to the tissues and ulti-mately must reach the mitochondria in order to play a part in oxidative processes. Carbon dioxide follows the reverse path. There are thus two distinct phases in the transport of gases, one through the tracheal system, known as air-tube diffusion, and one through the tissues in solution in the cytoplasm, known as tissue diffusion (Weis-Fogh, 1964b).

23.41 Diffusion

The rate of diffusion of a gas depends on a number of factors. It is inversely proportional to the square root of the molecular weight of the gas so that in air, oxygen, with a molecular weight of 16, diffuses 1·2 times faster than carbon dioxide, molecular weight 28. Diffusion also depends on the differences in concentration of the gas at the two ends of the system and in the absence of a difference in concentration there is no net movement of gas. The change in concentration, or partial pressure (p), with distance (x), that is the concentration gradient, is expressed as $\dfrac{\delta p}{\delta x}$. Finally the permeability of the substrate, in this case air or the tissues, through which the gas is diffusing affects the rate of diffusion. This factor is expressed in terms of the permeability constant, P, which is the flow of a substance through unit area per unit time when the concentration gradient is unity.

Hence the volume (J) of a given gas transported by diffusion at NTP can be represented by the equation

$$J = -P\frac{\delta p}{\delta x} \quad \text{(Weis-Fogh, 1964b)}.$$

The permeability constant for different substrates varies widely. That for oxygen in air at 20°C. is 11 ml./min./cm.²/atm./cm. whereas in water $P = 3\cdot4 \times 10^{-5}$ and in frog muscle $1\cdot4 \times 10^{-5}$ ml./min./cm.²/atm./cm. Hence oxygen in air diffuses more than 100,000 times faster than in water or the tissues so that although, in the insect, the path of oxygen through the tracheal system is very much longer than its path through the tissues, perhaps 10,000 times as long, it will take over 10 times as long for the gas to diffuse from the tracheole endings to the mitochondria, than from the spiracles to the tracheole endings.

Thus the length of the tissue diffusion path is likely to be a factor limiting the size of tissues and, in particular, of flight muscles with a high requirement for oxygen. With a partial pressure difference between the tracheole and the mitochondrion of 5% of an atmosphere a tracheole 1 μ in diameter would serve a muscle 7–15 μ in diameter if the oxygen uptake of the muscle was 1·5–3·0 ml./g./min., a level of uptake achieved in flight muscle (p. 225). Hence a muscle fibre in which the tracheoles are restricted to the outside of the fibres cannot exceed about 20 μ in diameter. The fibres of the flight muscles of dragonflies are of this type and are approaching their theoretical maximum size. On the other hand, if the tracheoles indent the muscle so as to become functionally internal, as they do in fibrillar muscle (p. 213), the muscle fibres can become much larger. In *Musca* (Diptera), for instance, the indenting tracheoles are only separated by distances of 3–5 μ so that, although individual fibres may be over one millimetre in diameter, they are well within the size limits imposed by tissue diffusion (Weis-Fogh, 1964b).

The inward diffusion of oxygen from the spiracles depends on the partial pressure within the tracheoles being lower than in the outside air and this will arise from the passage of oxygen into the tissues when it is utilised. A drop of 2% of an atmosphere is sufficient to ensure that enough oxygen diffuses to the tissues and a 5% drop ensures an adequate supply even to the extremities of the limbs. Such a difference also provides sufficient oxygen, by diffusion alone, for the flight muscles of small insects such as *Drosophila* (Diptera), but in larger insects diffusion by itself cannot meet the demands of highly active tissues.

Because of its greater solubility, the permeability constant of carbon dioxide in the tissues is 36 times greater than that for oxygen so that, despite its higher molecular weight, carbon dioxide travels more quickly than oxygen through the tissues for the same difference in partial pressure. Hence a system capable of bringing an adequate supply of oxygen to the tissues will also suffice to take the carbon dioxide away.

Carbon dioxide is more soluble and is present in higher concentrations in the tissues than oxygen. Thus some carbon dioxide, instead of passing directly into the tracheal system, might diffuse outwards through the tissues and enter the tracheae near the spiracles or pass out directly through the integument (p. 470). Such a shunt system is, however, unlikely to be of great importance if an adequate tracheal system exists because diffusion is so much more rapid in the gas phase. Carbonic anhydrase is present in insect tissues, but its role is not clear.

The exchange of gases between the tracheal system and the tissues is partly limited by the walls of the tracheae and tracheoles. The whole system may be permeable, with no marked difference between tracheoles and tracheae, but since the tracheoles are more closely associated with the tissues they will, in general, be more important than the tracheae in the transfer of oxygen to the tissues. The rate of exchange of gases also varies with the surface area through which they are diffusing. In some insects, the summed cross-sectional area of the tracheal system at different distances from the spiracles is believed to remain constant. Distally this area is made up of many small tubes, proximally of a few large ones so that the circumference or wall area/unit length is much greater distally than proximally. Although in *Bombyx* larva the summed cross-sectional area of the tracheoles is less than that of the tracheae, the wall area/unit length of the tracheoles is nevertheless greater (Buck, 1962). Since this is so it again follows that the tracheoles are generally a more important site of gaseous exchange with the tissues than are the more proximal tracheae.

23.42 Ventilation

In large, active insects diffusion alone does not bring sufficient oxygen to the tissues to meet their requirements and it is supplemented by convection produced by changes in the volume of the tracheal system. This is known as ventilation. Most tracheae are circular in cross-section and resist any change in form, but some, such as the longitudinal trunks of *Dytiscus* (Coleoptera) larvae, are oval in cross-section and are subject to collapse. The collapse of a trachea forces air out of the tracheal system, while its subsequent expansion sucks air in again. But changes in shape of the trachea only produce small volume changes. Much larger changes, and hence better gaseous exchange, are produced by the alternating collapse and expansion of air-sacs.

Compression of the system, causing expiration, results indirectly from muscular contractions, usually of the abdomen. These contractions lead to increased haemolymph pressure and movements of organs which press on the air-sacs, causing them to collapse. Expansion of the air-sacs and inspiration result from the reduction of pressure due to the muscular or elastic expansion of the abdomen. Changes in abdominal volume may be produced in various ways. In Heteroptera and Coleoptera the tergum moves up and down (Fig. 309A); in Odonata, Orthoptera, Hymenoptera and Diptera both tergum and sternum move (Fig. 309B), and this movement may be associated with telescoping movements of the abdominal segments (Fig. 309C); in Lepidoptera the movement is complex and involves movements of the pleural regions as well as terga and sterna.

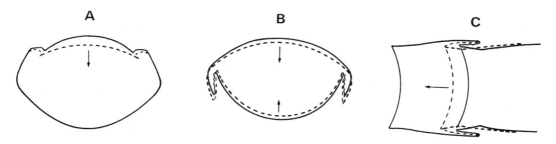

Fig. 309. Diagrammatic representations of types of abdominal ventilatory movements. Dashed lines indicate the contracted positions, arrows the directions of movement. A and B in transverse section, C in longitudinal section (from Snodgrass, 1935).

Alternate movements of compression and expansion pump air out from and in to the tracheal system through the spiracles. Air may flow in and out of each of the spiracles and such a movement of air is called a tidal flow. In many insects, however, opening and closing of certain spiracles is synchronised with the ventilatory pumping movements of the abdomen, so that air is sucked in through some spiracles and pumped out through others and a directed flow of air is produced. This is a more efficient form of ventilation than tidal flow since the 'dead' air, trapped in the inner parts of the system by tidal movements, is removed.

In most insects the flow of air is from front to back and in *Schistocerca* spiracles 1, 2 and 4 are open during inspiration, and then they close and spiracle 10 opens for expiration. When the insect is more active expiration takes place through spiracles 5 to 10. The spiracles for inspiration open immediately after the expiratory spiracles have closed and remain open for about 20% of the cycle while air is drawn in. Then they close and for a short time all the spiracles are closed (Fig. 310A). The abdomen starts to contract while the spiracles are still closed, so that the air in the tracheae is under pressure, this is known as the compression phase, and then the expiratory spiracles open and air is forced out. The expiratory spiracles are only open for some 5–10% of the cycle. During activity the frequency of ventilation and spiracular movements is increased. The times for which the spiracles open remain the same, but the period of closure is reduced and the compression phase eliminated (Fig. 310B) (Miller, 1960b).

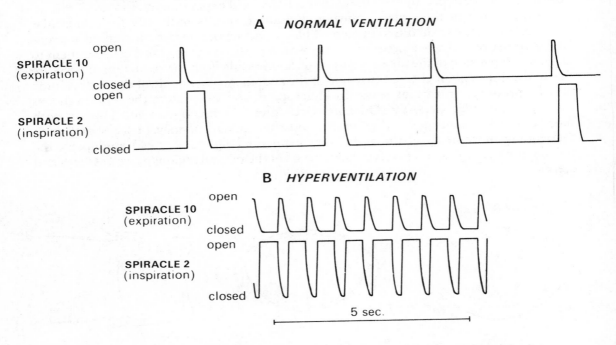

Fig. 310. Diagram illustrating the activity of the spiracles of *Schistocerca* in ventilation. A. Normal ventilation. B. Hyperventilation (after Miller, 1960b).

Ventilation in large insects, such as locusts, is continuous, although there may be periods of a minute or more without ventilation. After periods of activity abdominal ventilation is supplemented by other types of ventilation and in *Schistocerca* these involve protraction and retraction of the head on the prothorax, neck ventilation, and movement of the prothorax on the mesothorax, prothoracic ventilation (Miller, 1960a). These movements primarily ventilate the head so that they may be of considerable importance. The normal level of abdominal ventilation in *Schistocerca* pumps about 40 l.air/Kg./hr. through the body, about 5% of the air being exchanged at each movement, but this can be raised to 150 litres, with an exchange of about 20% of the volume at each stroke. Neck and prothoracic ventilation provide a further 50 l.air/Kg./hr. In *Dytiscus* 60% of the air is renewed with each compression and expansion.

Ventilation in flight

A stationary insect uses 0·6–3·0 litres O_2/Kg./hr. whereas in flight the figure rises to 15–180 litres O_2/Kg./hr., a 30- to 100-fold increase and the demands of the flight muscles themselves may increase up to 400-fold. During the flight of *Schistocerca* abdominal ventilation increases in frequency and amplitude, but still only supplies about 150 l.air/Kg./hr., which is not sufficient to supply the needs of the flight muscles. However, the distortion of the thorax, and in particular the raising and lowering of the notal sclerites, produces large volume changes in the extra-muscular air-sacs of the ptero-thoracic tracheal system (Fig. 300), while changes in the volumes of the muscles themselves compress the intramuscular air-sacs. This pterothoracic ventilation produces an airflow of about 350 l.air/Kg./hr. which is adequate for the needs of the flight muscles.

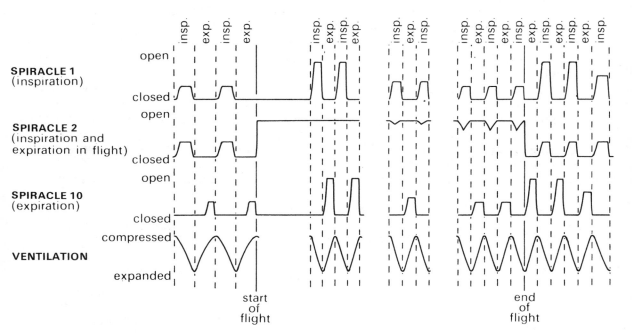

Fig. 311. Diagram illustrating the activity of some spiracles of *Schistocerca* synchronised with ventilatory movements during flight (after Miller, 1960c).

When *Schistocerca* starts to fly the pattern of opening of the spiracles also alters (Fig. 311). At first spiracles 1 and 4 to 10 close and then they open and close rhythmically, being synchronised with abdominal ventilation so that there is a good flow of air to the brain and the sense organs. Increased abdominal ventilation may also improve the blood circulation and hence the fuel supply to the flight muscles. Spiracles 2 and 3 remain wide open throughout flight and although they show some incipient closures after a time these do not affect the airflow through the spiracles. These spiracles supply the flight muscles, and since the tracheal system of these muscles is largely isolated and the spiracles remain open all the time there is a tidal flow of air in and out of them (Miller, 1960c).

Thoracic pumping is also important in flight in Odonata and probably in Lepi-doptera and Coleoptera, although in these two groups abdominal pumping is also important since the abdominal system is widely connected to the thoracic tracheal system. In Hymenoptera and Diptera changes in the thoracic volume during flight are not very large and abdominal pumping is of greater importance in maintaining the air supply to the flight muscles (Weis-Fogh, 1964a).

Control of ventilation

As in the control of spiracles, ventilatory movements are initiated by the accumulation of carbon dioxide and, to a lesser extent, the lack of oxygen, acting directly on centres in the ganglia of the central nervous system. Each abdominal ganglion produces rhythmical sequences of impulses controlling the movements, and the rhythm, once started, is autonomous. The third abdominal ganglion acts as a pacemaker and overrides the rhythms of the rest. In *Schistocerca* the pacemaker appears to be in the metathoracic ganglion, but this is a compound ganglion including the anterior abdominal ganglia.

Ventilatory movements are synchronous along the length of the abdomen and in the locust it is probable that a single interneuron transmits a signal from the metathoracic ganglion and initiates an expiratory stroke in each segment, at the same time inhibiting the inspiratory motor neuron. It is further suggested that the activity of the interneurons is rhythmically inhibited by a pacemaker neuron and this frees the inspiratory neurons from inhibition so that an inspiratory stroke occurs (Miller, 1966a). Centres sensitive to carbon dioxide are present in the head and thorax of *Schistocerca* and these

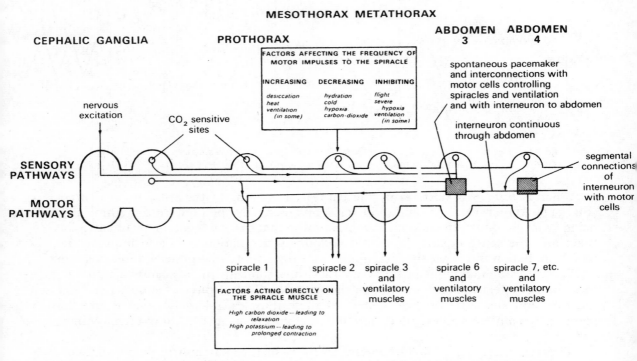

Fig. 312. A diagrammatic summary of the control of ventilation and the spiracles (modified after Miller, 1960a, 1964, 1966a).

modify the activity of the pacemaker, while the output is also modified by high temperature and nervous excitation generally (Fig. 312). Proprioceptors may play some part in the maintenance of the frequency of ventilation (Miller, 1960a).

The coordination of the spiracles with the ventilatory movements is brought about by motor patterns derived from the ventilatory centres.

23.43 Cyclic release of carbon dioxide

In some quiescent insects carbon dioxide is not released continuously from the spiracles, but is produced in bursts followed by long intervals in which very little carbon dioxide is liberated although the uptake of oxygen is continuous. This occurs during the diapause of some lepidopterous larvae and pupae, in some Coleoptera, and in immature and senile locusts. In *Hyalophora* pupae the period between bursts of carbon dioxide release may be as much as seven hours (Fig. 313), while in locusts the interburst period is only about three minutes and the bursts are synchronised with ventilatory

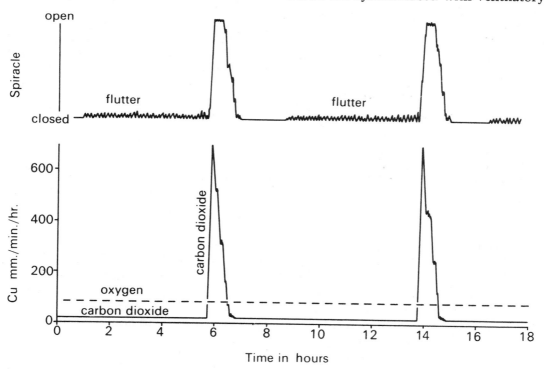

Fig. 313. Diagram to show the cyclic release of carbon dioxide and the associated activity of the spiracles (from Miller, 1964).

movements (Hamilton, 1964). During the bursts of carbon dioxide release the spiracles are wide open, while during the interburst period they repeatedly open very slightly and then close again, a phenomenon known as fluttering.

Cyclic release of carbon dioxide is usually observed when the oxygen requirements of an insect are low, but the oxygen in the tracheae is used up faster than it enters through the spiracles. At the end of a burst in a *Hyalophora* pupa the partial pressure of oxygen in the trachea is 18·2%. The spiracles close tightly and as the oxygen is used up the pressure falls by about 3·5 mm.Hg, and the partial pressure of oxygen is reduced to 2·9% within about ten minutes. At the same time there is a small rise in the partial pressure of carbon dioxide. In response to the low oxygen content of the tracheal air and tissues the spiracles open slightly, 5–10% of their maximum, and because of the low pressure in the tracheal system air rushes in. The bulk influx of air prevents the outward diffusion of carbon dioxide which therefore accumulates in the tracheae and the tissues. The influx of air temporarily raises the partial pressure of oxygen so that the spiracles close again, and the repeated lowering and raising of the oxygen level leads to the fluttering movement of the spiracle valves.

Slowly, in the course of the interburst period, carbon dioxide accumulates. Most of it is in the tissues, and in the pupa of *Agapema* (Lepidoptera) 90% of the carbon dioxide produced during the interburst is retained in the tissues. Nevertheless the concentration in the tracheal system rises and ultimately it reaches a level which promotes spiracle opening. In *Hyalophora* this occurs when the partial pressure of carbon dioxide reaches about 6·4% and then the spiracles open wide, releasing a burst of carbon dioxide. The bulk inward movement of air, while preventing the outward flow of carbon dioxide and carrying in oxygen also carries in a large volume of nitrogen and the inflow of this gas must be matched by its outward diffusion (Buck, 1962; and see Kanwisher, 1966).

The cyclic release of carbon dioxide may not, in itself, be important, but the prolonged periods of closure of the spiracles are important because they result in the restriction of water loss from the tracheal system. Kanwisher (1966) suggests that as a result of this mechanism water loss from the pupa of *Hyalophora* does not greatly exceed the production of metabolic water and the pupa only loses 5% of its weight over a four-month period. The cyclic release of CO_2 is not observed in pupae living in a moist environment, while in *Schistocerca* it is often associated with a lack of moisture (Hamilton, 1964).

23.44 Cutaneous respiration

Some gaseous exchange takes place through the cuticle of most insects, but this does not usually amount to more than a few percent of the total movement of gas. On the other hand, Protura and most Collembola have no tracheal system and must depend on cutaneous respiration together with transport from the body surface to the tissues by the haemolymph. Cutaneous respiration is also important in eggs (p. 339), aquatic insects, coupled with an apneustic tracheal system (p. 478), and endoparasitic insects. Cutaneous respiration without an associated apneustic tracheal system can only suffice for very small insects with a large surface/volume ratio.

The impermeability of most insect cuticles to oxygen arises from the epicuticle, but not from the wax layer which renders the cuticle impermeable to water (Buck, 1962). The permeability to carbon dioxide may be rather greater and the loss of this gas through the intersegmental membranes may be appreciable.

23.5 Other functions of the tracheal system

Apart from respiration the tracheal system has a number of other functions. The whole system, and in particular the air-sacs, lowers the specific gravity of the insect. In aquatic insects, but not in terrestrial ones, it also gives some degree of buoyancy and in the larvae of *Chaoborus* (Diptera) the tracheae form hydrostatic organs enabling the buoyancy to be adjusted.

Air-sacs, being collapsible, allow for the growth of organs within the body without any marked changes in body form. Thus at the beginning of an instar the tracheal system of *Locusta* (Orthoptera) occupies 42% of the body volume. By the end of the instar it only occupies 3·8% due to the growth of the other organs causing compression of the air-sacs (Clarke, 1957b).

When adult *Drosophila* emerge the air-sacs are collapsed, but subsequently they expand and at the same time there is a marked reduction in blood volume. Availability of oxidisable substrate, rather than shortage of oxygen, is likely to be a limiting factor in the activity of flight muscles and the air-sacs may indirectly improve the fuel supply by permitting a reduction in blood volume with a consequent increase in the concentration of fuels (Wigglesworth, 1963). Possibly intramuscular ventilation, causing marked changes in the volumes of the flight muscles, may also improve the blood supply to the muscles (Weis-Fogh, 1964b).

In some noctuids (Lepidoptera) tracheae form a reflecting tapetum beneath the eye (p. 549), and tympanal organs are usually backed by an air-sac which, being open to the outside air, allows the tympanum to vibrate freely with a minimum of damping (p. 608).

Expansion of the tracheal system may assist in inflation of the insect after a moult. Thus in dragonflies, spiracle closure, preventing the escape of gas from the tracheae, accompanies each muscular effort of the abdomen during expansion of the wings (Miller, 1964).

Some insects, such as *Aeschna* (Odonata), have an extensive development of air-sacs, apparently having no respiratory function, round the pterothoracic musculature. They probably serve an insulating function, helping to maintain the temperature of the flight muscles (Church, 1960b).

An important general function of tracheae and tracheoblasts is in acting as connective tissue, binding other organs together (Edwards, 1960).

CHAPTER XXIV

RESPIRATION IN AQUATIC AND ENDOPARASITIC INSECTS

Aquatic insects obtain oxygen directly from the air or from air dissolved in the water. The former necessitates some semi-permanent connection with the surface or frequent visits to the surface, but the frequency of surfacing may be reduced by increasing the size of the store of air with which they submerge. Insects which obtain air from the water nearly always retain the tracheal system so that the oxygen comes out of solution into the gaseous phase. This is important because the rate of diffusion in the gas phase is very much greater than in solution in the haemolymph. Often gaseous exchange takes place through thin-walled gills well supplied with tracheae, but in other cases a thin, permanent film of air is present on the outside of the body. The spiracles open into this film so that oxygen can readily pass from the water into the tracheae.

Like aquatic insects, endoparasitic insects may obtain their oxygen directly from the air outside the host or from that in the surrounding host tissues.

Insects rarely have respiratory pigments, but haemoglobin is present in a few aquatic and endoparasitic insects. It may provide a short-term store of oxygen or facilitate recovery from a period of oxygen lack.

For a general account of respiration see Wigglesworth (1965). Crisp (1964) and Thorpe (1950) review plastron respiration, while various studies on spiracular gills are reviewed by Hinton (1968, *Adv. Insect Physiol.* **5**).

24.1 Aquatic insects obtaining oxygen from the air

The majority of aquatic insects obtain their oxygen from the air and this usually necessitates periodic visits to the surface of the water to renew the gases in the tracheal system. A few insects, however, maintain a semi-permanent connection with the air via a long respiratory siphon or through the aerenchyma of certain aquatic plants.

Problems facing all insects which come to the surface are those of breaking the surface film when they surface and of preventing the entry of water into the spiracles when they submerge. The ease with which this is accomplished depends on the surface properties of the cuticle, and in particular its resistance to wetting. When a liquid rests on a solid or a solid dips into a liquid, the liquid/air interface meets the solid/air interface at a definite angle which is constant for the substances concerned. This angle, measured in the liquid, is known as the contact angle (Fig. 314). A high contact angle indicates that the surface of the solid is only wetted with difficulty and such surfaces are said to be hydrofuge. Under these conditions the cohesion of the liquid is greater than its adhesion to the solid so that, when an insect whose surface properties are such that the contact

472

angle is high comes to the surface, the water falls away leaving the body dry (Holdgate, 1955).

The whole surface of the cuticle may possess hydrofuge properties so that it is not readily wetted at all, or these properties may be restricted to the region around the spiracles, while the rest of the cuticle is easily wetted. In dipterous larvae, for instance,

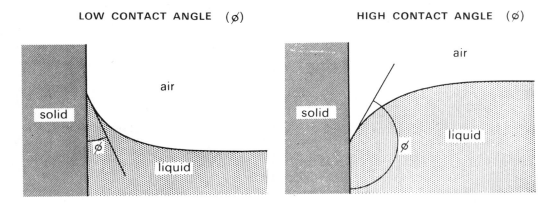

Fig. 314. Diagrams to illustrate low and high contact angles.

peristigmatic glands (p. 426) produce an oily secretion in the immediate neighbourhood of the spiracle. Often hydrofuge properties round the spiracle are associated with hairs, as in *Notonecta* (Heteroptera), or valves, as in mosquito larvae, which close when the insect dives, but open at the surface (Fig. 315), being spread out by the surface tension.

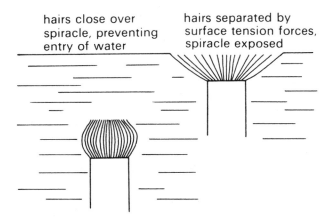

Fig. 315. Diagrams to show the movements of hydrofuge hairs surrounding a spiracle when the insect is submerged and at the surface. The movement of the hairs is entirely passive, depending on physical forces acting between the hairs and the water (modified after Wigglesworth, 1965).

In many of these insects only the posterior spiracles are functional and they are often carried on a siphon, as in larval Ephydridae and Culicidae, so that only the posterior part of the body penetrates the surface film, the rest remaining submerged, suspended from the surface film. In *Eristalis* (Diptera) the siphon is telescopic and can extend to a length of six centimetres or more in a larva only one centimetre long. By means of the siphon the larva can reach the surface with its posterior spiracles, while the body remains on the bottom mud (Fig. 316).

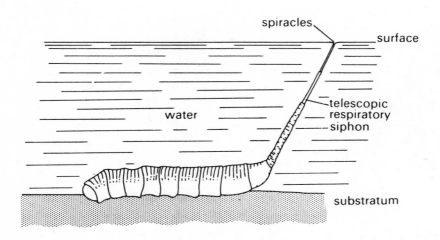

Fig. 316. Larva of *Eristalis* with the respiratory siphon partly extended (after Imms, 1947).

An increase in the number of functional spiracles often occurs in the last instar larva since this stage is commonly less strictly aquatic than earlier instars, leaving the water in order to pupate or, in hemimetabolous insects, to facilitate adult emergence. The number of functional spiracles never decreases from one instar to the next (Hinton, 1947).

24.11 Air stores

Some insects, such as mosquito larvae, can remain submerged only for as long as the supply of oxygen in the tracheae lasts, but some other insects have an extra-tracheal air store, carrying a bubble of air down into the water when they dive. The spiracles open into this bubble so that it provides a store of air, additional to that contained in the tracheal system, enabling the insects to remain submerged for longer periods than would be possible without it. The position of the store is characteristic for the species; in *Dytiscus* it is beneath the elytra, and removal of the hind wings, by increasing the space beneath the elytra, enables the insect to remain submerged for longer periods. In *Notonecta* air is held by long hydrofuge hairs on the ventral surface as well as in a store under the wings and in a thin film held by small bristles over the dorsal surface of the fore wing. The related *Anisops* (Heteroptera) has ventral and subelytral stores supplemented by oxygen loosely associated with haemoglobin in large tracheal cells just inside the abdominal spiracles (p. 488).

The air store also gives the insect buoyancy so that, as soon as it stops swimming or releases its hold on the vegetation, the insect floats to the surface. The position of the store is such that the insect breaks the surface suitably orientated to renew the air. *Dytiscus,* for instance, comes to the surface tail first and renews the subelytral air from the posterior end of the elytra (and see p. 160).

24.12 Physical gills

When an insect dives, the gases in its air store are in equilibrium with the gases dissolved in the water, assuming that this is saturated with air. Normally at the dive the bubble would contain approximately 21% oxygen and 79% nitrogen, while the water, because of the differing solubilities of the gases, will contain 33% oxygen, 64% nitrogen and 3% carbon dioxide. Carbon dioxide is very soluble so that there is never very much in the bubble.

Within a short period after diving the proportion of oxygen in the bubble will be reduced, since the oxygen is utilised by the insect, so that there is a corresponding increase in the proportion, and hence partial pressure, of nitrogen. This will disturb the equilibrium between the gases in the bubble and those in solution and movements of gases will occur tending to restore the equilibrium. Oxygen will tend to pass into the bubble from the surrounding medium, because the oxygen tension in the bubble is reduced, while nitrogen tends to pass out of the bubble into solution, because the nitrogen tension in the bubble is increased. Thus more oxygen will be made available to the insect than was originally present in the bubble, which is, in fact, acting as a gill.

This effect is enhanced by the fact that the oxygen passes into the bubble about three times more readily than nitrogen passes out into solution, so that there is a tendency for equilibrium to be restored by the movement of oxygen into the bubble rather than nitrogen out. As a result of this the insect is able to remain submerged for longer periods than would be the case if it depended solely on the oxygen initially available in its store.

The nitrogen, as a non-respiratory gas, is essential for the air bubble to act as a gill, since in its absence there is no change in partial pressure as the oxygen is utilised. For this reason an insect with a bubble of pure oxygen in water saturated with oxygen does not survive for very long if it is prevented from coming to the surface.

With small, inactive insects at low temperatures, that is when the rate of utilisation of oxygen is low, the air store may be sufficiently efficient as a gill for the insect to remain submerged for a long time. Thus *Hydrous* (Coleoptera) can remain submerged for some months during the winter (de Ruiter, *et al.,* 1952), but in larger, more active insects, with higher oxygen requirements, the bubble only lasts for a short time and the insect must come to the surface more frequently. If the temperature is above about 15°C. oxygen is utilised by *Notonecta* so much more rapidly than it enters the bubble that the gill effect is of negligible importance and the insect soon surfaces to replenish its airstore. At 10°C., however, it remains submerged for twice as long as would otherwise be possible and below 5°C. it can survive for a very long period without access to the surface (Popham, 1962).

The efficiency of the bubble as a gill depends on the oxygen content of the water adjacent to the gill. In water devoid of oxygen, or containing only a very little, the gas will tend to pass out of the bubble into solution and will be lost to the insect. Even if the oxygen tension in the water exceeds that in the bubble, the amount entering the bubble will depend on the difference in tension. Hence the higher the oxygen tension of the outside water, the more effective will the bubble be as a gill, and this must be true of any type of gill. Consequently the frequency with which an insect visits the surface will depend on the oxygen tension of the water (Fig. 317). If the water is still, that adjacent to the bubble

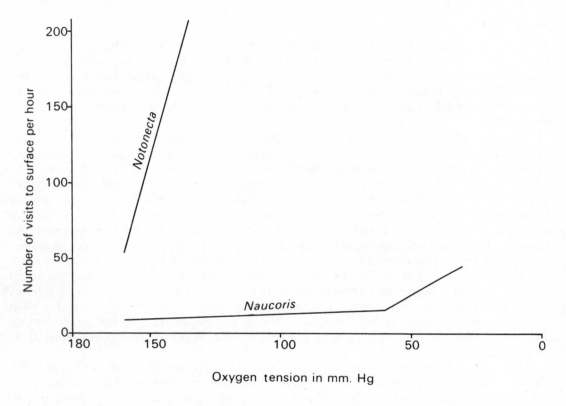

Fig. 317. The frequency with which insects using an air bubble as a physical gill visit the surface at different oxygen tensions. *Naucoris* at 20°C., *Notonecta* at 17°C. (data from de Ruiter *et al.*, 1952).

will soon be depleted in oxygen, and some insects direct a stream of water over the bubble so that this accumulation of 'spent' water does not occur. *Naucoris* (Heteroptera), for instance, holds on to the vegetation and makes swimming movements with its back legs so that a current is created, the movement apparently being stimulated by a high concentration of carbon dioxide in the tracheal system (de Ruiter, *et al.*, 1952).

24.13 Insects obtaining oxygen via the tissues of aquatic plants

A number of insects obtain oxygen by thrusting their spiracles into the aerenchyma of aquatic plants. This habit occurs in larval *Donacia* (Coleoptera) and *Chrysogaster* (Diptera), the larvae and puparia of *Notiphila* (Diptera) and the larvae and pupae of the mosquito *Mansonia*. With the exception of *Mansonia*, all of these live in mud containing very little free oxygen (Varley, 1937). The functional spiracles are at the tip of a sharp pointed post-abdominal siphon in larval forms (Fig. 318) and on the anterior thoracic horns of the pupae.

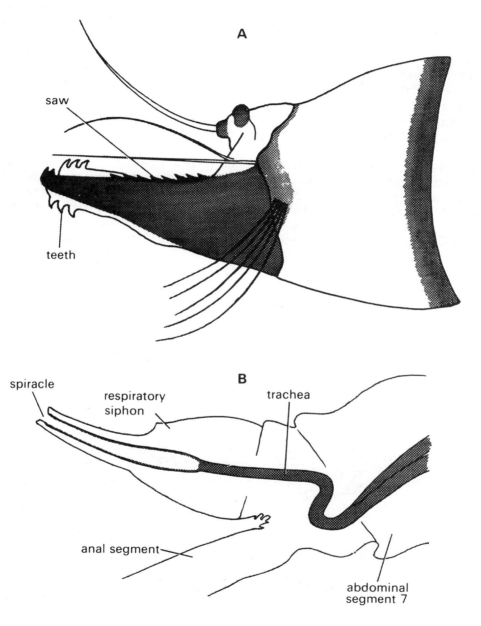

Fig. 318. A. Postabdominal respiratory siphon of *Mansonia* larva. B. Section of posterior end of larva to show tracheae and the terminal spiracle (after Keilin, 1944).

24.2 Insects obtaining oxygen from the water

In all insects living in water some inward diffusion of oxygen from the water takes place through the cuticle and in many larval forms gaseous exchange takes place solely in this way. Cutaneous diffusion depends on the permeability of the cuticle and a lower oxygen tension in the tissues as compared with the water. In many larval forms the cuticle is relatively permeable and in *Aphelocheirus* (Heteroptera), for instance, the cuticle of the last instar larva is about four times as permeable as that of the adult (Thorpe and Crisp, 1947b).

Some oxygen will pass through the cuticle into the blood of the insect and in very small larvae, such as the first instar larvae of *Simulium* (Diptera) and *Chironomus* (Diptera) in which the tracheal system is filled with fluid, this may meet the whole of the oxygen requirements of the insect. In general, however, the blood circulation is poor and the rate of diffusion through the blood is slow and would not suffice for most larger insects.

Hence the majority of insects which obtain their oxygen from water have a closed tracheal system, that is a system in which the spiracles are non-functional. Under these conditions the oxygen from the water diffuses through the cuticle and into the tracheal system within which it can rapidly diffuse round the body to the tissues. An incompressible tracheal system is essential for this type of gas movement to occur, otherwise as oxygen was used the tracheae would collapse under the pressure of the water.

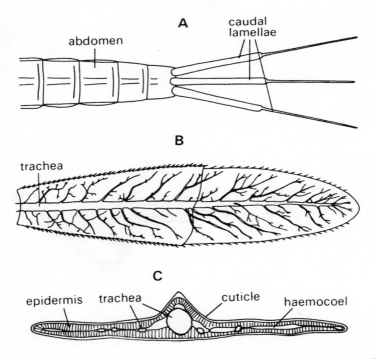

Fig. 319. Tracheal gills (caudal lamellae) of larval Zygoptera. A. Dorsal view of the posterior end of the abdomen of the larva of *Coenagrion*. B. Lateral view of one lamella (after Gardner, 1960). C. Transverse section of a caudal lamella of *Synlestes* (after Tillyard, 1917).

24.21 Tracheal gills

In some insects, such as *Simulium* larvae, there is a network of tracheoles close beneath the general body cuticle, but often there are leaf-like extensions of the body forming gills. These are covered by a very thin cuticle with a network of tracheoles immediately beneath (Fig. 319C) and they are known as tracheal gills. In most Zygoptera larvae there are three caudal gills (Fig. 319A, B) and Trichoptera larvae have filamentous abdominal gills, while in larval Plecoptera the gills are variable in position.

Larval Anisoptera have gills in the anterior part of the rectum (Fig. 320) and water is drawn in and out over these by muscular pumping. The pumping results largely from

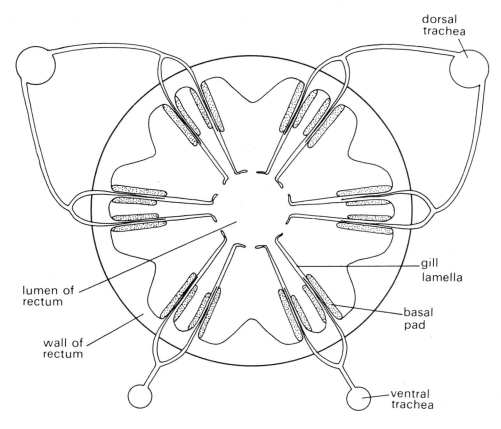

Fig. 320. Diagrammatic transverse section through the rectum of an anisopteran larva showing the rectal gills (after Tillyard, 1917).

the activity of muscles unconnected with the gut. Contraction of dorso-ventral muscles in the abdomen draws up the pleurites and arches the terga so that the volume of the abdomen is reduced. The haemocoel in the posterior part of the abdomen is isolated from the rest of the body cavity by a muscular diaphragm in the fifth abdominal segment and as a result the reduction in abdominal volume is transmitted to the rectum and water is forced out through the anus. Water is drawn in again when the dorso-ventral muscles relax and the volume of the abdomen is restored by the elasticity of the terga aided in some way which is not understood by a contraction of the muscles of the diaphragm and another transverse muscle in segment six.

Some 85% of the water in the rectum is renewed at each cycle of compression and relaxation and the frequency of pumping in *Aeschna* varies from about 25 to 50 cycles per minute. At the higher rates the interval between inspiration and expiration is reduced (Hughes and Mill, 1966).

It is also necessary to maintain a flow of water over external respiratory surfaces to prevent the accumulation of 'spent' water and the so-called gills of many Ephemeroptera are, in fact, fans which create a current of water over the respiratory surfaces. In *Ephemera*, for instance, the gills beat actively in water containing little oxygen and more slowly when the oxygen tension is high (Fig. 321) and in this way, by regulating the

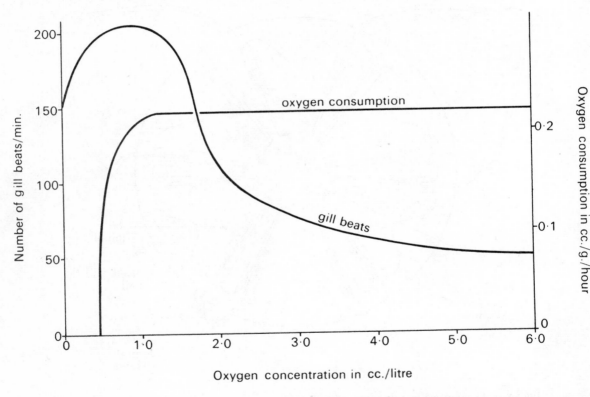

Fig. 321. The relationships of gill beat and oxygen uptake in the larva of *Ephemera* to the oxygen content of the water (after Eriksen, 1963).

flow of water over the respiratory surfaces, the uptake of oxygen is maintained at a constant level despite fluctuations in the oxygen tension in the water. When the oxygen content of the water is very low, however, the uptake does fall off (Eriksen, 1963). In *Ephemera* a good deal of gaseous exchange takes place through the gills, but in *Cloëon* they function almost entirely as paddles.

In general, although a good deal of gaseous exchange may take place through tracheal gills, and in *Agrion* (Odonata) larva 32–45% of the oxygen absorbed normally takes this route, the insects are able to survive without the gills under normal oxygen tensions. Where the oxygen tension of the water is low, however, they are of importance since they considerably increase the area available for gaseous exchange.

24.22 Plastron respiration

Some insects have specialised structures which hold a permanent thin film of air on the outside of the body in such a way that an extensive air/water interface is present for gaseous exchange. Such a film of gas is called a plastron (Thorpe, 1950) and the tracheae open into it so that oxygen can pass directly to the tissues.

The volume of the plastron is constant and usually small since it does not provide a store of air, but acts as a gill. The constant volume is maintained by various hydrofuge devices spaced very close together so that water only penetrates between them when under considerable pressure. Excess external pressures which may develop during the normal life of the insect are resisted. Such pressures may develop through the utilisation of oxygen from the plastron so that the internal pressure is reduced, or through the insect being in deep water and therefore subjected to high hydrostatic pressure.

In adult insects the plastron is held by a very close hair pile in which the hairs resist wetting as a result of their hydrofuge properties and their orientation. The most efficient resistance to wetting would be achieved by a system of hairs lying parallel with the surface of the body (Thorpe and Crisp, 1947a). *Aphelocheirus* approaches this condition in possessing hairs which are bent over at the tip (Fig. 322B); in other insects, such as

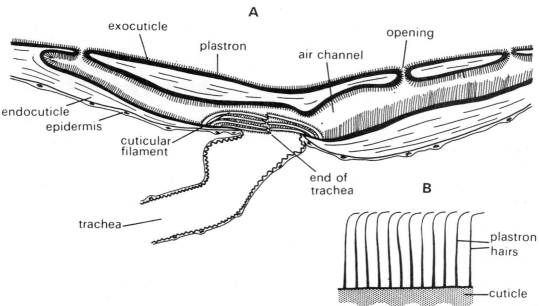

Fig. 322. A. Section through a spiracular rosette of *Aphelocheirus* showing the junction of the trachea with the system of channels in the cuticle. B. Part of the plastron highly enlarged, showing the form of the hairs (after Thorpe and Crisp, 1947a).

Elmis (Coleoptera) the hairs are sloping (Fig. 323B). The ability to withstand collapse depends on the hairs being slightly thickened at the base and also on their close packing. As a system of closely packed hairs is compressed the hairs become pressed together so that their overall resistance to compression increases.

In the adult *Aphelocheirus* the plastron covers the ventral and part of the dorsal surface of the body. The hairs which hold the air are 5–6 μ high and about 0·2 μ in diameter. They are packed very close together, about 2,500,000 per sq. mm., and are able to withstand a pressure of about four atmospheres before they collapse. Hence this is an extremely stable plastron which would only be displaced by water at excessive depths. The spiracles open into the plastron by small pores along a series of radiating canals in the cuticle (Fig. 322A). These canals are lined with hairs so that the entry of water into the tracheal system is prevented. The basal rate of oxygen utilisation at 20°C. is about 6 cu. mm./hr./individual and this is readily provided by the plastron so that, except in water poor in oxygen, the insect need never come to the surface.

The plastrons of other insects are generally less efficient than that of *Aphelocheirus* since they have a less dense hair pile from which the air is more readily displaced. However, a number of insects with a hair density of $3 \times 10^4 - 1\cdot5 \times 10^5$ per sq. mm., such as *Elmis*, have plastrons which are usually permanent and adequate for the needs of the insect. In these cases the more permanent plastron is often supplemented by a less permanent macroplastron. This consists of a thicker layer of air outside the plastron and held by longer hairs than the plastron, as in *Hydrophilus* (Coleoptera) (Fig. 323A), or

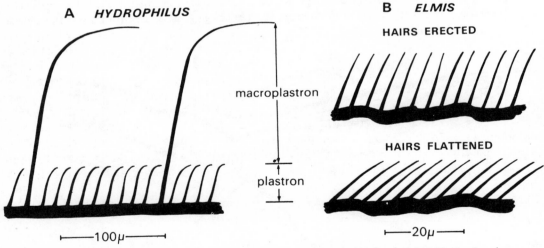

Fig. 323. Diagrams of the arrangement of hairs in (A) *Hydrophilus* and (B) *Elmis*, showing the mode of formation of a macroplastron (based on data in Thorpe and Crisp, 1949).

by the erection of the plastron hairs, as in *Elmis* (Fig. 323B). The macroplastron is an air store and acts as a physical gill. Consequently it is progressively reduced in size and finally eliminated, leaving only the plastron. The hairs holding the macroplastron are relatively long and flexible so that as the gas bubble is reduced they tend to clump, leaving patches of exposed cuticle which would be liable to wetting. To avoid this these insects groom their hair pile and in *Elmis* there are brushes on the legs for this purpose. These brushes are also used in capturing air bubbles and adding them to the macroplastron. Insects which only have a plastron do not make grooming movements of this type.

As with any form of gill, the water adjacent to the plastron tends to become depleted of oxygen. *Phytobius relatus* (Coleoptera) offsets this by directing a current of water over the plastron with its middle legs, while in *Aphelocheirus* and *Elmis*, both living in fast-flowing streams, the movement of the water obviates any such activity on the part of the insect.

A plastron forms an essential part of the respiratory apparatus of many insect eggs (p. 340), and also of the pupae of many aquatic insects. In the latter the plastron is held by spiracular gills.

24.23 Spiracular gills

A spiracular gill is an extension of the spiracle or the cuticle immediately surrounding it to form a long, partly hollow process. Such gills occur on the pupae of many Diptera and of some beetles of the family Psephenidae which live in aquatic habitats subject to drying up. Spiracular gills are functional in air and water. In water the plastron which they support presents a large gas/water interface for diffusion, while in air the interstices of the gill provide a direct route for the entry of oxygen, and water loss is limited because the gill opens into the atrium of the spiracle. Thus, in air, water loss through the spiracles would be little or no greater than in terrestrial insects (Hinton, 1964b).

In the tipulid *Taphrophila* the pupa has two spiracular gills, about 1·5 mm. long and with eight branches, connected to the prothoracic spiracles. The spiracular atrium extends into the gill and its branches, and where the atrium meets the wall of the gill it opens to the outside through a series of small pores, the aeropyles, about 4 μ in diameter (Figs. 324, 325). The atrium is flattened in cross-section with the two walls connected by cuticular struts so that it does not collapse even if the gills dry, and the hydrofuge properties of the struts prevent the entry of water into the atrium. Running from each aeropyle, on the outside of the gill, is a shallow canal about 4 μ wide which is crossed at intervals of about 1·0 μ by cuticular bridges about 0·5 μ wide (Fig. 326). The lining of the canals is strongly hydrofuge so that, in water, each canal holds a long cylinder of air, known as a plastron line, which is not easily displaced because of the cuticular bridges. The air is not displaced by the pressure of ten feet of water, although the pupae are not normally found below two feet.

The plastron lines provide a relatively large gas/water interface, 0·01 sq. cm. for each gill, over which gaseous exchange with the water can take place. In water the gills are turgid, due to the osmotic pressure of the blood which they contain and even after drying up the gills swell up again. This is important since if the gills are not turgid 'spent' water becomes trapped between the folds and the efficiency of the gills is reduced. In air the gill collapses, but the atrium does not so that it still provides a path along which air can diffuse to the spiracle.

The spiracular gills are everted at the larva/pupa moult and within eight hours of this pupa/adult apolysis occurs. Subsequently the pharate adult is served by the gills. At the pupa/adult apolysis the pupal cuticle becomes separated from the adult, but the lining and blood of the gills are not withdrawn. Instead they become cut off from the rest of the tissues by the basal occluding membrane (Fig. 324). The epithelium within the gills disintegrates and the cells form loose irregular clusters in the middle of the gill. This isolated tissue is important because it is able to repair damage to the surface of the gill, forming cuticular plugs in any holes which are produced and this facility is retained even after the gills have been strongly desiccated. Repairs to the gills are important because a damaged gill loses its high internal osmotic pressure and so becomes flaccid and inefficient when in the water (Hinton, 1957).

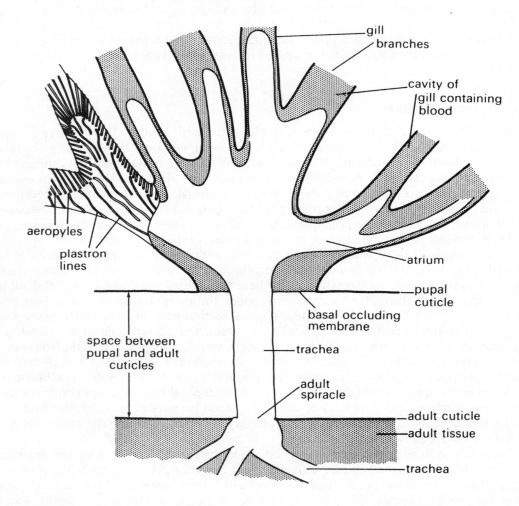

Fig. 324. The spiracular gill of the pharate adult of *Taphrophila*. The two left-hand branches represent the gill as seen from the outside, while the remainder represents a section to show the internal arrangement (modified after Hinton, 1957).

The spiracular gills of other insects are similar although the details of the plastron may vary. Thus in *Simulium* and *Eutanyderus* (Diptera) the gills are formed wholly from the body wall and do not contain extensions of the atrium as in *Taphrophila*. The plastron is held by hydrofuge cuticular struts running at right angles to the surface of the gill.

These struts branch at the apices and the branches of adjacent struts anastomose to form an open network. An extensive air/water interface thus exists in the interstices of the network. In these insects the plastron extends all over the gills and connects with the atrium of the spiracle only at the base of each gill.

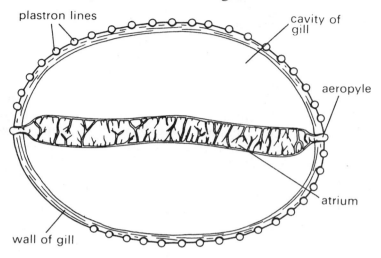

Fig. 325. Transverse section through a branch of a gill of pupal *Taphrophila* (after Hinton, 1957).

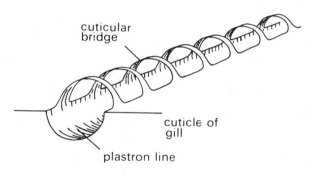

Fig. 326. Diagram of the cuticular bridges across a plastron line on the gill of *Taphrophila* (after Hinton, 1957).

At the base of each gill in *Simulium* is a thin membrane which bursts due to the intake of water resulting from the high osmotic pressure within the gills. The aperture so formed allows water to move freely in and out so that the shape of the gills is independent of the hydrostatic pressures exerted on them. Thus they are always fully expanded and the plastron fully exposed (Hinton, 1964b).

The spiracular gills of Psephenidae differ again in being extensions of the spiracle, not involving the adjacent body wall. Further, they are abdominal whereas nearly all the spiracular gills of dipterous pupae are prothoracic. In *Psephenoides volatilis*, for instance, they are on the second to seventh abdominal segments. Each gill has between four and ten long slender branches which maintain their shape in the water because two of their sides consist of very thick cuticle and these two sides are held together by stout cuticular struts. The cuticle on the other two sides is very thin and perforated by rows of small holes, 0.1–0.25 μ in diameter, which open directly into the cavity of the atrium (Hinton, 1966a). Since the atrium is gas-filled the holes provide the air/water interface.

In all these cases the spiracular gills provide for respiration in the pupa and subsequently in the pharate adult. Whether or not they do so efficiently depends on the rate of diffusion of oxygen into the plastron relative to the rate of utilisation by the insect. The rate of inward movement of oxygen depends on the area of the plastron and the differences in partial pressure of oxygen between the water and the atrium. In all cases so far investigated the dimensions of the plastron are such as to suggest that partial pressure differences are sufficient for oxygen to be drawn in over the whole of the plastron, but the area of the plastron may not always be adequate. Since oxygen consumption is generally proportional to weight, especially in immobile pupae, comparisons between insects can be made in terms of the area of plastron per unit body weight. In the pupa of *Simulium* the plastron area is 1.4×10^6 μ^2/mg., but in *Eutanyderus* it is only 1.5×10^4 μ^2/mg. Hinton (1966b) suggests that in the latter and other insects in which the relative area of the plastron is small plastron respiration is supplemented by cutaneous respiration.

24.3 Respiration in endoparasitic insects

Endoparasitic insects employ various methods of obtaining oxygen, generally comparable with those used by aquatic insects. The majority of endoparasites obtain some oxygen by diffusion through the cuticle from the host tissues. In many ichneumonid and braconid (Hymenoptera) larvae the tracheal system of the first instar is liquid-filled and even when it becomes gas-filled the spiracles remain closed until the last instar. Thus these insects and the young larvae of most parasitic Diptera depend entirely on cutaneous diffusion. In braconid larvae the hindgut is everted through the anus to form a caudal vesicle. This is variously developed in different species, but in some, such as *Apanteles*, it is relatively thin-walled and closely associated with the heart (Fig. 327) so that oxygen passing in is quickly carried round the body. In these insects the vesicles are responsible for about a third of the total gaseous exchange.

When the tracheal system becomes air-filled, networks of tracheoles may develop immediately beneath the cuticle, facilitating the diffusion of gases away from the surface. In *Cryptochaetum iceryae* (Diptera), a parasite of scale insects, there are two caudal filaments which, in the third instar larva, are ten times as long as the body and are packed with tracheae. Often these filaments get entangled with the host tracheae and so provide an easy path for the transfer of oxygen (Thorpe, 1930).

Other insects, and particularly older, actively growing larvae, with greater oxygen requirements communicate with the outside air either through the body wall of the host or via its respiratory system. The majority of these insects are metapneustic or amphipneustic, using the posterior spiracles to obtain their oxygen. Chalcid (Hymenoptera) larvae are connected to the outside from the first instar onwards by the hollow egg pedicel which projects through the body wall of the host. The posterior spiracles of the larva open into the funnel-shaped inner end of the pedicel and so make contact with the outside air. Many tachinid (Diptera) larvae, parasitic in other insects, tap the tracheal supply or pierce the body wall of the host, perforating the epidermis from within with their posterior spiracles. The host epidermis is stimulated to grow and spreads round the larva, almost completely enclosing it, and secreting a thin, cuticular membrane over its surface. The larva of *Melinda* (Diptera), parasitic in snails, respires by sticking its posterior spiracles out through the respiratory opening of the snail.

Parasites of vertebrates also often use atmospheric air. The larva of *Cordylobia* (Diptera) bores into the skin and produces a local swelling, but it always retains an opening to the outside into which the posterior spiracles are thrust. Similarly in the larva of the warble fly, *Hypoderma*, the warble opens to the outside, but in this case the larva bores its way out to the surface from within the host tissues (Keilin, 1944).

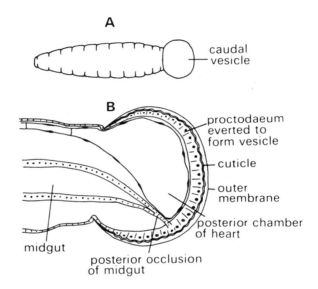

Fig. 327. A. Larva of *Apanteles* showing the caudal vesicle. B. Longitudinal section of the vesicle (from Wigglesworth, 1965).

24.4 Haemoglobin

The majority of insects have no respiratory pigments, but a few have haemoglobin in solution in the blood. The best known examples are the aquatic larvae of *Chironomus* and related insects, the aquatic bug *Anisops* and the endoparasitic larvae of *Gasterophilus* (Diptera).

The haemoglobin of *Chironomus* has a molecular weight of 31,400, that of *Gasterophilus* is about 34,000. This is about half the molecular weight of vertebrate haemoglobin and indicates that it contains only two haem groups. It has a much higher affinity for oxygen than vertebrate haemoglobin, being 50% saturated at tensions of less than 1·0 mm. of oxygen, compared with 27 mm. The haemoglobin of *Anisops* is different, however, having only a low affinity for oxygen, associated with the fact that it becomes unloaded during a dive even in well-aerated water.

Chironomus

Chironomus larvae live in burrows in the mud under stagnant water which is commonly poor in oxygen. A flow of water may be directed through the burrow by dorso-ventral undulating movements of the body and the current so produced provides food and oxygen. During such periods of irrigation the haemoglobin in the blood is fully saturated with oxygen and apparently has no function, but during the intervals between them the oxygen of the surrounding medium is quickly used up. The haemoglobin has a high affinity for oxygen and only dissociates when the tension in the tissues is very low as is soon the case during the pauses between irrigation movements. At this time the haemoglobin dissociates and gives up its oxygen to the tissues. Thus the haemoglobin provides a small store of oxygen for these periods, but the store only lasts for about nine minutes and since the pauses often last longer than this respiration during the rest of the time is anaerobic.

Haemoglobin in *Chironomus* is more important in facilitating rapid recovery from this oxygen lack when irrigation movements are resumed. The haemoglobin is able to take up oxygen and pass it to the tissues more quickly than is possible by simple solution in the haemolymph and this is especially true when the oxygen content of the water itself is low. Under these conditions the haemoglobin is continuously taking up oxygen from the water and transferring it to the tissues, so that it never becomes fully saturated with oxygen. It thus makes muscular activity more aerobic, and hence more efficient, than would be the case if physical solution alone was involved and it also permits filter feeding, which does not occur under anaerobic conditions, to continue at low oxygen tensions (Walshe, 1950).

Anisops

When *Anisops* dives it carries with it a small ventral air-store which is continuous with air under the wings. All the spiracles open into the air-store and the spiracles of abdominal segments 5–7 are very large and covered by sieve plates. From the atria of these spiracles several tracheae arise, branching repeatedly to form 'trees', the terminal branches of which indent large tracheal cells filled with haemoglobin. This haemoglobin is oxygenated when the bug is at the surface and deoxygenated during a dive, the supply of oxygen released at this time enabling the insect to remain submerged for longer than would otherwise be possible, while at the same time affecting its buoyancy.

When the insect first dives it is buoyant because of its ventral air-store, but as the store is used up this buoyancy is reduced until the density of the insect is roughly the same as water and it is able to float in mid water. This phase is maintained by the steady release of oxygen from the tracheal cells resulting from the reduction of partial pressure of oxygen in the store. After about five minutes, however, the haemoglobin is fully unloaded and the insect, now with a tendency to sink, swims to the surface and renews its air-store (Miller, 1966b).

Gasterophilus

The third instar larva of *Gasterophilus* is an internal parasite in the stomach of the horse. In the early instars the larvae contain haemoglobin dissolved in the blood, but in the third instar this becomes concentrated in large tracheal cells (p. 86). Running from the posterior spiracles are four pairs of tracheal trunks which taper and give off short branches at intervals along their lengths. Each branch breaks up into numerous tracheoles which are functionally, if not structurally, within a tracheal cell (Fig. 328).

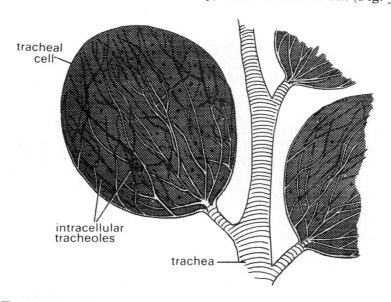

Fig. 328. Tracheal cells arising from a trachea in the larva of *Gasterophilus* (after Keilin, 1944).

Within the stomach of the horse the larva only receives an intermittent supply of air in gas bubbles with the food, and the haemoglobin of the tracheal cells enables the larva to take up more oxygen than is needed for its immediate requirements, to be used later when air is no longer available. The haemoglobin thus facilitates a more efficient use of the oxygen supply, but the store it provides is very small, lasting, at most, for four minutes (Keilin and Wang, 1946).

CHAPTER XXV

NITROGENOUS EXCRETION AND SALT AND WATER REGULATION

The activities of the cell are most efficiently carried out within a narrow range of conditions. It is therefore important that the environment within the cell and in the animal in general should be kept as nearly uniform as possible. This involves the maintenance of a constant level of salts and water and osmotic pressure in the haemolymph and the elimination of toxic nitrogenous wastes derived from protein and purine metabolism. In these activities the excretory system plays an essential part.

In most insects the Malpighian tubules and the rectum are concerned in excretion and salt and water regulation. Water and salts and excretory products pass into the Malpighian tubules from the haemolymph and controlled resorption takes place in the rectum. Nitrogen is usually excreted as uric acid since this is relatively non-toxic and insoluble. It can therefore be excreted with a minimum of water and the terrestrial insect is thus able to conserve water. Sometimes nitrogenous end products are stored in some relatively non-toxic form rather than being passed out of the body.

Terrestrial insects are subject to water loss from the respiratory and excretory systems, freshwater insects to an excessive intake of water, and brackish water insects may be subject to osmotic loss of water. The changes in water content will be accompanied by alterations in salt concentrations and the latter are also affected by the ionic concentrations of the food ingested. Terrestrial insects use various devices for gaining water, while some freshwater insects can absorb salts from the environment, but, in general, regulation in the different environments primarily involves differences in the amounts of water and salts resorbed in the rectum.

Nitrogenous excretion in insects is reviewed by Craig (1960) and Bursell (1967, *Adv. Insect Physiol.* **4**), and aspects of salt and water regulation by Barton-Browne (1964), Beament (1961, 1964), Edney (1957), Shaw and Stobbart (1963) and Stobbart and Shaw (1964).

25.1 Excretory organs

The typical insect excretory system consists of the Malpighian tubules, intestine and rectum. The intestine and rectum are described in Chapter III.

25.11 Malpighian tubules

The Malpighian tubules are long, thin, blindly ending tubes arising from the gut near the junction of midgut and hindgut (see Fig. 27) and lying freely in the body cavity. In some insects, such as *Necrophorus* (Coleoptera), the tubules clearly arise from the midgut, while in caterpillars they arise from the anterior hindgut. They may open independently into the gut or may join in groups at an ampulla or a more tubular ureter which then enters the gut (Fig. 332A). In *Carausius* (Phasmida) there are three distinct groups of Malpighian tubules; superior and inferior tubules arising at the junction of midgut and hindgut, and lateral tubules opening into the midgut. The different tubules show some histological differentiation and the inferior tubules are dilated distally (Fig. 340).

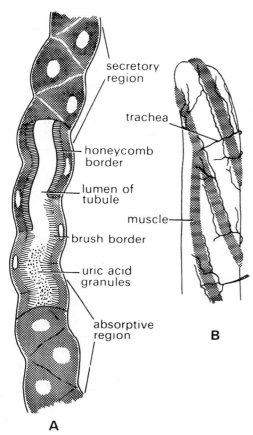

The wall of the tubule is one cell thick with one or a few cells encircling the lumen. The cells stand on a tough basement membrane outside which, in Orthoptera and some other insects, are strands of muscle forming wide spirals round the tubule (Fig. 329B). The Malpighian tubules of *Rhodnius* and Lepidoptera and Diptera in general have no muscles other than a series of circular longitudinal muscles proximally, while those of Coleoptera and Neuroptera have a continuous muscular sheath. These muscles produce writhing movements of the tubules in the haemolymph ensuring a maximum of contact with the blood and at the same time, perhaps, improving the movement of fluid in the tubules themselves. Outside the muscles is a peritoneal sheath formed from tracheoblasts.

The cells of the Malpighian tubules of *Rhodnius* and some other insects are of two types (Fig. 329A). In the more distal parts of the tubule, the free margins of the cells are produced into cytoplasmic filaments three to ten microns long and packed very close together, forming the so-called honeycomb border (Fig. 330A). The tips of the filaments are slightly swollen, especially during periods of active secretion. The more proximal cells have a typical brush border. This, too, is formed of cytoplasmic fila-

Fig. 329. A. Part of a Malpighian tubule of *Rhodnius* showing the junction of the more distal, secretory region of cells with honeycomb borders with the proximal region of absorptive cells with brush borders. B. End of a Malpighian tubule of *Apis* showing the spiral muscle strands and the tracheal supply (from Wigglesworth, 1965).

ments, but these are separated from each other by their own width or more and are less regularly arranged than the filaments of the honeycomb border (Fig. 330B). The filaments of the brush border vary in length at different times, ranging from $7\,\mu$ to $40\,\mu$ long. The plasma membrane of the basal regions of the cells is deeply invaginated within the cells, the invaginations being more complex in the cells with the honeycomb borders. Mitochondria are particularly conspicuous in the filaments of the honeycomb border, but in the more proximal cells they are most numberous within the basal folds of the plasma membrane. It is suggested that this difference in distribution might indicate different sites of maximum energy requirements with differences in the direction of active transport (see p. 498) (Wigglesworth and Salpeter, 1962a). The filaments of both types of cell also contain chains of vesicles which are parts of the endoplasmic reticulum.

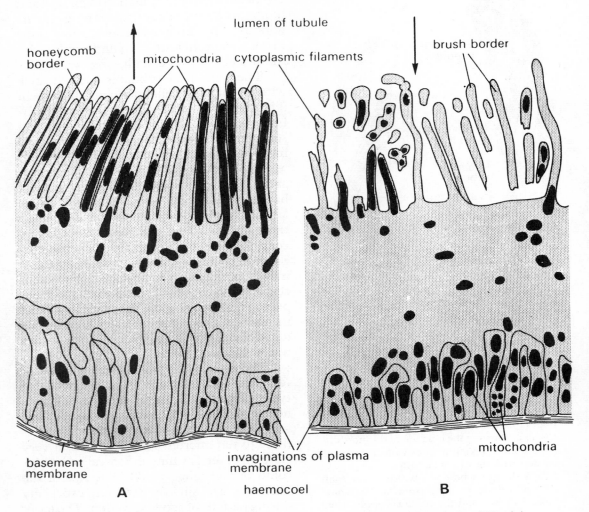

Fig. 330. A. Section of a cell from the distal region of a Malpighian tubule of *Rhodnius* showing the regular cytoplasmic filaments of the honeycomb border. B. Section of a cell from the proximal region showing the irregular filaments of the brush border. Some of the filaments are cut in transverse section. Arrows indicate the direction of secretion (after Wigglesworth and Salpeter, 1962a).

Malpighian tubules are absent from Collembola and aphids, and represented only by papillae in Diplura, Protura and Strepsiptera, but they are present in all other insects, varying in number from two in coccids to about 250 in *Schistocerca*. The number may increase during post-embryonic development (Fig. 331; and see p. 394). Because of the large number of tubules usually present their overall surface area is large, facilitating an exchange of materials with the haemolymph. In *Periplaneta*, with 60 tubules, their total surface area is about 132,000 sq. mm.

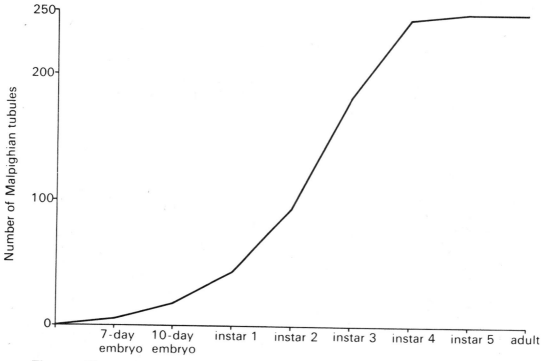

Fig. 331. The numbers of Malpighian tubules at the end of each stage of development of *Schistocerca* (from data in Savage, 1956).

In many Coleoptera and larval Lepidoptera the distal parts of the Malpighian tubules are closely associated with the rectum, forming a convoluted layer over its surface (Fig. 332A) (Ramsay, 1964; Saini, 1964). This is known as a cryptonephridial arrangement of the tubules. Commonly, as in *Tenebrio*, the tubules form a single layer, but in caterpillars they pass beneath the muscle layer of the rectum and then double back on themselves to form a more convoluted outer layer. Inner and outer layers of tubules are separated by a double membrane of thin cells and outside the outer layer is a single membrane, called the perinephric membrane, and the muscles of the rectum (Fig. 332B). The perinephric membrane is relatively impermeable, but in *Tenebrio*, at least, it is not fused with the alimentary canal anteriorly but forms a close-fitting sleeve so that water can seep out from the enclosed perirectal cavity into the haemocoel, but movement in the opposite direction is unlikely to occur. The cavity enclosed by the perinephric membrane may be divided by other membranes, but it is assumed that these do not form effective barriers. At intervals the tubules are attached to the perinephric membrane by specialised cells called leptophragmata over which, in *Tenebrio*, the outer lamina of the perinephric membrane is domed.

The cryptonephridial arrangement is concerned with improving the uptake of water from the rectum (p. 504) and is absent from the majority of aquatic forms.

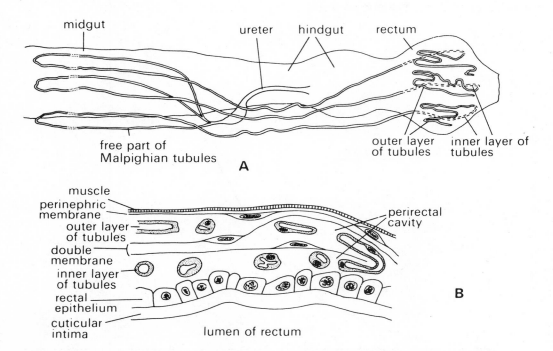

Fig. 332. Cryptonephridial arrangement of the Malpighian tubules of the larva of *Aglais urticae* (Lepidoptera). A. General arrangement showing the close association of the distal ends with the rectum. B. Section of rectum and associated tubules (from Wigglesworth, 1965).

25.12 Nephrocytes

Nephrocytes, or pericardial cells, are cells occurring singly or in groups in various parts of the body. They may be very large, as in dipterous larvae, or small and numerous and usually they contain more than one nucleus. In larval *Galleria* they are syncytial. They are usually present on the surface of the heart (see Fig. 456), or lie on the pericardial septum or the alary muscles. In larval Odonata they are scattered throughout the fat body and in *Pediculus* (Siphunculata), in addition, form a group on either side of the oesophagus. In larval Cyclorrhapha they form a conspicuous chain running between the salivary glands (Fig. 333).

The nephrocytes undergo cycles of development. In *Drosophila* they are seen to bud off pinosomes internally from the deeply invaginated plasma membrane and it is suggested that in this way materials too complex for immediate excretion are removed from the haemolymph. Within the cell, pinosomes are believed to coalesce and their contents crystallise. The crystals are then degraded and the products held in a large vacuole which is ultimately discharged into the haemolymph (Mills and King, 1965).

The effect of this suggested activity would be to transform the original waste materials into a form which could be dealt with by the normal metabolic pathways. Other authors believe the nephrocytes to play a part in protein and lipoprotein metabolism (see J. C. Jones, 1964).

Nephrocytes also take up dyes and probably colloidal particles from the haemolymph, and they play a part in the control of the heartbeat (p. 672).

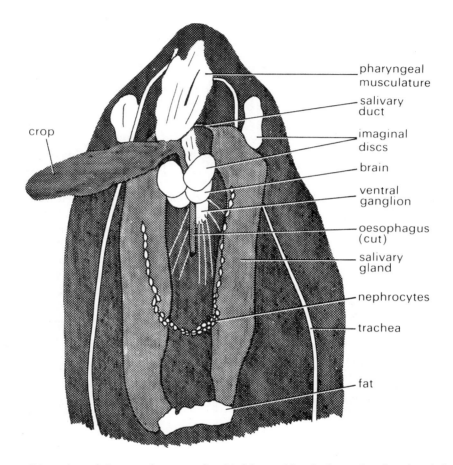

Fig. 333. Dissection of the anterior part of a third instar blowfly larva showing the chain of nephrocytes between the salivary glands. Oesophagus cut just behind brain.

25.13 Excretion by the gut

In *Periplaneta* the Malpighian tubules do not contain uric acid, but uric acid granules are present in the wall of the hind intestine and in the contents of the hindgut (Srivastava and Gupta, 1961). This suggests that the hindgut may have an excretory function. Uric acid also occurs in the midgut of larval Hymenoptera, in which the midgut is occluded from the hindgut, and in the midgut of larval *Lucilia* and various caterpillars, although in these cases its presence might be due to a forward seepage of urine from the Malpighian tubules.

Some insects excrete ammonia which appears to pass directly into the alimentary canal without involving the Malpighian tubules. In the blowfly larva, for instance, the ammonia is produced in the midgut and is then resorbed and passed via the haemolymph to the hindgut, while in aquatic insects the ammonia may be secreted directly into the rectum.

Dyes and various ions are also taken up from the haemolymph by parts of the gut in different insects (see Waterhouse and Day, 1953).

25.14 Other organs occasionally concerned in excretion

In Collembola, where the Malpighian tubules are absent, glands in the head which open at the base of the labium may be concerned in excretion. These consist of an upper saccule followed by a coiled labyrinth and have a gland opening into the outlet duct (Fig. 334). They take up dyes from the haemolymph and it is suggested that they may have an excretory function.

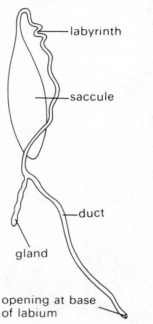

There is some evidence that the labial glands of adult *Hyalophora* might enable the insect to get rid of excess water, discharging through a median pore on the labium, and their secretion may also serve to soften the silk of the emergence tunnel of the cocoon (Edwards, 1964).

In *Blattella* and a few other cockroaches uric acid accumulates in a part of the male accessory glands. Here it is temporarily stored and then is poured out over the spermatophore during copulation (Roth and Dateo, 1965).

Fig. 334. Labial glands of a collembolan (from Wigglesworth, 1965).

25.2 Nitrogenous excretion

25.21 Excretory products

Ammonia is the primary end product of nitrogen metabolism, but it is highly toxic except in extreme dilutions. Consequently ammonia is only excreted in any quantity by insects with an ample supply of water, such as those living in fresh water and others, like blowfly larvae, which live in extremely moist environments (Table 3).

For most terrestrial insects water conservation is essential and the loss by excretion must be reduced to a minimum. Hence it is necessary to produce a less toxic substance than ammonia so that less water is required for safe elimination. This substance is uric acid, which, in addition to being relatively harmless, is also highly insoluble. As a result it tends to crystallise out of solution and can be retained as a solid, non-toxic waste substance for long periods. Further, uric acid contains less hydrogen per atom of nitrogen than any other nitrogenous end product produced by animals and since hydrogen may be derived from water this means that less water is needed in its production.

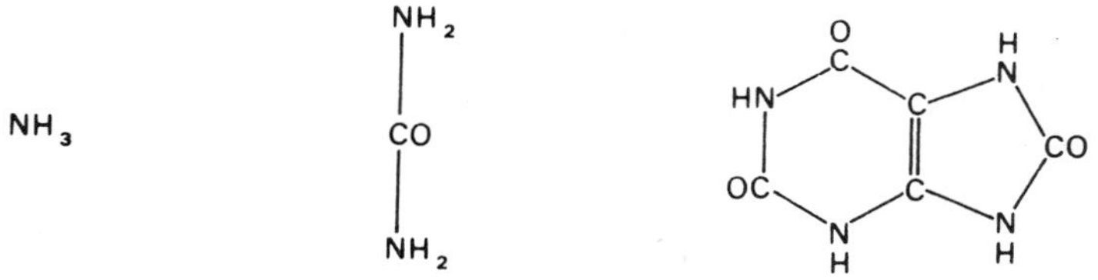

$$NH_3 \qquad \begin{array}{c} NH_2 \\ | \\ CO \\ | \\ NH_2 \end{array}$$

AMMONIA
H:N 3:1

UREA
H:N 2:1

URIC ACID
H:N 1:1

Arising from these various advantages, most terrestrial insects excrete 80–90% of their waste nitrogen as uric acid (Table 3).

TABLE 3

THE DISTRIBUTION OF NITROGEN IN THE EXCRETA OF INSECTS

(expressed as a percentage of the total nitrogen in the excreta)

Insect	Uric acid	Urea	Ammonia	Allantoin	Amino acids	Protein	
Rhodnius	90	+	—	—	+	—	Wigglesworth, 1931
Bombyx larva	86	—	—	—	—	—	Wigglesworth, 1965
Attacus	81	trace	1–8	—	9	—	Prosser and Brown, 1961
Aedes	47	12	6	—	4	11	Clements, 1963
Anopheles	42	9	8	—	5	9	Clements, 1963
Culex	47	8	10	—	5	10	Clements, 1963
Lucilia larva	—	—	90	10	—	—	Stobbart and Shaw, 1964
Aeschna larva	8	—	74	—	—	—	Staddon, 1959
Sialis larva	—	—	90	—	—	—	Staddon, 1955
Dysdercus larva	—	12	—	61	13	6	Berridge, 1965b

Uric acid is often present as the free acid, which, for instance, constitutes 80–90% of the uratic spheres formed in the Malpighian tubules of *Rhodnius*. In larval *Tinea* (Lepidoptera) ammonium urate occurs, while in the meconium of *Deilephila* (Lepidoptera) a good deal of potassium urate is present. Sodium and calcium urates may also occur.

Other substances may occasionally form the bulk of the nitrogenous waste, reflecting the circumstances of the particular insect. *Dysdercus* (Heteroptera), for instance, excretes a great deal of allantoin but no uric acid, although the latter is present in the haemolymph. Allantoic acid is often present in quantity in the meconium of Lepidoptera and more nitrogen may be excreted in this form than as uric acid (Razet, 1956). Urea is commonly present, but only in relatively small amounts.

Apart from these end products of metabolism other nitrogen-containing substances are sometimes present in the excreta. Thus in *Glossina* (Diptera), arginine and histidine from the blood of the host are excreted unchanged after absorption. These are substances with high nitrogen contents which would require a considerable expenditure of energy if they were to be metabolised along the normal pathways. Smaller amounts of other amino acids and proteins may be lost through not being fully resorbed in the rectum.

25.22 Mechanism of excretion

Uric acid passes into the Malpighian tubules along with other constituents of the haemolymph. It may be actively secreted, but this is not certain and it is probable that its movement is linked to the active movement of potassium (p. 507). In *Rhodnius* it is suggested that potassium urate is secreted. This occurs in the more distal parts of the tubules which are lined with the honeycomb border; in other insects, such as *Carausius*, the whole of the tubule is secretory.

Subsequently, in the more proximal parts of the system, water and salts are resorbed to a greater or lesser extent and uric acid or a urate may precipitate out. In *Rhodnius*, and other insects in which the tubules have an anatomical differentiation, this occurs in the proximal parts of the Malpighian tubules, uratic spheres first appearing at the bases of the filaments of the brush border. In *Carausius* the bulk of the uric acid only appears in the rectum since the whole of the tubules are concerned with secretion, while in dipterous larvae uric acid may appear throughout the tubules, suggesting either a change in the direction of secretion by the cells or the interspersion of different types of cell throughout the tubule. The separation of the uratic spheres is accompanied by a change in pH from weakly alkaline to weakly acid (Fig. 340).

A continuous flow of water down the Malpighian tubules to the rectum carries the uric acid with it so that ultimately the nitrogenous waste is excreted with the faeces via the anus. The rate at which fluid passes down the tubule depends on the rate at which water passes into it. The movement of water into the tubule may be active, but it is closely linked to the movement of potassium and it is suggested that there may be some frictional interaction between the molecules (Shaw and Stobbart, 1963). The rate of movement of potassium, and hence of water, is proportional to the concentration of potassium in the haemolymph.

25.3 Storage excretion

Waste materials may be retained in the body in a harmless form instead of being passed out with the urine. This is known as storage excretion. In the fat body of Collembola and *Periplaneta* there are specialised urate cells which accumulate uric acid (p. 85) and these cells are also present in the larva of *Apis* (Hymenoptera). In these insects the Malpighian tubules are absent or non-functional, but uric acid also accumulates in unspecialised cells of various tissues of insects in which the Malpighian tubules are functional. Thus uric acid crystals occur in the ordinary fat body cells of *Culex* (Diptera) and in the fat and epidermal cells of caterpillars. In these cases the uric acid may be the end product of metabolism of the individual cells. Subsequently, in the pupa, it is transferred to the Malpighian tubules and excreted with the meconium. Uric acid also accumulates in the epidermis of *Rhodnius* during moulting, being removed after each moult is completed.

In *Dysdercus* permanent stores of uric acid accumulate in the epidermis and contribute to the colour pattern of the insect. The progressive increase in uric acid throughout life accounts for the increase in the extent of the white markings in later instars of this insect (Berridge, 1965b). Similarly in *Pieris* (Lepidoptera) 80% of the uric acid produced during the pupal instar is stored, mainly in the scales of the wings, and the pterines (p. 113) are also stored in this way (Harmsen, 1966).

Phytophagous larvae of Diptera accumulate calcospherites in the fat, while *Rhodnius* stores iron from the haemoglobin in the gut epithelium and bilin in the nephrocytes. Nephrocytes in general accumulate particles of colloidal proportions (p. 494). The goblet cells in the midgut of caterpillars accumulate heavy metals as sulphides (p. 44).

25.4 Salt and water regulation

The water content of insects varies from about 50 to 90% of the body weight, but since this includes the cuticle, with a relatively low water content, the content of the living tissues is higher than this. Reduction of the water content ultimately leads to death, and *Rhodnius* and *Tenebrio*, for instance, die when their water content falls from about 75 to 60%. Inorganic salts are also important in the tissues and not only their absolute levels, but their relative concentrations may be important. Together, salts and water produce osmotic effects which will affect the distribution of water. Hence it is essential that the salt and water content of the tissues is regulated so as to maintain an optimal balance. The situation in the tissues is, in turn, related to that in the haemolymph and work on salt and water regulation in insects has been concerned with the haemolymph.

The problems of insects in regulating salts and water vary according to their habitat and so terrestrial insects, insects from fresh water and insects from salt water will be considered separately.

25.41 Terrestrial insects

Terrestrial insects lose water by evaporation from the general body surface and the respiratory surfaces, as well as in the urine. If they are to survive, these losses must be kept to a minimum and must be offset by water gained from other sources.

Water loss through the cuticle

The rate of evaporation of water from the insect cuticle at constant temperature is proportional to the saturation deficit of the air and to the wind speed. In still air local pockets of air with a low saturation deficit will accumulate round the insect, so reducing the rate of evaporation. Evaporation through the cuticle is largely independent of temperature up to a certain point known as the transition temperature but above this, in most insects, water is lost rapidly and continuously until the insect dies (Fig. 335). The transition temperature is usually well above the normal environmental temperatures which the insect is likely to meet: 30°C. for *Periplaneta*, 48°C. for *Schistocerca*.

Water loss through the cuticle is restricted by the presence of an orientated layer of wax molecules on the outside of the cuticulin layer of the epicuticle (p. 435). These molecules form a film one molecule thick, and hence called a monolayer, with their polar groups adsorbed on to the surface of the tanned cuticulin and the acetyl groups towards the outside. It is suggested (Beament, 1964) that the long chain molecules stand

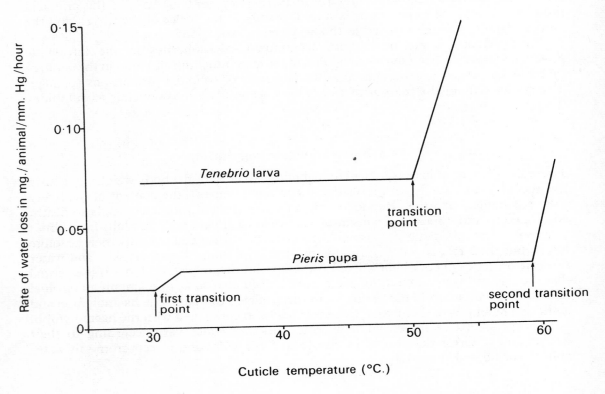

Fig. 335. The relationship between the rate of water loss through the cuticle and temperature in *Tenebrio* larvae and *Pieris* pupae (after Beament, 1959).

at an angle of about 25° to the perpendicular from the cuticle and are close-packed so that there are no spaces between them through which water could escape (Fig. 336A). Apart from being adsorbed on to the surface they are stabilised by van der Waals forces, cross-linking between the molecules. The molecules of wax outside the monolayer are believed to be randomly orientated.

At the transition temperature it is supposed that the van der Waals forces are overcome and the molecules become thermally agitated, vibrating about a mean vertical position so that spaces appear between them and water is able to escape (Fig. 336B). In species with higher transition temperatures the wax molecules are longer and so are more strongly bound by van der Waals forces so that higher temperatures are required to break the forces. Some species, such as *Rhodnius* and *Pieris* pupae, have two transition temperatures (Fig. 335), the upper one being due to a second monolayer at the outer

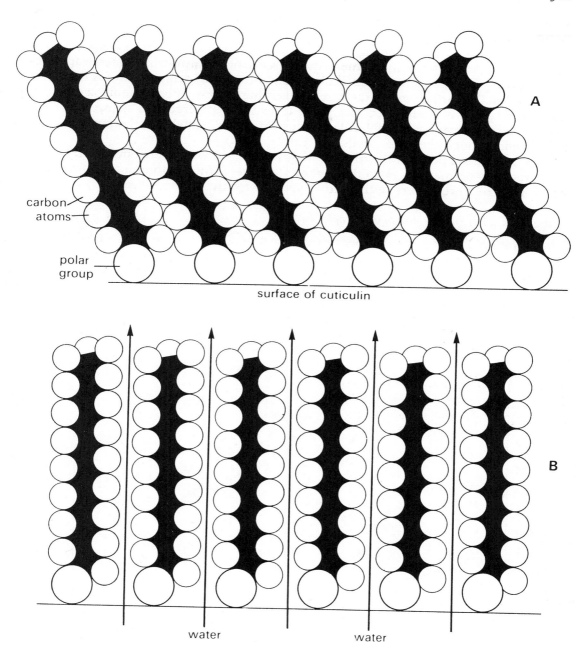

carbon
atoms

polar
group

surface of cuticulin

A

B

water   water

Fig. 336. Diagrammatic representation of the molecules of the wax monolayer providing the waterproofing layer of the insect cuticle. A. Molecules orientated at about 25° to the vertical with carbon atoms of adjacent chains interfitting so that there are no gaps between them. B. Molecules in the vertical position leaving gaps through which water can escape (after Beament, 1964).

surface of the wax, while it is possible that in highly waterproof insects the orientation of the molecules extends right through the thickness of the wax and is not restricted to one or two monolayers (Beament, 1959). The transition temperature is relatively low early in an instar and this may be due to the presence of a solvent which later evaporates off, hardening the wax. A different explanation of transition temperatures is called for if the wax on the surface and in the wax canals is in the form of lipid/liquid crystals (p. 439). In this case it is supposed that at the transition temperature a change of phase, that is a rearrangement of the molecules, occurs within the crystals and this permits water to pass out through the pore canals (see Locke, 1965).

The increase in permeability produced by heating the wax layer above its transition temperature is permanent, but although the wax layer is most important in preventing water loss, the lower layers of the cuticle are also relatively impermeable.

Water loss from the respiratory surfaces

The respiratory surfaces, being permeable, are a potential source of water loss and in *Gastrimargus* (Orthoptera), for instance, 70% of the normal water loss occurs from the tracheal system. The loss from this source is reduced by the invagination of the respiratory surfaces as the tracheal system (p. 449) and further by the spiracles which are opened for the minimum time consistent with efficient respiration (see sections 23.23 and 23.43). The efficiency of the spiracles in this respect is indicated if they are kept open constantly as they are in an atmosphere of 5% carbon dioxide (Fig. 337). Under these conditions the loss of water is excessive.

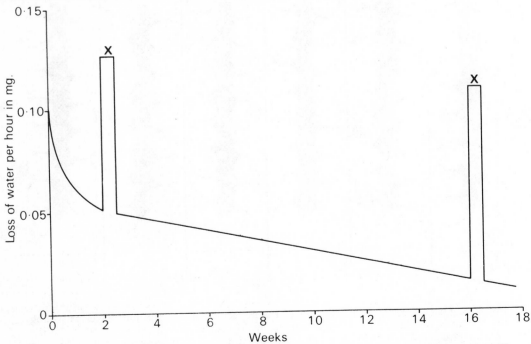

Fig. 337. The rate of water loss from starved *Tenebrio* larvae. At the points indicated by X the spiracles were kept open in 5% carbon dioxide (after Wigglesworth, 1965).

The total loss of water from the respiratory surfaces and the rest of the cuticle is probably normally less than 1% per hour of the initial water content of the body (Shaw and Stobbart, 1963).

Water loss in excretion

The other major source of water loss is in the urine and faeces. In *Carausius* urine is produced in the Malpighian tubules at the rate of about 6 cu. mm. per hour, implying a complete turnover of the water in the haemolymph every 24 hours (Ramsay, 1955). The rate of urine production, however, is not constant and in *Rhodnius* it is produced at a high rate immediately after feeding, but subsequently very much more slowly (Fig. 338) (Maddrell, 1964). At the end of diuresis the fed insect has lost about 40% of its

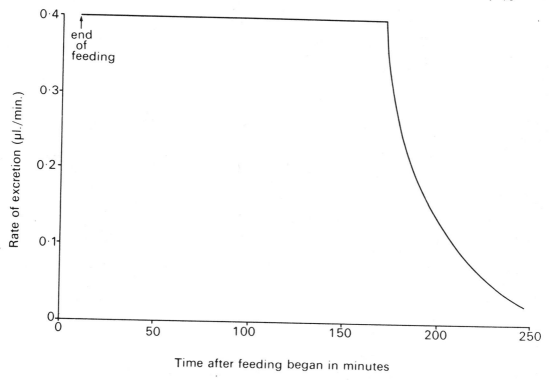

Fig. 338. The rate of excretion of *Rhodnius* immediately after feeding (after Maddrell, 1964).

weight and the osmotic concentration of the haemolymph is returned to normal after a brief period of depression. Hormones are concerned in the control of diuresis (see p. 712) and, in general, the rate of urine flow is less in dehydrated than in hydrated insects.

However, all the water passing down the Malpighian tubules is not lost to the insect; much of it is resorbed in the rectum and the volume of fluid passed out at the anus is related to the water content of the insect and perhaps to that of its environment. Insects living in a dry environment conserve most of their water and excrete dry faeces and solid uric acid, reabsorbing the water from faeces and urine in the rectum. In *Glossina* the water content of the faeces is about 75% at high humidities, but only about 35% in dry air, indicating a higher degree of absorption under the drier conditions (Bursell, 1960).

The uptake of water from the rectum of *Schistocerca* depends on active and passive processes. An active process moves water from the rectum to the haemolymph, while a passive osmotic movement also occurs, usually in the opposite direction since the active movement tends to produce a hypertonic urine. Hence the net flux of water across the rectal wall is a balance between active and passive movements and if the osmotic pressure of the rectal contents is too high, water is withdrawn from the haemolymph into the rectum. Usually this is not the case and water passes into the haemolymph (Phillips, 1964a, b). The degree to which the contents of the rectum are concentrated can be regulated according to the water requirements of the insect, but it is not known whether this is due to a change in the active uptake or to a change in the permeability of the rectal wall to the passive movement of water. In starved locusts, supplied only with water, almost the whole of the output of the Malpighian tubules, including salts, is resorbed (Phillips, 1964b). In *Dysdercus*, on the other hand, uptake from the rectum appears to be wholly passive and only occurs as long as the rectal fluid is hypotonic to the haemolymph (Berridge, 1965a).

In insects possessing a cryptonephridial arrangement of the Malpighian tubules the osmotic pressure of the fluid in the perirectal space assists in withdrawing water from the rectum. If the insect is living in a fairly moist environment the osmotic pressure in the perirectal space is similar to that of the haemolymph; some resorption of water from the rectum occurs, but the faeces remain moist. In a dry environment, however, potassium is actively pumped from the haemolymph into the perirectal parts of the Malpighian tubules, perhaps through the leptophragmata, so raising the osmotic pressure within the tubules. As a result water is withdrawn from the perirectal space and the osmotic pressure of the fluid in it rises until finally, due largely to a non-electrolyte, it becomes very much higher than that in the haemolymph. Thus a fluid of very high osmotic pressure surrounds the rectum and is separated from the haemolymph by a relatively impermeable membrane. This high osmotic pressure assists in the withdrawal of water from the faeces, decreasing the work necessary by the rectal epithelium (Ramsay, 1964).

Gain of water

To offset the inevitable loss by transpiration and excretion, water must be obtained from other sources. Most insects normally obtain sufficient water with their food and may select food with a high water content (Chapman, 1957). Others, with an efficient regulatory mechanism, require very little water, and food with a moisture content of only 1% is sufficient for the needs of *Tenebrio* larvae, for instance. There is also a suggestion that, if the moisture content of the food is very low, the insect may consume more food than it needs in order to extract the water from it. Thus *Ephestia* (Lepidoptera) and *Dermestes* (Coleoptera) larvae eat more food at low humidities, but it is clear that the bulk of their water is obtained as a result of the metabolism of this food rather than directly from its original water content (see p. 505) (Fraenkel and Blewett, 1944).

Many adult insects and the larvae of hemimetabolous insects drink water. *Phormia* has specific receptors for water in the tarsal and labellar sensilla and stimulation of these leads to drinking, but an overall control is exerted by internal mechanoreceptors which respond to distension or pressure. In *Lucilia*, however, it appears that the chloride ion concentration of the haemolymph to some extent governs drinking. In either case, a desiccated insect will tend to drink more than one which is fully hydrated.

Some insects, at least, are able to absorb water from a drop on the cuticle. This has been demonstrated in larval *Phlebotomus* (Diptera), in *Tetrix* (Orthoptera) and in *Periplaneta* and is an active process since water can be withdrawn from a drop of a nearly saturated salt solution (Beament, 1964). Absorption is most rapid in *Periplaneta* where the cuticle is thickest and it appears that the process is controlled by the epidermal cells which regulate the degree of hydration of the cuticle. The cuticle is asymmetrical with regard to the passage of water since water passes in more quickly than it passes out. The asymmetry possibly arises from the layer of wax on the outside of the cuticle. Again, if the wax is in the form of liquid crystals a change in phase of the crystals under moist conditions could account for the uptake of water (see Locke, 1965).

Some insects have special structures which are concerned with the absorption of water. The larva of *Epistrophe* (Diptera) can extrude an anal papilla into a drop of water and absorb it. In Collembola the ventral tube (Noble-Nesbitt, 1963a) and in *Campodea* (Diplura) the eversible vesicles on the abdomen have this function (Drummond, 1953).

A few insects, when desiccated, can obtain water from water vapour in the air. Larval *Tenebrio* and *Chortophaga* (Orthoptera) can remove water from the atmosphere at relative humidities above 90%, while *Thermobia* (Thysanura) and the prepupa of *Xenopsylla* (Siphonaptera) can obtain water at any humidity above 50%. The more the insect is desiccated the faster it gains moisture until it reaches a characteristic equilibrium with the ambient humidity and then it maintains a steady weight, water uptake matching water loss. Since the haemolymph is normally in equilibrium with a relative humidity of approximately 99% the movement of water from a lower humidity into the insect must be an active process involving the expenditure of energy.

Finally, water is an end product of oxidative metabolism and the water so produced is probably normally made use of by the insects, and some are dependent on this water for survival. The amount of metabolic water produced depends on the amount and nature of the food which is utilised and from this point of view fat is a more satisfactory substrate than carbohydrate since it produces more water per unit weight. The complete combustion of fat leads to the production of a weight of water greater than the weight of fat from which it is derived (100 g. of palmitic acid give 112 g. of water; 100 g. of glycogen only 56 g. of water).

The larvae of *Tribolium* (Coleoptera) and *Ephestia* (Lepidoptera) normally obtain much of their water from the oxidation of food, especially at low humidities. In order to produce this water these insects eat and metabolise greater quantities of food at the lower humidities (Fraenkel and Blewett, 1944). Metabolic water is also of particular importance to starved insects and it enables them to survive where otherwise they would die from desiccation.

The change in weight of a starved insect is a balance between the increase in weight due to oxygen intake and the loss in weight from water loss, carbon dioxide output and defaecation. In the case of starved *Tenebrio* larvae, defaecation does not occur and, since fat is metabolised and the respiratory quotient is low, loss in weight due to respiration is very slight. Hence any change in weight largely represents a balance between the metabolic water produced and water lost by transpiration and in respiration. At low temperatures and humidities water loss exceeds the water gained from metabolism so that the larvae lose weight, but in moist air at 30°C. the weight of water lost by transpiration is less than that produced in metabolism so that the larvae gain weight and their water content increases (Mellanby, 1932).

Fluid-feeding insects

Insects which feed on fluids are unusual amongst terrestrial insects in that, at least for a time after feeding, they contain an excess of water. In *Rhodnius* this excess is reduced by a rapid diuresis controlled by a hormone (p. 712). Other Heteroptera and some Homoptera have anatomical adaptations for the rapid elimination of water (Fig. 35), and Diptera and Lepidoptera store fluid in an impermeable crop so that the haemolymph does not become over-diluted.

Balance of salts

The balance of salts in the haemolymph of terrestrial insects is likely to be disturbed by salts absorbed in the food. This intake is balanced by output via the Malpighian tubules and subsequent selective resorption in the rectum. Many insects are able to regulate the composition of the haemolymph despite substantial alterations in the diet and in most the ionic composition of the haemolymph differs widely from that of the food (Table 4), indicating efficient regulation. To some extent this regulation may involve differential

TABLE 4

THE IONIC COMPOSITION OF THE DIET IN RELATION TO THAT OF THE HAEMOLYMPH IN SOME TERRESTRIAL INSECTS

(after Shaw and Stobbart, 1963)

Diet and insect	M.equiv./l.or/kg.wet weight			
	Na	K	Ca	Mg
human blood	87·0	51·1	3·0	2·5
Rhodnius	164·0	6·0	—	—
horse blood	84·8	31·4	1·7	3·3
Gasterophilus larva	175·0	11·5	5·7	32·0
lettuce leaves	13·0	86·2	—	—
Periplaneta	113·0	25·6	—	—
privet leaves	46·4	152·1	824·5	39·9
Carausius	8·7	27·5	16·2	142·0
carrot leaves	25·6	176·9	214·5	35·6
Papilio larva	13·6	45·3	33·4	59·8
potato leaves	trace	144·5	128·6	85·9
Leptinotarsa	3·5	65·1	47·5	188·3
Ribes leaves	trace	249·1	271·2	53·6
Pteronidea larva	1·6	43·4	17·5	60·5

absorption from the midgut, but no information is available on this. It appears that regulation is brought about largely by the excretory system.

The fluid which passes into the Malpighian tubules is iso-osmotic with the haemolymph, but it does not have the same ionic composition. The concentration of potassium is never less than six times as high in the tubules as in the haemolymph and a small increase in the haemolymph concentration results in a big increase in the tubule concentration. All the other inorganic ions, apart from phosphate, are present in concentrations proportional to, but lower than that in the haemolymph, and this is generally true also of sugars, amino acids and urea. The potassium is actively secreted into the tubule and this is probably true also of the sodium, despite its lower concentration in the tubules. Other substances pass passively into the tubules which, it appears, do not regulate the composition of the haemolymph, but indiscriminately remove all soluble substances of low molecular weight (Ramsay, 1958).

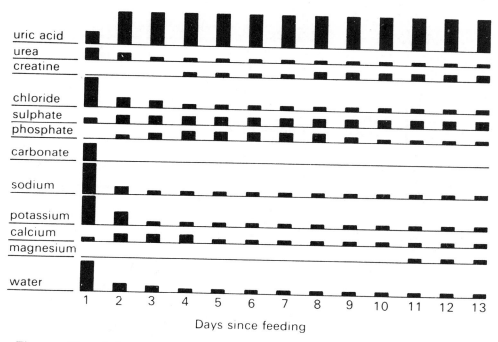

Fig. 339. The relative composition of the urine of *Rhodnius* on successive days after feeding (from Wigglesworth, 1965).

The composition of the tubule fluid may vary according to the food and state of feeding. This variation is particularly marked in insects, such as *Rhodnius*, which take large meals at infrequent intervals. Immediately after a blood meal the urine of this insect consists of water and salts with only a little uric acid. Then, as the amount of uric acid increases the fluid becomes first cloudy and then of a creamy consistency. At the same time the proportions of other constituents decline (Fig. 339).

Subsequently, water, salts and organic molecules are selectively resorbed from the urine. In *Rhodnius* some resorption takes place in the proximal region of the Malpighian tubules as well as in the rectum, but in *Carausius* only the rectum is involved.

The absorption of inorganic ions probably involves both active and passive transport and is proportional to the concentrations in the haemolymph (see p. 684). In *Carausius* about 95% of the sodium and 80% of the potassium in the urine may be resorbed, the rates of resorption depending on the concentrations in the rectum. The secretion and absorption of substances into and from the excretory system of *Rhodnius* and *Carausius* is summarised diagrammatically in Fig. 340.

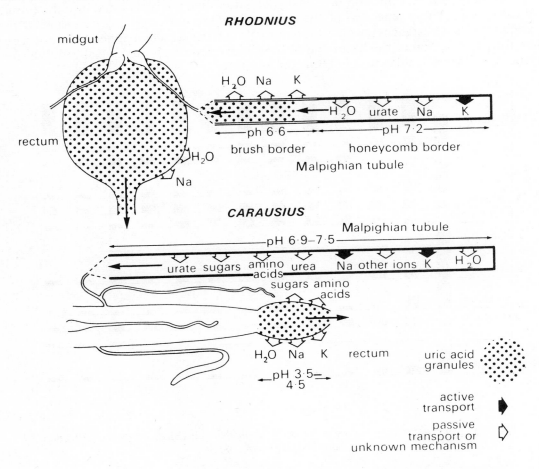

Fig. 340. Diagrammatic representation of the movement of inorganic ions and organic molecules into and out from the excretory system of *Rhodnius* and *Carausius* (after Stobbart and Shaw, 1964).

Calcium often crystallises out in the Malpighian tubules as calcium carbonate or oxalate. This, usually occurs in a particular part of the tubule and in *Carausius,* with a very high level of calcium in its diet (Table 4), involves the expanded terminal regions of the inferior tubules. In this insect the calcium carbonate is later resorbed into the haemolymph and deposited in the chorion of the eggs when these are produced. In the larva of *Cerambyx* (Coleoptera) the calcium carbonate passes forwards through the alimentary canal and is ejected through the mouth to form an operculum to the burrow in which the larva lives.

25.42 Freshwater insects

In insects living in fresh water the problems of salt and water regulation are quite different from those of terrestrial insects. Since the haemolymph is hypertonic to the water there is a tendency for water to pass into the insect through the cuticle, the permeability of which varies in different species. The cuticle of adult water beetles and aquatic Heteroptera is relatively impermeable, although much more permeable than in most terrestrial insects. This impermeability is produced by a wax monolayer with a low transition temperature, about 25°C. in *Dytiscus*. This is probably a reversed mono-layer on the outside of the wax with the acetyl groups adsorbed on to the mass of the wax and the polar groups towards the outside. Such a layer would account for the wettable nature of the cuticle (Beament, 1964). *Sialis* (Megaloptera) larva also has a relatively impermeable cuticle, and in these insects the osmotic uptake of water is not excessive, about 4% of the body weight per day. The majority of aquatic larval forms, however, have highly permeable cuticles without a lipid layer. Often the gills are even more permeable than the rest of the surface and in *Aedes aegypti*, where the anal papillae are very permeable, the osmotic uptake of water amounts to about 30% of the body weight per day. Some water is probably also taken in with the food, but there is no evidence that drinking substantially increases the amount of water taken in under normal conditions. *Sialis* larvae do drink if their haemolymph volume is artificially reduced.

This uptake of water by freshwater insects is offset by the production of a copious urine. Presumably relatively little water is resorbed in the rectum.

Freshwater insects tend to lose salts to the medium as a result of excretion and the permeability of the cuticle, but the amount lost by excretion is reduced to a very low level by resorption from the rectum. Sodium, potassium and chloride are known to be resorbed, the process being an active one in the case of sodium and chloride, at least, and being regulated in relation to the composition of the haemolymph (Shaw and Stobbart, 1963). The resorption of salts, but not of water, leads to the production of a rectal fluid which is hypotonic to the haemolymph. However, despite the almost complete resorption of the major ions the osmotic pressure of the rectal fluid may still be as much as 60% of that of the haemolymph. It is possible that this relatively high osmotic pressure is due to the presence of ammonia, probably as ammonium carbonate, which is secreted directly into the rectum.

Some salts will be gained from the food, but, in addition, some larvae are able to take up salts from very dilute solutions. This is true, for instance, of the larvae of *Aedes*, *Culex* and *Chironomus* in which the uptake occurs through the anal papillae. This is an active process and sodium, potassium, chloride and phosphate are known to be taken up in this way. Normal *Aedes aegypti* larvae are able to maintain a steady state in a medium containing only 6 μM/l. of sodium, indicating that they are able to take up salt from extremely dilute solutions. The size of the anal papillae is bigger in larvae from more dilute solutions (Fig. 341), the increased surface area presumably facilitating salt uptake. Salts are also taken up by the rectal gills of larval Anisoptera, but not all freshwater insects have this ability, and larval *Sialis*, for instance, are unable to take up chloride.

Some freshwater insects are able to offset changes in ionic concentrations in the haemolymph by compensating changes in the non-electrolyte fraction. Probably amino acids are produced from haemolymph proteins in sufficient quantity to maintain the osmotic pressure.

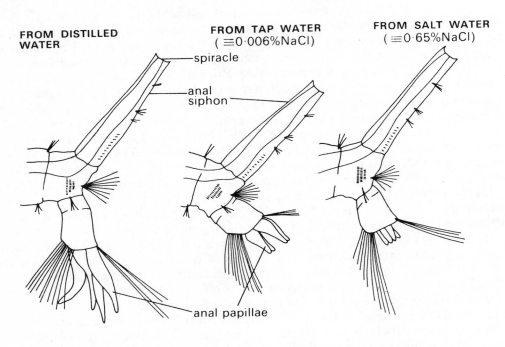

Fig. 341. Posterior end of larval *Culex pipiens* reared in different media showing the variation in size of the anal papillae (from Wigglesworth, 1965).

The ability of freshwater insects to regulate the composition and osmotic pressure of the haemolymph is good over the range of conditions to which they are normally subjected, but in hypertonic media the haemolymph rapidly becomes isotonic with the medium and regulation breaks down (Fig. 342, *Aedes aegypti*). Apparently they are unable to produce a fluid in the rectum which is hypertonic to the haemolymph.

25.43 Salt-water insects

Insects living in salt water are subject to the osmotic loss of water to the medium because the haemolymph is often hypotonic to the medium. More water is lost in the urine, but, as with terrestrial insects, some of this is resorbed in the rectum. The water lost is replaced by controlled drinking and absorption in the midgut, which in these species, but not in freshwater species, is able to withstand high salt concentrations without damage.

Salts are taken in by salt-water insects with the food and the excess is eliminated in the urine after controlled resorption from the rectum.

These insects are often subjected to widely fluctuating environmental salinities. *Aedes detritus*, for instance, occurs in salt marshes, and *Coelopa frigida* (Diptera) breeds in *Laminaria* washed up on the shore and in both these situations the salinity will vary widely according to the degree of inundation and desiccation. In keeping with this, salt-water insects exhibit very wide powers of osmotic regulation (Fig. 342). In fresh water, larval *Aedes detritus* produce a rectal fluid hypotonic to the haemolymph, but in salt water the rectal fluid is hypertonic. This is general for salt-water insects.

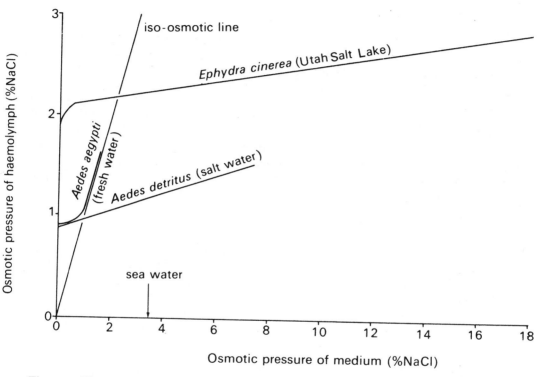

Fig. 342. The relationship between haemolymph osmotic pressure and that of the medium in some freshwater and salt-water larvae (from Shaw and Stobbart, 1963).

Ephydra cinerea (Diptera) is quite exceptional, living in the Utah Salt Lake which has a salinity equivalent to a 20% sodium chloride solution. This larva maintains the level of its haemolymph osmotic pressure, which is rather higher than in most other insects, with very little change irrespective of whether it is in distilled water or a 20% sodium chloride solution (Fig. 342).

25.5 Other functions of the Malpighian tubules

In a few insects the Malpighian tubules are modified for functions other than excretion. The tubules of larval *Chrysopa* (Neuroptera) become thickened distally and the nuclei of the cells become branched after the second instar. These regions produce silk which is used to form the pupal cocoon. Before this the tubules produce a proteinaceous substance which acts as an adhesive during locomotion and may, at the same time, be an excretory end product. Uric acid is stored in the cells of the fat body (p. 85) (Spiegler, 1962). Myrmeleontid larvae also produce silk in the Malpighian tubules and store it in the rectal sac. Chrysomelid beetles produce a sticky substance in the Malpighian tubules for covering the eggs.

Amongst cercopids (Homoptera) the proximal region of the larval tubules is enlarged, consisting of large cells with large nuclei, but without a brush border. These cells produce the spittle within which the larvae live (Marshall, 1964a). Some other cercopids build tubes, that of *Chaetophyes compacta* being conical and attached to the stem of the host plant. The proximal part of the Malpighian tubules in this insect is divided into two zones. Adjacent to the gut is a zone of cells which produce the fibrils forming the basis of the tube. The fibrils pass from the Malpighian tubules and out through the anus and are laid down by characteristic semicircular movements of the tip of the abdomen accompanied by radial pushes from the inside which push the tube into its polygonal form. More prolonged deposition at the corners produces protuberances in these positions. Other organic and inorganic material is deposited on the meshwork so formed (Marshall, 1965). The more distal zone of the proximal region of the Malpighian tubules produces spittle which is secreted at the mouth of the tube when the insect moults and in which the process of ecdysis is carried out (Marshall, 1964b).

In the larva of the fly *Bolitophila luminosa* the enlarged distal ends of the Malpighian tubules form luminous organs (p. 87).

SECTION E

The Nervous and Sensory Systems

CHAPTER XXVI
THE NERVOUS SYSTEM

The nervous system is a conducting system ensuring the rapid functioning and co-ordination of effectors, modifying their responses according to the input of peripheral sense organs. The basic elements in the nervous system are nerve cells which are produced into long processes, or axons, along which nerve impulses are conducted. The bodies of the nerve cells are aggregated to form ganglia while bundles of axons form the nerves. Within the nervous system the nerve cells are accompanied by other elements concerned with their nutrition and mechanical support. The central nervous system consists of a brain situated dorsally in the head and a ventral chain of segmental ganglia from which nerves run to the peripheral sense organs and muscle systems. A stomatogastric system, consisting of a number of small ganglia connected to the brain and their associated nerves, controls the movements of the alimentary canal.

Conduction along a nerve axon is an electrochemical process which is influenced by the composition of the fluid bathing the nerves. But the axons do not form a continuous system and successive axons are separated by small gaps. Transmission of an impulse across a gap to the next axon is believed to involve the movement of a chemical. Most impulses arise as the result of stimulation of a sense organ, but some nerve cells also discharge spontaneously.

The nervous system is not a simple relay, it also integrates the many activities of the body. The brain plays an important part in this, while at the cellular level the pathways and connections of axons within the system and the physiological and anatomical characteristics of the synapses are of great importance. Integration may involve inhibitory as well as stimulatory effects.

Finally, the central nervous system is concerned with learning, but very little is known of the central processes involved.

A general review of the insect nervous system is given by Horridge (1965). Smith and Treherne (1963) review the fine structure of the nervous system, Narahashi (1963, 1965), Colhoun (1963), Treherne (1966) and Boistel (1968, *Adv. Insect Physiol.* 5) consider aspects of its physiology. Neural integration is reviewed by Huber (1965) and Roeder (1963), while learning is considered by Schneirla (1953) and Thorpe (1963).

26.1 Structure of the nervous system

26.11 Nerve cell

The basic element in the nervous system is the nerve cell, or neuron. This consists of a cell body containing the nucleus, and long cytoplasmic projections which extend to make contact with other neurons. The cell body is known as the soma or perikaryon,

515

while the projections are known as axons. Frequently the axon has branches, collaterals, and ends in a terminal arborisation. Nerve impulses are conducted from one cell to the next along the axons. Part of each neuron is specialised for the reception of the stimuli which initiate conduction in the axon. This part, which is known as the dendrite, may arise directly from the perikaryon or represent the distal endings of an axon in which case there is no anatomical differentiation between axon and dendrite. The site at which neurons are closely apposed so that the activity of one is influenced by the other is called the synapse.

Most insect neurons are monopolar, having only a single axonal projection from the perikaryon (Fig. 343A), but the peripheral sense cells are bipolar with a short distal dendrite receiving stimuli from the environment and a proximal axon extending to the

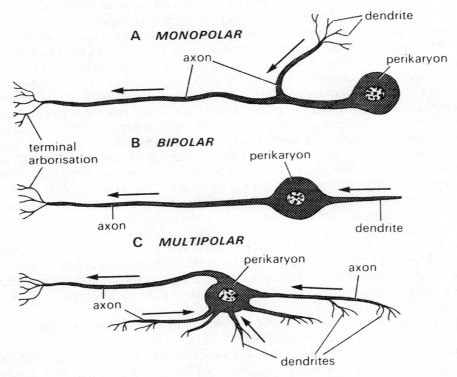

Fig. 343. Diagrammatic representations of the different types of neuron found in the insect nervous system. Arrows indicate the direction of conduction.

central ganglia (Fig. 343B). Some multipolar cells (Fig. 343C) occur in the hypocerebral and frontal ganglia and are also associated with stretch receptors (p. 617, and see also p. 518).

The sense cells concerned with the perception of stimuli are mostly peripheral with dendritic processes extending to the cuticle (see following chapters) and axons which conduct towards the central nervous system and hence are called afferent or sensory axons. Other axons conduct from the central nervous system to the effector organs and are called efferent or motor fibres. Their perikarya lie within the ganglia of the central nervous system. Afferent fibres may synapse directly with efferent fibres, but more frequently one or more neurons, known as internuncial neurons or interneurons, are interpolated between the two.

The neurons do not occur singly, but are aggregated to form the nervous system comprising the central nervous system with its peripheral nerves and the stomatogastric nervous system. Most adult insects, having a hard external cuticle, have no subepidermal nerve plexus, but in *Rhodnius* (Heteroptera), at least, neurosecretory axons from the ventral ganglionic mass run to the abdominal wall and penetrate the basement membrane of the epidermis. A subepidermal plexus does occur in soft-skinned larvae, where it is formed from the fibres of multipolar neurons.

26.12 Central nervous system

The perikarya of motor and internuncial neurons are aggregated to form ganglia within which they are grouped peripherally. The centres of the ganglia are occupied by the neuropile, a complex of afferent, internuncial and efferent fibres and their supporting glial elements (p. 527). Within the neuropile groups of fibres may be similarly orientated so as to form fibre tracts. There are no cell bodies in the neuropile (Fig. 344A).

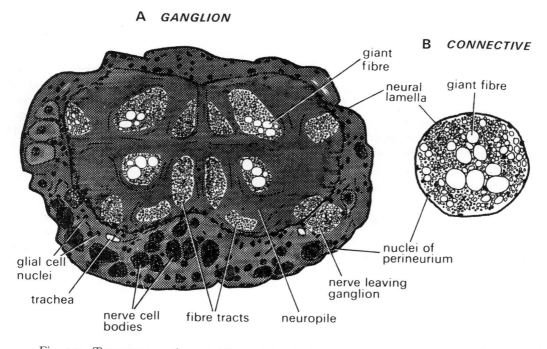

Fig. 344. Transverse sections of (A) an abdominal ganglion and (B) an abdominal interganglionic connective of *Periplaneta*. Not to same scale (after Roeder, 1953, 1963).

In many embryonic insects there is a paired ganglion in each segment of the body, but these always show some degree of fusion before the insect emerges from the egg. The most anterior ganglion is the brain or cerebral ganglion lying dorsal to the oesophagus in the head. It includes one or more segmental ganglia, how many is the subject of controversy, fused together with the primitive presegmental archecerebrum. From the brain the circumoesophageal connectives pass, one on either side of the oesophagus, to the first of a chain of ganglia lying ventrally in the haemocoel.

The ganglia are joined to each other longitudinally by connectives made up only of axons and supporting cells (Fig. 344B), while extending from each ganglion to the peripheral sense organs and effectors are the peripheral nerves. These are usually aggregations of both motor and sensory fibres (see Fig. 347) and in some cases, at least, the dorsal part of each nerve root contains only motor fibres, while the ventral part contains sensory fibres. A few nerves, such as that from the last abdominal ganglion to the cercus in the cockroach, contain only sensory fibres.

The axons from most insect sense organs are believed to extend to the ganglia of the central nerve cord without synapses, although the axons of a number of cells may fuse to form a single compound axon. This occurs, for instance, in the antenna of *Rhodnius* where the axons of some 4,000 to 5,000 sensilla of various sorts on the terminal antennal annulus fuse to give rise to about 300 compound axons. In the antennae of *Bombyx*, however, all the sensory axons remain separate (Boeckh, *et al.*, 1965). Unlike all the other receptors, it is suggested that the chemoreceptors on the palp of Neuroptera synapse with a multipolar neuron which then connects with the central nervous system (Eisner, 1953). Nerve cells thus interpolated between the receptor cells and the central nervous system are known as second order cells. (See also Steinbrecht, 1969, *J. Cell Sci.* 4.)

Brain

The brain is the principal association centre of the body, receiving sensory input from the sense organs of the head and, via ascending internuncial fibres, from the more posterior ganglia. Motor output from the brain supplies the antennal muscles and passes via descending premotor internuncial fibres to the posterior ganglia, controlling the activities of the rest of the nervous system to some extent (see p. 536). It is also the seat of many long-term organised behaviour patterns and governs their modification by learning (p. 541).

Three regions are recognised in the brain, a protocerebrum, deutocerebrum and tritocerebrum (Fig. 345).

Protocerebrum. The protocerebrum is bilobed and is continuous laterally with the optic lobes. In hypognathous insects it occupies a dorsal position in the head. It is the most complex part of the brain and, as with other ganglia, the perikarya are largely restricted to a peripheral zone while the central region is occupied by neuropile (p. 527). Anterodorsally, on either side of the midline, is a mass of cells forming the pars intercerebralis (Fig. 346). The anterior cells of the pars contribute fibres to the ocellar nerves, while fibres from the more lateral cells enter the protocerebral bridge (pons cerebralis), a median mass of neuropile connecting with many other parts of the brain apart from the corpora pedunculata. Also within the pars intercerebralis are neurosecretory cells, the axons of which decussate, cross over, within the brain and extend to the corpora cardiaca (p. 693 ; Fig. 474).

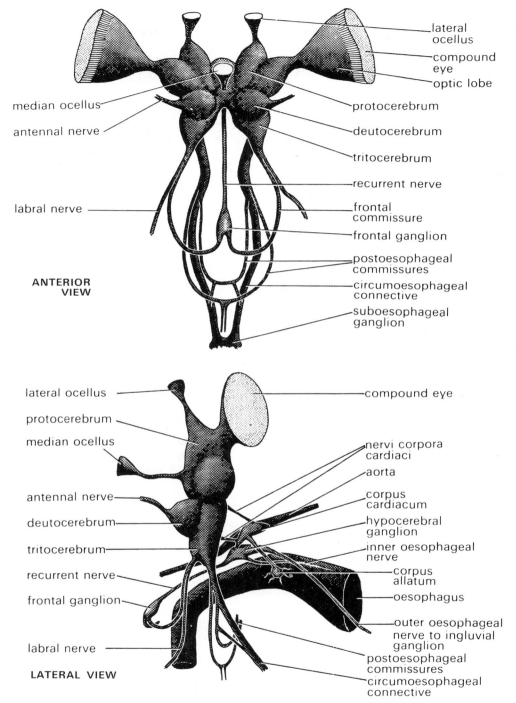

Fig. 345. Anterior and lateral views of the brain and stomatogastric nervous system of *Locusta* (Orthoptera) (after Albrecht, 1953).

At the sides of the pars intercerebralis are the corpora pedunculata, each with a group of cell bodies over a flattened cap of neuropile, the calyx, from which a stalk runs ventrally before dividing into two lobes, differentiated as α and β. The fibres in the corpora pedunculata are of two types. Those originating from the associated cells send branches to the calyx and the α and β lobes, but do not extend outside the corpus. The other types of fibres are those originating from cell bodies elsewhere in the brain, and through them the corpora pedunculata connect with many other parts (see Horridge, 1965). The connections to the calyx and α lobe appear to be largely sensory, while the endings in the β lobe synapse with premotor fibres, that is, with internuncial fibres which conduct to motor fibres.

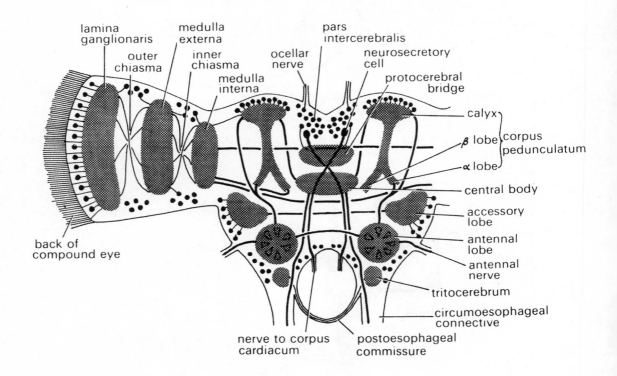

Fig. 346. Diagram of the brain showing the more important areas of neuropile (hatched) and a few of the main connections between these areas. Black dots represent zones containing perikarya.

The corpora pedunculata are believed to be the site of summation of simultaneous excitation from a number of different sources and are usually associated with complex behaviour. They are small in Collembola, Heteroptera, Diptera and Odonata, of medium size in Coleoptera, large in Orthoptera, Dictyoptera, Lepidoptera and solitary Hymenoptera, and most highly developed in social Hymenoptera.

In the centre of the protocerebrum a mass of neuropile forms the central body to which axons converge from many parts of the brain. It appears to be a major source of premotor outflow from the brain to the ventral cord. Ventro-laterally are the accessory lobes of neuropile also having widespread connections, the perikarya associated with each lobe lying laterally and in the pars intercerebralis. The two lobes are connected by transverse fibres.

Optic lobes. The optic lobes are lateral extensions of the protocerebrum to the compound eyes. Each consists of three neuropile masses, known as the lamina ganglionaris, medulla externa and medulla interna, together with their associated perikarya and connections (Fig. 346). Axons of the retinula cells pass through the basement membrane at the back of the eye and into the lamina ganglionaris where they synapse with large monopolar neurons, the axons of which extend to the medulla externa (see Fig. 366). There are also multipolar neurons with their perikarya in a layer behind the eye.

Some fibres, which may be the axons of mechanoreceptors on the surface of the eye, pass directly from the lamina ganglionaris to the protocerebrum, but the majority pass to the medulla externa, crossing over each other to form the external chiasma between the two neuropile layers. A second crossover, the internal chiasma, lies between the medulla externa and the medulla interna. Cell bodies, supplying axons to these systems, lie peripherally and in a group on the outside of the medulla externa.

Fibres from the medulla interna, which is divided into two parts in Lepidoptera and Diptera, pass to the protocerebrum, and anterior and posterior tracts connect the optic lobes of the two sides. Other axons pass directly to the ventral cord via both the ipsilateral and contralateral circumoesophageal connectives.

Deutocerebrum. The deutocerebrum contains the antennal lobes which are divided into dorsal sensory and ventral motor areas. The antennal nerves, which enter this part of the brain and contain both sensory and motor elements, are similarly divided. The sensory neuropile typically contains a number of dense areas (Fig. 346), the neuropiles of the two sides being connected by a commissure. Fibre tracts, both sensory and motor, connect the antennal lobes with the corpora pedunculata and other fibres pass to the tritocerebrum.

Tritocerebrum. This is a small part of the brain consisting of a pair of lobes beneath the deutocerebrum. From it the circumoesophageal connectives pass to the suboesophageal ganglion and the tritocerebral lobes of either side are connected by a commissure passing behind the oesophagus. Anteriorly nerves containing sensory and motor elements connect with the frontal ganglion and the labrum.

Ventral nerve cord

The first ganglion in the ventral chain is the suboesophageal. This is a compound ganglion, lying ventrally in the head, arising from the fusion of the ganglia of the mandibular, maxillary and labial segments. It sends mixed, motor and sensory, nerves to the mandibles, maxillae and labium and an additional one or two pairs to the neck and salivary glands. Typically there are three thoracic ganglia, each with some five or six nerves on each side which innervate the muscles and the sensilla of the thorax and its appendages (Fig. 347). The arrangement of nerves varies considerably, but usually the last nerve of one segment forms a common nerve with the first nerve of the next.

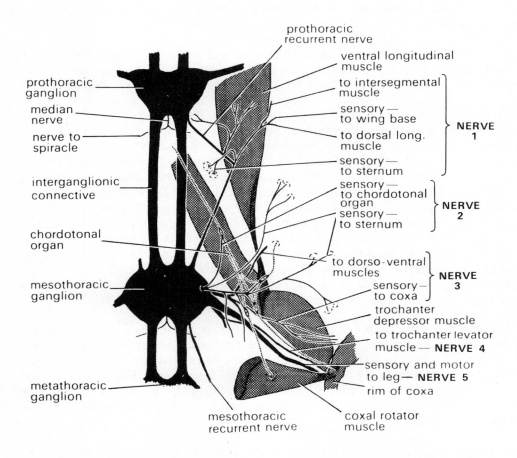

Fig. 347. Ventral view of part of the central nerve cord in the thorax of *Locusta* showing some of the nerves of the mesothoracic segment (after Campbell, 1961).

The largest number of abdominal ganglia occurring in larval or adult insects is eight, as in Thysanura, male *Pulex* (Siphonaptera) and many larval forms (Fig. 348A), but the last ganglion is always compound, being derived from the ganglia of the last four abdominal segments. In the majority of adult insects some further degree of fusion, particularly of the abdominal ganglia, occurs and in the extreme cases all the ventral ganglia may be fused together into one large ganglionic mass as in *Musca* (Diptera) (Fig. 348B).

The abdominal ganglia are smaller than those of the thorax and, in general, fewer peripheral nerves arise from each of them than arise from the thoracic ganglia. In addition the branching of the nerves is less diverse and variable, reflecting the relative simplicity of the abdominal musculature (see Schmitt, 1962). In most cases the muscles of a segment are innervated by fibres from the ganglion of the same segment, this being related to the overall autonomy of each segment, but, in the thorax at least, some innervation by axons arising in neighbouring ganglia also occurs. Some afferent fibres may also be intersegmental (see below).

Between the paired connectives joining the ganglia is a small median nerve which runs from the back of each ganglion and branches transversely to the spiracles and alary muscles (Fig. 347). In the thorax the median nerve does not extend beyond the origin of its lateral branches, but in the abdomen it forms a complete connective extending from one glanglion to the next. In the larva of *Aeschna* (Odonata) the median nerve contains four axons, two motor and two sensory. Each axon divides where the nerve branches so that each side of the body is innervated by each axon.

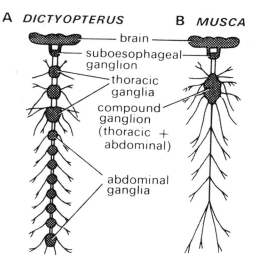

A DICTYOPTERUS — B MUSCA

brain
suboesophageal ganglion
thoracic ganglia
compound ganglion (thoracic + abdominal)
abdominal ganglia

Fig. 348. Two extreme arrangements of the ganglia in the central nervous system showing (A) minimal and (B) maximal degrees of fusion (from Horridge, 1965).

Giant fibres

Within the ventral nerve cord of cockroach, various Orthoptera, dragonfly larvae, *Drosophila* (Diptera) and possibly in all other insects are a number of axons which are much bigger than the majority, some being as much as 60 μ in diameter compared with a normal diameter of less than 5 μ (see Fig. 344). In the cockroach there are six to eight giant fibres, 20–60 μ in diameter, in each connective as well as 10 to 12 medium sized axons between 5 and 20 μ in diameter. The giant axons probably have a multicellular origin arising, in *Periplaneta* (Dictyoptera), from a number of cells in the last abdominal ganglion.

Giant fibres are interneurons, running for considerable lengths of the nerve cord without synapses. In *Periplaneta* the biggest fibres extend from the last abdominal ganglion to the metathoracic ganglion (Fig. 349); other smaller giants probably extend to the head.

They are believed, in general, to be concerned with the co-ordination of rapid evasive movements and are particularly fitted for this by their large diameter and lack of synapses, both features tending to increase the rate of nervous conduction (p. 534). Thus in the cockroach the giant fibres link the cercal nerves directly with motor nerves of the legs. A puff of air directed at a cercus elicits a quick escape movement by the insect. In the larva of *Anax* (Odonata) they co-ordinate the simultaneous action of effectors in many segments during the escape movement. In this insect the giant fibres have motor synapses in each segment, so that the legs are drawn up and simultaneous contraction of the abdominal muscles forces water out of the rectum, shooting the insect forwards.

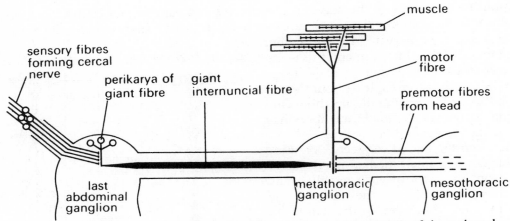

Fig. 349. Diagram of the nerve fibres concerned in the evasion response of the cockroach. Notice that abdominal ganglia 1–5 are omitted (after Roeder, 1953).

26.13 Stomatogastric nervous system

The stomatogastric nervous system consists of a number of small ganglia and their associated nerves. Above the oesophagus in front of the brain is the frontal ganglion which is connected by a nerve to the tritocerebral lobe on either side. Sometimes a median frontal nerve extends forwards from the ganglion to the wall of the pharynx and posteriorly a median recurrent nerve runs along the oesophagus beneath the brain, joining the hypocerebral ganglion just behind the brain (Fig. 345). Laterally the hypocerebral ganglion connects with the corpora cardiaca and axons pass to it from the brain via the nervi corpora cardiaci. It is sometimes also connected by a nerve to the suboesophageal ganglion and, in addition, one or two nerves leave it posteriorly running backwards over the surface of the alimentary canal to the ingluvial ganglia on the posterior end of the foregut. From the ingluvial ganglia and the nerves running to them other nerves spread over the surface of the foregut and may extend to the midgut (p. 50). In *Locusta* (Orthoptera) these nerves include three neurosecretory axons which probably have their origins in the brain (Strong, 1966).

The frontal ganglion contains the endings of axons from the brain and from the recurrent nerve and sends motor axons to the muscles of the gut wall. Thus it acts as a motor relay centre, co-ordinating local sensory input with premotor excitation from the brain. The frontal ganglion may control swallowing movements and the hypocerebral ganglion has some effect, but most of the movements of the foregut and midgut are directly controlled by the ingluvial ganglion. In *Locusta,* and probably in other insects, the frontal ganglion is concerned in controlling the release of secretion by the corpora cardiaca (p. 700).

26.14 Histology of nervous elements

The same basic units occur throughout the nervous system so that a detailed description of a segmental ganglion (Fig. 350) suffices for the whole system. Receptors are dealt with separately (Chapters XXVII, XXIX and XXX).

Nerve sheath

The whole of the nervous system is clothed in a non-nervous sheath which is differentiated into a non-cellular neural lamella and a cellular perineurium. The neural lamella comprises a thin outer homogeneous layer containing narrow orientated filaments, and a much thicker layer which consists of fibrils of a collagen-like protein in a structureless matrix, probably a neutral muco-polysaccharide. The collagen-like fibrils are randomly orientated, although parallel with the surface. The neural lamella is probably secreted by cells of the perineurium.

The neural lamella provides mechanical support for the central nervous system, holding the cells and axons together while permitting such flexibility as is necessitated by the movements of the insect. The lamella offers no resistance to diffusion (p. 681), but it probably does resist the hydrostatic pressures developed within the sheath as a result of the osmotic excess produced by a Donnan equilibrium across the sheath (p. 533).

The perineurium is a thin layer of cells beneath the neural lamella (Fig. 350). The cells contain abundant mitochondria, often in clusters, and they are concerned with the passage of organic substances and salts to the tissue beneath. They contain a great deal of glycogen which is probably obtained from the fat body cells associated with the outside of the nerve cord, and where an active movement of ions into the sheath occurs, as with sodium in *Carausius* (Phasmida) (p. 533), these cells are responsible.

The sheath surrounding peripheral nerves is thin and devoid of fibrils, resembling a typical basement membrane.

Glial cells

Each neuron is almost wholly invested by one or more cells which form an insulating, protective sheath round it. These cells are the glial cells. In the ganglia some of the glial cells are closely associated with the perikarya. The cell bodies of others are at the surface of the neuropile and from these processes extend inwards to invest the axons. The sheath which they form round an axon may consist of a single fold or the fold may coil round several times so that there are several layers forming the envelope (Fig. 350, axon A). The same effect may be achieved by several overlapping cells, while, in the case of small axons, several may be enclosed within one glial fold (Fig. 350, axon B).

The glial cells probably serve to insulate the axons from each other and it is believed that synapses only occur where glial folds are absent, although the absence of a glial fold does not necessarily indicate a synapse. In addition, the glial cells pass nutrient materials to the neurons, this being facilitated by finger-like inpushings of the glial cells into the neurons.

Between the glial cells are extracellular spaces. These are extensive peripherally, but much more restricted within the neuropile where they are continuous with the narrow spaces between the glial folds. These spaces show periodic lacunae which are characteristic of insect nerves (Fig. 350). The fluid in the extracellular spaces bathes the nervous elements directly and is therefore of great importance in nervous conduction (see p. 532). It differs in composition from the haemolymph, the concentrations of sodium and potassium being higher and that of chloride lower than in the haemolymph (Table 5). This results largely from a Donnan equilibrium across the neural sheath and the higher concentration of ions within the sheath causes an osmotic excess within the extracellular spaces so that a marked hydrostatic pressure develops within the neural lamella.

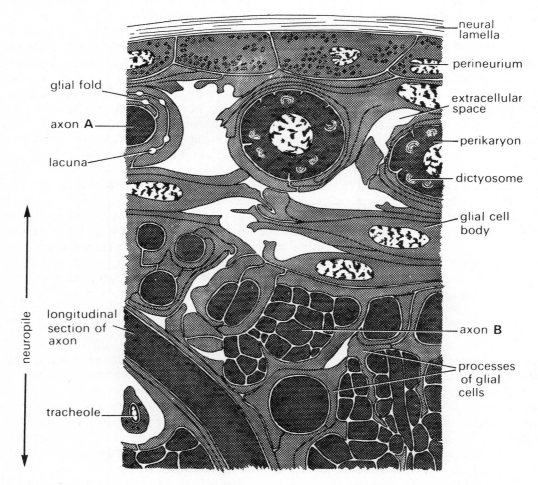

Fig. 350. Diagrammatic cross-section of part of an abdominal ganglion showing the arrangement of the various tissues (after Smith and Treherne, 1963).

Neurons

The cell bodies, perikarya, of the neurons are situated near the periphery of the ganglion, close beneath the perineurium. Within the perikarya, apart from the nucleus, there are abundant mitochondria, unattached ribosomes and ordered associations of membranes known as dictyosomes. These are often crescent-shaped and are associated with small vesicles. They may be concerned with the elaboration of cellular materials and secretions.

There is an abrupt change in the internal organisation of the neuron at the origin of the axon. The axoplasm contains mitochondria, but no dictyosomes or unattached ribosomes, while in addition, it contains neurofilaments. These are about 200 Å in diameter, sometimes appearing tubular, and they may form a link between the distal extremities of the axon and the perikaryon.

Neuropile

The neuropile consists of a mass of axons of all types and particularly their terminal arborisations, together with their investing glial elements and fine branches of the tracheal system. The glial material is reduced in the body of the neuropile and may be absent altogether so that adjacent axons are in contact with each other. It is believed that most synapses occur in the neuropile.

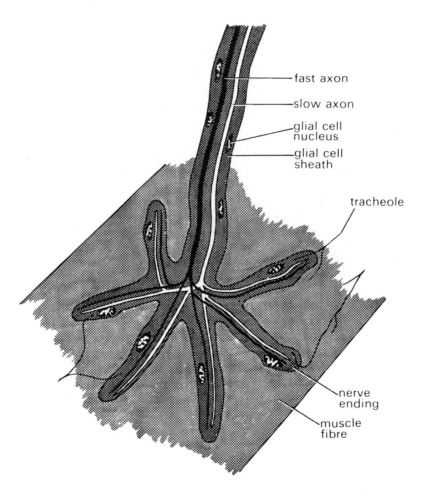

fast axon
slow axon
glial cell nucleus
glial cell sheath
tracheole
nerve ending
muscle fibre

Fig. 351. Diagram of a nerve/muscle junction in an orthopteran (after Hoyle, 1965a).

Synapses

Synapses occur where glial cells are absent so that the axons lie very close together, their membranes being separated only by a narrow synaptic gap. Synapses are believed to be characterised by foci of electron dense material in areas 150–500 mμ long close to the cell membrane where the two axons are adjacent. These foci are found particularly in what is presumed to be the presynaptic fibre. Also indicative of a synapse, although occurring elsewhere, are small synaptic vesicles, again usually found in the presynaptic fibre. These vesicles are of two types, some about 200 to 500 Å in diameter, which tend to aggregate in clusters and may contain the transmitter substance (p. 533), and others up to 1000 Å across which resemble neurosecretory droplets. Mitochondria are most abundant in axons where synaptic vesicles occur.

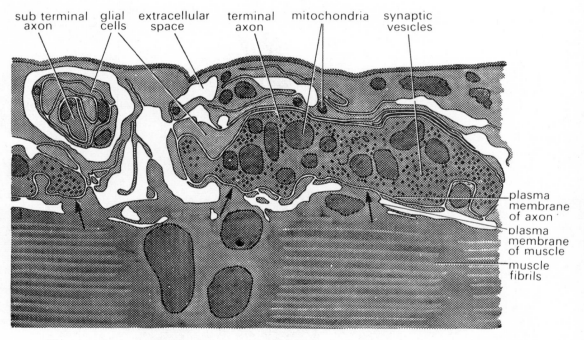

Fig. 352. A neuromuscular junction in *Apis* coxal muscle, from an electron micrograph. Arrows indicate points of apposition between neurilemma and sarcolemma (after Smith and Treherne, 1963).

Synapses of another type, perhaps involving electrical rather than chemical transmission, occur between the perikarya in the corpora pedunculata of *Formica* (Hymenoptera). There are gaps in the glial cells surrounding the perikarya so that the membranes of adjacent cells approach each other very closely, perhaps forming a compound membrane, but no accumulations of vesicles are present in the adjacent cytoplasm (Landolt and Ris, 1966).

Nerve muscle junctions

The motor nerve supplying an insect muscle makes contact with each muscle fibre at a number of points (p.210). The nature of the ending varies considerably. In the simplest form, such as occurs, for instance, in the flight muscles of Diptera, the fine nerve branches pass longitudinally over the surface of the muscle or sometimes, as in *Tenebrio* (Coleoptera), the terminal axon is completely invaginated into the muscle fibre so that it makes contact with the muscle all round its circumference. In Orthoptera the axon divides at the surface of the muscle and the branches, with their sheaths, form a claw-like structure (Fig. 351). Each junction may contain only one axon, as in *Tenebrio*, or more than one, as in *Blatta* (Dictyoptera). There is no known difference between the junctions of fast and slow axons (p. 216) and it is probable that multiaxonal junctions include both.

The fine structure appears to be similar in all these forms (Fig. 352). Glial cells are lacking along the nerve/muscle interface so that the axon and muscle fibre plasma membranes are close together, separated only by a synaptic gap of about 100 Å. The terminal axoplasm contains synaptic vesicles some 250–450 Å across (Smith, 1965c).

26.2 Physiology of the nervous system

Stimuli may be perceived in a number of ways depending on the nature of the stimulus and the characteristics of the sense organs. The energy received by the sense cell as a result of stimulation is then transformed (transduced) to electrical energy and this leads to the production of a nerve impulse which travels along the nerve axon to the central nervous system. Here the impulse crosses a synapse and, directly or via one or more interneurons, continues along a motor neuron, crossing a final synapse before producing some response from an effector organ, usually a muscle.

26.21 Reception and transduction of the stimulus

Different types of stimuli, mechanical, chemical or visual, are perceived in different ways and involve different sense organs. Mechanical stimuli appear to cause some mechanical distortion of the receptor dendrite (p.598); chemical stimuli may act in a number of unknown ways, but it is suggested that sugars form complexes with specific receptor molecules at the receptor site (p. 631); while visual perception probably involves the breakdown of some light sensitive pigment (p.553). Whatever the method of perception, the energy received by the sense cell is transformed to electrical energy. In some way not understood the stimulus affects the permeability of the plasma membrane of the dendrite so that it becomes depolarised (see below).

The potential produced in the dendrite by this depolarisation is called a receptor potential. It varies in size, or is graded, according to the strength of the stimulus, a weak stimulus producing only a weak receptor potential. The receptor potential leads to the development of a generator potential, although it is probable that in insects these are often not differentiated from each other. The generator potential is believed to arise in the region of the perikaryon. Like the receptor potential it is graded and if it exceeds a certain threshold value it triggers off the production of the all-or-none nerve impulse in the initial segment of the axon (Davis, 1961).

26.22 Nerve impulse

The production and conduction of a nerve impulse in insects is not fully understood, but it appears to be similar to the process in other animals (Narahashi, 1963, 1965). The account of the theory of conduction is therefore based to a large extent on the general concepts of nervous conduction (see *e.g.* Hodgkin, 1958; Keele and Neil, 1961).

Membrane potential

The ionic concentrations within an axon differ from those in the adjacent extracellular fluid despite the fact that the plasma membrane is freely permeable. Sodium is actively pumped out of the axon so that its concentration inside is much lower than outside and this movement is linked with an inward movement of potassium ions. Ionic movement is also influenced by large indiffusable organic anions within the axon and a Donnan equilibrium is set up across the plasma membrane with a high concentration of potassium ions inside the axon and a high concentration of chloride ions outside (Table 5). As a result of the equilibrium the inside of the axon becomes negatively charged with respect to the outside and the potential produced in this way is known as the membrane, or resting, potential. Its magnitude varies, but commonly nerve axons have a membrane potential of about —70 mV.

Action potential

Unlike the generator potential, which may vary in amplitude, the action, or spike, potential is of constant amplitude. It arises from a depolarisation of the axon membrane associated with a change in permeability. When a nerve impulse is initiated the change in permeability is produced by the generator potential, but as the impulse passes along the axon the change is self-regenerative.

The first change which occurs is a brief, but very marked, increase in permeability to sodium as a result of which sodium ions flow into the axon down the concentration gradient. This produces a rapid positive swing in the charge on the inside of the membrane, amounting to 80-100 mV. in the cockroach, representing the rising phase of the action potential (Fig. 353). Adjacent areas of axon are negatively charged so that a current flows in a local circuit away from the point of depolarisation inside the axon and towards it on the outside (Fig. 354). Where this current reaches an area of resting membrane it produces a slight depolarisation, of the order of 20 mV., so that the permeability to sodium rises and the charge on the inside of the fibre swings towards positive, becoming increasingly permeable as it does so. In this way a wave of increased permeability, and hence a nerve impulse, is propagated along the fibre without decrement.

The period of permeability to sodium is short-lived and is followed by a period of increased permeability to potassium as a result of which potassium flows out of the fibre which again becomes negatively charged on the inside. This is the falling phase of the action potential. Thus the total duration of the spike or action potential is very brief, only one or two milliseconds.

After the potential has returned to its resting level it overshoots slightly because of the high permeability to potassium. This is known as the positive phase and after it the potential swings back again to a level slightly higher than normal (Fig. 353). This phase, the negative after-potential, results from the potassium which is released in the falling phase of the action potential accumulating just outside the axon membrane so that the tendency for potassium to move out is reduced. The negative after-potential persists for several milliseconds, but finally the membrane potential returns to normal. In insects, the negative after-potential is short-lived compared with vertebrates, probably because the lacunae between the glial folds provide relatively large spaces into which the potassium can diffuse quickly.

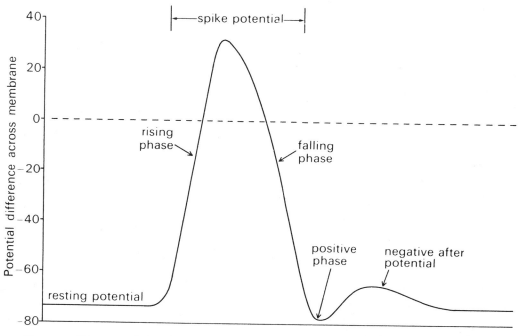

Fig. 353. Diagram of the changes in potential difference across the plasma membrane of an axon occurring during the passage of an impulse.

Following the development of an action potential the ionic composition within the axon is altered, the sodium concentration has increased and the potassium concentration decreased. The ionic quantities involved are very small and it has been estimated that an axon 500 μ in diameter loses about a millionth of its potassium ions in the passage of one impulse. Nevertheless, if the axon is to continue functioning over long periods a recovery mechanism is required to bring the ionic concentrations back to their original values. This involves the sodium pump which actively extrudes sodium ions, probably in exchange for potassium. In this way the concentration of sodium is slowly lowered, while that of potassium is raised to its original level.

Normally the stimulation of a nerve does not lead to the production of one nerve impulse, but of many. Since these are all of the same amplitude, information concerning the stimulus can only be conveyed in the number and frequency of the impulses, the latter being proportional to the size of the generator potential. There is, however, a limit to the frequency at which impulses can follow each other. In the presence of an action potential no further stimulation can initiate another impulse, nor can an impulse from elsewhere pass through the area. The period for which this is true is known as the absolute refractory period; it lasts for two or three milliseconds. Immediately after this an impulse can be produced, but only by a very strong stimulus and as the nerve recovers progressively weaker stimuli serve to produce impulses until the level of excitation returns to normal. This relative refractory period lasts for 10-15 msec.

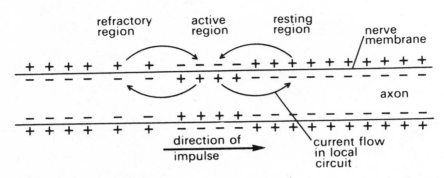

Fig. 354. Diagram of impulse conduction along a nerve axon. Conduction does not occur towards the left because the membrane is in a refractory state due to the recent passage of the nerve impulse (after Narahashi, 1965).

The velocity of conduction in a nerve fibre is proportional to its diameter. Giant fibres, with diameters of 8–50 μ, have conduction speeds of 3–7 m./sec.; normal fibres, of about 5 μ diameter, conduct at speeds of 1·5–2·3 m./sec. The velocity of conduction varies with temperature.

Effect of haemolymph composition on conduction

Since the passage of impulses in the nerve involves the movement of ions into and out from the axon it follows that this movement, and hence the impulse itself, is influenced by the concentration of ions in the medium bathing the axon (Treherne, 1965a). If the level of potassium in the external fluid is raised there is less tendency for potassium to flow out of the axon and hence the membrane potential is reduced. Similarly a low level of sodium in the external medium reduces the height of the action potential.

In many insects the concentration of sodium in the haemolymph is high, while the concentration of potassium is low (p. 683), but in some, particularly in herbivorous insects such as *Carausius*, the converse is true and there is much more potassium than sodium. It might be supposed that this would influence nervous conduction in some way, but this is not so because the concentrations of ions in the extracellular fluid within the nerve sheath are quite different from those in the haemolymph, the sodium concentration greatly exceeding the potassium concentration (Table 5). Even in *Periplaneta*, where there is more sodium than potassium in the haemolymph, the ionic concentrations within the nerve sheath are different. Thus the nervous tissue lies in its own microenvironment which resembles, in ionic composition, the body fluids of other animals.

The ionic concentrations within the nerve sheath of *Periplaneta* can be accounted for on the basis of a Donnan equilibrium between the fluid within the sheath and the haemolymph outside, but, apart from the calcium and magnesium concentrations, this is not the case in *Carausius*. Here sodium is actively pumped in from the haemolymph by the perineurium, but the mechanism by which potassium is maintained at a high level is not understood.

TABLE 5

IONIC CONCENTRATIONS (IN mM/LITRE) IN THE NERVE CORD AND
HAEMOLYMPH OF *CARAUSIUS* AND *PERIPLANETA*

(from Treherne, 1966)

Ion	Haemolymph conc.	Nerve cord concentrations (estimated)	
		Extracellular fluid	Cell water
Carausius			
Na	20	212	86
K	34	124	556
Ca	6	12	62
Mg	62	117	11
Periplaneta			
Na	157	284	67
K	12	17	225
Ca	4	18	14
Cl	184	107	—

Calcium is essential for efficient nerve conduction, being bound to molecules on the nerve membrane. When the calcium is displaced, as it is temporarily on stimulation, the permeability of the membrane increases. The calcium in the membrane is in equilibrium with that in the surrounding medium and lowering the level of external calcium results in progressive depolarisation of the membrane and complete nerve block. Thus calcium is an essential constituent of the haemolymph.

In *Carausius* magnesium is also an essential constituent of the haemolymph, possibly being able to replace sodium to some extent in the development of an action potential. In other species high concentrations of magnesium block conduction.

26.23 Transmission at the synapse

When an impulse has passed along an axon it must cross a synapse in order to stimulate another neuron or an effector. Transmission across the synapse involves a chemical and it is suggested that the substance concerned is stored in the synaptic vesicles. On the arrival of an impulse the membranes bounding the vesicles fuse with the cell membrane so that the transmitter substance is released into the synaptic gap (cf. Fig. 479). The transmitter substance becomes attached at receptor sites on the postsynaptic membrane and, through a change in permeability, causes it to become depolarised. The magnitude of the depolarisation is presumed to be proportional to the number of vesicles released. Normally they are released in small numbers in a random fashion, producing miniature potentials in the postsynaptic dendrite. These miniature potentials, which in insect muscle average only 0·25 mV. (Usherwood, 1963), are too small to initiate a nerve impulse or muscle contraction, but when a nerve impulse arrives at a synapse it is believed that large numbers of synaptic vesicles are released simultaneously so that the postsynaptic membrane is strongly depolarised. The resulting potential is normally big enough to initiate a nerve impulse or the activity of an effector (see p. 89, 214).

The depolarisation of the postsynaptic fibre is only short-lived because the chemical transmitter is rapidly hydrolysed by an appropriate enzyme. Within the nervous system the chemical transmitter is probably acetylcholine, but some other substance is involved at the nerve/muscle junctions. Acetylcholine is destroyed postsynaptically by the enzyme acetylcholine esterase; it is synthesised in the presynaptic fibre in a two-stage reaction, the second involving the acetylation of choline from acetyl coenzyme A in the presence of choline acetylase (Colhoun, 1963).

The postsynaptic receptor sites of insects appear to be less sensitive than those of other animals, requiring much higher concentrations of transmitter substances to effect transmission. This may reflect the high amino acid content of the extracellular fluid. Amino acids exert both inhibitory and excitatory effects on synapses and it is essential that transmission should only be effected by postsynaptic changes greater than those produced by the amino acids normally present (Treherne, 1966).

Relative to the rate of conduction in the axons, the impulse takes a long time to cross a synapse. Synaptic delay frequently varies from about one to five milliseconds and, for instance, in the cockroach the passage of the single synapse in the system from the tip of the cercus to the front end of the giant fibres (Fig. 349) takes about 25% (1·5 msec. in 5·8 msec.) of the total conduction time (Table 6). Delays may be much longer, as at the synapse between cockroach giant fibres and the motor fibres to the legs, where the average delay at the synapse is over twice as long as the total time taken for all the other events in the reflex.

TABLE 6

THE SEQUENCE OF EVENTS AND THEIR DURATIONS IN THE STARTLE RESPONSE OF THE COCKROACH (compare Fig. 349)

(from Huber, 1965)

	Event	Time in msec.
1.	Probable excitation time of cercal receptor	0·5
2.	Conduction time in cercal nerve	1·5
3.	Synaptic delay in afferent-giant junction	1·5
4.	Conduction time in giant fibre	2·8
5.	Estimated synaptic delay in giant-efferent junction	
	average	38·2
	minimum	13·0
6.	Conduction time in fast motor nerve	1·5
7.	Neuromuscular transmission	4·0
8.	Development of contraction	4·0

26.24 Spontaneous discharge

The production of an impulse in a nerve fibre normally results from stimulation of a sense cell, but many axons also discharge spontaneously in the absence of any sensory input. This discharge may be increased or decreased by sensory input, or it may remain unaffected, continuing in intermittent bursts over long periods. In some cases this spontaneous discharge may be concerned with the maintenance of muscle tonus, but in general its effect is probably to maintain the system in a highly active state so that it reacts readily to input and is more easily excited. Stimuli which would be subthreshold in an unexcited fibre may produce a response in a fibre already discharging spontaneously (see Roeder, 1963).

The rate of spontaneous discharge varies with temperature. For instance the output from an isolated ganglion of the cockroach increases with temperature up to a maximum and then falls off. The temperature at which the maximum occurs depends on the temperature to which the insects have been exposed previously, and the ganglia of insects kept at 22°C. have a maximum output at 22°C., while in insects kept at 31°C. the maximum is at 31°C. Sudden changes in temperature produce different effects in different fibres (see p. 637).

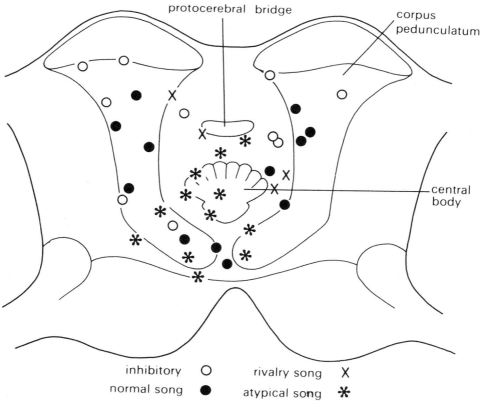

Fig. 355. Diagram of the brain of *Acheta* (Orthoptera). Stimulation at the points marked produces the different types of song and associated behaviour as indicated (from Horridge, 1965).

26.3 Integration in the nervous system

The nervous system does not act as a simple relay between receptors and effectors, it integrates the activities of different parts of the body so that appropriate behavioural responses and internal regulating changes are made. Thus, although the segmental ganglia are largely autonomous in their regulation of such activities as walking (p. 149) and respiration (p. 468), their output is modified by the input which they receive from other parts of the body and in this way the activities of the body as a whole are co-ordinated (Huber, 1965; Roeder, 1963).

The brain is important in integration, and the corpora pedunculata, in particular, have a significant role in the regulation of complex multisegmental behaviour, acting as a switch and controlling the temporal and spatial pattern of the behaviour. In the singing of crickets, for instance, they integrate the input from several receptors, such as the eyes and tympanal organs, and from the ventral nerve cord, signals from which indicate the presence or absence of a spermatophore. This determines whether or not singing will occur. The type of song produced depends on the stimulation of specific loci within the corpora pedunculata; stimulation of the calyx inhibits singing, while stimulation of the α and β lobes initiates the calling or rivalry songs with their appropriate behaviour (Fig. 355). In many cases output from the brain inhibits the activity of the more posterior ganglia (p. 538).

Integration between different motor units of the body depends to a large extent on the fact that some internuncial neurons pass through several segments and make synapses with a number of other neurons. For instance, one internuncial connecting with a number of afferent and efferent fibres can act as a relay in a number of different sensory/motor arcs (Fig. 356A). Alternatively, a single afferent fibre may ascend or

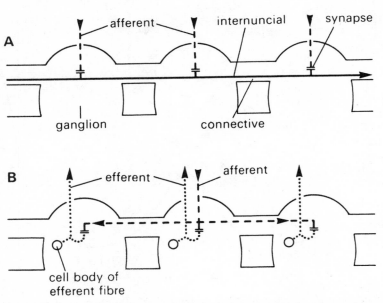

Fig. 356. Diagrams to illustrate some possible types of connection between different neurons (after Hughes, 1965b).

descend from one ganglion to the next making synaptic contact with an efferent fibre in each of the ganglia which it enters (Fig. 356B) and there are other variations on this theme (see Hughes, 1965b).

The physiological and anatomical nature of the synapse may also influence integration. For instance, it may happen that the postsynaptic potential produced by the arrival of a single impulse at a synapse may not be big enough to initiate an impulse and will slowly decay. If, however, a second impulse arrives at the synapse and causes a further depolarisation of the postsynaptic fibre before the first potential has completely decayed the total potential resulting from the two successive depolarisations may exceed the threshold and initiate an impulse (Fig. 357). This is temporal summation such as might occur where the synapse involves a 1:1 relationship between pre- and postsynaptic fibres (Fig. 358A). At some synapses, however, a number of afferent fibres synapse at one point with a single internuncial fibre (Fig. 358B). This is known as a convergent synapse and here spatial summation may occur. In this case the postsynaptic potential arising from the firing of one presynaptic fibre may be subthreshold, but if several fibres fire together the potential resulting from their combined effects will exceed the threshold and fire the postsynaptic fibre. The synapse of sensory fibres in the cockroach cercal nerve with a giant fibre (Fig. 349) is of the convergent type.

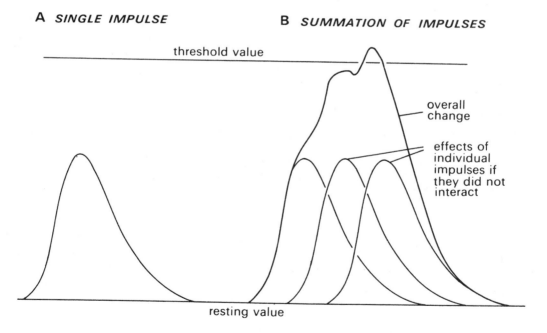

A *SINGLE IMPULSE*   **B** *SUMMATION OF IMPULSES*

threshold value

overall change

effects of individual impulses if they did not interact

resting value

Fig. 357. Diagram illustrating the changes in potential of a postsynaptic membrane. A. A single impulse in the presynaptic fibre produces a rise in the postsynaptic potential, but this does not reach the threshold value so that no action potential is produced. B. The increases in potential produced by three impulses arriving in rapid succession are summed so that a large overall increase is produced, exceeding the threshold and leading to the development of an action potential.

Integration may also occur at a synapse as the result of the convergence of fibres from different parts of the body. This occurs, for instance, at the anterior end of the cockroach giant fibre system where, in the metathoracic ganglion, the giant fibre/motor fibre synapse is also influenced by fibres from the head ganglia (Fig. 349). The output of these fibres excites the postsynaptic fibres so that they are more readily stimulated by impulses reaching them via the giant fibres.

Divergent synapses also occur (Fig. 358C) at which an impulse in the presynaptic fibre would produce a discharge in a number of postsynaptic fibres.

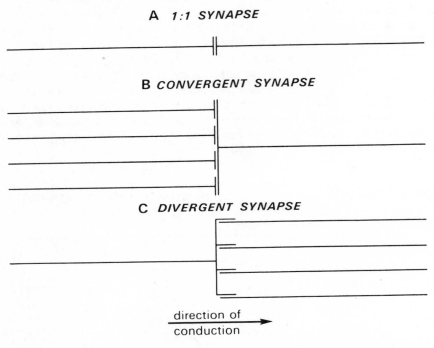

Fig. 358. Diagrammatic representation of different types of synapse (after Roeder, 1953).

The relationship between the discharge in pre- and post-synaptic fibres depends on the intrinsic properties of the cells. Although in many cases one impulse in the pre-synaptic fibre produces one impulse in the postsynaptic fibre, in some cases the response in the postsynaptic fibre is completely independent of the input, while in others there is some relationship, although not necessarily a direct one.

26.31 Inhibition

Integration does not involve only stimulation of neurons, inhibition also occurs. Inhibition may occur in one of two ways; either the normal stimulatory output from the central nervous system is abolished or inhibited, or an impulse passing from the central nervous system may inhibit the activity of an effector instead of stimulating it. These two phenomena are known respectively as central and peripheral inhibition.

Central inhibition is well known in insects. For instance, the spontaneous output of the last abdominal ganglion of the mantis is inhibited by the head ganglia. If the head is removed the output from the ganglion increases markedly and the male mantis makes continuous copulatory movements with the abdomen which were previously inhibited. Not only the ganglia of the head have inhibitory effects since, for instance, a prothoracic leg reflex in *Schistocerca* (Orthoptera) is inhibited from the meso- and meta-thoracic ganglia as well as from the suboesophageal ganglion (Rowell, 1964). Such central inhibition arising in the ganglia is probably of considerable importance in the regulation of many systems in the insect nervous system (Roeder, 1963).

In many cases, as with the inhibition of the output of the abdominal ganglion of the mantis, the inhibiting effect arises spontaneously in the brain or other ganglia. In other instances, the stimulation of a sense organ may lead to central inhibition. In *Phormia* (Diptera), for instance, the taste threshold of tarsal and labellar chemoreceptors (p. 630) rises soon after feeding. This is largely due to central inhibition resulting from the input of stretch receptors in the wall of the alimentary canal which are stimulated by the intake of food. If the oesophageal nerve, by which these receptors are innervated, is cut, inhibition is removed and the fly will continue to feed (see also Dethier and Gelperin, 1967). The degree of inhibition in instances such as this may vary and it is suggested that the likelihood of a particular activity being inhibited is greater when the input from other sources, not concerned with the activity, is high so that the insect is 'distracted'. Possibly this type of inhibition does not involve special inhibitory fibres (Rowell, 1964). On the other hand, some sense organs and the fibres running from them do appear to have a specific inhibiting function, the ocelli, for instance, inhibiting a spontaneous output from second order cells (see p. 571).

Peripheral inhibition is not well known in insects. In grasshoppers the extensor tibialis muscle of the hind leg is innervated by three nerves. One of these is the 'fast' fibre, another the 'slow' fibre (p. 216), while the third in *Romalea* is an inhibitor. Activity in this axon inhibits contraction of the muscle resulting from stimulation via the slow axon, and sometimes the inhibition is complete. This fibre also has some inhibitory effect in *Schistocerca*, but to a much lesser extent (Hoyle, 1965a).

Inhibition depends in some cases, at least, on the nature of the synaptic transmitter or on the postsynaptic membrane. The latter, on being stimulated by the transmitter, becomes hyperpolarised instead of depolarised so that there is a decrease in its excitability and no impulse is produced.

26.4 Learning

Neural mechanisms are concerned in learning, which may be defined as an adaptive change in individual behaviour as a result of experience. It can be conveniently classi-fied in a number of different categories which are briefly described (see Schneirla, 1953; Thorpe, 1963).

Habituation

Habituation is the term employed for learning not to respond to stimuli which tend to be without significance in the life of the animal. *Nemeritis* (Hymenoptera), for instance, moves away from the smell of cedarwood oil, but if it is continuously exposed to the smell it learns to tolerate it. Similarly if a cockroach is continually disturbed it ultimately learns to tolerate the disturbance without trying to escape from it.

Conditioning

An animal may learn to respond to a stimulus which was previously ineffective if the stimulus occurs repeatedly in the presence of an effective stimulus. The process is known as conditioning. For instance, bees do not usually respond to the smell of coumarin, but they can be trained to associate the odour with feeding by exposure to the smell while feeding on sugar water. Subsequently, after an average of only seven training periods, the odour alone is sufficient to elicit proboscis extension. Similarly newly emerged *Plusia* (Lepidoptera) locate the flowers on which they feed by scent only, but after a few experiences of feeding they learn to associate the appearance of the flower with feeding and subsequently employ both vision and olfaction in food finding.

Trial-and-error learning

An animal is said to learn by trial-and-error when a particular stimulus becomes associated with a motor action as a result of reinforcement in some subsequent behaviour. For instance, *Leptinotarsa* (Coleoptera) is at first not at all discriminating in selecting a mate. It does not differentiate members of other genera from its own species or differentiate head from tail. It recognises only the long axis of the body. Subsequently, however, as a result of various attempted copulations it learns to distinguish head from tail and also to pick out its own species.

Latent learning

Latent learning is the association of stimuli or situations having no particular significance and without any obvious or immediate reward. In insects latent learning often involves the recognition of landmarks by the insect in becoming familiar with its territory. *Philanthus* (Hymenoptera), for instance, learns the position of its nest by the landmarks surrounding it. These are learned on an orientation flight lasting about six seconds which the insect makes on leaving the nest. On returning, after an interval of perhaps 90 minutes, the insect recognises the landmarks and finds its way to the nest. If the landmarks are displaced it continues to orientate to them and is unable to find the nest. Recognition depends on the configuration of the landmarks rather than on their precise nature and number.

Apis (Hymenoptera) also learns to recognise the features of its home locality. In addition, the forager learns the position of the sun through the perception of polarised light (p. 569) and orientates the straight run of its dance appropriately on returning to the hive. Other workers in the hive learn the orientation of the dance and when they go out to forage base their subsequent orientation to polarised light on this knowledge (see von Frisch, 1950).

Time sense

Many insects have rhythms of activity based on previous experience which continue for a time under constant conditions. The cockroach, for instance, is normally active in the dark and continues to become active at the appropriate time even in continuous light (see Fig. 486). In *Periplaneta* this rhythm is based on a rhythmic production of neurosecretion from cells in the suboesophageal ganglion (p. 711) (Harker, 1964).

26.41 Neural basis of learning

Little is known about the neuronal changes which must be involved in these processes, but it is presumed that the brain, and especially the corpora pedunculata, are important. The corpora pedunculata are suggested on morphological grounds, being largest in insects with complex behaviour patterns and reaching a peak of development in the social Hymenoptera. In the workers of *Apis* they occupy 13·5% of the volume of the brain, compared with 9·2% in the queen and 5·6% in the drone. In ants, however, the corpora pedunculata are larger in the winged forms than in the workers. Ants can be trained to learn their way visually through a T-maze, but when the tracts from the corpora pedunculata are cut this ability is lost, although the insects are not blinded.

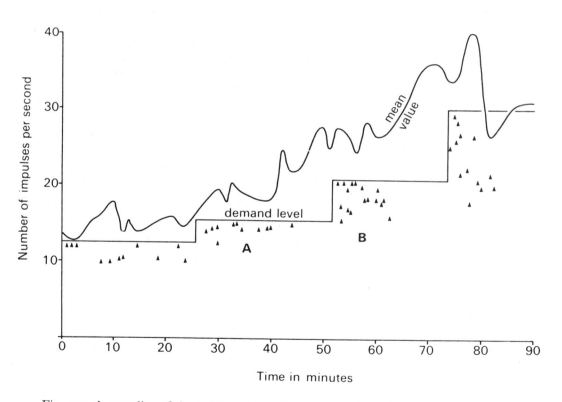

Fig. 359. A recording of the number of impulses per second arriving at the coxal adductor muscle of *Schistocerca*. Whenever the frequency fell below the arbitrarily fixed demand level the muscle was given an electric shock as indicated by the triangles. After a group of shocks, as at A and B, the frequency of impulses rose and remained high (modified after Hoyle, 1965b).

Habituation to repeated stimuli has been demonstrated at neuronal level in the cockroach. If the cerci are stimulated at half-minute intervals with a puff of air the number of impulses occurring in the ventral nerve cord in response to each stimulus falls off. It is therefore concluded that part of the mechanism resulting in the waning of the response to a puff of air occurs in the last abdominal ganglion (Hughes, 1965b).

Other evidence also indicates the part played in learning by the segmental ganglia. Thus headless *Schistocerca* can learn to keep a leg flexed so as to avoid electrical shocks. The raising is produced by the contraction of a number of muscles, but the coxal levators are of particular importance. Pinching the foot or an electric shock applied after a drop in the frequency of discharge to this muscle produce a maintained increase in the frequency of impulses in the motor nerve so that the muscle contracts and the leg is raised. By gradually increasing the level of discharge at which a shock is given a 300% increase in the motor frequency can be induced (Fig. 359). It is suggested as a generalisation that a burst of impulses in a sensory nerve following a change in frequency in a motor neuron induces a prolonged alteration in the output of the motor neuron in a direction counter to the original change so that further stimulation is avoided (Hoyle, 1965b).

In terms of the leg movement this means that a reduction in the nervous discharge to the adductor muscle leads to a reduction in muscle tension so that the leg drops. As a result it touches the surface of a liquid and receives a shock. The increased input due to the shock leads to an increased discharge in the motor nerve so that muscle tension increases and the leg is raised. Maintenance of the high rate of discharge in the motor nerve keeps the leg raised so that further shocks are avoided. Input from the proprioceptors of the leg is apparently of no significance in the response.

It is clear from this that the frequency of impulses to the coxal adductor muscles is determined in the metathoracic ganglion and that lasting changes of adaptive significance can occur in response to external events. The changes are readily reversed if the relationship to the environment changes.

CHAPTER XXVII
THE EYES AND VISION

Light is perceived by insects through a number of different sense organs, but the most important are the compound eyes. These consist of groups of units each of which is made up of a lens system and a small number of sense cells. The lens system focuses light on to a photosensitive element and the output from the sense cells travels back to the optic lobe of the brain. Here complex interconnections occur with other nerve cells having a wide variety of characteristics and the integrated signals are then fed back to the brain and ventral nerve cord.

The insect eye is well adapted to perceive movement, but complex form perception is also possible. The eye is not equally sensitive to all wavelengths, and further, its sensitivity varies under different conditions. Some species can discriminate between different colours, and some can perceive the plane of vibration of polarised light and may use this in steering. Insects may respond to light and other stimuli directionally or in a quantitative, but undirected, manner.

In addition to the compound eyes adult and larval hemimetabolous insects typically have three simple eyes, called ocelli, while larval holometabolous insects have no compound eyes, but have simple stemmata on the side of the head. The function of the ocelli is obscure; possibly they have a general stimulatory effect on the nervous system. Stemmata permit a limited amount of form perception.

General reviews of the structure and physiology of insect eyes are given by Burtt and Catton (1962b, 1966), Dethier (1963), Goldsmith (1964), Horridge (1965), Kuiper (1962) and Ruck (1964). The physiology of colour vision is dealt with by Burkhardt (1962, 1964), Jander (1963) reviews orientation in insects, and see also Fraenkel and Gunn (1940). See also Wolken (1963, *Symp. zool. Soc. Lond.* **23**).

27.1 Occurrence and structure of compound eyes

Most adult insects have a pair of compound eyes, one on either side of the head, which bulge out to a greater or lesser extent (Fig. 2) so that they give a wide field of vision in all directions. In *Notonecta,* for instance, the visual field extends through 246° in the horizontal plane and 360° in a vertical plane, the fields of the two eyes overlapping so as to give binocular vision in front, above and below the head. In some insects, such as Anisoptera and male Tabanidae and Syrphidae, the eyes extend dorsally and are contiguous along the midline, this being known as the holoptic condition.

The compound eyes are strongly reduced or absent in parasitic groups such as the Siphunculata, Siphonaptera and female coccids and this is also true of cave-dwelling forms.

Each compound eye is an aggregation of similar units known as ommatidia, the number of which varies from one in the worker of the ant *Ponera punctatissima* to over 10,000 in the eyes of dragonflies. When only a few ommatidia are present the facets which they present to the outside are separated from each other by narrow areas of cuticle and are round; more usually, with larger numbers, the facets are packed close together and assume a hexagonal form (Fig. 360).

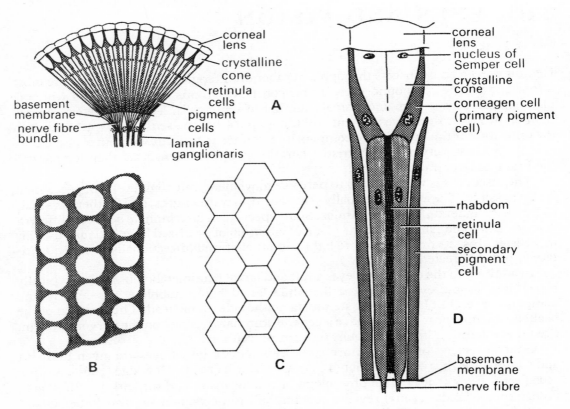

Fig. 360. Diagrams illustrating the structure of the compound eye. A. Section through part of an eye showing the arrangement of ommatidia. B. Surface view of part of the eye of an aphid which consists of a small number of ommatidia, showing the facets well separated by unmodified cuticle. C. Surface view of part of the eye of a syrphid which consists of a large number of ommatidia with the facets crowded together. D. Detail of a single ommatidium.

Ommatidia vary in size from insect to insect and within the Hymenoptera facet size is proportional to the square root of the height of the eye (Fig. 361). Variations also occur within one eye. In *Apis* the facets in the centre of the eye are about 22 μ in diameter whereas those at the top of the eye are about 17 μ in diameter (Barlow, 1952), and in dragonflies the dorsal facets may have twice the diameter of the ventral ones. In some other species the eye is sharply differentiated into a region with relatively large facets and another with much smaller facets, as in the male of *Bibio*. This separation is complete in the male of *Cloëon* (Ephemeroptera) where each eye is in two parts quite separate from each other. Not only are the ommatidia in these two parts different in size, they are also different in structure. Those of the dorsal part are relatively large and of the superposition type (p. 548), while in the lateral part the ommatidia are smaller and of the apposition type (p. 548). The eyes are also divided into two in the aquatic beetle *Gyrinus* (Coleoptera) where the dorsal eye is above the surface film when the insect is swimming and the ventral eye is below the surface.

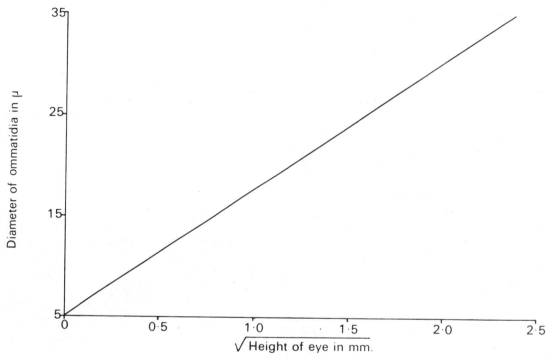

Fig. 361. The relationship between ommatidial diameter and the size of the eye in Hymenoptera (after Barlow, 1952).

27.11 Structure of an ommatidium

Each ommatidium consists essentially of an optical, light-gathering part and a sensory part, perceiving the radiation and transforming it into electrical energy.

The optical part of the system usually consists of two elements, a cuticular lens and a crystalline cone. The cuticle covering the eye is transparent and colourless and usually forms a biconvex corneal lens at the outer end of each ommatidium (Fig. 360D). It is these lenses which in surface view form the facets of the compound eye. In *Aleyrodes* all the lenses are not colourless, but each colourless one is surrounded by six yellow lenses. Some insects have the outer surface of the corneal lens produced into minute conical nipples about $0.2\ \mu$ high arranged in a hexagonal pattern with a $0.2\ \mu$ spacing. It is supposed that these projections decrease reflection from the surface of the lens and so increase the proportion of light transmitted through the facet. The cornea, like the rest of the cuticle, is secreted by epidermal cells, each lens being produced by two cells, the corneagen cells, which later become withdrawn to the sides of the ommatidium and form the primary pigment cells.

Beneath the cornea are four cells, the Semper cells, which, in most insects, produce the crystalline cone. This is a hard, clear intracellular structure bordered laterally by the primary pigment cells. Eyes in which the crystalline cone is present are called eucone eyes (but see p. 547).

Immediately behind the crystalline cone in eucone eyes are the sensory elements. These are elongate nerve cells known as retinula cells in each of which the margin nearest the ommatidial axis is differentiated to form a rhabdomere which extends the whole length of the cell. Primitively each ommatidium probably contained eight retinula cells arising from three successive divisions of a single cell. This number is found in some insects, such as *Apis,* but in many there is a tendency to reduction of this number to six or seven, the other one or two persisting as short basal cells in the proximal region of each ommatidium. The cytoplasm of the retinula cells contains pigment granules which are especially concentrated at the edge of the rhabdomere, but these granules do not contain the visual pigment. Arising from each cell is a nerve axon which passes out through the basement membrane at the back of the eye into the optic lobe.

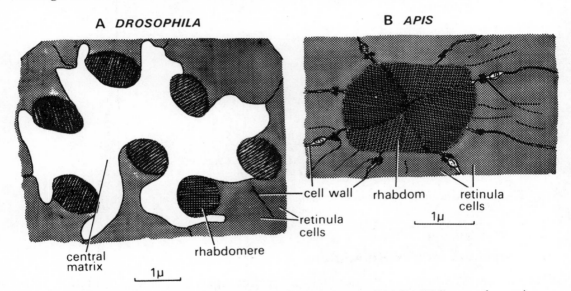

Fig. 362. Cross-section through the rhabdom of (A) *Drosophila* (after Wolken *et al.,* 1957) and (B) *Apis* (after Goldsmith, 1962).

The rhabdomere consists of close-packed microtubules or microvilli about 500 Å across, hexagonal in cross-section and extending towards the central axis of the ommatidium at right angles to the long axis of the retinula cell. The microtubules of each retinula cell are all parallel with each other and roughly aligned with those of the retinula cell opposite, but they are set at an angle to those of adjacent retinula cells (Fig. 362). In *Drosophila* each rhabdomere is 60 μ long and 1·2 μ in diameter (Wolken *et al.,* 1957), while in *Sarcophaga* their diameter is only about 0·5 μ (Goldsmith and Philpott, 1957).

Collectively the rhabdomeres of each ommatidium form the rhabdom. In Diptera the individual rhabdomeres remain separate, grouped around a central matrix which may have a fluid consistency (Wolken *et al.*, 1957) (Fig. 362A), but more often they are contiguous and may fuse together. In *Apis* (Fig. 362B) they are fused in pairs while in some Orthoptera all the rhabdomeres are fused into a single unit.

The retinula cells are shrouded by 12 to 18 secondary pigment cells which isolate each ommatidium from its neighbours (Fig. 360). Tracheae may pass between the ommatidia, but in *Apis* no tracheae penetrate the basement membrane of the eye.

27.12 Modifications of the ommatidial structure

In some Hemiptera, Coleoptera and Diptera the Semper cells do not form a crystalline cone, but become transparent and undergo only a little modification (Fig. 363B). Ommatidia of this type are described as acone ommatidia. The acone condition may be primitive and the eyes of many Apterygota are of this type. In other Apterygota, such as *Lepisma* (Thysanura) and *Orchesella* (Collembola), there is a very simple crystalline cone (Fig. 363A), while the Semper cells of most Diptera and some Odonata produce

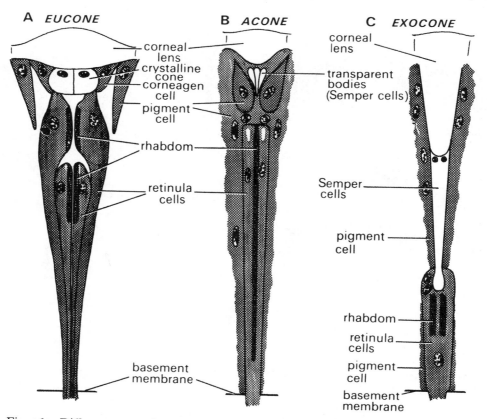

Fig. 363. Different types of ommatidia. A. Eucone ommatidium of *Lepisma* (Thysanura). B. Acone ommatidium of *Trichodes* (Coleoptera). C. Exocone ommatidium of *Lampyris* (Coleoptera) (from Eltringham, 1933).

cones which are liquid-filled or gelatinous rather than crystalline. Ommatidia of this type are described as pseudocone. Finally, in some beetles, such as *Lampyris*, the lens is formed from an inward extension of the cornea, not from the Semper cells which form a refractile structure between the cuticle and the retinula cells. This is an exocone ommatidium (Fig. 363C).

In the eyes of many insects the rhabdom is very long and extends from the back of the lens almost to the basement membrane. Because of the supposed method of image formation these are known as apposition eyes. In some Coleoptera and nocturnal Lepidoptera, on the other hand, the rhabdom is short and separated from the lenses by a space which is crossed by processes of the retinula cells surrounding an axial thread (Fig. 364). Eyes with this arrangement are said to be superposition eyes because of their supposed method of image formation (see p. 552).

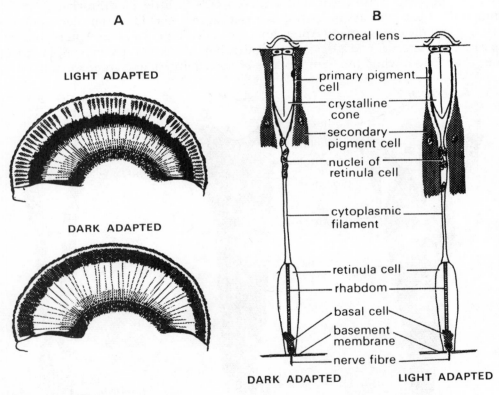

Fig. 364. A. Section through the eye of *Ephestia* in the light and dark adapted conditions. B. Detail of single ommatidia in light and dark adapted conditions (after Day, 1941).

Unlike the apposition eyes, the retinula cells of superposition eyes tend to increase in number and in *Ephestia* there are ten, nine of them with rhabdomeres. The tenth forms a short basal cell (Fig. 364B). In Noctuidae and some other moths with superposition eyes tracheae run through the eye parallel with the ommatidia and forming a layer round each one (Fig. 365). This layer may form a tapetum reflecting stray light back to the ommatidium.

Lepisma, the Collembola and some other insects have the retinula cells in two tiers, a distal tier usually of four cells and a proximal tier of three cells, so that there are two separate rhabdoms (Fig. 363A).

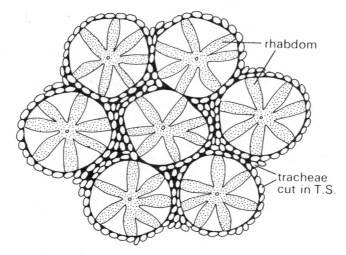

Fig. 365. Cross-section of a group of ommatidia of a moth showing the inter-ommatidial spaces packed with tracheae (from Imms, 1957).

27.13 Nervous connections from the eye

There is no optic nerve in insects, the eye connects directly with the optic lobe of the brain. This consists of three ganglionic layers, the lamina ganglionaris, medulla externa and medulla interna, connected to each other by chiasmata (see Fig. 346). Each ganglionic layer consists of an inner region of neuropile with the cell bodies at the periphery. Behind the eye the fibres from the retinula cells may decussate, as in *Calliphora,* or they may run in parallel strands, as in *Schistocerca.* Two kinds of axons run from the retinula cells, numerous short fibres to the lamina ganglionaris and occasional long fibres, perhaps from the basal cells, to the medulla externa (Fig. 366). The cells of the lamina ganglionaris are situated distally. They are monopolar and their axons pass inwards to the medulla externa, first making dendritic synapses with the retinula axons. There appears to be a good deal of convergence of the nerve fibres, fibres from several ommatidia connecting with each ganglion cell, but the degree of convergence differs in different parts of the eye (see also p. 554). Other fibres, arising from cells in the medulla externa, run, but do not necessarily conduct, centrifugally and make connections in the lamina ganglionaris.

27.2 Functioning of the eye

If the insect is to do more than differentiate between light and dark, that is if it has any degree of form vision, it must possess an optical system capable of forming a suitable image and a series of receptors capable of perceiving the image.

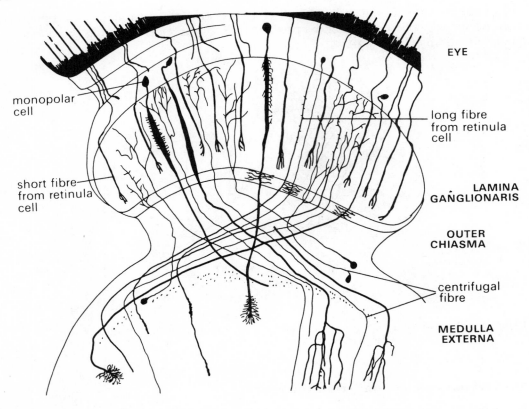

Fig. 366. Section through the back of the eye and part of the optic lobe of *Apis* illustrating some of the nervous connections (from Goldsmith, 1964).

27.21 Image formation by the optical system

Apposition eyes

The classical mosaic theory of insect vision supposes that each ommatidium forms an image of a limited part of the visual field. Each image has a given overall intensity which varies from one ommatidium to the next depending on the amount of light reflected from the object so that collectively the ommatidia produce a series of spots of light of different intensities which together form a picture of the object. In general, experimental evidence lends support to this theory, although with some modifications of detail.

Each ommatidium perceives light coming from a wide angle, which, in *Locusta* and *Calliphora*, is about 20° (Kuiper, 1962), and not simply from the field delimited by the ommatidial angle, the angle which the ommatidium subtends at the basement membrane, often 1 or 2°. Hence the visual fields of adjacent ommatidia overlap, but the amount of light transmitted through the lens system falls off sharply as the angle of incidence increases (Fig. 367) so that the greater part of the light entering each ommatidium does come from a limited area.

In the apposition eye, each lens system of corneal lens and crystalline cone is capable of forming an inverted image on the rhabdom. This image may have some significance, but Kuipér (1962) suggests that the function of the lens system is simply to concentrate the light into a narrow beam entering the rhabdom.

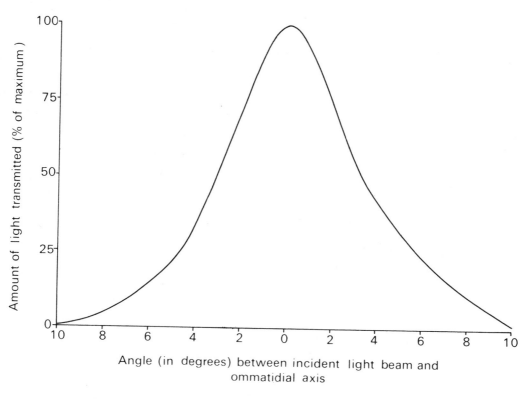

Fig. 367. The directional sensitivity of an ommatidium of *Apis* (after Kuiper, 1962).

The pigment cells of apposition eyes optically isolate the ommatidia so that little light passes from one to another, but the significance of this is not clear. It was believed that such isolation was necessary in order to obtain good resolution, but mutants of *Calliphora* which lack the screening pigment have equally good resolution of a moving pattern and are more sensitive than normal flies, requiring less incident light energy to produce a retinal response. This arises from the fact that light moving obliquely through the eye is not absorbed by the screening pigment as it is in normal eyes, so that it is able to stimulate adjacent ommatidia. This, however, leads to the rapid decay of the visual pigment and it may be that the function of the screening pigment normally present is to reduce the amount of light reaching the inner part of the eye so that the rate of decay of the visual pigment is reduced.

Superposition eyes

In the superposition eye the screening pigment moves. In the light it extends inwards and separates the ommatidia, but in the dark it condenses distally round the lenses. Not only does the pigment move within the secondary pigment cells, but the cells themselves also migrate proximally and distally to some extent (Fig. 364) (Day, 1941). The primary pigment cells do not move, nor does the pigment within them.

As a result of these pigment movements, the light-adapted eye, with the ommatidia separated from each other by pigment, functionally resembles an apposition eye. In poor light, however, when the pigment is contracted, light might pass obliquely through the eye without being absorbed. As a result each rhabdom might receive light from a number of lens systems, not only that of its own ommatidium, and the image formed as a result is called a superposition image. In this way more use is made of the available light since very little of it is absorbed by screening pigments. This is an advantage in crepuscular and nocturnal insects which are active when little light is available.

In *Lampyris* and some other beetles a single upright image is formed by the eye which, morphologically, is of the superposition type, but the image is formed below the basement membrane and so can have no functional value (Burtt and Catton, 1966). In other insects there is so little convergence of light from adjacent ommatidia that no image is formed. This, together with other evidence, suggests that superposition images, if they are formed at all, may not be important to insects and it is possible that superposition eyes form images by apposition. This would be facilitated by a refractile substance between the cone and the rhabdom acting as a wave guide and funnelling light to each rhabdom from its lens system. Such a guide might be provided by processes of the retinula cells (Fig. 364), or the Semper cells in *Lampyris* (Fig. 363C), which extend from the lens to the rhabdom, but they will not act in this way if their refractive index is low as seems likely.

If superposition images are not formed by these eyes, the observed pigment movements must have some significance other than that suggested above. Possibly the expanded condition in daylight affords protection to the visual pigments (and see p. 551), while contraction in the dark increases the sensitivity of the eye because less light is absorbed by the pigment.

Not all workers are agreed that superposition images are not formed since it has been shown that a series of images may be formed at progressively greater depths in the eye as a result of diffraction from the lens systems (Fig. 368). These diffraction images are

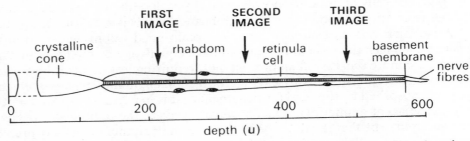

Fig. 368. Diagram of an ommatidium of *Locusta* showing the positions of the first three diffraction images (after Burtt and Catton, 1962b).

superposition images formed by groups of ommatidia acting together so that the effective diameter of the lens system is increased. It is suggested that this might form the basis of the insect's ability to discern stripes with a very low angular separation (p. 557) and, at the same time, would account for the great depth of the sensory system of the eye (Burtt and Catton, 1962a, b; Rogers, 1962). The image so formed may be extremely complex and distorted compared with the object, but it is possible that these patterns could be used as a means of recognition where this was not very precise (Burtt and Catton, 1966).

This theory is criticised on various grounds. McCann and MacGinitie (1965), for instance, suggest that small errors in the experimental pattern presented to the insect might cause small changes in the intensity of light falling on the eye, implying that the exceptional acuity associated with diffraction images is not a reality. Other criticisms are that diffraction images are only seen in bright light, otherwise the light deeper in the eye is absorbed by the pigments, and it is also doubtful if the insect can distinguish and utilise these images at the sensory level (see *e.g.* Goldsmith, 1964).

27.22 Reception of light

The rhabdom is presumed to be the site of photoreception and it probably acts as a wave guide, trapping most of the light which enters it. The refractive index of the rhabdom is higher than that of the surrounding cells ($1 \cdot 5 : 1 \cdot 33$) so that, unless the light enters it at a very oblique angle (as ray B in Fig. 369), the light is totally reflected at the interfaces (ray A in Fig. 369).

In vertebrates the conversion of light energy into a nerve impulse involves a photoreceptor pigment. This is a chromoprotein known as rhodopsin which consists of retinene, the aldehyde of vitamin A, conjugated with a protein. The production of rhodopsin is a continuous process, but in the light it is continually bleached and it dissociates, liberating retinene with an altered molecular configuration. This process leads to the production of a nerve impulse. In darkness no bleaching occurs so that the rhodopsin accumulates.

Evidence is accumulating which suggests that the process is basically similar in insects. Retinene has been isolated from the heads of Hymenoptera, Diptera and Orthoptera as well as other groups and it is reversibly converted to vitamin A by the action of a dehydrogenase. It has also been found that in the dark adapted head of *Apis* the ratio of retinene : vitamin A is 4 : 1 whereas in the light adapted head it is 1 : 4, suggesting that retinene is converted to vitamin A in the light (Goldsmith and Warner, 1964).

The absorption spectrum of the visual pigment may vary according to the protein with which the retinene is conjugated and it is probable that in some insects there are three pigments with different spectral sensitivities (p. 562).

27.23 Sensory system

However efficient the optical system of the eye may be, perception may be limited by the efficiency of the receptor mechanism and in particular by the number of sensory elements. A single element can perceive only a single sensory impression however complex the image falling on the element may be so that it is important to know if the rhabdom is a single functional unit or if the separate rhabdomeres function independently of each other.

The diffraction theory of vision and the theories of the basis of discrimination of colours (p. 562) and the plane of polarisation (p. 563) depend on the separate functioning of the rhabdomeres. In Diptera and Hemiptera the rhabdomeres are widely separated (see Fig. 362) and are presumed to function independently of each other, but in *Apis,* where the rhabdomeres are fused in pairs, there appear to be only four separate receptors and in some other cases there is apparently only one. If this is so, the sensory elements must be limiting factors in the vision of the species concerned.

Each retinula cell has its own nerve axon passing through the basement membrane at the back of the eye and these axons may decussate or remain in bundles (p. 549). Whether or not these axons remain separate or join together is difficult to determine, but in *Apis,* at least, there are fewer monopolar axons in the lamina ganglionaris than there are retinula cells in the eye, indicating that the axons from a number of retinula

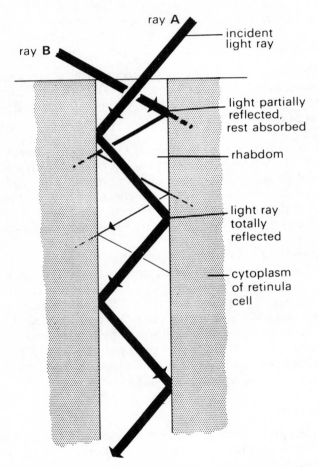

Fig. 369. Diagram illustrating the light-trapping effect of the rhabdom. The light ray entering on the right undergoes total internal reflection, but the ray entering very obliquely from the left is only partially reflected and becomes absorbed by the surrounding retinula cells (modified after Kuiper, 1962).

cells must synapse with each ganglion cell. Thus, despite the absence of detailed information on the connections in the optic lobe, it appears that, in general, the fibres from the individual retinula cells can remain separate for only a relatively short distance.

The cross connections between ommatidia which almost certainly occur in the optic lobe could account for the high level of acuity of the eye by the phenomenon of lateral inhibition (Hartline *et al.*, 1956). This occurs in *Limulus*, the king crab, where an illuminated ommatidium, apart from producing an afferent impulse, also inhibits the effect of other ommatidia. More strongly illuminated ommatidia inhibit the weakly illuminated more than the weakly illuminated inhibit the strongly illuminated, especially if they are close together. As a result differences are exaggerated and visual contrast is enhanced. This may be particularly important where the ommatidia have wide, overlapping visual fields.

27.24 Electrical responses resulting from excitation

The resting retinula cell has a potential of 25–70 mv., the inside being negative with respect to the outside. Light falling on the cell decreases the potential and, in the worker of *Apis,* the reduction in potential persists throughout the period of illumination. The degree of depolarisation increases with the intensity of illumination and at higher light intensities the cell is strongly depolarised at first so that the potential may at first fall almost to zero and then be maintained 20–30 mv. below the resting potential (Fig. 370A).

The sustained potential is regarded as the generator potential which may arise in the rhabdom and then spread across to the cell body, or the excitation of the rhabdom may be transmitted in some way to the cell body and the first change in potential may then take place (see Ruck, 1964). The spike potential may arise in the retinula cell axon.

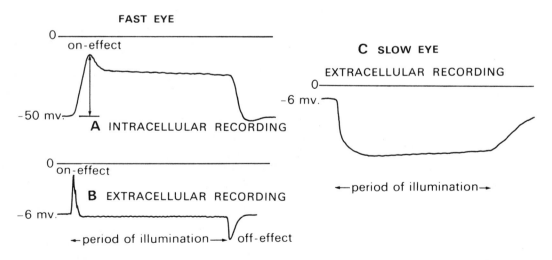

Fig. 370. Electrical responses of the eye. A. Intracellular recording in a retinula cell of *Calliphora*. B. Extracellular recording, electroretinogram, of same response. C. Electroretinogram from the eye of *Tachycines*. Notice that vertical scales differ in each case (modified after Autrum, 1958).

Responses of the eye as a whole are measured extracellularly, the recording being known as an electroretinogram. This is the sum of potentials arising in the eye and optic lobe and in these records the cornea is negative with respect to the retinula cells. Typically, when the eye is illuminated, the cornea rapidly assumes an even higher negative potential and this persists, slowly declining, throughout the period of illumination (Fig. 370C). This potential is derived from the retinula cells and probably represents the receptor generator potential. Superimposed on this may be a slight positive 'on' effect, that is a short-lived change in potential when the eye is first illuminated, which probably arises in the neurons of the lamina ganglionaris, and a negative 'off' effect, that is a transient change when illumination stops. The height of the 'on' effect varies with the intensity of stimulation and the level of adaptation of the eye.

On the basis of the electroretinogram eyes may be classified into two types (Autrum, 1958), although not all authors regard the differences as being real (see Dethier, 1963). In Orthoptera and Lepidoptera, relatively slow-flying insects, the electroretinogram is a sustained, slowly decaying response to illumination (Fig. 370C). These insects have poor discrimination of flicker (p. 567) with a flicker fusion frequency of about 40–50 per second. An eye with these characteristics is termed a slow eye. On the other hand in Diptera and Hymenoptera, fast-flying insects, there is a sharp positive 'on' effect, sometimes preceded by a slight negative potential, and then the potential returns to about the resting level except for a negative swing when the light is turned off (Fig. 370B). These eyes are less sensitive than slow eyes, but their flicker fusion frequency is about 300 per second. Eyes of this type are called fast eyes. It is suggested that the positive 'on' potential arising in the lamina ganglionaris of fast fliers prevents sustained depolarisation of the retinal cells so that they can respond to a much more rapid sequence of images than would be possible if they underwent a sustained depolarisation as in slow eyes.

Also arising in the optic lobe is a spontaneous rhythmic activity which is faster in fast eyes than in slow eyes. The amplitude of the excitation is related to the number of ommatidia illuminated, the intensity of light and the state of adaptation of the eye (p. 559). As illumination continues the amplitude slowly decreases, stopping when the stimulation is stopped (Dethier, 1963).

Recording from single nerve cells in the brain and optic lobes indicates a variety of different units reacting in different ways to changes in illumination of the eyes. For instance, some units fire continuously at low frequency in the dark, but are inhibited when the eyes are illuminated and have high frequency bursts at light-on and light-off. Others are silent in the dark and give a burst of spikes at light-on followed by a sustained discharge in continued illumination; others again are silent except for a burst of activity at light-on. Horridge et al. (1965) record some 20 different types of unit and these only represent the larger and less common units in the optic lobes and brain. They all represent second, or subsequent, order neurons and most of them are recognisable in the medulla externa.

Some of the effects in particular units are the result of inhibition by others and, for instance, the on-effect produced by one eye may be inhibited, wholly or partially, by on- or off-effects from the contralateral eye. Further, the sharp cut-off of some units on a change from light to dark, or vice versa, does not result simply from a failure of the stimulus, but also involves inhibition by other units (Blest and Collett, 1965).

From the optic lobe some fibres pass directly to the ventral nerve cord, others go to the brain where further integration occurs. Nearly all the units investigated in the protocerebrum of the locust respond to changes in visual stimuli, but sometimes only when these are in combination with other sensory modalities. A number of units are also known which respond to a variety of sensory modalities including vision. These are known as multimodal units.

27.25 Visual acuity

Behavioural experiments suggest that the insect eye is capable of resolving two objects with an angular separation of about 1°. Objects closer together than this are not differentiated from each other and the smallest resolvable angular separation is known as the minimum visual angle. Hence the minimum visual angle is a measure of visual acuity, which is the ability of the eye to separate two objects close together.

The resolving power of a lens system follows the formula

$$\theta = 1 \cdot 22 \frac{\lambda}{d}$$

where θ = smallest resolvable angular separation
λ = wavelength of light
d = diameter of the aperture

The eye of *Locusta* is most sensitive to light with a wavelength of about 500 mμ and the diameter of the lens is approximately 32 μ so that, on this basis, $\theta = 1 \cdot 09$. Even with

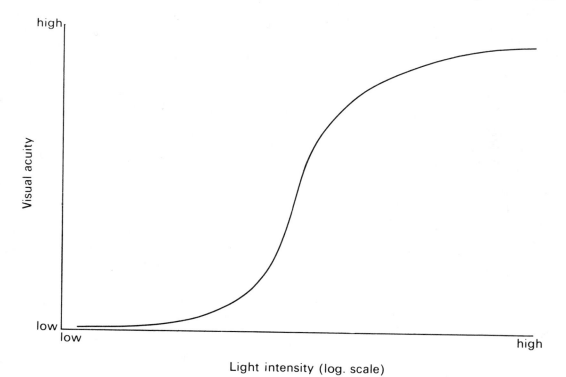

Fig. 371. The relationship between visual acuity of the eye of *Apis* and the intensity of illumination (from Dethier, 1963).

ultraviolet light, with $\lambda = 340$ mμ, $\theta = 0.74$. This suggests that, on physical grounds, the lens system of the eye cannot separate objects with an angular separation of much less than $1°$.

Recording the nervous output from the eye in the optic ganglion or the ventral nerve cord indicates, however, that both *Locusta* and *Calliphora* are capable of differentiating objects with an angular separation of only $0.3°$, although the insects do not respond behaviourally to such a separation. It is believed that this ability could result from the formation of diffraction images (p. 552). These are formed by groups of ommatidia acting together so that the effective diameter (d) of the lens system is increased. This has the effect of decreasing θ, the smallest resolvable angular separation, giving in the locust a value of $0.5°$ for the second image and $0.35°$ for the third (Burtt and Catton, 1962a). Lateral inhibition (p. 555) could also increase the resolving power of the insect eye.

Acuity is less good at low light intensities (Fig. 371). This may be due to the retinula cells of several ommatidia acting together as units so that sensitivity is improved (p. 570) and also depends on the ability of insects to discriminate between lights of different intensities. Most work suggests that their powers of intensity discrimination are poor. For instance, *Drosophila* can only separate two relatively low intensities when the brighter light has an intensity one hundred times that of the weaker light. At higher overall intensities differences of only two-and-a-half times may be detected. More refined experiments, however, indicate that discrimination may be very much better than this suggests, since *Musca* responds to a change of only 0.5% in the total illumination.

27.26 Sensitivity

The sensitivity of the insect eye depends on the characteristics of the visual pigment, the nervous interconnections behind the eye and the extent to which the eye is adapted to the prevailing light conditions.

In order to produce a response from the eye sufficient light must be absorbed by the visual pigment to generate a spike potential in the post-retinal nerve fibres. For flashes of very short duration, up to 0.08 seconds, the photochemical effect of light is proportional to its total energy, that is its intensity and duration, but over longer periods of illumination only the intensity is important so that the 'on' potential in the retinula cell is proportional to intensity (Fig. 372).

Clearly only those wavelengths which are absorbed will have this effect and most insects respond to a range which extends from the near ultraviolet, 300–400 mμ, up to a maximum of 600–650 mμ. Some butterflies and the firefly, *Photinus*, have a higher maximum, up to about 690 mμ, but the sensitivity of these species at the ultraviolet end of the spectrum has not been examined.

Sensitivity is not the same throughout the range and if the intensities of all the wavelengths are kept constant some wavelengths will appear brighter to the insect than others. Most insects have two peaks of maximum sensitivity, one in the near ultraviolet at about 350 mμ and a second in the blue-green, about 500 mμ, although the peaks tend to be flattened at higher intensities. The sensitivity to different wavelengths reflects the absorption characteristics of the visual pigment and in well-lit cells this is not influenced by the screening pigment (Burkhardt, 1962). On the other hand, weakly illuminated cells of *Calliphora* have a third peak of sensitivity at 616 mμ which probably does result from the characteristics of the screening pigments. These do not absorb light of long wavelengths as strongly as shorter wavelengths so that red light tends to move obliquely through the eye. In well illuminated eyes this has no particular significance, but if the illumination is poor a significant proportion of red light may reach each ommatidium obliquely through the screening pigments. This causes the peak of sensitivity to red. This peak does not reflect the absorption characteristics of the visual pigment, but indicates the presence of a large proportion of red light (Burkhardt, 1962; but see also Goldsmith, 1964).

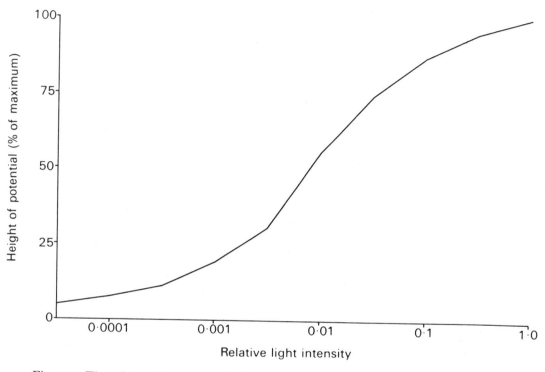

Fig. 372. The relationship between the intensity of white light and the height of the intracellular peak "on" potential in Fig. 370A (after Burkhardt, 1962).

Adaptation

The sensitivity of the eye varies, depending on whether the insect has recently been in the light or in the dark. After a period of illumination the eye is said to be light adapted and it becomes progressively less sensitive. In the dark, however, the eye gets more sensitive as it becomes dark adapted until a maximum sensitivity is reached. Thus in *Apis* there is a 1000-fold increase in sensitivity in the first 20 minutes in the dark, most of the increase occurring in the first minute (Fig. 373), but the longer the period of exposure to light the longer does it take for the insect to become fully dark adapted. A dark adapted insect is much more sensitive to light of low intensities than a light adapted insect.

This adaptation may involve a variety of different factors including the availability of the visual pigment, cytological changes in the eye and movements of the screening pigments. Adaptation may also occur within the nervous system.

The visual pigment is broken down in daylight as quickly or more quickly than it is produced so that after a period in the light an increasingly strong stimulus is required to maintain a given level of response: the insect is becoming light adapted. In the dark, on the other hand, sensitivity increases as the visual pigment accumulates: the insect becomes dark adapted.

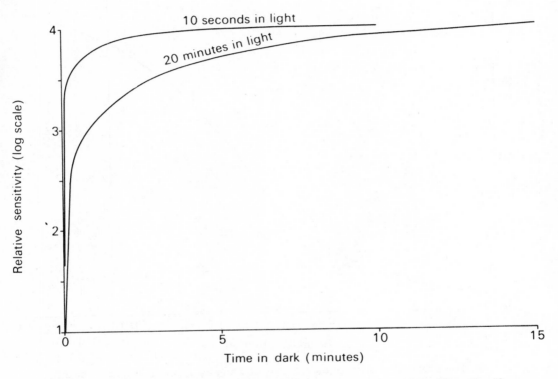

Fig. 373. Dark adaptation of the eye of *Apis* after different periods of light adaptation (from Goldsmith, 1964).

In addition, cytological changes occur in the eye of the locust when it is illuminated which affect its sensitivity. The rhabdom of the light adapted eye is surrounded by cytoplasm rich in mitochondria. This has a refractive index similar to that of the rhabdom so that light may pass freely out of the latter and be lost. After dark adaptation, however, the rhabdom is surrounded by lacunae of the endoplasmic reticulum, forming a palisade layer which has a refractive index lower than that of the rhabdom. As a result internal reflection of light occurs within the rhabdom so that nearly all the light is retained and the sensitivity of the eye is increased (Horridge and Barnard, 1965).

Adaptation of superposition eyes also involves movements of the screening pigments between the ommatidia (**Fig. 364**) so that the course of dark adaptation is in two phases. When first put in the dark there is a rapid increase in sensitivity due to the accumulation of the visual pigment then, beginning rather later, there is a further slow increase in sensitivity as the screening pigment moves to the dark adapted position (**Fig. 374**).

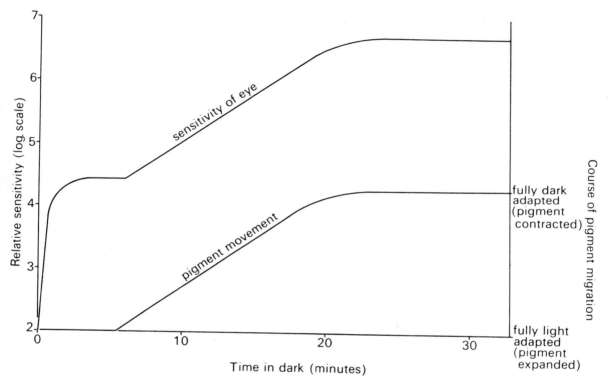

Fig. 374. Dark adaptation of the eye of *Cerapteryx* (Lepidoptera) showing the initial increase in sensitivity due to the accumulation of visual pigment and a further increase as the screening pigments migrate to the dark adapted condition (modified from Goldsmith, 1964).

In most nocturnal moths, the geometrids and noctuids, there is a rhythmical movement of the eye pigments. Thus the eye of the codling moth normally starts to become light adapted about half-an-hour before sunrise and dark adapted just before sunset, the process taking about an hour to complete. This rhythm continues for a time if the insects are kept in complete darkness and may be part of a general diurnal rhythm of activity. The factors controlling pigment movement are not understood. They do not appear to be hormonal, but may involve a nervous mechanism (Day, 1941).

There is also a rhythm of sensitivity in the eye of *Dytiscus*, but this is not wholly due to the movement of pigment. Thus the dark adapted night eye is 1000 times more sensitive than the dark adapted day eye although the distribution of pigments is the same, and similarly the light adapted day eye is more sensitive than the light adapted night eye.

27.27 Wavelength discrimination

The possession of different sensitivities to different wavelengths does not imply the ability to discriminate between wavelengths, but if an insect possesses two or more visual pigments with different spectral sensitivities then wavelength discrimination, that is colour vision, is possible (Burkhardt, 1964). *Calliphora* has three pigments which, apart from a common peak in the ultraviolet, have peak sensitivities at 470, 490 and 521 mμ respectively (Fig. 375). Thus it has the basis for colour vision and behaviour studies have shown that colour vision does occur in numbers of the Hymenoptera, Diptera, Coleoptera, Lepidoptera, Neuroptera, Heteroptera, Homoptera and Orthoptera.

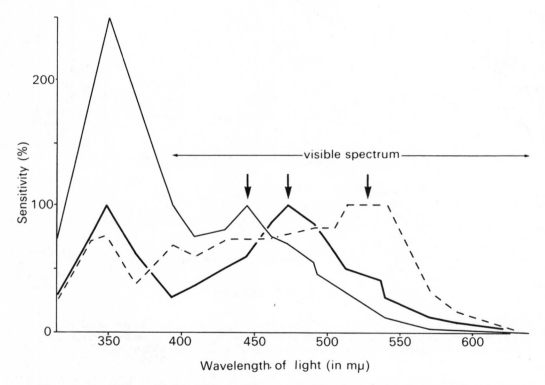

Fig. 375. Spectral sensitivities of three different cells from the eye of *Calliphora*. It is believed that the differences reflect the presence of three photosensitive pigments. Arrows indicate peak sensitivities in the part of the spectrum visible to man. Sensitivity expressed as a percentage of the maximum within the visible spectrum (after Burkhardt, 1962).

Apis can differentiate between six major categories of colour: yellow, blue-green, blue, violet, ultraviolet and bees' purple, a mixture of yellow and ultraviolet. Discrimination is not equally good throughout the range, but is best in the blue-green, violet and bees' purple ranges. The subject is less well studied in other insects, but, in general, blue and yellow tend to be distinguished as colours whereas red does not. The colours discriminated by the bee can be arranged in pairs of complementary colours to produce 'white' or uncoloured light for the bee (Fig. 376). It appears that the trichromatic theory of colour is valid for the bee, the sensation elicited by any single spectral colour also being elicited by an appropriate mixture of the three primary colours, which in this case are ultraviolet, blue and yellow.

Only some parts of the eye may be capable of discriminating between colours. Thus in *Calliphora* the ommatidia of the ventral region are able to distinguish colours while those of the dorsal region are not. In *Notonecta* the converse is true.

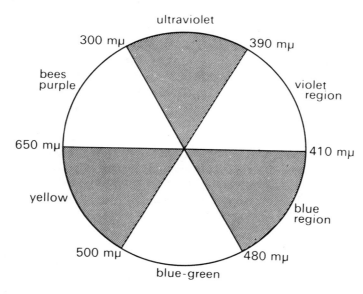

Fig. 376. Colour circle showing the colours which are differentiated by *Apis*. Hatched areas are primary colours (from Burkhardt, 1964).

A possible basis for colour discrimination has been found in *Calliphora*. Here the different visual pigments are associated with different cells which are found to occur roughly in the ratio:— 1 with maximum sensitivity to blue: 5 with maximum sensitivity to green: 1 with maximum sensitivity to yellow-green. This suggests that each ommatidium may have one retinula cell maximally sensitive to blue, five to green and one to yellow-green and that the output from each cell will differ depending on the wavelengths with which it is stimulated. The central nervous system must discriminate between these peripheral excitation patterns. Such a system presupposes that each of the retinula cells is acting independently of the others (p. 553).

27.28 Discrimination of the plane of vibration

Light waves vibrate in planes at right angles to the direction in which they are travelling. These planes of vibration may be equally distributed through 360° about the direction of travel or a higher proportion of the vibrations may occur in a particular plane. Such light is said to be polarised and if all the vibrations are in one plane the light is plane polarised.

Some insects, many Hymenoptera, *Drosophila* and *Sarcophaga,* are known to respond to the plane of polarisation of the light and to modify their responses, as by changing the direction of movement, if the plane of polarisation is rotated (von Frisch *et al.,* 1960). This ability is mediated by the compound eye, only involving the dorsal ommatidia in *Apis,* but in *Sarcophaga* the dorsal ocelli also play a part and in larval *Neodiprion* (Hymenoptera) the power resides in the lateral ocelli (Wellington, 1953). The ability of *Apis* to determine the plane of polarisation varies with the wavelength, being maximal between 300 and 400 mμ, while at wavelengths above 500 mμ there is no response.

It appears that the eye acts as a polarisation analyser, but there is nothing in the lens system favouring the transmission of light polarised in a particular plane. This suggests that the retinula cells are capable of perceiving the plane of polarisation and some work on intracellular potentials indicates that polarised light is a more effective stimulus than nonpolarised light and that the retinula cells have maximum sensitivities in different planes.

A suggested mechanism permitting this discrimination depends on the different orientations of the microtubules of the rhabdomeres in adjacent retinula cells (p. 546). Organic molecules tend to absorb light polarised in a plane parallel with their long axes and it is suggested that the molecules of visual pigment could be orientated to some extent with their axes along the microtubules of the rhabdomeres so that they would absorb light maximally in a plane parallel with the microtubules. This mechanism, however, remains largely hypothetical and there is some opposing evidence (Dethier, 1963; Goldsmith, 1964).

27.3 Visual responses

27.31 Taxes

A taxis is a movement of orientation to a source of stimulation, which may be light or any other stimulus (Jander, 1963; and see Carthy, 1958; Fraenkel and Gunn, 1940). Often the orientation is coupled with locomotion so that the animal may move towards or away from the source. Many insects, such as locusts, orientate towards a source of light, a positive phototaxis, so that if they walk they move towards the light; others, such as blowfly larvae, orientate and move away from a source of light, a negative phototaxis. This basic orientation depends on a tendency to maintain symmetrical stimulation of the two eyes, although some insects are still able to orientate with one eye blackened.

The normal taxis may be modified by other factors. At temperatures below 16°C. *Apis* is negatively phototactic; at higher temperatures it exhibits a positive response. High light intensities also tend to produce negative reactions. Often these changes are linked to the biology of the insect and may depend on the physiological condition. *Ips* (Coleoptera), for instance, reacts positively to light when about to fly and negatively when about to feed.

Under natural conditions the complex interaction of different factors probably means that simple phototactic reactions do not occur, but orientations to dark objects against a light background, sometimes differentiated as skototaxis, frequently do occur. This is involved in movements towards solid objects such as food plants (see section 27.34).

A taxis which is normally of some importance is the dorsal light reaction, the tendency to orientate the head so that the dorsal ommatidia of the two eyes are equally strongly illuminated. This reaction plays an important part in the maintenance of stability in the rolling plane during flight (p. 201). *Notonecta*, which normally swims on its back, has a ventral light reaction.

Some insects may orientate so that they move at a constant angle to the light source with the result that the sense organs of the two sides are unequally stimulated. If the light source is moved the insect alters its path so that its angle to the light source remains the same. This is called a menotaxis and is exhibited by ants and the caterpillar of *Aglais urticae* (Lepidoptera).

Menotaxis forms the basis of astrotaxis in which the orientation to the light source, in this case usually the sun, is constantly altered so as to compensate for the apparent movement of the sun. As a result the insect maintains a constant compass direction. Orientations of this type are learnt and bees, for instance, need to make several collecting trips before they learn to orientate accurately. An astrotaxis is important to social Hymenoptera as a means of finding the way back to the nest. In insects, such as *Melolontha* (Coleoptera), which have no nest, an astrotaxis probably serves merely to keep the individual insect on a steady course.

27.32 Kineses

Locomotory reactions which are not orientated, but in which the speed of movement or rate of turning are related to the intensity of stimulation are known as kineses. Locusts, for instance, are more active in the light than in the dark, while cockroaches are more active in the dark (Fig. 486). Under natural conditions changes in light intensity are nearly always associated with changes in temperature and the latter are probably of greater general importance, but photokinetic movements do occur. For instance, locusts begin to move about on the grass soon after it gets light, but before sunrise so that there is no corresponding increase in temperature. This movement is almost certainly a photokinesis to start with, although the influence of temperature soon becomes overriding (Chapman, 1959b).

27.33 Optomotor reaction

The optomotor reaction is a behavioural response to a pattern of stimulation moving over the eye. In experimental work the pattern usually consists of vertical stripes and the response of a turning movement tending to keep the images in the eye as stationary as possible. In the field the reaction is brought about by the apparent movement of environmental features as the insect moves. The passage of images across the eye from behind forwards indicates to the insect that it is moving backwards, while image movement from front to back indicates forward movement.

A flying insect appears to prefer images to pass over the eye from front to back at a certain moderate speed, it has a preferred retinal velocity. Usually if an insect flies downwind this velocity will be exceeded and so it turns and flies into the wind. An upwind orientation is maintained so long as it is able to make headway against the wind. If, however, the wind is too strong and the insect is carried backwards, as indicated by the forward movement of images in the eye, it lands (Kennedy, 1951). Hence orientation with respect to the wind involves an optomotor reaction although stimuli other than visual ones may also be important.

Some stream-dwelling insects hold their position in the current by an optomotor reaction. *Notonecta*, for instance, orientates upstream and swims strongly as the current tends to drift it downstream so that it tends to keep its visual field constant and as a result maintains its position. In a tank without any landmarks, or if the eyes are blackened, *Notonecta* is unable to keep station and is swept downstream.

27.34 Form perception

Behavioural responses indicate that insects are able to separate objects with an angular separation of 1 or 2° and it follows that larger objects should be clearly visible to most insects. *Locusta* responds to a pattern of black stripes on a white ground, being attracted to the edge of the stripe where white and black adjoin. Vertical stripes are preferred to oblique or wavy-edged lines and taller figures are preferred to short ones. If no vertical stripes are presented the more complex figure is preferred (Wallace, 1958). Such behaviour would be relevant to the locust in food finding. The ability to follow stripes is best developed in phytophagous insects.

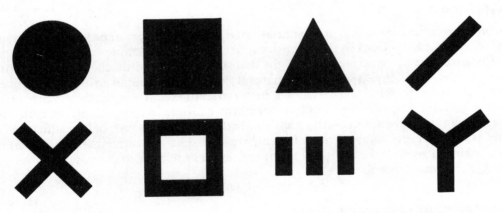

Fig. 377. Different symbols used in experiments on form perception by *Apis*. The shapes in the top row are not distinguished from each other, but are readily distinguished from those in the second row (from Wigglesworth, 1965).

Apis responds to shapes and can be trained to come to any mark which contrasts with the background. Solid figures of different shapes are not differentiated from each other, nor are broken figures, but *Apis* readily differentiates between solid and broken patterns (Fig. 377), showing a preference for broken figures which is not overcome by training. The number of visits paid by bees to a particular pattern is proportional to the length of its contour, suggesting that the choice depends on the frequency of change of retinal stimulation as the bee moves, that is on the flicker effect which the pattern produces in the eye. Related to this it is found that the settling of bees on flowers is improved if the flowers are moving slightly.

At least some insects, particularly hunting insects, must have rather better vision than this suggests. For instance, the spider-hunting wasp *Sceliphron* must be able to recognise spiders from some distance, although olfaction is probably also important at close quarters. *Philanthus* (Hymenoptera) recognises landmarks, such as pine cones, in the vicinity of its nest and the removal of such landmarks makes it difficult for it to find the nest. Its vision must presumably be of a high order for it to recognise such landmarks.

27.35 Movement perception

The insect eye appears to be better adapted for movement perception than for form perception (Burtt and Catton, 1962a). The system of small units, either ommatidia or rhabdomeres, which constitute the compound eye lends itself to the perception of changes in stimulation resulting from small movements of the object or the eye. Hence bees respond more readily to moving flowers than to stationary ones, dragonfly larvae respond to moving prey and most insects show a preference for more complex shapes causing more flicker.

But if an object vibrates too quickly its movement may not be observed because the sensory units need time in which to recover from the previous stimulus. The stimulation of the eye by a succession of stimuli is called a flicker effect and the highest number of separate stimuli which the eye can differentiate in unit time as the flicker threshold or the flicker fusion frequency. The flicker threshold varies with the type of eye. In slow eyes (p. 556) the threshold value lies between about 20/second in *Tachycines* (Orthoptera) and 60/second in *Aeschna* larva, while in the fast eyes of *Apis* and *Calliphora* the threshold frequency approaches 300/second, the value varying with the light intensity. A high flicker threshold is well suited to a fast-flying insect since it facilitates the perception of features of the terrain passing rapidly beneath it.

27.36 Distance perception

Most insects must be able to judge distances fairly accurately. This ability is obviously important in prey-catching insects and in grasshoppers jumping on to a perch, but it must also be important to most insects in making avoidance movements in the air and when they are landing. The ability to judge distances depends on binocular vision, and essentially on the simultaneous stimulation of ommatidia in the two eyes (Fig. 378, and see Mittelstaedt, 1962). If one eye is damaged the power is lost.

Errors can arise in the estimation of distance due to the size of the ommatidial angle, since this is important in determining acuity. Fig. 379 shows the error of estimation which might arise if the ommatidial angle was 2° and bigger ommatidial angles will result in bigger errors. Possibly related to this is the fact that dragonfly larvae have smaller ommatidia on the inside of the eye. These are the ommatidia used in judging the distance to the prey. Errors will also be larger if the distance of the insect from its prey is long relative to the distance between the eyes (Fig. 379), and in many carnivorous insects which hunt visually, such as mantids and Zygoptera, the eyes are wide apart, possibly tending to reduce errors arising in this way.

Insects, such as grasshoppers, which jump and need to judge distances accurately make peering movements while looking at their proposed perch. Peering movements are side to side swayings of the body with the feet still and the head vertical, but moving through an arc extending 10° or more on either side of the body axis. It is suggested that distance in this case is estimated by the extent of movement over the retina; big movements indicate that the object is close to the insect, while small movements show that it is at a greater distance (Wallace, 1959).

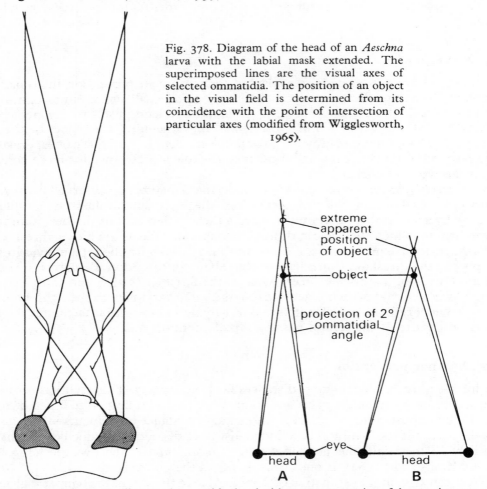

Fig. 378. Diagram of the head of an *Aeschna* larva with the labial mask extended. The superimposed lines are the visual axes of selected ommatidia. The position of an object in the visual field is determined from its coincidence with the point of intersection of particular axes (modified from Wigglesworth, 1965).

Fig. 379. Diagram to illustrate how a wider head with greater separation of the eyes improves the estimation of distance. If the supposed ommatidial angle is 2°, an object stimulating a single ommatidium might lie anywhere between the open circle and the black spot so that there could be a considerable error in distance estimation. In B the head is twice as wide and the possible error greatly reduced.

27.37 Colour vision

Colour is important in the lives of those insects which possess colour vision. Most flower-visiting insects, such as *Apis* and *Eristalis* (Diptera), exhibit preferences for blue or yellow and where red flowers are visited this may be because, as with the poppy, large amounts of ultraviolet light are reflected. It is also significant that the majority of flowers in the temperate zones, where the flowers are insect pollinated, are blue or yellow, with few pure reds, while in the tropics, where birds are common pollinators, red flowers are common. New Zealand with a sparse insect fauna is poor in indigenous coloured flowers. Colour is also important in the feeding of leaf-eating species, *Chrysomela* (Coleoptera) and various caterpillars being attracted to green.

The reactions of an insect to colour may vary depending on its physiological state. Thus female *Pieris* at first show a preference for blue, purple and yellow, the colours of the flowers from which they feed, but when they are mature the preferred colours are green and green-blue, corresponding with the tendency to oviposit on leaves. *Macroglossa* (Lepidoptera) females show a similar change of preference.

Colour vision also plays a part in the courtship behaviour of some insects (p. 123) and probably in the choice of backgrounds in cryptically coloured insects (p. 120).

27.38 Reactions to polarised light

The light coming from a blue sky is polarised, and the degree of polarisation and the plane of maximum polarisation of light from different parts of the sky varies and is correlated with the position of the sun (see Carthy, 1958). Consequently it is possible to determine the position of the sun, even when it is obscured, from the composition of polarised light from a patch of blue sky. Certain insects are able to make use of this information in performing an astrotaxis. It is particularly important in the homing of social Hymenoptera, and is best known in *Apis* where the communication dances of workers may be orientated with respect to the sun even when the sun is obscured (see *e.g.* von Frisch, 1950). In other insects where the ability to perceive polarised light exists it probably enables them to maintain a constant and steady orientation.

27.4 Dorsal ocelli

Dorsal ocelli are found in adult insects and the larvae of hemimetabolous insects. Typically there are three, forming an inverted triangle antero-dorsally on the head (Fig. 2), although in Diptera and Hymenoptera they occupy a more dorsal position on the vertex. The median ocellus shows evidence of a paired origin since the root of the ocellar nerve is double and the ocellus itself is bilobed in Odonata and *Bombus* (Hymenoptera). Frequently one or all of the ocelli are lost and they are often absent in wingless forms.

A typical ocellus has a single thickened cuticular lens (Fig. 380), but in *Machilis* and *Periplaneta* there is no cuticular thickening, only a transparent area of cuticle. In Ephemeroptera the lens is formed from a number of transparent cells, not from the cuticle. The epidermis beneath the lens is transparent and colourless, while beneath it are large numbers of nerve cells arranged in groups of two or more. Distally, within each group, the cells form rhabdomeres similar to those of the compound eyes. Pigment may occur between the groups of sense cells or round the outside of the eye, but in some insects, as in the cockroach, pigment is lacking. Instead, the cockroach ocellus is backed by a reflecting tapetum which is probably formed of urate crystals (Ruck, 1957). The fibres of the sense cells pass out at the back of the ocellus and extend at least halfway down the ocellar nerve, making repeated synaptic contacts with the axons of second order cells lying in the pars intercerebralis (p.518) of the brain (Ruck and Edwards, 1964). These second order axons form the bulk of the ocellar nerve. There are many more sense cells than there are second order axons so that there must be convergence at these first synapses. In *Sympetrum* (Odonata) there are about 675 nerve cells, while in the ocellar nerve there is one giant second order axon 30 μ in diameter, two 4–13 μ in diameter and probably some other much smaller axons (Ruck and Edwards, 1964). In *Periplaneta* there are 25 fibres in the ocellar nerve, four of them large ones.

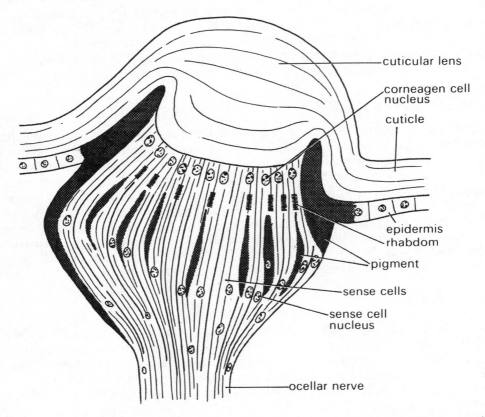

Fig. 380. Section through a dorsal ocellus of *Aphrophora* (Homoptera) (from Imms, 1957).

The lens system of a dorsal ocellus does produce an image, but, in the species studied, this image falls below the level of the sense cells. Thus the ocelli cannot be concerned with form vision. They are very sensitive to low light intensities and in the dragonfly an intensity as low as 10^{-5} foot-candles produces an electrical response in the ocellar nerve. This effect may be enhanced by the convergence of fibres from a number of sense cells on to a single second order axon.

In some insects, kept in darkness, there is a continuous discharge of impulses in the ocellar nerve and circumoesophageal connectives and there are also 'on' and 'off' effects when the light is switched on or off. In others, such as the cockroach, only the 'off' effect occurs. It is suggested that the continuous discharge in the locust ocellar nerve results from a spontaneous rhythmic activity of the second order cells. When the ocellus is illuminated this discharge is suppressed, possibly by a hyperpolarising effect produced by the sense cells of the ocellus.

Hence the ocelli are capable of perceiving changes in light intensity and in *Periplaneta,* which exhibits a diurnal rhythm of activity, being most active in the dark, the ocelli are essential for the maintenance of the response. The rhythm is lost if the ocelli are occluded. In other insects occlusion of the ocelli results in a less good response to visual stimuli involving the compound eyes and *Drosophila,* for instance, has a more rapid reaction to variation in intensity when the ocelli are intact. Experiments of this type suggest that the ocelli have a general stimulatory effect on the nervous system so that the insect responds more readily to outside stimulation (Dethier, 1963).

27.5 Stemmata

Stemmata are the only visual organs of larval holometabolous insects. They are sometimes called lateral ocelli, but this is better avoided since it leads to confusion with the dorsal ocelli. They occur laterally on the head and vary in number from one on each side in tenthredinid larvae to six on each side in lepidopterous larvae (Fig. 381).

In *Isia* (Lepidoptera) each of the stemmata has a cuticular lens formed largely of endocuticle (Fig. 381B). It is secreted by three epidermal cells and may show indications of its origins in consisting of three small, separate facets forming a tripartite lens. Beneath the cuticle is a crystalline lens secreted by three cells and this again may have a tripartite structure. Each lens system has seven heavily pigmented sense cells associated with it,

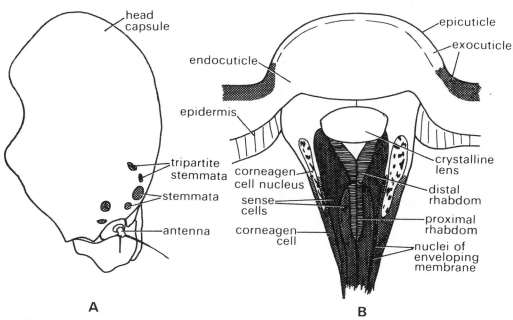

Fig. 381. A. Lateral view of the head of a caterpillar showing the positions of the stemmata. B. Section of a stemma (after Dethier, 1942, 1943).

three arching over distally to form a distal rhabdom and four proximal cells which form a proximal rhabdom. Round the outside of the sense cells is a thin cellular membrane which in turn is shrouded by an envelope formed by the extremely enlarged corneagen cells. The nerve fibres from the sense cells pass to the optic lobe of the brain (Dethier, 1942).

A good deal of variation from this basic form occurs. In tenthredinid larvae the stemmata are more like dorsal ocelli, each containing numerous groups of sense cells and lacking a crystalline lens. *Dytiscus* and *Sialis* (Megaloptera) larvae have similar stemmata, but with a crystalline lens. Finally, larval Cyclorrhapha have lost all external trace of the stemmata, but there are light sensitive spots, which are probably derived from the stemmata, internally on each side of the pharyngeal skeleton.

The lenses of the stemmata produce images which fall on the rhabdoms. If the object is closer to the eye than about 0·08 mm. the image falls on the proximal rhabdom, but if the object is any farther away than this the image is formed on the distal rhabdom (Dethier, 1943). Thus most objects will fall on the distal rhabdom and since this is only formed from three cells image reception cannot be at all efficient. Thus it is probable that the lens is important mainly in concentrating the light.

Each of the stemmata receives light from the area at which it is directed and, since the fields of adjacent stemmata do not overlap, a caterpillar with six stemmata on each side will perceive 12 points of light from different parts of the visual field. Hence it perceives a coarse mosaic which is improved by side to side movements of the head, enabling it to examine a larger field. It is known that caterpillars can differentiate shapes and orientate towards boundaries between black and white areas.

Larval *Neodiprion* (Hymenoptera) and tortricid caterpillars respond to the plane of polarisation of light. This response is mediated via the stemmata.

27.6 Dermal light sense

A number of insects, such as *Tenebrio* larvae, still respond to light when all the known visual receptors are occluded. There appear to be receptors in the general body surface, but no sense organs mediating this response have been located. Chitin lamellogenesis in *Schistocerca* is governed by a dermal light sense (Neville, 1967, *J. Insect Physiol.* **13**).

CHAPTER XXVIII

SOUND PRODUCTION

Sounds are produced by many insects using a variety of mechanisms. Some sounds, such as that resulting from the vibration of the wings in flight, may be adventitious and of no particular value to the insect, but usually they have some significance and special mechanisms are developed for their production. In many instances sounds are produced by scraping a ridge over a series of striations on some other part of the body which is thus caused to vibrate. Such frictional mechanisms are well known in Orthoptera and Coleoptera. In some Homoptera and Lepidoptera a specialised membrane is caused to vibrate by the direct action of a muscle.

The sounds produced by many insects appear to have some warning significance for other insects or perhaps serve to alarm a potential predator. In the latter case they often form part of a display which also involves the colour and movement of the insect. Sounds of this sort are irregular and extend over a wide range of frequencies.

Sounds which are of intraspecific significance are much more highly organised consisting of bursts of sound repeated in a regular manner. Some species have a number of different songs characterised by differences in the timing of the sounds and these are used in different situations. Intraspecific sounds are commonly used in courtship, but they may also be involved in sexual isolation, aggregation, and, in social insects, other behaviour which involves communication.

Insects only produce sounds under particular environmental conditions, the internal environment possibly being regulated by hormones. Given suitable conditions sound production is under nervous control, centres in the brain co-ordinating sensory input and signalling to centres in the segmental ganglia so that the appropriate songs are produced.

Sound production generally is reviewed by Haskell (1961, 1964) and Dumortier (1963a, b). Aspects of the control of sound production are dealt with by Huber (1963) and Loher and Huber (1966). See also Alexander (1967).

28.1 Mechanisms and the sounds produced

Sound with reference to insects may be defined as any mechanical disturbance which is potentially referable by the insect to an external and localised source (Pumphrey, 1950). Hence it includes not only vibrations carried through the air or water, but also vibrations transmitted through the substratum. The term stridulation is used in the sense of Haskell (1961) to mean any sound produced by an insect and implying nothing concerning the mode of sound production.

The characterisation of the sounds produced by insects is difficult and there is much

573

confusion in the literature (for discussion of terminology see Broughton, 1963). The sound may be continuous, as in the case of the noise produced by the vibration of the wings, but more usually it consists of discrete sounds separated by intervals of silence. The unitary sound perceived by the human ear is called a chirp and this may consist of a single pulse or, as in the cricket, of a series of pulses, a pulse being defined as a discrete train of sound waves. Each pulse may be produced by a single to and fro movement of the stridulatory apparatus or such a movement may produce a series of pulses (compare Figs. 382 and 387). A sequence of pulses which may be repeated in a regular manner is called a phrase (see Fig. 390, *Chorthippus parallelus*).

Many insects produce sounds and these may be divided into five categories according to the method used. They are: sounds produced as a by-product of some other activity; sounds produced by the impact of some part of the body against the substratum; sounds produced by frictional methods, rubbing two parts of the body together; sounds produced by a vibrating membrane; and sounds produced by a pulsed air stream.

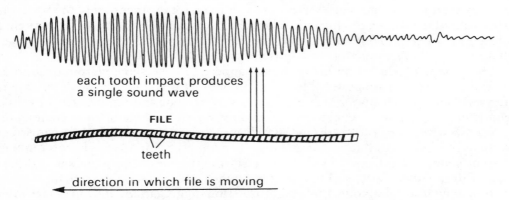

Fig. 382. Diagram of the file and oscillogram of a pulse of sound produced by the closing of the elytra of *Oecanthus* (after Pasquinelly and Busnel, 1955).

28.11 Sounds produced as a by-product of some other activity

Many sounds are produced by insects when they are feeding, cleaning or copulating, but there is no evidence that any of these sounds has any particular significance. Sounds produced in flight, however, may have some significance.

The vibration of the wings in flight causes waves of compression and rarefaction in the air and so produces a noise the fundamental frequency of which is the same as the frequency of the wingbeat (Sotavalta, 1963). However, other components may be added to this fundamental frequency as a result of the varied structure of different parts of the wing and the vibration of the thorax so that the overall sound produced is complex and its frequency may bear no simple relationship to the wingbeat frequency.

In insects such as Lepidoptera with a very low wingbeat frequency, of the order of 20 c./s., the sound produced is inaudible to man, but insects with a faster wingbeat produce clearly audible sounds. The flight tone of *Apis* is about 250 c./s. and that of culicine mosquitoes from 280 to 350 c./s. The frequency is relatively constant for a particular species, but it may vary with temperature, age and sex (see p. 190), while in general smaller species have a higher wingbeat frequency and flight tone than larger species. Hard bodied insects usually produce a higher intensity of sound than soft bodied insects.

The flight noise of a single locust (*Schistocerca*) is a complex sound with frequencies extending from 60–6400 c./s. although mainly falling between 3200 and 5000 c./s. Pulses of sound are produced at the rate of 17–20 per second, corresponding with the wingbeat frequency. A swarm of *Schistocerca* produces a sound with a widely spread spectrum resembling random noise (Haskell, 1957b).

Sounds are also produced by the wings of certain insects when they are not flying. *Bombus* produces a high frequency sound when it is collecting pollen and *Sceliphron* (Hymenoptera) makes a similar noise when collecting mud to build its nest. These noises are made by very small amplitude movements of the wings when they are folded.

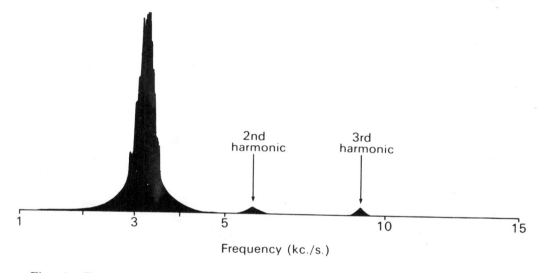

Fig. 383. Frequency spectrum of the song of *Oecanthus*. Note the difference in scale from Fig. 388 (after Dumortier, 1963b).

28.12 Sounds produced by the impact of part of the body against the substratum

Various insects produce sounds by striking the substratum, mostly without any related structural modifications, although female *Clothilla* (Psocoptera) have a small knob on the ventral surface of the abdomen with which they tap the ground. The death watch beetle, *Xestobium*, produces tapping sounds by bending its head down and banging it against the floor of its burrow in the wood seven or eight times a second. The sounds are produced when the insects are sexually mature. The grasshopper *Oedipoda* drums on the ground with its hind tibia at a rate, in the male, of about 12 beats per second. The female drums more slowly.

Some termites produce sounds by banging parts of the body against the substratum. Soldiers of *Zootermopsis* make vertical oscillating movements using the middle legs as a fulcrum so that the head rocks up and down banging the tips of the mandibles on the floor and, less frequently, the top of the head against the roof. Usually two or three taps are produced successively followed by an interval of about half-a-second before the taps are repeated. Workers and larvae produce a lower intensity sound by hitting their heads on the roof in similar vertical oscillating movements. The sound is produced as a result of outside stimulation, in particular vibration of the substratum, and leads to the release of oscillating movements and tapping by other individuals so that the behaviour is prolonged and spreads through the colony. The predominant frequency of the sound is about 1000 c./s., but this must vary to some extent according to the nature of the wood in which the termites are living (Howse, 1962a).

28.13 Sounds produced by frictional mechanisms

Many insects produce sounds by rubbing a roughened part of the body against another part. Often it is possible to distinguish a long ridged or roughened file (strigil) from a single scraper (plectrum). Movement of the scraper over the file causes the membrane to which the file is attached to vibrate so that a sound is produced. Frictional mechanisms for sound production are employed by many different orders of insects, but are particularly associated with Orthoptera, Heteroptera and Coleoptera and in one insect or another almost every part of the body has become modified to produce sound in this way.

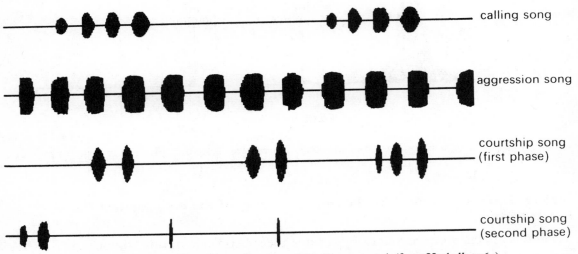

Fig. 384. Oscillograms of different songs of *Gryllus campestris* (from Haskell, 1964).

Orthoptera

In Orthoptera two main methods of stridulation are employed: elytral stridulation in Grylloidea and Tettigonioidea and femoro-elytral stridulation in Acridoidea. The more unusual methods of sound production are reviewed by Kevan (1955).

In male Grylloidea each elytron has a cubital vein near the base on its underside modified to form a toothed file while on the edge of the opposite elytron is a ridge forming the scraper. The right elytron overlaps the left so that only the right file and left scraper are functional. In producing the sound the elytra are raised at an angle of 15–40° to the body and then opened and closed so that the scraper rasps on the file causing the elytron to vibrate and produce a sound. Sound is produced on closure of the elytra, not when they are opened, each impact between the scraper and a tooth producing a single vibration of the elytral membrane. The membrane is thus driven by these impacts so that the frequency of the sound produced is the same as the frequency of impacts of the scraper on the teeth (Fig. 382). The elytral membrane is highly damped and its own natural frequency is not involved (Pierce, 1948; Walker, 1962; but see discussion in Dumortier, 1963b). As a result the sound produced is of relatively low frequency, within the range 2–10 kc./s. depending on the species, and is of a relatively pure tone with only a narrow frequency spectrum (Fig. 383). Each closure of the wings produces a single pulse of sound (Fig. 382), the frequency of which decreases at the end of each pulse due to a lower impact frequency. This results from the teeth at the end of the file being farther apart and may also involve a slowing down of the movement of the elytron towards the end of its stroke.

Each species of cricket has a number of different songs used in different situations (see p. 591). These songs can be differentiated by the frequency with which pulses of sound are produced, the pulse repetition frequency (Fig. 384), although the sound frequency remains more or less the same in all the songs. Different species are characterised by the frequency of the sound and the pulse repetition frequency,

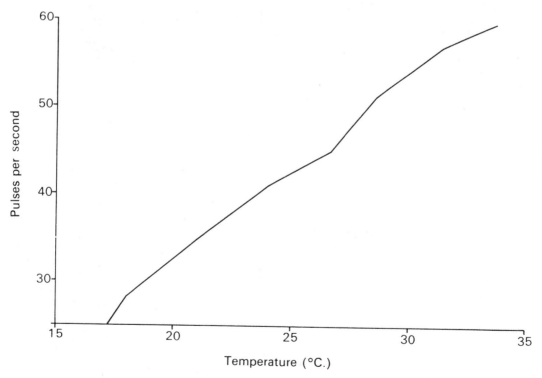

Fig. 385. Relationship between temperature and the pulse rate of the song of *Oecanthus* (after Walker, 1962).

although both of these parameters increase with temperature (Fig. 385). The increase in pulse repetiion frequency with temperature may result solely from a more rapid opening of the elytra so that more sound-producing closures are possible in unit time as in *Oecanthus*, or they may also involve a reduction in the number of file teeth employed so that short, rapid closing strokes of the elytra occur as in *Gryllus rubens*.

Female gryllids do not usually possess stridulatory apparatus, but male larvae of the later instars have the apparatus and may stridulate.

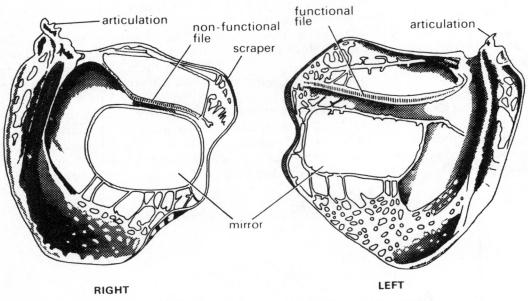

Fig. 386. Elytra of male *Ephippiger* from the ventral surface (after Dumortier, 1963a).

The stridulatory apparatus of Tettigonioidea is similar to that of gryllids, but the left elytron overlaps the right and, in most fully-winged forms, only the left file and the right scraper are present. In some species, however, in which the hind wings are absent and the elytra are short and rounded (Fig. 386), being retained only for the production of sound, a file and scraper are present on each elytron, although only the left file is functional. Close to the stridulatory apparatus on one or both elytra is an area of thin, clear cuticle known as the mirror and this may be surrounded by other areas of thin cuticle.

Tettigoniids produce very high frequency sounds, from about 5 to 100 kc./s., and here each tooth impact produces a damped train of sound waves (Fig. 387) so that the complete closure of the elytra produces a rapid series of pulses. Each tooth impact causes the elytron to vibrate with its own natural frequency producing a sound of corresponding frequency. The wide spectrum of frequencies produced (Fig. 388) suggests that a number of resonant systems are operating and it may be that the main sound generating process involves the whole of the elytron while the mirror and the surrounding parts of the elytron superimpose their individual effects on this general background (Broughton, 1964).

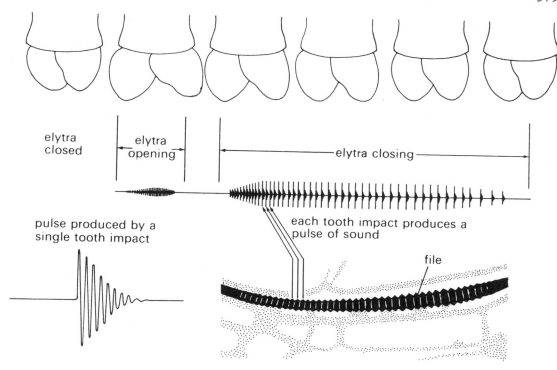

Fig. 387. Stridulation in *Ephippiger* showing the movements of the elytra in relation to sound production; detail of part of the left elytron showing the file and an oscillogram of a short train of sound waves (a pulse) produced by a single tooth impact (modified after Pasquinelly and Busnel, 1955).

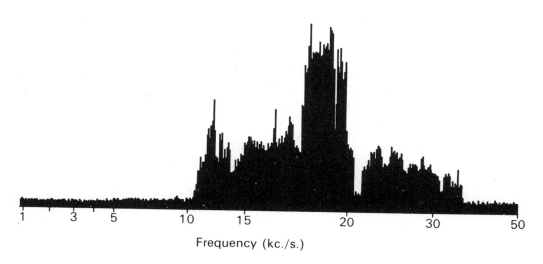

Fig. 388. Frequency spectrum of the song of *Ephippiger* (after Dumortier, 1963b).

Some female tettigoniids have stridulatory apparatus, but this is usually much less well developed than in males.

Sound is produced by most Acridoidea by rubbing the hind femora against the elytra. In Acridinae a ridge on the inside of the hind femur rasps against an irregular intercalary vein, while in Truxalinae a row of pegs on the femur is rubbed against ridged veins on the elytron (Fig. 389). This causes the elytra to vibrate with their natural frequency and so produce a sound, the frequency of which varies from 2–50 kc./s. To some extent the frequency of the sounds varies with the species, but even in a single insect a wide frequency spectrum results from the different resonances of different parts of the elytra. Each movement of the femur produces a single pulse of sound. Stridulatory apparatus is often present in the female as well as the male.

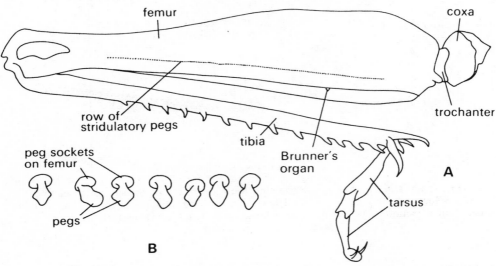

Fig. 389. A. Inside view of the left hind leg of a male *Stenobothrus* showing the position of the stridulatory pegs. B. Some of the stridulatory pegs much enlarged (after Roscow, 1963).

As with gryllids, each species has a series of different songs and different species may be differentiated by their pulse repetition frequencies (Fig. 390).

Many other stridulatory mechanisms occur in other Acridoidea and a single example from the Pneumoridae is given. Here the file consists of a series of radial ribs on the side of the third abdominal segment (Fig. 391). This is rubbed by a row of denticles on the inside of the hind femur, the dilated abdomen of these grasshoppers possibly acting as a sounding box and amplifying the sound (Kevan, 1955).

Heteroptera

Frictional mechanisms for stridulation occur widely amongst Pentatomomorpha where 15 different methods are recorded (Leston, 1957; Leston and Pringle, 1963). The most common mechanisms involve a file on the ventral surface rubbed by a scraper on the leg or a file on the wing rubbed against a scraper on the dorsal surface. For instance,

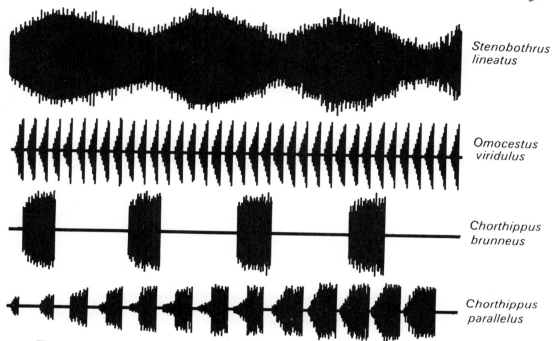

Fig. 390. Oscillograms of the calling or normal songs of the males of four common British grasshoppers. The oscillogram of *Chorthippus parallelus* represents one phrase of the song which is made up of a series of such phrases. Time scale for each trace about three seconds (after Haskell, 1957a).

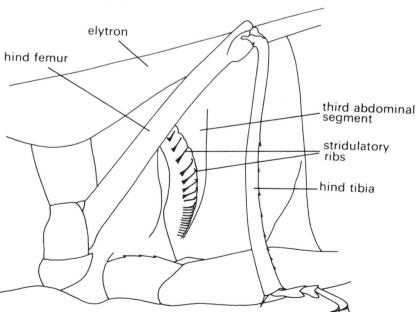

Fig. 391. Lateral view of the left side of the base of the abdomen of a male *Pneumora* showing the stridulatory apparatus (from Kevan, 1955).

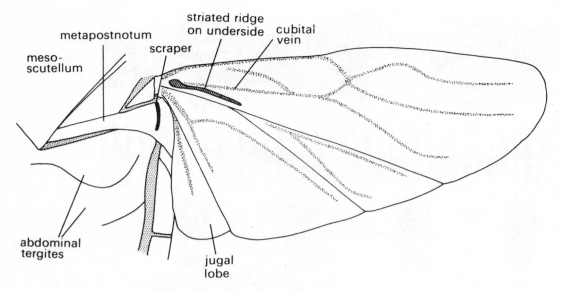

Fig. 392. The wing and part of the thorax and abdomen of *Kleidocerys resedae* from the dorsal surface showing the stridulatory apparatus (modified after Leston, 1957).

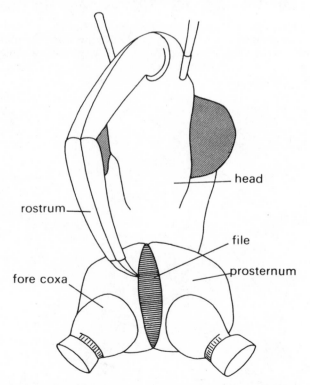

Fig. 393. Ventral view of the head and prosternum of *Coranus* (Heteroptera) showing the tip of the rostrum rasping against the intercoxal file (from Dumortier, 1963a).

both sexes of *Kleidocerys resedae* have a vein-like ridge on the underside of the hind wing. This ridge bears transverse striations about 1·7 μ apart and is rubbed on a scraper which projects from the lateral edge of the metapostnotum (Fig. 392). In general the Cimicomorpha do not stridulate, but the Reduvioidea nearly all have a file between the front legs which is rasped by the tip of the rostrum (Fig. 393). This apparatus is present in males, females and larvae.

Amphibicorisae are not known to stridulate, with the possible exception of Veliidae, but many Hydrocorisae, *Corixa* and *Notonecta*, for instance, are known to stridulate both in air and water.

Fig. 394. Oscillogram of the sound produced by a fourth instar larva of *Coranus*. Total trace lasting about 0·7 seconds (after Haskell, 1961).

The sounds produced by reduviids are of an irregular, unorganised nature (Fig. 394), but in other Heteroptera the songs are organised and show specific differences. Some, such as *Sehirus*, are known to have different songs with different pulse repetition frequencies. The fundamental frequency of the sound produced is the same as the natural frequency of the cuticular structure excited and the pulse repetition frequency equals the impact frequency of the file teeth.

Amongst Homoptera frictional methods of stridulation occur in *Toxoptera*, an aphid, and most Psyllidae.

Coleoptera

Stridulation using a frictional mechanism occurs in many beetles, especially amongst Carabidae, Scarabaeidae, Tenebrionidae and Curculionidae. Many different parts of the body are used to produce sounds in different species, but most commonly the elytra are involved. In *Oxycheila*, for instance, there is a striated ridge along the edge of the elytron which is rubbed by a ridged area on the hind femur.

Larval Lucanidae, Passalidae and Geotrupidae also stridulate, rubbing a series of ridges on the coxa of the middle legs with a scraper on the trochanter of the hind leg. In larval passalids the hind leg is greatly reduced to function as a scraper and is no longer used in locomotion (Fig. 395).

Lepidoptera

Some adult Lepidoptera, such as *Nymphalis io*, produce a sound by rubbing veins on the wings together (see p. 121). *Thecophora* has a specialised vein on the hind wing which is rasped by the modified tarsus of the hind leg and various other forms of stridulatory apparatus occur.

Three main types of stridulation occur in lepidopterous pupae, excluding the probably adventitious sounds produced by the movement of the pupa in the cocoon (Hinton, 1948a). In ten families, notably the Hesperiidae, Papilionidae, Lymantriidae and Saturniidae there are coarse transverse ridges on the anterior edges of certain abdominal segments against which fine tubercles on the posterior edges of the preceding segments are rubbed by movements of the abdomen. In Noctuidae the pupa may have rough areas on the head, thorax and abdomen which are rubbed against the inside of the cocoon or the inside of the cocoon itself may be ridged so that wriggling movements of the pupa produce a scraping sound. The pupa of *Gangara thyrsis,* a hesperiid, has a pair of transverse ridges on either side of the ventral midline of the fifth abdominal segment. The long proboscis extends between and beyond these ridges and is itself transversely striated so that when the abdomen contracts it rubs against the ridges and produces a hiss.

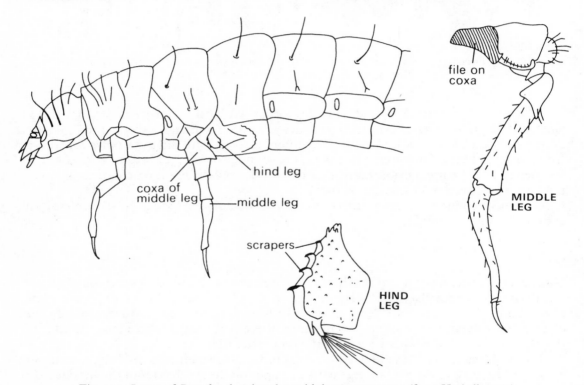

Fig. 395. Larva of *Passalus* showing the stridulatory apparatus (from Haskell, 1961).

Other groups

Relatively isolated instances of frictional stridulation are widespread in other groups of insects. A few examples will be given.

The larva of *Epiophlebia* (Odonata) has lateral ridged areas on abdominal segments three to seven. These are rubbed to produce a sound by the ridged inner side of the hind femur. Similarly, larval *Hydropsyche* (Trichoptera) have ridges on the side of the head and a scraper on the front femur (Johnstone, 1964). Amongst ants stridulation occurs in Ponerinae, Dorylinae and primitive Myrmicinae, striations at the base of the gaster being rubbed by a ridge on the petiole (Fig. 396). Finally in the Trypetidae (Diptera) stridulation is probably widespread. In the male of *Dacus tryoni* the cubito-anal area of each wing vibrates dorso-ventrally across two rows of 20–24 bristles on the third abdominal segment, thus producing a noise.

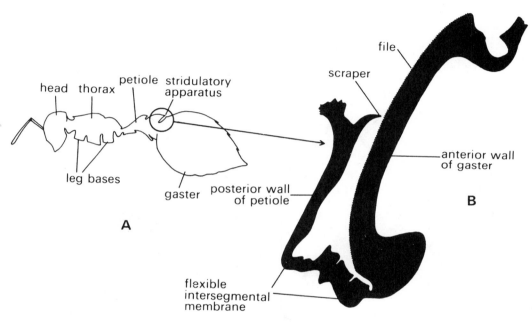

Fig. 396. A. Outline drawing of *Myrmica* showing the position of the stridulatory apparatus. B. Diagrammatic sagittal section through the cuticle of the stridulatory apparatus, highly magnified (from Dumortier, 1963a).

28.14 Sounds produced by a vibrating membrane

Sounds produced by the vibration of a membrane driven directly by muscles are common amongst Homoptera and also occur in some Heteroptera, Pentatomidae, and some Lepidoptera, Arctiidae. The mechanism is most fully studied in Cicadidae (Pringle, 1954) where it is normally restricted to the males, but is sometimes also functional in females.

In the dorso-lateral region of the first segment of *Platypleura* (Cicadidae) there is on each side an area of very thin cuticle supported by a thick cuticular rim and a series of dorso-ventral strengthening ribs. This area of cuticle forms the tymbal (Fig. 397) and it is protected by a forward extension of the abdomen forming the tymbal cover. Internally a cuticular compression strut runs from the ventral surface to the posterior edge of the supporting rim and a fibrillar tymbal muscle (p. 212), running parallel with the compression strut, arises ventrally and is inserted into an apodeme attached to the tymbal. The tymbal is backed by an air-sac which surrounds the muscle and communicates with the outside via the metathoracic spiracle. The presence of the air-sac leaves the tymbal free to vibrate with a minimum of damping.

Projecting back from the thorax on the ventral surface is the operculum which encloses a cavity containing the tympanum (see p. 611) and an area of thin, corrugated cuticle, the folded membrane, which separates the air-sacs from the cavity beneath the operculum. When the abdomen is raised the membrane is stretched.

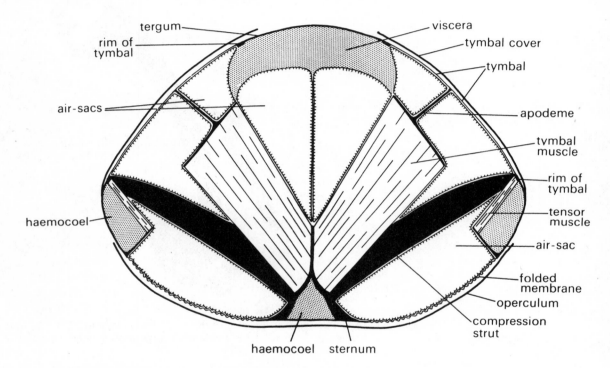

Fig. 397. Diagrammatic transverse section of the first abdominal segment of a cicada showing the main structures concerned with sound production (based on Pringle, 1954).

Sound is produced when the tymbal muscle contracts, pulling on the tymbal so that it buckles inwards producing a click as it does so. On relaxation of the muscle the tymbal returns to its original position by virtue of the elasticity of the surrounding cuticle and so produces a second click. Thus, under experimental conditions, a double click of sound is produced by each muscle contraction (Fig. 398), although the amplitude of the IN click is much lower than that of the OUT click. Under normal conditions, however, this is altered by changes in the tension of the tymbal so that the IN click becomes much stronger and the OUT is lost in the sound of the IN.

The tymbal muscle contracts myogenically (see p. 220) so that stimulation by a single nervous impulse produces a series of contractions and hence a series of sound pulses, the repetition frequency of which equals the frequency of muscle contraction.

In *Platypleura capitata* a stimulus frequency of 120/sec. produces a pulse repetition frequency of 390/sec. Contraction of the tymbal muscles is not myogenic in all cicadas, in *Magicicada* it is purely neurogenic, and in such cases the high pulse repetition frequency is achieved in other ways (see Aidley, 1969, *J. exp. Biol.* **51**).

The frequency of the sound produced is determined by the natural frequency of the tymbal, which in the case of *P. capitata* is about 4500 c./s., and in some species there are harmonics due to the complexity of the membrane. The air-sacs are approximately resonant to the frequency of the tymbal so that the intensity of the sound produced is increased.

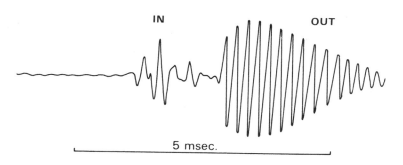

Fig. 398. Double click produced under experimental conditions by an IN-OUT movement of the tymbal of a cicada (after Pringle, 1954).

The mechanism is similar in all the species studied, but each has a different repetition frequency due to differences in the tension of the tymbal. Running from a backwardly projecting knob on the metathorax to the anterior rim of the tymbal is the tensor muscle. When this contracts it pulls the rim of the tymbal so that the curvature of the latter is increased, having the effect of raising the amplitude of the sound produced, but lowering the pulse repetition frequency. Contraction of the tensor muscle or of certain accessory muscles also raises the abdomen, stretching the folded membrane and increasing the space between the abdomen and the operculum. This alters the resonant frequency of the air-sacs so that they can be roughly tuned to the tymbal to increase the intensity of sound. Each species apparently has a characteristic and inherent pattern of activity of these different muscles so that, despite the possession of similar organs, each species produces its own characteristic song.

The two tymbals work synchronously. In the first instance this must be due to simultaneous nervous stimulation of the muscles, but they also remain in phase during the myogenic contractions of the tymbal muscles. Possibly this is a mechanical effect arising from the close proximity of the ventral attachments of the tymbal muscles of the two sides. While the insect is singing certain ventral muscles running to the sternum contract so as to crease the tympanum. In this way damage to the auditory system by the high intensity of sound is avoided.

Amongst other Homoptera a tymbal mechanism is present in the males of all the Auchenorrhyncha examined and in both sexes of Cercopidae and some Jassidae. In these insects the tymbals are not backed by air-sacs so that damping of the tymbals is very high and the intensity of sound produced very low (Ossiannilsson, 1949).

The tymbals of Pentatomidae are membranes on the dorso-lateral surfaces of the fused first and second abdominal terga with an air-sac beneath. Each tymbal is buckled by the contraction of a dorso-ventral muscle producing a click which, in *Carpocoris*, has a frequency of 150–200 c./s., and a pulse repetiton frequency of 9–12/sec. The tymbals usually occur in both sexes although often only those of the male are functional.

A comparable mechanism exists in some Arctiidae (Lepidoptera) where the tymbal is formed by a thin area of cuticle on the side of the metathorax (Fig. 399) (Blest, *et al.*, 1963). This is covered in scales posteriorly, but anteriorly has a band of parallel horizontal striations which vary in number in *Melese* from 15 to 20. In other species there may be as many as 60 striations. The main effector muscle is the coxo-basalar muscle

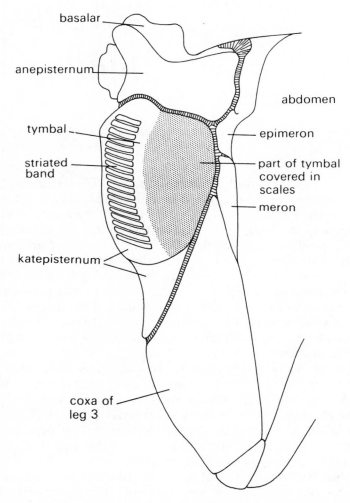

Fig. 399. Diagram of the left side of the metathorax of *Melese,* showing the position of the tymbal relative to the adjacent sclerites (after Blest *et al.*, 1963).

and when this contracts the tymbal buckles inwards, starting dorsally and proceeding along the length of the striated band, each stria being stressed to the point of buckling and then suddenly giving way. Thus each stria acts as a microtymbal and the buckling of each produces a pulse of sound so that the tymbal as a whole produces a sequence of 12–20 pulses. When the muscles relax the tymbal springs out due to the elasticity of the surrounding cuticle and a further series of pulses is produced. The sounds produced on the IN movement show a progressive fall in frequency, those on the OUT movement a progressive rise (Fig. 400). Such cycles of modulation occur in bursts of 1 to 20 with an average of 2·4 bursts per second. Most of the sound produced lies within a range of frequencies from 30–90 kc./s., but the overall spectrum extends from 11 to 160 kc./s.

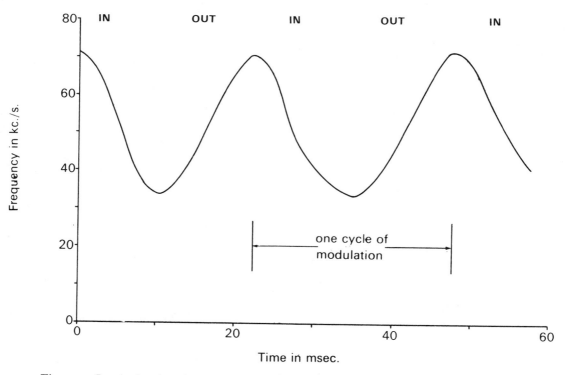

Fig. 400. Graph showing the cycles of modulation of the principal frequency component of the song of *Melese*. Each cycle is produced by an IN-OUT movement of the tymbal (after Blest *et al.*, 1963).

In quite a different category is the piping of queen bees. This sound is probably produced by vibration of the thoracic sclerites (Wenner, 1964) and so may be regarded as a vibrating membrane mechanism. The sound is only produced by virgin queens, the tendency to pipe being lost as the eggs mature, or by queens which are no longer ovipositing. The piping of free virgin queens consists of a phrase starting with a long pulse of sound followed by a series of short pulses with a fundamental frequency of 500 c./s. together with harmonics. Queens still enclosed in their larval cells also pipe, but their piping consists only of short pulses at a lower frequency.

28.15 Sound produced by a pulsed air stream

The only well documented example of a sound produced by a pulsed air stream is the stridulation of *Acherontia* (Lepidoptera). Air is sucked through the proboscis by dilation of the pharynx causing the epipharynx to vibrate and create a pulsed air stream (Fig. 401A). In this way a sound with a frequency of about 280 c./s. is produced. Contraction of the pharynx with the epipharynx held erect expels the air producing a high-pitched whistle (Fig. 401B). These sequences are repeated rapidly. The cockroach *Gromphadorhina* produces a hiss by forcing air out through the spiracles.

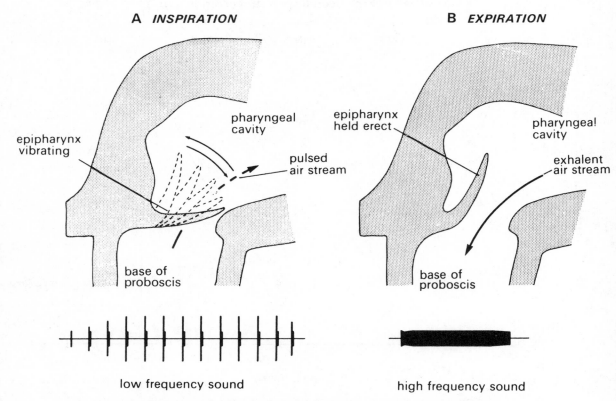

Fig. 401. Diagrammatic sagittal sections of the head of *Acherontia* showing the method of sound production, and oscillograms of the sound produced on inspiration and expiration (from Dumortier, 1963a).

28.16 Intensity of the sound produced

Relatively little work has been carried out on the intensities of the sounds produced by insects, but as some measure of this the distance over which a sound can be heard can be used. This distance will vary according to the sensitivity of the receiver, but the human ear can detect acridids at a distance of one or two metres, *Nemobius sylvestris* (Orthoptera) from eight metres, *Tettigonia viridissima* (Orthoptera) from 100 m. and *Gryllotalpa* (Orthoptera) from 350 m.

28.2 Significance of the sounds produced

The sounds produced by insects can be classified according to whether they represent signals to other species, that is they are extraspecific, or whether they are signals to other members of the same species, that is they are intraspecific.

28.21 Sounds having extraspecific significance

Sounds having extraspecific significance are usually unorganised sounds having no regular pulse repetition frequency (see Fig. 394) and covering a broad spectrum of frequencies. Usually they are produced by both males and females and sometimes also by the larvae. Sounds of this type, which include, for instance, the stridulation of reduviids, beetles and lepidopterous pupae, are presumed to be concerned with defence and warning, perhaps alarming a potential predator or warning other members of the species of the presence of a predator.

Sometimes warning stridulation accompanies other types of display as in the hissing noise produced by the opening of the wings of the peacock butterfly to display the eyespots (see p. 121). Similarly in Arctiidae sound production is associated with a display of warning colours. These are distasteful species and it is generally true that sounds are more readily elicited from the less distasteful species amongst them, these being the the forms which most need to reinforce their display if predators are to learn to avoid them. Noises associated with visual display are also produced by some mantids and grasshoppers.

There is also the suggestion that sound mimicry occurs. Not only do certain syrphids look like bees, they also sound like them (Sotavalta, 1963), and Lane and Rothschild (1965) suggest that the sounds produced by *Necrophorus* when it is disturbed are similar to those of a torpid bumble bee to which the beetle also bears a superficial visual resemblance.

It is suggested that the sounds produced by the tymbals of Arctiidae (p. 588) are added to the echoes of the sounds made by bats and so have the effect of disrupting the echolocation systems of the bats while they are hunting for moths (Blest *et al.*, 1963).

28.22 Sounds having intraspecific significance

Sounds having intraspecific significance are organised sounds with a regular pulse repetition frequency. Often they are concerned with courtship and in many of these cases only the males stridulate.

Courtship

The role of song in insect courtship has been most fully studied in Orthoptera, but is also important in Heteroptera and Cicadidae. The Orthoptera have five main classes of song concerned with calling, courtship, copulation, aggression and alarm, and differing from each other in the pulse repetition frequency and the form of the pulse (see Fig. 384). In the grasshoppers the female responds to the male only at certain times depending on her state of physiological development. She is not responsive until she is sexually mature or for a period of some 24 hours before oviposition, but the responsive state is regained soon after oviposition. Responsiveness is also inhibited by copulation, perhaps through some chemical factor associated with the sperm, but is recovered after an interval of some days. Responsiveness finally disappears a few days before death. The female only stridulates when she is in the responsive state.

The sexual behaviour of *Chorthippus brunneus* is fairly characteristic of that of the British grasshoppers. If a female in the responsive state hears the song of a male she sings in reply, her song being similar to the male's calling song. The two insects orientate and move towards each other, stopping to sing at intervals and thus carrying out a mutual search which eventually leads to their becoming visible to each other. When the male sees the female he starts to sing his courtship song, but if a second male intervenes during this period they sing an aggressive rivals song until one of the contestants leaves. During the courtship song the male makes hopping movements, finally hopping on to the female and attempting to copulate with her. If he is not accepted he starts the courtship song again. If the female becomes disturbed or starts to move during copulation the male sings his copulation song which has the effect of quietening her.

Other groups, such as the Pentatomomorpha and Trypetidae, are similar in that the song leads to a meeting of the sexes, but usually there is no female stridulation, only the male singing so that the female moves towards him. In mosquitoes the converse is true. The male of *Aedes aegypti* responds to the flight tone of the female and is attracted to her as a result. Immature females are not attractive, having a lower flight tone, but this reaches the attractive pitch as the female matures and subsequently she remains attractive for the rest of her life. The male can distinguish the female flight tone from a high level of background noise.

The knocking of *Xestobium* and the clicks of male *Oedipoda* in flight are also sexual signals.

Sexual isolation and aggregation

The different songs of different species of grasshoppers, crickets and cicadas have the effect of enhancing the isolation of species due to other factors. Usually, it is believed, the difference in song has arisen after species have become morphologically isolated, but in the two grasshoppers *Chorthippus brunneus* and *C. biguttulus* it is believed that the differences in song are of major importance in isolating the species from each other. These two species are very similar to each other and are only separated morphologically by a few small non-overlapping characters. They are not separated ecologically and have the same mating behaviour so that crossing readily occurs in the laboratory with the production of viable offspring. There is thus no morphological incompatibility, but very little crossing occurs in the field. The major difference between the species is in their songs which have a stimulating and orientating influence specific to their own species. For instance, in the presence of its own specific song a male moves faster and makes more attempts at copulation while a female is more ready to copulate than is the case in the presence of the song of the other species. These behavioural factors result in an effective isolation of the two species (Perdeck, 1958).

In some insects sounds lead to aggregation. This occurs in cicadas which have one song leading to aggregation of males and females, and resulting in a clumping of the species within a habitat so that particular trees may be occupied by a particular species. Thus in North America three species of *Magicicada* occur in the same habitat. In the laboratory interspecific crossing frequently occurs, but this is not the case in the field where aggregation of each species occurs as a result of their different songs and the tendency for the different species to sing in chorus mainly at different times of day (Fig. 402). In this way interspecific contacts are reduced and sexual isolation is achieved (Alexander and Moore, 1962). The cicadas of Ceylon have in general only one song, which is concerned with aggregation, but the North American species also have a courtship song.

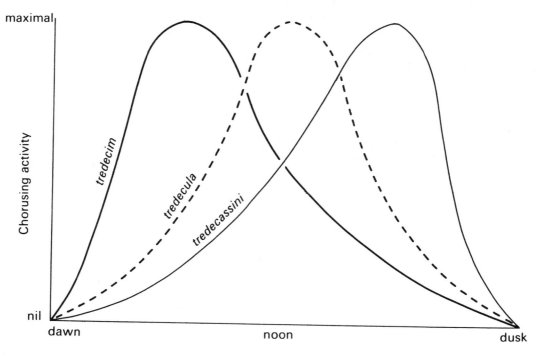

Fig. 402. Chorusing activity of three species of *Magicicada* living in the same habitat (after Alexander and Moore, 1962).

The songs of grasshoppers also lead to aggregation. If a male or female is isolated for 24 hours it orientates and moves towards a source emitting its own song, continuing to move until it is within sight of the singing group (Haskell, 1957a, 1958).

Aggressive stridulation

Aggressive stridulation is well illustrated by crickets. Each male of *Oecanthus* has a territory of some 50 sq. cm. in which he sings his normal song. If another cricket intrudes the male sings an aggressive song quite distinct from other songs (Fig. 384) and the intruding male replies. Fighting may occur, the males lashing each other with their antennae, sparring and biting until one male retires. The dominant males in a colony stridulate more in aggression than others less high in the hierarchy and at the end of an encounter the dominating male may continue to stridulate (Alexander, 1961). Larval passalids also exhibit aggressive stridulation (Alexander, *et al.*, 1963).

The rivalry song of grasshoppers is also aggressive and in the course of this the two males commonly chirp alternately in a regular manner. Such distinct alternation results from the song of one male temporarily inhibiting, and therefore delaying, the song of the other whose song, in turn, delays the next chirp of the first individual. In this way the alternating chirps become clearly separated and follow each other in a regular manner (M. D. R. Jones, 1966).

Aggressive stridulation probably has the effect of spacing the males over the largest possible area and at the same time reduces interference during mating (see p.302). The alternation of singing in some species may help an approaching female to locate the male by minimising background noise.

Sound communication in social and semi-social insects

In some social and semi-social insects sounds may be concerned in aspects of communication other than courtship and successful mating. *Apis* workers, for instance, produce a pulsed sound during the straight run of their dance and the number of pulses and total period of sound production is proportional to the distance from the food (Fig. 403). These sounds may be used, perhaps together with the number of waggles in the straight run, to indicate the distance of the food to other members of the colony. Sound

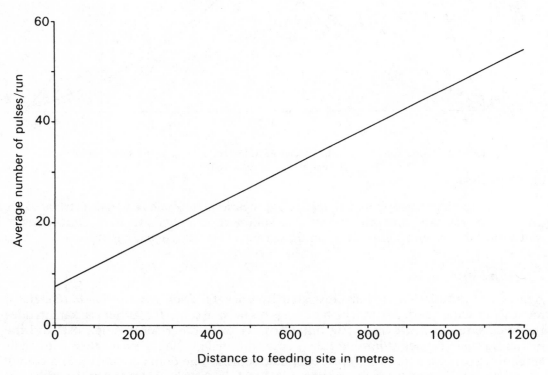

Fig. 403. Relationship between the average number of pulses produced by bees during the straight run of their dance and the distance of the feeding station from the hive (after Wenner, 1962).

might be more important than vision in the dark of the hive and since other workers tend to touch the thorax of the dancing bee they may be perceiving vibrations of the thorax which are perhaps concerned with sound production (Wenner, 1962, 1964).

Returning foragers of *Melipona* produce a characteristic buzz when they are given syrup and when they return to the hive. This sound might stimulate other bees not in physical contact with the returning forager. It may be perceived through vibration of the substratum rather than carriage through the air and experimental colonies in sound-proofed hives in which vibration was eliminated soon died out. This suggests that the sounds are playing an essential role in the transmission of information within the colony.

The piping of queen bees may be important in informing the colony of the presence of a virgin queen in the colony and indicating whether she is free or still enclosed within the cell.

In locusts the flight noise may be of some social significance. For instance, the noise of a passing swarm of *Schistocerca* may stimulate other, settled locusts to take off. Once in the air the swarm noise might have some effect in maintaining flight and possibly also in the maintenance of swarm cohesion. If a locust tends to stray away from the swarm it soon passes beyond the range, about five metres, at which it can hear the rest of the swarm. Unequal stimulation might result in the locust turning back towards the noise and so back into the swarm, but there is no doubt that other stimuli are also important in swarm cohesion (Haskell, 1957b). The noise of an individual locust is audible to others from a distance of two or three metres. Locusts in swarms seem to fly at a preferred distance from their fellows and it is possible that the sound of another individual locust might have a repelling effect and so stop locusts getting too close to each other.

The sounds produced by *Zootermopsis* (p. 575) are important as a warning to other members of the colony, being initiated by any disturbance and especially by vibration of the substratum. The sound leads to the retreat of other members of the colony to the remoter parts of the nest (Howse, 1962a).

28.3 Control of sound production

28.31 Initiation of sound production

Insects start to stridulate as a result of a balance between external and internal stimuli. The external stimuli include the physical factors of the environment. Temperature may be limiting; grasshoppers only sing when the air temperature is high or the solar radiation intense (Richards and Waloff, 1954). Light is also important in some species: some species of tettigoniid are nocturnal, others diurnal. Stridulation tends to be restricted to certain times of day in both North American and Ceylon cicadas (Fig. 402) and a rhythm may appear in the time of singing which, although not directly related to the environmental conditions, is derived from them.

Within the limits set by the physical environment biological factors are of great importance in initiating song. The most important external biological stimuli are visual, auditory and tactile. The sight or sound of another member of the species may lead to singing, the type of song, whether courtship or aggression, depending on the situation and sexes of the insects. Tactile stimuli are important in eliciting the warning stridulation of bugs and beetles.

Internal factors are also of great importance. Male grasshoppers only sing when they are sexually mature with a brief interruption of singing after copulation. In *Ephippiger* the interruption is much longer, lasting three to five days, while male *Gryllus campestris* only sing when they are carrying a spermatophore. After copulation, when the spermatophore is transferred to the female, singing stops until a new spermatophore is passed into the spermatophore sac.

Female grasshoppers only sing, when they are in a responsive state. Possibly this is under hormonal control since the removal of the ovaries of a mature female results in a loss of responsiveness, but responsiveness is restored following the injection of blood from another responsive female (Haskell, 1960a). In *Gomphocerus* a secretion from the corpora allata regulates responsiveness.

28.32 Nervous control of sound production

Ultimately, stridulation is controlled via the nervous system which controls and co-ordinates the muscles moving the stridulatory organs. In *Gryllus campestris* and *Gomphocerus* (Orthoptera) the brain is essential for stridulation to occur. The sensory stimuli initiating stridulation act via the corpora pedunculata which determine the beginning and end of singing since they may stimulate or inhibit sound production. Here the sensory input is co-ordinated, determining the type of song to be sung (see Fig. 355) and the information is passed to the central body (p. 521). Within the central body the stimulus is translated into pulse and sequence patterns of excitation related to the innate song rhythm of the species. The stimulus pattern now passes via the nerve cord to the thoracic ganglion controlling the stridulatory apparatus, the mesothoracic ganglion in *Gryllus* and the metathoracic ganglion in *Gomphocerus* (Huber, 1963).

Ewing and Hoyle (1965) suggest that there is a simple 'song centre' in the meso-thoracic ganglion of *Acheta* which co-ordinates muscle activity with reciprocating neural inhibition between the muscles opening and closing the elytra to produce sounds (compare Fig. 128). At first the muscles are activated only via the slow axons, but as excitation increases fast axons begin to fire, the muscles contract more strongly and the intensity of the song is increased. In the aggressive song excitation is maintained for longer than in calling by the presence of the intruding male so that each chirp consists of a greater number of pulses. The presence of a female, on the other hand, suppresses excitation and the fast axons are normally inactive so that the courtship song is of low intensity.

The muscles moving the wings of crickets in song production are the same as those employed in flight, but there is disagreement concerning the roles of individual muscles (Bentley and Kutsch, 1966; Ewing and Hoyle, 1965).

CHAPTER XXIX

MECHANORECEPTION

Treated in a broad sense mechanoreception includes the perception of any mechanical distortion of the body. This may result from touching an object or from the impact of vibrations borne through the air, water or the substratum, and thus mechanoreception includes the sense of hearing. It also includes distortions of the body which arise from the attitude of the insect and from the force exerted by gravity so that some mechanoreceptors are proprioceptors, others gravity receptors. To carry out this variety of functions a number of different sensilla are involved.

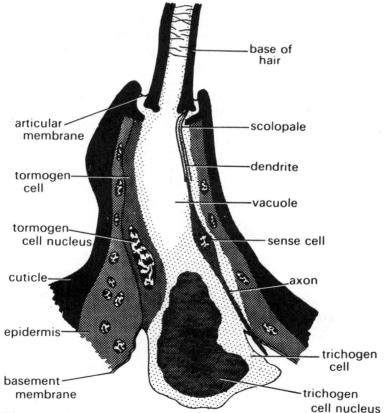

Fig. 404. Diagram of the base of a trichoid sensillum from the larva of *Aglais* (modified from Dethier, 1963).

Many of the hairs on the insect body are tactile organs and they may respond only during deformation or they may continue to respond throughout the period for which they are bent. The latter type commonly function as proprioceptors.

A second important class of mechanoreceptors are the chordotonal organs. These consist of single units or groups of units and occur in many parts of the body, recording changes in the positions of segments and also responding to vibrations from the environment. Associated with a tympanic membrane which is free to vibrate, these form the complex hearing organs found in a number of insects.

Campaniform sensilla respond to stresses in the cuticle, while internal proprioceptors are present in the form of stretch receptors.

Various aspects of mechanoreception are reviewed by Autrum (1963), Dethier (1963), Haskell (1961), Horridge (1965) and Schwartzkopff (1964). Thurm (1968, *Symp. zool. Soc. Lond.* **23**) reviews transducer processes of mechanoreceptors.

29.1 Trichoid sensilla

A trichoid sensillum is a hair-like projection of the cuticle articulated with the body wall by a membranous socket so that it is free to move. The hair is produced by a cell, the trichogen cell, and the socket by another, the tormagen cell, lying in the epidermis (Fig. 404). Associated with each hair is one or more nerve cells. Hairs concerned only with mechanoreception have only one neuron, but chemosensory hairs with a number of neurons (see Fig. 432) also often function as mechanoreceptors. Distally the sensory process or dendrite may be enclosed in a sheath of cuticular material which continues

to the surface of the cuticle at the base of the hair and is shed with the cuticle at moulting (Slifer *et al.*, 1957). This tube is called the scolopale (also known as the scolopoid sheath and cuticular sheath) and distally it may be capped by a scolopale cap or apical body. The dendrite may end in the scolopale cap or it may leave the scolopale and extend into the lumen of the hair. Commonly the end of the dendrite is inserted into the cuticle at one edge of the base of the hair. Movement of the hair results in mechanical deformation of the nerve ending leading to the production of a receptor potential. In some hairs, such as those along the edge of the prothorax of *Schistocerca*, a potential is produced when the hair is bent in any direction, but others, such as those in the hair beds (Fig. 407) on the face, only respond when they are bent in certain directions (Fig. 405).

The receptor potentials produced in the distal part of the dendrite differ in different types of hair. In the majority a potential only develops during movement of the hair,

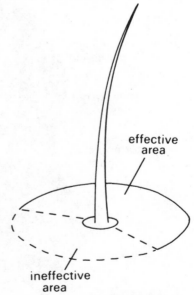

effective area

ineffective area

Fig. 405. Diagram to illustrate the directional sensitivity of a trichoid sensillum. Only bending towards the effective area leads to the development of a nervous impulse (after Haskell, 1960b).

bending or straightening (Fig. 406A), a phasic response, but in others the potential is maintained all the time the hair is bent, adapting only very slowly (Fig. 406B). This is known as a tonic response.

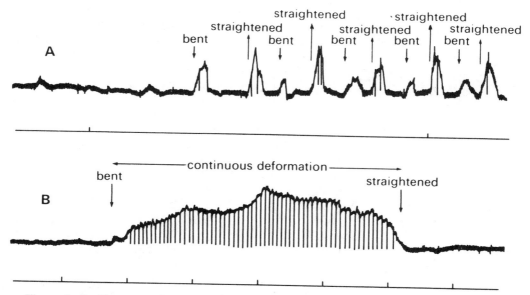

Fig. 406. Oscillograms of the responses to deformation of two types of mechanosensory hairs. A. On the wing of *Sarcophaga* responding only to movement of the hair. B. On the clasper of a male *Phormia* giving a continuous response to continuous deformation. Time marker 0·2 seconds (after Wolbarsht, 1960).

Phasic receptors

Hairs showing phasic responses function as tactile receptors, occurring particularly on the antennae, the tarsi and wherever the insect touches the substratum. They may also respond to vibration of the substratum and in some cases to sounds carried through the air if these are of high intensity.

Hairs responding to sounds in the range 32–1000 c./sec. occur over the body of caterpillars and stimulation by high intensity sounds causes convulsive contractions of the longitudinal muscles so that the insects make writhing movements with their heads. Similar hairs are present on the ventral surface of the abdomen and on the cerci of grasshoppers, while the cercal hairs of *Periplaneta* respond to frequencies up to 3000/sec. At low frequencies the impulses in the cercal nerve of *Periplaneta* are synchronous with the stimulus frequency, but they become completely asynchronous at a stimulus frequency of about 800 c./sec. It is doubtful if the cercal hairs of grasshoppers are of any importance in perceiving stridulation, but the hairs on the abdomen might be important when the intensity of sound is high as during the later stages of courtship with the insects only a few centimetres apart.

Apart from sounds, air moving at only 4 cm./sec. is sufficient to stimulate the cercal hairs of the locust. The cockroach, but not the locust, makes rapid evasive movements when these hairs are stimulated by a puff of air (see p. 523).

Tonic receptors

Hairs which exhibit a tonic response to bending occur between the joints of the legs, on the prothorax and genitalia, and in many other situations on the body, often associated with joints. They serve different functions according to their positions, but, since their output adapts only slowly and so provides continuous information, they are often proprioceptors. Sometimes these hairs are grouped together to form hair beds. These occur on the face of the locust (Fig. 407), on the cervical sclerites, at the junction of the coxa with the thorax and the trochanter with the coxa, at the joints of the palps, at the base of the abdomen and elsewhere (see *e.g.* Markl, 1962). They serve different functions according to their positions.

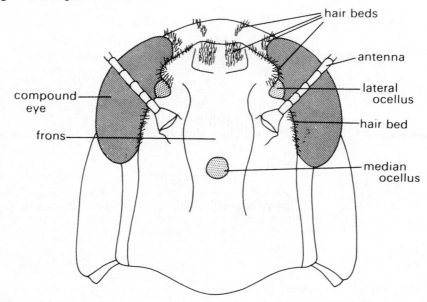

Fig. 407. Frontal view of the head capsule of *Schistocerca* showing the positions of the hair beds (after Weis-Fogh, 1949).

The facial hair beds of the locust are stimulated by air blowing on to the face at speeds of two metres/second or more. They show directional sensitivity and are orientated so that they respond to air passing along the axis of the insect. Thus they enable the insect to orientate to wind while on the ground and help to control yaw (p. 202) while it is flying, since asymmetrical stimulation of the hair beds of the two sides leads to variable oscillation of the wings. Stimulation of the facial hair beds also initiates a flight reflex resulting in the drawing up of the legs into the flight position and the maintenance of flight (see p. 197).

Where hair beds occur at joints in the skeleton they are stimulated by contact with adjoining surfaces (Fig. 408) so that they function as proprioceptors. The hair beds on the first cervical sclerite, for instance, provide the insect with information on the position of its head. This is important in the mantis during feeding and aids the stability of the locust in flight when the head is orientated by a dorsal light reaction and the thorax is aligned with the head (see p. 201).

Hair beds are also important in orientating to gravity. The ability to orientate to gravity must be important to most insects, but is particularly important in the communication dances of *Apis*. The head of *Apis* is suspended from the thorax by two cuticular processes which extend forwards from the episterna and articulate with the occipital condyles. There is a hair bed on the outside of each of these processes so placed that when the bee is standing on a horizontal surface the hairs are in even contact with the head capsule. The centre of gravity of the head is below its point of articulation with the thorax so that when the bee crawls upwards the head nods down and the ventral hairs of the cervical hair beds are stimulated more strongly than those dorsally in the group. On a less inclined slope the forces acting on these hairs are reduced, while on crawling downwards the ventral part of the head would hang down, away from the thorax, so that the dorsal hairs of the hair beds are stimulated more strongly than the ventral ones. Side to side turning on a vertical surface will be indicated by forces of different intensity acting on the two sides. Other setal fields on the petiole, the antenna and elsewhere also play a part, but are less important. The response to gravity is a response to the combined output of these receptors, individually the hair beds function as proprioceptors (Lindauer, 1961).

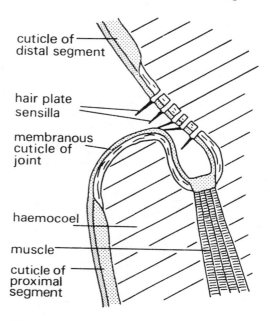

cuticle of distal segment

hair plate sensilla

membranous cuticle of joint

haemocoel

muscle

cuticle of proximal segment

Fig. 408. Diagram to show the manner in which the sensilla of a hair plate are stimulated by coming into contact with adjacent cuticle.

The larger tactile setae on the legs of *Periplaneta,* and possibly of other insects, function in an entirely different way from typical trichoid sensilla. At the base of each seta, where it joins the membrane of the socket, is a single campaniform sensillum, $10-15 \mu$ across. Movement of the spine is unlikely to deform the sensillum because of the flexibility of the socket membrane, but possibly the movement causes the membrane to fold up and press on the sensillum so that it is stimulated (Chapman, K., 1965).

29.2 Chordotonal organs

Chordotonal, or scolopophorus, organs consist of single units or groups of similar units called scolopidia. They are subcuticular, often with no external sign of their presence, and are attached to the cuticle at one or both ends. Each scolopidium consists essentially of three cells arranged in a linear manner: the neuron, an enveloping, or scolopale cell, and an attachment, or cap cell. The scolopidia in the locust tympanal organ also possess a fibrous sheath-cell round the base of the dendrite (Fig. 409). In this case, at least, the dendrite ends in a cilium-like process containing a peripheral ring of nine double filaments and with roots extending proximally within the dendrite. The tip of the cilium lies in a hollow of the extracellular scolopale cap. Within the scolopale cell is the

602

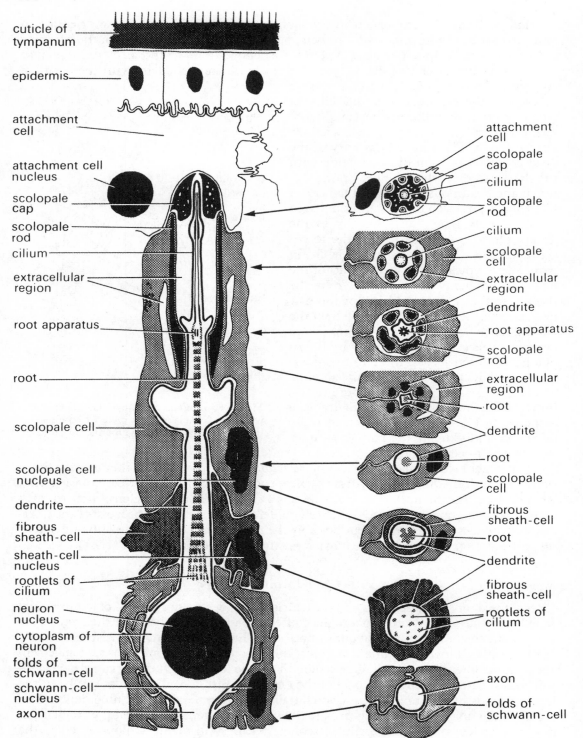

cuticle of tympanum
epidermis
attachment cell
attachment cell nucleus
scolopale cap
scolopale rod
cilium
extracellular region
root apparatus
root
scolopale cell
scolopale cell nucleus
dendrite
fibrous sheath-cell
sheath-cell nucleus
rootlets of cilium
neuron nucleus
cytoplasm of neuron
folds of schwann-cell
schwann-cell nucleus
axon

attachment cell
scolopale cap
cilium
scolopale rod
cilium
scolopale cell
extracellular region
dendrite
root apparatus
scolopale rod
extracellular region
root
dendrite
root
scolopale cell
fibrous sheath-cell
root
dendrite
fibrous sheath-cell
rootlets of cilium
axon
folds of schwann-cell

Fig. 409. Diagrammatic longitudinal section through a scolopidium from the tympanum of *Locusta* with transverse sections at the levels indicated (after Gray, 1960).

tubular scolopale. In *Locusta* this is made up of five to seven rods of fibrous material arranged in a ring and enclosing an extracellular space round the cilium. The contents of the extracellular space are not known. The attachment cell connects the sensillum to the epidermis (Gray, 1960). See also Howse (1968, *Symp. zool. Soc. Lond.* **23**).

Chordotonal organs occur throughout the peripheral regions of the body of the insect. In larval *Drosophila* there are 90 such organs, each containing from one to five scolopidia, arranged in a segmental pattern and suspended between points on the body wall so that they function as proprioceptors (Fig. 410). In *Melanoplus* (Orthoptera)

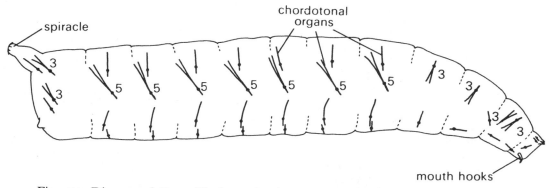

Fig. 410. Diagram of *Drosophila* larva showing the arrangement of chordotonal organs. The numbers indicate the number of scolopidia in each sense organ; those not numbered have one (from Horridge, 1965).

there are 76 pairs. In the thorax of many insects there are large chordotonal organs, containing about 20 scolopidia; these record the movements of the head on the thorax. Others in the wing bases of some insects, but not Orthoptera, record some of the forces which the wings exert on the body. In *Apis* there are three such organs, each with 15–30 scolopidia, at the base of the radial and subcostal veins and in the lumen of the radial vein.

Typically four chordotonal organs occur in each leg. The first is attached proximally within the femur and distally is inserted into the knee joint. In *Machilis* this organ contains seven scolopidia; in grasshoppers there are about 300. Proximally in the tibia is the subgenual organ (see below) and distally another chordotonal organ, which in *Apis* contains about 60 scolopidia, arises in the connective tissue of the tibia and is inserted into the tibio-tarsal articulation. Finally, a small organ with only about three scolopidia extends from the tarsus to the pretarsus. These organs function as proprioceptors monitoring the positions of the leg joints.

29.21 Subgenual organs

The subgenual organ is a chordotonal organ usually containing between 10 and 40 scolopidia in the proximal part of the tibia. It is not associated with a joint. Processes from the accessory cells at the distal ends of the scolopidia are packed together as an attachment body which is fixed to the cuticle at one point, while the proximal ends are supported by a trachea (Fig. 411). Often the organ is in two parts, one more proximal, called the true subgenual organ by Debaisieux (1938), and the other slightly more distal. Both are present in Odonata, Dictyoptera and Orthoptera where in Tettigonioidea and Grylloidea the distal organ probably gives rise to the intermediate organ and the crista acoustica (p. 609). In Homoptera, Heteroptera, Neuroptera and Lepidoptera only the distal organ is present, while in *Machilis*, Coleoptera and Diptera no subgenual organ is present at all (Debaisieux, 1938).

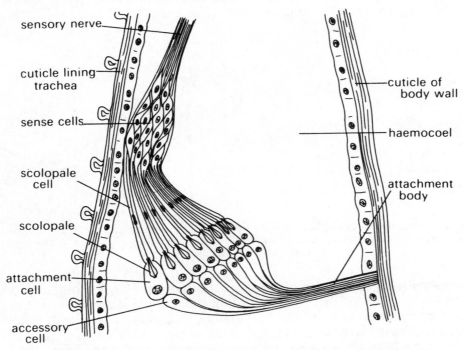

Fig. 411. Diagram of the subgenual organ of an ant (from Horridge, 1965).

These organs are sensitive to vibrations of the substratum and to airborne sounds if these are of sufficiently high intensity to cause the leg or substratum to vibrate. They are extremely sensitive and in *Periplaneta*, for instance, respond to a displacement of only $10^{-9}–10^{-7}$ cm. The subgenual organs of *Periplaneta* are sensitive to vibrations at frequencies up to 8 kc./sec., with an optimum at 1500 c./sec. *Calliphora*, which has no subgenual organs, on the other hand, only responds to displacements greater than 10^{-5} cm. within the frequency range 50–1000 c./sec. In this case the sensilla which respond to vibration are the tibio-tarsal chordotonal organ, the tarsal hairs and hair beds between the joints of the legs.

The response of the subgenual organs of *Periplaneta* is synchronous with the stimulus frequency up to 50 c./sec. (Howse, 1964), but at higher frequencies is asynchronous. In nature it is unlikely that pure tones occur, rather the insect is subject to pulse-like vibrations transmitted through the substratum and including the high frequencies as transients. Hence it is important that the organs should be able to perceive the high frequencies.

The mechanism by which the subgenual organs are stimulated is not understood. Possibly vibrations of the leg create vortices in the haemolymph within the leg and these move the chordotonal organ so that the sense organ is stimulated. Alternatively, the vibrations of the leg may cause the organ to vibrate with its own natural frequency, but, because the attachment cells are bound together and attached to the cuticle, they have a different natural frequency from the scolopale cells which are relatively free. Hence the proximal and distal parts of the organ will vibrate at different frequencies so that rapid and complex changes occur in the forces acting at the junction between the two parts and these rapid changes serve to stimulate the sense cells (Howse, 1962b).

29.22 Johnston's organ

Johnston's organ is a chordotonal organ lying in the second segment of the antenna with its distal insertion in the articulation between the second and third segments. It occurs in all adult insects except Collembola and Diplura, and, in a simplified form, is present in many larvae. It consists of a single mass or several groups of scolopidia and is most highly developed in the males of Culicidae and Chironomidae where the pedicel is enlarged to house the organ. In Culicidae the base of the antennal flagellum forms a plate from which processes extend for the insertion of the scolopidia (Fig. 412). The latter are arranged in two rings all round the axis of the antenna and in addition there are three single scolopidia which extend from the scape to the flagellum.

Johnston's organ perceives movements of the antennal flagellum. In *Calliphora* most of the sensilla comprising the organ give phasic responses, potentials only developing during and immediately after the movement so that a single to and fro movement of the flagellum produces an 'on' and an 'off' response. The amplitude of the 'on' response increases with stimulus intensity due to different units having different thresholds and, if the stimulus is of very short duration, the 'off' response may be completely suppressed. Hence at high frequencies of stimulation small changes in stimulus pattern may produce major changes in excitation. Some of the sensilla respond to movement in any direction, others only if they are moved in a particular direction, stretching being the effective stimulus (Burkhardt, 1960). Since movement of the flagellum may result from a number of causes Johnston's organ may serve a variety of functions in any one insect.

In *Calliphora* Johnston's organ acts as a flight speed indicator and is concerned with the maintenance and control of flight speed. Wind blowing on the face causes the arista to act as a lever, rotating the third antennal segment on the second (see Fig. 8D). This stimulates Johnston's organ which, because of the phasic nature of most of the sensilla, responds primarily to changes in the degree of rotation of the third segment. Even in a steady airflow the antenna trembles, perhaps because of the setting up of eddies, so that Johnston's organ is stimulated. Since with an increased angle of rotation more scolopidia are stimulated it is possible that, as a result of the trembling of the antenna causing continuous restimulation, Johnston's organ might give a measure of the degree of static deflection of the third antennal segment as well as changes in its position (Burkhardt, 1960).

Johnston's organ also perceives sounds carried through the air to *Calliphora,* but its use as an organ of hearing is best known in Chironomidae and Culicidae where it enables the males to locate the females by their flight tone (p. 592). The males of these insects have plumose antennae with many fine, long hairs arising from each annular joint. These hairs are caused to vibrate by sound waves and their combined action produces a movement of the flagellum. The amplitude of flagellar movement is greatest near its own natural frequency which approximately corresponds to the flight tone of the mature female and stimulation at this frequency leads to the seizing and clasping response in mating. *Aedes aegypti* males are most readily induced to mate by frequencies between about 400 and 650 c./sec., but the limits to which they respond become wider as the insect gets older and are wider in unmated than in mated males. Sounds at other frequencies and high intensities produce a variety of reactions:—cleaning movements, jerking, flight or freezing (Roth, 1948).

In order to find the female, the stimulated male must be able to determine the direction from which the sound is coming. It is suggested that if the sound waves are parallel with the flagellum the basal plate (Fig. 412) is pushed in and out. The sensilla of the inner ring of Johnston's organ respond when they are stretched, that is when the plate is pushed in, so that their output frequency will be the same as the stimulus fre-

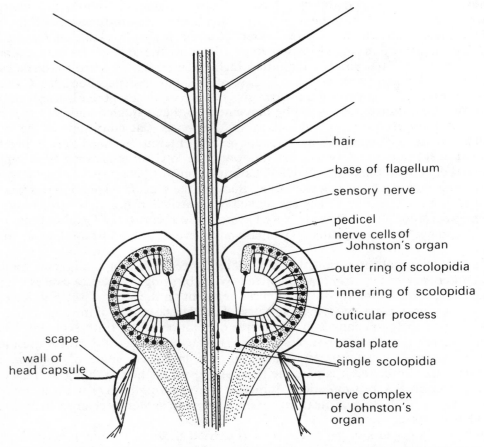

Fig. 412. Diagram of the basal part of the antenna of a male mosquito showing Johnston's organ (from Autrum, 1963).

quency. The output of the outer ring of sensilla, however, will be double this because some cells will respond to the 'in' movement, others to the 'out'. Hence the overall action potential will contain the basic stimulus frequency and its first harmonic. If the sound waves are at right angles to the flagellum, the latter rocks on its axis so that the output from both rings of sensilla will be double the basic frequency. At intermediate positions the output will vary, the basic frequency progressively disappearing as the parallel component of the sound waves becomes less. By this means the insect might be able to orientate to the sound (see *e.g.* Autrum, 1963).

The dominant forces acting on the antenna of ants are perceived by Johnston's organ, as presumably they are in any insect, and this may play a part in their orientation to gravity.

Johnston's organ is concerned with the orientation of *Notonecta* in the water. An air bubble extends between the head and the antenna so that when the insect is correctly orientated on its back the antenna is deflected away from the head. If, however, the insect is the wrong way up the antenna is drawn towards the head and Johnston's organ registers the position. Gyrinid beetles are able to perceive ripples on the water surface, apparently due to displacements of the antennal flagellum, so that they are able to avoid

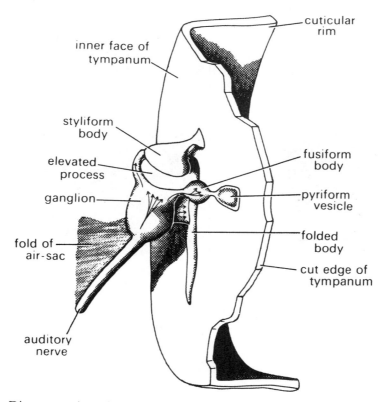

Fig. 413. Diagram to show the method of attachment of the auditory ganglion to the inner surface of the tympanum of *Locusta*. The folded body, styliform body and elevated process are cuticular structures. The orientations of the scolopidia are indicated by the arrows (after Gray, 1960).

collisions with other insects and, by echolocating by means of their own ripples, also avoid the sides of their container. In order to do this the insect must also be able to detect the direction from which the ripples are coming.

Where Johnston's organ is well developed other chordotonal organs are absent from the antennae, but in most insects additional organs occur in the basal and terminal antennal segments where they function as proprioceptors.

29.3 Tympanal organs

29.31 Structure and occurrence of tympanal organs

Tympanal organs are specialised chordotonal organs. Each consists of a thin area of cuticle, the tympanic membrane, backed by an air-sac so that it is free to vibrate. Attached to the inside of the membrane or adjacent to it is a chordotonal organ which contains from one scolopidium in *Plea* (Heteroptera) to about 1500 in Cicadidae. Tympanal organs occur on the prothoracic legs in Grylloidea and Tettigonioidea, on the mesothorax of some Hydrocorisae, such as *Corixa* and *Plea*, on the metathorax in Noctuoidea, and on the abdomen in Acrididae, Cicadidae, Pyralidoidea and Geometroidea (Lepidoptera).

In Acrididae there is a tympanum in a recess on either side of the first abdominal segment. The tympanum of *Locusta* is about 2·5 × 1·5 sq. mm. in area and at the front edge is a spiracle which leads into the air-sac beneath the tympanum (Fig. 414). The chordotonal organ, attached to the centre of the tympanic membrane, is complex, containing about 80 neurons with the cell bodies aggregated into a ganglion (Fig. 413).

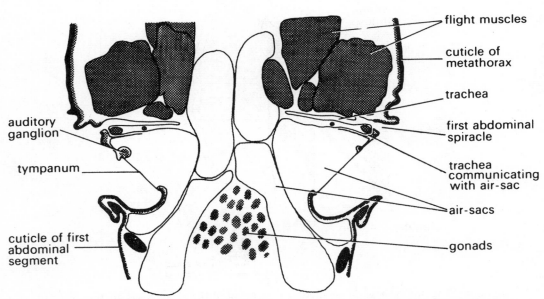

Fig. 414. Diagrammatic horizontal section through the base of the abdomen of a grasshopper, *Oedipoda*, showing the positions of the tympanic membranes, the air-sacs and the associated spiracles (after Schwabe, 1906).

From the ganglion the sensory units connect with the tympanum in four separate groups, which are attached to thickenings or invaginations of the cuticle. The scolopidia are joined to the epidermis by the attachment cells (see Fig. 409). The whole chordotonal organ and the auditory nerve which runs from it to the metathoracic ganglion are enclosed in folds of the air-sacs which are continuous right across the body (Fig. 414). Tracheoles extend to the epidermis and attachment cells, but none occurs in the body of the ganglion. Two muscles are attached to the edge of the tympanum, but their function is unknown.

The tympanal organs of Grylloidea and Tettigonioidea are similar to each other, being situated in the base of the fore tibia which is slightly dilated and typically has a tympanum on either side. Often the outer tympanum is bigger than the inner one and sometimes, as in *Gryllotalpa,* only the outer organ is present. In most Tettigonioidea the tympanic membranes are protected by forwardly projecting folds of the tibial cuticle (Fig. 415). The whole cavity of the leg between the two tympanic membranes is occupied by a trachea divided into two by a rigid membrane, the blood space of the leg being restricted to canals anteriorly and posteriorly. The main chordotonal organ, the crista acoustica, in *Decticus* contains 40 scolopidia. The more proximal seven of these are associated with the intermediate organ, another chordotonal organ (Fig. 416), but the remainder lie parallel with each other in a vertical row, the sensilla becoming progressively smaller towards the distal end. The whole organ lies between the tracheoblast cells and what is presumably the basement membrane of these cells, the cap cells of the scolopidia adjoining the basement membrane (Schwabe, 1906). The nerve from the crista acoustica also receives a branch from the intermediate organ and another from the subgenual organ, but the latter has another nerve joining the main nerve to the

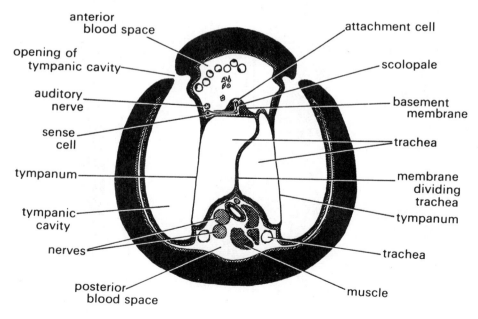

Fig. 415. Transverse section through the base of the fore tibia of a tettigoniid, *Decticus,* showing the arrangement of the tympanal organs (after Schwabe, 1906).

610

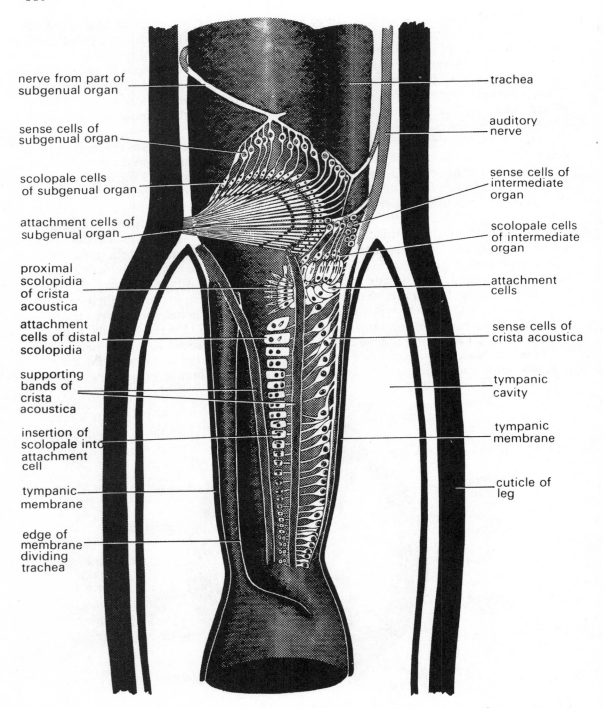

nerve from part of
subgenual organ

sense cells of
subgenual organ

scolopale cells
of subgenual organ

attachment cells of
subgenual organ

proximal
scolopidia
of crista
acoustica

attachment
cells of distal
scolopidia

supporting
bands of
crista
acoustica

insertion of
scolopale into
attachment
cell

tympanic
membrane

edge of
membrane
dividing
trachea

trachea

auditory
nerve

sense cells of
intermediate
organ

scolopale cells
of intermediate
organ

attachment
cells

sense cells of
crista acoustica

tympanic
cavity

tympanic
membrane

cuticle of
leg

Fig. 416. Longitudinal section of the fore tibia of a tettigoniid, *Decticus*, showing the arrangement of the tympanal organs and associated chordotonal organs (after Schwabe, 1906).

leg. The significance of the intermediate chordotonal organ is unknown. In these insects, as in the Acrididae, tympanal organs are present in all the instars, but they probably only become functional in the later larval instars and adults.

The tympanal organs of the Noctuoidea occupy the posterior part of the metathorax (Fig. 417) and the tympanic membrane faces into a cavity between the thorax and abdomen roofed over by the alula of the hind wing. Lateral to the tympanum and separated from it by a sclerotised ridge, the epaulette, is a soft white membrane, the conjunctiva, while medially there is a second membrane, resembling the tympanic membrane, but without a sense organ. This second membrane is the counter tympanic membrane which is probably an accessory resonating structure. The sense organ, which is attached to the back of the tympanum, contains only two scolopidia which are supported by an apodemal ligament and an invagination of the tympanal frame known as the Bügel (Roeder and Treat, 1957).

In cicadas the two tympanic membranes are situated ventro-laterally on the posterior end of the first abdominal segment behind the folded membrane (p. 586) and beneath the operculum. The air-sacs by which they are backed are continuous right across the abdominal cavity. Each chordotonal organ contains about 1500 scolopidia enclosed in a cuticular tympanic capsule and attached to the posterior rim of the tympanum by an apodeme.

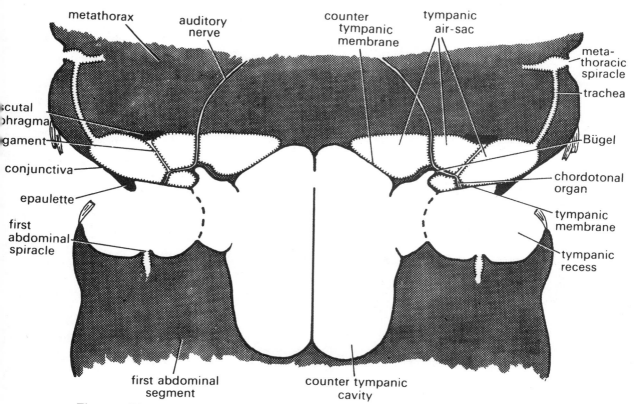

Fig. 417. Diagrammatic horizontal section through the metathorax and base of the abdomen of a noctuid moth showing the tympanal organs (modified after Roeder and Treat, 1957).

29.32 Functioning of the tympanal organs

Auditory receptors may function by perceiving the pressure pulses which emanate from the sound source or by perceiving the displacements of the air which its vibration causes. The two types of receptors are called, respectively, pressure and displacement receivers (see Haskell, 1961). Insect tympanal organs, as well as other organs sensitive to sound, are displacement receivers.

It is essential for the functioning of a displacement receiver that the tympanum should be free to vibrate without any constraint and that both sides of the tympanum should be exposed to the sound. In insects damping of the tympanic membrane is reduced to a minimum by the air-sacs which back it, while the two sides of the tympanum are exposed to the sound, either by free access between the air-sac and the outside air through an adjacent spiracle, as in Acrididae (see Fig. 414) and Cicadidae, or by having two membranes back to back as in Grylloidea, Tettigonioidea and Lepidoptera (see Figs. 415 and 417).

Sound impinging on the tympanic membrane sets the membrane in motion. This movement stimulates the sense cells of the chordotonal organ so that impulses are produced in the auditory nerve. The method by which vibration of the membrane is transduced so as to produce electrical changes in the sense cells is not known.

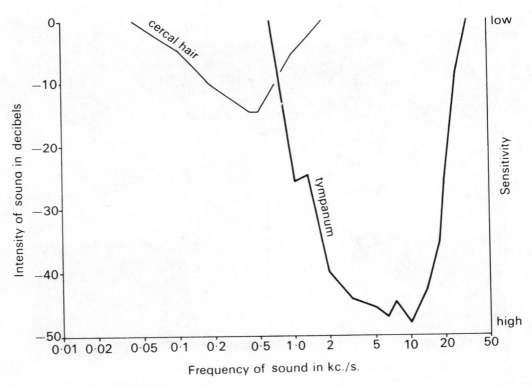

Fig. 418. The intensity of sound at different frequencies necessary to produce a response in the nerves from the cercal hairs and tympanal organs of *Oxya* (after Katsuki and Suga, 1960).

The tympanal organs of different groups of insects respond to a wide range of frequencies which, in general, correspond with the frequencies of the sound produced by stridulation (see p. 577). Acrididae respond to sounds with frequencies from 100 c./sec. to 50 kc./sec., tettigoniids from 1 to 100 kc./sec., gryllids from 200 c./sec. to 15 kc./sec., noctuids from 1 to 240 kc./sec., and cicadas from 100 c./sec. to 15 kc./sec.

In general, insects are unable to discriminate between sounds of different frequencies. In *Schistocerca* and *Locusta*, however, the impulses in the auditory nerve are not quite independent of the stimulus frequency and further discrimination may occur in the metathoracic ganglion which has a differential response favouring certain frequencies (Horridge, 1961). The tympanal organ of *Gampsocleis* (Orthoptera) has two types of neurons with maximum sensitivity to different frequencies (Katsuki and Suga, 1960). Thus some frequency discrimination in the tympanal organ is possible, but only to a very limited extent and it cannot be of great significance in the life of the animal (Horridge, 1961). It is, however, possible that a rough form of frequency discrimination could result from the different sensitivities of different sense organs. For instance, the cercal hairs of *Oxya* (Orthoptera) have a maximal response to stimulus frequencies of about 500 c./sec., while the tympanal organs respond maximally from about two to 15 kc./sec. (Fig. 418) (Katsuki and Suga, 1960). In general, tympanal organs are more sensitive to high frequency stimulation than to low frequencies.

The amplitude of the impulses in the auditory nerve is proportional to the intensity of sound since the scolopidia have a range of thresholds at which they respond and the greater the intensity of sound the more scolopidia are stimulated. Following from this, it is found that insects can perceive amplitude modulations. Volleys of spikes occur in the auditory nerve synchronous with pulses of sound and hence the pulse repetition frequency of insect songs is probably an important factor in their recognition (see p. 591). It is also possible that transients, sudden changes in intensity, are important in song recognition (for discussion and references see Haskell, 1956, 1961) and the output of the auditory nerve of *Tettigonia* can follow transients up to a frequency of 400 per second. The steeper the transient, the greater the response in the nerve.

Directional sensitivity

A characteristic of displacement sound receivers is that they show directional sensitivity, being most sensitive to sound waves striking the tympanum at right angles to the plane of its surface. Hence insects are able to locate sources of sound. A possible method by which location may occur has been described in tettigoniids where sensitivity is minimal to sounds coming from directly in front of the leg. On either side of this zone sensitivity increases sharply. As the insect walks forwards, obliquely towards a source of sound, the front leg on the side nearest the sound continues to move until the intensity of stimulation begins to change rapidly. At this point the leg stops moving, but the tympanic membranes on the contralateral leg are so placed that such rapid changes in the intensity of stimulation do not occur and the leg continues to move forwards. As a result the insect is pivoted about its stationary leg towards the sound source and this sequence of events is repeated until the insect is facing directly towards the source. At this stage the stimulation of the two legs is the same.

Differences in stimulation of the two legs are enhanced by a central contrast mechanism in *Gampsocleis*. Impulses in the auditory nerve evoke spikes in a large interneuron which extends from the metathoracic ganglion to the head, a continuous train of impulses from the tympanum producing only an 'on' response in the interneuron. Stimulation of the tympanum of one side excites the ipsilateral interneuron, so that the number of spikes produced is increased, but inhibits the contralateral fibre. As a result, any asymmetrical stimulation of the tympanal organs of the two legs is accentuated in the central nervous system. In addition, the discharge in the ipsilateral interneuron is synchronous with the sound pulses, but there is a delay in spike production in the contralateral fibre. In this way the information about the sound source received by the insect is increased (Suga and Katsuki, 1961).

Noctuids are able to locate a source of high frequency sound when they are flying so that they have the problem of localisation in a vertical as well as a horizontal direction. At low intensities of sound there is a difference in the response from the two tympanic membranes when they are asymmetrically stimulated so that a basis for horizontal location of the source is available. In addition, the wings tend to screen the tympani so that there is a marked difference in the responses of the two organs to asymmetrical stimulation when the wings are raised, but when the wings are in the lower half of their beat there is little difference between the two sides. There are thus cycles of sensitivity to asymmetrical sound stimulation and this may serve to assist in the location of the source (Roeder, 1965). Vertical localisation of the sound source also appears to depend on cyclical changes in the sensitivity of the tympanal organs in the course of a wing beat. Thus when the wings are down the insect is more sensitive to sounds coming from below it than to sounds from above, and a sound coming from below and in front would appear to be increasing in intensity during the downstroke.

During flight the auditory input from low intensity sounds of high frequency will thus vary cyclically and in different ways according to the position of the sound source. When the source is immediately behind the moth, however, no cyclical changes occur because the wings do not screen the tympanal organs, and this might provide a basis for the observed movements of moths away from low intensity sound sources (Roeder and Payne, 1966).

29.33 Functions of tympanal organs

The tympanal organs play an important part in mating behaviour in insects which stridulate, auditory stimuli serving to locate and signal to the opposite sex (see p. 591). They are also important in the aggregation of Acrididae and Cicadidae (p. 592).

One of the functions of the tympanal organs of Lepidoptera is the detection of the sounds produced by bats. Insectivorous bats, such as *Myotis*, produce very short pulses of sound, about 0·5 msec. long, separated by intervals of 5–6 msec., when they are hunting. The frequency of each pulse is modulated, starting at about 100 kc./sec. and falling to 30 kc./sec. or below (Griffin *et al.*, 1960). The tympanal organ of noctuids is sensitive over the whole of this range with a maximum sensitivity between 15 and 60 kc./sec. Unlike the tympanal organ of Orthoptera, it adapts rapidly to a continuing stimulus and has an after discharge which has the effect of amplifying any stimulus of short duration so that it is well suited to the reception of the sounds produced by bats.

Moths can detect bats about 100 ft. away and at such distances, where the intensity of stimulation is low, tend to turn away from the source of sound (see above). At high intensities of sound, such as would occur when the bat was within about 20 ft. of the moth, the response from the two tympanal organs is such that location of a sound source could not occur and at these intensities the moth takes violent evasive action. It may close its wings and drop to the ground, or power dive to the ground, or follow an erratic, weaving course. This behaviour is probably elicited by a time interval of less than 2·5 msec. between the impulses produced in the auditory nerve. The frequency of impulses increases with the intensity of sound so that as the bat approaches the impulse frequency in the auditory nerve increases, until finally the impulses are so close together that the moth is stimulated to take avoiding action. It has been shown that this avoiding action does have survival value (Roeder, 1965; Roeder and Treat, 1961).

The tympanal organs of a moth also respond to the sound of the wingbeats of another moth if this is within a few feet, but whether or not this has any significance for the moth is not known.

29.4 Campaniform sensilla

Campaniform sensilla are areas of thin cuticle, domed and usually oval in shape, having a long diameter of 20–30 μ (Fig. 419). The dome is thickened along its long diameter and inserted into it is the dendrite of a single neuron, often enclosed in a scolopale. These

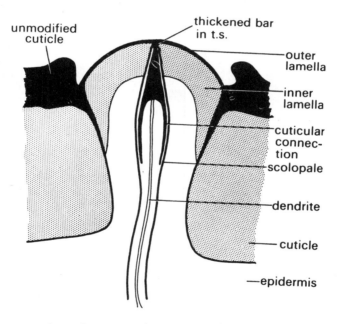

Fig. 419. Diagrammatic section through a campaniform sensillum (from Snodgrass, 1935).

sensilla often occur in groups, all those within a group having the same orientation and possibly connecting to the same nerve fibre so that they function as a unit. They occur in all parts of the body subject to stress and are concentrated near the joints as at the base of the wing or the haltere in Diptera (see Figs. 112, 113). On the leg of the cockroach there are four groups on the trochanter, each containing 15–20 sensilla, one at the base of the femur, another at the base of the tibia and one on each of the tarsal segments.

In the insect skeleton all stresses can be expressed as shearing stresses in the plane of the surface. Such stresses produce changes in the shape of the campaniform sensilla and, because of the thickened bar across the dome, compression forces along the length of the sensillum raise the dome while extension in the same direction lowers the dome. The nerve is stimulated when the dome is raised, that is by compression forces along the length of the sensillum and, for instance, most or all of the campaniform sensilla on the leg are so orientated that they are stimulated when the foot is on the ground and the leg bears the weight of the insect. The longer the axis of the dome the greater the sensitivity of the sensillum and in groups of campaniform sensilla there is usually a range of sizes, perhaps giving a range of sensitivity (Pringle, 1938b).

The response of campaniform sensilla is determined by the properties of the cuticle: its elasticity, thickness and curvature; by the forces exerted on the cuticle by muscles; and by the pattern of forces due to gravity or inertia. They thus function as proprioceptors, but, unlike vertebrate proprioceptors, they do not respond to the movements of individual muscles, but to the resultants of a variety of contending strains on the cuticle. Thus some campaniform sensilla monitor the movements of the wings and halteres, others are concerned in the control of leg movement as, for instance, in *Periplaneta* where the leg depressor reflex is initiated by stimulation of the campaniform sensilla of the trochanter. Like all proprioceptors they are slow adapting (Fig. 420).

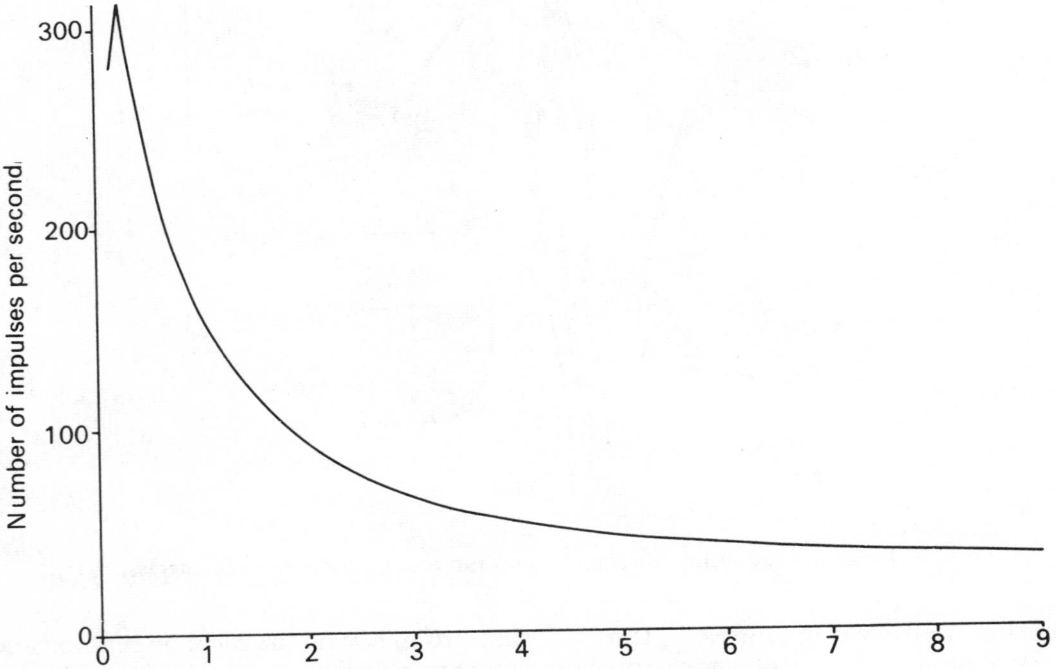

Fig. 420. The frequency of impulses in the nerves from a group of campaniform sensilla on the maxillary palp of *Periplaneta* showing the initial high level followed by a long period during which the frequency of impulses is maintained at a lower level with very little adaptation (after Pringle, 1938a).

29.5 Stretch receptors

Stretch receptors differ from other insect sensilla in consisting of a multipolar neuron with free nerve endings, while all the others contain a bipolar neuron with a dendrite associated with the cuticle. These types of neuron are differentiated as Type II and Type I neurons respectively.

Stretch receptors occur in connective tissue or associated with muscles. In *Periplaneta* there is a pair in the dorsal region of each of abdominal segments two to seven above the bands of longitudinal muscle. The neuron is embedded in fibrous connective tissue which is connected to an intersegmental membrane at one end and to the dorsal body wall and the dorsal muscles at the other. In *Blaberus* (Dictyoptera) the ends of the dendrites inside the connective tissue are not sheathed in Schwann cells, as is the rest of the neuron, and are only 0·1–0·2 μ in diameter. The connective tissue consists of a matrix with fibrils embedded in it, but without any limiting membrane so that it is in direct contact with the haemolymph, and plasmatocytes (p. 676) are closely applied to the surface. The inelastic fibrils serve to support the neuron and, perhaps, prevent it from being stretched too far (Osborne, 1963).

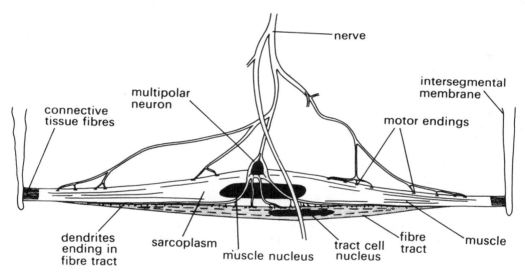

Fig. 421. Diagram of a stretch receptor from the larva of *Antheraea* (based on Finlayson and Lowenstein, 1958).

Acrididae also have stretch receptors dorsally in the abdomen, but the dendritic endings are associated with a slender muscle fibre which runs from the anterior end of one segment to the anterior end of the next, forming a part of the dorsal longitudinal muscles. Stretch receptors associated with muscles also occur in Lepidoptera larvae, pupae and adults, and in Trichoptera and Neuroptera, but here the muscle strand is separated from the other muscles and has a separate innervation. It contains typical muscle fibrils, but these are sparse in the centre of the fibre which contains a large amount of sarcoplasm and a giant nucleus (Fig. 421). Attached to the muscle and partly embedded in it is a tube of connective tissue known as the fibre tract, which contains reinforcing fibres set in a matrix. These fibres are secreted by the tract cell which lies within the connective tissue and also has a giant nucleus. The neuron gives rise to two to four main dendrites which run along the length of the fibre tract, remaining free at the centre, but bound to the tract by connective tissue at the ends. From these main dendrites side branches, which at the tips are not clothed in Schwann cells, pass to the outside, and insinuate their way inside the fibre tract (Osborne and Finlayson, 1965).

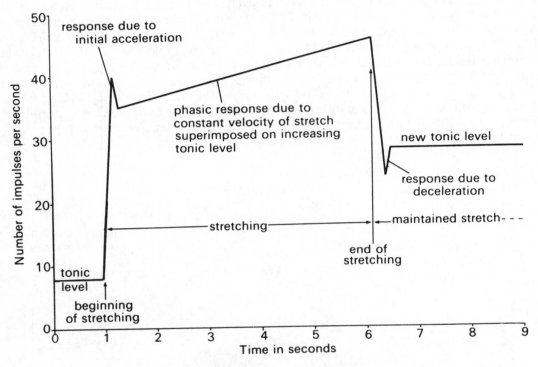

Fig. 422. The frequency of impulses in the nerve from a stretch receptor in the larva of *Antheraea* before, during and after a period of steady stretching (after Weevers, 1966a).

Larval *Antheraea* (Lepidoptera) have a pair of stretch receptors in the first nine abdominal segments just above the dorsal longitudinal muscles. At metamorphosis the dorsal longitudinal muscles of larval Lepidoptera disappear, but, except for those in the eighth and ninth abdominal segments, the stretch receptors persist. They do undergo a metamorphosis which involves dedifferentiation and subsequent rediffer-entiation of the associated muscles (Finlayson and Mowat, 1963).

These sensilla are proprioceptors and are stimulated by stretching. In the complete absence of tension there is no output, but under normal tension an output of 5–10 impulses per second is maintained for hours. With further stretching the impulse frequency rises and the adapted frequency is proportional to the length of the receptor. The muscle thus has a tonic response, but superimposed on this is a phasic response which appears while the length of the receptor is changing. The impulse frequency increases with the velocity of stretch and, in addition, a burst of spikes is produced by any acceleration of stretching, either at the start or in the course of stretch. When stretching is complete the impulse frequency falls to its new tonic level (Fig. 422).

The stretch receptor can thus, through its tonic output, provide information on the position of one part of the body with respect to another, while the phasic response signals changes in these positions. Since at low frequencies, up to about five per second, the output is synchronised with stretching these receptors may also monitor relatively slow rhythmic movements such as ventilatory movements (p. 464) (Osborne, 1963).

The frequency with which the receptor responds to cyclical stimulation may be limited by the viscosity of the connective tissue matrix in which the dendrites end, but the muscle associated with the lepidopteran stretch receptor may offset this effect to some extent by taking up the slack when the receptor is suddenly released. Relaxation causes a drop in the output of the receptor and this leads to a brief increase in the frequency of impulses to the muscle so that it contracts. Conversely, when the stretch receptor is stimulated the tonic stimulation of the muscle is inhibited so that it relaxes. This perhaps has the effect of preventing overstimulation of the receptor during rapid stretching (Weevers, 1966b).

29.6 Statocysts

Well-developed statocysts are unusual in insects, but in *Dorymyrmex* (Hymenoptera) there is a statocyst on the metathorax just above the coxa. It consists of an invagination of the cuticle lined with tactile hairs. Within the cavity are one or two sand grains which become supported by two cuticular projections in such a way that, although they cannot make large movements, they are free to move if the insect changes its orientation. As a result of a change in orientation they press on some of the hairs, different hairs being stimulated with different orientations so that the organs function as gravity receptors. Comparable organs occur in the head of *Anoplotermes* (Isoptera), and another, but with a cuticular statolith instead of a sand grain, on the prosternum of *Dorymyrmex* (Marcus, 1956).

An organ, known as Palmen's organ, which may function as a statocyst occurs in the head of larval and adult Ephemeroptera. This consists of a cuticular nodule at the junction of four tracheae mid-dorsally behind the eyes. No special innervation of this organ is known, but behaviour is disturbed if it is destroyed.

29.7 Pressure receptors

Most aquatic insects are buoyant because of the air which they carry down under the water when they submerge, but *Aphelocheirus* (Heteroptera), living on the bottoms of streams and respiring by a plastron is not buoyant. Although the plastron can withstand considerable pressures (see p. 482) it only functions efficiently in water with a high oxygen content such as normally occurs in relatively shallow water. Hence some mechanism of depth perception is an advantage to *Aphelocheirus*, although it is unnecessary in the majority of other, buoyant insects.

On the ventral surface of the second abdominal segment of *Aphelocheirus* is a shallow depression containing hydrofuge hairs which are much larger than the hairs of the plastron. They are inclined at an angle of about 30° to the surface of the cuticle and dispersed amongst them are thin-walled sensory hairs (Fig. 423). The volume of air trapped by these hairs depends on the balance between the pressure of air inside and the pressure of water outside. If the insect moves into deep water the increase in water pressure reduces the volume of air so that the hairs are bent over, carrying with them the sensilla which are thus stimulated. The insect responds to such an increase in pressure by swimming up, but there is no response to a decrease in pressure.

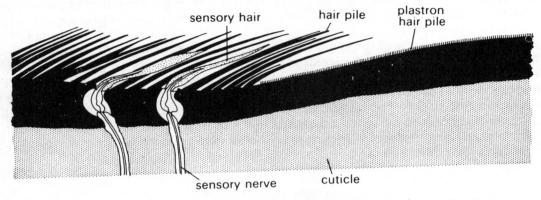

Fig. 423. Section through the edge of a pressure sense organ of *Aphelocheirus* (after Thorpe and Crisp, 1947b).

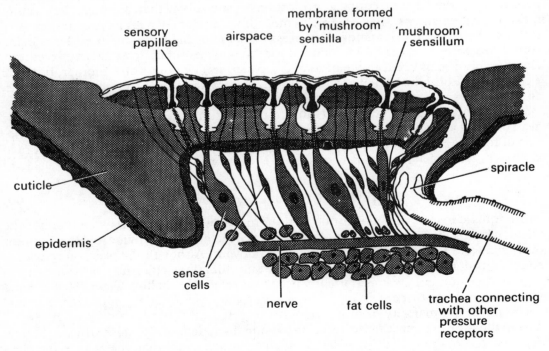

Fig. 424. Section of a pressure sense organ of *Nepa* (after Thorpe and Crisp, 1947b).

Changes in the gas tension in the water, by influencing the exchange of gases, may also influence the pressure in the tracheal system and hence could affect the volume of air trapped by the hydrofuge hairs. However, it is possible that such small changes may be damped out by compensating expansion or contraction of an air-sac on the trachea near the spiracle leading into the depression housing the receptor (Thorpe and Crisp, 1947b).

Pressure receptors are also present in *Nepa* (Heteroptera) which has a pair on the sterna of each of abdominal segments three to five. Each consists of a number of mushroom-shaped plates enclosing an airspace (Fig. 424). Nerve endings occur in the plates, and sensory papillae on the inner wall of the airspace are stimulated by the plates pressing on them. A spiracle opens into the space so that the spaces in the three organs of one side are connected through the tracheal system. The receptors give no general response to an increase in pressure, but differential stimulation of the organs of one side produces a response. If the head is tilted upwards the air in the system of pressure receptors tends to rise towards the head end and as a result the anterior mushroom-shaped plates will tend to be pushed out while those on the posterior organ will collapse against the papillae so that the organ is stimulated (Fig. 425). The converse is true if the head is tilted downwards and in this way the insect obtains information on its orientation (Thorpe and Crisp, 1947b).

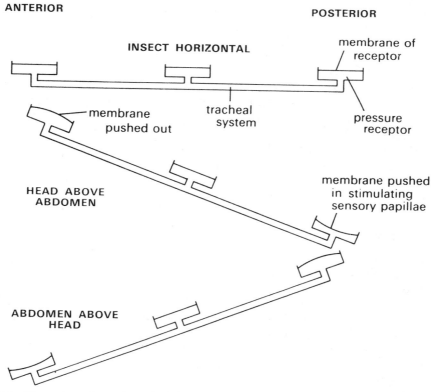

Fig. 425. Diagram to show the principle of action of the pressure receptors of *Nepa* (after Thorpe and Crisp, 1947b).

CHAPTER XXX

CHEMORECEPTION

Stimulation by chemicals can occur in different ways. First, if the chemicals are present in a gaseous state in relatively low concentrations they may be perceived as smells and the mechanism of perception is known as olfaction. Second, they may be perceived as a result of direct contact if they are present in the liquid state or in solution at relatively high concentrations. This is known as contact chemoreception and it is not clearly separated from olfaction. Finally, insects have a common chemical sense by which they perceive high concentrations of irritant substances such as ammonia.

The sensilla concerned with chemoreception are widespread, but are particularly abundant on the antennae, mouthparts and legs, and they are generally characterised by having fine nerve endings exposed through gaps in the cuticle. Olfactory receptors often have many sense cells each of which responds to a range of substances and which are sometimes specialised for the perception of chemicals of particular importance to the insect. Contact chemoreceptors have a smaller number of sense cells each responding to a different class of chemicals.

The perception of chemicals is important in many aspects of the life of insects. For instance, smell may assist insects in finding food or a mate, while contact chemoreception may be of importance in final recognition of the food, an oviposition site or a mate.

Chemoreception is reviewed by Boeckh *et al.* (1965), Dethier (1953, 1962, 1963), Dethier and Chadwick (1948) and Hodgson (1958, 1964). The fine structure of insect chemoreceptors has been studied in particular by Slifer and her associates: see Slifer (1970, *A. Rev. Ent.* **15**).

30.1 Olfaction

30.11 Receptors

The identification of olfactory receptors is often uncertain because it is based only on the results of ablation experiments. Nevertheless, it is reasonably certain that thin-walled basiconic pegs and coeloconic pegs are olfactory receptors.

The thin-walled basiconic pegs on the antenna of *Melanoplus* are 12–20 μ long with a dark, permeable spot at the base on one side. From this spot the scolopale extends inwards, ending above the nerve cell bodies (Fig. 426). The number of neurons varies from a few to over 50 and the size of the peg varies proportionally. The dendrites of these cells pass into the scolopale and at the point of entry a short segment of each assumes a cilium-like structure with nine pairs of peripheral fibrils. These do not extend distally into the dendrite, but are replaced by numerous neurofilaments. At the top of the scolopale the dendrites pass out into the lumen of the peg through a number of small holes and then divide into finer branches which pass close beneath the surface of the peg. From these branches tufts of finger-like filaments resembling microvilli extend out to end in small pores about 0·1 μ in diameter in the cuticle of the peg so that the tips of the filaments are exposed to the atmosphere. Locke (1965a) suggests that these filaments are not nerve endings but lipid/water crystals and such an arrangement would facilitate the trapping of oil soluble molecules. See also Ernst (1969, *Z. Zellforsch. Mikroskop. Anat.* **94**). A vacuole occupies the interior of the peg and the cells forming the sensillum are enclosed by fibres on the outer surface of the tormogen cell which surrounds the other cells (Slifer, 1961; Slifer *et al.*, 1959; Slifer and Sekhon, 1964b).

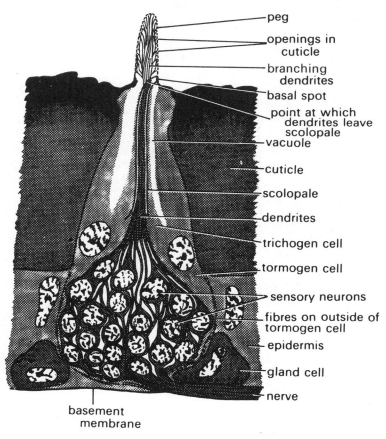

Fig. 426. Diagram of a thin-walled basiconic peg from the antenna of a grasshopper (after Slifer *et al.*, 1959).

Similar sensilla occur on the antenna of insects in all the major orders (Slifer and Sekhon, 1964c). Some variation occurs as, for instance, in *Lygaeus* (Heteroptera) in which the cilium-like regions of the dendrites are more extensive, reaching almost to the top of the scolopale, while at the base of the cilium are basal bodies and rootlets extending proximally into the dendrite.

Coeloconic pegs are known to occur on the grasshopper antenna and the mandibles of bees. In the grasshopper they consist of short pegs about 8 μ long, resembling thick-walled basiconic pegs (p. 635), but sunk into a cavity below the general level of the surface of the cuticle. The cavity, about 20 μ in diameter, is broadly open to the outside (Fig. 427). Each sensillum contains three or four neurons with the tips of the dendrites exposed at the top of the peg.

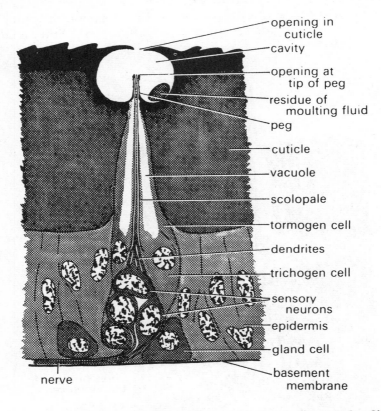

Fig. 427. Diagram of a coeloconic peg from the antenna of a grasshopper (after Slifer *et al.*, 1959).

Comparable organs, but with each pit containing many sensilla, occur on the third antennal segments of cyclorrhaphous flies and on the labial palps of Lepidoptera and Neuroptera. In *Sarcophaga* there are about 50 of these olfactory pits on each antenna of the male, but over 250 on each in the female; in *Phormia* there are 9–11 in males and 11–16 in females. The entrance to each pit is guarded by spines which prevent the entry of dust and the larger pits in *Sarcophaga* contain 200–300 sensory pegs. The pits on the median and dorso-lateral faces of the antenna contain mainly bottle-shaped pegs about 8 μ long (Fig. 428). Associated with each peg are two neurons, the dendrites of which have a cilium-like structure for part of their length. Distally the dendrites branch irregularly so that they fill the lumen of the peg, filaments from the branches passing to

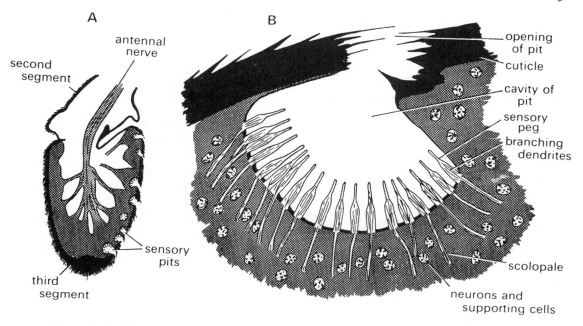

Fig. 428. A. Diagrammatic longitudinal section of the antenna of *Sarcophaga* showing the positions of the sensory pits. B. Detail of a single sensory pit (based on Slifer and Sekhon, 1964a).

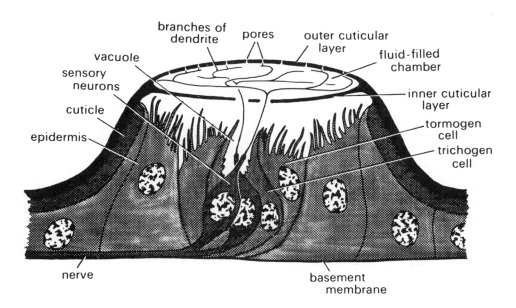

Fig. 429. Diagram of a plate organ from the antenna of an aphid (after Slifer *et al.*, 1964).

pores in the distal wall of the peg as they do in the thin-walled basiconic peg (p. 622). Other olfactory pits on the dorso-lateral surfaces of the antennae contain other types of sensilla (Slifer and Sekhon, 1964a).

Another type of sensillum which may have an olfactory function is the plate organ (Fig. 429). Organs of this type occur on the two basal segments of the antenna of aphids and consist of oval areas of transparent cuticle with long diameters ranging, in *Megoura*, from 60 to 250 μ. The cuticle of the plate is thin, about 0·35 μ thick, and about 2 μ below it is a second layer of cuticle with holes in it so that a fluid-filled space between the two layers is continuous with the vacuole formed by the trichogen cell. A few neurons are associated with each sensillum and the dendrites, each with a cilium-like segment, extend towards the surface cuticle through the perforations in the inner layer. In the fluid-filled chamber they branch repeatedly and from the finer branches close beneath the surface tufts of filaments pass into pores in the outer layer of cuticle. These pores appear to be open in newly moulted individuals, but it is not certain that they are in older insects (Slifer *et al.*, 1964). Plate organs also occur on the antenna of *Apis*, but here it is not certain that there are perforations in the cuticle and dendrites do not approach the surface. See also Schneider and Steinbrecht (1968, *Symp. zool. Soc. Lond.* **23**).

30.12 Functioning of olfactory receptors

Most olfactory sensilla have a number of sense cells and, at least in some cases, each cell responds in a particular way to a spectrum of odours. Some odours may elicit a response from a cell, while others may have no effect or may depress the activity of a cell which is already active. Different cells respond to different spectra of odours, although these may overlap. Other cells respond to particular odours which are significant for the species. For instance, certain cells in the sensilla of male *Antheraea* are stimulated by the female pheromone, but do not respond to that of the related *Bombyx*; none of the cells in the female receptors gives this response (Boeckh *et al.*, 1965).

The response of the antenna as a whole is often measured as the electroantennogram which probably represents the summed generator potentials of the sense cells. This is a sustained potential which may be either depolarising or hyperpolarising, that is inhibiting (see p. 538). In adult male *Bombyx* a sustained depolarising potential is produced by stimulation with the scent of the female and, although a similar response does occur to the odours of various saturniid moths, the potential which develops in response to conspecific stimulation is generally larger. The amplitude of the electro-antennogram increases as the concentration of female scent increases and there may be an associated change in behaviour. Stimulation with other substances such as xylene produces an electroantennogram of a quite different form.

For a response to occur a given number of molecules of the stimulating odour must impinge on the receptor sites and this is facilitated by the large numbers of sensilla usually present, by the presence in each sensillum of a number of sensory neurons and by the multiplication of nerve endings in the wall of the sensory peg. Correlated with this it appears that thresholds to smells are lowest when the number of sensilla present is highest, and, perhaps also reflecting differences in the numbers of sensilla, the different organs of an insect have different sensitivities. In *Phormia* for instance, the antennae are more sensitive to odours than are the palps and these in turn are more sensitive than the labellum.

30.13 Behavioural responses to odours

The effect of stimulation by odours is to promote activity; some substances attract insects, some lead to a rejection or an attempted avoidance of the stimulus, while in some cases the response varies with the concentration of the odour.

Whether a stimulating odour is attractive or repellant is determined by the genetical constitution of the insect. Hence carrion feeders react positively to the smell of ammonia which is associated with decaying meat, and female blowflies, which oviposit on meat, are more strongly attracted than males. Many insects, on the other hand, are repelled by ammonia at all concentrations. Similarly the specific response of male insects to female scents is genetically controlled.

Some modification of genetically controlled responses may occur as a result of conditioning. For instance, *Nemeritis* (Hymenoptera) is normally parasitic on *Ephestia*, the female parasites ovipositing in the host larvae which they locate largely by olfaction. Adult *Nemeritis* reared normally on *Ephestia* do not respond to the smell of *Meliphora* (Lepidoptera) larvae, but if, before they are tested, they are exposed to the smell of *Meliphora* for a day or more the parasites are subsequently attracted by the smell. The attraction is not so marked as the attraction to *Ephestia*, which always remains dominant, and unless conditioning is continued they cease to be attracted to *Meliphora* after a few days.

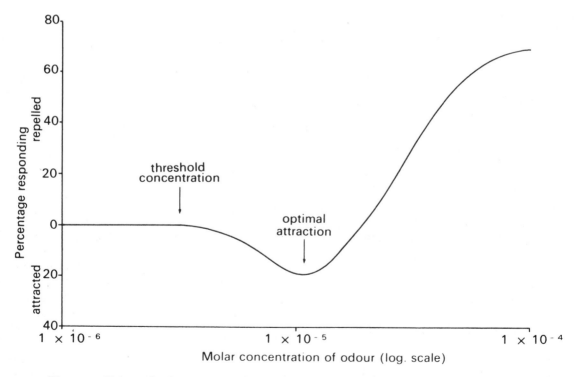

Fig. 430. Changes in the response of adult *Musca* (Diptera) to different concentrations of the odour of iso-valeraldehyde. Concentrations are low to the left of the figure (from Dethier, 1963).

Conditioning during the larval stage is also of some importance. *Nemeritis* can be induced to oviposit in *Meliphora* and the parasites develop normally. The emerging adults are then attracted by the smell of *Meliphora*, although *Ephestia* is still preferred, but the attraction wanes if the adult parasites are not also conditioned. Continued breeding for up to eight generations on the abnormal host made no significant improvement in the response to *Meliphora* (Thorpe and Jones, 1937).

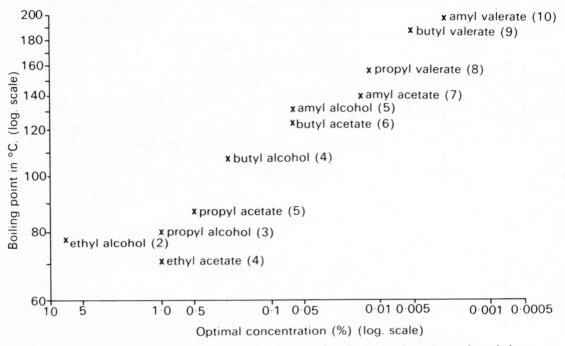

Fig. 431. Relationship between the boiling points of various organic compounds and the optimal concentrations which attract flies. Notice that concentrations are low to the right of the figure. Numbers in brackets indicate the number of carbon atoms in each compound, giving an indication of chain length (after Cook, 1926).

Apart from the influence of the intrinsic make up of the insect responsiveness is affected by its physiological state. For instance, blowfly larvae are attracted by the smell of ammonia during their feeding period, but when feeding ends in the third instar, at a time when the larvae normally leave the food in order to pupate, the response to ammonia is reversed. The state of feeding also influences the response of *Schistocerca* larvae to the smell of food. Fully fed larvae do not respond to food smells, but after being starved for a few hours they make directed movements towards the source of smell (Haskell, Paskin and Moorhouse, 1962).

Further, the response varies with the concentration of the stimulating odour. In general the intensity of response, either attraction or repulsion, increases with the concentration, but some substances which are attractive at low concentration are rejected when their concentration becomes too high (Fig. 430). Other behavioural changes may result from increased concentrations of odour and, for instance, the pheromone from female *Bombyx* evokes an orientation response from the male at low concentrations, but at high concentrations it causes the male to make mating responses.

The sensitivity of insects to different odours is related to the physical characteristics of the odour and hence to its chemical composition. Thus within an homologous series of organic chemicals flies and moths are stimulated by increasingly lower concentrations as the chain lengths of the chemicals increase (Fig. 431) and an increase in the length of the acid side of a molecule, such as an ester, is more effective than an increase on the alcohol side. Chain length is proportional to boiling point and inversely proportional to the solubility of the substance in water.

Insects can differentiate between smells as is indicated by their specific responses to pheromones and the fact that starved female *Xenopsylla* (Siphonaptera) respond positively to the smell of white rats, but not to the smells of other rodents (Shulov and Naor, 1964). *Apis,* which has been most fully studied, can differentiate an essential oil derived from oranges from 23 other scents including three other oils derived from citrus fruits, although it does confuse the citrus oils to some extent. It can also detect very small changes in scents. Thus bees trained to the odour of 1% benzyl acetate can separate this from a mixture containing 119 parts of 1% benzyl acetate to one part of 1% linalol (Ribbands, 1955).

30.14 Significance of odour perception

Olfactory stimulation is of considerable importance to many insects in locating their food. Carrion-feeding species such as *Necrophorus* (Coleoptera) are attracted by the smell of ammonia and *Leptinotarsa* (Coleoptera) responds positively to the smell of acetaldehyde from the potato. *Philanthus* only responds to insects having the smell of bees (p. 24). In *Apis* flower scents on the bodies of returning foragers help other workers to recognise the source of food and this is further facilitated by the habit of marking the flowers which are visited with the colony odour.

Female insects are commonly attracted to suitable oviposition sites by smell. Fertilised females of *Lucilia sericata* (Diptera) are attracted by the smell of wool. This species commonly oviposits on live sheep, but the related *L. caesar, L. illustris* and *Calliphora vomitoria,* which do not normally attack sheep in Britain, are not attracted to wool to any marked extent (Cragg and Cole, 1956). The parasite *Rhyssa* (Hymenoptera) is able to detect the larva of its host *Sirex* (Hymenoptera) through several inches of wood as a result of olfactory stimulation.

Odours, in the form of pheromones, are of great importance in many species in promoting the meeting of the sexes (p. 737) and in some cases are important in the later stages of courtship. In social insects the colony odour is important in recognition of members of the colony and the differentiation of intruders.

There is no evidence that insects can follow gradients of smell and it is unlikely that, under natural conditions with air turbulence, such gradients can be stable over any but very short distances. Thus it is improbable that smell provides a directing influence, but it may stimulate the insect to orientate to some other factor. Thus *Schistocerca* larvae tend to drift slowly downwind, but when stimulated by the smell of food they orientate into the wind and so, by moving upwind, arrive in the neighbourhood of the source of smell. Moths and bees responding to sexual pheromones also orientate to the wind (p. 737).

30.2 Contact chemoreception

30.21 Receptors

The most fully studied contact chemoreceptors are the trichoid sensilla on the legs and mouthparts of *Phormia*. They are from 30 to 300 μ long. From the tip the scolopale is invaginated, and is confluent with one wall of the hair so that the lumen of the hair is divided into two (Fig. 432A). The scolopale extends down to the level of the perikarya where its wall is invaginated so that the dendrites are separated from each other (Fig. 432B). Associated with each sensillum are four to six neurons, but the dendrite of one of these ends at the base of the hair, functioning as a mechanoreceptor, so that only three to five dendrites extend along the lumen of the scolopale to the tip of the hair where, in *Stomoxys* (Diptera), at least, they are exposed to the atmosphere. Up to their point of entry into the scolopale the dendrites are clothed in a membrane, but this is absent within the scolopale. A membrane also forms a partial diaphragm across the base of the hair,

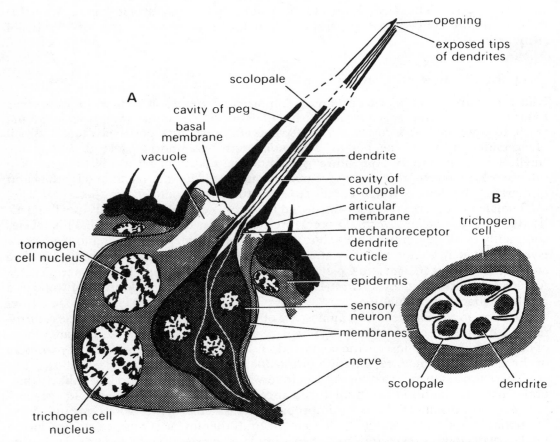

Fig. 432. A. Diagram of a chemosensory trichoid sensillum from *Phormia* (modified after Dethier, 1955; and Larsen, 1962). B. Transverse section through the scolopale of a trichoid sensillum just proximal to the base of the hair showing the invaginations of the scolopale between the dendrites (after Larsen, 1962).

perhaps serving to transmit movement of the hair to the dendrite concerned with mechanoreception. The trichogen cell is the largest in the complex forming the sensillum. It contains a large vacuole and a membrane outside it encloses all the cells including the tormogen cell which only envelops the trichogen cell distally (Dethier, 1963; Larsen, 1962). Sensilla of this type are found on the tarsi and mouthparts of many insect and on the ovipositors of such insects as ichneumonids and gryllids.

Also on the mouthparts of *Phormia* are interpseudotracheal papillae, of which there are about 150 on the oral surface of the labellum, projecting between the plates supporting the pseudotracheae. These are short pegs, about 10 μ long, on a broad base, and are heavily sclerotised except at the tip. The lumen of the peg contains an extension of the vacuole of the trichogen cell and the dendrites from four neurons extend into the scolopale, presumably being exposed at the tip of the peg, although this is not certainly known (Larsen, 1963).

30.22 Functioning of contact chemoreceptors

These sensilla are stimulated by contact with chemical substances. In order to stimulate the sensillum the substance concerned must produce a depolarisation of the membrane of the dendrite. It is not known how this is brought about, but it is suggested that in the case of sugars the sugar molecule combines with a specific receptor site, which must have a good fit for the sugar configuration, by weak forces such as van der Waal's. The complex so formed depolarises the membrane and the sugar is removed by a shift in the concentration gradient. The fact that the latent period between the time of application of the stimulus and the appearance of the first impulse is different for sugar and salt receptors (see below) suggests that the mechanisms of excitation by sugars and salts are different. See also Rees (1970, *Proc. R. Soc.* B. **174**).

The receptor potential produced by stimulation probably also serves as a generator potential giving rise to the spike potential near the perikaryon. The impulses produced are conducted in both directions, but only pass for a short distance up the dendrite. The number of impulses produced is proportional to the concentration of the stimulating substance, but the receptor adapts rapidly suggesting that the relevant information regarding the stimulus is supplied to the central nervous system within the first second from the time of stimulation.

Electrophysiological studies show that each of the nerve fibres reaching the tip of a trichoid sensillum reacts to a particular class of compounds. In *Phormia* one responds to stimulation by sugars, another responds to salts and a third to water, while the function of the fourth fibre when it is present is unknown. Not all the hairs respond in the same way, some giving a more vigorous response than others to stimulation by a particular substance. In the larva of *Bombyx* one of the sense cells of the maxillary sensilla responds to bitter substances while others respond to sugars, water, salts and acids.

30.23 Behavioural responses to contact chemoreception

Behavioural responses tie in closely with the electrophysiological evidence, indicating that insects are able to differentiate between sweet, salt, acid and bitter substances, and that further differentiation between different bitter tastes may also occur. Comprehensive studies have been made on *Phormia* which responds to stimulation of the trichoid sensilla with sugar or water by extending the proboscis. The response varies with different sugars and in general the α-glucosides are the most stimulating. Thus in *Phormia* and *Calliphora* the lowest acceptance thresholds are those for sucrose, maltose and trehalose of the disaccharides and fructose, fucose and glucose of the mono-saccharides. Some sugars fail to stimulate altogether while others have an inhibiting effect. Polysaccharides also fail to stimulate.

Species differ in their acceptance of sugars, and blowflies for instance are more catholic than *Apis*. This also applies to different sensilla on a single insect and mannose is an effective stimulus for the interpseudotracheal sensilla of *Phormia,* although it does not stimulate the trichoid sensilla. Mixtures of sugars have different effects because inhibition or synergism may occur.

The response to water is most readily elicited by water free of salts. High osmotic pressure or the presence of inorganic electrolytes inhibit the response in varying degrees, and the effects of electrolytes are specific; calcium chloride, for instance, inhibits the response at lower concentrations than does sodium chloride.

Stimulation of the trichoid sensilla of *Phormia* with inorganic salts leads to proboscis withdrawal or the inhibition of extension. In general, inorganic cations are more effective if they have high ionic mobilities. Thus their stimulating or inhibiting power follows the series: $H^+ > NH_4^+ > K^+ > Ca^{++} > Mg^{++} > Na^+$. With anions the situation is more complex and is different for mono- and di-valent ions. In *Periplaneta* the stimulating power of anions follows the sequence: $OH' > NO_3' > I' > Br' > Cl' = SO_4'' > Ac' > PO_4'''$. With organic electrolytes the hydrogen ions are important, but the anion also contributes to the stimulating power. Thresholds for stimulation are lower with longer chain lengths.

Similarly in any series of aliphatic organic compounds stimulating power is proportional to chain length, and thus to their solubility in lipoids and the boiling point, and inversely proportional to the vapour pressure. The relationship is not linear for any one series of compounds, but shows a sharp break in the region of a certain chain length which is characteristic for the series (Fig. 433). Replacement of the hydrogen atoms in the molecule by various other groups, such as chloride or a hydroxyl group, alters the stimulating power of the compound. It is suggested that surface energy relationships are involved in stimulation by these substances.

The inhibition of proboscis extension in *Phormia* by hydrocarbons and other substances may result from the stimulation of a rejection fibre, but Steinhardt *et al.* (1966) suggest that the effects may be to inhibit the activity of the other receptors. They found that alcohols and amines had no stimulating effect, but they inhibited the output from salt, sugar and water receptors at certain concentrations, causing a complete loss of responsiveness. Similarly, mannose does not stimulate a rejection receptor, but interferes with the stimulation of the sugar receptor by fructose, and rhamnose inhibits the response to glucose in the same way.

The responses of the insect to a substance are not constant, but vary depending on the physiological condition of the insect, the state of feeding being especially important. Thresholds for stimulation are lower after a period without food. Further, the sensitivity of different parts of the body also varies and in *Apis*, for instance, the proboscis is more sensitive than the antennae which, in turn, are more sensitive than the legs.

Integration may occur within the central nervous system. *Phormia,* for instance, responds to lower concentrations of sugar if two tarsi are stimulated instead of one.

This suggests central summation of the stimuli, although the results could be accounted for by chance alone (see Dethier, 1963). Central summation is also suggested by the response to stimulation of one tarsus with an acceptable substance, such as a sugar, and of a contralateral tarsus with an unacceptable substance.

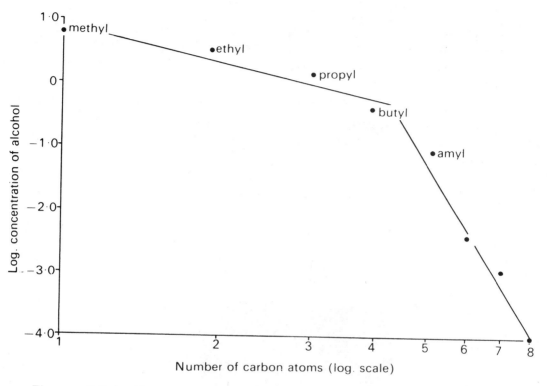

Fig. 433. Relationship between the number of carbon atoms in various primary alcohols and the concentrations required to cause rejection by 50% of the flies tested. Concentrations are lowest at the bottom of the figure (from Dethier, 1963).

30.24 Significance of contact chemoreception

Contact chemoreception is of particular importance in the control of feeding. In *Phormia*, for instance, stimulation of the tarsi with sugar leads to proboscis extension. This brings the labellar hairs into contact with the food so that this is subjected to a further test. The labellar hairs are more sensitive than the tarsal hairs and so are able to detect substances, perhaps unsuitable, which are present in concentrations too low to stimulate the tarsal hairs. If the substance still proves to be suitable the labellar lobes are spread out and the insect starts to suck up the sugar. The entry of sugar into the pseudotracheal system immediately stimulates the interpseudotracheal pegs providing a final check on the suitability of the food. Continuous sensory input is necessary for feeding to continue (Dethier *et al.*, 1956). In a similar way the sensilla on the palps and mouthparts of locusts and other insects presumably control feeding.

Insects usually respond positively to substances in their normal food, but acceptance of a substance does not necessarily imply that it is of any nutritive value to the insect. *Calliphora*, for instance, will accept cellobiose, although this is of no value to it as food.

Contact chemoreception may also be important in the control of oviposition. Thus *Locusta*, which oviposits in moist sand, digging a hole with the tip of the abdomen, can detect various inorganic salts in the sand. If the concentration of salts is high the insect withdraws its abdomen without ovipositing and the higher the concentration the more often is the sand rejected as an oviposition site (Woodrow, 1965). Chemoreceptors on the ovipositor are also important in parasitic insects.

30.3 Common chemical sense

Insects respond through the common chemical sense to high concentrations of irritant substances such as ammonia, chlorine and essential oils by making avoidance reactions. It is a characteristic of the sense that the sensilla by which it is mediated are widely

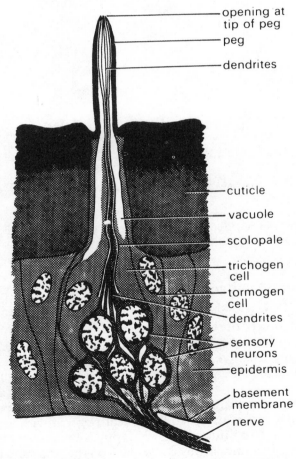

opening at
tip of peg
peg
dendrites
cuticle
vacuole
scolopale
trichogen cell
tormogen cell
dendrites
sensory neurons
epidermis
basement membrane
nerve

Fig. 434. Diagram of a thick-walled basiconic peg of a grasshopper (after Slifer *et al.*, 1957).

distributed over the insect and the response persists even after all the known olfactory receptors have been destroyed.

The receptors concerned with the perception of irritant substances are not certainly known, but it is suggested (Slifer *et al.*, 1957) that in grasshoppers the thick-walled basiconic pegs are important in this. These sensilla are up to 50 μ long and are blunt at the tip from which a scolopale extends down through the peg, narrowing proximally and ending just above the level of the sense cells (Fig. 434). The scolopale is partly enclosed by the trichogen cell which produces the peg and the scolopale at the moult. Subsequently the trichogen cell withdraws from the peg, the lumen of which is occupied by a fluid-filled vacuole which extends down between the trichogen and tormogen cells. Associated with each peg are from four to six bipolar neurons with their dendrites passing into the scolopale and extending to the tip of the peg. This is perforated by an opening about 2 μ in diameter so that at this point the ends of the dendrites are exposed to the atmosphere. These thick-walled basiconic sensilla are widely distributed over the body, being particularly abundant on the antennae, palps, legs and elytra.

CHAPTER XXXI
TEMPERATURE AND HUMIDITY

Water forms a large proportion of insect tissues and survival depends on the ability to maintain the balance of water in the body (p. 499); enzymes function efficiently only within a limited range of temperatures and for these reasons environmental humidity and temperature are of great importance in the lives of all insects. Relatively little is known about the receptors involved with the perception of these phenomena, but since insects are poikilothermic, their temperatures approximating to and varying with ambient temperature, the nervous system must be directly influenced by changes in body temperature. In general, body temperature is probably more important than ambient temperature in controlling insect behaviour since it influences the nervous system and enzyme activity directly. It represents a balance between the heat gained from metabolic activities and from the environment and the heat lost by evaporation and convection.

There is little physiological control of body temperature, but behavioural adaptations tend to maintain the temperature as near to an overall optimum for metabolic activity as environmental conditions allow. Responses to humidity also tend to keep the insect within an optimal range and in both cases the response may vary according to the previous treatment of the insect.

Insects develop only within a limited range of temperature which is characteristic of the species and they are killed by temperatures outside this range. There is no limiting range of humidity and most insects can develop at any humidity provided they are able to control their water balance. A few insects are known which can withstand complete desiccation of all or some of their tissues.

Various aspects of temperature in relation to insects and other animals are reviewed by Asahina (1966; 1969, *Adv. Insect Physiol.* **6**), Bursell (1964a), Clarke (1967), Murray (1962), R. W. Salt (1961; 1969, *Symp. Soc. exp. Biol.* **23**) and Wigglesworth (1965), while Stower and Griffiths (1966) make a detailed study of body temperature in the locust. Responses of insects to humidity are reviewed by Bursell (1964b) and Wigglesworth (1965).

31.1 Temperature

31.11 Temperature reception

There is no good evidence that insects possess specialised temperature receptors. Thick-walled trichoid sensilla on the antennae of *Rhodnius* have been identified as temperature receptors and ablation experiments suggest the presence of temperature sensitive sensilla on the antennae of other insects, but no electrophysiological information is available. In grasshoppers the sensitivity to temperature is widely distributed over the body, although the antennae and tarsi are more sensitive than other parts.

Electrophysiological work shows that in *Periplaneta* the output from the tarsal nerve varies with temperature, suggesting a receptor in the tarsus, but none has been identified. Similarly, the labellar chemoreceptors of *Phormia* are temperature sensitive, their output increasing with temperature, and it is possible that they are involved in temperature reception, having a dual function. Unspecialised nerve endings in the integument may be concerned in the peripheral reception of temperature.

Since insects are poikilothermic the central nervous system itself is subject to temperature changes and the spontaneous output from the ganglia varies with temperature. In *Periplaneta* the units in the central nervous system fall into four categories with respect to their responses to temperature. In the first type, output is directly proportional to temperature (Fig. 435A). The output of the second type is also directly proportional to temperature, but in addition shows a transient decrease in output when the temperature rises and a transient increase when the temperature falls (Fig. 435B). The third type of unit is a 'cold receptor', being more active at low than at high temperatures (Fig. 435C) and, finally, the output of the fourth type is uninfluenced by temperature (Fig. 435D).

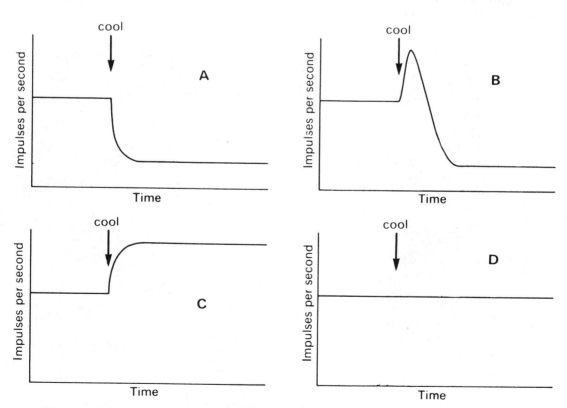

Fig. 435. Diagrammatic representation of the response elicited by a sudden decrease in temperature from four different types of nerve cells in the cockroach nerve cord (after Kerkut and Taylor, 1958).

Thus the response of the insect as a whole is determined by the external temperature influencing the sensory input and by the body temperature which modifies the output from the central nervous system. Changes in internal body temperature will be slower than peripheral changes so that most often the central nervous system will only be affected by relatively persistent changes in the outside temperature.

There is little evidence that insects are able to perceive or orientate to radiant heat. This is true even in blood-sucking species in which temperature is important in host-finding, but in *Melanophila* (Coleoptera) sensory pits on the underside of the meso-thorax are reported to be sensitive to infra red radiation (Evans, 1964). See also Callahan (1965a, 1965b).

Insects can perceive small differences in air temperature. *Cimex* (Heteroptera), for instance, is sensitive to changes of less than 1°C., and bees can be trained to one of two temperatures differing by only 2°C.

31.12 Body temperature

While some behaviour, as in host-finding, is probably a straightforward response to environmental temperature, the body temperature of the insect is of great importance because of its effect on metabolism and its direct effect on the central nervous system.

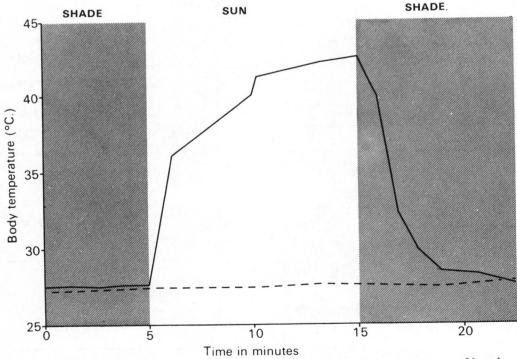

Fig. 436. The effect of the absorption of solar radiation on the body temperature of larval *Locusta*. Full line indicates the temperature of a larva at first in the shade, then in sunlight and then in shade again; broken line the temperature of a larva in continuous shade (from Uvarov, 1948).

In general, the body temperature is close to the ambient temperature, but the precise relationship varies, being a balance between the heat lost and gained by the insect. As a result of differences in this balance, body temperature may differ widely from air temperature.

Heat gain

The heat produced by metabolic activities, and especially by muscular activity, increases the body temperature so that individual insects tend to be slightly warmer than their environment, especially at high humidities where evaporative cooling is reduced. Flight, which may involve a 50-fold increase in the metabolic rate (p. 223), is particularly important in this respect and the thoracic temperature of a moth in flight may be more than 10°C. above ambient. Since the thorax is largely isolated from the head and abdomen in many insects, it is much hotter in flight than the rest of the body and in *Bombus* the thorax may be 10°C. hotter than the abdomen, only 5–15% of the heat generated being conducted to the head and abdomen (Church, 1960b). This insulation of the thorax is important in maintaining the temperature of the flight muscles which only function efficiently within a limited range of temperatures (p. 229).

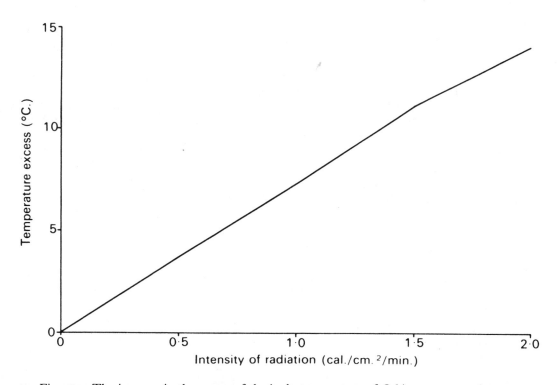

Fig. 437. The increase in the excess of the body temperature of *Schistocerca* over air temperature with increasing intensity of radiation. A maximum value for the intensity of radiation from the sun is about 1·5 cal./cm.²/min. (after Digby, 1955).

A second factor tending to raise the body temperature above ambient is solar radiation. Thus a locust larva in the shade is much cooler than another fully exposed to the sun (Fig. 436), the amount by which the body temperature exceeds air temperature, the temperature excess, being directly proportional to the intensity of radiation (Fig. 437). For a given size of insect the temperature excess in the thorax of Hymenoptera and Diptera, in which conduction to the head and abdomen from the thorax is reduced by the narrowness of the connections, is greater than in Orthoptera (Digby, 1955). The temperature excess is reduced in high winds because of the increase in evaporation and convection (see below).

Colour affects the amount of radiation absorbed so that, in bright sunlight, gregarious locust larvae which are black and orange in colour may be 6°C. hotter than solitary larvae which are green, although the differences are often much less marked than this (Stower and Griffiths, 1966).

If the insect is cooler than its immediate environment it may also gain some heat by long wave radiation from the surroundings.

Heat loss

Evaporation has the effect of cooling because the latent heat of vaporisation is withdrawn from the body. In stationary insects this is the most important source of heat loss and, for instance, in the range 10–30°C. some 80–100% of the heat lost by *Anomala* (Coleoptera) is lost through evaporation. Hence factors affecting evaporation will also affect heat loss.

The rate of evaporation from a body is limited by the humidity of the immediate environment. If environmental humidity is high little evaporation occurs so that there will be little heat loss by this route. In dry air, on the other hand, evaporation is much faster and the body temperature of an insect in dry air may be 3–4°C. below ambient. Evaporation may be reduced by local accumulations of water vapour round the body and this effect may be enhanced by hairs and scales which tend to hold a layer of still air adjacent to the body. Similarly, closure of the spiracles, by restricting evaporation from the tracheal system, tends to maintain the body temperature so that in *Glossina* (Diptera), for instance, the body temperature with the spiracles open averages 0·6°C. lower than that of insects with the spiracles closed. Air movement tends to remove local accumulations of water vapour and so to increase evaporation. Thus at higher wind speeds body temperature is reduced (Fig. 438).

Evaporation is generally slight at low air temperatures so that, even in the absence of radiation, body temperature slightly exceeds air temperature because of the heat produced by its metabolism. At higher temperatures evaporation is increased and body temperature falls below ambient. For instance, in *Gastrimargus* (Orthoptera) at a constant relative humidity of 60% the temperature excess at 10°C. is 0·6°C., at 20°C. it is 0·4°C., while at 30°C. body temperature is 0·2°C. below ambient.

Heat loss by convection through the spiracles is probably negligible, but convection from the body surface may be a major source of heat loss as in larval *Schistocerca* and adult *Locusta* in flight. In the latter 60–80% of the heat loss results from convection and only some 10% from evaporation and 10–15% by long wave radiation. Convection is increased at higher wind speeds.

Conduction is probably unimportant as a means of heat loss or gain except in the transfer of heat between the body and the layer of air immediately adjacent to it.

Heat loss from the body is reduced by insulation at the surface. The hairs and scales of *Bombus* and *Noctua* (Lepidoptera) hold an insulating layer of air adjacent to the body and the same effect is achieved in dragonflies by a layer of air-sacs at the surface of the thorax. The effectiveness of the insulation depends on the density of hairs, but in general the temperature excess of flying insects is increased by 50–100% by their insulation, amounting to about 9°C. in a hawk moth.

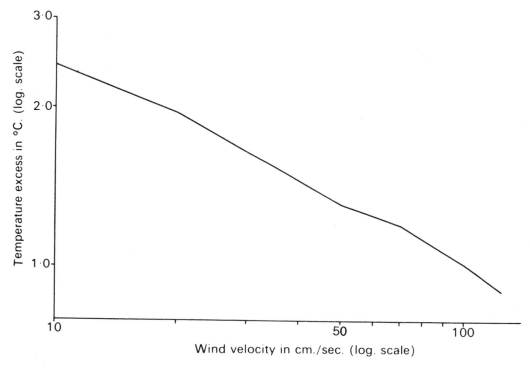

Fig. 438. The effect of wind velocity on the temperature excess of *Drosophila* exposed to constant radiation with an intensity of 1·5 cal./cm.²/min. (after Digby, 1955).

31.13 Temperature control

At least some insects are capable of exerting some measure of control over their temperature. Thus, if air temperature increases, the body temperature of a locust also increases, but only after a short time lag so that the insect becomes a little cooler than its environment (Fig. 439, stage I). After this, in a fully fed insect, body temperature increases at about the same rate as air temperature so that the difference between the two remains roughly constant (Fig. 439, stage II), but after a time it starts to increase more rapidly so that the difference between the two is reduced (Fig. 439, stage III). Finally, when the air temperature stops rising body temperature continues to rise until it is higher than ambient (Fig. 439, stage IV). In starved locusts, on the other hand, the body temperature does not increase as rapidly as air temperature and the difference between the two steadily increases. Further, when the air temperature stops rising body temperature does not overshoot it. It is suggested that normally the stimulation of peripheral receptors leads to the release of a substance into the haemolymph which stimulates some metabolic processes so that the temperature of the insect increases more rapidly than if it depended only on conduction from the air. This mechanism brings the insect into equilibrium with its environment more rapidly than would otherwise be the case and also enables it to make the maximum use of transient temperature increases. In starved locusts the metabolic process is disturbed and the insect is unable to maintain its temperature (Clarke, 1960).

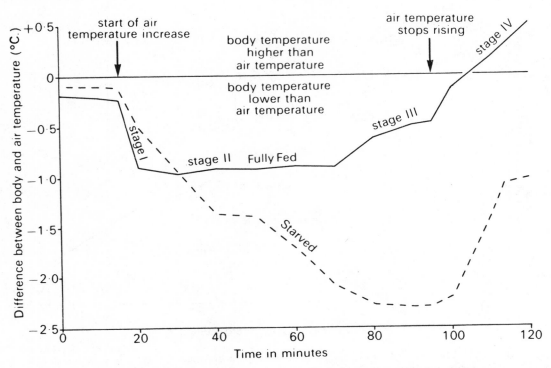

Fig. 439. The difference between the body temperature of *Locusta* and air temperature when air temperature is steadily increased from 20 to 35°C. (after Clarke, 1960).

Physiological regulation of temperature may also occur in *Kosciuscola* (Orthoptera) as a result of colour changes. At low temperatures the insects are darker so that they absorb more radiation (see p. 117).

In general in insects the control of body temperature involves some behavioural mechanism. Extreme temperatures are avoided. At temperatures over 44°C., approaching the upper lethal temperature, *Schistocerca* larvae become highly active. Similarly, movement into an area of low temperature promotes a brief burst of activity. This activity is undirected, but may tend to take the insect out of the immediately unfavourable area so that it is neither killed by extreme heat nor trapped at temperatures too low for its metabolism to continue efficiently (Chapman, 1965).

Within the normal range of temperature insects have a preferred range in which, given the choice, they tend to remain for relatively long periods. The preferred temperature range is towards the upper end of the normal range of temperatures and in *Schistocerca*, for instance, extends from 35 to 45°C. with a peak at 40–41°C. (Fig. 440). The tendency to remain still in this preferred range may be regarded as a mechanism tending to keep the insects within a range of temperatures which is optimal for most metabolic processes.

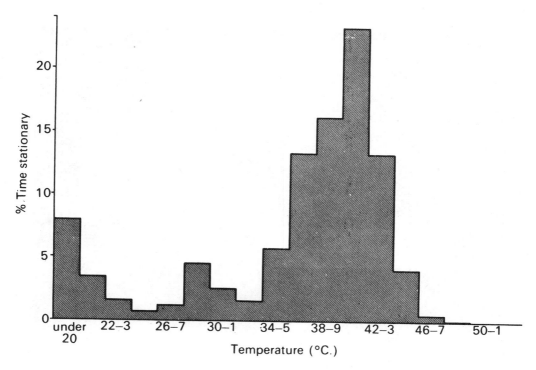

Fig. 440. The temperature preference of *Schistocerca* as shown by the amount of time spent stationary at different temperatures (after Chapman, 1965).

In the field behaviour may be varied so as to keep the body temperature within the preferred range. Thus at low temperatures *Schistocerca* sits broadside to the sun and, if it is on the ground, it lies over on its side so that its lateral surface is perpendicular to the sun's rays, exposing the maximum surface area. When the body temperature is within the range 39–43°C. the insect turns to face the sun, so exposing a smaller surface. In a larval locust the ratio of the surfaces exposed in these two positions, known as flanking and facing, is 6:1 and as a result of this change in position the temperature excess of the body is reduced. At still higher temperatures the legs are extended so as to raise the body off the ground into the stilted position (Fig. 441). This permits a free circulation of air all round the body and at the same time avoids the excessive temperatures at the surface of the ground. For example, on one occasion with a ground temperature of 56°C., air temperature at 6 mm. was only 40°C. and the body temperature of a stilting locust 43°C. If temperatures on the ground become excessive the locust climbs up the vegetation where it may be shaded and where convective and evaporative cooling by the wind are increased. This effect may be further increased by orientating across the wind. In the evening as temperature falls the locust crouches close to the ground, gaining heat by conduction (Waloff, 1963). The effect of these various activities is to keep the body temperature between 35 and 41°C. for as long as possible, employing methods of warming at lower temperatures and cooling at higher temperatures.

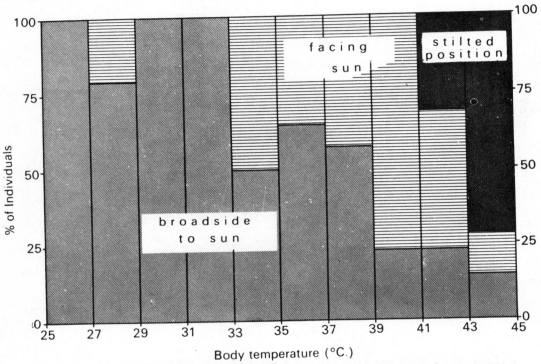

Fig. 441. The orientation of *Schistocerca* with respect to the sun at different body temperatures (based on Waloff, 1963).

Other insects show comparable behaviour. *Argynnis* (Lepidoptera), for instance, spreads its wings and orientates to the sun so that it may achieve a temperature excess of as much as 17°C. It varies the degree of opening of the wings to maintain a body temperature of 32–37°C. and if the temperature becomes too high it closes its wings over its back and ultimately retreats to the shade (Vielmetter, 1958).

Many insects, such as locusts and moths, are able to raise the temperatures of their bodies by fanning, fluttering the wings without flight. This behaviour is most frequently observed if the insects are disturbed at temperatures suboptimal for flight and the increase in temperature produced may be such that flight becomes possible. In *Saturnia* (Lepidoptera), for instance, fanning can increase the body temperature to 26°C. at an air temperature of 18°C. *Geotrupes* (Coleoptera) achieves the same effect by contractions of the wing muscles, but without moving the wings.

Temperature regulation is most highly developed in social insects. Ants, for instance, carry their larvae about the nest to the most favourable situations. On warm days in summer the older larvae are brought near to the surface, while in winter they may be a foot or more below the surface so as to avoid frosts. On hot days *Formica* (Hymenoptera) blocks the entrance to its nest with nest materials so as to stop the entry of warm air.

Temperature control is well known in *Apis*. At high temperatures workers stand at the entrance of the hive fanning with their wings so as to create a draught through the nest. This is sufficiently effective to keep the temperature of the brood down to 36°C. when the hive is heated to 40°C. Water may also be carried in to help cool the hive by evaporation and at excessively high temperatures the bees leave the combs and cluster outside so that further heating due to their metabolism is avoided. On the other hand in winter when there is little or no brood the bees cluster together on and between a small number of combs. This behaviour is seen when the temperature drops below 15°C. and the heat of their metabolism maintains the inside of the cluster at 20–25°C. By packing closer when the temperature is very low and spreading out when it is higher, the bees are able to regulate this temperature.

31.14 Metabolism

These regulating devices tend to enable metabolic processes, which are greatly influenced by temperature, to proceed optimally. In general, an increase in temperature

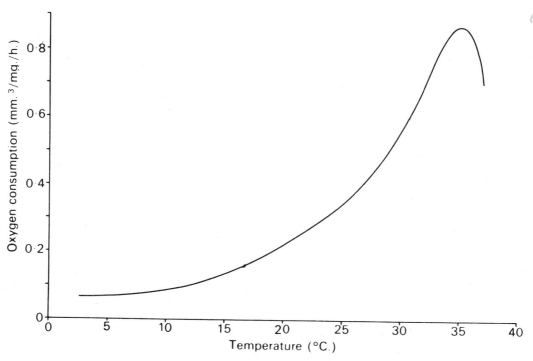

Fig. 442. The oxygen consumption of *Periplaneta* at different temperatures (from Keister and Buck, 1964).

increases the metabolic rate as indicated by the increased oxygen consumption (Fig. 442), but at temperatures approaching the upper lethal limit the rate of metabolism falls off. Some insects do not exhibit this simple relationship with temperature and in *Apis* oxygen consumption is maximal at 10°C., decreasing at higher and lower temperatures (Fig. 443). Similarly in diapause development (see p. 726), as in the egg of *Austroicetes* (Orthoptera), there is no development at 25°C. and emergence from the egg is most successful at 10°C. (see Fig. 496).

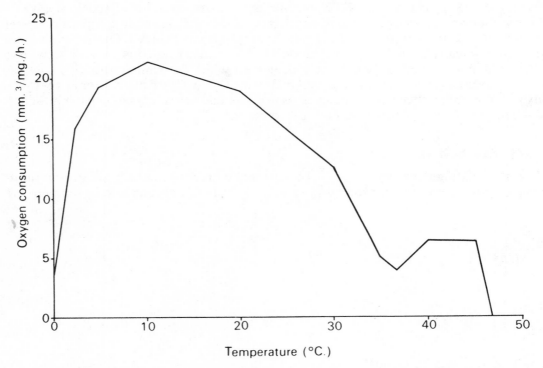

Fig. 443. The oxygen consumption of *Apis* at different temperatures (from Wigglesworth, 1965).

The normal increase in metabolic rate with increasing temperature is reflected in an increased rate of development. Thus the larval development of *Locusta* occupies 40 days at 27°C., but only 20 days at 43°C., and the pupal period of *Tenebrio* lasts for 320 hours at 21°C., but only 140 hours at 33°C. The range in which development occurs varies, being 5–28°C. in *Ptinus* (Coleoptera) and 15–40°C. in *Tribolium* (Coleoptera), while in *Astagobius*, a cave-dwelling beetle, the environmental temperature ranges from only 1·0 to −1·7°C.

There is also a general tendency for insects to be more active at higher temperatures as in *Nomadacris* larvae which spend some 5% of their time in activity at 16°C., but about 15% at 34°C. (Fig. 444). The effects of temperature changes and temperature preference are superimposed on this general tendency.

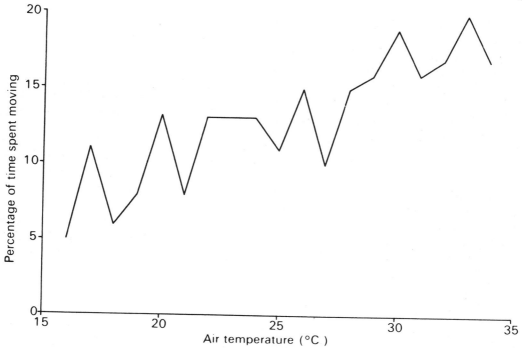

Fig. 444. Showing the increase in the activity of solitary larvae of *Nomadacris* at higher temperatures (after Chapman, 1959b).

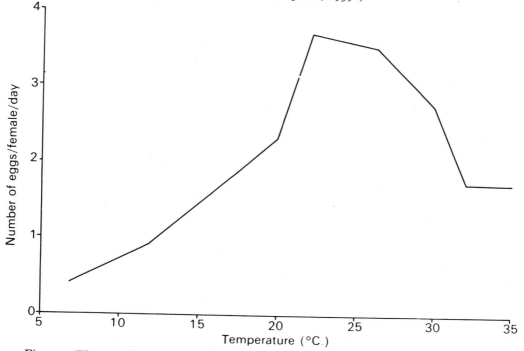

Fig. 445. The rate of oviposition of *Toxoptera* at different temperatures (from Bursell, 1964a).

Most processes have an optimum temperature at which they proceed most favourably or most rapidly, falling off at higher and lower temperatures, but it is possible to base the optimum on a number of different criteria. For instance, it is possible to regard as optimal the temperature at which the least fuel consumption occurs in the completion of a certain stage of development. Thus in the pupa of *Glossina* (Diptera) least fat is utilised at 22–24°C. At higher temperatures the consumption of fat is increased without any corresponding reduction in the pupal period, while at lower temperatures there is a great lengthening of the pupal period with no corresponding decrease in fat consumption. Alternatively the temperature at which development is most rapid or that at which the largest number of insects successfully complete their development may be regarded as optimal. In adults, longevity and egg production also have their independent optima. Longevity is usually greatest at the lowest temperature at which an insect can feed normally; presumably at such temperatures the basic expenditure of energy is at a minimum. Egg production is mostly maximal at about the middle of the normal range of temperature, in *Toxoptera* at 25°C. in a range of 5–35°C. (Fig. 445). This perhaps represents a balance between the utilisation of reserves in the metabolism of the adult insect and their use in yolk production.

31.15 Acclimation

Responses to temperature are not static, but vary according to the previous experience of the insect. Such modification is known as acclimatisation or acclimation. For instance,

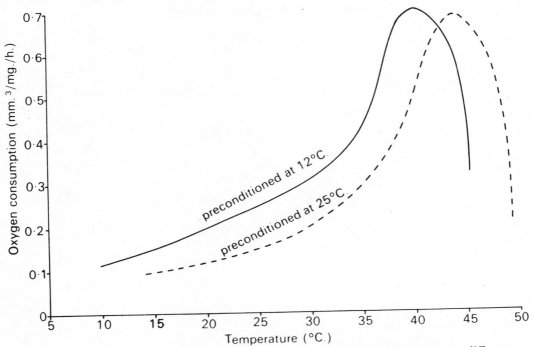

Fig. 446. The effect on oxygen consumption of preconditioning *Melasoma* at different temperatures (from Wigglesworth, 1965).

the oxygen consumption of *Melasoma* (Coleoptera) adults increases with temperature, but the level of consumption depends on the temperature at which the insects were kept before the experiment and for any given temperature the oxygen consumption is higher in insects acclimatised to lower temperatures (Fig. 446). The temperature at which maximum oxygen consumption occurs is also lower in the insects preconditioned at the lower temperature. Similarly the spontaneous output from the central nervous system is related to preconditioning temperature (Kerkut and Taylor, 1958) as is the level of

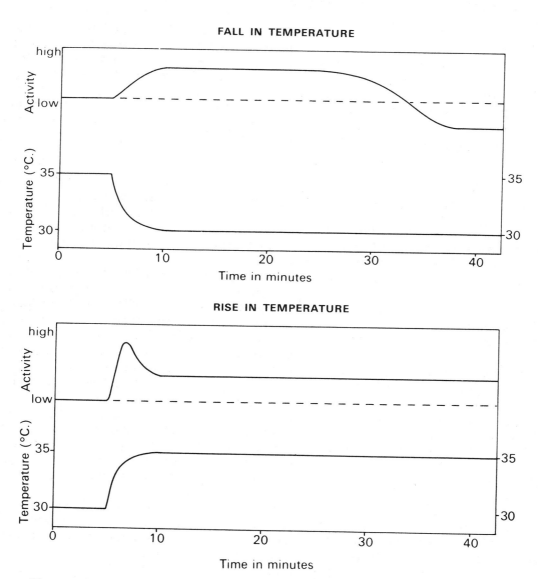

Fig. 447. Diagram of the effect on activity of a sharp change of temperature (after Kennedy, 1939).

activity of the whole insect. Thus, adults of *Ptinus* previously maintained at 15°C. are less active at all temperatures than others previously maintained at 28°C. (Gunn and Hopf, 1942). Not all insects are so adaptable and some species of *Drosophila* which are restricted in distribution do not acclimate to different rearing temperatures (Hunter, 1966).

An increase in activity occurs after a change in temperature from that to which the insect is acclimatised, irrespective of whether the temperature increases or decreases. These increases in activity are only transient and subsequently activity returns to a level appropriate to the final temperature (Fig. 447). For instance, *Nomadacris* (Orthoptera) is stimulated to take off by the sun appearing from behind a cloud increasing its temperature, or by gusts of cold wind before a dust storm lowering its temperature. In the first case the insect may keep flying, but in the second it lands after a few minutes (Chapman, 1959a). Corresponding transients occur in the activity of the central nervous system (see Fig. 435B).

Acclimation is a continuous process and in the field its importance lies in tending to fit the insect to the prevailing conditions. The process continues at the extremes of the temperature range which may be extended as a result (see below).

31.16 Upper lethal temperature

At the upper end of the temperature range, above the preferred temperature, insects show a sharp rise in activity. At still higher temperatures this is followed by an inability to move, a phase known as heat stupor, and then by death. The temperature at which death occurs depends on the species, the duration of exposure and interaction with other factors, in particular with humidity.

Large insects are cooled by evaporation so that, for short periods of exposure of an hour or so, they can withstand higher air temperatures if the air is dry. *Periplaneta*, for instance, dies at 38°C. at high humidities, but can survive up to 48°C. if the air is dry.

For long-term exposures humidity has the opposite effect because at low humidities the insects die from the effects of desiccation. Thus *Blatta* can survive for 24 hours at 37–39°C. if the air is moist, but dies as a result of similar exposure in dry air. In small insects such as lice, the humidity does not affect the lethal temperature since the volume of water available for evaporation is small while the surface taking up heat is relatively large.

For many insects the lethal temperature for short-term exposures is within the range 40–50°C., but for insects from particular habitats lethal temperatures may be very different. Thus *Grylloblatta* (Grylloblattodea), living at high altitudes in the Rocky Mountains, dies at 20°C., *Thermobia* (Thysanura), the fire brat, at 51°C., and in chironomid larvae living in hot springs at 49–51°C. the lethal temperature must be even higher.

Some modification of the upper lethal temperature occurs, depending on the previous experience of the insect. Thus *Drosophila* reared at 15°C. and maintained at 15°C. as adults, survive for about 50 minutes in dry air at 33·5°C., but if they are maintained at 25°C. beforehand they survive for about 130 minutes. If the larvae are also reared at the higher temperature the period of exposure which they can survive is still further increased to 140 minutes in adults maintained at 15°C. and to 180 minutes in adults maintained at 25°C. Thus two types of acclimation can be recognised; long

lasting acclimation due to conditions during development and short-term physiological acclimation depending on the more immediate conditions and easily reversible.
The effect of physiological acclimation is more marked in dry conditions than in wet,
indicating that this type of acclimation gives increased resistance to desiccation rather
than to higher temperatures (Maynard Smith, 1957).

Death at high temperatures may result from various factors. Proteins may be
denatured or the balance of metabolic processes may be disturbed so that toxic products
accumulate. Thus blowfly larvae kept at high temperatures accumulate organic and
inorganic phosphates and adenyl pyrophosphate in the haemolymph. In some cases
food reserves may be exhausted and *Pediculus* (Siphunculata), for instance, survives
better at high temperatures if it has recently fed. Sometimes, particularly over long
periods, death at high temperatures may result from desiccation.

31.17 Lower lethal temperature

At temperatures below the preferred range insects become increasingly less active until
finally they are unable to move, or do so only with difficulty. They may remain alive
under these conditions for a considerable time, but if they are unable to feed they
ultimately starve to death. This is the case, for instance, with *Locusta* which does not
feed below about 20°C. At lower temperatures death occurs much more rapidly from
other causes, but in different insects the lower lethal temperature varies considerably
(Salt, 1961).

Insects from warm environments often die quite quickly even at temperatures above
freezing. *Glossina*, for instance, survives for only a few hours at 5°C. This may result
from the accumulation of toxic products or some other metabolic disturbance. In *Apis*
the absorption of sugars from the gut, where they are stored, is prevented below 8°C.
so that the insects effectively starve. Some acclimation occurs in these insects. Thus
Blatta reared at 30°C. goes into a state of cold stupor at 7·5°C. and soon dies at −5°C.,
but after 20 hours at 15°C. they are active down to 2°C. and survive for nine hours at
−5°C.

At temperatures below freezing the majority of insects die as a result of the tissues
freezing. The temperature at which this occurs is usually well below 0°C. because the
freezing point is lowered by the electrolytes in the haemolymph and tissues (see p. 684),
but also because supercooling occurs. The temperature to which insects supercool is
not fixed, but is influenced by many factors controlling the production of ice crystals.
Crystals start to form round a nucleus and once this happens the whole of the body rapidly
freezes. Food in the gut may provide such a nucleus so that feeding insects are much less
cold-hardy than non-feeding insects and the supercooling point of *Ephestia* larvae is
lower during the period of the moult when they contain no food. The greater hardiness of
diapausing and hibernating insects also results partly from the absence of food in the
alimentary canal.

Water droplets on the outside of the insect may also form nuclei for ice crystal
formation, while, on the other hand, body fluids with a high viscosity tend to inhibit
nucleation by reducing molecular travel. Viscosity increases as the temperature gets
lower. Increased cold hardiness is often associated with some degree of desiccation of
the tissues and in *Popillia* (Coleoptera) hardiness increases as the water content is
lowered. This is not always true, however, and the apparent correlation could be
fortuitous.

Many insects in which the supercooling point is low have glycerol in the haemo-lymph, sometimes in high concentrations. Thus in the hibernating stages of *Bracon cephi* (Hymenoptera) glycerol accounts for 25% of the fresh weight and forms a 5M solution in the haemolymph. Acting as an electrolyte this lowers the freezing point of the haemolymph to about $-15°C$. It also greatly increases the viscosity, and the super-cooling temperature of the insect may be as low as $-47°C.$, but factors other than the glycerol are also involved in this.

Glycerol is commonly formed only immediately before or during hibernation, dis-appearing again afterwards. In the larva of *Monema* (Lepidoptera) glycerol is produced from glycogen, but its synthesis is dependent on temperature and is optimal at $10°C$. Such a phenomenon could account for the fact that in some insects mild chilling often improves cold hardiness; perhaps during chilling conditions favour the synthesis of a protective substance (Asahina, 1966).

Cold hardiness is particularly important in hibernating insects in temperate and subarctic regions where they must survive long periods below $0°C$. In many of these the supercooling temperature is about $-30°C.$, but the temperature at which freezing of the tissues occurs tends to rise the longer the period of exposure. Once the tissues freeze the insects die. The causes of death are not certainly known, but probably involve mechanical damage to the tissues by the ice crystals, especially if they are intracellular, an increase in the concentration of electrolytes so that they become lethal, and possibly also dehydration.

A few insects can tolerate ice formation provided this is restricted to the extracellular fluids. They are mostly lepidopterous larvae and pupae which hibernate in localities where the air temperature falls below the limit of supercooling. Intracellular ice forma-tion destroys the cells, and if many cells are affected the insect dies when it thaws. In avoiding intracellular freezing any mechanism which reduces the rate of cooling at the surface of the cells is important. Thus the freezing of a large amount of the extra-cellular body fluids beforehand is beneficial and layers of blood containing high con-centrations of salts round the ice crystals may limit the propagation of freezing and prevent the contact of the crystals with the cell surfaces. The ability to withstand extra-cellular freezing may involve partial dehydration of the tissues or the production of a protective substance such as glycerol, but these are not the only factors and resistance may also involve some structural change in the cytoplasm. Prolonged extracellular freezing kills even these frost-resistant insects, perhaps due to some metabolic im-balance occurring below a certain temperature (Asahina, 1966).

31.2 Humidity

31.21 Humidity receptors

Humidity receptors have been identified by ablation experiments and are variable in form. In *Tenebrio* they are thin-walled basiconic pegs (see p. 622) and similar structures in *Tribolium* are branched (Fig. 448B). Coeloconic pegs (p. 624) are the probable humi-dity receptors in *Melanoplus*, while in *Pediculus* the structures concerned are tufts of four small hairs innervated by several neurons (Fig. 448A).

In most cases the humidity receptors have been identified on the antennae, but the palps are also sometimes implicated and in *Drosophila* larvae the receptors are on the underside of the anterior body segments. In *Glossina* the guard hairs of the spiracles are sensitive to humidity and, because of their position, they are influenced not only by the ambient humidity, but also by the humidity of the air leaving the spiracles. Impulses from these receptors produce central inhibition of locomotion (Bursell, 1957).

The mode of functioning of humidity receptors is not understood, but various possibilities exist. They may respond simply to water molecules impinging on the surface in the same way that chemoreceptors are presumed to act. Alternatively they may function as hygroreceptors, containing some substance with hygroscopic properties which absorbs water in proportion to the amount of water vapour in the

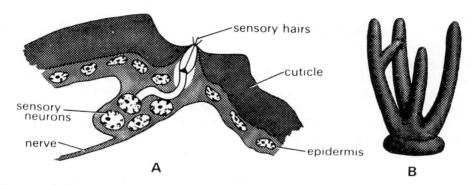

Fig. 448. A. Tuft organ from the antenna of *Pediculus*. B. Branched humidity receptor from the antenna of *Tribolium* (from Carthy, 1958).

atmosphere. Finally, water loss from the sensillum may produce temperature differences due to evaporation or it may change the internal environment of the receptor cell, altering the chemical composition and osmotic pressure of the cytoplasm as a result of which the cell initiates an impulse.

It has been suggested that insects have two types of humidity receptors, one mediating the reaction to moisture and the other the reaction to dryness. The evidence, however, is not conclusive (see discussion in Syrjämäki, 1962).

31.22 Responses to humidity

Humidity may affect the metabolism and hence the rate of development of insects. For instance, *Ptinus* eggs take 15 days to develop at 20°C. and a relative humidity of 30%, but at 90% humidity the incubation period is reduced to 10 days. Similarly the rate of oviposition of most insects increases at high humidities. The low metabolic rates at low humidities implied by these differences may result from an increased water loss leading to a generally low water content. In some cases, however, humidity does not have this effect. The eggs of *Cimex* and other insects living in dry environments are not influenced by humidity, while in *Locusta* larval development is fastest at about 70% relative humidity, being slower at lower and higher humidities.

Humidity also affects behaviour, most insects having a range of preferred humidities in which they are relatively inactive, while outside this range they become more active. In *Schistocerca* larvae the preferred zone is between 60 and 70% relative humidity. Adult *Tenebrio* on the other hand, always choose the driest of two humidities even showing a slight, but distinct, preference for 5% over 10% relative humidity (Pielou and Gunn, 1940). Conversely, *Agriotes* (Coleoptera) larvae choose the wettest parts of the ranges. These differences reflect differences in the degree of waterproofing of the insects' cuticles; that of *Tenebrio* is relatively impermeable, while the cuticle of *Agriotes* larvae is freely permeable to water.

The intensity of reaction to different humidities varies in different parts of the range, but most insects have the greatest sensitivity at high humidities. *Tenebrio*, for instance, always shows a preference for the drier of any two humidities to which it is exposed, but below 70% relative humidity the intensity of the reaction is slight even when the two humidities differ by as much as 40%. Above 70% relative humidity, however, the reaction becomes much more marked and differences of 5% and less produce very strong reactions. In the upper part of the range *Agriotes* larvae respond to differences of 0·5% relative humidity.

The preferred range of humidity of any one insect may vary due to differences in its water content. Thus *Tribolium* normally has a preference for dry conditions, but after three or four days without food or water a preference for higher humidities develops, the speed of the change in preference being related to the rate of water loss.

Some insects, such as *Tribolium,* make directed movements towards areas of high humidity and others perform avoidance reactions when they pass out of the favourable zone. Thus *Tenebrio* on passing from the drier to the wetter side of a choice chamber sometimes stops and makes movements with its antennae and then turns back into the drier zone. *Agriotes* larvae make avoidance reactions in passing from wet to dry conditions.

Reactions of this type will tend to keep the insect within its preferred range of humidities and will account to some extent for the micro-environments occupied by the insects in the field. Other than in the soil, where, apart from the upper layers, humidity is fairly high and uniform, there are big differences in humidity between different micro-environments and there may also be marked temporal fluctuations (see *e.g.* Cloudsley-Thompson, 1962; Lewis, 1962; F. L. Waterhouse, 1950).

31.23 Humidity and survival

The time of survival at different relative humidities depends largely on the ability of the insect to maintain its water content. If this falls too low the insect dies, although there are exceptions to this (see below). If, as in the egg and pupa, the insect is unable to replenish its water the duration of survival is inversely proportional to the rate of water loss and hence, roughly, to the saturation deficit. The more permeable the cuticle, the lower the saturation deficit at which the insect will die. For instance, the puparium of *Glossina brevipalpis* loses water at the rate of 10·2 mg./cm./h./mm.Hg and mortality is high in a saturation deficit of 5 mm. Hg (Fig. 449). The puparium of *G. swynnertoni*, on the other hand, loses water much more slowly, 1·6 mg./cm./h./mm. Hg, and mortality is slight even at a saturation deficit of 20 mm. Hg.

When the insect can replace the water which it loses it can usually withstand extremes of humidity. Thus there is no range outside which the insect cannot survive as there is with temperature. But there may be mortality at low humidities even with an ample supply of water, possibly because the energy expended in maintaining the water content exerts a metabolic strain on the insect. Similarly death may occur at excessively high humidities because the insect is unable to get rid of its excess water quickly enough. This apparently occurs with *Tenebrio* at humidities over 70% and temperatures over 30°C.

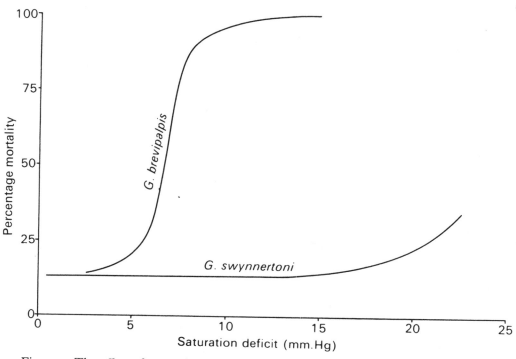

Fig. 449. The effect of saturation deficit on pupal survival in *Glossina brevipalpis* and *G. swynnertoni* (from Bursell, 1964b).

31.3 Cryptobiosis

Cryptobiosis is the term used to describe the state of an organism when it shows no visible signs of life and metabolic activity is brought reversibly to a standstill. The only insect in which this is known to occur is the larva of *Polypedilum* (Diptera), a chironomid living in pools on unshaded rocks in Nigeria. In the dry season these pools dry up and the surface temperatures of the rock probably reach 70°C. Active larvae of *Polypedilum* die after an exposure of one hour at 43°C., but if they are dehydrated so that their water content is less than 8% of its original value they can survive extreme temperatures for long periods. Some recovery occurs even after one minute at 102°C. or several days in liquid air at −190°C. At room temperatures larvae can withstand total dehydration for three years and some showed a temporary recovery after ten years (Hinton, 1960b).

There is some evidence that the larva of a species of *Sciara* (Diptera) and some ceratopogonid larvae also exhibit cryptobiosis and other insects may possess some tissues which exhibit the phenomenon, although the insect as a whole may not. For instance, the blood cells in the gills of *Taphrophila* (Diptera) pupae (p. 484) and *Sialis* larvae can be desiccated for long periods, but when rehydrated show some vital activities such as clotting.

SECTION F

The Blood, Hormones and Pheromones

CHAPTER XXXII

THE CIRCULATORY SYSTEM

Insects have an open blood system in which circulation is produced by the activity of a dorsal longitudinal vessel comprising a posterior heart and an anterior aorta. When the heart relaxes blood passes into it through valved openings, while waves of contraction, which normally start at the back, pump the blood forwards and out through the aorta. The heart is usually cut off from the major part of the body cavity by a muscular diaphragm, while in some insects a second diaphragm overlies the nerve cord. These diaphragms, together with accessory pulsatile organs associated with the appendages, supplement the activity of the dorsal vessel.

The frequency with which the heart contracts varies in different species, but also with the stage of development and physiological condition of the individual insect. Sometimes the contractions may start at the front instead of the back of the heart, or it may stop beating altogether for short periods. In some cases the activity of the heart is myogenic, but in most insects it is uncertain whether the beat is myogenic or neurogenic. Possibly a myogenic beat is modulated by the nervous input. Extrinsic activities, such as feeding, may modify the frequency of the heartbeat through the release of a hormone from the corpora cardiaca.

Aspects of the structure and physiology of the circulatory system are reviewed by Beard (1953), Davey (1964), J. C. Jones (1964), Krijgsman (1952), Richards (1963) and Wigglesworth (1965), McCann (1970, *A. Rev. Ent.* **15**).

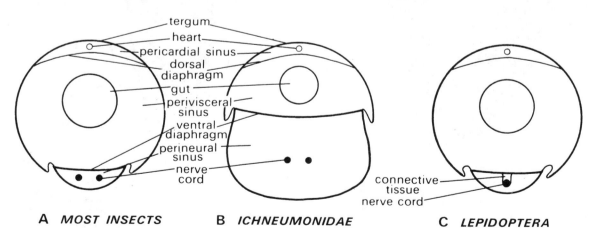

A *MOST INSECTS* **B** *ICHNEUMONIDAE* **C** *LEPIDOPTERA*

Fig. 450. Diagrammatic cross-sections of various insects showing the main sinuses of the haemocoel and the positions of heart, alimentary canal and nerve cord (after Richards, 1963).

32.1 **Structure**

Insects have an open blood system with the blood occupying the general body cavity which is thus known as a haemocoel. Blood is circulated mainly by the activity of a contractile longitudinal vessel which opens into the haemocoel and which usually lies in a

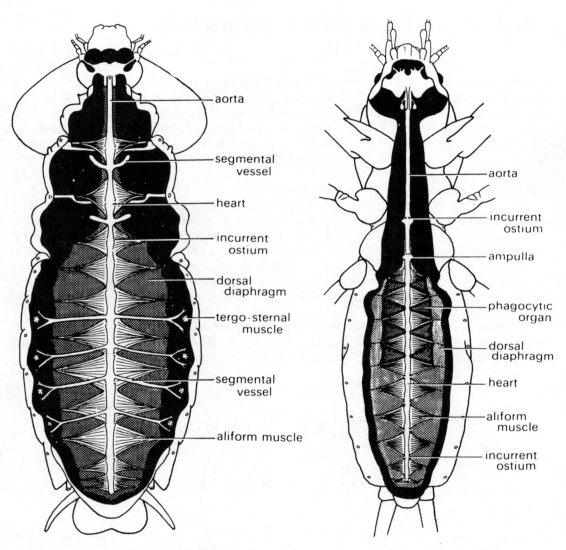

Fig. 451. Ventral dissection of *Blaberus* to show the dorsal and segmental vessels. The dorsal diaphragm and aliform muscles are continuous over the ventral wall of the heart and vessels, but are omitted from the diagram for clarity (after Nutting, 1951).

Fig. 452. Ventral dissection of *Gryllotalpa* to show the dorsal vessel and phagocytic organs. The dorsal diaphragm is continuous over the ventral wall of the heart, but is omitted in the diagram for clarity (after Nutting, 1951).

dorsal pericardial sinus, cut off by a dorsal diaphragm from the perivisceral sinus which contains the viscera (Fig. 450A). Sometimes there is also a ventral diaphragm above the nerve cord which cuts off a ventral perineural sinus from the perivisceral sinus. The perineural sinus is normally only a small part of the haemocoel, but in Ichneumonidae it may form half the body cavity because the sterna, to which the ventral diaphragm is attached, are extended upwards (Fig. 450B).

32.11 Dorsal Vessel

The dorsal vessel runs along the dorsal midline, just below the terga, for almost the whole length of the body. Anteriorly it leaves the dorsal wall and is more closely associated with the alimentary canal, passing under the cerebral ganglion just above the oesophagus. The dorsal vessel is divided into two regions: a posterior heart in which the wall of the vessel is perforated by incurrent and sometimes also by excurrent ostia; and an anterior aorta which is a simple, unperforated tube (Figs. 451, 452). It is open anteriorly, but closed posteriorly except in Ephemeroptera nymphs where three vessels diverge to the caudal filaments from the end of the heart.

The wall of the dorsal vessel in the heart and the aorta is contractile and consists of a single layer of cells in which circular or spiral muscle fibrils are differentiated. In Heteroptera longitudinal muscle strands are also present, especially round the aorta. These cells are bounded on both sides by a homogeneous membrane and on the outside there is usually some connective tissue. A network of tracheoles is often present, especially round the posterior part of the heart.

Heart

The heart is often restricted to the abdomen, but may extend as far forwards as the prothorax as in Dictyoptera. In orthopteroids it has a chambered appearance due to the fact that it is slightly enlarged into ampullae at the points where the ostia pierce the wall (Nutting, 1951). These ampullae are often more prominent in the thorax. In the larvae of Odonata and *Tipula* (Diptera) the heart is divided into chambers by valves in front of each pair of incurrent ostia and in other cases, as in *Cloëon* (Ephemeroptera) larvae, the ostial valves themselves are so long that they meet across the lumen. The heart may be directly bound to the dorsal body wall or suspended from it by elastic filaments.

Incurrent ostia

The incurrent ostia are vertical, slit-like openings occurring laterally in the heart wall. There may be nine pairs of incurrent ostia in the abdomen and up to three pairs in the thorax. All 12 pairs are present in Dictyoptera, but there are only five pairs in aculeate Hymenoptera and three pairs in *Musca* (Diptera). Mallophaga, Siphunculata and Geocorisae also have only two or three pairs of ostia and the heart is restricted to the posterior abdominal segments. The anterior and posterior lips of each ostium are reflexed into the heart so that they form a valve permitting the flow of blood into the heart at diastole, but preventing its outward passage at systole. The action of the valves is shown in Fig. 453. During diastole the lips are forced apart by the inflowing blood (A). When diastole is complete the lips are forced together by the pressure of blood in the heart (B) and they remain closed throughout systole. Towards the end of systole the valves tend to become evaginated by the pressure (C), but they are prevented from turning completely inside out by a unicellular thread attached to the inside of the heart. In *Bombyx* (Lepidoptera) only the hind lip of each ostium is extended as a flap within the heart (Fig. 454). During systole this is pressed against the wall of the heart so that the escape of blood is prevented.

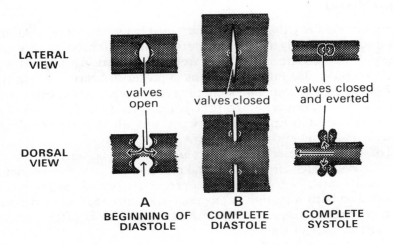

Fig. 453. Incurrent ostial valves in the larva of *Chaoborus* at different phases of the heartbeat. Lateral view above, dorsal below. Arrows indicate the directions of blood flow (from Wigglesworth, 1965).

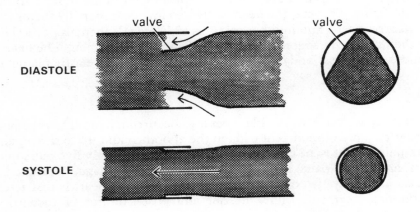

Fig. 454. Diagrammatic representation of the incurrent ostial valves as found in *Bombyx* seen in horizontal (left) and transverse (right) sections of the heart. Arrows indicate the direction of blood flow.

Excurrent ostia

Nutting (1951) has described excurrent ostia in the orthopteroids and also in Thysanura. These are usually paired ventro-lateral openings in the wall of the heart without any internal valves. The number of excurrent ostia varies, but Acridoidea have two thoracic and five abdominal pairs. Externally each opening is surrounded by a papilla of spongiform multinucleate cells which expands when the heart contracts, so that blood passes out, and contracts when the heart relaxes, so that the entry of blood is prevented. The excurrent ostia of Phasmida open into the pericardial sinus, but in Acridoidea the papillae penetrate the dorsal diaphragm so that the ostia open into the

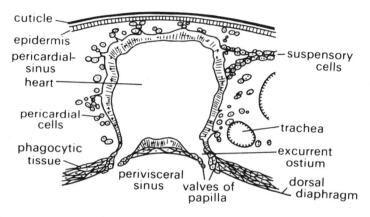

Fig. 455. Transverse section of the heart of *Taentopoda* showing the excurrent ostia opening directly to the periviseral sinus (after Nutting, 1951).

periviseral sinus (Fig. 455). In Tettigonioidea the ostia open between two layers of the dorsal diaphragm so that blood leaving the heart is channelled laterally before it enters the general body cavity. There are unpaired excurrent ostia in the heart of Plecoptera and Embioptera.

Segmental vessels

Most Dictyoptera have no excurrent ostia, but there are definite segmental vessels by which the blood leaves the heart (Fig. 451) (Nutting, 1951). In Blattaria there are two thoracic and four abdominal vessels, but only the latter are present in Mantodea. They pass out between the aliform (alary) muscles, branching distally and disappearing as fine ramifications in the fat (Fig. 456). At the origin of each vessel is a group of loosely packed cells which functions as a valve only permitting the outward flow of blood from the heart. The walls of the vessels are non-muscular, but there is a suggestion that they may contract independently of the heart. It is possible that the small amount of muscle in the valve could cause a wave of contraction to pass down the rest of the vessel.

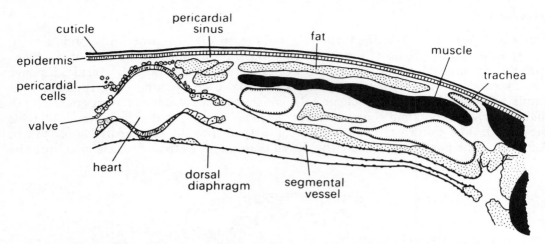

Fig. 456. Transverse section through the pericardial sinus in the abdomen of *Blaberus* showing a segmental vessel arising from the heart and discharging into fatty tissue distally (after Nutting, 1951).

Phagocytic organs

The phagocytic organs are found in the anterior part of the abdomen of Tettigonioidea and Grylloidea. They are flattened triangular sacs opening ventro-laterally from the heart by narrow connections, at which there are excurrent valves, and then fanning out between the aliform muscles (Fig. 452). Two to four pairs may be present. The ventral wall of these organs is formed by the dorsal diaphragm, the dorsal wall by phagocytic cells which are multinucleate and occupy part of the lumen of each sac (Fig. 457). These organs appear to act as filters removing dyes and particles from the blood which is forced into them; the blood itself is presumed to percolate through the dorsal diaphragm.

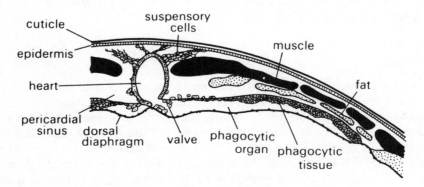

Fig. 457. Transverse section through the pericardial sinus in the abdomen of *Gryllotalpa* showing a phagocytic organ and phagocytic tissue. Pericardial cells form supporting elements (suspensory cells) for the heart dorsally (after Nutting, 1951).

Aorta

In front of the heart the dorsal vessel continues as the aorta. This is a simple tube without ostia, but in Odonata, Orthoptera, Coleoptera and Lepidoptera there may be diverticula extending from it dorsally. These diverticula are often connected with the pulsatile organs which are concerned with blood circulation through the wings. The aorta of orthopteroids extends below the cerebral ganglion as an open gutter; in other groups it ends more abruptly either discharging into the body cavity or, in *Rhodnius* (Heteroptera), into a sinus which runs forwards beneath the brain. In *Bombyx* the aorta dilates into a sac in front of the brain and from this vessels diverge to the maxillae, antennae and eyes (Gerould, 1938).

32.12 Aliform muscles and dorsal diaphragm

Closely associated with the heart are the aliform, or alary, muscles. These stretch from one side of the body to the other just below the heart. Usually they fan out from a restricted origin on the tergum, the muscles of each side meeting in a broad zone at the midline (Figs. 451, 452), but sometimes, as in Acridoidea, the origin of the muscles is also broad. In most orthopteroids, at least, only the proximal part near the point of origin is contractile, the rest and greater part of the 'muscle' being made up of bundles of connective tissue which branch and anastomose. Some of the connective tissue fibres form a plexus which extends to the heart wall, but in some insects, such as dipterous larvae, the aliform muscles are inserted directly into the walls of the heart instead of meeting beneath it. Orthopteroids may have as many as ten abdominal and two thoracic pairs of aliform muscles, but in other insects the number is reduced. Geocorisae, for instance, have from four to seven pairs.

The aliform muscles form an integral part of the dorsal diaphragm which spreads between them as a fenestrated connective tissue membrane. It is usually incomplete laterally so that the pericardial sinus is broadly continuous with the perivisceral sinus in this region. The lateral limits are often indefinite and are determined by the presence of muscles or tracheae or the origins of the aliform muscles.

32.13 Ventral diaphragm

The ventral diaphragm is a horizontal septum just above the nerve cord cutting off the perineural sinus from the main perivisceral sinus (Fig. 450). It is present in both larvae and adults of Odonata, Orthoptera, Hymenoptera and Neuroptera, but is only found in adults of Mecoptera and the lower Diptera (Richards, 1963). No ventral diaphragm is present in the other orders of insects except in Lepidoptera where it is unusual in having the nerve cord bound to its ventral surface by connective tissue (Fig. 450C). Laterally it is attached to the sternum, usually at only one point in each segment so that there are broad gaps along the margins where perivisceral and perineural sinuses are continuous, but in the Lepidoptera there are several points of attachment in each segment.

In several orders the ventral diaphragm is restricted to the abdomen, but in Orthoptera it is also present in the thorax. Posteriorly it does not extend beyond the posterior end of the nerve cord.

The structure of the ventral diaphragm varies. For instance, in the thorax of grasshoppers it is a delicate membrane with little or no muscle, but in the abdomen it becomes a solid muscular sheet. Its structure may also vary with age and in *Corydalis* it forms a solid sheet in the larva, but a fenestrated membrane in the adult.

The contractions of the ventral diaphragm are probably myogenic and are propagated by tension, while nervous inhibition reduces the frequency with which contractions occur.

32.14 Accessory pulsatile organs

In addition to the dorsal vessel there are often other pulsating structures connected with the haemocoel which are concerned with maintaining a circulation through the appendages. In the mesothorax and sometimes also in the metathorax there is a pulsatile organ concerned with the circulation through the wings. The veins of the posterior part of the wing connect with a blood space beneath the tergum via the axillary cord. In Odonata (Whedon, 1938) the blood space, or reservoir, opens through a terminal ostium into an ampulla at the end of a dorsal diverticulum of the aorta (Fig. 458). Contraction

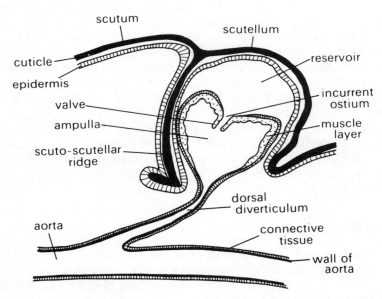

Fig. 458. Sagittal section of the mesothorax of *Anax* showing the pulsatile organ (after Whedon, 1938).

of this ampulla drives blood into the dorsal vessel; when it relaxes the ostium opens, drawing blood in from the reservoir beneath the tergum and hence, indirectly, from the wings. In many Lepidoptera the dorsal vessel itself loops up to the dorsal surface of the thorax and forms the so-called pulsatile organ (Fig. 459). A reservoir is cut off beneath the tergum by a muscular membrane and this connects with the heart by a pair of ostia at the top of the loop. At diastole blood is drawn into the heart from the reservoir, while at systole it is pumped forwards in the normal way and at the same time the muscular diaphragm falls, drawing in a fresh supply of blood from the wings and thorax. Gerould (1938) maintains that the muscular membrane moves passively, but Brocher (1919) regards the membrane as actively forcing blood through the ostia.

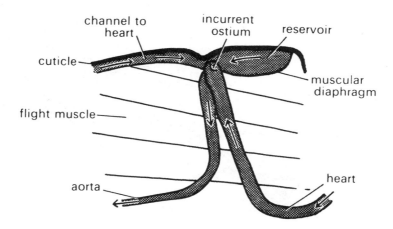

Fig. 459. Sagittal section of the mesothorax of *Bombyx* showing the dorsal loop of the heart resembling a pulsatile organ (after Gerould, 1938).

The circulation of blood through the wings is also often aided by pulsatile membranes in the veins. For instance, in each wing of *Drosophila* there are four such membranes in the veins which conduct centripetally and one in a vein conducting centrifugally. The structure and mode of action of these membranes is not understood, but their activity is probably dependent on the activity of the thoracic pulsatile organ (see J. C. Jones, 1964).

Orthoptera and probably many other insects have a small ampulla at the base of each antenna. This communicates with the haemocoel by a valved opening and extends as a vessel into the antenna. When the ampulla expands blood is drawn into it from the haemocoel; when it contracts blood is forced into the antenna. Other pulsating organs occur in the legs of Heteroptera.

32.15 Innervation of the heart

In some insects, such as *Anopheles,* the heart is entirely without any nerve supply although there are segmental nerves to the aliform muscles (J. C. Jones, 1954a). On the other hand the heart of *Periplaneta* is innervated from three sources. Nerves from the corpora cardiaca and from the segmental ganglia combine to form a longitudinal nerve on either side of the heart from which nerve endings ramify in the wall of the heart and the aliform muscles. In addition, supposedly sensory fibres arise from the heart and join the sensory nerves in the dorsal body wall (Fig. 460). Between these two extremes are various intermediate degrees of innervation and *Prodenia*, for instance, has only segmental nerves. In the cockroach, and probably in most orthopteroids, scattered nerve cells, known as ganglion cells, occur along the lateral heart nerves, but these are not always present in other insects.

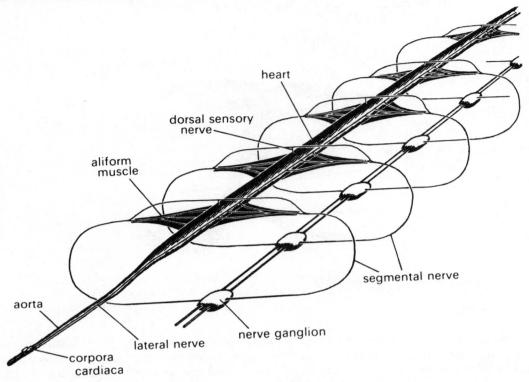

Fig. 460. Diagrammatic representation of the innervation of the heart in an insect, such as *Periplaneta*, with a well-developed innervation.

32.2 Circulation

32.21 The course of circulation

In normal circulation the blood is pumped forwards through the heart at systole, passing out of the heart via the excurrent ostia and, anteriorly, from the aorta (Fig. 461). The valves on the incurrent ostia prevent the escape of blood through these openings. The blood driven forwards by the heart increases the blood pressure anteriorly in the perivisceral sinus so that in this sinus blood tends to pass backwards along a pressure gradient. Blood percolates down to the perineural sinus where it is agitated by movements of the ventral diaphragm which assist the blood supply to the nervous system and possibly produce a backward flow of blood. The dorsal diaphragm is usually convex above so that contraction of the alary muscles tends to flatten it. This flattening increases the volume of the pericardial sinus at the expense of the perivisceral sinus so that blood passes up into the pericardial sinus and then at diastole is drawn into the heart through the incurrent ostia.

Many insects have a well-defined, but variable, circulation through the wings, although in some, apparently, circulation only occurs in the young adult. Normally blood passes out along the anterior veins, back to the posterior veins via cross veins and smaller tissue spaces and then back to the body via the posterior veins and the axillary cord. Changes in pressure modify the wing circulation by pumping blood into spaces which were previously empty or stagnant, but the general course of the circulation remains the same. If, however, the pressure changes in the thorax are very marked the direction of blood flow along the veins may be reversed, particularly in the anterior veins.

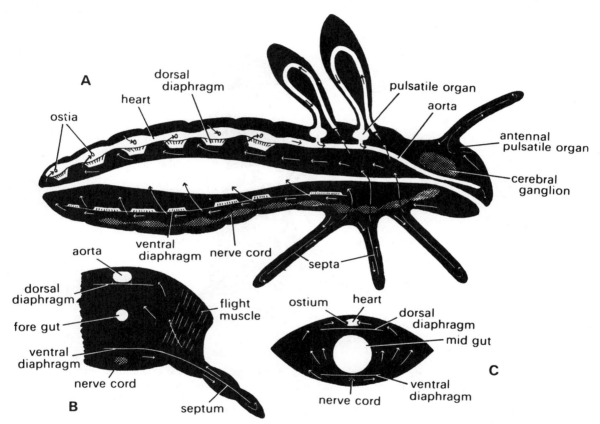

Fig. 461. Diagrammatic representation of the blood circulation in an insect with a fully developed circulatory system. Arrows indicate the course of circulation. A. Longitudinal section. B. Transverse section of thorax. C. Transverse section of abdomen (from Wigglesworth, 1965).

The flow at the base of the wings is directed by the fusion of the dorsal and ventral articular membranes so that the space between them is largely occluded. Anteriorly the membranes are held apart by the axillary sclerites so that they contain a space, the anterior sinus (Fig. 462), which is continuous anteriorly with the perivisceral sinus. Behind the axillary sclerites the membranes are fused except for a few small, irregular channels so that blood from the anterior sinus is mostly directed back to the perivisceral sinus or out along the anterior veins. Posteriorly the anal veins connect with the axillary cord via channels between the two fused membranes and from here it is aspirated by the pulsatile organ in the thorax (Clare and Tauber, 1942). In this way the normal circulation in the wings is maintained although in *Anopheles* the contractions of the pulsatile organ are very irregular (J. C. Jones, 1954a). The circulation is reduced when the wings are folded because of the occlusion of the channels in the articular membrane. In the absence of the wing circulation the tracheae in the wings of *Blattella* collapse, and the wing structure becomes dry and brittle.

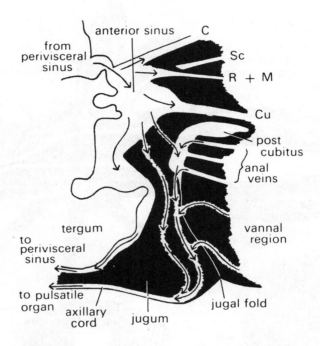

Fig. 462. Diagrammatic representation of the circulation in the base of the fore wing of *Blattella*. Areas in which the two membranes of the wing are fused together are black. Well-defined channels between the membranes, *e.g.* veins, have a regular outline, less definite channels have an irregular outline. Axillary sclerites are omitted (after Clare and Tauber, 1942)

Pulsatile organs also pump blood into the antennae and in Heteroptera serve to aspirate blood from the legs. In most insects the cavity of the legs is divided into anterior and posterior channels by a longitudinal septum. Blood passes down the posterior channel from the perineural sinus and up the anterior channel to the spaces between the wing muscles in the perivisceral sinus. It is thought that pressure differences between these two sinuses maintain the direction of flow.

The circulation is affected in an irregular manner by movements of the alimentary canal and by respiratory movements. Any activity which tends to induce pressure differences in different parts of the body must affect the circulation.

32.22 Heartbeat

Systole, the contraction phase of the heartbeat, results from the contractions of the muscles in the heart wall which start posteriorly and spread forwards as a wave. Diastole, the relaxation phase, results from relaxation of the muscles assisted by the elastic filaments supporting the heart and, in some cases, by the contraction of the aliform muscles, whether these are inserted directly into the heart wall or are only indirectly connected to it by connective tissue. The contractions of the aliform muscles are in anti-phase with the contractions of the heart (Fig. 463) although they may not coincide exactly with diastole. After diastole there is a third phase in the heart cycle, known as diastasis, in which the heart rests in the expanded condition. Increases in the frequency of the heartbeat result from reductions in the period of diastasis.

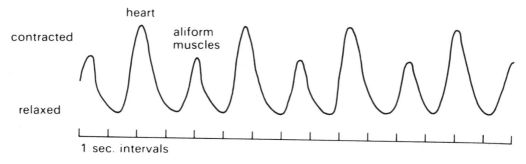

Fig. 463. A mechanical trace showing the alternating contractions of heart and aliform muscles in the larva of *Cossus cossus* (after de Wilde, 1947).

In a mechanical recording of heart activity there is often a slight dip in the trace immediately before systole indicating a slight expansion before the contraction (Fig. 464). This dip is known as the presystolic notch and probably results from an increase in hydrostatic pressure within the heart due to the start of systole in the more posterior segments.

Rate of heartbeat

The frequency with which the heart contracts varies considerably. Beard (1953) gives a range of from 14 beats per minute in the larva of *Lucanus* to 150 beats per minute in *Campodea*. In general the frequency of beating is higher in early than in later instar larvae and also depends on the age within an instar, becoming very low just before moulting. In the larva of *Sphinx* the rate drops from over 80 beats per minute in the first instar to less than 50 in the fifth; just before moulting it drops to 30 per minute and in the pupa is only about 22 beats per minute. The heart of the young pupa of *Anopheles* sometimes stops beating altogether and in old pupae no beating is observed (Jones, 1954). The heart beats faster in the adult than in immature stages: 150 beats per minute compared with 100–130 in *Anopheles*. Other factors also affect the rate of heartbeat; high temperature and activity increase it, strong movements of the gut may slow it or even stop it for short periods. In general, the heart stops beating at temperatures below

1–5°C. or above 45–50°C., but it is interesting that the heart of *Periplaneta* continues to beat when the insect is in a state of cold stupor.

The heart may undergo periodic reversals in which contractions start at the front and move backwards. This occurs particularly in late larval instars, pupae and adult insects, and in female *Anopheles* 31% of the beats start at the front of the heart (J. C. Jones, 1954a). Often the frequency of the heartbeat is lower than normal during these periods of reversal. With a reversed beat blood is forced out of the excurrent ostia and Nutting (1951) records powerful currents passing out of the subterminal incurrent ostia in the heart of *Gryllotalpa*.

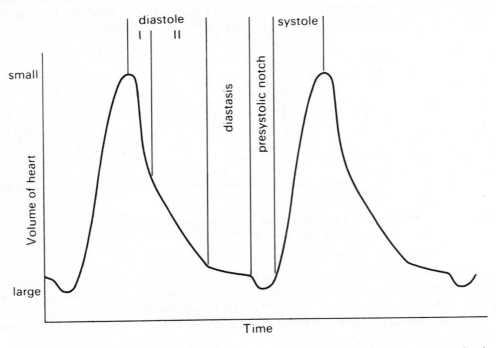

Fig. 464. Changes in volume of a section of the heart during beating as indicated by a mechanical trace. The first phase of diastole results from the elasticity of the heart wall, the second phase from contraction of the aliform muscles.

Control of heartbeat

Since the heart sometimes has no nerve supply, in these instances the contractions of the heart muscle must be myogenic. Where a nerve supply to the heart is present it is not clear whether the beat is myogenic or neurogenic. Since, in a number of insects, the heart continues to beat after removal of connections to all parts of the nervous system a myogenic beat is suggested, but it is possible in these cases that there are intrinsic ganglion cells on or near the heart as in *Periplaneta*. Pharmacological evidence is conflicting, but possibly favours a neurogenic origin for the beat. Krijgsman (1952) concludes that the heart muscle contracts myogenically, but often has neurogenic pacemakers. The pacemaker cell has cholinergic properties and acts via motor fibres with adrenergic properties. In turn the pacemaker cell may be stimulated and its output varied by sensory input from extrinsic fibres and possibly also by sensory fibres from the heart itself (Fig. 465). When contraction is purely myogenic activity may be initiated by contraction of the aliform muscles, as in *Chironomus* larva, but this is not always so because the heart will beat with all the aliform muscles cut and de Wilde (1947) suggests that in Lepidoptera it is the heartbeat which initiates contraction of the aliform muscles.

The heart is caused to beat faster by a substance from the corpora cardiaca which is presumably normally released into the blood. This substance promotes the activity of the pericardial cells which enlarge and become vacuolated, producing a second substance which acts on the muscles of the heart. Release of the first substance from the corpora cardiaca is known to be induced in *Periplaneta* by feeding on glucose. As this is ingested sensilla on the labrum are stimulated and impulses pass from them to the corpora cardiaca via the brain and the frontal ganglion. Other activities probably affect the corpora cardiaca through different sensilla. There is no evidence that this role of the pericardial cells is a general phenomenon, while there is some evidence that hormones may act directly on the heart (see Novák, 1966).

A beat can be initiated in any part of the heart (Beard, 1953), but normally contraction starts posteriorly so that it moves forwards. The direction of beat may be related to the distribution of blood pressures. If pressure at the front of the heart becomes so high that a back pressure is set up the heartbeat is reversed. The direction

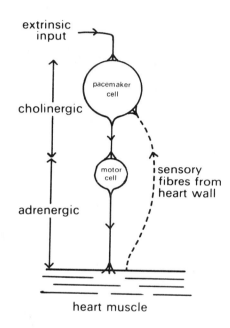

Fig. 465. Diagrammatic representation of the possible mechanism of nervous control of the heart (after Krijgsman, 1952).

of beat after transection of the heart adds support to this suggestion and possibly the prevalence of a reversed beat in pupal insects results from the blockage of excurrent ostia by the abundant fat and histolysed tissue present at this time. In *Anopheles* the direction of heartbeat is sometimes correlated with abdominal ventilation. If ventilation starts posteriorly the heart beats forwards; if ventilation starts anteriorly the heart beats backwards. These changes might well be due to differences in pressure.

Alternatively or additionally the direction of heartbeat might be related to the availability of oxygen. In the absence of a good oxygen supply the rate of heartbeat is strongly reduced indicating the need for an adequate supply for normal working. The larva of *Bombyx* has a better tracheal supply to the posterior end of the heart than to the anterior end. Thus the posterior end has a better oxygen supply and so might be dominant, producing the normal forward heartbeat. If, however, the posterior spiracles are occluded so that the oxygen supply is reduced the direction of heartbeat is reversed since the anterior part now has the better oxygen supply. In the pupa the tracheal system of the whole heart is poor and the rate of beating is low with reversals, while in the adult the tracheal system is dense both anteriorly and posteriorly and the heartbeat is rapid, again with reversals (see also discussion in J. C. Jones, 1964).

CHAPTER XXXIII

THE HAEMOLYMPH

The blood or haemolymph of insects consists of a fluid plasma in which nucleated cells are suspended. Several different types of blood cells occur and the number in circulation varies considerably, sometimes due to real changes in the numbers present, but also because they may adhere in large numbers to various tissues so that they do not circulate. Their functions include phagocytosis, wound healing and perhaps storage and intermediate metabolism.

Blood cells may be involved in connective tissue formation, but in many cases connective tissue is formed by the cells of other tissues. The functions of connective tissue include supporting and binding tissues together and in this the tracheal system may play an important role, but it is also possible that some connective tissue serves to conduct secretions from their origins to the target cells.

The volume of blood may vary at different stages in the life cycle and according to the physiological condition of the insect. The plasma contains various inorganic ions, of which sodium and chloride may be the most important, but insects differ from other animals in that other ions may be present in higher concentrations than these two. Organic substances are also present and in higher insects amino acids make a considerable contribution to the total osmolar concentration of the haemolymph. Proteins are also present and vary in concentration in the course of the life history.

The plasma serves primarily as a means by which substances may be transported round the body, although it plays little part in respiration. It may also provide a store of substances such as sugars and proteins, while its water acts as a reservoir for the maintenance of the tissue fluids. The hydrostatic pressure of the haemolymph is important in the movements of soft-bodied larvae, in expansion after moulting and in other ways.

The structure and functions of the blood cells are reviewed by J. C. Jones (1962, 1964) and Wigglesworth (1959a), and the reactions to parasites and coagulation are dealt with by G. Salt (1963, 1968), and Beard (1950) and Grégoire (1951, 1964) respectively. The chemical composition, biochemistry and functions of the plasma are reviewed by Buck (1953), Florkin and Jeuniaux (1964), Sutcliffe (1963) and G. R. Wyatt (1961). The functions of blood in general are reviewed by Mellanby (1939). Ashhurst (1968) reviews the structure and functions of connective tissue.

33.1 Haemocytes

The blood or haemolymph circulates round the body cavity between the various organs, bathing them directly. It consists of a fluid plasma in which are suspended the blood cells or haemocytes.

675

33.11 Types of haemocyte

Many different types of haemocyte have been described, but a comprehensive classification is difficult because individual cells can have very different appearances under different conditions and a variety of techniques have been used in their study. J. C. Jones (1962, 1964) recognises four main types of cell, which are found in most of the insects studied.

1. Prohaemocytes (Fig. 466A) are small rounded cells with relatively large nuclei and intensely basophilic cytoplasm. They divide at frequent intervals and give rise to other types of cell.

2. Plasmatocytes are frequently the most abundant cell type. They are variable in form, phagocytic and with a basophilic cytoplasm (Fig. 466B).

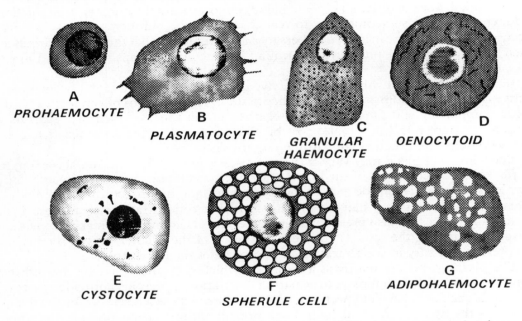

Fig. 466. Diagrammatic representation of various types of haemocyte as seen under phase contrast. All approx. × 2000. (A, D and G after Rizki, 1953; B after Jones, 1954b; C and F after Jones, 1956; E after Grégoire, 1951).

3. Granular haemocytes are also phagocytic, but are characterised by the possession of acidophilic granules in the cytoplasm (Fig. 466C).

4. Cystocytes (coagulocytes) which, when viewed with the phase contrast microscope, have a small, sharply defined nucleus and a pale, hyaline cytoplasm containing scattered black granules (Fig. 466E), while other types of haemocytes have a larger, paler nucleus and darker cytoplasm. The cystocytes are probably specialised granular haemocytes.

In addition there are other types of cell which only occur in certain insects. The commonest of these are oenocytoids, spherule cells and adipohaemocytes. Oenocytoids are found in Coleoptera, Lepidoptera and some Diptera and Heteroptera. They are usually large, thick, basophilic cells containing canaliculi, strands of granules or crystals (Fig. 466D) (Jones, 1962). Spherule cells, found in Lepidoptera and Diptera, are round or oval cells with large, non-refringent, usually acidophilic inclusions filling the whole cell (Fig. 466F). Adipohaemocytes (spheroidocytes) have been found in all the Lepidoptera and Diptera so far studied and in some representatives of various other groups. They are characterised by refringent fat droplets and other inclusions (Fig. 466G).

It is not clear if these different types of haemocyte represent different stages in the development of individual cells, but it seems probable that most of them are derived independently from prohaemocytes.

33.12 Origin of haemocytes

Haemocytes are derived from the embryonic mesoderm and in some insects it appears that subsequently no new blood cells are formed other than by division of existing prohaemocytes. The incidence of mitosis may vary with the stage of development so that the number of blood cells present may also change. However, in larval Lepidoptera and some other groups there are haemopoietic organs. In caterpillars there are four of these behind the prothoracic spiracles, each consisting of a mass of rounded cells connected together by an intercellular reticulum and enclosed in a capsule. They are discrete organs, not simply aggregations of cells, and have a discrete tracheal supply. The haemopoietic organs get bigger throughout larval life associated with frequent divisions of the contained cells and by the third larval instar all types of differentiating blood cells are recognisable. The definitive haemocytes escape through gaps in the capsule until finally, in the pupa, the haemopoietic organs disintegrate and large numbers of haemocytes are released into the blood.

Similar organs, but without a limiting capsule, occur in the larva of *Musca* which has no free cells in circulation (Arvy, 1954). In general it appears to be true that haemopoietic organs release their cells at metamorphosis in insects where there are few or no cells already in circulation. Perhaps these cells assist in the histolysis which occurs at this time. *Calliphora*, however, is exceptional since in this species the blood cells are released from the haemopoietic organs in the second instar larva. Haemopoietic organs are not known to occur in adult insects.

33.13 Numbers of haemocytes present

The number of haemocytes present in the blood can fluctuate considerably over short periods because normally not all the cells are free in the circulation; many of them may adhere to the surfaces of tissues in the haemocoel, only appearing in the circulation at certain times. The number of cells in a unit volume of blood is also influenced by changes in the blood volume, but marked changes in the total numbers of blood cells are known to occur. Some insects, such as the larvae of *Musca* and *Chironomus plumosus*, normally have no haemocytes in circulation, while in others, like *Periplaneta*, there may be several million free blood cells.

In general the number of circulating cells increases before a moult and decreases again after it. In *Sarcophaga* the blood cell count rises from about 8000/mm.^{3} in the larva to 34,000/mm.^{3} just before pupation, possibly following the release of cells from haemopoietic organs. In the early pupa the number drops to 12,000/mm.^{3} probably as a result of many cells adhering to the tissues (J. C. Jones, 1956). These changes are largely due to alterations in the numbers of granular haemocytes, very few of which are present at the beginning of the last larval instar.

Differential changes in the types of cell present are common. In *Sialis* granular haemocytes first appear in the last larval instar, reaching a peak and disappearing again before pupation (Selman, 1962). Similarly, the adipohaemocytes in *Prodenia* (Yeager, 1945) and the spherule cells in *Sarcophaga* (called oenocytoids by Dennell, 1947, but not homologous with oenocytoids elsewhere) reach a peak just before pupation. In *Prodenia* the most abundant cell types vary throughout the life of the insect and in holometabolous insects generally many of the cells break down at pupation and a new generation arises in the adult by division of the prohaemocytes.

33.14 Functions

Phagocytosis

The most common function of haemocytes is phagocytosis of foreign particles, micro-organisms and tissue debris. Many cells are capable of phagocytosis but probably the plasmatocytes are most important. Injection of micro-organisms sometimes results in an increase in the numbers of free blood cells and these often confer some degree of non-specific immunity on the insect. In the habitual host, phagocytosis of protozoans and fungi is not normally successful, but these organisms rarely survive in unusual hosts. The reaction against bacteria depends on the condition of host and parasite, any factors adverse to the insect tending to the success of the bacterium, and probably, in general, the plasma is more important than the haemocytes in combating bacteria.

The increase of phagocytes which occurs at metamorphosis may be associated with the phagocytosis of tissue debris, but this is not always true since in *Rhodnius*, for instance, phagocytosis does not occur at this time. Phagocytosed material may be digested in the cell or fully laden phagocytes may be encapsulated by other phagocytes. In some insects phagocytes aggregate to form well-defined phagocytic organs (see p. 664).

Encapsulation

Particles such as metazoan parasites which are too large to phagocytose are encapsulated. The haemocytes congregate round the parasite and become flattened. More adhere to the outside so that the capsule becomes smooth and consolidated (Fig. 467) (G. Salt, 1963). After some hours or days, depending on the species, the capsule differentiates into two layers. The outer layer consists of semi-opaque, flattened, but distinct cells which retain their capacity to return to the blood and many of these cells do leave the capsule with the result that it becomes much smaller. For instance, the capsule formed round the larva of *Nemeritis* by larval *Diataraxia* shrinks to about one tenth of its original size and mass movements of the cells may change the shape of the capsule. The inner layer is more translucent and the cells break down to some extent so that a continuous layer of homogeneous cytoplasm with nuclei at intervals is formed. Subsequently this part of the capsule is transformed to non-living connective tissue formed either from the cells themselves or from their secretions. Ultimately this is all that remains of the capsule and it is normally retained for the rest of the life of the insect either free in the body cavity or attached to the tissues. Only a poor reaction is produced if the host is unhealthy or young.

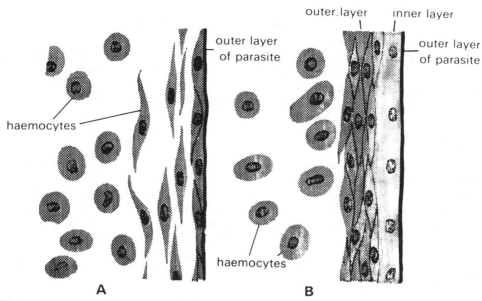

Fig. 467. A. Haemocytes aggregating on the outside of a parasite. B. Later stage with the inner layer of the enclosing capsule differentiated, but the cells of the outer layer retaining their identities (after Salt, 1963).

Encapsulation normally occurs if the parasite is in an unusual host and generally the parasite dies through lack of oxygen. In an habitual host encapsulation may or may not occur. Some parasitic Hymenoptera are able to resist encapsulation by making vigorous movements and older tachinid larvae have a respiratory funnel connected to the host tracheal system so that encapsulation does not impair their respiration. Some parasites, such as encysted metacercariae, are unaffected by encapsulation, apparently because of their low oxygen requirements. The majority of Hymenoptera in their habitual hosts do not evoke encapsulating behaviour by the haemocytes and G. Salt (1961) has shown that the response of the haemocytes to foreign objects is related to the surface properties of the object. In *Nemeritis* a substance is added to the outside of the eggs in the region of the calyx which alters the surface properties of the egg so that the haemocytes of *Ephestia,* its habitual host, are not activated (G. Salt, 1965).

Secretion and metabolism

Haemocytes may be concerned in the formation of connective tissue (section 33.2) and Wigglesworth (1956) has shown that they are important in normal basement membrane formation in *Rhodnius.* When the epidermal cells are growing at the moult the haemocytes spread underneath the epidermis. They contain inclusions of mucopolysaccharide and these are secreted to form the membranes while the blood cells them-selves may break down. Similar cells may form sheaths round muscle fibres, insinuating themselves between the fibres and spreading over them before secreting their products. Jones (1965) questions the evidence for the secretory activity of these cells.

There is evidence that in some insects haemocytes are concerned in the activation of the prothoracic glands before moulting. If the phagocytes of *Rhodnius* are immobi-lised experimentally before the critical period of the moult the prothoracic glands do not become fully activated for the production of the moulting hormone and moulting is delayed. Normally the phagocytes become associated with the gland at the critical period and they increase in size and become vacuolated suggesting that they secrete some material which is necessary for full activation of the gland. Vacuolated haemocytes are also found in the corpora cardiaca of *Mimas* when these are releasing neurosecretory material (Highnam, 1958b).

Some haemocytes may be involved in the formation of the fat body (p. 84) and are concerned in intermediate metabolism. This is true of the spherule cells of *Sarcophaga* which are most abundant just before pupation. They contain tyrosinase which is im-portant in the hardening and darkening of the larval cuticle to form the puparium (p. 443). Before the moult the level of tyrosinase builds up rapidly in the cells which aggre-gate beneath the epidermis and along the tracheae. Then they break down, releasing the tyrosinase into the plasma. The enzyme does not, however, immediately react with the tyrosine already present, apparently because it is inhibited by the low redox potential of the haemolymph. At the time of pupation the redox potential increases sharply. Jones (1962), however, has shown that the spherule cells are not essential for normal hardening and darkening of the puparium to occur.

Haemocytes are probably involved in other aspects of intermediate metabolism as yet unknown. They are also concerned in the transfer of nutrient materials round the body. Glycogen builds up in these cells in larval *Prodenia*, but is depleted at meta-morphosis when it is utilised. Fat inclusions also occur if the insect is fed on a fatty diet.

In some instances the cells themselves break down to provide nutriment for other tissues and J. C. Jones (1956) accounts for the disappearance of granular haemocytes from the pupa of *Sarcophaga* in this way. In *Ephestia* blood cells adhere in large numbers to the membranes of the developing wings and the cell contents pass into the epidermal cells, providing nutriment.

Wound healing and coagulation

The blood cells are concerned in wound healing. Damaged tissues are phagocytosed and the plasmatocytes extend processes which join with those of other cells to form a cellular network. The plasma may coagulate in this network so that the wound is effectively plugged until the epidermis regenerates.

Beard (1950) considers that coagulation might result either from agglutination of the haemocytes or from coagulation of the plasma, but Grégoire (1951, 1964) regards all coagulation as resulting from cellular reactions. Two types of coagulation occur, both being variations of the same process and involving the cystocytes (hyaline haemo-cytes of Grégoire). In *Gryllotalpa* and many other insects when the blood is exposed the cystocytes stop moving and their cytoplasm expands rapidly and becomes vacuolated. Round each cystocyte a thin fog of particles appears in the plasma (Fig. 468A), progressively increasing in amount and density. This material coagulates so that the cystocytes are surrounded by areas of coagulation in which other types of haemocyte may become trapped. The second type of coagulation occurs, for instance, in many lepidopteran larvae and Scarabaeidae. Here there are no islands of coagulation, but the cystocytes send out straight, thread-like pseudopodia which stick to interfaces and foreign particles, forming a meshwork of threads (Fig. 468B). Slowly the fluid contained

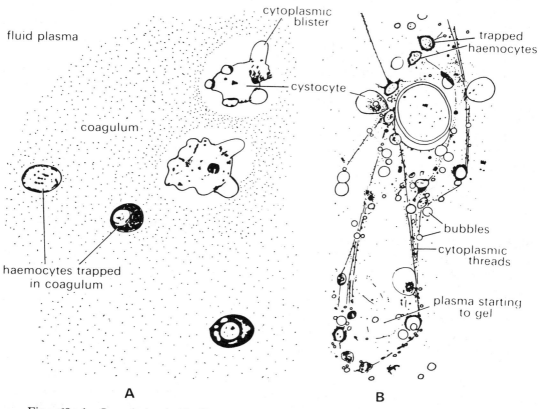

Fig. 468. A. Coagulation in *Gryllotalpa*. The coagulum (dotted) round two cystocytes has trapped three other haemocytes. B. Coagulation in *Cychrus*. The cystocytes have produced a meshwork of cytoplasmic threads to which other haemocytes and foreign bodies adhere. Between the threads the plasma gels (after Grégoire, 1951).

within the meshes becomes jelly-like and coagulates. Other types of haemocytes may stick to the pseudopodia or become trapped during coagulation. This reaction has more widespread effects than the first. In some Coleoptera and Hymenoptera, coagulation is a combination of these two types.

It is not known if the cystocytes which produce these different reactions belong to the same category. The differences may result from the release of larger or smaller amounts of the substance inducing coagulation or they might reflect differences in the composition of the coagulating plasma.

Commonly the cystocytes constitute 50% of the blood cells, but the numbers vary and, in general, reflect the readiness with which the plasma coagulates. However, cystocytes are present in the blood of many Heteroptera and adult Diptera which does not coagulate (Grégoire, 1964).

33.2 Connective tissue

Insects do not possess a cellular connective tissue comparable with that of vertebrates, but nevertheless connective tissues are present which bind together and suspend other tissues in the body cavity. The tracheal system plays an important part in binding tissues, such as the ovary, together, but in addition to this most organs in the haemocoel are bounded by a usually non-cellular membrane. Most such membranes are extremely delicate, but in some specialised regions they are much more strongly developed. This is especially true of the neural lamella (see Fig. 350), and in adult Lepidoptera this is thickened dorsally and serves for the attachment of the muscles of the ventral diaphragm (Fig. 450C).

The connective tissue bounding different organs is often continuous. For instance, the basement membrane of the epidermis is continuous with the sarcolemma surrounding the muscles, and the sarcolemma is continuous with the neurilemma where the muscles are innervated.

In many cases the connective tissue is a secretion of the underlying cells. This is true, for instance, of the neural lamella and the tunica propria which is secreted by the follicular tissue, but in some cases, at least, plasmatocytes add mucopolysaccharide to the substance of the membrane. This has been observed to occur at the basement membrane of the epidermis and the sarcolemma of developing muscles. The relative importance of the haemocytes and the cells of the underlying tissue in these instances is unknown.

A neutral mucopolysaccharide forms a major part of the connective tissue and sometimes embedded in this are fibres of a collagen-like substance. These occur in the neural lamella, in the connective tissue of the auditory ganglion of *Locusta,* and sometimes in the basement membrane of the Malpighian tubules. A lipid is also present in the neural lamella of Lepidoptera.

Connective tissue membranes break down in the pupa and in the neural lamella of *Galleria,* at least, this process is aided by haemocytes (Shrivastava and Richards, 1965). The connective tissue membranes of the adult are not produced until the underlying tissues are complete and they are characteristically absent from dividing tissues (Whitten, 1962).

The commonest functions of connective tissue are those of supporting and binding tissues together. The elastic properties of the tunica propria assist ovulation (p. 295), while in the larvae of higher Diptera and in *Leucophaea* the connective tissue membranes may serve to conduct secretions from their sites of origin to the target organs. For instance, in the larva of *Sarcophaga* the pericardial cells are attached to the heart by strands of connective tissue. Fine channels run through these strands, originating as a series of converging channels in the limiting membrane of the pericardial cells and running to the wall of the heart (Fig. 469). Probably the substance concerned in the control of the heartbeat (p. 673) is conducted to the heart in this way. Similar channels connect the ring gland (p. 696) with the heart, suggesting that the products of the former may be conducted to the heart so that they are distributed round the body with the blood with a maximum of efficiency. Channels are also present in some other membranes, but are absent from the majority, apparently occurring only where secretory cells are present. Such a system facilitates the rapid and uniform transport of secretions to their target organs (Whitten, 1964).

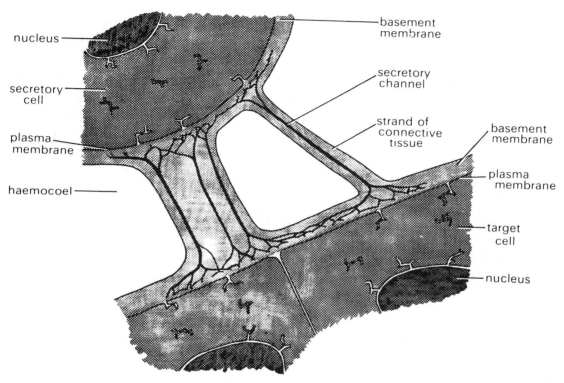

Fig. 469. Diagram showing the channels in connective tissue running from a secretory cell to target cells (after Whitten, 1964).

It has been suggested that the connective tissue membranes may form barriers round tissues, preventing the free access of materials in the blood, but if these membranes are comparable with the neural lamella they offer no resistance to diffusion (p. 525).

33.3 Plasma

33.31 Blood volume

About 90% of the insect blood is water, but the volume of water varies. Just before a moult the blood volume increases, partly because less water is excreted and partly by the removal of water from the tissues. Afterwards the volume decreases again (Fig. 470), water being returned to the actively growing tissues and some being excreted (Lee, 1961). The reduction after the moult is necessary because too high a blood volume during active periods would be a hindrance by creating too high a turgor pressure and so damping movements of the appendages.

Shorter-term changes in volume may also occur and there is probably a daily cycle related to feeding behaviour and the amount of desiccation. Thus, *Nomadacris* adults contain very little blood on a hot afternoon, but in the evening after feeding the blood volume increases and remains high until the following morning (Chapman, 1958).

Various inorganic and organic substances are dissolved in the plasma (G. R. Wyatt, 1961).

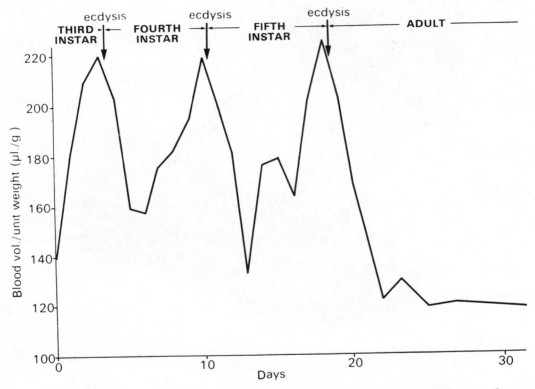

Fig. 470. Changes in the haemolymph volume during the life cycle of *Schistocerca* (after Lee, 1961).

33.32 Inorganic constituents

Chloride is the most abundant inorganic anion in insect blood. The concentration of chloride is high in Apterygota and hemimetabolous insects, but is characteristically low, usually amounting to less than 10% of the total osmolar concentration, in holometabolous forms (Sutcliffe, 1963). Other inorganic anions present are carbonate and phosphate, but these are rarely found in any quantity. Phosphates are important in *Carausius* and *Anabrus* (Orthoptera).

The most abundant cation is usually sodium, but in Lepidoptera, Hymenoptera and some Coleoptera there is relatively little and it contributes only about 10% of the total osmolar concentration (Fig. 473). The absolute concentration of potassium is usually lower than that of sodium, 2–10% of the total osmolar concentrations, but the Na/K ratio varies considerably (see Table 4). In *Petrobius* Na/K = 40 and relatively high values occur in Odonata, Orthoptera, Diptera and some Coleoptera, but in phytophagous Coleoptera, Hymenoptera and Lepidoptera Na/K is much lower and may be less than one. It is suggested that these last groups evolved with the angiosperms which contained relatively little sodium and the adaptation of the insects to a lower Na/K ratio reduced the amount of regulation necessary to maintain a more or less constant level in the blood. Hoyle (1954) has shown that the level of potassium in the blood influences the activity of locusts. A low level of potassium raises the muscle resting potential. As a result the action potential arising from stimulation is higher, the twitch tension of the muscle is increased and the insect will jump farther or much more readily than when the potassium concentration is high (Ellis and Hoyle, 1954). Ellis and Hoyle suggested that feeding raised the potassium level in the blood and hence produced the characteristic period of quiescence after a meal, but field work suggests that the potassium concentration in the blood is influenced more by changes in the blood volume than by the potassium concentration in the food (Chapman, 1958). The potassium concentration increases markedly before moulting and this is probably responsible for much of the inactivity occurring at this time (Hoyle, 1956).

The concentration of magnesium in the blood is often relatively high. In phytophagous insects this to some extent reflects the high level of magnesium in the diet, since it is a constituent of chlorophyll, and in Lepidoptera the level in the blood falls when the larvae stop feeding. A good deal of magnesium still occurs, however, and all insects appear to concentrate this metal. In Phasmida it almost completely replaces sodium. Calcium is usually less important than the previous metallic elements but is essential for the development of the end plate potential at the muscle (Hoyle, 1955b).

TABLE 7

CONCENTRATIONS, IN MILLI-EQUIVALENTS/LITRE, OF THE MAJOR INORGANIC CATIONS IN THE HAEMOLYMPH OF TWO INSECTS IN DIFFERENT STAGES OF DEVELOPMENT

(from Florkin and Jeuniaux, 1964)

Insect	Stage	Cation			
		Na	K	Ca	Mg
Bombyx	larva	15	46	24	101
	pupa*	11	41	24	69
		22	55	29	87
	adult	14	36	14	47
Vespula	larva*	26	56	19	24
		48	41	—	—
	pupa	23	61	11	19
	adult*	93	18	2	3
		153	22	2	1

* estimates by different authors

In many insects the ionic concentrations in the blood are roughly similar in larval and adult stages, although adult Lepidoptera have less magnesium than the larvae (see above). There is relatively little information, however, on different stages of holometabolous insects and in *Vespula* the concentrations change markedly between the pupal and adult stages, the sodium concentration increasing, while all the other cations decrease (Table 7).

Various metallic trace elements are also found in the blood. The most frequent are copper, which is a constituent of tyrosine, iron, present in the cytochromes, zinc and manganese.

It is possible that the metallic elements do not exist wholly as free ions, but that a proportion is bound in organic complexes. In *Antheraea* there is no evidence for any binding of potassium, but 15–20% of calcium and magnesium is bound to macromolecules.

33.33 Organic constituents

Insect blood is characterised by the very high level of amino acids present in the plasma. Most of the known amino acids have been recognised in various insects, but they vary considerably both qualitatively and quantitatively from one species to another and in different stages of the same species. To some extent the amino acids present depend on those available in the food.

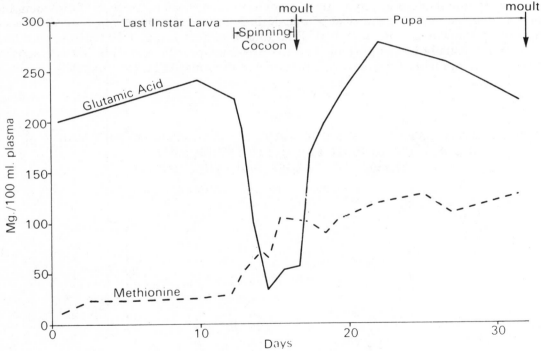

Fig. 471. Changes in the concentrations of two amino acids during cocoon formation and metamorphosis of *Bombyx*. Glutamic acid is involved in silk production, methionine is not (from Florkin and Jeuniaux, 1964).

In general, members of the more primitive insect orders possess fewer amino acids. Most insects have high concentrations of glutamine, which may be concerned in uric acid synthesis, proline and one or more of arginine, lysine and histidine. Amino acids constitute 35–65% of the non-protein nitrogen present in the blood.

The concentrations of amino acids may change at different stages in the life cycle. Tyrosine, for instance, commonly accumulates before each moult and then decreases sharply as it is used in tanning and melanisation of the new cuticle (p. 443). Similarly in the larva of *Bombyx* the amino acids, such as glutamic acid and aspartic acid, which are concerned with silk production fall to a very low level while the larva is spinning its cocoon, increasing again when this is complete (Fig. 471). Others, such as methionine, are not concerned with silk production, but increase at the time of the pupal moult as a result of the histolysis of the larval tissues (but see p. 417). In *Rhodnius*, however, the amino acid concentration in the haemolymph rises after feeding, but then remains constant right through the period of moulting. It appears that in this insect the utilisation of amino acids is offset by the slow, continuous digestion of the stored blood meal (Coles, 1965).

Other non-protein nitrogen in the plasma is mainly in the form of the end products of nitrogen metabolism. Uric acid is always present and in addition there may be allantoin, urea and ammonia. Apart from metabolic end products, amino sugars and peptides occur, the former sometimes constituting half the total carbohydrate in the blood.

Numerous proteins are present in the haemolymph; 19 are recorded from *Drosophila* and 21 from *Locusta*. They are not all present at the same time, but there are progressive changes through the life cycle of the insects. For instance, the first instar larva of *Locusta* emerges from the egg with seven different haemolymph protein fractions (Fig. 472). Within a day or two more fractions (16 and 17 in Fig. 472) have developed and these increase in concentration, but before the end of the instar four of the original fractions have disappeared (1, 4, 6 and 11 in Fig. 472). These probably represent the remains of yolk proteins which are being utilised (McCormick and Scott, 1966a). Another protein band regularly reaches a maximum at the time of moulting and then disappears again (14 in Fig. 472) (McCormick and Scott, 1966b; and see Chen and Levenbook, 1966).

The significance of the haemolymph proteins is not always clear. In the early larva of *Malacosoma* none of these proteins is detectable in the tissues, but at the onset of pupation they are selectively and differentially absorbed by the fat body, the wall of the midgut and the muscles of the heart. Similarly in *Hyalophora* a haemolymph protein which develops in the female pupa is selectively absorbed by the oocytes (see p. 291). The uptake of these proteins at metamorphosis and in oogenesis may be under hormonal control (p. 708).

Other proteins, which do not appear in the tissues, may be broken down to provide a source of amino acids which are then resynthesised *in situ* in the tissues, while others may be enzymes. Just before puparium formation in *Sarcophaga* the enzyme tyrosinase is released into the plasma from the blood cells (see above). Trehalase and other carbohydrases are also present as well as various other enzymes, some of which probably leak out from the surrounding tissues.

Non-amino organic acids may be present in some quantity in the plasma. Citrate is usually present in high concentration, although this varies considerably from one species to another, and there is consistently more in the larva than in the adult. In *Prodenia* the level of citrate is not markedly affected by diet so that it must be endogenous in origin

(Levenbook and Hollis, 1961). The organic phosphate concentration in insect blood is also usually high and in *Hyalophora* α-glycerophosphate and phosphocholine, in particular, contribute to this.

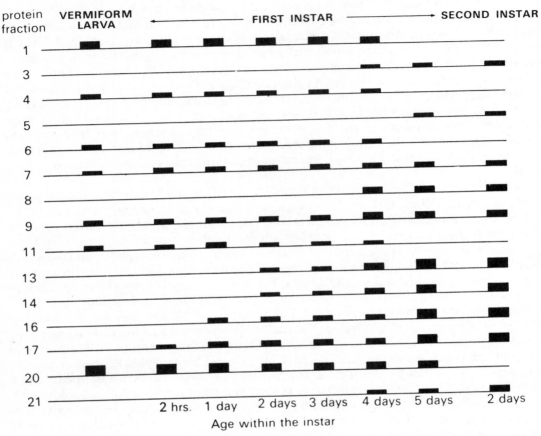

Fig. 472. Diagrammatic representation of an electropherogram showing the proteins present in the haemolymph of *Locusta*. The intensity of staining of the bands, which is influenced by the concentration of protein, is represented by their thickness in the diagram (after McCormick and Scott, 1966a).

There is characteristically a high concentration of trehalose, a non-reducing di-saccharide, in insect blood. Trehalose is a source of energy so that its level in the blood is reduced by starvation and also by activity, such as flight (Howden and Kilby, 1960), but it is increased after feeding because other sugars are converted to it (p. 67). *Apis* is exceptional in having high concentrations of glucose and fructose in the blood.

Glycerol, or some equivalent, is probably always present, sometimes in very high concentrations, in insects which are able to tolerate freezing (p. 652) (R. W. Salt, 1961). It is well known that glycerol helps to preserve living tissues in the frozen state, although the way in which it acts is uncertain.

33·34 Variations in plasma in different insect orders

Sutcliffe (1963) groups the plasma of pterygote insects into three broad categories:
1. Sodium and chloride account for most of the osmolar concentration (Fig. 473A).
This is probably the basic type of insect blood and is similar to that in most other arthropods. This type occurs in Ephemeroptera, Odonata, Plecoptera, Orthoptera and Homoptera.
2. Chloride is low relative to sodium which constitutes 21–48% of the total osmolar concentration (Fig. 473B). Amino acids are also present in high concentration. This type is found in Trichoptera, Diptera, Megaloptera, Neuroptera, Mecoptera and most Coleoptera.

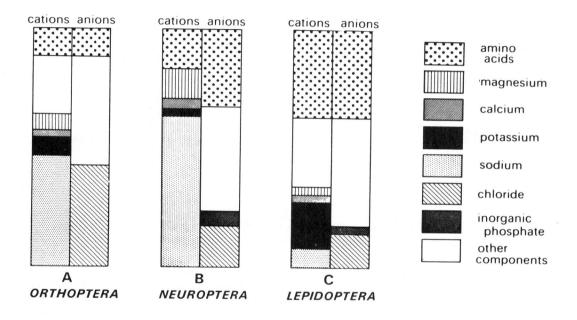

Fig. 473. Osmotic components of the haemolymph in different groups of insects expressed as percentages of the total osmolar concentration. Each vertical column represents 50% of the total concentration (after Sutcliffe, 1963).

3. Amino acids account for about 40% of the total osmolar concentration (Fig. 473C). There is a large unknown factor, but none of the other substances accounts for more than 10% of the total. Lepidoptera and Hymenoptera have this type of blood.

33·35 Pigments

Apart from *Chironomus* larvae in which haemoglobin is present in solution in the plasma, respiratory pigments do not occur in insect blood. The blood may, nevertheless, assume a variety of colours due to various pigments. Commonly the blood is green due to the presence of insectoverdin, a mixture of carotenoid and bile pigment. Insectoverdin is present in the blood of Lepidoptera and in solitary locusts, but in locusts it becomes altered with starvation as the pigments are metabolised and if the insects are crowded together the insectoverdin is replaced by blue mesobiliverdin (Nickerson, 1956). In the blood of *Bombyx* larva carotene, xanthophyll and flavines are present; in the pupa of *Hyalophora* are α-carotene, taraxanthin, riboflavine and chlorophyll. Aphids frequently have a purplish-red pigment in the blood in large quantities, up to 2% of the wet weight. This pigment is protoaphin belonging to a class of pigments, the aphins, so far found only in members of the Aphididae and the genus *Adelges* (Cromartie, 1959) (p. 116).

33.36 Properties of the plasma

Osmotic pressure

Although there may be active regulation of water movement between the blood and the tissue fluids, osmotic pressures will also influence this movement. Hence the osmotic pressure of the blood is important in controlling the water content of the cells. It is generally believed that the osmotic pressures of blood and tissue fluids are roughly the same. In many insects the osmotic pressure of the blood is about 7–8 atmospheres (Buck, 1953), but this figure varies in different stages of development and in xerophytic insects is often higher, about 12 atmospheres.

pH

In most insects the blood has a slightly acid reaction, pH 6·0–7·0, but in some, such as *Chironomus*, it is distinctly alkaline, pH 7·2–7·7. There is usually a slight rise in pH at moulting.

Most enzymes only work efficiently within a limited range of pH so that its control is important. During normal activity there is a tendency for the blood to become markedly acid due to the liberation of acid metabolites, including carbon dioxide. This tendency to change is offset, or buffered, by substances in the blood. The buffering capacity of insect blood, that is, its ability to prevent change of pH, is minimal in the normal physiological range, but increases sharply on either side of this range. Levenbook (1950b) suggests that this arrangement is associated with tracheal respiration. Carbon dioxide passes from the tissues to the tracheae via the blood and if the insect is active it accumulates in the blood. This accumulation leads to opening of the spiracles and ventilatory movements, but the carbon dioxide only diffuses slowly from the blood to the gas phase because there is no carbonic anhydrase in insects to catalyse the reaction. This inefficiency of the system could result in very large changes in pH, but as the buffering capacity of the blood increases as the pH varies from the normal range these changes will be limited.

Within the normal physiological range bicarbonates and phosphates are the most important buffers. On the acid side of this range the carboxyl groups of organic acids such as citric acid are important while on the alkaline side the amino groups of various amino acids are most significant. Proteins buffer over a wide range of pH.

33.37 Functions of the plasma

Plasma is important in the transport of various materials about the body. Nutritive materials are carried from the alimentary canal and storage tissues to the sites at which they are to be metabolised; excretory products from their places of origin to the Malpighian tubules; and hormones from the endocrine organs to their sites of action. The blood is normally unimportant in the transport of oxygen to the tissues because these are supplied directly by the tracheae. It normally contains much more carbon dioxide than oxygen. This partly reflects the much greater solubility of carbon dioxide, but the carbon dioxide in solution only accounts for about 20% of the total in the blood. The remainder is bound in some form, mainly as bicarbonate (Levenbook, 1950a). Oxygen is only present in solution. The much greater affinity of the blood for carbon dioxide than for oxygen is probably important in the cyclic release of carbon dioxide which occurs in some insects (Buck, 1958) (p. 469).

The plasma acts as a store for some substances, although sometimes only for relatively short periods. Trehalose is stored as a source of energy and although the supply can be replenished relatively rapidly from the fat body, the amount immediately available in the blood is a limiting factor in the flight of *Phormia* (Clegg and Evans, 1961). Amino acids are stored for use in the production of proteins which may, for instance, contribute to yolk formation (Hill, 1962) and tyrosine, used for quinone production in the cuticle, builds up before moulting.

Water storage is also important and by drawing on the plasma an insect can maintain the level of its cell fluids if the food is dry (Lee, 1961). The water itself also functions as a hydrostatic skeleton in forms, such as many larvae, where the cuticle is soft and provides little support for the insect. At moulting the hydrostatic properties are used in the expansion of the appendages and the ptilinum in cyclorrhaphous Diptera, while the amount of fluid present at this time can influence the ultimate size of the insect. Larval *Lucilia* with access to more moisture produce bigger adults, and wing size in *Orgyia* is greater if the emerging adult has a greater blood volume (Mellanby, 1939). Increases in hydrostatic pressure as a result of muscular activity are also responsible for the eversion of various organs such as the penis in male insects and the osmeterium, a fleshy, bifurcate defensive device, on the prothoracic segment of larval Papilionidae.

Reflex bleeding also results from an increase in hydrostatic pressure. In this case plasma is forced through weak spots or pores in the cuticle and in species exhibiting this behaviour the blood always contains some caustic or repellant substance so that this is presumed to be a defensive mechanism. In the grasshopper *Dictyophorus* the blood is mixed with air as it is forced out so that it produces a nauseous froth on the outside of the insect. In the bloody-nosed beetle, *Timarcha*, the red blood is forced out round the mouth. In general the blood is not lost to the insect, but the bulk is withdrawn into the haemocoel when the pressure is relaxed.

CHAPTER XXXIV
THE ENDOCRINE ORGANS AND HORMONES

The endocrine organs produce hormones which travel, usually in the blood, to various organs of the body, co-ordinating their longer term activities. The endocrine system is thus complementary to the nervous system.

Endocrine organs are of two types: neurosecretory cells in the central nervous system, and specialised endocrine glands. The neurosecretory cells, which may be modified motor neurons, form a link between the endocrine system and the nervous system. Both types of organ produce hormones which are generally released directly, or indirectly via storage organs, into the blood, but in some instances the hormones produced by neurosecretory cells are conveyed to the target organs along the axons of the cells. Nervous stimuli commonly lead to the release of the hormones. In some cases it is fairly certain that the hormones act directly on the nuclei of the target cells so that appropriate biochemical changes occur in the cells, but in other instances the effects of the hormones are indirect.

The hormones of insects are many and various in their effects and even hormones from a single organ may have a variety of effects. Among others, activities which are affected by hormones are moulting, metamorphosis, oocyte production, colour change and diurnal rhythms of activity. Insect hormones generally are reviewed by Novák (1966) and neurosecretion by Gabe (1966) and van der Kloot (1960). Reviews of particular aspects of endocrinology are given by Cazal (1948), Gilbert (1964), Gilbert and Schneiderman (1961), Highnam (1964), Wigglesworth (1954b, 1959b, 1964) and de Wilde (1964b) and Engelmann (1968).

34.1 Endocrine organs

The endocrine organs of insects are of two types: neurosecretory cells within the central nervous system, and specialised endocrine glands, such as the corpora cardiaca, corpora allata and prothoracic glands.

34.11 Neurosecretory cells

Neurosecretory cells normally occur in the ganglia of the central nervous system. They resemble typical nerve cells with axons, but they are characterised by showing cytological evidence of secretion. The secretion is granular with characteristic staining properties and the granules pass down the axons. Several types of cell, designated A, B, C and D, can be differentiated by their staining reactions, but these types are not always comparable in the works of different authors and may sometimes represent successive stages in a cycle of secretion (Delphin, 1965). It is probable that the visible secretion is only a carrier, possibly a large protein molecule, to which the smaller hormone molecule is attached. When the hormone is finally released it becomes separated from the carrier and is then free to enter the blood. It is assumed that whenever the carrier is visible it is accompanied by the hormone (see Schreiner, 1966).

The amount of granular material in a cell at any one time is the result of a balance between its rate of production and the rate of dissipation. Some authorities regard a cell full of granular material as actively secreting, while others regard such a cell as an inactive one accumulating material. It is probable that both points of view could be correct under different circumstances.

The endocrine activity of neurosecretory cells may take one of two forms. Either the cells may produce hormones which act directly on effector organs or they may act on other endocrine organs, which, in turn, are stimulated to produce hormones. In this case the neurosecretory cells act as intermediaries between the nervous system and the endocrine glands, responding to the overall situation perceived and analysed by the nervous system (Scharrer, 1959).

Large numbers of neurosecretory cells may be present in the nervous system, but it is possible that they do not all produce hormones.

Neurosecretory cells of the brain

Typically there are two groups of neurosecretory cells on each side of the brain. One group is in the pars intercerebralis, near the midline. The axons from these cells pass backwards through the brain and some or all of them cross over to the opposite side, emerging from the brain as a nerve which runs back to the corpus cardiacum. Most of the fibres end here, but a few pass through the corpus cardiacum to the corpus allatum and, in the locust, to the foregut and ingluvial ganglion (Strong, 1966) (Fig. 474). In most Apterygota these median neurosecretory cells are contained in separate capsules of connective tissue, known as the lateral frontal organs, on the dorsal side of the brain, but in Machilidae the cells are usually intercerebral as in Pterygota. *Petrobius* occupies an intermediate position with some neurosecretory cells in the lateral frontal organs and others in an adjacent frontal zone of the brain (Watson, 1963).

The second group of cells is variable in position. Sometimes it is medial to the corpora pedunculata, sometimes between the latter and the optic lobes. In some Diptera and Hymenoptera the cells corresponding with these are grouped with the other neurosecretory cells in the pars intercerebralis. From these cells a second nerve passes through the brain to the corpus cardiacum and in *Schistocerca* some fibres also extend to the corpus allatum (Highnam, 1964).

The products of the neurosecretory cells of the brain pass along the axons, usually to the corpora cardiaca or allata. Here they may be stored or released, or it is suggested that they may provide the raw materials from which specific hormones are produced in the various organs. The secretions of the neurosecretory cells in the pars intercerebralis promote the functioning of the prothoracic glands, stimulate protein synthesis and possibly control water loss, oocyte development and activity. It is not known whether these different effects are all produced by a single hormone or whether there are a number of separate hormones, but there are a number of different neurosecretory cell types, suggesting that several different secretions are possible.

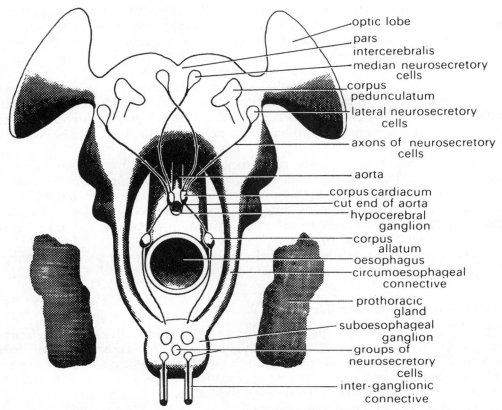

Fig. 474. Diagrammatic representation of the relationships of the main endocrine organs.

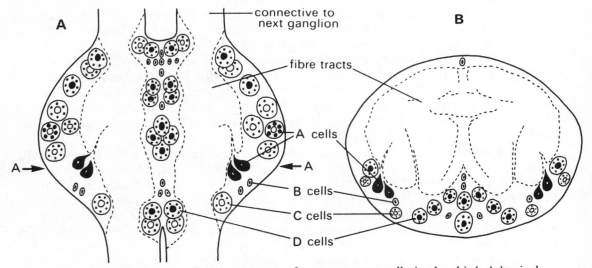

Fig. 475. Distribution of different types of neurosecretory cells in the third abdominal ganglion of *Schistocerca*. A. Dorsal view. B. Transverse section at AA (after Delphin, 1965).

Neurosecretory cells of other ganglia

Large numbers of neurosecretory cells occur in the ventral ganglia of the nerve cord. In *Bombyx* there are more secretory cells in the ventral ganglia than in the brain, but this is not true in *Schistocerca* (Delphin, 1965). Different cell types are widely distributed in different ganglia (Fig. 475), but some types are restricted to particular ganglia. The secretions from these cells can pass along the interganglionic connectives in either direction and also outwards along the peripheral nerves. Presumably the secretory products are liberated into the blood in this way or they may sometimes be carried direct to the effector organs.

The functions of these cells in general is unknown, but in some cases they are known to be concerned with activity (p. 713) and in others with water regulation (p. 712).

34.12 Corpora cardiaca

The corpora cardiaca are a pair of organs often closely associated with the aorta, and forming part of its wall (Fig. 474, 476). In higher groups such as Lepidoptera, Coleoptera and some Diptera they become separated from the aorta. Corpora cardiaca are not known to be present in Collembola. Each organ contains the endings of axons from cells in the brain and other axons passing through to the corpora allata. In addition there are glial cells (p. 525), with a clear, vacuolated cytoplasm, nerve cells, which constitute part of the stomatogastric system, and intrinsic secretory cells with long cytoplasmic projections extending towards the periphery of the organ. The projections probably serve for the release of secretions into the blood.

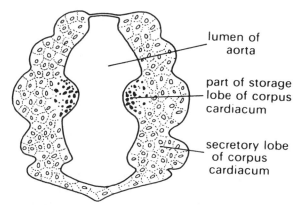

lumen of
aorta

part of storage
lobe of corpus
cardiacum

secretory lobe
of corpus
cardiacum

Fig. 476. Transverse section through the posterior parts of the corpora cardiaca of *Schistocerca* (after Highnam, 1961).

The corpora cardiaca store and release hormones from the neurosecretory cells of the brain to which they are connected by one or two pairs of nerves. In addition, the intrinsic secretory cells produce hormones which are concerned with the regulation of the heartbeat (p. 673) and have other physiological effects. Sometimes storage and secretory cells are intermingled, but in *Schistocerca* (Fig. 476) and some Heteroptera one part of the corpus cardiacum is concerned with secretion and another part with storage (Cazal, 1948).

34.13 Corpora allata

The corpora allata are glandular bodies, usually one on either side of the oesophagus (Fig. 474) although they may be fused to a single median organ as in higher Diptera. Each is connected with the corpus cardiacum of the same side by a nerve which carries fibres from the neurosecretory cells of the brain. In addition, a fine nerve connects each corpus allatum with the suboesophageal ganglion. This is a major nerve in Ephemeroptera where the nerve from the corpus cardiacum is absent. In Thysanura, the corpora allata are in the bases of the maxillae and in addition to a fine nerve direct from the suboesophageal ganglion they are innervated by branches from the mandibular and maxillary roots of the suboesophageal ganglion.

In Thysanura and Phasmida the corpora allata are hollow balls of cells, with gland cells forming the walls. Elsewhere they are solid organs of glandular, secretory cells, often with lacunae between the cells. The secretory cells in the inactive gland of *Leucophaea* (Dictyoptera) are stellate with processes at right angles to the periphery, but in the active gland the cell membranes tend to straighten out. The corpora allata show cycles of secretion associated with which are changes in size. As they get bigger nuclear division also increases, but even so the ratio of nuclear volume to cytoplasmic volume decreases. As the glands decrease in size the nuclei break down and the ratio of nuclear volume to cytoplasmic volume increases. It is not known if each cell only undergoes one cycle of activity before breaking down, but the cells are certainly short-lived.

The corpora allata produce juvenile hormone regulating metamorphosis (p. 704) and yolk deposition in the eggs (p. 708). The same or different hormones have a variety of other functions.

34.14 Prothoracic glands

The prothoracic, or thoracic, glands are a pair of diffuse glands at the back of the head or in the thorax (Fig. 474), but in Thysanura they are in the base of the labium. Each gland has a rich tracheal supply and often a nerve supply, but this is absent in some Heteroptera and Coleoptera.

The glands show cycles of development associated with secretion. At rest the nuclei are small and oval, but in the active gland they become enlarged and lobulated and the cell has more extensive and deeply staining cytoplasm. The numbers of mitochondria round the nucleus also increase and the endoplasmic reticulum becomes more extensive. At first intense RNA synthesis takes place in the nucleus and subsequently the RNA passes into the cytoplasm where protein synthesis occurs. This presumably reflects the production of enzymes engaged in the synthesis of ecdyson (p. 702). Towards the end of a cycle the nuclei become small again.

The prothoracic glands produce moulting hormone, ecdyson (p. 702) and, except in Thysanura, which moult as adults, and solitary locusts, the prothoracic glands break down soon after the final moult to adult.

34.15 Ring gland

In the larvae of cyclorrhaphous Diptera the ring gland surrounds the aorta just above the brain (Fig. 477). It is formed from the corpora allata, corpora cardiaca and prothoracic glands all fused together, although the component elements can still be identified. The ring gland is connected to the brain by a pair of nerves and it also has a connection with the recurrent nerve.

The larvae of Nematocera have completely separate endocrine glands, but larval Brachycera approach the cyclorrhaphan condition, although the corpus allatum tends to be separated from the rest as a single median lobe.

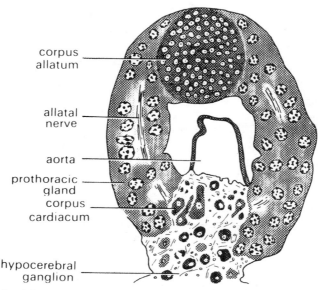

corpus
allatum

allatal
nerve

aorta

prothoracic
gland

corpus
cardiacum

hypocerebral
ganglion

Fig. 477. Ring gland from the early pupa of *Eristalis* (Diptera). Here the ring gland is fused with the hypocerebral ganglion, but this is not always the case (after Cazal, 1948).

34.2 Dispersal of hormones

Hormones produced in the neurosecretory cells pass along the axons of these cells as a result of the intra-axonal flow of cytoplasm or possibly along minute tubules which run the length of the axon. In this way the hormones may pass directly to their target organs or they may ultimately be released into the blood.

Direct transfer along the axons probably occurs in *Aphis* (Homoptera) (Fig. 478) where two large neurosecretory cells in the protocerebrum have extensive branching axons which pass to various parts of the body (B. Johnson, 1962, 1963). Similarly, neurosecretory axons pass from the corpora cardiaca of *Calliphora* and other insects to the pericardial cells and the control of the corpora allata and corpora cardiaca by the neurosecretory cells of the brain also involves the carriage of hormones along the axons of the cells.

Where the hormones are released into the blood specialised neurohaemal organs may or may not be involved. For instance, the corpora cardiaca serve for the release and sometimes for the storage of the brain hormone, and the position of these organs adjacent to the aorta may facilitate dispersal of the hormone. On the other hand, in *Nebria* (Coleoptera) some neurosecretory axons in the brain end near the front end of the aorta so that their secretions are dispersed without the intervention of the corpora cardiaca (Ganagarajah, 1965). Similarly in *Rhodnius* the diuretic hormone which is produced in neurosecretory cells of the ventral ganglion passes out along the axons and then is released into the blood via numerous short lateral branches. These branches are swollen terminally and end close beneath the nerve sheath which may be thinner at these points than elsewhere. The large number of endings facilitates the rapid release of the hormone (Maddrell, 1966b).

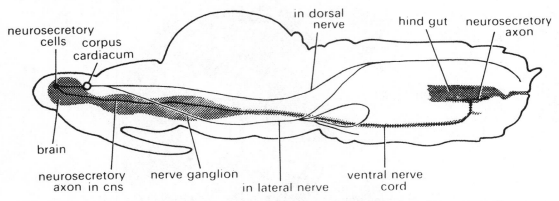

Fig. 478. Pathways of axons which carry neurosecretion from the brain and corpora cardiaca in the aphid *Drepanosiphum* (Homoptera) (after Johnson, 1962).

In *Calliphora* the areas at which the hormones are believed to be released into the blood or adjacent tissues resemble synapses (see p. 528). These areas have clusters of small vesicles and electron dense material close to the plasma membrane at points where the latter is separated from the blood only by a basement membrane or where it is adjacent to the plasma membrane of other cells. The vesicles are much smaller than the neurosecretory granules with which they are associated, and may be derived from them so that they contain the hormone. Such clusters of vesicles have been observed within and at the periphery of the corpus cardiacum, in the axons running from the corpus cardiacum to the corpus allatum and in axons in the wall of the heart. It is suggested that some of the release sites are permanent, while others are only transient (B. Johnson, 1966).

The mechanism of release of the hormone at these points is not understood. Axons of neurosecretory cells in some animals are known to conduct nerve impulses, and this probably also applies to insect neurosecretory cells. It is suggested that the arrival of a nerve impulse might lead to the release of any small vesicles containing the hormone which are adjacent to the plasma membrane in much the same way that an impulse in a typical nerve leads to the release of vesicles containing acetylcholine at the synapse (p. 533). Further, the action potential lasts for longer than in a typical nerve and this could allow more time for the escape of the hormone.

Smith and Smith (1966), however, believe that in the corpus cardiacum of *Carausius* the neurosecretion is released directly from the neurosecretory droplets or granules. These are bounded by a membrane and it is supposed that this membrane comes into contact and fuses with the plasma membrane of the cell so that the contents of the droplet are discharged into the extracellular space (Fig. 479).

Hormones from the prothoracic glands and corpora allata are produced in glandular cells and discharged directly into the blood.

Whitten (1964) suggests that some hormones may be transported from their organ of origin to the target organs or site of release in channels in the connective tissue membrane (p. 682). There are, for instance, channels in the basement membrane of the ring gland in larval *Sarcophaga* which connect with other channels in the connective tissue so that secretions are carried directly from the ring gland to the heart and so into the blood at a point where they are most readily dispersed.

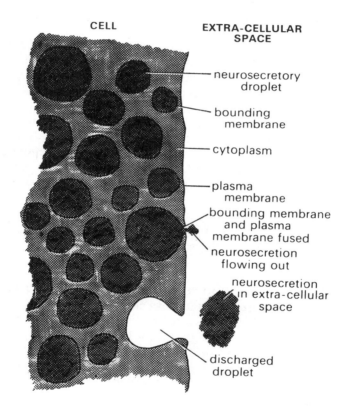

Fig. 479. Diagram showing the manner in which a neurosecretory droplet might discharge to the outside (based on Smith and Smith, 1966).

34.3 Mode of action of hormones

The manner in which hormones produce their effects is not well understood. Ecdyson (p. 702) rapidly accumulates in the nuclei of epidermal cells and it is probable that it acts directly on the nuclei. In the giant chromosomes of dipterous larvae characteristic swellings (puffs) occur which appear to indicate activity of particular genes. When the larva of *Chironomus* moults to a pupa a new puff appears on one chromosome and another disappears. The injection of ecdyson into a larva between moults has the same effect, the first puff appearing within about 15 minutes of the injection and reaching a maximum in about two hours. A little later a second puff forms and two or three days later another characteristic pattern of puffs appears. This suggests that the changing biochemical activities in cells at the time of moulting may be caused by the differential activation or suppression of different sets of genes by the ecdyson (Beermann and Clever, 1964; Gilbert and Schneiderman, 1961).

Under normal conditions the genes are not actively producing RNA because their activity is inhibited by repressors, possibly the histone with which the DNA of the gene is associated. The effect of the hormone is to free the gene from this repression so that specific messenger RNA is produced. This passes into the cytoplasm and protein synthesis follows.

The freeing of the gene from repression may result from the direct action of the hormone with the repressor or it may result indirectly from a change in the environment within the nucleus. Possibly the hormone modifies the activity of the sodium pump which controls the sodium/potassium ratio in the nucleoplasm and the change in puffing pattern is a response to the altered ratio.

Not all the gene activity which follows the activity of ecdyson results from such direct action, however. Some of the puffs which appear later in the puffing pattern are not specific to the moulting periods and the activity of these genes depends on the protein synthesis which follows the activation of the first genes (Clever, 1965; Karlson and Sekeris, 1966; Kroeger and Lezzi, 1966). The following sequence of events is thus suggested:—

$$\text{Ecdyson} \rightarrow ? \rightarrow \begin{array}{c}\text{Activation of}\\\text{specific genes}\end{array} \rightarrow \text{mRNA} \rightarrow \begin{array}{c}\text{Protein}\\\text{synthesis}\end{array} \rightarrow ? \rightarrow \begin{array}{c}\text{Further}\\\text{genes}\\\text{activated}\end{array}$$

Juvenile hormone is also known to act at the cellular level and since the quantity present is important it is suggested that it plays some quantitative part in metabolism. The enzyme system in the cell must assume one set of properties in the presence of juvenile hormone, leading to the development of larval characters, and another set of properties in its absence, resulting in the development of adult characters. Wigglesworth (1957b) suggests that the juvenile hormone may be a coenzyme which favours the activity of the enzymes for larval development or it may selectively affect permeability so that the enzymes responsible for larval characters are brought into action. Alternatively, it is possible that the juvenile hormone acts directly on the nucleus, modifying the effect of ecdyson. This is suggested by the fact that in the larval moults of *Chironomus* the first two chromosomal puffs observed are the same as those occurring at the larva/pupa moult, but the later puffs are quite different (Clever, 1965).

Whether or not the hormones act via the genes their effect is often, if not always, to promote the synthesis or activity of proteins. Ecdyson, for instance, initiates the *de novo* synthesis of DOPAdecarboxylase and also activates the enzyme which catalyses the synthesis of a phenol oxidase from its proenzyme. Thus essential enzymes for tanning the cuticle are made available (Karlson, 1963). In other cases hormones appear to be directly concerned with the activation of phosphorylases.

34.4 Structure of hormones

The brain hormone is believed to be a lipid by some authorities, while others believe it to be a peptide (see Gilbert, 1964). The neurosecretion of vertebrates is a polypeptide together with a large protein molecule which acts as a carrier.

Ecdyson is a steroid with the formula:

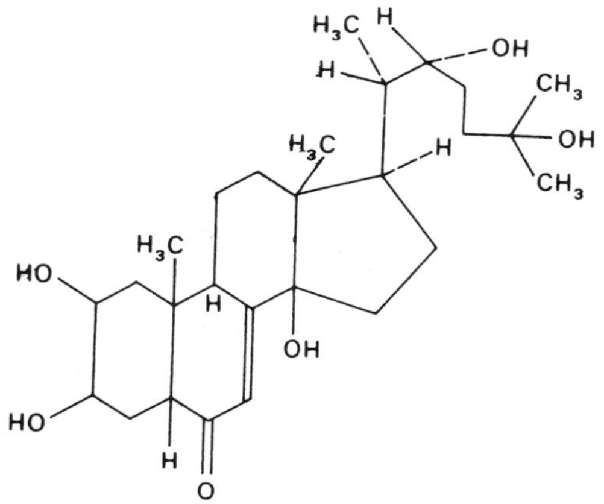

The ecdyson extracted from *Bombyx* can be separated into five different fractions each of which is active in promoting moulting. Insects are unable to synthesise steroids (p.73) and ecdyson is probably derived from cholesterol or some related steroid obtained with the diet.

Juvenile hormone is probably a nonsterolic lipid. Various substances are known which produce the same effects as juvenile hormone, the best known being the terpene farnesol. This is present in insects, and it seems likely that the juvenile hormone is farnesol or a derivative of it.

34.5 Hormones and their functions

Insect hormones are at present receiving a great deal of attention by many workers so that this study is in a state of flux and is correspondingly complex. The following account is consequently extremely simplified and selective.

34.51 Growth and moulting

Growth in insects is largely limited by the rigid cuticle which must be shed from time to time if continued growth is to occur. Hence growth and moulting must be very closely related and will be considered together.

Before a moult the epidermal cells and cells in certain other tissues, such as the sternal intersegmental muscles of *Rhodnius*, become active. Their nucleoli enlarge, RNA in the cytoplasm increases and the mitochondria increase in size and number. These changes are produced and co-ordinated throughout the body by a hormone which at the same time activates the cells so that they are ready to divide. Whether or not they do then divide depends on the environment of the cells; the hormone does not cause the cells to divide.

Much of the work in this field has been carried out on the blood-sucking bug *Rhodnius* (Wigglesworth, 1954b, 1957b, 1959b). This insect normally takes only a single large blood meal in each instar which results in very great distension of the abdomen. The changes described above start in the cells within six hours of feeding, and moulting follows about 15 days later.

The changes are initiated by a secretion from the median neurosecretory cells which passes to the corpora cardiaca and then is liberated into the blood. The secretion stimulates the prothoracic glands to produce the moulting hormone, ecdyson, which initiates changes in the cells concerned with ecdysis (Fig. 480). The brain factor does not have a

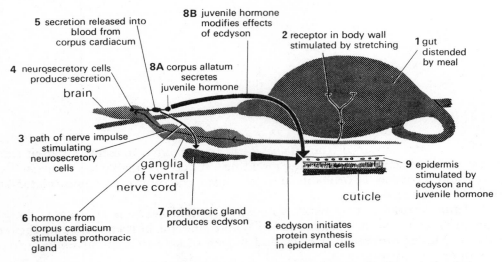

Fig. 480. Diagrammatic representation of the sequence of events leading to stimulation of the epidermis and moulting in *Rhodnius*. At the final moult to adult, juvenile hormone (stages 8A and 8B) would be absent.

simple triggering effect on the prothoracic glands, but its continuous presence is necessary for two-and-a-half to three days for the continued activity of these glands and it is possible that it is contributing some essential component to the ecdyson. The period for which the brain hormone is necessary is known as the critical period and its removal during this period, as by decapitation, results in a failure to moult. Decapitation after the critical period does not inhibit moulting. An essentially similar sequence of events occurs in other insects.

In *Rhodnius*, the initial secretion of the brain factor is caused by the distension of the abdomen which results from feeding. The distension stimulates receptors in the wall of the abdomen and these stimulate the neurosecretory cells via the nerve cord. At the same time impulses, at the rate of about three per second, pass down the previously silent nerves to the corpora cardiaca, possibly leading to the release of neurosecretory material.

In other insects which feed continuously the position appears to be rather different. In *Locusta*, for instance, stretch receptors in the pharyngeal wall are stimulated during feeding and lead to the release of the brain hormone. This occurs throughout the instar, but production of the moulting hormone is not initiated, possibly because the prothoracic glands are relatively insensitive and because the brain hormone is utilised in metabolic processes. Towards the end of the instar the insect stops feeding but movements of the foregut continue due first to its emptying and then, as the time of the moult approaches, to the swallowing of air. Hence there is a continued release of neurosecretion, but the hypothesis suggests that this is not now utilised in metabolising the products of digestion since feeding has stopped. Hence the brain hormone accumulates and reaches a concentration high enough to stimulate the prothoracic glands so that a moult is induced (Clarke and Langley, 1963; and see Schneiderman and Gilbert, 1964). It does not follow from these examples that stretch receptors are necessarily always involved in activating the median neurosecretory cells.

Apart from Thysanura, adult insects do not moult and the prothoracic glands degenerate. In *Rhodnius* degeneration starts within 24 hours of the final moult and is complete within 48 hours. In other insects the process takes rather longer. At the time of moulting to the adult stage the gland receives some hormonal stimulus causing it to degenerate, but this stimulus is only effective if the gland has passed through a moulting cycle in the absence of the juvenile hormone (see p. 704). In other words the gland itself must undergo some sort of metamorphosis.

34.52 Diapause

The failure of growth in the absence of hormones is suggestive of diapause and diapause may, in fact, result from the failure of the endocrine activity of the brain. The moth *Hyalophora* has a pupal diapause which results from the failure of the median neurosecretory cells to release secretion so that no ecdyson is produced by the prothoracic glands. Injection of ecdyson leads to a resumption of growth and the emergence of the adult moth.

The lime hawk moth, *Mimas*, has a pupal diapause controlled by the prothoracic glands in the same way as *Hyalophora*, but in this species the corpora allata are active during the first three weeks of diapause. Highnam (1958b) suggests that during this period the corpora allata are secreting a hormone inducing diapause and other authors believe that diapause in various larval insects is actively maintained by the presence of a hormone secreted by the corpora allata, this hormone perhaps inhibiting the secretion of the brain hormone (see *e.g.* Gilbert, 1964).

Diapause is not always dependent on the absence of brain hormone. The diapause in the egg of the bivoltine race of *Bombyx* depends on the temperature and light conditions during the incubation of the eggs of the previous generation (see p. 721). These conditions, acting via the brain, stimulate or inhibit the neurosecretory cells in the suboesophageal ganglion of the parent female. If the cells are stimulated they produce a hormone which is released into the blood and acts on the eggs in the ovary so that when they are laid they undergo diapause. One of the effects of the hormone is to facilitate the passage of blood sugars into the ovaries so that diapausing eggs have a greater reserve of glycogen than nondiapausing eggs (Hasegawa and Yamashita, 1965). In the absence of the hormone nondiapause eggs are laid.

Diapause in adult insects manifests itself in a failure to mature. This results from the inactivity of the corpora allata which are normally responsible for maturation (p. 708).

34.53 Metamorphosis

When a hemimetabolous insect moults it may moult to another, essentially similar larval form or it may undergo a more complete change in body form, usually associated with the development of wings, to become the adult insect. Wigglesworth (1961) regards the progressive development of larval characters and the final metamorphosis to adult as two distinct types of differentiation. The first only takes place in the presence of the juvenile hormone which is normally secreted throughout all the larval instars except the last and which is responsible for the retention of larval characters. Differentiation of larval characters occurs at a certain rate so that the changes occurring at successive moults are controlled by the timing and quantity of moulting hormone secreted.

Other authors regard the stages of development as resulting from a progressive reduction in the concentration of juvenile hormone. Although the corpora allata increase in size throughout larval development they do so more slowly than the body as a whole and this suggests that the concentration of juvenile hormone will be much lower in later larval instars than in the early instars. For a consideration of this point of view see Novák (1966).

Metamorphosis to the adult is fundamentally different from larval development in that, according to Wigglesworth, the moult takes place in the absence of juvenile hormone. It is thus believed that the effect of juvenile hormone is to modify the reaction of the target cells to the moulting hormone. Probably in its presence one set of genes, giving rise to larval characters, is activated, while in its absence a second set, producing adult characters, is activated. The juvenile hormone by itself has no effect.

In holometabolous insects the position is believed to be similar except that an intermediate concentration of juvenile hormone leads to the activation of a third group of genes which produce pupal characteristics.

The final moult to the adult takes place in the absence of any juvenile hormone, but it is not known why the corpora allata do not produce hormone at this time. They are not autonomous since it can be shown experimentally that they do not produce juvenile hormone for a definite number of moults and then stop. Adult corpora allata also produce juvenile hormone and it is only during the last larval instar that none is produced. It is suggested that the nervous system exerts a restraining influence on the corpora allata, while at other times they are stimulated by a neurosecretion from the brain (see Wigglesworth, 1964).

Novák (1966), on the other hand, believes that the juvenile hormone is never completely absent, but that the larval tissues only grow when the concentration of juvenile hormone exceeds a certain value. The corpora allata undergo cycles of development in each instar and, because of their progressive decrease in relative size (see above), the critical concentration is reached progressively later in each instar. This allows more time for the development of the adult tissues, which Novák believes grow in the absence of juvenile hormone, but less time for the growth of larval tissues. Finally a stage is reached in which the concentration of hormone does not reach the critical level so that only adult tissues develop, and at the next moult metamorphosis occurs. On this hypothesis the corpora allata do not stop producing juvenile hormone in the last larval instar and there is some experimental evidence in support of this point of view.

If the corpora allata are removed during the critical period so that they do not produce any juvenile hormone an insect will undergo a precocious metamorphosis at the next moult. The degree of perfection of the adult structures formed depends to some extent on the competence of the tissues to produce them at this time. Some organs, such as the genitalia, may be well developed, but in *Rhodnius* the wings are not well formed in a precocious adult because they contain too few cells to produce the extensive wings of the adult. Other organs vary in their ability to form precocious adult structures.

34.54 Polymorphism

Wigglesworth suggests that larva, pupa and adult represent different forms of a polymorphic organism, and that polymorphism in adult insects may be similarly determined by differences in hormone balance.

Imbalance of the hormones can arise in two ways. Either the influence of the juvenile hormone may be excessive, in which case juvenile characters will persist in the adult (metathetely or neoteny) or the influence of the juvenile hormone may be depressed, leading to a precocious development of adult characters in the larva (prothetely or paedogenesis). Metathetely in particular often results in the failure of the wings to develop fully and brachypterous adults are formed. This is the case in *Gryllus campestris* (Orthoptera) where the short wings are the result of a slight predominance of juvenile hormone in the later stages. Experimental adjustment of the hormone balance in favour of ecdyson leads to the development of fully winged forms. Conversely in *Locusta* (Orthoptera) prothetely may occasionally occur, a fourth instar larva developing incomplete adult characters and becoming sexually mature.

The hormone balance may be disturbed by a variety of external factors. In aphids winged and wingless forms, alatae and apterae, occur, the wingless forms being more juvenile in appearance with less sclerotisation of the thorax and fewer sense organs on the antennae. This appearance and the lack of wings is the result of an excess of juvenile hormone. In *Megoura* the activity of the corpora allata is regulated in the late embryo, and this determines the type of development which will follow. If the parent is in a crowd a hormone from her head activates the corpora allata of the embryo so that no wings develop, but if the parent is isolated the embryonic corpora allata are not activated and the offspring develops wings. In other species, such as *Macrosiphum* and *Aphis*, winglessness is determined later, crowding or isolating the early instars having a direct effect on wing development (Lees, 1966, 1967).

Wigglesworth found that low temperature upsets the hormone balance slightly in favour of the juvenile hormone whereas high temperature slightly favours ecdyson. If *Rhodnius* is bred at low temperatures it is slightly neotenous whereas at high temperatures it exhibits slight prothetely. Southwood (1961) has suggested that brachyptery in Heteroptera may arise from breeding at relatively low temperatures. This could be true of montane forms, since temperature is lower at higher altitudes, and in the first generation of bivoltine species, where this generation is subjected to lower temperatures during its development than is the second. On the other hand *Dolichonabis limbatus* has only four larval instars whereas most Heteroptera have five and Southwood suggests that in this case brachyptery arises as a result of prothetely.

Termite castes

Caste determination in termites is more complex, but is similarly under hormonal control with the juvenile hormone probably playing an important part (Lüscher, 1960). In a colony of *Kalotermes* a number of different forms occur:— larvae of various instars, pseudergates (a larval form functionally equivalent to the worker caste in other species), nymphs (the conventional term for termite larvae with obvious wing buds), white- or pre-soldiers, soldiers and a king and queen, the only reproductive stages. In the absence of the king or queen replacement reproductives develop and at certain seasons immature, winged reproductives (imagos) are produced. The relationships of these forms are shown in figure 481. The pseudergate is a central form from which various others can

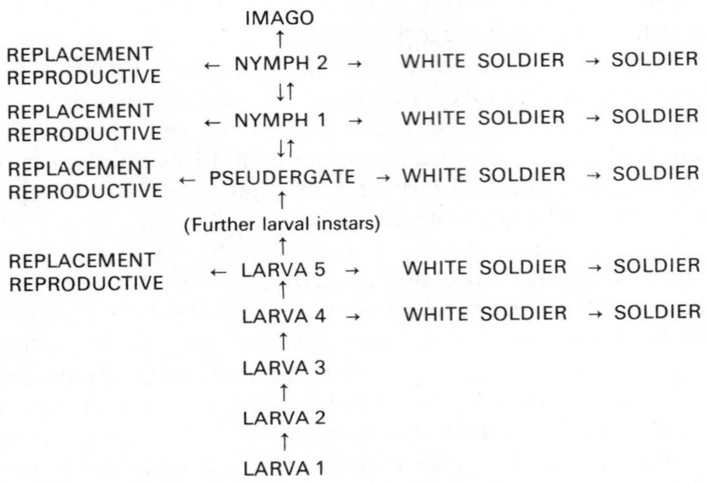

```
                                    IMAGO
                                      ↑
   REPLACEMENT              ←  NYMPH 2  →      WHITE SOLDIER  → SOLDIER
   REPRODUCTIVE                     ↓↑
   REPLACEMENT              ←  NYMPH 1  →      WHITE SOLDIER  → SOLDIER
   REPRODUCTIVE                     ↓↑
   REPLACEMENT              ←  PSEUDERGATE →  WHITE SOLDIER  → SOLDIER
   REPRODUCTIVE                     ↑
                            (Further larval instars)
                                    ↑
   REPLACEMENT              ←  LARVA 5  →      WHITE SOLDIER  → SOLDIER
   REPRODUCTIVE                     ↑
                               LARVA 4  →      WHITE SOLDIER  → SOLDIER
                                    ↑
                               LARVA 3
                                    ↑
                               LARVA 2
                                    ↑
                               LARVA 1
```

Fig. 481. The course of development of *Kalotermes flavicollis* (after Lüscher, 1960).

be derived and which can also undergo stationary moults, retaining its form. Nymphs may undergo regressive moults, changing back into pseudergates.

The development of the various castes is controlled so as to meet the needs of the colony by a series of pheromones (p. 745) produced by the reproductive and soldier castes. The pheromones act via the endocrine system and Lüscher supposes that they inhibit secretion by the brain neurosecretory cells. In the absence of pheromones the neurosecretory cells activate the prothoracic glands so that the insect moults. The result of this moult depends in part on the existing stage of development and in part on the timing of the moult relative to the secretory cycle of the corpora allata.

The corpora allata are presumed to show two peaks of secretion during a cycle (Fig. 482), the first bringing the insect into a state of competence to differentiate and the second leading to the retention of more juvenile characters in the usual manner of the juvenile hormone. In the complete absence of pheromone due to the absence of the king and queen the neurosecretory cells of a pseudergate become active and ecdyson is secreted at an early stage during the first phase of corpus allatum activity. This leads to the secretion of a gonadotropic hormone, supposedly distinct from juvenile hormone, with the result that the pseudergate moults to a replacement reproductive (Fig. 482B). Under more normal conditions in the presence of the king and queen the pseudergate might receive some gonadotropic hormone from them in the course of trophallaxis.

If this occurs during the first phase of activity of the corpora allata these glands stop producing juvenile hormone and produce gonadotropic hormone instead. At the next moult a white soldier is produced (Fig. 482C).

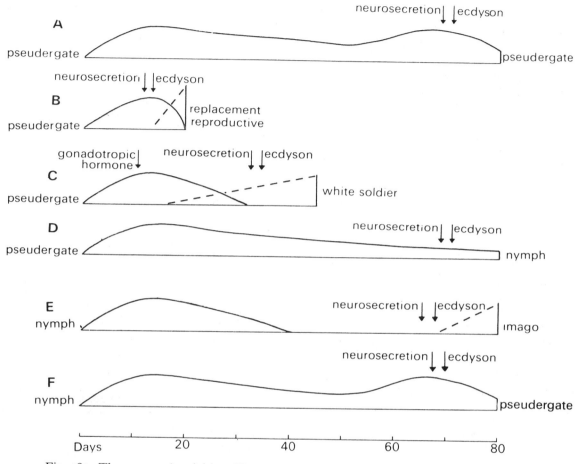

Fig. 482. The supposed activities of hormones in caste differentiation in *Kalotermes*. The continuous curves represent the juvenile hormone titre; the broken lines indicate production of gonadotropic hormone by the corpora allata (after Lüscher, 1960).

If, in the presence of the king and queen, the pseudergate does not receive any gonadotropic hormone its development at the moult depends on the amount of juvenile hormone produced during the second cycle of activity and this is related to nutrition. In the presence of abundant food the amount of juvenile hormone produced is reduced and the pseudergate moults to a nymph (Fig. 482D), but if food is scarce the corpora allata become active and the insect undergoes a stationary moult to another pseudergate (Fig. 482A). The moulting of nymphs is controlled in a similar way. With abundant food corpus allatum activity is completely suppressed and the insect becomes a winged imago (Fig. 482E), but with little food a good deal of juvenile hormone is produced and the insect may undergo a regressive moult back to pseudergate (Fig. 482F).

Locust phases

As a final instance of hormonal control of polymorphism locust phases may be considered. Locusts have two extreme phases, *solitaria* and *gregaria,* whose differences arise as a result of differences in nervous stimulation which in turn affect the endocrine system. Kennedy (1956) suggests that the solitary locust is a more juvenile form and this suggestion is supported by the persistence of the prothoracic glands in the adult solitary locust, but not in adults of the gregarious phase. The corpora allata are also larger in mature solitary than in gregarious locusts (Carlisle and Ellis, 1962) and these glands, together with the prothoracic glands, promote the development of the green colour and the morphometrics which are characteristic of solitary locusts (p. 711).

It is clear from these examples, although they are not yet fully understood, that polymorphism in insects is sometimes controlled in the same way as normal metamorphosis by differences in the balance between the moulting and the juvenile hormones.

34.55 Maturation of oocytes

In most insects the corpora allata play an important part in controlling normal oocyte development. Generally the corpora allata are activated by a secretion from the median neurosecretory cells and the hormone which they release results in the laying down of yolk in the oocytes. Various stimuli acting via the nervous system control secretion by the median neurosecretory cells so that the corpora allata only become active when such factors as daylength, temperature and the state of nutrition of the insect are suitable. In *Schistocerca* the neurosecretory cells are stimulated by copulation, by the male pheromone (p. 741) or simply by enforced activity. In *Aedes* (Diptera) distension of the gut as a result of feeding acts as a stimulus. Sometimes, however, the activity of the corpora allata is restrained (see below) and in the viviparous cockroaches the removal of this restraint, as by cutting the nerves to the corpora allata, is sufficient to induce secretion. Nevertheless, stimulation of the corpora allata is necessary for them to become fully effective.

The effect of the corpus allatum hormone is not simply to promote protein development in the haemolymph and so make it available for yolk formation. In *Schistocerca* females from which the corpora allata have been removed, no yolk formation occurs although there is ample protein in the haemolymph. This suggests that the corpus allatum hormone acts directly on the oocyte or the follicle cells controlling the movement of protein into the oocyte.

In *Calliphora* and *Schistocerca* the median neurosecretory cells are not only concerned with the control of the corpora allata, but the hormone they produce is essential for protein synthesis. This is not true in all insects, however, since normal development of the oocytes of *Rhodnius* occurs even if these cells are extirpated.

As the deposition of yolk proceeds the corpora allata become inactive again. This is necessary since otherwise the second series of oocytes would start to mature before the first was laid. It is not known what controls these changes in activity of the corpora allata. In *Iphita* (Heteroptera) it is possible that they are inhibited by a hormone from the fully developed oocytes, but in other species this does not occur and the neurosecretory cells, which control the corpora allata, are probably restrained by the nervous system.

In *Diploptera* and some other cockroaches the eggs are retained in the uterus during the period of embryonic development. The wall of the brood sac is stretched by the ootheca and receptors in the wall are stimulated. These act via the central nervous system to inhibit the corpora allata so that no hormone is produced and no more oocytes mature. During gestation the receptors in the wall of the brood sac or the central nervous system itself slowly become adapted to the stimulation by the ootheca so that by the time of parturition the inhibition of the corpora allata has been almost completely lifted and more oocytes start to mature. In this way cycles of development of the oocytes are produced at the shortest possible intervals (Fig. 483).

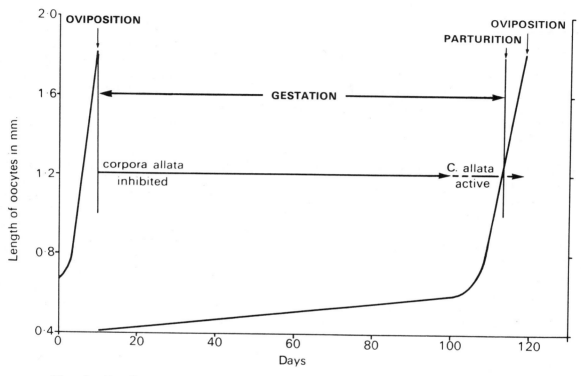

Fig. 483. Development of the oocytes in *Diploptera*, a viviparous cockroach (after Roth and Stay, 1961).

It is probable that the hormone concerned in the control of oocyte development is the same as the juvenile hormone. Only in the caste determination of *Kalotermes* do two separate hormones appear to be necessary to account for the observed development (p. 706), but even in this case it is possible that only differences in the concentration of a single hormone are involved (Wigglesworth, 1964).

The humoral control of oocyte development provides a means of gearing egg production to suitable environmental conditions, but in Phasmida and adult Lepidoptera the corpora allata are not important in this respect. *Carausius* is parthenogenetic and feeding and egg production are continuous so that perhaps there is no need for humoral regulation. The Lepidoptera which have so far been studied are species in which the eggs are all produced in one batch, being laid down during pupal development and it is suggested that in these the ovaries are rendered competent to develop while they are still influenced by juvenile hormone in the larva and early pupa. It may be that in other species of Lepidoptera in which the eggs are produced in the adult the corpora allata play a part comparable with that in other insects.

34.56 Other functions of hormones

Metabolism

The action of hormones is often associated with a rise in oxygen consumption due to increased synthesis and possibly in some cases to a direct effect on oxidative phosphorylation. The corpus allatum hormone often has a stimulating effect on basal metabolism and in *Leptinotarsa* (Coleoptera) allatectomy results in disintegration of the flight muscle sarcosomes. It is also believed that the effect of the moulting hormone may be to stimulate specific protein metabolism (p. 700) and in some cases hormones are known to affect protein metabolism directly. In *Calliphora* and larval *Tenebrio* (Coleoptera) there is an increase in protease activity in the midgut after feeding, the production of protease being directly influenced by a hormone from the median neurosecretory cells of the brain (Thomsen and Møller, 1963). The hormone is released by the ingestion of protein and its effect is to increase the digestion of protein and so facilitate further protein metabolism.

In *Schistocerca* a hormone from the median neurosecretory cells, released via the corpora cardiaca, controls the level of protein in the haemolymph. In the presence of the hormone proteins are produced from the amino acids in the blood and the protein concentration rises; in the absence of the hormone the protein concentration falls (Hill, 1962). Clarke and Gillott (1967a, b) show that in *Locusta* some protein synthesis occurs even in the absence of the hormone and they suggest that the genes concerned in the control of protein synthesis are normally active although largely inhibited by feed-back from their metabolic products. Release of the hormone from the corpora cardiaca suppresses this inhibition so that synthesis occurs at a much higher rate.

Colour and colour change

Locust nymphs exist in a green or yellow solitary form with relatively little superimposed pattern, and a gregarious form with a yellow background and extensive black patterning. Nickerson (1956) postulates that the colour is governed by two hormones, one responsible for the background colour, producing green when in high concentration and yellow when in low concentration, and the other responsible for the pattern, the amount of black pigment increasing with the concentration of hormone. Hence the green solitary form results from a high titre of background hormone and a low titre of pattern hormone; the gregarious form results from a decrease of the former and an increase of the latter (Fig. 484).

It has been shown that the corpora allata and prothoracic glands are concerned in these colour differences (Ellis and Carlisle, 1961; Carlisle and Ellis, 1962). For instance, removal of part of the prothoracic gland from a green fourth instar solitary larva results in a fifth instar larva with extensive areas of black over a yellow/cream background. This suggests that the prothoracic gland governs pigment metabolism and controls changes in balance with another hormone as suggested above.

Other insects show environmental differences. For instance the larvae of *Acrida* (Orthoptera) are green in a damp environment, but brown in a dry habitat. These differences are controlled by the corpora allata.

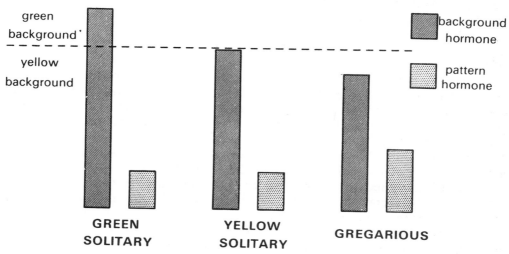

Fig. 484. Supposed concentrations of hormones controlling colour in different types of locust larvae (after Nickerson, 1956).

Physiological colour change (p. 117) may also be due to hormonal activity. Brown specimens of the stick insect, *Carausius* (Phasmida), become black at night, resuming their brown colour in daylight. The change results from movements of pigment granules in the epidermal cells and in particular from the movement of large brown-black granules. In the light these granules are concentrated in the lower parts of the cells, in the dark they move up close to the surface above the yellow-orange pigment in the middle of the cell (Fig. 485). This causes the insect to get darker. These changes are

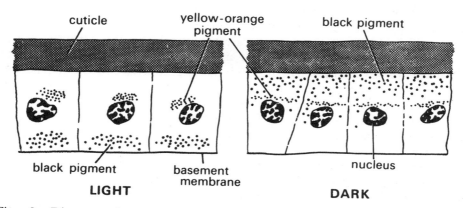

Fig. 485. Diagrammatic representations of the distribution of yellow-orange and black pigments in the epidermis of *Carausius* in the light and in the dark (after Dupont-Raabe, 1957).

controlled by a secretion from neurosecretory cells in the tritocerebrum which passes back along the nerve cord to be liberated into the haemolymph. Most of the secretion is liberated at the suboesophageal ganglion. The corpora cardiaca also release a substance causing moderate pigment migration with the development of intermediate colouration. This substance is probably derived from the brain secretion (Dupont-Raabe, 1957).

Water balance

There is some evidence that the excretion of water is controlled by a hormone. Immediately after a blood meal *Rhodnius* excretes a large amount of water so that the food is concentrated and Maddrell (1962) found that the excretory activity of the Malpighian tubules was controlled directly by a hormone coming from the mesothoracic ganglionic mass. Diuresis begins within three minutes of the onset of feeding and the rapid transport of the hormone necessary to facilitate this is produced by an increased rate of blood circulation due to strong contractions of the gut.

A diuretic hormone regulating water content is produced in the brain of *Anisotarsus* (Coleoptera). Its secretion is stimulated via the central nerve cord and there may be sense organs in the abdominal ganglia sensitive to the water content of the haemolymph. There is also some evidence for a diuretic hormone being produced by the neurosecretory cells in *Iphita*, *Blaberus*, *Periplaneta*, *Carausius* and *Schistocerca*, although it is possible that this effect is only apparent, resulting from hormonal effects on other metabolic processes (Highnam, *et al.*, 1965).

There is also some evidence for an antidiuretic hormone in some insects. Thus in *Schistocerca* some of the neurosecretory cells in the abdominal ganglia discharge their secretions under conditions of water loss (Delphin, 1965) and antidiuretic hormones are also reported from *Iphita*, *Periplaneta* and *Blaberus*.

The release of the diuretic hormone in *Rhodnius*, *Anisotarsus* and *Periplaneta* appears to be controlled by sensory information received from the abdomen (Maddrell, 1966b).

Nervous activity and behaviour

There is some evidence that hormones affect the level of spontaneous discharge in the central nervous system. Spontaneous discharges occur in the isolated nerve cord of *Periplaneta*, but an extract of the corpora cardiaca reduces this activity. In the whole animal the extract reduces co-ordination and results in more stereotyped locomotory behaviour (Ozbas and Hodgson, 1958). Similarly receptivity of the female cockroach (p. 302) is probably controlled by the neurosecretory cells of the brain, their secretion presumably acting via the nervous system (Roth, 1964).

In *Schistocerca*, on the other hand, allatectomy reduces activity and it is possible that the corpora allata normally regulate the nervous system so that various aspects of behaviour are affected (Odhiambo, 1966). Haskell and Moorhouse (1963) suggest that the relative inactivity of solitary locusts may also be due to hormone activity. Ecdyson increases the spontaneous discharge in the central nervous system, but reduces the discharge in the motor nerves and an extract of the prothoracic glands injected into gregarious locusts reduces their activity. This supports the suggestion that the main differences between the phases are due to differences in the way in which information is utilised in the central nervous system as a result of differences in hormone balance. Hormone balance is itself influenced by sensory input acting on centres in the brain.

Diurnal rhythms of activity

Many insects show recurrent temporal patterns of activity. Thus, *Schistocerca* is active during daylight and almost completely inactive at night, while, conversely, many insects are wholly nocturnal in their flight activity (Lewis and Taylor, 1965). *Periplaneta* normally becomes fully active just after it gets dark, but the stimulus promoting activity is not simply the change from light to dark because the insect shows an increase in activity just before it gets dark (Fig. 486).

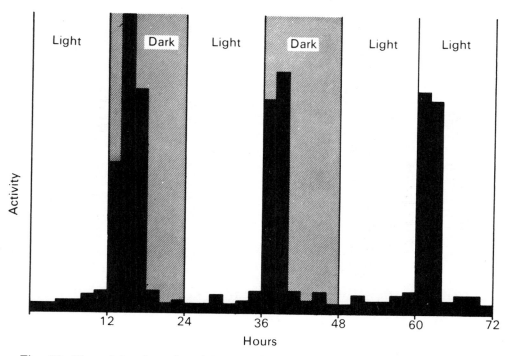

Fig. 486. The activity of a cockroach in alternating light and darkness and then in continuous light (modified after Harker, 1960).

In some insects, as in *Schistocerca*, the periodicity of activity disappears if the insect is kept in constant light or darkness (Odhiambo, 1966); such periodicity is clearly controlled directly by exogenous environmental factors. In other cases, as in *Periplaneta*, activity continues to occur rhythmically even under constant environmental conditions (Fig. 486): it is controlled endogenously and, since bursts of activity commonly occur at roughly 24-hour intervals, the insects are said to exhibit a circadian rhythm. Under field conditions any periodicity of activity will be the result of interaction between exogenous and endogenous factors.

The timing of activity in an endogenous rhythm is determined initially by an environmental stimulus, often the change from light to dark, as in the activity rhythm of *Periplaneta* and the oviposition rhythm of *Aedes*. Populations of *Drosophila* have a rhythm of emergence from the puparium and here a flash of light of only 0·005 seconds is sufficient to set the timing of emergence, although normally, of course, the light period is much more prolonged. The compound eyes are of the greatest importance in perceiving the phase-setting light stimulus.

If the light conditions are constant, a change in temperature will determine phase setting and presumably, in the field, light, temperature and other factors interact. It is, however, significant that, once entrained, the circadian periodicity of activity is virtually independent of temperature.

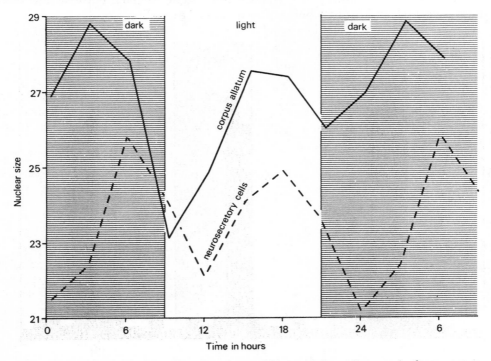

Fig. 487. Changes in the nuclear sizes (sum of long and short diameters) of neurosecretory cells in the pars intercerebralis and corpus allatum cells of *Drosophila* in relation to photoperiod (after Rensing, 1964).

There has been considerable controversy concerning the mechanism by which persistent rhythmic activity is regulated (see Brady, 1969, *Nature, Lond.* **223**). Earlier evidence appeared to indicate that the internal clock mechanism resided in neurosecretory cells and that information was conveyed to other parts of the body by hormones (Harker, 1964). Subsequent workers were not able to repeat this work (see Brady, 1967a, 1967b; Roberts, 1966), and later evidence suggests that neurons in the optic lobes are of primary importance and that information is transmitted electrically via the nervous system (Nishiitsutsuji-Uwo and Pittendrigh, 1968, *Z. vergl. Physiol.* **58**). Rhythms of activity of neurosecretory cells do occur (Fig. 487) (Rensing, 1964, *Science, N.Y.* **144**), but these cells are not the primary oscillators.

Corbet (1966, *Symp. R. ent. Soc. Lond.* **3**) considers that endogenous rhythms of activity are to be regarded as adaptations to tropical conditions where the physical factors of the environment are predictable and remain suitable for long periods each day. By limiting activity to certain periods of the day, rhythms can reduce interspecific competition. Further from the equator, however, the weather is less predictable and may impose severe limits on activity. Here the necessity of making maximum use of suitable periods of weather is overriding; opportunism becomes dominant and endogenous rhythms of activity will tend not to occur.

34.57 Sex hormones

There is no evidence that the gonads of insects produce hormones which affect the secondary sexual characters (Novák, 1966), but there are a few instances in which a hormone from the gonads appears to influence behaviour or some physiological process. For instance, ovariectomy of female grasshoppers leads to a failure to respond to male singing, but the response reappears following the injection of blood from a normal female. Presumably a factor in the blood produced by the ovaries is responsible for this. The behaviour of male grasshoppers, however, is not affected by castration (Haskell, 1960a).

There is also evidence in a few insects for a type of sex hormone controlling the corpora allata (p. 708). In *Iphita* this comes from mature oocytes and in *Leucophaea* from the ootheca, in both cases indirectly depressing the activity of the corpora allata so that further oocyte production is inhibited.

34.58 Hormones in embryogenesis

In the embryo of *Locustana* (Orthoptera) the embryonic moult (p. 362) is controlled in the same way as a normal moult by the neurosecretory cells and prothoracic glands, but active cell division occurs in the epidermis before the prothoracic glands are fully developed. Because of this B. M. Jones (1956a) suggests that the hormone from the prothoracic glands is only concerned with the retraction of the epidermis from the cuticle, but subsequently its presence is necessary for further development and cell differentiation (but see p. 367). The same hormone stimulates the pleuropodia to produce the enzymes which digest the serosal cuticle before eclosion (B. M. Jones, 1956b).

In the embryo of *Periplaneta* neurosecretory cells first appear in the brain about 12 days before eclosion. Subsequently neurosecretion accumulates in the cells and then is lost before eclosion. A similar cycle occurs in the corpora cardiaca, but in the corpora allata the accumulation of neurosecretory material is maximal at eclosion and then declines in the newly hatched larva. There is thus a phase of neurosecretion before eclosion suggesting some similarity between eclosion and moulting (Khan and Fraser, 1962).

34.6 The rabbit flea and hormones

The ovaries of the rabbit flea, *Spilopsyllus cuniculi*, only mature if the insect feeds on a pregnant female rabbit or a nestling rabbit less than a week old. In fleas feeding on rabbits in other stages, development of the ovaries does not occur. This effect is due to several of the host hormones produced during pregnancy acting directly on the flea. The most important of these hormones are the corticosteroids from the adrenal glands. Apart from maturation of the ovaries, the salivary gland and alimentary canal enlarge and the rate of defaecation increases, indicating an increase in feeding. The male is also affected, although the production of sperm is not controlled by the host hormones.

Fleas tend to mass on a pregnant doe rabbit and do not readily detach or move to another host, but a few hours after the young rabbits are born the fleas become active and move on to the young ones. This activity is probably initiated by a change in the hormonal balance of the female rabbit. On the young rabbits, which also have a high level of corticosteroid in the blood, feeding and copulation occur and the fleas leave the host to lay eggs in the nest which is fouled by the blood defaecated by the parent fleas. This blood provides an important source of food for the larvae. As the level of hormone in the host blood declines the fleas stop laying eggs and the ovaries regress until another pregnant host is found (Rothschild, 1965).

Mead-Briggs (1964) suggests that the rabbit hormones lead to the release of hormone from the median neurosecretory cells in the brain of the flea. This activates the corpora allata and so leads to the laying down of yolk in the oocytes, while at the same time enzyme activity is stimulated so that more metabolites are available for vitellogenesis.

CHAPTER XXXV

DIAPAUSE

One of the major functions of insect hormones is the control of morphogenesis and if their production is retarded prolonged delays in development result. During such delays the insect, or its reproductive system, remains dormant, and this type of dormancy, which is known as diapause, is an adaptation which enables the insect to survive regularly occurring adverse conditions.

Diapause is common in insects from temperate regions and it may occur obligatorily in every generation or only in response to environmental signals which prelude the coming of adverse conditions. Diapause is usually restricted to one stage in the life history, but commonly an earlier stage is the recipient of the environmental signals initiating the delay in development, and as a result the insect is able to increase its reserves of nutriment and become dormant before conditions become unsuitable. Daylength is particularly important as an indicator of the season and in most insects from temperate regions diapause is induced by exposure to short days.

The metabolic rate is very low during diapause and probably some biochemical changes occur. These are unusual in many insects in that they occur most readily at low temperatures and ultimately they lead to the reactivation of the humoral system so that growth is resumed. In the silkmoth and possibly in other insects the delay in development is produced by a diapause-inducing hormone.

Diapause in general is reviewed by Andrewartha (1952), Danilevskii (1965), Lees (1955) and de Wilde (1962). Harvey (1962) discusses the biochemical aspects of diapause and Norris (1964) reviews reproductive diapause.

35.1 Diapause and its significance

Diapause is a delay in development which, although its effect is usually to facilitate survival during unfavourable periods, is not immediately referable to the adverse environmental conditions. This is an adaptive phenomenon, comparable with migration, and it enables the insect to live in areas which at times are unsuitable for it. Diapause and migration may occur in the same insect, as in *Coccinella* which migrates to winter quarters before entering diapause (p. 252). Thus diapause may be contrasted with quiescence which is a state of delayed development directly referable to environmental conditions.

In temperate regions diapause is generally concerned with survival during the cold winters when normal growth is not possible; in the tropics it may facilitate survival during the dry season which is characterised by a lack of moisture and food.

Diapause thus results in the synchronisation of active stages of morphogenesis with suitable environmental conditions of temperature and food. If this did not occur and the insect relied only on quiescence for survival, considerable or even complete loss of the population would occur. For instance, in Britain grasshoppers overwinter as eggs in a state of diapause. The eggs are laid from August to October and, being buried in the ground, are protected from low temperatures and excessive water loss. When the larvae emerge in the following May or June there is abundant fresh grass and temperatures are suitable for activity and growth. In the absence of a diapause some eggs might hatch in the autumn, but the resulting larvae would soon be subjected to temperatures too low for their normal activity and would die.

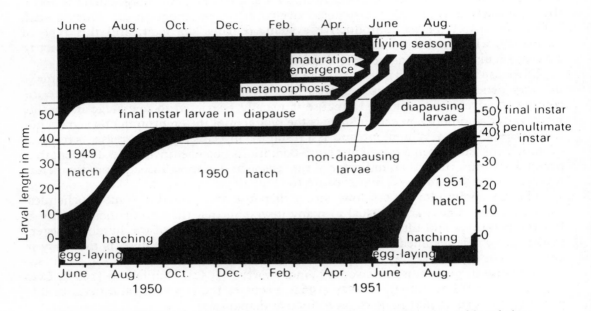

Fig. 488. The life history of *Anax imperator* showing the very wide range of larval sizes present at any one time. Despite this, adult emergence is restricted to a brief period because of the diapause in the last larval instar. A few individuals, entering the last larval instar early in the season, develop without a diapause (after Corbet *et al.*, 1960).

Diapause also results in the synchronising of adult emergence so that the chances of finding a mate are considerably improved. This is particularly necessary in long-lived species like *Anax*. Larval development of this dragonfly usually extends over two summers and during this time individual rates of development vary so that at any one time a wide variety of larval size is present (Fig. 488). This might clearly lead to the emergence of adults over a long period, but any larvae reaching the last instar after May do not undergo an immediate metamorphosis, instead, they remain in diapause until the following April. Thus although larvae may enter the last instar at any time between June and September they will all emerge as adults at the same time.

35.2 Occurrence of diapause

Probably most insects living in temperate regions where winter temperatures are too low for development enter a state of diapause at some stage of the life history, but the occurrence of diapause in insects from warmer regions depends on the severity of their environment and the conditions in their particular micro-habitat. Many tropical insects are able to survive without a diapause.

In the majority of diapausing insects only one stage, characteristic of the species, enters diapause, although the stage may differ in closely related insects. *Austroicetes* and *Melanoplus differentialis* both have an egg diapause in which development is delayed before katatrepsis. *Melanoplus mexicanus* eggs enter diapause when the embryo is fully developed. Larval diapause is commonly restricted to the last larval instar, as in the codling moth *Cydia*. A pupal diapause is common in Lepidoptera, such as *Saturnia*, while an adult diapause occurs in individual species of most orders of insects, but especially in Heteroptera and Coleoptera (Norris, 1964).

Sometimes every individual in every generation enters diapause. This is obligatory diapause and as a result there is usually only one generation each year, a univoltine cycle. This is the case with the eggs of *Orgyia* which are laid in late summer and autumn and do not hatch until the following May. There is a single generation of adults on the wing from July to October. Alternatively, in other species, some generations may be completely free of diapause while in other generations some or all of the insects may enter diapause. This is facultative diapause and as a rule there are two or more generations per year, a multivoltine cycle. Facultative diapause is well suited to regions with a long developmental season since it enables the insect to make the best use of the time available. If, however, the season is short so that there would not be time for a complete second generation an obligatory diapause is advantageous.

35.3 Initiation of diapause

Before diapause begins most insects lay down increased reserves in the fat body. This, as well as the onset of diapause itself, occurs while the prevailing conditions are still suitable for morphogenesis. In insects undergoing an obligatory diapause the onset of diapause in a particular stage is determined genetically, but where a facultative diapause occurs it is clear that the changes in metabolism must be initiated by some signal from the environment which, although not unfavourable in itself, indicates the advent of unfavourable conditions.

Experimental work, however, suggests that the difference between obligatory and facultative diapause is only one of degree. Insects with an obligatory diapause apparently respond to such a wide range of environmental factors that they invariably undergo diapause, but in the laboratory it may be possible to avoid diapause by using extreme conditions. Conversely, although facultative diapause is largely controlled by environmental factors, different races of a species may become genetically differentiated with respect to diapause so that their behaviour is not readily altered experimentally. This is best known in *Bombyx mori* where univoltine, bivoltine and quadrivoltine strains are known as well as a strain entirely free of diapause, and each of these responds differently to environmental factors (and see Fig. 493).

The effects of these internal and external phenomena are integrated in the nervous system which controls the activity of the neurosecretory system (see p. 702).

The most reliable and consistent indicator of seasons is daylength or photoperiod and this is the most important of the sign stimuli initiating diapause. Other possible indicators are temperature, the state of the food, and the age of the parent.

35.31 Photoperiod

Outside the tropics, long days occur in summer and short days in winter with increasing or decreasing daylength in spring or autumn. The relatively short days of autumn herald the approach of winter and for many species they act as a stimulus initiating diapause. The pupae of *Acronycta*, for instance, do not undergo a diapause if the daylength during the larval period exceeds 16 hours, but do diapause if the daylength is less than 16 hours (Fig. 489A). In Britain daylength exceeds 16 hours for a few weeks in midsummer so

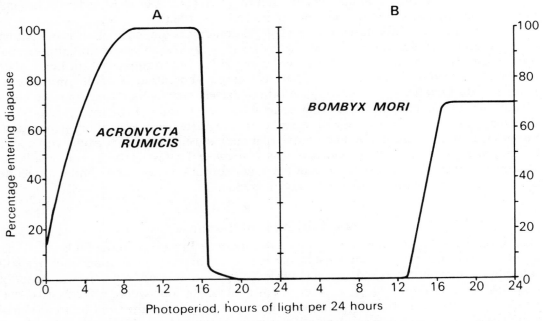

Fig. 489. The effect of photoperiod on the incidence of diapause in (A) *Acronycta*, a long-day insect, at 27–28°C. and (B) the bivoltine race of *Bombyx*, a short-day insect, at 15°C. In *Acronycta* exposure of larvae to short photoperiod induces diapause in the pupae; in *Bombyx* exposure of eggs to long photoperiod induces diapause in eggs of the next generation (from Lees, 1955).

that only larvae passing through the sensitive stage (see below) during this time develop without diapause. The adults from overwintering pupae emerge in May, June and July so that the bulk of their offspring are not influenced as larvae by the long midsummer days with the result that the pupae enter diapause and the next generation of adults does not emerge until the following year. However, a few larvae, the offspring of early emerging adults, may pass through their sensitive period in midsummer so that when they pupate they develop without any delay and a second generation of moths emerges in late August and September.

Essentially similar reactions occur in many other insects in temperate regions, there being a critical daylength around which small differences in photoperiod can produce a complete change in the type of development. Since they develop without diapause under long-day conditions they are known as long-day insects.

Photoperiod interacts with temperature and in long-day insects the critical daylength, below which diapause occurs, is often longer at lower temperatures. For instance, the critical daylength inducing pupal diapause in *Acronycta* is about 16 hours at 25°C., but almost 19 hours at 15°C. (Fig. 490). For this reason the date of the onset of diapause varies from year to year despite the constancy of seasonal changes in daylength. In *Pieris*, however, the critical daylength is not influenced by temperature.

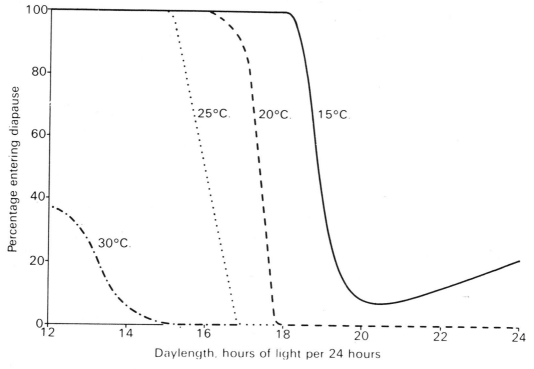

Fig. 490. The effect of temperature on the critical daylength for diapause development in *Acronycta* (from Danilevskii, 1965).

A characteristic feature of long-day insects is that under extreme short-day conditions they again develop without a diapause (Fig. 489A). This phenomenon only occurs in experiments and can have no ecological significance because such short photoperiods are only observed in winter at high latitudes at times when insects are already inactive.

Bombyx is one of the few insects in which exposure to long days initiates diapause (Fig. 489B). Here exposure of the eggs of the bivoltine race to long days, ensures that the eggs of the next generation will enter diapause. Eggs exposed to a short photoperiod of less than 14 hours lead to non-diapausing eggs in the next generation. Thus the long-day conditions of spring acting on the eggs leads to the production of diapause eggs in the autumn, but these eggs, being subjected to short days, will ensure that the eggs of the next generation, which are laid the following spring, develop without diapause. Such insects which develop without diapause when the sensitive stage is exposed to short days are called short-day insects.

An unusual intermediate type of development occurs in a few insects, such as *Euproctis*. Larval diapause in this insect results from exposure to either short or extremely long photoperiods, but development occurs without any delay if the daylength is between about 16 and 20 hours (Fig. 491).

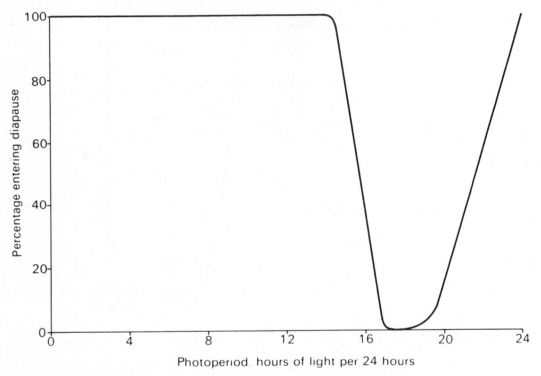

Fig. 491. The effect of postperiod on the incidence of larval diapause in *Euproctis* (from Danilevskii, 1965).

The response of many animals to photoperiod involves the perception of small changes in daylength rather than the actual duration of the light period, but in insects this is not the case. Most insects respond to the absolute length of the photoperiod. A few cases in which the insect is believed to respond to changes in daylength are recorded, but even these can be accounted for in terms of reactions to the absolute daylength. For instance, there is evidence which suggests that larval *Anax* develop without a diapause if, during the critical period, they are exposed to photoperiods increasing by only three minutes each day, but Danilevskii (1965) suggests that this insect exhibits an intermediate type of response to daylength comparable with that of *Euproctis*. He suggests that at the beginning of May daylength is in the intermediate range so that development proceeds without diapause, but by the end of May the longer days induce diapause in later developing larvae (Fig. 488). The intermediate daylengths recur in the autumn, but they do not lead to development without a delay because the larvae are already in diapause.

The adult diapause of *Nomadacris* might also be interpreted as a response to shortening daylength, but Norris (1965) suggests that the effect results from stimulation by different daylengths at different stages of development. In the course of larval and early adult development of this insect the daylength decreases from 13 to 12 hours, and experiments show that rearing the larvae in a 13-hour photoperiod, even when this is constant intensifies the effect of a constant 12-hour photoperiod in inducing diapause in the adult.

Sensitivity to light

The intensity of light during the photoperiod is not important provided that it exceeds a very low threshold value. This varies with the species, but commonly is about 1·0 ft.-candle or less. Hence daily fluctuations in light intensity due to clouds have no effect on photoperiod and the 'effective daylength' includes the periods of twilight. As a result of this high sensitivity, insects inside fruit and even the pupa of *Antheraea* inside its cocoon are affected by photoperiod. In some cases the sensitivity is such that the insect could be stimulated by moonlight (about 0·5 ft.-candles) which might, therefore, contribute to the effective daylength. However, this effect might be offset by the relatively low temperatures occurring at night (de Wilde, 1962).

In most insects only the short wavelengths are concerned in the photoperiodic reaction.

Neither the compound eyes nor the ocelli of adult insects act as receptors of photoperiod. In larvae, the stemmata may be involved, but possibly the light acts directly on the central nervous system. Lees (1964) working on *Megoura* has suggested a direct influence on the neurosecretory cells of the brain.

35.32 Temperature

Temperature also plays a part in the induction of diapause and in general in temperate regions high temperature suppresses and low temperature enhances any tendency to enter diapause. Temperature and photoperiod interact and if *Diataraxia*, a long-day insect, is bred under experimental conditions of light and temperature short day length is dominant and induces diapause irrespective of temperature unless the latter is very high (Fig. 492A). On the other hand with long photoperiod temperature is dominant, low temperature inducing diapause and high temperature preventing it.

In the course of the seasons temperature and photoperiod will reinforce each other because high temperature is associated with long days and low temperature with short days. With changes in latitude, however, this reinforcement does not occur since at higher latitudes, although summer days are longer, the temperatures are lower than they are nearer the equator. Hence species with extensive geographical distribution are differently adapted to photoperiod in different parts of their range. For instance, in southern Russia *Acronycta* enters diapause only when the daylength falls below 15

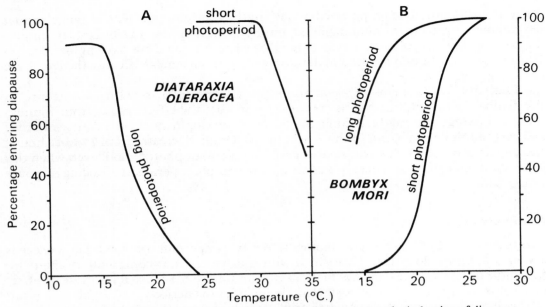

Fig. 492. The combined action of temperature and photoperiod on the induction of diapause in (A) *Diataraxia* and (B) *Bombyx* (from Lees, 1955).

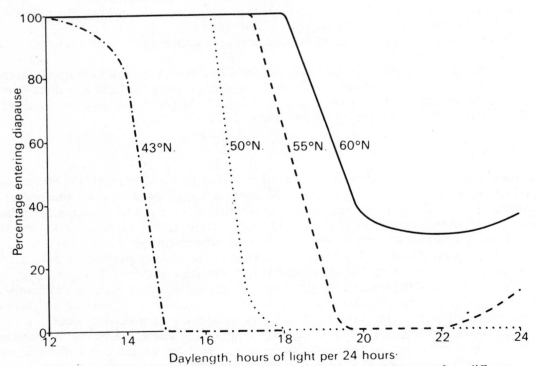

Fig. 493. The critical daylength for diapause development in races of *Acronycta* from different latitudes. All experiments were carried out at 23°C. (from Danilevskii, 1965).

hours, but with increasing latitude there is an increase in the critical daylength so that specimens from Leningrad almost invariably enter diapause. At this latitude diapause is only avoided when the photoperiod exceeds 18 hours (Fig. 493). These differences are inherited characteristics of the populations.

Because of these differences the life history of the species varies in different parts of its range. In the south (latitude 43°N.) three partly overlapping generations occur and only in the last do the pupae undergo diapause. Farther north (latitude 50°N.) two generations occur, the whole of the second being determined for diapause, while round Leningrad (latitude 60°N.) only a very small number of individuals avoid diapause and the species is largely univoltine. Comparable differences in the life histories are known in other insects.

Bombyx again differs from most other insects in that high temperature induces diapause and low temperature prevents it (Fig. 492B).

In *Mormoniella* temperature acts independently of photoperiod, and chilling the female causes her to lay eggs which will give rise to diapausing larvae (Schneiderman and Horwitz, 1958).

Lees (1955) and Danilevskii (1965) suggest that temperature, like photoperiod, acts as a sign stimulus, but de Wilde (1962) considers that it has some metabolic effect.

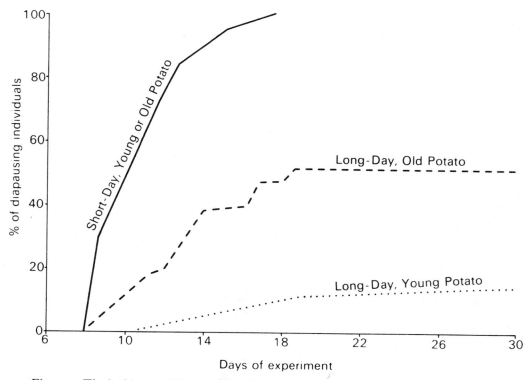

Fig. 494. The incidence of diapause in adult *Leptinotarsa* subjected to different photoperiods and with different types of food (from Danilevskii, 1965).

35.33 Food

There is evidence in a few cases that the amount or quality of the food can influence diapause. Starvation or feeding on senescent leaves induce diapause in adult *Leptinotarsa* even in long days (Fig. 494) and starvation also has some effect in *Mormoniella* (Schneiderman and Horwitz, 1958). In many cases the effects of diet are apparent only when the daylength is close to the critical photoperiod. With longer or shorter days the effects of photoperiod are dominant.

Most evidence indicates that photoperiod acts directly on insects and not via changes in the food plants, but there are some cases where the food plant is influenced by the photoperiod and in turn influences the insects. This appears to be true of larvae of the cabbage rootfly, *Erioischia,* which respond to short days even though the soil in which they are living is shaded (Hughes, 1960).

35.34 Physiology of parent

There are a number of instances where the physiology of the parent is known to affect the incidence of diapause in the following generation. For instance, rearing conditions affect the physiology of adult *Locustana* and, in turn, the incidence of diapause in the eggs which these insects lay. Thus phase *solitaria* females lay 100% diapausing eggs compared with only 42% by phase *gregaria* females. Further, old *gregaria* females lay more diapausing eggs than young females. Ageing has a similar effect in *Mormoniella.*

Numerous instances are known in which the exposure of females to particular conditions of photoperiod or temperature influences the incidence of diapause in their offspring (Ring, 1967).

35.35 Sensitive stages

The environmental factors initiating diapause act before the onset of unfavourable conditions and they may act some time before diapause begins. As a result, these stimuli may operate on a different stage from that which undergoes diapause, and, for instance, in *Diataraxia* stimulation of the fourth instar larva by appropriate photoperiods induces diapause in the pupa. *Bombyx* is an extreme example where appropriate stimulation of the egg causes diapause in the eggs of the next generation.

The period of sensitivity to stimulation also varies in different species. *Diataraxia* larvae are only sensitive to photoperiod for two days while in *Bombyx,* although the well-developed embryo is the most sensitive stage, the first three larval instars are also sensitive to decreasing extents. Further, a number of photoperiodic cycles are necessary in order to produce an effect. The larva of *Dendrolimus,* for instance, must be subjected to about 20 short-day impulses to induce diapause, while 15 and 11 short-day impulses are required respectively to induce diapause in pupal *Acronycta* and *Pieris.* This number varies, however, under the influence of temperature and nutrition.

35.4 Diapause development

Except in the adult, a delay in morphogenesis is characteristic of diapause. Adult diapause is a reproductive delay, characterised by the failure of oocytes to develop or, in species which enter diapause more than once as adults, such as *Dytiscus* and *Leptinotarsa,* degeneration of the oocytes before yolk deposition occurs. Larval and adult forms usually become quiescent and do not feed during diapause, as in *Leptinotarsa* adults which bury themselves in the ground, but in other cases adults remain active throughout the period. Their activity, however, tends to be reduced and feeding is at a very low level.

Before the insects become inactive there is usually a build up of reserve food substances, particularly in the fat body, with a consequent reduction in the proportion of water in the body. Comparison of different forms determined for diapause or non-diapause shows that those destined for diapause build up bigger food reserves. Sometimes, as in female *Culex pipiens,* these stores are used up during diapause, but often this is not so. In the eggs of *Melanoplus differentialis,* for instance, 50% of the fat content of the yolk is used up in 40 days of active growth, but there is no depletion during three or four months of diapause development. This reflects the very low level of metabolism during this period, as is indicated also by the very low oxygen consumption (Fig. 495).

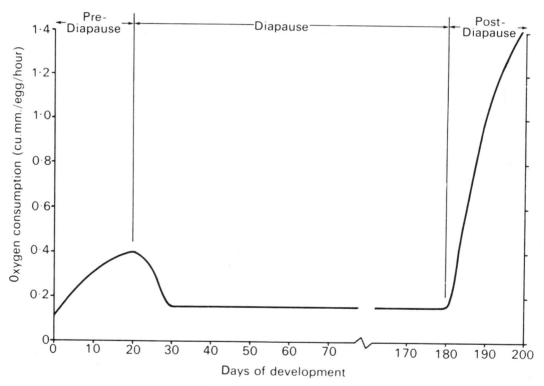

Fig. 495. The oxygen consumption of the egg of *Melanoplus differentialis* during diapause and pre- and post-diapause development (from Lees, 1955).

It was believed, mainly as a result of work on the pupal diapause of *Hyalophora,* that the terminal enzyme system involved in oxidation was not complete (Williams; refs. in *e.g.* Harvey, 1962), but it is now known that even in this species the enzyme system is complete. Electron transfer follows the normal path from NAD and succinate through the cytochromes, although it is limited by the very low levels of cytochromes b and c. There is no evidence that the autoxidisable cytochrome b_5 is the terminal oxidase as has been suggested (Gilmour, 1961; Harvey, 1962).

It is not clear how the cytochrome system is controlled. Harvey (1962) suggests that energy demands are low because of the lack of effector activity and as a consequence of this there is little breakdown of ATP to ADP. ADP, which is a phosphate acceptor, is therefore in short supply and this in itself sets a limit on the amount of oxidative metabolism which can occur. Hence reduced nicotinamide-adenine dinucleotide phosphate, which normally passes electrons to the cytochromes (see p. 91), accumulates. Diminished electron transport will, in turn, lead to a reduction in the level of the cytochromes and this too will limit the level of metabolism.

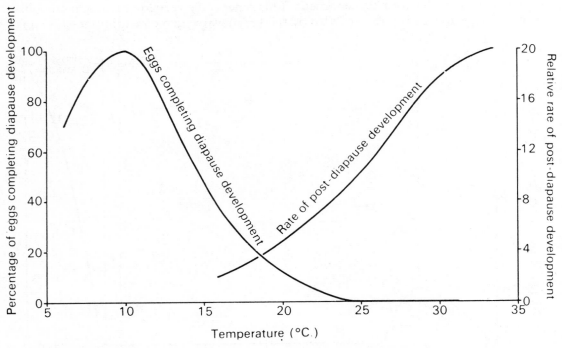

Fig. 496. The influence of temperature on diapause development and postdiapause morphogenesis in *Austroicetes*. The optimum for diapause development is about 10°C., that for morphogenesis is over 30°C. (after Andrewartha, 1952)

Although morphogenesis is at a standstill during diapause physiological changes do occur and Andrewartha (1952) refers to this physiological development as diapause development. Danilevskii (1965), however, believes the phenomena occurring during diapause to remove a block which inhibits development, and he refers to the processes occurring as a reactivation.

Once diapause development, or reactivation, is complete morphogenesis is resumed, provided the environmental conditions are suitable. If they are not the insect remains in a state of quiescence until conditions become more favourable.

As with other physiological processes diapause development occurs most rapidly under certain environmental conditions of which temperature is often of overriding importance. The range of temperatures at which diapause development occurs, unlike that for morphogenesis, varies with the geographical distribution of the species and in temperate regions the optimum temperature for diapause development is commonly within the range 0–10°C., well below the temperature necessary for morphogenesis (Figs. 496, 497). At higher or lower temperatures diapause development proceeds more slowly and in the extremes stops altogether. On the other hand in tropical species, where diapause is concerned with survival of the dry season, the temperature range for diapause development is often little, if any, lower than the range for morphogenesis (Fig. 497)

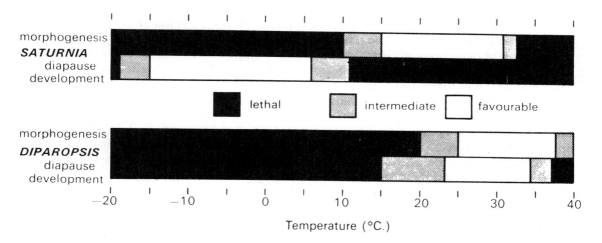

Fig. 497. The thermal requirements for morphogenesis and diapause development in a Palaearctic moth (*Saturnia*) and a tropical moth (*Diparopsis*) (adapted from Lees, 1955).

Diapause is commonly associated with a relatively low water content of the tissues. This probably enhances the ability of the insect to survive periods of extremely low temperature, but the role of water in diapause development is not clear. In the eggs of many species of Orthoptera morphogenesis is not resumed until water is available, but this water is only effective after a period of diapause development has been completed. Hence, although water is essential for the resumption of morphogenesis, as is true even of eggs developing without diapause (p. 343), it is not immediately concerned in the process of diapause. A similar restoration of the water balance accompanying reactivation after diapause is known to occur also in other insects in other stages of development.

In a few cases diapause development is directly affected by the photoperiod. For instance, the larva of *Dendrolimus* resumes its growth after a delay of only two weeks if the days during diapause are long, but remains dormant for twice as long in short days. In the vast majority of insects, however, photoperiod is of no importance once diapause has been initiated.

The duration of diapause development varies considerably with conditions and from species to species. Under optimal conditions the diapause development of *Gryllulus commodus* is completed in 15 days; on the other hand *Cephus* requires a minimum of 90–100 days.

35.5 Control of diapause

Diapause in the larva and pupa, and probably also in late embryonic stages, results from a deficiency of ecdyson so that growth and moulting do not occur. In adult diapause lack of the corpus allatum hormone results in a failure of the oocytes to develop. The activity of both the prothoracic glands and the corpora allata are controlled by the neurosecretory cells of the brain (p.703) and their failure to function during diapause results from the inactivity of the neurosecretory cells.

Various hypotheses have been put forward to account for the inactivity of the neuro-secretory cells during diapause and their subsequent activation which leads to a resumption of development. Danilevskii (1965) suggests that the activity of the neuro-secretory cells before diapause results from the direct and independent action of light, temperature and other stimuli. It is presumed that long photoperiod or high tempera-ture, either in the light or dark phase, may activate the neurosecretory cells so that development continues without interruption. Short photoperiod and low temperatures fail to activate the neurosecretory cells so that diapause follows. It is known that in aphids light acts directly on the brain (Lees, 1964) and the brain of *Hyalophora* is directly affected by low temperature during diapause development (see papers by Williams cited in *e.g.* Danilevskii, 1965).

Andrewartha (1952), on the other hand, supposes that the neurosecretory cells are stimulated indirectly by breakdown products of the fat body or the yolk in the case of embryos. In his food mobilisation hypothesis he suggests that in individuals destined for diapause the food reserves accumulate so that the neurosecretory cells are not stimu-lated. The food reserves can only be broken down after diapause development and only then are the neurosecretory cells stimulated and morphogenesis resumed. The physio-logical evidence does not favour this hypothesis (Lees, 1955).

According to Schneiderman and Horwitz (1958) diapause development involves a complex of synthetic reactions with several different phases—aerobic and anaerobic, reversible and irreversible. In addition there is a breakdown reaction which is probably enzymatic and results in the destruction of products of the reversible phase of the syn-thetic reactions. Low temperature during diapause development slows down the break-down reaction so that the substance produced by the synthetic reactions accumulates. Earlier work on the brain of *Hyalophora* pupae suggested that the accumulating sub-stance was acetylcholine and this was associated with the absence of cholinesterase and all electrical activity from the brain. Subsequent work, however, indicates that this is not the case and electrical activity persists in the brain throughout diapause (see *e.g.* Mansingh and Smallman, 1967).

Diapause in eggs which are only just beginning to develop must involve a com-pletely different mechanism because they have no endocrine system at this time. In *Bombyx* eggs the diapause is caused by a diapause-inducing hormone produced by the neurosecretory cells in the suboesophageal ganglion of the parent. In addition an antagonistic hormone is secreted by the parental corpora allata which inhibits the diapause-inducing hormone. The release of the two secretions is controlled by the brain and differences in the balance between the two hormones are responsible for the differences between the races of *Bombyx*.

There is some evidence for a diapause-inducing hormone in other insects in stages other than the egg. For instance, de Wilde and de Boer (1961) suggest that such a hormone may be involved in the diapause of adult *Leptinotarsa*.

The resumption of activity of the neurosecretory cells after a period of diapause development might be due to the removal of some inhibiting substance or possibly to stimulation by the products of diapause development.

CHAPTER XXXVI

PHEROMONES

Hormones are concerned with regulation within the organism. Comparable chemical substances, called pheromones, are concerned with the co-ordination of individuals in a population. They are produced by various ectodermal glands on the abdomen, or associated with the mandibles of Hymenoptera or on the wings of many male Lepidoptera.

In many insects, but especially the Lepidoptera, pheromones function as sexual attractants, enabling one sex to detect and seek out the other, often from considerable distances. These sexual attractants are often relatively specific and, in their chemical structure, they appear to strike a balance between the need for specifity and the need to be relatively volatile. Sometimes a high concentration of the attractant stimulates copulation, but in other cases aphrodisiac pheromones are produced, usually by the males. In locusts pheromones lead to a synchronisation of maturation throughout the population.

Pheromones are particularly important in social insects where they are used in communication between workers and in the maintenance of colony structure.

Insect pheromones in general are reviewed by Butler (1967) and Karlson and Butenandt (1959). Various aspects of pheromones in sexual processes are dealt with by Butler (1964b), Jacobson (1965) and Schneider (1966), while E. O. Wilson (1963a, 1963b) discusses pheromones in ants. The maintenance of colony structure in bees has been studied in particular by Butler (see *e.g.* Butler, 1967) and in termites by Lüscher (1961). Alarm pheromones are reviewed by Blum (1969, *A. Rev. Ent.* **14**).

36.1 The nature of pheromones

Pheromones are substances which are secreted to the outside by animals and which, if passed to another individual of the same species, cause it to respond in a particular manner (Karlson and Butenandt, 1959). They are thus concerned with the co-ordination of individuals and are, therefore, often important in sexual behaviour and in regulating the behaviour and physiology of social and subsocial insects.

Some pheromones, such as sexual attractants in Lepidoptera, are perceived as scents by olfactory receptors and affect the recipient via the central nervous system. In other cases the pheromones are ingested by the recipient. These may be perceived by the sense of taste so that their action is comparable with olfactory pheromones, or the pheromone, once ingested, may be absorbed and play some part in a biochemical reaction within the recipient. It is not know which of these alternatives is the correct one.

36.2 Glands producing pheromones

Although some pheromones, such as that inducing maturation in *Schistocerca* (p. 741), are produced by the epidermal cells, in many cases they originate in definite glands. There is a great variety of these and only a few selected examples will be given.

36.21 Lepidoptera

Male Lepidoptera are often able to produce aphrodisiac scents from glands which are commonly associated with scales. These scales, known as androconia, often occur on the wings, as in Pieridae, and they may be either scattered or grouped together. Scent scales often have an elongated form and terminate in a row of processes or fimbriae (Fig. 498). Glandular cells in the wing membrane are presumed to connect with the base of the scale, but it is not clear how the scent is discharged from the scale. Bourgogne (1951) says that the products of the glands pass into the cavity of the scale and either diffuse out or pass through small terminal openings in the fimbriae, but Dixey (1932) does not consider that these terminal openings exist. Dickens (1936) is unable to decide whether or not pores are present. Alternatively, the glandular product may simply spread over the surface of the scale (Bourgogne, 1951), presumably from a basal pore. In any case the effect of the frilled margin of the scale will be to increase the surface area from which evaporation occurs.

Comparable scales may occur on the legs or abdomen. In *Ephestia kühniella*, for instance, the male has a dorso-lateral tuft of androconia on each side of the eighth abdominal segment. Normally these are hidden from view by being telescoped inside segment seven, but they are exposed by extension of the abdomen, releasing their scent.

In the males of some species the scent secreting zone is separated from the dispensing zone. The males of *Amauris niavius* have a small scent patch on each of the hind wings. These patches contain highly modified scales, called scent cups by Eltringham (1913), which arise from the upper surface of the wing as dome-shaped eruptions with

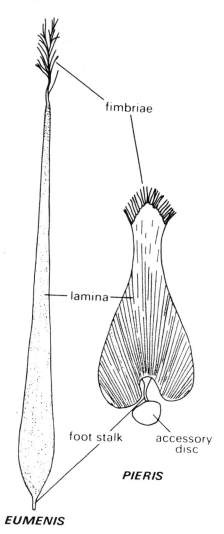

Fig. 498. Scent scales from the wings of *Eumenis* (from South, 1941) and *Pieris* (from Imms, 1957).

a small median pore (Fig. 499). Small multicellular glands in the wing open by the pore and the whole area occupied by the scent cups is roofed over by small, but normally shaped, scales.

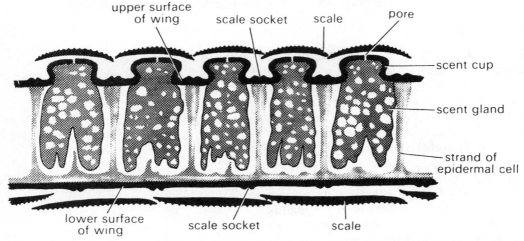

Fig. 499. Transverse section through part of the hind wing of *Amauris* showing the scent cups and glands (after Eltringham, 1913).

The scent from these scent patches is dispersed by scent brushes associated with the genitalia. Each brush consists of a group of long hairs arising from the proximal end of a sac which can be everted by blood pressure so that the hairs project as a tuft. The sac is retracted by a muscle. In order to disperse the scent the insect lands with its wings spread and then bends the abdomen towards one of the scent patches, everting the scent brush as it does so (Lamborn, 1911). The scent organs are brushed with the hairs which presumably raise the covering of scales and come into contact with the scent cups. The scent is then dispersed from the expanded brush and the movement is repeated. The scent dispersed in this way has been shown to be a sexual attractant in *Euploea core*. In

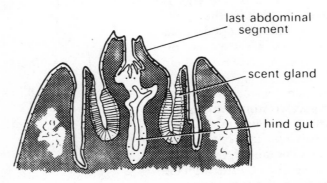

Fig. 500. Horizontal section through the tip of the abdomen of the female *Plodia* showing the integumental scent glands (from Wigglesworth, 1965).

Danaus Brower and Jones (1965) have shown that the scent brushes themselves produce a scent, but that this is enhanced after the brushes have made contact with the glands on the wing. The scent is dispersed by similar brushes on the abdomen of many Sphingidae and some Noctuidae.

The scent glands of the female are usually in the form of glandular epithelium near the tip of the abdomen. In *E. kühniella* the intersegmental membrane between segments eight and nine is deeply infolded on the ventral side and the epidermal cells are large and conspicuous. The cuticle above them is thicker than elsewhere, but it is not perforated by pores since its properties are such that the secretion of the glands can diffuse through it (Dickens, 1936). The area is exposed and dispersal of the scent promoted by extension of the abdomen.

In other species there are invaginated glands lined by cuticle and opening either intersegmentally, as in *Plodia* (Fig. 500), or on either side of the genital pore, as in *Ephestia cautella*. The walls of these glands consist of a single layer of columnar cells with, in *Bombyx*, the outer plasma membrane thrown into deep folds. The scent is disseminated via the terminal opening, or, in some cases, by an evagination of the gland. Only occasionally, as in the females of *Triphaena* and *Gonepteryx*, are such glands associated with hairs to facilitate dissemination.

36.22 Hymenoptera

Apis mellifera

Honey bees have two important glands producing pheromones: the mandibular glands in the head and Nassanoff's gland in the abdomen.

The mandibular gland is sac-like with an epithelium of secretory cells lined by a thin cuticular intima. The duct from the gland opens at the base of the mandible into a groove which runs into a depression on the inner face of the mandible (Fig. 501). These glands are well developed in the queen and worker, but greatly reduced in the drone. They are present in nearly all Hymenoptera.

Nassanoff's gland is beneath the intersegmental membrane between abdominal tergites six and seven (Fig. 502). It is made up of a number of large cells each of which has a narrow duct leading to the exterior through the cuticle. Normally it is concealed beneath tergite six, but it can be exposed by depressing the tip of the abdomen. Nassanoff's gland is well developed in workers, but is absent from drones and opinions differ as to whether or not one is present in queens (see Snodgrass, 1956).

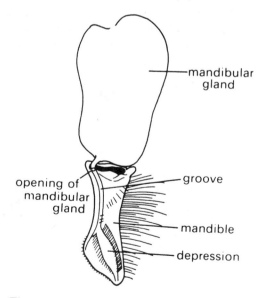

Fig. 501. Inner view of the mandible and mandibular gland of a worker honey bee (after Snodgrass, 1956).

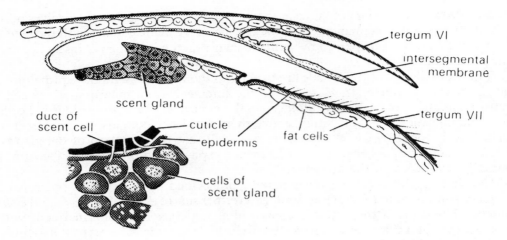

Fig. 502. Longitudinal section through the base of tergum VII of the abdomen of a worker honeybee showing the position of the scent gland. Enlargement showing a group of scent cells and their ducts (after Snodgrass, 1956).

Ants

Ants have mandibular glands similar to *Apis*. Other sources of pheromone are the poison gland and Dufour's gland, both of which are absent in males since they are associated with the sting, and Pavan's gland which opens on the ventral surface of the abdomen above the sixth abdominal sternite. The poison gland consists of a pair of glandular tubules which unite to form a convoluted duct opening into a reservoir (Fig. 503). Dufour's gland opens into the poison duct near the base of the sting. It is a small, simple sac with thin glandular walls and a delicate muscular sheath.

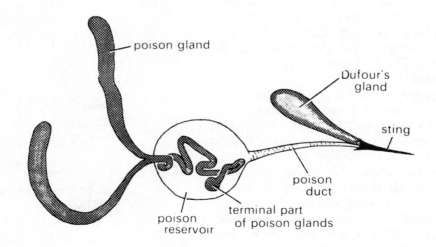

Fig. 503. Poison glands and Dufour's gland of a worker ant (after Wheeler, 1926).

36.3 Pheromones as sex attractants

Pheromones are employed by a large number of insects in bringing the sexes together for mating. These pheromones are known as sex attractants. They are widespread amongst the Lepidoptera and are also known to occur in some Dictyoptera, Coleoptera, Hymenoptera and some other orders (see Jacobson, 1965). In most cases the pheromone is produced by the female to attract the male, while less frequently a male pheromone attracts the female, or both sexes may be lured by the odour.

Pheromones which attract males

Usually the glands producing the female sex attractant are between the more posterior segments of the abdomen and the insect regulates the release of the scent by exposing or covering the glands by movements of the abdomen, or by everting and retracting the glands if they are of the eversible type. Normally scent is only released at particular times of day which are characteristic for the species. For instance, males of *Lobesia* (Lepidoptera) are only attracted by the female from about 21.00 hours to midnight, while *Heliothis* (Lepidoptera) males are attracted to the females from 04.00 hours to daylight. Other species, such as *Ephestia,* however, appear to release the pheromone at any time.

Commonly females do not release the pheromone for a day or two after emergence and then they produce it until they are mated. Sometimes, however, the attractant is produced before the female emerges and males of *Megarhyssa* (Hymenoptera) may congregate on the tree trunks occupied by females, waiting for them to emerge. They are attracted by the female pheromone despite the fact that she has not yet emerged from the host in which she pupated. After mating the attractiveness of the female wanes in many species. This is the case in *Bombyx,* for instance, which only mates once, although the precursor of the pheromone is still present in the cells of the glands (Schneider, 1966). In other species, such as *Trichoplusia* (Lepidoptera), which mate several times the release of pheromone may continue undiminished after mating.

The scent is perceived by olfactory receptors on the antennae of the male and it is significant that the antennae of many male Lepidoptera which are attracted by scent are strongly pectinate (see Fig. 8C). Stimulation of the antennal sense organs by the female scent produces a characteristic pattern in the output from the antennal nerve even in very low concentrations. The effect of the scent is to excite the male and to promote take-off. In the presence of the scent, flight is directed upwind and this brings the male to the vicinity of the female. Such attraction may occur over very long distances and there is a record of a male *Actias selene* coming to a female from 11 km. away. It is difficult to assess whether the males are attracted from such distances or if attraction occurs only when they come closer to the female as a result of chance flight. *Porthetria dispar* males are known to have come to a female after release 3·8 km. away and on theoretical grounds E. O. Wilson (1963b) has calculated that gyplure, the pheromone produced by female *Porthetria,* is an effective attractant over a distance of 4·5 km. with a wind of 100 cm./sec. The effective distance is reduced at higher wind speeds by increased turbulence and under natural conditions must be greatly reduced by topography and local air movements. At very high concentrations of scent the male becomes very excited, extruding the claspers and attempting to copulate with the source of pheromone which now functions as an aphrodisiac.

The queen of *Apis mellifera* also attracts males by a pheromone, the principal component of which is 9-oxodecenoic acid produced in the mandibular glands. In the absence of stimulation the males fly about randomly, but when stimulated by the attractant they fly upwind to the vicinity of its source, the queen. This attraction only occurs from 20–30 metres (Butler, 1964a) and when the queen is more than 15 feet above the ground; below this males are not attracted to her. Having arrived close to the queen as a result of her scent the final approach is probably visual. Sometimes males overshoot the queen on their upwind flight. In this case they fly on for 20–30 feet and then fly round at random with the result that they may soon reappear on the lee side of the queen and are able to reorientate to her.

The sex attractants of Lepidoptera are not species specific, but rather are group specific. In Saturniidae, for instance, all the species in a genus respond equally well to the attractant of one species. Members of some closely related genera also make a full response, but in others the response is less marked. More distantly related genera make no response at all (Fig. 504). This pattern of responses also occurs in other families (Schneider, 1966).

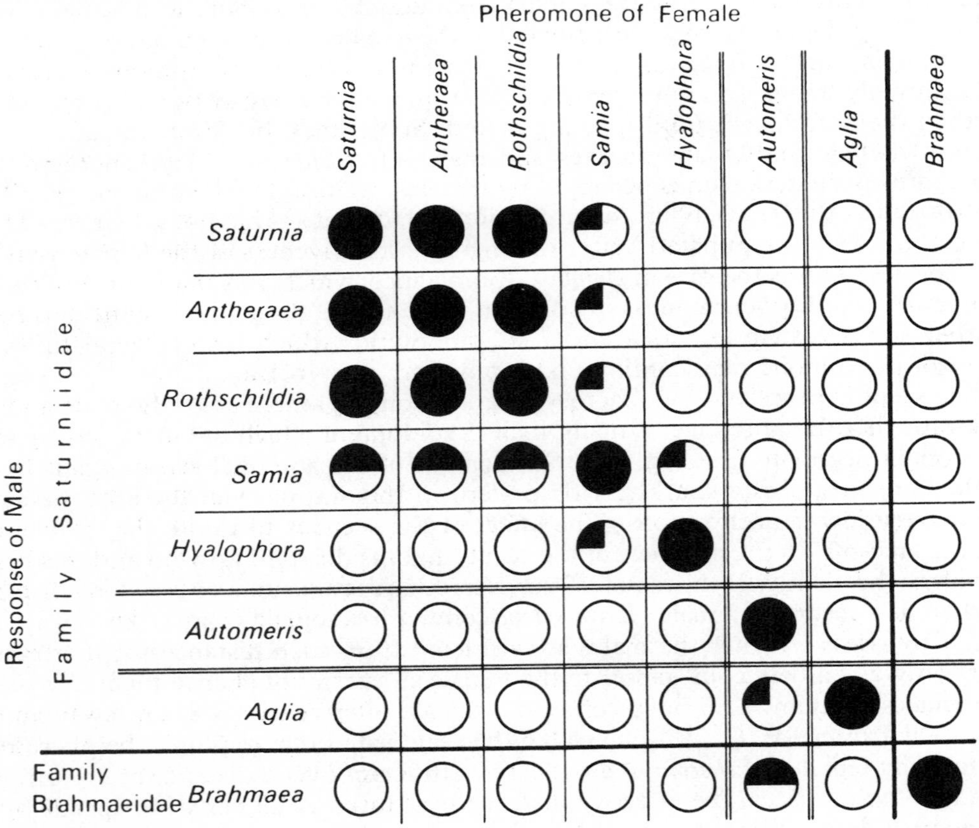

Fig. 504. Diagram to illustrate the specificity of the sex attractants of female Saturniidae, based on the electroantennogram responses of the males. Black disc indicates maximal response to the pheromone of the species indicated; white disc, no response; partially blackened disc, intermediate response (from Schneider, 1966).

This degree of specifity can only be achieved with relatively large molecules which permit some degree of variation. With a small molecule only a very limited number of variations is possible. At the same time, an essential feature of a sex attractant is that it should be volatile and volatility falls off with molecular weight so that this factor opposes the increase in size demanded by specifity. Hence molecular size of the sex attractant pheromones will represent a balance between these two opposing needs, while a limit will also be set by the ability of the insect to synthesise the molecule (E. O. Wilson, 1963b).

The sex attractants have been chemically isolated in a few cases. The molecules contain 10–17 carbon atoms and have molecular weights between 180 and 300. Bombykol, the sex attractant of *Bombyx,* is an unsaturated alcohol with the formula:

$$H-\underset{\underset{H}{|}}{\overset{\overset{H}{|}}{C}}-\underset{\underset{H}{|}}{\overset{\overset{H}{|}}{C}}-\underset{\underset{H}{|}}{\overset{\overset{H}{|}}{C}}-\overset{\overset{H}{|}}{C}=\overset{\overset{H}{|}}{C}-\overset{\overset{H}{|}}{C}=\overset{\overset{H}{|}}{C}-\underset{\underset{H}{|}}{\overset{\overset{H}{|}}{C}}-\underset{\underset{H}{|}}{\overset{\overset{H}{|}}{C}}-\underset{\underset{H}{|}}{\overset{\overset{H}{|}}{C}}-\underset{\underset{H}{|}}{\overset{\overset{H}{|}}{C}}-\underset{\underset{H}{|}}{\overset{\overset{H}{|}}{C}}-\underset{\underset{H}{|}}{\overset{\overset{H}{|}}{C}}-\underset{\underset{H}{|}}{\overset{\overset{H}{|}}{C}}-\underset{\underset{H}{|}}{\overset{\overset{H}{|}}{C}}-OH$$

Pheromones which attract females

There are a few instances of males producing sexual attractants. This is true of the beetle *Anthonomus* and of *Harpobittacus* (Mecoptera). In the latter, after the male has caught his prey and started to feed, two vesicles are everted from between the posterior abdominal tergites. These vesicles are expanded and contracted and the scent released in this way attracts the female. On her approach the male copulates with her and presents her with the remains of his prey.

Pheromones which attract both sexes

Sometimes both sexes are attracted by a pheromone. The virgin female of *Dendroctonus* produces a scent which attracts males and other females, and a similar scent is produced by male *Ips*. In the latter the pheromone is produced in the cells of the ileum so that the frass which is pushed out of the burrow is attractive to other beetles. Both *Dendroctonus* and *Ips* are timber boring beetles and the effect of the pheromone, as well as bringing the sexes together, is to attract other members of the species to suitable food since in neither case is the pheromone produced until the insect is feeding on suitable timber.

The male *Lycus loripes* (Coleoptera) also emits a scent which attracts other beetles of both sexes with the result that aggregations are formed on the flowers of the food plant *Melilotus*. Mating occurs in these groups, but grouping is important for another reason. *Lycus* is a distasteful beetle with a yellow colour which birds learn to avoid (Eisner and Kafatos, 1962). Distasteful insects with aposematic colouration frequently form groups and it is believed that as a result of grouping, which makes them more conspicuous, predators learn to avoid them more quickly and wastage of the population is reduced. In this case, at least, grouping is promoted by a pheromone. Scent also plays a part in producing hibernating swarms of Coccinellidae in which mating subsequently occurs before the insects disperse.

Sexual attraction in Bombus

It is possible that sexual attraction in *Bombus* involves pheromones, but here it takes a different form from that recorded in other insects. In *B. terrestris*, for instance, the male has a definite circuit round which he continually flies (Free and Butler, 1959). At intervals the route is marked by a scent produced in the mandibular glands. This is applied by the bee by grasping the object to be marked in the mandibles and gnawing at its surface. Marking is carried out once in the morning and the scent then persists for the rest of the day while the male flies round the circuit. Each time he comes to a marked point he hovers for a short period before flying on to the next point. Females are said to be attracted by the scent so that they fly into the region of the circuit and the frequent passage of the male ensures that he will meet any female arriving (but see Butler, 1967).

The lengths of such circuits vary, and larger, stronger bees tend to have longer circuits. One recorded circuit of *B. terrestris* was 275 m. long with 27 visiting places. The male flew round this circuit 35 times in 90 minutes. The same circuit is retained on successive days, but in the morning when the route is re-marked some previous stopping points may be omitted and new ones included. The circuits of different males of the same species may overlap so that several males may use one marked stopping point.

The scents used to mark these circuits are species specific and this specificity is enhanced by the tendency of different species to fly at different heights. *B. lapidarius* makes its circuit at tree-top level, *B. agrorum* about six feet above the ground and *B. terrestris* two to three feet above the ground. Comparable scent routes are also made by male *Psithyrus* and *Anthophora*.

36.4 Aphrodisiacs

The sexual attractants of some Lepidoptera lead to copulation when they are in high concentration, but in many insects special scents are employed to induce copulation after the two sexes have been brought together by other means. Such aphrodisiac scents are often produced by male Lepidoptera, usually from androconia on the wings. For instance, in *Eumenis semele* the male follows the female visually and ultimately, if she is a virgin, the female lands. The male has scent scales in a patch on the upper side of the fore wing (Fig. 505) and courtship is completed by the male standing in front of the female and bowing towards her with the wings partly open so that the female's

position of scent patch

Fig. 505. Male *Eumenis semele* showing the position of the scent patches on the upper side of the fore wings (from South, 1941; and Tinbergen, 1951).

antennae come into contact with the scent areas (Fig. 506). The female then allows the male to move round and copulate. Males with the scent scales removed have great difficulty in acquiring a mate.

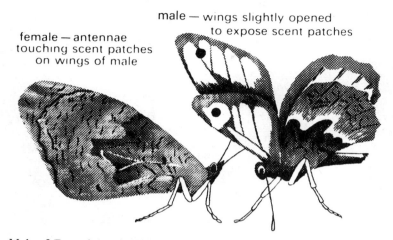

female — antennae touching scent patches on wings of male

male — wings slightly opened to expose scent patches

Fig. 506. Male of *Eumenis* bowing towards the female during courtship so that the female's antennae touch his scent patches (from Tinbergen, 1951).

Glands which may produce aphrodisiac scents also occur in various Neuroptera, Trichoptera, Diptera and Hymenoptera, sometimes in the male, sometimes in the female. Some male cockroaches produce a substance from a dorsal abdominal or thoracic gland which is fed on by the female and induces her to mount on the back of the male, so facilitating copulation (p. 303).

36.5 Pheromones of locusts

Locusts are, in a sense, semi-social insects and they produce certain pheromones which are concerned with the co-ordination of the population.

Mature male *Schistocerca*, which are bright yellow in colour, accelerate the maturation of other, less mature locusts of either sex. The pheromone responsible for this is possibly produced in the epidermal cells, which in a mature male become vacuolated and columnar (Fig. 507), and then passes on to the surface of the cuticle via epidermal glands or pore canals (Loher, 1960). Other individuals may perceive the pheromone either as a scent or by bodily contact, the latter being more effective. As a mature male approaches, other locusts become excited, vibrating first the antennae, then the palpi and finally the hind femora. The mode of action of the pheromone is not understood, but its effect is to stimulate the activity of the corpora allata, probably via the nervous system. This leads to maturation of the gonads and development of the yellow colour in males. Not only does the pheromone accelerate maturation, but it also leads to some synchronisation of maturation throughout the population.

There is also evidence that immature adult locusts, females less than eight days old for instance, retard maturation in others. A retarding pheromone is suggested, although none has been isolated. This, with the accelerating pheromone, results in the synchroni-sation of maturation since mature individuals tend to speed the maturation of immature insects, while the latter retard the development of those that are already mature (Norris, 1962).

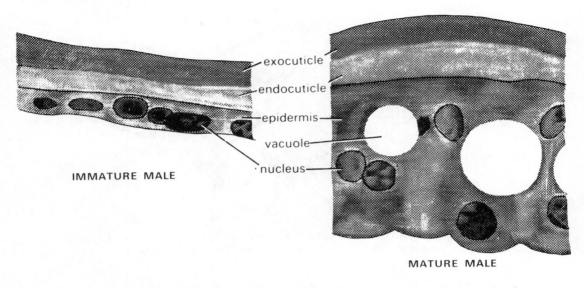

Fig. 507. Sections of the integument of immature and mature male *Schistocerca* showing the changes in the epidermis on maturation (after Loher, 1960).

Females of *Schistocerca* tend to lay their eggs in groups and the most powerful stimulus leading to the cohesion of these groups is a pheromone. It is produced by both sexes, whether they are mature or immature and is important mainly as a contact stimu-lus (Norris, 1963).

36.6 Pheromones of social insects

The pheromones of social insects fall roughly into two categories according to their functions:—those concerned with communication between workers and those con-cerned with the maintenance of colony structure. Some selected topics are considered below.

36.61 Communication in ants

Ant trails

Many ant species lay scent trails by which they are able to find their way about. The scent is produced in Dufour's gland or the poison gland in Myrmicinae, from Pavan's gland in .Dolichoderinae, and from the hind gut in Ponerinae, Dorylinae and Formicinae. Hence it may be dispensed via the sting, the edge of abdominal sternite 6, or the anus.

The trail initially consists of a series of scent spots produced by a worker ant touching the ground with its abdomen as it runs along. In *Solenopsis* these spots are not visible, but in *Lasius fuliginosus* drops of fluid are deposited. Subsequently, if the trail is used by many ants, the spots which they produce may merge into a continuous streak. The marking scents of many ants are species specific, but where the pheromone comes from the poison gland, as in Attini, this may not be so (see Blum, 1966).

Some trails are concerned in exploration, others in the recruitment of workers to a source of food. Exploratory trails are produced by army ants (Ponerinae, Dorylinae) and are laid more or less continuously by the blind workers as they forage. These species do not have permanent nests, but form temporary bivouacs from which they forage in columns. The scent trail laid by the individual is insignificant, but the accumulated trail of a whole column of ants is considerable and may last for several weeks in dry conditions. By means of the trails foragers are able to find their way back to the bivouac with food and it is also suggested that the male after its initial flight is able to find a trail and follow it to a bivouac where the new queens, which in these species are wingless, occur.

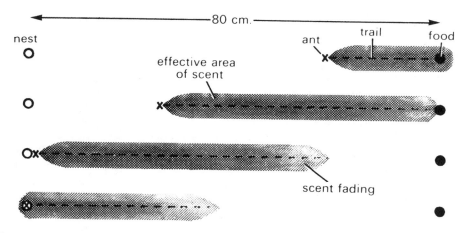

Fig. 508. Diagrammatic representations at successive time intervals of an ant laying a trail from a food source to the nest. The effective area of the scent is the area over which the scent is attractive to other ants (after Wilson, 1963b).

Recruitment trails are only laid by workers returning to the nest after finding a source of food or a more suitable nest site. These trails are laid by some members of the Myrmicinae, Dolichoderinae and Formicinae and, unlike the exploratory trails of army ants, are ephemeral, depending on constant use for their maintenance.

If a worker of *Solenopsis* finds food which it cannot carry it returns to the nest laying a trail (E. O. Wilson, 1962). On encountering a fellow worker it rushes towards the second ant and may briefly climb on it, apparently bringing the trail substance to its attention. Such recruited workers follow the trail, usually back towards the food, although directions to and from the nest are not indicated by the trail and workers may follow it in either direction. If the food is within 50 cm. of the nest the recruited workers may reach it, but if it is at a greater distance the first laid parts of the trail may have evaporated before the workers get to the end (Fig. 508). Feeding elicits trail laying so that any recruits which do reach the food deposit pheromone on their way back to the nest so that the original trail is reinforced. The pheromone itself is sufficient to elicit the following response in other workers so that if the food is close to the nest a rapid build up of foragers at the feeding site occurs. As the food supply diminishes fewer workers lay trails as they return to the nest so that less recruits are obtained and finally the trail fades out altogether.

At greater distances, although part of the initial trail evaporates, workers reaching the end of the trail continue searching and many rediscover the food. In this way a series of tracks are laid which, as more and more foragers are attracted, build up into a definite trail. Thus trails to more distant food depend on numbers of workers for their establishment because of the volatility of the pheromone. Related to this it is found that the distance foraged depends on the number of workers available; large colonies are able to find food more rapidly and at greater distances than small ones and there is a maximum distance beyond which a colony of a given size will not be able to produce a lasting trail.

Workers of *Solenopsis* often excavate along their trails and form irregular roofs over them so that trails to old food finds may be maintained over long periods. In this way the foraging field of a colony may be enlarged.

Alerting behaviour

If an ant in a colony is attacked the other members of the colony respond by assuming aggressive postures or attacking the intruder. The workers are stimulated by a pheromone from the mandibular or anal glands which is released by any individual being attacked. Sometimes these alerting substances are attractive at low concentrations so that workers are attracted to the scene of disturbance where the high concentration of pheromone causes them to become aggressive. These substances are highly volatile so that they are quickly dissipated; if this was not the case colonies might be in an almost continually disturbed state. Sometimes the alerting pheromone also functions as a defensive substance. This is the case with the formic acid produced by *Formica*, but in most cases defensive substances and alerting pheromones are quite different.

In *Acanthomyops claviger* the alerting substance is a mixture of citronellal and citral in the ratio 9:1.

There is evidence for the existence in ants of other pheromones which induce the gathering and settling of workers, grooming other workers and food exchange. Larvae also produce substances which affect the behaviour of workers.

36.62 Communication in Apis mellifera

Worker bees are attracted to each other by a scent from Nassanoff's gland. This scent is dispersed by depressing the tip of the abdomen so that the gland is exposed and sometimes the wings are vibrated at the same time, creating an air current over the gland. The scent is released in various situations, at syrup dishes where the bees have been feeding, for instance, or during recruitment to a new colony site. In the latter case workers which have successfully returned may stand by the entrance to the hive, fanning their wings and with Nassanoff's gland exposed so that the scent is dispersed. As a result of this behaviour returning foragers can orientate correctly even after their first flight (Ribbands and Spiers, 1953).

The scent produced in Nassanoff's gland is species specific, but not colony specific. In addition, bees do have a specific colony odour. This is an acquired, composite odour involving the secretion from Nassanoff's gland and the odours of substances with which the insect has been in contact and which have become absorbed in the wax covering the cuticle. Such substances include other members of the colony, the combs, larvae and the flowers visited by the bees. Thus the odour will vary with the particular circumstances of the colony and different colonies will have different odours. The colony odour facilitates the recognition of other members of the colony and workers are attracted to flowers marked with the scent of their own colony, rather than with that of another colony. This leads to greater constancy in foraging behaviour than would otherwise be the case (Kalmus and Ribbands, 1952).

36.63 Maintenance of colony structure

Isoptera

The differentiation of castes in termites appears to be regulated by a series of pheromones, although the pheromones have yet to be isolated. Most work has been carried out on *Kalotermes* (p. 706) (Lüscher, 1961).

Regulation in the numbers of a particular caste is brought about by the production and elimination of members of the caste concerned. For instance, in the absence of the king and queen, replacement reproductives are produced within a week. Usually an excess of replacements is produced and these are eaten by the pseudergates so as to leave only one pair. All this is believed to be controlled by pheromones produced by the reproductives.

Normally a queen *Kalotermes* produces a substance which inhibits the further development of female pseudergates (Fig. 509A). In the absence of this substance any female pseudergates that are competent to do so become replacement reproductives (p. 707). The male produces a comparable pheromone which inhibits the development of male pseudergates (Fig. 509B), and the production of this pheromone is stimulated in some unknown manner by the presence of the queen (Fig. 509C). The production of inhibitor by the queen is stimulated by the male to a lesser extent (Fig. 509D). These inhibitory pheromones are produced in the head or thorax and then pass via the alimentary canal to the anus. They are picked up by some pseudergates as a result of proctodaeal feeding and then passed on to others during mutual feeding. If a female pseudergate receives the female inhibiting substance it is believed that this is absorbed, but if she receives male inhibiting substance this is passed on unchanged to other members of the colony (Fig. 509E). Conversely males absorb male inhibiting substance, but merely serve to distribute the female inhibitor (Fig. 509F). This is important because the pheromones, as in the bees, are only active for a short time and so must be continually circulating round the colony in order to prevent the development of replacement reproductives.

The male produces a further substance which, in the absence of the female inhibitor, stimulates the production of females (Fig. 509G). If a comparable substance is produced by the queen it is very weak. Finally, the behaviour of the pseudergates is affected by other pheromones which lead the insects to eat any excess replacement reproductives which may be produced. The male produces a substance leading to the elimination of excess males (Fig. 509H), the female one leading to the elimination of excess females (Fig. 509J). These pheromones are possibly secreted through the cuticle and stimulate the pseudergates via their antennae. As a result of this complex of substances the colony is maintained with one male and one female reproductive.

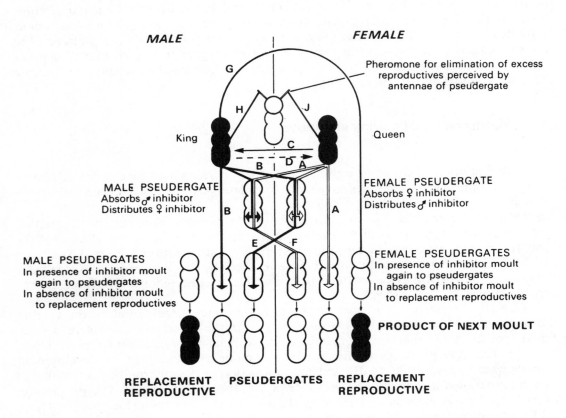

Fig. 509. Tenative representation of pheromone actions controlling the production and elimination of replacement reproductives in *Kalotermes*. Reproductives are shown in black, pseudergates in white. For explanation of the lettering see text (after Lüscher, 1961).

The production of soldiers is probably controlled in a similar way. This is suggested by observations on colony structure. In large colonies of *Kalotermes* there are, on the average, three soldiers for every 100 individuals in the colony. If soldiers are removed others develop in their place. Conversely when a colony is producing alates the number of individuals and hence the number of soldiers increases, but when the alates swarm the population of the colony suddenly decreases leaving an excess of soldiers. The excess is eliminated, being eaten by the pseudergates.

The pheromones in some way act on the nervous system which in turn produces changes in the endocrine system leading to moulting and differentiation (p. 707).

Apis mellifera

The queen honey bee produces several pheromones which play a part in controlling the social structure of her colony. If a queen is removed from a colony her absence is very soon perceived by the workers who become restless within about 30 minutes of her removal. A few hours later they start to build emergency queen cells, worker cells which are enlarged and reshaped so that the larvae within them can, with appropriate feeding, develop into queens. In the presence of the queen this behaviour is inhibited by a pheromone, known as queen substance, produced in her mandibular glands. The major component of the queen substance is 9-oxodecenoic acid, which is also the principal component of the sex attractant (p. 738). As with the termites, it is essential for the pheromone to be continually circulated round the colony in order to inhibit emergency queen cell building and again mutual feeding amongst the workers is involved. From the mandibular glands the pheromone becomes distributed over the whole body of the queen and is licked off by the workers. Mutual feeding is a common occurrence in *Apis* colonies, but workers who have recently licked the queen are even more ready to offer food to other workers than is usually the case. As a result the substance is very quickly distributed round the colony.

Emergency queen cell production is also inhibited by a volatile scent which acts with 9-oxodecenoic acid. The combined effect of the two substances in experiments is still less than that of a live queen so that in all probability at least one other inhibiting substance is involved.

Young virgin queens are unable to inhibit queen rearing. At first they produce no 9-oxodecenoic acid, but even after the first week, when this substance is formed, inhibition is poor, probably due to the absence of the inhibiting scent (Butler and Paton, 1962).

Queen rearing may take place in colonies with mature queens if the workers do not receive sufficient inhibitor. This can occur in two ways:—the output of pheromone by an ageing queen may be reduced or, alternatively, if a colony becomes very large and crowded the distribution of the pheromone may become inefficient so that some workers do not receive an adequate amount. In either case queen cells may be built and queen rearing follows. Such behaviour will result in the development of more queens and subsequently in the supersedure of the existing queen by one of the new ones, or in a part of the colony leaving the hive as a swarm. In a small colony whether supersedure or swarming occurs depends, at least to some extent, on the prevailing environmental conditions.

In the absence of the queen the ovaries of some of the workers develop, this depending in part also on adequate amounts of protein and carbohydrate in the diet. This ovary development is normally inhibited by the pheromones inhibiting queen cell building, but in this case scent is less effective.

Another pheromone produced by the mandibular glands is 9-hydroxydecenoic acid. This is a scent which is attractive to workers and plays a part in the maintenance of swarm clusters.

Other Hymenoptera

In ants there is some evidence for a substance comparable with queen substance since, at least in *Formica pratensis* and *Myrmica rubra*, the queen inhibits queen production.

On the other hand the failure of worker ovaries to develop in bumblebees, wasps and some other ants is apparently not due to pheromones. It is possible that the insect with the best developed ovaries, normally the queen, so harrasses the others that development of their ovaries is retarded (Butler, 1964b).

REFERENCES

AGRELL, I. (1964). Physiological and biochemical changes during insect development. *in* Rockstein, M. (Ed.), *The physiology of Insecta*. vol. 1. Academic Press, New York.

ALBRECHT, F. O. (1953). *The anatomy of the migratory locust*. Athlone Press, London.

ALBRECHT, F. O. (1955). La densité des populations et la croissance chez *Schistocerca gregaria* (Forsk.) et *Nomadacris septemfasciata* (Serv.); la mue d'adjustement. *J. Agric. trop. Bot. appl.* 11: 109–192.

ALBRECHT, F. O. (1956). The anatomy of the red locust, *Nomadacris septemfasciata* Serville. *Anti-Locust Bull.* no. 23, 9 pp. + figs.

ALEXANDER, R. D. (1961). Aggressiveness, territoriality, and sexual behaviour in field crickets (Orthoptera: Gryllidae). *Behaviour* 17: 130–223.

ALEXANDER, R. D. (1964). The evolution of mating behaviour in arthropods. *Symp. R. ent. Soc. Lond.* 2: 78–94.

ALEXANDER, R. D. (1967). Acoustical communication in arthropods. *A. Rev. Ent.* 12: 495–526.

ALEXANDER, R. D. and MOORE, T. E. (1962). The evolutionary relationships of 17-year and 13-year cicadas, and three new species (Homoptera, Cicadidae, *Magicicada*). *Misc. Publs. Mus. Zool. Univ. Mich.* no. 121, 59 pp.

ALEXANDER, R. D., MOORE, T. E. and WOODRUFF, R. E. (1963). The evolutionary differentiation of stridulatory signals in beetles (Insecta: Coleoptera). *Anim. Behav.* 11: 111–115.

ANDERSEN, S. O. and WEIS-FOGH, T. (1964). Resilin. A rubberlike protein in arthropod cuticle. *Adv. Ins. Physiol.* 2: 1–66.

ANDERSON, D. S. (1960). The respiratory system of the egg-shell of *Calliphora erythrocephala*. *J. Insect Physiol.* 5: 120–128.

ANDERSON, D. S. (1965). Observations on female accessory glands of some Acridoidea, with particular reference to *Pyrgomorpha dispar* I. Bolivar. *Entomologist's mon. Mag.* 101: 16–17.

ANDERSON, D. S. (1966). The developmental anatomy and histology of the reproductive system in Acridoidea. Ph.D. Thesis, University of London.

ANDERSON, D. T. (1962). The embryology of *Dacus tryoni* (Frogg.) (Diptera, Trypetidae (= Tephritidae)), the Queensland fruit-fly. *J. Embryol. exp. Morph.* 10: 248–292.

ANDERSON, D. T. (1964). The embryology of *Dacus tryoni* 3. Origins of imaginal rudiments other than the principal discs. *J. Embryol. exp. Morph.* 12: 65–75.

ANDERSON, D. T. (1966). The comparative embryology of the Diptera. *A. Rev. Ent.* 11: 23–46.

ANDERSON, E. (1964). Oocyte differentiation and vitellogenesis in the roach *Periplaneta americana*. *J. Cell Biol.* 20: 131–155.

ANDERSON, J. M. (1950). A cytological and histological study of the testicular cyst-cells in the Japanese beetle. *Physiol. Zoöl.* 23: 308–316.

ANDERSON, T. F. and RICHARDS, A. G. (1942). An electron microscope study of some structural colours of insects. *J. appl. Phys.* 13: 748–758.

ANDREWARTHA, H. G. (1952). Diapause in relation to the ecology of insects. *Biol. Rev.* 27: 50–107.

APPLEBAUM, S. W., JANKOVIĆ, M., GROZDANOVIĆ, J. and MARINKOVIĆ, D. (1964). Compensation for temperature in the digestive metabolism of *Tenebrio molitor* larvae. *Physiol. Zoöl.* 37: 90–95.

ARVY, L. (1954). Données sur la leucopoièse chez *Musca domestica* L. *Proc. R. ent. Soc. Lond.* A, 29: 39–41.

ASAHINA, E. (1966). Freezing and frost resistance in insects. *in* Meryman, H. T. (Ed.), *Cryobiology.* Academic Press, London.

ASHHURST, D. E. (1965). The connective tissue tissue sheath of the locust nervous system: its development in the embryo. *Q. Jl microsc. Sci.* 106: 61–74.

ASHHURST, D. E. (1968). The connective tissues of insects. *A. Rev. Ent.* 13: 45–74.

AUCLAIR, J. L. (1963). Aphid feeding and nutrition. *A. Rev. Ent.* 8: 439–490.

AUTRUM, H. (1958). Electrophysiological analysis of the visual systems in insects. *Expl. Cell Res.* suppl. 5: 426–439.

AUTRUM, H. (1963). Anatomy and physiology of sound receptors in invertebrates. *in* Busnel, R.-G. (Ed.), *Acoustic behaviour of animals.* Elsevier Publishing Co., Amsterdam.

BADE, M. L. (1964). Biosynthesis of fatty acids in the roach *Eurycotis floridana*. *J. Insect Physiol.* 10: 333–342.

BAKER, J. M. (1963). Ambrosia beetles and their fungi with particular reference to *Platypus cylindrus*, Fab. *Symp. Soc. gen. Microbiol.* 13: 232–265.

BALDWIN, E. (1949). *Dynamic aspects of biochemistry.* Cambridge University Press.

BARETH, C. (1964). Structure et dépôt des spermatophores chez *Campodea remyi.* *C. r. hebd. Séanc. Acad. Sci., Paris* 259: 1572–1575.

BARLOW, H. B. (1952). The size of ommatidia in apposition eyes. *J. exp. Biol.* 29: 667–674.

BARNES, O. L. (1955). Effect of food plants on the lesser migratory grasshopper. *J. econ. Ent.* 48: 119–124.

BARRASS, R. (1960). The courtship behaviour of *Mormoniella vitripennis* Walk. (Hymenoptera, Pteromalidae). *Behaviour* 15: 185–209.

BARTON-BROWNE, L. B. (1964). Water regulation in insects. *A. Rev. Ent.* 9: 63–82.

BASTOCK, M. and MANNING, A. (1955). The courtship of *Drosophila melanogaster.* *Behaviour* 8: 85–111.

BATELLI, F. and STERN, L. (1913). Intensität des respiratorischen Gaswechsels der Insekten. *Biochem. Z.* 56: 50–58.

BAWA, S. R. (1964). Electron microscope study of spermiogenesis in a fire-brat insect, *Thermobia domestica* Pack. I. Mature spermatozoon. *J. Cell Biol.* 23: 431–446.

BEAMENT, J. W. L. (1946a). The formation and structure of the chorion of the egg in an hemipteran, *Rhodnius prolixus*. *Q. Jl microsc. Sci.* 87: 393–439.

BEAMENT, J. W. L. (1946b). The waterproofing process in eggs of *Rhodnis prolixus* Stähl. *Proc. R. Soc.* B, 133: 407–418.

BEAMENT, J. W. L. (1947). The formation and structure of the micropylar complex in the egg-shell of *Rhodnius prolixus* Stähl. (Heteroptera Reduviidae). *J. exp. Biol.* 23: 213–233.

BEAMENT, J. W. L. (1959). The waterproofing mechanism of arthropods. I. The effect of temperature on cuticle permeability in terrestrial insects and ticks. *J. exp. Biol.* 36: 391–422.

BEAMENT, J. W. L. (1960). Wetting properties of insect cuticle. *Nature, Lond.* 186: 408–409.

BEAMENT, J. W. L. (1961). The waterproofing mechanism of arthropods. II. The permeability of the cuticle of some aquatic insects. *J. exp. Biol.* 38: 277–290.

BEAMENT, J. W. L. (1964). The active transport and passive movement of water in insects. *Adv. Ins. Physiol.* 2: 67–130.

BEARD, R. L. (1950). Experimental observations on coagulation of insect haemolymph. *Physiol. Zoöl.* 23: 47–57.

BEARD, R. L. (1953). Circulation; in Roeder, K. D. (Ed.), *Insect physiology*. Wiley and Sons, New York.

BEARD, R. L. (1963). Insect toxins and venoms. *A. Rev. Ent.* 8: 1–18.

BEENAKKERS, A. M. T. (1965). Transport of fatty acids in *Locusta migratoria* during sustained flight. *J. Insect Physiol.* 11: 879–888.

BEERMANN, W. and CLEVER, W. (1964). Chromosome puffs. *Scient. Am.* 210, no. 4: 50–58.

BENNET-CLARK, H. C. and LUCEY, E. C. A. (1967). The jump of the flea: A study of the energetics and a model of the mechanism. *J. exp. Biol.* 47: 59–76.

BENTLEY, D. R. and KUTSCH, W. (1966). The neuromuscular mechanism of stridulation in crickets (Orthoptera: Gryllidae). *J. exp. Biol.* 45: 151–164.

BERLAND, L. and GRASSÉ, P.-P. (1951). Super-ordre des Neuroptéroides. *in* Grassé, P.-P. (Ed.), *Traité de Zoologie* vol. 10. Masson et Cie., Paris.

BERRIDGE, M. J. (1965a). The physiology of excretion in the cotton stainer, *Dysdercus fasciatus* Signoret I. Anatomy, water excretion and osmoregulation. *J. exp. Biol.* 43: 511–521.

BERRIDGE, M. J. (1965b). The physiology of excretion in the cotton stainer, *Dysdercus fasciatus* Signoret III. Nitrogen excretion and excretary metabolism. *J. exp. Biol.* 43: 535–552.

BICK, G. H. and SULZBACH, D. (1966). Reproductive behaviour of the damselfly, *Hetaerina americana* (Fabricius) (Odonata: Calopterygidae). *Anim. Behav.* 14: 156–158.

BILLARD, G. and BRUYANT, C. (1905). Sur un mode particulier de locomotion de certains *Stenus*. *C. r. Séanc. Soc. Biol.* 59: 102–103.

BISHOP, D. W. (1962). Sperm motility. *Physiol. Rev.* 42: 1–59.

BLACKITH, R. E., DAVIES, R. G. and MOY, E. A. (1963). A biometric analysis of development in *Dysdercus fasciatus* Sign. (Hemiptera: Pyrrhocoridae). *Growth* 27: 317–334.

BLEST, A. D. (1957). The function of eyespot patterns in the Lepidoptera. *Behaviour* 11: 209–256.

BLEST, A. D. and COLLETT, T. S. (1965). Micro-electrode studies of the medial protocerebrum of some Lepidoptera—I. Responses to simple, binocular visual stimulation. *J. Insect Physiol.* 11: 1079–1103.

BLEST, A. D., COLLETT, T. S. and PYE, J. D. (1963). The generation of ultrasonic signals by a New World arctiid moth. *Proc. R. Soc.* B, 158: 196–207.

BLOCH, D. P. and BRACK, S. D. (1964). Evidence for the cytoplasmic synthesis of nuclear histone during spermiogenesis in the grasshopper *Chortophaga viridifasciata* (De Geer). *J. Cell Biol.* 22: 327–340.

BLUM, M. S. (1966). The source and specificity of trail pheromones in *Termitopone, Monomorium* and *Huberia,* and their relation to those of some other ants. *Proc. R. ent. Soc. Lond.* A, 41: 155–160.

BODENSTEIN, D. (1950). The postembryonic development of *Drosophila*. *in* Demerec, M. (Ed.), *Biology of Drosophila*. Wiley & Sons, New York.

BOECKH, J., KAISSLING, K. E. and SCHNEIDER, D. (1965). Insect olfactory receptors. *Cold Spring Harbor Symp. Quant. Biol.* 30: 263–280.

BOETTIGER, E. G. (1960). Insect flight muscles and their basic physiology. *A. Rev. Ent.* 5: 1–16.

BONHAG, P. F. (1956). The origin and distribution of periodic acid-Schiff-positive substances in the oocyte of the earwig, *Anisolabis maritima* (Géné). *J. Morph.* 99: 433–463.

BONHAG, P. F. (1958). Ovarian structure and vitellogenesis in insects. *A. Rev. Ent.* 3: 137–160.

BONHAG, P. F. and ARNOLD, W. J. (1961). Histology, histochemistry and tracheation of the ovariole sheaths in the American cockroach, *Periplaneta americana* (L.). *J. Morph.* 108: 107–129.

BONHAG, P. F. and WICK, J. R. (1953). The functional anatomy of the male and female reproductive systems of the milkweed bug, *Oncopeltus fasciatus* (Dallas) (Heteroptera: Lygaeidae). *J. Morph.* 93: 177–283.

BOURGOGNE, J. (1951). Ordre des Lépidoptères. *in* Grassé, P.-P. (Ed.), *Traité de Zoologie.* vol. 10. Masson et Cie., Paris.

BRADY, J. (1967a). Control of the circadian rhythm of activity in the cockroach. I. The role of the corpora cardiaca, brain and stress. *J. exp. Biol.* 47: 153–163.

BRADY, J. (1967b). Control of the circadian rhythm of activity in the rockroach. II. The role of the sub-oesophageal ganglion and ventral nerve cord. *J. exp. Biol.* 47: 165–178.

BRIAN, M. V. and BRIAN, A. D. (1952). The wasp *Vespula sylvestris* Scopoli: feeding, foraging and colony development. *Trans. R. ent. Soc. Lond.* 103: 1–26.

BRINKHURST, R. O. (1959a). Alary polymorphism in the Gerroidea (Hemiptera-Heteroptera). *J. Anim. Ecol.* 28: 211–230.

BRINKHURST, R. O. (1959b). Studies on the functional morphology of *Gerris najas* De Geer (Hem. Het. Gerridae). *Proc. zool. Soc. Lond.* 133: 531–559.

BRINKHURST, R. O. (1963). Observations on wing-polymorphism in the Heteroptera. *Proc. R. ent. Soc. Lond.* A, 38: 15–22.

BROCHER, F. (1919). Les organs pulsatile méso—et métatergaux des Lépidoptères. *Archs Zool. exp. gén.* 58: 149–171.

BROOKS, M. A. (1963a). The microorganisms of healthy insects. *in* Steinhaus, E. A. (Ed.), *Insect pathology* vol. 1. Academic Press, New York.

BROOKS, M. A. (1963b). Symbiosis and aposymbiosis in arthropods. *Symp. Soc. gen. Microbiol.* 13: 200–231.

BROUGHTON, W. B. (1963). Method in bio-acoustic terminology. *in* Busnel, R.-G. (Ed.), *Acoustic behaviour of animals.* Elsevier, Amsterdam.

BROUGHTON, W. B. (1964). Function of the 'mirror' in tettigonioid Orthoptera. *Nature, Lond.* 201: 949–950.

BROUGHTON, W. B. (Ed.) (1965). *Colour and Life.* Institute of Biology, London.

BROWER, L. P. and JONES, M. A. (1965). Precourtship interaction of wing and abdominal sex glands in male *Danaus* butterflies. *Proc. R. ent. Soc. Lond.* A, 40: 147–151.

BROWN, A. W. A. (1958). Factors which attract *Aedes* mosquitoes to humans. *Proc. Xth Int. Congr. Ent.* 3: 757–764.

BROWN, E. S. (1965). Notes on the migration and direction of flight of *Eurygaster* and *Aelia* species (Hemiptera, Pentatomoidea) and their possible bearing on invasions of cereal crops. *J. Anim. Ecol.* 34: 93–108.

BROWN, R. G. B. (1965). Courtship in the *Drosophila obscura* group. II. Comparative studies. *Behaviour* 25: 281–323.

BROWNING, T. O. (1965). Observations on the absorption of water, diapause and embryogenesis in the eggs of the cricket *Teleogryllus commodus* (Walker). *J. exp. Biol.* 43: 433–439.

BROWNING, T. O. and FORREST, W. W. (1960). The permeability of the shell of the egg of *Acheta commodus* Walker (Orthoptera, Gryllidae). *J. exp. Biol.* 37: 213–217.

BRUES, C. T. (1946). *Insect dietary. An account of the food habits of insects.* Harvard University Press, Cambridge, Mass.

BRUNET, P. C. J. (1952). The formation of the ootheca by *Periplaneta americana* II. The structure and function of the left colleterial gland. *Q. Jl microsc. Sci.* 93: 47–69.

BÜCHER, Th. (1965). Formation of the specific structural and enzymic pattern of the insect flight muscle. *in* Goodwin, T. W. (Ed.), *Aspects of insect biochemistry.* Academic Press, London.

BUCHTHAL, F., WEIS-FOGH, T. and ROSENFALCK, P. (1957). Twitch contractions of isolated flight muscle of locusts. *Acta physiol. scand.* 39: 246–276.

BUCK, J. B. (1948). The anatomy and physiology of the light organ in fireflies. *Ann. N.Y. Acad. Sci.* 49: 397–483.

BUCK, J. B. (1953). Physical properties and chemical composition of insect blood. *in* Roeder, K. (Ed.), *Insect physiology.* Wiley and Sons, New York.

BUCK, J. (1958). Cyclic CO_2 release in insects. IV. A theory of mechanism. *Biol. Bull. mar. biol. Lab., Woods Hole* 114: 118–140.

BUCK, J. (1962). Some physical aspects of insect respiration. *A. Rev. Ent.* 7: 27–56.

BUCK, J. and KEISTER, M. (1955). Further studies of gas-filling in the insect tracheal system. *J. exp. Biol.* 32: 681–691.

BURKHARDT, D. (1960). Action potentials in the antennae of the blowfly (*Calliphora erythrocephala*) during mechanical stimulation. *J. Insect Physiol.* 4: 138–145.

BURKHARDT, D. (1962). Spectral sensitivity and other response characteristics of single visual cells in the arthropod eye. *Symp. Soc. exp. Biol.* 16: 86–109.

BURKHARDT, D. (1964). Colour discrimination in insects. *Adv. Ins. Physiol.* 2: 131–174.

BURSELL, E. (1956). The polypneustic lobes of the tsetse larva (*Glossina*, Diptera). *Proc. R. Soc. B*, 144: 275–286.

BURSELL, E. (1957). The effect of humidity on the activity of tsetse flies. *J. exp. Biol.* 34: 42–51.

BURSELL, E. (1960). Loss of water by excretion and defaecation in the tsetse fly. *J. exp. Biol.* 37: 689–697.

BURSELL, E. (1961). Post-teneral development of the thoracic musculature in tsetse flies. *Proc. R. ent. Soc. Lond.* A, 36: 69–74.

BURSELL, E. (1964a). Environmental aspects: temperature. *in* Rockstein, M. (Ed.), *The physiology of Insecta.* vol. 1. Academic Press, New York.

BURSELL, E. (1964b). Environmental aspects: humidity. *in* Rockstein, M. (Ed.), *The physiology of Insecta.* vol. 1. Academic Press, New York.

BURSELL, E. and JACKSON, C. H. N. (1957). Notes on the choriothete and milk gland of *Glossina* and *Hippobosca* (Diptera). *Proc. R. ent. Soc. Lond.* A, 32: 30–34.

BURTT, E. D. and UVAROV, B. P. (1944). Changes in wing pigmentation during the adult life of Acrididae (Orthoptera). *Proc. R. ent. Soc. Lond.* A, 19: 7–8.

BURTT, E. T. and CATTON, W. T. (1962a). A diffraction theory of insect vision. I. An experimental investigation of visual acuity and image formation in the compound eyes of three species of insects. *Proc. R. Soc. B*, 157: 53–82.

BURTT, E. T. and CATTON, W. T. (1962b). The resolving power of the compound eye. *Symp. Soc. exp. Biol.* 16: 72–85.

BURTT, E. T. and CATTON, W. T. (1966). Image formation and sensory transmission in the compound eye. *Adv. Ins. Physiol.* 3: 2–46.

BUTLER, C. G. (1962). *The world of the honeybee.* Collins, London.

BUTLER, C. G. (1964a). Recent work on the swarm cluster and on the behaviour of honeybee drones in the field. *Proc. R. ent. Soc. Lond.* C, 29: 12–13.

BUTLER, C. G. (1964b). Pheromones in sexual processes in insects. *Symp. R. ent. Soc. Lond.* 2: 66–77.

BUTLER, C. G. (1965). Sex attraction in *Andrena flavipes* Panzer (Hymenoptera: Apidae) with some observations on nest-site restriction. *Proc. R. ent. Soc. Lond.* A, 40: 77–80.

BUTLER, C. G. (1967). Insect pheromones. *Biol. Rev.* 42: 42–87.

BUTLER, C. G. and PATON, P. N. (1962). Inhibition of queen rearing by queen honey-bees (*Apis mellifera* L.) of different ages. *Proc. R. ent. Soc. Lond.* A, 37: 114–116.

BUXTON, P. A. (1955). *The natural history of tsetse flies.* Lewis & Co., London.

CALLAHAN, P. S. (1965). A photoelectric-photographic analysis of flight behaviour in the corn earworm, *Heliothis zea*, and other moths. *Ann. ent. Soc. Amer.* 58: 159–169.

CALLAHAN, P. S. (1965a). Intermediate and far infrared sensing of nocturnal insects. Part I. Evidences for a far infrared (FIR) electromagnetic theory of communication and sensing in moths and its relationship to the limiting biosphere of the corn earworm. *Ann. ent. Soc. Amer.* 58: 727–745.

CALLAHAN, P. S. (1965b). Intermediate and far infrared sensing of nocturnal insects. Part II. The compound eye of the corn earworm, *Heliothis zea*, and other moths as a mosaic optic-electromagnetic thermal radiometer. *Ann. ent. Soc. Amer.* 58: 746–755.

CAMPBELL, J. I. (1961). The anatomy of the nervous system of the mesothorax of *Locusta migratoria migratorioides* R. & F. *Proc. zool. Soc. Lond.* 137: 403–432.

CANDY, D. J. and KILBY, B. A. (1962). Studies on chitin synthesis in the desert locust. *J. exp. Biol.* 39: 129–140.

CARAYON, J. (1953a). Organe de Ribaga et fécondation hémocoelienne chez les *Xylocoris* du groupe *galactinus* (Hemipt. Anthocoridae). *C. r. hebd. Séanc. Acad. Sci., Paris* 236: 1099–1101.

CARAYON, J. (1953b). Existence d'un double orifice génital et d'un tissu conducteur des spermatozoïdes chez les Anthocorinae (Hemipt. Anthocoridae). *C. r. hebd. Séanc. Acad. Sci., Paris* 236: 1206–1208.

CARAYON, J. (1964). Un cas d'offrande nuptiale chez les Heteroptères. *C. r. hebd. Séanc. Acad. Sci., Paris* 259: 4815–4818.

CARLISLE, D. B. and ELLIS, P. E. (1962). Endocrine glands and phase in locusts. *Symp. genet.* 10: 219–224.

CARPENTER, G. D. H. and FORD, E. B. (1933). *Mimicry.* Methuen, London.

CARSON, H. L. (1945). A comparative study of the apical cell of the insect testis. *J. Morph.* 77: 141–155.

CARTHY, J. D. (1958). *An introduction to the behaviour of invertebrates.* Allen and Unwin, London.

CAZAL, P. (1948). Les glandes endocrines rétro-cérébrales des insectes (étude morphologique). *Bull. biol. Fr. Belg.* suppl. 32: 227 pp.

CHADWICK, L. E. (1953a). The motion of the wings. *in* Roeder, K. D. (Ed.), *Insect physiology.* Wiley & Sons, New York.

CHADWICK, L. E. (1953b). Aerodynamics and flight metabolism. *in* Roeder, K. D. (Ed.), *Insect physiology.* Wiley & Sons, New York.

CHANDLEY, A. C. (1966). Studies on oogenesis in *Drosophila melanogaster* with ^{3}H-thymidine label. *Expl. Cell Res.* 44: 201–215.

CHAO, H.-F. (1953). The external morphology of the dragonfly *Onychogomphus ardens* Needham. *Smithson. misc. Collns.* 122, no. 6: 1–56.

CHAPMAN, K. M. (1965). Campaniform sensilla on the tactile spines of the legs of the cockroach. *J. exp. Biol.* 42: 191–203. no. 6: 1–56.

CHAPMAN, R. F. (1957). Observations on the feeding of adults of the red locust (*Nomadacris septemfasciata* (Serville)). *Br. J. Anim. Behav.* 5: 60–75.

CHAPMAN, R. F. (1958). A field study of the potassium concentration in the blood of the red locust, *Nomadacris septemfasciata* (Serv.), in relation to its activity. *Anim. Behav.* 6: 60–67.

CHAPMAN, R. F. (1959a). Observations on the flight activity of the red locust, *Nomadacris septemfasciata* (Serville). *Behaviour* 14: 300–334.

CHAPMAN, R. F. (1959b). Field observations on the behaviour of hoppers of the red locust (*Nomadacris septemfasciata* Serville). *Anti-Locust Bull.* no. 33, 51 pp.

CHAPMAN, R. F. (1959c). Some observations on *Pachyophthalmus africa* Curran (Diptera: Calliphoridae), a parasite of *Eumenes maxillosus* De Geer (Hymenoptera: Eumenidae). *Proc. R. ent. Soc. Lond.* A, 34: 1–6.

CHAPMAN, R. F. (1961). Some experiments to determine the methods used in host-finding by the tsetse fly, *Glossina medicorum* Austen. *Bull. ent. Res.* 52: 83–97.

CHAPMAN, R. F. (1964). The structure and wear of the mandibles in some African grasshoppers. *Proc. zool. Soc. Lond.* 142: 107–121.

CHAPMAN, R. F. (1965). The behaviour of nymphs of *Schistocerca gregaria* (Forskal) (Orthoptera, Acrididae) in a temperature gradient, with special reference to temperature preference. *Behaviour* 24: 283–317.

CHAPMAN, R. F. and ROBERTSON, I. A. D. (1958). The egg pods of some tropical African grasshoppers. *J. ent. Soc. Sth. Afr.* 21: 85–112.

CHEFURKA, W. (1965a). Intermediary metabolism of carbohydrates in insects. *in* Rockstein, M. (Ed.), *The physiology of Insecta.* vol. 2. Academic Press, New York.

CHEFURKA, W. (1965b). Intermediary metabolism of nitrogenous and lipid compounds in insects. *in* Rockstein, M. (Ed.), *The physiology of Insecta.* vol. 2. Academic Press, New York.

CHEFURKA, W. (1965c). Some comparative aspects of the metabolism of carbohydrates in insects. *A. Rev. Ent.* 10: 345–382.

CHEN, P. S. (1966). Amino acid and protein metabolism in insect development. *Adv. Ins. Physiol.* 3: 53–132.

CHEN, P. S. and BACHMANN-DIEM, C. (1964). Studies on the transamination reactions in the larval fat body of *Drosophila melanogaster.* *J. Insect Physiol.* 10: 819–830.

CHEN, P. S. and LEVENBOOK, L. (1966). Studies on the haemolymph proteins of the blowfly *Phormia regina*—I. Changes in ontogenetic patterns. *J. Insect Physiol.* 12: 1595–1609.

CHEN, S. H. (1946). Evolution of the insect larva. *Trans. R. ent. Soc. Lond.* 97: 381–404.

CHURCH, N. S. (1960a). Heat loss and the body temperatures of flying insects. I. Heat loss by evaporation of water from the body. *J. exp. Biol.* 37: 171–185.

CHURCH, N. S. (1960b). Heat loss and the body temperatures of flying insects. II. Heat conduction within the body and its loss by radiation and convection. *J. exp. Biol.* 37: 186–212.

CLARE, S. and TAUBER, O. E. (1942). Circulation of haemolymph in the wings of the cockroach *Blatella germanica* L. III. Circulation in the articular membrane: the significance of this membrane, the pteralia, and wing folds as directive and speed controlling mechanisms in wing circulation. *Iowa St. Coll. J. Sci.* 16: 349–356.

CLARKE, K. U. (1957a). On the increase in linear size during growth in *Locusta migratoria* L. *Proc. R. ent. Soc. Lond.* A, 32: 35–39.

CLARKE, K. U. (1957b). On the role of the tracheal system in the post-embryonic growth of *Locusta migratoria* L. *Proc. R. ent. Soc. Lond.* A, 32: 67–79.

CLARKE, K. U. (1960). Studies on the relationships between air temperature and the internal body temperature of *Locusta migratoria.* *J. Insect Physiol.* 5: 23–36.

CLARKE, K. U. (1967). Insects and temperature. *in* Rose, A. H. (Ed.), *Thermobiology.* Academic Press, London.

CLARKE, K. U. and GILLOTT, C. (1967a). Studies on the effects of the removal of the frontal ganglion in *Locusta migratoria* L. I. The effect on protein metabolism. *J. exp. Biol.* 46: 13–25.

CLARKE, K. U. and GILLOTT, C. (1967b). Studies on the effects of the removal of the frontal ganglion in *Locusta migratoria* L. II. Ribonucleic acid synthesis. *J. exp. Biol.* 46: 27–34.

CLARKE, K. U. and LANGLEY, P. A. (1963). Studies on the initiation of growth and moulting in *Locusta migratoria migratorioides* R. & F. IV. The relationship between the stomatogastric nervous system and neurosecretion. *J. Insect Physiol.* 9: 423–430.

CLAUSEN, C. P. (1940). *Entomophagous insects*. McGraw Hill, New York.

CLEGG, J. S. and EVANS, D. R. (1961). The physiology of blood trehalose and its function during flight in the blowfly. *J. exp. Biol.* 38: 771–792.

CLEMENTS, A. N. (1959). Studies on the metabolism of locust fat body. *J. exp. Biol.* 36: 665–675.

CLEMENTS, A. N. (1963). *The physiology of mosquitoes*. Pergamon Press, Oxford.

CLEVER, U. (1965). The effect of ecdysone on gene activity patterns in giant chromosomes. in Karlson, P. (Ed.), *Mechanisms of hormone action*. Academic Press, London.

CLOUDSLEY-THOMPSON, J. L. (1962). Bioclimatic observations in the Red Sea hills and coastal plain, a major habitat of the desert locust. *Proc. R. ent. Soc. Lond.* A, 37: 27–34.

COLES, G. C. (1965). The haemolymph and moulting in *Rhodnius prolixus* Stål. *J. Insect Physiol.* 11: 1317–1323.

COLHOUN, E. H. (1963). The physiological significance of acetylcholine in insects and observations upon other pharmacologically active substances. *Adv. Ins. Physiol.* 1: 1–46.

COLLINS, H. R. and RICHTER, K. M. (1961). Ordinary and electron microscope studies on mitochondrial ultrastructural transformations attending spermatogenesis in the notonectid, *Buenea* sp. *Anat. Rec.* 139: 297–298.

COMSTOCK, J. H. (1918). *The wings of insects*. Comstock publishing Co., New York.

COOK, W. C. (1926). The effectiveness of certain paraffin derivatives in attracting flies. *J. agric. Res.* 32: 347–358.

CORBET, P. (1962). *A biology of dragonflies*. Witherby Ltd., London.

CORBET, P. S. and HADDOW, A. J. (1962). Diptera swarming high above the forest canopy in Uganda, with special reference to Tabanidae. *Trans. R. ent. Soc. Lond.* 114: 267–284.

CORBET, P. S., LONGFIELD, C. and MOORE, N. W. (1960). *Dragonflies*. Collins, London.

COTT, H. B. (1957). *Adaptive coloration in animals*. Methuen, London.

COTTRELL, C. B. (1962a). The imaginal ecdysis of blowflies. Observations on the hydrostatic mechanisms involved in digging and expansion. *J. exp. Biol.* 39: 431–448.

COTTRELL, C. B. (1962b). The imaginal ecdysis of blowflies. Evidence for a change in the mechanical properties of the cuticle at expansion. *J. exp. Biol.* 39: 449–458.

COTTRELL, C. B. (1964). Insect ecdysis with particular emphasis on cuticular hardening and darkening. *Adv. Ins. Physiol.* 2: 175–218.

COUNCE, S. J. (1961). The analysis of insect embryogenesis. *A. Rev. Ent.* 6: 295–312.

COUNCE, S. J. (1963). Developmental morphology of polar granules in *Drosophila* including observations on pole cell behaviour and distribution during embryogenesis. *J. Morph.* 112: 129–145.

CRAGG, J. B. and COLE, P. (1956). Laboratory studies on the chemosensory reactions of blowflies. *Ann. appl. Biol.* 44: 478–491.

CRAIG, R. (1960). The physiology of excretion in the insect. *A. Rev. Ent.* 5: 53–68.

CRISP, D. J. (1964). Plastron respiration. *Recent Prog. Surf. Sci.* 2: 377–425.

CROMARTIE, R. I. T. (1959). Insect pigments. *A. Rev. Ent.* 4: 59–76.

CROMBIE, A. C. (1942). On oviposition, olfactory conditioning and host selection in *Rhizopertha dominica* Fab. (Insecta, Coleoptera). *J. exp. Biol.* 18: 62–79.

CROWSON, R. A. (1960). The phylogeny of Coleoptera. *A. Rev. Ent.* 5: 111–134.

DADD, R. H. (1960a). The nutritional requirements of locusts. I. Development of synthetic diets and lipid requirements. *J. Insect Physiol.* 4: 319–347.

DADD, R. H. (1960b). The nutritional requirements of locusts. II. Utilisation of sterols.

J. Insect Physiol. 5: 161–168.

DADD, R. H. (1960c). The nutritional requirements of locusts. III. Carbohydrate requirements and utilisation. *J. Insect Physiol.* 5: 301–316.

DADD, R. H. (1961a). The nutritional requirements of locusts. IV. Requirements for vitamins of the B complex. *J. Insect Physiol.* 6: 1–12.

DADD, R. H. (1961b). The nutritional requirements of locusts. V. Observations on essential fatty acids, chlorophyll, nutritional salt mixtures, and the protein or amino acid components of synthetic diets. *J. Insect Physiol.* 6: 126–145.

DADD, R. H. (1961c). Observations on the effects of carotene on the growth and pigmentation of locusts. *Bull. ent. Res.* 52: 63–81.

DADD, R. H. (1963). Feeding behaviour and nutrition in grasshoppers and locusts. *Adv. Ins. Physiol.* 1: 47–111.

DADD, R. H. (1964). A study of carbohydrate and lipid nutrition in the wax moth, *Galleria mellonella* (L.), using partially synthetic diets. *J. Insect Physiol.* 10: 161–178.

DANILEVSKII, A. S. (1965). *Photoperiodism and seasonal development of insects.* Oliver & Boyd, Edinburgh.

DAS, C. C., KAUFMANN, B. P. and GAY, H. (1964). Histone-protein transition in *Drosophila melanogaster.* I. Changes during spermatogenesis. *Expl Cell Res.* 35: 507–514.

DASS, C. M. S. and RIS, H. (1958). Submicroscopic organisation of the nucleus during spermiogenesis in the grasshopper. *J. biophys. biochem. Cytol.* 4: 129–132.

DAVEY, J. T. (1959). The African migratory locust (*Locusta migratoria migratorioides* Rch. and Frm., Orth.) in the Central Niger Delta. Part two. The ecology of *Locusta* in the semi-arid lands and seasonal movements of populations. *Locusta* 7: 1–180.

DAVEY, K. G. (1958). The migration of spermatozoa in the female of *Rhodnius prolixus* Stal. *J. exp. Biol.* 35: 694–701.

DAVEY, K. G. (1960). The evolution of spermatophores in insects. *Proc. R. ent. Soc. Lond.* A, 35: 107–113.

DAVEY, K. G. (1964). The control of visceral muscles in insects. *Adv. Ins. Physiol.* 2: 219–245.

DAVEY, K. G. (1965a). *Reproduction in the insects.* Oliver and Boyd, Edinburgh.

DAVEY, K. G. (1965b). Copulation and egg-production in *Rhodnius prolixus*: the role of the spermathecae. *J. exp. Biol.* 42: 373–378.

DAVEY, K. G. and TREHERNE, J. E. (1963a). Studies on crop function in the cockroach (*Periplaneta americana* L.) I. The mechanism of crop-emptying. *J. exp. Biol.* 40: 763–773.

DAVEY, K. G. and TREHERNE, J. E. (1963b). Studies on crop functions in the cockroach (*Periplaneta americana* L.) II. The nervous control of crop-emptying. *J. exp. Biol.* 40: 775–780.

DAVEY, P. M. (1954). Quantities of food eaten by the desert locust, *Schistocerca gregaria* (Forsk.), in relation to growth. *Bull. ent. Res.* 45: 539–551.

DAVID, W. A. L. and GARDINER, B. O. C. (1962). Oviposition and the hatching of the eggs of *Pieris brassicae* (L.) in a laboratory culture. *Bull. ent. Res.* 53: 91–109.

DAVIES, L. (1965). On spermatophores in Simuliidae (Diptera). *Proc. R. ent. Soc. Lond.* A, 40: 30–34.

DAVIES, R. G. (1966). The postembryonic development of *Hemimerus vicinus*, Rehn & Rehn (Dermaptera: Hemimeridae). *Proc. R. ent. Soc. Lond.* A, 41: 67–77.

DAVIS, H. (1961). Some principles of sensory receptor action. *Physiol. Rev.* 41: 391–416.

DAVIS, N. T. (1964). Studies on the reproductive physiology of Cimicidae (Hemiptera)— I. Fecundation and egg maturation. *J. Insect Physiol.* 10: 947–963.

DAY, M. F. (1941). Pigment migration in the eyes of the moth, *Ephestia kuehniella* Zeller. *Biol. Bull. mar. biol. Lab., Woods Hole* 80: 275–291.

DAY, M. F. and WATERHOUSE, D. F. (1953). The mechanism of digestion. *in* Roeder,

K. D. (Ed.), *Insect physiology*. Wiley and Sons, New York.

DEBAISIEUX, P. (1938). Organes scolopidiaux des pattes d'insectes. *Cellule* 47: 77–202.

DELPHIN, F. (1965). The histology and possible functions of neurosecretory cells in the ventral ganglia of *Schistocerca gregaria* Forskål (Orthoptera: Acrididae). *Trans. R. ent. Soc. Lond.* 117: 167–214.

DENIS, R. (1949). Sous-classe des Aptérygotes. *in* Grassé, P.-P. (Ed.), *Traité de Zoologie*. vol. 9. Masson et Cie., Paris.

DENNELL, R. (1946). A study of an insect cuticle: the larval cuticle of *Sarcophaga falculata* Pand. (Diptera). *Proc. R. Soc.* B, 133: 348–373.

DENNELL, R. (1947). A study of an insect cuticle: the formation of the puparium of *Sarcophaga falculata* Pand. (Diptera). *Proc. R. Soc.* B, 134: 79–110.

DENNELL, R. and MALEK, S. R. A. (1955). The cuticle of the cockroach *Periplaneta americana* II. The epicuticle. *Proc. R. Soc.* B, 143: 239–257.

DETHIER, V. G. (1942). The dioptric apparatus of the lateral ocelli. I. The corneal lens. *J. cell. comp. Physiol.* 19: 301–313.

DETHIER, V. G. (1943). The dioptric apparatus of the lateral ocelli. II. Visual capacities of the ocellus. *J. cell. comp. Physiol.* 22: 115–126.

DETHIER, V. G. (1947a). The response of hymenopterous parasites to chemical stimulation of the ovipositor. *J. exp. Zool.* 105: 199–207.

DETHIER, V. G. (1947B). *Chemical insect attractants and repellants*. Lewis & Co., London.

DETHIER, V. G. (1953). Chemoreception. *in* Roeder, K. D. (Ed.), *Insect physiology*. Wiley & Sons, New York.

DETHIER, V. G. (1962). Chemoreceptor mechanisms in insects. *Symp. Soc. exp. Biol.* 16: 180–196.

DETHIER, V. G. (1963). *The physiology of insect senses*. Methuen, London.

DETHIER, V. G. (1966). Feeding behaviour. *Symp. R. ent. Soc. Lond.* 3: 46–58.

DETHIER, V. G. and CHADWICK, L. E. (1948). Chemoreception in insects. *Physiol. Rev.* 28: 220–254.

DETHIER, V. G., EVANS, D. R. and RHOADES, M. V. (1956). Some factors controlling the ingestion of carbohydrates by the blowfly. *Biol. Bull. mar. biol. Lab., Woods Hole* 111: 204–222.

DETHIER, V. G. and GELPERIN, A. (1967). Hyperphagia in the blowfly. *J. exp. Biol.* 47: 191–200.

DICKINS, G. R. (1936). The scent glands of certain Phycitidae (Lepidoptera). *Trans. R. ent. Soc. Lond.* 85: 331–362.

DIGBY, P. S. B. (1955). Factors affecting the temperature excess of insects in sunshine. *J. exp. Biol.* 32: 279–298.

DIGBY, P. S. B. (1958a). Flight activity in the blowfly, *Calliphora erythrocephala*, in relation to light and radiant heat, with special reference to adaptation. *J. exp. Biol.* 35: 1–19.

DIGBY, P. S. B. (1958b). Flight activity in the blowfly, *Calliphora erythrocephala*, in relation to wind speed, with special reference to adaptation. *J. exp. Biol.* 35: 776–795.

DIXEY, F. A. (1932). The plume-scales of the Pierinae. *Trans. ent. Soc. Lond.* 80: 57–75.

DOWNES, J. A. (1955). Observations on the swarming flight and mating of *Culicoides* (Diptera: Ceratopogonidae). *Trans. R. ent. Soc. Lond.* 106: 213–236.

DOWNES, J. A. (1958). The feeding habits of biting flies and their significance in classification. *A. Rev. Ent.* 3: 249–266.

DRUMMOND, F. H. (1953). The eversible vesicles of *Campodea* (Thysanura). *Proc. R. ent. Soc. Lond.* A, 28: 145–148.

DUMORTIER, B. (1963a). Morphology of sound emission apparatus in Arthropoda. *in* Busnel, R.-G. (Ed.), *Acoustic behaviour of animals*. Elsevier, Amsterdam.

DUMORTIER, B. (1963b). The physical characteristics of sound emissions in Arthropoda.

in Busnel, R.-G. (Ed.), *Acoustic behaviour of animals*. Elsevier, Amsterdam.

DUPONT-RAABE, M. (1957). Les mécanismes de l'adaptation chromatique chez les insectes.' *Arch. Zool. exp. gén.* 94: 61–294.

DUPORTE, E. M. (1946). Observations on the morphology of the face in insects. *J. Morph.* 79: 371–417.

DUPORTE, E. M. (1957). The comparative morphology of the insect head. *A. Rev. Ent.* 2: 55–70.

EASSA, Y. E. E. (1953). The development of imaginal buds in the head of *Pieris brassicae* Linn. (Lepidoptera). *Trans. R. ent. Soc. Lond.* 104: 39–50.

EASTHAM, L. E. S. (1930). The formation of germ layers in insects. *Biol. Rev.* 5: 1–29.

EASTHAM, L. E. S. and EASSA, Y. E. E. (1955). The feeding mechanism of the butterfly *Pieris brassicae* L. *Phil. Trans. R. Soc.* B, 239: 1–43.

EDNEY, E. B. (1957). *The water relations of terrestrial arthropods*. Cambridge University Press.

EDWARDS, G. A. (1953). Respiratory metabolism. *in* Roeder, K. D. (Ed.), *Insect physiology*. Wiley and Sons, New York.

EDWARDS, G. A. (1960). Insect micromorphology. *A. Rev. Ent.* 5: 17–34.

EDWARDS, G. A., RUSKA, H. and HARVEN, E. de (1958). The fine structure of insect tracheoblasts, tracheae and tracheoles. *Arch. Biol.* 69: 351–369.

EDWARDS, J. S. (1961). On the reproduction of *Prionoplus reticularis* (Coleoptera, Cerambycidae), with general remarks on reproduction in the Cerambycidae. *Q. Jl microsc. Sci.* 102: 519–529.

EDWARDS, J. S. (1963). Arthropods as predators. *Viewpoints in Biology* 2: 85–114.

EDWARDS, J. S. (1964). Diuretic function of the labial glands in adult giant silk moths, *Hyalophora cecropia. Nature, Lond.* 203: 668–669.

EDWARDS, R. L. (1955). The host-finding and oviposition behaviour of *Mormoniella vitripennis* (Walker) (Hym., Pteromalidae), a parasite of muscoid flies. *Behaviour* 7: 88–112.

EISNER, T. (1953). The histology of a sense organ in the labial palps of Neuroptera. *J. Morph.* 93: 109–121.

EISNER, T. and KAFATOS, F. C. (1962). Defence mechanisms of arthropods. X. A pheromone promoting aggregation in an aposematic distasteful insect. *Psyche, Camb.* 69: 53–61.

ELLIS, P. E. (1951). The marching behaviour of hoppers of the African migratory locust (*Locusta migratoria migratorioides* R. & F.) in the laboratory. *Anti-Locust Bull.* no. 7, 46 pp.

ELLIS, P. E. and CARLISLE, D. B. (1961). The prothoracic gland and colour change in locusts. *Nature, Lond.* 190: 368–369.

ELLIS, P. E. and HOYLE, G. (1954). A physiological interpretation of the marching of hoppers of the African migratory locust (*Locusta migratoria migratorioides* R. & F.). *J. exp. Biol.* 31: 271–279.

ELTRINGHAM, H. (1913). On the scent apparatus in the male of *Amauris niavius* Linn. *Trans. ent. Soc. Lond.* 1913, 399–406.

ELTRINGHAM, H. (1933). *The senses of insects*. Methuen, London.

EMDEN, F. I. van (1946). Egg-bursters in some more families of polyphagous beetles and some general remarks on egg-bursters. *Proc. R. ent. Soc. Lond.* A, 21: 89–97.

ENGELMANN, F. (1968). Endocrine control of reproduction in insects. *A. Rev. Ent.* 13: 1–27.

ERIKSEN, C. H. (1963). Respiratory regulation in *Ephemera simulans* (Walker) and *Hexagenia limbata* (Serville) (Ephemeroptera). *J. exp. Biol.* 40: 455–468.

ESCHENBERG, K. M. and DUNLAP, H. L. (1966). The histology and histochemistry of oogenesis in the water strider, *Gerris remigis* Say. *J. Morph.* 118: 297–316.

EVANS, A. C. (1939). The utilisation of food by certain lepidopterous larvae. *Trans. R. ent. Soc. Lond.* 89: 13–22.

EVANS, W. A. L. and PAYNE, D. W. (1964). Carbohydrases of the alimentary tract of the desert locust, *Schistocerca gregaria* Forsk. *J. Insect Physiol.* 10: 657–674.

EVANS, W. G. (1964). Infra-red receptors in *Melanophila acuminata* DeGeer. *Nature, Lond.* 202: 211.

EWING, A. W. (1964). The influence of wing area on the courtship behaviour of *Drosophila melanogaster*. *Anim. Behav.* 12: 316–320.

EWING, A. and HOYLE, G. (1965). Neuronal mechanisms underlying control of sound production in a cricket: *Acheta domesticus*. *J. exp. Biol.* 43: 139–153.

FAHMY, O. G. (1952). The cytology and genetics of *Drosophila subobscura*. VI. Maturation, fertilisation and cleavage in normal eggs and in the presence of the *cross-over suppressor* gene. *J. Genet.* 50: 486–506.

FINLAYSON, L. H. and LOWENSTEIN, O. (1958). The structure and function of abdominal stretch receptors in insects. *Proc. R. Soc. B*, 148: 433–449.

FINLAYSON, L. H. and MOWAT, D. J. (1963). Variations in histology of abdominal stretch receptors of saturniid moths during development. *Q. Jl microsc. Sci.* 104: 243–251.

FLANDERS, S. E. (1942). Oosorption and ovulation in relation to oviposition in the parasitic Hymenoptera. *Ann. ent. Soc. Am.* 35: 251–266.

FLORKIN, M. and JEUNIAUX, C. (1964). Haemolymph: composition. *in* Rockstein, M. (Ed.), *The physiology of Insecta*. vol. 3. Academic Press, New York.

FOX, D. L. (1953). *Animal biochromes and structural colours*. Cambridge University Press.

FOX, H. M. and VEVERS, G. (1960). *The nature of animal colours*. Sidgwick and Jackson, London.

FRAENKEL, G. and BLEWETT, M. (1944). The utilisation of metabolic water in insects. *Bull. ent. Res.* 35: 127–139.

FRAENKEL, G. S. and GUNN, D. L. (1940). *The orientation of animals*. Oxford University Press.

FRAENKEL, G. and HSIAO, C. (1965). Bursicon, a hormone which mediates tanning of the cuticle in the adult fly and other insects. *J. Insect Physiol.* 11: 513–556.

FREE, J. B. and BUTLER, C. G. (1959). *Bumblebees*. Collins, London.

FRENCH, R. A. (1965). Long range dispersal of insects in relation to synoptic meteorology. *Proc. XIIth. Int. Congr. Ent.* 418–419.

FRIEND, W. G. (1958). Nutritional requirements of phytophagous insects. *A. Rev. Ent.* 3: 57–74.

FRIEND, W. G., SALKELD, E. H. and STEVENSON, I. L. (1959). Nutrition of onion maggots, larvae of *Hylemya antiqua* (Meig.), with reference to other members of the genus *Hylemya*. *Ann. N.Y. Acad. Sci.* 77: 384–393.

FRINGS, H. and FRINGS, M. (1949). The loci of contact chemoreceptors in insects. *Am. Midl. Nat.* 41: 602–658.

FRISCH, K. von (1950). *Bees. Their vision, chemical senses, and language*. Cornell University Press, New York.

FRISCH, K. von, LINDAUER, M. and DAUMER, K. (1960). Über die Wahrnehmung polarisierten Lichtes durch das Bienenauge. *Experientia* 16: 289–301.

GABE, L. (1966). *Neurosecretion*. Pergamon Press, London.

GANAGARAJAH, M. (1965). The neuro-endocrine complex of adult *Nebria brevicollis* (F.) and its relation to reproduction. *J. Insect Physiol.* 11: 1377–1388.

GANGWERE, S. K. (1960). Notes on drinking and the need for water in Orthoptera. *Can. Ent.* 92: 911–915.

GARDNER, A. E. (1960). A key to the larvae of the British Odonata. *in* Corbet, P. S., Long-field, C. and Moore, N. W., *Dragonflies*. Collins, London.

GERE, G. (1956). Investigations concerning the energy turn-over of the *Hyphantria cunea* Drury caterpillars. *Opusc. zool. Bpest.* 1: 29–32.

GEROULD, J. H. (1938). Structure and action of the heart of *Bombyx mori* and other insects. *Acta zool., Stockh.* 19: 297–352.

GETTRUP, E. (1962). Thoracic proprioceptors in the flight systems of locusts. *Nature, Lond.* 193: 498–499.

GETTRUP, E. (1963). Phasic stimulation of a thoracic stretch receptor in locusts. *J. exp. Biol.* 40: 323–333.

GETTRUP, E. (1965). Sensory mechanisms in locomotion. The campaniform sensilla of the insect wing and their function during flight. *Cold Spring Harb. Symp. quant. Biol.* 30: 615–622.

GETTRUP, E. (1966). Sensory regulation of wing twisting in locusts. *J. exp. Biol.* 44: 1–16.

GEYER-DUSZYŃSKA, I. (1959). Experimental research on chromosome elimination in Cecidomyidae (Diptera). *J. exp. Zool.* 141: 391–447.

GHILAROV, M. S. (1949). *The peculiarities of the soil as an environment and its significance in the evolution of insects.* (in Russian). Moskva, Leningrad.

GILBERT, L. I. (1964). Physiology of growth and development: endocrine aspects. *in* Rockstein, M. (Ed.), *The physiology of Insecta.* vol. 1. Academic Press, New York.

GILBERT, L. I. and SCHNEIDERMAN, H. A. (1961). Some biochemical aspects of insect metamorphosis. *Am. Zoologist* 1: 11–51.

GILBY, A. R. (1965). Lipids and their metabolism in insects. *A. Rev. Ent.* 10: 141–160.

GILL, K. S. (1964). Epigenetics of the promorphology of the egg in *Drosophila melanogaster*. *J. exp. Zool.* 155: 91–104.

GILLETT, J. D. and WIGGLESWORTH, V. B. (1932). The climbing organ of an insect, *Rhodnius prolixus* (Hemiptera; Reduviidae). *Proc. R. Soc. B,* 111: 364–376.

GILMOUR, D. (1961). *The biochemistry of insects.* Academic Press, New York and London.

GILMOUR, D. (1965). *The metabolism of insects.* Oliver and Boyd, Edinburgh.

GILMOUR, D. and ROBINSON, P. M. (1964). Contraction in glycerinated myofibrils of an insect (Orthoptera, Acrididae). *J. Cell Biol.* 21: 385–396.

GIVEN, B. B. (1954). Evolutionary trends in the Thynninae with special reference to feeding habits of Australian species. *Trans. R. ent. Soc. Lond.* 105: 1–10.

GOLDSMITH, T. H. (1962). Fine structure of the retinulae in the compound eye of the honey-bee. *J. Cell Biol.* 14: 489–494.

GOLDSMITH, T. H. (1964). The visual system of insects. *in* Rockstein, M. (Ed.), *The physiology of Insecta.* vol. 1. Academic Press, New York.

GOLDSMITH, T. H. and PHILPOTT, D. E. (1957). The microstructure of the compound eyes of insects. *J. biophys. biochem. Cytol.* 3: 429–438.

GOLDSMITH, T. H. and WARNER, L. T. (1964). Vitamin A in the vision of insects. *J. Gen. Physiol.* 47: 433–441.

GOODCHILD, A. J. P. (1963a). Some new observations on the intestinal structures concerned with water disposal in sap-sucking Hemiptera. *Trans. R. ent. Soc. Lond.* 115: 217–237.

GOODCHILD, A. J. P. (1963b). Studies on the functional anatomy of the intestines of Heteroptera. *Proc. zool. Soc. Lond.* 141: 851–910.

GOODCHILD, A. J. P. (1966). Evolution of the alimentary canal in the Hemiptera. *Biol. Rev.* 41: 97–140.

GOODHUE, D. (1963). Some differences in the passage of food through the intestines of the desert and migratory locusts. *Nature, Lond.* 200: 288–289.

GOODMAN, L. J. (1960). The landing responses of insects. 1. The landing response of the fly, *Lucilia sericata*, and other Calliphorinae. *J. exp. Biol.* 37: 854–878.

GOODMAN, L. J. (1965). The role of certain optomotor reactions in regulating stability in the rolling plane during flight in the desert locust, *Schistocerca gregaria. J. exp. Biol.* 42: 385–408.

GOODWIN, T. W. (1952). The biochemistry of locust pigmentation. *Biol. Rev.* 27: 439–460.

GORDON, H. T. (1959). Minimal nutritional requirements of the German roach *Blattella germanica* L. *Ann. N.Y. Acad. Sci.* 77: 290–351.

GRASSÉ, P.-P. (1949). Ordre des Isoptères ou termites. *in* Grassé, P.-P. (Ed.), *Traité de Zoologie.* vol. 9. Masson et Cie., Paris.

GRASSÉ, P.-P. (1952a). La symbiose flagellés—termites. *in* Grassé, P.-P. (Ed.), *Traité de Zoologie.* vol. 1. Masson et Cie., Paris.

GRASSÉ, P.-P. (1952b). Roles des flagellés symbiotiques chez les blattes et les termites. *Tijdschr. Ent.* 95: 70–80.

GRASSÉ, P.-P. and GHARAGOZLOU, I. (1963). L'ergastoplasme et la genèse des protéines dans le tissu adipeux royal du termite à cou jaune. *C. r. hebd. Séanc. Acad. Sci., Paris* 257: 3546–3548.

GRASSÉ, P.-P. and GHARAGOZLOU, I. (1964). Sur une nouvelle sorte de cellules du tissu adipeux royal de *Calotermes flavicollis* (Insecte isoptère): l'endolophocyte. *C. r. hebd. Séanc. Acad. Sci., Paris* 258: 1045–1047.

GRAY, E. G. (1960). The fine structure of the insect ear. *Phil. Trans. R. Soc.* B, 243: 75–94.

GRAY, J. (1944). Studies in the mechanics of the tetrapod skeleton. *J. exp. Biol.* 20: 88–116.

GRAY, J. (1953). Undulatory propulsion. *Q. Jl microsc. Sci.* 94: 551–578.

GRÉGOIRE, C. (1951). Blood coagulation in arthropods. II. Phase contrast microscopic observations on haemolymph coagulation in sixty-one species of insects. *Blood* 6: 1173–1198.

GRÉGOIRE, C. (1964). Haemolymph coagulation. *in* Rockstein, M. (Ed.), *The physiology of Insecta.* vol. 3. Academic Press, New York.

GREGORY, G. E. (1965). The formation and fate of the spermatophore in the African migratory locust *Locusta migratoria migratorioides* Reiche and Fairmaire. *Trans. R. ent. Soc. Lond.* 117: 33–66.

GRESSITT, J. L., COATSWORTH, J. and YOSHIMOTO, C. M. (1962). Air-borne insects trapped on 'Monsoon expedition'. *Pacif. Insects* 4: 319–323.

GRIFFIN, D. R., WEBSTER, F. A. and MICHAEL, C. R. (1960). The echolocation of flying insects by bats. *Anim. Behav.* 8: 141–154.

GUNN, D. L. and HOPF, H. S. (1942). The biology and behaviour of *Ptinus tectus* Boie. (Coleoptera, Ptinidae), a pest of stored products. II. The amount of locomotory activity in relation to experimental and to previous temperatures. *J. exp. Biol.* 18: 278–289.

GUNN, D. L. and HUNTER-JONES, P. (1952). Laboratory experiments on phase differences in locusts. *Anti-Locust Bull.* no. 12: 1–29.

HACKMAN, R. H. (1953). Chemistry of insect cuticle. 1. The water-soluble proteins. *Biochem. J.* 54: 362–367.

HACKMAN, R. H. (1964). Chemistry of the insect cuticle. *in* Rockstein, M. (Ed.), *The physiology of Insecta.* vol. 3. Academic Press, New York.

HADDOW, A. J. (1961). Entomological studies from a high tower in Mpanga Forest, Uganda. VII. The biting behaviour of mosquitoes and tabanids. *Trans. R. ent. Soc. Lond.* 113: 315–335.

HADDOW, A. J. and CORBET, P. S. (1961). Entomological studies from a high tower in Mpanga Forest, Uganda. V. Swarming activity above the forest. *Trans. R. ent. Soc. Lond.* 113: 284–300.

HAGAN, H. R. (1951). *Embryology of the viviparous insects.* Ronald Press Co., New York.

HAGEN, K. S. (1962). Biology and ecology of predaceous Coccinellidae. *A. Rev. Ent.* 7: 289–326.

HAMAMURA, Y., HAYASHIYA, K., NAITO, K., MATSUURA, K. and NISHIDA, J. (1962). Food selection by silkworm larvae. *Nature, Lond.* 194: 754–755.

HAMILTON, A. G. (1936). The relation of humidity and temperature to the development of three species of African locusts—*Locusta migratoria migratorioides* (R. and F.), *Schistocerca gregaria* (Forsk.), *Nomadacris septemfasciata* (Serv.). *Trans. R. ent. Soc. Lond.* 85: 1–60.

HAMILTON, A. G. (1950). Further studies on the relation of humidity and temperature to the development of two species of African locusts—*Locusta migratoria migratorioides* (R. and F.) and *Schistocerca gregaria* (Forsk.). *Trans. R. ent. Soc. Lond.* 101: 1–58.

HAMILTON, A. G. (1955). Parthenogenesis in the desert locust (*Schistocerca gregaria* Forsk.) and its possible effect on the maintenance of the species. *Proc. R. ent. Soc. Lond.* A, 30: 103–114.

HAMILTON, A. G. (1964). The occurrence of periodic and continuous discharge of carbon dioxide by male desert locusts (*Schistocerca gregaria* Forskål) measured by an infra-red gas analyser. *Proc. R. Soc.* B, 160: 373–395.

HARKER, J. E. (1960). Internal factors controlling the suboesophageal ganglion neuro-secretory cycle in *Periplaneta americana* L. *J. exp. Biol.* 37: 164–170.

HARKER, J. E. (1961). Diurnal rhythms. *A. Rev. Ent.* 6: 131–146.

HARKER, J. E. (1964). *The physiology of diurnal rhythms.* Cambridge University Press.

HARKER, J. E. (1965). The effect of a biological clock on the development rate of *Drosophila* pupae. *J. exp. Biol.* 42: 323–337.

HARMSEN, R. (1966). The excretory role of pteridines in insects. *J. exp. Biol.* 45: 1–13.

HARTLEY, J. C. (1961). The shell of acridid eggs. *Q. Jl microsc. Sci.* 102: 249–255.

HARTLEY, J. C. (1962). The egg of *Tetrix* (Tetrigidae, Orthoptera), with a discussion on the probable significance of the anterior horn. *Q. Jl microsc. Sci.* 103: 253–259.

HARTLEY, J. C. (1965). The structure and function of the egg-shell of *Deraeocoris rubar* L. (Heteroptera, Miridae). *J. Insect Physiol.* 11: 103–109.

HARTLINE, H. K., WAGNER, H. G. and RATLIFF, F. (1956). Inhibition in the eye of *Limulus. J. gen. Physiol.* 39: 651–673.

HARVEY, W. R. (1962). Metabolic aspects of insect diapause. *A. Rev. Ent.* 7: 57–80.

HARVEY, W. R. and HASKELL, J. A. (1966). Metabolic control mechanisms in insects. *Adv. Ins. Physiol.* 3: 133–206.

HASEGAWA, K. and YAMASHITA, O. (1965). Studies on the mode of action of the diapause hormone in the silkworm, *Bombyx mori* L. VI. The target organ of the diapause hormone. *J. exp. Biol.* 43: 271–277.

HASKELL, P. T. (1956). Hearing in certain Orthoptera. II. The nature of the response of certain receptors to natural and imitation stridulation. *J. exp. Biol.* 33: 767–776. 1.

HASKELL, P. T. (1957a). Stridulation and associated behaviour in certain Orthoptera. 1. Analysis of the stridulation of, and behaviour between, males. *Anim. Behav.* 5: 139–148.

HASKELL, P. T. (1957b). The influence of flight noise on behaviour in the desert locust *Schistocerca gregaria* (Forsk.). *J. Insect Physiol.* 1: 52–75.

HASKELL, P. T. (1958). Stridulation and associated behaviour in certain Orthoptera. 2. Stridulation of females and their behaviour with males. *Anim. Behav.* 6: 27–42.

HASKELL, P. T. (1960a). Stridulation and associated behaviour in certain Orthoptera. 3. The influence of the gonads. *Anim. Behav.* 8: 76–81.

HASKELL, P. T. (1960b). The sensory equipment of the migratory locust. *Symp. zool. Soc. Lond.* 3: 1–23.

HASKELL, P. T. (1961). *Insect sounds.* Witherby, London.

HASKELL, P. T. (1964). Sound production. *in* Rockstein, M. (Ed.), *The physiology of Insecta*. vol. 1. Academic Press, New York.

HASKELL, P. T. (1966). Flight behaviour. *Symp. R. ent. Soc. Lond.* 3: 29–45.

HASKELL, P. T. and MOORHOUSE, J. E. (1963). A blood-borne factor influencing the activity of the central nervous system of the desert locust. *Nature, Lond.* 197: 56–58.

HASKELL, P. T., PASKIN, M. W. J. and MOORHOUSE, J. E. (1962). Laboratory observations on factors affecting the movements of hoppers of the desert locust. *J. Insect Physiol.* 8: 53–78.

HATHAWAY, D. S. and SELMAN, G. G. (1961). Certain aspects of cell lineage and morphogenesis studied in embryos of *Drosophila melanogaster* with an ultra-violet microbeam. *J. Embryol. exp. Morph.* 9: 310–325.

HAYWARD, K. J. (1953). Migration of butterflies in Argentina during the spring and summer of 1951–52. *Proc. R. ent. Soc. Lond.* A, 28: 63–73.

HEATH, J. E. and ADAMS, P. A. (1965). Temperature regulation in the sphinx moth during flight. *Nature, Lond.* 205: 309–310.

HENSON, H. (1932). The development of the alimentary canal in *Pieris brassicae* and the endodermal origin of the Malpighian tubules of insects. *Q. Jl microsc. Sci.* 75: 283–305.

HENSON, H. (1944). The development of the Malpighian tubules of *Blatta orientalis* (Orthoptera). *Proc. R. ent. Soc. Lond.* A, 19: 73–91.

HENSON, H. (1946). The theoretical aspect of insect metamorphosis. *Biol. Rev.* 21: 1–14.

HERING, E. M. (1951). *Biology of leaf miners*. Junk, 's-Gravenhage.

HEROLD, R. C. and BOREI, H. (1963). Cytochrome changes during honeybee flight muscle development. *Devl Biol.* 8: 67–79.

HEUVAL M. J. van den (1963). The effect of rearing temperature on the wing length, thorax length, leg length and ovariole number of the adult mosquito, *Aedes aegypti* (L.). *Trans. R. ent. Soc. Lond.* 115: 197–216.

HEWITT, C. G. (1914). *The house-fly, Musca domestica Linn*. Cambridge University Press.

HEYWOOD, R. B. (1965). Changes occurring in the central nervous system of *Pieris brassicae* L. (Lepidoptera) during metamorphosis. *J. Insect Physiol.* 11: 413–430.

HIGHNAM, K. C. (1958a). Activity of the brain/corpora cardiaca system during pupal diapause 'break' in *Mimas tiliae* (Lepidoptera). *Q. Jl microsc. Sci.* 99: 73–88.

HIGHNAM, K. C. (1958b). Activity of the corpora allata during pupal diapause in *Mimas tiliae* (Lepidoptera). *Q. Jl microsc. Sci.* 99: 171–180.

HIGHNAM, K. C. (1961). The histology of the neurosecretory system of the adult female desert locust, *Schistocerca gregaria*. *Q. Jl microsc. Sci.* 102: 27–38.

HIGHNAM, K. C. (1964). Endocrine relationships in insect reproduction. *Symp. R. ent. Soc. Lond.* 2: 26–42.

HIGHNAM, K. C., HILL, L. and GINGELL, D. J. (1965). Neurosecretion and water balance in the male desert locust (*Schistocerca gregaria*). *J. Zool.* 147: 201–215.

HIGHNAM, K. C., LÜSIS, O. and HILL, L. (1963). Factors affecting oöcyte resorption in the desert locust *Schistocerca gregaria* (Forskål). *J. Insect Physiol.* 9: 827–837.

HILDRETH, P. E. and LUCHESI, J. C. (1963). Fertilisation in *Drosophila*. I. Evidence for the regular occurrence of monospermy. *Devl Biol.* 6: 262–278.

HILL, L. (1962). Neurosecretory control of haemolymph protein concentration during ovarian development in the desert locust. *J. Insect Physiol.* 8: 609–619.

HINTON, H. E. (1946). A new classification of insect pupae. *Proc. zool. Soc. Lond.* 116: 282–328.

HINTON, H. E. (1947). On the reduction of functional spiracles in the aquatic larvae of the Holometabola, with notes on the moulting process of spiracles. *Trans. R. ent. Soc. Lond.* 98: 449–473.

HINTON, H. E. (1948a). Sound production in lepidopterous pupae. *Entomologist* 81: 254–269.

HINTON, H. E. (1948b). On the origin and function of the pupal stage. *Trans. R. ent. Soc. Lond.* 99: 395–409.

HINTON, H. E. (1955). On the structure, function, and distribution of the prolegs of the Panorpoidea, with a criticism of the Berlese-Imms theory. *Trans. R. ent. Soc. Lond.* 106: 455–545.

HINTON, H. E. (1957). The structure and function of the spiracular gill of the fly *Taphrophila vitripennis*. *Proc. R. Soc.* B, 147: 90–120.

HINTON, H. E. (1959). How the indirect flight muscles of insects grow. *Sci. Prog., Lond.* 47: 321–333.

HINTON, H. E. (1960a). Plastron respiration in the eggs of blowflies. *J. Insect Physiol.* 4: 176–183.

HINTON, H. E. (1960b). Cryptobiosis in the larva of *Polypedilum vanderplanki* Hint. (Chironomidae). *J. Insect Physiol.* 5: 286–300.

HINTON, H. E. (1961a). The structure and function of the respiratory horns of the eggs of some flies. *Phil. Trans. R. Soc.* B, 243: 45–73.

HINTON, H. E. (1961b). The structure and function of the egg-shell in the Nepidae (Hemiptera). *J. Insect Physiol.* 7: 224–257.

HINTON, H. E. (1962a). The fine structure and biology of the egg-shell of the wheat bulb fly *Leptohylemyia coarctata*. *Q. Jl microsc. Sci.* 103: 243–251.

HINTON, H. E. (1962b). Respiratory systems of insect egg-shells. *Sci. Prog., Lond.* 50: 96–113.

HINTON, H. E. (1963a). The ventral ecdysial lines of the head of endopterygote larvae. *Trans. R. ent. Soc. Lond.* 115: 39–61.

HINTON, H. E. (1963b). The origin and function of the pupal stage. *Proc. R. ent. Soc. Lond.* A, 38: 77–85.

HINTON, H. E. (1964a). Sperm transfer in insects and the evolution of haemocoelic insemination. *Symp. R. ent. Soc. Lond.* 2: 95–107.

HINTON, H. E. (1964b). The respiratory efficiency of the spiracular gill of *Simulium*. *J. Insect Physiol.* 10: 73–80.

HINTON, H. E. (1966a). Respiratory adaptions of the pupae of beetles of the family Psephenidae. *Phil. Trans. R. Soc.* B, 251: 211–245.

HINTON, H. E. (1966b). The spiracular gill of the fly *Eutanyderus* (Tanyderidae). *Aust. J. Zool.* 14: 365–369.

HINTON, H. E. and COLE, S. (1965). The structure of the egg-shell of the cabbage root fly, *Erioischia brassicae*. *Ann. appl. Biol.* 56: 1–6.

HOCKING, B. (1953). The intrinsic range and speed of flight of insects. *Trans. R. ent. Soc. Lond.* 104: 223–345.

HODGKIN, A. L. (1958). Ionic movements and electrical activity in giant nerve fibres. *Proc. R. Soc.* B, 148: 1–37.

HODGSON, E. S. (1958). Chemoreception in arthropods. *A. Rev. Ent.* 3: 19–36.

HODGSON, E. S. (1964). Chemoreception. *in* Rockstein, M. (Ed.), *The physiology of Insecta*. vol. 1. Academic Press, New York.

HOLDGATE, M. W. (1955). The wetting of insect cuticles by water. *J. exp. Biol.* 32: 591–617.

HOLLICK, F. S. J. (1941). The flight of the dipterous fly *Muscina stabulans* Fallén. *Phil. Trans. R. Soc.* B, 230: 357–390.

HOPKINS, C. R. (1964). The histochemistry and fine structure of the accessory nuclei in the oocyte of *Bombus terrestris*. *Q. Jl microsc. Sci.* 105: 475–480.

HOPKINS, C. R. and KING, P. E. (1964). Egg resorption in *Nasonia vitripennis* (Walker)

(Hymenoptera: Pteromalidae). *Proc. R. ent. Soc. Lond.* A, 39: 101–107.

HOPKINS, C. R. and KING, P. E. (1966). An electron-microscopical and histochemical study of the oocyte periphery in *Bombus terrestris* during vitellogenesis. *J. Cell Sci.* 1: 201–216.

HOPKINS, G. H. E. (1950). The host-associations of the lice of mammals. *Proc. zool. Soc. Lond.* 119: 387–604.

HORRIDGE, G. A. (1956). The flight of very small insects. *Nature, Lond.* 178: 1334–1335.

HORRIDGE, G. A. (1961). Pitch discrimination in locusts. *Proc. R. Soc.* B, 155: 218–231.

HORRIDGE, G. A. (1965). The Arthropoda. *in* Bullock, T. H. and Horridge, G. A. *Structure and function in the nervous systems of invertebrates.* Freeman & Co., San Francisco.

HORRIDGE, G. A. and BARNARD, P. B. T. (1965). Movement of palisade in locust retinula cells when illuminated. *Q. Jl microsc. Sci.* 106: 131–135.

HORRIDGE, G. A., SCHOLES, J. H., SHAW, S. and TUNSTALL, J. (1965). Extracellular recordings from single neurones in the optic lobe and brain of the locust. *in* Treherne, J. E. and Beament, J. W. L. (Eds.), *The physiology of the insect central nervous system.* Academic Press, London.

HOUSE, H. L. (1959). Nutrition of the parasitoid *Pseudosarcophaga affinis* (Fall.) and other insects. *Ann. N.Y. Acad. Sci.* 77: 394–405.

HOUSE, H. L. (1961). Insect nutrition. *A. Rev. Ent.* 6: 13–26.

HOUSE, H. L. (1963). Nutritional diseases. *in* Steinhaus, E. A. (Ed.), *Insect pathology.* vol. 1. Academic Press, New York.

HOUSE, H. L. (1965a). Digestion. *in* Rockstein, M. (Ed.), *The physiology of Insecta.* vol. 2. Academic Press, New York.

HOUSE, H. L. (1965b). Insect nutrition. *in* Rockstein, M. (Ed.), *The physiology of Insecta.* vol. 2. Academic Press, New York.

HOUSE, H. L. (1966). Effects and interactions of varied levels of temperature, amino acids, and a vitamin on the rate of larval development in the fly *Pseudosarcophaga affinis. J. Insect Physiol.* 12: 1493–1501.

HOWDEN, G. F. and KILBY, B. A. (1960). Biochemical studies on insect haemolymph—I. Variations in reducing power with age and the effect of diet. *J. Insect Physiol.* 4: 258–269.

HOWE, R. W. (1967). Temperature effects on embryonic development in insects. *A. Rev. Ent.* 12: 15–42.

HOWSE, P. E. (1962a). Certain aspects of intercommunication in *Zootermopsis angusticollis* and other termites. Ph.D. Thesis, University of London.

HOWSE, P. E. (1962b). The perception of vibration by the subgenual organ in *Zootermopsis angusticollis* Emerson and *Periplaneta americana. Experientia* 18: 457–458.

HOWSE, P. E. (1964). An investigation into the mode of action of the subgenual organ in the termite, *Zootermopsis angusticollis* Emerson, and in the cockroach, *Periplaneta americana* L. *J. Insect Physiol.* 10: 409–424.

HOYLE, G. (1954). Changes in the blood potassium concentration of the African migratory locust (*Locusta migratoria migratorioides* R. & F.) during food deprivation and the effect on neuromuscular activity. *J. exp. Biol.* 31: 260–270.

HOYLE, G. (1955a). Neuromuscular mechanisms of a locust skeletal muscle. *Proc. R. Soc.* B, 143: 343–367.

HOYLE, G. (1955b). The effects of some common cations on neuromuscular transmission in insects. *J. Physiol., Lond.* 127: 90–103.

HOYLE, G. (1956). Sodium and potassium changes occurring in the haemolymph of insects at the time of moulting and their physiological consequences. *Nature, Lond.* 178: 1236–1237.

HOYLE, G. (1960). The action of carbon dioxide gas on an insect spiracular muscle. *J. Insect Physiol.* 4: 63–79.

HOYLE, G. (1961). Functional contracture in a spiracular muscle. *J. Insect Physiol.* 7: 305–314.

HOYLE, G. (1964). Exploration of neuronal mechanisms underlying behaviour in insects. *in* Reiss, R. F. (Ed.), *Neural theory and modeling.* Stanford University Press.

HOYLE, G. (1965a). Neural control of skeletal muscle. *in* Rockstein, M. (Ed.), *The physiology of Insecta.* vol. 2. Academic Press, New York.

HOYLE, G. (1965b). Neurophysiological studies on 'learning' in headless insects. *in* Treherne, J. E. and Beament, J. W. L. (Eds.), *The physiology of the insect central nervous system.* Academic Press, London.

HUBER, F. (1963). The role of the central nervous system in Orthoptera during the co-ordination and control of stridulation. *in* Busnel, R.-G. (Ed.), *Acoustic behaviour of animals.* Elsevier, Amsterdam.

HUBER, F. (1965). Neural integration (central nervous system). *in* Rockstein, M. (Ed.), *The physiology of Insecta.* vol. 2. Academic Press, New York.

HUDSON, B. N. A. (1956). The behaviour of the female mosquito in selecting water for oviposition. *J. exp. Biol.* 33: 478–492.

HUGHES, G. M. (1952). The co-ordination of insect movements. I. The walking movements of insects. *J. exp. Biol.* 29: 267–284.

HUGHES, G. M. (1958). The co-ordination of insect movements. III. Swimming in *Dytiscus, Hydrophilus,* and a dragonfly nymph. *J. exp. Biol.* 35: 567–583.

HUGHES, G. M. (1965a). Locomotion: terrestrial. *in* Rockstein, M. (Ed.), *The physiology of Insecta.* vol. 2. Academic Press, New York.

HUGHES, G. M. (1965b). Neuronal pathways in the insect central nervous system. *in* Treherne, J. E. and Beament, J. W. L. (Eds.), *The physiology of the insect central nervous system.* Academic Press, London.

HUGHES, G. M. and MILL, P. J. (1966). Patterns of ventilation in dragonfly larvae. *J. exp. Biol.* 44: 317–334.

HUGHES, R. D. (1960). Induction of diapause in *Erioischia brassicae* Bouche (Diptera, Anthomyidae). *J. exp. Biol.* 37: 218–223.

HUNTER, A. S. (1966). Effects of temperature on *Drosophila* III. Respiration of *D. willistoni* and *D. hydei* grown at different temperatures. *Comp. Biochem. Physiol.* 19: 171–177.

HUNTER-JONES, P. (1964). Egg development in the desert locust (*Schistocerca gregaria* Forsk.) in relation to the availability of water. *Proc. R. ent. Soc. Lond.* A, 39: 25–33.

HUNTER-JONES, P. (1966). Studies on the genus *Schistocerca* with special reference to development. Ph.D. Thesis, University of London.

HUSSEIN, M. (1937). The effect of temperature on locust activity. *Bull. Minist. Agric. Egypt tech. scient. Serv.* no. 184, 55 pp.

HUSSEY, P. B. (1927). Studies on the pleuropodia of *Belostoma flumineum* Say and *Ranatra fusca* Palisot de Beauvois, with a discussion of these organs in other insects. *Entomologica am.* 7: 1–81.

HUXLEY, A. F. and HUXLEY, H. E. (1964). A discussion on the physical and chemical basis of muscular contraction. *Proc. R. Soc.* B, 160: 434–542.

HUXLEY, H. E. (1965). The mechanism of muscular contraction. *Scient. Am.* 213, no. 6: 18–27.

HUXLEY, H. E. and HANSON, J. (1960). The molecular basis of contraction in cross-striated muscles. *in* Bourne, G. H. (Ed.), *The structure and function of muscle.* vol. 1. Academic Press, London.

IKEDA, K. and BOETTIGER, E. G. (1965). Studies on the flight mechanism of insects. III. The innervation and electrical activity of the basalar fibrillar flight muscle of the beetle, *Oryctes rhinoceros. J. Insect Physiol.* 11: 791–802.

IMMS, A. D. (1940). On the antennal musculature in insects and other arthropods. *Q. Jl microsc. Sci.* 81: 273–320.

IMMS, A. D. (1947). *Insect natural history*. Collins, London.

IMMS, A. D. (1957). *A general textbook of entomology*. 9th edition revised by Richards and Davies. Methuen, London.

JACKSON, D. J. (1952). Observations on the capacity for flight of water beetles. *Proc. R. ent. Soc. Lond.* A, 27: 57–70.

JACKSON, D. J. (1958). Egg-laying and egg-hatching in *Agabus bipustulatus* L., with notes on oviposition in other species of *Agabus* (Coleoptera: Dytiscidae). *Trans. R. ent. Soc. Lond.* 110: 53–80.

JACKSON, D. J. (1960). Observations on egg-laying in *Ilybius fuliginosus* Fabricius and *I. ater* Degeer (Coleoptera: Dytiscidae), with an account of the female genitalia. *Trans. R. ent. Soc. Lond.* 112: 37–52.

JACKSON, D. J. (1966). Observations on the biology of *Caraphractus cinctus* Walker (Hymenoptera: Mymaridae), a parasitoid of the eggs of Dytiscidae (Coleoptera) III. The adult life and sex ratio. *Trans. R. ent. Soc. Lond.* 118: 23–49.

JACOBSON, M. (1965). *Insect sex attractants*. Wiley & Sons, New York.

JAGO, N. D. (1963). Some observations on the life cycle of *Eyprepocnemis plorans meridionalis* Uvarov, 1921, with a key for the separation of nymphs at any instar. *Proc. R. ent. Soc. Lond.* A, 38: 113–124.

JANDER, R. (1963). Insect orientation. *A. Rev. Ent.* 8: 95–114.

JEANNEL, R. (1949). Ordre des Coléoptèroïdes. *in* Grassé, P.-P. (Ed.), *Traité de Zoologie*. vol. 9. Masson et Cie., Paris.

JENKIN, P. M. (1966). Apolysis and hormones in the moulting cycles of Arthropoda. *Annls Endocr.* 27: 331–341.

JENKIN, P. M. and HINTON, H. E. (1966). Apolysis in arthropod moulting cycles. *Nature, Lond.* 211: 871–872.

JENSEN, M. (1956). Biology and physics of locust flight. III. The aerodynamics of locust flight. *Phil. Trans. R. Soc.* B, 239: 511–552.

JENSEN, M. and WEIS-FOGH, T. (1962). Biology and physics of locust flight. V. Strength and elasticity of locust cuticle. *Phil. Trans. R. Soc.* B, 245: 137–169.

JEWELL, B. R. and RÜEGG, J. C. (1966). Oscillatory contraction of insect fibrillar muscle after glycerol extraction. *Proc. R. Soc.* B, 164: 428–459.

JOHANNSEN, O. A. and BUTT, F. H. (1941). *Embryology of insects and myriapods*. McGraw-Hill, New York.

JOHANNSON, A. S. (1964). Feeding and nutrition in reproductive processes in insects. *Symp. R. ent. Soc. Lond.* 2: 43–55.

JOHNSON, B. (1957). Studies on the degeneration of the flight muscles of alate aphids—I. A comparative study of the occurrence of muscle breakdown in relation to reproduction in several species. *J. Insect Physiol.* 1: 248–256.

JOHNSON, B. (1959). Studies on the degeneration of the flight muscles of alate aphids—II. Histology and control of muscle breakdown. *J. Insect Physiol.* 3: 367–377.

JOHNSON, B. (1962). Neurosecretion and the transport of secretory material from the corpora cardiaca in aphids. *Nature, Lond.* 196: 1338–1339.

JOHNSON, B. (1963). A histological study of neurosecretion in aphids. *J. Insect Physiol.* 9: 727–739.

JOHNSON, B. (1966). Ultrastructure of probable sites of release of neurosecretory materials in an insect *Calliphora stygia* Fabr. (Diptera). *Gen. comp. Endocrin.* 6: 99–108.

JOHNSON, C. G. (1954). Aphid migration in relation to weather. *Biol. Rev.* 29: 87–118.

JOHNSON, C. G. (1965). Migration. *in* Rockstein, M. (Ed.), *The physiology of Insecta*.

vol. 2. Academic Press, New York.

JOHNSON, C. G. (1966). A functional system of adaptive dispersal by flight. *A. Rev. Ent.* 11: 233–260.

JOHNSON, C. G. and TAYLOR, L. R. (1957). Periodism and energy summation with special reference to flight rhythms in aphids. *J. exp. Biol.* 34: 209–221.

JOHNSTONE, G. W. (1964). Stridulation by larval Hydropsychidae, (Trichoptera). *Proc. R. ent. Soc. Lond.* A, 39: 146–150.

JONES, B. M. (1956a). Endocrine activity during insect embryogenesis. Function of the ventral head glands in locust embryos (*Locustana pardalina* and *Locusta migratoria*, Orthoptera). *J. exp. Biol.* 33: 174–185.

JONES, B. M. (1956b). Endocrine activity during embryogenesis. Control of events in development following the embryonic moult (*Locusta migratoria* and *Locustana pardalina*, Orthoptera) *J. exp. Biol.* 33: 685–696.

JONES, J. C. (1954a). The heart and associated tissues of *Anopheles quadrimaculatus* Say (Diptera: Culicidae). *J. Morph.* 94: 71–123.

JONES, J. C. (1954b). A study of mealworm hemocytes with phase contrast microscopy. *Ann. ent. Soc. Am.* 47: 308–315.

JONES, J. C. (1956). The hemocytes of *Sarcophaga bullata* Parker. *J. Morph.* 99: 233–257.

JONES, J. C. (1962). Current concepts concerning insect hemocytes. *Am. Zoologist* 2: 209–246.

JONES, J. C. (1964). The circulatory system of insects. *in* Rockstein, M. (Ed.), *The physiology of Insecta.* vol. 3. Academic Press, New York.

JONES, J. C. (1965). The hemocytes of *Rhodnius prolixus* Stål. *Biol. Bull. mar. biol. Lab., Woods Hole* 129: 282–294.

JONES, J. C. and WHEELER, R. E. (1965). Studies on spermathecal filling in *Aedes aegypti* (Linnaeus). I. Description. *Biol. Bull. mar. biol. Lab., Woods Hole* 129: 134–150.

JONES, M. D. R. (1964). Inhibition and excitation in the acoustic behaviour of *Pholidoptera*. *Nature, Lond.* 203: 322–323.

JONES, M. D. R. (1966). The acoustic behaviour of the bush cricket *Pholidoptera griseoaptera*. I. Alternation, synchronism and rivalry between males. *J. exp. Biol.* 45: 15–30.

JUDSON, C. L. and HOKAMA, Y. (1965). Formation of the line of dehiscence in aedine mosquito eggs. *J. Insect Physiol.* 11: 337–345.

JUDSON, C. L., HOKAMA, Y. and HAYDOCK, I. (1965). The physiology of hatching of aedine mosquito eggs: some larval responses to the hatching stimulus. *J. Insect Physiol.* 11: 1169–1177.

KALMUS, H. and HOCKING, B. (1960). Behaviour of *Aedes* mosquitoes in relation to blood-feeding and repellants. *Entomologia exp. appl.* 3: 1–26.

KALMUS, H. and RIBBANDS, C. R. (1952). The origin of the odours by which honeybees distinguish their companions. *Proc. R. Soc.* B 140: 50–59.

KANWISHER, J. W. (1966). Tracheal gas dynamics in pupae of the cecropia silkworm. *Biol. Bull. mar. biol. Lab., Woods Hole* 130: 96–105.

KARLSON, P. (1963). Chemistry and biochemistry of insect hormones. *Angew. Chem.* 2: 175–182.

KARLSON, P. and BUTENANDT, A. (1959). Pheromones (ectohormones) in insects. *A. Rev. Ent.* 4: 39–58.

KARLSON, P. and SEKERIS, C. E. (1966). Ecdysone, an insect steroid hormone, and its mode of action. *Recent Prog. in Hormone Res.* 22: 473–493.

KATSUKI, Y. and SUGA, N. (1960). Neural mechanism of hearing in insects. *J. exp. Biol.* 37: 279–290.

KAYE, J. S. (1962). Acrosome formation in the house cricket. *J. Cell Biol.* 12: 411–431.

KAYE, J. S. and McMASTER-KAYE, R. (1966). The fine structure and chemical composition of nuclei during spermiogenesis in the house cricket. I. Initial stages of differentiation and the loss of nonhistone protein. *J. Cell Biol.* 31: 159–179.

KEELE, C. A. and NEIL, E. (1961). *Samson Wright's applied physiology*. Oxford University Press, London.

KEILIN, D. (1916). Sur la viviparité chez les Diptères et sur les larves de Diptères vivipares. *Archs. Zool. exp. gén.* 55: 393–415.

KEILIN, D. (1944). Respiratory systems and respiratory adaptations in larvae and pupae of Diptera. *Parasitology* 36: 1–66.

KEILIN, D. and WANG, Y. L. (1946). Haemoglobin of *Gastrophilus* larvae. Purification and properties. *Biochem. J.* 40: 855–866.

KEISTER, M. L. (1948). The morphogenesis of the tracheal system of *Sciara*. *J. Morph.* 83: 373–424.

KEISTER, M. and BUCK, J. (1964). Respiration: some exogenous and endogenous effects on rate of respiration. *in* Rockstein, M. (Ed.), *The physiology of Insecta*. vol. 2. Academic Press, New York.

KENNEDY, J. S. (1939). The behaviour of the desert locust (*Schistocerca gregaria* (Forsk.)) (Orthopt.) in an outbreak centre. *Trans. R. ent. Soc. Lond.* 89: 385–542.

KENNEDY, J. S. (1951). The migration of the desert locust (*Schistocerca gregaria* Forsk.). *Phil. Trans. R. Soc.* B, 235: 163–290.

KENNEDY, J. S. (1956). Phase transformation in locust biology. *Biol. Rev.* 31: 349–370.

KENNEDY, J. S. and BOOTH, C. O. (1951). Host alternation in *Aphis fabae* Scop. I. Feeding performances and fecundity in relation to the age and kind of leaves. *Ann. appl. Biol.* 38: 25–64.

KENNEDY, J. S. and BOOTH, C. O. (1963a). Free flight of aphids in the laboratory. *J. exp. Biol.* 40: 67–85.

KENNEDY, J. S. and BOOTH, C. O. (1963b). Co-ordination of successive activities in an aphid. The effect of flight on the settling responses. *J. exp. Biol.* 40: 351–369.

KENNEDY, J. S. and STROYAN, H. L. G. (1959). Biology of aphids. *A. Rev. Ent.* 4: 139–160.

KERR, W. E. (1962). Genetics of sex determination. *A. Rev. Ent.* 7: 157–176.

KESSEL, R. G. (1961). Cytological studies on the suboesophageal body cells and pericardial cells in embryos of the grasshopper, *Melanoplus differentialis differentialis* (Thomas). *J. Morph.* 109: 289–321.

KETTLEWELL, H. B. D. (1961). The phenomenon of industrial melanism in Lepidoptera. *A. Rev. Ent.* 6: 245–262.

KEVAN, D. K. McE. (1955). Méthodes inhabituelles de production de son chez les Orthoptères. *in* Busnel, R.-G. (Ed.), *Colloques sur l'acoustique des Orthoptères. Annls Épiphyt.* fasc. hors. série.

KEY, K. H. L. and DAY, M. F. (1954a). A temperature-controlled physiological colour response in the grasshopper *Kosciuscola tristis* Sjost. (Orthoptera: Acrididae). *Aust. J. Zool.* 2: 309–339.

KEY, K. H. L. and DAY, M. F. (1954b). The physiological mechanism of colour change in the grasshopper *Koscuiscola tristis* Sjost. (Orthoptera: Acrididae). *Aust. J. Zool.* 2: 340–363.

KHALIFA, A. (1949). The mechanism of insemination and the mode of action of the spermatophore in *Gryllus domesticus*. *Q. Jl microsc. Sci.* 90: 281–292.

KHALIFA, A. (1950a). Spermatophore production in *Galleria mellonella* L. (Lepidoptera). *Proc. R. ent. Soc. Lond.* A, 25: 33–42.

KHALIFA, A. (1950b). Spermatophore production in *Blatella germanica* L. (Orthoptera: Blattidae). *Proc. R. ent. Soc. Lond.* A, 25: 53–61.

KHAN, T. R. and FRASER, A. (1962). Neurosecretion in the embryo and later stages of the cockroach (*Periplaneta americana* L.). *Mem. Soc. Endocr.* 12: 349–369.

KILBY, B. A. (1963). The biochemistry of insect fat body. *Adv. Ins. Physiol.* 1: 112–174.

KIM, C.-W. (1959). The differentiation centre inducing the development from larval to adult leg in *Pieris brassicae* (Lepidoptera). *J. Embryol. exp. Morph.* 7: 572–582.

KIMMINS, D. E. (1950). Ephemeroptera. *Handbk Ident. Br. Insects* 1, part 9.

KING, P. E. (1962). The structure and action of the spermatheca in *Nasonia vitripennis* (Walker) (Hymenoptera: Pteromalidae). *Proc. R. ent. Soc. Lond.* A, 37: 73–75.

KING, R. C. (1964). Studies on early stages of insect oogenesis. *Symp. R. ent. Soc. Lond.* 2: 13–25.

KING, R. C. and AGGARWAL, S. K. (1965). Oogenesis in *Hyalophora cecropia*. *Growth* 29: 17–83.

KLOOT, W. G. van der (1960). Neurosecretion in insects. *A. Rev. Ent.* 5: 35–52.

KOCH, E. A. and KING, R. C. (1966). The origin and early differentiation of the egg chamber of *Drosophila melanogaster*. *J. Morph.* 119: 283–303.

KRAUSE, G. and SANDER, K. (1962). Ooplasmic reaction systems in insect embryogenesis. *Adv. Morphogenesis* 2: 259–303.

KRIJGSMAN, B. J. (1952). Contractile and pacemaker mechanisms of the heart of arthropods. *Biol. Rev.* 27: 320–346.

KROEGER, H. and LEZZI, M. (1966). Regulation of gene action in insect development. *A. Rev. Ent.* 11: 1–22.

KROGH, A. and WEIS-FOGH, T. (1951). The respiratory exchange of the desert locust (*Schistocerca gregaria*), before, during and after flight. *J. exp. Biol.* 28: 342–357.

KUIPER, J. W. (1962). The optics of the compound eye. *Symp. Soc. exp. Biol.* 16: 58–71.

KUK-MEIRI, S., LICHTENSTEIN, N., SHULOV, A. and PENER, M. P. (1966). Cathepsin-type proteolytic activity in the developing eggs of the African migratory locust (*Locusta migratoria migratorioides* R. and F.). *Comp. Biochem. Physiol.* 18: 783–795.

LAI-FOOK, J. (1967). The structure of developing muscle insertions in insects. *J. Morph.* 123: 503–528.

LAMBORN, W. A. (1911). Instances of mimicry, protective resemblance, etc. from the Lagos district. *Proc. ent. Soc. Lond.* 1911: 46–47.

LANDOLT, A. M. and RIS, H. (1966). Electron microscope studies on soma-somatic interneuronal junctions in the corpus pedunculatum of the wood ant (*Formica lugubris* Zett.). *J. cell Biol.* 28: 391–403.

LANE, C. and ROTHSCHILD, M. (1965). A case of Müllerian mimicry of sound. *Proc. R. ent. Soc. Lond.* A, 40: 156–158.

LARSEN, J. R. (1962). The fine structure of the labellar chemosensory hairs of the blowfly, *Phormia regina* Meig. *J. Insect Physiol.* 8: 683–691.

LARSEN, J. R. (1963). Fine structure of the interpseudo-tracheal papillae of the blowfly. *Science, N.Y.* 139: 347.

LAWRENCE, P. A. (1966a). Development and determination of hairs and bristles in the milkweed bug, *Oncopeltus fasciatus* (Lygaeidae) (Hemiptera). *J. Cell Sci.* 1: 475–498.

LAWRENCE, P. A. (1966b). The hormonal control of the development of hairs and bristles in the milkweed bug, *Oncopeltus fasciatus* Dall. *J. exp. Biol.* 44: 507–522.

LEE, R. M. (1961). The variation of blood volume with age in the desert locust (*Schistocerca gregaria* Forsk.). *J. Insect Physiol.* 6: 36–51.

LEES, A. D. (1955). *The physiology of diapause in arthropods.* Cambridge University Press.

LEES, A. D. (1961). Clonal polymorphism in aphids. *Symp. R. ent. Soc. Lond.* 1: 68–79.

LEES, A. D. (1964). The location of the photoperiodic receptors in the aphid *Megoura viciae* Buckton. *J. exp. Biol.* 41: 119–134.

LEES, A. D. (1966). The control of polymorphism in aphids. *Adv. Ins. Physiol.* 3: 207–277.

LEES, A. D. (1967). The production of the apterons and alate forms in the aphid *Megoura viciae* Buckton, with special reference to the role of crowding. *J. Insect Physiol.* 13: 289–318.

LESTON, D. (1957). The stridulatory mechanisms in terrestrial species of Hemiptera Heteroptera. *Proc. zool. Soc. Lond.* 128: 369–386.

LESTON, D. and PRINGLE, J. W. S. (1963). Acoustic behaviour of Hemiptera. *in* Busnel, R.-G. (Ed.), *Acoustic behaviour of animals.* Elsevier, Amsterdam.

LEVENBOOK, L. (1950a). The physiology of carbon dioxide transport in insect blood. Part I. The form of carbon dioxide present in *Gastrophilus* larva blood. *J. exp. Biol.* 27: 158–174.

LEVENBOOK, L. (1950b). The physiology of carbon dioxide transport in insect blood. Part III. The buffer capacity of *Gastrophilus* blood. *J. exp. Biol.* 27: 184–191.

LEVENBOOK, L. and HOLLIS, V. W. (1961). Organic acid in insects. I. Citric acid. *J. Insect Physiol.* 6: 52–61.

LEVINSON, Z. H. (1962). The function of dietary sterols in phytophagous insects. *J. Insect Physiol.* 8: 191–198.

LEWIS, T. (1962). The effects of temperature and relative humidity on mortality in *Limothrips cerealium* Haliday (Thysanoptera) overwintering in bark *Ann appl. Biol.* 50: 313–326.

LEWIS, T. and TAYLOR, L. R. (1965). Diurnal periodicity of flight by insects. *Trans. R. ent. Soc. Lond.* 116: 393–479.

LIN, N. (1963). Territorial behaviour in the cicada killer wasp, *Sphecius speciosus* (Drury) (Hymenoptera: Sphecidae). I. *Behaviour* 20: 115–133.

LINDAUER, M. (1961). *Communication among social bees.* Harvard University Press, Cambridge, Mass.

LINLEY, J. R. (1966). The ovarian cycle of *Culicoides barbosai* Wirth & Blanton and *C. furens* (Poey) (Diptera, Ceratopogonidae). *Bull. ent. Res.* 57: 1–17.

LIPKE, H. and FRAENKEL, G. (1956). Insect nutrition. *A. Rev. Ent.* 1: 17–44.

LIU, Y. S. and LEO, P. L. (1960). Histological studies on the sense organs and the appendages of the Oriental migratory locust, *Locusta migratoria manilensis* Meyen. (In Chinese with English summary). *Acta ent. sin.* 10: 243–260.

LOCKE, M. (1959). The cuticular pattern in an insect, *Rhodnius prolixus* Stål. *J. exp. Biol.* 36: 459–477.

LOCKE, M. (1960). The cuticle and wax secretion in *Calpodes ethlius* (Lepidoptera, Hesperidae). *Q. Jl microsc. Sci.* 101: 333–338.

LOCKE, M. (1961). Pore canals and related structures in insect cuticle. *J. biophys. biochem. Cytol.* 10: 589–618.

LOCKE, M. (1964). The structure and formation of the integument in insects. *in* Rockstein, M. (Ed.), *The physiology of Insecta.* vol. 3. Academic Press, New York.

LOCKE, M. (1965a). Permeability of insect cuticle to water and lipids. *Science, N.Y.* 147: 295–298.

LOCKE, M. (1965b). The hormonal control of wax secretion in an insect, *Calpodes ethlius* Stoll (Lepidoptera, Hesperiidae). *J. Insect Physiol.* 11: 641–658.

LOHER, W. (1960). The chemical acceleration of the maturation process and its hormonal control in the male of the desert locust. *Proc. R. Soc. B,* 153: 380–397.

LOHER, W. and HUBER, F. (1966). Nervous and endocrine control of sexual behaviour in a grasshopper (*Gomphocerus rufus* L., Acridinae). *Symp. Soc. exp. Biol.* 20: 381–400.

LONG, D. B. (1953). Effects of population density on larvae of Lepidoptera. *Trans. R. ent. Soc. Lond.* 104: 543–584.

LONGFIELD, C. (1949). *The dragonflies of the British Isles.* Warne & Co., London.

LOUGHTON, B. G. and WEST, A. S. (1965). The development and distribution of haemolymph proteins in Lepidoptera. *J. Insect Physiol.* 11: 919–932.

LÜSCHER, M. (1960). Hormonal control of caste differentiation in termites. *Ann. N.Y. Acad. Sci.* 89: 549–563.

LÜSCHER, M. (1961). Social control of polymorphism in termites. *Symp. R. ent. Soc. Lond.* 1: 57–67.

LŪSIS, O. (1963). The histology and histochemistry of development and resorption in the terminal oocytes of the desert locust, *Schistocerca gregaria. Q. Jl microsc. Sci.* 104: 57–68.

MACAN, T. T. (1961). A key to the nymphs of the British species of Ephemeroptera. *Freshwater Biol. Assoc. Sci. Publ.* no. 20, 63 pp.

MADDRELL, S. H. P. (1962). A diuretic hormone in *Rhodnius prolixus* Stål. *Nature, Lond.* 194: 605–606.

MADDRELL, S. H. P. (1964). Excretion in the blood-sucking bug, *Rhodnius prolixus* Stål. II. The normal course of diuresis and the effect of temperature. *J. exp. Biol.* 41: 163–176.

MADDRELL, S. H. P. (1966a). Nervous control of the mechanical properties of the abdominal wall at feeding in *Rhodnius. J. exp. Biol.* 44: 59–68.

MADDRELL, S. H. P. (1966b). The site of release of the diuretic hormone in *Rhodnius*— a new neuro-haemal system in insects. *J. exp. Biol.* 45: 499–508.

MAHOWALD, A. P. (1962). Fine structure of pole cells and polar granules in *Drosophila melanogaster. J. exp. Zool.* 151: 201–215.

MAHOWALD, A. P. (1963a). Ultrastructural differentiations during formation of the blastoderm in the *Drosophila melanogaster* embryo. *Devl Biol.* 8: 186–204.

MAHOWALD, A. P. (1963b). Electron microscopy of the formation of the cellular blastoderm in *Drosophila melanogaster. Expl Cell Res.* 32: 457–468.

MAKIELSKI, S. K. (1966). The structure and maturation of the spermatozoa of *Sciara coprophila. J. Morph.* 118: 11–41.

MAKINGS, P. (1958). The oviposition behaviour of *Achroia grisella* (Fabricius) (Lepidoptera: Galeriidae). *Proc. R. ent. Soc. Lond.* A, 33: 136–148.

MANNING, A. (1959). The sexual isolation between *Drosophila melanogaster* and *Drosophila simulans. Anim. Behav.* 7: 60–65.

MANNING, A. (1966). Sexual behaviour. *Symp. R. ent. Soc. Lond.* 3: 59–68.

MANSINGH, A. and SMALLMAN, B. N. (1967). The cholinergic system in insect diapause. *J. Insect Physiol.* 13: 447–467.

MANTON, S. M. (1953). Locomotory habits and the evolution of the larger arthropodan groups. *Symp. Soc. exp. Biol.* 7: 339–376.

MANTON, S. M. (1964). Mandibular mechanisms and the evolution of arthropods. *Phil. Trans. R. Soc.* B, 247: 1–183.

MARCUS, H. (1956). Über Sinnesorgane bei Articulaten. *Z. Wiss. Zool.* 159: 225–254.

MARKL, H. (1962). Borstenfelder an den Gelenken als Schwaresinnesorgane bei Ameisen und anderen Hymenopteren. *Z. vergl. Physiol.* 45: 475–569.

MARSHALL, A. T. (1964a). Spittle-production and tube-building by cercopoid nymphs (Homoptera). 1. The cytology of the Malpighian tubules of spittle-bug nymphs. *Q. Jl microsc. Sci.* 105: 257–262.

MARSHALL, A. T. (1964b). Spittle-production and tube-building by cercopoid nymphs (Homoptera). 2. The cytology and function of the granule zone of the Malpighian tubules of tube-building nymphs. *Q. Jl microsc. Sci.* 105: 415–422.

MARSHALL, A. T. (1965). Spittle-production and tube-building by cercopoid nymphs (Homoptera). 3. The cytology and function of the fibril zone of the Malpighian tubules of tube-dwelling nymphs. *Q. Jl microsc. Sci.* 106: 37–44.

MARSHALL, J. F. (1938). *The British mosquitoes.* Brit. Mus., London.

MARUYAMA, K. (1965). The biochemistry of the contractile elements of insect muscle.

in Rockstein, M. (Ed.), *The physiology of Insecta.* vol. 2. Academic Press, New York.

MASON, C. W. (1923). Structural colours in feathers. II. *J. phys. Chem., Ithaca* 27: 401–447.

MASON, C. W. (1926). Structural colours in insects. I. *J. phys. Chem., Ithaca* 30: 383–395.

MASON, C. W. (1927a). Structural colours in insects. II. *J. phys. Chem., Ithaca* 31: 321–354.

MASON, C. W. (1927b). Structural colours in insects. III. *J. phys. Chem., Ithaca* 31: 1856–1872.

MATSUDA, R. (1963). Some evolutionary aspects of the insect thorax. *A. Rev. Ent.* 8: 59–76.

MATSUDA, R. (1965). Morphology and evolution of the insect head. *Mem. Am. ent. Inst.* no. 4, 334 pp.

MATTHÉE, J. J. (1951). The structure and physiology of the egg of *Locustana pardalina* (Walk). *Bull. Dep. Agric. For. Un. S. Afr.* no. 316, 83 pp.

MAYNARD SMITH, J. (1957). Temperature tolerance and acclimatization in *Drosophila subobscura. J. exp. Biol.* 34: 85–96.

McCANN, G. D. and MacGINITIE, G. F. (1965). Optomotor response studies of insect vision. *Proc. R. Soc.* B, 163: 369–401.

McCORMICK, F. W. and SCOTT, A. (1966a). Changes in haemolymph proteins in first instar locusts. *Archs. int. Physiol. Biochim.* 124: 442–448.

McCORMICK, F. W. and SCOTT, A. (1966b). A protein fraction in locust hemolymph associated with the moulting cycle. *Experientia* 22: 228–229.

McELROY, W. D. (1965). Insect bioluminescence. *in* Rockstein, M. (Ed.), *The physiology of Insecta.* vol. 1. Academic Press, New York.

McFARLANE, J. E. (1966). The permeability of the cricket eggshell to water. *J. Insect Physiol.* 12: 1567–1575.

MEAD-BRIGGS, A. R. (1964). A correlation between development of the ovaries and of the midgut epithelium in the rabbit flea *Spilopsyllus cuniculi. Nature, Lond.* 201: 1303–1304.

MELLANBY, K. (1932). The effect of atmospheric humidity on the metabolism of the fasting mealworm (*Tenebrio molitor* L., Coleoptera). *Proc. R. Soc.* B, 111: 376–390.

MELLANBY, K. (1939). The functions of insect blood. *Biol. Rev.* 14: 243–260.

MERCER, E. H. and BRUNET, P. C. J. (1959). The electron microscopy of the left colleterial gland of the cockroach. *J. biophys. biochem. Cytol.* 5: 257–262.

MERCER, E. H. and DAY, M. F. (1952). The fine structure of the peritrophic membranes of certain insects. *Biol. Bull. mar. biol. Lab., Woods Hole* 103: 384–394.

MIALL, L. C. (1922). *The natural history of aquatic insects.* MacMillan, London.

MICHENER, C. D. (1961). Social polymorphism in Hymenoptera. *Symp. R. ent. Soc. Lond.* 1: 43–56.

MILES, P. W. (1959). The salivary secretions of a plant-sucking bug, *Oncopeltus fasciatus* (Dall.) (Heteroptera: Lygaeidae). I. The types of secretion and their roles during feeding. *J. Insect Physiol.* 3: 243–255.

MILES, P. W. (1960). The salivary secretions of a plant-sucking bug, *Oncopeltus fasciatus* (Dall.) (Heteroptera: Lygaeidae). III. Origins in the salivary glands. *J. Insect Physiol.* 4: 271–282.

MILES, P. W. (1964). Studies on the salivary physiology of plant bugs: the chemistry of formation of the sheath material. *J. Insect Physiol.* 10: 147–160.

MILLER, P. L. (1960a). Respiration in the desert locust. I. The control of ventilation. *J. exp. Biol.* 37: 224–236.

MILLER, P. L. (1960b). Respiration in the desert locust. II. The control of the spiracles. *J. exp. Biol.* 37: 237–263.

MILLER, P. L. (1960c). Respiration in the desert locust. III. Ventilation and the spiracles during flight. *J. exp. Biol.* 37: 264–278.

MILLER, P. L. (1964). Respiration—aerial gas transport. *in* Rockstein, M. (Ed.), *The physiology of Insecta.* vol. 3. Academic Press, New York.

MILLER, P. L. (1966a). The regulation of breathing in insects. *Adv. Ins. Physiol.* 3: 279–344.

MILLER, P. L. (1966b). The function of haemoglobin in relation to the maintenance of neutral buoyancy in *Anisops pellucens* (Notonectidae, Hemiptera). *J. exp. Biol.* 44: 529–544.

MILLS, R. P. and KING, R. C. (1965). The pericardial cells of *Drosophila melanogaster. Q. Jl microsc. Sci.* 106: 261–268.

MILLS, R. R. and NIELSEN, D. J. (1967). Hormonal control of tanning in the American cockroach—V. Some properties of the purified hormone. *J. Insect Physiol.* 13: 273–280.

MITTELSTAEDT, H. (1962). Control systems of orientation in insects. *A. Rev. Ent.* 7: 177–198.

MUCKENTHALER, F. A. (1964). Autoradiographic study of nucleic acid synthesis during spermatogenesis in the grasshopper, *Melanoplus differentialis. Expl Cell Res.* 35: 531–547.

MUELLER, N. S. (1963). An experimental analysis of molting in embryos of *Melanoplus differentialis. Devl Biol.* 8: 222–240.

MUIR, F. and SHARP, D. (1904). On the egg-cases and early stages of some Cassididae. *Trans. ent. Soc. Lond.* 1904, 1–23.

MÜLLER, H. J. (1955). Die Saisonformenbildung von *Arachnia levana*, ein photoperiodisch gesteuerter Diapause-Effekt. *Naturwissenschaften* 42: 134–135.

MURRAY, R. W. (1962). Temperature receptors in animals. *Symp. Soc. exp. Biol.* 16: 245–266.

MUSGRAVE, A. J. (1964). Insect mycetomes. *Can. Ent.* 96: 377–389.

NACHTIGALL, W. (1965). Locomotion: swimming (hydrodynamics) of aquatic insects. *in* Rockstein, M. (Ed.), *The physiology of Insecta.* vol. 2. Academic Press, New York.

NAIR, K. S. S. and GEORGE, J. C. (1964). A histological and histochemical study of the larval fat body of *Anthrenus vorax* Waterhouse (Dermestidae, Coleoptera). *J. Insect Physiol.* 10: 509–517.

NARAHASHI, T. (1963). The properties of insect axons. *Adv. Ins. Physiol.* 1: 175–256.

NARAHASHI, T. (1965). The physiology of insect axons. *in* Treherne, J. E. and Beament, J. W. L. (Eds.), *The physiology of the insect central nervous system.* Academic Press, London.

NEKRUTENKO, Y. P. (1965). 'Gynandromorphic effect' and the optical nature of hidden wing-pattern in *Gonepteryx rhamni* L. (Lepidoptera, Pieridae). *Nature, Lond.* 205: 417–418.

NEVILLE, A. C. (1963). Growth and deposition of resilin and chitin in locust rubber-like cuticle. *J. Insect Physiol.* 9: 265–278.

NEVILLE, A. C. (1965a). Chitin lamellogenesis in locust cuticle. *Q. Jl microsc. Sci.* 106: 269–286.

NEVILLE, A. C. (1965b). Circadian organisation of chitin in some insect skeletons. *Q. Jl microsc. Sci.* 106: 315–325.

NEVILLE, A. C. (1965c). Energy and economy in insect flight. *Sci. Prog., Lond.* 53: 203–220.

NEVILLE, A. C. and WEIS-FOGH, T. (1963). The effect of temperature on locust flight muscle. *J. exp. Biol.* 40: 111–121.

NICKERSON, B. (1956). Pigmentation of hoppers of the desert locust (*Schistocerca gregaria* Forskål) in relation to phase colouration *Anti-Locust Bull.* no. 24, 34 pp.

NIELSEN, E. T. (1958). The initial stage of migration in saltmarsh mosquitoes. *Bull. ent. Res.* 49: 305–313.

NIELSEN, E. T. (1959). Copulation of *Glyptotendipes* (*Phytotendipes*) *paripes* Edwards. *Nature, Lond.* 184: 1252–1253.

NIELSEN, E. T. (1961). On the habits of the migratory butterfly *Ascia monuste* L. *Biol. Meddr.* 23: 1–81.

NIELSEN, E. T. and NIELSEN, H. T. (1958). Observations on mosquitoes in Iraq. *Ent. Meddr.* 28: 282–321.

NOBLE-NESBITT, J. (1963a). A site of water and ionic exchange with the medium in *Podera aquatica* L. (Collembola, Isotomidae). *J. exp. Biol.* 40: 701–711.

NOBLE-NESBITT, J. (1963b). The fully formed intermoult cuticle and associated structures of *Podura aquatica* (Collembola). *Q. Jl microsc. Sci.* 104: 253–270.

NOBLE-NESBITT, J. (1963c). The cuticle and associated structures of *Podura aquatica* at the moult. *Q. Jl microsc. Sci.* 104: 369–392.

NORRIS, M. J. (1933). Contributions towards the study of insect fertility. III. Experiments on the factors influencing fertility of *Ephestia kühniella* Z. (Lepidoptera, Phycitidae). *Proc. zool. Soc. Lond.* 1933, 903–934.

NORRIS, M. J. (1962). Group effects on the activity and behaviour of adult males of the desert locust (*Schistocerca gregaria* Forsk.) in relation to sexual maturation. *Anim. Behav.* 10: 275–291.

NORRIS, M. J. (1963). Laboratory experiments on gregarious behaviour in ovipositing females of the desert locust (*Schistocerca gregaria* (Forsk.)). *Entomologia exp. appl.* 6: 279–303.

NORRIS, M. J. (1964). Environmental control of sexual maturation in insects. *Symp. R. ent. Soc. Lond.* 2: 56–65.

NORRIS, M. J. (1965). The influence of constant and changing photoperiods on imaginal diapause in the red locust (*Nomadacris septemfasciata* Serv.). *J. Insect Physiol.* 11: 1105–1119.

NOVÁK, V. J. A. (1966). *Insect hormones*. Methuen and Co., London.

NUR, U. (1962). Sperms, sperm bundles and fertilisation in a mealy bug, *Prendococcus obscurus* Essig. (Homoptera: Coccoidea). *J. Morph.* 111: 173–199.

NUTTING, W. L. (1951). A comparative anatomical study of the heart and accessory structures of the orthopteroid insects. *J. Morph.* 89: 501–597.

ODHIAMBO, T. R. (1966). The metabolic effects of the corpus allatum hormone in the male desert locust. II. Spontaneous locomotor activity. *J. exp. Biol.* 45: 51–63.

OLDROYD, H. (1949). Diptera. 1. Introduction and key to families. *Handbk. Ident. Br. Insects* 9, part 1.

OLDROYD, H. (1964). *The natural history of flies.* Weidenfeld and Nicolson, London.

OSBORNE, M. P. (1963). An electron microscope study of an abdominal stretch receptor of the cockroach. *J. Insect Physiol.* 9: 237–245.

OSBORNE, M. P. and FINLAYSON, L. H. (1965). An electron microscope study of the stretch receptor of *Antheraea pernyi* (Lepidoptera, Saturniidae). *J. Insect Physiol.* 11: 703–710.

OSSIANNILSSON, F. (1949). Insect drummers. *Opusc. ent.* suppl. 10: 1–146.

OZBAS, S. and HODGSON, E. S. (1958). Action of insect neurosecretion upon central nervous system in vitro and upon behaviour. *Proc. natn. Acad. Sci. U.S.A.* 44: 825–830.

PAINTER, T. S. (1966). The role of the E-chromosomes in Cecidomyiidae. *Proc. natn. Acad. Sci. U.S.A.* 56: 853–855.

PASQUINELLY, F. and BUSNEL, M.-C. (1955). Études preliminaires sur les mécanismes de la production des sons par les Orthoptères. in Busnel, R.-G. (Ed.), *Colloques sur l'acoustique des Orthoptères. Annls. Épiphyt.* fasc. hors série.

PASSAMA-VUILLAUME, M. (1965). Étude de l'irridiation lumineuse, facteur essentiel du brunissement de *Mantis religiosa* (L.). *C. r. hebd. Séanc. Acad.'Sci., Paris* 261: 3683–3685.

PASSONNEAU, J. V. and WILLIAMS, C. M. (1953). The moulting fluid of the cecropia silkworm. *Q. Jl microsc. Sci.* 30: 545–560.

PAYNE, D. W. and EVANS, W. A. L. (1964). Transglycosylation in the desert locust, *Schistocerca gregaria* Forsk. *J. Insect Physiol.* 10: 675–688.

PAYNE, F. (1966). Some observations on spermatogenesis in *Gelastocoris oculatus* (Hemiptera) with the aid of the electron microscope. *J. Morph.* 119: 357–381.

PAYNE, M. A. (1933). The structure of the testis and movement of sperms in *Chortophaga viridifasciata* as demonstrated by intravitam technique. *J. Morph.* 54: 321–345.

PAYNE, M. A. (1934). Intravitam studies on the hemipteran, *Leptocoris trivittatus*. A description of the male reproductive organs and the aggregation and turning of the sperms. *J. Morph.* 56: 513–531.

PERDECK, A. C. (1958). The isolating value of specific song patterns in two sibling species of grasshoppers (*Chorthippus brunneus* Thunb. and *C. biguttulus* L.). *Behaviour* 12: 1–75.

PESSON, P. (1951a). Ordre des Homoptères. *in* Grassé, P.-P. (Ed.), *Traité de Zoologie*. vol. 10. Masson et Cie., Paris.

PESSON, P. (1951b). Ordre des Thysanoptera. *in* Grassé, P.-P. (Ed.), *Traité de Zoologie*. vol. 10. Masson et Cie., Paris.

PETERSON, A. (1960). *Larvae of insects. Part II. Coleoptera, Diptera, Neuroptera, Siphonaptera, Mecoptera, Trichoptera*. Columbus, Ohio.

PETERSON, A. (1962). *Larvae of insects. Part I. Lepidoptera and plant infesting Hymenoptera*. Columbus, Ohio.

PFADT, R. E. (1949). Food plants as factors in the ecology of the lesser migratory grasshopper, *Melanoplus mexicanus* (Sauss.). *Bull. Wyoming agric. Exp. Stn.* no. 290, 51 pp.

PHILLIPS, D. M. (1966). Observations on spermiogenesis in the fungus gnat *Sciara coprophila*. *J. Cell Biol.* 30: 477–497.

PHILLIPS, J. E. (1964a). Rectal absorption in the desert locust, *Schistocerca gregaria* Forskål. I. Water. *J. exp. Biol.* 41:15–38.

PHILLIPS, J. E. (1964b). Rectal absorption in the desert locust, *Schistocerca gregaria* Forskål. II. Sodium, potassium and chloride. *J. exp. Biol.* 41: 15–38.

PHIPPS, J. (1962). The ovaries of some Sierra Leone Acridoidea (Orthoptera) with some comparisons between East and West African forms. *Proc. R. ent. Soc. Lond.* A, 37: 13–21.

PIEK, T. (1964). Synthesis of wax in the honeybee (*Apis mellifera* L.). *J. Insect Physiol.* 10: 563–572.

PIELOU, D. P. and GUNN, D. L. (1940). The humidity behaviour of the mealworm beetle, *Tenebrio molitor* L. 1. The reaction to differences of humidity. *J. exp. Biol.* 17: 286–294.

PIERCE, G. W. (1948). *The songs of insects*. Harvard Yniversity Press.

POPHAM, E. J. (1952). A preliminary investigation into the locomotion of aquatic Hemiptera and Coleoptera. *Proc. R. ent. Soc. Lond.* A, 27: 117–119.

POPHAM, E. J. (1962). A repetition of Ege's experiments and a note on the efficiency of the physical gill of *Notonecta* (Hemiptera—Heteroptera). *Proc. R. ent. Soc. Lond.* A, 37: 154–160.

POPHAM, E. J. (1965). The functional morphology of the reproductive organs of the common earwig (*Forficula auricularia*) and other Dermaptera with reference to the natural classification of the order. *J. Zool.* 146: 1–43.

POPOV, G. B. (1958). Ecological studies on oviposition by swarms of the desert locust (*Schistocerca gregaria* Forskål) in Eastern Africa. *Anti-Locust Bull.* no. 31, 70 pp.

POVLOVSKY, E. N. (1922). On the biology and structure of the larva of *Hydrophilus caraboides* L. *Q. Jl microsc. Sci.* 66: 627–655.

PRINGLE, J. A. (1938). A contribution to the knowledge of *Micromalthus debilis* Le C.

(Coleoptera). *Trans. R. ent. Soc. Lond.* 87: 271–286.

PRINGLE, J. W. S. (1938a). Proprioception in insects. I. A new type of mechanical receptor. from the palps of the cockroach. *J. exp. Biol.* 15: 101–113.

PRINGLE, J. W. S. (1938b). Proprioception in insects. II. The action of the campaniform sensilla on the legs. *J. exp. Biol.* 15: 114–131.

PRINGLE, J. W. S. (1938c). Proprioception in insects. III. The function of the hair sensilla at the joints. *J. exp. Biol.* 15: 467–473.

PRINGLE, J. W. S. (1940). The reflex mechanism of the insect leg. *J. exp. Biol.* 17: 8–17.

PRINGLE, J. W. S. (1948). The gyroscopic mechanism of the halteres of Diptera. *Phil. Trans. R. Soc.* B, 233: 347–384.

PRINGLE, J. W. S. (1954). A physiological analysis of cicada song. *J. exp. Biol.* 31: 525–560.

PRINGLE, J. W. S. (1957). *Insect flight.* Cambridge University Press.

PRINGLE, J. W. S. (1965). Locomotion: flight. *in* Rockstein, M. (Ed.), *The physiology of Insecta.* vol. 2. Academic Press, New York.

PROSSER, C. L. and BROWN, F. A. (1961). *Comparative animal physiology.* Saunders Company, Philadelphia.

PUMPHREY, R. J. (1950). Hearing. *Symp. Soc. exp. Biol.* 4: 3–18.

RAGGE, D. R. (1955). *The wing-venation of the Orthoptera Saltatoria.* British Museum, London.

RAGGE, D. R. (1965). *Grasshoppers, crickets and cockroaches of the British Isles.* Warne & Co., London.

RAINEY, R. C. (1958). Some observations on flying locusts and atmospheric turbulence in eastern Africa. *Q. Jl R. met. Soc.* 84: 334–354.

RAINEY, R. C. (1963). Meteorology and the migration of desert locusts. Applications of synoptic meteorology in locust control. *Anti-Locust Mem.* no. 7, 115 pp.

RAMSAY, J. A. (1955). The excretory system of the stick insect, *Dixippus morosus* (Orthoptera, Phasmidae). *J. exp. Biol.* 32: 183–199.

RAMSAY, J. A. (1958). Excretion by the malpighian tubules of the stick insect, *Dixippus morosus* (Orthoptera, Phasmidae): amino acids, sugars and urea. *J. exp. Biol.* 35: 871–891.

RAMSAY, J. A. (1964). The rectal complex of the mealworm *Tenebrio molitor*, L. (Coleoptera, Tenebrionidae). *Phil. Trans. R. Soc.* B, 248: 279–314.

RAVEN, C. P. (1961). *Oogenesis.* Pergamon Press, London.

RAZET, P. (1956). Sur l'élimination simultanée d'acide urique et d'acide allantoïques chez les insectes. *C. r. hebd. Séanc. Acad. Sci., Paris* 243: 185–187.

RIBBANDS, C. R. (1953). *The behaviour and social life of honeybees.* Bee research association, London.

RIBBANDS, C. R. (1955). The scent perception of the honeybee. *Proc. R. Soc.* B, 143: 367–379.

RIBBANDS, C. R. and SPEIRS, N. (1953). The adaptability of the homecoming honeybee. *Br. J. Anim. Behav.* 1: 59–66.

RICHARDS, A. G. (1951). *The integument of arthropods.* University of Minnesota Press, Minneapolis.

RICHARDS, A. G. (1957). Cumulative effects of optimum and suboptimum temperatures on insect development. *in* Johnson, F. H. (Ed.), *Influence of temperature on biological systems.* Amer. Physiol. Soc.

RICHARDS, A. G. (1958). The cuticle of arthropods. *Ergebn. Biol.* 20: 1–26.

RICHARDS, A. G. (1963). The ventral diaphragm of insects. *J. Morph.* 113: 17–47.

RICHARDS, A. G. and BROOKS, M. A. (1958). Internal symbiosis in insects. *A. Rev. Ent.* 3: 37–56.

RICHARDS, O. W. (1927). Sexual selection and allied problems in the insects. *Biol. Rev.* 2: 298–364.

RICHARDS, O. W. (1949). The relation between measurements of the successive instars of insects. *Proc. R. ent. Soc. Lond.* A, 24: 8–10.

RICHARDS, O. W. (1953). *The social insects.* Macdonald & Co., London.

RICHARDS, O. W. (1956). Hymenoptera. Introduction and key to families. *Handbk Ident. Br. Insects* 6, part 1.

RICHARDS, O. W. and WALOFF, N. (1954). Studies on the biology and population dynamics of British grasshoppers. *Anti-Locust Bull.* no. 17, 182 pp.

RING, R. A. (1967). Maternal induction of diapause in the larva of *Lucilia caesar* L. (Diptera: Callophoridae). *J. exp. Biol.* 46: 123–136.

RIZKI, M. T. M. (1953). The larval blood cells of *Drosophila willistoni. J. exp. Zool.* 123: 397–411.

ROBERTS, S. K. de F. (1966). Circadian activity rhythms in cockroaches. III. The role of endocrine and neural factors. *J. cell. Physiol.* 67: 473–486.

ROBISON, W. G. (1966). Microtubules in relation to the motility of a sperm syncytium in an armoured scale insect. *J. Cell Biol.* 29: 251–265.

ROCKSTEIN, M. and BHATNAGAR, P. L. (1965). Age changes in size and number of the giant mitochondria in the flight muscle of the common housefly (*Musca domestica* L.). *J. Insect Physiol.* 11: 481–491.

ROEDER, K. D. (1953). Electric activity in nerves and ganglia. *in* Roeder, K. D. (Ed.), *Insect physiology.* Wiley & Sons, New York.

ROEDER, K. D. (1963). *Nerve cells and insect behaviour.* Harvard University Press, Cambridge, Mass.

ROEDER, K. D. (1965). Moths and ultrasound. *Scient. Am.* 212, no. 4: 94–102.

ROEDER, K. D. and PAYNE, R. S. (1966). Acoustic orientation of a moth in flight by means of two sense cells. *Symp. Soc. exp. Biol.* 20: 251–272.

ROEDER, K. D. and TREAT, A. E. (1957). Ultrasonic reception by the tympanic organ of noctuid moths. *J. exp. Zool.* 134: 127–157.

ROEDER, K. D. and TREAT, A. E. (1961). The detection and evasion of bats by moths. *Am. Scient.* 49: 135–148.

ROFFEY, J. (1963). Observations on night flight in the desert locust (*Schistocerca gregaria* Forskål). *Anti-Locust Bull.* no. 39, 32 pp.

ROGERS, G. L. (1962). A diffraction theory of insect vision. II. Theory and experiments with a simple model eye. *Proc. R. Soc.* B, 157: 83–98.

ROONWAL, M. L. (1937). Studies on the embryology of the African migratory locust, *Locusta migratoria migratorioides* Reiche and Frm. (Orthoptera, Acrididae) II—Organogeny. *Phil. Trans. R. Soc.* B, 227: 175–244.

ROONWAL, M. L. (1954). The egg-wall of the African migratory locust, *Locusta migratoria migratorioides* Reiche and Frm. (Orthoptera, Acrididae). *Proc. natn. Inst. Sci. India* 20: 361–370.

ROSCOW, J. M. (1963). The structure, development and variation of the stridulatory file of *Stenobothrus lineatus* (Panzer) (Orthoptera: Acrididae). *Proc. R. ent. Soc. Lond.* A, 38: 194–199.

ROTH, L. M. (1948). A study of mosquito behaviour. *Am. Midl. Nat.* 40: 265–352.

ROTH, L. M. (1964). Control of reproduction in female cockroaches with special reference to *Nauphoeta cinerea*—I. First pre-oviposition period. *J. Insect Physiol.* 10: 915–945.

ROTH, L. M. (1968). Öothecae of the Blattaria. *Ann. ent. Soc. Amer.* 61: 83–111.

ROTH, L. M. and BARTH, R. H. (1964). The control of sexual receptivity in female cockroaches. *J. Insect Physiol.* 10: 965–975.

ROTH, L. M. and DATEO, G. P. (1965). Uric acid storage and excretion by accessory sex glands of male cockroaches. *J. Insect Physiol.* 11: 1023–1029.

ROTH, L. M. and STAY, B. (1961). Oocyte development in *Diploptera punctata.* (Esch-scholtz) (Blattaria). *J. Insect Physiol.* 7: 186–202.

ROTH, L. M. and WILLIS, E. R. (1956). Parthenogenesis in cockroaches. *Ann. ent. Soc. Amer.* 49: 195–204.

ROTH, L. M. and WILLIS, E. R. (1958). An analysis of oviparity and viviparity in the Blattaria. *Trans. Am. ent. Soc.* 83: 221–238.

ROTH, T. F. and PORTER, K. R. (1964). Yolk protein uptake in the oocyte of the mosquito *Aedes aegypti* L. *J. Cell Biol.* 20: 313–332.

ROTHSCHILD, M. (1965). The rabbit flea and hormones. *Endeavour* 24: 162–167.

ROWELL, C. H. F. (1964). Central control of an insect segmental reflex. I. Inhibition by different parts of the central nervous system. *J. exp. Biol.* 41: 559–572.

RUCK, P. R. (1957). The electrical responses of dorsal ocelli in cockroaches and grass-hoppers. *J. Insect Physiol.* 1: 109–123.

RUCK, P. (1964). Retinal structures and photoreception. *A. Rev. Ent.* 9: 83–102.

RUCK, P. and EDWARDS, G. A. (1964). The structure of the insect dorsal ocellus. I. General organisation of the ocellus in dragonflies. *J. Morph.* 115: 1–25.

RUDALL, K. M. (1963). The chitin/protein complexes of insect cuticles. *Adv. Ins. Physiol.* 1: 257–314.

RUDALL, K. M. (1965). Skeletal structure in insects. *in* Goodwin, T. W. (Ed.), *Aspects of insect biochemistry.* Academic Press, London.

RUITER, L. de (1955). Countershading in caterpillars. *Archs néerl. Zool.* 11: 1–57.

RUITER, L. de, WOLVEKAMP, H. P., TOOREN, A. J. van and VLASBLOM, A. (1952). Experiments on the efficiency of the 'physical gill' (*Hydrous piceus* L., *Naucoris cimicoides* L., and *Notonecta glauca* L.). *Acta physiol. pharmac. néerl.* 2: 180–213.

SACKTOR, B. (1961). The role of mitochondria in respiratory metabolism of flight muscle. *A. Rev. Ent.* 6: 103–130.

SACKTOR, B. (1965). Energetics and respiratory metabolism of muscular contraction. *in* Rockstein, M. (Ed.), *The physiology of Insecta.* vol. 2. Academic Press, New York.

SAINI, R. S. (1964). Histology and physiology of the cryptonephridial system of insects. *Trans. R. ent. Soc. Lond.* 116: 347–392.

SALT, G. (1963). The defence reaction of insects to metazoan parasites. *Parasitology* 53: 527–642.

SALT, G. (1961). The haemocytic reaction of insects to foreign bodies. *in* Ramsay, J. A. and Wigglesworth, V. B. (Eds.), *The cell and the organism.* Cambridge University Press.

SALT, G. (1965). Experimental studies in insect parasitism. XIII. The haemocytic reaction of a caterpillar to eggs of its habitual parasite. *Proc. R. Soc.* B, 162: 303–318.

SALT, G. (1968). The resistance of insect parasitoids to the defence reactions of their hosts. *Biol. Rev.* 43: 200–232.

SALT, R. W. (1961). Principles of insect cold-hardiness. *A. Rev. Ent.* 6: 55–74.

SANDERSON, A. R. (1961). The cytology of a diploid bisexual spider beetle, *Ptinus clavipes* Panzer and its triploid gynogenetic form *mobilis* Moore. *Proc. R. Soc. Edinb.* 67: 333–350.

SANG, J. H. (1959). Circumstances affecting the nutritional requirements of *Drosophila melanogaster. Ann. N.Y. Acad. Sci.* 77: 352–365.

SAUNDERS, D. S. (1964). Age-changes in the ovaries of the sheep ked, *Melophagus ovinus* (L.) (Diptera: Hippoboscidae). *Proc. R. ent. Soc. Lond.* A, 39: 68–72.

SAVAGE, A. A. (1956). The development of the Malpighian tubules of *Schistocerca gregaria* (Orthoptera). *Q. Jl microsc. Sci.* 97: 599–615.

SCHARRER, B. (1959). The role of neurosecretion in neuro-endocrine integration. *in* Gorbman, A. (Ed.), *Comparative endocrinology.* Wiley & Sons, New York.

SCHMITT, J. B. (1962). The comparative anatomy of the insect nervous system. *A. Rev. Ent.* 7: 137–156.

SCHNEIDER, D. (1964). Insect antennae. *A. Rev. Ent.* 9: 103–122.

SCHNEIDER, D. (1966). Chemical sense communication in insects. *Symp. Soc. exp. Biol.* 20: 273–297.

SCHNEIDER, F. (1962). Dispersal and migration. *A. Rev. Ent.* 7: 223–242.

SCHNEIDERMAN, H. A. and GILBERT, L. I. (1964). Control of growth and development in insects. *Science, N.Y.* 143: 325–333.

SCHNEIDERMAN, H. A. and HORWITZ, J. (1958). The induction and termination of facultative diapause in the chalcid wasps, *Mormoniella vitripennis* (Walker) and *Tritneptis klugii* (Ratzeburg). *J. exp. Biol.* 35: 520–551.

SCHNEIRLA, T. C. (1953). Modifiability in insect behaviour. *in* Roeder, K. D. (Ed.), *Insect physiology.* Wiley & Sons, New York.

SCHREINER, B. (1966). Histochemistry of the A cell neurosecretory material in the milkweed bug, *Oncopeltus fasciatus* Dallas (Heteroptera: Lygaeidae), with a discussion of the neurosecretory material/carrier substance problem. *Gen. comp. Endocrin.* 6: 388–400.

SCHWABE, J. (1906). Beiträge zur Morphologie und Histologie der tympanalen Sinnesapparate der Orthopteren. *Zoologica, Stuttg.* 20, no. 50: 1–154.

SCHWARTZKOPFF, J. (1964). Mechanoreception. *in* Rockstein, M. (Ed.), *The physiology of Insecta.* vol. 1. Academic Press, New York.

SCOTT, A. (1941). Reversal of sex production in *Micromalthus*. *Biol. Bull. mar. biol. Lab., Woods Hole* 81: 420–431.

SCUDDER, G. G. E. (1959). The female genitalia of the Heteroptera: morphology and bearing on classification. *Trans. R. ent. Soc. Lond.* 111: 405–467.

SCUDDER, G. G. E. (1961). The comparative morphology of the insect ovipositor. *Trans. R. ent. Soc. Lond.* 113: 25–40.

SÉGUY, E. (1951a). Ordre des Anoploures ou poux. *in* Grassé, P.-P. (Ed.), *Traité de Zoologie.* vol. 10. Masson et Cie., Paris.

SÉGUY, E. (1951b). Ordre des Diptères. *in* Grassé, P.-P. (Ed.), *Traité de Zoologie.* vol. 10. Masson et Cie., Paris.

SELMAN, B. J. (1962). The fate of the blood cells during the life history of *Sialis lutaria* L. *J. Insect Physiol.* 8: 209–214.

SESHACHAR, B. R. and BAGGA, S. (1963). A cytochemical study of oogenesis in the dragonfly *Pantala flavescens* (Fabricius). *Growth* 27: 225–246.

SHARPLIN, J. (1963). A flexible cuticle in the wing bases of Lepidoptera. *Can. Ent.* 95: 96–100.

SHAUMAR, N. (1966). Anatomie du système nerveux et analyse des facteurs externes pouvant intervenir dans le déterminisme du sexe chez les Ichneumonidae Pimplinae. *Annls Sci. nat. Zool.* 8: 391–493.

SHAW, J. and STOBBART, R. H. (1963). Osmotic and ionic regulation in insects. *Adv. Ins. Physiol.* 1: 315–399.

SHRIVASTAVA, S. C. and RICHARDS, A. G. (1965). An autoradiographic study of the relation between hemocytes and connective tissue in the wax moth, *Galleria mellonella* L. *Biol. Bull. mar. biol. Lab., Woods Hole* 128: 337–345.

SHULOV, A. and NAOR, D. (1964). Experiments on the olfactory responses and host-specificity of the Oriental rat flea (*Xenopsylla cheopis*) (Siphonaptera: Pulicidae). *Parasitology* 54: 225–232.

SIKES, E. K. and WIGGLESWORTH, V. B. (1931). The hatching of insects from eggs and the appearance of air in the tracheal system. *Q. Jl microsc. Sci.* 74: 165–192.

SINGH, T. (1958). Ovulation and corpus luteum formation in *Locusta migratoria migra-*

torioides Reiche and Fairmaire and *Schistocerca gregaria* (Forskål). *Trans. R. ent. Soc. Lond.* 110: 1–20.

SLIFER, E. H. (1961). The fine structure of insect sense organs. *Int. Rev. Cytol.* 2: 125–159.

SLIFER, E. H., PRESTAGE, J. J. and BEAMS, H. W. (1957). The fine structure of the long basiconic sensory pegs of the grasshopper (Orthoptera, Acrididae) with special reference to those on the antenna. *J. Morph.* 101: 359–397.

SLIFER, E. H., PRESTAGE, J. J. and BEAMS, H. W. (1959). The chemoreceptors and other sense organs on the antennal flagellum of the grasshopper, (Orthoptera: Acrididae). *J. Morph.* 105: 145–191.

SLIFER, E. H. and SEKHON, S. S. (1963). The fine structure of the membranes which cover the egg of the grasshopper, *Melanoplus differentialis,* with special reference to the hydropyle. *Q. Jl microsc. Sci.* 104: 321–334.

SLIFER, E. H. and SEKHON, S. S. (1964a). Fine structure of the sense organs on the antennal flagellum of a flesh fly, *Sarcophaga argyrostoma* R.-D. (Diptera, Sarcophagidae). *J. Morph.* 114: 185–207.

SLIFER, E. H. and SEKHON, S. S. (1964b). The dendrites of the thin-walled olfactory pegs of the grasshopper (Orthoptera, Acrididae). *J. Morph.* 114: 393–409.

SLIFER, E. H. and SEKHON, S. S. (1964c). Fine structure of the thin-walled sensory pegs on the antenna of a beetle, *Popilius disjunctus* (Coleoptera: Passalidae). *Ann. ent. Soc. Amer.* 57: 541–548.

SLIFER, E. H., SEKHON, S. S. and LEES, A. D. (1964). The sense organs on the antennal flagellum of aphids (Homoptera), with special reference to the plate organs. *Q. Jl microsc. Sci.* 105: 21–30.

SMALLEY, A. E. (1960). Energy flow of a salt marsh grasshopper population. *Ecology* 41: 785–790.

SMITH, D. S. (1961). The structure of insect fibrillar flight muscle. *J. biophys. biochem. Cytol.* 10, suppl. 123–158.

SMITH, D. S. (1963). The organization and innervation of the luminescent organ in a firefly, *Photuris pennsylvanica* (Coleoptera). *J. Cell Biol.* 16: 323–359.

SMITH, D. S. (1965a). The flight muscles of insects. *Scient. Am.* 212, no. 6: 76–89.

SMITH, D. S. (1965b). The organisation of flight muscle in an aphid, *Megoura viciae* (Homoptera). With a discussion of the structure of synchronous and asynchronous striated muscle fibres. *J. Cell Biol.* 27: 379–393.

SMITH, D. S. (1965c). Synapses in the insect nervous system. *in* Treherne, J. E. and Beament, J. W. L. (Eds.), *The physiology of the insect central nervous system.* Academic Press, London.

SMITH, D. S. (1966). The organisation of flight muscle fibres in the Odonata. *J. Cell Biol.* 28: 109–126.

SMITH, D. S., GUPTA, B. L. and SMITH, U. (1966). The organisation and myofilament array of insect visceral muscles. *J. Cell Sci.* 1: 49–57.

SMITH, D. S. and TREHERNE, J. E. (1963). Functional aspects of the organisation of the insect nervous system. *Adv. Ins. Physiol.* 1: 401–484.

SMITH, J. N. (1955). Detoxication mechanisms in insects. *Biol. Rev.* 30: 455–475.

SMITH, U. and SMITH, D. S. (1966). Observations on the secretory processes in the corpus cardiacum of the stick insect, *Carausius morosus. J. Cell Sci.* 1: 59–66.

SNODGRASS, R. E. (1927). Morphology and mechanism of the insect thorax. *Smithson misc. Collns* 80, no. 1, 108 pp.

SNODGRASS, R. E. (1928). Morphology and evolution of the insect head and its appendages. *Smithson. misc. Collns* 81, no. 3, 158 pp.

SNODGRASS, R. E. (1935). *Principles of insect morphology.* McGraw-Hill, New York.

SNODGRASS, R. E. (1944). The feeding apparatus of biting and sucking insects affecting men and animals. *Smithson. misc. Collns* 104, no. 7, 113 pp.

SNODGRASS, R. E. (1947). The insect cranium and the 'epicranial suture'. *Smithson. misc. Collns* 107, no. 7, 52 pp.

SNODGRASS, R. E. (1952). *A textbook of arthropod anatomy.* Cornell Univ. Press, Ithaca.

SNODGRASS, R. E. (1954). Insect metamorphosis. *Smithson. misc. Collns* 122, no. 9, 124 pp.

SNODGRASS, R. E. (1956). *Anatomy of the honey bee.* Constable and Co., London.

SNODGRASS, R. E. (1957). A revised interpretation of the external reproductive organs of male insects. *Smithson. misc. Collns* 135, no. 6, 60 pp.

SNODGRASS, R. E. (1958). Evolution of arthropod mechanisms. *Smithson. misc. Collns* 138, no. 2, 77 pp.

SNODGRASS, R. E. (1960). Facts and theories concerning the insect head. *Smithson. misc. Collns* 142: 1–61.

SOTAVALTA, O. (1963). The flight-sounds of insects. *in* Busnel, R.-G. (Ed.), *Acoustic behaviour of animals.* Elsevier, Amsterdam.

SOUMALAINEN, E. (1962). Significance of parthenogenesis in the evolution of insects. *A. Rev. Ent.* 7: 349–366.

SOUTH, R. (1941). *The butterflies of the British Isles.* Warne and Co., London.

SOUTHWOOD, T. R. E. (1956). The structure of the eggs of the terrestrial Heteroptera and its relationship to the classification of the group. *Trans. R. ent. Soc. Lond.* 108: 163–221.

SOUTHWOOD, T. R. E. (1961). A hormonal theory of the mechanism of wing polymorphism in Heteroptera. *Proc. R. ent. Soc. Lond.* A, 36: 63–66.

SOUTHWOOD, T. R. E. (1962). Migration of terrestrial arthropods in relation to habitat. *Biol. Rev.* 37: 171–214.

SOUTHWOOD, T. R. E. and LESTON, D. (1959). *Land and water bugs of the British Isles.* Warne and Co., London.

SPICKETT, S. G. (1963). Genetic and developmental studies of a quantitative character. *Nature, Lond.* 199: 870–873.

SPIEGLER, P. E. (1962). Uric acid and urate storage in the larva of *Chrysopa carnea* Stephens (Neuroptera, Chrysopidae). *J. Insect Physiol.* 8: 127–132.

SPIELMAN, A. (1964). The mechanics of copulation in *Aedes aegypti. Biol. Bull. mar. biol. Lab., Woods Hole* 127: 324–344.

SRIVASTAVA, P. N. and GUPTA, P. D. (1961). Excretion of uric acid in *Periplaneta americana* L. *J. Insect Physiol.* 6: 163–167.

SRIVASTAVA, U. S. and KHARE, M. K. (1966). The development of Malpighian tubules and associated structures in *Philosamia ricini* (Lepidoptera, Saturnidae). *J. Zool.* 150: 145–163.

STADDON, B. W. (1955). The excretion and storage of ammonia by the aquatic larva of *Sialis lutaria* (Neuroptera). *J. exp. Biol.* 32: 84–94.

STADDON, B. W. (1959). Nitrogen excretion in nymphs of *Aeshna cyanea* (Müll.) (Odonata, Anisoptera). *J. exp. Biol.* 36: 566–574.

STAY, B. and GELPERIN, A. (1966). Physiological basis of ovipositional behaviour in the false ovoviviparous cockroach *Pycnoscelus surinamensis* (L.). *J. Insect Physiol.* 12: 1217–1226.

STEINHARDT, R. A., MORITA, H. and HODGSON, E. S. (1966). Mode of action of straight chain hydrocarbons on primary chemoreceptors of the blowfly, *Phormia regina. J. cell. Physiol.* 67: 53–62.

STOBBART, R. H. and SHAW, J. (1964). Salt and water balance: excretion. *in* Rockstein, M. (Ed.), *The physiology of Insecta.* vol. 3. Academic Press, New York.

STOWER, W. J. (1959). The colour patterns of hoppers of the desert locust (*Schistocerca gregaria* Forskål). *Anti-Locust Bull.* no. 32, 75 pp.

STOWER, W. J. and GRIFFITHS, J. F. (1966). The body temperature of the desert locust (*Schistocerca gregaria*). *Entomologia exp. appl.* 9: 127–178.

STRANGWAYS-DIXON, J. (1959). Hormonal control of selective feeding in female *Calliphora erythrocephala* Meig. *Nature, Lond.* 184: 2040–2041.

STRIDE, G. O. (1957). Investigations into the courtship behaviour of the male of *Hypolimnas misippus* L. (Lepidoptera, Nymphalidae), with special reference to the role of visual stimuli. *Br. J. Anim. Behav.* 5: 153–167.

STRONG, L. (1966). On the occurrence of neuroglandular axons within the sympathetic nervous system of a locust, *Locusta migratoria migratorioides*. *J. R. micros. Soc.* 86: 141–149.

STUART, D. C. and EDWARDS, G. A. (1958). Intercellular bars at myochitin junctions. *N.Y. State Dept. Health Ann. Rept. Div. Labs. and Research* (1958), 49–50.

SUGA, N. and KATSUKI, Y. (1961). Central mechanism of hearing in insects. *J. exp. Biol.* 38: 545–558.

SUTCLIFFE, D. W. (1963). The chemical composition of haemolymph in insects and some other arthropods, in relation to their phylogeny. *Comp. Biochem. Physiol.* 9: 121–135.

SYMMONS, P. and CARNEGIE, A. J. M. (1959). Some factors affecting breeding and oviposition of the red locust, *Nomadacris septemfasciata* (Serv.). *Bull. ent. Res.* 50: 333–353.

SYRJÄMÄKI, J. (1962). Humidity perception in *Drosophila melanogaster*. *Suomal. eläin-ja Kasvit. Seur. van Julk.* 23, no. 3, 74 pp.

TELFER, W. H. (1965). The mechanism and control of yolk formation. *A. Rev. Ent.* 10: 161–184.

THOMAS, J. G. (1954). The post-embryonic development of the dorsal part of the pterothoracic skeleton and certain muscles of *Locusta migratoria migratorioides* (Reiche & Fairm.). *Proc. zool. Soc. Lond.* 124: 229–238.

THOMAS, J. G. (1965). The abdomen of the female desert locust (*Schistocerca gregaria* Forskål) with special reference to the sense organs. *Anti-Locust Bull.* no. 42, 20 pp. + figs.

THOMSEN, E. and MØLLER, I. (1963). Influence of neurosecretory cells and of corpus allatum on intestinal protease activity in the adult *Calliphora erythrocephala* Meig. *J. exp. Biol.* 40: 301–321.

THORPE, W. H. (1930). The biology, post-embryonic development, and economic importance of *Cryptochaetum iceryae* (Diptera, Agromyzidae) parasitic on *Icerya purchasi* (Coccidae, Monophlebini). *Proc. zool. Soc. Lond.* 1930, 929–971.

THORPE, W. H. (1950). Plastron respiration in aquatic insects. *Biol. Rev.* 25: 344–390.

THORPE, W. H. (1963). *Learning and instinct in animals.* Methuen & Co., London.

THORPE, W. H. and CRISP, D. J. (1947a). Studies on plastron respiration. I. The biology of *Aphelocheirus* (Hemiptera, Aphelocheiridae (Naucoridae)) and the mechanism of plastron retention. *J. exp. Biol.* 24: 227–269.

THORPE, W. H. and CRISP, D. J. (1947b). Studies on plastron respiration. III. The orientation responses of *Aphelocheirus* (Hemiptera, Aphelocheiridae (Naucoridae)) in relation to plastron respiration; together with an account of specialised pressure receptors in aquatic insects. *J. exp. Biol.* 24: 310–328.

THORPE, W. H. and CRISP, D. J. (1949). Studies on plastron respiration. IV. Plastron respiration in the Coleoptera. *J. exp. Biol.* 26: 219–260.

THORPE, W. H. and JONES, F. G. W. (1937). Olfactory conditioning in a parasitic insect and its relation to the problem of host selection. *Proc. R. Soc.* B, 124: 56–81.

THORSTEINSON, A. J. (1960). Host selection in phytophagous insects. *A. Rev. Ent.* 5: 193–218.

TICE, L. W. and SMITH, D. S. (1965). The localisation of myofibrillar ATPase activity in the flight muscles of the blowfly, *Calliphora erythrocephala*. *J. Cell Biol.* 25: 121–136.

TIEGS, O. W. (1955). The flight muscles of insects—their anatomy and histology; with some observations on the structure of striated muscle in general. *Phil. Trans. R. Soc. B*, 238: 221–348.

TILLYARD, R. J. (1917). *The biology of dragonflies.* Cambridge University Press.

TILLYARD, R. J. (1918). The panorpoid complex. I. The wing-coupling apparatus, with special reference to the Lepidoptera. *Proc. Linn. Soc. N.S.W.* 43: 286–319.

TINBERGEN, N. (1951). *The study of instinct.* Oxford University Press.

TINDALL, A. R. (1963). The skeleton and musculature of the thorax and limbs of the larva of *Limnephilus* sp. (Trichoptera, Limnephilidae). *Trans. R. ent. Soc. Lond.* 115: 409–477.

TINDALL, A. R. (1964). The skeleton and musculature of the larval thorax of *Triaenodes bicolor* Curtis. (Trichoptera: Limnephilidae). *Trans. R. ent. Soc. Lond.* 116: 151–210.

TÓTH, L. (1952). The role of nitrogen-active micro-organisms in the nitrogen metabolism of insects. *Tijdschr. Ent.* 95: 43–62.

TRAGER, W. (1953). Nutrition. *in* Roeder, K. D. (Ed.), *Insect physiology.* Wiley & Sons, New York.

TREHERNE, J. E. (1962). The physiology of absorption from the alimentary canal in insects. *Viewpoints in Biology.* 1: 201–241.

TREHERNE, J. E. (1965a). The chemical environment of the insect central nervous system. *in* Treherne, J. E. and Beament, J. W. L. (Eds.), *The physiology of the insect central nervous system.* Academic Press, London.

TREHERNE, J. E. (1965b). The distribution and exchange of inorganic ions in the central nervous system of the stick insect *Carausius morosus. J. exp. Biol.* 42: 7–28.

TREHERNE, J. E. (1965c). Active transport in insects. *in* Goodwin, T. W. (Ed.), *Aspects of insect biochemistry.* Academic Press, London.

TREHERNE, J. E. (1966). *The neurochemistry of arthropods.* Cambridge University Press.

TREHERNE, J. E. (1967). Gut absorption. *A. Rev. Ent.* 12: 43–58.

TUXEN, S. L. (1956). *Taxonomist's glossary of genitalia in insects.* Munksgaard, Copenhagen.

ULLMANN, S. L. (1964). The origin and structure of the mesoderm and the formation of the coelomic sacs in *Tenebrio molitor* L. (Insecta, Coleoptera). *Phil. Trans. R. Soc. B,* 248: 254–277.

URQUHART, F. A. (1960). *The monarch butterfly.* University of Toronto Press.

USHERWOOD, P. N. R. (1963). Spontaneous miniature potentials from insect muscle fibres. *J. Physiol., Lond.* 169: 149–160.

UVAROV, B. P. (1948). Recent advances in acridology: anatomy and physiology of Acrididae. *Trans. R. ent. Soc. Lond.* 99: 1–75.

UVAROV, B. P. (1966). *Grasshoppers and locusts.* Cambridge University Press.

VARLEY, G. C. (1937). Aquatic insect larvae which obtain oxygen from the roots of plants. *Proc. R. ent. Soc. Lond.* A, 12: 55–60.

VIELMETTER, W. (1958). Physiologie des Verhaltens zur Sonnenstrahlung bei dem Tagfalter *Argynnis paphia* L. I. Untersuchungen im Freiland. *J. Insect Physiol.* 2: 13–37.

VOGEL, S. (1966). Flight in *Drosophila.* I. Flight performance of tethered flies. *J. exp. Biol.* 44: 567–578.

WADDINGTON, C. H. (1941). The genetic control of wing development in *Drosophila. J. Genet.* 41: 75–139.

WADDINGTON, C. H. (1956). *Principles of embryology.* Allen & Unwin, London.

WALKER, P. A. (1965). The structure of the fat body in normal and starved cockroaches as seen with the electron microscope. *J. Insect Physiol.* 11: 1625–1631.

WALKER, T. J. (1962). Factors responsible for intraspecific variation in the calling songs of crickets. *Evolution, Lancaster, Pa.* 16: 407–428.

WALLACE, G. K. (1958). Some experiments on form perception in the nymphs of the desert locust, *Schistocerca gregaria* Forsk. *J. exp. Biol.* 35: 765–775.

WALLACE, G. K. (1959). Visual scanning in the desert locust *Schistocerca gregaria* Forskål. *J. exp. Biol.* 36: 512–525.

WALLS, G. L. (1942). *The vertebrate eye.* Cranbrook Press, Michigan.

WALOFF, Z. (1946). A long-range migration of the desert locust from southern Morocco to Portugal, with an analysis of concurrent weather conditions. *Proc. R. ent. Soc. Lond.* A, 21: 81–84.

WALOFF, Z. (1953). Flight in desert locusts in relation to humidity. *Bull. ent. Res.* 43: 575–580.

WALOFF, Z. (1963). Field studies on solitary and *transiens* desert locusts in the Red Sea area. *Anti-Locust Bull.* no. 40, 93 pp.

WALOFF, Z. and RAINEY, R. C. (1951). Field studies on factors affecting the displacements of desert locust swarms in eastern Africa. *Anti-Locust Bull.* no. 9, 1–50.

WALSH, E. O'F. (1961). *An introduction to biochemistry.* English Universities Press, London.

WALSHE, B. M. (1950). The function of haemoglobin in *Chironomus plumosus* under natural conditions. *J. exp. Biol.* 27: 73–95.

WATERHOUSE, D. F. (1957). Digestion in insects. *A. Rev. Ent.* 2: 1–18.

WATERHOUSE, D. F. and DAY, M. P. (1953). Function of the gut in absorption, excretion, and intermediary metabolism. *in* Roeder, K. D. (Ed.), *Insect physiology.* Wiley & Sons, New York.

WATERHOUSE, D. F. and WRIGHT, M. (1960). The fine structure of the mosaic midgut epithelium of blowfly larvae. *J. Insect Physiol.* 5: 230–239.

WATERHOUSE, F. L. (1955). Microclimatological profiles in grass cover in relation to biological problems. *Q. Jl R. met. Soc.* 81: 63–71.

WATSON, J. A. L. (1963). The cephalic endocrine system in the Thysanura. *J. Morph.* 113: 359–373.

WAY, M. J. (1950). The structure and development of the larval cuticle of *Diataraxia oleracea* (Lepidoptera). *Q. Jl microsc. Sci.* 91: 145–182.

WEBB, J. E. (1948). The origin of the atrial spines in the spiracles of sucking lice of the Genus *Haematopinus* Leach. *Proc. zool. Soc. Lond.* 118: 582–587.

WEEVERS, R. de G. (1965). Proprioceptive reflexes and the co-ordination of locomotion in the caterpillar of *Antheraea pernyi* (Lepidoptera). *in* Treherne, J. E. and Beament, J. W. L. (Eds.), *The physiology of the insect central nervous system.* Academic Press, London.

WEEVERS, R. de G. (1966a). The physiology of a lepidopteran muscle receptor. I. The sensory response to stretching. *J. exp. Biol.* 44: 177–194.

WEEVERS, R. de G. (1966b). The physiology of a lepidopteran muscle receptor. II. The function of the receptor muscle. *J. exp. Biol.* 44: 195–208.

WEIR, J. S. (1959). The influence of worker age on trophogenic larval dormancy in the ant *Myrmica. Insectes soc.* 6: 271–290.

WEIS-FOGH, T. (1949). An aerodynamic sense organ stimulating and regulating flight in locusts. *Nature, Lond.* 164: 873.

WEIS-FOGH, T. (1952). Fat combustion and metabolic rate of flying locusts (*Schistocerca gregaria* Forskål). *Phil. Trans. R. Soc.* B, 237: 1–36.

WEIS-FOGH, T. (1956a). Biology and physics of locust flight. II. Flight performance of the desert locust (*Schistocerca gregaria*). *Phil. Trans. R. Soc.* B, 239: 459–510.

WEIS-FOGH, T. (1956b). Biology and physics of locust flight. IV. Notes on sensory mechanisms in locust flight. *Phil. Trans. R. Soc.* B, 239: 553–584.

WEIS-FOGH, T. (1961). Power in flapping flight. *in* Ramsay, J. A. and Wigglesworth,

V. B. (Eds.), *The cell and the organism*. Cambridge University Press.

WEIS-FOGH, T. (1964a). Functional design of the tracheal system of flying insects as compared with the avian lung. *J. exp. Biol.* 41: 207–227.

WEIS-FOGH, T. (1964b). Diffusion in insect wing muscle, the most active tissue known. *J. exp. Biol.* 41: 229–256.

WEIS-FOGH, T. (1964c). Control of basic movements in flying insects. *Symp. Soc. exp. Biol.* 18: 343–361.

WEIS-FOGH, T. and JENSEN, M. (1956). Biology and physics of locust flight. I. Basic principles in insect flight. A critical review. *Phil. Trans. R. Soc.* B, 239: 415–458.

WEITZ, B. (1964). Feeding habits of tsetse flies. *Endeavour* 23: 38–42.

WELLINGTON, W. G. (1945). Conditions governing the distribution of insects in the free atmosphere. III. Thermal convection. *Can. Ent.* 77: 44–49.

WELLINGTON, W. G. (1953). Motor responses evoked by the dorsal ocelli of *Sarcophaga aldrichi* Parker, and the orientation of the fly to plane polarised light. *Nature, Lond.* 172: 1177–1179.

WENDLER, G. (1966). The co-ordination of walking movements in arthropods. *Symp. Soc. exp. Biol.* 20: 229–250.

WENNER, A. M. (1962). Sound production during the waggle dance of the honey bee. *Anim. Behav.* 10: 79–95.

WENNER, A. M. (1964). Sound communication in honeybees. *Scient. Am.* 210: 116–124.

WHEDON, A. D. (1938). The aortic diverticula of the Odonata. *J. Morph.* 63: 229–261.

WHEELER, W. M. (1922). *Social life among the insects*. Constable & Co., London.

WHEELER, W. M. (1926). *Ants. Their structure, development and behaviour*. Columbia University Press, New York.

WHITE, M. J. D. (1954). *Animal cytology and evolution*. Cambridge University Press.

WHITE, M. J. D. (1964). Cytogenetic mechanisms in insect reproduction. *Symp. R. ent. Soc. Lond.* 2: 1–12.

WHITE, R. H. (1961). Analysis of the development of the compound eye in the mosquito, *Aedes aegypti*. *J. exp. Zool.* 148: 223–239.

WHITING, P. W. (1945). The evolution of male haploidy. *Q. Rev. Biol.* 20: 231–260.

WHITTEN, J. M. (1957). The supposed pre-pupa in cyclorrhaphous Diptera. *Q. Jl microsc. Sci.* 98: 241–249.

WHITTEN, J. M. (1962). Breakdown and formation of connective tissue in the pupal stage of an insect. *Q. Jl microsc. Sci.* 103: 359–367.

WHITTEN, J. M. (1964). Connective tissue membranes and their apparent role in transporting neurosecretory and other secretory products in insects. *Gen. Comp. Endocrin.* 4: 176–192.

WIGGLESWORTH, V. B. (1931). The physiology of excretion in a blood-sucking insect, *Rhodnius prolixus* (Hemiptera, Reduviidae). *J. exp. Biol.* 8: 411–427.

WIGGLESWORTH, V. B. (1942). The storage of protein, fat, glycogen and uric acid in the fat body and other tissues of mosquito larvae. *J. exp. Biol.* 19: 56–77.

WIGGLESWORTH, V. B. (1952). Symbiosis in blood-sucking insects. *Tijdschr. Ent.* 95: 63–69.

WIGGLESWORTH, V. B. (1954a). Growth and regeneration in the tracheal system of an insect, *Rhodnius prolixus* (Hemiptera). *Q. Jl microsc. Sci.* 95: 115–137.

WIGGLESWORTH, V. B. (1954b). *The physiology of insect metamorphosis*. Cambridge University Press.

WIGGLESWORTH, V. B. (1956). The haemocytes and connective tissue formation in an insect, *Rhodnius prolixus* (Hemiptera). *Q. Jl microsc. Sci.* 97: 89–98.

WIGGLESWORTH, V. B. (1957a). The physiology of insect cuticle. *A. Rev. Ent.* 2: 37–54.

WIGGLESWORTH, V. B. (1957b). The action of growth hormones in insects. *Symp. Soc.*

exp. Biol. 11: 204–226.

WIGGLESWORTH, V. B. (1959a). Insect blood cells. *A. Rev. Ent.* 4: 1–16.

WIGGLESWORTH, V. B. (1959b). *The control of growth and form.* Cornell University Press, Ithaca.

WIGGLESWORTH, V. B. (1959c). The role of the epidermal cells in the migration of tracheoles in *Rhodnius prolixus* (Hemiptera). *J. exp. Biol.* 36: 632–640.

WIGGLESWORTH, V. B. (1961). Some observations on the juvenile hormone effect of farnesol in *Rhodnius prolixus* Stål (Hemiptera). *J. Insect Physiol.* 7: 73–78.

WIGGLESWORTH, V. B. (1963). A further function of the air sacs in some insects. *Nature, Lond.* 198: 106.

WIGGLESWORTH, V. B. (1964). The hormonal regulation of growth and reproduction in insects. *Adv. Ins. Physiol.* 2: 247–336.

WIGGLESWORTH, V. B. (1965). *The principles of insect physiology.* Methuen & Co., London.

WIGGLESWORTH, V. B. and BEAMENT, J. W. L. (1950). The respiratory mechanisms of some insect eggs. *Q. Jl microsc. Sci.* 91: 429–452.

WIGGLESWORTH, V. B. and SALPETER, M. M. (1962a). Histology of the Malpighian tubules of *Rhodnius prolixus* Stål (Hemiptera). *J. Insect Physiol.* 8: 299–307.

WIGGLESWORTH, V. B. and SALPETER, M. M. (1962b). The aeroscopic chorion of the egg of *Calliphora erythrocephala* Meig. (Diptera) studied with the electron microscope. *J. Insect Physiol.* 8: 635–641.

WILDE, J. de (1947). Contribution to the physiology of the heart of insects with special reference to the alary muscles. *Archs. néerl. Physiol.* 28: 530–542.

WILDE, J. de (1962). Photoperidism in insects and mites. *A. Rev. Ent.* 7: 1–26.

WILDE, J. de (1964a). Reproduction. *in* Rockstein, M. (Ed.), *The physiology of Insecta.* vol. 1. Academic Press, New York.

WILDE, J. de (1964b). Reproduction—endocrine control. *in* Rockstein, M. (Ed.), *The physiology of Insecta.* vol. 1. Academic Press, New York.

WILDE, J. de and BOER, J. A. de (1961). Physiology of diapause in the adult colorado beetle II. Diapause as a case of pseudo-allatectomy. *J. Insect Physiol.* 6: 152–161.

WILLIAMS, C. B. (1930). *The migration of butterflies.* Oliver and Boyd, Edinburgh.

WILLIAMS, C. B. (1951). Seasonal changes in flight direction of migrant butterflies in the British Isles. *J. Anim. Ecol.* 20: 180–190.

WILLIAMS, C. B. (1958). *Insect migration.* Collins, London.

WILLIAMS, J. R. (1951). The factors which promote and influence the oviposition of *Nemeritis canescens* Grav. (Ichneumonidae, Ophioninae). *Proc. R. ent. Soc. Lond.* A, 26: 49–58.

WILSON, D. M. (1962). Bifunctional muscles in the thorax of grasshoppers. *J. exp. Biol.* 39: 669–677.

WILSON, D. M. (1964). Relative refractoriness and patterned discharge of locust flight motor neurons. *J. exp. Biol.* 41: 191–205.

WILSON, D. M. (1965a). Proprioceptive leg reflexes in cockroaches. *J. exp. Biol.* 43: 397–410.

WILSON, D. M. (1965b). The nervous co-ordination of insect locomotion. *in* Treherne, J. E. and Beament, J. W. L. (Eds.), *The physiology of the insect central nervous system.* Academic Press, London.

WILSON, D. M. (1966a). Insect walking. *A. Rev. Ent.* 11: 103–122.

WILSON, D. M. (1966b). Central nervous mechanisms for the generation of rhythmic behaviour in arthropods. *Symp. Soc. exp. Biol.* 20: 199–228.

WILSON, D. M. and GETTRUP, E. (1963). A stretch reflex controlling wingbeat frequency in grasshoppers. *J. exp. Biol.* 40: 171–185.

WILSON, D. M. and WEIS-FOGH, T. (1962). Patterned activity of co-ordinated motor units, studied in flying locusts. *J. exp. Biol.* 39: 643–667.

WILSON, D. M. and WYMAN, R. J. (1963). Phasically unpatterned nervous control of dipteran flight. *J. Insect Physiol.* 9: 859–865.

WILSON, E. O. (1962). Chemical communication among workers of the fire ant *Solenopsis saevissima* (Fr. Smith) 1. The organisation of mass-foraging. *Anim. Behav.* 10: 134–164.

WILSON, E. O. (1963a). The social biology of ants. *A. Rev. Ent.* 8: 345–368.

WILSON, E. O. (1963b). Pheromones. *Scient. Am.* 208, no. 4: 2–11.

WOLBARSHT, M. L. (1960). Electrical characteristics of insect mechanoreceptors. *J. gen. Physiol.* 44: 105–122.

WOLFE, L. S. (1954a). The deposition of the third instar larval cuticle of *Calliphora erythrocephala. Q. Jl microsc. Sci.* 95: 49–66.

WOLFE, L. S. (1954b). Studies of the development of the imaginal cuticle of *Calliphora erythrocephala. Q. Jl microsc. Sci.* 95: 67–78.

WOLKEN, J. J., CAPENOS, J. and TURANO, A. (1957). Photoreceptor structures. III. *Drosophila melanogaster. J. biophys. biochem. Cytol.* 3: 441–447.

WOODROW, D. F. (1963). Egg laying behaviour in locusts. Ph.D. Thesis, University of London.

WOODROW, D. F. (1965). The responses of the African migratory locust, *Locusta migratoria migratorioides* R. & F. to the chemical composition of the soil at oviposition. *Anim. Behav.* 13: 348–356.

WYATT, G. R. (1961). The biochemistry of insect haemolymph. *A. Rev. Ent.* 6: 75–102.

WYATT, I. J. (1961). Pupal paedogenesis in the Cecidomyiidae (Diptera). I. *Proc. R. ent. Soc. Lond.* A, 36: 133–143.

WYATT, I. J. (1963). Pupal paedogenesis in the Cecidomyiidae (Diptera). II. *Proc. R. ent. Soc. Lond.* A, 38: 136–144.

YEAGER, J. F. (1945). The blood picture of the southern army worm (*Prodenia uridania*). *J. agric. Res.* 71: 1–40.

YOUNG, E. C. (1965a). The incidence of flight polymorphism in British Corixidae and description of the morphs. *J. Zool.* 146: 567–576.

YOUNG, E. C. (1965b). Flight muscle polymorphism in British Corixidae: ecological observations. *J. Anim. Ecol.* 34: 353–390.

ZEBE, E. C. and McSHAN, W. H. (1957). Lactic acid α-glycerophosphate dehydrogenases in insects. *J. gen. Physiol.* 40: 779–790.

ZHUZHIKOV, D. P. (1964). Function of the peritrophic membrane in *Musca domestica* L. and *Calliphora erythrocephala* Meig. *J. Insect Physiol.* 10: 273–278.

ZIEGLER-GÜNDER, I. (1956). Pterine: Pigmente und Wirkstoffe im Tierreich. *Biol. Rev.* 31: 313–348.

TAXONOMIC INDEX

Some indication of the subject dealt with by each page reference may be obtained by cross-reference to the following table of contents.

Italicised page numbers denote illustrations. The major orders are omitted.

SUBJECT INDEX

Page numbers in bold refer to a major reference or an illustration.

Puparium, **405**, 415, 419, 441, 680, 687
Purine, 85, 113, 124
Pygidial gland, 158
Pylorus, **38–9**, 49
Pyrrole, **115**
Pyruvate, 90, 95, 101

Quadrate plate, 325, **332–3**
Queen,
    ant,
        determination, 36, 78, 747
        location of, 743
    bee,
        determination, 36, 78, 747
        pheromones of, 51–2, 738, 747
    termite, 86, 706–7, 745–6
Quiescence, 85, 469, **717–8**, 728
    egg, 368
    prepupa, 404
Quinone,
    cuticular, 443–7
    oothecal, 248
    pigments, 111–2, **116–7**
    salivary sheath, 54

Radiant heat, 229, **638–9**, 640, 642
Radial vein, **166**, 168, 176–7, 179
Raffinose, 72
Rake, **35–6**
Raptorial legs, **24**, 139
Rebound effect, **149–50**
Receptivity of female, 302–3, 596, 712
Receptor potential, 529, 598, 631
Rectal,
    gills, **479**
    pads, 49–50, 68
    sac, 512
Rectum, 38, **50–1**
    resorption in, 67–9, **493–4**, 504, 507
    secretion by, 496
    tracheal supply, 50, 479
Recurrent nerve, 50, **519**, 524
Redox potential, **65**
Reflex bleeding, 691
Refractory period, 198, **532**
Regenerative cells, **44**, 394, 415
Regulation egg, **350**
Relative wind, **192–5**, 197
Remigium, **169–70**
Remotion, 142
Replete, 35
Reproductive,
    behaviour, **298–322**
    caste, 36, 173, 706, 745
    diapause, 703, **726–7**
    potential, 377, 380
    system, see also Genitalia
        development, **364–6**
        female, **280–97**
        male, **270–80**
Resilin, 153, 178, 187, **434–5**
Resonance, see Natural frequency
Resorption of oocytes, **295**
Respiration,
    aquatic insects, 260, 406, 470, **472–86**
    egg, 284, **339–41**, 470
    endoparasites, **486–7**
    larval *Glossina*, 374–5
    pupal, 406, 483–6
    terrestrial insects, **449–71**

Respiratory,
    horn, 328, 335, **339–40**
    metabolism, **90–6**, 105–6, 115, 226, 276
    pigment, 487–9
    quotient, **105**, 366, 505
    siphon, 260, **474, 477**
    system, **449–63**
Resting potential, see Membrane potential
Retinaculum,
    Collembolan, **153–4**, 264
    wing coupling, **175–6**
Retinene, 74, 113, 553
Retinula cell, **544**, 546–9, 560, 564
    connections, 521, **550**, 554–6, 558, 563
Retraction, 142, 146–8, 161
Rhabdom, **546–9**, 551–3, 555, 560
    of stemma, **571–2**
Rhabdomere, **546–8**, 553–4, 567
    of ocellus, 569
Rhodopsin, 553
Rhythm,
    activity, 34, 540–1, 561, 571, **713–4**
    nervous, 541, 556, 713–4
    oviduct contraction, 318
    pigment movement, 561, 711
    singing, 595
Ribonucleic acid, see RNA
Ribose-5-phosphate, 103
Ribosome, 290, 348, 526
Ring gland, 682, **696–7**
Rivalry song, 301, 536, 592, 594
RNA,
    dietary, 71, 75–6
    synthesis, 71, 102, 275, 290, 395, 696
    in yolk synthesis, 290–2
Rolling, 163, **200–2, 204–5**
Rotation of genital segments, 306, **310–11**

Saliva,
    action, 30–1, 52–3, 55
    in courtship, 303
    enzymes, 41, 52–3, 55–7
    injection, 19, 30–1
    secretion, 17, 54, 85, 304
    trophallaxis, 37, 55
Salivarium, **6–7**, 17, 19, 52
Salivary duct, 7, 19, 20, 52
Salivary gland, 30, **52–4, 495**
    endomitosis, 394
    water regulation, 46
Salivary pump, 20, 30, **52–3**
Salivary reservoir, 52
Salivary sheath, 30, **54**
Salt,
    buffering by, **64**
    dietary requirements, 75
    regulation, 50, **499–511**
Salt water insects, **510–11**
Sarcolemma, **207**, 213
    elasticity, 187, 226
    metamorphosis, 408, 415
    muscle attachment, 426, 682
    in muscle autolysis, 232
Sarcomere, 208, **209**
    fibrillar muscles, 213
    shortening, **214–6**
Sarcoplasm, 207–8, 211
Sarcoplasmic reticulum, 207, 212, 214, 220
Sarcosome, 208
Saturation deficit, see Humidity